CHAIN SAW SERVICE MANUAL

(EIGHTH EDITION)

Allis-Chalmers	Husqvarna	ProKut
Alpina	Jonsered	Redmax
Castor	Lombard	Remington
Clinton	Massey-Ferguson	Roper
Danarm	McCulloch	Sachs-Dolmar
John Deere	Olympyk	Shindaiwa
Echo	Partner	Solo
Frontier	Pioneer	Stihl
The Green Machine	Pioneer-Partner	Tanaka
Homelite	Poulan	

Published by
INTERTEC PUBLISHING CORPORATION
P.O. BOX 12901, OVERLAND PARK, KS 66212

Cover photo courtesy of:
Stihl, Inc.
536 Viking Drive
Virginia Beach, VA 23452

1

CONTENTS

DUAL DIMENSIONS

This service manual provides specifications in both the U.S. Customary and Metric (SI) systems of measurement. The first specification is given in the measuring system perceived by us to be the preferred system when servicing a particular component, while the second specification (given in parenthesis) is the converted measurement. For instance, a specification of "0.011 inch (0.28 mm)" would indicate that we feel the preferred measurement, in this instance, is the U.S. system of measurement and the metric equivalent of 0.011 inch is 0.28 mm.

Intertec Publishing thanks the following firms for their cooperation and technical assistance:
  Alpina, Griffith, Indiana
  Beaird-Poulan, Inc., Shreveport, Louisiana
  Echo Incorporated, Lake Zurich, Illinois
  EMAB Canada, Ontario, Canada
  HMC, Long Beach, California
  Homelite Division of Textron, Inc., Charlotte, North Carolina
  Husqvarna Power Products Company, Itasca, Illinois
  Jonsered, Sweden
  Komatsu Zenoah America, Inc., Norcross, Georgia
  McCulloch Corporation, Lake Havasu City, Arizona
  Sachs-Dolmar Division, Shreveport, Louisiana
  Shindaiwa, Inc., Tualatin, Oregon
  Solo Motors, Inc., Newport News, Virginia
  Stihl Inc., Virginia Beach, Virginia
  Tanaka Kogyo (USA) Co., Bothell, Washington
  Tilton Equipment Company, Rye, New Hampshire

Saw Chain, Guide Bars and Sprockets

SAW CHAIN

CHAIN NOMENCLATURE

Note component parts of chain shown in Fig. CM1 exploded view. The cutters remove material being sawed while saw chain is driven by engagement of drive links with engine sprocket. Side links connect drive links and ride against bar. Special chain types such as anti-kickback or ripping chain may use components designed as a safety feature or for specialized cutting.

CHAIN SIZE

Saw chain size is determined by chain pitch and gage. Pitch is the distance between alternate chain rivets divided by half as shown in Fig. CM2. Common pitch sizes are ¼, 3/8, 0.404, 7/16 and ½ inch. Gage is the drive link thickness measured at the tang as shown in Fig. CM3. Common gage sizes are 0.050, 0.058 and 0.063 inch.

Chain size must be matched with engine drive sprocket and bar sprocket, if so equipped. Mismatching chain and sprocket will result in damage to both components as well as possible damage to engine should chain break.

CHAIN TYPES

The two common types of chain cutters are chipper and chisel. Note in Fig. CM4 that cutting edge of chipper cutter is round while cutting edge of chisel cutter is square. Different configurations of chisel and chipper cutters may be used to meet specific cutting requirements. Refer to subsequent CHAIN SHARPENING section for procedures and tools used when sharpening chipper and chisel chain types.

Anti-kickback saw chain uses drive links or side links which extend as they travel around tip of bar thereby preventing contact between cutter link and wood. Refer to Fig. CM5. Possibility of saw kickback is lessened if cutter contact is prevented as chain travels around bar nose.

CHAIN BREAK IN, TENSION AND LUBRICATION

BREAKING IN A NEW CHAIN. As with any machine or accessory containing moving parts, the first hour or so of operation can make a great difference to the length of life. Careful attention to the instructions for breaking in and making tension adjustments can greatly add to the life of the chain.

The following instructions are important and will add to the life of saw chain:

1. If possible, soak chain in oil bath before use and between uses.
2. Install chain properly with recommended chain tension.
3. Run chain at slow speed for about 5 minutes, giving it plenty of oil.
4. Stop engine and readjust chain tension.
5. Recheck tension until chain is fully broken in.
6. Keep chain well lubricated when in use.
7. Keep chain sharp. Always use a new file on a new chain.
8. Correct chain tension, especially on bar lengths of 32 inches and over, is important to prevent the chain jumping the bar and causing damage to the equipment and loss of time to the operator.

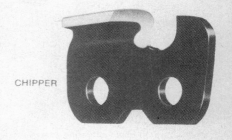

CHIPPER

CHISEL

Fig. CM4—View of chipper and chisel cutters.

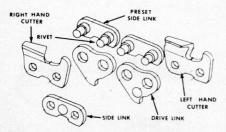

RIGHT HAND CUTTER
RIVET
PRESET SIDE LINK
SIDE LINK
DRIVE LINK
LEFT HAND CUTTER

Fig. CM1—Exploded view of typical section of saw chain.

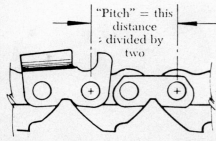

"Pitch" = this distance ÷ divided by two

Fig. CM2—Chain pitch is measured between rivet pins as shown above.

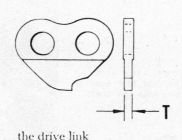

the drive link

Fig. CM3—Saw chain gage size is thickness of drive link tang (T).

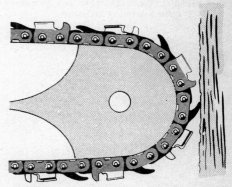

Fig. CM5—Protruding drive links of anti-kickback chain prevent cutter contact with wood as cutters travel around bar nose.

Fig. CM6—Loosen bar retaining nuts prior to chain adjustment.

CHAIN TENSION ADJUSTMENTS. Correct tension is very important. It will increase the life of the saw and chain. Loose tension is a major cause of saw chain problems; it ruins chain, bar and sprocket. Check chain tension often, but make adjustments only when the attachments have cooled off. To insure correct tension follow steps shown in Figs. CM6, CM7, CM8, CM9, CM10 and CM11.

It is well known that over-tension, or a tight chain, will lead to excessive wear on both the guide bar and the side links of the chain, thus shortening the life of the bar and chain. The chain can also damage the guide bar if it is too loose. The chain will damage the guide bar immediately behind the stellite tip by a pounding operation. Further damage at the tail end of the bar can be caused by excessive pounding as the chain arcs off the sprocket. These pounding forces will cause stress in the chain components, which may eventually break, or the pounding may cause the chain to have stiff links. A loose chain may jump off of the bar, damaging the drive links, or wear the rails of the guide bar itself.

LUBRICATION. The importance of proper lubrication of the chain and guide bar cannot be over-stressed. Each rivet in the chain should be considered as a bearing and must be lubricated. This is particularly important in direct drive or high speed chains. The same applies to bearing surface between the chain and the guide bar.

Clean chain in solvent before and after filing, then give chain an oil bath for proper lubrication. DO NOT leave it all to the oil pump. Be sure to use the correct weight of clean oil (not reclaimed crankcase oil) to allow maximum chain lubrication under all cutting conditions and varying temperatures. Good quality chain oil winter or summer grade is recommended. A good grade SAE 10 to SAE 40 motor oil may also be used, depending upon prevailing temperature.

Adequate lubrication is essential to assure the maximum life of the chain. Be generous with the application of oil to the bar and chain. Thin the oil with kerosene or fuel oil in cold weather.

CHAIN MAINTENANCE

The chain saw engine may be perfectly maintained, but, if the chain does not function properly, it is impossible to obtain satisfactory results. The power head exists merely as a convenient method of moving a saw chain in

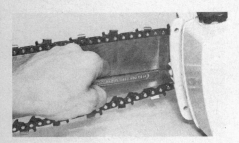

Fig. CM7—Tighten chain adjusting screw.

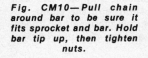

Fig. CM10—Pull chain around bar to be sure it fits sprocket and bar. Hold bar tip up, then tighten nuts.

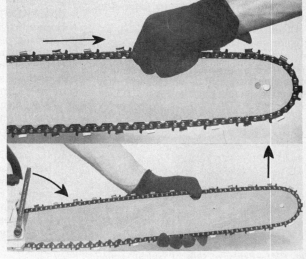

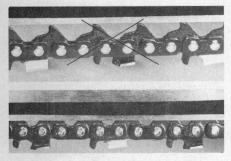

Fig. CM8—For correct tension tighten chain adjusting screw until chain just touches bottom bar rails. Chain on roller and sprocket nose bars must be tighter.

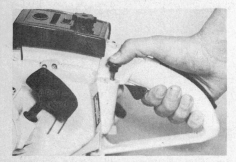

Fig. CM9—Make sure chain is always properly lubricated.

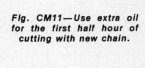

Fig. CM11—Use extra oil for the first half hour of cutting with new chain.

order to cut wood. Correct maintenance and operating conditions are essential to insure the proper functioning of your chain and hence the chain saw.

CHAIN SHARPENING

CHIPPER CHAIN. A full round file (not a rat tail) is used to sharpen the chipper-type chains. For good results, the procedures shown in Figs. CM12, CM13. CM14 and CM15 should be adopted.

For average sawing, maintain the filing angles shown in Figs. CM16 and CM17 by holding the file in the position shown in Figs. CM12 through CM15. Do not allow the file to drag on the backstroke, and rotate the file occasionally to increase file life. Approximately 1/10th of the file diameter should be above the cutting edge of the cutter. If the distance is less than this, the cutting edge will be too blunt; if distance is greater, a rapidly wearing feather edge will result. For convenience, file alternate (either all right hand or left hand) cutters; then reverse the chain in the vise or turn the saw around and file the remaining cutters. All cutters must be filed alike and the same amount to keep the cutting edges at the same height. Check this by laying a file or straightedge across the tops of the cutters. Continue filing high cutters in normal manner until all cutters are same height.

Suggested file sizes for standard (chipper-type) chain:

Chain Pitch	Round File Size
¼"	1/8"
3/8"	3/16"
.404"	7/32"
7/16", ½"	¼"

Different size and design chain will require different file sizes. If manufacturer's recommendations are not available, refer to the above chart.

After filing the cutting edges, check the depth gages, or riders as they are sometimes called, for correct distance below the cutting edges (Fig. CM18). Depth gages are generally checked with a tool that is pre-set for the desired distance, as the one shown in Figs. CM19 and CM20, or a tool with an adjustable setting.

Average depth gage (joint) setting for standard chain:

Chain Pitch	Depth Gage Setting
¼"	.020"
3/8"	.020"
.404"	.030"
7/16"	.030"
½"	.030"-.040"

The normal top plate filing angle of 35° and the depth gage distances for different pitch chain have been determined to be the most satisfactory for general sawing. However, the woodsman may, through trial and error, find the most suitable depth gage distance for a particular condition. No specific figures can be given due to the variety of sawing conditions, but the following

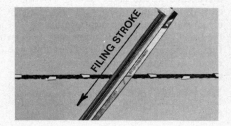

Fig. CM15—Sharpen all cutters on one side of chain. Move to other side and file all cutters on opposite side of chain.

Fig. CM12—File from inside to outside of cutter.

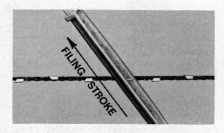

Fig. CM13—Place file holder on cutter; keep mark on holder parallel with chain.

Fig. CM14—Hold file level. Press against cutter and make 2 or 3 light strokes forward.

CORRECT

WRONG

TOO HIGH   **TOO LOW**

Fig. CM16—Correct shape of cutter will help chain to cut faster and remain sharp longer. Back slope is caused by file held too high. Hooked edge is caused by file held too low.

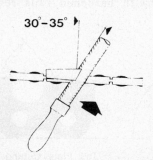

Fig. CM17—Angle of cutting face should be 35 degrees as shown. Insufficient top angle causes chain to cut roughly and dull very quickly. Excessive top angle causes side thrust and wear on sides of drive lugs.

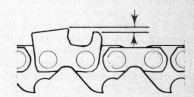

Fig. CM18—Depth gage clearance is measured as shown. This is also known as joint clearance.

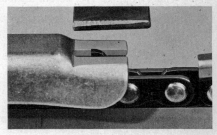

Fig. CM19—If depth gage projects above tool, file depth gage level with tool.

Fig. CM20—Round off front corner of depth gage. Tilt tool to protect top of cutter.

information can be used as a guide.

A. On larger horsepower saws and saws with slow chain speeds, the depth gage distance may be increased, which will allow the cutter to take a larger chip. The depth gage distance should be decreased on small saws and direct drive saws.

B. When cutting continually in soft woods, the depth gage distance can be increased somewhat.

C. When cutting hard woods, frozen or resin timber, the depth gage distance should be decreased.

When sharpening the cutting edges on the saw chain, the drive link tangs should also be sharpened to keep the guide groove clean, and any burrs on the sides of the drive link tangs should be removed.

CHISEL. Refer to Fig. CM4 for view of chisel type saw chain. To sharpen chisel chain a bevel or round file is used, depending on manufacturer. Hold file at a 10° angle as shown in View B of Fig. CM21. Note top and side plate angles in Fig. CM22. Refer to CHIPPER CHAIN section for depth gage settings.

GULLETS. The gullet is the open area between the depth gage and the side plate. The gullet should be cleaned out with a round file before every fifth sharpening. This will keep the gullet open and allow better chip clearance and more efficient side plate cutting action. Hold file level as shown in Fig. CM23 and at a 20° angle with cutter.

REPAIRS

Saw chain repairs are accomplished by removing damaged links and installing new links which requires disconnecting chain (chain breaking). Use of a chain breaker is the preferred method of removing chain rivets when disconnecting a chain. When a chain breaker is not available, such as at the work site, file off the rivet head and drive out the rivet using a sharp punch. A small chisel or screwdriver may be used to spread side links if rivet is not completely cleared.

Rivet spinning tools are available to install rivets when assembling chain links. If a spinner is not available, then a ball peen hammer may be used if special care is taken. DO NOT strike the rivet head too hard. This can cause a fracture in the rivet drum. The rivet can be peened over on the outside circumference with light taps of the hammer. The rivet should not have a flat appearance caused by pounding the rivet and making it spread from the center. Rivets that are pounded flat will not have enough strength around the circumference. See Figs. CM24 and CM25.

CHAIN TROUBLE DIAGNOSIS

If the chain is not performing satisfactorily:

1. Remove chain from bar.
2. Clean with solvent to remove pitch and resin.
3. Compare chain with the illustrations and list shown in accompanying table.
4. Repair as indicated.

GUIDE BARS

SOLID NOSE BARS

Guide rails are sometimes split from the bar being pinched while the saw is hung up in a cut. Splits of two inches long or less can be repaired by using ordinary welding methods on bars with non-hardened rails. Repairing splits on bars with hardened rails requires special equipment for re-hardening the rails.

Small kinks or bends in guide bars can be removed by laying the bar on the large true anvil or other similar work surface and using light hammer blows to bring the bar back into shape. See Fig. CM26. Technique is very similar to straightening other flat metal pieces.

Use a file to funnel the entrance to the guide rail groove of the bar as

Fig. CM23—Before every fifth sharpening, clean out gullets with round file. Hold file level and at 20 degree angle to cutter.

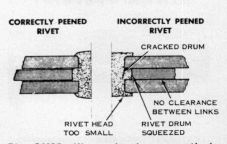

Fig. CM24—Rivets can be installed using a ball peen if carefully done.

Fig. CM21—Hold file level for chipper chain as shown in View A. File must be held at 10 degrees for chisel chain as shown in View B.

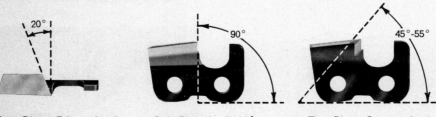

Top Plate Filing Angle 20°. Gradually increase angle as cutter is filed back.

Side Plate Angle 90°.

Top Plate Cutting Angle 45°-55°.

Fig. CM22—View of top and side plate specifications for chisel chain.

CORRECTLY PEENED RIVET

INCORRECTLY PEENED RIVET

CRACKED DRUM

NO CLEARANCE BETWEEN LINKS

RIVET HEAD TOO SMALL

RIVET DRUM SQUEEZED

Fig. CM25—Views showing correctly installed rivet and rivet damaged by incorrect installation.

common problems found with CUTTERS and LINKS

	FAILURE	CAUSE	REMEDY		FAILURE	CAUSE	REMEDY
	Concave side link and cutter bottoms.	Chain run too tight. Insufficient lubrication. Cutters dull.	Decrease chain tension. Check oiler, file cutters.		Side wear.	Abrasive cutting condition.	Check for grit in timber being cut. Lubricate well.
	Heel wear on cutters and side links.	Chain run too loose. Too much joint. Cutters dull.	Increase chain tension. Maintain basic .025" joint. File cutters.		Back nicked.	Chain run too loose.	Increase tension.
	Slight heel wear cutters and side links.	Back slope on cutters—chain slightly tight. Cutters dull.	Remove back slope. Decrease chain tension. File cutters.		Back rounded to bottom.	Worn sprocket. Chain run too loose.	Increase tension. Renew sprocket.
	Excessive bottom wear on cutters and side links.	Insufficient joint—chain run tight, filing blunt—no undercut, cutters dull.	Increase joint to .025". Decrease tension—refer to filing instr. File cutters.		Back and front of link peened.	Worn or wrong pitch sprocket.	Renew sprocket. Increase tension.
	Severe side wear and abrasive damage.	Caused by striking stone or nails, etc. Cutters dull.	All visible abrasion must be removed by filing cutters back. File cutters.		Back peened.	Worn sprocket. Dull cutters.	Renew sprocket. File cutters.
	Crack under rear rivet.	Cutters dull or hooked.	Refer to filing instructions.		Bottom peened and worn.	Link riding on bottom of bar groove. Bar rails worn. Dull cutters.	Renew bar. File cutters.
	Crack under front rivet.	Insufficient joint.	Increase joint to basic .025".		Bottom point rolled up.	Link bottoming in worn sprocket. Dull cutters.	Renew sprocket. File cutters.
	Cracks under both rivets.	Chain run dull and tight—insufficient joint.	Refer to filing instr. Increase joint to basic .025".		Bottom rough and broken off.	Chain run too tight causes stretch and climbs up on sprocket teeth.	Renew worn chain or sprocket. Run chain with less tension.
	Bottom peened and burred.	Hooked cutters—dull—no undercut causes chain to pound on rails.	Eliminate hook. Refer to filing instructions.		Drive lugs worn on sides.	Excessive face angle of cutters causes side thrust.	Refer to filing instructions.
	Front peened.	Chain run too slack—crowds at bar entry.	Increase tension.		Drive lugs worn on one side.	Excessive face angle of cutters on one side.	Cutters must have equal face angles.
	Clearance notch peened.	Sprocket teeth worn.	Renew sprocket.		Chain jumps out of bar groove.	Uneven filing. Chain run too loose.	Increase chain tension. Refer to filing instructions.

shown in the "right" view in Fig. CM27. If the guide rails are as in the "wrong" view in this illustration, damage to the chain can occur as the chain enters the groove.

Check the fit of the chain to the guide bar as shown in Fig. CM28. If the tangs of the drive links touch the bottom of the guide rail groove, poor cutting and damage to the chain will result. The side links of the chain should ride on the rails and the tangs should clear the bottom of the guide groove. When replacing a chain or a guide bar, the length of the tang and the guide bar groove depth should be checked.

If the guide rails are worn or rough, they can be ground smooth and the groove deepened on a special bar grinding machine.

ROLLER AND SPROCKET NOSE BARS

LUBRICATION. The precision bearings in the roller and sprocket nose bar must be lubricated regularly for efficient operation and long life. Grease nose bearing every time saw is refueled. Always grease the bearing after a day's use. Grease bearing by cleaning oil hole and inserting grease with any good type hand grease gun with a needle nozzle. Insert nozzle into hole in center of roller as shown in Fig. CM29 and pump gun until grease flows from rim of roller or sprocket. A lighter grease may be necessary for winter operation.

ROLLER SIDE PLATE CARE. Refer to Fig. CM30. Remove burrs that form on side plate of roller with a flat file. Pump bearing full of grease before filing. File away from slot so filings will not get into bearing. Wipe filings from inside and outside of roller before mounting chain.

ROLLER AND SPROCKET RENEWAL. Roller and sprocket may be removed by drilling or punching out retaining rivets in end of guide bar. Remove roller or sprocket and install new roller or sprocket with new retaining rivets. Care should be taken not to damage rivets or mounting holes when peening or driving out rivets.

NOTE: Be sure sprocket size is matched to chain size. Mismatched sprocket and chain will cause excessive wear.

SPROCKETS AND CLUTCHES

SPROCKETS

Two types of chain drive sprockets are used: The integral star and the self-aligning rim sprocket shown in Fig. CM31. The integral star sprocket is permanently attached to the clutch drum. The self-aligning rim sprocket assembly shown in Fig. CM32 consists of a splined hub fastened to the clutch drum and the rim sprocket is located over the splined hub. The sprocket is permitted to float on the splined hub and automatically align with groove in the guide bar. Sprockets for gear drive saws fit on the output shaft instead of a hub on the clutch drum.

FAILURES AND CAUSES. Drive sprockets are, like any moving part subject to extreme friction, subject to wear. A worn sprocket can quickly damage the bar and the chain. The illustrations in Fig. CM31 are typical examples of worn sprockets which should be renewed to keep from damaging the bar and chain. Wear on the sprocket teeth can be caused by any of the following:
1. Wrong pitch chain.
2. Insufficient chain lubrication.
3. Excessive chain tension.
4. Improper chain filing and jointing.
5. A badly worn and possibly stretched chain has a slight varia-

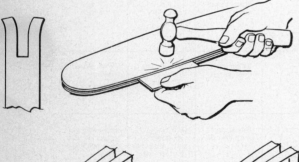

Fig. CM26—Use steel shim 0.004 inch thicker than drive link tangs to close spread bar rails.

Fig. CM27—Cut funnel shaped opening to guide groove with file.

WRONG   RIGHT

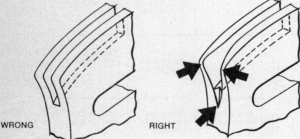

Fig. CM28—Guide groove too shallow in cross section view of left. Tang must clear bottom of groove as in cross section view at right.

Fig. CM29—Lubricate roller or sprocket nose bar.

Fig. CM30—Remove burrs from roller side plates.

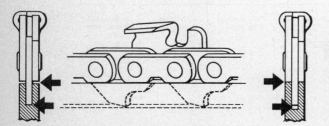

tion in pitch which will contribute to rapid wear of sprocket teeth.

6. A badly worn bar will contribute to rapid wear of the chain which will cause the sprocket to wear. Rapid deterioration and wear on chain drive lugs, side links and cutters will result from installing a new chain. Never install a new chain on a worn sprocket or bar.

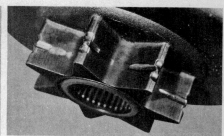

Fig. CM31—View of self-aligning sprocket (left) and worn integral star sprocket (right).

CLUTCH

CLUTCH BEARING. The clutch drum and sprocket can rotate freely (or stop) when the clutch is disengaged. A caged needle roller bearing is located between the clutch drum hub and the shaft. The bearing on most models uses the shaft as the inner race and the clutch drum hub as the outer race and can be removed by hand without any special tools.

Clutch needle bearing failure is often caused by storing the saw after operating under extremely wet conditions. The water will penetrate the needle bearing, form rust and cause the needles to become locked. It is recommended that the clutch drum be removed periodically (depending on local conditions) and the bearing repacked with a good grade of water-resistant grease (not water pump grease).

CLUTCH DRUM AND SHOES. Rapid clutch drum wear, shoe glazing

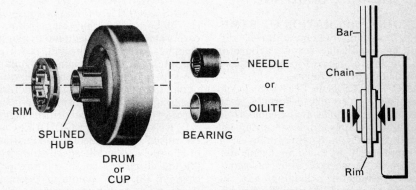

Fig. CM32—View of typical self-aligning sprocket and clutch assembly. Note that sprocket can float on splined hub to align with bar groove.

or grooving may be caused by any of the following:

1. Improper filing. Hooked cutters and excessive joint will especially cause the clutch to slip.
2. Chain pinched in cut causing clutch to slip. Throttle should be released immediately when chain becomes pinched.
3. Oil soaked or worn clutch shoes. Clutch shoes should be inspected periodically. Glazing can be removed by wire brushing or other similar method.

CARBURETOR SERVICE

GENERAL CARBURETOR SERVICE

TROUBLE-SHOOTING

ENGINE OPERATIONAL SYMPTOMS. Normally encountered difficulties resulting from carburetor malfunction, along with possible causes of difficulty, are as follows:

A. CARBURETOR FLOODS. Could be caused by: (1), dirt or foreign particles preventing inlet fuel needle from seating; (2), diaphragm lever spring not seated correctly on diaphragm lever; or (3), improperly installed metering diaphragm. Also, when fuel tank is located above carburetor, flooding can be caused by leaking fuel pump diaphragm.

B. ENGINE RUNS LEAN. Could be caused by: (1), fuel tank vent plugged; (2), leak in fuel line or fittings between fuel tank and carburetor; (3), filter screen in carburetor or filter element in fuel pickup head plugged; (4), fuel orifice plugged; (5), hole in fuel metering diaphragm; (6) metering lever not properly set; (7), dirt in carburetor fuel channels or pulse channel to engine crankcase plugged; or (8), leaky gaskets between carburetor and crankcase intake port. Also, check for leaking crankshaft seals, porous or cracked crankcase or other cause for air leak into crankcase. When fuel tank or fuel lever is below carburetor, lean operation can be caused by hole in fuel pump diaphragm or damaged valve flaps on pump diaphragm. On Walbro series SDC carburetor with diaphragm type accelerating pump, a leak in accelerating pump diaphragm will cause lean operation.

C. ENGINE WILL NOT ACCELERATE SMOOTHLY. Could be caused by: (1), inoperative accelerating pump, on carburetors so equipped, due to plugged channel, leaking diaphragm, stuck piston, etc.; (2), idle or main fuel mixture too lean on models without accelerating pump; (3), incorrect setting of metering diaphragm lever; (4), diaphragm gasket leaking; or (5), main fuel orifice plugged.

D. ENGINE WILL NOT IDLE. Could be caused by: (1), incorrect adjustment of idle fuel and/or idle speed stop screw; (2), idle discharge or air mixture ports clogged; (3), fuel channel clogged; (4), dirty or damaged main orifice check valve; (5), Welch (expansion) plug covering idle ports not sealing properly allowing engine to run with idle fuel needle closed; or (6), throttle shutter not properly aligned on throttle shaft causing fast idle.

E. ENGINE RUNS RICH. Could be caused by: (1), plug covering main nozzle orifice not sealing; (2), when fuel level is above carburetor, leak in fuel pump diaphragm; worn or damaged adjustment needle and seat.

PRESSURE TESTING. With engine stopped and cooled, first set carburetor low speed and high speed mixture screws at chain saw manufacturer's initial recommendation. Remove fuel tank cap and withdraw fuel line out fuel tank opening. Remove strainer on end of fuel line and connect a suitable pressure tester as shown in Fig. CS1. Pressurize system until 7 psi (0.5 bar) is read on pressure gage. Pressure reading must remain constant. If not, remove components as needed and connect pressure tester directly to carburetor inlet fitting as shown in Fig. CS2. Pressurize system until 7 psi (0.5 bar) is read on pressure gage. If pressure reading now remains constant, the fuel line is defective. If pressure reading decreases, then carburetor must be removed for further testing.

Connect pressure tester directly to carburetor inlet fitting and submerge carburetor assembly into a suitable container filled with a nonflammable solution or water as shown in Fig. CS3. Pressurize system until 7 psi (0.5 bar) is read on pressure gage. Observe carburetor and note location of leaking air bubbles. If air bubbles escape from around jet needles or venturi, then inlet needle

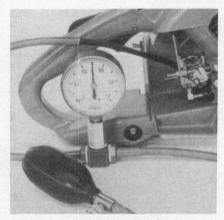

Fig. CS2 — View showing connection of pressure tester directly to carburetor inlet fitting. Refer to text.

Fig. CS1 — View showing connection of pressure tester to fuel tank fuel line. Refer to text.

Fig. CS3 — Submerge carburetor into a suitable container filled with a nonflammable solution or water and pressure test as outlined in text.

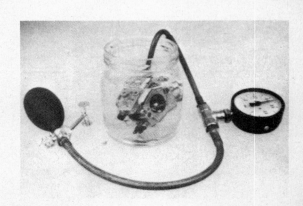

or metering mechanism is defective. If air bubbles escape at impulse opening, then pump diaphragm is defective. If air bubbles escape from around fuel pump cover, then cover gasket or pump diaphragm is defective.

To check inlet needle and metering mechanism, first rotate low and high speed mixture screws inward until seated. Pressurize system until 7 psi (0.5 bar) is read on pressure gage. Use a suitable length and thickness of wire, and reach through hole in metering diaphragm cover. Slowly depress metering diaphragm. A slight drop in pressure reading should be noted as metering chamber becomes pressurized. If no drop in pressure reading is noted, then inlet needle is sticking. If pressure does not hold after a slight drop, then a defective metering mechanism or leaking high or low speed Welch plugs is indicated. To determine which component is leaking, submerge carburetor as previously outlined. Pressurize system until 7 psi (0.5 bar) is read on pressure gage, then depress metering diaphragm as previously outlined. If bubbles escape around metering diaphragm cover, then metering diaphragm or gasket is defective. If bubbles escape from hole in metering diaphragm cover, then metering diaphragm is defective. If bubbles escape from within venturi, then determine which discharge port the air bubbles are escaping from to determine which welch plug is leaking.

If low or high speed running problems are noted, the passage beneath the respective welch plug may be restricted. To test idle circuit, adjust low speed mixture screw to recommended initial setting and rotate high speed mixture screw inward to seat. Pressurize system until 7 psi (0.5 bar) is read on pressure gage. Depress metering diaphragm as previously outlined. If pressure reading does not drop off or drops off very slowly, then a restriction is indicated. To test high speed circuit, adjust high speed mixture screw to recommended initial setting and rotate low speed mixture screw inward to seat. Pressurize system and depress metering diaphragm as previously outlined and note pressure gage. If pressure reading does not drop off or drops off very slowly, then a restriction is indicated.

Refer to specific carburetor service section and repair defect or renew defective component as needed.

ADJUSTMENT

Initial setting for the mixture adjustment needles is listed in the specific engine sections of this manual. Make final carburetor adjustment with engine warm and running. Adjust idle speed screw so that engine is idling at just below clutch engagement speed; do not try to make engine idle any slower than this. Adjust idle fuel needle for best engine idle performance, keeping the mixture rich as possible (turn needle out to richen mixture). If necessary, readjust idle speed screw. Adjust main fuel needle while engine is under cutting load so that engine runs at highest speed without excessive smoke.

If idle mixture is too lean and cannot be properly adjusted, consider the possibility of plugged idle fuel passages, expansion plug for main fuel check valve loose or missing, main fuel check valve not seating, improperly adjusted inlet control lever, leaking metering diaphragm or malfunctioning fuel pump.

If idle mixture is too rich, check idle mixture screw and its seat in carburetor body for damage. Check causes for carburetor flooding.

If high speed mixture is too lean and cannot be properly adjusted, check for dirt or plugging in main fuel passages, improperly adjusted inlet control lever, malfunctioning diaphragm or main fuel check valve. Also check for damaged or missing packing for high speed mixture screw and for malfunctioning fuel pump.

If high speed mixture is too rich, check high speed mixture screw and its seat for damage. Check causes for carburetor flooding.

Setting or adjusting the inlet control lever (metering diaphragm lever height) necessitates disassembly of the carburetor. Refer to the following carburetor sections for adjusting the lever height.

BING

Model 48B102

Bing carburetor Model 48B102 is a diaphragm type carburetor with an integral fuel pump.

OPERATION. Operation of Bing carburetor Model 48B102 is typical of other diaphragm type carburetors.

OVERHAUL. Clean carburetor externally prior to disassembly. Refer to Fig. CS5 and disassemble carburetor. Clean and inspect all components. Inspect metering diaphragm (25) and fuel pump diaphragm (3) for punctures or tears which may affect operation. Examine fuel inlet valve (18) and seat. Inlet valve is renewable, but carburetor body

Fig. CS5 — Exploded view of Bing Model 48B102 carburetor.

1. Fuel pump cover	13. Retainer clip
2. Gasket	14. Spring
3. Fuel pump diaphragm & check valves	15. Friction ball
4. Body	15. Throttle plate
5. Spring	16. Throttle shaft
6. Throttle shaft	18. Fuel inlet valve
7. Throttle plate	19. Spring
8. Spring	20. Lever pin
9. Idle speed screw	21. Diaphragm lever
10. Spring	22. Circuit plate diaphragm
11. Low speed mixture screw	23. Circuit plate
12. High speed mixture screw	24. Gasket
	25. Metering diaphragm
	26. Cover

Fig. CS7 — Exploded view of Dell'Orto Model FTR-16-12 carburetor.

1. Cover
2. Metering diaphragm
3. Gasket
4. Metering block
5. Low speed mixture screw
6. High speed mixture screw
7. Gasket
8. Screen
9. High speed valve
10. Body
11. Diaphragm lever
12. Pin
13. Spring
14. Fuel inlet valve
15. Throttle plate
16. Throttle shaft
17. Bushing
18. Return spring
19. Bushing
20. Retainer
21. Fuel inlet fitting
22. Screen
23. Fuel pump diaphragm & check valves
24. Idle speed screw
25. Metering diaphragm
26. Fuel pump cover
27. Plate

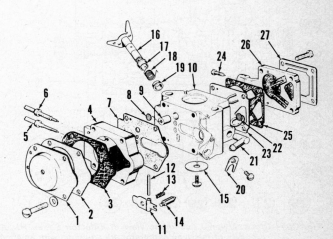

must be renewed if needle seat is excessively worn or damaged. Sharp objects should not be used to clean orifices or passages as fuel flow may be altered. Fuel mixture screws (11 and 12) must be renewed if grooved or broken. Inspect mixture needle seats in carburetor body and renew body if seats are damaged or excessively worn.

To reassemble carburetor, reverse order of disassembly. Renew gaskets (2 and 24). Diaphragm lever (21) should be flush with circuit plate (23).

DELL'ORTO

Model FTR-16-12

Dell'Orto carburetor Model FTR-16-12 is a diaphragm type carburetor with an integral fuel pump.

OPERATION. Operation of Dell'Orto carburetor Model FTR-16-12 is typical of other diaphragm type carburetors. Inlet needle valve (14 – Fig. CS7), low and high speed mixture screws (5 and 6) and metering diaphragm (2) are incorporated into metering block (4) which can be separated from carburetor body (10).

OVERHAUL. Clean carburetor externally prior to disassembly. Refer to Fig. CS7 and disassemble carburetor. Clean and inspect all components. Inspect metering diaphragm (2) and fuel pump diaphragm (23) for punctures or tears which may affect operation. Examine fuel inlet valve (14) and seat. Inlet

valve is renewable, but metering block (4) must be renewed if needle seat is excessively worn or damaged. Sharp objects should not be used to clean orifices or passages as fuel flow may be altered. Fuel mixture screws (5 and 6) must be renewed if grooved or broken. Inspect mixture needle seats in metering block (4) and renew metering block if seats are damaged or excessively worn.

To reassemble carburetor, reverse order of disassembly. Renew gaskets (3, 7 and 25). Diaphragm lever (11) should be flush with chamber floor.

TILLOTSON

Models HC, HJ And HL

Tillotson Model HC, HJ and HL carburetors are diaphragm type carburetors with Model HL having an integral diaphragm fuel pump. Operation and servicing of these carburetors is similar and covered in the following paragraphs.

OPERATION. Operation of Model HL carburetor is outlined in the following paragraphs. Operation of HC and HJ carburetors is similar to HL but they are not equipped with a diaphragm fuel pump.

A cross-sectional schematic view of a typical Tillotson Series HL diaphragm type carburetor with integral fuel pump is shown in Fig. CS9. The top of the pump diaphragm is vented to the engine

crankcase through the channel (8). As the diaphragm pulsates, fuel is drawn into the carburetor through inlet (1), screen (28) and pump inlet valve (3A). The fuel is then pumped through outlet valve (3B) into supply channel (17). Engine suction through main jet (15) and idle jets (10) is transmitted to the top of the carburetor diaphragm (25) and atmospheric pressure through vent (23) pushes upward on the diaphragm (25) overcoming spring (20) pressure and unseating inlet needle (18) allowing fuel to flow into diaphragm chamber (6).

When starting an engine, closing choke disc (16) increases the vacuum in the carburetor throat so the carburetor will function at the low cranking rpm.

When the engine is idling, the throttle disc is almost completely closed and there is not enough air passing through venturi (14) to create any vacuum on main jet (15). A vacuum is created at primary idle jet (10A), however, and the fuel necessary for running the engine is drawn through that jet.

As the throttle disc is opened, enough vacuum is created on secondary idle jet port (10B) so fuel is drawn through that port also. At a certain point, the throttle disc is open far enough so the velocity of air passing through the venturi is sufficient to lower the pressure at main fuel discharge port (15) so fuel will flow through this port also. Opening the throttle disc farther results in, higher air velocities and lower venturi pressures

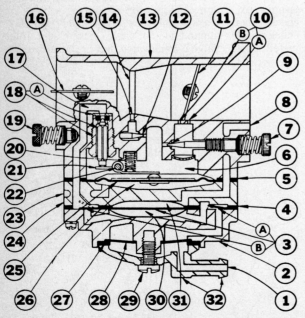

1. Fuel inlet
2. Pump body
3. Pump diaphragm
3A & B. Pump valves
4. Gasket
5. Gasket
6. Metering chamber
7. Idle needle
8. Impulse channel
9. Idle fuel orifice
10. Idle ports
11. Throttle shutter
12. Main fuel orifice
13. Body
14. Venturi
15. Main fuel port
16. Choke shutter
17. Inlet channel
18. Inlet valve
19. Main needle
20. Spring
21. Diaphragm lever
22. Fulcrum pin
23. Vent hole
24. Cover
25. Diaphragm
26. Atmospheric chamber
27. Gasket
28. Screen
29. Screw
30. Fuel chamber
31. Pulse chamber
32. Strainer cover

Fig. CS9—Cross-sectional schematic view of Tillotson Series HL diaphragm carburetor. Some models of this type carburetor are equipped with an accelerator pump.

Fig. CS10—Exploded view of Tillotson Model HC carburetor. Model HJ is similar.

1. Throttle plate
2. Lever pin
3. Body
4. Return spring
5. Throttle shaft
6. Choke shaft
7. Choke plate
8. Idle mixture screw
9. High speed mixture screw
10. Choke friction pin
11. Fuel inlet valve assy.
12. Spring
13. Diaphragm lever
14. Idle speed screw
15. Gasket
16. Metering diaphragm
17. Cover

that increase the flow of fuel out of the discharge ports.

Any vacuum created at idle discharge ports (10) or main fuel discharge port (15) is transferred through metering chamber (6) to diaphragm (25). Air pressure entering through atmospheric vent hole (23) pushes against the diaphragm because of the vacuum and overcomes pressure applied by spring (20) through control lever (21). This releases inlet needle valve (18) and allows fuel to enter the metering chamber in a direct relationship to the vacuum created at the fuel discharge ports. The higher the vacuum, the greater the movement of the diaphragm and the larger the opening of the needle valve. Thus, fuel is metered into the carburetor to meet the needs of the engine.

Some HL carburetors are equipped with governor valve (25–Fig. CS11) which enrichens the fuel mixture at the governed speed and prevents engine overspeeding. Original governor assembly is tuned for each engine and cannot be renewed. A disc may be installed in place of governor assembly.

Fig. CS11 — Exploded view of Tillotson Model HL carburetor. On some HL carburetors, pump diaphragm (19) and valves (20) are one-piece. Governor valve (25) is not used on all carburetors.

1. Throttle plate
2. Lever pin
3. Body
4. Throttle return spring
5. Idle mixture screw
6. Drain plug
7. High speed mixture screw
8. Choke detent
9. Gasket
10. Fuel inlet valve assy.
11. Spring
12. Diaphragm lever
13. Idle speed screw
14. Choke plate
15. Gasket
16. Metering diaphragm
17. Diaphragm cover
18. Gasket
19. Fuel pump diaphragm
20. Fuel pump valves
21. Pump body
22. Screen
23. Gasket
24. Fuel inlet
25. Governor valve
26. Diaphragm lever pin

OVERHAUL. Since the Model HL carburetor is the most widely used carburetor, overhaul procedures for the Model HL will be covered. Overhaul of Models HC and HJ is similar to the HL carburetor with the exception of the fuel pump. Refer to Figs. CS10 and CS11.

DISASSEMBLY. Clean carburetor and inspect for signs of external damage. Remove idle speed screw and inspect screw, washer and spring. Inspect threads in carburetor body for damage and repair with a Heli-Coil insert, if necessary.

Remove the filter cover, cover gasket, and filter screen. Clean filter screen by flushing with solvent and dry with compressed air. The cover gasket should be renewed whenever filter screen is serviced. Clean all dirt from plastic cover before assembly.

Remove the six body screws, fuel pump cover casting, fuel pump diaphragm and gasket. Diaphragm should be flat and free from holes. The gasket should be renewed if there are holes or creases in the sealing surface.

Remove the diaphragm cover casting, metering diaphragm and diaphragm gasket. Inspect the diaphragm for holes, tears and other imperfections.

Remove the fulcrum pin, inlet control lever and inlet tension spring. Care must be used while removing parts due to spring pressure on inlet control lever. The spring must be handled carefully to prevent stretching or compressing. Any alteration to the spring will cause improper carburetor operation. If in doubt as to its condition, renew it.

Remove inlet needle. Remove inlet seat assembly using a 5/16 inch thin wall socket. Remove the inlet seat gasket.

Inlet needles and seats are in matched sets and should not be interchanged. Needle and seat assembly must be clean for proper performance. Use a new gasket when installing the insert cage. Do not force cage as threads may be stripped or the cage distorted. Use a torque wrench and tighten cage to 25-30 in.-lbs. (2.8-3.4 N·m).

Remove both high speed and idle mixture screws and inspect points. Notice the idle mixture screw point has the step design to minimize point and casting damage. The mixture screws may be damaged from being forced into the casting seat or possibly broken off in the casting. They may be bent. If damage is present be sure to inspect condition of casting. If adjustment seats are damaged, a new body casting is required.

ASSEMBLY. Install the main nozzle ball check valve if this part was found to be defective. Do not overtighten as distortion will result. Install new Welch

plugs if they were removed. Place the new Welch plugs into the casting counterbore with convex side up and flatten it to a tight fit using a 5/16 inch flat end punch. If the installed Welch plug is concave, it may be loose and cause an uncontrolled fuel leak. The correctly installed Welch plug is flat.

Install inlet seat and tighten to 25-30 in.-lbs. (2.8-3.4 N·m). Install inlet needle. Install inlet tension spring, inlet control lever, fulcrum pin and fulcrum pin retaining screw. The inlet control lever must rotate freely on the fulcrum pin. Adjust inlet control lever so the center of the lever that contacts the metering diaphragm is flush to the metering chamber floor as shown in Fig. CS12.

Place metering diaphragm gasket on the body casting. Install metering diaphragm next to gasket. Reinstall diaphragm cover casting over metering diaphragm and gasket. Install pump gasket on diaphragm cover first, then the fuel pump diaphragm should be assembled next to the gasket and the flap valve member next to the fuel pump diaphragm so that the flap valves will seat against the fuel pump cover. Reinstall fuel pump cover and attach with six body screws. The above parts must be assembled in the proper order or the carburetor will not function properly.

Install filter screen on fuel pump cover. Install gasket on filter screen and replace filter cover over filter screen and gasket and attach with center screw.

Install high speed and idle mixture screws in their respective holes being careful not to damage points.

Welch plugs seal the idle bypass ports and main nozzle ball check valve from the metering chamber. Removal of these plugs is seldom necessary because of lack of wear in these sections and any dirt that may accumulate can usually be blown out with compressed air through the mixture screw holes. If removal of the welch plugs is necessary, drill through the Welch plug using a 1/8 inch drill bit. Allow the drill bit to just break through the Welch plug. If the drill bit travels too deep into the cavity, the casting may be ruined. Pry the Welch plug out of its seat using a small punch.

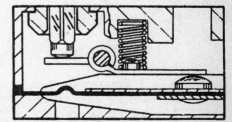

Fig. CS12 — Diaphragm lever should be flush with diaphragm chamber floor.

Inspect the idle bypass holes to ensure they are not plugged. Do not push drill bits or wires in to the metering holes. This may damage the flow characteristics of the holes and damage carburetor performance. Blow out plugged holes with compressed air. Remove main nozzle ball check assembly with a screwdriver of correct blade width. If ball check is defective, engine idling will be hampered unless high speed mixture screw is shut off or there will be poor high speed performance with the high speed mixture screw adjusted at 1¼ turns open. Replace the ball check if defective.

Removing choke and throttle plates before cleaning the body is not necessary if there is no evidence of wear. Indication of wear will require the removal of plates to check the casting. To remove the plates, first mark the position of the plates on their respective shafts to assure correct reassembly. The plates are tapered for exact fit in the carburetor bore. Remove two screws and pull the plate out of the carburetor body. Remove the throttle shaft clip and pull the shaft out of the casting. Examine both the shaft and body bearing areas for wear. Should either part show wear then either the shaft or the body or both will have to be renewed. Remove the choke shaft from the body carefully so the friction ball and spring will not fly out of the casting. Inspect the shaft and bushings for wear.

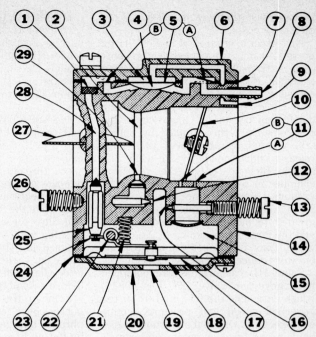

Fig. CS-14 — Cross-sectional view of typical Series HS Tillotson diaphragm type carburetor.

1. Filter screen
2. Venturi
3. Pulse chamber
4. Fuel chamber
5. Pump diaphragm
5A. Inlet valve
5B. Outlet valve
6. Pump body
7. Gasket
8. Inlet fitting
9. Impulse channel
10. Throttle plate
11. Primary (A) & secondary (B) idle ports
12. Main fuel orifice
13. Idle fuel needle
14. Carburetor body
15. Metering chamber
16. Idle fuel orifice
17. Metering diaphragm
18. Atmospheric chamber
19. Vent hole
20. Diaphragm cover
21. Spring
22. Fulcrum pin
23. Gasket
24. Diaphragm lever
25. Inlet valve
26. Main fuel needle
27. Choke disc
28. Inlet channel
29. Main fuel port

Model HK

Tillotson Model HK carburetor is a diaphragm type with an integral diaphragm type fuel pump.

OPERATION. Operation of Tillotson Model HK is basically similar to that described for the Tillotson HL carburetor in preceding section, the main difference being that the Series HK carburetor is a compactly designed unit usually used on lightweight, small displacement engines.

OVERHAUL. Carburetor may be disassembled after inspecting unit and referral to exploded view in Fig. CS13. Clean components using a suitable solvent and compressed air. Do not attempt to clean metered passages with drill bits or wire as carburetor performance may be affected.

Inspect inlet lever spring (20) and renew if stretched or damaged. Inspect diaphragms for tears, cracks or other damage. Renew idle and high speed adjusting needles if needle points are grooved or broken. Carburetor body must be renewed if needle seats are damaged. Fuel inlet needle has a rubber tip and seats directly on a machined orifice in circuit block (19). Inlet needle or circuit block should be renewed if excessively worn.

With circuit block components installed, note height of long end of diaphragm lever (21). Lever end should be flush with chamber floor in circuit block. Bend lever adjacent to spring to obtain correct lever height.

Models HS And HU

Tillotson Model HS and HU carburetors are diaphragm type with integral diaphragm type fuel pumps. Operation and servicing of HS and HU carburetors is similar and covered in the following paragraphs.

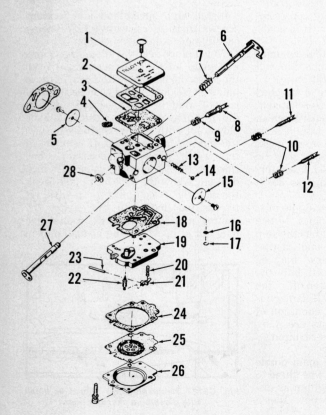

Fig. CS13 — Exploded view of Tillotson Model HK carburetor.

1. Pump cover
2. Gasket
3. Fuel pump diaphragm & valves
4. Screen
5. Throttle plate
6. Throttle shaft
7. Throttle return spring
8. Idle speed screw
9. Spring
10. Spring
11. Idle mixture screw
12. High speed mixture screw
13. Spring
14. Detent ball
15. Choke plate
16. Screen
17. Retainer
18. Gasket
19. Circuit block
20. Spring
21. Diaphragm lever
22. Fuel inlet needle
23. Lever pin
24. Gasket
25. Metering diaphragm
26. Cover
27. Choke shaft
28. "E" ring

OPERATION. In Fig. CS14, a cross-sectional schematic view of a Tillotson Series HS carburetor is shown. Operation is basically similar to that described for the Tillotson HL carburetor in OPERATION section of Models HC, HJ and HL section, the main difference being that the Series HS carburetor is a compactly designed unit usually used on lightweight, small displacement engines. Due to similarity, discussion of operation of HS carburetor will also apply to Model HU. Some Model HS carburetors are equipped with governor valve (26–Fig. CS15) which resonates at a desired engine speed and directs excess fuel into carburetor bore to prevent overspeeding. Governor valve is designed for specific engines and should not be altered.

OVERHAUL. Carburetor may be disassembled after inspecting unit and referring to exploded view in Figs. CS15 or CS16. Clean filter screen (4–Fig. CS17). Welch plugs (Fig. CS18) may be removed by drilling plug with a suitable size drill bit and prying out as shown in Fig. CS19. Care must be taken not to drill into carburetor body. Some HS carburetors are equipped with check valve (29–Fig. CS15) in place of components (16, 17 and 18).

Inspect inlet lever spring (15–Fig. CS15 or 19–Fig. CS16) and renew if stretched or damaged. Inspect diaphragms for tears, cracks or other damage. Renew idle and high speed adjusting needle if needle points are grooved or broken. Carburetor body must be renewed if needle seats are damaged. Fuel inlet needle has a rubber tip and seats directly on a machined orifice in carburetor body. Inlet needle or carburetor body should be renewed if worn excessively.

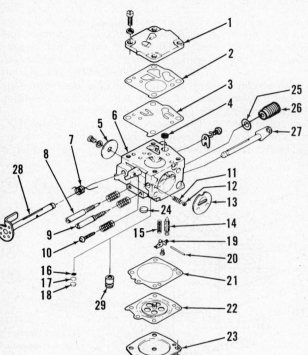

Fig. CS15 — Exploded view of Tillotson Model HS carburetor.

1. Pump cover
2. Gasket
3. Fuel pump diaphragm & valves
4. Screen
5. Throttle plate
6. Body
7. Throttle return spring
8. Idle mixture screw
9. High speed mixture screw
10. Idle speed screw
11. Spring
12. Choke friction ball
13. Choke plate
14. Fuel inlet valve
15. Spring
16. Screen
17. Screen retainer
18. Welch plug
19. Diaphragm lever
20. Lever pin
21. Gasket
22. Metering diaphragm
23. Cover
24. Welch plug
25. Gasket
26. Governor
27. Choke shaft
28. Throttle shaft
29. Check valve

Fig. CS18 — View showing location of Welch plugs (18 & 24 — Fig. CS15).

Fig. CS17 — Be sure to clean filter screen (4 — Fig. CS15 or CS16) when servicing carburetor.

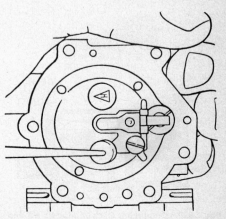

Fig. CS16 — Exploded view of Tillotson Model HU carburetor. Note difference in idle speed screw location used on fuel pump covers (3 and 3A) of some carburetors. Idle speed screw (25) may be located in cover (24).

1. Idle speed screw
2. Friction ball
3. & 3A. Fuel pump cover
4. Screen
5. Gasket
6. Fuel pump diaphragm & valves
7. Throttle plate
8. Return spring
9. Throttle shaft
10. Body
11. "E" ring
12. Idle mixture screw
13. High speed mixture screw
14. Nozzle check valve
15. Screen
16. Retainer
17. Cup plug
18. Fuel inlet valve
19. Spring
20. Diaphragm lever
21. Lever pin
22. Gasket
23. Metering diaphragm
24. Cover
25. Idle speed screw
26. Idle speed screw
27. Welch plug

Fig. CS19 — A punch can be used to remove Welch plugs as shown.

Carburetor may be reassembled by reversing disassembly procedure. Adjust position of inlet control lever so lever is flush with diaphragm chamber floor as shown in Fig. CS20. Bend lever adjacent to spring to obtain correct lever position.

WALBRO

Models HD, HDA, HDB, HDC And SDC

Walbro carburetor Models HD, HDA, HDB, HDC and SDC are diaphragm type carburetors with integral diaphragm type fuel pumps. Some carburetors are also equipped with an accelerator pump. Model number on Model HD, HDA, HDB or HDC carburetor is found on side of carburetor adjacent to fuel mixture adjusting screws. Model number on Model SDC carburetors is stamped on bottom of carburetor.

OPERATION. In Fig. CS21, a cross-sectional schematic view of a Walbro Series SDC carburetor is shown. Operation of Models HD, HDA, HDB and HDC is similar to Model SDC and discussion will also apply to Models HD, HDA, HDB and HDC except for explanation of Model HDC accelerator pump.

Except for some models, Model SDC carburetor is equipped with an accelerator pump. When throttle is open, indexing hole in throttle shaft (25 – Fig. CS21) opens pulse passage (4) to accelerator pump passage (8). Pressure against pump diaphragm (9) compresses spring (10) and pressurizes fuel passage (11), ejecting excess fuel from main nozzle (27). When throttle is closed, or partially closed, indexing hole closes pulse passage and accelerator pump spring returns diaphragm to original position, drawing fuel back up passage (11) to recharge accelerator pump.

At idle speed, air is drawn into carburetor through air bleed hole (13) and mixed with fuel from idle fuel passage in what is called the "emulsion channel." More air enters idle fuel cavity through the two idle holes (24) nearest venturi and the fuel:air mixture is ejected from the third idle hole. Air cannot enter the main fuel nozzle (27) as the check valve (15) closes against its seat when engine is idling. Note that idle fuel supply must first pass main (high speed) metering needle (14) before it reaches idle fuel needle (22).

Model HDC carburetors with accelerator pump, except HDC 70, have a pulse passage (P – Fig. CS22) in carburetor body which allows crankcase pulsations to enter idle fuel circuit. The pulse passage is opened and closed by throttle shaft (S). Passage is closed when throttle is closed and open when throttle is open. When pulse passage is open, crankcase pulsations pass by idle fuel needle (IN) and act directly on fuel in main fuel circuit (MF). If throttle is opened rapidly, engine will tend to "bog" because vacuum in carburetor bore is insufficient to pull fuel from main fuel orifice. Pressure of crankcase pulsations is sufficient to force fuel out main fuel orifice (O) to feed engine and remove bogging tendency. The relative strength of the crankcase pulsations is such that they will affect engine operation only when there is a low vacuum condition such as previously described.

The accelerator pump of Model HDC 70 uses a rubber bladder which accumulates fuel. Fuel in the bladder is

1. Fuel inlet
2. Surge chamber
3. Inlet check valve
4. Crankcase pulse channel
5. Fuel pump diaphragm
6. Outlet check valve
7. Fuel filter
8. Accelerator pulse channel
9. Accelerator diaphragm
10. Accelerator spring
11. Accelerator fuel channel
12. Choke disc
13. Idle air bleed channel
14. Main (high speed) fuel needle
15. Main orifice check valve
16. Inlet needle
17. Metering lever
18. Metering diaphragm
19. Atmospheric vent
20. Metering diaphragm spring
21. Idle fuel channel
22. Idle fuel needle
23. Idle fuel passage
24. Idle air and fuel holes
25. Throttle shaft
26. Throttle disc
27. Main fuel orifice

Fig. CS21 – Cross-sectional schematic view of Walbro Series SDC carburetor with accelerator pump. Some models are not equipped with accelerator pump and passages (8 and 11) are plugged. Fuel cavity above metering diaphragm extends to cavity shown at tip of main fuel needle (14).

Fig. CS20 – Diaphragm lever on Models HS and HU should be flush with diaphragm chamber floor as shown above.

Fig. CS22 – Cross-sectional view of Walbro Model HDC carburetor showing accelerator pump pulse passage (P). Refer to text for operation.

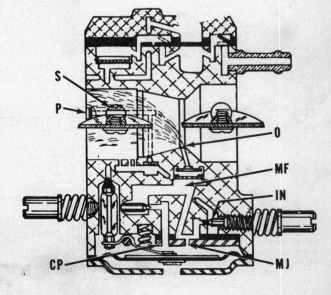

ejected through the main fuel orifice when low vacuum occurs in the carburetor bore. Operation is similar to SDC carburetor previously described.

Model HDC circuit plate (CP–Fig. CS22) may have a hole (MJ) to serve as main jet. High speed adjustment needle on these models is used only to enrich high speed mixture. Main fuel supply is fully adjustable with high speed adjustment needle on all other models as hole (MJ) is nonexistent.

OVERHAUL. Carburetor may be disassembled after inspection of unit and referral to exploded views in Figs. CS23, CS24, CS25 or CS26. Care should be taken not to lose ball and spring which will be released when choke shaft is withdrawn.

Clean and inspect all components. Inspect diaphragms for defects which may affect operation. Examine fuel inlet needle and seat. Inlet needle is renewable, but carburetor body must be renewed if needle seat is excessively worn or damaged. Sharp objects should not be used to clean orifices or passages as fuel flow may be altered. Compressed air should not be used to clean main nozzle as check valve may be damaged. A check valve repair kit is available to renew a damaged valve. Fuel mixture needles must be renewed if grooved or broken.

Inspect mixture needle seats in carburetor body and renew body if seats are damaged or excessively worn. Screens should be clean.

To reassemble carburetor, reverse disassembly procedure. Fuel metering lever should be flush with a straightedge laid across carburetor body of Model

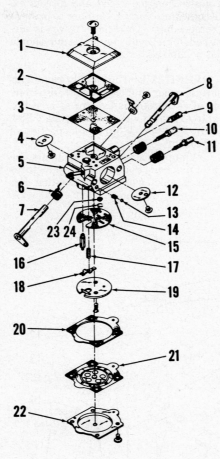

Fig. CS24 — Exploded view of Walbro Model HDB and HDC carburetors.

1. Pump cover
2. Gasket
3. Fuel pump diaphragm & valves
4. Throttle plate
5. Body
6. Return spring
7. Throttle shaft
8. Choke shaft
9. Idle speed screw
10. Idle mixture screw
11. High speed mixture screw
12. Choke plate
13. Choke friction ball
14. Spring
15. Gasket
16. Fuel inlet valve
17. Spring
18. Diaphragm lever
19. Circuit plate
20. Gasket
21. Metering diaphragm
22. Cover
23. Check valve screen
24. Retainer

Fig. CS23 — Exploded view of Walbro Model HD and Model HDA carburetor.

1. Cover
2. Metering diaphragm
3. Gasket
4. Circuit plate
5. Gasket
6. Diaphragm lever
7. Pin
8. Fuel inlet valve
9. Spring
10. Retainer
11. Check valve screen
12. Choke friction ball
13. Spring
14. Body
15. Throttle shaft
16. Throttle plate
17. Return spring
18. Fuel inlet
19. High speed mixture screw
20. Low speed mixture screw
21. Idle speed screw
22. Choke plate
23. Choke shaft
24. Throttle stop
25. Fuel inlet screen
26. Fuel pump diaphragm & valves
27. Gasket
28. Pump cover

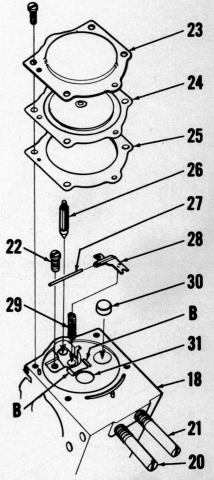

Fig. CS25 — Exploded view of metering diaphragm assembly used on Walbro Model SDC. Refer to Fig. CS26 for other carburetor components.

B. Bosses
18. Body
20. High speed mixture screw
21. Idle mixture screw
22. Lever pin screw
23. Cover
24. Diaphragm
25. Gasket
26. Fuel inlet valve
27. Lever pin
28. Diaphragm lever
29. Spring
30. Idle passage plug
31. Main channel plug

HDA, HDB or HDC as shown in Fig. CS27. On Model SDC, lever should be flush with bosses (B—Fig. CS28) on chamber floor. Be sure lever spring correctly contacts locating dimple on lever before measuring lever height. Bend lever to obtain correct lever height.

Models WA, WB, WJ, WS And WT

Walbro carburetor Models WA, WB, WJ, WS and WT are diaphragm type carburetors with integral fuel pumps.

OPERATION. Operation of WA, WB, WJ, WS or WT carburetors is similar to Walbro SDC carburetor discussed in preceding section although an accelerator pump is not used. Model WJ and some Model WS carburetors are equipped with governor valve (13—Fig. CS31 and Fig. CS32) which resonates at a desired engine speed and directs excess fuel into carburetor bore to prevent overspeeding. Governor valve is designed for specific engines and should not be altered.

OVERHAUL. Thoroughly clean carburetor prior to disassembly. Disassembly of carburetor is evident after referral to exploded view (Figs. CS29, CS30, CS31, CS32 or CS35) and inspection of carburetor.

Clean and inspect all components. Inspect metering diaphragm for punctures or tears which may affect operation. Ex-

amine fuel inlet needle and seat. Inlet needle is renewable, but carburetor body must be renewed if needle seat is excessively worn or damaged. Sharp objects should not be used to clean orifices or passages as fuel flow may be altered. Fuel mixture needles must be renewed if grooved or broken. Inspect mixture needle seats in carburetor body and renew body if seats are damaged or excessively worn. Fuel screen should be cleaned. On WS and WT models, do not direct compressed air through main nozzle check valve (18—Fig. CS32 or CS35) as check valve will be damaged.

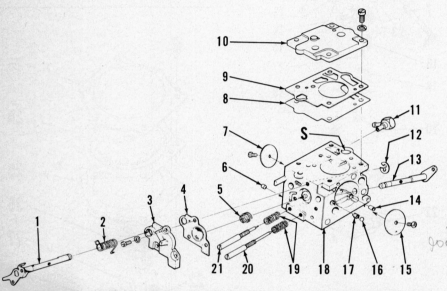

Fig. CS26—Exploded view of Walbro Model SDC carburetor with accelerator pump assembly. Refer to Fig. CS25 for metering diaphragm assembly.

S. Fuel screen	6. Limiting plug	17. Spring
1. Throttle shaft	7. Throttle plate	18. Body
2. Return spring	8. Fuel pump diaphragm	19. Springs
3. Pump cover	9. Gasket	20. High speed mixture screw
4. Accelerator	10. Pump cover	21. Idle mixture screw
5. Spring	11. Elbow fitting	
	12. "E" ring	
	13. Choke shaft	
	14. Idle air jet	
	15. Choke plate	
	16. Detent ball	

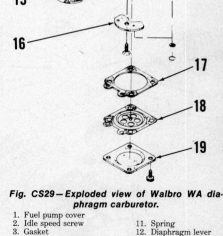

Fig. CS29—Exploded view of Walbro WA diaphragm carburetor.

1. Fuel pump cover	
2. Idle speed screw	11. Spring
3. Gasket	12. Diaphragm lever
4. Fuel pump diaphragm	13. Pin
5. Throttle plate	14. Gasket
6. Throttle shaft	15. Circuit plate diaphragm
7. Idle mixture screw	16. Circuit plate
8. High speed mixture screw	17. Gasket
9. Springs	18. Metering diaphragm
10. Fuel inlet valve	19. Cover

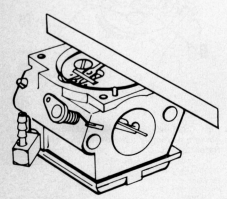

Fig. CS27—Diaphragm lever on Model HDB or HDC should just touch a straightedge laid on carburetor body as shown.

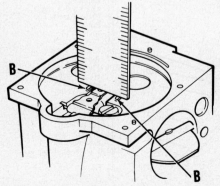

Fig. CS28—Diaphragm lever on Model SDC should just touch straightedge placed on bosses (B) adjacent to lever.

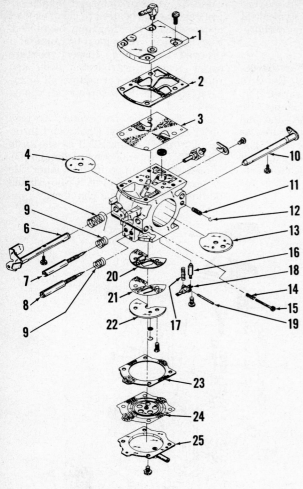

1. Fuel pump cover
2. Gasket
3. Diaphragm
4. Throttle plate
5. Spring
6. Throttle shaft
7. Idle mixture screw
8. High speed mixture screw
9. Springs
10. Choke shaft
11. Spring
12. Choke friction ball
13. Choke plate
14. Spring
15. Idle speed screw
16. Fuel inlet valve
17. Spring
18. Diaphragm lever
19. Pin
20. Gasket
21. Circuit plate valve
22. Circuit plate
23. Gasket
24. Metering diaphragm
25. Cover

To reassemble carburetor, reverse order of disassembly. On Models WA, WJ and WS, fuel metering lever should be flush with circuit plate as shown in Fig. CS33. On Model WT, fuel metering lever should be flush with carburetor body. To measure height of fuel metering lever on Model WB, lay a straight-edge across carburetor body with diaphragm gasket removed. Gap between fuel metering lever and straightedge should be 3/64-1/16 inch (1.2-1.6 mm) (See Fig. CS34). Gently bend lever to obtain desired lever height.

Model MDC

Walbro carburetor Model MDC is a diaphragm type carburetor with an integral fuel pump.

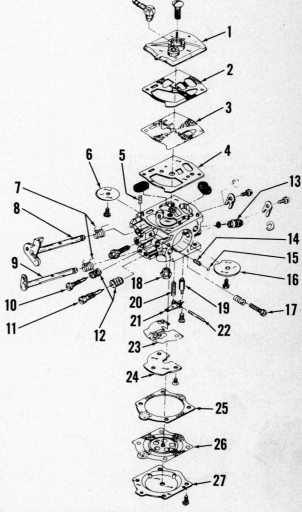

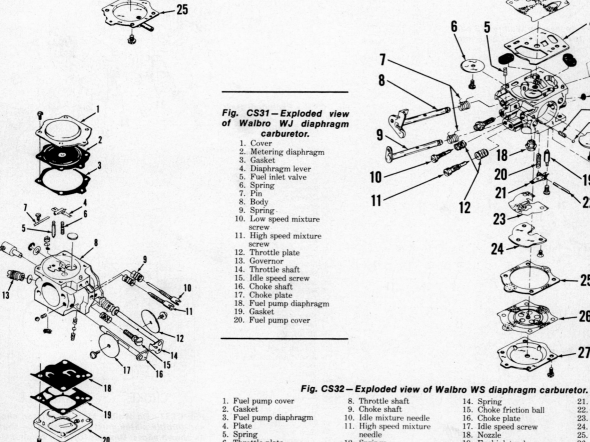

Fig. CS31 — Exploded view of Walbro WJ diaphragm carburetor.

1. Cover
2. Metering diaphragm
3. Gasket
4. Diaphragm lever
5. Fuel inlet valve
6. Spring
7. Pin
8. Body
9. Spring
10. Low speed mixture screw
11. High speed mixture screw
12. Throttle plate
13. Governor
14. Throttle shaft
15. Idle speed screw
16. Choke shaft
17. Choke plate
18. Fuel pump diaphragm
19. Gasket
20. Fuel pump cover

Fig. CS32 — Exploded view of Walbro WS diaphragm carburetor.

1. Fuel pump cover	8. Throttle shaft	14. Spring	21. Diaphragm lever
2. Gasket	9. Choke shaft	15. Choke friction ball	22. Pin
3. Fuel pump diaphragm	10. Idle mixture needle	16. Choke plate	23. Gasket
4. Plate	11. High speed mixture needle	17. Idle speed screw	24. Circuit plate
5. Spring	12. Springs	18. Nozzle	25. Gasket
6. Throttle plate	13. Governor	19. Fuel inlet valve	26. Metering diaphragm
7. Springs		20. Spring	27. Cover

Fig. CS33 — Diaphragm lever on Walbro WA, WJ and WS carburetors should be flush with circuit plate.

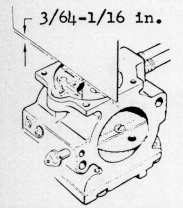

Fig. CS34 — Diaphragm lever on Walbro WB carburetor should be 3/64 to 1/16 inch (1.2-1.6 mm) from carburetor body.

OPERATION. Operation of Walbro carburetor Model MDC is typical of other Walbro diaphragm type carburetors.

OVERHAUL. Clean carburetor externally prior to disassembly. Refer to Fig. CS36 and disassemble carburetor. Clean and inspect all components. Inspect metering diaphragm (22) and fuel pump diaphragm (25) for punctures or tears which may affect operation. Examine fuel inlet valve (19) and seat. Inlet valve is renewable, but carburetor body must be renewed if valve seat is excessively worn or damaged. Sharp objects should not be used to clean orifices or passages as fuel flow may be altered. Fuel mixture screws must be renewed if grooved or broken. Inspect mixture screw seats in carburetor body and renew body if seats are damaged or excessively worn. Fuel screen (29) should be cleaned.

To reassemble carburetor, reverse order of disassembly. Choke and throttle plate must be installed as shown in Fig. CS37. Note location of dimple (D). Dimple must be in position on inner side of plate. Lever (17–Fig. CS36) should be flush with metering chamber.

Fig. CS36 — Exploded view of Walbro MDC carburetor.

1. Spring
2. Idle speed screw
3. Idle mixture screw
4. High speed mixture screw
5. Spring
6. Choke shaft
7. Throttle shaft
8. Throttle plate
9. Choke plate
10. Choke friction ball
11. Spring
12. Valve
13. Seat
14. Plug
15. Plug
16. Spring
17. Fuel inlet lever
18. Lever pin
19. Inlet needle valve
20. Screw
21. Gasket
22. Diaphragm
23. Fuel pump body
24. Gasket
25. Diaphragm
26. Cover
27. Vent screen
28. Retainer
29. Inlet screen

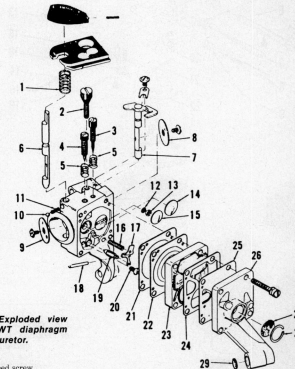

Fig. CS35 — Exploded view of Walbro WT diaphragm carburetor.

1. Cover
2. Spring
3. Idle speed screw
4. Diaphragm
5. Gasket
6. Diaphragm
7. Screen
8. Governor
9. Spring
10. Bushing
11. Choke shaft
12. Spring
13. Ball
14. Choke plate
15. Spring
16. Inlet needle valve
17. Plug
18. Seat
19. Metering lever
20. Pin
21. Spring
22. High speed screw
23. Low speed screw
24. Spring
25. Spring
26. Throttle shaft
27. Accelerator diaphragm
28. Washer
29. Spring
30. Plug
31. Screen
32. Spring
33. "O" ring
34. Piston
35. Throttle plate
36. Gasket
37. Metering diaphragm
38. Cover

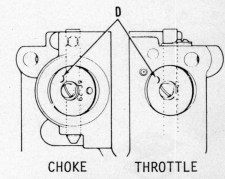

Fig. CS37 — On Walbro MDC carburetor, choke and throttle plates must be installed on shafts as shown above. Dimples (D) must be on inside of plate.

ZAMA

Models C1, C1S, C2, C2S, C3A M1, Z1 And Z1A

Zama carburetor Models, C1, C1S, C2, C2S, C3A, M1, Z1 and Z1A are diaphragm type carburetors with integral fuel pumps.

OPERATION. Operation of Zama carburetor Models C1, C1S, C2, C2S, C3A, M1, Z1 and Z1A is typical of other diaphragm type carburetors.

OVERHAUL. Clean carburetor externally prior to disassembly. Refer to appropriate exploded view and disassemble carburetor. Clean and inspect all components. Inspect metering

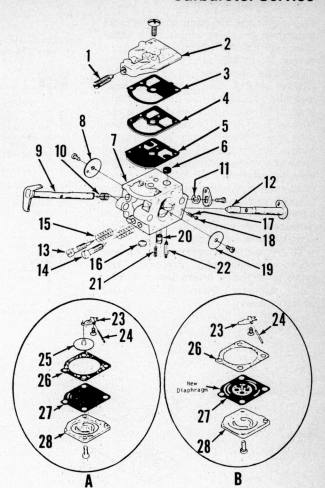

Fig. CS40—Exploded view of Zama C1S carburetor. Note differences in diaphragm assembly. "A" shows the old type diaphragm assembly and "B" shows the new type diaphragm assembly.

1. Idle speed screw
2. Fuel pump cover
3. Gasket
4. Plate
5. Fuel pump diaphragm
6. Screen
7. Body
8. Throttle plate
9. Throttle shaft
10. Spring
11. "E" clip
12. Choke shaft
13. Idle mixture screw
14. High speed mixture screw
15. Spring
16. Plug
17. Spring
18. Detent ball
19. Choke plate
20. Check valve
21. Spring
22. Fuel inlet valve
23. Metering lever
24. Pin
25. Metering disc
26. Gasket
27. Metering diaphragm
28. Cover

Fig. CS39—Exploded view of Zama C1 carburetor.

1. Cover
2. Metering diaphragm
3. Gasket
4. Welch plug
5. Check valve nozzle assy.
6. Screen
7. Metering lever
8. Pin
9. Spring
10. Body
11. Spring
12. Spring
13. High speed mixture screw
14. Low speed mixture screw
15. Throttle shaft
16. Return spring
17. "E" clip
18. Throttle plate
19. Fuel pump diaphragm & check valves
20. Gasket
21. Fuel pump cover
22. Fuel inlet valve
23. Idle speed screw

Fig. CS41—Exploded view of Zama C2 carburetor.

1. Cover
2. Metering diaphragm
3. Gasket
4. Pin
5. Screw
6. Screen
7. Metering lever
8. Spring
9. Check valve nozzle assy.
10. Choke shaft
11. Welch plug
12. "E" clip
13. High speed mixture screw
14. Low speed mixture screw
15. Choke plate
16. Ball
17. Spring
18. Spring
19. Spring
20. Throttle shaft
21. Return spring
22. Fuel inlet valve
23. Throttle plate
24. Fuel pump diaphragm & check valves
25. Plate
26. Gasket
27. Fuel pump cover
28. Body

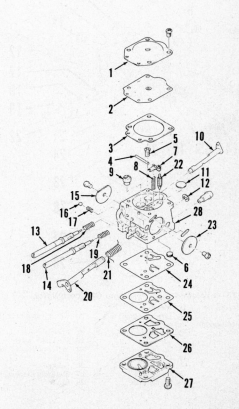

diaphragm and fuel pump diaphragm for punctures or tears which may affect operation. On early model carburetors, except Model M1, note the new design diaphragm assembly (B–Fig. CS40). Always install the new diaphragm assembly. Examine fuel inlet valve and seat. Inlet valve is renewable, but carburetor body must be renewed if valve seat is excessively worn or damaged. Sharp objects should not be used to clean orifices or passages as fuel flow may be altered. Fuel mixture screws must be renewed if grooved or broken. Inspect mixture screw seats in carburetor body and renew body if seats are damaged or excessively worn. Fuel screen should be cleaned.

To reassemble carburetor, reverse order of disassembly. Note the two types of metering levers shown in Fig. CS46. Adjust clearance "A" to 0-0.012 inch (0-0.3 mm).

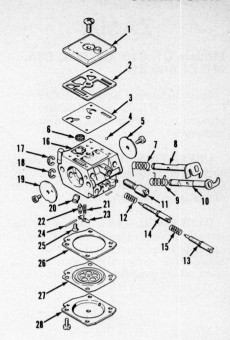

Fig. CS43 — Exploded view of Zama C3A carburetor.

1. Fuel pump cover
2. Gasket
3. Fuel pump diaphragm & check valves
4. Ball
5. Throttle plate
6. Screen
7. Return spring
8. Throttle shaft
9. Return spring
10. Choke shaft
11. Idle speed screw
12. Spring
13. High speed mixture screw
14. Low speed mixture screw
15. Spring
16. Body
17. "E" clip
18. "E" clip
19. Choke plate
20. Check valve nozzle assy.
21. Spring
22. Fuel inlet valve
23. Metering lever
24. Pin
25. Screw
26. Gasket
27. Metering diaphragm
28. Cover

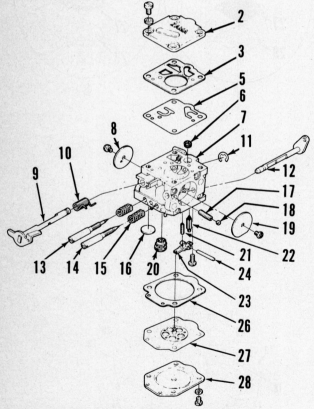

Fig. CS42 — Exploded view of Zama C2S carburetor.

2. Fuel pump cover	12. Choke shaft	20. Check valve nozzle assy.
3. Gasket	13. Low speed mixture screw	21. Spring
5. Fuel pump diaphragm & check valves	14. High speed mixture screw	22. Fuel inlet valve
6. Screen	15. Spring	23. Metering lever
7. Body	16. Plug	24. Pin
8. Throttle plate	17. Spring	26. Gasket
9. Throttle shaft	18. Check ball	27. Metering diaphragm
10. Spring	19. Choke plate	28. Cover
11. "E" clip		

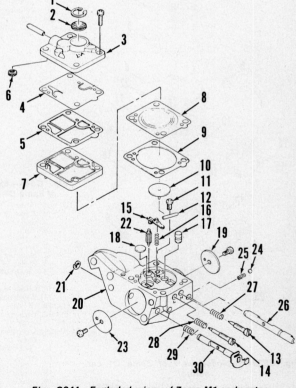

Fig. CS44 — Exploded view of Zama M1 carburetor.

1. Snap ring	12. Pin	21. "E" clip
2. Screen	13. High speed mixture screw	22. Fuel inlet valve
3. Fuel pump cover	14. Low speed mixture screw	23. Throttle plate
4. Fuel pump diaphragm & check valves	15. Metering lever	24. Ball
5. Gasket	16. Spring	25. Spring
6. Screen	17. Check valve nozzle assy.	26. Choke shaft
7. Metering block	18. Welch plug	27. Spring
8. Metering diaphragm	19. Choke plate	28. Spring
9. Gasket	20. Body	29. Return spring
10. Disc		30. Throttle shaft
11. Screw		

Fig. CS45 — Exploded view of Zama Z1 and Z1A carburetor.

1. Fuel pump cover
2. Idle speed screw
3. Plate
4. Gasket
5. Fuel pump diaphragm & check valves
6. Screen
7. Body
8. Throttle shaft
9. Return spring
10. Throttle plate
11. Spring
12. Spring
13. High speed mixture screw
14. Low speed mixture screw
15. Collar
16. Retainer
17. Welch plug
18. Spring
19. Screw
20. Metering lever
21. Pin
22. Fuel inlet valve
23. Gasket
24. Metering diaphragm
25. Cover

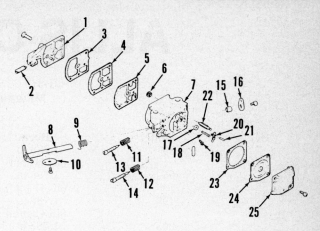

Fig. CS46 — Note position of metering lever in the different carburetor castings. Metering lever in right view must be flush as shown. Adjust metering lever in left view so distance "A" is 0.000-0.012 inch (0.0.3 mm).

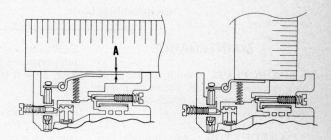

ALLIS-CHALMERS

DEUTZ-ALLIS
P.O. Box 512
Milwaukee, Wisconsin 53201

Model	Bore	Stroke	Displ.	Drive Type
85	1.788 in.	1.437 in.	3.6 cu. in.	Gear*
	(45.41 mm)	(36.49 mm)	(59 cc)	
95	1.788 in.	1.437 in.	3.6 cu. in.	Direct
	(45.41 mm)	(36.49 mm)	(59 cc)	
195	1.788 in.	1.437 in.	3.6 cu. in.	Direct
	(45.41 mm)	(36.49 mm)	(59 cc)	
295	1.788 in.	1.437 in.	3.6 cu. in.	Direct
	(45.41 mm)	(36.49 mm)	(59 cc)	

*Reciprocating blade.

MAINTENANCE

SPARK PLUG. Recommended spark plug is Champion CJ8. Spark plug electrode gap should be 0.025 inch (0.63 mm).

CARBURETOR. All models are equipped with a Tillotson Model HS diaphragm carburetor. Initial idle and high speed mixture settings are one turn open. Adjust idle speed screw so that engine idles at engine speed just below clutch engagement speed. Adjust idle mixture screw so that engine will accelerate without lagging or faltering. Adjust high speed mixture screw to give optimum performance under cutting load. It may be necessary to readjust idle mixture screw after adjusting high speed screw. Be sure mixture settings are not too lean as engine damage may result.

Refer to Tillotson section of CARBURETOR SERVICE section for carburetor operation and overhaul.

MAGNETO AND TIMING. A flywheel magneto is used on all models. Breaker point gap should be 0.015 inch (0.38 mm) for Model 95 and 0.017 inch (0.43 mm) for all other models. Ignition timing is fixed but incorrect breaker point gap will affect timing. Magneto air gap should be 0.012 inch (0.30 mm).

LUBRICATION. All engines are lubricated by mixing oil with fuel. Fuel:oil ratio is 16:1. Oil should be a good quality SAE 30 oil designed for chain saw or air-cooled two-stroke engines.

All models are equipped with a manual chain oiler except Model 85 which is equipped with a blade in place of the chain. Models 195 and 295 are also equipped with an automatic chain oiler. Fill oil reservoir with a good quality

SAE 30 Service MS oil if ambient temperature is above 40°F (4°C) or SAE 10W if temperature is below 40°F (4°C).

CARBON. Carbon deposits should be removed from muffler and exhaust ports at regular intervals. When scraping carbon, be careful not to damage engine cylinder. Do not allow loosened carbon to enter cylinder.

REPAIRS

CYLINDER. All models are equipped with a chrome plated cylinder. Renew

Fig. A1 — Exploded view of Model 95 engine. Refer to Fig. A2 for parts identification except: 26. Muffler; 27. Muffler Baffle; 28. Cover.

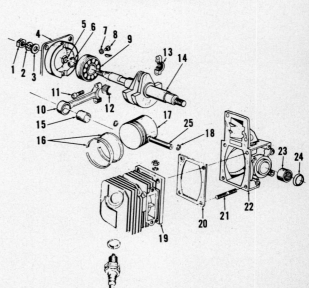

Fig. A2 — Exploded view of engine used on Models 85, 195 and 295. Carrier (4) is a partial view of rear of bearing carrier (15 — Fig. A6).

1. Nut
2. Lockwasher
3. Washer
4. Bearing carrier
5. Seal
6. Snap ring
7. Washer
8. Cap screw
9. Bearing
10. Connecting rod
11. Socket head screw
12. Bearing rollers (25)
13. Rod cap
14. Crankshaft
15. Bearing
16. Piston rings
17. Piston
18. Snap ring
19. Cylinder
20. Gasket
21. Stud
22. Crankcase
23. Bearing
24. Seal
25. Piston pin

cylinder if cylinder is scored, cracked or excessively worn. Only standard size piston and rings are available.

PISTON, PIN AND RINGS. All models are equipped with two piston rings. Piston rings are retained by pins in ring grooves and must be aligned with pins when cylinder is installed. Install piston so ring locating pins are on magneto side of engine. Piston wrist pin has one closed end, which must be towards exhaust port. Heat piston to about 200°F (93°C) to aid in pin installation. Piston pin snap rings should be installed so sharp edge is out.

Pistons and rings are available in standard size only. Manufacturer does not specify piston or piston ring clearances.

CONNECTING ROD. Connecting rod may be removed after removing cylinder and piston. Unscrew connecting rod screws and remove rod and cap being careful not to lose loose bearing rollers. There are 25 bearing rollers in Model 85, 95, 195 and 295 connecting rod. Connecting rod small end bearing must be pressed out of rod. Be sure rod is properly supported when removing or installing bearing.

Use heavy grease to hold roller bearings in rod and cap. Match marks on sides of rod and cap must be aligned during installation.

CRANKSHAFT AND CRANK-CASE. Crankshaft is supported in antifriction bearings at both ends. Flywheel end of crankshaft on Model 95 is supported by a needle roller bearing (23 – Fig. A1) in the crankcase while a ball bearing (9 – Fig. A2) contained in bearing carrier (4) is used to support flywheel end of crankshaft on all other models. Clutch end of crankshaft on Model 95 is supported by a ball bearing (3 – Fig. A3) in bearing carrier (7) while a needle roller bearing (23 – Fig. A2) in crankcase (22) supports clutch end of crankshaft on all other models.

Fuel, oil, ignition, starter and clutch assemblies must be removed from engine to remove crankshaft. Remove cylinder piston and connecting rod. On Models 85, 195 and 295, remove bearing carrier (4 – Fig. A2), bearing (9) and crankshaft (14) from crankcase. Unscrew retaining cap screws (8) and separate bearing (9) and crankshaft from carrier (4). Remove snap ring (6) and pull bearing (9) off crankshaft. To remove crankshaft on Model 95, unscrew bearing carrier (7 – Fig. A3) screws and remove bearing carrier and crankshaft from crankcase. Remove crankshaft from bearing (3). Unscrew two retaining screws (1) and separate

bearing from carrier (7). To reassemble, reverse disassembly procedure. Install ball bearing with groove in outer race adjacent to crankshaft counterweight. Bearing holder (4 – Fig. A2) and bearing carrier (7 – Fig. A3) must be heated to 200°F (93°C) before installing bearing.

CLUTCH. Clutch hub is equipped with left hand threads. Clutch hub bearing is available for all models. Refer to Figs. A3, A4 or A7 for exploded view of clutch.

REED VALVE. All models are equipped with reed valve induction with four reed petals on a pyramid reed cage. Inspect reed valve for nicks, chips or burrs. Be sure reed petal lays flat against seat.

AUTOMATIC CHAIN OILER. Models 195 and 295 are equipped with an automatic chain oiler. Oil pump is driven by cam (18 – Fig. A4) on engine crankshaft. Inspect bronze gear (19) and renew if gear teeth are broken or ex-

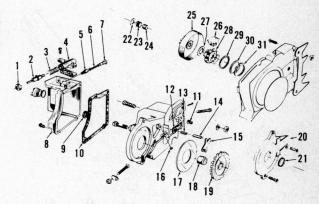

Fig. A3 – Exploded view of clutch and bearing housing carrier used on Model 95.

1. Cap screw
2. Washer
3. Bearing
4. "O" ring
5. Oil line
6. Oil fitting
7. Bearing housing carrier
8. Oil line
9. Seal
10. Sleeve
11. Clutch cover
12. Clutch shoe
13. Clutch hub
14. Spring
15. Thrust washer
16. Bearing race
17. Clutch drum
18. Bearing
19. Washer
20. Washer
21. Nut

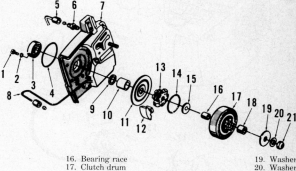

Fig. A4 – Exploded view of Model 195 and Model 295 manual and automatic oil pump and clutch assemblies.

1. Plunger
2. Plunger rod
3. Spring
4. Manual oil pump housing
5. Intake valve
6. Spring
7. Oil pump button
8. Oil tank
9. Gasket
10. Gasket
11. Oil outlet valve
12. Washer
13. Spring
14. Piston
15. Lever
16. Quad ring
17. Disc.
18. Cam
19. Gear
20. Automatic oil pump cover
21. Seal
22. Thrust washer
23. Bearing
24. Bearing race
25. Clutch drum
26. Clutch shoe
27. Thrust washer
28. Clutch hub
29. Clutch spring
30. Retaining ring
31. Spirolox

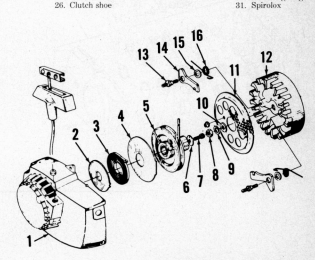

Fig. A5 – Exploded view of Model 95 rewind starter.

1. Starter housing
2. Spring plate
3. Rewind spring
4. Spring cover
5. Rope pulley
6. Washer
7. Screw
8. Flywheel nut
9. Lockwasher
10. Washer
11. Flywheel cover
12. Flywheel
13. Stud
14. Starter dog
15. Washer
16. Spring

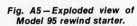

cessively worn. If button on lever (15) is worn, renew lever. Pack oil pump cavity with a suitable grease before reassembly. Install seal (21) in cover and carefully install cam (18) in seal with

step of cam towards seal until seal seats against shoulder of cam. Be careful not to damage seal. Install pump lever (15) in cover and gear (19) on cam (18). Place thrust washer (12), spring (13), piston

(14) and quad ring (16). Install cover (20) and pump components in cover on crankshaft.

REWIND STARTER. Refer to Figs. A5 and A6 for exploded views of rewind starters. Rewind spring on Model 95 should be wound in clockwise direction when viewed installed in housing. Rewind spring should be wound in counterclockwise direction on Models 85, 195 and 295. Starter rope on Model 95 should be wound on a rope pulley in clockwise direction when viewed installed in starter housing. Starter rope should be wound in counterclockwise direction on Models 85, 195 and 295. Turn rope pulley sufficient turns to place tension on rewind spring before passing rope through outlet so rope will rewind into housing.

TRANSMISSION. Model 85 is equipped with a transmission to drive the saw blade. To disassemble transmission, remove blade, clutch cover and clutch. Remove snap ring (21–Fig. A7) and unscrew transmission cover (22) screws. Remove cover and inspect bearings (24), bearing (27) and seal (25) for wear or damage. Remove snap ring (17). If plunger (14) is to be removed, remove cap (34) and withdraw plunger. Remove screws retaining guide (13) and withdraw transmission assembly. Disassembly of remainder of transmission is self-evident.

Inspect components for wear or damage. Counterweight (10) and counterweight rod (12) are available only as a unit assembly. To reassemble, reverse disassembly procedure and note the following:

Forty needle rollers are used between counterweight rod (12) and driven gear (20). Hold rollers in place with heavy grease. Recess on counterweight rod (12) should be adjacent to gear (20). Note difference in seal (35 and 36) assembly between early and late models. Earlier models used three seals (35) and a metal retainer (36). Later models use two interlocking type seals and a metal back seal. Interlocking seals should have lips inward while metal back seal should have lip out. Install metal back seal so it stands out from housing about 1/16 inch (1.58 mm). Early models should have later seal assembly installed. Install seal (25) so metal back stands out 1/32 inch (0.79 mm) from outside of housing.

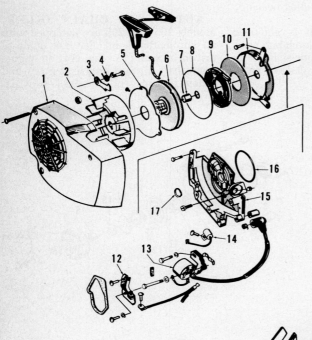

Fig. A6—Exploded view of recoil starter and ignition assembly used on Models 85, 195 and 295.

1. Fan housing
2. Flywheel
3. Starter dog
4. Spring
5. Plate
6. Rope pulley
7. Bearing
8. Spring plate
9. Rewind spring
10. Spring plate
11. Starter housing
12. Breaker-points
13. Coil & armature
14. Condenser
15. Side cover
16. "O" ring
17. Seal

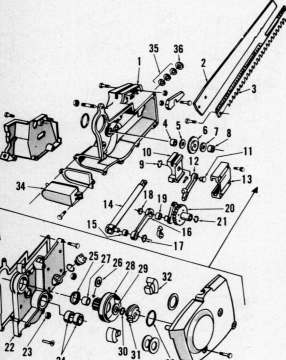

Fig. A7—Exploded view of gear drive assembly used on Model 85. Later models use interlocking seals and a metal back seal in place of seals (35) and retainer (36) shown. Refer to text.

1. Housing
2. Bar
3. Blade
4. Bearing
5. Washer
6. Idler gear
7. Washer
8. Bearing
9. Snap ring
10. Counterweight
11. Pin
12. Counterweight rod
13. Retaining guide
14. Plunger
15. Bearing
16. Connecting rod
17. Snap ring
18. Snap ring
19. Bearing
20. Driven gear
21. Snap ring
22. Cover
23. Nut
24. Bearings
25. Seal
26. Washer
27. Bearing
28. Clutch drum
29. Washer
28. Clutch drum
29. Washer
30. Seal
31. Clutch hub
32. Clutch shoe
33. Clutch spring
34. Cap
35. Seals
36. Retainer

ALLIS-CHALMERS

Model	Bore	Stroke	Displ.	Drive Type
65	1.375 in. (32.92 mm)	1.250 in. (31.75 mm)	1.86 cu. in. (30.5 cc)	Direct

MAINTENANCE

SPARK PLUG. Recommended spark plug is Champion CJ8. Spark plug electrode gap should be 0.025 inch (0.63 mm).

CARBURETOR. Model 65 is equipped with a Tillotson Model HU diaphragm carburetor. Refer to Tillotson section of CARBURETOR SERVICE section for exploded view and service of carburetor.

Initial adjustment of idle mixture screw is one turn open. Carburetor has a fixed main fuel jet so high speed fuel mixture is not adjustable. Adjust idle mixture screw so that engine will accelerate without faltering. Adjust idle speed screw so engine idles just below clutch engagement speed.

MAGNETO AND TIMING. A flywheel magneto is used. The ignition coil is located adjacent to the flywheel while the breaker-points are located on the right crankcase half.

Breaker-point gap should be 0.020-0.022 inch (0.51-0.56 mm) for new points and 0.017 inch (0.43 mm) for used points. Ignition timing is not adjustable and breaker-point gap must be set correctly or ignition timing will be affected. Air gap between coil legs and flywheel should be 0.010 inch (0.25 mm).

LUBRICATION. The engine is lubricated by mixing oil with fuel. Recommended fuel:oil ratio is 16:1. Oil should be a good quality oil designed for use in chain saws or air-cooled two-stroke engines. Regular gasoline is recommended.

Model 65 is equipped with a manual and automatic chain oil pumps. The manual oil pump is operated by pushing plunger (18–Fig. A10). The automatic oil pump is operated by crankcase pulsations through impulse line (10). Check valve (11) in end of impulse line (10) prevents entrance of oil into crankcase. Check valve must be located in slot just forward of filler hole in upper part of oil tank to prevent immersion of check valve in oil. Automatic oil pump (14) is available only as a unit assembly.

REPAIRS

CYLINDER, PISTON, PIN AND RINGS. Cylinder can be removed after detaching fan housing, flywheel, carburetor, front handle, chain bar and muffler. Care must be used when handling piston and rod assembly to prevent rod from slipping off bearing rollers (12–Fig. A11) as rollers may fall into crankcase.

Cylinder has a chrome bore which should be inspected for flaking, scoring or other damage. Be sure piston is properly supported when removing piston pin to prevent damage to connecting rod. Piston pin rides directly in connecting rod. Check fit by inserting piston pin in small end of connecting rod and renew pin and rod if excessively worn. Tighten cylinder base nuts evenly to 100-110 in.-lbs. (11.3-12.4 N·m).

CONNECTING ROD, CRANKSHAFT AND CRANKCASE. Connecting rod is one-piece and rides on 12 loose bearing rollers (12-Fig. A11). Be careful not to lose any loose bearing rollers during diassembly. Bearing rollers can be removed after rod is slid off rollers. Bearing rollers may be held in place with petroleum jelly or heavy grease when installing connecting rod.

The crankshaft is supported by a needle roller bearing at each end. Install bearings so end of bearing is

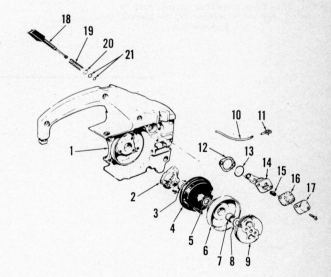

Fig. A10—Exploded view of right crankcase half.

1. Right crankcase half
2. Ignition breaker points
3. Seal
4. Breaker point cover
5. Spacer
6. Clutch drum
7. Bushing
8. Washer
9. Clutch assy.
10. Impulse line
11. Check valve
12. Gasket
13. "O" ring
14. Automatic oil pump
15. Filter
16. Gasket
17. Cover
18. Manual oil pump plunger
19. Spring
20. Washer
21. "O" rings

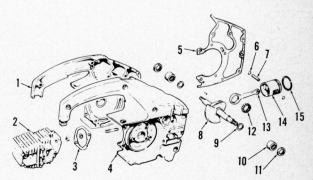

Fig. A11—Exploded view of engine.

1. Left crankcase half
2. Cylinder
3. Gasket
4. Right crankcase half
5. Gasket
6. Pin retainer
7. Piston pin
8. Crankshaft
9. Washer
10. Needle roller bearing
11. Seal
12. Bearing rollers (12)
13. Connecting rod
14. Piston
15. Piston ring

0.6225-0.6265 inch (15.81-15.91 mm) from machined gasket surface. Washer (9–Fig. A11) must be installed with beveled edge nearest crankpin. Ignition coil-to-breaker point wire must be routed through crankcase halves and trigger assembly installed before crankcase impulse line and fuel pickup lines are properly located and not pinched. Be sure a fiber washer (2–Fig. A12) is installed on long crankcase screw. Absence of washer will result in oil leakage. Tighten crankcase screws to 30-35 in.-lbs. (3.4-3.9 N·m).

CLUTCH. Clutch hub has left hand threads. Clutch hub, shoes and spring are available only as a unit assembly.

Clutch drum (6–Fig. A10) and bushing (7) are available separately.

REWIND STARTER. The rewind starter is located on the left end of the crankshaft. Starter pawls are located on back side of flywheel (3–Fig. A13). Starter pawls are not available separate from flywheel but must be serviced as a unit assembly. Rope pulley (6) rides on needle roller bearing (5). Care should be used if rewind spring is removed to pre-

vent spring from uncoiling uncontrolled. Install rewind spring (7) in rope pulley so outer end of spring is pointing in a clockwise direction. Wind rope around puley in counterclockwise direction as viewed from flywheel side of pulley. Lubricate rope pulley bearing. Apply tension to rewind spring by turning rope pulley three turns clockwise before passing rope through rope outlet. Be sure spacer (4) is installed or starter pawls will rub against rope pulley. Align dot on flywheel shown in Fig. A14 with keyway in crankshaft when installing flywheel. This will align key in crankshaft with corresponding slot in flywheel. Tighten flywheel nut to 8-10 ft.-lbs. (10.9-13.6 N·m).

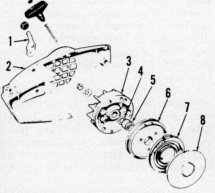

Fig. A13–Exploded view of rewind starter.

1. Choke plate
2. Left side cover
3. Flywheel
4. Spacer
5. Needle roller bearing
6. Rope pulley
7. Rewind spring
8. Spring plate

Fig. A12–Long crankcase screw must be installed with fiber washer (2) to prevent oil leakage.

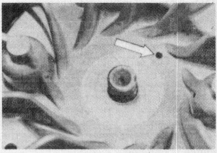

Fig. A14–Align dot on flywheel with crankshaft keyway to assist in mating key with flywheel slot.

ALLIS-CHALMERS

Model	Bore	Stroke	Displ.	Drive Type
75, 75A	1.4375 in. (36.51 mm)	1.3125 in. (33.34 mm)	2.1 cu. in. (34.4 cc)	Direct

MAINTENANCE

SPARK PLUG. Recommended spark plug is Champion CJ8. Spark plug electrode gap should be 0.025 inch (0.63 mm).

CARBURETOR. Models 75 and 75A are equipped with a Tillotson Model HU diaphragm carburetor. Refer to Tillotson section of CARBURETOR SERVICE for operation and overhaul of carburetor.

Initial setting idle mixture screw and high speed mixture screw is one turn open. Adjust idle speed screw until engine will idle just below clutch engagement speed. Adjust idle mixture screw so that engine will accelerate without lagging or faltering. High speed mixture screw should be adjusted to obtain optimum performance with engine operating under cutting load. Be sure mixture settings are not too lean as engine damage may result.

MAGNETO AND TIMING. A conventional flywheel magneto ignition system is used on Models 75 and 75A. Breaker point gap should be 0.017 inch (0.43 mm). Ignition timing is fixed but incorrect breaker point gap will affect timing.

Magneto air gap should be 0.010-0.014 inch (0.25-0.35 mm). Magneto air gap is adjusted by loosening screws (2 – Fig. A20) and placing 0.012 inch (0.30 mm) shim stock between lamination legs and

flywheel magnets. Move coil assembly until lamination legs contact shim stock and tighten screws (2). Recheck air gap. Flywheel nut should not be tightened to 13-15 ft.-lbs. (17.7-20.4 N·m).

LUBRICATION. Engines on Models 75 and 75A are lubricated by mixing oil with fuel. Fuel:oil ratio is 16:1. Oil should be a good quality SAE 30 oil designed for chain saw or air-cooled two-stroke engines.

All models are equipped with a manual chain oiler while Model 75A is equipped with automatic chain oiler. Fill oil reservoir with a good quality SAE 30 Service MS oil if ambient temperature is above 40°F (4°C) or SAE 10W Service MS oil if temperature is below 40°F (4°C).

CARBON. Carbon deposits should be removed from muffler and exhaust ports at regular intervals. Be careful not to damage engine cylinder, piston or exhaust port when scraping carbon. Do not allow loosened carbon to enter cylinder.

REPAIRS

CYLINDER. Cylinder has a chrome bore which should be inspected and renewed if chrome is scored, cracked or

excessively worn. Check for ring ridge at top of piston travel which may cause piston ring land to break when a new piston ring is installed.

PISTON, PIN AND RINGS. Piston should be heated to approximately 200° F (93°C) to aid in piston pin removal and installation. Closed end of piston pin must be towards exhaust port of cylinder. Snap ring on exhaust side of piston is sunk in retaining groove and will require use of a sharp hook type tool for removal. It may be necessary to drill a ⅛ inch hole into groove to gain access to snap ring. Manufacturer recommends discarding piston if a hole must be drilled to remove snap ring.

Piston is equipped with two piston rings. Piston rings are retained by a pin in each ring groove. Be sure piston rings are correctly aligned with pins and do not overlap pins when cylinder is installed. Install piston with ring locating pins on magneto side of engine. Piston and rings are available in standard sizes only.

CONNECTING ROD, CRANKSHAFT AND CRANKCASE. Crankcase halves (1 and 20 – Fig. A22) must be separated to remove crankshaft and to

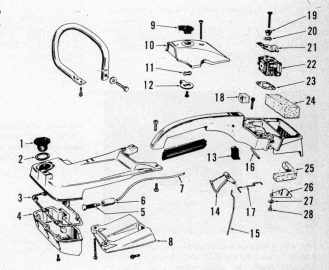

Fig. A21 – Exploded view of handle and gas tank assemblies.

1. Gas cap
2. Gasket
3. Gasket
4. Gas tank
5. Fuel pick-up weight
6. Filter
7. Fuel line
8. Cylinder shroud
9. Choke knob
10. Cover
11. Wave washer
12. Choke lever
13. Manual oil pump button
14. Trigger
15. Oil pump rod
16. Trigger pin
17. Throttle link
18. Throttle link boot
19. Spacer
20. Wave washer
21. Choke shutter
22. Carburetor
23. Gasket
24. Air filter
25. Dust seal
26. Reed valve petal
27. Washer
28. Screw

Fig. A20 – View of flywheel and coil assembly on Models 75 and 75A. Note that washer (3) must have outer diameter contacting flywheel.

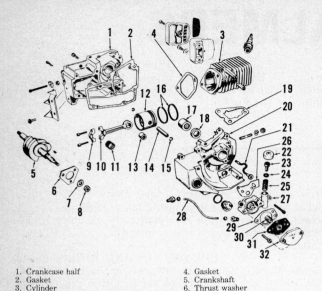

1. Crankcase half
2. Gasket
3. Cylinder
4. Gasket
5. Crankshaft
6. Thrust washer

Fig. A22 — Exploded view of Model 75 and 75A engine. Automatic oil pump shown in not used on Model 75.

7. Washer
8. Nut
9. Rod cap
10. Connecting rod
11. Bearing rollers (28)
12. Piston
13. Bearing
14. Piston pin
15. Snap rings
16. Piston rings
17. Bearing
18. Seal
19. Gasket
20. Crankcase half
21. Intake oil line & valve
22. Cap
23. Manual pump plunger
24. "O" ring
25. Spring
26. Gasket
27. Pump housing
28. Exhaust oil line
29. Gasket
30. Spring
31. Diaphragm & piston
32. Cover

remove connecting rod from crankshaft. Be careful during disassembly not to nick or damage mating surfaces.

Unscrew connecting rod screws and remove rod and cap being careful not to lose loose bearing rollers (11). There are 28 bearing rollers in connecting rod bearing. Connecting rod small end bearing must be pressed out of rod. Be sure rod is properly supported when removing or installing bearing. Use heavy grease to hold bearing rollers (11) in rod and cap when installing connecting rod

on crankshaft. Match marks on sides of rod and cap must be aligned during installation. Tighten connecting rod screws to 55-60 in.-lbs. (6.2-6.8 N·m).

Crankshaft is supported by a needle roller bearing (17) in each crankcase half. Crankcase bearings must be pressed out of crankcase using a suitable driver. Install bearings by pressing bearings into crankcase until bearings are 1/32 inch (0.79 mm) below inner surface of crankcase. Thrust washers (6) may be installed with either side up and are held in place with a light coat of grease. Use a suitable seal protector when passing crankshaft end through crankcase seals. Be sure thrust washers (6) do not dislodge during assembly. Tighten crankcase screws to 55-60 in.-lbs. (6.2-6.8 N·m).

CLUTCH. Refer to Fig. A23 for exploded view of clutch assembly. Clutch hub has left hand threads. Inspect clutch drum (6) and clutch shoes (5) for excessive wear or overheating and renew if required. Press clutch bushing (7) out of clutch drum and inspect bushing for roughness and wear.

REED VALVE. Models 75 and 75A are equipped with a single reed valve petal (26 – Fig. A21) beneath the carburetor. Reed valve is retained by screw (28) and washer (27). Sharp edge of washer (27) must be against reed petal. Tighten screw to 8-12 in.-lbs. (0.9-1.3 N·m). Reed petal should not stand open more than 0.010 inch (0.25 mm) from seat. Inspect reed petal for cracks and seat for burrs.

AUTOMATIC CHAIN OILER. Model 75A is equipped with automatic chain oil pump shown in Fig. A22. Crankcase pulsations pass through impulse hole (1 – Fig. A24) and actuate diaphragm and piston (31 – Fig. A22) which forces chain oil out discharge line (28). Inspect pump components for wear or damage which may cause pump malfunction. Diaphragm piston (31) should move freely in hole of pump housing (27) for a stroke of approximately ¼ inch (6.35 mm). Piston hole may be cleaned using a 0.063 inch drill bit in a hand drill. Do not use an electric drill. Do not insert drill bit more than 9/16 inch into hole. Be sure hole in diaphragm (31) for impulse passage in housing is aligned with passage as shown in Fig. A24 during assembly.

REWIND STARTER. Refer to Fig. A25 for exploded view of rewind starter used on Models 75 and 75A. To disassemble starter, remove starter housing (17). Remove rope handle and allow rope to wind into rope pulley (15). Unscrew retaining screw (13) and remove rope pulley (15) being careful not to dislodge rewind spring (16). Rewind spring (16) can now be removed if necessary, but precaution should be taken not to allow spring to uncoil uncontrolled.

Rewind spring is wound in clockwise direction in housing. Wind rope on rope pulley (15) in clockwise direction when viewing pulley as installed in housing. Turn pulley (15) 1½-2 turns before passing rope through rope outlet in housing (17).

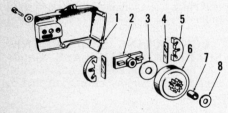

Fig. A23 — Exploded view of clutch assembly.

1. Housing
2. Clutch hub
3. Disc
4. Spring
5. Clutch shoe
6. Clutch drum
7. Bushing
8. Washer

Fig. A24 — View of installation of diaphragm and piston in housing (2). Note use of wire (3) to align impulse hole in diaphragm with impulse passage (1).

Fig. A25 — Exploded view of ignition and rewind starter assemblies used on Models 75 and 75A.

9. Base plate
10. Breaker point assy.
11. Cover
12. Flywheel
13. Screw
14. Washer
15. Rope pulley
16. Rewind spring
17. Starter housing
18. Ignition coil
19. High tension wire

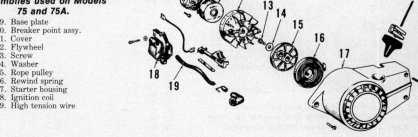

ALPINA

**ALPINA
P.O. Box 777
Griffith, IN 46319**

Model	Bore	Stroke	Displ.	Drive Type
A330, A432	36.5 mm (1.44 in.)	30.4 mm (1.2 in.)	32 cc (1.9 cu. in.)	Direct
A380, A438	39.7 mm (1.56 in.)	30.4 mm (1.2 in.)	38 cc (2.3 cu. in.)	Direct

MAINTENANCE

SPARK PLUG. Recommended spark plug is Champion CJ7Y for all models. Spark plug electrode gap should be 0.5 mm (0.020 in.).

CARBURETOR. Models A330 and A380 are equipped with a Walbro WA diaphragm type carburetor. Models A432 and A438 are equipped with a Dell'Orto diaphragm type carburetor. Refer to Walbro and Dell'Orto sections of CARBURETOR SERVICE section for service procedures and exploded views.

High speed mixture is not adjustable on Models A330 and A380. Initial setting of low speed mixture screw is 1⅜ turns open on Model A330 and 1½ turns open on Model A380. Initial setting on Models A432 and A438 is 1¾ turns open for low speed mixture screw and 1½ turns open for high speed mixture screw.

Final adjusment should be made with engine running at operating temperature. Adjust engine idle speed to just below clutch engagement speed. Adjust low speed mixture so engine will accelerate cleanly without hesitation. Adjust high speed ixture to obtain maximum no-load speed of 11,200 rpm on Model A432 and 11,700 rpm on Model A438.

IGNITION. All models are equipped with a breakerless electronic ignition system. Ignition coil and all electronic circuitry are contained in a one-piece ignition module. Ignition timing is not adjustable. Air gap between ignition module legs and flywheel magnets should be 0.35 mm (0.014 in.). Loosen ignition module mounting screws and move module to adjust air gap. Use a suitable thread locking solution on module screws to prevent screws from vibrating loose. If flywheel requires removal, use Alpina tool 3630260 or a suitable equivalent to withdraw flywheel. Tighten flywheel nut to 34.3 N·m (26 ft.-lbs.).

LUBRICATION. The engine is lubricated by mixing oil with the fuel. Use a good quality oil designed for use in air-cooled two-stroke engines. Fuel:oil ratio is 16:1 for all models. Use a separate container when mixing fuel and oil.

Models A330 and A380 are equipped with an automatic oil pump which utilizes crankcase pulsations to pressurize oil tank. Pump output is adjustable. Models A432 and A438 are equipped with an automatic plunger type oil pump driven by a worm gear on engine crankshaft. Pump output is not adjustable. Refer to OIL PUMP under REPAIRS section for service procedures and exploded views.

Use clean automotive oil for saw chain lubrication. On Models A330 and A380, oil viscosity must be chosen according to ambient temperature. For example, use SAE 30 for warm weather operation and SAE 15 for cold weather operation.

REPAIRS

CYLINDER, PISTON PIN AND RINGS. Cylinder is chrome plated and should be renewed if cracking, scoring or other damage is noted in cylinder bore.

NOTE: Piston aligns connecting rod on rod bearing rollers (25 – Fig. AP1). Excessive piston movement during or after cylinder removal may allow rod bearing rollers to fall into crankcase.

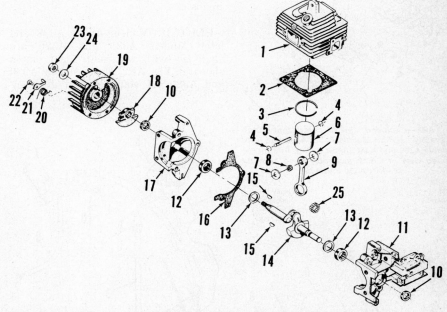

Fig. AP1—Exploded view of engine assembly typical of all models noting counterweight (18) is absent on Models A432 and A438. Two pawl assemblies (20, 21 and 22) are used.

1. Cylinder	8. Bearing rollers	14. Crankshaft	20. Spring
2. Gasket	9. Connecting rod	15. Key	21. Pawl
3. Piston ring	10. Seal	16. Gasket	22. Pin
4. Snap ring	11. Right crankcase half	17. Left crankcase half	23. Nut
5. Piston pin	12. Main bearing	18. Counterweight	24. Washer
6. Piston	13. Thrust washer	19. Flywheel	25. Bearing rollers
7. Thrust washer			

Piston and cylinder are marked during production to obtain desired piston-to-cylinder clearance of 0.02 mm (0.0008 in.). Original piston and cylinder are marked "A." Factory renewal piston and cylinder assemblies are marked "B." Piston or cylinder marked "C" is 0.127 mm (0.005 in.) oversize while piston or cylinder marked "D" is 0.127 mm (0.005 in.) undersize. Piston and cylinder markings should match, however, a new piston marked "B" can be installed in a used cylinder marked "A."

NOTE: Do not install a new piston marked "B" or "C" into a new cylinder marked "A."

Piston is equipped with one piston ring. A locating pin is present in ring groove to prevent ring rotation. Maximum allowable piston ring end gap is 1.0 mm (0.039 in.). Piston pin (5–Fig. AP1) rides on 18 loose bearing rollers (8). Use Alpina tool 4180010 or a suitable equivalent with proper size drivers to remove and install piston pin. Hold bearing rollers (8) in place with heavy grease and place thrust washer (7) on each side of rod before installing piston. Install piston with arrow on piston crown facing toward exhaust side of cylinder. Make certain piston ring end gap is properly positioned around locat-

ing pin in ring groove before installing cylinder. Tighten cylinder screws to 8.8 N·m (78 in.-lbs.).

CRANKSHAFT, CONNECTING ROD AND CRANKCASE. Crankshaft (14–Fig. AP1) is supported at both ends with caged roller bearings (12). Bearings (12) locate in crankcase halves (11 and 17). To split crankcase halves, first remove cylinder and crankcase halves mounting screws. Insert a screwdriver or similar tool between crankcase and crankshaft counterweight. Carefully pry crankcase halves apart being careful not to damage crankcase mating surfaces.

NOTE: Crankshaft runout can be checked before disassembly of engine. To check runout, remove clutch and flywheel. Mount a dial indicator on both ends of crankshaft as close as possible to bearings (12). Check runout while rotating crankshaft. Runout should not exceed 0.07 mm (0.0027 in.).

Connecting rod rides on 12 loose bearing rollers (25). Connecting rod can be removed from crankshaft after crankcase halves are separated. Hold bearing rollers on crankpin with heavy grease when installing connecting rod. Note location of thrust washers (13). Counterweight (18) is used on Models A330 and A380 only. Do not use gasket sealing compounds on crankcase gasket (16). Tighten crankcase screws using a crisscross pattern to 6.9 N·m (61 in.-lbs.).

CLUTCH. Models A432, A438 and later Models A330 and A380 are equipped with the centrifugal clutch shown in Fig. AP2. Early Models A330 and A380 are equipped with the cen-

trifugal clutch shown in Fig. AP3. Complete clutch assemblies are interchangeable, although, individual components are not. Clutch hubs (2–Figs. AP2 and AP3) have left-hand threads. Inspect shoes, hub, drum and needle bearing for excessive wear or damage due to overheating. Clutch shoes are available only as a complete set. Tighten clutch hub to 18.6 N·m (14 ft.-lbs.).

OIL PUMP. Models A330 and A380 are equipped with the pressure-type chain oiling system shown in Fig. AP4. Impulse hose (3) connects to crankcase. Crankcase pulsations pressurize oil tank (1). Check valve (4) prevents chain oil from entering crankcase. Pump output is regulated by rotating screw (8). Clockwise rotation decreases output. Shut-off valve (10) is linked to throttle trigger, preventing oil flow at idle speed.

Oil tank (1) must hold pressure for proper operation of system. Pressurize oil tank to 34.5 kPa (5.0 psi) to check for leakage in tank or leak-back of check

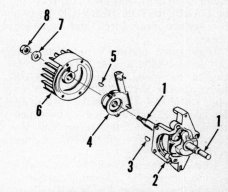

Fig. AP5–View showing location of automatic oil pump used on Models A432 and A438. Refer to Fig. AP6 for exploded view of oil pump assembly (4).

1. Crankshaft
2. Left crankcase half
3. Oil pump key
4. Oil pump assy.
5. Flywheel key
6. Flywheel
7. Washer
8. Nut

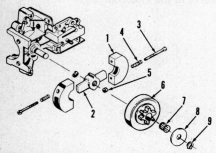

Fig. AP2–Exploded view of centrifugal clutch assembly used on Models A432, A438 and later Models A330 and A380. Refer to Fig. AP3 for exploded view of clutch assembly used on early Models A330 and A380.

1. Shoe
2. Hub
3. Screw
4. Spring
5. Nut
6. Drum
7. Needle bearing
8. Washer
9. Snap ring

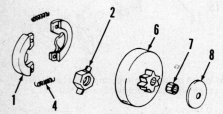

Fig. AP3–Exploded view of centrifugal clutch assembly used on early Models A330 and A380. Refer to legend in Fig. AP2 for component identification.

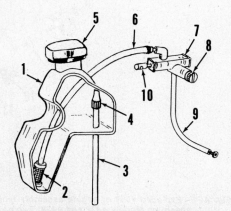

Fig. AP4–View showing automatic oiling system used on Models A330 and A380.

1. Oil tank
2. Oil filter
3. Impulse hose
4. Check valve
5. Cap
6. Hose
7. Metering valve assy.
8. Adjusting screw
9. Discharge hose
10. Shut-off valve

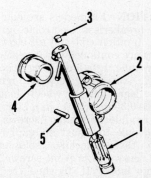

Fig. AP6–Exploded view of automatic oil pump assembly used on Models A432 and A438.

1. Plunger
2. Pump body
3. Plug
4. Worm gear
5. Cam pin

valve (4). Malfunctions are often due to check valve (4) stuck closed preventing crankcase pulsations from entering oil tank.

Models A432 and A438 are equipped with the automatic oil pump shown in Figs. AP5 and AP6. Pump output is not adjustable. Plunger (1–Fig. AP6) is rotated by worm gear (4) on engine crankshaft. Oil is pumped by plunger (1) as plunger reciprocates in pump body (2) due to cam pin (5) riding in oblique groove in plunger.

Remove flywheel (6–Fig. AP5) to gain access to oil pump. Withdrawn cam pin (5–Fig. AP6) to remove plunger (1). Inspect all components for excessive wear or damage and renew if needed. Tighten flywheel nut (8–Fig. AP5) to 34.3 N·m (26 ft.-lbs.).

REWIND STARTER. Models A330 and A380 are equipped with the rewind starter shown in Fig. AP7. Models A432 and A438 are equipped with the rewind starter shown in Fig. AP8.

On all models, remove starter housing (7–Figs. AP7 and AP8) to disassemble starter. Withdraw housing (7) sufficiently to disconnect ignition switch wires then remove housing. Remove rope handle and allow rope to slowly wind into starter housing to relieve tension on rewind spring. Remove screw (1) and carefully remove rope pulley (4). If rewind spring (6) must be removed, care should be taken to prevent personal injury due to uncontrolled uncoiling of spring.

Install rewind spring (6) into housing (7) in a clockwise direction starting with outer coil end. Wrap starter rope around rope pulley in a clockwise direction as viewed from flywheel side of pulley. To preload rewind spring, pull out a loop of rope from notch in rope pulley and rotate pulley ½ turn clockwise. Rope handle should be snug against housing with rope retracted. With rope fully extended, rope pulley should be able to rotate an additional ½ turn to prevent rewind spring breakage.

On all models, starter pawls (21–Fig. AP1) are secured on flywheel with pins (22). Drive pins out from inside of flywheel to remove pawls. Use Alpina tool 3630260 or a suitable equivalent to remove flywheel. Use a suitable thread locking solution on pins (22) when reassembling pawls. Tighten flywheel nut to 34.3 N·m (26 ft.-lbs.).

CHAIN BRAKE. Some models are equipped with the chain brake system shown in Fig. AP9. Chain brake is actuated when operator's hand strikes hand guard (15). Forward movement of actuator (13) trips latch (11) allowing spring (4) to pull brake band (2) tight around clutch drum (6). Pull back hand guard (15) to reset chain brake.

To adjust chain brake, disengage brake by pulling hand guard (15) to rearmost position (toward engine). Install guide bar and saw chain and properly adjust chain tension. Rotate brake tension adjustment screw (between brake arm mounting studs at front of actuator) clockwise, while pulling saw chain around guide bar, until chain movement becomes difficult. Back off adjustment screw (counterclockwise) until chain moves freely around guide bar. Make certain brake band does not contact clutch drum with brake in the disengaged position.

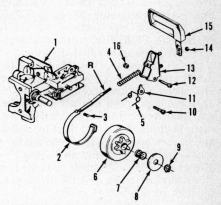

Fig. AP9 – Exploded view of chain brake system used on some models. Brake tension screw (not shown) is located at front of actuator (13) between hand guard (15) mounting studs.

1. Right crankcase half	10. Screw
2. Brake band	11. Latch
3. Pin	12. Shoulder screw
4. Spring	13. Actuator
5. Spring	14. Nut
6. Drum	15. Hand guard
7. Needle bearing	16. Nut
8. Washer	R. Rod
9. Snap ring	

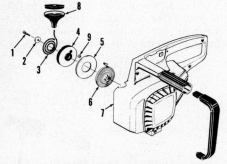

Fig. AP7 – Exploded view of rewind starter used on Models A330 and A380.

1. Screw	
2. Washer	
3. Rope	6. Rewind spring
4. Rope pulley	7. Housing
5. Spring cover	8. Rope handle
	9. Eyelet

Fig. AP8 – Exploded view of rewind starter used on Models A432 and A438. Refer to Fig. AP7 for component identification except cover (10) and screw (11).

ALPINA

Model	Bore	Stroke	Displ.	Type
A40, A40E, Pro 40, Pro 41	40 mm (1.57 in.)	31.5 mm (1.24 in.)	40 cc (2.44 cu. in.)	Direct
Pro 45, Pro 45E	41 mm (1.61 in.)	33.8 mm (1.33 in.)	45 cc (2.74 cu. in.)	Direct

MAINTENANCE

SPARK PLUG. Recommended spark plug for all models is Champion CJ7Y. Electrode gap should be 0.5 mm (0.020 in.).

CARBURETOR. Models A40, A40E, Pro 40 and early Pro 45 and Pro 45E models are equipped with a Tillotson HU diaphragm carburetor. All other models are equipped with a Dell'Orto C16.12 diaphragm carburetor. Refer to Tillotson and Dell'Orto sections of CARBURETOR SERVICE section for service procedures and exploded views.

Initial adjustment on Models A40, A40E and Pro 40 is 1¼ turns open for low speed mixture screw and ¾ turn open for high speed mixture screw. Initial adjustment on Model Pro 41 is 2⅛ turns open for low speed mixture screw and ¾ turn open for high speed mixture screw. Initial adjustment on Models Pro 45 and Pro 45E is 1¾ turns open for low speed mixture screw and 1¼ turns open for high speed mixture screw.

Final adjustment should be made with engine running at operating temperature. Adjust idle speed to just below clutch engagement speed. Adjust low speed mixture screw so engine will accelerate cleanly without hesitation. Adjust high speed mixture screw to obtain maximum no-load speed of 11,700 rpm on Models A40, A40E and Pro 40, 12,000 rpm on Model Pro 41 and 12,400 rpm on Models Pro 45 and Pro 45E.

IGNITION. Models A40 and Pro 45 manufactured prior to 1981 are equipped with a breaker-point ignition system. Refer to Fig. AP15. Breaker-point gap should be 0.45-0.50 mm (0.018-0.020 in.). Air gap between ignition coil and flywheel magnets should be 0.45 mm (0.018 in.). Ignition timing is not adjustable, however, breaker-point gap will affect timing. Be certain point gap is

adjusted correctly as a gap too wide will advance timing and a gap too close will retard timing.

All other models, including Models A40 and Pro 45 manufactured after 1980, are equipped with a breakerless electronic ignition system. Refer to Fig. AP16. Ignition coil and all electronic circuitry are contained in a one-piece ignition module (8). Ignition timing is not adjustable. Air gap between ignition module and flywheel magnets should be 0.35 mm (0.014 in.).

On all models, use Alpina tool 4180100 or a suitable equivalent bolt-type puller to remove flywheel. Remove starter pawl bolts (4) to accommodate puller bolts. Use a suitable thread locking solution on pawl bolts during reassembly. Tighten flywheel nut to 28.4 N·m (21 ft.-lbs.). Use a suitable threat locking solution on ignition coil/module attaching screws if air gap is adjusted.

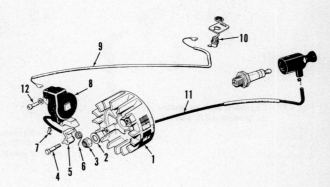

Fig. AP16 — Exploded view of electronic ignition system used on all models except Models A40 and Pro 45 manufactured prior to 1981. Two pawl assemblies (4, 5 and 6) are used.

1. Flywheel
2. Washer
3. Nut
4. Bolt
5. Pawl
6. Spring
7. Clamp
8. Ignition module
9. Primary lead
10. Ignition switch
11. High tension lead
12. Screw

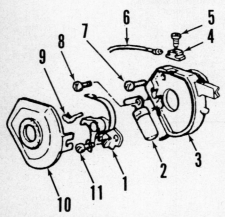

Fig. AP15 — Exploded view of breaker-point ignition system used on Models A40 and Pro 45 manufactured prior to 1981.

1. Breaker points
2. Condenser
3. Breaker box
4. Insulator
5. Screw
6. Primary lead
7. Screw
8. Screw
9. Felt wick
10. Cover
11. Screw

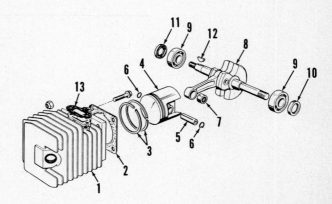

Fig. AP17 — Exploded view of engine assembly used on all models.

1. Cylinder
2. Gasket
3. Piston rings
4. Piston
5. Piston pin
6. Snap ring
7. Needle bearing
8. Crankshaft & connecting rod assy.
9. Main bearings
10. Seal
11. Seal
12. Key
13. Gasket

LUBRICATION. The engine is lubricated by mixing oil with the fuel. Use a good quality oil designed for use in air-cooled two-stroke engines. Fuel:oil mixture should be a 16:1 ratio. Use a separate container when mixing fuel and oil.

All models are equipped with the automatic oil pump shown in Fig. AP23. Pump output is not adjustable. Use clean automotive oil for saw chain lubrication.

REPAIRS

CYLINDER, PISTON, PIN AND RINGS. Cylinder bore is chrome plated and should be renewed if cracking, scoring or other damage is noted in cylinder bore.

Piston and cylinder are marked during production to obtain desired piston-to-cylinder clearance of 0.02 mm (0.0008 in.). Original equipment piston and cylinder are marked "A." Factory renewal piston and cylinder assemblies are marked "B." Piston or cylinder marked "C" is 0.127 mm (0.005 in.) oversize. Piston or cylinder marked "D" is 0.127 mm (0.005) undersize. Piston and cylinder markings should match, however a new piston marked "B" can be installed into a used cylinder marked "A."

NOTE: Do not install a new piston marked "B" or "C" into a new cylinder marked "A."

Piston is equipped with two piston rings. Piston ring end gap should not exceed 1.0 mm (0.039 in.). Locating pins are present in ring grooves to prevent ring rotation. Make certain ring end gaps are properly postioned around locating pins when installing cylinder.

Piston pin (5–Fig. AP17) rides in needle bearing (7) and is retained with two snap rings (6). Use Alpina tool 4180010 or a suitable equivalent to press out pin. Piston may be heated to approximately 110°-120° C (230°-248° F) to ease installation of piston pin.

NOTE: Use electric oven or hot oil bath to heat piston. Do not use an open flame.

Install piston into cylinder with arrow on piston crown facing toward exhaust port.

CRANKSHAFT, CONNECTING ROD AND CRANKCASE. Crankshaft and connecting rod are available as a unit assembly only. Check rotation of connecting rod around crankpin and renew crankshaft assembly if roughness, excessive play or other damage is noted. Check crankshaft

runout by supporting crankshaft assembly between two counter points – such as a lathe. Make certain no damage exists to centering holes at each end of crankshaft. Maximum allowable runout is 0.08 mm (0.0031 in.).

NOTE: Crankshaft runout can be checked while still assembled in crankcase. Remove clutch and flywheel and mount dial indicators on both sides of

crankshaft as close to main bearings as possible. Measure runout while rotating crankshaft. Renew crankshaft assembly if runout exceeds 0.07 mm (0.0027 in.), when measured in this manner.

Crankshaft is supported at both ends by ball-type main bearings (9 – Fig. AP17) that locate in crankcase halves (2 and 3 – Figs. AP18, AP19 and AP20). Use the proper drivers to re-

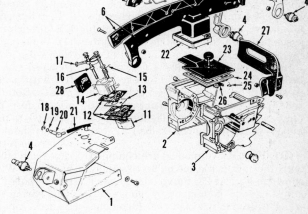

Fig. AP18—Exploded view of crankcase, handle assemblies, carburetor and related components used on A40, A40E and Pro 40 models.

1. Cylinder cover
2. Left crankcase half
3. Right crankcase half
4. Vibration isolator
5. Front handle
6. Rear grip assy.
7. Throttle trigger
8. Throttle rod
9. Throttle rod
10. Throttle trigger
11. Intake spacer
12. Gaskets
13. Heat shield
14. Carburetor
15. Spring
16. Spacer
17. Choke valve
18. "E" ring
19. "O" ring
20. Fitting
21. Fuel hose
22. Seal
23. Cover
24. Air filter
25. Retainer
26. Air filter support
27. Hand guard
28. Seal

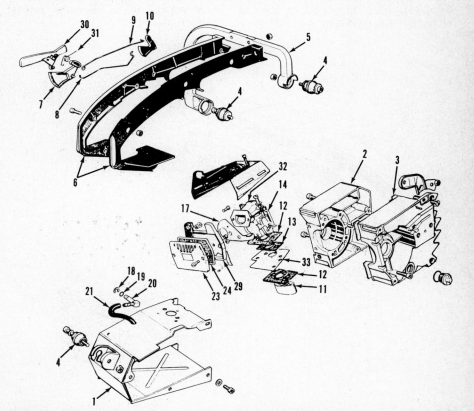

Fig. AP19—Exploded view of crankcase, handle assemblies, carburetor and related components used on Model Pro 41. Refer to legend in Fig. AP18 for component identification except for air filter base (29), safety lever (30), spring (31), air intake (32) and gasket (33).

move and install main bearings. Use Alpina tool 4180900 to install crankshaft assembly into main bearing. Refer to Fig. AP21. Do not use gasket sealer on crankcase gasket. On Models A40, A40E and Pro 40, make certain air filter support (26–Fig. AP18) is in position before assembling crankcase halves. Tighten crankcase screws using a crisscross pattern to 6.9 N·m (61 in.-lbs.).

CLUTCH. All models are equipped with the centrifugal clutch assembly shown in Fig. AP22. Clutch hub (1) has left-hand threads. On some early model clutch assemblies, hub (1) has 9 mm (0.354 in.) mounting threads while all later model (after 1978) clutch assemblies use 10 mm (0.394 in.) mounting threads.

Inspect shoes (2), drum (7), needle bearing (6) and bushing (5) for excessive wear or damage due to overheating and renew if needed. Shoes (2) are available only as a complete set. Tighten clutch hub (1) to 28.4 N·m (21 ft.-lbs.).

OIL PUMP. All models are equipped with the automatic oil pump assembly shown in Fig. AP23. Pump output is not adjustable. Oil is pumped by plunger (2) which is driven by worm gear (3) on end of engine crankshaft. Pump plunger (2) reciprocates in pump body (1) due to cam bolt (14) riding in oblique groove in plunger. Plunger can be removed from housing after removing cam bolt (14) and bushing (4). Inspect worm gear (3), plunger (2) and pump body (1) for excessive wear or damage. Always renew seal (12) and washers (18) during reassembly of pump.

REWIND STARTER. Refer to Fig. AP24 for exploded view of rewind starter used on all models.

To disassemble starter, remove starter housing (1) from saw. Remove rope handle (3) and carefully allow rope to wind into housing (1). Remove nut (6) and washer (5). Rope pulley (4) and rewind spring and case assembly (2) can now be removed from housing.

Install rewind spring (2) into housing (1) with open side of case facing housing (1). Wind rope onto rope pulley (4) in a clockwise direction as viewed from flywheel side of pulley. Lubricate shaft (S) with a suitable low temperature grease. Rotate rope pulley ½ turn clockwise before passing rope through rope guide (G) to preload rewind spring. Rope handle should be snug against housing with rope retracted. If not, lift a loop of rope from pulley and place into notch (N) in pulley. While holding rope in notch, rotate pulley clockwise to increase rewind spring tension. With rope fully extended, rope pulley should be able to rotate ½ turn further. If not, repeat above procedure, only rotate pulley counterclockwise to decrease rewind spring tension.

Refer to Fig. AP16 for exploded view of starter pawl assemblies. Use a suitable thread locking solution on pawl bolts (4). Tighten flywheel nut to 28.4 N·m (21 ft.-lbs.).

CHAIN BRAKE. Some Pro 41, Pro 45 and Pro 45E models are equipped with a chain brake system designed to quickly stop chain movement should kickback occur. Refer to Fig. AP25 for exploded view of chain brake system used. Chain brake is activated when operator's hand strikes chain brake lever (1), disengaging latch (7) and allowing spring (14) to pull brake band (10) tight around clutch drum. Pull back chain brake lever to reset mechanism.

Disassembly for repair or component renewal is evident after inspection of unit and referral to Fig. AP25. No adjustment of chain brake system is required.

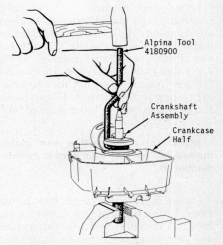

Fig. AP21 — View showing installation procedure of crankshaft and connecting rod assembly into crankcase using Alpina tool 4180900. Main bearing (9 — Fig. AP17) is pressed into crankcase half prior to installation of crankshaft assembly.

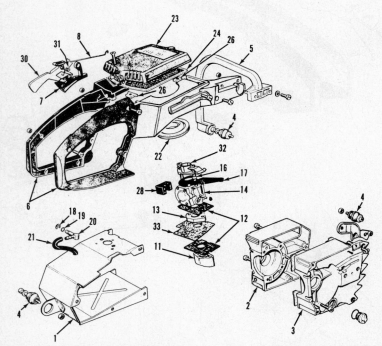

Fig. AP20 — Exploded view of crankcase, handle assemblies, carburetor and related components used on Models Pro 45 and Pro 45E. Refer to legend in Fig. AP18 for component identification except for safety lever (30), spring (31), air intake (32) and gasket (33).

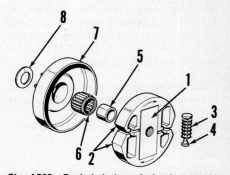

Fig. AP22 — Exploded view of clutch assembly used on all models manufactured after 1978. Early model clutch assembly is similar except hub (1) has 9 mm (0.354 in.) mounting threads. Late model hub has 10 mm (0.394 in.) mounting threads.

1. Hub	5. Bushing
2. Shoes	6. Needle bearing
3. Spring	7. Drum
4. Spring guide	8. Washer

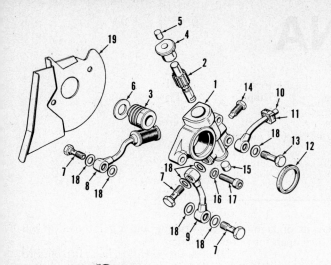

Fig. AP23 — Exploded view of automatic oil pump used on all models.

1. Pump body
2. Plunger
3. Worm gear
4. Bushing
5. Felt plug
6. Thrust washer
7. Banjo bolt
8. Pickup & filter assy.
9. Suction line
10. Oil line
11. Seal
12. Seal
13. Banjo bolt
14. Cam bolt
15. Plug
16. Washer
17. Screw
18. Washers
19. Plate

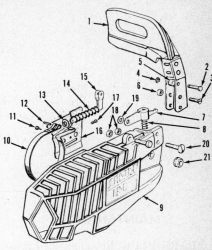

Fig. AP25 — Exploded view of chain brake assembly used on so equipped Pro 41, Pro 45 and Pro 45E models.

1. Chain brake lever
2. Pin
3. Screw
4. "E" ring
5. Spacer
6. Nut
7. Latch
8. Spring
9. Housing
10. Brake band
11. Screw
12. Pin
13. Washer
14. Spring
15. Arm
16. Guide plate
17. Screw
18. Nuts
19. Washer
20. Screw
21. Nut

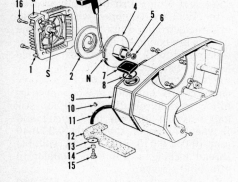

Fig. AP24 — Exploded view of rewind starter, left engine cover and fuel tank assembly and related components. Refer to Fig. AP16 for view of flywheel and starter pawls.

G. Rope guide
N. Notch
S. Shaft
1. Starter housing
2. Rewind spring & case assy.
3. Rope handle
4. Rope pulley
5. Washer
6. Nut
7. Fuel cap
8. Seal
9. Left engine cover & fuel tank assy.
10. Clamp
11. Fuel hose
12. Felt
13. Washer
14. Fuel screen
15. Fuel pickup

ALPINA

Model	Bore	Stroke	Displ.	Drive Type
Pro 55, Pro 55E, Pro 56	44 mm (1.73 in.)	36 mm (1.42 in.)	49 cc (3.4 cu. in.)	Direct
Pro 65, Pro 65E, Pro 66	47 mm (1.85 in.)	37.3 mm (1.47 in.)	65 cc (4.0 cu. in.)	Direct

MAINTENANCE

SPARK PLUG. Recommended spark plug for all models is Champion CJ7Y. Electrode gap should be 0.5 mm (0.020 in.).

CARBURETOR. All models are equipped with a Tillotson HK diaphragm carburetor. Refer to Tillotson section of CARBURETOR SERVICE section for service procedure and exploded view.

Initial adjustment of low speed mixture screw is 1½ turns open on Models Pro 55, Pro 55E and Pro 56 and 1⅜ turns open on Models Pro 65, Pro 65E

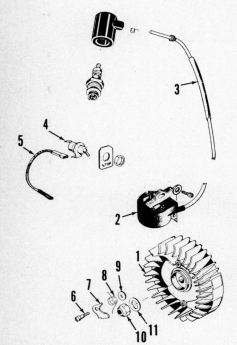

Fig. AP35 — Exploded view of breakerless electronic ignition system used on Models Pro 56 and Pro 66. Other models are similar. Refer to text.

1. Flywheel
2. Ignition module/coil
3. High tension lead
4. Ignition switch
5. Primary lead
6. Pawl bolt
7. Pawl
8. Spring
9. Washer
10. Nut
11. Washer

and Pro 66. Initial adjustment of high speed mixture screw is ¾ turn open for all models.

Final adjustment should be made with engine running at operating temperature. Adjust idle speed to just below clutch engagement speed. Adjust low speed mixture screw so engine will accelerate cleanly without hesitation. Adjust high speed mixture screw to obtain maximum no-load speed of 12,000 rpm for Models Pro 55, Pro 55E and Pro 56 and 11,600 rpm for Models Pro 65, Pro 65E and Pro 66.

IGNITION. Model Pro 55 manufactured prior to 1985 and Model Pro 65 manufactured prior to 1984 are equipped with a breaker-point ignition system. Breaker-point gap should be 0.45-0.50 mm (0.018-0.020 in.). Air gap between ignition coil legs and flywheel magnets should be 0.45 mm (0.018 in.). Loosen coil attaching screws and move coil to adjust air gap. Use a suitable thread locking solution on coil attaching screws. Ignition timing is not adjustable, however, breaker-point gap will affect timing. Be sure breaker-point gap is adjusted correctly as a gap too wide will

advance timing and a gap too close will retard timing.

Models Pro 55E, Pro 65E, Pro 56, Pro 66 and Model Pro 55 manufactured after 1984 and Model Pro 65 manufactured after 1983 are equipped with a breakerless electronic ignition system. Some models are equipped with a standard ignition coil with an electronic module located behind flywheel. On other models, ignition coil and all electronic circuitry are contained in a one-piece ignition module/coil (2 – Fig. AP35). Air gap between ignition module/coil and flywheel magnets should be 0.35-0.40 mm (0.014-0.016 in.). Use a suitable thread locking solution on module/coil attaching screws.

On all models, use Alpina tool 4180140 to remove flywheel. If Alpina tool 4180140 is not available, remove starter pawl assemblies (6, 7, 8 and 9) to accomodate a bolt-type puller. Use a suitable thread locking solution on pawl bolts (6) during reassembly. Tighten flywheel nut (10) to 34.8 N·m (26 ft.-lbs.).

LUBRICATION. The engine is lubricated by mixing oil with the fuel. Use a

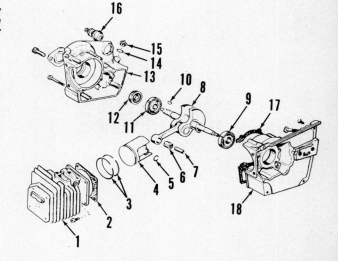

Fig. AP36 — Exploded view of engine assembly used on Model Pro 56. All other models are similar.

1. Cylinder
2. Gasket
3. Piston rings
4. Piston
5. Retainer
6. Needle bearing
7. Piston pin
8. Crankshaft & connecting rod assy.
9. Right main bearing
10. Woodruff key
11. Left main bearing
12. Seal
13. Left crankcase half
14. Seal
15. Oil cap
16. Vibration isolator
17. Gasket
18. Right crankcase half

good quality oil designed for use in air-cooled two-stroke engines. Fuel:oil mixture should be a 16:1 ratio. Use a separate container when mixing fuel and oil.

All models are equipped with an automatic chain oil pump. Oil pump is driven by a worm gear coupled to clutch drum. Pump output is not adjustable. Refer to OIL PUMP under REPAIRS section for service and exploded view. Use clean automotive oil for saw chain lubrication.

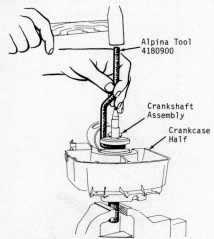

Fig. AP37 — View showing installation of crankshaft and connecting rod assembly into crankcase using Alpina tool 4180900. Main bearing (9 — Fig. AP36) is pressed into crankcase half prior to installation of crankshaft assembly.

Fig. AP38 — Exploded view of rear grip and front handle assemblies, crankcase, fuel tank assembly and related components used on Model Pro 56. Other models are similar.

1. Right crankcase half
2. Left crankcase half
3. Gasket
4. Vibration isolator
5. Cylinder cover
6. Rear grip assy.
7. Bushing
8. Safety lever
9. Spring
10. Trigger
11. Throttle rod
12. Carburetor support
13. Oil pickup assy.
14. Clamp
15. Fuel tank assy.
16. Air filter cover
17. Front handle assy.
18. Trigger lock assy.
19. Spring
20. Clamp
21. Fuel hose
22. Air filter
23. Choke rod

REPAIRS

CYLINDER, PISTON, PIN AND RINGS. Cylinder bore is chrome plated and should be renewed if cracking, scoring or other damage is noted in cylinder bore.

Piston and cylinder are marked during production to obtain desired piston-to-cylinder clearance of 0.02 mm (0.0008 in.). Original equipment piston and cylinder are marked "A." Factory renewal piston and cylinder assemblies are marked "B." Piston or cylinder marked "C" is 0.127 mm (0.005 in.) oversize. Piston or cylinder marked "D" is 0.127 mm (0.005 in.) undersize. Piston and cylinder markings should match, however, a new piston marked "B" can be installed into a used cylinder marked "A."

NOTE: Do not install a new piston marked "B" or "C" into a new cylinder marked "A."

Piston is equipped with two piston rings. Piston ring end gap should not exceed 1.0 mm (0.039 in.). Locating pins are present in ring grooves to prevent ring rotation. Make certain ring end gaps are properly positioned around locating pins when installing cylinder.

Piston pin (7 – Fig. AP36) rides in needle bearing (6) and is retained with two snap rings (5). Use Alpina tool 4180010 or a suitable equivalent to press out pin. Piston may be heated to approximately 110°-120° C (230°-248° F) to ease piston pin installation.

NOTE: Use electric oven or hot oil bath to heat piston. Do not use an open flame.

Install piston into cylinder with arrow on piston crown facing toward exhaust port.

CRANKSHAFT, CONNECTING ROD AND CRANKCASE. Crankcase and connecting rod (8 – Fig. AP36) are available as a unit assembly only. Check rotation of connecting rod around crankpin and renew crankshaft assembly if roughness, excessive play or other damage is noted. Check crank-

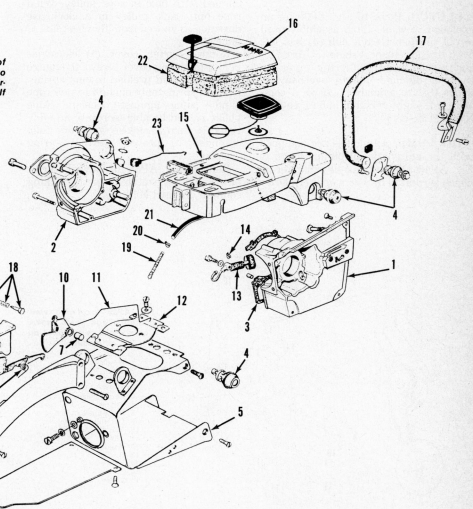

shaft runout by supporting crankshaft assembly between two counter points such as a lathe. Make certain no damage exists to centering holes at each end of crankshaft. Maximum allowable runout is 0.08 mm (0.0031 in.).

NOTE: Crankshaft runout can be checked while still assembled in crankcase. Remove clutch and flywheel and mount dial indicators on both sides of crankshaft as close to main bearings as possible. Measure runout while rotating crankshaft. Renew crankshaft assembly if runout exceeds 0.07 mm (0.0027 in.) when measured in this manner.

Crankshaft is supported at both ends with ball-type main bearings (9 and 11). Main bearings are located in crankcase halves (13 and 18). Use the proper size drivers to remove and install main bearings. Use Alpina tool 4180900 to install crankshaft assembly into main bearing. Refer to Fig. AP37. Do not use gasket sealer on crankcase gasket (17–Fig. AP36). Tighten crankcase screws using a crisscross pattern to 6.4 N·m (57 in.-lbs.).

CLUTCH. Refer to Fig. AP39 for an exploded view of clutch assembly used on all models. Clutch hub (4) has left hand threads. Inspect shoes (5), drum (3) and needle bearing (2) for excessive wear or damage due to overheating. Shoes (5) are available only as a complete set. Tighten clutch hub (4) to 41.2 N·m (31 ft.-lbs.).

OIL PUMP. All models are equipped with the automatic oil pump shown in Fig. AP40. Oil is pumped by plunger (6) which is rotated by worm gear (1). Drive

lugs (L) on worm gear (1) engage clutch drum, therefore oil is pumped only when saw chain is rotating.

To disassemble pump, remove cam bolt (5), plug (8) and bushing (7). Plunger (6) can now be removed for inspection or renewal. Carefully inspect seal (2) and seal surface on worm gear (1). Note that slight wear on seal or worm gear may allow pump to draw air causing pump malfunction. It is recommended to renew seal (2) any time pump is disassembled.

REWIND STARTER. All models are equipped with the rewind starter shown in Fig. AP41. To disassemble starter, remove starter housing (5) from saw. Remove rope handle (4) and carefully allow rope to wind into starter, relieving tension on rewind spring (2). Starter drive (6) is a press fit in rope pulley (3). Remove rope and tap drive (6) out of pulley (3) toward flywheel side of housing (5) using a proper size punch and hammer.

Rewind spring (2) is retained in a plastic case. Install spring with open side of case toward starter cover (1). Install starter drive (6) with hole in drive aligned with hole in rope pulley. Wind rope onto rope pulley in a clockwise direction as viewed from flywheel side of pulley.

Rotate starter cover (1) clockwise before installing cover screws to engage rope pulley and preload rewind spring. Preload spring only enough to pull rope handle snug against housing. Rope pulley should be able to rotate an additional ½ turn clockwise with rope fully extended to prevent rewind spring breakage.

Refer to Fig. AP35 for view of starter pawls. Use a suitable thread locking solution on pawl bolts (6).

CHAIN BRAKE. Some models are equipped with a chain brake system designed to stop chain movement should kickback occur. Chain brake is activated when operator's hand strikes hand guard (12–Fig. AP39), tripping lever (16) and allowing spring (15) to draw brake band (14) tight around clutch drum (3). Pull back hand guard to reset mechanism.

Disassembly is evident after inspection of unit and referral to exploded view. Renew any component excessively worn or damaged. Chain brake should be clean and free of sawdust and dirt accumulation. No adjustment of chain brake is required.

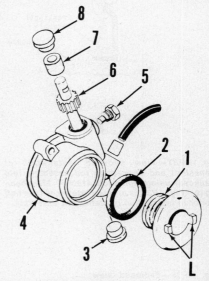

Fig. AP40—Exploded view of automatic oil pump assembly.

1. Worm gear	
2. Seal	6. Plunger
3. Plug	7. Bushing
4. Housing	8. Plug
5. Cam bolt	L. Drive lugs

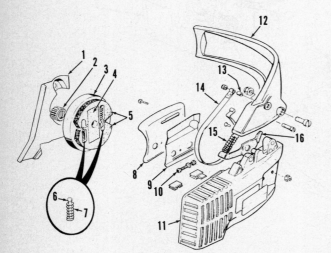

Fig. AP39—Exploded view of clutch and chain brake. Chain brake is optional on all models.

1. Plate
2. Needle bearing
3. Drum
4. Hub
5. Shoes
6. Spring guide
7. Spring
8. Inner guide plate
9. Outer guide plate
10. Bar adjusting screw
11. Cover
12. Hand guard
13. Spacer
14. Brake band
15. Spring
16. Lever

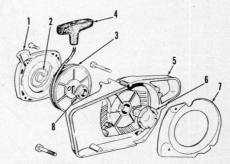

Fig. AP41—Exploded view of rewind starter assembly.

1. Starter cover	5. Housing
2. Rewind spring	6. Starter drive
3. Rope pulley	7. Baffle
4. Rope handle	8. Bushing

ALPINA

Model	Bore	Stroke	Displ.	Drive Type
070, 070S, A70, Super Pro 70	51 mm (2.0 in.)	34.5 mm (1.36 in.)	70 cc (4.3 cu. in.)	Direct
Super Pro 90	54 mm (2.13 in.)	39.1 mm (1.54 in.)	90 cc (5.5 cu. in.)	Direct
Super Pro 120	58 mm (2.28 in.)	45.5 mm (1.79 in.)	120 cc (7.3 cu. in.)	Direct

MAINTENANCE

SPARK PLUG. Recommended spark plug for all models is Champion CJ7Y. Electrode gap should be 0.5 mm (0.020 in.).

CARBURETOR. All models are equipped with a Tillotson HS diaphragm carburetor. Refer to Tillotson section of CARBURETOR SERVICE section for service and exploded views.

Initial adjustment of low speed mixture screw is 1⅞ turns open on Super Pro 120, 2 turns open on Super Pro 90 and 1¾ turns open on all other models. Initial adjustment of high speed mixture screw is ⅞ turn open on Super Pro 120 and ¾ turn open on all other models. Final adjustment should be made with engine running at operating temperature. Adjust idle speed to just below clutch engagement speed. Adjust low speed mixture screw so engine will accelerate cleanly without hesitation. Adjust high speed mixture screw to obtain maximum speed of 10,300 rpm on Super Pro 120, 9,700 rpm on Super Pro 90 and 10,500 rpm on all other models.

IGNITION. Models 070 and 070S manufactured prior to 1984 are equipped with a breaker-point ignition system. All other models, including Models 070 and 070S manufactured after 1983, are equipped with a breaker-less electronic ignition system.

Breaker-Point Ignition. Breaker-point gap should be 0.45-0.50 mm (0.018-0.020 in.). Air gap between ignition coil lamination and flywheel magnets should be 0.45 mm (0.018 in.). Use a suitable thread locking solution on coil attaching screws. Ignition timing is not adjustable, however, breaker-point gap will affect timing. Be sure breaker-point gap is adjusted correctly.

Electronic Ignition. Refer to Fig. AP51 for exploded view of electronic ignition system used on Models A70, Super Pro 70 and so equipped Models 070 and 070S. Note that coil (8) is located outside of flywheel (1) while ignition module (13) is located behind flywheel (1). Super Pro 90 and Super Pro 120 models are equipped with electronic ignition system shown in Fig. AP52. Ignition coil and all electronic circuitry are contained in one-piece ignition module (13).

Except for faulty wiring or wiring connections, repair of ignition system malfunctions is accomplished by component renewal.

On Super Pro 90 and Super Pro 120 models, air gap between ignition module and flywheel magnets should be 0.65 mm (0.026 in.). Air gap between ignition coil and flywheel magnets on all other models should be 0.40 mm (0.016 in.). Use a suitable thread locking solution on module (or coil) attaching screws. Ignition timing is not adjustable on all models.

Starter pawl assemblies (2, 3, 4 and 7 – Fig. AP51) can be removed to accomodate a suitable bolt-type puller to remove flywheel on all models. Use a suitable thread locking solution on bolts (2) when reassembling pawls. Tighten flywheel nut to 39.2 N·m (29 ft.-lbs.) on Super Pro 90 and Super Pro 120 models and 28.4 N·m (21 ft.-lbs.) on all other models.

LUBRICATION. The engine is lubricated by mixing oil with the fuel. Use a good quality oil designed for use in air-cooled two-stroke engines. Fuel:oil mixture should be a 16:1 ratio. Use a separate container when mixing fuel and oil.

Models 070S and Super Pro 70 are equipped with a manual and automatic chain oil pump. All other models are only equipped with an automatic chain oil

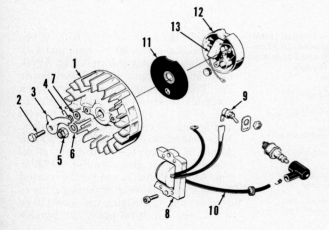

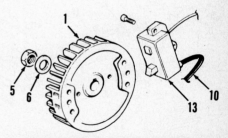

Fig. AP51 — Exploded view of electronic ignition system used on Models A70, Super Pro 70, and Models 070 and 070S manufactured after 1983. Two pawl assemblies (2,3, 4 and 7) are used.

1. Flywheel
2. Bolt
3. Pawl
4. Spring
5. Nut
6. Washer
7. Washer
8. Ignition coil
9. Ignition switch
10. High tension lead
11. Cover
12. Module case
13. Module

Fig. AP52 — Exploded view of electronic ignition system used on Super Pro 90 and Super Pro 120 models. Refer to Fig. AP51 for component identification.

pump. Automatic oil pump output is only adjustable on Super Pro 90 and Super Pro 120 models. Refer to OIL PUMP under REPAIRS for service and exploded views of manual and automatic oil pump assemblies. Use clean automotive oil for saw chain lubrication.

REPAIRS

CYLINDER, PISTON, PIN AND RINGS. Cylinder bore is chrome plated and should be renewed if cracking, scoring or other damage is noted in cylinder bore. Note that cylinder used on Super Pro 90 and Super Pro 120 models is equipped with decompression valve (28–Fig. AP54) to ease starting.

Piston and cylinder are marked during production to obtain desired piston-to-cylinder clearance of 0.02 mm (0.0008 in.). Original equipment piston and cylinder are marked "A." Factory renewal piston and cylinder assemblies are marked "B." Piston or cylinder marked "C" is 0.127 mm (0.005 in.) oversize. Piston or cylinder marked "D" is 0.127 mm (0.005 in.) undersize. Piston and cylinder markings should match, however, a new piston marked "B" can be installed into a used cylinder marked "A."

NOTE: Do not install a new piston marked "B" or "C" into a new cylinder marked "A."

Piston is equipped with two piston rings. Piston should be inspected and renewed if cracking or scoring is noted. Maximum allowable piston ring end gap is 1.0 mm (0.039 in.). Locating pins are present in ring grooves to prevent ring rotation. Be certain ring end gaps are properly positioned around locating pins when installing cylinder. Tighten cylinder screws to 11.8 N·m (9 ft.-lbs.) on all models.

On Models 070, 070S, A70 and Super Pro 70, piston pin (8–Fig. AP53) is a press fit in connecting rod small end. Piston rides in needle bearings (7) installed in each side of piston. Piston pin is retained with two snap rings (9). Use Alpina tool 4180020 or a suitable equivalent press to remove and install piston pin. Be sure piston is properly supported to prevent damage to piston.

On all other models, piston pin (8–Fig. AP54) is a press fit in piston and rides in one needle bearing (7) installed in connecting rod small end. Piston pin is retained with two wire clips (9). Use Alpina tool 4180010 or a suitable equivalent to remove and install

piston pin. Piston may be heated to approximately 110°-120° C (230°-248° F) to ease installation of piston pin.

NOTE: Use electric oven or hot oil bath to heat piston. Do not use an open flame.

On all models, install piston into cylinder with arrow on piston crown facing toward exhaust port.

CRANKSHAFT, CONNECTING ROD AND CRANKCASE. Crankshaft and connecting rod are available as a unit assembly only. Check rotation of connecting rod around crankpin and renew crankshaft assembly if roughness, excessive play or other damage is noted. Check crankshaft runout by supporting crankshaft between two counter points such as a lathe. Make certain no damage is present in centering holes at each end of crankshaft. Renew crankshaft assembly if runout exceeds 0.08 mm (0.0031 in.).

NOTE: Crankshaft runout can be checked while still assembled in crankcase. Remove clutch and flywheel and mount dial indicators on each side of crankshaft as close to main bearings as possible. Measure runout while rotating crankshaft. Renew crankshaft assembly if runout exceeds 0.07 mm (0.0027 in.) when measured in this manner.

Crankshaft is supported with ball-type main bearings (12–Fig. AP53) or (24 and 25–Fig. AP54) at both ends. Main bearings are a press fit into crankcase halves. Use the proper size drivers to remove and install main bearings. Use Alpina tool 4180900 or a suitable equivalent to install crankshaft assembly into crankcase. Refer to Fig. AP57. Do not use gasket sealer on crankcase gasket. Tighten crankcase screws using a crisscross pattern to 7.8 N·m (69 in.-lbs.) on Super Pro 90 and Super Pro 120 models and 7.3 N·m (69 in.-lbs.) on Super Pro 90 and Super Pro 120 models and 7.3 N·m (65 in.-lbs.) on all other models.

CLUTCH. Late Models 070, 070S, A70 and Super Pro 70 are equipped with the clutch assembly shown in Fig. AP58. Late Models Super Pro 90 and Super Pro 120 are equipped with the clutch assembly shown in Fig. AP60. Refer to Fig. AP59 for view of shoes (4), hub (5) and spring (3) used on all early models. Note that hub (5–Figs. AP58, AP59 and AP60) is keyed to crankshaft on all models. Inspect shoes (4–Fig. AP58 or Fig. AP60), drum (7) and needle bearing (9) for excessive wear or damage due to overheating. Use Alpina tool 4180110 or a suitable bolt-type puller to remove

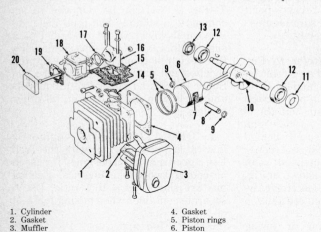

1. Cylinder
2. Gasket
3. Muffler
4. Gasket
5. Piston rings
6. Piston

Fig. AP53–Exploded view of engine assembly, carburetor and related components used on all models except Super Pro 90 and Super Pro 120. Two needle bearings (7) are used. Refer to text.

7. Needle bearing
8. Piston pin
9. Snap ring
10. Crankshaft & connecting rod assy.
11. Seal
12. Main bearing
13. Seal
14. Gasket
15. Gasket
16. Intake manifold
17. Gasket
18. Carburetor
19. Plate
20. Screen

Fig. AP54–Exploded view of engine assembly used on Super Pro 90 and Super Pro 120 models.

1. Cylinder
4. Gasket
5. Piston rings
6. Piston
7. Needle bearing
8. Piston pin
9. Wire clip
10. Crankshaft & connecting rod assy.
21. Right crankcase half
22. Gasket
23. Seal
24. Main bearing
25. Main bearing
26. Seal
27. Left crankcase half
28. Decompression valve

clutch. Nut (12) has right-hand threads. Clutch shoes (4) are available only as a complete set. Tighten nut (12) to 45.1 N·m (33 ft.-lbs.) on Super Pro 90 and Super Pro 120 models and 35.3 N·m (26 ft.-lbs.) on all other models.

OIL PUMP. Refer to Fig. AP61 for exploded view of manual chain oil pump used on Models 070S and Super Pro 70.

Disassembly for repair or component renewal is evident after inspection of unit and referral to Fig. AP61. Hoses (4) must be renewed if pump is disassembled. Be sure clamps (3) are tight and properly installed to prevent leakage.

Refer to Fig. AP62 for exploded view of automatic oil pump used on Models 070, 070S, A70 and Super Pro 70. Oil is pumped by piston (5) which is rotated by

drive plate (10). Drive plate is cycled up and down by plunger (15) which rides on cam of engine crankshaft. Piston (5) rotates one notch with each down stroke of drive plate (10). Spring (12) forces piston brake (13) against piston (5), preventing piston (5) from backing up during drive plate (10) return stroke.

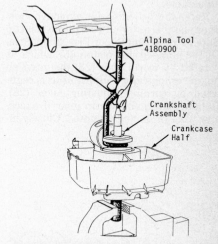

Fig. AP57 — View showing installation procedure of crankshaft and connecting rod assembly into crankcase half using Alpina tool 4180900. Main bearing is pressed into crankcase half prior to installation of crankshaft assembly.

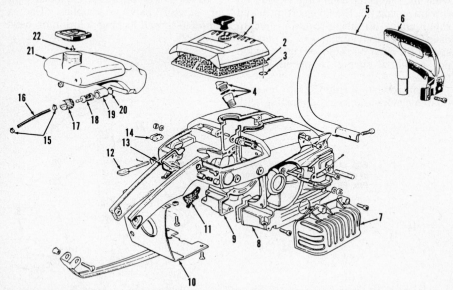

Fig. AP55 — Exploded view of crankcase, front handle assembly, fuel tank and related components used on Models 070, 070S and A70.

1. Cover	7. Muffler cover	12. Choke lever	17. Screen
2. Air filter	8. Right crankcase half	13. Throttle rod	18. Fuel pickup
3. Snap ring	9. Left crankcase half	14. Grommet	19. Filter
4. Oil tank cap assy.	10. Cylinder cover	15. Clamp	20. "O" ring
5. Front handle	11. Trigger	16. Fuel hose	21. Fuel tank
6. Hand guard			22. Vent valve

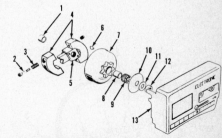

Fig. AP58 — Exploded view of new design clutch used on late 070, 070S, A70 and Super Pro 70 models.

1. Bushing	
2. Screw	8. Bushing
3. Spring	9. Needle bearing
4. Shoes	10. Washer
5. Hub	11. Washer
6. Woodruff key	12. Nut
7. Drum	13. Cover

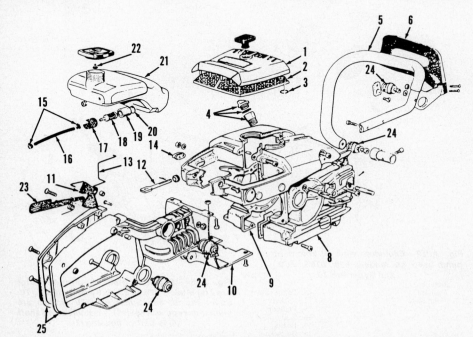

Fig. AP56 — Exploded view of crankcase, front handle assembly, rear grip assembly, fuel tank and related components used on Model Super Pro 70. Refer to legend in Fig. AP55 for component identification except, safety lever (23), vibration isolator (24) and rear grip assembly (25). Super Pro 90 and Super Pro 120 models are similar.

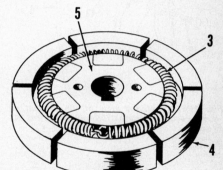

Fig. AP59 — View showing clutch shoes (4), hub (5) and spring (3) used on all early models.

Plunger (15) is 31 mm (1.22 in.) long when new. Renew plunger if worn shorter than 30.3 mm (1.193 in.). Renew drive plate (10) if wear at piston contact area exceeds 1.5 mm (0.059 in.) when compared with a new drive plate. Reservoir (R) should be filled with high temperature lithium base grease and capped with felt plug (20). Pump output is not adjustable.

Refer to Fig. AP63 for exploded view of adjustable automatic oil pump used on Super Pro 90 and Super Pro 120 models. Oil is pumped by piston (5) which is rotated by worm gear (23) mounted on engine crankshaft. Pump output is regulated by turning adjusting lever (28). Renew piston and worm gear if excessive wear or damage is noted. Closely inspect seal (30) and seal surface on worm gear (23). Note that slight wear on seal or worm gear may allow pump to draw air causing pump malfunction. It is recommended to renew seal (30) any time pump is disassembled.

REWIND STARTER. To disassemble starter, remove rope handle (10–Fig. AP64) and carefully allow rope to wind into housing, relieving tension on rewind spring (5). Remove screw (9) and rope pulley (6) using caution not to dislodge rewind spring (5). If rewind spring (5) must be removed, use caution not to allow spring to uncoil uncontrolled.

Install rewind spring (5) into housing (2) in a clockwise direction starting with outer coil. Install rope onto rope pulley (6) in a clockwise direction as viewed from flywheel side of pulley. Rotate pulley (6) clockwise to apply tension on rewind spring. Apply only enough tension on rewind spring (5) to pull rope handle snug against housing. Rope pulley should be able to rotate an additional ½ turn with rope completely extended.

Refer to Fig. AP51 for exploded view of starter pawl assemblies. Use a suitable thread locking solution on pawl bolts (2).

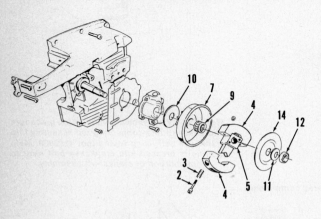

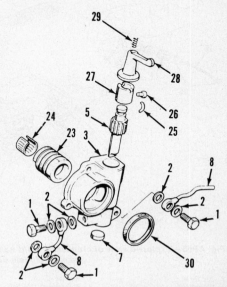

Fig. AP60—Exploded view of clutch used on later Super Pro 90 and Super Pro 120 models.

2.	Screw
3.	Spring
4.	Shoes
5.	Hub
7.	Drum
9.	Needle bearing
10.	Washer
11.	Washer
12.	Nut
14.	Washer

Fig. AP63—Exploded view of adjustable automatic oil pump used on Super Pro 90 and Super Pro 120 models.

1.	Banjo bolt	24.	Collar
2.	Washers	25.	Pin
3.	Pump body	26.	Pin
5.	Piston	27.	Bushing
7.	Plug	28.	Adjusting lever
8.	Tube	29.	Spring
23.	Worm gear	30.	Seal

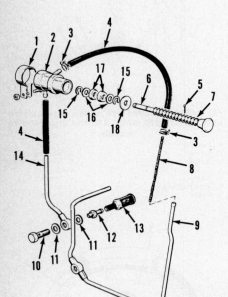

Fig. AP61—Exploded view of the manual oil pump used on Models 070S and Super Pro 70.

1.	Clamp	10.	Bolt
2.	Pump body	11.	Washer
3.	Clamp	12.	Fitting
4.	Hose	13.	Oil pickup
5.	Cotter pin	14.	Tube
6.	Piston	15.	"E" ring
7.	Spring	16.	Washers
8.	Spring	17.	Seals
9.	Tube	18.	Washer

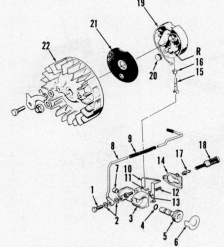

Fig. AP62—Exploded view of automatic oil pump used on Models 070, 070S, A70 and Super Pro 70.

1.	Banjo bolt	13.	Piston brake
2.	Washers	14.	Gasket
3.	Pump body	15.	Plunger
4.	"O" ring	16.	Seal
5.	Piston	17.	Fitting
6.	Cover	18.	Oil pickup
7.	Plug	19.	Module case
8.	Tube	20.	Felt plug
9.	Hose	21.	Cover
10.	Drive plate	22.	Flywheel
11.	Pin	R.	Reservoir
12.	Spring		

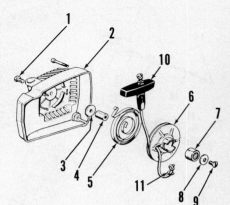

Fig. AP64—Exploded view of rewind starter used on Models 070, 070S, A70 and Super Pro 70. Super Pro 90 and Super Pro 120 models are similar except, washer (11) is not used and shaft (4) is part of housing (2).

1.	Bolt	7.	Needle bearing
2.	Housing	8.	Washer
3.	Washer	9.	Screw
4.	Shaft	10.	Rope handle
5.	Rewind spring	11.	Washer
6.	Rope pulley		

CASTOR

CONSUMER DIVISION OF ALPINA
P.O. Box 777
Griffith, IN 46319

Model	Bore	Stroke	Displ.	Drive Type
330, 432	36.5 mm (1.44 in.)	30.4 mm (1.2 in.)	32 cc (1.9 cu. in.)	Direct
380, 438	39:7 mm (1.56 in.)	30.4 mm (1.2 in.)	38 cc (2.3 cu. in.)	Direct

MAINTENANCE

SPARK PLUG. Recommended spark plug is Champion CJ7Y for all models. Spark plug electrode gap should be 0.5 mm (0.020 in.).

CARBURETOR. Models 330 and 380 are equipped with a Walbro WA diaphragm type carburetor. Models 432 and 438 are equipped with a Dell'Orto diaphragm type carburetor. Refer to Walbro and Dell'Orto sections of CARBURETOR SERVICE section for service procedures and exploded views.

High speed mixture is not adjustable on Models 330 and 380. Initial setting of low speed mixture screw is 1⅜ turns open on Model 330 and 1½ turns open on Model 380. Initial setting on Models 432 and 438 is 1¾ turns open for low speed mixture screw and 1½ turns open for high speed mixture screw.

Final adjustment should be made with engine running at operating temperature. Adjust engine idle speed to just below clutch engagement speed. Adjust low speed mixture so engine will accelerate cleanly without hesitation. Adjust high speed mixture to obtain maximum no-load speed of 11,200 rpm on Model 432 and 11,700 rpm on Model 438.

IGNITION. All models are equipped with a breakerless electronic ignition system. Ignition coil and all electronic circuitry are contained in a one-piece ignition module. Ignition timing is not adjustable. Air gap between ignition module legs and flywheel magnets should be 0.35 mm (0.014 in.). Loosen ignition module mounting screws and move module to adjust air gap. Use a suitable thread locking solution on module screws to prevent screws from vibrating loose. If flywheel requires removal, use Castor tool 3630260 or a suitable equivalent to withdraw flywheel. Tighten flywheel nut to 34.3 N·m (26 ft.-lbs.).

LUBRICATION. The engine is lubricated by mixing oil with the fuel. Use a good quality oil designed for use in air-cooled two-stroke engines. Fuel:oil ratio is 16:1 for all models. Use a separate container when mixing fuel and oil.

Models 330 and 380 are equipped with an automatic oil pump which utilizes crankcase pulsations to pressurize oil tank. Pump output is adjustable. Models 432 and 438 are equipped with an automatic plunger type oil pump driven by a worm gear on engine crankshaft. Pump output is not adjustable. Refer to OIL PUMP under REPAIRS section for service procedures and exploded views.

Use clean automotive oil for saw chain lubrication. On Models 330 and 380, oil viscosity must be chosen according to ambient temperature. For example, use SAE 30 for warm weather operation and SAE 15 for cold weather operation.

REPAIRS

CYLINDER, PISTON, PIN AND RINGS. Cylinder is chrome plated and should be renewed if cracking, scoring or other damage is noted in cylinder bore.

NOTE: Piston aligns connecting rod on rod bearing rollers (25—Fig. CR1). Excessive piston movement during or after cylinder removal may allow rod bearing rollers to fall into crankcase.

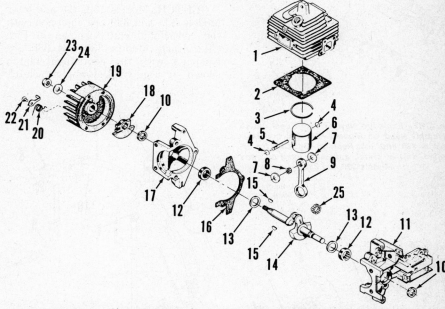

Fig. CR1 — Exploded view of engine assembly typical of all models noting counterweight (18) is absent on Models 432 and 438. Two pawl assemblies (20, 21 and 22) are used.

1. Cylinder	8. Bearing rollers	14. Crankshaft	20. Spring
2. Gasket	9. Connecting rod	15. Key	21. Pawl
3. Piston ring	10. Seal	16. Gasket	22. Pin
4. Snap ring	11. Right crankcase half	17. Left crankcase half	23. Nut
5. Piston pin	12. Main bearing	18. Counterweight	24. Washer
6. Piston	13. Thrust washer	19. Flywheel	25. Bearing rollers
7. Thrust washer			

Piston and cylinder are marked during production to obtain desired piston-to-cylinder clearance of 0.02 mm (0.0008 in.). Original piston and cylinder are marked "A." Factory renewal piston and cylinder assemblies are marked "B." Piston or cylinder marked "C" is 0.127 mm (0.005 in.) oversize while piston or cylinder marked "D" is 0.127 mm (0.005 in.) undersize. Piston and cylinder markings should match, however, a new piston marked "B" can be installed in a used cylinder marked "A."

NOTE: Do not install a new piston marked "B" or "C" into a new cylinder marked "A."

Piston is equipped with one piston ring. A locating pin is present in ring groove to prevent ring rotation. Maximum allowable piston ring end gap is 1.0 mm (0.039 in.). Piston pin (5 – Fig. CR1) rides on 18 loose bearing rollers (8). Use Castor tool 4180010 or a suitable equivalent with proper size drivers to remove and install piston pin. Hold bearing rollers (8) in place with heavy grease and place thrust washer (7) on each side of rod before installing piston. Install piston with arrow on piston crown facing toward exhaust side of cylinder. Make certain piston ring end gap is properly positioned around locating pin in ring groove before installing

cylinder. Tighten cylinder screws to 8.8 N·m (78 in.-lbs.)

CRANKSHAFT, CONNECTING ROD AND CRANKCASE. Crankshaft (14 – Fig. CR1) is supported at both ends with caged roller bearings (12). Bearings (12) are located in crankcase halves (11 and 17). To split crankcase halves, first remove cylinder and crankcase halves mounting screws. Insert a screwdriver or similar tool between crankcase and crankshaft counterweight. Carefully pry crankcase halves apart being careful not to damage crankcase mating surfaces.

NOTE: Crankshaft runout can be checked before disassembly of engine. To check runout, remove clutch and flywheel. Mount a dial indicator on both ends of crankshaft as close as possible to bearings (12). Check runout while rotating crankshaft. Runout should not exceed 0.07 mm (0.0027 in.).

Connecting rod rides on 12 loose bearing rollers (25). Connecting rod can be removed from crankshaft after crankcase halves are separated. Hold bearing rollers on crankpin with heavy grease when installing connecting rod. Note location of thrust washers (13). Counterweight (18) is used on Models 330 and 380 only. Do not use gasket sealing compounds on crankcase gasket (16). Tighten crankcase screws using a crisscross pattern to 6.9 N·m (61 in.-lbs.).

CLUTCH. Models 432, 438 and later Models 330 and 380 are equipped with the centrifugal clutch shown in Fig. CR2. Early Models 330 and 380 are equipped with the centrifugal clutch shown in Fig. CR3. Complete clutch

assemblies are interchangeable, although, individual components are not. Clutch hubs (2 – Figs. CR2 and CR3) have left-hand threads. Inspect shoes, hub, drum and needle bearing for excessive wear or damage due to overheating. Clutch shoes are available only as a complete set. Tighten clutch hub to 18.6 N·m (14 ft.-lbs.).

OIL PUMP. Models 330 and 380 are equipped with the pressure-type chain oiling system shown in Fig. CR4. Impulse hose (3) connects to crankcase. Crankcase pulsations pressurize oil tank (1). Check valve (4) prevents chain oil from entering crankcase. Pump output is regulated by rotating screw (8). Clockwise rotation decreases output. Shut-off valve (10) is linked to throttle trigger, preventing oil flow at idle speed.

Oil tank (1) must hold pressure for proper operation of system. Pressurize oil tank to 34.5 kPa (5.0 psi) to check for leakage in tank or leak-back of check valve (4). Malfunctions are often due to check valve (4) stuck closed preventing crankcase pulsations from entering oil tank.

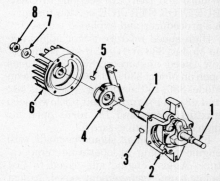

Fig. CR5 – View showing location of automatic oil pump used on Models 432 and 438. Refer to Fig. CR6 for exploded view of oil pump assembly (4).

1. Crankshaft	5. Flywheel key
2. Left crankcase half	6. Flywheel
3. Oil pump key	7. Washer
4. Oil pump assy.	8. Nut

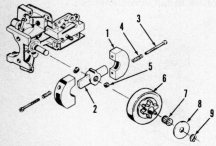

Fig. CR2 – Exploded view of centrifugal clutch assembly used on Models 432, 438 and later Models 330 and 380. Refer to Fig. CR3 for exploded view of clutch assembly used on early Models 330 and 380.

1. Shoe	
2. Hub	
3. Screw	6. Drum
4. Spring	7. Needle bearing
5. Nut	8. Washer
	9. Snap ring

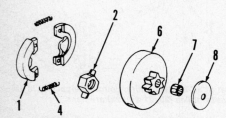

Fig. CR3 – Exploded view of centrifugal clutch assembly used on early Models 330 and 380. Refer to legend in Fig. CR2 for component identification.

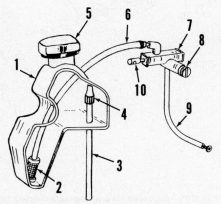

Fig. CR4 – View showing automatic oiling system used on Models 330 and 380.

1. Oil tank	6. Hose
2. Oil filter	7. Metering valve assy.
3. Impulse hose	8. Adjusting screw
4. Check valve	9. Discharge hose
5. Cap	10. Shut-off valve

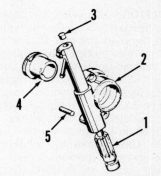

Fig. CR6 – Exploded view of automatic oil pump assembly used on Models 432 and 438.

1. Plunger	
2. Pump body	4. Worm gear
3. Plug	5. Cam pin

Models 432 and 438 are equipped with the automatic oil pump shown in Figs. CR5 and CR6. Pump output is not adjustable. Plunger (1–Fig. CR6) is rotated by worm gear (4) on engine crankshaft. Oil is pumped by plunger (1) as plunger reciprocates in pump body (2) due to cam pin (5) riding in oblique groove in plunger.

Remove flywheel (6–Fig. CR5) to gain access to oil pump. Withdraw cam pin (5–Fig. CR6) to remove plunger (1). Inspect all components for excessive wear or damage and renew if needed. Tighten flywheel nut (8–Fig. CR5) to 34.3 N·m (26 ft.-lbs.).

REWIND STARTER. Models 330 and 380 are equipped with the rewind starter shown in Fig. CR7. Models A432 and A438 are equipped with the rewind starter shown in Fig. CR8.

On all models, remove starter housing (7–Figs. CR7 and CR8) to disassemble starter. Withdraw housing (7) sufficiently to disconnect ignition switch wires then remove housing. Remove rope handle and allow rope to slowly wind into starter housing to relieve tension on re-

wind spring. Remove screw (1) and carefully remove rope pulley (4). If rewind spring (6) must be removed, care should be taken to prevent personal injury due to uncontrolled uncoiling of spring.

Install rewind spring (6) into housing in a clockwise direction starting with outer coil end. Wrap starter rope around rope pulley in a clockwise direction as viewed from flywheel side of pulley. To preload rewind spring, pull out a loop of rope from notch in rope pulley and rotate pulley ½ turn clockwise. Rope handle should be snug against housing with rope retracted. With rope fully extended, rope pulley should be able to rotate an additional ½ turn to prevent rewind spring breakage.

On all models, starter pawls (21–Fig. CR1) are secured on flywheel with pins (22). Drive pins out from inside of flywheel to remove pawls. Use Castor tool 3630260 or a suitable equivalent to remove flywheel. Use a suitable thread locking solution on pins (22) when reassembling pawls. Tighten flywheel nut to 34.3 N·m (26 ft.-lbs.).

CHAIN BRAKE. Some models are equipped with the chain brake system shown in Fig. CR9. Chain brake is actuated when operator's hand strikes hand guard (15). Forward movement of actuator (13) trips latch (11) allowing spring (4) to pull brake band (2) tight around clutch drum (6). Pull back hand guard (15) to reset chain brake.

To adjust chain brake, disengage brake by pulling hand guard (15) to rearmost position (toward engine). Install guide bar and saw chain and properly adjust chain tension. Rotate brake tension adjustment screw (between brake arm mounting studs at front of actuator) clockwise, while pulling saw chain around guide bar, until chain movement becomes difficult. Back off adjustment screw (counterclockwise) until chain moves freely around guide bar. Make certain brake band does not contact clutch drum with brake in the disengaged position.

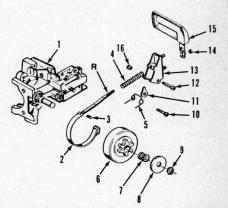

Fig. CR9—Exploded view of chain brake system used on some models. Brake tension screw (not shown) is located at front of actuator (13) between hand guard (15) mounting studs.

1. Right crankcase half
2. Brake band
3. Pin
4. Spring
5. Spring
6. Drum
7. Needle bearing
8. Washer
9. Snap ring
10. Screw
11. Latch
12. Shoulder screw
13. Actuator
14. Nut
15. Hand guard
16. Nut
R. Rod

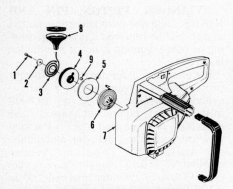

Fig. CR7—Exploded view of rewind starter used on Models 330 and 380.

1. Screw
2. Washer
3. Rope
4. Rope pulley
5. Spring cover
6. Rewind spring
7. Housing
8. Rope handle
9. Eyelet

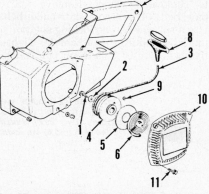

Fig. CR8—Exploded view of rewind starter used on Models 432 and 438. Refer to Fig. CR7 for component identification except cover (10) and screw (11).

CASTOR

Model	Bore	Stroke	Displ.	Drive Type
CP41	40 mm (1.57 in.)	3.15 mm (1.24 in.)	40 cc (2.44 cu. in.)	Direct
CP45	41 mm (1.61 in.)	33.8 mm (1.33 in.)	45 cc (2.74 cu. in.)	Direct

MAINTENANCE

SPARK PLUG. Recommended spark plug for both models is Champion CJ7Y. Electrode gap should be 0.5 mm (0.020 in.).

CARBURETOR. Early Model CP45 is equipped with a Tillotson HU diaphragm carburetor. Model CP41 and late Model CP45 are equipped with a Dell'Orto C16.12 diaphragm carburetor. Refer to Tillotson and Dell'Orto sections of CARBURETOR SERVICE section for service procedures and exploded views.

Initial adjustment on Model CP41 is 2⅛ turns open for low speed mixture screw and ¾ turn open for high speed mixture screw. Initial adjustment on Model CP45 is 1¾ turns open for low speed mixture screw and 1¼ turns for high speed mixture screw.

Final adjustment should be made with engine running at operating tempera-ture. Adjust idle speed to just below clutch engagement speed. Adjust low speed mixture screw so engine will ac-celerate cleanly without hesitation. Adjust high speed mixture screw to obtain maximum no-load speed of 12,000 rpm on Model CP41 and 12,400 rpm on Model CP45.

IGNITION. Both models are equipped with a breakerless electronic ignition system. Refer to Fig. CR16. Ig-nition coil and all electronic circuitry are contained in a one-piece ignition module (8). Ignition timing is not adjustable. Air gap between ignition module and fly-wheel magnets should be 0.35 mm (0.014 in.).

On all models, use Castor tool 4180100 or a suitable equivalent bolt-type puller to remove flywheel. Remove starter pawl bolts (4) to accomodate puller bolts. Use a suitable thread locking solution on pawl bolts during reassembly. Tighten flywheel nut to 28.4 N·m (21 ft.-lbs.).

Use a suitable thread locking solution on ignition coil/module attaching screws if air gap is adjusted.

LUBRICATION. The engine is lubricated by mixing oil with the fuel. Use a good quality oil designed for use in air-cooled two-stroke engines. Fuel:oil mixture should be a 16:1 ratio. Use a separate container when mixing fuel and oil.

Both models are equipped with the automatic oil pump shown in Fig. CR23. Pump output is not adjustable. Use clean automotive oil for saw chain lubrication.

REPAIRS

CYLINDER, PISTON, PIN AND RINGS. Cylinder bore is chrome plated and should be renewed if cracking, scor-ing or other damage is noted in cylinder bore.

Piston and cylinder are marked during protection to obtain desired piston-to-cylinder clearance of 0.02 mm (0.0008 in.). Original equipment piston and cylinder are marked "A." Factory renewal piston and cylinder assemblies are marked "B." Piston or cylinder marked "C" is 0.127 mm (0.005 in.) over-size. Piston or cylinder marked "D" is 0.127 mm (0.005 in.) undersize. Piston and cylinder markings should match, however, a new piston marked "B" can be installed into a used cylinder marked "A."

NOTE: Do not install a new piston marked "B" or "C" into a new cylinder marked "A."

Piston is equipped with two piston rings. Piston ring end gap should not ex-ceed 1.0 mm (0.039 in.). Locating pins are present in ring grooves to prevent ring rotation. Make certain ring end gaps are properly positioned around locating pins when installing cylinder.

Piston pin (5 – Fig. CR17) rides in nee-dle bearing (7) and is retained with two snap rings (6). Use Castor tool 4180010 or a suitable equivalent to press out pin. Piston may be heated to approximately

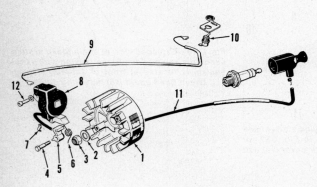

Fig. CR16 – Exploded view of electronic ignition system. Two pawl assem-blies (4, 5 and 6) are used.

1. Flywheel
2. Washer
3. Nut
4. Bolt
5. Pawl
6. Spring
7. Clamp
8. Ignition module
9. Primary lead
10. Ignition switch
11. High tension lead
12. Screw

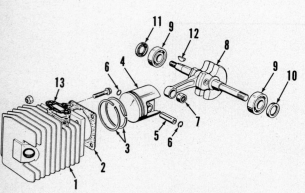

Fig. CR17 – Exploded view of engine assembly.

1. Cylinder
2. Gasket
3. Piston rings
4. Piston
5. Piston pin
6. Snap ring
7. Needle bearing
8. Crankshaft & connecting rod assy.
9. Main bearings
10. Seal
11. Seal
12. Key
13. Gasket

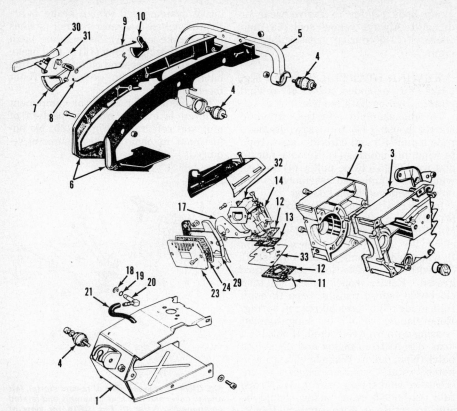

Fig. CR19—Exploded view of crankcase, handle assemblies, carburetor and related components used on Model CP41.

1. Cylinder cover	8. Throttle rod	23. Cover
2. Left crankcase half	9. Throttle rod	24. Air filter
3. Right crankcase half	10. Throttle trigger	29. Air filter base
4. Vibration isolator	11. Intake spacer	30. Safety lever
5. Front handle	12. Gasket	31. Spring
6. Rear grip assy.	13. Heat shield	32. Air intake
7. Throttle trigger	14. Carburetor	33. Gasket
	17. Choke valve	
	18. "E" ring	
	19. "O" ring	
	20. Fitting	
	21. Fuel hose	

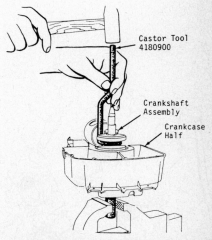

Fig. CR20—Exploded view of crankcase, handle assemblies, carburetor and related components used on Model CP45. Refer to legend in Fig. CR19 for component identification except for spacer (16), seal (22), support (26) and seal (28).

110°-120° C (230°-248° F) to ease installation of piston pin.

NOTE: Use electric oven or hot oil bath to heat piston. Do not use an open flame.

Install piston into cylinder with arrow on piston crown facing toward exhaust port.

CRANKSHAFT, CONNECTING ROD AND CRANKCASE. Crankshaft and connecting rod are available as a unit assembly only. Check rotation of connecting rod around crankpin and renew crankshaft assembly if roughness, excessive play or other damage is noted. Check crankshaft runout by supporting crankshaft assembly between two counter points—such as a lathe. Make certain no damage exists to centering holes at each end of crankshaft. Maximum allowable runout is 0.08 mm (0.0031 in.).

NOTE: Crankshaft runout can be checked while still assembled in crankcase. Remove clutch and flywheel and mount dial indicators on both sides of crankshaft as close to main bearings as possible. Measure runout while rotating crankshaft. Renew crankshaft assembly if runout exceeds 0.07 mm (0.0027 in.), when measured in this manner.

Crankshaft is supported at both ends by ball-type main bearings (9–Fig. CR17) that locate in crankcase halves (2 and 3–Figs. CR19 and CR20). Use the proper size drivers to remove and install main bearings. Use Castor tool 4180900 to install crankshaft assembly into main bearing. Refer to Fig. CR21. Do not use

Fig. CR21—View showing installation procedure of crankshaft and connecting rod assembly into crankcase using Castor tool 4180900. Main bearing (9 – Fig. CR17) is pressed into crankcase half prior to installation of crankshaft assembly.

gasket sealer on crankcase gasket. Tighten crankcase screws using a crisscross pattern to 6.9 N·m (61 in.-lbs.).

CLUTCH. Both models are equipped with the centrifugal clutch assembly shown in Fig. CR22. Clutch hub (1) has left-hand threads.

Inspect shoes (2), drum (7), needle bearing (6) and bushing (5) for excessive wear or damage due to overheating and renew if needed. Shoes (2) are available only as a complete set. Tighten clutch hub (1) to 28.4 N·m (21 ft.-lbs.).

OIL PUMP. Both models are equipped with the automatic oil pump assembly shown in Fig. CR23. Pump output is not adjustable. Oil is pumped by plunger (2) which is driven by worm gear (3) on end of engine crankshaft. Pump plunger (2) reciprocates in pump body (1) due to cam bolt (14) riding in oblique groove in plunger. Plunger can be removed from housing after removing cam bolt (14) and bushing (4). Inspect worm gear (3), plunger (2) and

pump body (1) for excessive wear or damage. Always renew seal (12) and washers (18) during reassembly of pump.

REWIND STARTER. Refer to Fig. CR24 for exploded view of rewind starter used on both models.

To disassemble starter, remove starter housing (1) from saw. Remove rope handle (3) and carefully allow rope to wind into housing (1). Remove nut (6) and washer (5). Rope pulley (4) and rewind spring and case assembly (2) can now be removed from housing.

Install rewind spring (2) into housing (1) with open side of case facing housing (1). Wind rope onto rope pulley (4) in a clockwise direction as viewed from flywheel side of pulley. Lubricate shaft (S) with a suitable low temperature grease. Rotate rope pulley ½ turn clockwise before passing rope through rope guide (G) to preload rewind spring. Rope handle should be snug against housing with rope retracted. If not, lift a loop of rope from pulley and place into notch (N) in pulley. While holding rope in notch, rotate pulley clockwise to increase rewind spring tension. With rope fully extended, rope pulley should be able to rotate ½ turn further. If not, repeat above procedure, only rotate pulley counterclockwise to decrease rewind spring tension.

Refer to Fig. CR16 for exploded view or starter pawl assemblies. Use a suitable thread locking solution on pawl bolts (4). Tighten flywheel nut to 28.4 N·m (21 ft.-lbs.).

CHAIN BRAKE. Both models are equipped with a chain brake system designed to quickly stop chain movement should kickback occur. Refer to Fig. CR25 for exploded view of chain

brake system used. Chain brake is activated when operator's hand strikes chain brake lever (1), disengaging latch (7) and allowing spring (14) to pull brake band (10) tight around clutch drum. Pull back chain brake lever to reset mechanism.

Disassembly for repair or component renewal is evident after inspection of unit and referral to Fig. CR25. No adjustment of chain brake system is required.

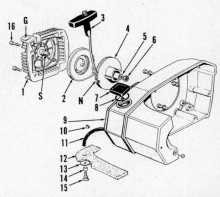

Fig. CR24 — Exploded view of rewind starter, left engine cover and fuel tank assembly and related components. Refer to Fig. CR16 for view of flywheel and starter pawls.

G. Rope guide	7. Fuel cap
N. Notch	8. Seal
S. Shaft	9. Left engine cover &
1. Starter housing	fuel tank assy.
2. Rewind spring &	10. Clamp
case assy.	11. Fuel hose
3. Rope handle	12. Felt
4. Rope pulley	13. Washer
5. Washer	14. Fuel screen
6. Nut	15. Fuel pickup

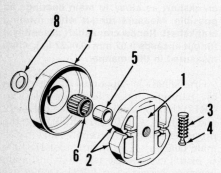

Fig. CR22 — Exploded view of centrifugal clutch assembly.

1. Hub	5. Bushing
2. Shoes	6. Needle bearing
3. Spring	7. Drum
4. Spring guide	8. Washer

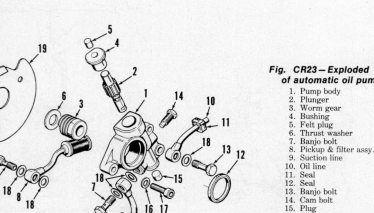

Fig. CR23 — Exploded view of automatic oil pump.

1. Pump body
2. Plunger
3. Worm gear
4. Bushing
5. Felt plug
6. Thrust washer
7. Banjo bolt
8. Pickup & filter assy.
9. Suction line
10. Oil line
11. Seal
12. Seal
13. Banjo bolt
14. Cam bolt
15. Plug
16. Washer
17. Screw
18. Washers
19. Plate

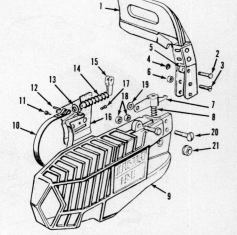

Fig. CR25 — Exploded view of chain brake assembly.

1. Chain brake lever			
2. Pin		12. Pin	
3. Screw		13. Washer	
4. "E" ring		14. Spring	
5. Spacer		15. Arm	
6. Nut		16. Guide plate	
7. Latch		17. Screw	
8. Spring		18. Nuts	
9. Housing		19. Washer	
10. Brake band		20. Screw	
11. Screw		21. Nut	

CASTOR

Model	Bore	Stroke	Displ.	Drive Type
CP55	44 mm (1.73 in.)	36 mm (1.42 in.)	49 cc (3.4 cu. in.)	Direct
CP65	47 mm (1.85 in.)	37.3 mm (1.47 in.)	65 cc (4.0 cu. in.)	Direct

MAINTENANCE

SPARK PLUG. Recommended spark plug for both models is Champion CJ7Y. Electrode gap should be 0.5 mm (0.020 in.).

CARBURETOR. Both models are equipped with a Tillotson HK diaphragm carburetor. Refer to Tillotson section of CARBURETOR SERVICE section for service procedure and exploded view.

Initial adjustment of low speed mixture screw is 1½ turns open on Model CP55 and 1⅜ turns open on Model CP65. Initial adjustment of high speed mixture screw is ¾ turn open for both models.

Final adjustment should be made with engine running at operating temperature. Adjust idle speed to just below clutch engagement speed. Adjust low speed mixture screw so engine will accelerate cleanly without hesitation. Adjust high speed mixture screw to obtain maximum no-load speed of 12,000 rpm for Model CP55 and 11,600 rpm for Model CP65.

IGNITION. Model CP55 manufactured prior to 1985 and Model CP65 manufactured prior to 1984 are equipped with a breaker-point ignition system. Breaker-point gap should be 0.45-0.50 mm (0.018-0.020 in.). Air gap between ignition coil legs and flywheel magnets should be 0.45 mm (0.018 in.). Loosen coil attaching screws and move coil to adjust air gap. Use a suitable thread locking solution on coil attaching screws. Ignition timing is not adjustable, however, breaker-point gap will affect timing. Be sure breaker-point gap is adjusted correctly as a gap too wide will advance timing and a gap too close will retard timing.

Model CP55 manufactured after 1984 and Model CP65 manufactured after 1983 are equipped with a breakerless electronic ignition system. Some models are equipped with a standard ignition coil with an electronic module located behind flywheel. On other models, ignition coil and all electronic circuitry are contained in a one-piece ignition module/coil (2 – Fig. CR35). Air gap between ignition module/coil and flywheel magnets should be 0.35-0.40 mm (0.014-0.016 in.). Use a suitable thread locking solution on module/coil attaching screws.

On both models, use Castor tool 4180140 to remove flywheel. If Castor tool 4180140 is not available, remove starter pawl assemblies (6, 7, 8 and 9) to accomodate a bolt-type puller. Use a suitable thread locking solution on pawl bolts (6) during reassembly. Tighten flywheel nut (10) to 34.8 N·m (26 ft.-lbs.).

LUBRICATION. The engine is lubricated by mixing oil with the fuel. Use a good quality oil designed for use in air-cooled two-stroke engines. Fuel:oil mixture should be 16:1 ratio. Use a separate container when mixing fuel and oil.

Both models are equipped with an automatic chain oil pump. Oil pump is driven by a worm gear coupled to clutch drum. Pump output is not adjustable. Refer to OIL PUMP under REPAIRS section for service and exploded view. Use clean automotive oil for saw chain lubrication.

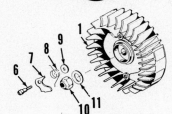

Fig. CR35 – Exploded view of breakerless electronic ignition system typical of type used. Refer to text.

1. Flywheel
2. Ignition module/coil
3. High tension lead
4. Ignition switch
5. Primary lead
6. Pawl bolt
7. Pawl
8. Spring
9. Washer
10. Nut
11. Washer

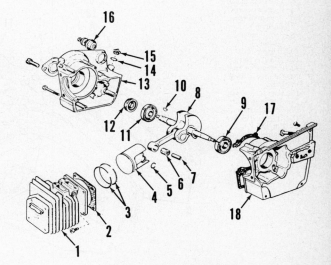

Fig. CR36 – Exploded view of typical engine assembly.

1. Cylinder
2. Gasket
3. Piston rings
4. Piston
5. Retainer
6. Needle bearing
7. Piston pin
8. Crankshaft & connecting rod assy.
9. Right main bearing
10. Woodruff key
11. Left main bearing
12. Seal
13. Left crankcase half
14. Seal
15. Oil cap
16. Vibration isolator
17. Gasket
18. Right crankcase half

REPAIRS

CYLINDER, PISTON, PIN AND RINGS. Cylinder bore is chrome plated and should be renewed if cracking, scoring or other damage is noted in cylinder bore.

Piston and cylinder are marked during production to obtain desired piston-to-cylinder clearance of 0.02 mm (0.0008

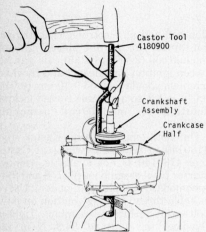

Fig. CR37—View showing installation of crankshaft and connecting rod assembly into crankcase using Castor tool 4180900. Main bearing (9—Fig. CR36) is pressed into crankcase half prior to installation of crankshaft assembly.

in.). Original equipment piston and cylinder are marked "A." Factory renewal piston and cylinder assemblies are marked "B." Piston or cylinder marked "C" is 0.127 mm (0.005 in.) oversize. Piston and cylinder marked "D" is 0.127 mm (0.005 in.) undersize. Piston and cylinder markings should match, however, a new piston marked "B" can be installed into a used cylinder marked "A."

NOTE: Do not install a new piston marked "B" or "C" into a new cylinder marked "A."

Piston is equipped with two piston rings. Piston ring end gap should not exceed 1.0 mm (0.039 in.). Locating pins are present in ring grooves to prevent ring rotation. Make certain ring end gaps are properly positioned around locating pins when installing cylinder.

Piston pin (7—Fig. CR36) rides in needle bearing (6) and is retained with two snap rings (5). Use Castor tool 4180010 or a suitable equivalent to press out pin.

Piston may be heated to approximately 110°-120° C (230°-248° F) to ease piston pin installation.

NOTE: Use electric oven or hot oil bath to heat piston. Do not use and open flame.

Install piston into cylinder with arrow on piston crown facing toward exhaust port.

CRANKSHAFT, CONNECTING ROD AND CRANKCASE. Crankshaft and connecting rod (8—Fig. CR36) are available as a unit assembly only. Check rotation of connecting rod around crankpin and renew crankshaft assembly if roughness, excessive play or other damage is noted. Check crankshaft runout by supporting crankshaft assembly between two counter points such as a lathe. Make certain no damage exists to centering holes at each end of crankshaft. Maximum allowable runout is 0.08 mm (0.0031 in.).

NOTE: Crankshaft runout can be checked while still assembled in

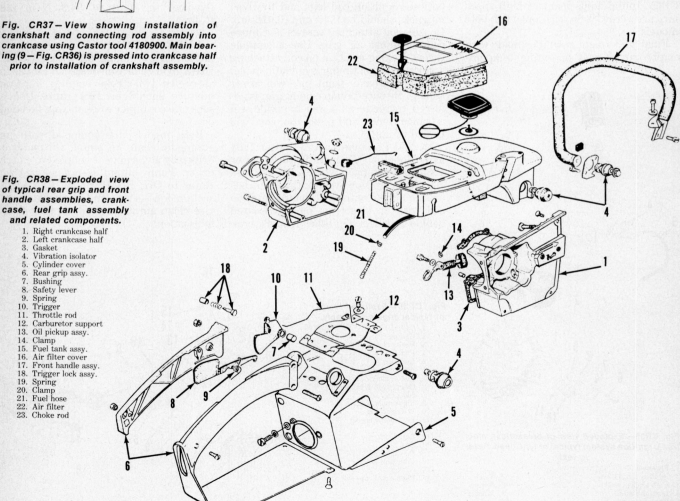

Fig. CR38—Exploded view of typical rear grip and front handle assemblies, crankcase, fuel tank assembly and related components.

1. Right crankcase half
2. Left crankcase half
3. Gasket
4. Vibration isolator
5. Cylinder cover
6. Rear grip assy.
7. Bushing
8. Safety lever
9. Spring
10. Trigger
11. Throttle rod
12. Carburetor support
13. Oil pickup assy.
14. Clamp
15. Fuel tank assy.
16. Air filter cover
17. Front handle assy.
18. Trigger lock assy.
19. Spring
20. Clamp
21. Fuel hose
22. Air filter
23. Choke rod

crankcase. Remove clutch and flywheel and mount dial indicators on both sides of crankshaft as close to main bearings as possible. Measure runout while rotating crankshaft. Renew crankshaft assembly if runout exceeds 0.07 mm (0.0027 in.) when measured in this manner.

Crankshaft is supported at both ends with ball-type main bearings (9 and 11). Main bearings located in crankcase halves (13 and 18). Use the proper size drivers to remove and install main bearings. Use Castor tool 4180900 to install crankshaft assembly into main bearing. Refer to Fig. CR37. Do not use gasket sealer on crankcase gasket (17–Fig. CR36). Tighten crankcase screws using a crisscross pattern to 6.4 N·m (57 in.-lbs.).

CLUTCH. Refer to Fig. CR39 for an exploded view of clutch assembly used on both models. Clutch hub (4) has left hand threads. Inspect shoes (5), drum (3) and needle bearing (2) for excessive wear or damage due to overheating. Shoes (5) are available only as a complete set. Tighten clutch hub (4) to 41.2 N·m (31 ft.-lbs.).

OIL PUMP. Both models are equipped with the automatic oil pump shown in Fig. CR40. Oil is pumped by plunger (6) which is rotated by worm gear (1). Drive lugs (L) on worm gear (1) engage clutch drum, therefore oil is pumped only when saw chain is rotating.

To disassemble pump, remove cam bolt (5), plug (8) and bushing (7). Plunger (6) can now be removed for inspection or renewal. Carefully inspect seal (2) and seal surface on worm gear (1). Note that slight wear on seal or worm gear may allow pump to draw air causing pump malfunction. It is recommended to renew seal (2) any time pump is disassembled.

REWIND STARTER. All models are equipped with the rewind starter shown in Fig. CR41. To disassemble starter, remove starter housing (5) from saw. Remove rope handle (4) and carefully allow rope to wind into starter, relieving tension on rewind spring (2). Starter drive (6) is a press fit in rope pulley (3). Remove rope and tap drive (6) out of pulley (3) toward flywheel side of housing (5) using a proper size punch and hammer.

Rewind spring (2) is retained in a plastic case. Install spring with open side of case toward starter cover (1). Install starter drive (6) with hole in drive aligned with hole in rope pulley. Wind rope onto rope pulley in a clockwise direction as viewed from flywheel side of pulley.

Rotate starter cover (1) clockwise before installing cover screws to engage rope pulley and preload rewind spring. Preload spring only enough to pull rope handle snug against housing. Rope pulley should be able to rotate an additional ½ turn clockwise with rope fully extended to prevent rewind spring breakage.

Refer to Fig. CR35 for view of starter pawls. Use a suitable thread locking solution on pawl bolts (6).

CHAIN BRAKE. Some models are equipped with a chain brake system designed to stop chain movement should kickback occur. Chain brake is activated when operator's hand strikes hand guard (12–Fig. CR39), tripping lever (16) and allowing spring (15) to draw brake band (14) tight around clutch drum (3). Pull back hand guard to reset mechanism.

Disassembly is evident after inspection of unit and referral to exploded view. Renew any component excessively worn or damaged. Chain brake should be clean and free of sawdust and dirt accumulation. No adjustment of chain brake is required.

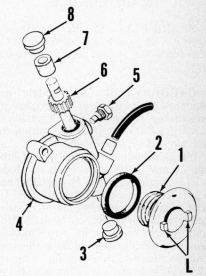

Fig. CR40—Exploded view of automatic oil pump assembly.

1. Worm gear	
2. Seal	6. Plunger
3. Plug	7. Bushing
4. Housing	8. Plug
5. Cam bolt	L. Drive lugs

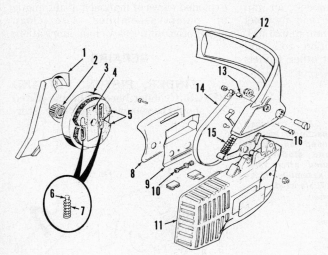

Fig. CR39—Exploded view of clutch and chain brake. Chain brake is optional on both models.

1. Plate
2. Needle bearing
3. Drum
4. Hub
5. Shoes
6. Spring guide
7. Spring
8. Inner guide plate
9. Outer guide plate
10. Bar adjusting screw
11. Cover
12. Hand guard
13. Spacer
14. Brake band
15. Spring
16. Lever

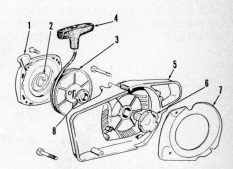

Fig. CR41—Exploded view of rewind starter assembly.

1. Starter cover	5. Housing
2. Rewind spring	6. Starter drive
3. Rope pulley	7. Baffle
4. Rope handle	8. Bushing

CASTOR

Model	Bore	Stroke	Displ.	Drive Type
C70, CP70S	51 mm (2.0 in.)	34.5 mm (1.36 in.)	70 cc (4.3 cu. in.)	Direct
CP90	54 mm (2.13 in.)	39.1 mm (1.54 in.)	90 cc (5.5 cu. in.)	Direct
CP120	58 mm (2.28 in.)	45.5 mm (1.79 in.)	120 cc (7.3 cu. in.)	Direct

MAINTENANCE

SPARK PLUG. Recommended spark plug for all models is Champion CJ7Y. Electrode gap should be 0.5 mm (0.020 in.).

CARBURETOR. All models are equipped with a Tillotson HS diaphragm carburetor. Refer to Tillotson section of CARBURETOR SERVICE section for service and exploded views.

Initial adjustment of low speed mixture screw is 1⅞ turns open on Model CP120, 2 turns open on Model CP90 and 1¾ turns open on all other models. Initial adjustment of high speed mixture screw is ⅞ turn open on Model CP120 and ¾ turn open on all other models. Final adjustment should be made with engine running at operating temperature. Adjust idle speed to just below clutch engagement speed. Adjust low speed mixture screw so engine will accelerate cleanly without hesitation. Adjust high speed mixture screw to obtain maximum speed of 10,300 rpm on Model CP120, 9,700 rpm on Model CP90 and 10,500 rpm on all other models.

IGNITION. Model C70 manufactured prior to 1984 is equipped with a breaker-point ignition system. All other models, including Model C70 manufactured after 1983, are equipped with a breakerless electronic ignition system.

Breaker-Point Ignition. Breaker-point gap should be 0.45-0.50 mm (0.018-0.020 in.). Air gap between ignition coil lamination and flywheel magnets should be 0.45 mm (0.018 in.). Use a suitable thread locking solution on coil attaching screws. Ignition timing is not adjustable, however, breaker-point gap will affect timing. Be sure breaker-point gap is adjusted correctly.

Electronic Ignition. Refer to Fig. CR51 for exploded view of electronic ignition system used on Model CP70S and so equipped C70 models. Note that coil (8) is located outside of flywheel (1) while ignition module (13) is located behind flywheel (1). Models CP90 and CP120 are equipped with the electronic ignition system shown in Fig. CR52. Ignition coil and all electronic circuitry are contained in a one-piece ignition module (13).

Except for faulty wiring or wiring connections, repair of ignition system malfunctions is accomplished by component renewal.

On CP90 and CP120 models, air gap between ignition module and flywheel magnets should be 0.65 mm (0.026 in.). Air gap between ignition coil and flywheel magnets on all other models should be 0.40 mm (0.016 in.). Use a suitable thread locking solution on module (or coil) attaching screws. Ignition timing is not adjustable on all models.

Starter pawl assemblies (2, 3, 4 and 7 – Fig. CR51) can be removed to accomodate a suitable bolt-type puller to remove flywheel on all models. Use a suitable thread locking solution on bolts (2) when reassembling pawls. Tighten flywheel nut to 39.2 N·m (29 ft.-lbs.) on CP 90 and CP120 models and 28.4 N·m (21 ft.-lbs.) on all other models.

LUBRICATION. The engine is lubricated by mixing oil with the fuel. Use a good quality oil designed for use in air-cooled two-stroke engines. Fuel:oil mixture should be a 16:1 ratio. Use a separate container when mixing fuel and oil.

Model CP70S is equipped with a manual and automatic chain oil pump. All other models are only equipped with an automatic chain oil pump. Automatic oil pump output is only adjustable on CP90 and CP120 models. Refer to OIL PUMP under REPAIRS section for service and exploded views of manual and automatic oil pump assemblies. Use clean automotive oil for saw chain lubrication.

REPAIRS

CYLINDER, PISTON, PIN AND RINGS. Cylinder bore is chrome plated and should be renewed if cracking, scor-

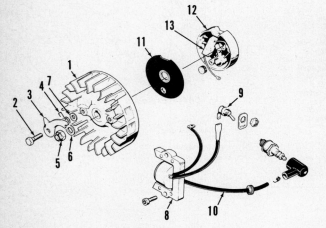

Fig. Fig. CR51—Exploded view of electronic ignition system used on Model CP70S and Model C70 manufactured after 1983. Two pawl assemblies (2,3,4 and 7) are used.

1. Flywheel
2. Bolt
3. Pawl
4. Spring
5. Nut
6. Washer
7. Washer
8. Ignition coil
9. Ignition switch
10. High tension lead
11. Cover
12. Module case
13. Module

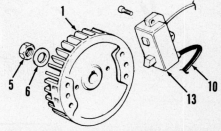

Fig. CR52 — Exploded view of electronic ignition system used on CP90 and CP120 models. Refer to Fig. CR51 for component identification.

ing or other damage is noted in cylinder bore. Note that cylinder used on CP90 and CP120 models is equipped with decompression valve (28–Fig. CR54) to ease starting.

Piston and cylinder are marked during production to obtain desired piston-to-cylinder clearance of 0.02 mm (0.0008 in.). Original equipment piston and cylinder are marked "A." Factory renewal piston and cylinder assemblies are marked "B." Piston or cylinder marked "C" is 0.127 (0.005 in.) oversize. Piston or cylinder marked "D" is 0.127 mm (0.005 in.) undersize. Piston and cylinder markings should match, however, a new piston marked "B" can be installed into used cylinder marked "A."

NOTE: Do not install a new piston marked "B" or "C" into a new cylinder marked "A."

Piston is equipped with two piston rings. Piston should be inspected and renewed if cracking or scoring is noted. Maximum allowable piston ring end gap is 1.0 mm (0.039 in.). Locating pins are present in ring grooves to prevent ring rotation. Be certain ring end gaps are properly positioned around locating pins when installing cylinder. Tighten cylinder screws to 11.8 N·m (9 ft.-lbs.) on all models.

On Models C70 and CP70S, piston pin (8–Fig. CR53) is a press fit in connecting rod small end. Piston pin rides in needle bearings (7) installed in each side of piston. Piston pin is retained with two snap rings (9). Use Castor tool 4180020 or a suitable equivalent press to remove and install piston pin. Be sure piston in properly supported to prevent damage to piston.

On all other models, piston pin (8–Fig. CR54) is a press fit in piston and rides in one needle bearing (7) installed in connecting rod small end. Piston pin is retained with two wire clips (9). Use Castor tool 4180010 or a suitable equivalent to remove and install piston pin. Piston may be heated to approximately 110°-120° C (230°-248° F) to ease installation of piston pin.

NOTE: Use electric oven or hot oil bath to heat piston. Do not use an open flame.

On all models, install piston into cylinder with arrow on piston crown facing toward exhaust port.

CRANKSHAFT, CONNECTING ROD AND CRANKCASE. Crankshaft and connecting rod are available as a unit assembly only. Check rotation of connecting rod around crankpin and renew crankshaft assembly if rough-

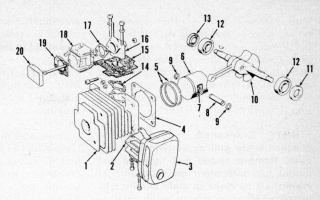

Fig. CR53 – Exploded view of engine assembly, carburetor and related components used on Models C70 and CP70S. Two needle bearings (7) are used. Refer to text.

1. Cylinder
2. Gasket
3. Muffler
4. Gasket
5. Piston rings
6. Piston
7. Needle bearing
8. Piston pin
9. Snap ring
10. Crankshaft & connecting rod assy.
11. Seal
12. Main bearing
13. Seal
14. Gasket
15. Gasket
16. Intake manifold
17. Gasket
18. Carburetor
19. Plate
20. Screen

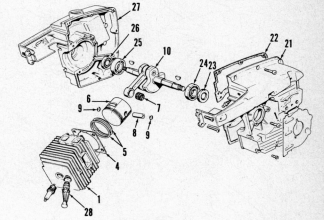

Fig. CR54 – Exploded view of engine assembly used on Models CP90 and CP120.

1. Cylinder
4. Gasket
5. Piston rings
6. Piston
7. Needle bearing
8. Piston pin
9. Wire clip
10. Crankshaft & connecting rod assy.
21. Right crankcase half
22. Gasket
23. Seal
24. Main bearing
25. Main bearing
26. Seal
27. Left crankcase half
28. Decompression valve

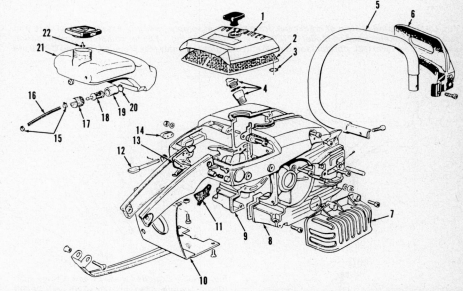

Fig. CR55 – Exploded view of crankcases, front handle assembly, fuel tank and related components used on Model C70.

1. Cover
2. Air filter
3. Snap ring
4. Oil tank cap assy.
5. Front handle
6. Hand guard
7. Muffler cover
8. Right crankcase half
9. Left crankcase half
10. Cylinder cover
11. Trigger
12. Choke lever
13. Throttle rod
14. Grommet
15. Clamp
16. Fuel hose
17. Screen
18. Fuel pickup
19. Filter
20. "O" ring
21. Fuel tank
22. Vent valve

ness, excessive play or other damage is noted. Check crankshaft runout by supporting crankshaft between two counter points such as a lathe. Make certain no damage is present in centering holes at each end of crankshaft. Renew crankshaft assembly if runout exceeds 0.08 mm (0.0031 in.).

NOTE: Crankshaft runout can be checked while still assembled in crankcase. Remove clutch and flywheel and mount dial indicators on each side of crankshaft as close to main bearings as possible. Measure runout while rotating

crankshaft. **Renew crankshaft assembly if runout exceeds 0.07 mm (0.0027 in.) when measured in this manner.**

Crankshaft is supported with ball-type main bearings (12–Fig. CR53) or (24 and 25–Fig. CR54) at both ends. Main bearings are a press fit into crankcase halves. Use the proper size drivers to remove and install main bearings. Use Castor tool 4180900 or a suitable equivalent to install crankshaft assembly into crankcase. Refer to Fig. CR57. Do not use gasket sealer on crankcase gasket. Tighten crankcase screws using a

crisscross pattern to 7.8 N·m (69 in.-lbs.) on CP90 and CP120 models and 7.3 N·m (65 in.-lbs.) on all other models.

CLUTCH. Late Models C70 and CP70S are equipped with the clutch assembly shown in Fig. CR58. Late Models CP90 and CP120 are equipped with the clutch assembly shown in Fig. CR60. Refer to Fig. CR59 for view of shoes (4), hub (5) and spring (3) used on all early models. Note that hub (5–Figs. CR58, CR59 and CR60) is keyed to crankshaft on all models. Inspect shoes (4–Fig. CR58 or Fig. CR60), drum (7) and needle bearing (9) for excessive wear or damage due to overheating. Use Castor tool 4180110 or a suitable bolt-type puller to remove clutch. Nut (12) has right-hand threads. Clutch shoes (4) are available only as a complete set. Tighten nut (12) to 45.1 N·m (33 ft.-lbs.) on CP90 and CP120 models and 35.3 N·m (26 ft.-lbs.) on all other models.

OIL PUMP. Refer to Fig. CR61 for exploded view of manual chain oil pump used on Model CP70S. Disassembly for repair or component renewal is evident after inspection of unit and referral to Fig. CR61. Hoses (4) must be renewed if pump is disassembled. Be sure clamps (3) are tight and properly installed to prevent leakage.

Refer to Fig. CR62 for exploded view of automatic oil pump used on Models C70 and CP70S. Oil is pumped by piston (5) which is rotated by drive plate (10). Drive plate is cycled up and down by plunger (15) which rides on cam of engine crankshaft. Piston (5) rotates one notch with each down stroke of drive plate (10). Spring (12) forces piston brake (13) against piston (5), preventing piston (5) from backing up during drive plate (10) return stroke.

Plunger (15) is 31 mm (1.22 in.) long when new. Renew plunger if worn shorter than 30.3 mm (1.193 in.). Renew drive plate (10) if wear at piston contact area exceeds 1.5 mm (0.059 in.) when

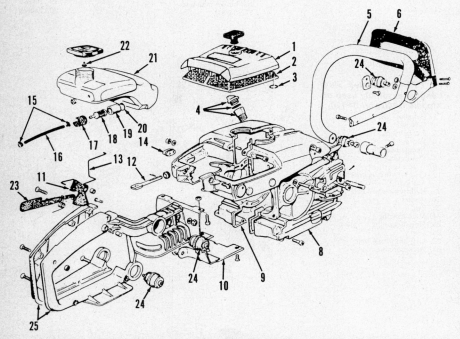

Fig. CR56—Exploded view of crankcase, front handle assembly, rear grip assembly, fuel tank and related components used on Model CP70S. Refer to legend in Fig. CR55 for component identification except, safety lever (23), vibrator isolator (24) and rear grip assembly (25). Models CP90 and CP120 are similar.

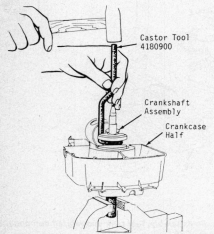

Fig. CP57—View showing installation procedure of crankshaft and connecting rod assembly into crankcase half using Castor tool 4180900. Main bearing is pressed into crankcase half prior to installation of crankshaft assembly.

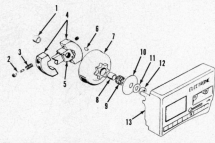

Fig. CR58—Exploded view of new design centrifugal clutch used on late C70 and CP70S models.

1. Bushing
2. Screw
3. Spring
4. Shoes
5. Hub
6. Woodruff key
7. Drum
8. Bushing
9. Needle bearing
10. Washer
11. Washer
12. Nut
13. Cover

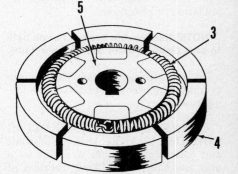

Fig. CR59—View showing clutch shoes (4), hub (5) and spring (3) used on all early models.

compared with a new drive plate. Reservoir (R) should be filled with high temperature lithium base grease and capped with felt plug (20). Pump output is not adjustable.

Refer to Fig. CR63 for exploded view of adjustable automatic oil pump used on CP90 and CP120 models. Oil is pumped by piston (5) which is rotated by worm gear (23) mounted on engine crankshaft. Pump output is regulated by turning adjusting lever (28). Renew piston and worm gear if excessive wear or damage is noted. Closely inspect seal (30) and seal surface on worm gear (23). Note that slight wear on seal or worm gear may allow pump to draw air causing pump malfunction. It is recommended to renew seal (30) any time pump is disassembled.

REWIND STARTER. To disassemble starter, remove rope handle (10 – Fig. CR64) and carefully allow rope to wind into housing, relieving tension on rewind spring (5). Remove screw (9) and rope pulley (6) using caution not to dislodge rewind spring (5). If rewind spring (5) must be removed, use caution not to allow spring to uncoil uncontrolled.

Install rewind spring (5) into housing (2) in a clockwise direction starting with outer coil. Install rope onto rope pulley (6) in a clockwise direction as viewed from flywheel side of pulley. Rotate pulley (6) clockwise to apply tension on rewind spring. Apply only enough tension on rewind spring (5) to pull rope handle snug against housing. Rope pulley should be able to rotate an additional ½ turn with rope completely extended.

Refer to Fig. CR51 for exploded view of starter pawl assemblies. Use a suitable thread locking solution on pawl bolts (2).

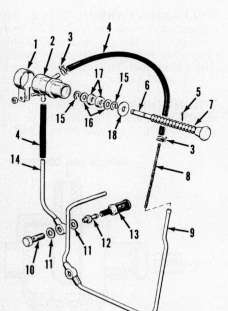

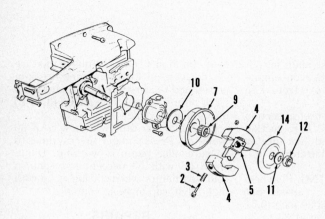

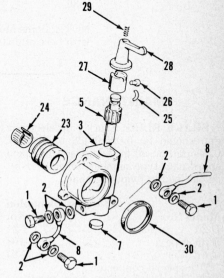

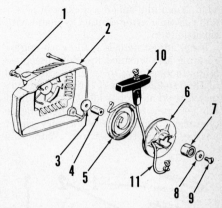

Fig. CR60 — Exploded view of centrifugal clutch used on later CP90 and CP120 models.

2. Screw
3. Spring
4. Shoes
5. Hub
7. Drum
9. Needle bearing
10. Washer
11. Washer
12. Nut
14. Washer

Fig. CR63 — Exploded view of adjustable automatic oil pump used on CP90 and CP120 models.

1. Banjo bolt	24. Collar
2. Washers	25. Pin
3. Pump body	26. Pin
5. Piston	27. Bushing
7. Plug	28. Adjusting lever
8. Tube	29. Spring
23. Worm gear	30. Seal

Fig. CR61 — Exploded view of manual oil pump used on Model CP70S.

1. Clamp	10. Bolt
2. Pump body	11. Washer
3. Clamp	12. Fitting
4. Hose	13. Oil pickup
5. Cotter pin	14. Tube
6. Piston	15. "E" ring
7. Spring	16. Washers
8. Spring	17. Seals
9. Tube	18. Washer

Fig. CR62 — Exploded view of automatic oil pump on Models C70 and CP70S.

1. Banjo bolt	13. Piston brake
2. Washers	14. Gasket
3. Pump body	15. Plunger
4. "O" ring	16. Seal
5. Piston	17. Fitting
6. Cover	18. Oil pickup
7. Plug	19. Module case
8. Tube	20. Felt plug
9. Hose	21. Cover
10. Drive plate	22. Flywheel
11. Pin	R. Reservoir
12. Spring	

Fig. CR64 — Exploded view of rewind starter used on Models C70 and CP70S. Models CP90 and CP120 are simlar except, washer (11) is not used and shaft (4) is part of housing (2).

1. Bolt	
2. Housing	7. Needle bearing
3. Washer	8. Washer
4. Shaft	9. Screw
5. Rewind spring	10. Rope handle
6. Rope pulley	11. Washer

CLINTON

**CLINTON ENGINES
CORPORATION
Clark & Maple Streets
Maquoketa, Iowa 52060**

Model	Bore	Stroke	Displ.	Drive Type
D-25	1-7/8 in.	1-5/8 in.	4.48 cu. in.	Direct
	(47.6 mm)	(41.3 mm)	(78.4 cc)	
D-35	2-1/8 in.	1-5/8 in.	5.78 cu. in.	Direct
	(53.9 mm)	(41.3 mm)	(94.7 cu. in.)	

NOTE: Some Model D-25 saws were equipped with 5.78 cu. in. (94.7 cc) engine with bore and stroke shown for Model D-35.

MAINTENANCE

SPARK PLUG. Spark plug electrode gap should be 0.025-0.028 inch (0.63-0.71 mm) on all models. Use Champion spark plug type number, or equivalent, as outlined in following chart:

Model No.	Champion Type No.
D-25	TJ-8J, CJ-8*
D-35, type A	H-10J
All other types	J-8J

*With special connector.

CARBURETOR. Models D-25 and D-35 are equipped with a Tillotson HC-11A diaphragm carburetor and a separate fuel pump as shown in Fig. CL2.

For initial adjustment on all models, open main jet adjustment screw 1¼ turns and idle jet adjustment screw ¾ turn. Turn idle speed adjustment screw one full turn after contact is made with throttle stop.

Final adjustment is made with engine running and warmed up. Set idle speed adjustment screw to give an idle speed of 1800 to 2200 rpm. (Clutch should stay disengaged at proper idle speed.) Adjust idle jet screw to obtain smoothest engine operation; then open jet a very slight amount over this setting. With saw

under cutting load, adjust main jet adjustment screw to obtain even engine speed. This setting will vary from 1 to 1½ turns open.

Refer to Tillotson carburetor section in CARBURETOR SERVICE section for exploded view and carburetor overhaul on Tillotson carburetors.

MAGNETO AND TIMING. Flywheel type Clinton magneto is used. Set breaker contact gap to 0.020 inch (0.51 mm). Spark timing is fixed at 33 to 35 degrees and is nonadjustable. Armature air gap is 0.005 to 0.007 inch (0.13-0.18 mm). Edge gap (distance between trailing edge of flywheel magnet and edge of coil lamination core after magnet has passed coil lamination core) is ⅛ to ¼ inch (3.18-6.35 mm). Condenser capacity is 0.13 to 0.14 mfd. Spark should jump ⅛ inch (3.18 mm) gap at cranking speed and a 1-1/16 inch (27 mm) gap at engine operating speed.

CAUTION: Check gap at running speed for a brief instant only, to avoid damage to coil.

LUBRICATION. Recommended fuel:oil mixture for Model D-25 is ¾ pint (0.35 L) oil mixed with one gallon (3.78 L) of regular gasoline. SAE 30 MM or MS motor oil or outboard oil should be

used. On Model D-35, the above mixture should be used for the engine break-in period and then reduced to ½ pint (0.24 L) of oil mixed with one gallon (3.78 L) of regular gasoline.

Fill chain oiler tank with new SAE 30 motor oil. Press plunger several times to be sure oiler pump is working. Dilute chain oil with 50 percent kerosene in cold weather, or when cutting wood with high pitch, sap or resin content.

REPAIRS

CLEANING CARBON. To clean the exhaust valve ports, remove muffler and turn engine so that piston is below ports. Clean the exhaust ports by scraping with a blunt tool. Take care not to score the top of the piston.

TIGHTENING TORQUES. Graphite should be applied to threads of all screws which thread into die cast parts.

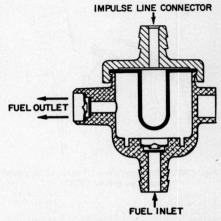

Fig. CL2 — Cross-sectional view of fuel pump used with Tillotson carburetor. Renew fuel pump assembly if inoperative; component parts are not serviceable.

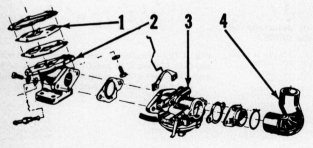

Fig. CL1 — Induction system of Clinton chain saw engine.

1. Reed plate
2. Induction bracket
3. Carburetor
4. Carburetor to air cleaner hose

Fastener Location	Torque Value
Guide bar mounting studs	125-175 in.-lbs. (14.1-19.8 N·m)
Sprocket nut	33-37 ft.-lbs. (44.9-50.3 N·m)
Reduction housing to block	150-175 in.-lbs. (16.9-19.8 N·m)
Clutch to crankshaft (1st nut)	110-120 in.-lbs. (12.4-13.6 N·m)
(2nd nut, where used)	190-210 in.-lbs. (21.5-23.7 N·m)
Induction bracket to block	30-50 in.-lbs. (3.4-5.6 N·m)
Carburetor to induction bracket	30-50 in.-lbs. (3.4-5.6 N·m)
Bearing plate to block	80-90 in.-lbs. (9.0-10.2 N·m)
Flywheel nut	31-35 ft.-lbs. (42.2-47.6 N·m)
Stator plate to bearing plate	50-60 in.-lbs. (5.6-6.8 N·m)
Blower housing to bearing plate	80-90 in.-lbs. (10.0-10.2 N·m)
Spark plug	230-270 in.-lbs. (26.0-30.5 N·m)
Cap to connecting rod	*

Fastener Location	Torque Value
Muffler body to block	60-70 in.-lbs. (6.8-7.9 N·m)
Air deflectors to cylinder block	15-20 in.-lbs. (1.7-2.2 N·m)
Tubular handle	60-80 in.-lbs. (6.8-9.0 N·m)
Starter to blower housing	30-40 in.-lbs. (3.4-4.5 N·m)
Reed plate to induction bracket	20-25 in.-lbs. (2.2-2.8 N·m)
Condenser	10-15 in.-lbs. (1.1-1.7 N·m)
Tank strap to block	20-25 in.-lbs. (2.2-2.8 N·m)
Cover to transmission casting	20-25 in.-lbs. (2.2-2.8 N·m)
Spike to casting	120-130 in.-lbs. (13.6-14.7 N·m)

*See CONNECTING ROD paragraph.

BEARING PLATE. Because of the pressure and vacuum pulsations in crankcase, bearing plate and gasket must form an air-tight seal when installed. Make sure gasket surfaces are not cracked, nicked or warped, that oil passages in crankcase, gasket and plate are aligned and that correct number and thickness of thrust washers are used. Also check to be sure the right cap screws are installed when engine is reassembled.

CAUTION: Cap screws (1 — Fig. CL5) may bottom in threaded holes (2) if incorrect screws are used. When long screws are tightened, damage to cylinder walls can result.

CONNECTING ROD. Piston and connecting rod assembly are removed from bottom of the crankcase after first removing the crankshaft. The long sloping side of the piston is the exhaust side; place this side of piston to exhaust port when installing piston and connecting rod assembly.

On Model D-25, an aluminum connecting rod, with a cast-in bronze insert is used. Crankpin diameter is 0.7788-0.7795 inch (19.781-19.799 mm). Desired clearance between crankpin and connecting rod is 0.0021-0.0037 inch (0.053-0.094 mm). Renew connecting rod and/or crankshaft if clearance exceeds 0.005 inch (0.13 mm).

On Model D-35, crankpin bearing consists of 25 uncaged needle bearings. Either a steel connecting rod or a forged aluminum connecting rod with renewable steel bearing liner is used. The aluminum rod and bearing liner are interchangeable with the steel rod. Renew crankshaft, steel rod or bearing liner if bearing surfaces show signs of wear or are scored. When installing connecting rod to crankpin, place 13 needle rollers between crankpin and rod. Apply low temperature grease to rod cap and stick the remaining 12 rollers to cap.

On all models, place cap on connecting rod with mating marks aligned and torque rod cap screws to proper torque value as follows:

Model D-25 . . . . .55-65 in.-lbs. (6.2-7.3 N·m)
Model D-35:
  Aluminum rod . . . . .80-90 in.-lbs. (9.0-10.2 N·m)
  Steel rod . . . . .100-110 in.-lbs. (11.3-12.4 N·m)

PISTON, PIN AND RINGS. On Model D-25, piston is fitted with two pinned piston rings. On Model D-35, the

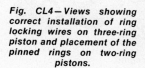

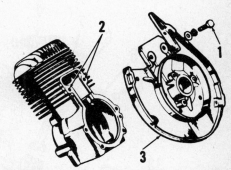

Fig. CL5—If cap screws (1) which thread into holes (2) are too long, they may bottom and damage cylinder walls.

Fig. CL4—Views showing correct installation of ring locking wires on three-ring piston and placement of the pinned rings on two-ring pistons.

PISTONS and RINGS

Fig. CL3—Exploded view of Clinton magneto and related parts.

1. Stator cover & gasket
2. Condenser
3. Magneto cam
4. Breaker-points
5. Stator plate, coil & armature
6. Crankshaft seal
7. Crankcase side plate
8. Main needle bearing
9. Starter housing
10. Rewind spring
11. Rope pulley
12. Pawl
13. Pawl spring
14. Actuator spring
15. Actuator
16. Retaining ring
17. Blower cover
18. Starter cup
19. Flywheel

aluminum alloy piston is fitted with three compression rings. A ring lock wire is placed in a small groove at the bottom of each ring groove to prevent rings from moving into the port holes. To install lock wires refer to Fig. CL4 and proceed as follows: Hold piston with intake side facing right. (The sharp contoured side of the piston is the intake side.) Place the three lock wires over the piston with the lock ring tab to the right of the locating hole on top and bottom ring, and to the left of locating hole on center ring. When placing rings on the piston, be sure that recess in ring gap is placed over lock wire ring tab, so ring gap can close when piston is inserted in the cylinder. Use piston ring compressor when installing piston.

Ring end gap should be 0.007 inch (0.18 mm) with wear limit to 0.017 inch (0.43 mm). Ring side clearance should not be more than 0.002 inch (0.05 mm). Pistons and rings are available in 0.010 inch (0.25 mm) and 0.020 inch (0.51 mm) oversizes as well as in standard size.

The piston pin must be installed with closed end inserted into intake side of piston. The piston pin is available in one size only and should be renewed when the connecting rod is renewed.

CYLINDER. Cylinder block is die cast with integral cast iron cylinder liner. Clearance between piston skirt

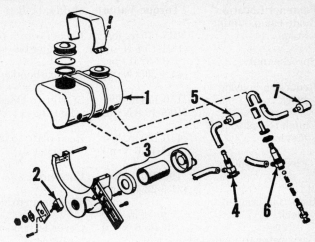

Fig. CL7 — View identifies fuel-chain oil tank assembly and related components, air cleaner assembly and magneto grounding switch.

1. Fuel-chain oil tank
2. Magneto grounding switch
3. Air cleaner
4. Fuel shut-off valve
5. Fuel pickup
6. Oiler pump
7. Oil pickup

and cylinder wall measured at right angle to piston pin and below ports should be 0.0045 to 0.0050 inch (0.114-0.127 mm) with wear limit of 0.007 inch (0.178 mm). If worn beyond the 0.007 inch (0.178 mm) wear limit when checked with a new piston, hone to the next oversize and leave the cross-hatch pattern in the cylinder wall to provide piston lubrication. Do not polish cylinder wall.

CRANKSHAFT. On Model D-25, the flywheel end of the crankshaft is sup-

ported in a sleeve type bushing. Desired bushing to crankshaft main journal clearance is 0.0013-0.0030 inch (0.033-0.076 mm), maximum allowable clearance is 0.0040 inch (0.102 mm). Crankshaft journal diameter (new) is 0.7495-0.7502 inch (19.037-19.055 mm); renew crankshaft if journal is worn to a diameter of 0.7475 inch (18.986 mm) or less. Bushing is renewable in bearing plate; ream bushing to a diameter of 0.7515-0.7525 inch (19.088-19.113 mm) after installation.

On Model D-35, flywheel end of crankshaft is supported in a needle bearing. Renew the crankshaft if bearing surface shows signs of wear or is scored. Renew the needle bearing if any roller has flat spots or if any two rollers can be separated the width of one roller. Install needle bearing by pressing on lettered end of bearing cage only.

Drive end of crankshaft is supported in a ball bearing on all models. Crankshaft end play is controlled by the ball bearing which is a snug fit in crankcase and on crankshaft. The ball bearing (12 – Fig. CL6) is held in place in the crankcase with two snap rings (15 and 16) and on the crankshaft with a snap ring (13). On early production models, shims were used between the bearing and outer snap ring (15) to remove any side play of the bearing outer race between the snap rings. Shims are not required on late production units.

To remove the crankshaft, proceed as follows: Remove the carburetor adapter (23) and reed plate (20); then, remove the connecting rod cap (27) and needle bearing rollers (on models so equipped). Push the piston and connecting rod unit to top of cylinder. Remove bearing plate (33). Then, remove oil seal (14) from pto end of crankshaft to allow removal of snap ring (13). Turn crankshaft so that throw will clear connecting rod and push crankshaft from crankcase. Reinstall by reversing removal procedures.

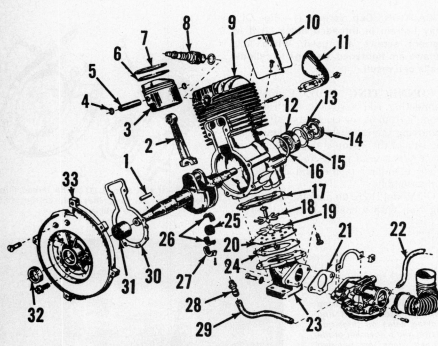

Fig. CL6 — View of typical Clinton chain saw engine.

1. Flywheel key	9. Cylinder	18. Reed stop	26. Bearing liners
2. Connecting rod	10. Baffle	19. Valve reed	27. Rod cap
3. Piston	11. Exhaust	20. Reed plate	28. Fitting
4. Snap rings	12. Ball bearing	21. Gasket	29. Impulse line
5. Piston pin	13. Snap ring	22. Fuel line	30. Gasket
6. Ring lock wires (3)	14. Crankshaft seal	23. Carburetor adapter	31. Needle bearing
7. Piston rings (3)	15 & 16. Snap rings	24. Gasket	32. Crankshaft seal
8. Spark plug	17. Gasket	25. Needle rollers	33. Bearing plate

CRANKSHAFT SEALS. Seals must be maintained in good condition because of leakage through seals would cause loss of power. It is important therefore to carefully inspect the seals and to exercise extreme care when renewing seals to prevent their being damaged. Use seal protector over ends of crankshaft or tape shaft to prevent seal damage.

REED VALVE. The reed valve unit can be inspected after removing carburetor and induction bracket as a single unit. Renew reed plate if petal is broken, cracked, warped or rusted, or if seat for petal is not smooth. Reed petal and plate are available only as an assembly.

CLUTCH A roller type clutch is used. There is no adjustment to the clutch, but if it does not engage and disengage properly, it should be inspected for worn or broken parts or for incorrect assembly. The clutch is shown in Fig. CL8.

Rollers, clutch hub, and band asembly are available as individual replacement parts or as an assembly. Refer to Fig. CL8 for correct assembly of clutch.

The clutch drum (2–Fig. CL8) on Model D-25 is fitted with a renewable bushing that rides on the engine crankshaft. Desired clearance of bushing to crankshaft is 0.0010-0.0035 inch (0.025-0.089 mm); renew bushing if clearance exceeds 0.004 inch (0.102 mm). On Model D-35, the clutch drum is equipped with a renewable needle bearing.

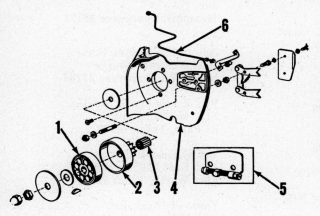

Fig. CL8 — Exploded view of drive clutch and bar mounting plate on direct drive models. Item (3) is a bushing on Model D-35.

1. Clutch assy.
2. Clutch drum & chain sprocket
3. Clutch drum needle bearing
4. Bar mounting plate
5. Bar adjusting plate
6. Chain oiler tube

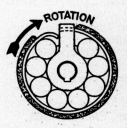

Fig. CL9 — Showing assembly of clutch.

CLINTON CENTRAL PARTS DISTRIBUTORS
(Arranged Alphabetically by States)

**These franchised firms carry extensive stocks of repair parts. Contact them
for name and address of nearest service distributor who may have the parts you need.**

Auto Electric & Carburetor Co.
2625-4th Avenue South
P.O. Box 2246
Birmingham, Alabama 35201

Charlie C. Jones Battery & Electric Co.
P.O. Box 6654
2440 West McDowell Road
Phoenix, Arizona 85005

Garden Equipment Co.
6600 Cherry Avenue
Long Beach, California 90805

Air Cooled Engines
1076 N. 10th St.
San Jose, California 95112

Kee Manufacturing Parts Div.
P.O. Box 2195
1211-44th Avenue East
Bradenton, Florida 33503

Radco Distributors Co.
4909 Victor St.,
P.O. Box 5459
Jacksonville, Florida 32207

Rogers Engines
3330 West 45th Street
West Palm Beach, Florida 33407

Blalock Machinery & Equipment Co.,
 Inc.
P.O. Box 490379
5112 Blalock Ind. Blvd.
College Park, Georgia 30349

Midwest Engine Warehouse
515 Romans Road
Elmhurst, Illinois 60126

Mid-East Power Equipment Co.
185 Lisle Road
P.O. Box 658
Lexington, Kentucky 40505

Yazoo Of Louisiana, Inc.
2615 Airline Highway
Box 52979
Baton Rouge, Louisiana 70805

Springfield Auto Electric Service, Inc.
117 West Gardner St.,
Springfield, Massachusetts 01105

Automotive Products Co.
520 First St.,
Menominee, Michigan 49858

Engine Parts Supply Co.
1220-24 Harmon Place
Minneapolis, Minnesota 55403

Johnson Big Wheel Mowers, Inc.
P.O. Box 717
Ridgeland, Mississippi 39157

Electrical & Magneto Service Co.
1600 Campbell
Kansas City, Missouri 64108

Medart Engines & Parts
100 Larkin Williams Ind. Court
Fenton, Missouri 63026

A & I Distributors
P.O. Box 1999
2112-4th Avenue North
Billings, Montana 59103

A & I Distributors
317 Second Street South
Box 1159
Great Falls, Montana 59403

Carl A. Anderson, Inc. of Neb.
7410 "L" Street
P.O. Box 27139
Omaha, Nebraska 68127

Central Motive Power, Inc.
3740 Princeton Drive N.E.
Albuquerque, New Mexico 87103

John Reiner & Co., Inc.
946 Spencer St., Box 183
Syracuse, New York 13204

E. J. Smith & Sons Co.
4250 Golf Acres Drive
Box 668887
Charlotte, North Carolina 28266

United Power Equipment
2031 E. Lee Avenue
Box 1077
Bismarck, North Dakota 58502

V. E. Petersen Company
28101 East Broadway
Walbridge (Toledo), Ohio 43465

Victory Motors, Inc.
605 Cherokee
Muskogee, Oklahoma 74001

Brown & Wiser, Inc.
9991 S.W. Avery St., Box 119
Tualatin, Oregon 97062

McCullogh Distributing Co.
5613-19 Tulip Street
Philadelphia, Pennsylvania 19124

R. K. Mickel Equipment Co.
401-03 Bell Avenue
Altoona, Pennsylvania 16602

Locke Auto Electric Service, Inc.
231 North Dakota Avenue
P.O. Box 1165
Sioux Falls, South Dakota 57101

RCH Distributors, Inc.
3140 Carrier Street
Box 173
Memphis, Tennessee 38101

Automobile Electric Service
1008 Charlotte Avenue
Nashville, Tennessee 37203

Wes Kern's Repair Service
2423 East Missouri
El Paso, Texas 79901

McCoy Sales & Service
4045 East Belknap Street
Fort Worth, Texas 76111

Yazoo of Texas, Inc.
1409 Telephone Road
Houston, Texas 77023

A-1 Engine & Mower Company
437 East 9th South
Salt Lake City, Utah 84111

R.B.I. Corporation
P.O. Box 25369
Richmond, Virginia 23260

Hunt Auto Supply
1300 Monticello Avenue
Norfolk, Virginia 23510

Fremont Electric Company
744 N. 34th St.
Box 31640
Seattle, Washington 98103

CANADA
Loveseth, Ltd.
9570-58th Avenue
**Edmonton, Alberta, Canada
T6E 0B6**

Western Air Cooled Engines, Ltd.
1205 East Hastings
**Vancouver, B.C., Canada
V6A 1S5**

Yetman's, Ltd.
949 Jarvis Avenue
**Winnipeg, Manitoba, Canada
R2X 0A1**

Longwood Equipment Company
1940 Ellesmere Road, Unit 8
**Scarborough, Ontario, Canada
M1H 2V7**

DANARM

DANARM, LTD.
Slad Road
Stroud, Gloucestershire, England

Model	Bore	Stroke	Displ.	Drive Type
1-36, 36AV, 1-36 Mk11	1-7/16 in. (36.5 mm)	1.28 in. (32.5 mm)	2.1 in. (34.4 cc)	Direct

MAINTENANCE

SPARK PLUG. Recommended spark plug is Champion CJ6. Spark plug electrode gap should be 0.025 inch (0.63 mm).

CARBURETOR. All models are equipped with a Tillotson Model HU diaphragm type carburetor. Refer to Tillotson section of CARBURETOR SERVICE section for service procedures and exploded views.
Initial adjustment of idle mixture screw and high speed mixture screw is 1 turn open.

Final adjustment of high speed mixture screw should be made with engine warm and engine under cutting load. High speed mixture must not be adjusted too lean as engine may be damaged.

MAGNETO AND TIMING. All models are equipped with a conventional flywheel magneto ignition system. Refer to Fig. DA3 for exploded view of ignition assembly.
Breaker point gap for all models should be 0.015 inch (0.38 mm). Ignition timing is fixed but breaker point gap will affect ignition timing and should be set correctly.

LUBRICATION. Engine is lubricated by mixing oil with fuel. Recommended fuel:oil ratio is 16:1. A good quality SAE 30 oil designed for chain saw engines should be used.

Fill chain oil tank with SAE 30 motor oil. Chain oil may be diluted up to 50 percent for winter usage by adding kerosene or diesel fuel to chain oil.

CARBON. Carbon should be removed from exhaust system and cylinder periodically. Loose carbon should not be allowed to enter cylinder and care should be taken not to damage cylinder or piston.

REPAIRS

CYLINDER, PISTON, PIN AND RINGS. Cylinder (16–Fig. DA1) is also upper crankcase half. Crankshaft is loose in crankcase when cylinder is removed. Care must be taken not to nick or scratch crankcase mating surfaces during disassembly.

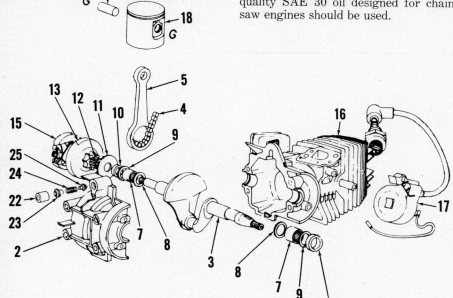

Fig. DA1 — Exploded view of engine.

Fig. DA2 — Exploded view of manual oil pump and front housing.

2. Crankcase	9. Retaining ring	15. Clutch assy.
3. Crankshaft	10. Seal	16. Cylinder
4. Roller bearings	11. Thrust washer	17. Ignition coil
5. Connecting rod	12. Bearing	18. Piston
7. Needle bearing	13. Clutch drum	19. Piston ring
8. Washer		

20. Piston pin	
21. Pin retainer	
22. Spacer	
23. Spring seat	
24. Spring	
25. Pulse valve	

1. Piston	6. Pump body	11. Front cover
2. "O" ring	7. Screen	12. Spring
3. Spring	8. Front housing	13. Spring
4. Spring seat	9. Fuel hose	14. Oil outlet valve
5. Ball	10. Filter	15. Nut

Cylinder head is integral with cylinder and cylinder must be removed to remove piston. Piston is equipped with a single piston ring and a floating type piston pin (20). It may be necessary to heat piston to remove or install piston pin. Piston, pin and ring are available in standard size only. Cylinder bore is chrome and should be inspected to determine if chrome is scored, peeling or excessively worn. Renew cylinder and piston if damaged or excessively worn.

Refer to CRANKSHAFT section for proper assembly of crankcase and cylinder.

CONNECTING ROD. To remove connecting rod, remove cylinder (16–Fig. DA1). Note that cylinder is also upper crankcase half and crankshaft assembly is loose when cylinder is removed. Connecting rod (5) is one-piece and supported on crankpin by 11 loose bearing rollers (4). Be careful not to lose loose rollers that may fall out during

disassembly. Rollers can be removed by sliding rod off rollers. To install rod bearing, hold rollers in place with heavy grease or petroleum jelly and position rod over rollers. Be sure rollers do not fall out during assembly of crankcase.

NOTE: Early and late model piston and connecting rod are not individually interchangeable. Later model piston and rod are available only as a unit assembly and may be installed in early model saws. Early piston and rod are no longer available.

CRANKSHAFT AND SEALS. Crankshaft is supported by needle roller bearings (7–Fig. DA1) at both ends. Crankshaft assembly may be removed after removing stator plate, clutch and cylinder assemblies. Care should be taken when removing cylinder as crankshaft will be loose in crankcase and connecting rod may slide off bearing rollers allowing them to fall into crankcase.

Before reassembling crankcases, apply a light coat of nonhardening sealant to crankcase mating surface. Be sure mating surfaces are not damaged during assembly. Retaining rings (9) must fit in ring grooves of crankcase and cylinder.

CLUTCH. A two-shoe centrifugal type clutch is used on all models. Clutch hub has left hand thread. Clutch bearing (12–Fig. DA1) should be inspected for excessive wear or damage. Inspect clutch shoes and drum for signs of excessive heat.

OIL PUMP. All models are equipped with a manual oil pump and automatic oiling system. Refer to Fig. DA2 for exploded view of manual oil pump. Automatic oiling is accomplished by crankcase pulsations which pressurize oil tank and force oil to bar. A one-way valve (25–Fig. DA1) prevents oil from entering crankcase.

NOTE: Later models are equipped with a duckbill type valve in place of valve components (22, 23, 24 and 25).

RECOIL STARTER. Refer to Fig. DA3 for exploded view of pawl type starter used on all models. Care should be taken if necessary to remove rewind spring (12) to prevent spring from uncoiling uncontrolled.

Rewind spring (12) should be wound in clockwise direction in housing. Wind starter rope in clockwise direction around rope pulley (11) as viewed in starter housing (4).

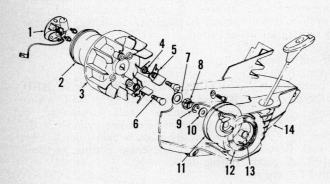

Fig. DA3 — Exploded view of ignition and rewind starter.

1. Stator plate
2. Cover
3. Flywheel
4. Spring
5. Pawl
6. Pivot pin
7. Washer
8. Nut
9. Snap ring
10. Thrust washer
11. Rope pulley
12. Rewind spring
13. Bushing
14. Starter housing

DANARM

Model	Bore	Stroke	Displ.	Drive Type
1-71-SS	2.0 in. (50.8 mm)	1.38 in. (35.0 mm)	4.3 cu. in. (70.5 cc)	Direct
76	1-13/16 in. (46.0 mm)	1-7/16 in. (36.5 mm)	3.7 cu. in. (60.6 cc)	Direct

MAINTENANCE

SPARK PLUG. Recommended spark plug is Champion CJ6 or equivalent. Spark plug electrode gap should be 0.025 inch (0.63 mm).

CARBURETOR. A Tillotson Model HU diaphragm type carburetor is used. Refer to Tillotson section of CARBURETOR SERVICE section for carburetor overhaul and exploded views.

Initial adjustment of carburetor on Model 1-71-SS is 7/8 turn open for idle and high speed mixture screws. Initial adjustment of carburetor on Model 76 is 1-1/8 turns open for idle mixture screw and 1 turn open for high speed mixture screw. Final adjustments should be made with engine warm. High speed mixture screw should be adjusted with engine under cutting load to obtain optimum performance. Do not adjust high speed mixture too lean as engine damage may result.

MAGNETO AND TIMING. A conventional flywheel magneto is used on both models. Breaker-point gap is 0.018-0.020 inch (0.46-0.51 mm) for Model 1-71-SS and 0.015 inch (0.38 mm) for Model 76. Ignition timing on Model 76 is fixed. Ignition timing on Model 1-71-SS may be adjusted by unscrewing breaker-point box retaining screws and rotating breaker-point box retaining screws and rotating breaker-point box

(7–Fig. DA5). Ignition timing on Model 1-71-SS should occur with piston 30-31 degrees or 0.115-0.120 inch (2.92-3.05 mm) before top dead center (BTDC). If ignition timing tools are not available, ignition timing should be close if arrow on bottom of breaker-point box (7) is aligned with mark on crankcase. Magneto air gap should be 0.015 inch (0.38 mm) on Model 1-71-SS and 0.005-0.010 inch (0.13-0.25 mm) on Model 76.

LUBRICATION. The engine is lubricated by mixing oil with fuel. Oil designed for use in two-stroke air-cooled engines is recommended. Fuel:oil ratio is 16:1 and should be increased during engine break-in.

REPAIRS

CYLINDER HEAD. Cylinder head is separate from cylinder on Model 1-71-SS while cylinder head on Model 76 is integral with cylinder. Cylinder head on Model 1-71-SS is retained by six screws which should be tightened in a crisscross pattern.

PISTON, PIN, RINGS AND CYLINDER. The piston is equipped with two piston rings which are pinned to prevent rotation. Piston pin rides in a roller bearing in the small end of the connecting rod. Heat must be applied to the piston for piston pin removal.

The cylinder bore on Model 76 is chrome plated while the cylinder bore on Model 1-71-SS is iron. Inspect cylinder bore of Model 76 for scoring, flaking, cracking or other signs of damage or excessive wear. Cylinder on Model 1-71-SS may be rebored to fit oversize pistons of 0.015 inch (0.38 mm) or 0.030 inch (0.76 mm).

Piston pin on Model 76 must be installed in piston with closed end of pin toward exhaust port. Pistons on both models must be installed with "EXH" on piston crown toward exhaust port.

CRANKSHAFT, CONNECTING ROD AND CRANKCASE. Connecting rod on Model 76 may be removed without removing crankshaft. Be careful not to lose any of the 31 loose bearing rollers around crankpin. Connecting rod and cap have match marks

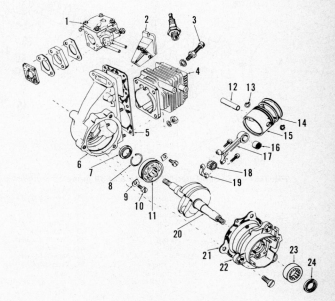

Fig. DA6 — Exploded view of Model 76 engine assembly.

1. Carburetor
2. Reed valve assy.
3. Compression release valve
4. Gasket
5. Gasket
6. Crankcase
7. Seal
8. Retainer
9. Bearing retainer
10. Screw
11. Ball bearing
12. Piston pin
13. Snap ring
14. Piston rings
15. Piston
16. Needle bearing
17. Connecting rod
18. Bearing rollers (31)
19. Rod cap
20. Crankshaft
21. Gasket
22. Bearing housing
23. Roller bearing
24. Seal

Fig. DA5 — View of ignition breaker point assembly used on Model 1-71-SS

1. Retainer
2. Cover
3. Gasket
4. Moveable breaker-point
5. Fixed breaker-point
6. Cam felt
7. Breaker-point box

which must be aligned during assembly. The connecting rod on Model 1-71-SS is one-piece and rides around a crankpin which is pressed into the crankshaft halves. Separate components are not available and connecting rod and crankshaft must be serviced as a unit assembly.

Both main bearings on Model 76 are a press fit on the crankshaft. Crankcases should be heated to aid in removal and installation of crankshaft and main bearings. Right main bearing on Model 76 is secured by retainers (9–Fig. DA6). Groove around outer race of bearing (11) must be adjacent to crankpin. Coat threads of retainer screws (10) with Loctite and be sure screws do not contact crankshaft when shaft is turned.

Crankshaft counterweight size was increased on Models 1-71-SS after serial number 3000. Note counterweight change in Fig. DA8. Crankcase was also changed to accommodate larger counterweight. Early crankshaft may be used in early or late crankcase but late crankshaft will not fit in early crankcase.

REED VALVE. Model 76 is equipped with a reed valve induction system (2–Fig. DA6). Inspect reed petals for cracks or other damage. Inspect reed valve seats for pitting or other damage which may prevent petals from seating properly. Reed petals and seat are available only as a unit assembly.

CLUTCH. Refer to Fig. DA9 or Fig. DA10 for an exploded view of the clutch. Renew any components which are damaged or excessively worn. Remove glaze from clutch shoes and clutch drum with emery cloth. Tighten clutch nut on Model 1-71-SS to 160-170 in.-lbs. (18.1-19.2 N·m).

AUTOMATIC CHAIN OILER. Both models are equipped with an automatic chain oiler. Chain oil in oil tank of Model 76 is pressurized by crankcase pressure and metered to the chain. A check valve is located at the end of the crankcase pressure line to prevent chain oil from entering the engine crankcase. Be sure the check valve is operating correctly.

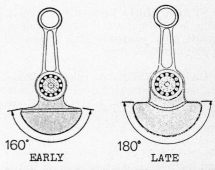

Fig. DA8 – Note larger crankshaft counterweight on late Model 1-71-SS. See text.

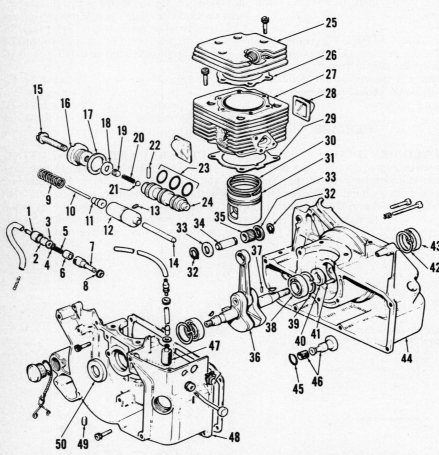

Fig. DA7 – Exploded view of engine and oil pump assemblies used on Model 1-71-SS.

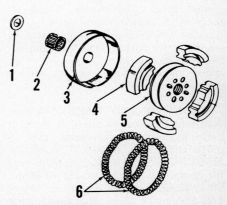

Fig. DA9 – Exploded view of clutch used on Model 76.

1. Washer	4. Clutch shoes
2. Bearing	5. Clutch hub
3. Clutch drum	6. Garter springs

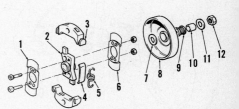

Fig. DA10 – Exploded view of clutch used on Model 1-71-SS. Guide plates (1 and 6) were not used on early models.

1. Clutch plate	7. Washer
2. Clutch hub	8. Clutch drum
3. Clutch shoes	9. Bearing
4. Spring plate	10. Inner race
5. Spring	11. Washer
6. Guide plate	12. Clutch nut

1. Fule tank vent cap	14. Push rod	27. Cylinder	38. Ball bearing
2. Filter	15. Adjusting screw	28. Transfer port cover	39. Snap ring
3. Plate	16. Gland nut	29. Gasket	40. Oil pump cam
4. "O" ring	17. Gasket	30. Piston rings	41. Dowel pin
5. Spring	18. Washer	31. Piston	42. Snap ring
6. Valve	19. Set screw	32. Snap ring	43. Seal
7. Vent body	20. Spring	33. Thrust washer	44. Right crankcase half
8. Grommet	21. Ball	34. Piston pin	45. "O" ring
9. Spring	22. Pin	35. Needle bearing	46. Oil filter
10. Plunger rod	23. "O" rings	36. Crankshaft & rod	47. Fuel pickup
11. Oil pump plunger	24. Pump body	assy.	48. Left crankcase half
12. Bushing	25. Cylinder head	37. Oil pump cam drive	49. Set screw
13. Set screw	26. Gasket	pin	50. Seal

Model 1-71-SS is equipped with the plunger type automatic oil pump shown in Fig. DA7. To remove oil pump, unscrew gland nut (16) and withdraw oil pump assembly. Unscrew set screw (13) and remove bushing (12). The crankshaft must be removed for access to oil pump cam (40). Oil pump output is adjusted by turning adjusting screw (15).

REWIND STARTER. Refer to Fig. DA11 or Fig. DA12 for an exploded view of rewind starter. To disassemble starter, remove starter housing, remove rope handle and allow rope to wind into starter housing. Unscrew retaining screw or "E" ring and remove rope pulley, being careful not to dislodge rewind spring. If necessary, remove rewind spring using care not to allow spring to uncoil uncontrolled. During reassembly, rewind spring is wound in clockwise direction in housing while rope is wound on pulley in clockwise direction when viewing pulley installed in housing. Place tension on rewind spring by turning rope pulley two turns clockwise before passing rope through rope outlet.

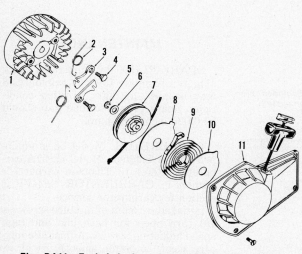

Fig. DA11—Exploded view of starter used on Model 76.

1. Flywheel
2. Pawl spring
3. Pawl
4. Pawl screw
5. "E" ring
6. Washer
7. Rope pulley
8. Inner spring plate
9. Rewind plate
10. Outer spring plate
11. Starter housing

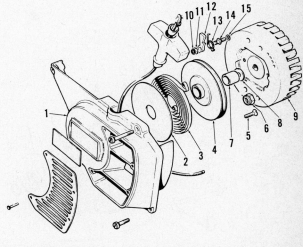

Fig. DA12—Exploded view of starter used on Model 1-71-SS.

1. Starter housing
2. Spring plate
3. Rewind spring
4. Rope pulley
5. Screw
6. Flywheel nut
7. Pulley bushing
8. Washer
9. Flywheel
10. Snap ring
11. Washer
12. Starter dog
13. Spring
14. Stud
15. Lockwasher

DANARM

Model	Bore	Stroke	Displ.	Drive Type
55	1.750 in. (44.4 mm)	1.375 in. (34.9 mm)	2.3 cu. in. (54.1 cc)	Direct

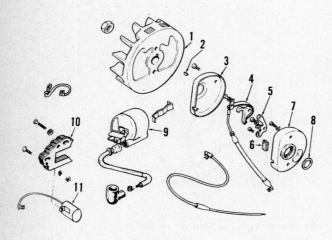

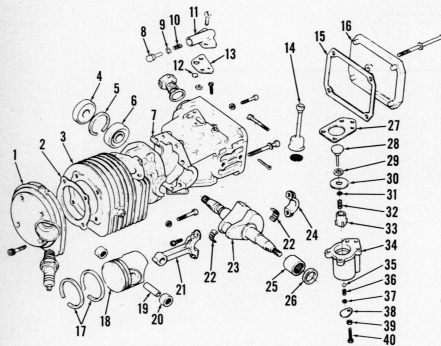

Fig. DA20—Exploded view of ignition system.

1. Flywheel
2. Key
3. Cover
4. Moveable breaker-point
5. Stationary breaker-point
6. Wick
7. Breaker-point box
8. Seal
9. Coil
10. Laminations
11. Condenser

Fig. DA21—Exploded view of Model 55 engine.

1. Cylinder head	11. Manual oil pump housing	21. Connecting rod
2. Gasket	12. Valve	22. Bearing roller (20)
3. Cylinder	13. Gasket	23. Crankshaft
4. Seal	14. Oil pickup	24. Rod cap
5. Snap ring	15. Gasket	25. Bearing
6. Bearing	16. Oil tank cover	26. Seal
7. Crankcase	17. Piston rings	27. Gasket
8. Plunger	18. Piston	28. Piston
9. "O" ring	19. Piston pin	29. Seal washer
10. Spring	20. Bearing	30. Piston ring
		31. "O" ring

32. Spring
33. Adjustment sleeve
34. Automatic oil pump housing
35. Outlet ball valve
36. Spring
37. "O" ring
38. Valve cover
39. Locknut
40. Adjusting screw

MAINTENANCE

SPARK PLUG. Recommended spark plug is Champion CJ6. Champion CJ8 may be used for light working conditions. Spark plug electrode gap should be 0.025 inch (0.63 mm).

CARBURETOR. Model 55 is equipped with a Tillotson Model HS57A carburetor. Refer to Tillotson carburetor section in CARBURETOR SERVICE section for carburetor service.

Initial adjustment of mixture screws is 7/8 turn open for both idle and high speed adjusting screws. Adjust idle mixture screw to obtain smooth, rapid acceleration without hesitation. Adjust idle speed stop screw so engine idles just below clutch engagement speed. High speed mixture screw should be adjusted with saw under cutting load.

MAGNETO AND TIMING. A conventional flywheel magneto ignition system is used on Model 55. Breaker points are contained in a breaker-box behind the flywheel. Breaker-point gap should be 0.018 inch (0.46 mm). Ignition timing is fixed so breaker point gap should be accurately set to 0.018 inch (0.46 mm) for correct ignition timing.

Clearance between flywheel and legs of coil laminations is adjustable. Loosen coil mounting screws and adjust coil position so clearance is 0.010 inch (0.25 mm). Retighten coil screws.

LUBRICATION. The engine is lubricated by mixing oil with the fuel. Recommended fuel is regular gasoline. Fuel:oil ratio should be 16:1. Use a good quality oil designed for air-cooled two-stroke engines.

Model 55 is equipped with manual and automatic chain oilers. Fill oil tank with clean automotive type oil.

CARBON. Carbon should be periodically removed from exhaust system and cylinder. Loose carbon should not be allowed to enter cylinder and care should be taken not to damage cylinder or piston.

REPAIRS

CYLINDER HEAD. The cylinder head is removable on Model 55. To remove cylinder head, remove bar, rewind starter, air filter and carburetor. Unscrew handle/tank unit retaining screws and disconnect ignition switch wire. Remove handle/tank unit while noting insulating plate between handle/tank unit and cowling. Remove cowling. Unscrew cylinder head retaining screws and separate head from engine.

Install cylinder head by reversing removal procedure. Using a crisscross pattern, tighten cylinder head screws to 120-130 in.-lbs. (13.6-14.7 N·m).

CRANKCASE. The crankcase must be separated from cylinder for access to internal engine components. Proceed as follows to separate crankcase: Remove cylinder head as previously outlined then remove clutch, flywheel and breaker-box assembly. If necessary, drain oil tank and remove oil tank cover (16–Fig. DA21). Remove the four interior and four exterior cylinder retaining cap screws and separate crankcase from cylinder. Refer to appropriate section for component service.

When assembling cylinder and crankcase, apply a light coat of sealant on mating surfaces. Be sure snap ring (5) is located in groove. Tighten four interior cap screws to 70-75 in.-lbs. (7.9-8.5 N·m) and four exterior cap screws to 35-40 in.-lbs. (3.9-4.5 N·m).

PISTON, PIN, RINGS AND CYLINDER. To remove piston, refer to CRANKCASE section and separate crankcase and cylinder. Piston may be removed from rod after driving out wrist pin.

Cylinder has cast iron liner which may be bored to accomodate 0.015 inch (0.38 mm) and 0.030 in. (0.76 mm) oversize pistons. Piston clearance in cylinder is 0.003-0.005 inch (0.08-0.13 mm) measured at bottom of piston skirt. Two piston rings are used on piston. Piston ring end gap should be 0.008-0.012 inch (0.20-0.30 mm).

If piston pin bearings must be renewed, place a support between piston pin bosses. Support must have a hole larger than bearing outer diameter. Press bearing toward inside of piston and remove; then remove remaining bearing using same method. Bearings should not be reused. Install new piston pin bearings so inner ends are flush with inner edges of piston pin bosses.

Piston must be installed so "EX" on piston crown is toward exhaust port. Be sure piston rings are properly located in grooves when sliding cylinder over piston.

CONNECTING ROD. Removal of connecting rod requires separating cylinder and crankcase as outlined in CRANKCASE section. Remove the rod cap screws and remove rod and piston from crankshaft. Do not lose any of the 20 loose rollers. Support piston boss on a suitably sized deep socket and using a driver smaller than piston pin, press piston pin from rod.

Inspect connecting rod for worn or scored bearing surfaces, bends or twists. If any defects are found, renew rod.

To reassemble, reverse removal procedure. Install rod on crankshaft with pips on rod and cap aligned. Use grease to hold rollers in crankshaft end of rod. Tighten rod cap screws to 55-60 in.-lbs. (6.2-6.8 N·m) with oiled threads.

CRANKSHAFT. The crankshaft is supported by a ball bearing at flywheel end and a needle bearing at clutch end. Crankshaft should be discarded if it shows uneven or excessive wear, or any other signs of damage. When installing

bearing on crankshaft, place shielded side of ball bearing next to counterweight of crankshaft and press bearing on shaft until it bottoms. When crankshaft and piston assembly is positioned in cylinder, be sure inner end of needle bearing is positioned 1/8 inch (3.2 mm) away from counterweight of crankshaft and that shaft seals are installed with lips facing inward. Tighten the four interior crankcase bolts to 70-75 in.-lbs. (7.9-8.5 N·m) and the four exterior crankcase bolts to 35-40 in.-lbs. (3.9-4.5 N·m).

AUTOMATIC OILER. Model 55 has manual and automatic chain oil pumps as shown in Fig. DA21.

Automatic oil pump is operated by crankcase pulsations. Chain oil is routed first through the automatic oiler before it exists at the bar pad. This allows the manual oiler to be used independently as well as providing priming for the automatic oiler. The oil pump is contained within the oil tank and may be removed after draining oil tank and removing tank cover. Oil pump should be cleaned and inspected for damage or excessive wear. Be sure all oil passages are open and clean and renew piston disc if warped or cracked. Before starting chain saw, prime automatic oil pump by operating manual oiler several times.

Automatic oil pump output is adjusted by turning screw (40–Fig. DA21) on bottom of pump.

CLUTCH. To remove clutch, remove clutch guard and starter assembly, bar, chain and fan (flywheel) housing. Lock flywheel using a suitable flywheel holding tool. Unscrew clutch retaining nut and pull clutch from crankshaft. Remove clutch drum and bearing, and thrust washer. Refer to Fig. DA22.

Inspect all parts for signs of excessive wear or other damage. Clutch shoes must be renewed as a unit. Clutch spring(s) should also be renewed. Renew clutch rotor if it allows excessive play of

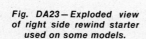

Fig. DA22 – Exploded view of Model 55 clutch.

1. Thrust washer	
2. Bearing	7. Clutch hub
3. Sprocket & drum	8. Retainer
4. Key	9. Starter pawl
5. Shoes	10. Spring
6. Springs	11. Rivet

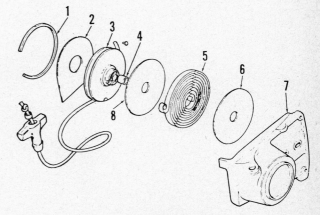

Fig. DA23 – Exploded view of right side rewind starter used on some models.

1. Snap ring
2. Plate
3. Rope pulley
4. Bushing
5. Rewind spring
6. Plate
7. Starter housing
8. Plate

clutch shoes. Renew thrust washer if grooved or damaged. Inspect sprocket starter pawls on models equipped with recoil starter on clutch side of saw. Pawls can be renewed by removing rivets and installing new pawls and rivets. Tighten clutch nut to 160-170 in.-lbs. (18.1-19.2 N·m).

REWIND STARTER. Chain saw may be equipped with a rewind starter mounted on right or left side. Refer to Fig. DA23 for exploded view of rewind starter mounted on right side of chain saw. Rewind spring is wound in counterclockwise direction in housing and rope is wound in counterclockwise direction around rope pulley as viewed installed in housing.

Place tension on rope by pulling rope handle then hold rope pulley so notch on outer edge of pulley aligns with rope outlet. Pull loose rope into housing and rotate rope pulley one or two turns in counterclockwise direction. Release rope and check starter operation.

Left hand starter shown in Fig. DA24 is used on some models. Rewind spring is wound in clockwise direction in housing. Rope is wound on rope pulley in clockwise direction as viewed with pulley installed in housing. Place tension on rope by pulling rope handle and then hold rope pulley so notch on outer edge of pulley aligns with rope outlet. Pull loose rope into housing and rotate rope pulley one or two turns in clockwise direction. Release rope and check starter operation.

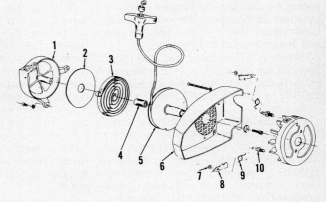

Fig. DA24—Exploded view of left side rewind starter used on some models.

1. Starter housing
2. Plate
3. Rewind spring
4. Bushing
5. Rope pulley
6. Side cover
7. Retainer
8. Pawl
9. Spring
10. Stud

DANARM

Model	Bore	Stroke	Displ.	Drive Type
110	2.50 in. (63.5 mm)	1.36 in. (34.5 mm)	6.7 cu. in. (109.8 cc)	Direct
125	2.50 in. (63.5 mm)	1.563 in. (39.7 mm)	7.6 cu. in. (124.5 cc)	Direct

MAINTENANCE

SPARK PLUG. Recommended spark plug is Champion RJ8. Spark plug electrode gap should be 0.018-0.020 inch (0.46-0.51 mm).

CARBURETOR. A Tillotson Model HL172B carburetor is used. Refer to Tillotson carburetor section in CARBURETOR SERVICE section for carburetor service.

Initial adjustment of mixture screws is ¾ turn open for idle mixture screw and 1 turn open for high speed adjusting screw. Adjust idle mixture screw to obtain smooth, rapid acceleration without hesitation. Adjust idle speed stop screw so that engine idles just below clutch engagement speed. High speed mixture screw should be adjusted with saw under cutting load.

MAGNETO AND TIMING. A conventional breaker-point type flywheel magneto ignition system is used. Breaker-points are attached to a stator plate mounted on left side of engine crankcase. Breaker-point gap should be 0.018 inch (0.46 mm).

Ignition timing is adjusted by loosening stator plate (3 – Fig. DA30) retaining screws and rotating stator plate. Ignition timing should occur with piston 26 degrees BTDC or 0.082-0.087 inch (2.08-2.21 mm) BTDC on Model 110 and 0.098-0.102 inch (2.49-2.59 mm) BTDC on Model 125. Ignition timing should be correct when mark on stator plate is aligned with mark on fan housing. Tighten flywheel nut to 280-300 in.-lbs. (31.6-33.9 N·m).

LUBRICATION. The engine is lubricated by mixing oil with the fuel. Recommended fuel is regular gasoline. Fuel:oil ratio should be 16:1. Use a good quality oil designed for air-cooled two-stroke engines.

Models 110 and 125 are equipped with manual and automatic chain oil pumps. Fill oil tank with clean automotive type oil.

CARBON. Carbon should be periodically removed from exhaust system and cylinder. Loose carbon should not be allowed to enter cylinder and care should be taken not to damage cylinder or piston.

REPAIRS

CYLINDER HEAD. Cylinder head is removeable on Models 110 and 125. To remove cylinder head, detach cowling and shroud and disconnect spark plug lead. Unscrew cylinder head screws and remove cylinder head.

When reinstalling cylinder head, tighten cylinder head screws in a crisscross pattern to 120-130 in.-lbs. (13.6-14.7 N·m).

CYLINDER, PISTON AND CONNECTING ROD. To remove cylinder, remove cowling, shroud, front handlebar and muffler. Unscrew cylinder retaining screws and carefully slide cylinder up and off of piston and away from crankcase. Extract piston pin and remove piston. To remove connecting rod, unscrew rod screws and carefully lift rod off crankshaft while noting any bearing roller which may fall into crankcase. Remove rod cap, bearing roller and cages. Be sure 12 bearing rollers are removed.

Inspect and renew, if necessary, connecting rod small end bearing. Press on

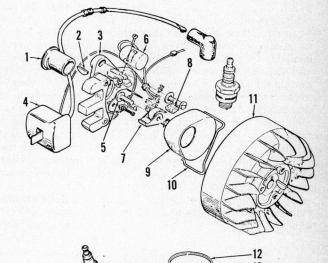

Fig. DA30 — Exploded view of ignition system.
1. Cam
2. Key
3. Stator plate
4. Coil
5. Stationary breaker-point
6. Condenser
7. Moveable breaker-point
8. Wick
9. Cover
10. Retainer
11. Flywheel

Fig. DA31 — Exploded view of Model 110 or 125 engine.
1. Cylinder head
2. Gasket
3. Cylinder
4. Nut
5. Washer
6. Seal
7. Snap ring
8. Bearing
9. Crankcase
10. Crankshaft
11. Piston
12. Piston rings
13. Piston pin
14. Snap ring
15. Bearing
16. Connecting rod
17. Bearing cage
18. Rod cap
19. Bearing rollers (12)
20. Bearing
21. Snap ring
22. Seal
23. Gasket
24. Flywheel housing
25. Washer
26. Nut

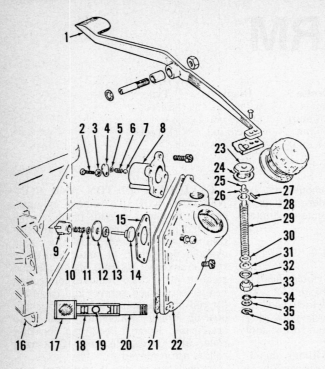

Fig. DA32 — View of manual and automatic oil pump components. Nipple (20) screws into cover (22).

1. Manual pump lever
2. Adjusting screw
3. Locknut
4. Valve cover
5. "O" ring
6. Spring
7. Outlet ball valve
8. Automatic oil pump housing
9. Adjustment sleeve
10. Spring
11. "O" ring
12. Piston ring
13. Teflon washer
14. Plunger
15. Gasket
16. Crankcase
17. Filter
18. Pickup tube
19. Check ball
20. Nipple
21. Gasket
22. Cover
23. Gland nut
24. Washer
25. Rod
26. "O" ring
27. Pin
28. Washer
29. Spring
30. Washer
31. Washer
32. "O" ring
33. Piston
34. "O" ring
35. Washer
36. Clip

(11.3-12.4 N·m). Install crankshaft seals with lip toward crankcase.

AUTOMATIC OILER. Models 110 and 125 are equipped with manual and automatic oil pumps as shown in Fig. DA32.

The automatic oil pump is operated by crankcase pulsations against pump plunger (14). The oil pump is contained in oil tank and may be serviced after removing cover (22). Clean and inspect all pump components and check for blocked oil passages. Be sure check ball (19) operates properly in pickup tube.

Automatic oil pump output is adjusted by turning screw (2 – Fig. DA32). Be sure to lock adjustment screw setting with nut (3).

CLUTCH. To remove the clutch, detach the right side cover, bar and chain. Remove clutch springs and unscrew clutch retaining nut. Use a suitable puller to remove clutch hub (8 – Fig. DA33).

Inspect components for excessive wear or damage. Place a small amount of grease on bushing (2). Install clutch hub (8) with tapped holes out. Tighten clutch nut to 220-240 in.-lbs. (24.9-27.1 N·m).

REWIND STARTER. Refer to Fig. DA34 for an exploded view of rewind starter. Sharp edge of pawls (10) marked "DA" should be toward closed side of brake lever (7) as shown. The sharp edge should be filed to 27 degrees. The pawls may catch in the starter cup (1) if edge is too sharp or if cup surface is rough. Starter may slip if starter pawls are dull or if fiber washers (6) are oil soaked. Rewind spring and rope are coiled in a clockwise direction when viewed installed in starter housing (16). To preload rewind spring, turn starter housing against spring tension two turns before installing retaining screws.

lettered end of bearing when installing in rod.

The cylinder on Models 110 and 125 has an iron bore which may be machined to accept oversize pistons and rings available from Danarm. Connecting rod and cap are fractured with irregular mating surfaces which must be in proper mesh when assembling rod on crankshaft. Be sure 12 bearing rollers and cages are installed correctly and tighten rod screws to 75 in.-lbs. (8.5 N·m).

Gently heat piston prior to installing piston pin. Install piston rings so end gaps are 180 degrees from each other and on piston pin centerline. Tighten cylinder retaining nuts to 85-90 in.-lbs. (9.6-10.2 N·m).

CRANKSHAFT AND CRANKCASE. To remove crankshaft, remove clutch, ignition and intake assemblies. Remove rear handle components then refer to previous section and remove cylinder, piston and connecting rod. Unscrew four crankcase screws then heat flywheel housing (24 – Fig. DA31) and separate housing from crankcase. It may be necessary to use a suitable puller to separate flywheel housing and crankcase. Gently tap on end of crankshaft and remove crankshaft from crankcase bearing.

Inspect bearings, seals and crankshaft for damage or excessive wear. When installing crankshaft, center crankpin in middle of cylinder opening. Tighten crankcase screws to 100-110 in.-lbs.

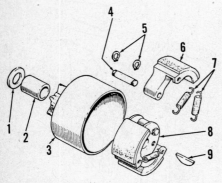

Fig. DA33—Exploded view of clutch.

1. Washer
2. Bushing
3. Sprocket & drum
4. Pin
5. Snap rings
6. Shoe
7. Springs
8. Clutch hub
9. Key

Fig. DA34—Exploded view of rewind starter.

1. Starter cup
2. "E" ring
3. Washer
4. Spring
5. Brake washers
6. Fiber washers
7. Brake lever
8. Spring retainer
9. Spring
10. Starter pawls
11. Rope pulley
12. Rewind spring
13. Starter adapter
14. Plate
15. Spindle
16. Starter housing

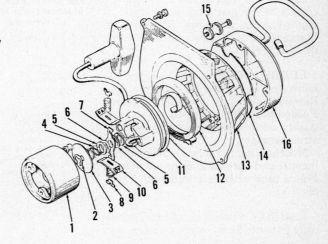

JOHN DEERE

DEERE & COMPANY
Moline, Illinois 61265

Model	Bore	Stroke	Displ.	Drive Type
61, 81, 81 Electric Start, 91	1.5 in. (38.1 mm)	1.2 in. (30.5 mm)	2.1 cu. in. (34.4 cc)	Direct
18	1.81 in. (46.0 mm)	1.38 in. (35.0 mm)	3.6 cu. in. (59.0 cc)	Direct
19	1.91 in. (48.5 mm)	1.38 in. (35.0 mm)	4.0 cu. in (65.5 cc)	Direct
23	2.06 in. (52.3 mm)	1.50 in. (38.1 mm)	5.0 cu. in. (82.0 cc)	Direct

MAINTENANCE

SPARK PLUG. Recommended spark plug is Champion CJ6 or AC CS-42. Spark plug electrode gap should be 0.025 (0.63 mm).

CARBURETOR. All models are equipped with a Model HS or HU Tillotson diaphragm carburetor. Initial adjustment of high and low speed mixture screws is one turn open from a lightly seated position. Final adjustment should be made with engine running at operating temperature. Adjust low speed mixture so engine will accelerate cleanly without hesitation.

NOTE: High speed mixture on Models 61, 81, 81 Electric Start and 91 is preset at factory.

Adjust high speed mixture on Models 18, 19 and 23 to obtain optimum full throttle performance under cutting load. Do not adjust high speed mixture too lean as overheating and engine damage could result. Adjust idle speed to just below clutch engagement speed.

Refer to Tillotson section of CARBURETOR SERVICE section for carburetor operation and overhaul.

MAGNETO AND TIMING. A flywheel magneto is used on all models. Breaker-point gap should be 0.015 inch (0.38 mm). Ignition timing is fixed. Be sure breaker-point gap is correct as incorrect gap setting will affect ignition timing. Breaker-points are located under flywheel. Flywheel may be removed using a suitable flywheel puller.

Magneto air gap should be 0.010 inch (0.25 mm). Adjust air gap by loosening coil mounting screws and installing 0.010 inch (0.25 mm) shim stock between coil legs and flywheel. Move coil legs against shim stock and tighten coil mounting screws. Remove shim stock.

LUBRICATION. Engine is lubricated by mixing oil with the fuel. Recommended fuel:oil ratio is 16:1. Type of oil should be a good quality SAE 30 oil designed for chain saw or air-cooled two-stroke engines.

A manual chain oil pump is used on all models. Models 18, 19, 23, 81, 81 Electric Start and 91 are also equipped with an automatic chain oiler. Oil in oil tank is pressurized by engine crankcase pulsations to force chain oil to the chain. Oil output on Models 23, 81, 81 Electric Start and 91 is adjusted by turning adjusting screw located near trigger on rear grip. Oil output on Models 18 and 19 is adjusted by turning metering screw located at the base of front handle on the right hand side. A mixture of half SAE nondetergent oil and half kerosene is recommended by manufacturer for chain saw oil.

CARBON. Carbon deposits should be removed from muffler and exhaust ports at regular intervals. Do not allow loose carbon to enter cylinder. Be careful not to damage piston or cylinder.

REPAIRS

TIGHTENING TORQUES. Recommended tightening torques are listed in the following table.

Models 18, 19 and 23

Connecting rod screws . . . . . . 55 in.-lbs. (6.2 N·m)
Cylinder base nuts . . . . 70 in.-lbs. (8.0 N·m)
Starter cup nut . . . . 175 in.-lbs. (19.8 N·m)
Clutch nut . . . . 160 in.-lbs. (18.1 N·m)
Carburetor mounting screws . 50 in.-lbs. (5.6 N·m)
Muffler screws . . . . 100 in.-lbs. (11.3 N·m)

Models 61, 81, 81 Electric Start and 91

Connecting rod screws . . . . . . 35 in.-lbs. (4.0 N·m)
Cylinder base screws . . . . 60 in.-lbs. (6.8 N·m)
Starter cup nut . . . . 150 in.-lbs. (17.0 N·m)
Clutch nut . . . . 150 in.-lbs. (17.0 N·m)
Carburetor mounting screws . 45 in.-lbs. (5.1 N·m)
Muffler screws . . . . 60 in.-lbs. (6.8 N·m)

CYLINDER, PISTON, PIN AND RINGS. To remove cylinder on Models 18, 19 and 23, remove starter housing, clutch, flywheel and stator. Remove carburetor and disconnect oil lines. Disconnect impulse line on Models 18 and 19. Detach rear handle cover and remove compression release rod on Models 19 and 23. Remove rear handle assembly. Detach right crankcase cover (19 – Fig. JD5), unscrew cylinder base nuts and remove cylinder.

To remove cylinder on Models 61, 81, 81 Electric Start and 91, remove chain guard, starter housing and carburetor cover. Disconnect choke linkage and ignition switch wire. Disconnect throttle linkage and fuel line and remove carburetor. Remove rear handle assembly while pulling linkage through grommets. Unscrew coil mount screw in cylinder head. Unscrew cylinder base screws and remove cylinder.

Cylinder on all models is chrome plated and oversize pistons and rings are not available. Inspect cylinder for excessive wear, cracking, scoring or flaking of chrome bore. Install piston rings with bevel edge on ring toward top of piston. Install piston so "EXH" marking on piston crown is toward exhaust port of cylinder. Be sure piston ring end gap is correctly positioned around piston ring locating pin when installing cylinder.

CONNECTING ROD. Remove cylinder and piston to detach connecting rod from crankshaft. Unscrew connecting rod screws and remove connecting rod and cap being careful not to lose loose bearing rollers (14 – Fig. JD4 or JD5). Twenty-eight bearing rollers are used on Models 18 and 19. All other models are equipped with twenty-four bearing rollers. Manufacturer recommends renewing rollers whenever connecting rod is removed. Connecting rod is fractured and has match marks on one side of rod and cap. Be sure rod and cap are correctly meshed and match marks are aligned during assembly.

CRANKSHAFT AND CRANKCASE. Crankshaft removal on Models 61, 81, 81 Electric Start and 91 requires removing clutch, starter housing and flywheel assemblies. Clutch has left hand threads. Remove cylinder, piston

and connecting rod as previously outlined. Remove front handle, detach crankcase cover (1 – Fig. JD4) and remove crankshaft.

Crankshaft is supported by roller bearings (3) in crankcase cover (1) and crankcase (8). Press seals (2) and roller bearings (3) out of crankcase cover and crankcase and inspect for damage and excessive wear. Check crankshaft for damaged bearing surfaces or discoloration.

Crankshaft roller bearings must be installed so numbered side of bearing will be toward connecting rod. Press on numbered side of bearing until bearing is 0.010 inch (0.25 mm) below surface of casting. Press seals into cover (1) or crankcase (8) until flush with surface. Crankshaft end play should be 0.008-0.022 inch (0.20-0.56 mm).

To remove crankshaft on Models 18, 19 and 23, remove cylinder, piston and connecting rod as previously outlined. Crankshaft can not be removed from crankcase. Crankcase can be separated from fuel tank on Models 18, 19 and 23.

Inspect bearings and seals for damage or excessive wear. Crankshaft bearings

should be installed so numbered side of bearing is inward. Press on inward side of bearing so bearing is 0.010 inch (0.25 mm) below surface of casting. Seals should be flush with surface. Crankshaft end play should be 0.005-0.015 inch (0.13-0.38 mm).

AUTOMATIC CHAIN OILER. All models are equipped with an automatic chain oiling system. Crankcase pulsations are directed through check valve (C – Fig. JD6) to oil tank. Oil in tank is pressurized and metered to chain by adjusting screw. Check valve (C) is renewable and should be inspected if spark plug is fouling due to excessive oil or engine exhaust smoke indicates excessive oil burning. Defective check valve may allow pressurized oil in oil tank to flow through crankcase impulse passage into crankcase.

Models 18, 19 and 23 are equipped with an oil shut-off valve which is actuated by a link connected to the throttle trigger which shuts off oil output when engine is idling.

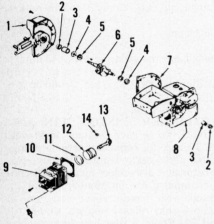

Fig. JD4 — Exploded view of engine used on Models 61, 81, 81 Electric Start and 91. Some models use a bushing in place of bearing (5).

1. Crankcase cover
2. Seal
3. Bearing
4. Thrust washer
5. Thrust bearing
6. Crankshaft
7. Gasket
8. Crankcase
9. Cylinder
10. Gasket
11. Piston rings
12. Piston
13. Connecting rod & cap
14. Bearing

Fig. JD6 — View showing location of check valve (C) in oil tank on Models 18 and 19. Model 23 is similar except check valve is located on right side of oil tank. On all other models equipped with automatic oil pump, check valve is located in impulse line fitting at oil tank.

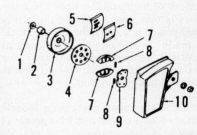

Fig. JD7 — Exploded view of clutch assembly used on Models 61, 81, 81 Electric Start and 91.

1. Thrust washer
2. Bearing
3. Clutch drum
4. Cover
5. Inner bar guide
6. Outer bar guide
7. Clutch shoe
8. Spring
9. Clutch hub
10. Cover

Fig. JD5 — Exploded view of engine used on Models 18, 19 and 23. Refer to Fig. JD4 for component identification except, bearing (15), piston pin (16), retainer (17), "O" ring (18) and right crankcase cover (19).

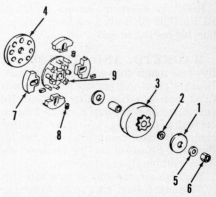

Fig. JD8 — Exploded view of clutch assembly used on Models 18, 19 and 23.

1. Washer
2. Bearing
3. Clutch drum
4. Cover
5. Washer
6. Nut
7. Clutch shoe
8. Spring
9. Clutch hub

MANUAL CHAIN OIL PUMP. All models are equipped with a manual plunger type oil pump. Pump assembly on 61, 81, 81 Electric Start and 91 models is mounted on inside of oil tank cover which must be removed for access to pump assembly. Pump assembly is mounted in rear handle grip on Models 18, 19 and 23. Inspect oil pump components wear or damage which may cause leakage or decreased oil output.

CLUTCH. Refer to Fig. JD7 for exploded view of centrifugal clutch used on Models 61, 81, 81 Electric Start and 91. Refer to Fig. JD8 for exploded view of centrifugal clutch used on Models 18, 19 and 23. Clutch hub (9) is screwed on crankshaft with left-hand threads. Inspect clutch and renew any components found to be excessively worn or damaged.

REED VALVE. A reed valve induction system is used on 18, 19 and 23 models with the reed valve assembly located between rear handle and air box assembly and crankcase. Inspect reed petal for cracks or chips and reed valve seat for damage which may prevent satisfactory reed valve operation.

REWIND STARTER. Refer to Fig. JD9 for exploded view of rewind starter. To disassemble starter, remove starter housing from saw. Detach rope handle and allow rope to rewind into starter. Unscrew retaining screw or pry off "E" clip (11), if so equipped, and remove friction shoe assembly. Remove rope pulley (6) being careful not to disturb rewind spring. Be careful not to allow spring to uncoil uncontrolled.

To reassemble starter, reverse disassembly procedure. Install rewind spring so coils are in clockwise direction starting with outer coil. Grease pulley post in housing (2) lightly. Wrap rope around pulley (6) in clockwise direction as viewed with pulley in housing. Be sure inner hook of rewind spring (4) engages pulley. Place tension on rewind spring by turning pulley three turns clockwise before passing rope through hole in housing. Components in friction shoe assembly (9) are not available individually. Friction shoe components must be assembled as shown in Fig. JD10. One edge of each friction shoe must be sharp to properly engage starter cup. Note in Fig. JD9 the location of sharp edges (S) for correct starter assembly. Renew fiber washers (8 and 10) if glazed or oil soaked.

ELECTRIC STARTER. Model 81 Electric Start is equipped with an electric motor to start engine. The electric motor is driven by an external 12 volt battery which may be recharged. Starter mechanism is gear driven by electric motor as shown in Fig. JD11.

Wires for electric starter should be connected as follows: One white lead of battery connector (6) should be connected to rear pole of switch (4) while other white lead should be connected to positive " + " terminal of starter motor. A black wire should be connected between negative " − " terminal of starter motor and middle pole of switch (4). A green wire should be connected to middle poles of switch (4) and grounded to starter housing (5). A blue wire should be connected to front pole of switch (4) and the ignition coil primary wire.

Battery should be discarded if minimum voltage level of 12.8 volts is not attained after 48 hours of charging. The battery charger may be checked by connecting a voltmeter to battery connector if charger-exposed pin is negative. With battery charger plugged into a 110 volt circuit, battery charger output should be in excess of 7.5 volts. If battery and charger operate satisfactorily, remove starter cover and note if starter motor will turn freely. If starter motor is not binding, connect battery to starter housing plug and using a voltmeter and appropriate voltage checks, determine if starter switch, starter motor or wiring is defective.

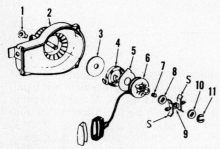

Fig JD9 — Exploded view of rewind starter typical of all models. Spring shield (3) and dust shield (5) are not used on Models 61, 81, 81 Electric Start and 91. Some models use a screw in place of "E" ring (11).

1. Rope bushing
2. Starter housing
3. Spring shield
4. Rewind spring
5. Dust shield
6. Rope pulley
7. Brake spring
8. Fiber washer
9. Friction shoe assy.
10. Fiber washer
11. "E" ring

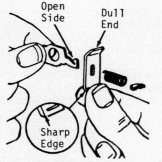

Fig. JD10 — Friction shoe assembly (9 — Fig. JD9) must be assembled as shown above. Refer to text.

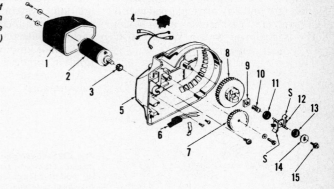

Fig. JD11 — Exploded view of electric starter used on Model 81 Electric Start. Note position of sharp edges (S) of friction shoes.

1. Cover
2. Starter motor
3. Pinion gear
4. Starter switch
5. Starter housing
6. Battery connector
7. Idler gear
8. Starter gear
9. Drive washer
10. Spring
11. Fiber washer
12. Friction shoe assy.
13. Fiber washer
14. Washer
15. SEMS screw

JOHN DEERE

Model	Bore	Stroke	Displ.	Drive Type
28, 30	1.457 in. (37 mm)	1.102 in. (28 mm)	1.83 cu. in. (30.1 cc)	Direct
40V	1.575 in. (40 mm)	1.102 in. (28 mm)	2.15 cu. in. (35.2 cc)	Direct
50V	1.68 in. (42 mm)	1.28 in. (32 mm)	2.7 cu. in. (44.3 cc)	Direct
55V	1.68 in. (42 mm)	1.42 in. (36 mm)	3.05 cu. in. (49.9 cc)	Direct
60V	1.81 in. (46 mm)	1.42 in. (36 mm)	3.65 cu. in. (59.8 mm)	Direct
70V	1.97 in. (50 mm)	1.42 in. (36 mm)	4.31 cu. in. (70.7 cc)	Direct
80EV	2.03 in. (52 mm)	1.46 in. (37 mm)	4.8 cu. in. (78.6 cc)	Direct

MAINTENANCE

SPARK PLUG. Recommended spark plug is Champion CJ8 or NGK BM-6A for Models 28, 30, 40V, 50V and 55V. Recommended spark plug for all other models is Champion CJ7Y or NGK BPM-7A. On all models, spark plug electrode gape should be 0.025 inch (0.63 mm).

CARBURETOR. Models 28, 30 and 40V are equipped with a Walbro WA diaphragm type carburetor. A Tillotson HU carburetor is used on 50V models prior to serial number 017521 while a Walbro WA carburetor is used after serial number 017520. A Walbro HDB carburetor is used on 55V models while Models 60V and 70V are equipped with a Tillotson HS carburetor and Model 80EV is equipped with a Walbro SDC carburetor. Refer to Tillotson or Walbro section of CARBURETOR SERVICE section for carburetor overhaul and exploded views.

Initial setting of idle and high speed mixture screws is one turn open from a lightly seated position. Make final carburetor adjustments with engine running at operating temperature. Adjust idle mixture screw so engine will accelerate without stumbling. Adjust high speed mixture screw to obtain optimum performance with saw under cutting load. Adjust idle speed screw so engine idles just under clutch engagement speed.

IGNITION. Model 80EV is equipped with a breakerless capacitor discharge ignition system. Repair of ignition system malfunction except for faulty wiring connections is accomplished by renewal of ignition system components. Ignition timing is not adjustable.

All other models are equipped with a conventional flywheel magneto ignition system having breaker-points located under the flywheel. Breaker-point gap should be 0.014 inch (0.35 mm). Magneto air gap should be 0.016 inch (0.40 mm) on all models.

Correct ignition timing is 30 degrees BTDC. Reference marks are located on flywheel and crankcase to set ignition timing. With flywheel turning counterclockwise, first mark "F" on flywheel periphery indicates ignition point when aligned with crankcase mark while second mark "T" indicates top dead center. Ignition timing on Models 28, 30, 40V, 50V and 55V is adjusted by altering breaker-point gap while timing on Models 60V and 70V is adjusted by rotating stator plate. Tighten flywheel nut on Models 28, 30, 40V, 50V and 55V to 14.5-17 ft.-lbs. (19.7-23.1 N·m) and on Models 60V and 70V to 24-26 ft.-lbs. (32.6-35.4 N·m).

LUBRICATION. The engine is lubricated by mixing oil with the fuel. Fuel:oil ratio is 40:1 when using John Deere

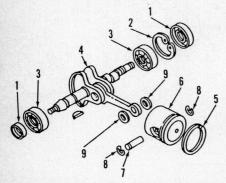

Fig. JD20 — Exploded view of engine assembly used on Model 28.

1. Seal
2. Snap ring
3. Ball bearing
4. Crankshaft & rod assy.
5. Piston ring
6. Piston
7. Piston pin
8. Pin retainer
9. Spacers

Fig. JD21 — Exploded view of engine assembly typical of all models except Model 28. Flywheel side snap ring (11) is absent on 55V models.

1. Seal
2. Clutch side snap ring
3. Ball bearing
4. Crankshaft & rod assy.
5. Piston rings
6. Piston
7. Piston pin
8. Pin retainer
10. Needle bearing
11. Flywheel side snap ring

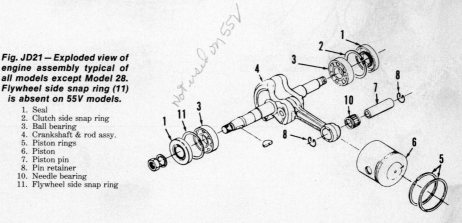

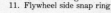

2-Cycle Engine Oil. If John Deere 2-Cycle Engine oil is not available, a good quality oil designed for two-stroke air-cooled engines may be used when mixed at a 32:1 ratio. Use a separate container when mixing the oil and gas.

Clean SAE 10 or SAE 30 automotive oil may be used to lubricate chain and bar. Cut oil with up to 33 percent kerosene during cold weather to aid lubrication.

REPAIRS

CYLINDER, PISTON, PIN AND RINGS. Cylinder bore is chrome plated on all models and oversize pistons and rings are not available. Inspect cylinder bore for scoring, flaking or other damage to chrome surface.

Install piston with arrow on piston crown toward exhaust port. Install piston pin with closed end toward exhaust port. Piston rings are pinned in ring grooves to prevent rotation. Be sure piston ring end gaps are properly positioned around piston ring locating pins when installing cylinder. On 55V models, tighten cylinder base nuts to 75-85 in.-lbs. (8.5-9.6 N·m). On all other models, tighten cylinder base nuts to 65-75 in.-lbs. (7.3-8.5 N·m).

CRANKSHAFT, CONNECTING ROD AND CRANKCASE. All models are equipped with a crankshaft and con-

necting rod unit assembly which is supported in the crankcase by ball bearings at both ends. Crankshaft and connecting rod are not available separately.

Check crankshaft runout by supporting crankshaft at points (A–Fig. JD22) and measure at points (B). Maximum allowable runout is 0.002 inch (0.05 mm). Side clearance between rod big end and crankshaft should be 0.0098-0.0118 inch (0.25-0.30 mm).

Crankshaft main bearings are located in crankcase by snap rings (2 and 11–Fig. JD21) on all models except 28 and 55V models. The clutch side main bearing of 28 and 55V models is located by a snap ring but flywheel side main bearing is located by a shoulder in the crankcase. Install oil seals with open side toward inside of crankcase.

A needle bearing (10–Fig. JD21) is used in connecting rod small end of all models except Model 28 which supports piston pin directly in rod. Note spacers (9–Fig. JD20) used on Model 28.

CLUTCH. Note that clutch nut and clutch hub have left-hand threads on all models.

Refer to Fig. JD23 for view of clutch used on Models 28, 30 and 40V. Clutch hub and shoes (1) are available only as a unit assembly. Be sure washer (2) is installed between clutch hub and drum.

Models 50V, 55V and 60V are equipped with the three-shoe clutch shown in Fig. JD25 while Models 70V and 80EV are equipped with the six-shoe clutch shown in Fig. JD24. The clutch drum on all models rides on a renewable needle roller bearing. Be sure washer (W–Fig. JD25) on Model 60V is installed between clutch hub and drum.

OIL PUMP. All models are equipped with an automatic oil pump. Refer to Fig. JD26. The pump is operated by a cam on the crankshaft which actuates plunger (6).

When installing oil pump, proceed as follows: If removed, install dowel (8) on Models 30 and 50V. On all models, screw oil pump assembly (3) into crankcase until lightly seated. Remove bar and chain so oil port is exposed then start and run saw at half throttle. Turn oil pump counterclockwise so maximum oil flow is obtained then continue counterclockwise rotation until oil flow is small but not stopped. Install spring washer (7) over dowel (8) on Models 30 and 50V.

Install dial (2) when applicable, so dial can only be turned clockwise and install screw (1).

A manual oil pump is used on Models 50V, 60V, 70V and 80EV. The manual oil pump consists of pump mechanism and two check valves. Check valves are located just above clutch drum and must function freely for proper pump operation.

REWIND STARTER. To disassemble rewind starter, remove starter housing, remove rope handle and allow rope

Fig. JD25—Exploded view of clutch used on Models 50V, 55V and 60V. Washer (W) is used only on Model 60V.

1. Dust seal	6. Sprocket
2. Clutch hub	7. Needle bearing
3. Clutch shoes	8. Washer
4. Garter spring	9. Nut
5. Clutch drum	

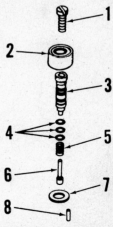

Fig. JD26—Exploded view of automatic oil pump typical of all models. Spring washer (7) and dowel (8) are used only on Models 30 and 50V.

1. Set screw	5. Spring
2. Adjusting dial	6. Plunger
3. Pump body	7. Spring washer
4. "O" rings	8. Dowel

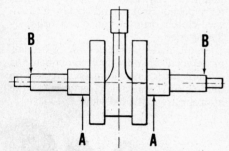

Fig. JD22—Measure crankshaft by supporting crankshaft at points (A). Maximum runout measured at points (B) should not exceed 0.002 inch (0.05 mm).

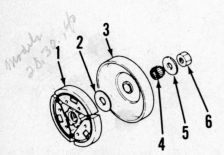

Fig. JD23—Exploded view of clutch used on Models 28, 30 and 40V.

1. Hub & shoe assy.	4. Needle bearing
2. Washer	5. Washer
3. Clutch drum	6. Nut

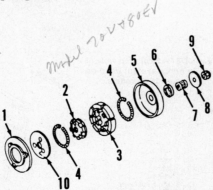

Fig. JD24—Exploded view of clutch used on Models 70V and 80EV.

1. Dust seal	6. Sprocket
2. Clutch hub	7. Needle bearing
3. Clutch shoes	8. Washer
4. Garter spring	9. Nut
5. Clutch drum	10. Washer

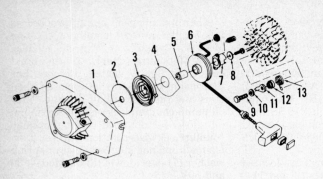

Fig. JD27 — Exploded view of rewind starter used on Models 30 and 50V. Models 40, 55V, 60V, 70V and 80EV are similar.

1. Starter housing
2. Plate
3. Rewind spring
4. Plate
5. Bushing
6. Rope pulley
7. Starter cup
8. Washer
9. Screw
10. Washer
11. Pawl
12. Spacer
13. Spring

to rewind into housing. Unscrew rope pulley screw and carefully remove rope pulley (6 – Fig. JD27 or Fig. JD28), being careful not to dislodge rewind spring (3). If necessary to remove rewind spring, care should be used not to allow spring to uncoil uncontrolled.

Install rewind spring (3) into starter housing (1) with coils wrapped in a clockwise direction from outer end of spring.

Wind rope around pulley in a clockwise direction as viewed from flywheel side of pulley. Turn pulley three or four turns clockwise before passing rope through outlet. Check starter operation. It should be possible to pull rope to its full extension and still turn rope pulley approximately ½ turn clockwise. If rewind spring binds before rope is fully extended, reduce pre-tension on rope by

pulling rope up into notch in rope pulley and allowing pulley to rotate one turn counterclockwise. Recheck starter operation.

COMPRESSION RELEASE VALVE. Models 60V, 70V and 80EV are equipped with a compression release valve which is located adjacent to exhaust port in cylinder. When servicing valve, clean all components of carbon being sure hole in valve body (4 – Fig. JD29) is clean. After assembling valve, stake nut (1) to valve (6).

CHAIN BRAKE. Some models are equipped with an optional chain brake system designed to stop chain movement should kickback occur. The chain brake system available for Models 30, 40, 50V, 60V and 70V uses a spring-loaded set of brake shoes located inside clutch/brake drum to stop the chain when the operator's hand strikes the chain brake lever. Pull back chain brake lever to reset mechanism. No adjustment of brake mechanism is required.

The optional chain brake system for Model 55V is activated when the operator's hand strikes chain brake lever (1 – Fig. JD30) thereby forcing actuating cam (4) to release spring (3). Spring (3) then draws brake band tight around clutch drum to stop chain. Chain brake operation is similar on 80EV models. On 55V and 80EV models, brake band is adjusted by rotating adjuster (9 – Fig. JD30 or 17 – Fig. JD31) as required. Brake band should not contact clutch drum when chain brake is disengaged.

On all models, disassembly for repair or renewal of individual components is evident after inspection of unit and on Models 55V and 80EV, referral to the appropriate exploded view.

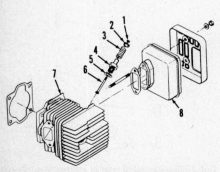

Fig. JD28 — Exploded view of rewind starter used on Model 28.

1. Starter housing	9. Spacer
2. Rewind spring case	11. Spring
3. Rewind spring	12. Pawl
6. Rope pulley	13. Flywheel
8. Washer	15. Screw

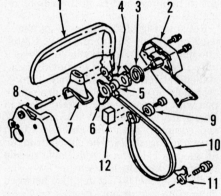

Fig. JD30 — Exploded view of chain brake system used on some 55V models.

1. Chain brake lever	7. Dust cover
2. Shield	8. Pivot pin
3. Spring	9. Brake band adjuster
4. Actuating cam	10. Brake band
5. Spacer	11. Brake band retainer
6. Brake band lever	12. Dust seal

JD29 — Exploded view of compression release valve used on Models 60V, 70V and 80EV.

1. Nut	5. Seal
2. Washer	6. Valve
3. Spring	7. Cylinder
4. Valve body	8. Muffler

Fig. JD31 — Exploded view of chain brake system used on some 80EV models.

1. Hand guard
2. Chain brake lever
3. Dust cover
4. Nut
5. Spring
6. Washer
7. Spacer
8. Actuating lever
9. Washer
10. Shield
11. Dust seal
12. Brake band lever
13. Washer
14. Spring
15. Sleeve
16. Brake band
17. Brake band adjuster

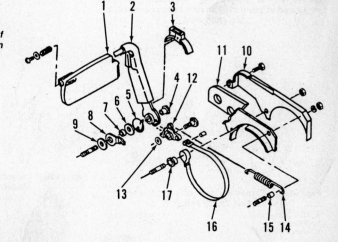

ECHO

ECHO INCORPORATED
400 Oakwood Road
Lake Zurich, IL 60047

Model	Bore	Stroke	Displ.	Drive Type
CS-60S	48 mm (1.89 in.)	34 mm (1.34 in.)	61.5 cc (3.75 cu. in.)	Direct
CS-100	57 mm (2.24 in.)	40 mm (1.57 in.)	102 cc (6.23 cu. in.)	Direct

MAINTENANCE

SPARK PLUG. Recommended spark plug for Model CS-60S is NGK BM-6A. Recommended spark plug for Model CS-100 is NGK B-7S. Electrode gap for both models should be 0.024-0.028 inch (0.61-0.71 mm).

CARBURETOR. Model CS-60S is equipped with a Tillotson Model HS diaphragm carburetor while Model CS-100 is equipped with a Tillotson Model HL diaphragm carburetor. Refer to Tillotson section of CARBURETOR SERVICE section for an exploded view and service information on carburetors.

Initial setting of idle mixture screw is one turn open and high speed mixture screw is ¾ turn open. Make final adjustments with engine warm and running. Adjust idle speed screw so engine idles just below clutch engagement speed. Adjust idle mixture screw so engine will accelerate without stumbling. Adjust high speed mixture screw to obtain optimum performance with saw under a cutting load. Do not adjust mixture screws too lean as engine damage may result.

IGNITION. Both models are equipped with a flywheel magneto ignition system. Breaker point gap should be 0.012-0.016 inch (0.30-0.40 mm). Correct ignition timing for Model CS-60S is 25 degrees BTDC. Correct ignition timing for Model CS-100 is 30 degrees BTDC. Reference marks are provided on cylinder and flywheel to set ignition timing. With flywheel turning counterclockwise, first mark on flywheel periphery indicates ignition point when aligned with mark on cylinder. Second mark indicates Top Dead Center when aligned with mark on cylinder. Adjust ignition timing by rotating stator plate. When reinstalling flywheel, tighten nut to 330-365 in.-lbs. (37.3-41.2 N·m).

LUBRICATION. The engine is lubricated by oil mixed with fuel.

Regular grade automotive gasoline is recommended. Recommended oil is Echo air-cooled two-stroke engine oil mixed with fuel at a 50:1 ratio. If Echo air-cooled two-stroke engine oil is not available, use a good quality oil designed for use in air-cooled two-stroke engines mixed with fuel at a 32:1 ratio.

Clean SAE 20 or SAE 30 automotive oil may be used to lubricate chain and bar. Dilute oil with up to 50 percent kerosene during cold weather to aid lubrication.

REPAIRS

CYLINDER HEAD. Model CS-100 is equipped with a removeable cylinder head. Do not damage cylinder head or cylinder mating surfaces. Inspect cylinder head surface for warpage. Tighten cylinder head screws to 95-130 in.-lbs. (10.8-14.7 N·m).

CYLINDER, PISTON, RINGS AND PIN. Cylinder head on Model CS-100 is removeable as indicated in previous paragraph while cylinder head on Model

CS-60S is integral with cylinder. Cylinder bore is chrome plated on both models and oversize piston and rings are not available. Maximum piston ring end gap is 0.02 inch (0.5 mm), and maximum

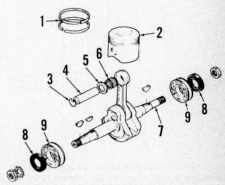

Fig. E2 — Exploded view of Model CS-60S crankshaft, rod and piston assembly.

1. Piston rings	6. Bearing
2. Piston	7. Crankshaft & rod assy.
3. Pin retainer	8. Seal
4. Piston pin	9. Ball bearing
5. Spacer (2)	

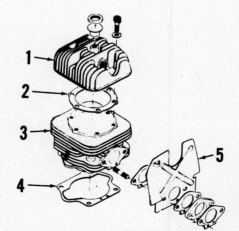

Fig. E1 — Exploded view of cylinder assembly used on Model CS-100. Model CS-60S is similar but does not have a removeable cylinder head.

1. Cylinder head	
2. Gasket	4. Gasket
3. Cylinder	5. Shroud

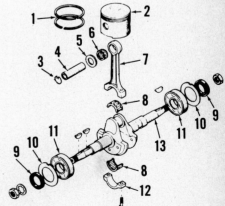

Fig. E3 — Exploded view of Model CS-100 crankshaft, rod and piston assembly.

1. Piston rings	
2. Piston	8. Roller bearing
3. Pin retainer	9. Seal
4. Piston pin	10. Washer
5. Spacer	11. Ball bearing
6. Bearing	12. Rod cap
7. Connecting rod	13. Crankshaft

ring side clearance is 0.004 inch (0.10 mm).

Inspect cylinder bore for scoring, flaking or other damage to the chrome surface. Install piston so arrow on piston crown is toward exhaust port. Piston rings are pinned to prevent rotation. Be sure piston ring end gaps are properly positioned around piston ring locating pins when installing cylinder.

CRANKSHAFT CONNECTING ROD AND CRANKCASE. Crankshaft is supported at both ends by ball bearings. Connecting rod and crankshaft on Model CS-60S are available only as a unit assembly. Connecting rod and crankshaft on Model CS-100 are available separately. Connecting rod rides on a caged roller bearing (6 – Fig. E2 or E3). Inspect connecting rod, bearing and crankpin for excessive wear or damage.

Check crankshaft runout by supporting crankshaft at points (A – Fig. E4) and measure at points (B). Maximum allowable runout is 0.002 inch (0.05 mm).

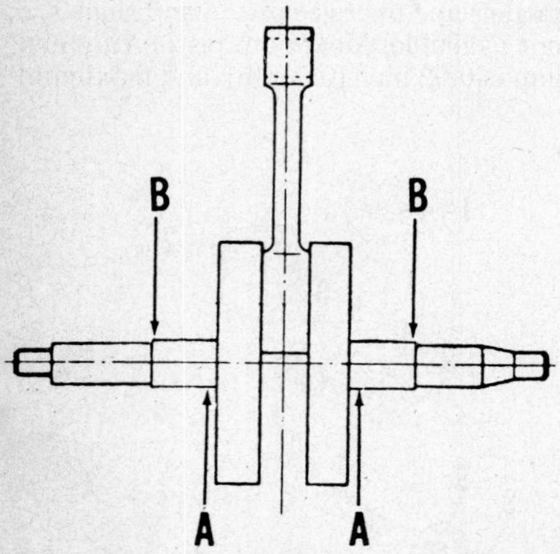

CLUTCH. Model CS-60S is equipped with the six-shoe centrifugal clutch shown in Fig. E5, while Model CS-100 is equipped with the four-shoe centrifugal clutch shown in Fig. E6. The clutch drum on both models rides on a caged needle roller bearing. Inspect clutch drum and shoes for excessive wear or damage due to overheating.

REWIND STARTER. Refer to Fig. E7 for an exploded view of rewind starter. To disassemble starter, remove rope handle and allow rope to wind into starter housing. Care should be used when disassembling starter to prevent rewind spring from uncoiling uncontrolled.

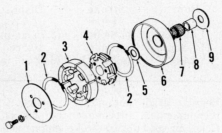

Fig. E5 — Exploded view of Model CS-60S clutch.

1. Cover
2. Garter spring
3. Clutch shoes
4. Clutch hub
5. Washer
6. Clutch drum
7. Bearing
8. Inner race
9. Washer

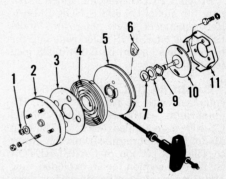

Fig. E7 — Exploded view of rewind starter used on Models CS-60S and CS-100.

1. "E" ring
2. Spring housing
3. Plate
4. Rewind spring
5. Rope pulley
6. Pawl
7. "E" ring
8. Washer
9. Spring washer
10. Spindle
11. Starter cup

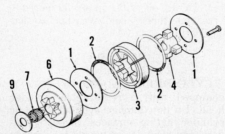

Fig. E6 — Exploded view of Model CS-100 clutch. Refer to Fig. E5 for parts identification.

Fig. E4 — Support crankshaft at points (A) and measure runout at points (B). Runout must not exceed 0.002 inch (0.05 mm).

ECHO

Model	Bore	Stroke	Displ.	Drive Type
CS-302, CS-315	37 mm (1.46 in.)	28 mm (1.10 in.)	30.1 cc (1.83 cu. in.)	Direct
CS-302S	39 mm (1.53 in.)	28 mm (1.10 in.)	33.4 cc (2.04 cu. in.)	Direct
CS-351, CS-351VL	40 mm (1.57 in.)	28 mm (1.10 in.)	35.2 cc (2.14 cu. in.)	Direct
CS-451, CS-451VL, CS-452, CS-452VL	42 mm (1.65 in.)	32 mm (1.26 in.)	44.3 cc (2.69 cu. in.)	Direct
CS-601, CS-602, CS-602VL	46 mm (1.81 in.)	36 mm (1.42 in.)	59.8 cc (3.65 cu. in.)	Direct
CS-701, CS-702, CS-702VL, CS-702EVL	50 mm (1.97 in.)	36 mm (1.42 in.)	70.7 cc (4.32 cu. in.)	Direct
CS-750, CS-750VL, CS-750EVL	52 mm (2.03 in.)	37 mm (1.46 mm)	78.6 cc (4.8 cu. in.)	Direct

---

MAINTENANCE

SPARK PLUG. Recommended spark plug is NGK BPM–7A for Models CS-602, CS-602VL, CS-702, CS-702VL, CS-702EVL, CS-750, CS-750VL and CS-750EVL. Recommended spark plug for all other models is NGK BM-6A. Electrode gap should be 0.024-0.028 inch (0.61-0.71 mm).

CARBURETOR. Models CS-750, CS-750VL and CS-750EVL are equipped with a Walbro SDC carburetor. All other models are equipped with either a Walbro WA, Tillotson HU or Tillotson HS carburetor. Refer to CARBURETOR SERVICE section for carburetor overhaul.

Initial setting of idle and high speed mixture screws is one turn open. Make final carburetor adjustments with engine at operating temperature. Adjust idle mixture screw so engine will accelerate without stumbling. Adjust high speed mixture screw to obtain optimum performance with saw under cutting load. Adjust idle speed screw so engine idles just under clutch engagement speed.

IGNITION. Models CS-702EVL and CS-750EVL are equipped with a breakerless capacitor discharge ignition system. Repair of ignition system malfunction except for faulty wiring connections is accomplished by renewal of ignition system components. Ignition timing is fixed at 30 degrees BTDC and is not adjustable.

All other models are equipped with a flywheel magneto ignition system using breaker points. Breaker point gap should be 0.012-0.016 inch (0.30-0.40 mm). Correct ignition timing is 30 degrees BTDC. Reference marks are provided on crankcase and flywheel to set ignition timing. With flywheel turning counterclockwise, first mark on flywheel periphery indicates ignition point when aligned with mark on crankcase. On some models the flywheel mark is lettered "M" or "F." A second flywheel mark when aligned with the crankcase mark indicates piston is at TDC. Adjust ignition timing by rotating stator plate on Models CS-601, CS-602, CS-602VL, CS-701, CS-702, CS-702VL, CS-750 and CS-750VL. On all other breaker-point models, adjust timing by increasing or decreasing breaker-point gap.

On all models, air gap between flywheel magnets and ignition module or magneto core legs should be 0.012-0.016 inch (0.30-0.40 mm).

LUBRICATION. The engine is lubricated by mixing oil with fuel. Regular grade automotive gasoline is recommended. Recommended oil is Echo air-cooled two-stroke engine oil mixed with fuel at a 50:1 ratio. If Echo air-cooled two-stroke engine oil is not available, use a good quality oil designed for use in air-cooled two-stroke engines mixed with fuel at a 32:1 ratio.

Clean SAE 20 or SAE 30 automotive oil may be used to lubricate chain and bar. Dilute oil with up to 50 percent kerosene during cold weather to aid lubrication. Automatic oil pump output is adjusted by turning knob located on top side of saw near front handle.

REPAIRS

CYLINDER, PISTON, PIN AND RINGS. Cylinder bore is chrome plated on all models and oversize pistons and rings are not available. Inspect cylinder bore for scoring, flaking or other damage to chrome surface.

Piston ring end gap should be 0.004-0.012 inch (0.10-0.30 mm); maximum allowable ring end gap is 0.020 inch (0.51 mm). Piston ring side clearance should be 0.002 inch (0.05 mm) with a maximum allowable side clearance of 0.004 inch (0.10 mm).

Install piston with arrow on piston crown toward exhaust port. On Models CS-602, CS-602VL, CS-702, CS-702VL, CS-750, CS-750VL and CS-750EVL, install piston pin with closed end toward exhaust port. Piston rings are pinned in ring grooves to prevent rotation. Be sure piston end gaps are properly positioned around piston ring locating pins when installing cylinder. Tighten cylinder base nuts to 70-80 in.-lbs. (7.9-9.0 N·m) on Models CS-302 and CS-302S. Tighten cylinder base nuts to 30-35 in.-lbs. (3.4-3.9 N·m) on Model CS-315, 45-50 in.-lbs. (5.1-5.6 N·m) on Models CS-451, CS-451VL, CS-452 and CS-452VL and 65-75 in.-lbs. (7.4-8.4 N·m) on all other models.

CRANKSHAFT CONNECTING ROD AND CRANKCASE. All models are equipped with a crankshaft and connecting rod unit assembly which is supported in the crankcase by ball bearings at both ends. Crankshaft and connecting rod are not available separately.

Check crankshaft runout by supporting crankshaft at points (A–Fig. E12) and measure at points (B). Maximum allowable runout is 0.002 inch (0.05 mm).

Crankshaft main bearings are located in crankcase by snap rings (2–Fig. E11) on all models except CS-315. The clutch side main bearing of Model CS-315 is located by a snap ring but flywheel side main bearing is located by a shoulder in the crankcase. Some models may be equipped with a lubrication passage designed to lubricate oil pump cam and plunger. Make certain snap ring (2–Fig. E11 or Fig. E11A) does not obstruct passage when installed (snap ring gap should surround oil passage hole). Install

crankshaft seals, open sides toward each other, flush with outer face of crankcase.

A needle bearing is used in connecting rod small end of all models except Model CS-315 which supports piston pin directly in rod. Note spacers (10–Fig. E11A) used on Model CS-315.

CLUTCH. Models CS-302, CS-302S, CS-315, CS-351 and CS-351VL are equipped with the clutch assembly

shown in Fig. E13. Rivets (R) must be removed to separate clutch shoes and hub. Refer to Fig. E14 for exploded view of clutch used on Models CS-701, CS-702, CS-702VL, CS-702EVL, CS-750, CS-750VL and CS-750EVL. Clutch used on all other models is shown in Fig. E13A.

Clutch nut and hub have left-hand threads. Clutch drum on Model CS-315 is retained by a snap ring. On all models, the clutch drum rides on a roller bearing. Bearing should be periodically inspected and lubricated with a suitable

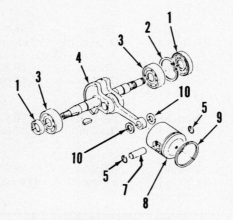

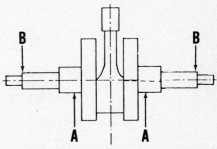

Fig. E12—Measure crankshaft by supporting crankshaft at points (A). Maximum runout measured at points (B) should not exceed 0.002 inch (0.05 mm).

Fig. E11A—Exploded view of crankshaft assembly used on Model CS-315. Refer to Fig. E11 for parts identification except for: 10. Spacers.

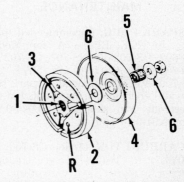

Fig. E13—Exploded view of clutch used on Models CS-302, CS-302S, CS-315, CS-351 and CS-351VL. Remove rivets (R) to separate clutch shoe components. Refer to Fig. 13A for parts identification.

Fig. E10—Exploded view of cylinder and compression release valve on Models CS-601, CS-602, CS-602VL, CS-701, CS-702, CS-702VL, CS-702EVL, CS-750, CS-750VL and CS-750EVL.

1. Cylinder
2. Compression release valve
3. Valve seat
4. Spring
5. Muffler

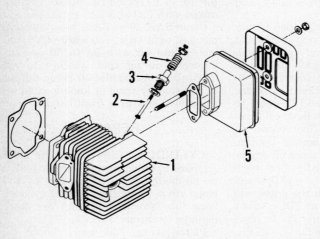

Fig. E11—Exploded view of crankshaft assembly used on all models except CS-315.

1. Seal
2. Snap ring
3. Ball bearing
4. Crankshaft & rod assy.
5. Pin retainer
6. Needle roller bearing
7. Piston pin
8. Piston
9. Piston rings

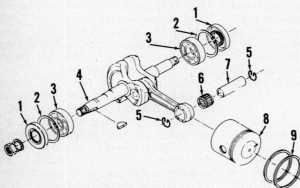

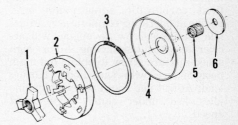

Fig. E13A—Exploded view of clutch used on Models CS451, CS451VL, CS-452, CS-452VL and CS-601. Clutch used on Models CS-602 and CS-602VL is similar.

1. Clutch hub
2. Clutch shoes
3. Garter spring
4. Clutch drum
5. Needle roller bearing
6. Washer

high temperature grease. Inspect clutch shoes and drum for damage due to over-heating. Renew excessively worn or damaged components.

OIL PUMP. All models are equipped with an automatic plunger type chain oil pump. The plunger on all models except CS-601 and CS-701 is actuated by a cam on the crankshaft as shown in Fig. E15. The plunger on Models CS-601 and CS-701 is actuated by cam follower (16—Fig. E16) which rides on a cam attached to the clutch drum. Refer to Fig. E17 or E18 for an exploded view of the automatic oil pump.

When installing pump body, screw body in until lightly seated then run saw at medium speed and unscrew pump body approximately ½ to 1 turn until maximum oil output is obtained. Mark pump body for future reference then install adjusting knob so it is against stop for maximum oil output and must be turned counterclockwise to decrease oil output.

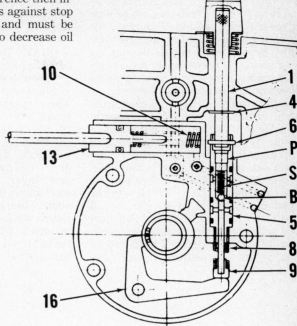

Fig. E16—Cross-sectional view of manual and automatic oil pumps used on Models CS-601 and CS-701. Note location of plunger (P), spring (S) and ball (B) in pump body (5—Fig. E18). Refer to Fig. E18 for parts identification.

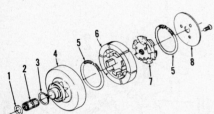

Fig. E14—Exploded view of clutch used on Models CS-701, CS-702, CS-702VL, CS-702EVL, LCS-750, CS-750VL and CS-750EVL.

1. Washer	5. Garter spring
2. Needle roller bearing	6. Clutch shoes
3. Snap ring	7. Clutch hub
4. Clutch drum	8. Washer

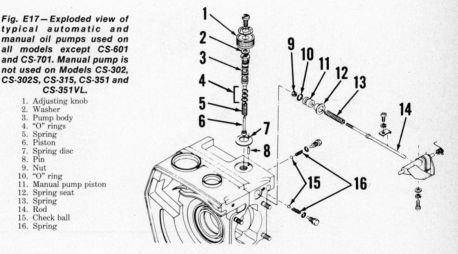

Fig. E17—Exploded view of typical automatic and manual oil pumps used on all models except CS-601 and CS-701. Manual pump is not used on Models CS-302, CS-302S, CS-315, CS-351 and CS-351VL.

1. Adjusting knob
2. Washer
3. Pump body
4. "O" rings
5. Spring
6. Piston
7. Spring disc
8. Pin
9. Nut
10. "O" ring
11. Manual pump piston
12. Spring seat
13. Spring
14. Rod
15. Check ball
16. Spring

Fig. E15—Typical cross-sectional view of automatic oil pump used on all models except CS-601 and CS-701. Note location of plunger (P), spring (S) and ball (B) in pump body (3—Fig. E17). Refer to Fig. E17 for identification of components (3, 5 and 6).

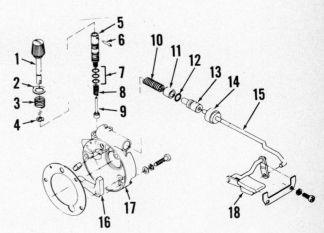

Fig. E18—Exploded view of automatic and manual oil pumps used on Models CS-601 and CS-701.

1. Adjuster
2. Spring disc
3. Spring
4. "E" ring
5. Pump body
6. Pin
7. "O" rings
8. Spring
9. Automatic pump piston
10. Spring
11. Spring seat
12. "O" ring
13. Manual pump piston
14. Rod cap
15. Rod
16. Cam follower
17. Pump housing
18. Manual pump actuator

REWIND STARTER. To disassemble rewind starter, remove starter housing, remove rope handle and allow rope to rewind into housing. Unscrew rope pulley screw and carefully remove rope pulley being careful not to dislodge rewind spring. If necessary to remove rewind spring, care should be used not to allow spring to uncoil uncontrolled.

Install rewind spring in starter housing or spring case with coils wrapped in a clockwise direction from outer end of spring. Wind rope around pulley in a clockwise direction as viewed from flywheel side of pulley. Turn pulley three or four turns clockwise before passing rope through outlet. Check starter operation. It should be possible to pull rope to its full extension and still turn rope pulley approximately ½ turn clockwise. If rewind spring coil binds before rope is fully extended, reduce pre-tension on rope by pulling rope up into notch in rope pulley and allowing pulley to rotate one turn counterclockwise. Recheck starter operation.

CHAIN BRAKE. Some models may be equipped with a chain brake system designed to stop chain movement should kickback occur. Chain brake is activated when operator's hand strikes chain brake lever and hand guard assembly (1–Fig. E21) tripping dog (10), releasing latch (7) and allowing spring (5) to pull brake band (4) tight around clutch drum. Pull back chain brake hand guard and lever assembly (1) to reset mechanism. Rotate adjusting cam (6) to adjust brake band (4). Brake band should not contact clutch drum after adjustment. Disassembly and component renewal is evident after inspection of unit and referral to Fig. E21.

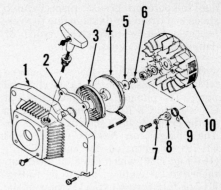

Fig. E20—Exploded view of rewind starter used on Model CS-315.

1. Starter housing
2. Spring case
3. Rewind spring
4. Rope pulley
5. Washer
6. Screw
7. Spacer
8. Starter pawl
9. Spring
10. Flywheel

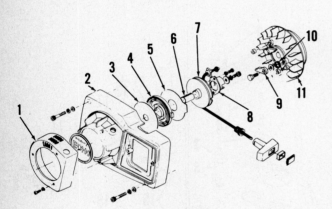

Fig. E19—Exploded view of typical rewind starter used on all models except Model CS-315.

1. Cover
2. Starter housing
3. Washer
4. Rewind spring
5. Washer
6. Bushing
7. Rope pulley
8. Starter cup
9. Pawl
10. Spring
11. Flywheel

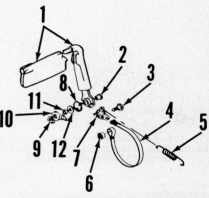

Fig. E21—Exploded view of chain brake system used on so equipped models.

1. Hand guard & lever assy.
2. Nut
3. Pivot screw
4. Brake band
5. Spring
6. Adjusting cam
7. Latch
8. Spring
9. Stop
10. Dog
11. Spacer
12. Washer

ECHO

Model	Bore	Stroke	Displ.	Drive Type
CS-280E, CS-280EP, CS-290EVL, CS-290EVLP	35 mm (1.378 in.)	29 mm (1.142 in.)	27.9 cc (1.703 cu. in.)	Direct

MAINTENANCE

SPARK PLUG. Recommended spark plug for all models is Champion CJ8Y. Spark plug electrode gap should be 0.6-0.7 mm (0.024-0.028 in.).

CARBURETOR. A Zama C1S-K1, C1S-K1A or C1S-K1B diaphragm type carburetor type carburetor is used on all models. Refer to Zama section of CARBURETOR SERVICE section for service and exploded views.

Initial adjustment of low and high speed mixture screws is 1⅛ turns open from a lightly seated position. Make final adjustment with engine warm and running. Adjust idle speed screw so engine idles just below clutch engagement speed. Adjust low speed mixture screw so engine will accelerate cleanly without hesitation. Adjust high speed mixture screw to obtain optimum performance under cutting load.

IGNITION. All models are equipped with a capacitor discharge ignition system. Refer to Fig. E24. Ignition timing is fixed at 30 degrees BTDC and is not adjustable. Air gap between flywheel magnets and ignition module core should be 0.3-0.4 mm (0.012-0.016 in.).

LUBRICATION. Engine is lubricated by mixing engine oil with fuel.

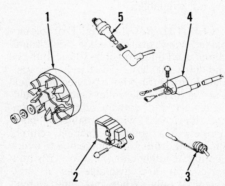

Fig. E24 — View of Models CS-290EVL and CS-290EVLP ignition components. Models CS-280E and CS-280EP are similar.

1. Flywheel
2. Ignition module
3. Stop switch
4. Ignition coil
5. Spark plug

Regular grade automotive gasoline is recommended. Recommended oil is Echo air-cooled two-stroke oil mixed with fuel at a 50:1 ratio. If Echo oil is not available, a good quality oil designed for air-cooled two-stroke engines may be used when mixed with fuel at a 32:1 ratio. Use a separate container when mixing the oil and gas.

All models are equipped with an automatic chain oil pump. Clean automotive oil may be used. Oil viscosity should be chosen according to ambient temperature. Oil pump output is adjustable. Refer to OIL PUMP section for service and adjustment procedures.

REPAIRS

CYLINDER, PISTON, PIN AND RINGS. Cylinder bore is chrome plated on all models and oversize pistons and

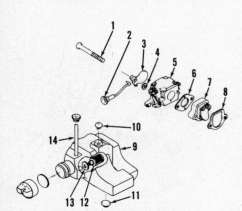

Fig. E23 — Exploded view of fuel tank and related components.

1. Screw
2. Choke knob
3. Choke shutter
4. Spacer
5. Carburetor
6. Gasket
7. Reed valve assy.
8. Gasket
9. Fuel tank
10. Tank vent
11. Cushion
12. Fuel filter
13. Washer
14. Fuel hose

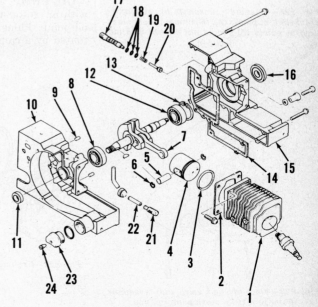

Fig. E25 — Exploded view of engine and automatic oil pump.

1. Cylinder
2. Gasket
3. Piston ring
4. Piston
5. Piston pin
6. Wire retainer
7. Crankshaft & rod assy.
8. Main bearing
9. Dowel
10. Left crankcase half
11. Seal
12. Main bearing
13. Snap ring
14. Gasket
15. Right crankcase half
16. Seal
17. Oil pump housing
18. "O" ring
19. Spring
20. Pump plunger
21. Oil filter
22. Oil hose
23. Oil filler cap
24. Oil tank vent

rings are not available. Inspect cylinder bore for scoring, flaking or other damage to chrome surface.

Piston has a single piston ring. Maximum allowable ring end gap is 0.5 mm (0.020 in.). Maximum allowable piston ring in ring groove side clearance is 0.1 mm (0.004 in.). A locating pin is present in piston ring groove to prevent piston ring rotation. Be sure ring end gap is around locating pin when installing cylinder.

The floating type piston pin is retained by wire retainers and rides directly in the small end of connecting rod. Be sure piston is properly supported when removing or installing piston pin to prevent damage. Arrow on piston crown must point toward exhaust port when installing piston.

CRANKSHAFT, CONNECTING ROD AND CRANKCASE. All models are equipped with a crankshaft and connecting rod unit assembly which is supported in the crankcase by ball bearings at both ends. Crankshaft and connecting rod are not available separately.

Check crankshaft runout by supporting crankshaft at points (A – Fig. E26)

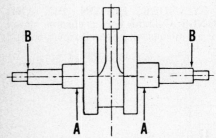

Fig. E26 — Measure crankshaft by supporting crankshaft at points (A). Maximum runout measured at points (B) should not exceed 0.05 mm (0.002 in.).

and measuring at points (B). Maximum allowable runout is 0.05 mm (0.002 in.).

Flywheel side main bearing (8 – Fig. E25) is held in position by a shoulder in crankcase half (10) while a snap ring (13) retains clutch side main bearing (12). Snap ring (13) should be installed in crankcase so open end of ring is around oil hole and snap ring does not obstruct lubrication passage. Install crankshaft seals (11 and 16), open sides toward each other, flush with outer face of crankcase.

REED VALVE. Reed valve (7 – Fig. E23) should be inspected whenever carburetor is removed. Reed petal (P – Fig. E28) should seat very lightly against insulator block (B) throughout its entire length with the least possible tension. Tip of reed petal must not stand open more than 0.3 mm (0.012 in.). Reed stop (S) opening should be 6 mm (0.24 in.). Individual reed valve components are not available.

CLUTCH. Refer to Fig. E29 for exploded view of three-shoe centrifugal clutch used on all models. Clutch hub (1) and nut (8) have left-hand threads. Clutch drum (5) rides on a needle roller bearing (6). Needle roller bearing should be inspected for damage or discoloration and lubricated with a suitable high temperature grease. Inspect clutch shoes and drum for damage due to overheating. Clutch hub (1), shoes (2) and spring (3) are available as a unit assembly only. When installing clutch, clutch hub should be positioned with chamfered thread opening side towards crankshaft. Tighten clutch hub (1) to 27.6-31.6 N·m (20-23 ft.-lbs.) and nut (8) to 13-15 N·m (9-11 ft.-lbs.).

OIL PUMP. All models are equipped with an automatic, plunger type chain oil pump. Plunger (20 – Fig. E25) is actuated by a cam on the crankshaft. Oil

pump output is adjusted by rotating the pump housing (17). Oil pump may be disassembled for cleaning or renewal of individual components after removing the air filter and withdrawing oil pump assembly from crankcase.

When installing pump, screw housing (17) in until lightly seated. Run saw at medium speed and unscrew pump housing approximately one turn until maximum oil output is obtained. Pump housing location should be marked when at maximum output for future reference. Rotate pump housing counterclockwise from maximum output position to decrease oil output.

REWIND STARTER. To disassemble rewind starter, remove starter housing (14 – Fig. E30), remove rope handle and allow rope to rewind into housing. Unscrew rope pulley screw (10) and carefully remove rope pulley (12) being careful not to dislodge rewind spring. If necessary to remove rewind spring, care should be used not to allow spring to uncoil uncontrolled.

Install rewind spring in starter housing with coils wrapped in a clockwise direction from outer end of spring. Wind rope around pulley in a clockwise direction as viewed from flywheel side of pulley. Turn pulley three turns clockwise before passing rope through outlet. Check starter operation. It should be possible to pull rope to its full extension and still turn rope pulley approximately ½ turn clockwise. If rewind spring coil binds before rope is fully extended, reduce pre-tension on rope by pulling rope up into notch in rope pulley and allowing pulley to rotate one turn counterclockwise. Recheck starter operation.

CHAIN BRAKE. Models CS-280EP and CS-290EVLP are equipped with a

Fig. E28 — View of reed valve unit assembly. Refer to text for service information.

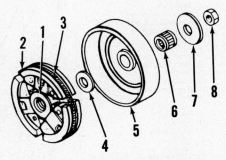

Fig. E29 — Exploded view of clutch assembly.

1. Hub
2. Shoe
3. Spring
4. Washer
5. Drum
6. Needle bearing
7. Washer
8. Nut

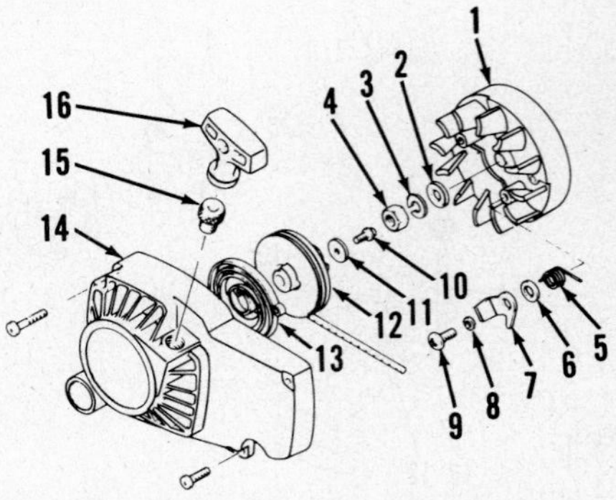

Fig. E30 — Exploded view of typical rewind starter assembly.

1. Flywheel
2. Lockwasher
3. Spring washer
4. Nut
5. Pawl spring
6. Washer
7. Pawl
8. Spacer
9. Screw
10. Screw
11. Washer
12. Rope pulley
13. Rewind spring
14. Starter housing
15. Rope guide
16. Rope handle

chain brake system designed to stop chain movement should kickback occur. Chain brake is activated when operator's hand strikes hand guard (1–Fig. E31) tripping brake lever (2), releasing brank band case (10) and allowing brake spring (6) to draw brake band (5) tight around clutch drum. Brake band (5), brake band case (10) and brake spring (6) are removed and renewed as an assembly. If brake spring (6) is removed or renewed, Echo special tool 566834 can be used to hold brake spring (6) in piston on brake band case (10) while reassembling unit. No adjustments of chain brake system is required. Make certain clutch drum turns freely with chain brake in off position after reassembly of chain brake system.

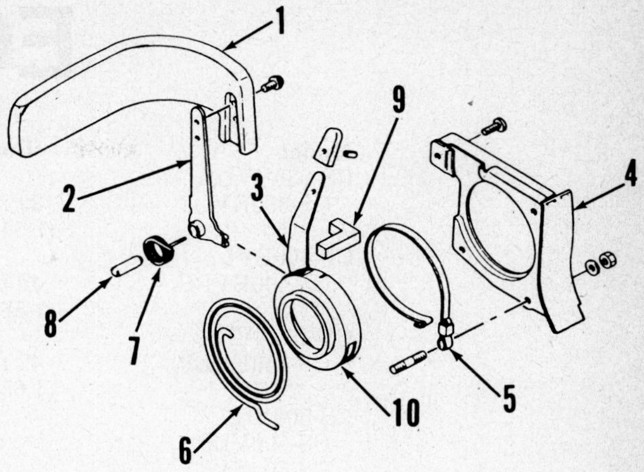

Fig. E31 — Exploded view of chain brake system used on Models CS-280EP and CS-290EVLP.

1. Hand guard
2. Brake lever
3. Reset lever
4. Brake cover
5. Brake band
6. Brake spring
7. Spring
8. Shaft
9. Seal
10. Brake band case

ECHO

Model	Bore	Stroke	Displ.	Drive Type
CS-330EVL, CS-330EVLP	39 mm (1.54 in.)	28 mm (1.10 in.)	33.4 cc (2.04 cu. in.)	Direct
CS-400EVL, CS-400EVLP	40 mm (1.58 in.)	32 mm (1.26 in.)	40.2 cc (2.45 cu. in.)	Direct
CS-440EVL ✓ CS-440EVLP	42 mm (1.65 in.)	32 mm (1.26 in.)	33.4 cc (2.70 cu. in.)	Direct
CS-500VL, CS-500VLP, CS-500EVL, CS-500EVLP, CS-510EVL, CS-510EVLP	42 mm (1.65 in.)	36 mm (1.42 in.)	49.9 cc (3.04 cu. in.)	Direct
CS-550EVL, CS-550EVLP	44 mm (1.73 in.)	36 mm (1.42 in.)	54.7 cc (3.34 cu. in.)	Direct
CS-650EVL, CS-650EVLP, CS-660EVL, CS-660EVLP	47 mm (1.85 in.)	37 mm (1.46 in.)	64.2 cc (3.92 cu. in.)	Direct

MAINTENANCE

SPARK PLUG. Recommended spark plug is Champion CJ8 or equivalent for Models CS-330EVL and CS-330EVLP and Champion CJ8Y for Models CS-400EVL, CS-400EVLP, CS-500VL, CS-500VLP, CS-500EVL and CS-500EVLP. Recommended spark plug for all other models is Champion CJ7Y or equivalent. Spark plug electrode gap should be 0.6-0.7 mm (0.024-0.028 in.) on all models.

CARBURETOR. Models CS-330EVL and CS-330EVLP are equipped with a Zama C1S type carburetor. Models CS-

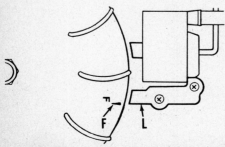

Fig. E33—Ignition on CS-500VL and CS-500VLP models should occur when flywheel mark (F) is aligned with leading pole outer edge (L).

400EVL, CS-400EVLP, CS-440EVL and CS-440EVLP are equipped with a Walbro WA type carburetor. Models CS-510EVL, CS-510EVLP, CS-550EVL and CS-550EVLP are equipped with a Walbro HDA type carburetor. All other models are equipped with a Walbro HDB carburetor. Refer to Zama or Walbro section of CARBURETOR SERVICE section for carburetor overhaul procedures and exploded views.

Initial setting of both low and high speed mixture screws on CS-330EVL models is 1¼ turns open from a lightly seated position. Initial setting for Models CS-400EVL, CS-400EVLP, CS-440EVL and CS-440EVLP is ¾-1¼ turns open for high speed mixture screw and one turn open for low speed mixture screw. On Models CS-500VL, CS-500VLP, CS-500EVL and CS-500EVLP, initially adjust high speed mixture screw to ¼-1 turn open and low speed mixture screw to 1-1¼ turns open. On all other models except CS-650EVL and CS-650EVLP, adjust high speed mixture screw to ¾ turn open and low speed mixture screw to 1⅛ turns open.

On CS-650EVL models, initial adjustment of low speed mixture screw is 1⅛ turns open. Initial high speed mixture needle adjustment may be ½ or 1¼

turns open due to carburetor design differences. Check carburetor setting decal located externally on saw for proper initial adjustment. Should decal be absent, set high speed mixture needle one turn open and observe performance. Reset to approximately ¼ turn open if required. Do not adjust high speed mixture needle too lean as engine may be damaged.

On all models, perform final carburetor adjustments with engine at operating temperature and running. Adjust idle speed screw just below clutch engagement speed. Adjust low speed mixture screw so engine will accelerate cleanly without hesitation. Adjust high speed mixture screw to obtain optimum performance under cutting load.

IGNITION. Models CS-500VL and CS-500VLP are equipped with a conventional flywheel magneto ignition system using breaker-points while all other models are equipped with a breakerless electronic ignition system.

On CS-500VL and CS-500VLP models, breaker-point gap should be 0.3-0.4 mm (0.012-0.016 in.). Correct ignition timing is 30 degrees BTDC. A reference mark is provided on flywheel to set ignition timing. With flywheel turning counterclockwise, first mark (F—Fig. E33) on flywheel periphery indicates ignition point when aligned with outer edge of leading magneto core pole (L). Adjust ignition timing by varying breaker-point gap. Air gap between flywheel magnets and magneto coil legs should be 0.4 mm (0.016 in.). Loosen magneto mounting screws and move magneto to adjust air gap.

On all other models, ignition timing is not adjustable. Air gap between flywheel magnets and ignition module or coil core should be 0.4 mm (0.016 in.). Repair of electronic ignition system malfunction is accomplished by renewal of ignition components. Be sure wiring is properly connected.

LUBRICATION. Engine is lubricated by mixing engine oil with fuel. Regular grade automotive gasoline is recommended. Recommended oil is Echo air-cooled two-stroke oil mixed with fuel at a 50:1 ratio. If Echo oil is not available, a good quality oil designed for air-cooled two-stroke engines may be used when mixed with fuel at a 32:1 ratio. Use a separate container when mixing the oil and gas.

All models are equipped with an automatic chain oil pump. Clean automotive oil may be used. Oil viscosity should be chosen according to ambient temperature. Oil pump output is adjustable. Refer to OIL PUMP section for service and adjustment procedures.

REPAIRS

CYLINDER, PISTON, PIN AND RINGS. Cylinder bore is chrome plated on all models and oversize pistons and rings are not available. Inspect cylinder bore for scoring, flaking or other damage to chrome surface.

The piston is equipped with two piston rings. Maximum allowable ring end gap is 0.5 mm (0.020 in.). Maximum allowable piston ring in ring groove side clearance is 0.1 mm (0.004 in.). Renew rings, piston or cylinder as required when service limits are exceeded. A locating pin is present in piston ring grooves to prevent piston ring rotation. Be sure ring end gap is around locating pin when installing cylinder.

The piston pin is retained by wire retainers and rides in needle roller bearing in small end of connecting rod. Be sure piston is properly supported when removing or installing piston pin to prevent damage to connecting rod. Arrow on piston crown must point toward exhaust port when installing piston.

CRANKSHAFT, CONNECTING ROD AND CRANKCASE. All models are equipped with a crankshaft and connecting rod unit assembly which is supported in the crankcase by ball bearings at both ends. Crankshaft and connecting rod are not available separately.

Check crankshaft runout by supporting crankshaft at points (A – Fig. E35) and measure at points (B). Maximum allowable runout is 0.05 mm (0.002 in.).

Flywheel side main bearing (11 – Fig. E34) is held in position by a shoulder in crankcase half (14) while snap ring (16) retains clutch side main bearing (15). Some models may be equipped with a lubrication passage designed to lubricate oil pump cam and plunger. Make certain snap ring (16) does not obstruct passage when installed (snap ring gap should surround oil passage hole). Install crankshaft seals (13 and 17), open sides toward each other, flush with outer face of crankcase.

OIL PUMP. All models are equipped with an automatic plunger type chain oil pump. The plunger (25 – Fig. E34) is actuated by a cam on the crankshaft. Oil pump output is adjusted by rotating knob (21) which is secured to pump housing (22) by screw (20). Oil pump may be disassembled for cleaning or renewal of individual components after removing output adjustment knob (21) and unscrewing pump housing (22) from crankcase.

When installing pump housing, screw housing in until lightly seated. Run saw at medium speed and unscrew pump housing approximately ½ to 1 turn until maximum oil output is obtained. Mark pump housing for future reference then install adjusting knob so it is against

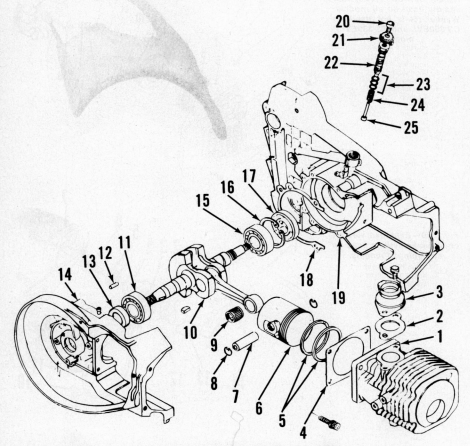

Fig. E34 — Exploded view of Model CS-500EVL engine assembly. Other models are similar.

1. Cylinder
2. Gasket
3. Intake manifold
4. Gasket
5. Piston rings
6. Piston
7. Piston pin
8. Pin retainer
9. Needle bearing
10. Crankshaft & rod assy.
11. Bearing
12. Guide pin
13. Seal
14. Left crankcase half
15. Bearing
16. Snap ring
17. Seal
18. Gasket
19. Right crankcase half
20. Screw
21. Knob
22. Oil pump housing
23. "O" ring
24. Spring
25. Oil pump plunger

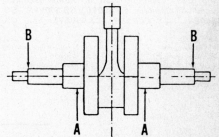

Fig. E35 — Measure crankshaft by supporting crankshaft at points (A). Maximum runout measured at points (B) should not exceed 0.05 mm (0.002 in.).

stop for maximum oil output and must be turned counterclockwise to decrease oil output.

CLUTCH. Some models are equipped with the clutch assembly shown in Fig. E37. Clutch hub, shoes and garter spring (1) are a unit assembly and are not available separately on early model saws. Individual clutch components are available on late model saws. Refer to Fig. E38 for exploded view of clutch used on all other models. Individual clutch components are available.

On all models, clutch nut and hub have left-hand threads. Clutch drum rides on a needle roller bearing. Inspect clutch shoes and drum for damage due to overheating. Renew excessively worn or damaged components. Clutch hub and

nut should be tightened to 20.2-23.7 N·m (14.9-17.5 ft.-lbs.).

REWIND STARTER. To disassemble rewind starter, remove starter housing, remove rope handle and allow rope to rewind into housing. Unscrew rope pulley screw and carefully remove rope pulley, being careful not to dislodge rewind spring. If necessary to remove rewind spring, care should be used not to allow spring to uncoil uncontrolled.

Install rewind spring in starter housing with coils wrapped in a clockwise direction from outer end of spring. Wind rope around pulley in a clockwise direction as viewed from flywheel side of pulley. Turn pulley three turns clockwise before passing rope through outlet. Check starter operation. It should be possible to pull rope to its full extension and still turn rope pulley approximately ½ turn clockwise. If rewind spring coil binds before rope is fully extended, reduce pretension on rope by pulling rope up into notch in rope pulley and

allowing pulley to rotate one turn counterclockwise. Recheck starter operation.

CHAIN BRAKE. Some models are equipped with a chain brake system designed to stop chain movement should kickback occur. Chain brake is activated when operator's hand strikes chain brake lever (1 – Fig. E40) tripping actuating cam (4), allowing spring (5) to draw brake band (11) tight around clutch drum. Pull back chain brake lever (1) to reset mechanism.

Disassembly for repair and component renewal is evident after referral to Fig. E40 and inspection of unit. Chain brake system should be periodically cleaned and inspected for excessive were or other damage to clutch drum, brake band or linkage.

To adjust chain brake, loosen screw (8) and rotate adjusting cam (9). Make certain clutch drum turns freely and chain brake band does not contact clutch drum when chain brake is disengaged.

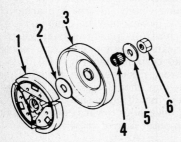

Fig. E37 – Exploded view of typical clutch assembly used on all models except CS-500VL, CS-500VLP, CS-500EVL, CS-500EVLP, CS-650EVL and CS-650EVLP models. Only Models CS-330EVL and CS-330EVLP use washer (2).

1. Hub & shoe assy.
2. Washer
3. Drum
4. Needle bearing
5. Washer
6. Clutch nut

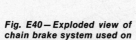

Fig. E39 – Exploded view of typical rewind starter assembly used on all models. Washer (5) is not used on CS-330EVL and CS-330EVLP models.

1. Starter housing
2. Washer
3. Rope handle
4. Rope guide
5. Washer
6. Rewind spring
7. Washer
8. Rope pulley
9. Washer
10. Screw
11. Cap screw
12. Washer
13. Pawl
14. Spacer
15. Spring
16. Nut
17. Flywheel

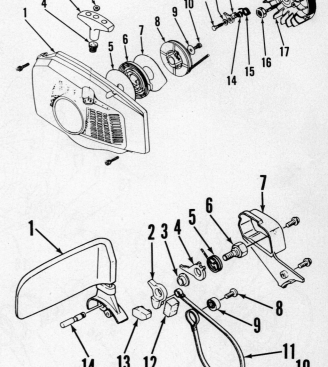

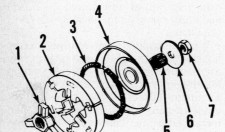

Fig. E38 – Exploded view of clutch assembly used on Models CS-500VL, CS-500VLP, CS-500EVL, CS-500EVLP, CS-650EVL and CS-650EVLP.

1. Hub
2. Clutch shoes
3. Garter spring
4. Clutch drum
5. Needle roller bearing
6. Washer
7. Clutch nut

Fig. E40 – Exploded view of chain brake system used on so equipped models.

1. Chain brake lever
2. Brake band lever
3. Spacer
4. Actuating cam
5. Spring
6. Pivot screw
7. Cover
8. Screw
9. Adjusting cam
10. Brake band retainer
11. Brake band
12. Dust seal
13. Rubber bumper
14. Pin

ECHO

Model	Bore	Stroke	Displ.	Drive Type
CS-900EVL, CS-900EVLP	54 mm (2.126 in.)	40 mm (1.575 in.)	91.6 cc (5.59 cu. in.)	Direct

MAINTENANCE

SPARK PLUG. Recommended spark plug is NGK BPM7A or equivalent. Spark plug electrode gap should be 0.6-0.7 mm (0.024-0.028 in.).

CARBURETOR. A Walbro SDC diaphragm type carburetor is used. Refer to Walbro section of CARBURETOR SERVICE section for carburetor overhaul and exploded views.

Initial adjustment for both low speed and high speed mixture screws is one turn open from a lightly seated position. Make final adjustment with engine warm and running. Adjust idle speed screw so engine idles just below clutch engagement speed. Adjust low speed mixture screw so engine will accelerate cleanly without hesitation. Adjust high speed mixture screw to obtain optimum performance under cutting load. Do not adjust high speed mixture too lean as engine may be damaged.

IGNITION. Both models are equipped with a two-piece breakerless capacitor discharge ignition system. Refer to Fig. E41. Repair of ignition system malfunction except for faulty wiring connections, is accomplished by renewal of ignition system components. Ignition timing is not adjustable but should be checked periodically to ensure correct ignition module operation.

To check ignition timing, first remove the spark plug and starter housing from saw. Locate ignition timing reference marks provided on crankcase and flywheel periphery (Fig. E42). Insert a dial indicator into spark plug opening, then position piston at exactly TDC. Crankcase stationary mark (M) and flywheel mark "T" (TDC) should be aligned. If marks do not align, remove flywheel and renew flywheel key as required. Reinstall flywheel, then rotate flywheel counterclockwise until first mark "F" (30 degrees BTDC) is aligned with stationary mark (M). Ensure marks are aligned, then paint similar marks on ignition module and flywheel fin. Marks must be visible when starter housing is installed. Install starter housing and

connect a suitable power timing light. Start and run saw at idle speed and observe timing marks. If marks do not align, renew ignition module and retest.

Air gap between flywheel magnets and ignition module core should be 0.3-0.4 mm (0.012-0.016 in.). Tighten flywheel nut to 32.3-36.2 N·m (23.8-26.7 ft.-lbs.).

LUBRICATION. Engine is lubricated by mixing engine oil with fuel. Regular grade automotive gasoline is recommended. Recommended oil is Echo air-cooled two-stroke oil mixed with fuel at a 50:1 ratio. If Echo oil is not available, a good quality oil designed for air-cooled two-stroke engines may be used when mixed with fuel at a 32:1 ratio. Use a separate container when mixing the oil and gas.

A manual and automatic chain oil pump is used. Clean automotive oil may be used. Oil viscosity should be chosen according to ambient temperature. Oil pump output is adjustable. Refer to OIL PUMP section for service and adjustment procedures.

REPAIRS

CYLINDER, PISTON, PIN AND RINGS. The vertical cylinder has a chrome plated bore and oversize piston and rings are not available. Inspect

cylinder bore for scoring, flaking or other damage to chrome surface.

The piston is equipped with two piston rings. Maximum allowable ring end gap is 0.5 mm (0.020 in.). Maximum allowable piston ring in ring groove side clearance is 0.1 mm (0.004 in.). Renew rings, piston or cylinder as required when service limits are exceeded. A locating pin is present in piston ring grooves to prevent piston ring rotation. Be sure ring end gap is around locating pin when installing cylinder.

The piston pin is retained by wire retainers and rides in needle roller bearing in small end of connecting rod. Be sure piston is properly supported when removing or installing piston pin to prevent damage. Arrow on piston crown must point toward exhaust port when installing piston.

CRANKSHAFT, CONNECTING ROD AND CRANKCASE. The crankshaft, crankpin and connecting rod are pressed together and are available only as a complete assembly. Crankshaft assembly is supported in the crankcase by ball bearings at both ends.

Check crankshaft runout by supporting crankshaft at points (A – Fig. E44) and measuring at points (B). Maximum allowable runout is 0.05 mm (0.002 in.).

Crankshaft main bearings are located in crankcase by snap rings (10 and 15 –

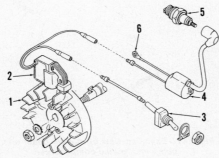

Fig. E41—Illustrated view of ignition components.

1. Flywheel
2. Ignition module
3. Stop switch
4. Ignition coil
5. Spark plug

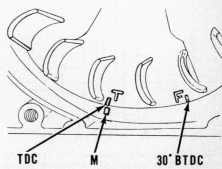

Fig. E42—View of ignition timing reference marks. Refer to text.

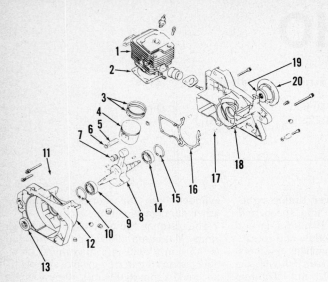

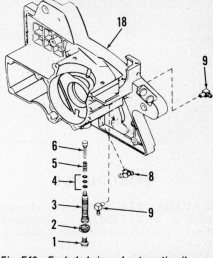

Fig. E43 — Exploded view of engine assembly.
1. Cylinder
2. Gasket
3. Piston rings
4. Piston
5. Piston pin
6. Pin retainer
7. Needle bearing
8. Crankshaft & rod assy.
9. Bearing
10. Snap ring
11. Guide pin
12. Left crankcase half
13. Seal
14. Bearing
15. Snap ring
16. Gasket
17. Guide pin
18. Right crankcase half
19. Seal
20. Seal retainer

Fig. E46 — Exploded view of automatic oil pump assembly. Connector (8) and elbow connectors (9) are also shown in Fig. E45.

1. Adjusting screw	6. Pump plunger
2. Adjusting stop	8. Connector
3. Oil pump housing	9. Elbow connector
4. "O" ring	18. Right crankcase half
5. Spring	

Fig. E43). Right crankcase half (18) has a lubrication passage designed to lubricate oil pump cam and plunger. Make certain snap ring (15) does not obstruct passage when installed (snap ring gap should surround oil passage hole). Install crankshaft seals (13 and 19), open sides toward each other, flush with outer face of crankcase half (12) and seal retainer (20).

OIL PUMP. Both models are equipped with manual and automatic chain oiler pumps. Refer to Fig. E45 for exploded view if manual oil pump and related components. Check balls (10) must move freely for proper pump operation. Renew "O" ring (4) and hoses as required when signs of hardening or cracking are evident.

Refer to Fig. E46 for exploded view of automatic oil pump. The plunger (6) is actuated by a cam on the crankshaft. Oil pump output is adjusted by rotating screw (1) located underneath saw. Oil pump may be disassembled for cleaning or renewal of individual components

after removing pump cover plate, adjusting screw (1), adjustment stop (2) and unscrewing pump housing (3) from crankcase.

When installing pump housing, screw housing in until lightly seated. Remove saw chain, guide bar and side plates so oil pump output may be observed. Run saw at medium speed and unscrew pump housing approximately ½ to 1 turn until maximum oil output is obtained. Mark pump housing for future reference, then install adjustment stop (2) so it is against stop for maximum oil output and must be turned counterclockwise to decrease oil output.

CLUTCH. Both models are equipped with the four-shoe centrifugal clutch shown in Fig. E48. Clutch nut (14) has

left hand threads. Clutch hub (4) is a snug fit on crankshaft. A Woodruff key prevents independent rotation of hub and crankshaft. It may be necessary to use a puller to withdraw clutch hub and shoe assembly. Individual clutch components are available.

Clutch drum rides on a caged needle roller bearing. Inspect clutch drum and shoes for excessive wear or damage due to overheating. Renew excessively worn or damaged components. Clutch nut should be tightened to 19.9-23.7 N·m (15.17 ft.-lbs.).

REWIND STARTER. To disassemble rewind starter (Fig. E49), remove starter housing and rope handle then allow rope to rewind into housing. Unscrew rope pulley screw and carefully

Fig. E44 — Measure crankshaft by supporting crankshaft at points (A). Maximum runout measured at points (B) should not exceed 0.05 mm (0.002 in.).

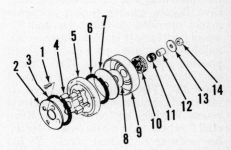

Fig. E45 — Exploded view of manual chain oiler pump and related components.

1. Button	7. Oil pickup
2. Bushing	8. Connector
3. Plunger	9. Elbow connector
4. "O" ring	10. Check ball
5. Spring	11. Spring
6. Housing	13. Oil outlet fitting

Fig. E48 — Exploded view of clutch assembly.

1. Screw	8. Washer
2. Washer	9. Clutch
3. Garter spring	10. Sprocket
4. Clutch hub	11. Needle bearing
5. Clutch shoes	12. Spacer
6. Garter spring	13. Washer
7. Washer	14. Nut

remove rope pulley being careful not to dislodge rewind spring. If necessary to remove rewind spring, care should be used not to allow spring to uncoil uncontrolled.

Install rewind spring in starter housing with coils wrapped in a clockwise direction from outer end of spring. Wind rope around pulley in a clockwise direction as viewed from flywheel side of pulley. Turn pulley three turns clockwise before passing rope through outlet. Check starter operation. It should be possible to pull rope to its full extension and still turn rope pulley approximately

½ turn clockwise. If rewind spring coil binds before rope is fully extended, reduce pre-tension on rope by pulling rope up into notch in rope pulley and allowing pulley to rotate one turn counterclockwise. Recheck starter operation.

CHAIN BRAKE. Model CS-900EVLP is equipped with a chain brake system designed to stop chain movement should kickback occur. The chain brake system is activated when the operator's hand strikes the chain brake lever (1 – Fig. E50) thereby forcing actuating cam (8) to release spring (9).

Brake band is adjusted by rotating adjuster (12). Brake band should not contact clutch drum when chain brake is disengaged.

Disassembly for repair or renewal of individual components is evident after inspection of unit and referral to the exploded view.

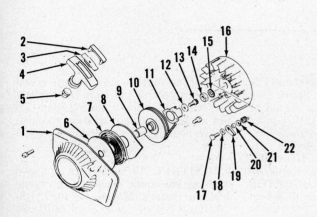

Fig. E49 — Exploded view of rewind starter assembly.

1. Starter housing
2. Cover
3. Insert
4. Rope handle
5. Rope guide
6. Washer
7. Rewind spring
8. Washer
9. Bushing
10. Rope pulley
11. Starter cup
12. Washer
13. Screw
14. Nut
15. Washer
16. Flywheel
17. Cap screw
18. Washer
19. Pawl
20. Spacer
21. Washer
22. Spring

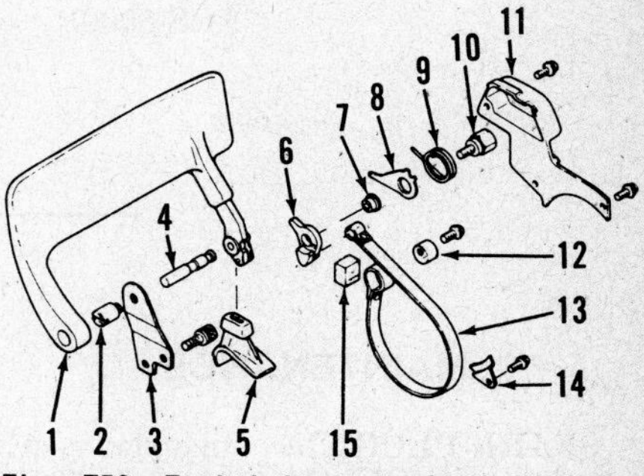

Fig. E50 — Exploded view of chain brake assembly used on Model CS-900EVLP.

1. Chain brake lever
2. Pivot pin
3. Support
4. Pivot pin
5. Dust cover
6. Brake band lever
7. Spacer
8. Actuating cam
9. Spring
10. Cap screw
11. Shield
12. Brake band adjuster
13. Brake band
14. Brake band retainer
15. Dust seal

ECHO

Model	Bore	Stroke	Displ.	Drive Type
CS-4000, CS-4000P	40.0 mm (1.575 in.)	31.0 mm (1.220 in.)	39.0 cc (2.377 cu. in.)	Direct
CS-4500, CS-4500P	43.0 mm (1.693 in.)	31.0 mm (1.220 in.)	45.0 cc (2.747 cu. in.)	Direct
CS-8000, CS-8000P	52.0 mm (2.047 in.)	38.0 mm (1.496 in.)	80.7 cc (4.925 cu. in.)	Direct

MAINTENANCE

SPARK PLUG. Recommended spark plug for Models CS-4000, CS-4000P, CS-4500 and CS-4500P is Champion CJ6Y or equivalent. Recommended

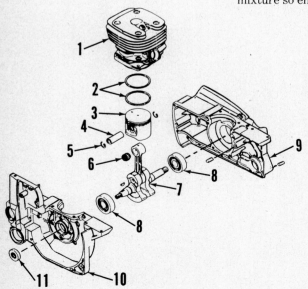

Fig. E57 — View of ignition timing reference marks. Refer to text.

Fig. E58 — Exploded view of engine assembly.
1. Cylinder
2. Piston rings
3. Piston
4. Piston pin
5. Piston pin retainer
6. Needle roller bearing
7. Crankshaft & connecting rod assy.
8. Ball bearings
9. Right crankcase half
10. Left crankcase half
11. Crankcase seal

spark plug for Models CS-8000 and CS-8000P is Champion CJ7Y. Spark plug electrode gap for all models should be 0.6-0.7 mm (0.024-0.028 in.).

CARBURETOR. All models are equipped with a Walbro HDA diaphragm type carburetor. Refer to Walbro section of CARBURETOR SERVICE section for overhaul and exploded views.

Initial adjustment for Models CS-4000, CS-4000P, CS-4500 and CS-4500P is one turn open from a lightly seated position on both high and low speed mixture screws. On Models CS-8000 and CS-8000P, initial adjustment is one turn open for high speed mixture screw and 1¼ turns open for low speed mixture screw.

Make final adjustment with engine running at operating temperature. Adjust idle speed to just below clutch engagement speed. Adjust low speed mixture so engine will accelerate cleanly without hesitation. Adjust high speed mixture to obtain optimum full throttle performance under a cutting load. Do not adjust high speed mixture too lean as overheating and engine damage could occur.

IGNITION. All models are equipped with an electronic capacitor discharge ignition system. Models CS-4000, CS-4000P, CS-4500 and CS-4500P are equipped with a separate ignition coil and ignition module while Models CS-8000 and CS-8000P are equipped with a one-piece ignition coil and module assembly. Except for faulty wiring and connections, repair of ignition system malfunctions is accomplished by component renewal. Ignition timing is not adjustable but should be checked periodically to ensure proper operation of ignition module.

To check ignition timing, first remove sprocket cover, saw chain, guide bar and spark plug. Position piston at top dead center (TDC), then scribe a mark (M – Fig. E57) on clutch shoe and an adjacent mark (T) on engine body. On Models CS-4000, CS-4000P, CS-4500 and CS-4500P, scribe another mark (A) on engine body a distance (D) of 15 mm (0.59 in.) counterclockwise of TDC mark (T). On Models CS-8000 and CS-8000P, distance (D) should be 16 mm (0.63 in.). Install spark plug and connect a suitable power timing light. Start engine and allow to warm-up to normal operating temperature. Operate engine above 5000 rpm and observe timing marks. Marks (M) and (A) should be aligned if ignition timing is operating properly. If marks (M) and (A) do not align, check for sheared or damaged flywheel key or damaged flywheel keyway. If no damage to key or keyway is noted, renew ignition module and recheck ignition timing.

Air gap between ignition module and flywheel magnets should be 0.3-0.4 mm (0.012-0.016 in.).

LUBRICATION. Engine is lubricated by mixing engine oil with fuel. Regular grade automotive gasoline is recommended. Recommended oil is Echo air-cooled two-stroke engine oil mixed with fuel at a 50:1 ratio. If Echo air-cooled two-stroke engine oil is not available, use a good quality oil designed for use in air-cooled two-stroke engines mixed with fuel at a 32:1 ratio. Use a separate container when mixing the oil and gas.

All models are equipped with an automatic chain oil pump. Some models are equipped with an optional manual oil pump. Clean automotive oil may be used. Viscosity should be chosen according to ambient temperature. Oil pump output is adjustable. Refer to OIL PUMP section for service and adjustment procedures.

REPAIRS

CYLINDER, PISTON, PIN AND RINGS. The vertical cylinder has a chrome plated bore and oversize piston and rings are not available. Cylinder should be renewed if scoring, flaking or other damage is noted in cylinder bore.

The piston is equipped with two piston rings. Maximum allowable piston ring in ring groove side clearance is 0.1 mm (0.004 in.). Maximum allowable piston ring end gap is 0.5 mm (0.020 in.). Renew rings, piston or cylinder as required if service limits are exceeded. Locating pins are present in piston ring grooves to prevent ring rotation. Make certain piston ring end gap is around locating pin when installing cylinder.

Piston pin (4–Fig. E58) rides in needle roller bearing (6) in small end of connecting rod and is held in place by two wire retainers (5). Needle roller bearing (6) is color coded to match small end of connecting rod. Make certain piston is properly supported when removing or installing piston pin (4) to prevent damage. Echo piston holder 897719-02830 and piston pin tool 897702-30130 should be used to ease piston pin removal and installation.

Arrow on piston crown must point toward front of saw when installing piston.

CRANKSHAFT, CONNECTING ROD AND CRANKCASE. Crankshaft and connecting rod (7–Fig. E58) are a unit assembly and are not available

separately. The crankshaft is supported by two ball bearings (8) which locate into position by shoulders in crankcase halves (9 and 10). Use Echo puller 897502-19830 or a suitable equivalent to separate crankcase halves. Use care not to damage crankcase mating surfaces. Ball bearings (8) should be renewed if removed from crankshaft.

Check crankshaft runout by supporting crankshaft at points (A–Fig. E59) and measure at points (B). Maximum allowable runout is 0.05 mm (0.002 in.).

Bearing bores in crankcase halves (9 and 10–Fig. E58) should be heated to ease reassembly. Do not exceed 150° C (302° F) or use open flame to heat bearing bores. If ball bearings (8) are renewed, install bearings in crankcase halves then heat inner bearing races to ease installation of crankshaft. Make certain crankshaft is centered in crankcase and turns freely. Install starter side crankcase seal (11) flush with crankcase. Clutch side crankcase seal (4–Figs. E61 and E62) is contained in automatic oil pump body (3).

OIL PUMP. All models are equipped with an automatic chain oil pump. Some

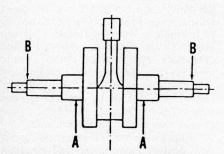

Fig. E59—Measure crankshaft runout by supporting at points (A). Maximum runout measured at points (B) should not exceed 0.05 mm (0.002 in.).

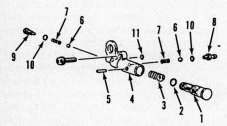

Fig. E60—Exploded view of manual chain oil pump used on some models.

1. Plunger
2. "O" ring
3. Plunger spring
4. Pump body
5. Roll pin
6. Check ball
7. Spring
8. Inlet fitting
9. Plug
10. "O" ring
11. "O" ring

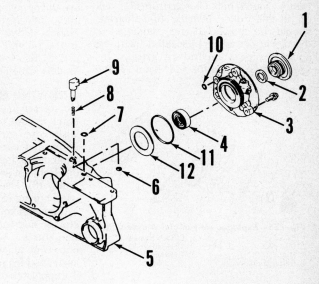

Fig. E61—Exploded view of automatic chain oil pump used on Models CS-4000, CS-4000P, CS-4500 and CS-4500P.

1. Worm gear
2. Washer
3. Oil pump assy.
4. Crankcase seal
5. Right crankcase half
6. "E" clip
7. "O" ring
8. Spring
9. Adjusting knob
10. "O" ring
11. "O" ring
12. Plate

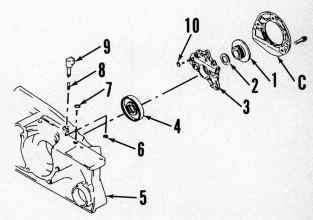

Fig. E62—Exploded view of automatic chain oil pump used on Models CS-8000 and CS-8000P. Refer to legend in Fig. E61 for component identification except for cover (C).

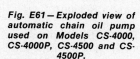

models are equipped with an optional manual chain oil pump. Refer to Fig. E60 for exploded view of manual oil pump. Check balls (6) must move freely for proper operation.

Models CS-4000, CS-4000P, CS-4500 and CS-4500P are equipped with the automatic oil pump shown in Fig. E61. Models CS-8000 and CS-8000P are equipped with the automatic oil pump shown in Fig. E62. Pump plunger is driven by worm gear (1 – Figs. E61 and Fig. E62) and pump output is adjusted by rotating knob (9).

NOTE: Late style automatic oil pump plunger has fewer teeth than early style plunger. If an early style plunger is found to be excessively worn or damaged, then renew plunger and worm gear as a set using late style components.

When installing washer (2) make certain beveled side faces inward.

CLUTCH. All models are equipped with the three-shoe centrifugal clutch shown in Fig. E63. Clutch hub (3) has left-hand threads. Use Echo special tool 897505-16130 or a suitable equivalent to remove clutch hub. Clutch drum (7) rides on needle roller bearing (6). Bearing should be inspected for damage or discoloration and lubricated with a suitable high temperature grease. Inspect clutch shoes (5) and drum (7) for

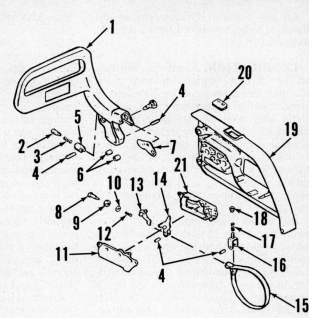

Fig. E65 — Exploded view of chain brake system used on Models CS-4000P, CS-4500P and CS-8000P.

1. Chain brake lever
2. Stopper
3. Spring
4. Pin
5. Holder
6. Spacers
7. Lever
8. Screw
9. Nut
10. Washer
11. Cover
12. Spring
13. Stopper
14. Lever
15. Brake band
16. Clevis
17. Spring
18. Nut
19. Chain guard
20. Cover
21. Brake cover

excessive wear or damage due to overheating. Renew excessively worn or damaged components.

When installing clutch assembly, make certain clutch shoe side plates (2) are facing inward. Tighten clutch hub to 19.8-22.6 N·m (175-200 in.-lbs.) on Models CS-4000, CS-4000P, CS-4500 and CS-4500P. Tighten clutch hub to 27.7-31.6 N·m (245-280 in.-lbs.) on Models CS-8000 and CS-8000P.

REWIND STARTER. To disassemble starter assembly, pull out rope until notch in rope pulley (8 – Fig. E64) aligns with rope guide (2). Place rope into notch and carefully allow pulley to rewind, releasing tension on rewind spring (5). Remove screw (10) and lift out rope pulley (8). Use caution not to allow rewind spring (5) to unwind uncontrolled.

If rewind spring is removed, wind into starter housing (1) in a clockwise direction starting with outer coil. Wind rope onto rope pulley in a clockwise direction as viewed from inside of starter housing. To apply tension on rewind spring, pull

out a length of rope and locate in notch in rope pulley. Holding rope in notch, turn pulley several turns clockwise then carefully allow pulley to rewind. Rope handle (3) should be tight against housing. If not, repeat procedure one additional turn clockwise. When installing starter assembly on saw, slowly pull rope to engage pawls (14) on flywheel.

CHAIN BRAKE. Models CS-4000P, CS-4500P and CS-8000P are equipped with a chain brake system designed to stop chain movement should kickback occur. Chain brake is activated when operator's hand strikes chain brake lever (1 – Fig. E65) drawing brake band (15) tight around clutch drum. Disassembly for repair and component renewal is evident after referral to exploded view and inspection of unit.

Adjust brake band (15) by rotating nut (18) located under cover (20) on chain guard (19). Adjustment is correct when chain will not move with chain brake engaged.

HEATED HANDLES. Some models are equipped with a front and rear handle heating system. A generator coil located under flywheel supplies an electrical current to heating coils in front and rear handles. To test handle heating coils, connect ohmmeter probes to heating coil leads. Meter should read 3.5-4.5 ohms for front handle and 1.0-1.3 ohms for rear handle. Heating coils and handles must be renewed as a unit assembly. To test generator coil, connect one ohmmeter probe to generator coil lead and remaining ohmmeter probe to a good engine ground. Renew generator coil if reading is not 1.0-1.8 ohms.

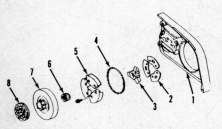

Fig. E63 — Exploded view of clutch assembly.

1. Cover
2. Side plates
3. Hub
4. Garter spring
5. Clutch shoes
6. Needle roller bearing
7. Drum
8. Sprocket

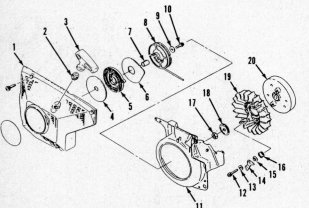

Fig. E64 — Exploded view of rewind starter assembly.

1. Housing
2. Rope guide
3. Rope handle
4. Washer
5. Rewind spring
6. Washer
7. Bushing
8. Rope pulley
9. Washer
10. Screw
11. Fan cover
12. Screw
13. Washer
14. Pawl
15. Spacer
16. Pawl spring
17. Nut
18. Washer
19. Fan
20. Flywheel

ECHO

Model	Bore	Stroke	Displ.	Drive Type
CST-610EVL, CST-610EVLP	36.0 mm (1.417 in.)	30.0 mm (1.181 in.)	61.0 cc (3.72 cu. in.)	Direct

MAINTENANCE

SPARK PLUG. Recommended spark plug is NGK BPM7A or Champion CJ6Y. Recommended electrode gap is 0.55-0.65 mm (0.022-0.026 in.).

CARBURETOR. A Walbro HDA diaphragm type carburetor is used. Refer to Walbro section of CARBURETOR SERVICE for service and exploded views.

Initial adjustment for both high and low speed mixture screws is 1⅛ to 1¼ turns open from a lightly seated position. Make final adjustment with engine running at operating temperature. Adjust low speed mixture so engine will accelerate cleanly without hesitation. Adjust high speed mixture to obtain optimum full throttle performance under a cutting load. Do not adjust high speed mixture too lean as overheating and engine damage could result.

IGNITION. An electronic capacitor discharge ignition system is used. Refer to Fig. E75. Note two separate ignition coils (4) which fire both cylinders simultaneously. Ignition module (5) contains a built in electronic ignition timing advance system. Except for faulty wiring and connections, repair of ignition system malfunctions is accomplished by renewal of ignition system components. Ignition timing is not adjustable but should be checked periodically to ensure proper operation of ignition module.

To check ignition timing it will be necessary to first lock clutch drum (5–Fig. E79) to crankshaft. Remove spark plug leads and properly ground. Remove chain guard, saw chain, guide bar, nut (8) and washer (7).

NOTE: Nut (8) has left-hand threads.

Install Echo special washer tool 900600-00010 (W–Fig. E76) or equivalent washer with a 10 mm (0.393 in.) inner diameter, 22 mm (0.866 in.) outer diameter and 1.5 mm (0.059 in.) thickness on crankshaft end and tighten nut (8–Fig. E79) to 19.8-23.7 N·m (175-210 in.-lbs.). Remove starter housing. Rotate flywheel to align "F" mark on flywheel with mark on crankcase. Scribe reference marks (M–Fig. E76) on clutch drum and chain brake cover. Install starter housing, reattach spark plug leads and connect a suitable power timing light. Start engine and allow to warm-up to normal operating temperature. Operate engine at 7,000 rpm and observe timing marks. Reference marks (M) should be aligned. If reference marks (M) do not align, check for sheared or damaged flywheel key or damaged flywheel keyway. If no damage to key or keyway is noted, renew ignition module and recheck ignition timing. Remove clutch drum locking washer and reassemble components. Tighten nut (8–Fig. E79) to 19.8-23.7 N·m (175-210 in.-lbs.).

Air gap between ignition module (5–Fig. E75) and flywheel magnets (1) should be 0.3 mm (0.012 in.). Incorrect adjustment will affect ignition timing.

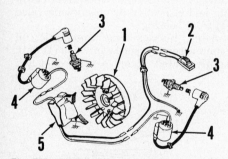

Fig. E75 – Exploded view of electronic ignition system.

1. Flywheel
2. Ignition switch
3. Spark plug
4. Ignition coil
5. Ignition module

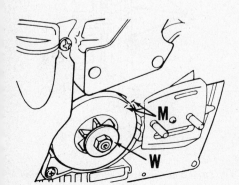

Fig. E76 – View showing positioning of timing reference marks (M) and Echo special washer tool 900600-00010. Refer to text.

Fig. E77 – Exploded view of two-cylinder engine assembly.

1. Right crankcase half
2. Crankcase seal
3. Gaskets
4. Cylinder
5. Cylinder gasket
6. Piston rings
7. Piston
8. Piston pin
9. Piston pin retainer
10. Needle roller bearing
11. Left crankcase half
12. Crankcase seal
13. Snap ring
14. Ball bearing
15. Crankshaft & connecting rods assy.

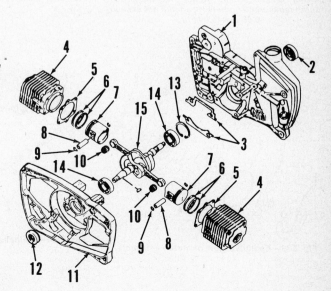

LUBRICATION. Engine is lubricated by mixing engine oil with fuel. Regular grade automotive gasoline is recommended. Recommended oil is Echo air-cooled two-stroke engine oil mixed with fuel at a 50:1 ratio. If Echo air-cooled two-stroke engine oil is not available, use a good quality oil designed for use in air-cooled two-stroke engines mixed with fuel at a 32:1 ratio. Use a separate container when mixing the oil and gas.

Both models are equipped with automatic and manual chain oil pumps. Clean automotive oil may be used. Oil viscosity should be chosen according to ambient temperatures. Automatic oil pump output is adjustable. Refer to OIL PUMP section for service and adjustment procedures.

REPAIRS

CYLINDERS, PISTONS, PINS AND RINGS. Cylinder bores are chrome plated and oversize pistons and rings are not available. Inspect cylinder bore for scoring, flaking or other damage to chrome surface.

Pistons are equipped with two piston rings. Maximum allowable ring end gap is 0.5 mm (0.020 in.). Maximum allowable piston ring in ring groove side clearance is 0.1 mm (0.004 in.). Renew cylinders, pistons and piston rings as required if service limits are exceeded. When installing piston rings, install semi-keystone ring in top piston ring groove and rectangular piston ring in second ring groove. Locating pins are present in ring grooves to prevent piston ring rotation. Make certain ring end gaps are around locating pins when installing cylinders.

Piston pin (8 – Fig. E77) rides in needle roller bearing (10) and is held in place by two wire retainers (9). To remove piston pin, remove wire retainers, properly support piston then carefully tap out piston pin using a suitable driver. Echo special tool 8977102-04320 should be used to remove and install piston pins.

When installing pistons, make certain triangular mark on piston crown faces downward toward cylinder exhaust port.

CRANKSHAFT, CONNECTING RODS AND CRANKCASE. Crankshaft and connecting rods (15 – Fig. E77) are a unit assembly and are not available separately. Crankshaft is supported by two ball bearings (14). Clutch side ball bearing is retained in position by snap ring (13) while flywheel side ball bearing is held in position by a shoulder in crankcase half.

Check crankshaft runout by supporting crankshaft at points (A – Fig. E78) and measuring at points (B). Maximum allowable runout is 0.05 mm (0.002 in.).

Crankcase ball bearing bores should be heated with a heat gun or heat lamp to ease reassembly. Do not use an open flame. Make certain crankshaft turns freely before final tightening of crankcase cap screws. Tighten crankcase cap screws to 7.9-9.0 N·m (70-80 in.-lbs.).

REED VALVE. The reed valve assembly should be inspected whenever the carburetor is removed. Reed petals should seat lightly against insulator block. Renew reed valve assembly if reed petals are cracked, warped or damaged.

CLUTCH. Refer to Fig. E79 for an exploded view of three-shoe centrifugal clutch used. Clutch hub (2) and nut (8) have left-hand threads. Clutch drum (5) rides on needle roller bearing (6). Inspect clutch shoes (4) and drum (5) for excessive wear or damage due to overheating. Inspect needle roller bearing for damage or discoloration. Install clutch with side plates (1) facing inward. Tighten clutch hub to 19.8-23.7 N·m (175-210 in.-lbs.). Tighten clutch nut to 22.6-27.1 N·m (200-240 in.-lbs.).

OIL PUMP. All models are equipped with automatic and manual chain oil pumps. Refer to Fig. E80 for exploded view of manual oil pump. Check balls (8) must move freely for proper pump operation. Renew "O" ring (4) and hoses as required when signs of hardening and cracking are found.

Refer to Fig. E81 for cross-sectional view of automatic oil pump. Plunger (4) is actuated by cam (5) on crankshaft. Pump output is adjusted by rotating valve (1). Oil pump is removed for cleaning and inspection by unscrewing valve (1) from housing.

After reassembling automatic oil pump assembly, screw in valve (1) until lightly seated. Remove saw chain and

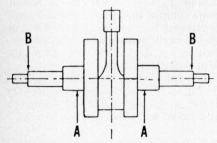

Fig. E78 — Measure crankshaft runout by supporting crankshaft at points (A). Maximum runout measured at points (B) should not exceed 0.05 mm (0.002 in.).

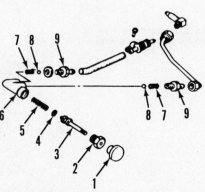

Fig. E79 — Exploded view of clutch assembly.

1. Side plates
2. Hub
3. Garter spring
4. Shoes
5. Drum
6. Needle roller bearing
7. Washer
8. Nut

Fig. E80 — Exploded view of manual oil pump.

1. Button
2. End cap
3. Plunger
4. "O" ring
5. Spring
6. Housing
7. Spring
8. Check ball
9. Fitting

Fig. E81 — Cross-sectional view of automatic oil pump.

1. Valve
2. "O" rings
3. Spring
4. Plunger
5. Cam
6. Check ball
7. Spring

guide bar and run engine at half throttle. Rotate valve (1) counterclockwise until maximum oil output is obtained (approx. ¾ turn). Mark top of valve (1) adjacent to housing stop tab for future reference, then install oiler adjustment knob assembly so valve (1) can only be turned counterclockwise to decrease oil pump output.

REWIND STARTER. To disassemble rewind starter, remove rope handle (3–Fig. E82) and allow rope to slowly rewind into starter housing (1). Remove screw (12) and carefully lift out rope pulley (8) noting how rope pulley engages rewind spring (5). If necessary to remove rewind spring, care must be taken not to allow spring to uncoil uncontrolled.

Install rewind spring into starter housing in a clockwise direction starting with outer coil. Wind rope on rope pulley in a clockwise direction as viewed from flywheel side of pulley. Install rope pulley into starter housing making sure pulley properly engages rewind spring. Rotate pulley four turns clockwise before passing rope through rope guide (2) and installing rope handle (3). Tension on rewind spring is correct when rope handle is tight against starter housing and rope pulley can be rotated ½ turn clockwise when rope is fully extended.

CHAIN BRAKE. Model CST-610EVLP is equipped with a chain brake system designed to stop chain movement should kickback occur. Chain brake is activated when operator's hand strikes chain brake lever (1–Fig. E83), tripping latch (11) and allowing spring (12) to draw brake band (6) tight around clutch drum. Pull back chain brake lever to reset mechanism. Disassembly for service and component renewal is evident after referral to exploded view and inspection of unit. To adjust brake band, loosen screw (9) and rotate adjusting cam (8). Adjust brake band so saw chain will not move with chain brake engaged. Brake band should not contact clutch drum with chain brake disengaged.

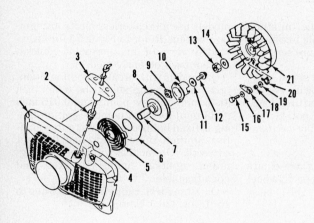

Fig. E82 — Exploded view of rewind starter assembly.

1. Starter housing
2. Rope guide
3. Rope handle
4. Washer
5. Rewind spring
6. Washer
7. Bushing
8. Rope pulley
9. Clip
10. Starter cup
11. Washer
12. Screw
13. Nut
14. Washer
15. Cap screw
16. Washer
17. Pawl
18. Spacer
19. Washer
20. Pawl spring
21. Flywheel

Fig. E83 — Exploded view of chain brake system used on Model CST-610EVLP.

1. Chain brake lever	8. Adjusting cam
2. Dust cover	9. Screw
3. Pivot pin	10. Spacer
4. Brake band lever	11. Latch
5. Dust seal	12. Spring
6. Brake band	13. Cap screw
7. Brake band retainer	14. Shield

FRONTIER

EMAB CANADA
P.O. Box 549
Huron Park, Ontario, Canada N0M 1Y0

Model	Bore	Stroke	Displ.	Drive Type
Mark I, Mark I V.I.P.	1-7/16 in. (36.5 mm)	1.28 in. (32.5 mm)	2.1 cu. in. (34.4 cc)	Direct
F-35, F-35 V.I.P.	1-7/16 in. (36.5 mm)	1.28 in. (32.5 mm)	2.1 cu. in. (34.4 cc)	Direct
FB-35, FB-35 V.I.P.	1-7/16 in. (36.5 mm)	1.28 in. (32.5 mm)	2.1 cu. in. (34.4 cc)	Direct

MAINTENANCE

SPARK PLUG. Recommended spark plug is Champion CJ6. Spark plug electrode gap should be 0.025 inch (0.63 mm).

CARBURETOR. A Tillotson Model HU diaphragm carburetor or a Walbro Model WA diaphragm carburetor may be used. Refer to Tillotson or Walbro section of CARBURETOR SERVICE section for service procedures and exploded view.

Initial adjustment of idle mixture screws is 1½ turns open while initial adjustment of high speed mixture screw is 1⅛ turns open.

Final adjustment of high speed mixture screw should be made with engine warm and engine under cutting load. High speed mixture must not be adjusted too lean as engine may be damaged.

IGNITION. Early models are equipped with a breaker-point type flywheel magneto ignition system while later models use a breakerless electronic ignition system. Refer to Fig. FR3 for an exploded view of breaker-point ignition system used on early models.

On models with breaker-point ignition, breaker-point gap should be 0.018 inch (0.45 mm) for new points and 0.015 inch (0.38 mm) for used points. Ignition timing is fixed but breaker-point gap will affect ignition timing and should be set correctly. On models with electronic ignition, ignition timing is fixed and nonadjustable.

On all models, tighten flywheel nut to 15 ft.-lbs. (20.4 N·m).

LUBRICATION. The engine is lubricated by mixing oil with the fuel. Recommended fuel:oil ratio is 16:1. A good quality oil designed for chain saw engines should be used.

Fill chain oil tank with SAE 30 motor oil. Chain oil may be diluted up to 50 percent for winter usage by adding kerosene or diesel fuel to chain oil.

CARBON. Carbon should be removed from exhaust system and cylinder periodically. Loose carbon should not be allowed to enter cylinder and care should be taken not to damage cylinder or piston.

REPAIRS

CYLINDER, PISTON, PIN AND RINGS. Cylinder (16–Fig. FR1) on all models is also upper crankcase half. Crankshaft is loose in crankcase when cylinder is removed. Care must be taken not to nick or scratch crankcase mating surfaces during disassembly.

Cylinder head is integral with cylinder and cylinder must be removed to remove piston. Piston is equipped with a single piston ring and a floating type piston pin (20). Piston, pin and ring are available in

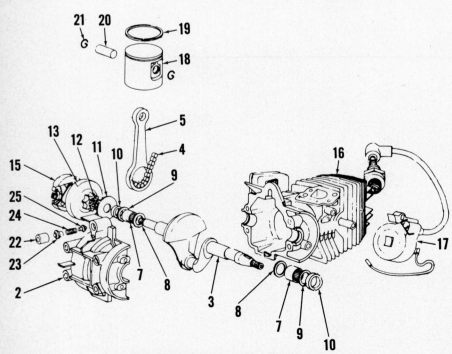

Fig. FR1 – Exploded view of engine used on all models.

2. Crankcase	9. Retaining ring	20. Piston pin
3. Crankshaft	10. Seal	21. Pin retainer
4. Roller bearing	11. Thrust washer	22. Spacer
5. Connecting rod	12. Bearing	23. Spring seat
7. Needle bearing	13. Clutch drum	24. Spring
8. Washer	15. Clutch assy.	25. Pulse valve
	16. Cylinder	
	17. Ignition oil	
	18. Piston	
	19. Piston ring	

standard size only. Cylinder bore is chrome and should be inspected to determine if chrome is scored, peeling or excessively worn. Renew cylinder and piston if damaged or excessively worn.

Refer to CRANKSHAFT section for proper assembly of crankcase and cylinder. Tighten cylinder retaining screws to 50-55 in.-lbs. (5.6-6.2 N·m)

CONNECTING ROD. To remove connecting rod, remove cylinder (16—Fig. FR1). Note that cylinder is also upper crankcase half and crankshaft assembly is loose when cylinder is removed. Connecting rod (5) is one-piece and supported on crankpin by 11 loose bearing rollers (4). Be careful not to lose loose rollers that may fall out during disassembly. Rollers can be removed by sliding rod off rollers. To install rod bearing, hold rollers in place with heavy

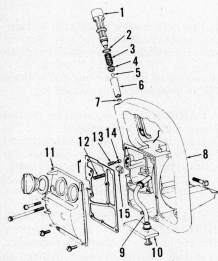

Fig. FR2—Exploded view of manual oil pump and front housing.

1. Piston	9. Fuel hose
2. "O" ring	10. Filter
3. Spring	11. Front cover
4. Spring seat	12. Spring
5. Ball	13. Spring
6. Pump body	14. Oil outlet valve
7. Screen	15. Nut
8. Front housing	

grease or petroleum jelly and position rod over rollers. Be sure rollers do not fall out during assembly of crankcase.

CRANKSHAFT AND SEALS. Crankshaft is supported by needle roller bearings (7—Fig. FR1) at both ends. Crankshaft assembly may be removed after removing stator plate, clutch and cylinder assemblies. Care should be taken when removing cylinder as crankshaft will be loose in crankcase and connecting rod may slide off bearing rollers allowing them to fall into crankcase.

Before reassembling crankcases, apply a light coat of nonhardening silicone sealant to crankcase mating surface. Be sure mating surfaces are not damaged during assembly. Retaining rings (9) must fit in ring grooves of crankcase and cylinder.

CLUTCH. A two-shoe centrifugal type clutch is used on all models. Clutch hub has left-hand threads. Clutch bearing (12—Fig. FR1) should be inspected for excessive wear or damage. Inspect clutch shoes and drum for signs of excessive heat.

OIL PUMP. All early models are equipped with a manual oil pump and automatic oiling system. Refer to Fig. FR2 for an exploded view of manual oil pump. Automatic oiling is accomplished by crankcase pulsations which pressur-

ize oil tank and force oil to bar. A one-way valve (25—Fig. FR1) prevents oil from entering crankcase.

NOTE: Later models equipped with manual oil pump and automatic oiling system are equipped with a duckbill type valve in place of valve components (22, 23, 24 and 25).

Later model saws are equipped with a positive displacement oil pump assembly located behind flywheel. Oil pump assembly is driven by a worm gear on crankshaft. Remove oil pump plunger retaining roll pin and withdraw plunger, gear and spring to service. Use suitable tools to pry worm gear off crankshaft. Renew any component that is excessively worn or damaged. Plunger is available only with complete oil pump assembly.

REWIND STARTER. Refer to Fig. FR3 for an exploded view of pawl type starter used on all models. Care should be taken while removing rewind spring to prevent spring from uncoiling uncontrolled.

Rewind spring (12) should be wound in clockwise direction in housing. Wind starter rope in clockwise direction around pulley (11) as viewed in starter housing (14). Place tension on rope by turning rope pulley three turns clockwise before passing rope end through rope outlet.

Fig. FR3—Exploded view of rewind starter used on all models. Breaker-point ignition (1) is used on early models.

1. Stator plate
2. Cover
3. Flywheel
4. Spring
5. Pawl
6. Pivot pin
7. Washer
8. Nut
9. Snap ring
10. Thrust washer
11. Rope pulley
12. Rewind spring
13. Bushing
14. Starter housing

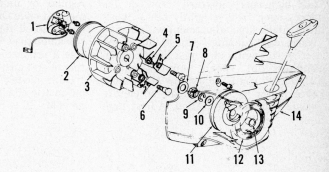

THE GREEN MACHINE

HMC
P.O. Box 560
Long Beach, CA 90801-0560

Model	Bore	Stroke	Displ.	Drive Type
7200	35 mm (1.38 in.)	33 mm (1.30 in.)	31.7 cc (1.9 cu. in.)	Direct
7400	38 mm (1.50 in.)	33 mm (1.30 in.)	37.4 cc (2.3 cu. in.)	Direct

MAINTENANCE

SPARK PLUG. Recommended spark plug is Champion CJ8Y for both models. Electrode gap should be 0.6 mm (0.024 in.).

CARBURETOR. A Walbro WA diaphragm type carburetor is used on both models. Refer to Walbro section of CARBURETOR SERVICE for service and exploded views of carburetor.

Initial adjustment for both low speed and high speed mixture screws is 1½ turns open from a lightly seated position. Make final adjustment with engine warm and running. Adjust idle speed screw so engine idles just below clutch engagement speed (approximately 2700-3100 rpm). Adjust low speed mixture screw so engine will accelerate cleanly without hesitation. Adjust high speed mixture screw to obtain optimum performance under cutting load.

IGNITION. Both models are equipped with a breakerless electronic ignition system. Ignition timing is not adjustable. Air gap between ignition module/coil assembly (1–Fig. GR11) legs and flywheel should be 0.5 mm (0.020 in.).

LUBRICATION. Engine is lubricated by mixing engine oil with regular or unleaded gasoline. Recommended oil is One-Mix or a good-quality oil designed for use in air-cooled two-stroke engines mixed at a ratio of 25:1. Use a separate container when mixing the oil and gas.

Both models are equipped with an automatic chain oil pump. Recommended chain oil is SAE 10W-30 oil. Oil output on both models is adjusted by turning control knob on top of saw. Four oil delivery settings are provided: Positions "A," "B," "C" and "D." Position "A" is minimum oil output setting and position "D" is maximum oil output setting.

CARBON. Carbon should be cleaned from muffler and exhaust ports at regular intervals. When scraping carbon, be careful not to damage the chamfered edges of the exhaust ports.

REPAIRS

CYLINDER, PISTON, PIN AND RING. Cylinder (13–Fig. GR12) bore is chrome plated and should be renewed if cracking, flaking or other damage to cylinder bore is noted. Oversize piston and rings are not available. During disassembly, note direction of piston (10) in cylinder. Make sure piston is reinstalled in same direction. Piston (10) is equipped with one piston ring (11). A locating pin is present in ring groove to

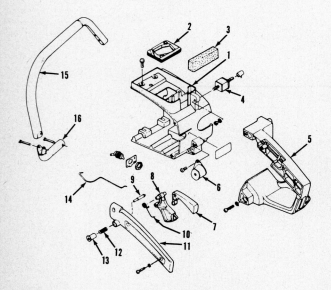

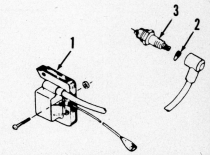

Fig. GR10—Exploded view of trigger assembly, front and rear handle assemblies and related components.

1. Engine cover
2. Seal
3. Air filter
4. Vibration damper
5. Rear handle
6. Vibration damper
7. Trigger lock
8. Trigger
9. Stopper
10. Spring
11. Cover
12. Spring
13. Stop knob
14. Throttle link
15. Front handle
16. Handle mount

Fig. GR11—View of breakerless electronic ignition system.

1. Ignition module/ coil assy.
2. Terminal
3. Spark plug

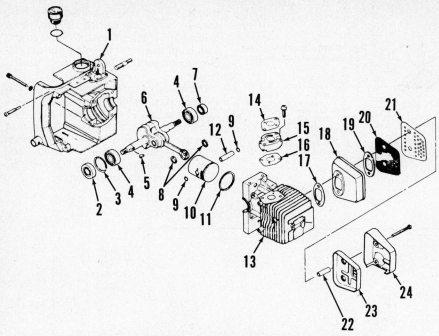

Fig. GR12 — Exploded view of engine, intake and muffler assemblies.

1. Lower crankcase half & oil tank
2. Seal
3. Snap ring
4. Bearing
5. Key
6. Crankshaft & connecting rod assy.
7. Seal
8. Thrust washer
9. Retainer clip
10. Piston
11. Piston ring
12. Piston pin
13. Cylinder & upper crankcase half
14. Gasket
15. Insulator block
16. Gasket
17. Gasket
18. Base
19. Plate
20. Spark arrestor
21. Baffle
22. Spacer
23. Inner cover
24. Outer cover

ing rod (6 – Fig. GR12) are a unit assembly and supported at both ends with ball type main bearings (4). Rotate connecting rod around crankpin and renew assembly if roughness, excessive play or other damage is noted.

New seals (2 and 7) should be installed on crankshaft when reassembling upper and lower crankcase halves. Use a suitable form-in-place gasket compound on mating surfaces of upper and lower crankcase halves. Be sure mating surfaces are not damaged during assembly.

CLUTCH. A two-shoe centrifugal type clutch is used on both models. Clutch hub (6 – Fig. GR13) has left-hand threads. Clutch needle bearing (2) should be inspected for excessive wear or damage. Inspect clutch shoes and drum for signs of excessive heat.

AUTOMATIC CHAIN OILER. Both models are equipped with an automatic chain oil pump assembly. Control valve assembly (1 – Fig. GR14) is renewable only as a complete assembly. Four oil output settings are provided. Refer to LUBRICATION under MAINTENANCE section.

REWIND STARTER. Refer to Fig. GR15 for exploded view of pawl type starter used on both models. Care should be exercised when handling rewind spring (3) to prevent spring from uncoiling uncontrolled.

During reassembly, do not apply any more tension on rewind spring than required to properly draw rope handle up against starter housing in relaxed position.

CHAIN BRAKE. All models are equipped with a chain brake designed to stop the saw chain quickly should kickback occur. Chain brake is activated when operator's hand strikes hand

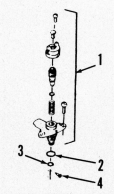

Fig. GR13 — Exploded view of two-stroke clutch assembly.

1. Washer
2. Needle bearing
3. Drum
4. Washer
5. Washer
6. Hub
7. Shoe
8. Spring

prevent ring rotation. Make certain ring end gap is properly positioned around locating pin before installing cylinder. A floating type piston pin (12) is used and is retained in position with two wire retainer clips (9). Once removed, wire clips should not be reused.

CRANKSHAFT AND CONNECTING ROD. Crankshaft is loose in crankcase when cylinder is removed. Cylinder and upper crankcase half are a unit assembly. Crankshaft and connect-

Fig. GR14 — Exploded view of chain oil output control valve.

1. Control valve assy.
2. "O" ring
3. "O" ring
4. Bladder valve

Fig. GR15 — Exploded view of rewind starter.

1. Housing
2. Rope guide
3. Rewind spring & cassette
4. Rope pulley
5. Rope
6. Handle
7. Washer
8. Screw
9. Nut
10. Lockwasher
11. Flat washer
12. Pivot
13. Pawl
14. Spring
15. Flywheel

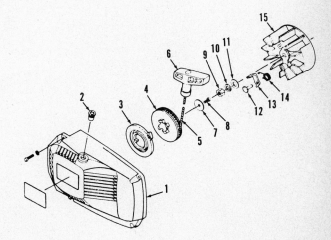

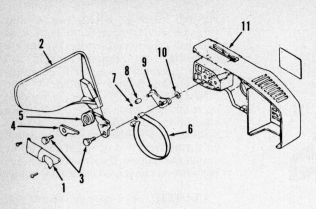

guard (2 – Fig. GR16), releasing latch (4) thereby allowing spring (5) to draw brake band (6) tight around clutch drum. Pull hand guard (2) to reset mechanism. No adjustment of brake mechanism is required.

Disassembly for inspection or repair is evident after referral to exploded view and inspection of unit. Renew any component found to be excessively worn or damaged. Chain brake mechanism should be clean and free of sawdust and dirt accumulation. Lightly lubricate all moving parts and pivot points.

THE GREEN MACHINE

Model	Bore	Stroke	Displ.	Drive Type
7600	44 mm (1.73 in.)	35 mm (1.38 in.)	53.2 cc (3.25 cu. in.)	Direct
7700	47.5 mm (1.87 in.)	35 mm (1.38 in.)	62 cc (3.78 cu. in.)	Direct

MAINTENANCE

SPARK PLUG. Recommended spark plug is Champion CJ7Y. Electrode gap should be 0.6 mm (0.024 in.).

CARBURETOR. All models are equipped with a Walbro HDA diaphragm type carburetor. Refer to Walbro section of CARBURETOR SERVICE section for service procedures and exploded views.

Initial adjustment is 1½ turns open for low speed mixture screw and 1⅝ turns open for high speed mixture screw. Mixture screws should be adjusted from a lightly seated position.

Final adjustment should be made with engine running at operating temperature. Adjust idle speed to 2,300-2,800 rpm. Adjust low speed mixture screw to obtain highest idle speed, plus an additional ¼ turn open. Readjust idle speed to 2,300-2,800 rpm. Repeat procedure until optimum idle condition is obtained. Adjust high speed mixture screw to obtain optimum performance under cutting load. Readjust idle speed to 2,300-2,800 rpm.

IGNITION. A breakerless electronic ignition system is used. Ignition coil and all electronic circuitry are contained in a one-piece ignition module (4 – Fig. GR20) located outside of flywheel. Ignition timing is not adjustable. Air gap between ignition module core lamination (4) and flywheel (1) magnets should be 0.4-0.5 mm (0.016-0.020 in.).

Ignition module can be tested with an ohmmeter. Coil primary resistance should be 0.72-0.98 ohm. Coil secondary resistance should be 4880-7320 ohms.

Renew module if recommended specifications are not noted. Flywheel nut should be tightened to 14.7-19.6 N·m (11-14 ft.-lbs.).

LUBRICATION. The engine is lubricated by mixing oil with the fuel. Recommended oil is One-Mix or a good-quality oil designed for use in air-cooled two-stroke engines. Recommended fuel is regular or unleaded gasoline. Mix fuel and oil at a 25:1 ratio. Use a separate container when mixing fuel and oil.

All models are equipped with an adjustable automatic chain oil pump. Refer to OIL PUMP under REPAIRS section for service and exploded view.

Oil pump output is adjusted by rotating adjusting knob located at top

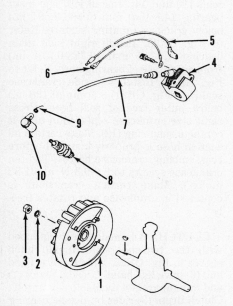

Fig. GR20—Exploded view of ignition system used.

1. Flywheel	6. Ground lead	
2. Washer	7. Secondary lead	
3. Nut	8. Spark plug	
4. Ignition module	9. Terminal	
5. Primary lead	10. Boot	

Fig. GR21—Exploded view of engine assembly.

1. Cylinder	9. Crankshaft & connecting rod assy.	12. Snap ring
2. Gasket	10. Seal	13. Main bearing
3. Piston rings	11. Right crankcase half	14. Seal
4. Piston		15. Gasket
5. Piston pin		16. Left crankcase half
6. Wire clip		
7. Needle bearing		
8. Thrust washer		

right cylinder cover. Clockwise rotation decreases pump output. Recommended chain oil is clean SAE 10W-30 oil.

REPAIRS

CYLINDER, PISTON, PIN AND RINGS. Cylinder (1–Fig. GR21) bore is chrome plated and should be inspected and renewed if cracking, flaking or other damage is noted. Oversize piston and rings are not available. Piston (4) is equipped with two piston rigns (3). Maximum piston ring end gap is 0.6 mm (0.024 in.) on Model 7600 and 0.7 mm (0.028 in.) on Model 7700. Maximum allowable piston ring side clearance is 0.13 mm (0.005 in.) for all models. Locating pins are present in ring grooves to prevent ring rotation. Make certain ring end gaps are properly positioned around locating pins before installing cylinder. Piston pin (5) rides in needle bearing (7) and is retained in position with two wire clips (6). Once removed, wire clips (6) should not be reused. Install new wire clips with end gaps facing upward. It should be possible to push piston pin (5) out with hand pressure. If pin is tight, tap out with hammer and punch while properly supporting piston to prevent damage to connecting rod. Install piston in cylinder with arrow on piston crown toward exhaust ports. Note location of thrust washers (8) when installing piston on connecting rod. Tighten cylinder screws to 6.9-8.8 N·m (61-78 in.-lbs.).

CRANKSHAFT, CONNECTING ROD AND CRANKCASE. Crankcase halves (11 and 16–Fig. GR21) must be split to remove crankshaft and connect-

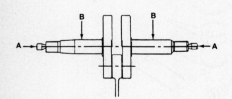

Fig. GR22—Measure crankshaft runout by supporting crankshaft at points (A). Maximum allowable runout measured at points (B) is 0.1 mm (0.004 in.).

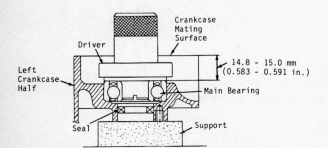

Fig. GR23—View showing installation of left side main bearing.

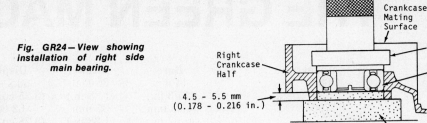

Fig. GR24—View showing installation of right side main bearing.

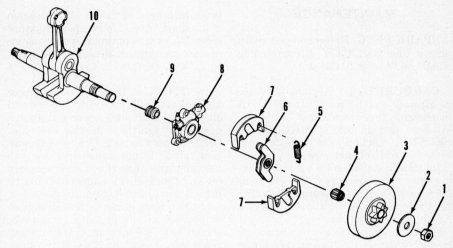

Fig. GR25—View showing crankshaft and connecting rod assembly, worm gear, oil pump and exploded view of centrifugal clutch.

1. Nut	4. Needle bearing	7. Clutch shoe	9. Worm gear
2. Washer	5. Spring	8. Oil pump	10. Crankshaft & connecting rod assy.
3. Clutch drum	6. Clutch hub		

ing rod assembly (9). Use a soft-faced mallet to tap crankcase halves apart. Do not damage crankcase mating surfaces. Crankshaft and connecting rod are a unit assembly and are not available separately. Rotate connecting rod around crankpin and renew assembly if roughness, excessive play or other damage is noted. Crankshaft is supported at both ends with ball type main bearings (13).

Check crankshaft runout by supporting crankshaft at points (A–Fig. GR22) and measuring at points (B). Runout should not exceed 0.1 mm (0.004 in.).

Use a press and the proper size drivers and supports when removing and install-

ing main bearings (13–Fig. GR21) and seals (10 and 14). Install left side main bearing 14.8-15.0 mm (0.583-0.591 in.) below crankcase mating surface. Refer to Fig. GR23. Install right side main bearing 4.5-5.5 mm (0.178-0.216 in.) from outer face of bearing bore. Refer to Fig. GR24. Install left side crankcase seal (14–Fig. GR21) 3.5 mm (0.138 in.) below outer face of seal bore. Press right side crankcase seal (10) in until it contacts snap ring (12). Make certain oil suction hose is properly installed before reassembling crankcase halves. Tighten crankcase screws to 6.9-9.3 N·m (61-82 in.-lbs.). Make certain crankshaft is centered in crankcase and rotates freely.

CLUTCH. All models are equipped with the two-shoe centrifugal clutch shown in Fig. GR25. Clutch nut (1) and hub (6) have left-hand threads. Shoes (7) and hub (6) are not available separately. Clutch drum (3) rides on needle bearing (4). Inspect shoes, drum, needle bearing and bearing surface on crankshaft for excessive wear or damage due to overheating. Renew any component found to be excessively worn or damaged. Tighten clutch hub to 24.5-29.4 N·m (18-22 ft.-lbs.) and clutch nut to 14.7-19.6 N·m (11-14 ft.-lbs.).

OIL PUMP. All models are equipped with an adjustable automatic chain oil pump. Oil pump output is adjusted by rotating adjusting shaft (8–Fig. GR26). Pump is driven by worm gear (11) located on engine crankshaft. Inspect pump plunger and worm gear for excessive wear or damage. Pump plunger is not available separately from pump body. Inspect suction and discharge hoses and renew hoses if cracking or any other damage is noted. Apply a suitable grease on teeth of pump plunger and worm gear during reassembly. Oil tank vent valve is located behind ignition module and retained in tank with a snap ring.

REWIND STARTER. All models are equipped with the rewind starter shown in Fig. GR27. To disassemble starter, remove rope handle (14) and carefully allow rope to wind into starter housing (12) relieving tension on rewind spring (11). Remove screw (7) and lift out rope pulley (9) noting how pulley engages inner coil of rewind spring. If rewind spring must be removed, use caution not to allow spring to uncoil uncontrolled. Renew any component found to be excessively worn or damaged.

Lightly lubricate rewind spring and rope pulley shaft in starter housing with a suitable low temperature grease. Wind rewind spring into spring case (10) in a counterclockwise direction starting with outer coil as viewed from spring side of case. Assemble rope pulley into rewind spring case making certain hook on inner coil of rewind spring properly

engages slot in rope pulley. Install rope pulley with rewind spring and case into starter housing and install washer (8) and screw (7). Securely tighten screw (7). Make certain pulley turns freely. Pass rope through rope guide (13). Place rope into notch in outer edge of rope pulley and rotate pulley clockwise until spring is coil bound. Back off pulley one full turn and carefully allow pulley to rewind rope onto pulley. If spring tension is correct, rope pulley should be able to

rotate an additional 1½ to 2 turns clockwise with rope fully extended.

CHAIN BRAKE. Some models are equipped with a chain brake system designed to quickly stop chain movement should kickback occur. Chain brake is activated when operator's hand strikes hand guard (1–Fig. GR28). Forward movement of brake lever (5) causes stopper (4) to disengage arm (11) allowing spring (10) to draw brake band (9) tight around clutch drum. Pull back hand guard to reset mechanism.

Disassembly for inspection or repair is evident after referral to exploded view and inspection of unit. Renew any component found to be excessively worn or damaged. Lightly lubricate pivot points with a suitable grease. No adjustment of chain brake system is required.

Fig. GR27 – Exploded view or rewind starter used on all models.

1. Flywheel	5. Pivot screw	9. Rope pulley	12. Starter housing
2. Spring	6. Cover	10. Rewind spring case	13. Rope guide
3. Washer	7. Screw	11. Rewind spring	14. Rope handle
4. Pawl	8. Washer		15. Washer

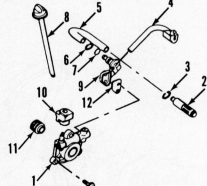

Fig. GR26 – Exploded view of automatic oil pump.

1. Oil pump assy.	7. "O" ring
2. Pickup filter	8. Adjusting shaft
3. Clip	9. Connector
4. Discharge hose	10. Grommet
5. Suction hose	11. Worm gear
6. Clip	12. Gasket

Fig. GR28 – Exploded view of chain brake system used.

1. Hand guard
2. Cover
3. "E" ring
4. Stopper
5. Lever
6. Spring
7. Pin
8. Pin
9. Brake band
10. Spring
11. Arm
12. "E" ring
13. Shoulder screw

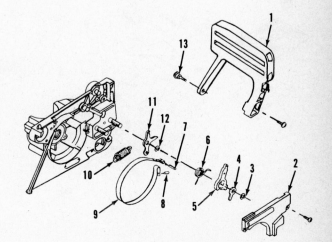

HOMELITE

HOMELITE DIVISION OF TEXTRON, INC.
P.O. Box 7047
14401 Carowinds Blvd.
Charlotte, NC 28217

Model	Bore	Stroke	Displ.	Drive Type
EZ	1.4375 in. (36.5 mm)	1.3 in. (33.0 mm)	2.1 cu. in. (34.4 cc)	Direct
Super EZ Automatic	1.5625 in. (39.7 mm)	1.3125 in. (33.3 mm)	2.5 cu. in. (40.9 cc)	Direct

MAINTENANCE

SPARK PLUG. A Champion DJ-6J spark plug with tapered seat is used; no gasket is required. Adjust electrode gap to 0.025 inch (0.63 mm).

CARBURETOR. A Walbro Model HDC diaphragm type carburetor is used on all models. Refer to Walbro section of CARBURETOR SERVICE section for overhaul and exploded view of carburetor.

For initial carburetor adjustment, back idle speed adjusting screw out until throttle valve will completely close, then turn screw back in until it contacts idle stop plus ½ turn additional. Turn both fuel adjusting needles in until lightly seated, then back main fuel needle (located to left and marked "HI" on grommet when viewing adjustment needle side of throttle handle) out about one turn and back idle ("LO") needle out about ¾ turn. Start engine, readjust idle speed and fuel needles so engine idles at just below clutch engagement speed.

With engine running at full throttle under load, readjust main fuel needle so engine will run at highest obtainable speed without excessive smoke.

To adjust starting speed (speed at which engine will run with throttle latch engaged), stop engine and remove chain, guide bar, air filter cover and air filter. Open trigger adjusting screw ⅛ turn clockwise. With trigger latched, start engine and run at half throttle (not at high speed) for 30-50 seconds to warm it up. Release throttle trigger, then latch it while engine is running. If engine stops, restart it. With throttle trigger latched, gently hold trigger down and slowly back trigger adjusting screw out counterclockwise until engine falters, then turn screw back in 1/16 turn clockwise. Squeeze and release trigger to idle engine, then shut engine off with stop switch. Try to restart engine; if hard to start, open screw another 1/16 turn at a time until enough for consistent starting. When starting speed is satisfactorily adjusted, stop engine and reinstall guide bar, chain, air filter and filter cover. If engine will start readily and saw chain does not turn or only turns slowly, adjustment is correct. If chain turns rapidly with throttle latched, repeat adjustment procedure to set starting speed slower.

MAGNETO AND TIMING. A conventional flywheel type magneto ignition system is used on early models while later Super EZ Automatic models are equipped with solid-state ignition. The solid-state ignition system is serviced by renewing the spark plug and/or ignition module. Air gap between ignition module and flywheel is adjustable. Adjust air gap by loosening module retaining screws and place a 0.015 inch (0.38 mm) shim stock between flywheel and module. Remove shim stock.

Note the following on breaker-point equipped models: Breaker-points are contained in a breaker-box under the flywheel. Ignition timing is not adjustable. Breaker-point gap should be 0.015 inch (0.38 mm) and must be correct or ignition timing will be affected. Condenser capacity should be approximately 0.2 mfd. Air gap between flywheel and coil should be 0.015 inch (0.38 mm).

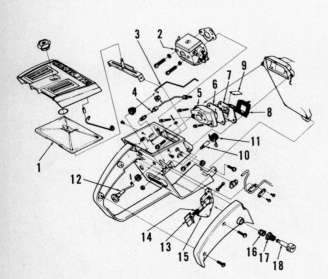

Fig. HL1 — Exploded view of handle assembly and related assemblies.

1. Air filter
2. Carburetor
3. Throttle rod
4. Oil line
5. Spacer
6. Gasket
7. Reed valve seat
8. Reed retainer
9. Reed petals
10. Spring post
11. Spring
12. Choke rod
13. Throttle stop
14. Spring
15. Trigger
16. Bushing
17. Spring
18. Throttle latch

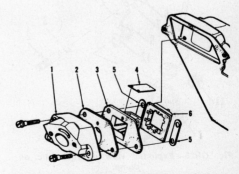

Fig. HL2 — View showing reed valve and spacer used prior to assembly shown in Fig. HL1.

1. Reed spacer
2. Gasket
3. Reed seat
4. Valve reeds
5. Spacers
6. Reed retainer

CARBON. Carbon deposits should be removed from muffler and exhaust ports at regular intervals. When scraping carbon, be careful not to damage chamfered edges of exhaust ports or scratch piston. A wooden scraper should be used. Turn engine so piston is at top dead center to prevent carbon from falling into cylinder. Do not attempt to run engine with muffler removed.

LUBRICATION. The engine is lubricated by mixing oil with unleaded gasoline. Recommended oil is Homelite two-stroke oil mixed at ratio as designated on oil container. If Homelite oil is not available, a good quality oil designed for two-stroke engines may be used when mixed at a 16:1 ratio, however, an antioxidant fuel stabilizer (such as Sta-Bil) should be added to fuel mix. Antioxidant fuel stabilizer is not required with Homelite® oils as they contain fuel stabilizer so the fuel mix will stay fresh up to one year.

Fill chain oiler reservoir with Homelite® Bar and Chain oil or with light weight motor oil (not over SAE 30). In cold weather, thin oil with kerosene until it will flow freely.

The clutch needle roller bearing should be cleaned and relubricated after each 100 hours of use. A high temperature grease such as Homelite® ALL-TEMP Multipurpose Grease or equivalent should be used.

REPAIRS

TIGHTENING TORQUES. Recommended tightening torques are listed in the following table.

4/40 Flange bearing . . . . 5-6 in.-lbs.
(0.6-0.7 N·m)

6/32 Compression release
clamp . . . . 20-24 in.-lbs.
(2.3-2.7 N·m)

6/32 Compression release
post nut . . . . 20-24 in.-lbs.
(2.3-2.7 N·m)

6/32 Breaker-box . . . . 20-24 in.-lbs.
(2.3-2.7 N·m)

6/32 Breaker-point
adjustable arm . . . . 20-24 in.-lbs.
(2.3-2.7 N·m)

6/32 Condenser . . . . 20-24 in.-lbs.
(2.3-2.7 N·m)

8/32 Air filter bracket . . . . . 25-30 in.-lbs.
(2.8-3.4 N·m)

8/32 Connecting rod . . . . . . 55-66 in.-lbs.
(6.2-7.5 N·m)

8/32 Throttle handle
cover . . . . 35-42 in.-lbs.
(3.9-4.7 N·m)

8/32 Rewind spring
cover . . . . 35-42 in.-lbs.
(3.9-4.7 N·m)

8/32 Intake manifold
(reed spacer) . . . . 20-24 in.-lbs.
(2.3-2.7 N·m)

8/32 Coil assembly . . . . . . 20-24 in.-lbs.
(2.3-2.7 N·m)

8/32 Automatic oiler
pump . . . . 35-42 in.-lbs.
(3.9-4.7 N·m)

8/32 Fuel tank . . . . 35-42 in.-lbs.
(3.9-4.7 N·m)

10/32 Main bearing
retainer screws . . . . 50-60 in.-lbs.
(5.6-6.8 N·m)

10/32 Stack muffler . . . . . . 50-60 in.-lbs.
(5.6-6.8 N·m)

10/32 Muffler body . . . . 50-60 in.-lbs.
(5.6-6.8 N·m)

10/32 Muffler cap . . . . 35-42 in.-lbs.
(3.9-4.7 N·m)

10/32 Starter housing . . . . . 50-60 in.-lbs.
(5.6-6.8 N·m)

10/32 Carburetor . . . . 20-24 in.-lbs.
(2.3-2.7 N·m)

10/32 Starter pawl
studs . . . . 50-60 in.-lbs.
(5.6-6.8 N·m)

10/32 Handle bar . . . . 50-60 in.-lbs.
(5.6-6.8 N·m)

12/24 Throttle handle . . . . . 80-96 in.-lbs.
(9.0-10.8 N·m)

12/24 Fuel tank to
crankcase . . . . 75-90 in.-lbs.
(8.5-10.2 N·m)

12/24 Drivecase . . . . 75-90 in.-lbs.
(8.5-10.2 N·m)

1/4-28 Cylinder nuts . . . . 100-120 in.-lbs.
(11.3-13.6 N·m)

5/16-24 Rotor (flywheel)
nut . . . . 100-120 in.-lbs.
(11.3-13.6 N·m)

14 mm Spark plug . . . . . 120-144 in.-lbs.
(11.3-16.3 N·m)

Clutch . . . . 180-216 in.-lbs.
(20.3-24.4 N·m)

SPECIAL SERVICE TOOLS. Special service tools which may be required are listed as follows:

Tool No.	Description & Model Usage
24299 –	Anvil, crankshaft installation.
24300 –	Sleeve, crankshaft bearing.
24294 –	Plug, needle bearing assembly.
24292 –	Plug, seal removal.
24298 –	Plug, bearing and seal.
24320 –	#3 Pozidriv screwdriver bit.
24982-1 –	Torx driver bit.
A-24290 –	Bracket, rotor remover.
A-24060 –	Wrench, clutch spanner.
A-24309 –	Jackscrew, crankshaft and bearing.
23136-1 –	Body for A-24309.
24295 –	Bearing collar for A-24309.
24291 –	Sleeve, drivecase seal.

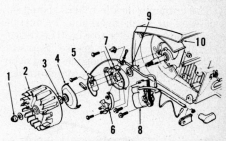

Fig. HL5— Exploded view of ignition assembly. Felt seal (3) is cemented to breaker-box cover (4).

1. Nut
2. Flywheel
3. Felt seal
4. Box cover
5. Condenser
6. Breaker-points
7. Breaker-box
8. Ignition coil
9. Felt seal
10. Fuel tank

Fig. HL3— Before tightening screws retaining air filter bracket in throttle handle, place air filter element on bracket stud and align filter with edges of air box.

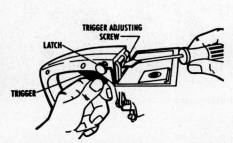

Fig. HL4— Refer to text for procedures to adjust starting speed.

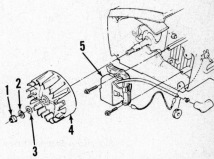

Fig. HL6— Exploded view of solid-state ignition used on later Super EZ Automatic models.

1. Nut
2. Lockwasher
3. Washer
4. Flywheel
5. Ignition module

24297—Sleeve, crankcase seal.
JA-31316-4—Test spark plug.
17789—Carburetor repair tool kit.
A-93791—Wrench, "S" clutch.
94197—Carburetor tester.
94194—Compression gage.

COMPRESSION PRESSURE. For optimum performance of Model Super EZ Automatic, cylinder compression pressure should be 155-185 psi (1069-1275 kPa) with engine at normal operating temperature. Engine should be inspected and repaired when compression pressure is 90 psi (620 kPa) or below.

CONNECTING ROD. Connecting rod and piston assembly can be detached from crankshaft after removing cylinder; refer to Fig. HL8. Be careful to remove all of the 28 loose needle bearing rollers.

Renew connecting rod if bent, twisted or if crankpin bearing surface shows visible wear or is scored. The needle roller bearing for piston pin should be renewed if any roller shows flat spots or if worn so that any two rollers can be separated the width equal to thickness of one roller and if rod is otherwise serviceable. Press on lettered side of bearing cage only when removing and installing bearing.

The crankpin needle rollers should be renewed at each overhaul. To install connecting rod, refer to Fig. HL8. Stick 14 rollers in cap with grease. Support rod cap in crankcase, then place rod over crankpin and to cap with match marks

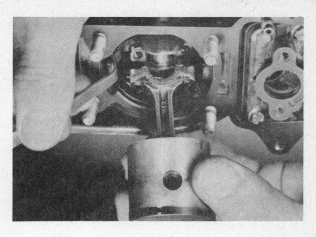

Fig. HL8—Installing piston and connecting rod assembly using locally made tool to hold rod cap in position. Tool can be made from flat strip of metal. Using grease, stick 14 rollers in cap and 14 rollers in rod; make sure that match marks on rod and cap are aligned.

aligned and install new retaining cap screws.

PISTON, PIN AND RINGS. The piston has two pinned piston rings. The rings should be renewed whenever engine is disassembled for service.

Piston pin is retained in piston by "Rulon" plastic plugs. Insert a plug at each end of pin in piston bore and be sure piston pin and plugs are centered in piston.

Assemble piston to connecting rod so piston ring locating pin is toward intake side (away from exhaust port).

CYLINDER. The cylinder can be unbolted and removed from crankcase after removing starter housing and throttle handle. Be careful not to let piston strike crankcase as cylinder is removed.

The cylinder bore is chrome plated and cylinder should be renewed if the chrome plating has worn through exposing the softer base metal. Also inspect for cracks and damage to compression release valve bore.

CRANKSHAFT, BEARINGS AND SEALS. Crankshaft is supported by a roller bearing (19—Fig. HL7) mounted in crankcase bore and by a ball bearing (23) mounted in drivecase (18).

To remove crankshaft, first remove clutch assembly, automatic oil pump on models so equipped, starter housing, magneto rotor, throttle handle, cylinder, piston and connecting rod assembly and the fuel/oil tank assembly. Remove retaining screws and separate drivecase and crankshaft from crankcase.

NOTE: Use "Pozidriv" or "Torx" screwdriver bit, according to type of screw head, only when removing drivecase to fuel tank cover screw (25).

Remove the two main bearing retaining screws (21) and bearing retainers (22), then push crankshaft and ball bearing (23) from drivecase. Remove snap ring (24) and press crankshaft from ball bearing.

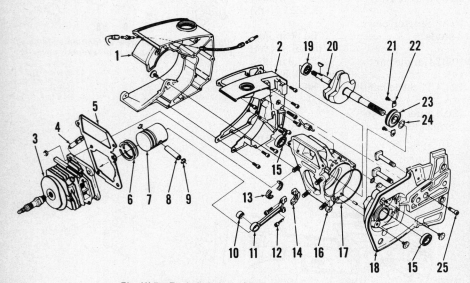

Fig. HL7—Exploded view of typical engine assembly.

1. Fuel tank	14. Connecting rod cap
2. Oil tank	15. Seal
3. Cylinder	16. Crankcase
4. Compression release valve	17. "O" ring
5. Gasket	18. Drivecase
6. Piston rings	19. Roller bearing
7. Piston	20. Crankshaft
8. Piston pin	21. Screw
9. Pin retainer	22. Bearing retainer
10. Needle bearing	23. Ball bearing
11. Connecting rod	24. Snap ring
12. Cap screw	25. Screw
13. Bearing rollers (28)	

Fig. HL9—Roller type main bearing used at flywheel end of crankshaft is marked on one side, "PRESS OTHER SIDE." Be sure to observe this precaution when installing bearing in crankcase.

Illustrations Courtesy Homelite Div. of Textron, ©1987

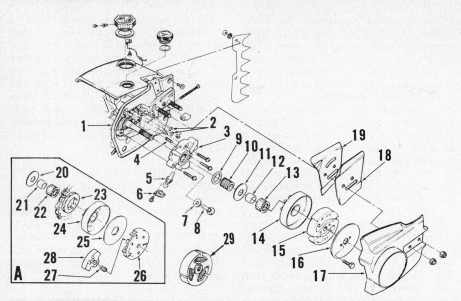

Fig. HL10 — Exploded view of automatic oil pump and clutch assemblies. Inset A shows three-shoe type clutch. Sprocket (23) and clutch drum (24) are integral on some models. Clutch assembly (29) is later three-shoe type.

1. Drivecase
2. "O" rings
3. Oil pump body
4. Tube
5. Gear
6. Cap
7. Gasket
8. Cam screw
9. Seal
10. Worm gear
11. Thrust washer
12. Inner race
13. Bearing
14. Clutch drum
15. Hub
16. Cover
17. Drivecase cover
18. Outer guide plate
19. Inner guide plate
20. Thrust washer
21. Inner race
22. Bearing
23. Sprocket
24. Clutch drum
25. Thrust washer
26. Clutch hub
27. Spring
28. Clutch shoe
29. Clutch assy.

Fig. HL10A — View of correct installation of "S" type clutch hub in drum.

When reassembling, be sure groove in outer race of ball bearing is towards crankpin and that retaining snap ring is seated in groove on crankshaft. Install new seals (15) with lip of seal inward. Using protector sleeve to prevent damage to seal, press the crankshaft and ball bearing into drivecase and install new retaining screws and washers. Assemble crankcase to crankshaft and drivecase using new "O" ring (17) and protector sleeve to prevent damage to crankcase seal. Be sure bar studs are in place before installing fuel tank.

COMPRESSION RELEASE. When throttle lock is pushed in, a lever connected to throttle lock lifts away from compression release valve (4 – Fig.

HL7). When engine is cranked, compression forces valve open and compression is partly relieved through port in cylinder. Squeezing throttle trigger after engine is running releases throttle lock, allowing spring (11 – Fig. HL1) to snap lever against release valve, closing the valve.

Service of compression release valve usually consists of cleaning valve seat and port in cylinder as carbon may gradually fill the port.

When overhauling engine, cylinder should be inspected for any damage to compression release port.

PYRAMID REED VALVE. A "Delrin" plastic pyramid type reed intake valve seat and four reeds are used. Reeds are retained on pins projecting from the reed seat by a moulded retainer. Inspect reed seat, retainer and reeds for any distortion, excessive wear or other damage.

To reinstall, use a drop of oil to stick each reed to the plastic seat, then push reed retainer down over the seat and reeds. Then install the assembly in crankcase; never install retainer, then attempt to install reed seat and reeds.

AUTOMATIC CHAIN OILER PUMP. Refer to Fig. HL10 for exploded view showing automatic chain oiler pump installation. After removing clutch, the pump can be removed from crankshaft and drivecase. The pump body, flange and plunger are available as a complete pump assembly, less worm gear, only. Check valve parts, cam screw and worm gear are available separately. If pump body and/or plunger are scored or excessively worn, it will be necessary to install a new pump.

CLUTCH. Refer to Fig. HL10 for exploded view of types of clutches used. Early models were equipped with three-shoe clutch shown in Inset A. "S" type clutch (15) was used next and later

Fig. HL11 — View showing easy method of installing clutch shoes and springs. Model EZ clutch is not shown; however, method is same.

Fig. HL12 — Exploded view of rewind starter used on early models.

1. Stud
2. Spring
3. Pawl
4. Washer
5. Nut
6. Flywheel
7. Cover
8. Spring shield
9. Spring lock
10. Rewind spring
11. Spring shield
12. Snap ring
13. Rope pulley
14. Washer
15. Bushing
16. Screen
17. Starter housing
18. Rope handle

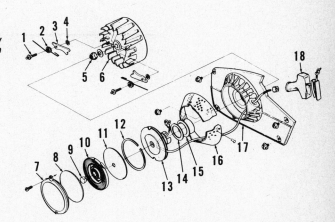

models are equipped with three-shoe clutch (29).

The clutch hub on all types has left hand threads. Special tool A-93791 may be used when removing or installing "S" type clutch while tool A-24060 may be used when removing or installing three-shoe type clutch.

Clean and inspect clutch hub, drum and bearing for damage or excessive wear. Inspect crankshaft for wear or damage caused by a defective clutch bearing. Refer to Fig. HL10A for correct installation of "S" type clutch. Tighten "S" clutch hub to 100 in.-lbs. (11.3 N·m).

Install clutch shoes on early three-shoe clutch as shown in Fig. HL11. Install either three-shoe clutch so "OFF" on hub faces out. Tighten early three-shoe clutch hub (26 – Fig. HL10) to 180 in.-lbs. (20.3 N·m). Tighten later clutch hub (29) to 250-300 in.-lbs. (28.2-33.9 N·m).

REWIND STARTER. Exploded view of early production rewind starter is shown in Fig. HL12 and late production rewind starter is shown in Fig. HL13. Starter can be removed as a complete unit by removing housing retaining screws.

To disassemble starter on early models, hold cover (7 – Fig. HL12) while removing retaining screws, then allow cover to turn slowly until spring tension is released. Remainder of disassembly is evident from inspection of unit and with reference to exploded view.

To disassemble starter on late models, pull starter rope fully out, hold starter pulley (8 – Fig. HL13) from turning, pull all slack in rope out inner side of fan housing and allow pulley to unwind slowly until spring tension is relieved. Remainder of disassembly is evident from inspection of unit and with reference to exploded view.

Fig. HL14 shows correct installation of starter dogs on flywheel for early models, late models will be similar. When installing a new starter rope, knot rope ends and coat with Duxseal, then trim excess rope next to knot. Rewind spring is wound in clockwise direction in cover (7 – Fig. HL12) or housing (11 – Fig. HL13).

Set rewind spring tension as follows: On early models, turn cover (7 – Fig. HL12) in a clockwise direction to pull rope handle against starter housing, then continue turning cover three more times.

On late models, hook rope in notch on flywheel side of pulley (8 – Fig. 13), then pull up loop of cord between notch and housing (11). Turn pulley in a clockwise direction three turns and hold. Pull rope handle, removing all slack in rope and disengage rope from notch. Release rope handle. If handle is not snug against starter housing, repeat tensioning procedure turning pulley only one turn at a time.

MUFFLER. Some later Super EZ Automatic models may experience vapor lock due to exhaust gas directed toward drivecase cover. The air filter and carburetor may be discolored due to heat. Muffler #A96580 with deflector (D – Fig. HL15) may be installed to prevent hot exhaust gas from reaching drivecase cover.

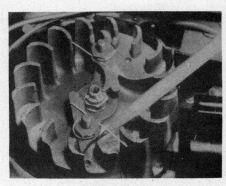

Fig. HL14 – View showing proper installation of pawl springs.

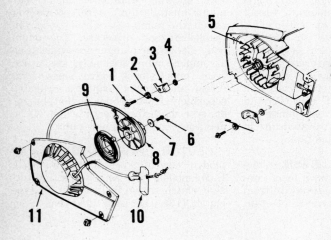

Fig. HL13 – Exploded view of rewind starter used on late models.

1. Stud
2. Spring
3. Pawl
4. Washer
5. Flywheel
6. Screw
7. Washer
8. Rope pulley
9. Rewind spring
10. Rope handle
11. Starter housing

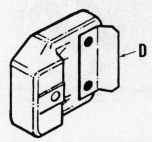

Fig. HL15 – View of Super EZ Automatic muffler #A96580 with exhaust gas deflector (D).

Illustrations Courtesy Homelite Div. of Textron, ©1987

HOMELITE

Model	Bore	Stroke	Displ.	Drive Type
XL-12	1¾ in. (44.4 mm)	1⅜ in. (34.9 mm)	3.3 cu. in. (54.1 cc)	Direct
Super XL Automatic	1-13/16 in. (46.0 mm)	1⅜ in. (34.9 mm)	3.55 cu. in. (58.2 cc)	Direct

MAINTENANCE

SPARK PLUG. Model XL-12 is equipped with a Champion CJ8 spark plug while Model Super XL Automatic uses a CJ6. For heavy duty service, a Champion UTJ11P gold-paladium tip spark plug can be used.

For all models, set spark plug electrode gap to 0.025 inch (0.63 mm).

CARBURETOR. A Tillotson HS, Walbro SDC or Zama diaphragm carburetor is used. Refer to CARBURETOR SERVICE section for service procedures and exploded views.

Initial adjustment of idle mixture screw is 1¾ turns open and for high speed mixture screw is 1¼ turns open. Adjust idle mixture screw and idle speed screw so engine idles just below clutch engagement speed. Make high speed mixture adjustment with engine warm and under cutting load. It may be necessary to readjust one mixture screw after adjusting the other mixture screw as the functions of the idle and high speed mixture screws are related.

MAGNETO AND TIMING. A Wico or Phelon flywheel type magneto with external armature is used on early models while late models are equipped with solid state ignition. The solid state ignition system is serviced by renewing the spark plug and/or ignition module. Air gap between ignition module and flywheel is adjustable. Adjust air gap by loosening module retaining screws and place a 0.015 inch (0.38 mm) shim stock between flywheel and module. Remove shim stock.

Note the following on breaker-point equipped models: Units equipped with Phelon magneto will have a letter "P" stamped after the serial number. The Wico and Phelon magnetos are similarly constructed, so care should be taken to properly identify magneto before ordering service parts. Breaker-points and condenser are located behind flywheel.

Armature core and stator plate are riveted together and are serviced only as a unit. Stator plate fits firmly on shoulder of crankcase; hence, armature air gap is nonadjustable.

Late production Wico magneto stator plates are built to retain a felt seal (5 – Fig. HL33); the seal cannot be used with early production Wico stator plates. All Phelon stator plates are built to retain the felt seal (5).

Magneto stator plate has slotted mounting holes, and should be rotated as far clockwise as possible before tightening mounting screws to obtain correct ignition timing of 30 degrees BTDC. Set breaker point gap to 0.015 inch (0.38 mm). Condenser capacity should test 0.16-0.20 mfd.

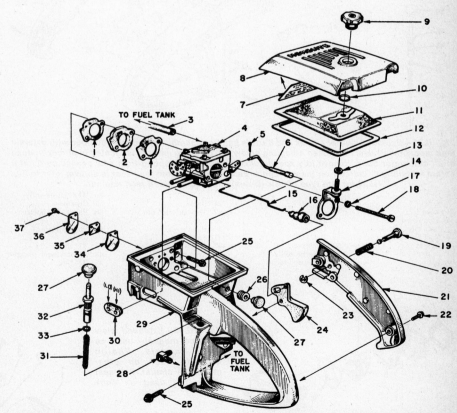

Fig. HL30 — Exploded view of air box (throttle handle) and related parts on models with flat reed intake valve (34). Refer to Fig. HL31 for models equipped with pyramid reed valve.

1. Gasket	10. Snap ring	19. Throttle latch pin	29. Air box
2. Insulator	11. Filter element	20. Spring	30. Grommet
3. Fuel line	12. Gasket	23. Snap ring	31. Spring
4. Carburetor	13. Gasket	24. Throttle trigger	32. Pump plunger
5. Cotter pin	14. Bracket	26. Grommet	33. "O" ring
6. Choke rod	15. Throttle rod	27. Choke button	34. Reed valve
8. Filter cover	16. Boot	28. Check valve	35. Reed back-up
9. Nut			36. Reed stop

CAUTION: Be careful when installing breaker-points not to bend tension spring any more than necessary; if spring is bent excessively, spring tension may be reduced causing improper breaker-point operation. Late Wico units have a retaining clip and flat washer to secure breaker arm on pivot post.

LUBRICATION. The engine is lubricated mixing oil with unleaded gasoline. Recommended oil is Homelite® two-stroke oil mixed at ratio as designated on oil container. If Homelite® oil is not available, a good quality oil designed for two-stroke engines may be used when mixed at a 16:1 ratio, however, an antioxidant fuel stabilizer (such as Sta-Bil) should be added to fuel mix. Antioxidant fuel stabilizer is not required with Homelite® oils as they contain fuel stabilizer so the fuel mix will stay fresh up to one year.

Fill chain oiler reservoir with Homelite® Bar and Chain oil or a light weight oil (no heavier than SAE 30). In cold weather, chain oil can be diluted with kerosene to allow easier flow of oil through pump and lines.

CARBON. Muffler and cylinder exhaust ports should be cleaned periodically to prevent loss of power due to carbon build up. Remove muffler and scrape free of carbon. With muffler removed, turn engine so that piston is at top dead center and carefully remove carbon from exhaust ports with a wooden scraper. Be careful not to damage chamfered edges of exhaust ports or to scratch piston. **Do not** run engine with muffler removed.

REPAIRS

TIGHTENING TORQUE VALUES. Tightening torque values are as follows:

4/40 Reed & stop to
   chamber . . . . .5-6 in.-lbs.
                 (0.6-0.7 N·m)

4/20 Oil line plate or
   shield to tank . . . . .5-6 in.-lbs.
                 (0.6-0.7 N·m)

8/32 Throttle handle
   cover . . . . .40-48 in.-lbs.
                 (4.5-5.4 N·m)

8/36 Connecting rod . . . . . .55-66 in.-lbs.
                 (6.2-7.5 N·m)

10/32 Muffler cap . . . . .50-60 in.-lbs.
                 (5.6-6.8 N·m)

10/32 Bearing retainer . . . .55-66 in.-lbs.
                 (6.2-7.5 N·m)

10/32 Screen to rotor . . . . .50-60 in.-lbs.
                 (5.6-6.8 N·m)

10/32 Drivecase cover . . . . .55-66 in.-lbs.
                 (6.2-7.5 N·m)

Fig. HL31 — Exploded view of air box and throttle handle assembly for models equipped with pyramid reed type intake valve. Idle speed adjusting screw (23) on some models, is located in air box instead of on carburetor body; remove idle speed adjusting screw and spring from new service carburetor before installing carburetor on these models. Early type aluminum reed seat is shown; refer to Fig. HL32 for late type plastic (Delrin) seat and moulded reed retainer.

1. Gaskets	11. Gasket	24. Boot	36. "Out" check valve
2. Spacer	14. Cover	27. Throttle latch pin	37. Grommet
3. Reed seat	17. Filter	28. Spring	38. Plug (AO models)
4. Valve reeds (4)	18. Gasket	29. Handle cover	39. Gasket
5. Retaining plates	19. Bracket	31. Snap ring	40. Spring (manual
7. Fuel line	20. Choke rod	32. Throttle trigger	oiler)
8. Gasket	21. Throttle rod	33. Grommet	41. "O" ring
9. Carburetor	23. Idle speed screw	35. "In" check valve	43. Manual pump plunger
10. Air box			43. "O" ring

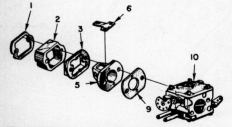

Fig. HL32 — View showing late type Delrin plastic reed seat (5) and moulded reed retainer (3). Reeds (6) are held on pins protruding from seat by the retainer. Refer to text for assembly instructions.

1. Gasket	
2. Spacer	
3. Reed retainer	6. Reeds (4)
5. Reed seat	9. Gasket
	10. Carburetor

Fig. HL33 — Exploded view of Wico magneto used on some models. Phelon magneto used on other models is similar. Felt seal (5) is not used on early models.

1. Flywheel
2. Cover
3. Gasket
4. Breaker-points
5. Felt seal
6. Gasket
7. Condenser
8. Ignition coil
9. Coil clip
10. Armature core
11. Stator plate

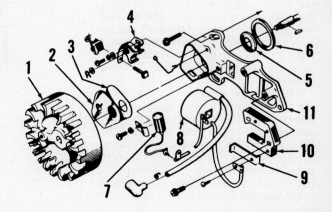

Illustrations Courtesy Homelite Div. of Textron, ©1987

10/32 Pulley to fan
housing . . . . .50-60 in.-lbs.
(5.6-6.8 N·m)

10/32 Flanged inner
race for pulley . . . . .55-66 in.-lbs.
(6.2-7.5 N·m)

10/32 Carburetor to
chamber . . . . .50-60 in.-lbs.
(5.6-6.8 N·m)

12/24 Handle bar to
fuel tank . . . . .80-96 in.-lbs.
(9.0-10.8 N·m)

12/24 Bracket to
drivecase . . . . .80-96 in.-lbs.
(9.0-10.8 N·m)

12/24 Stator to crankcase
and cylinder . . . . .80-96 in.-lbs.
(9.0-10.8 N·m)

12/24 Drivecase to
crankcase . . . . .80-96 in.-lbs.
(9.0-10.8 N·m)

12/24 Carburetor
chamber to fuel tank . . . .80-96 in.-lbs.
(9.0-10.8 N·m)

12/24 Muffler to cylinder . .80-96 in.-lbs.
(9.0-10.8 N·m)

1/4-20 Fuel tank to
crankcase . . . . .80-96 in.-lbs.
(9.0-10.8 N·m)

12/24 Fan housing to
fuel tank . . . . .80-96 in.-lbs.
(9.0-10.8 N·m)

1/4-28 Cylinder nuts . . . .100-120 in.-lbs.
(11.3-13.6 N·m)

12/24 Pawl studs to
rotor . . . . .80-96 in.-lbs.
(9.0-10.8 N·m)

1/4-20 Handle bar to
bracket . . . . .100-120 in.-lbs.
(11.3-13.6 N·m)

1/4-20 Bumper screws . . . .80-96 in.-lbs.
(9.0-10.8 N·m)

3/8-24 Clutch nut . . . . . . .150-180 in.-lbs.
(16.9-20.3 N·m)

5/8-32 Clutch . . . . .150-180 in.-lbs.
(16.9-20.3 N·m)

5/16-24 Rotor nut . . . . . . .150-180 in.-lbs.
(16.9-20.3 N·m)

1/2-20 Clutch to
crankshaft . . . . .150-180 in.-lbs.
(16.9-20.3 N·m)

14 mm Spark plug . . . . .250-300 in.-lbs.
(28.2-33.9 N·m)

Clutch spider . . . . .180-216 in.-lbs.
(20.3-24.4 N·m)

HOMELITE SERVICE TOOLS.

Listed below are Homelite tool numbers, tool description and model application of tools for servicing.

Tool No.   Description & Model Usage
04197 – Carburetor tester
17789 – Carburetor repair tool kit.
22820-1 – Bearing collar for A-23137.
23136 – Body for A-23137.
23756 – Plug, connecting rod bearing removal and installation, all models.
23757 – Plug, needle roller type main bearing installation, all models.
23758 – Plug, crankcase seal installation, all models; drivecase seal installation, Model XL-12.
23759 – Sleeve, crankcase seal protector, all models; drivecase seal protector, Model XL-12.

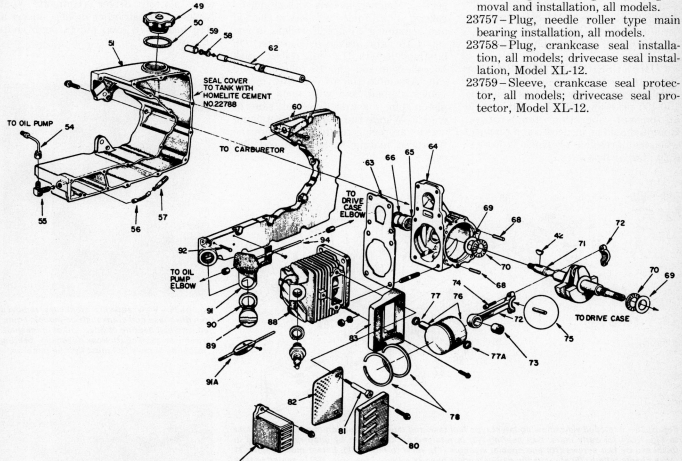

Fig. HL34 – Exploded view showing power head and fuel tank construction of Model XL-12; refer to Fig. HL35 for Model Super XL Automatic. Dowel pin (68) are used on later models. Refer to text. Single or two-piece muffler may be used. Shield (91) is not used on later models.

42. Woodruff key	58. Fuel pickup	66. Crankshaft seal	80. Muffler cap
49. Fuel tank cap	59. Fuel filter	68. Dowel pins	81. Special studs	73. Needle bearing	78. Piston rings
50. Gasket	60. Tank cover (late)	69. Thrust washers	82. Baffle	74. Rod cap screws	90. Gasket
51. Fuel tank	62. Flexible fuel line	70. Thrust bearings	83. Muffler body	75. Needle rollers	91. Shield
54. Oil line	63. Gasket	71. Crankshaft	83A. Muffler	76. Piston & pin	91A. Plate
55. Check valve	64. Crankcase	72. Connecting rod &	88. Cylinder	77. Snap ring	92. Cotter pin
56. Oil line	65. Needle bearing	cap	89. Oil cap	77A. Snap ring	(breather)
57. Oil filter					94. Oil line

23800 – Sleeve, crankcase seal installation, all models; drivecase seal installation. Model XL-12.

23819 – Plug, clutch drum needle bearing installation, all direct drive models.

23843 – Sleeve, drive seal installation, Model Super XL Automatic.

23844 – Sleeve, drive seal protector, Model Super XL Automatic.

23845 – Plug, drivecase seal installation, Model Super XL Automatic.

23846 – Anvil, crankshaft installation, Model Super XL Automatic.

23884 – Sleeve, bearing and shaft, Model Super XL Automatic.

94194 – Compression gage.

A-23137 – Jackscrew, crankshaft assembly and installation, all models except XL-12.

A-23841-A – Wrench, guide bar stud insert, Model Super XL Automatic.

A-23934 – Wrench, clutch plate removal and installation, all late production.

A-23949 – Remover, piston pin with Spirol pin at exhaust side of piston.

A-23960 – Remover and locking bracket, rotor (flywheel), all models.

JA-31316-4 – Test spark plug.

COMPRESSION PRESSURE. For optimum performance on all models, cylinder compression pressure should be 130-155 psi (896-1069 kPa) with engine at normal operating temperature. Engine should be inspected and repaired when compression pressure is 90 psi (620 kPa) or below.

CONNECTING ROD. Connecting rod and piston assembly can be removed after removing cylinder from crankcase. Refer to Fig. HL39. Be careful to remove all of the loose needle rollers when detaching rod from crankpin. Early models have 28 loose needle rollers; starting with serial number 207-1277, 31 needle rollers are used.

NOTE: A different crankshaft and connecting rod are used on late models with 31 needle rollers.

Renew connecting rod if bent or twisted, or if crankpin bearing surface is scored, burned or excessively worn. The caged needle roller piston pin bearing can be renewed by pressing old bearing out and pressing new bearing in with Homelite tool 23756. Press on lettered end of bearing cage only.

It is recommended that the crankpin needle rollers be renewed as a set whenever engine is disassembled for service. On early models with 28 needle rollers, stick 14 needle rollers in the rod and remaining 14 needle rollers in rod cap with light grease or beeswax. On late models with 31 needle rollers, stick 16 rollers in rod and 15 rollers in rod cap. Assemble rod to cap with match marks aligned, and with open end of piston pin towards flywheel side of engine. Wiggle the rod as cap retaining screws are being tightened to align the fractured mating surfaces of rod and cap.

PISTON, PIN AND RINGS. The piston is fitted with two pinned compression rings. Renew piston if scored, cracked or excessively worn, or if ring side clearance in top ring groove exceeds 0.0035 inch (0.089 mm).

Recommended piston ring end gap is 0.070-0.080 inch (1.78-2.03 mm); maximum allowable ring end gap is 0.085 inch (2.16 mm). Desired ring side clearance in groove is 0.002-0.003 inch (0.05-0.08 mm).

Piston, pin and rings are available in standard size only. Piston and pin are available in a matched set, and are not available separately.

Piston pin has one open and one closed end and may be retained in piston with snap rings or a Spirol pin. A wire retaining ring is used on exhaust side of piston on some models and should be removed.

To remove piston pin on all models, remove the snap ring at intake side of piston. On piston with Spirol pin at exhaust side, drive pin from piston rod with slotted driver (Homelite tool A-23949). On all other models, insert a 3/16 inch (4.76 mm) pin through snap

Fig. HL36 – View showing crankcase removed from drivecase and crankshaft on models equipped with ball bearing at drive end of crankshaft. To remove crankshaft from drivecase, bearing retaining screws (70) must first be removed.

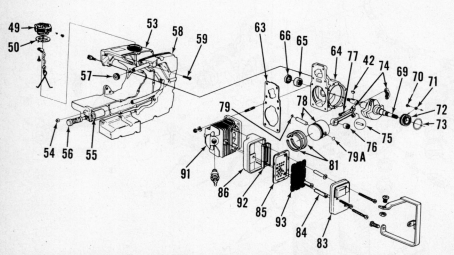

Fig. HL35 – Exploded view showing latest type fuel tank and later construction of power head; refer to Fig. HL34 for early units. Ball bearing (72) is retained on crankshaft by snap ring (73) and in drivecase by two screws (70) and special washers (71); refer to Fig. HL36. Latest models have 31 loose needle rollers (75) at crankpin; earlier models have 28 rollers. Tank cover (58) is sealed to tank (53) with cement (Homelite part 22788) and is retained with 16 screws (59). Later tanks are permanently bonded.

Fig. HL38 – Be sure the steel thrust washers (26) are to outside of thrust bearings (27) when installing crankshaft on Model XL-12. Model Super XL Automatic does not use thrust washers or thrust bearings.

42. Woodruff key	59. Screws (16)	72. Ball bearing
49. Fuel tank cap	63. Gasket	73. Snap ring
50. Gasket	64. Crankcase	74. Connecting rod
53. Fuel tank	65. Needle bearing	75. Needle rollers
54. Pipe plug	66. Crankshaft seal	76. Needle bearing
55. Fuel filter	69. Crankshaft	77. Rod cap screws
56. Pick-up head	70. Bearing screws	78. Piston & pin
57. Grommet	71. Special washers	79. Snap ring
58. Fuel tank cover		

79A. Snap ring	
81. Piston rings	
83. Muffler cap	
84. Special studs	
85. Baffle	
86. Muffler body	
91. Cylinder	
92. Plate	
93. Spark arrestor	

ring at exhaust side and drive piston pin out as shown in Fig. HL40.

When reassembling piston to connecting rod, be sure to install closed end of piston pin towards exhaust side of piston (away from piston ring locating pin). Fit the Waldes Truarc snap ring in groove of pin bore with sharp edge out and turn ring gap towards closed end of piston.

CRANKSHAFT AND BEARINGS. On Model XL-12 the crankshaft is supported in two caged needle roller bearings and crankshaft end play is controlled by a roller bearing and hardened steel thrust washer on each end of the shaft. Refer to Fig. HL38. On Model Super XL Automatic, flywheel end of crankshaft is supported in a needle bearing in crankcase and drive end is supported in a ball bearing located in drivecase; end play is controlled by the ball bearing.

Maximum allowable crankshaft end play on models with thrust bearings (Fig. HL38) is 0.020 inch (0.51 mm); renew thrust bearings if end play is excessive. Normal end play is approximately 0.010 inch (0.25 mm).

Renew the crankshaft if any of the main bearing, crankpin bearing or thrust bearing surfaces or sealing surfaces are scored, burned or excessively worn. Renew the drivecase ball bearing

if excessively loose or rough. Also, reject crankshaft if flywheel keyway is beat out or if threads are badly damaged.

CYLINDER. The cylinder bore is chrome plated. Renew the cylinder if chrome plating is worn away exposing the softer base metal.

CRANKCASE, DRIVECASE AND SEALS. On all models, crankshaft seals can be renewed without disassembling crankcase, drivecase and crankshaft unit. With magneto armature and core assembly removed, pry seal from crankcase. Install new seal over crankshaft with lip of seal inward, then using driver sleeve, drive seal into crankcase. Seal in drivecase can be pried out after removing clutch assembly and, on models so equipped, the automatic chain oiler pump. Install seal with lip inward and drive into position with sleeve.

NOTE: Use of seal protectors is recommended; if protectors are not available, wrap threads on crankshaft with thin plastic tape to prevent damage to seal lips.

Crankcase can be removed from crankcase and drivecase after removing cylinder, piston and connecting rod and removing retaining screws. On Model XL-12, crankshaft can be withdrawn from drivecase. On Model Super XL Automatic, remove the two bearing retaining screws (70—Fig. HL35) special washers (71), then press crankshaft and ball bearing (72) from drivecase. Remove snap ring (73), then press crankshaft out of the ball bearing.

Inspect the needle roller bearing in crankcase, and on Model XL-12, the needle roller bearing in drivecase. Bearings should be renewed if any needle roller has flat spots or is otherwise damaged, or if rollers are worn so any two rollers can be separated a width equal to thickness of one roller. Always press against lettered end of bearing cage when removing and installing needle roller bearings. Needle roller bearings

should be installed using appropriate installation plug.

Install new ball bearing on crankshaft using jackscrew or by supporting crankshaft at crank throw and installing bearing in a press. Groove in outer race of bearing must be toward crankpin.

Renew crankshaft seals before assembling crankshaft, crankcase and drivecase. Using installation plug, press seal into position with lip to inside of crankcase. On Model XL-12, install thrust bearings on crankshaft next to crankpin throw, then install the hardened steel rust washers at outer side of each thrust bearing. On Model Super XL Automatic, first assemble crankshaft and drivecase by placing seal protector on crankshaft, then pulling crankshaft and ball bearing into drivecase with jackscrew and adapters. Install two NEW bearing retaining screws and lockwashers. On Model XL-12, place seal protector on crankshaft and insert crankshaft in crankcase. Then, on all models, assemble crankcase to drivecase using new gasket.

NOTE: On early production, crankcase was sealed to drivecase with an "O" ring; however, use of "O" ring has been discontinued and a gasket, rather than an "O" ring, should be used on all models.

On all late production models, crankcase is fitted with dowel pins to provide a more positive alignment of crankcase and drivecase. Service crankcases are drilled for dowel pins, but dowel pins are not installed so crankcase can be used with early type drivecase not drilled for dowels. If renewing late type crankcase fitted with dowel pins, two new dowel pins must be obtained and installed in new crankcase; install dowel pins so they protrude 0.165-0.180 inch (4.19-4.57 mm) from crankcase.

PYRAMID REED VALVE. All models are equipped with a pyramid reed type intake valve with four reeds. Early production reed seat was made of

Fig. HL39 — Piston and connecting rod assembly can be removed from crankpin after removing cylinder from crankcase. Note piston ring locating pin on intake side of piston.

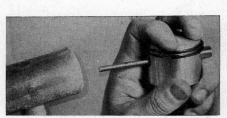

Fig. HL40 — After removing snap rings the piston pin can be tapped out using a 3/16 inch (4.76 mm) rod as shown or, on pistons with Spirol pin at exhaust side, by driving piston pin out with slotted driver (Homelite tool A23949).

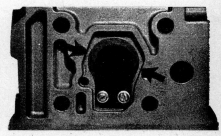

Fig. HL41 — When installing reed valve on air box (models with flat reed intake valve only), be sure reed is centered between the two points indicated by arrows.

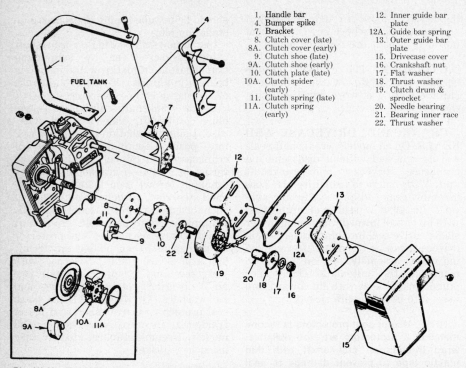

1. Handle bar	12. Inner guide bar plate
4. Bumper spike	12A. Guide bar spring
7. Bracket	13. Outer guide bar plate
8. Clutch cover (late)	15. Drivecase cover
8A. Clutch cover (early)	16. Crankshaft nut
9. Clutch shoe (late)	17. Flat washer
9A. Clutch shoe (early)	18. Thrust washer
10. Clutch plate (late)	19. Clutch drum & sprocket
10A. Clutch spider (early)	20. Needle bearing
11. Clutch spring (late)	21. Bearing inner race
11A. Clutch spring (early)	22. Thrust washer

Fig. HL42 — Exploded view of typical direct drive clutch assembly. Late type clutch assembly (items 8, 9, 10 & 11) is interchangeable as a unit with early production clutch shown in inset at lower left corner.

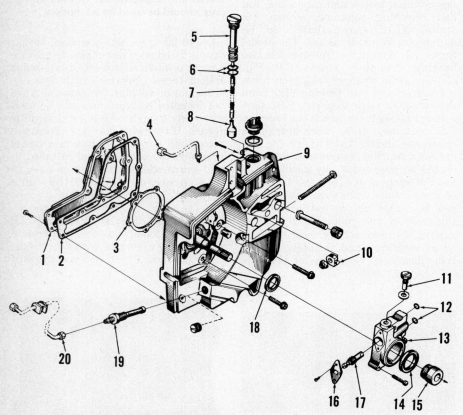

Fig. HL43 — Exploded view of automatic chain oil pump on models so equipped.

1. Oil reservoir cover	6. "O" rings	10. Bar adjusting pin	14. Felt seal
2. Gasket	7. Oil line	11. Cam screw	15. Worm gear
3. Gasket	8. Oil filter	12. "O" rings	16. Flange
4. Oil line	9. Drivecase	13. Pump body	17. Plunger
5. Oil line tube			18. Crankshaft seal

aluminum and reeds were retained to seat by spring plates and screws.

Late production reed seat (see Fig. HL32) is made of Delrin plastic. The reeds fit onto pins protruding from the plastic seat and are held in place by a molded retainer, eliminating the retaining spring plates and screws.

Reeds, spring plates and retaining screws are available for servicing the early type aluminum reed seat. However, if the seat is worn or damaged beyond further use, the Delrin seat and molded retainer is used as replacement.

When assembling reeds to aluminum seat, apply Loctite to retaining screws to keep them from working loose. Renew the spacer gaskets and carburetor gasket and install the spacer, reed seal assembly and carburetor as in Fig. HL31.

To assemble and install Delrin reed seat and reeds, proceed as follows: Fit reed retainer (3 – Fig. HL32) into spacer (2) so the pin on retainer clears cut-out in spacer. Using a drop of oil under each reed, stick the reeds to pyramid seat so holes in reeds fit over the pins molded into seat. Place the retainer and spacer over the reeds and seat so all parts are locked together, then install the valve assembly and carburetor with new gaskets (1 and 8).

CLUTCH. Refer to Fig. HL42 for exploded view of typical clutch assembly. Illustration shows late type clutch assembly using three compression springs (11) to hold shoes retracted in plate (10) and in insets at lower left corner, the early type clutch using garter type springs (11A) to hold shoes to spider (10A). The early type clutch (inset) and late type clutch are interchangeable as an assembly. Clutch plate (10) or spider (10A) is threaded to crankshaft.

If clutch will not disengage (chain continues to turn) with engine at idle speed, check for broken, weak or improperly installed clutch springs. If clutch slips under load and engine continues to run at high speed, excessive wear of clutch shoes is indicated.

On early production Model XL-12, clutch drum was equipped with an Oilite bushing. All later clutch drums, including service clutch drum for early XL-12, are fitted with caged needle roller bearings. When renewing early bushing type clutch drum, a new needle bearing inner race must also be installed.

Renew needle roller bearing inner race if wear marks are visible. Renew bearing in clutch drum if any roller has flat spots or is damaged, or if worn to extent that any two rollers can be separated the width equal to the thickness of one roller. Using installer plug, press against lettered side of needle bearing cage when installing bearing.

Refer to Fig. HL47 for assembly of late type clutch.

AUTOMATIC CHAIN OILER PUMP.
Refer to Fig. HL43 for exploded view of typical automatic oiler pump installation, and to Fig. HL44 for schematic view showing pump operation.

The automatic oiler pump pump is accessible after removing the clutch assembly from crankshaft and disconnecting oil lines. Pump plunger (17–Fig. HL43) and body (13) are available as a complete assembly only which includes flange (16), cam screw (11), gasket, "O" rings (12), sealing felt (14) and flange retaining screws; however, all parts except plunger and body are available separately.

Inspect tip of cam screw (11) and cam groove on plunger (17) for wear and plunger bore in body and piston portion of plunger for scoring or wear. Renew pump assembly if body and/or piston is worn or damaged beyond further use.

REWIND STARTER. Refer to Fig. HL49 or HL50 for an exploded view of early or late rewind starter. There were some models equipped with the early starter that used some of the components shown on the later starter. Service procedures for all of these starters are the same.

To disassemble starter, pull starter rope fully out, hold starter pulley from turning, pull all slack in rope out inner side of fan housing and allow pulley to unwind slowly until spring tension is relieved. Remove the slotted hex head screw retaining pulley to post and remove starter pulley and cup with flat retaining washer. Remove the rewind spring and, if so equipped, the spring

shields, from fan housing. Remove rope from pulley and handle.

Starter pulley post in fan housing is not renewable; a new fan housing must be installed if post is broken loose, or on mid-range production models without starter post bushing, if post is worn so that pulley is not held in proper position. Renew flanged bushing on early production models if bushing is worn excessively and fan housing is serviceable. Renew rope bushing if worn.

To reassemble, proceed as follows: Do not lubricate starter spring, but apply light oil sparingly to starter post, bushing (if used) and bore of starter pulley. Place outer shield (if used) in fan housing, then install rewind spring with

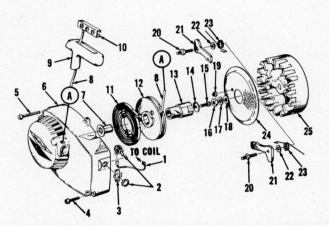

Fig. HL44 — Automatic oil pump worm gear (W) driven by crankshaft turns plunger (P) at 1/20 engine speed. As plunger turns, cam on end of plunger engages cam screw (C) causing the plunger to go back and forth. Flat end of plunger acts as inlet and outlet valve.

Fig. HL47 — View showing easy method for installing late type clutch shoes and springs on clutch plate.

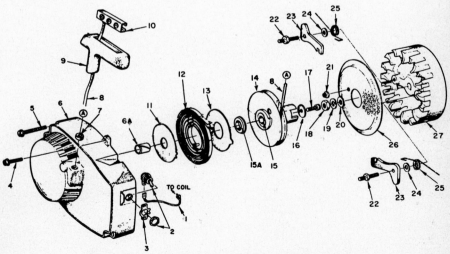

Fig. HL49 — Exploded view of early rewind starter components and related parts. Starter unit is mounted on shaft (starter post) which is an integral part of the blower housing.

1. Ground wire
2. Ignition switch
6. Blower (fan) housing
7. Bushing
8. Starter rope
9. Hand grip
10. Insert
11. Rewind spring
12. Rope pulley
13. Starter cup
14. Washer
15. Socket head screw
16. Flywheel nut
17. **Lockwasher**
18. Flat washer
20. Pawl studs
21. Pawls
22. Washers
23. Pawl springs
24. Rotating screen
25. Flywheel

Fig. HL50 — Exploded view of later production rewind starter.

1. Ground lead	10. Insert	16. Retaining washer
2. "ON-OFF" switch	11. Inner spring shield	17. Hex head screw
3. Switch plate	12. Rewind spring	18. Crankshaft nut
6. Fan housing	13. Outer spring shield	19. Lockwasher
6A. Bushing	14. Starter pulley	20. Flat washer
7. Rope bushing	15. Spring lock	21. Screen retaining nuts
8. Starter rope	15A. Spring lock bushing	22. Pawl studs
9. Starter handle		23. Starter pawls
		24. Washers
		25. Pawl springs
		26. Air screen
		27. Rotor (flywheel)

Illustrations Courtesy Homelite Div. of Textron, ©1987

Fig. HL51— When installing starter pawls (21), be sure pawl return springs (23) are located in flywheel vanes so they are parallel to the pawls as shown.

loop in outer end over spring post in fan housing and install inner spring shield (if used). Attach starter cord to pulley, insert rope through rope bore or bushing in fan housing and attach handle and insert to outer end of rope. Wind rope on-to starter pulley. Place pulley and starter cup (with spring lock and spring lock bushing if integral pulley and lock are used) on starter post and be sure spring lock or pulley is properly engaged with rewind spring. Install retaining washer and hex head screw and tighten screw to 50 in.-lbs. (5.6 N·m). Pull rope out about two feet and hold pulley from turning. Locate notch in pulley at cord insert in housing and pull up loop of cord between notch and housing. Holding on-to pulley, wind cord three more turns onto pulley by turning pulley, then let spring rewind pulley until handle is pulled against fan housing.

HOMELITE

Model	Bore	Stroke	Displ.	Drive Type
C-72	2 in. (50.8 mm)	1-9/16 in. (39.7 mm)	4.9 cu. in. (80.3 cc)	Direct*
S1050 Automatic	2-3/16 in. (55.6 mm)	1-5/8 in. (41.3 mm)	6.1 cu. in. (100.0 cc)	Direct
S1130G	2-3/16 in. (55.6 mm)	1-5/8 in. (41.3 mm)	6.1 cu. in. (100.0 cc)	†
Super 2100 Automatic	2-1/4 in. (57.1 mm)	1-3/4 in. (44.4 mm)	7.0 cu. in. (114.7 cc)	Direct

*Convertible to planetary gear drive.
†Three gear transmission with optional ratios of 2:1 and 3:1.

MAINTENANCE

SPARK PLUG. Recommended spark plug on Model C-72 is a Champion J6J. Recommended spark plug on all other models is a Champion CJ6. Recommended spark plug electrode gap on all models is 0.025 inch (0.63 mm).

CARBURETOR. A Tillotson HL diaphragm carburetor is used on all models except the S1050 and S1130G which may equipped with a Tillotson HL or Walbro SDC carburetor. Refer to Tillotson or Walbro section of CARBURETOR SERVICE section for carburetor overhaul and exploded views.

Initial adjustment for C-72 saws is ½-¾ turns open for idle high speed mixture screws. Initial adjustment for all other models is one turn open for idle and high speed adjustment screws (later S1050 Auto models are not equipped with high speed mixture screw). Note that on early Model S1050 Automatic and S1130G saws, idle speed is adjusted by turning air screw (5–Fig. HL53) in intake manifold. Turning screw clockwise will increase idle speed while turning screw counterclockwise will decrease idle speed. Initial setting is ⅜ turn open. Make final adjustments with engine at running temperature. Adjust high speed screw, on models so equipped, to obtain optimum performance with engine under cutting load.

MAGNETO AND TIMING. All saws are equipped with a conventional flywheel type magneto. Refer to Fig. HL56 or HL57 for exploded view of magneto.

Timing is correct when stator plate (breaker-box) is turned as far clockwise as possible before tightening mounting screws and breaker-point gap is adjusted to specified value.

Condenser capacity should be 0.16-0.20 mfd. for Model Super 2100 Automatic and 0.18-0.22 mfd. for all other models. Adjust breaker-point gap to 0.015 inch (0.38 mm) for all models.

LUBRICATION. The engine is lubricated by mixing oil with unleaded gasoline. Recommended oil is Homelite® two-stroke oil mixed at ratio as designated on oil container. If Homelite® oil is not available, a good quality oil designed for two-stroke engines may be used when mixed at a 16:1 ratio, however, an antioxidant fuel stabilizer (such as Sta-Bil) should be added to fuel

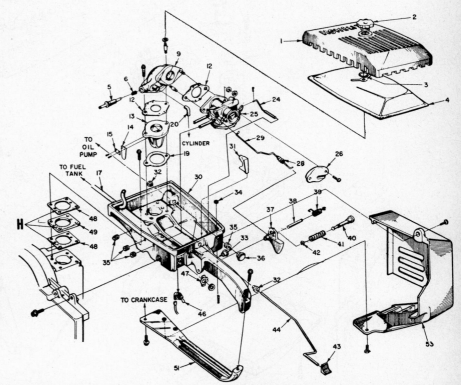

Fig. HL53—Exploded view of air box assembly for S1050 Automatic and S1130G. Note idler air (speed) adjusting screw (5) in elbow (intake manifold) (9). Tube (20) is connected between intake manifold and cylinder transfer port. Align holes (H) in gaskets (48) and spacer (49) with holes in air box and crankcase as shown. Air filter element (4) has integral air box sealing gasket.

H. Holes	14. Reed valves	31. Stop
1. Cover	15. Retainers	32. Grommet
2. Cover knob	19. Gasket	33. Bushing
3. Retainer	20. Idle air tube	34. Felt
4. Air filter	24. Choke rod	35. Grommets
5. Idle air screw	25. Carburetor	36. Choke button
6. Spring	26. Air deflector	37. Throttle trigger
9. Intake manifold	28. Grommet	38. Pivot pin
12. Gaskets	29. Throttle rod	39. Return spring
13. Reed valve seat	30. Air box	40. Throttle latch pin

41. Spring
42. Snap ring
43. Oiler button
44. Oiler rod
46. Ignition switch
47. On-off plate
48. Gaskets
49. Spacer
51. Brace
53. Muffler shield

mix. Antioxidant fuel stabilizer is not required with Homelite® oils as they contain fuel stabilizer so the fuel mix will stay fresh up to one year.

Fill chain oil reservoir with Homelite® Bar and Chain oil or a light oil (up to SAE 30 motor oil).

The planetary drive assembly or the clutch drum and sprocket assembly should be removed and the needle bearing in the clutch drum lubricated occasionally.

Check oil level in gear drive after each day of use. With saw setting on level surface, oil should be level with filler cap opening. Drain and flush gearcase with kerosene after each 100 hours of use. Refill with Homelite® 55291-C gear oil.

CARBON. Muffler and cylinder exhaust ports should be cleaned periodically to prevent loss of power due to carbon build up. Remove muffler and scrape

free of carbon. With muffler removed, turn engine so that piston is at top dead center and carefully remove carbon from exhaust ports with a wooden scraper. Be careful not to damage edges of the exhaust ports or to scratch piston. Do not run engine with muffler removed.

REPAIRS

TIGHTENING TORQUES. Recommended minimum tightening torques are as follows:

4/40 Reed to adapter ....5-6 in.-lbs. (0.6-0.7 N·m)
4/40 Flange bearing, oil pump ....5-6 in.-lbs. (0.6-0.7 N·m)
#6 Oil reservoir cover .....25-30 in.-lbs. (2.8-3.4 N·m)

Automatic oiler cam screw ....70-84 in.-lbs. (7.9-9.5 N·m)
8/32 Connecting rod .....55-66 in.-lbs. (6.2-7.5 N·m)
8/32 Condenser screw ....15-18 in.-lbs. (1.7-2.0 N·m)
8/32 Oiler pump to drivecase ....40-48 in.-lbs. (4.5-5.4 N·m)
10/32 Connecting rod .....70-84 in.-lbs. (7.9-9.5 N·m)
10/32 Carburetor air deflector..............50-60 in.-lbs. (5.6-6.8 N·m)
10/32 Starter pulley ......50-60 in.-lbs. (5.6-6.8 N·m)
10/24 Stator to crankcase . .40-48 in.lbs. (4.5-5.4 N·m)
10/24 High tension lead clamp ....25-30 in.-lbs. (2.8-3.4 N·m)
10/24 Cylinder shield .....50-60 in.-lbs. (5.6-6.8 N·m)

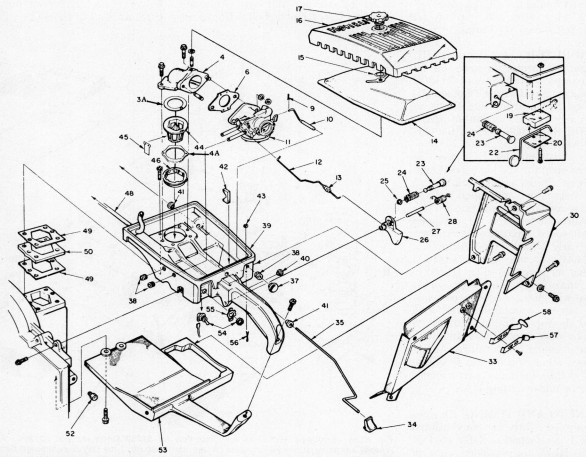

Fig. HL54—Exploded view of typical air box and throttle assembly used on Model Super 2100 Automatic. Compression release and throttle lock mechanism is shown in inset at upper right. Early models did not use gaskets (3A and 4A); do not install gaskets on early models unless a new intake manifold is also installed.

3A. Gasket	22. Compression release lever	40. Bushing	50. Spacer
4. Intake manifold		30. Muffler shield	52. Spacer
4A. Gasket	13. Boot	33. Cylinder shield	53. Brace
6. Gasket	14. Air filter element	34. Oiler button	54. Ignition switch
9. Cotter pin	15. Snap ring	35. Oil pump rod	55. Switch plate
10. Choke rod	16. Air filter cover	37. Choke button	56. Cotter pin
11. Carburetor	17. Cover nut	38. Grommet	57. Upper lever clamp
12. Throttle rod	19. Lever guide	39. Throttle handle	58. Lower lever clamp
	20. Guide plate	22. Compression release lever	42. Pump rod stop
	23. Throttle latch pin	28. Trigger spring	44. Reed valve seat
	24. Spring	41. Bushing	45. Valve reeds
	25. Snap ring		46. Reed retainer
	26. Throttle trigger		48. Fuel line
	27. Throttle shaft		49. Gasket

12/24 Fuel tank . . . . 80-96 in.-lbs.
(9.0-10.8 N·m)

12/24 Muffler cap . . . . 50-60 in.-lbs.
(5.6-6.8 N·m)

12/24 Muffler to cylinder . . 60-72 in.-lbs.
(6.8-8.1 N·m)

12/24 Pistol grip bracket . . 80-96 in.-lbs.
(9.0-10.8 N·m)

12/24 Recoil starter
assembly . . . . 80-96 in.-lbs.
(9.0-10.8 N·m)

12/24 Air shroud . . . . 80-96 in.-lbs.
(9.0-10.8 N·m)

12/24 Carburetor chamber
to crankcase . . . . 80-96 in.-lbs.
(9.0-10.8 N·m)

12/24 Reed valve
assembly . . . . 80-96 in.-lbs.
(9.0-10.8 N·m)

12/24 Drivecase to
crankcase . . . . 80-96 in.-lbs.
(9.0-10.8 N·m)

12/24 Gearcase cover . . . . 70-84 in.-lbs.
(7.9-9.5 N·m)

12/24 Chain guard . . . . 80-96 in.-lbs.
(9.0-10.8 N·m)

12/24 Mounting bracket . . . 80-96 in.-lbs.
(9.0-10.8 N·m)

12/24 Idler gear post . . . . . 80-96 in.-lbs.
(9.0-10.8 N·m)

1/4-20 Main bearing
retainer . . . . 80-96 in.-lbs.
(9.0-10.8 N·m)

1/4-28 Check valve caps . . . 25-30 in.-lbs.
(2.8-3.4 N·m)

5/16-18 Handle bar . . . . . 180-216 in.-lbs.
(20.3-24.4 N·m)

3/8-24 Clutch nut . . . . . . 250-300 in.-lbs.
(28.2-33.9 N·m)

7/16-24 Rotor (flywheel)
nut . . . . 250-300 in.-lbs.
(28.2-33.9 N·m)

1/2-20 Idler gear nut . . . . 200-240 in.-lbs.
(22.6-27.1 N·m)

1/2-20 Sprocket nut . . . . . 250-300 in.-lbs.
(28.2-33.9 N·m)

14 mm Spark plug . . . . . 250-300 in.-lbs.
(28.2-33.9 N·m)

Clutch spider . . . . 180-216 in.-lbs.
(20.3-24.4 N·m)

SPECIAL SERVICES TOOLS.
The following special tools will aid servicing.

Tool No.   Description & Model Usage

A-23809 – Plug connecting rod bearing, C-72.

23874 – Plug, connecting rod bearing, 1050 & 1130G.

24206-1 – Plug, connecting rod bearing, Super 2100 Automatic.

22828 – Pliers, piston pin snap ring, all models.

AA-22560 – Remover, rotor, C-72.

A-24028 – Remover, rotor, S1050 & S1130G.

A-23762 – Jackscrew, ball main bearing, all models.

23136 – Body for A-23762.

22820-2 – Bearing collar for A-23762.

23670 – Aligning plate, crankshaft, C-72, S1050, S1130G.

24207-1 – Aligning plate, crankshaft, Super 2100 Automatic.

A-23858 – Fixture, drivecase, Super 2100 Automatic.

23373-4 – Bearing collar, Super 2100 Automatic.

23382 – Crankshaft spacer, Super 2100 Automatic.

24210-1 – Collar, Super 2100 Automatic.

23233-1 – Plug, crankcase seal, all models.

23671 – Plug, drivecase seal, all models.

23693 – Sleeve, drivecase seal, C-72 S1050, S1130G.

23876 – Plug, drive case bearing, C-72 S1050.

23391-2 – Plug, drivecase bearing, C-72.

23391-3 – Plug, drivecase bearing, S1130G.

23384 – Plug, drivecase seal, Super 2100 Automatic.

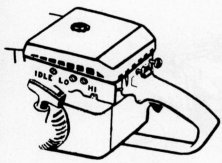

Fig. HL55 – View showing carburetor adjustment points for early Model S1050 Automatic and S1130G. Refer to exploded view in Fig. HL53 for view showing idle adjusting screw (5), spring (6), and intake manifold (9).

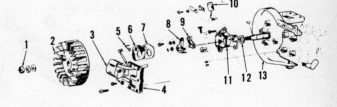

Fig. HL57 – Exploded view of magneto used on some later models.

1. Nut
2. Flywheel
3. Ignition coil
4. Armature laminations
5. Retainer
6. Breaker-box cover
7. Gasket
8. Moveable breaker-point
9. Fixed breaker-point
10. Condenser
11. Stator plate
12. Seal
13. Crankcase

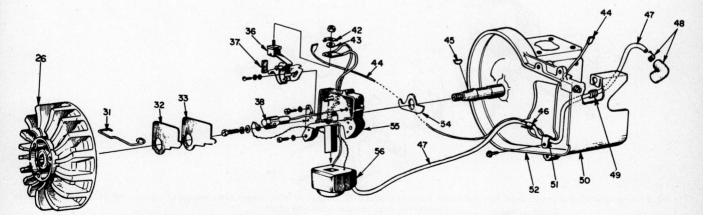

Fig. HL56 – Exploded view of flywheel magneto assembly used on some models. Refer to Fig. HL57 for magneto which is also used on some models.

26. Rotor
31. Retainer
32. Breaker-box cover
33. Gasket

36. Breaker-points
37. Cam wiper
38. Condenser

42. Ground tab
43. Terminal washer
44. Switch lead

45. Rotor key
46. Sleeve
47. Spark plug wire

48. Terminal
49. Grommet
50. Cylinder shield
51. Clamp

52. Crankcase
54. Seal
55. Breaker-box & core
56. Ignition coil

23390 – Sleeve, crankshaft assembling, Super 2100 Automatic.

A-24138 – Reamer, compression release valve seat, Super 2100 Automatic.

23420 – Plug, clutch drum bearing, S1050.

23139 – Plug, clutch drum bearing, C-72 & Super 2100 Automatic.

A-23137 – Jackscrew, clutch, Super 2100 Automatic.

A-23696 – Remover, spider, sun gear, all models.

23678 – Tool, starter bearing, C-72.

A-23679 – Remover, starter bearing, C-72.

A-23713 – Sprocket holder, C-72.

23725A – Plug, planetary bearing, C-72.

23726A – Plug planetary drum, C-72.

23913 – Plug, ball bearing & seal, S1130G.

22750 – Sprocket locking tool, S1130G.

23228 – Plug, sprocket shaft bearing, S1130G.

23528 – Wrench, connecting rod screw, S1050, S1130G, Super 2100 Automatic.

A-23960 – Puller, magneto, Super 2100 Automatic.

JA-31316-4 – Test spark plug.

17789 – Carburetor repair tool kit.

94197 – Carburetor tester.

94194 – Compression gage.

COMPRESSION PRESSURE. For optimum performance of Models S1050 Automatic and S1130G, cylinder compression pressure should be 155-185 psi (1069-1275 kPa) with engine at normal operating temperature. Engine should be inspected and repaired when compression pressure is 90 psi (620 kPa) or below.

CONNECTING ROD. Connecting rod and piston assembly can be removed from crankpin after removing cylinder from crankcase. Be careful to remove all the loose needle rollers from crankcase.

Model C-72 is equipped with 27 rollers, Models S1050 Automatic and S1130G have 31 rollers and Model Super 2100 Automatic has 26 rollers.

Renew connecting rod if bent or twisted, or if crankpin bearing surface is scored, burned or excessively worn.

Latest connecting rods are 1/16 inch (1.59 mm) wider than early rods (at piston pin end). The caged needle roller piston pin bearing can be renewed by pressing old bearing out of rod and pressing new bearing in. Press on lettered side of bearing cage during installation. Recommended Homelite® tools are listed in SPECIAL TOOLS section.

Renew the crankpin needle rollers as a set if any roller has flat spots, or is scored or worn. New needle rollers are serviced in a strip; wrap the strip around crankpin. If reusing needle rollers, use beeswax or light grease to stick rollers to rod and cap. Install piston and rod assembly ring retaining pin in piston away from exhaust port side of cylinder. Be sure match marks on rod and cap are aligned and secure rod to cap with new socket head screws.

PISTON, PIN AND RINGS. On all models, piston is fitted with two pinned compression rings. Renew piston if scored, cracked or excessively worn, or if ring side clearance in top ring groove exceeds 0.004 inch (0.10 mm).

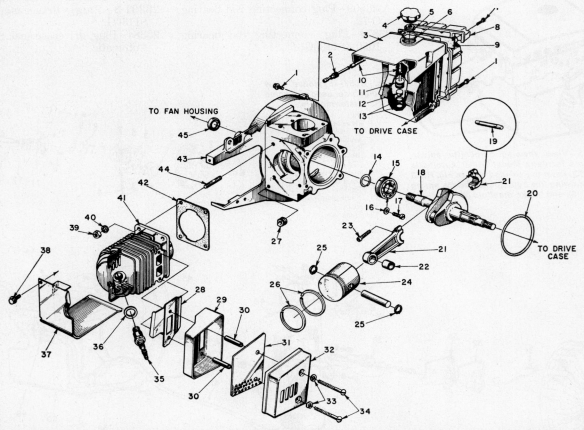

Fig. HL58 — Exploded view of power head and fuel tank similar to Model C-72. Gasket (9) is no longer used. Homelite® cement 22788 is used in place of gasket to seal between tank and cover.

2. Fuel fitting	9. Gasket (no longer used)	15. Ball bearing
3. Fuel tank	10. Flexible hose	16. Lockwashers (2)
4. Filler cap	11. Fuel pickup	17. Screws (2)
5. Relief valve	12. Fuel filter	18. Crankshaft
6. Gasket	13. Bumpers	19. Needle rollers (27)
8. Fuel tank cover	14. Snap ring	

20. "O" ring	26. Piston rings	32. Muffler cap
21. Connecting rod	27. Grommet (Sleeve now used)	35. Spark plug
22. Needle bearing	28. Air deflector	41. Cylinder
24. Piston & pin assy.	29. Muffler body	42. Gasket
25. Snap rings (2)	31. Baffle	43. Crankcase
		45. Seal

Recommended piston ring end gap is 0.070-0.080 inch (1.78-2.03 mm); maximum allowable ring end gap is 0.085 inch (2.16 mm). Desired ring side clearance in groove is 0.002-0.003 inch (0.05-0.08 mm).

Several different methods of retaining piston pin have been used; pin may be retained by two Waldes Truarc snap rings, by a nonremovable Spirol pin at exhaust side and a Waldes Truarc snap ring at intake side, by two Rulon plastic plugs that snap into pin bore, or by a wire section snap ring at exhaust side and a Waldes Truarc snap ring at intake side of piston.

On all pistons with Truarc snap ring, remove snap ring from intake side using special pliers (Homelite® tool 22828), then push pin out toward intake side. On models with snap ring at exhaust side, push pin out with a plain rod inserted through the snap ring. On models with Spirol pin, use slotted remover (Homelite® tool A-23950). On models with Rulon plugs, pry plugs out, then remove piston pin.

When reassembling piston to connecting rod on models with Rulon plugs, install piston pin, then snap plugs into pin bore at each end of pin. Be sure pin and plugs are centered in piston.

When reassembling piston to connecting rod using snap rings or snap ring and spirol pin, be sure closed end of pin is toward exhaust side of piston (away from piston ring locating pin or toward the Spirol or wire section retaining ring). Be sure the Waldes Truarc snap ring, or rings are installed with sharp edge out and turn end gap of ring toward closed end of piston.

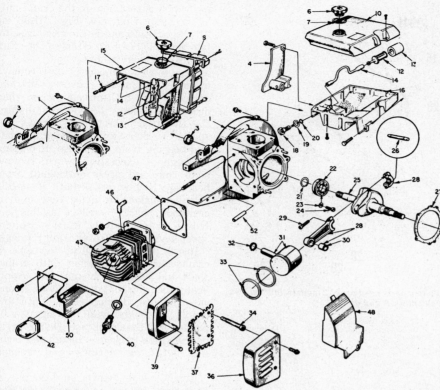

Fig. HL59—Exploded view showing Model S1050 Automatic and Model S1130G engine assembly. View shows fuel tank construction for both the direct and gear drive models.

1. Crankcase	16. Fuel tank	26. Needle rollers (31)
3. Crankshaft seal	17. Fitting	27. Gasket
4. Handle brace	18. Fitting	28. Connecting rod
6. Filler cap	19. Gasket	29. Screws
7. "O" ring	20. "O" ring	30. Needle bearing
9. Tank cover	21. Snap ring	31. Piston & pin
10. Tank cover	22. Ball bearing	32. Snap ring
12. Fuel pickup	23. Lockwashers (2)	33. Piston rings
13. Filter	24. Screws (2)	34. Muffler studs
14. Flex hose	25. Crankshaft	36. Muffler cap
15. Fuel tank		

37. Baffle	
39. Muffler body	
40. Spark plug	
42. Spark plug cap	
43. Cylinder	
46. Idle tube (20 – Fig. HL53)	
47. Gasket	
48. Heat exchanger (optional)	
49. Cylinder shield	

CRANKSHAFT, MAIN BEARINGS AND SEALS.
The crankshaft of Models C-72, S1050 Automatic and S1130G is

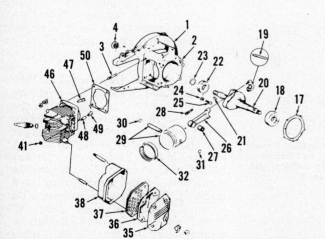

Fig. HL60—Exploded view of power head similar to type used on Model Super 2100 Automatic. An "O" ring is used in place of gasket (17).

1. Crankcase	27. Needle bearing
2. Dowel pins	28. Rod cap screws
3. Cylinder studs	29. Piston & pin
4. Crankshaft seal	30. Snap ring
17. Gasket	31. Snap ring
18. Ball bearing	32. Piston rings
19. Needle rollers	35. Muffler cover
20. Crankshaft	36. Spark arrester
21. Woodruff key	37. Muffler baffle
22. Ball bearing	38. Muffler body
23. Snap ring	41. Self-locking nut
24. Special washers	46. Cylinder
25. Bearing screws	47. Compression release valve
26. Connecting rod	48. Spring post
	49. Spring
	50. Cylinder gasket

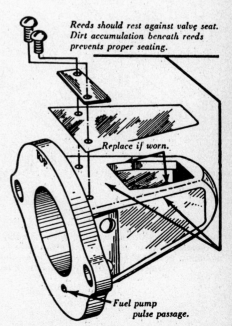

Reeds should rest against valve seat. Dirt accumulation beneath reeds prevents proper seating.

Replace if worn.

Fuel pump pulse passage.

Fig. HL61—Pyramid type reed valve showing proper installation for models with metal reed seat.

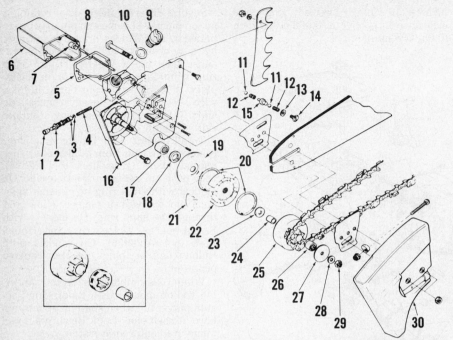

Fig. HL62 — Exploded view of direct-drive clutch and related parts used on C-72 models. Inset shows the other available splined type sprocket and drum.

1. Connector	9. Oil filler cap	17. Needle bearing	24. Bearing race
2. Oil pump plunger	10. "O" ring	18. Crankshaft seal	25. Clutch drum &
3. "O" ring	11. Check ball	19. Clutch cover	sprocket assy.
4. Spring	12. Spring	20. Clutch springs	26. Needle bearing
5. Gasket	13. Gasket	21. Clutch shoe	27. Thrust washer
6. Oil tank	14. Check valve cap	22. Clutch hub	28. Washer
7. Oil filter	15. Valve seat	23. Thrust washer	29. Nut
8. Oil line	16. Drivecase		30. Cover

Fig. HL64 — Exploded view of gear drive assembly used on Model S1130G. Refer to Fig. HL65 for view of opposite side of gearcase and chain drive sprocket. Ratios of 2:1 and 3:1 can be obtained by changing gear (13) and repositioning idler gear assembly to accommodate the different gear diameter. The 2:1 ratio gear has 42 teeth and the 3:1 ratio gear has 64 teeth.

1. Oil seal		21. Oil filter (manual)	31. Spring
2. Gearcase		22. Oil line	32. Clutch shoe
3. Filler cap	12. Snap ring	23. Oil filter (auto)	33. Clutch spider
4. "O" rings	13. Gear	24. Flange bearing	34. Spring
5. Ball bearing	14. Snap ring	25. Plunger & gear	35. Clutch cover
6. Cam screw	15. Ball bearing	26. Needle bearing	36. Washer
7. Oil pump housing	16. Idler gear	27. Oil seal	37. Nut
8. Worm gear	17. Ball bearing	28. Thrust washer	38. Gasket
9. Sprocket shaft	18. Snap ring	29. Sleeve bearing	39. Cover
10. Sprocket shaft	19. Nut	30. Clutch drum	40. Filler cap
11. Idler gear post	20. Bushing		

supported in a caged needle roller bearing at drivecase end of shaft and a ball bearing at flywheel end. End play of the crankshaft is controlled by the ball bearing which is retained on the crankshaft by a snap ring (14–Fig. HL58 or 21–Fig. HL59) and in the crankcase by two screws (17–Fig. HL58 or 24–Fig. HL59) and lockwashers.

To remove crankshaft, first remove cylinder, piston and rod assembly and drivecase or transmission case, then proceed as follows: Remove and discard the two bearing retaining screws and special washers and press crankshaft and bearing from crankcase. If bearing is rough or excessively worn, remove snap ring and press crankshaft from bearing. Renew crankshaft if needle bearing surface at drive case end or crankpin bearing surface is burned, scored or excessively worn. Also, inspect keyways and threads for damage.

Install new seal with lip to inside of crankcase. Press bearing onto crankshaft and secure with snap ring. Apply heat to bearing seat in crankcase, taking care not to damage seal, until the crankshaft with main bearing can be pushed into the crankcase. Do not press bearing into crankcase. Install new bearing retaining screws and special washers.

Renew needle bearing in drivecase, if necessary, by removing seal (18–Fig. HL62 or 1–Fig. HL64) and pressing bearing from casting. Press new bearing into case and install new seal with lip on inside. Place large "O" ring, or gasket on the drivecase, place seal protector (or tape) over keyways, threads and shoulder; and install drivecase on crankshaft and crankcase. Tighten the retaining screws alternately.

On Super 2100 Automatic engines, both ends of crankshaft are supported in ball bearings. Ball bearing (22–Fig. HL60) at magneto side is retained in crankcase by two screws (25) and special washers (24). Ball bearing (18) at drive clutch end should be a press fit on crankshaft and a snug fit in drivecase.

REED VALVE. (Models C-72, S1050 Automatic and S1130G). The reed inlet valve on Model C-72 is attached to the carburetor adapter elbow (9–Fig. HL53) and is serviced as a complete assembly only. A pyramid reed valve is used on Models S1050 Automatic and S1130G. Refer to Fig. HL61 for service information on the pyramid reed valve assembly. When installing new reeds on pyramid seat, throughly clean all threads and apply Loctite to threads on screws before installing. Be sure reeds are centered on seats before tightening screws.

Be sure that pulse passage holes in gaskets (48 – Fig. HL53 or 49 – Fig. HL54) and spacer (49 – Fig. HL53 or 50 – Fig. HL54) are located as shown.

Reed lift distance on Model C-72 should be 0.172-0.177 inch (4.37-4.49 mm). The pyramid structure reeds on other models have no reed stops.

REED VALVE. (Model Super 2100 Automatic). A Delrin plastic pyramid reed seat (44 – Fig. HL54) with six inlet reeds is used. The stainless steel reeds fit onto pins molded in plastic seat and are held in position by a retainer (46). The reed nearest carburetor is shorter than the remaining five reeds. Renew reed seat if worn or damaged and renew any broken or distorted reeds.

To assemble reeds to the Delrin plastic seat, stick the reeds to seat with a drop of oil under each reed. Be sure the short reed is on the small reed opening in seat and the reeds are properly located on the pins. Push retainer down over the reeds and seat, then install the seat, reeds and retainer as a unit.

COMPRESSION RELEASE VALVE. Model Super 2100 Automatic is equipped with a compression release valve (47 – Fig. HL60). Valve is operated by lever (22 – Fig. HL54).

Service of the compression release valve usually consists of cleaning the valve seat as the release port may gradually fill with carbon while engine is running with compression release valve open. A special service tool (Homelite® tool A-24138) can be used to ream carbon from the valve seat and bore.

CLUTCH. All models are equipped with a six-shoe clutch. Hold crankshaft from turning and turn clutch hub in a clockwise direction. If Homelite® tools are not available, suitable spanner wrenches may be used.

TRANSMISSION. Model S1130G is equipped with a gear transmission as shown in Fig. HL64. Except for renewal of the crankshaft needle bearing, transmission can be serviced after cover (39) is removed.

To service transmission, drain oil from chain oil tank and transmission case, then remove handlebar and cover (39). Tap cover lightly, if necessary, to loosen cover. Install a ¼ inch lock pin through hole in bottom of blower housing to hold

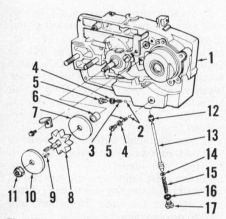

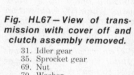

Fig. HL65 – View showing chain drive sprocket and manual oiler pump components removed on Model S1130G.

1. Gearcase
2. Check ball
3. Spring
4. Gasket
5. Cap
6. Spacer
7. Washer, inner
8. Sprocket
9. Keys
10. Washer, outer
11. Nut
12. Bushing
13. Plunger
14. "O" ring
15. Spring
16. Washer
17. Cap

Fig. HL67 – View of transmission with cover off and clutch assembly removed.

31. Idler gear
35. Sprocket gear
69. Nut
70. Washer
71. Clutch cover
72. Clutch spring
73. Clutch
74. Clutch shoe
75. Thrust washer
76. Clutch drum

Fig. HL68 – View of gearcase with clutch, idler gear and sprocket gear removed.

C. Clutch assy.
I. Idler gear assy.
P. Idler gear post
S. Sprocket gear
OP. Oil pump (chain)

Fig. HL66 – When removing clutch spider, use lock pin (LP) inserted as shown and turn clutch spider clockwise using a Homelite® spanner wrench A-23969 (S).

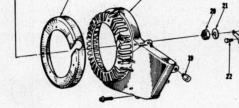

Fig. HL72—Exploded view of pawl type starter used on all models.

2. Starter cover
3. Rope bushing
4. Spring bushing
5. Starter rope
6. Hand grip
7. Insert
8. Inner spring shield
9. Rewind spring
10. Outer spring shield
11. Spring lock
12. Starter pulley
13. Starter cup
14. Retaining washer
15. Self locking screw
16. Sawdust shield
17. Air screen
18. Fan housing
19. Spacer
20. Crankshaft nut
21. Flat washer
22. Pawl stud
23. Starter pawl
24. Washer
25. Pawl spring
26. Rotor (flywheel)

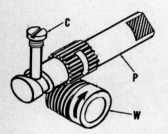

Fig. HL74—View showing operation of automatic chain oiler pump. Worm (W) mounted on crankshaft or sprocket shaft turns the plunger (P). As the plunger turns, it is moved back and forth by the cam groove cut in plunger riding on the cam screw (C). Flat on piston end of plunger acts as inlet and outlet valve as the plunger turns past inlet and outlet ports.

flywheel, then use a spanner wrench (Homelite® A-23969) and turn clutch clockwise to remove it from crankshaft. See Fig. HL66 and HL67. Thrust bearing (75) and clutch drum (76) can now be removed. Drum sleeve and bearing (29–Fig. HL64) can be removed if necessary. Turn nut (19) clockwise to remove and lift idler gear assembly (16) off idler post (11). Bearing (17) can be removed from idler gear after removing snap ring (18). Remove retaining ring (14) and pull sprocket gear (13) from sprocket shaft (10). See Fig. HL68.

NOTE: Sprocket shaft gear can be removed without removing idler gear should it be necessary for service only on the sprocket gear, sprocket shaft and bearings or the automatic chain oiler pump (OP) which is located behind the sprocket gear.

To remove the sprocket shaft, unbolt and remove the oil pump housing and discard the two "O" rings (4–Fig. HL64). Hold sprocket (8–Fig. HL65) from turning and remove nut (11), outer washer (10), sprocket and keys, inner washer (7), spacer (6), then push sprocket shaft from gearcase. Worm gear (9–Fig. HL64) can now be removed from shaft.

If sprocket shaft outer (pilot) bearing requires renewal, heat cover (39) until bearing will drop out. To remove sprocket shaft inner bearing, remove oil seal and press bearing out toward clutch side of gearcase using Homelite® tool 23228, or equivalent.

If crankshaft needle (main) bearing (26–Fig. HL64) is to be renewed, remove gearcase and using Homelite® tool 23931-3, press bearing out toward clutch side. When reinstalling bearing, install from engine side of gearcase and press only on lettered end of bearing. Use protector sleeve, Homelite® tool 23963, over crankshaft when installing gearcase to engine.

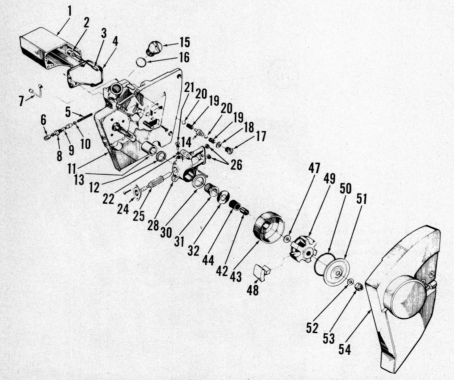

Fig. HL75—Exploded view of Model S1050 Automatic chain oiler pump and related parts; other models are similar except for ball bearing main instead of needle bearing. Refer to Fig. HL74 for view showing pump operation.

1. Oil reservoir
2. Oil pickup
3. Flexible tube
4. Gasket
5. Spring
6. Connector
7. Oil line
8. Plunger (manual)
9. "O" ring
10. "O" ring
11. Drivecase
12. Seal
13. Needle bearing
14. Valve seat
15. Filler cap
16. Gasket
17. Check valve cap
18. Gasket
19. Spring
20. Check ball
21. Cam screw
22. Gasket
23. Flange bearing
24. Flange bearing
25. Plunger & gear
26. "O" rings
28. Pump housing
30. Felt seal
31. Worm gear
32. Thrust washer
42. Inner race
43. Sprocket & drum
44. Needle bearing
47. Thrust washer
48. Clutch shoes
49. Clutch hub
50. Clutch springs
51. Clutch cover
52. Washer
53. Nut
54. Drivecase cover

Reassemble by reversing disassembly procedure. Use new oil seals and install with open side next to bearing. Use new "O" rings between gearcase and oil pump housing. Use Loctite on idler gear retaining nut and tighten nut to 200 in.-lbs. (22.6 N·m). Tighten clutch spider and nut (37) to a minimum of 300 in.-lbs. (33.9 N·m) and sprocket nut to 250 in.-lbs. (28.2 N·m).

REWIND STARTER. All models are equipped with the pawl type clutch assembly shown in Fig. HL72. Rewind spring (9) is would in cover (2) in clockwise direction. Tension is placed on rewind spring by turning cover (2) in clockwise direction approximately three turns before installing cover retaining screws.

AUTOMATIC CHAIN OILER. Gear drive Model S1130G is equipped with an automatic chain oil system and pump located in gearcase shown in Fig. HL68. Refer also to exploded view in Fig. HL64.

Models S1050 Automatic and Super 2100 Automatic are equipped with automatic oil pump shown in Fig. HL75.

To service pump on gear drive models, drain chain oil tank and transmission case, then remove cover (39 – Fig. HL64). Remove retaining ring (14) and pull gear (13) from sprocket shaft (10). Unbolt and remove pump body (7) from gearcase. Discard "O" rings (4) and use new "O" rings during installation. Pump plunger (25) can be removed from body after removing the flanged bearing (24).

If necessary to remove worm (9), remove chain sprocket and spacer (6 – HL65), push shaft from gearcase and remove spacer if so equipped and worm (9 – Fig. HL64) from shaft.

NOTE: Spacer is used only with a short (11/16 inch long) worm which was used in some saws. If saw is equipped with a long (13/16 inch) worm, the spacer is not used.

To service pump on direct drive models, first remove the clutch assembly, clutch drum and sprocket and the drive worm (31 – Fig. HL75). The pump can then be removed from crankcase cover (11).

Clean and inspect all parts and renew parts as necessary. Reassemble by reversing the disassembly procedure.

HOMELITE

Model	Bore	Stroke	Displ.	Drive Type
XL-923	2-1/16 in. (52.4 mm)	1½ in. (38.1 mm)	5.01 cu. in. (82.1 cc)	Direct
SXL-925	2-1/16 in. (52.4 mm)	1½ in. (38.1 mm)	5.01 cu. in. (82.1 cc)	Direct
VI-944	2-1/16 in. (52.4 mm)	1½ in. (38.1 mm)	5.01 cu. in. (82.1 cc)	Direct
VI-955	2-1/16 in. (52.4 mm)	1½ in. (38.1 mm)	5.01 cu. in. (82.1 cc)	Direct

MAINTENANCE

SPARK PLUG. Models so equipped with a solid-state, one-piece ignition module (above lot number C246) use a Champion DJ6Y spark plug. Early models (below lot number C246) use Champion CJ6, or Champion UJ11G for heavy duty operation. It will be necessary to pull the plug wire further out of the retaining clip in the air box when using UJ11G spark plug. Set electrode gap to 0.025 inch (0.63 mm) on all models.

CARBURETOR. All models are equipped with a Tillotson Model HS diaphragm carburetor. Refer to Tillotson section of CARBURETOR SERVICE section for carburetor overhaul and exploded views.

Initial setting of idle speed mixture screw and high speed mixture screw shown in Fig. HL76 is one turn open (later Model SXL-925 is not equipped with a high speed mixture screw). Make final adjustments with engine warm. Adjust idle mixture screw so that engine idles smoothly and will accelerate cleanly. Adjust high speed mixture screw, on models so equipped, to obtain optimum performance with saw under cutting load. Do not adjust high speed screw too lean as engine may be damaged.

On models with Simplex starting system (decompression valve and adjustable starting speed), speed at which engine runs with throttle latch engaged can be adjusted by turning eccentric throttle trigger pivot pin (28 – Fig. HL79).

MAGNETO. Three types of magnetos are used. Models XL-923 and VI-944 are equipped with a conventional flywheel type magneto. Models VI-955 and early SXL-925 are equipped with a capacitor discharge (CD) magneto. Later SXL-925 models are equipped with a one-piece solid-state ignition. Refer to appropriate following paragraph for service information on each type magneto.

CONVENTIONAL (BREAKER POINT) MAGNETO. Refer to Fig. HL81 for exploded view of magneto. Breaker-points and condenser are accessible after removing starter housing, flywheel and breaker-box cover. Adjust breaker-point gap to 0.015 inch (0.38 mm). Condenser capacity should test 0.18-0.22 mfd. After reinstalling flywheel, check armature air gap which should be 0.005-0.007 inch (0.13-0.18 mm). To adjust air gap loosen core retaining screws, turn flywheel so magnets are below legs of armature core and place plastic shim (Homelite® part 23987) between armature and magnets. Push flywheel toward core legs and tighten armature retaining screws, then remove shim.

CAPACITOR DISCHARGE (CD) MAGNETO. Refer to Fig. HL84 for exploded view of the capacitor discharge (CD) magneto used on all early and some later SXL-925 and VI-955 models.

The capacitor discharge magneto can be considered OK if spark will jump a ⅜ inch (9.5 mm) gap when turning engine at cranking speed. If magneto fails to

Fig. HL76 – Drawing showing locations of fuel mixture adjustment needles, idle speed needle and throttle stop lever.

(Labels in figure: THROTTLE STOP LEVER; IDLE SPEED ADJUSTMENT SCREW; IDLE MIXTURE ADJUSTMENT (LO SPEED) NEEDLE; MAIN MIXTURE ADJUSTMENT (HI SPEED) NEEDLE)

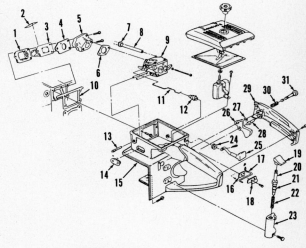

Fig. HL79 – Typical exploded view of air box and manual oil pump assemblies used on Models XL-923 and SXL-925.

1. Reed retainer
2. Reed petal
3. Reed valve seat
4. Gasket
5. Intake manifold
6. Gasket
7. Grommet
8. Fuel line
9. Carburetor
10. Gasket
11. Throttle rod
12. Boot
13. Idle speed screw
14. Grommet
15. Air box
16. Plate
17. Compression release lever
18. Clamp
19. Manual oiler button
20. Oil pump plunger
21. "O" rings (2)
22. Spring
23. Oil pump body
24. Grommet
25. Choke rod
26. Throttle trigger
27. "E" ring
28. Eccentric pin
29. Handle cover
30. Spring
31. Throttle latch pin

produce spark, service consists of locating and renewing inoperative unit; no maintenance is necessary.

To check magneto with volt-ohmmeter, proceed as follows: Remove starter housing and disconnect wire from ignition switch. Check to be sure there is no continuity through switch when in "ON" position to be sure a grounded switch is not cause of trouble and inspect wiring to be sure it is not shorted.

CAUTION: Be sure storage capacitor is discharged before touching connections; flip ignition switch to "OFF" position or ground switch lead (S).

Resistance through secondary (high tension) winding of transformer coil should be 2400 to 2900 ohms and resistance through primary winding should be 0.2-0.4 ohms. Connect ohmmeter leads between high tension (spark plug wire and ground, then between input terminal and ground. If transformer coil does not test within specifications,

renew coil and recheck for spark at cranking speed. If magneto still does not produce spark, check generator as follows:

Remove rotor (flywheel) and disconnect lead from generator to generator (G) terminal on module (3) and switch lead (S) at ignition switch. Connect negative lead of ohmmeter to ground wire from generator and the positive lead of ohmmeter to generator (G) wire. The ohmmeter should register showing continuity through generator. Reverse leads from ohmmeter; ohmmeter should

then show no continuity (infinite resistance) through generator. Renew generator is continuity is noted with ohmmeter leads connected in both directions. A further check can be made using voltmeter if continuity checked correctly. Remove spark plug and reinstall rotor leaving wire (G) from generator disconnected. Connect positive (red) lead from voltmeter to wire (G) from generator and negative (black) lead of voltmeter to magneto back plate; wires must be routed so starter can be reinstalled. A firm pull on starter rope

Fig. HL81—Exploded view of conventional flywheel type magneto. Coil clip retaining screw location is shown by letter "B." Condenser lead and ignition coil primary lead are attached to terminal block (28) at "D."

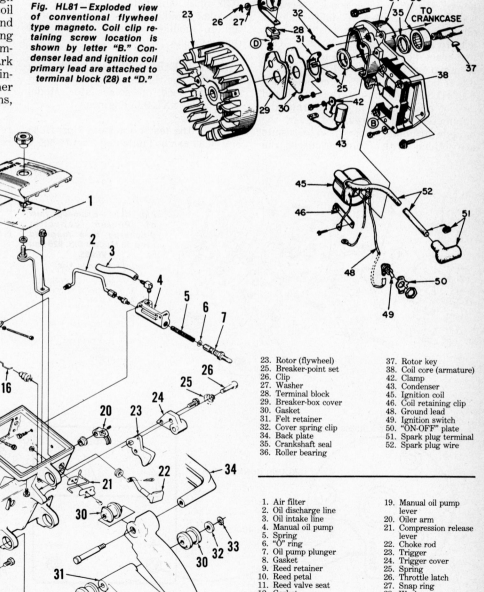

23. Rotor (flywheel)	37. Rotor key
25. Breaker-point set	38. Coil core (armature)
26. Clip	42. Clamp
27. Washer	43. Condenser
28. Terminal block	45. Ignition coil
29. Breaker-box cover	46. Coil retaining clip
30. Gasket	48. Ground lead
31. Felt retainer	49. Ignition switch
32. Cover spring clip	50. "ON-OFF" plate
34. Back plate	51. Spark plug terminal
35. Crankshaft seal	52. Spark plug wire
36. Roller bearing	

1. Air filter	19. Manual oil pump lever
2. Oil discharge line	20. Oiler arm
3. Oil intake line	21. Compression release lever
4. Manual oil pump	22. Choke rod
5. Spring	23. Trigger
6. "O" ring	24. Trigger cover
7. Oil pump plunger	25. Spring
8. Gasket	26. Throttle latch
9. Reed retainer	27. Snap ring
10. Reed petal	28. Washer
11. Reed valve seat	29. Shaft
12. Gasket	30. Vibration bushing
13. Intake manifold	31. Handle
14. Gasket	32. Washer
15. Carburetor	33. Snap ring
16. Throttle rod	34. Mounting arm
17. Frame	
18. Idle speed stop screw	

Fig. HL80—Exploded view of Models VI-944 and VI-955. Note vibration isolating bushings (30).

should spin engine at about 500 rpm and voltmeter should show minimum reading of 4 volts. If both generator and transformer coil tested OK, a faulty ignition module (3) should be suspected.

A partial check of ignition module can be made using ohmmeter. With ohmmeter set to R X 1000 scale, connect positive (red) lead of ohmmeter to module terminal marked "Gen." and negative ohmmeter lead to module ground connection (see Fig. HL85). An instant deflection of ohmmeter needle should be noted; if not, reverse ohmmeter leads and observe needle. If no deflection of needle is noted with ohmmeter leads connected in either direction, module is faulty and should be renewed. If needle deflection is observed, select R X 1 (direct reading) scale of ohmmeter and connect positive (red) lead to module terminal marked "Gen." and place negative (black) lead against terminal marked "Trans." Place a screwdriver across the two trigger poles (see Fig. HL85); the ohmmeter needle should deflect and remain deflected until the ohmmeter lead is released from the module terminal. If the desired results are obtained with ohmmeter checks, the

module is probably OK; however, as this is not a complete check and other magneto components and wiring check OK, renew module if no ignition spark can be obtained.

SOLID-STATE IGNITION. Later SXL-925 models are equipped with a one-piece solid-state ignition module (27 – Fig. HL86). The solid-state ignition system is serviced by renewing the spark plug or ignition module, however, be sure all wires are connected properly and the ignition switch functions correctly before renewing ignition module. Air gap between ignition module and flywheel is adjustable. Loosen module retaining screws and place a 0.015 inch (0.38 mm) shim between flywheel and module. Hold module against shim, tighten module retaining screws and remove shim.

THREE-PIECE SOLID-STATE IGNITION. The three-piece solid-state ignition is used on some later Model VI-955 and SXL-925 engines.

NOTE: The tester shown in Figs. HL88 and HL89 can be fabricated from 70-500 V

neon tester (Radio Shack number 272-201) and two leads with alligator clips.

Refer to Fig. HL87 and test for spark as shown. If weak spark or no spark is observed, refer to Fig. HL88 and test coil as follows: Remove spark plug and fan housing. Disconnect primary ignition wire from coil table "A." Connect one tester lead to the switch terminal and connect the other test lead to a good ground on the engine block. Temporarily reinstall the starter and fan housing. Move the switch to "ON" or "RUN" and spin the engine with the starter. A good coil will light the tester with a bright, pulsing glow. Replace the coil if other results are observed.

To test the trigger module, refer to Fig. HL89 and connect one of the tester leads to the disconnected coil primary wire and other tester lead to a good ground on the engine block. Reinstall the starter and fan housing. Move the switch to "ON" or "RUN" and spin the engine with the starter. If the tester glows brightly, the trigger circuit is functioning. Remove the flywheel and replace the trigger module if other results are oserved.

When reinstalling the flywheel, torque the flywheel nut to 150 in.-lbs. (17 N·m). Adjust coil-to-flywheel air gap to 0.015 inch (0.38 mm) using the black plastic feeler gage (part 24306). Tighten coil holddown screws to 20 in.-lbs. (2.25 N·m).

LUBRICATION. The engine is lubricated by mixing oil and unleaded gasoline. Recommended oil is Homelite®

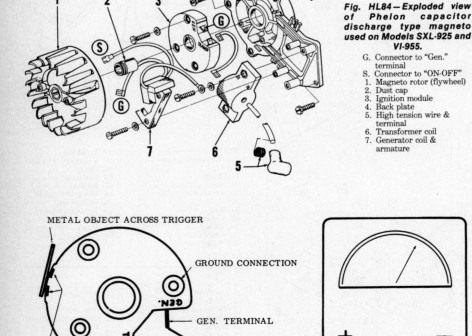

Fig. HL84 — Exploded view of Phelon capacitor discharge type magneto used on Models SXL-925 and VI-955.

G. Connector to "Gen." terminal
S. Connector to "ON-OFF"
1. Magneto rotor (flywheel)
2. Dust cap
3. Ignition module
4. Back plate
5. High tension wire & terminal
6. Transformer coil
7. Generator coil & armature

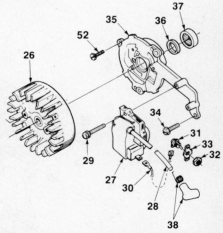

Fig. HL86 — View of one-piece solid-state ignition used on later SXL-925 models.

26. Flywheel	33. Indicating plate
27. Ignition module	34. Screw
28. High tension wire	35. Back plate
29. Sems screws	36. Crankshaft seal
30. Ground lead	37. Roller bearing
31. Ignition switch	38. Spark plug terminal
32. Nut	52. Screw

Fig. HL85 — Drawing showing volt-ohmmeter to ignition module (3 – Fig. HL84) for checking module. It should be noted that this is not a conclusive test and module should be renewed in event of spark failure when other magneto components test OK.

two-stroke oil mixed at ratio as designated on the oil container. If Homelite® oil is not available, a good quality oil designed for two-stroke engines may be used when mixed at a 16:1 ratio, however, and antioxidant fuel stabilizer (such as Sta-Bil) should be added to fuel mix. Antioxidant fuel stabilizer is not required with Homelite® oils as they contain fuel stabilizer so the fuel mix will stay fresh up to one year.

Fill chain oiler reservoir with Homelite® Bar and Chain oil or a light oil (no heavier than SAE 30). In cold weather, chain oil can be diluted with kerosene to allow easier flow of oil through pump and lines.

The clutch drum and sprocket should be removed and the needle roller bearing and inner race be cleaned and greased occasionally.

CARBON. Muffler and cylinder exhaust ports should be cleaned periodically to prevent loss of power due to carbon build up. Remove muffler cover and baffle plate and scrape muffler free of carbon. With muffler cover removed, turn engine so piston is at top dead center and carefully remove carbon from exhaust ports with wooden scraper. Be careful not to damage the edges of exhaust ports or to scratch piston. Do not attempt to run engine with muffler baffle plate or cover removed.

REPAIRS

TIGHTENING TORQUE VALUES.
Tightening torque values are as follows:
8/32 Connecting rod......55-66 in.-lbs. (6.2-7.5 N·m)
3/8-24 Clutch nut.......150-180 in.-lbs. (16.9-20.3 N·m)
3/8-24 Rotor nut.......150-180 in.-lbs. (16.9-20.3 N·m)
1/4-28 Cylinder nuts....100-120 in.-lbs. (11.3-13.6 N·m)
14 mm Spark plug......150-180 in.-lbs. (16.9-20.3 N·m)

RECOMMENDED SERVICE TOOLS.
Special tools which will aid servicing are as follows:
Tool No. Description & Model Usage
23987 – Shim, magneto air gap, all models except with capacitor magneto.
24306 – Shim, capacitor discharge magneto air gap.
23955 or 23955-I – Plug, connecting rod bearing installation, all models.
A-23965 – Jackscrew, crankshaft and bearing.
23136-1 – Jackscrew body.
22820-4 – Collar, main bearing installation.
23971 – Sleeve, crankcase seal protector.
23972 – Sleeve, crankcase seal installation, all models.

23957 – Plug, crankshaft seal installtion, all models.
A-23696-A – Wrench, clutch spider, all models with 6-shoe spring type clutch.
A-17146 – Wrench, clutch plate, all models with 3-shoe type clutch.
A-23960 – Puller, flywheel (magneto rotor) all models.
23420 – Plug, sprocket bearing, all models.
23956 – Plug, back plate bearing and seal, Model XL-923.
A23962 – Jackscrew, back plate bearing, all models.
23846-2 – Anvil, back plate bearing, all models.
A-23951 – Remover, piston pin, piston with Spirol pin.
22828 – Pliers, piston pin snap ring, all models except with Rulon plastic pin retaining plugs.
23846-1 – Anvil, crankshaft installation, all models.
23846-2 – Anvil, back plate bearing, all models.
24006-1 – Aligning plate, crankshaft installation, all models.
24304 – "Pozidriv" screwdriver bit.
24230 – "Pozidriv" hand screwdriver.
24982-01 – "Torx" bit, 1/4 in. shank.
24982-02 – "Torx" bit, 5/16 in. shank.
24302 – Plug, backplate seal, models SXL-925, VI-944 and VI-955.
23528 – Wrench, connecting rod, all models.
JA-31316-4 – Test spark plug.
17789 – Carburetor tool kit.
14197 – Carburetor tester.
94194 – Compression gage.

COMPRESSION PRESSURE. For optimum performance of Model SXL-925, cylinder compression pressure should be 155-185 psi (1069-1275 kPa) with engine at normal operating temperature. Engine should be inspected and repaired when compression pressure is 90 psi (620 kPa) or below.

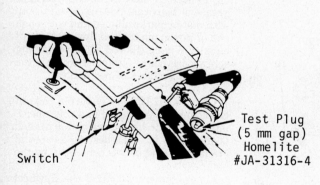

Switch

Test Plug (5 mm gap) Homelite #JA-31316-4

Fig. HL87 — Test for proper spark with a test plug as shown for models with three-piece solid-state ignition.

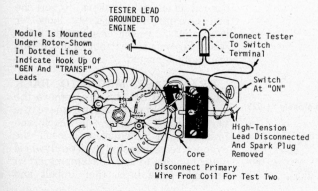

Module Is Mounted Under Rotor-Shown In Dotted Line to Indicate Hook Up Of "GEN And "TRANSF" Leads

TESTER LEAD GROUNDED TO ENGINE

Connect Tester To Switch Terminal

Switch At "ON"

High-Tension Lead Disconnected And Spark Plug Removed

Core

Disconnect Primary Wire From Coil For Test Two

Fig. HL88 — Test coil with a neon tester connected as shown for models with three-piece solid-state ignition.

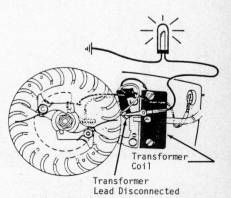

Transformer Coil

Transformer Lead Disconnected

Fig. HL89 — Test trigger module (under flywheel) with a neon tester as shown for models with three-piece solid-state ignition.

COMPRESSION RELIEF VALVE. Models XL-923 and VI-944 are equipped with a compression relief (decompression) valve. The poppet type relief valve is mounted in a port adjacent to exhaust port as shown in Fig. HL90. The valve is opened as throttle lock plunger is depressed to lock position. If valve fails to close when throttle lock plunger is released, either remove valve and clean using a carbon solvent or renew the valve assembly. Copper sealing washer is available separately.

CYLINDER. The cylinder bore is chrome plated. Renew cylinder if chrome plating is worn away exposing the softer base metal.

To remove cylinder, first remove the blower (fan) housing, carburetor and air box (handle) assemblies and remove the screw retaining magneto back plate to flywheel side of cylinder. The cylinder can then be unbolted from crankcase and removed from the piston.

PISTON, PIN AND RINGS. All models are equipped with piston fitted with two pinned compression rings. Desired ring side clearance in groove is 0.002-0.003 inch (0.05-0.08 mm), renew the piston if side clearance in top groove with new ring is 0.0035 inch (0.089 mm)

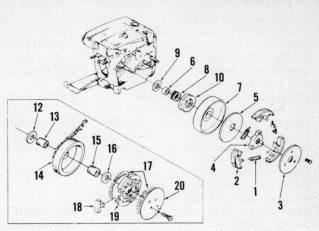

Fig. HL91 — Models may be equipped with clutch components (1 through 10) or clutch components (12 through 20).

1. Spring
2. Clutch shoe
3. Cover
4. Hub
5. Thrust washer
6. Inner race
7. Drum
8. Bearing
9. Thrust washer
10. Sprocket
12. Thrust washer
13. Inner race
14. Drum
15. Bearing
16. Thrust washer
17. Spring
18. Clutch shoe
19. Hub
20. Cover

or more. Recommended piston ring end gap is 0.070-0.080 inch (1.78-2.03 mm); maximum allowable ring end gap is 0.085 inch (2.16 mm). Piston, pin and rings are available in standard size only. Pin and piston are available as a fitted set only.

When installing piston pin, be sure closed and is toward exhaust side of piston (away from piston ring locating pin). Insert piston pin snap rings using special pliers; sharp edge of snap ring must be out and locate end gap towards closed end of piston.

CONNECTING ROD. Connecting rod and piston assembly can be removed after removing cylinder from crankcase. Be careful to remove all of the 28 loose needle rollers when detaching rod from crankpin.

Renew connecting rod if bent or twisted, or if crankpin bearing surface is scored, burned or excessively worn. The caged needle roller piston pin bearing can be renewed by pressing old bearing out and pressing new bearing in with Homelite® tool 23955 or 23955-1. Press on lettered end of bearing cage only.

It is recommended that crankpin needle rollers be renewed as a set whenever engine is disassembled for service. Stick 14 needle rollers in rod and the remaining 14 needle rollers in rod cap with light grease or beeswax. Assemble rod to cap with match marks aligned and with open end of piston pin toward flywheel side of engine. Wiggle the rod as cap retaining screws are being tightened to align the fractured surfaces of rod and cap.

CRANKSHAFT. Flywheel end of crankshaft is supported in a roller bearing in magneto back plate and drive end is supported in a ball bearing located in crankcase. End play is controlled by the ball bearing.

Renew the crankshaft if the flywheel end main bearing or crankpin bearing surface or sealing surfaces are scored, burned or excessively worn. Renew the ball bearing if excessively loose or rough. Also, reject crankshaft if flywheel keyway is beat out or if threads are badly damaged.

CRANKCASE MAGNETO BACK PLATE AND SEALS. To remove the magneto back plate, first remove the blower (fan) housing, flywheel and breaker-point assemblies. Loosen the cylinder retaining stud nuts on flywheel side of engine to reduce clamping effect on back plate boss, then unbolt and

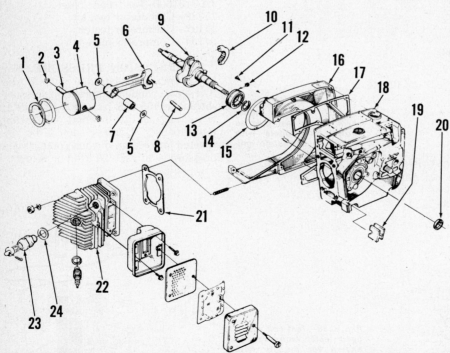

Fig. HL90 — Exploded view of engine assembly. Compression relief valve is used on Models XL-923 and VI-944.

1. Piston rings
2. Snap ring
3. Piston pin
4. Piston
5. Thrust washer
6. Connecting rod
7. Needle bearing
8. Bearing rollers (28)
9. Crankshaft
10. Rod cap
11. Screw
12. Bearing retainer
13. Bearing
14. Snap ring
15. "O" ring
16. Fuel tank
17. Gasket
18. Crankcase
19. Grommet
20. Seal
21. Gasket
22. Cylinder
23. Compression relief valve
24. Washer

remove the back plate assembly from crankcase.

To remove crankshaft from crankcase, first remove the cylinder, connecting rod and piston assembly and the magneto backplate as previously outlined. Remove the drive clutch assembly and, on models so equipped, the automatic chain oiler drive worm and pump from drive end of crankcase and shaft. Then, remove the two ball bearing retaining screws (11 – Fig. HL90) from inside of crankcase and remove the crankshaft and ball bearing assembly from crankcase. Remove snap ring (14) and press crankshaft from bearing if necessary.

REED VALVES. All models are equipped with pyramid reed valves. The pyramid seat is of "Delrin" plastic and the 0.004 inch (0.10 mm) thick reeds are located by pins molded in the seat. The reeds are held in place by a molded retainer that also serves as a gasket between reed seat and crankcase. When installing intake elbow and "Delrin" seat assembly, insert reed retainer into crankcase first. Stick reeds to seat with oil, then insert seat with reeds.

CLUTCH. Model SXL-925 is equipped with either a three- or six-shoe clutch while all other models are equipped with a six-shoe clutch. See Fig. HL91.

To remove clutch, first remove screws retaining clutch cover to clutch hub and remove cover. Torx screws are used on three-shoe clutch and may be removed with tools 24982-01 or 24982-02. Unscrew clutch hub (L.H. thread) from crankshaft using a spanner wrench (Homelite® tool A-17146) for three-shoe clutch or tool A-23696-A for six-shoe clutch). The clutch drum, bearing and inner race can then be removed from crankshaft.

Clutch shoes and springs on all models should be renewed as a set. When reassembling six-shoe clutch, be sure the identifying marks on the shoes are all to same side of the assembly. Inspect bearing and lubricate with Homelite ALL-TEMP Multipurpose Grease (# 24551) or a lithium base grease.

CHAIN OILER. Saws may be equipped with manual chain oiler pump only or with both a manual pump and an automatic chain oiler pump.

The manual oiler pump is installed as shown in Fig. HL79 or Fig. HL80; these illustrations show exploded view of the pump assembly. Usually, service of the manual pump consists of renewing the plunger and shaft "O" rings.

To service the automatic chain oiler pump, the clutch drum and spider must first be removed from the crankshaft as outlined in a preceding paragraph. Refer to Fig. HL93 for operational diagram of pump and to Fig. HL92 for exploded view of pump assembly.

REWIND STARTER. Refer to Fig. HL94 for exploded view of rewind starter. To disassemble starter after removing fan housing and starter assembly from saw, proceed as follows:

On models with slotted rope pulley, pull rope fully out, hold pulley from turning and pry knot end of rope from pulley. Allow pulley to rewind slowly.

On models without slot in pulley, pull rope outward a short distance, hold rope, pry retainer from starter handle and untie knot in outer end of rope. Allow pulley to rewind slowly.

Then, on all models, remove the socket head screw, flat washer cup and rope pulley.

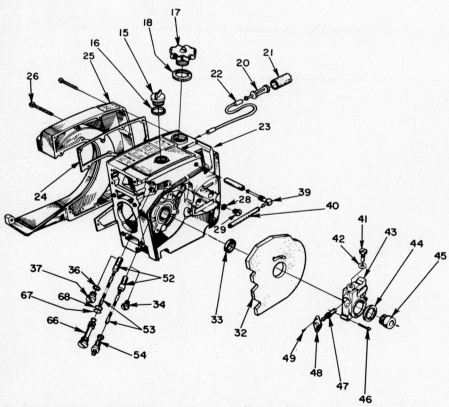

Fig. HL92—Exploded view showing automatic chain oiler pump, manual and automatic oil pick-ups, crankcase and oil reservoir and fuel tank. Automatic oil pump plunger (47) and pump body (43) are available as a matched set only. Plug (34) is used to seal opening when saw is not equipped with manual chain oiler; plug (37) and washer (36) are used on models not equipped with automatic chain oiler.

15. Chain oil cap	25. Fuel tank	39. Elbow	47. Pump gear/plunger
16. Gasket	26. Tank cover screws	40. Fuel line	48. Flanged bearing
17. Fuel tank cap	28. Gasket	41. Oil pump cam	49. Screws
18. Gasket	29. Cap	42. Gasket	52. Oil pickups
20. Pickup head	32. Saw dust shield	43. Oil pump body	53. Flexible oil lines
21. Fuel filter	33. Crankshaft seal	44. Felt seal	54. Connector
22. Flexible line	34. Plug	45. Worm gear	66. Oil line tube
23. Crankcase	36. Sealing washer	46. Pump retaining	67. Gasket
24. Gasket	37. Plug	screws	68. "O" ring

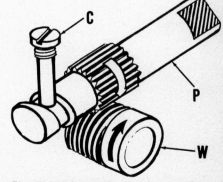

Fig. HL93—Schematic diagram of automatic chain oiler pump operation. Worm gear (W) on crankshaft drives (rotates) pump plunger (P). Cam cut in plunger rides against cam screw (C) causing plunger to move back and forth as it rotates. Flat on plunger acts as a valve as it opens intake port on downward stroke and outlet port on upward stroke.

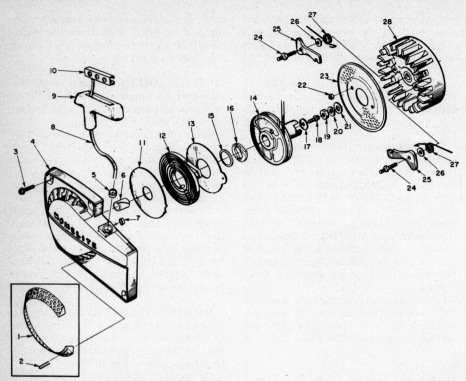

CAUTION: Rewind spring may be dislodged and can cause injury if allowed to uncoil uncontrolled. Rope bushing, starter post bushing, and/or rewind spring bushing in housing should be renewed if worn.

When reassembling starter, lubricate starter post lightly and install spring dry except for a small amount of lithium base grease on edges of spring.

Reassemble starter using exploded view in Fig. HL94 as a guide. Prewind spring about 2-4 turns.

1. Screen
2. Fastener clips
3. Hex head screws
4. Fan housing
5. Rope bushing
6. Starter post bushing
7. Rewind spring bushing
8. Starter rope
9. Handle
10. Rope retainer
11. Inner spring shield
12. Rewind spring
13. Outer spring shield
14. Starter pulley
15. Spring lock bushing
16. Spring lock
17. Retaining washer
18. Hex head screw
19. Flywheel (rotor) nut
20. Lockwasher
21. Flat washer
22. Lock nuts
23. Rotating screen
24. Pawl studs
25. Starter pawls
26. Washers
27. Pawl springs
28. Flywheel (rotor)

Fig. HL94 — Exploded view of starter. An air flow ring is used in place of screen (23) on some models.

Illustrations Courtesy Homelite Div. of Textron, ©1987

HOMELITE

Model	Bore	Stroke	Displ.	Drive Type
150 Automatic	1-9/16 in. (39.7 mm)	1⅜ in. (34.9 mm)	2.64 cu. in. (43.3 cc)	Direct

MAINTENANCE

SPARK PLUG. Recommended spark plug is Champion DJ-7J. Spark plug electrode gap should be 0.025 inch (0.63 mm). Note that spark plug has a tapered seat and does not require a gasket.

CARBURETOR. Model 150 Automatic may be equipped with a Walbro HDC or Tillotson HK diaphragm carburetor. Refer to Tillotson or Walbro section of CARBURETOR SERVICE section for carburetor overhaul and exploded views.

Initial carburetor adjustment is idle mixture needle ¾ turn open and high speed mixture needle 1 turn open. Adjust idle speed screw so that clutch is not engaged at idle speed. Turn idle mixture needle until engine will accelerate cleanly. Adjust high speed needle to obtain optimum performance with saw under cutting load. Do not set mixture needle position too lean as engine may be damaged.

MAGNETO AND TIMING. A conventional flywheel type magneto ignition system is used on early models while late models are equipped with solid-state ignition. Breaker-point models may be converted to solid-state ignition without removing breaker-box by using kit #A-97026.

The solid-state ignition system is serviced by renewing the spark plug and/or ignition module, however, be sure all wires are connected properly and the ignition switch functions correctly before renewing ignition module. Air gap between ignition module and flywheel is adjustable. Adjust air gap by loosening module retaining screws and placing a 0.015 inch (0.38 mm) shim stock between flywheel and module. Tighten module screws and remove shim stock.

Note the following on breaker-point equipped models: Breaker-points are contained in a breaker-box under the flywheel. Ignition timing is not adjustable. Breaker-point gap should be 0.015 inch (0.38 mm) and must be correct or ignition timing will be affected. Condenser capacity should be 0.15-0.19 mfd. Air gap between flywheel and coil should be 0.015 inch (0.38 mm) and is adjusted in the same manner as the solid-state ignition previously outlined.

LUBRICATION. The engine is lubricated by mixing oil with unleaded gasoline. Reocmmended oil is Homelite® two-stroke oil mixed at ratio as designated on oil container. If Homelite® oil is not available, a good quality oil designed for two-stroke engines may be used when mixed at a 16:1 ratio, however, an anti-oxidant fuel stabilizer (such as Sta-Bil) should be added to fuel mix. Anti-oxidant fuel stabilizer is not required with Homelite® oils as they contain fuel stabilizer so the fuel mix will stay fresh up to one year.

Chain oil tank should be filled with Homelite® Bar and Chain Oil or a good quality SAE 30 oil. It may be necessary to use SAE 10 oil or oil mixed with kerosene if temperature is below 40°F (4°C).

Clutch needle bearing should be removed, cleaned and lubricated periodically with Homelite® All-Temp Multi-purpose Grease.

CARBON. Carbon deposits should be removed from muffler and exhaust ports at regular intervals. Be careful not to damage ports or piston or to allow loose carbon to enter cylinder.

REPAIRS

TIGHTENING TORQUES. Recommended tightening torques are listed in following table.

Flywheel nut	200 in.-lbs. (22.6 N·m)
Spark plug	150 in.-lbs. (16.9 N·m)
Clutch hub	100 in.-lbs. (11.3 N·m)
Connecting rod screws	60 in.-lbs. (6.8 N·m)
10-24 Engine housing	45 in.-lbs. (5.1 N·m)
10-24 Front handle	45 in.-lbs. (5.1 N·m)
8-32 Socket Head, Cylinder-to-crankcase	40 in.-lbs. (4.5 N·m)
8-32 Muffler	36 in.-lbs. (4.1 N·m)
8-32 Intake manifold	36 in.-lbs. (4.1 N·m)
8-32 Oil pump mounting screws	36 in.-lbs. (4.1 N·m)
8-32 Cylinder-to-crankcase	36 in.-lbs. (4.1 N·m)
8-32 Oil pump spring screw	36 in.-lbs. (4.1 N·m)
8-32 Starter housing	36 in.-lbs. (4.1 N·m)

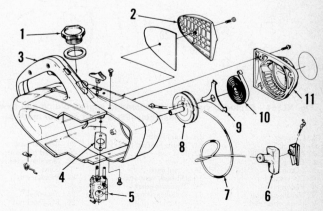

Fig. HL150 — View of engine housing and rewind starter.
1. Gas cap
2. Air filter
3. Engine housing
4. Gasket
5. Carburetor
6. Rope handle
7. Rope
8. Rope pulley
9. Spring retainer
10. Rewind spring
11. Starter housing

COMPRESSION PRESSURE. For optimum performance of all models, cylinder compression pressure should be 120-140 psi (827-965 kPa) with engine at normal operating temperature. Engine should be inspected and repaired when compression pressure is 90 psi (620 kPa) or below.

CYLINDER, PISTON, PIN AND RINGS. Refer to Fig. HL151 for exploded view of engine. To remove cylinder, remove chain, bar, starter, carburetor, engine housing, clutch, flywheel and ignition assembly. Remove chain and dirt guards. Remove oil tank and unscrew cylinder-to-crankcase screws. Note that there are four socket head screws in bottom of crankcase. Be careful when removing cylinder as crankshaft assembly will be loose in crankcase. Care should be taken not to scratch or nick mating surfaces of cylinder and crankcase.

Cylinder bore is chromed and should be inspected for excessive wear which may expose soft base metal underneath. Also inspect bore for scoring, flaking, or chipping of chrome surface.

Piston pin retaining ring on exhaust side of piston does not have a removal notch and opposite retaining ring must be removed to push pin out of piston. Piston pin is a snug fit in piston and has a closed end which must be installed on exhaust side of piston. Piston rings are retained in position by locating pins. Install piston on connecting rod so piston ring locating pins will be toward flywheel side of engine when cylinder is installed.

Be sure piston rings are correctly positioned around ring locating pins while installing cylinder. Refer to CRANKSHAFT AND CRANKCASE section to install cylinder on crankcase.

CONNECTING ROD. Connecting rod can be removed after removing cylinder as previously outlined. Connecting rod has a needle roller bearing in small end and 18 loose bearing rollers in big end. Big end is fractured and rod and cap must have serrations correctly mated. Rod and cap have aligning marks as shown in Fig. HL152 which must be aligned to correctly assemble connecting rod. Bearing rollers may be held in place during assembly with grease or beeswax on new bearing roller strip. Homelite® tool 24294 and Spacer 24548 can be used to remove and install small end needle bearing.

CRANKSHAFT AND CRANKCASE. Disassemble engine as outlined previously. Care should be taken not to scratch or damage mating surface between cylinder and crankcase.

Crankshaft is supported at both ends by roller bearings which are retained in crankcase by a retaining ring in a groove at either end. Crankshaft seals are installed with seal lip to inside. Mating surfaces of cylinder and crankcase should be cleaned then coated with room temperature-vulcanizing silicone sealer before assembly. Be sure crankshaft bearings, retaining rings and seals sit squarely in crankcase before sliding cylinder on piston. If crankshaft is cocked or cylinder is not installed squarely with crankcase, piston ring ends may catch in ports and be broken.

CLUTCH. Clutch hub has left hand threads and must be installed as shown in Fig. HL153. Clean and inspect clutch hub, drum and bearing for damage or excessive wear. Inspect crankshaft for wear or damage caused by clutch bearing. Lubricate clutch bearing with Homelite® ALL-TEMP Multipurpose Grease.

AUTOMATIC CHAIN OILER. Model 150 Automatic is equipped with a crankcase pulse-actuated automatic chain oiler pump. Refer to exploded view of oiler pump shown in Fig. HL154. Crankcase pulses actuate diaphragm and plunger to force oil out oil outlet.

To remove oil pump, remove recoil starter, engine housing and drain oil tank. Disconnect high tension lead from spark plug and clamp. Unscrew four screws and separate oil tank from crankcase. Remove oil pump from crankcase and disassemble pump. Clean and inspect pump components and passages. Note that there is a bleed hole on clutch side of crankcase which must be clear to vent tank. Air vent seal (15 – Fig. HL151) has been changed from packing felt to foam rubber.

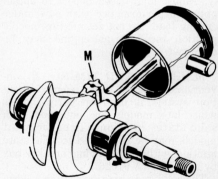

Fig. HL152 — View of connecting rod match marks (M).

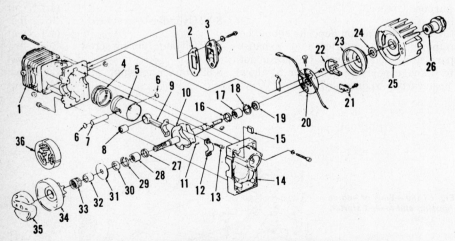

Fig. HL151 — Exploded view of 150 Automatic engine, clutch and flywheel assemblies. Clutch hub assembly (36) is used on later models.

1. Cylinder	10. Crankshaft	19. Seal	27. Thrust bearing
2. Gasket	11. Roller bearing (18)	20. Breaker plate	28. Roller bearing
3. Intake manifold	12. Rod cap	21. Fixed breaker-point	29. Retaining ring
4. Piston rings	13. Screw	22. Movable breaker-	30. Seal
5. Piston	14. Crankcase	point	31. Thrust washer
6. Pin retainers	15. Oil tank vent seal	23. Breaker-box	32. Bearing race
7. Piston pin	16. Thrust washer	24. Seal	33. Roller bearing
8. Needle bearing	17. Roller bearing	25. Flywheel	34. Clutch drum
9. Connecting rod	18. Retaining ring	26. Flywheel nut	35. Clutch hub
			36. Clutch assy.

Fig. HL153 — View of correct installation of clutch hub in drum.

Note the following specifications: Plunger (4–Fig. HL154) length should be 0.620-0.630 inch (15.7-16.0 N·m) measured from collar to end of plunger as shown in Fig. HL157. Plunger guide in pump body (7–Fig. HL154) should be 0.125-0.155 inch (3.17-3.94 N·m) from face of pump body as shown in Fig. HL158. Plunger guide is not available separately from housing. Mating surfaces of oil pump and crankcase must be flat and can be dressed using #180 grit emery paper on a surface plate. Pressure check pump by attaching a pressure tester to oil inlet line; pump and inlet line must be full of oil during test. Pump should maintain pressure of 8-10 psi (55-60 kPa). Oil tank gasket surface

should be flat and can be dressed with emery paper to remove roughness. Crankcase gasket sealing surface has ridges that cannot be dressed and must be in good condition. Apply a thin coat of RTV silastic sealer to gasket sealing surfaces of crankcase and oil tank. Note gray and black areas of crankcase shown in Fig. HL155 which must be coated. On older models, do not apply sealer in oil crossover hole or allow excess sealer to enter hole. Oil tank should maintain 6-8 psi (41-55 kPa) pressure if tested after assembly.

Model 150 saws prior to serial number 42411584 should be modified as follows to use later style pump components. Using later pump components and modify-

ing pump will stop pump oil output when engine idles. Remove oil pump and discard diaphragm and plunger (4–Fig. HL154) and gaskets. New style diaphragm and plunger is 0.025 inch (0.63 mm) thick and does not require gaskets. Refer to Fig. HL156. Remove then discard rubber sleeve attached to post. Shorten post by breaking or filing so top of post is 7/64 inch (2.8 mm) below diaphragm sealing surface. Clean old vent hole and block hole with RTV plastic sealer. Drill a new vent hole as shown in Fig. HL156 using a 0.070-0.090 inch (1.8-2.3 mm) drill bit; be careful not to

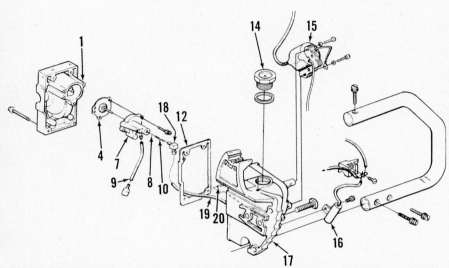

Fig. HL154–Exploded view of oil tank and related assemblies. On models equipped with solid-state ignition, condenser (16) is not used and ignition module is located in place of ignition coil (15).

1. Crankcase		17. Oil tank
4. Diaphragm & plunger	9. Oil intake	18. Elbow fitting
7. Oil pump body	10. Spring	19. Hose
8. Ball	12. Gasket	20. Outlet fitting
	14. Oil tank cap	
	15. Ignition coil or module	
	16. Condenser	

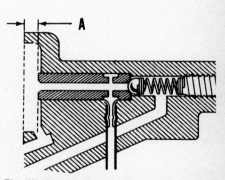

Fig. HL157 – Plunger length must be 0.620-0.630 inch (15.7-16.0 N·m) from collar to end.

Fig. HL158 – Plunger guide should be 0.125-0.155 inch (3.17-3.93 mm) (A) from end of guide to face of oil tank.

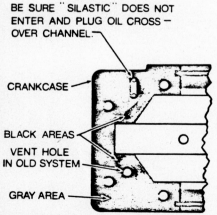

IMPORTANT

BE SURE "SILASTIC" DOES NOT ENTER AND PLUG OIL CROSS – OVER CHANNEL.

CRANKCASE

BLACK AREAS

VENT HOLE IN OLD SYSTEM

GRAY AREA

Fig. HL155 – Apply RTV silastic sealer to gray and black areas of crankcase as shown.

Fig. HL156 – View showing modifications of crankcase when installing later oil pump components on early models. See text.

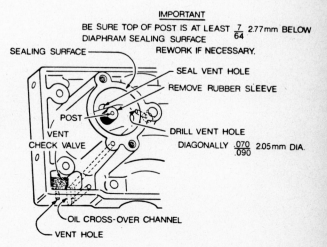

IMPORTANT

BE SURE TOP OF POST IS AT LEAST 7/64 2.77mm BELOW DIAPHRAM SEALING SURFACE REWORK IF NECESSARY.

SEALING SURFACE

SEAL VENT HOLE

REMOVE RUBBER SLEEVE

POST

VENT

CHECK VALVE

DRILL VENT HOLE

DIAGONALLY .070/.090 2.05mm DIA.

OIL CROSS-OVER CHANNEL

VENT HOLE

allow metal chips to enter crankcase. Assemble and pressure check pump and oil tank as previously outlined.

REWIND STARTER. To remove recoil starter, insert a screwdriver between air intake slots to hold rope pulley (8 – Fig. HL150) in starter housing during removal. Unscrew starter housing screws and remove starter. Pull starter rope and hold rope pulley with notch in pulley adjacent to rope outlet. Pull rope back through outlet so that it engages notch in pulley and allow pulley to completely rewind. Lift out rope pulley and carefully remove spring retainer (9) by pressing down in center of retainer while freeing retainer legs. Care must be taken if rewind spring is allowed to uncoil uncontrolled.

Rewind spring is wound in clockwise direction in starter housing. Rope is wound on rope pulley in clockwise direction as viewed with pulley in housing. To place tension on rewind spring, pass rope through rope outlet in housing and install rope handle. Pull rope out and hold rope pulley so notch on pulley is adjacent to rope outlet. Pull rope back through outlet between notch in pulley and housing. Turn rope pulley clockwise to place tension on spring. Release pulley and check starter action. Do not place more tension on rewind spring than is necessary to draw rope handle up against housing.

Illustrations Courtesy Homelite Div. of Textron, ©1987

HOMELITE

Model	Bore	Stroke	Displ.	Drive Type
Super WIZ 55	2 in. (50.8 mm)	1⅜ in. (34.9 mm)	4.32 cu. in. (70.8 cc)	Gear
Super WIZ 66	2 in. (50.8 mm)	1½ in. (38.1 mm)	4.7 cu. in. (77.0 cc)	Gear
Super WIZ 80	2-3/16 in. (55.6 mm)	1-35/64 in. (39.3 mm)	5.8 cu. in. (95.0 cc)	Gear

MAINTENANCE

SPARK PLUG. Recommended spark plug is Champion J6J for Super WIZ 55 and Super WIZ 66 and Champion UJ11G for Super WIZ 80. Electrode gap should be 0.025 inch (0.63 mm). In high temperatures or for heavy duty operation, use UJ7G plug in place of J6J or UJ11G. In extremely cold weather, a UJ12 plug may be used to avoid cold fouling and improve starting.

CARBURETOR. All models are equipped with a Tillotson Model HL diaphragm type carburetor. Carburetor model number is stamped on carburetor mouting flange. Refer to Tillotson section of CARBURETOR SERVICE section for carburetor overhaul and exploded views.

For initial starting equipment, close both fuel mixture needles lightly (turn clockwise), then open idle fuel needle ¾ turn counterclockwise and main fuel needle one to 1¼ turns counterclockwise. Back idle speed stop screw out until throttle disc will fully close, then turn screw back in until it contacts throttle shaft arm plus one additional turn.

Make final adjustment with engine warm and running. Adjust idle speed screw so that engine will run at just below clutch engagement speed, then adjust idle fuel mixture needle so engine runs smoothly. Readjust idle speed stop screw if necessary. With engine running at full throttle under load (stall chain in cut), adjust main fuel needle so engine runs at highest obtainable speed without excessive smoke. Idle fuel needle is left, main fuel needle is to right.

THROTTLE CONNECTIONS. The throttle trigger is not directly connected with the carburetor throttle shaft arm.

When throttle trigger is released, the throttle shaft arm should be held against the idle speed stop screw. Squeezing throttle trigger moves the throttle rod or lever away from carburetor shaft arm allowing the throttle opening spring (nongoverned models) or governor spring to move throttle to wide open

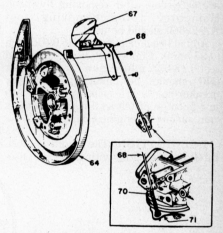

Fig. HL211 — View showing governor hookup used on Super WIZ 66 and Super WIZ 80. Refer to Fig. HL215; throttle rod is connected at hole numbered (3). Governor spring (70) is compressed between bracket (71) and shoulder on governor rod.

64. Back plate
67. Governor assy.
68. Governor rod
70. Governor spring
71. Spring bracket

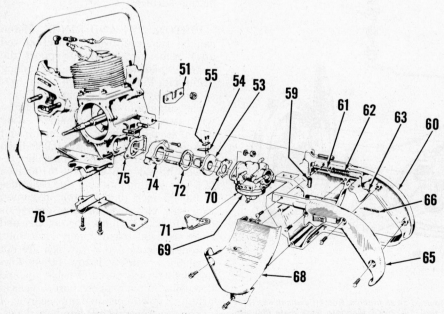

Fig. HL202 — Exploded view showing typical throttle controls and carburetor mounting.

51. Fuel tank strap
53. Pyramid reed seat
54. Inlet reeds
55. Reed clamps
59. Throttle rod sleeve
60. Throttle handle
61. Throttle rod
62. Throttle spring
63. Throttle trigger
65. Handle cover
66. Throttle latch spring
68. Carburetor shield
69. Carburetor
70. Gasket
71. Spring bracket
72. Gasket
74. Pyramid reed spacer
75. Gasket
76. Brace

Fig. HL215 — View showing throttle shaft arm typical of all carburetors. It is important that throttle opening or governor spring and/or link be hooked into proper hole. Refer also to Fig. HL211.

position. Check action of throttle linkage, carburetor throttle shaft and throttle opening or governor spring with engine stopped.

GOVERNOR. All models except Super WIZ 55 are equipped with an air vane type governor to prevent over-speeding of engine when saw is out of cut. Maximum no-load engine speed should be 7500 rpm; engine peak horsepower is obtained at about 6000 rpm.

With engine not running, check to see that governor spring will fully open throttle when throttle trigger is squeezed to wide open position. With engine warm and running at no load, governor should limit engine speed to about 7500 rpm by closing carburetor throttle. Check governor air vane and linkage for free operation and renew governor if worn or damaged.

MAGNETO. Refer to Fig. HL217 for exploded view of typical REPCO magneto. Breaker points, coil and condenser are accessible after removing flywheel. Homelite® rotor removing tool AA-22560 should be used.

Adjust breaker-point gap to 0.015 inch (0.38 mm). Condenser capacity should test 0.18-0.22 mfd. A new cam wiper felt (53) should be installed whenever breaker-points are being renewed. Adjust position of felt so it lightly contacts cam surface of engine crankshaft.

LUBRICATION. The engine is lubricated by mixing oil with unleaded gasoline. Recommended oil is Homelite® two-stroke oil mixed at ratio as designated on oil container. If Homelite® oil is not available, a good quality oil designed for two-stroke engines may be used when mixed at a 16:1 ratio, however, an anti-oxidant fuel stabilizer (such as Sta-Bil) should be added to fuel mix. Anti-oxidant fuel stabilizer is not required with Homelite® oils as they contain fuel stabilizer so the fuel mix will stay fresh up to one year.

Maintain oil level in gearcase to arrow on inspection window using Homelite® Gear Oil or SAE 90 gear lubricant. Check oil level with saw setting on level surface. Do not overfill.

Chain oiler tank should be filled with Homelite® Bar and Chain Oil or SAE 30 motor oil. In low temperatures, dilute chain oil with one part of kerosene to four parts of oil.

CARBON REMOVAL. Carbon deposits shoud be removed from exhaust ports and muffler at regular intervals. Use a wood scraper and be careful not to damage edges of exhaust ports. Piston should be at top dead center when removing carbon. Do not attempt to start engine with muffler removed.

REPAIRS

CONNECTING ROD. Connecting rod and piston assembly can be removed after removing cylinder from crankcase. Be careful to remove all of the loose needle rollers when detaching rod from crankpin. Models Super WIZ 55 and Super WIZ 66 and 27 needle rollers while Super WIZ 80 has 31 loose needle rollers.

Renew connecting rod if bent or twisted, or if crankpin bearing surface is scored, burned or excessively worn or if Formica thrust washers are deeply grooved or are not completely bonded to rod. The caged needle roller piston pin bearing can be renewed by pressing old bearing out and new bearing in using Homelite® tool A-23809. Press on lettered end of bearing cage only.

Homelite recommends renewing the crankpin needle rollers at each overhaul. New needle rollers are supplied in a wax strip; wrap the strip around crankpin, then assemble connecting rod cap on the crankpin. When reassembling engine after inspection, use light grease or beeswax to stick 16 rollers to rod and cap. Install piston and connecting rod assembly so pinned ends of piston rings are away from exhaust port (muffler) side of engine.

On Models Super WIZ 55 and Super WIZ 66, tighten the connecting rod cap screws to 55-60 in.-lbs. (6.2-6.8 N·m). On Model Super WIZ 80, tighten rod cap screws to a torque of 70-80 in.-lbs. (7.9-9.0 N·m). Wiggle rod and cap as the screws are tightened to align fracture mating surfaces.

PISTON, PIN AND RINGS. Piston can be removed from connecting rod after removing cylinder. Support the piston while removing and installing piston pin. Pin is retained in piston by a snap ring at each end of pin.

The aluminum alloy piston is fitted with two pinned piston rings. Ring width is 0.037 inch (0.94 mm) and end gap should be 0.070-0.080 inch (1.78-2.03 mm). Rings should be renewed if end gap exceeds 0.100 inch (2.54 mm). Minimum ring side clearance is 0.0025 inch (0.063 mm); maximum ring side clearance in ring groove is 0.004 inch (0.10 mm). Piston, pin and rings are available in standard size only.

Renew piston and pin, which are not available separately, if any of the following defects are noted: Visible up and down play of pin in piston bore, cracks in piston or hole in piston dome, scoring of piston accompanied by aluminum deposits in cylinder bore, piston ring locating pin worn to half of original thickness, or if side clearance of new ring exceeds 0.004 inch (0.10 mm). Refer to CYLIN-

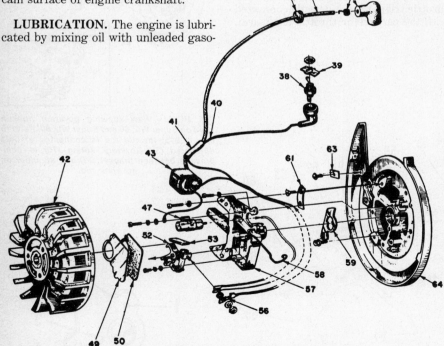

Fig. HL217—Exploded view of typical REPCO magneto used on all models. Rotor (flywheel) has three tapped holes for installation of remover (Homelite® tool AA-22560). Magneto back plate (64) supports crankshaft seal and needle bearing.

35. Plug terminal	40. Ground wire	49. Breaker cover	57. Armature core
36. High tension wire	41. Sleeve	50. Gasket	58. Cover clip
37. Grommet	42. Rotor	52. Breaker points	59. Sealing felt
38. "ON-OFF" switch	43. Ignition coil	53. Cam wiper felt	61. Wire clamp, inner
39. Switch plate	47. Condenser	56. Ground wire tab	63. Wire clamp, outer

DER paragraph for information from cylinder bore.

Assemble piston to connecting rod or install piston and rod assembly so piston ring locating pin side of piston is toward intake side of cylinder (away from exhaust ports). Always use new piston pin retaining snap rings.

CYLINDER. Cylinder bore is chrome plated; plating is light gray in color and does not have appearance of polished chrome. Because cylinder is honed after plating, the chrome bore looks much like the base metal of the aluminum cylinder. If plating has been penetrated by scoring or other causes, the aluminum exposed will appear as a bright area. These bright areas are usually, but not always, located at edges of cylinder ports. If further checking, as outlined in following paragraph, shows that chrome has been penetrated, the cylinder should be renewed.

In some instances, particles of metal from scored piston are deposited on the cylinder bore. This condition is indicated by a rough appearance and deposits can be removed using a rubber impregnated grinding wheel mounted in a ¼ inch electric drill. If a screwdriver will scratch the cleaned surface, chrome plating has been worn away and the cylinder should be renewed. Also, renew the cylinder if cracked or if more than three critical cooling fins are broken off.

When installing both a new piston and a new cylinder, clean and oil both parts and place piston in cylinder bore without rings or connecting rod. The piston should fall freely when cylinder is turned up. If not, select a new piston or a new cylinder that will give this desired fit.

CRANKSHAFT, BEARINGS AND SEALS. The drive end of the crankshaft is supported in a ball bearing (24 – Fig. HL219) which is retained in crankcase by two screws (26) and special washers (25) which engage groove in ball bearing outer race. Crankshaft is held in position by a snap ring (23) at outer side of bearing. The flywheel end crankshaft journal rotates in a caged needle roller bearing supported in magneto back plate (64 – Fig. HL217).

To remove crankshaft, first remove cylinder, piston and connecting rod assembly, clutch spider and drum, flywheel (magneto rotor) and magneto back plate.

NOTE: On models with governor, be sure to disconnect governor linkage before attempting to remove back plate.

Remove the two bearing retaining screws (26 – Fig. HL219) and washers (25), then bump or push crankshaft and bearing from crankcase. To remove ball bearing, remove snap ring (23) and press crankshaft from bearing.

Renew magneto end needle bearing if any roller shows visible wear or flat spot, or if rollers can be separated more than width of one roller. Renew drive end ball bearing if bearing is rough or has perceptible wear. Inspect crankshaft magneto end and crankpin journals and renew crankshaft if wear marks are visible. Also, renew crankshaft if tapered end fits loosely in magneto rotor or if keyway is enlarged. Crankshaft runout should not exceed 0.003 inch (0.08 mm).

New crankshaft seals and sealing gasket should always be installed when reassembling engine. Install new seal in crankcase with lip of seal inward (toward main bearing position). Install ball bearing on crankshaft with retaining groove in outer race toward crankshaft throw, then install retaining snap ring. Soak new gasket in oil, then position gasket in crankcase. Install crankshaft and bearing using seal protector sleeve and jackscrew, then secure bearing in position using new special washers and screws. Install new seal in back plate with new gasket.

Homelite® special tools for installing bearings, crankshaft seals and crankshaft are as follows:

A-23137 – Jackscrew, crankshaft and bearing.
23136 – Jackscrew body.
22820-1 – Collar, crankshaft and bearing.
22812-1 – Plate, shaft aligning.
23233 – Plug, back plate & crankcase seal.
23232 – Sleeve, crankshaft seal.
23391-1 – Plug, back plate bearing.

CRANKCASE. With crankshaft and bearing removed, check bearing bore. A lapped appearance indicates that the bearing outer race has been turning in the bore. If bearing fits loose in bore, renew the crankcase and/or bearing as necessary to obtain a tight fit. New ball bearing special retaining washers and screws should always be used when reassembling.

REED VALVE. The reed valve should be inspected whenever carburetor is removed. All models are equipped with a pyramid reed type valve which has renewable reeds. Refer to Fig. HL221.

CLUTCH. A shoe type clutch is used on all models and clutch hub is threaded to engine crankshaft. All models have right hand threads. Refer to Fig. HL225 for exploded view.

On Models Super WIZ 55 and Super WIZ 66, standard clutch shoes are ⅝ inch (15.8 mm) wide; optional heavy duty clutch shoes are ¾ inch (19.0 mm) wide. Standard and heavy duty clutch components are not individually

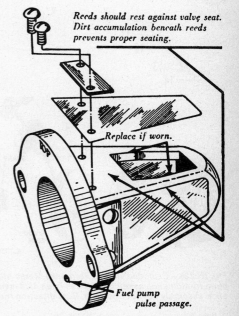

Fig. HL221 – Inspection points for pyramid reed seat and reeds.

Reeds should rest against valve seat. Dirt accumulation beneath reeds prevents proper seating.

Replace if worn.

Fuel pump pulse passage.

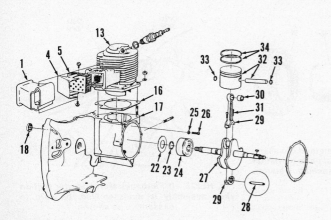

Fig. HL219 – Exploded view of typical engine.

1. Heat damper
4. Exhaust cap
5. Muffler element
13. Cylinder
16. Gasket
17. Crankcase
18. Crankshaft seal
22. Gasket
23. Snap ring
24. Ball bearing
25. Special washers
26. Special screws
27. Crankshaft
28. Needle rollers
29. Connecting rod & cap
30. Needle bearing
31. Connecting rod screws
32. Piston & pin
33. Snap rings
34. Piston rings

interchangeable; also, a different gear case cover is required with heavy duty clutch. Clutch drum bushing is renewable on all models.

Homelite® tool A-23696 can be used with wrench to remove clutch spider. When assembling clutch, be sure end loops of springs are closed and are located at the center of a clutch shoe. If installing new clutch drum, wash off protective coating with petroleum solvent.

TRANSMISSION. All models have a two-gear transmission as shown in Fig. HL225.

To service transmission, first drain oil from transmission case, then remove the screws retaining cover to case. Tap cover lightly, if necessary, to loosen gasket seal and remove the cover.

To disassemble transmission, remove nut (1 – Fig. HL225) from crankshaft, remove washer and clutch cover (3) and using Homelite® special tool A-23696, turn clutch hub counterclockwise while holding engine from turning to remove the spider and shoe assembly. Remove clutch drum (7) and thrust washers (8) from crankshaft. Remove sprocket nut (10), sprocket (12) and related parts, then using soft mallet, bump sprocket shaft (20) and gear from case. Remove snap ring (18), then press bearing from case using Homelite® special tool 23228. Renew the Formica seal (16) before installing new bearing. Remove retaining screws, then remove output gear (19) from sprocket shaft. Reverse disassembly procedure and use Fig. HL225 as a guide to reassemble. Reinstall cover with new gasket and fill transmission to proper level with lubricant.

REWIND STARTER. Refer to Fig. HL228 for exploded view of starter. When installing rewind spring, pulley and rope, spring should be pretensioned so pulley will rewind all rope and pull rope handle lightly against starter housing. If spring is tensioned too tightly, or if starter rope is too long, spring can be damaged by being wound too tightly when starter rope is pulled out. Friction shoe assembly (8) is available as a unit assembly only. If friction shoes have been disassembled, they must be reassembled as shown in Fig. 229. Be sure that starter is properly placed on starter pulley so sharp edges of clutch shoes are pointing in direction shown in Fig. HL228.

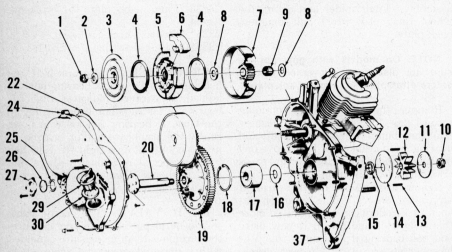

Fig. HL225 — Exploded view of transmission. One standard and two optional gear ratios are available. Standard gear ratio of 3.57:1 is provided by output gear with 75 teeth and clutch drum with 21 teeth. Optional 2.84:1 ratio requires output (driven) gear with 71 teeth and clutch drum gear with 25 teeth. On 2:1 optional gear ratio, output gear has 64 teeth and clutch drum gear has 32 teeth.

1. Crankshaft nut		24. Transmission cover
2. Flat washer	9. Bronze bushing	25. "O" ring
3. Clutch cover	10. Sprocket shaft nut	26. Window
4. Clutch springs	11. Sprocket washer	27. Window plate
5. Clutch spider	12. Chain sprocket	29. Filler cap
6. Clutch shoes	13. Sprocket keys	30. Gasket
7. Clutch drum & gear	14. Sprocket washer	37. Crankcase & gear
8. Thrust washer	15. Sprocket spacer	case
	16. Formica seal	
	17. Ball bearing	
	18. Snap ring	
	19. Driven (output) gear	
	20. Sprocket shaft	
	22. Gasket	

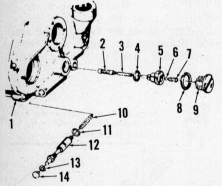

Fig. HL226 — Exploded view of typical manual oil pump assembly.

1. Fuel tank	8. Gasket
2. Oil filter	9. Plug
3. Oil line	10. Spring
4. Gasket	11. "O" ring
5. Valve seat	12. Pump plunger
6. Check ball	13. "O" ring
7. Check valve spring	14. Button

CCW ROTATION

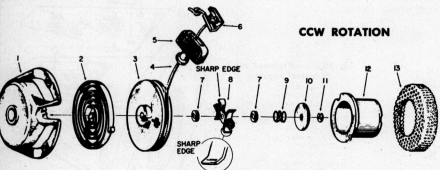

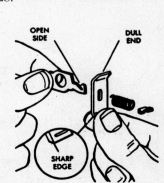

Fig. HL228 — Exploded view of Fairbanks-Morse starter. Fig. HL229 shows proper method of assembling friction shoe assembly if it has been disassembled for some reason; individual parts of friction shoe assembly are not available. Note direction for shaft edges of shoes when reassembling starter.

1. Cover		
2. Rewind spring	5. Handle grip	8. Friction shoe assy.	11. Retaining ring
3. Rope pulley	6. Grip insert	9. Brake spring	12. Starter cup
4. Starter rope	7. Brake washers	10. Retaining washer	13. Starter screen

Fig. HL229 — If Fairbanks-Morse starter friction shoe assembly is disassembled, be sure to reassemble as shown.

HOMELITE

Model XEL 8, XEL 10, XEL 12, XEL 14	Volts 110-120	Current/Hz AC/60	Amps 11	HP 1.5	Drive Type Gear

ELECTRICAL REQUIREMENTS

The XEL series electric saw is designed to be used on electrical circuits with 115-120 volt alternating current. The XEL series electric saw is double-insulated and does not require a ground wire. A two-wire extension cord is recommended but a three-wire cord may be used if ground wire is not connected to saw. A UL or similarly approved extension cord should be used. It is necessary that the correct wire gauge be matched to cord length and line current. Using an undersized cord may result in power loss and overheating.

MAINTENANCE

LUBRICATION. Oilite bushings (8, 10 and 11 – Fig. HL230) and rear bearing (15) do not require lubrication. Drive gear (9 or 9A) should have 2½ to 3 ounces (74-89 mL) of Homelite® grease, part 17237, around gear teeth.

Saw chain is lubricated by oil from a manual oil pump. Recommended chain oil is Homelite® Bar and Chain Oil. Clean SAE 30 oil may be used for temperatures above 40°F and progressively lighter weight oils for temperatures below 40°F.

BRUSHES. Brushes may be renewed without major disassembly of unit. Position saw so housing cover (23 – Fig. HL230) is up, then remove cover. Insert the tip of a narrow screwdriver under brush holder (22) between the commutator and housing and pry up to unsnap holder. Disconnect brush lead, then carefully withdraw brush assembly.

When reinstalling, make certain brush holder is snapped fully into place and brush leads are positioned properly.

DRIVE SPROCKET. The XEL 12 and XEL 14 models are equipped with a slipper drive sprocket (3 through 6 – Fig. HL230) designed to absorb shock loads transmitted through the chain to the motor. Adjustment is required when sprocket slips under light loads.

To adjust, first remove sprocket cover (2), chain and guide bar. Using a suitable tool to prevent sprocket (6) from turning, tighten retaining nut (3) to 30-35 in.-lbs. (3.4-3.9 N·m) or back nut (3) off and retighten until snug, then rotate nut ³/₈ inch turn further. Do not overtighten retaining nut. Overtightening slipper sprocket assembly will reduce its effectiveness and may cause motor damage.

REPAIR

Major component disassembly and reassembly procedures are evident after inspection of unit and referral to exploded view in Fig. HL230.

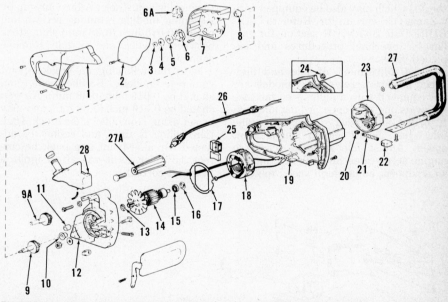

Fig. HL230 — Exploded view of XEL electric chain saw. Components 6A, 9A and 27A are used on XEL 8 and XEL 10 saws.

1. Handle cover	8. Bushing	22. Brush holder
2. Sprocket cover	9. Slipper drive gear	23. Housing cover
3. Nut	9A. Drive gear	24. Lock ring
4. Belleville washer	10. Bushing	25. Switch
5. Washer	11. Bushing	26. Power cord
6. Slipper sprocket	12. Drivecase	27. Handle bar
6A. Sprocket	13. Thrust washer	27A. Handle
7. Drivecase cover	14. Armature	28. Oil tank
	15. Bearing	
	16. Spring washer	
	17. Fan baffle	
	18. Field	
	19. Motor housing	
	20. Brush	
	21. Spring	

HOMELITE

Model	Bore	Stroke	Displ.	Drive Type
XL, XL2	1-5/16 in. (33.34 mm)	1-3/16 in. (30.16 mm)	1.6 cu. in. (26.2 cc)	Direct
Super 2, VI Super 2, VI Super 2SL	1-7/16 in. (36.51 mm)	1-3/16 in. (30.16 mm)	1.9 cu. in. (31.2 cc)	Direct

MAINTENANCE

SPARK PLUG. Recommended spark plug is Champion DJ7J. Spark plug electrode gap should be 0.025 inch (0.63 mm).

CARBURETOR. The VI Super models are equipped with a Walbro HDC diaphragm carburetor while all remaining models may have a Walbro HDC or Tillotson HK carburetor, except the XL which may also be equipped with a Zama C2S carburetor. Refer to CARBURETOR SERVICE section for carburetor overhaul procedures and exploded views.

Initial adjustment of idle and high speed mixture screws (early models are not equipped with a high speed mixture screw) is one turn open. Adjust idle mixture and idle speed screws so engine idles just below clutch engagement speed. Adjust idle mixture screw so engine accelerates smoothly. On models so equipped, adjust high speed mixture screw to obtain optimum performance under cutting load. Final adjustments should be made with engine warm.

MAGNETO AND TIMING. A conventional flywheel type magneto ignition system is used on early models while later models are equipped with solid-state ignition. The solid-state ignition system is serviced by renewing the spark plug and/or ignition module. Air gap between ignition module and flywheel is adjustable. Adjust air gap by loosening module retaining screws and place a 0.015 inch (0.38 mm) shim stock between flywheel and module. Remove shim stock.

Note the following on breaker-point equipped models: Breaker-point gap should be 0.015 inch (0.38 mm). Air gap should be 0.015 inch (0.38 mm) and may be set using Homelite® shim stock. Ignition timing is fixed and cannot be adjusted. Breaker-point gap must be correct, however, as it will affect ignition timing if correct.

LUBRICATION. The engine is lubricated by mixing oil with unleaded gasoline. Recommended oil is Homelite® two-stroke oil mixed at ratio as designated on oil container. If Homelite® oil is not available, a good quality oil designed for two-stroke engines may be used when mixed at a 16:1 ratio, however, an antioxidant fuel stabilizer (such as Sta-Bil) should be added to fuel mix. Antioxidant fuel stabilizer is not required with Homelite® oils as they contain fuel stabilizer so the fuel mix will stay fresh up to one year.

Saw chain is lubricated by oil from an automatic oil pump. Recommended chain oil is Homelite® Bar and Chain Oil or clean SAE 30 oil. Dilute SAE 30 oil with kerosene if ambient temperature is below 40°F (4°C).

MUFFLER. Outer screen of muffler should be cleaned of debris every week or as required. Carbon should be removed from muffler and engine ports to prevent excessive carbon buildup and power loss. Do not allow loose carbon to enter cylinder and be careful not to damage exhaust port or piston.

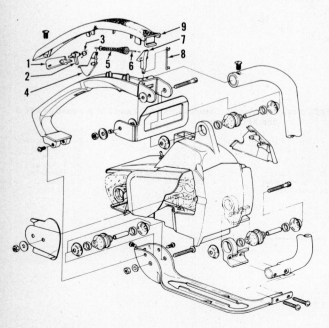

Fig. HL240—Exploded view of trigger mechanism and associated parts used on VI Super models.

1. Throttle safety lever
2. Throttle safety stop
3. Spring
4. Trigger
5. Spring
6. Trigger rod
7. Throttle lever
8. Throttle rod
9. Handle cover

REPAIRS

TIGHTENING TORQUE VALUES. Tightening torque values are listed in following table.

Flywheel	100 in.-lbs. (11.3 N·m)
Clutch hub	100 in.-lbs. (11.3 N·m)
Spark plug	150 in.-lbs. (16.9 N·m)
Crankcase screws socket head	35 in.-lbs. (3.9 N·m)
Starter pulley screw	35 in.-lbs. (3.9 N·m)
Carburetor retaining screws	35 in.-lbs. (3.9 N·m)

COMPRESSION PRESSURE. For optimum performance of all models, cylinder compression pressure should be 115-145 psi (793-1000 kPa) with engine at normal operating temperature. Engine should be inspected and repaired when compression pressure is 90 psi (620 kPa) or below.

CYLINDER, PISTON, PIN AND RINGS. Cylinder may be removed after unscrewing socket head cap screws in bottom of crankcase (25–Fig. HL247). Be careful when removing cylinder as crankshaft assembly will be loose in crankcase. Care should be taken not to scratch or nick mating surfaces of cylinder and crankcase.

Inspect crankshaft bearings and renew if scored or worn. Thrust washers (15–Fig. HL243) should be installed with shoulder to outside. Crankshaft seals are installed with seal lip to inside. Cylinder and crankcase mating surfaces should be flat and free of nicks and scratches. Mating surfaces should be cleaned then coated with room temperature vulcanizing (RTV) silicone sealer before assembly.

Early model cylinders are equipped with an open exhaust port while a bridged exhaust port is used on late model cylinders. Early model piston is equipped with a piston ring locating pin in the piston ring groove. Piston ring installed on early model piston must be positioned so end gap indexes with locating pin in ring groove. Install early model piston so piston ring locating pin is opposite exhaust port. Late model piston does not have piston ring locating pin and piston ring should be installed so end gap is opposite exhaust port.

Bearings, seals and thrust washers must be positioned correctly on crankshaft before final assembly. Use the following procedure for crankshaft installation: With piston assembly installed on rod, insert piston in cylinder being sure piston ring is aligned on locating pin. Install thrust washers (15), bearings (14), seal spacers (13) and seals (12) on crankshaft. Place 0.015 inch (0.38 mm) thick shims shown in Fig.

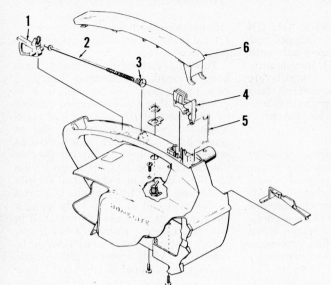

Fig. HL241 — View showing dual trigger mechanism.
1. Rear trigger
2. Trigger rod
3. Spring
4. Front trigger
5. Throttle rod
6. Handle cover

Fig. HL242 — View of later model case assembly.
1. Handle cover
2. Rear trigger
3. Trigger rod
4. Spring
5. Front trigger
6. Case assy.
7. Air filter cover
8. Chain guard
9. Guide bar plate
10. Hand guard

Fig. HL243 — Exploded view of cylinder, crankshaft and clutch assemblies. Clutch hub assembly (17) is used on later models.
1. Ignition coil
2. Cylinder
3. Retainer
4. Piston pin
5. Piston
6. Piston ring
7. Snap ring
8. Washer
9. Clutch hub
10. Bearing
11. Clutch drum
12. Seal
13. Seal spacer
14. Bearing
15. Thrust washer
16. Crankshaft assy.
17. Clutch assy.

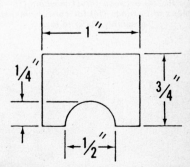

Fig. HL244 — Shims used in crankshaft assembly may be made by cutting 0.015 inch (0.38 mm) thick plastic, metal or other suitable material in the outline shown above. Refer to Fig. HL245 and text.

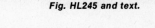

HL244 between thrust washers and bearings as shown in Fig. HL245. Gently push seals toward crankshaft counterweights until assemblies are snug. Remove shims and complete assembly being careful not to disturb position of thrust washers, bearings and seals; do not tighten crankcase screws. Gently tap crankshaft at both ends, then tighten crankcase screws.

CLUTCH. Clutch hub has left hand threads and must be installed as shown in Fig. HL246. Clean and inspect clutch hub, drum and bearing for damage or excessive wear. Inspect crankshaft for wear or damage caused by defective clutch bearing. Clutch bearing contains 21 needle rollers which will fall out when bearing is removed if the following procedure is not followed. Roll a tube of paper approximately the size of the crankshaft and slide the clutch drum and bearing off the crankshaft and on to the rolled paper. The roll of paper will prevent the bearing needle rollers from falling out and the drum and bearing can be installed by reversing the procedure. If bearing is removed without using the above procedure, the needle bearings will fall out and a new bearing must be installed as needle rollers are too small.

NOTE: Be sure all 21 needle rollers are present in bearing race.

Fig. HL245 — View showing placement of shims (Fig. HL244) between thrust washers (15 — Fig. H243) and bearings (14) for correct crankshaft assembly. Refer to text.

Fig. HL246 — View of correct installation of clutch hub in drum.

New bearings can be installed without using above procedure since wear has not yet loosened rollers.

AUTOMATIC CHAIN OILER SYSTEM. All models are equipped with a crankcase pulse actuated automatic chain oil pump except XL models after serial number 772776001 which are equipped with a pressurized oil tank system. Refer to the appropriate following paragraphs to service automatic chain oiler systems.

Diaphragm Type Pump. A defective oiler pump may cause excessive smoke during operation, hydraulic lock preventing starting of engine or oil leaking from guide bar pad while engine idles or is shut off. If any of these conditions exist and excessive smoke is not due to improperly mixed fuel, proceed as follows: Attach a suitable carburetor tester to pickup line as shown in Fig. HL248 and pressurize to 5-8 psi (34-55 kPa). If system does not hold pressure, then oil is leaking past pump body (6 – Fig. HL247) and crankcase (25), renew pump body.

To remove pump body, remove pump cover (2), spring (3) and diaphragm and plunger (5). Seal off pressure and pulse passages in crankcase and insert a small wad of paper in pump body bore. Two methods of detaching pump body are recommended. One method is to drill into pump body bore with a 7/64 inch drill bit approximately ½ inch (12.7 mm), then tap a #2 "easy out" into bore. Twist

and pull pump body from crankcase. The other method is to drill and tap pump body bore with a 10-32 thread and use a suitable puller to withdraw pump body from crankcase. Make certain check ball (7) and spring (8) are not lost when pump body is removed.

Thoroughly clean all parts and pump bore in crankcase. Measure length of new pump body and related bore in crankcase, then install required number of Homelite® 0.015 inch thick gaskets 69596 to position diaphragm end of pump body 0.000-0.015 inch (0.00-0.38 mm) above diaphragm chamber floor as shown at (A – Fig. HL248). Insert spring (8 – Fig. HL247) and check ball (7) into crankcase. Check ball may also be placed in ball seat end of pump body using a small amount of grease to hold ball in position. Using a suitable arbor press, insert pump body halfway into crankcase. Apply a bead of RTV silastic sealer around upper third of body, then continue pressing body into crankcase until it seats in bore. Wipe off excess sealer. Insert diaphragm and plunger and work it against check ball several times making sure it operates freely. Allow RTV sealer to dry. Pressure test pump as previously outlined to check repair. If system does not hold pressure then pump bore in crankcase is damaged or defective and renewal of crankcase assembly is required. If system holds pressure, reassemble remaining components and fill oil tank.

With bar and chain removed, start and run saw at wide open throttle in 15

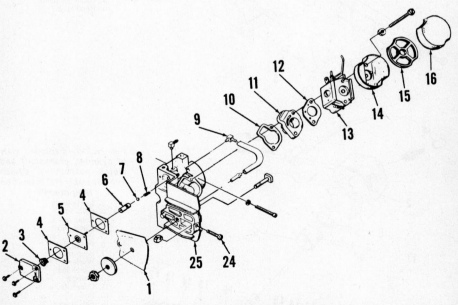

Fig. HL247 — Exploded view of Model XL-2 crankcase and oil pump assemblies. Other models are similar.

1. Bar plate	6. Oil pump cylinder	15. Retainer
2. Pump cover	7. Check ball	16. Air filter
3. Spring	8. Spring	24. Chain tension
4. Gasket	9. Oil line	11. Intake manifold	adjusting screw
5. Diaphragm & plunger	10. Gasket	12. Gasket	25. Crankcase
		13. Carburetor	
		14. Filter housing	

second intervals. Oil pump should deliver 12-17 cc/min. during test and 5-12 cc/min. under actual operating conditions. Shut off engine and check for leaks.

Pressurized Oil Tank System. Crankcase pulses pressurize the oil tank forcing oil directly from the oil tank to the outlet. In temperatures below 32°F (0°C), it is necessary to dilute chain oil with one part of kerosene to four parts of oil to allow system operation.

If chain oil flow is inadequate or has stopped completely, proceed as follows: Check condition of oil filter cap, cap must allow oil tank to pressurize. Make sure oil level is not above the duck bill check valve and oil pickup is at bottom of tank. Check condition of oil filter on pickup line and renew as required. Check diameter of oil metering orifice located in oil pickup line above oil filter. Diameter of orifice should not be less than 0.0465 inch (1.181 mm). Oil pickup line should be 4-4⅛ inches (101.6-104.8 mm) long on outside of tank and positioned under the carburetor throttle stop. Check for a pinched or restricted oil pickup line using a suitable carburetor tester with test cap attached. Pressurize tank to 4-5 psi (28-34 kPa) and check for free flowing oil at guide bar. With pressure tester still attached, start and run saw at wide open throttle. Tank should pressurize to 2½-6 psi (17-41 kPa). While engine idles or is shut off, pressure should drop to zero after approximately 5 seconds. If tank fails to pressurize, check condition of crankcase pulse line by submerging the duck bill check valve shown in Fig. HL249 in oil and running saw. Constant bubbles

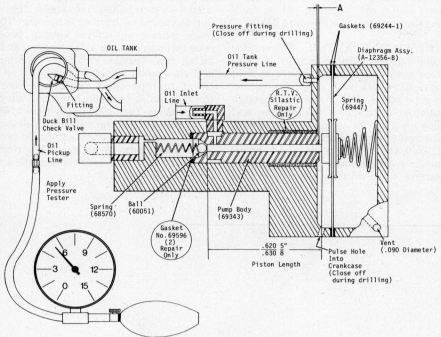

Fig. HL248 — Diagram showing pressure tester hook-up and diaphragm oil pump components.

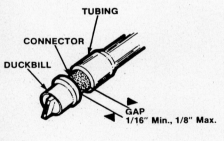

Fig. HL249 — Gap between duck bill valve and tubing end must be 1/16-1/8 inch (1.59-3.17 mm).

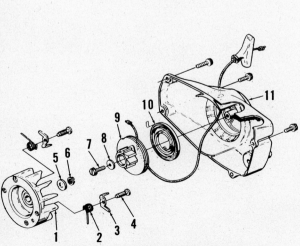

Fig. HL250 — Exploded view of rewind starter.

1. Flywheel
2. Spring
3. Starter pawl
4. Pawl pin
5. Washer
6. Nut
7. Cap screw
8. Washer
9. Rope pulley
10. Rewind spring
11. Housing

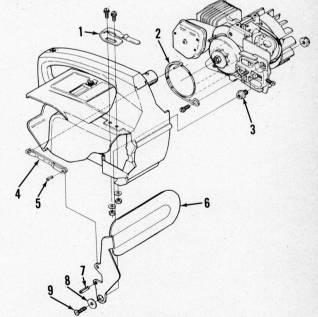

Fig. HL251 — Exploded view of chain brake used on some models.

1. Clip
2. Brake band
3. Post
4. Pivot link
5. Spring pin
6. Lever
7. Roll pin
8. Washer
9. Screw

should emit from check valve with slight bubbling from porous connector between check valve and line. A connector that is too porous will not maintain the required 2½ psi (17 kPa) minimum for oiling.

If chain oil flow is excessive or continues to flow after saw is shut off, proceed as follows: Over-oiling may be caused by incorrect installation of duck bill check valve. There should be a gap of 1/16-1/8 inch (1.59-3.17 mm) (see Fig. HL249) between duck bill check valve and pulse line thereby allowing porous connector to bleed off pressure while engine idles or is shut off. A good connector will bleed off pressure in approximately 5 seconds. Oil may also be

siphoning from tank to outlet after engine is shut off and can be corrected by installing Homelite® Oil Filter A-78889 which contains a check valve that shuts off oil flow when tank pressure drops below 2 psi (14 kPa).

REWIND STARTER. To service recoil starter, remove starter housing from saw. Pull starter rope and hold rope pulley with notch in pulley adjacent to rope outlet. Pull rope back through outlet so it engages notch in pulley and allow pulley to completely unwind. Unscrew pulley retaining screw (7 – Fig. HL250) and remove rope pulley being careful not to dislodge rewind spring in housing. Care must be taken if rewind

spring is removed to prevent injury if spring is allowed to uncoil uncontrolled.

Rewind spring is wound in clockwise direction in starter housing. Rope is wound on rope pulley in clockwise direction as viewed with pulley in housing. To place tension on rewind spring, pass rope through rope outlet in housing and install rope handle. Pull rope out and hold rope pulley so notch on pulley is adjacent to rope outlet. Pull rope back through outlet between notch in pulley and housing. Turn rope pulley clockwise to place tension on spring. Release pulley and check starter action. Do not place more tension on rewind spring than is necessary to draw rope handle up against housing.

Illustrations Courtesy Homelite Div. of Textron, ©1987

HOMELITE

Model	Bore	Stroke	Displ.	Drive Type
350, 350B, 350HG, 350SL Automatic	1.75 in. (44.4 mm)	1.44 in. (36.6 mm)	3.5 cu. in. (57 cc)	Direct
360, 360HG, 360SL, 360W Automatic	1.75 in. (44.4 mm)	1.44 in. (36.6 mm)	3.5 cu. in. (57 cc)	Direct

MAINTENANCE

SPARK PLUG. Recommended spark plug is Champion DJ6J. Spark plug electrode gap should be 0.025 inch (0.63 mm).

CARBURETOR. A Walbro Model HDC-16, HDC-21 or HDC-23 diaphragm carburetor may be used on 350 series saws while a Walbro HDC-39 carburetor is used on 360 series saws. Refer to Walbro section of CARBURETOR SERVICE section for Walbro carburetor overhaul and an exploded view of carburetor.

Correct carburetor adjustment procedure is determined by type of high speed fuel delivery system in carburetor. Model HDC-16 carburetors were originally designed with a 0.037 inch main jet in the circuit plate and the high speed adjustment needle was used to enrichen the high speed fuel mixture. Later Model 350 saws are equipped with Model HDC-21 carburetors which have a 0.033 inch main jet in the circuit plate.

Note location of carburetor adjusting screws in Fig. HL260 and refer to following paragraphs for carburetor adjustment.

Model HDC-16 and HDC-21 carburetors with fixed main jets are adjusted as follows: Turn high speed adjusting screw fully clockwise until closed and turn idle mixture screw one turn open (counterclockwise). Start saw and allow to idle. If necessary, increase idle speed with idle speed screw until saw will idle without stalling. Turn idle mixture screw slowly clockwise and note where idle speed drops off. Turn idle mixture screw in opposite direction until engine speed drops off again. Set idle mixture screw halfway between these two positions. Readjust idle speed screw by turning it clockwise until chain turns, then counterclockwise ½ turn. Normal position of high speed mixture screw is

closed. To determine best position of high speed mixture screw, idle saw and open screw (CCW) one turn. Slowly close screw approximately ⅛ turn at a time until saw runs fastest and has most power. High speed mixture screw will probably be closed or almost closed for best power.

To adjust Model HDC-23 or Models HDC-16 and HDC-21 that have been modified to provide full adjustment, proceed as follows: Be sure all components including chain and filters are installed and chain is properly tensioned and lubricated.

NOTE: Engine must not be placed under load during adjustments and nothing should come in contact with chain.

Initial settings are 1¼ turns open for high speed mixture screw and 1-3/16 turns open for idle mixture screw. Turn screw counterclockwise to open screw. Start engine and increase idle speed by turning idle speed screw if necessary to prevent stalling. Run engine under no load until it reaches operating temperature and then momentarily at full throttle to clear engine out. If necessary, turn idle speed screw counterclockwise until chain rotation stops. Turn idle mixture screw clockwise to find fastest engine speed. Squeeze trigger rapidly to check for smooth acceleration. If engine stumbles or hesitates, open idle mixture screw slightly, but not beyond initial setting of 1-3/16 turns open. Engine should idle smoothly at lowest possible speed (approximately 2500-2800 rpm) and not fluctuate when attitude of saw is changed.

To adjust Walbro Model HDC-39 carburetor, proceed as follows: Set initial adjustment of idle and high speed mixture screws at 1¼ turns open. Start and run engine until operating temperature is reached. Adjust idle mixture screw so engine accelerates cleanly and idles

smoothly. Turn idle speed screw so engine idles just below clutch engagement speed. Turn fast idle speed screw located adjacent to fast idle latch so engine will idle at a suitable fast idle for starting. Adjust high speed mixture screw to obtain optimum engine performance while under cutting load.

Maximum no-load speed of saws equipped with fully adjustable carburetors is 12,500 rpm and should be adjusted to operate in a no load range of 11,000-12,500 rpm. A tachometer is necessary to accurately adjust high speed mixture screw. If no-load speed at full throttle is below 11,000 rpm, turn high speed mixture screw clockwise.

NOTE: Final high speed mixture screw position should not be less than 7/8 turn open at altitudes below 5000 feet.

Components required to convert fixed main jet carburetors to fully adjustable are available from Homelite in kit A-12958.

A thin coat of suitable RTV silicone rubber sealant should be applied to both sides of intake gasket (6 – Fig. HL267).

MAGNETO AND TIMING. A solid state ignition is used on all models. The

Fig. HL260 — View of carburetor idle speed screw (I), high speed mixture screw (H) and idle mixture screw (L).

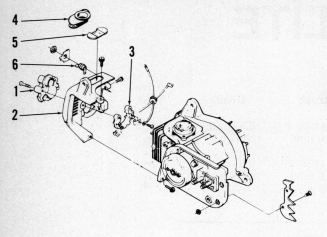

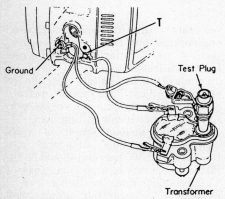

Fig. HL261 — Exploded view of cylinder shield assembly. Heat exchanger (4) is used in place of plug (5) in cold weather to warm carburetor air box.

1. Transformer
2. Cylinder shield
3. Transformer receptacle
4. Heat exchanger
5. Plug
6. Ignition switch

Fig. HL262 — A test plug may be used to determine if ignition system is operating correctly. Refer to text.

cally each working day by removing chain and forcing a good quality grease such as Homelite® ALL-TEMP Multipurpose Grease through lube hole in nose of bar. Bar should be warm before applying grease. Force grease into nose of bar until dirty grease is forced out and fresh grease is evident.

Lubricate clutch needle bearing after every 100 hours of operation with Homelite® ALL-TEMP Multipurpose Grease.

MUFFLER. Muffler should be disassembled and periodically cleaned. Carbon should be removed from muffler and exhaust port to prevent excessive carbon build-up and power loss. Do not allow loose carbon to enter cylinder.

VIBRATION ISOLATORS. All models are equipped with cushion type vibration isolators (12 – Fig. HL265) between power head and housing assembly (13). Isolators can be renewed as follows:

Remove air filter cover, filter, drive case cover and guide bar. Remove handle brace (11 – Fig. HL265). Unscrew two screws securing carburetor and

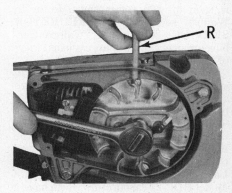

Fig. HL264 — Removal of flywheel or clutch is facilitated by preventing flywheel rotation with a ¼ inch (6.35 mm) rod stuck through hole in back plate into notch in flywheel.

ignition module is mounted adjacent to the flywheel while the high tension transformer is mounted on the cylinder shield as shown in Fig. HL261 and covers the spark plug. The transformer must be removed for access to the spark plug.

The ignition system is serviced by replacing the spark plug, ignition module, high tension transformer or wires with new components. The ignition system can be checked using a test plug or spark plug with the side electrode removed as follows: Remove the high tension transformer and install the test plug and connect test wires as shown in Fig. HL262. Test wire should be inserted behind receptacle tab (T). Push ignition switch to run position and briskly operate starter. If test plug sparks then ignition system is operating satisfactorily and the spark plug should be checked. If no spark is seen at test plug then another transformer should be checked. If no spark is seen when another transformer is checked, then suspect a faulty ignition module, faulty ignition switch or loose connections.

Air gap between ignition module and flywheel is adjustable. Adjust air gap by

loosening module retaining screws and place 0.015 inch (0.38 mm) shim stock between flywheel and module as shown in Fig. HL263.

LUBRICATION. The engine is lubricated by mixing oil with unleaded gasoline. Recommended oil is Homelite® two-stroke oil mixed at ratio as designated on oil container. If Homelite® oil is not available, a good quality oil designed for two-stroke engines may be used when mixed at a 16:1 ratio, however, an antioxidant fuel stabilizer (such as Sta-Bil) should be added to fuel mix. Antioxidant fuel stabilizer is not required with Homelite® oils as they contain fuel stabilizer so the fuel mix will stay fresh up to one year.

Saw chain is lubricated by oil from an automatic chain oil pump. Recommended chain saw oil is Homelite® Bar and Chain Oil. Clean automotive oil may also be used if the former is not available. SAE 30 oil should be used in warm temperatures and cut with 20 percent kerosene in cold temperatures. A light weight oil such as SAE 10 may also be used in cold temperatures.

A sprocket nose bar is used on all models and should be lubricated periodi-

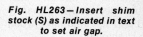

Fig. HL263 — Insert shim stock (S) as indicated in text to set air gap.

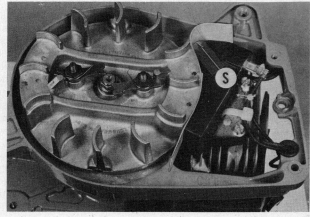

disconnect pulse line at rear of carburetor. Lift and angle carburetor and grommet on carburetor adjustment screws to gain access to two screws in floor of air box. Remove screws. Remove isolator pins (8) and lift upward on throttle grip and gently slide engine housing (13) free of power head until it is possible to remove rear isolators. Disconnect oil line (Fig. HL275) and slide housing further off power head for access to front isolators.

Reverse isolator removal procedure to reassemble saw. Apply a thin coat of RTV silicone rubber sealant to both sides of intake gasket (6–Fig. HL267). Carburetor pulse line should be routed around rear of air box and over carburetor control rods before connecting pulse line to carburetor. Tighten carburetor retaining screws to 45 in.-lbs. (5.1 N·m) and isolator pins (8–Fig. HL265) to 80 in.-lbs. (9 N·m). Tighten handle brace (11) screws to 45 in.-lbs. (5.1 N·m).

REPAIRS

TIGHTENING TORQUES. Tightening torque values are as follows:

Spark plug ....150 in.-lbs.
(16.9 N·m)
Clutch plate, "S" clutch
and cover ....350 in.-lbs.
(39.5 N·m)
Flywheel nut ....250-300 in.-lbs.
(28.2-33.9 N·m)
Back plate screws ....45 in.-lbs.
(5.1 N·m)
Cylinder screws ....80 in.-lbs.
(9.0 N·m)
Connecting rod screws .....60 in.-lbs.
(6.8 N·m)
Starter housing screws .....45 in.-lbs.
(5.1 N·m)
Muffler to cylinder
screws ....45 in.-lbs.
(5.1 N·m)
Ignition module screws .....35 in.-lbs.
(3.9 N·m)

Transformer coil screws .....27 in.-lbs.
(3.0 N·m)
Air deflector screws ....45 in.-lbs.
(5.1 N·m)
Air box to carburetor
connector screws ....45 in.-lbs.
(5.1 N·m)
Carburetor mounting
screws ....45 in.-lbs.
(5.1 N·m)
Vibrator isolator pins ......80 in.-lbs.
(9.0 N·m)
Starter pawl studs ....60-70 in.-lbs.
(6.8-7.9 N·m)

HOMELITE SERVICE TOOLS.

Listed below are Homelite tool numbers and descriptions:

Tool No.   Description & Model Usage

A-17146–Clutch wrench (3-shoe; 360 Series).
A-23696-A–Clutch wrench ("S" clutch).
A-23934–Clutch wrench (3-shoe; 350 Series).
A-24290–Flywheel puller.
A-24871–Piston pin removal & installation.
23136-6–Crankcase seal removal.
23759–Crankcase seal installation.
23846-1–Crankcase bearing removal.
23846-2–Backplate bearing & seal removal.
24826–Seal installation plug.
24827–Bearing & seal removal & installation.
14868–Oil pump alignment plug.
A-24994–Ignition tester.
JA-31316-4–Test spark plug.
17789–Carburetor repair tool kit.
94197–Carburetor tester.
94194–Compression gage.

COMPRESSION PRESSURE. For optimum performance of all models, cylinder compression pressure should be 140-170 psi (966-1173 kPa) with engine

Fig. HL265 — Exploded view of engine housing assembly. Some housings will use a threaded elbow fitting (18) on oil pickup tube as shown in inset.

1. Filter cover	6. Gasket	20. Handle bar
2. Air filter	7. Flange bushing	11. Handle brace
3. Spring plate	8. Isolator pins	12. Vibration isolators
4. Flange bushing	9. Handle bar bracket	13. Engine housing
5. Carburetor		

14. Oil cap	
15. Duckbill valve	
16. Bronze filter	
17. Fuel cap	
18. Elbow fitting	

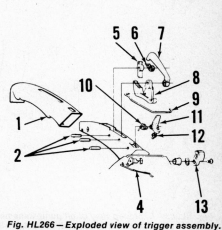

Fig. HL266 — Exploded view of trigger assembly.

1. Handle grip	8. Trigger
2. Dowel pin	9. Throttle rod
4. Choke rod	10. Spring
5. Trigger lock lever	11. Trigger latch
6. Spring	12. Screw
7. Trigger lock	13. Choke knob

at normal operating temperature. Engine should be inspected and repaired when compression pressure is 90 psi (620 kPa) or below.

CYLINDER, PISTON, PIN AND RINGS. Cylinder can be removed using the following procedure: Remove handle bar and chain guide bar and then using

procedure in VIBRATION ISOLATORS section, remove housing assembly (13–Fig. HL265) from power head. Remove starter housing, disconnect wires from ignition module and remove high voltage transformer coil and cylinder shield (2–Fig. HL261). Detach muffler from power head. Remove intake manifold. Unscrew socket head screws retaining cylinder and remove cylinder.

Cylinder has chrome bore which should be inspected for excessive wear or damage. Piston is equipped with two piston rings and is available in standard size only. Piston pin pressed in rod and rides in two needle roller bearings in piston. Piston and bearings are available only as a unit. Piston must be installed with side of piston indicated by arrow on piston pin boss marked "EXH" toward exhaust port. Refer to Fig. HL268.

CONNECTING ROD. Connecting rod may be removed after removing cylinder as previously outlined. Connecting rod is fractured type secured by two socket head screws. Connecting rod rides on 25 loose needle bearings around crankpin. Marks (M–Fig. HL268) at big end of rod must be aligned and cap and rod properly mated during reassembly. Needle bearings may be held in place around crankpin with a suitable grease.

CRANKSHAFT, CRANKCASE AND SEALS. To disassemble crankcase, remove clutch as outlined in CLUTCH section and then remove starter housing and flywheel assemblies. Remove connecting rod as previously outlined. Remove screw securing back plate (22–Fig. HL267) to crankcase (12). Bearings and seals may be pressed out of back plate and crankcase using Homelite® tools previously listed. In-

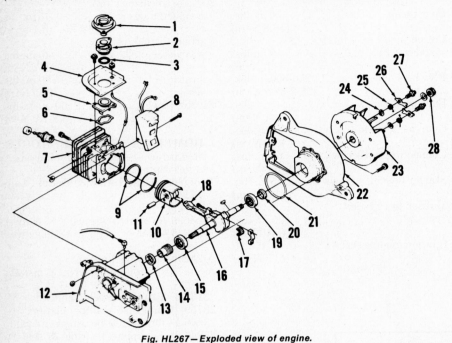

Fig. HL267 — Exploded view of engine.

1. Carburetor flange	8. Ignition module	15. Roller bearing	22. Back plate
2. Connector	9. Piston rings	16. Crankshaft	23. Flywheel
3. Garter spring	10. Piston & bearings	17. Needle bearing	24. Lockwasher
4. Air deflector	11. Piston pin	18. Connecting rod	25. Spring
5. Intake manifold	12. Crankcase	19. Roller bearing	26. Starter pawl
6. Gasket	13. Seal	20. Seal	27. Pawl stud
7. Cylinder	14. Oil pump worm gear	21. "O" ring	28. Nut

Fig. HL268 — Alignment marks (M) on rod must match and arrow adjacent to "EXH" on piston pin boss must point towards exhaust port for proper installation of piston and connecting rod.

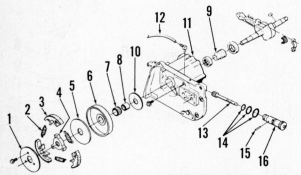

Fig. HL269 — Exploded view of oil pump assembly used on later 360 series and clutch used on some later 360 models.

1. Cover	7. Bearing	12. Oil line
2. Spring	8. Inner race	13. Oil pump plunger
3. Shoe	9. Worm gear	14. "O" rings
4. Hub	10. Washer	15. Pin
5. Washer	11. Crankcase	16. Pump body
6. Clutch drum		

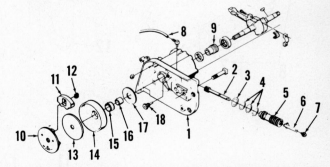

Fig. HL270 — Exploded view of oil pump used on all 350 and early 360 models and clutch used on later 350 and early 360 models.

1. Crankcase	7. Sems screw	13. Washer
2. Oil pump plunger	8. Oil line	14. Clutch drum
3. "O" rings	9. Oil pump worm gear	15. Bearing
4. "O" rings	10. Clutch hub	16. Bearing race
5. Pump body	11. Clutch shoe	17. Washer
6. Adjusting lever	12. Spring	18. Cam screw

spect crankshaft bearings, seals and "O" rings (21) for damage or excessive wear. Be sure "O" ring is properly seated during assembly of crankcase.

CLUTCH. Models are equipped either with the three-shoe centrifugal clutch shown in Fig. HL269, HL270 or HL271 or a one-piece "S" configuration clutch similar to that shown in Fig. HL272. Clutch can be removed by holding flywheel with a ¼ inch (6.35 mm) rod (Fig. HL264) and turning clutch hub clockwise as shown in Fig. HL273.

CHAIN OIL PUMP. All models are equipped with a plunger type automatic chain oil pump as shown in Fig. HL269 or HL270. The pump is driven by worm (9) on the engine crankshaft.

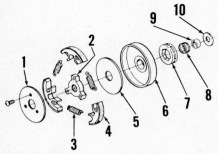

Fig. HL271 — Exploded view of clutch assembly used on late Model 360 series.

1. Cover plate	6. Clutch drum
2. Hub	7. Sprocket
3. Spring	8. Bearing
4. Shoe	9. Inner race
5. Washer	10. Washer

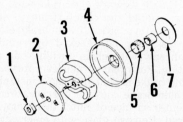

Fig. HL272 — View of "S" clutch used on some models. Cover (2) is threaded on some models and nut (1) is not used. Note correct installation of hub (3) in upper view.

1. Nut	5. Bearing
2. Cover	6. Inner race
3. Hub	7. Washer
4. Clutch drum	

All 350 series models and early 360 series models are equipped with oil pump shown in Fig. HL270. Crankcase (1) can be identified by number 12061-A stamped in crankcase. Oil output is adjusted by turning adjusting lever shown in Fig. HL274. Oil pump assembly can be withdrawn after unscrewing cam screw (P – Fig. HL275). Measure depth

Fig. HL273 — Clutch hub is removed by unscrewing clockwise as indicated on hub. Refer to Fig. HL264.

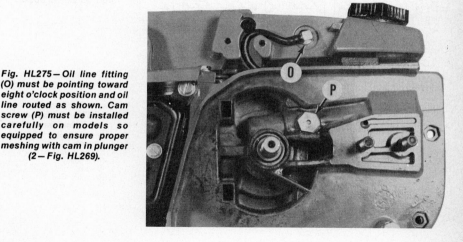

Fig. HL274 — Oil pump output on all 350 series and early 360 series saws is adjusted by turning lever (L) counterclockwise to increase oil flow or clockwise to decrease oil flow.

Fig. HL275 — Oil line fitting (O) must be pointing toward eight o'clock position and oil line routed as shown. Cam screw (P) must be installed carefully on models so equipped to ensure proper meshing with cam in plunger (2 – Fig. HL269).

of cam screw pin as shown in Fig. HL276. Depth should be 0.553-0.557 inch (14.05-14.18 mm) and can be adjusted by driving pin in or out of cam screw. Incorrect pin depth will affect engagement with slot in plunger. Measure depth of plug (P – Fig. HL277) in pump bore. Plug should be 2.011-2.016 inches (51.08-51.21 mm) from end of pump as shown in Fig. HL277. Lubricate pump components prior to assembly. Align cam groove in plunger with slot in pump body using tool 24868. Carefully install pump assembly in housing to prevent plunger from moving out of alignment with pump body slot. Screw cam screw (P – Fig. HL275) into housing being sure cam screw pin properly engages slot in pump body (5 – Fig. HL270) and cam groove in plunger (2). Do not tighten cam screw with a wrench until final turns are reached.

Late 360 series saws are equipped with automatic chain oil pump shown in Fig. HL269. Oil pump output is not adjustable.

Oil tank cap has a bronze filter and one-way valve to admit air into the oil tank. If filter is dirty or valve is defective, oil in tank will not flow to oil pump. Valve and filter in oil tank cap can be checked by operating with oil tank cap tight and then loose. If oil output is increased when cap is loose, filter and valve should be inspected.

Oil output fitting on oil tank should point in an eight o'clock direction as shown in Fig. HL275 to properly route oil tube. Reduced oil output may also be due to a clogged oil strainer at end of the oil tube in oil tank or by leaking or blocked oil lines.

REWIND STARTER. Refer to Fig. HL278 for an exploded view of starter used on all models. Starter can be

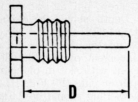

Fig. HL276 — Depth (D) of cam screw pin in cam screw must be 0.553-0.557 inch (14.05-14.18 mm) when mesured as shown above. Adjust pin depth by driving pin in or out of cam screw.

Fig. HL279 — Exploded view of chain brake and muffler on Model 350SL.
1. Exhaust plate
2. Baffle
3. Spark arrestor
4. Gasket
5. Power head
6. Drive cover
7. Brake lever
8. Guide bar adjuster
9. Chain tension adjusting screw
10. Pin
11. Gear cover
12. Spring
13. Chain brake band
14. Washer

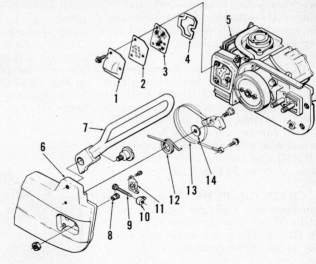

disassembled without removing housing (1) except to remove and install bushing (2).

To disassemble starter, unscrew cover (8) screws and allow cover to rotate until tension in rewind spring is relieved. Remove cover with spring (6), shield (5), and post (7). Untie knot in end of rope, remove rope handle and remove rope pulley (4) and rope. Inspect bushing (2) and remove housing (1) if it is necessary to remove bushing. Bushing is a press fit in housing.

If old bushing is to be retained, lubricate bushing with oil. Note direction spring (6) is wound in Fig. HL278. A new spring should be lightly lubricated on its edges with Homelite® ALL-TEMP Multipurpose Grease or a suitable lithium base grease before installing spring in cover. Do not over-lubricate. Place spring post (7) in center of spring and snap shield (5) into cover (8). Install rope end through pulley and housing and install rope handle. Turn pulley clockwise until rope is wound on pulley. Install

Fig. HL280 — Exploded view of chain brake mechanism used on Model 360SL.
1. "E" ring
2. Roller
3. Sleeve
4. Actuating lever
5. Washer
6. Spring
7. Washer
8. Latch
9. Shoulder screw
10. "E" ring
11. Brake band
12. Dowel pin
13. Screw
14. Washer
15. Spring
16. Sleeve
17. Cover

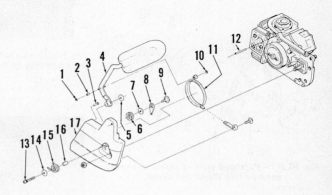

spring washer (3) with concave side towards pulley. Install spring and cover assembly on housing but do not install cover screws. Be sure spring post (7)

engages hole in pulley (4). To place tension on rewind spring, turn cover (8) clockwise until rope handle is held against housing (1). Do not turn cover excessively or spring may break when rope is pulled to its full length. Install cover screws and check starter operation.

CHAIN BRAKE. Models 350SL and 360SL are equipped with a chain brake mechanism to stop saw chain motion in the event of kickback. In the event of kickback, the operator's left hand will force brake lever (7–Fig. HL279 or 4–HL280) forward and brake band will wrap around the clutch drum to stop clutch drum rotation. Chain brake effectiveness may be checked by running chain saw with chain turning but not cutting. Push chain brake lever forward. Chain brake should stop chain instantly. If chain brake does not operate correctly, outer surface of clutch drum may be glazed. Remove glaze with emery cloth being sure to clean drum afterwards. Clutch drum and brake band must not be bent or nicked. On Model 360SL, dowel pin (12–Fig. HL280) must be driven into crankcase so 0.375 inch (9.52 mm) of pin stands out from crankcase.

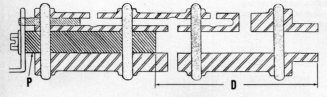

Fig. HL277 — Plug (P) in pump bore must be 2.011-2.016 inches (51.08-51.21 mm) (D) from end of pump bore as shown above.

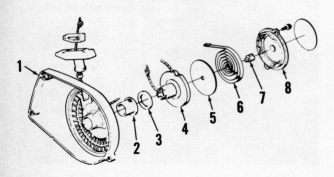

Fig. HL278 — Exploded view of rewind starter.
1. Starter housing
2. Bushing
3. Spring washer
4. Rope pulley
5. Washer
6. Rewind spring
7. Spring post
8. Cover

HOMELITE

Model	Bore	Stroke	Displ.	Drive Type
650	2.125 in. (54 mm)	1.720 in. (43.7 mm)	6.1 cu. in. (100 cc)	Direct
750, 750E	2.250 in. (57.2 mm)	1.720 in. (43.7 mm)	6.8 cu. in. (112 cc)	Direct

MAINTENANCE

SPARK PLUG. Recommended spark plug is Champion CJ4 for Model 650 and CJ3 for Model 750. Spark plug electrode gap should be 0.025 inch (0.63 mm).

CARBURETOR. All models are equipped with a Walbro WB diaphragm carburetor. Refer to CARBURETOR SERVICE section for carburetor service.

Initial adjustment of idle and high speed mixture screws is one turn open. Adjust idle speed screw so that engine idles at approximately 2400-2600 rpm.

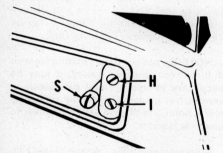

Fig. HL290— View showing location of carburetor high speed mixture screw (H), idle mixture screw (I) and idle speed screw (S).

Adjust idle mixture screw to obtain maximum engine speed at idle. If necessary, readjust idle speed screw to obtain engine idle speed of approximately 2400-2600 rpm.

To adjust high speed mixture screw, proceed as follows: Run saw at idle until engine reaches operating temperature. Turn high speed mixture needle counterclockwise approximately 1/8-1/4 turn. Check performance of saw. Engine should accelerate without hesitation and should not exceed 12,000 rpm at full throttle under no load. When high speed no-load rpm has been adjusted within the correct range, maximum power should occur at desired cutting speed.

Models 650 and 750E are equipped with a trigger latch mechanism coupled to a compression release valve to aid engine starting. Starting speed is adjusted by turning slotted head adjustment screw (13 – Fig. HL292) at top and front of saw handle. Turning screw clockwise raises starting speed while turning screw counterclockwise lowers starting speed. Adjust starting speed by latching trigger in start position, start engine and turn screw until desired engine speed is obtained. Stop engine and restart to check starting speed.

MAGNETO AND TIMING. A solid state ignition is used on all models. The ignition module is mounted adjacent to the flywheel while the high tension transformer covers the spark plug and is mounted on the cylinder shield. The high tension transformer must be removed for access to spark plug.

The ignition system is serviced by replacing the spark plug, ignition module, high tension transformer or wires with new components. The ignition system can be checked using a test plug or spark plug with the side electrode removed as follows: Remove the high tension transformer and install the test plug and connect test wires as shown in Fig. HL291. Test wire should be inserted behind receptacle tab (T). Push ignition switch to run position and briskly operate starter. If test plug sparks then ignition system is operating satisfactorily and the spark plug should be checked. If no spark is seen at test plug then another transformer should be checked. If no spark is seen when another transformer is checked, then suspect a faulty ignition module, faulty ignition switch or loose connections.

High tension transformer and leads may be checked by disconnecting wires

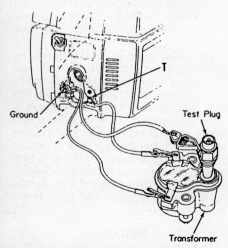

Fig. HL291— A test plug may be used to determine if ignition system is operating correctly. Refer to text.

Fig. HL292— Exploded view of handle components. Inset shows trigger lock mechanism used on Model 750E to aid in cold starting.

1. Throttle trigger
2. Throttle rod
3. Cover
4. Spring
5. Compression release cam
6. Pivot pin
7. Snap ring
8. Trigger pin
9. Spring
10. Choke lever
11. Choke rod
12. Pivot pin
13. Set screw
14. Spring
15. Compression release arm
16. Shoulder screw
17. Compression release valve
18. Spring

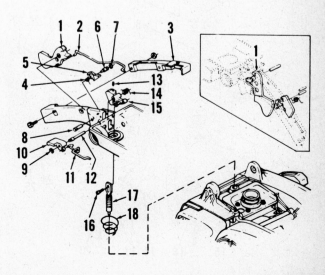

at ignition module which lead from ignition module to transformer receptacle and connecting an ohmmeter to end of wires. There should be continuity between wire ends. If continuity does not exist, disassemble rear of saw until access is possible to two transformer receptacle leads and disconnect leads. Check continuity of each wire and terminal.

To check ignition switch and lead, connect one probe of ohmmeter to switch terminal and ground other probe to ignition module core. Check continuity of ignition switch and lead with switch in "RUN" and "STOP" positions. If continuity exists when switch is in "RUN" position, switch or lead is shorted and must be replaced. Continuity should exist with switch in "STOP" position. If continuity is not present in "STOP" position, check connection of switch lead and replace switch if necessary.

Air gap between ignition module and flywheel is adjustable. Adjust air gap by loosening module retaining screws and place 0.015 inch (pink) (0.38 mm) shim stock between flywheel and module.

If the flywheel is removed using Homelite® tool A-17106-B, which attaches to starter pawl studs, the starter pawl studs must be retightened to 70-90 in.-lbs. (7.9-10.2 N·m) to restore any possible torque loss.

LUBRICATION. The engine is lubricated by mixing oil with unleaded gasoline. Recommended oil is Homelite® two-stroke oil mixed at ratio as designated on oil container. If Homelite® oil is not available, a good quality oil designed for two-stroke engines may be used when mixed at a 16:1 ratio, however, an anti-oxidant fuel stabilizer (such as Sta-Bil) should be added to fuel mix. Anti-oxidant fuel stabilizer is not required with Homelite® oils as they contain fuel stabilizer so the fuel mix will stay fresh up to one year.

Saw chain is lubricated by oil from an automatic or manual chain oil pump. Recommended saw chain oil is Homelite® Bar and Chain Oil. Clean automotive oil may also be used if the former is not available. SAE 30 oil should be used in warm temperatures above 40°F (4°C) and cut with 20 percent kerosene in cold temperatures. A light weight oil such as SAE 10 or SAE 5 may also be used in cold temperatures.

Automatic chain oil pump is designed to leave approximately 3 ounces (88.7 mL) of oil in oil tank when one tankful of fuel is consumed after oil and fuel tanks had been full.

A sprocket nose bar is used and should be lubricated periodically by removing chain and forcing a good quality grease such as Homelite® ALL-TEMP Multi-purpose Grease through lube hole in nose of bar. Bar should be warm before applying grease. Force grease into nose of bar until dirty grease is forced out and fresh grease is evident.

VIBRATION ISOLATORS. All models are equipped with vibration isolators between engine and engine housing. Use the following procedure to remove vibration isolators:

Remove drivecase cover chain and bar, and bumper spikes. Remove throttle handle brace (15 – Fig. HL293) and handle bar. Remove air filter cover and filter and disconnect choke rod from choke lever. Unscrew carburetor mounting screws and remove air intake tube (5). Lift metal shield (6) off air box and pull carburetor free of adjustment needle grommet. Disconnect pulse line and fuel line from carburetor. Disconnect manual oil pump lines at pump end. Unscrew four screws in front wall of air box which secure front and rear assemblies together. Disconnect manual oil line from fitting at automatic oil pump housing.

Unscrew two front vibration isolators screws (16) and with a screwdriver, work isolators (17) clear of their sockets in drivecase wall and back plate. Remove fuel and oil tanks and disconnect oil line from oil tank. Unscrew vibration isolators (17) from tank.

NOTE: Do not continue twisting isolator if it will not unscrew easily. It may be necessary to use a small pin punch or screwdriver placed against the rubber-to-metal bond and tapped with a hammer to unscrew isolator.

Remove shoulder screw (16 – Fig. HL292) and disconnect compression release valve (17) and arm (15). Remove heat insulating spacer. Push rubber carburetor flange through floor of air box and using technique previously described, remove two rear vibration isolators.

Vibration isolators are retained by threaded inserts pressed into castings. Threads of inserts and isolator should be sprayed with "LPS" prior to installation of a new or used isolator. If insert is loose or damaged, screw an isolator into insert and pull isolator and insert out as a unit. Both the insert recess in casting and the insert must be cleaned with Locquic Grade N Primer before installing insert. Apply Loctite Grade AA Sealant to outer surface of insert and press insert into casting.

REPAIRS

TIGHTENING TORQUES. Tightening torque values are as follows:

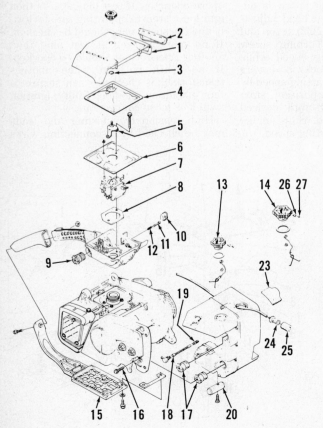

Fig. HL293 – View of induction, fuel and oil assemblies.

1. Air filter cover
2. Air intake
3. Retaining ring
4. Air filter
5. Bracket
6. Air box shield
7. Carburetor
8. Spacer plate
9. Rear vibration isolator
10. Grommet
11. Idle speed screw
12. Spring
13. Oil tank cap
14. Fuel tank cap
15. Handle brace
16. Vibration isolator screw
17. Front vibration isolator
18. Oil line
19. Oil pickup
20. Chain stop
23. Fuel tank bumper
24. Fuel pickup
25. Fuel filter
26. Check valve
27. Filter

Spark plug . . . . .150 in.-lbs.
(16.9 N·m)

Clutch plate . . . . .180 in.-lbs.
(20.3 N·m)

Clutch cover screws . . . . .35 in.-lbs.
(3.9 N·m)

Flywheel nut . . . . .250-300 in.-lbs.
(28.2-33.9 N·m)

Back plate screws . . . . .45 in.-lbs.
(5.1 N·m)

Cylinder screws . . . . .80 in.-lbs.
(9.0 N·m)

Connecting rod screws . . . .70-80 in.-lbs.
(7.9-9.0 N·m)

Starter housing screws . . . . . .35 in.-lbs.
(3.9 N·m)

COMPRESSION PRESSURE. For optimum performance, cylinder compression pressure at normal engine operating temperature should be 155-185 psi (1069-1275 kPa) on 650 models and 135-165 psi (931-1138 kPa) on 750 and 750E models. Engine should be inspected and repaired when compression pressure is 90 psi (620 kPa) or below.

CYLINDER, PISTON, PIN AND RINGS. Cylinder has chrome bore which should be inspected for wear or damage. Piston and rings are available in standard sizes only. Piston pin is pressed in rod and rides in two needle roller bearings in piston. Homelite® tool A-24871 may be used to remove or install piston pin. Piston and bearings are available as a unit assembly only.

Note that one piston pin boss is marked with an arrow and "EXH." Install piston with side indicated by arrow toward exhaust port.

CONNECTING ROD. Connecting rod is fractured type secured by two socket head screws. Connecting rod rides on a split caged needle bearing at big end. Marks at big end of rod must be aligned and cap and rod properly mated during reassembly. Needle bearings may be held around crankpin with a suitable grease to aid in assembly.

CRANKSHAFT, CRANKCASE AND SEALS. Crankshaft on 750 and 750E models is supported by roller bearing (19 – Fig. HL294) and ball bearing (32). Crankshaft on 650 models is supported by roller bearings (19) in the back plate and crankcase. Crankcase on 650 models may be removed after unscrewing crankcase screws. To remove crankcase on 750 models, unscrew crankcase screws and remove crankcase (31). Remove bearing retainers (33), heat back plate (no more than 300°F [149°C]) and remove crankshaft with bearing (32). Wrap tape around crankshaft end to protect crankshaft and remove snap ring (34). Press bearing (32) off crankshaft.

On all models, roller bearings and seals may be pressed out of crankcase and back plate using Homelite® or other suitable tools. When removing crankcase seal (30), force oil pump worm (29) and seal (30) to outside of crankcase by inserting driver from inside of crankcase. Force bearing (19) to inside of crankcase for removal.

Inspect bearings, seals and "O" ring (20) for damage or excessive wear. When reassembling crankcase, be sure

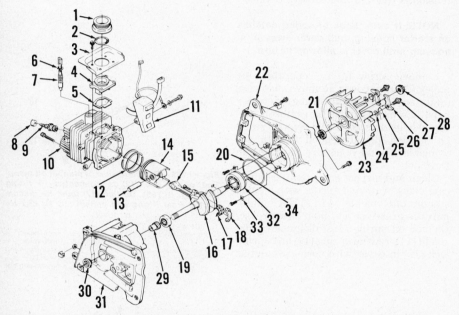

Fig. HL294 — Exploded view of Models 750 and 750E engine. Model 650 is similar except second roller bearing (19) is used in place of components (32, 33 and 34).

1. Rubber carburetor flange
2. Garter spring
3. Air deflector
4. Intake manifold
5. Gasket
6. Snap ring
7. Compression relief valve
8. Grommet
9. Spark plug
10. Cylinder
11. Ignition module
12. Piston rings
13. Piston pin
14. Piston
15. Connecting rod
16. Crankshaft
17. Split cage bearing
18. Rod cap
19. Roller bearing
20. "O" ring
21. Seal
22. Back plate
23. Flywheel
24. Lockwasher
25. Spring
26. Starter pawl
27. Pawl stud
28. Roller bearing
29. Oil pump worm
30. Seal
31. Crankcase
32. Ball bearing
33. Bearing retainer
34. Snap ring

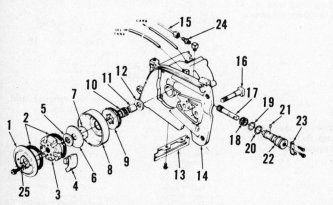

Fig. HL295 — Exploded view of clutch and oil pump assemblies.

1. Cover
2. Clutch spring
3. Clutch hub
4. Clutch shoe
5. Thrust washer (1 in.)
6. Thrust washer (2 in.)
7. Thrust washer (1⅛ in.)
8. Clutch drum
9. Sprocket
10. Bearing
11. Bearing race
12. Thrust washer (1⅛ in.)
13. Heat shield
14. Crankcase
15. Manual discharge line
16. Guide bar stud
17. Oil pump plunger
18. "O" rings
19. "O" ring
20. "O" ring
21. Cam pin
22. Oil pump body
23. Fitting
24. Fitting
25. Belleville washer

Fig. HL295A — Exploded view of late model clutch assembly.

1. Cover
2. Clutch spring
3. Clutch hub
4. Clutch shoe
5. Thrust washer
6. Thrust washer
7. Thrust washer
8. Clutch drum
9. Sprocket
10. Bearing
11. Bearing race
12. Thrust washer

Illustrations Courtesy Homelite Div. of Textron, ©1987

"O" ring (20) is properly seated. Install bearings so unstamped side is toward inside of crankcase and back plate.

CLUTCH. Refer to Fig. HL295 or HL295A for exploded view of clutch assembly. To remove clutch, prevent flywheel rotation by inserting 3/16 inch rod through hole located in bottom of back plate into notch in flywheel. Using a Homelite® clutch spanner or a suitable tool, unscrew clutch hub (3) in clockwise direction as shown by arrow on hub.

Inspect bearing and lubricate with Homelite® ALL-TEMP Multipurpose Grease (#24551) or a lithium base grease. Clutch shoes (4) should be renewed as a complete set.

AUTOMATIC CHAIN OIL PUMP. All models are equipped with an automatic oil pump driven by worm (29–Fig. HL294) on crankshaft. Oil is pumped by plunger (17–Fig. HL296) as it reciprocates due to cam pin (21) located in cam groove (G). Oil enters pump through port (A) and passes around pump body (22) to enter plunger bore through port (B). Oil exists through ports (C, D and E) to saw chain. Oil may be pumped through port (F) and fitting (24) to manual oil pump. Oil is also routed through ports (H and J) to cam groove to reduce back pressure on oil plunger.

To disassemble automatic oil pump, unscrew oil pump bracket screw and gently withdraw oil pump body (22–Fig. HL295). Do not lose cam pin (21) which is loose in pump body. Remove pin (21) and slide pump plunger out of pump body. Inspect pump plunger, body and "O" rings for excessive wear or damage. An excessively loose fit between pump plunger and pump body will cause low pump output. Oil "O" rings before installation in grooves of pump body. "O" rings must be straight in grooves and not twisted. Oil "O" rings before inserting pump body and plunger assembly into pump housing.

If oil pump operates correctly but oil output is insufficient, disconnect and clean oil lines and fittings (Fig. HL295). Install outlet elbow in oil tank wall to provide an angle of as close to 90 degrees as shown in Fig. HL298 without pinching line. Elbow threads should be coated with thread sealant.

REWIND STARTER. Refer to Fig. 301 for an exploded view of starter assembly. Starter pawl components attached to flywheel are shown in Fig. HL294.

To disassemble starter, hold cover (14–Fig. HL301) and unscrew retaining screws. Allow cover to turn until spring tension is relieved and remove cover.

NOTE: If outer hook of spring catches on starter housing, pull cover away from housing until cover is allowed to turn.

Remove screw (4) to separate rope pulley (7) from cover. Remove snap ring (8) for access to rewind spring. If starter pawl assemblies must be removed, unscrew housing screws and remove starter housing (2). Threaded inserts are available if stud holes are damaged in flywheel.

Clean and inspect components. Lubricate sides of rewind spring with a small amount of Homelite® ALL-TEMP Multipurpose grease or a lithium base grease. Do not oil spring. Install inner spring shield (11), rewind spring (10) and spring lock (12) in cover with spring wound as

shown in Fig. HL302. Install outer spring shield (9–Fig. HL301) and snap ring (8). Insert bushings (6 and 13) in rope pulley (7) being sure knobs on bushings align with notches in pulley.

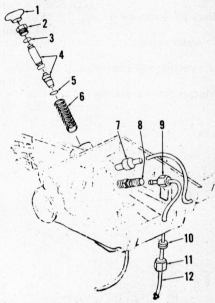

Fig. HL299—Exploded view of manual oil pump. End of oil line (12) is connected to fitting (24–Fig. HL296). Oil line (12) must be disconnected from fitting and pulled into air box for removal.

1. Button	
2. Plunger nut	7. Check valve
3. "O" ring	8. Check valve
4. Plunger assy.	9. Compression nut
5. "O" ring	10. Grommet
6. Spring	11. Compression nut

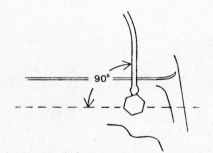

Fig. HL298—Oil line and fitting in oil tank must be angled close to 90 degrees as shown above.

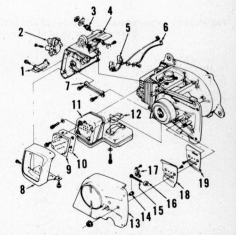

Fig. HL300—Exploded view of exhaust and chain tensioning assemblies.

1. Rear snubber	13. Cover
2. High tension coil	14. Guide bar adjuster gear
3. Ignition switch	
4. Cylinder shield	15. Chain tension adjuster screw
5. Coil receptacle	
6. Ground lead	16. Pin
7. Brace	17. Gear cover
8. Muffler shield	18. Outer guide bar plate
9. Muffler cap	
10. Spark arrestor	19. Inner guide bar plate
11. Muffler	
12. Gasket	

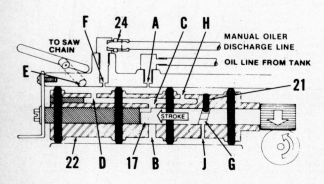

Fig. HL296—Cross-section of oil pump. Refer to text for operation.

Slide pulley onto post in cover and check to be sure splines on pulley engage splines in spring lock. Install and tighten cap screw (4) to 45 in.-lbs. (5.1 N·m). Wind rope around pulley in clockwise direction as viewed from screw end of pulley. Set cover in housing. Pull rope handle and then allow rope to rewind so starter pawls will be forced open and pulley hub can slide between them into place. Turn cover clockwise 2 or 3 turns to preload rewind spring, snap plastic screen into place and install cover screws. Check starter operation.

COMPRESSION RELEASE. All models are equipped with a compression release to aid starting. A leaking compression release valve may be repaired by cleaning valve seat with Homelite® tool A-24884. This tool is designed to remove carbon without removing metal from valve seat. Piston must be at TDC and engine positioned with valve side down to prevent debris from entering cylinder.

Inspect valve stem for wear which may not allow valve to seat properly and renew valve if valve stem is excessively worn. Examine pin connecting valve link to stem and renew assembly if pin is worn or loose.

Install compression release valve with sharp side of snap ring (6 – Fig. HL294) out. Push compression release valve and snap ring down into valve bore making sure snap ring fully engages snap ring groove. Homelite® tool A-24876 may be used to seat snap ring in groove.

Later Model 750 is equipped with a cylinder having a smaller compression release hole and a matching compression release valve. Later compression release valve is identified by a groove located as shown in Fig. HL303. Early and late cylinders and compression release valves are not interchangeable.

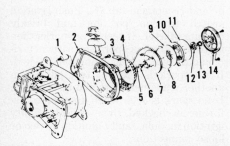

Fig. HL301 – Exploded view of rewind starter.

1. Spacer	8. Snap ring
2. Starter housing	9. Outer spring shield
3. Screen	10. Rewind spring
4. Capscrew	11. Inner spring shield
5. Lockwasher	12. Spring lock
6. Bushing	13. Bushing
7. Rope pulley	14. Cover

Fig. HL302 – View of rewind spring installation in starter cover. Hook outer loop (A) of spring in notch as shown. Inner loop (B) of spring must be curved inward to engage notch of spring lock.

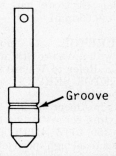

Fig. HL303 – The compression release valve on later Model 750 is identified by the groove shown above.

HOMELITE

Model	Bore	Stroke	Displ.	Drive Type
450, 450W				
450HG, 450SL	1.875 in.	1.625 in.	4.5 cu. in.	Direct
	(47.6 mm)	(41.3 mm)	(74 cc)	
550, 550W, 550SL	2.00 in.	1.625 in.	5.1 cu. in.	Direct
	(51 mm)	(41.3 mm)	(84 cc)	

MAINTENANCE

SPARK PLUG. Recommended spark plug is Champion DJ6J for all models. Spark plug electrode gap should be 0.025 inch (0.63 mm).

CARBURETOR. All models are equipped with a Walbro SDC diaphragm carburetor. Refer to Walbro section of CARBURETOR SERVICE section for carburetor service.

Initial adjustment of idle and high speed mixture screws is one turn open except on 450, 450W, 450HG and 450SL which has a fixed high speed jet and high speed mixture is not adjustable. Adjust idle speed screw so engine idles at approximately 2400-2600 rpm. Adjust idle mixture screw so engine will accelerate cleanly without bogging. If necessary, readjust idle speed screw to obtain engine idle speed of approximately 2400-2600 rpm.

To adjust high speed mixture screw on 550, 550W and 550SL, proceed as follows: Run saw at idle until engine reaches operating temperature. Turn high speed mixture needle to obtain optimum performance with saw under cutting load.

Starting speed is adjusted by turning slotted head adjustment screw in fast idle latch. See Fig. HL311. Turning screw clockwise raises starting speed while turning screw counterclockwise lowers starting speed. Adjust starting speed by latching trigger in start position, start engine and turn screw until desired engine speed is obtained. Stop engine and restart to check starting speed.

MAGNETO AND TIMING. A solid state ignition is used on all models. The ignition module is mounted adjacent to the flywheel while the high tension transformer covers the spark plug and is mounted on the cylinder shield. The high tension transformer must be removed for access to spark plug. The ignition module on 450, 450W, 450HG and 450SL uses an electronic governor to prevent overspeeding of engine.

The ignition system is serviced by replacing the spark plug, ignition module, high tension transformer or wires with new components. The ignition system can be checked using a test plug or spark plug with the side electrode removed as follows: Remove the high tension transformer and install the test plug and connect test wires as shown in Fig. HL312. Test wire should be inserted behind receptacle tab (T). Push ignition switch to run position and briskly operate starter. If test plug sparks then ignition system is operating satisfactorily and the spark plug should be checked. If no spark is seen at test plug then another transformer should be checked. If no spark is seen when another transformer is checked, then suspect a faulty ignition module, faulty ignition switch or loose connections.

High tension transformer and leads may be checked by disconnecting wires at ignition module which lead from ignition module to transformer receptacle

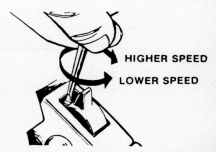

Fig. HL311—View showing location of fast idle screw.

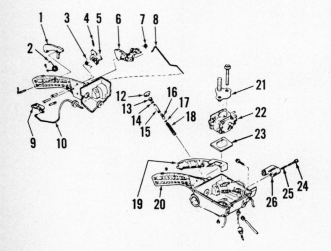

Fig. HL310—Exploded view of handle, air box and manual oil pump assemblies.

1. Lockout
2. Spring
3. Spring
4. Fast idle screw
5. Throttle latch
6. Throttle trigger
7. Spring
8. Throttle rod
9. Choke lever
10. Choke rod
12. Oil pump button
13. Nut
14. "O" ring
15. Rod
16. Plunger
17. "O" ring
18. Spring
19. Handle cover
20. Handle & air box
21. Bracket
22. Carburetor
23. Spacer
24. Idle speed screw
25. Spring
26. Grommet

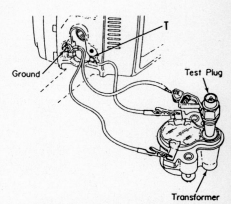

Fig. HL312—A test plug may be used to determine if ignition system is operating correctly. Refer to text.

and connecting an ohmmeter to end of wires. There should be continuity between wire ends. If continuity does not exist, disassemble rear of saw until access is possible to two transformer receptacle leads and disconnect leads. Check continuity of each wire and terminal.

To check ignition switch and lead, connect one probe of ohmmeter to switch terminal and ground other probe to ignition module core. Check continuity of ignition switch and lead with switch in "RUN" and "STOP" positions. If continuity exists when switch is in "RUN" position, switch or lead is shorted and must be replaced. Continuity should exist with switch in "STOP" position. If continuity is not present in "STOP" position, check connection of switch lead and replace lead and switch if necessary.

Air gap between ignition module and flywheel is adjustable. Adjust air gap by loosening module retaining screws and place 0.015 inch (0.38 mm) (pink) shim stock between flywheel and module.

LUBRICATION. The engine is lubricated by mixing oil with unleaded gasoline. Recommended oil is Homelite® two-stroke oil mixed at ratio as designated on oil container. If Homelite® oil is not available, a good quality oil designed for two-stroke engines may be used when mixed at a 16:1 ratio, however, an antioxidant fuel stabilizer (such as Sta-Bil) should be added to fuel mix. Antioxidant fuel stabilizer is not required with Homelite® oils as they contain fuel stabilizer so the fuel mix ill stay fresh up to one year.

Saw chain is lubricated by oil from an automatic or manual chain oil pump. Recommended saw chain oil is Homelite® Bar and Chain Oil. Clean auto-

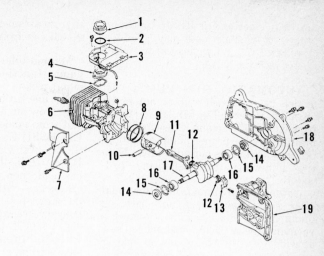

Fig. HL314 — Exploded view of engine.

1. Connector
2. Garter spring
3. Air deflector & seal
4. Intake manifold
5. Gasket
6. Cylinder
7. Shield
8. Piston rings
9. Piston
10. Piston pin
11. Connecting rod
12. Bearing
13. Rod cap
14. Seal
15. Snap ring
16. Bearing
17. Crankshaft
18. Back plate
19. Crankcase

motive oil may be used if the former is not available. SAE 30 oil should be used in warm temperatures above 40°F (4°C) and cut with 20 percent kerosene in cold temperatures. A light weight oil such as SAE 10 or SAE 5 may also be used in cold temperatures.

REPAIRS

TIGHTENING TORQUE VALUES. Tightening torque values are as follows:

Connecting rod . . . . 65-78 in.-lbs.
(7.3-8.8 N·m)

Crankcase retaining
screws . . . . 60-72 in.-lbs.
(6.8-8.2 N·m)

Starter housing . . . . 45-54 in.-lbs.
(5.1-6.1 N·m)

COMPRESSION PRESSURE. For optimum performance, cylinder compression pressure at normal operating temperature should be 160-190 psi (1104-1311 kPa) on 450, 450W, 450HG and 450SL models and 125-155 psi (863-1069 kPa) on 550, 550W and 550SL models. Engine should be inspected and repaired when compression pressure is 90 psi (620 kPa) or below.

CYLINDER, PISTON, PIN AND RINGS. The cylinder may be separated from crankcase after removing screws securing cylinder to crankcase. Care should be used when separating cylinder and crankcase as crankshaft may be dislodged from crankcase. Inspect cylinder bore and discard cylinder if excessively worn or damaged. Cylinder may not be bored for oversize pistons and oversize cylinders are not available. Refer to CONNECTING ROD, CRANKSHAFT AND CRANKCASE. section when installing cylinder.

The piston is equipped with two piston rings. Oversize pistons and rings are not available. The piston pin rides in non-renewable needle bearings in piston. Piston and bearings are available only as a unit assembly.

CONNECTING ROD, CRANKSHAFT AND CRANKCASE. Refer to preceding section and remove cylinder. Separate crankshaft assembly from crankcase and disassemble as required. Inspect components and renew any which are damaged.

Connecting rod (11 – Fig. HL314) rides on twelve caged bearing rollers (12). The crankshaft is supported by roller bearings (16) which are installed so lettered end is toward snap rings (15).

Tighten connecting rod screws to 65-75 in.-lbs. (7.3-8.4 N·m). When assembling crankcase and cylinder, use a suitable sealant on mating surfaces. Be sure components are properly assembled and snap rings (15) engage grooves in cylinder and crankcase. Before final tightening of crankcase screws, lightly

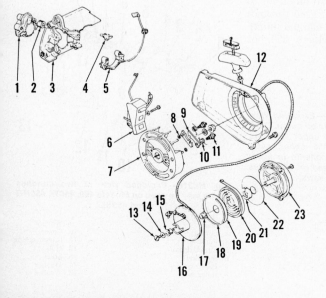

Fig. HL313 — Exploded view of ignition system and rewind starter.

1. Transformer
2. Grommet
3. Shield
4. Ignition switch
5. Transformer receptacle
6. Ignition module
7. Flywheel
8. Lockwasher
9. Starter pawl
10. Spring
11. Stud
12. Starter housing
13. Screw
14. Washer
15. Bushing
16. Rope pulley
17. Bushing
18. Snap ring
19. Outer spring shield
20. Rewind spring
21. Spring lock
22. Inner spring shield
23. Cover

tap both ends of crankshaft to obtain proper crankshaft end play. Tighten crankcase retaining screws to 60-70 in.-lbs. (6.8-7.9 N·m).

AUTOMATIC OIL PUMP. All models are equipped with an automatic oil pump. Refer to Fig. HL315 for an exploded view of oil pump. Check ball must move freely for proper pump operation. Oil pump output is not adjustable. Note the following troubleshooting procedure:

Automatic oil pump fails but manual oiler functions: Check automatic oil pump pickup for blockage. Connect a vacuum gage to pickup line and run saw at wide-open throttle under no load or while cutting and note vacuum gage reading. A good pump will develop 25-28 inches of vacuum (Mercury). Remove oil pump cover (1 – Fig. HL315) and check for cracks, and on early models, be sure lead shot plug in cover is sealing properly, otherwise, the pump cover must be renewed. Lightly push on plunger (2) and note if plunger is lifting ball check valve (6) off its seat. Also check for binding of plunger in bore and for a defective diaphragm. Plunger must not turn in diaphragm. There must be sufficient oil film in pump body (4) so "O" ring on plunger of later models does not drag. Pulse and vent holes must be open. Blow air through system from strainer end of pickup; air should exist through plunger bore of pump body (4). With plunger inserted in pump body, pressurize pickup line at strainer end and check for leaks in line or between pump body (4) and plunger. Pressurize delivery side of automatic oil pump at manual oil pump fitting so air exits from guide bar pad, then plug guide bar pad hole. Check that check ball (6) is seating and pump body "O" rings (5) do not leak. Using a suitable tool (an old plunger may be reduced in diameter by 0.020 in.), lift check ball (6) off its seat to check for free flow through delivery end of pump body. With check ball lifted off its seat, blow air into strainer end of pickup line; air should exit from guide bar pad.

Manual oiler fails but automatic oil pump functions: Check manual oil pump pickup for blockage. Disconnect outlet line fitting from manual oil pump then blow air into outlet line; air should exit from guide bar pad. DO NOT USE EXCESSIVE AIR PRESSURE AS SEAL AT CRANKCASE MAY BE DAMAGED. If air does not exit from bar pad then blockage exists in line, crankcase fitting or in crankcase passage prior to joining common delivery passage with auto oil pump. This test will also reveal leaks in line and fittings. Pressurize pickup line at strainer end and check for leaks in line, fittings and around pump plunger "O" rings (14 and 17 – Fig. HL310). Remove manual oil pump and inspect components and be sure all parts operate freely. Be sure spring returns pump to full up/intake position.

Automatic and manual oil pumps malfunction: Be sure oil tank is filled with proper oil. Operate manual oil pump. If manual oil pump operates freely, check for blocked oil pickup strainers and improperly positioned pickup lines. Reinstall oil tank cap, but do not tighten. Operate both oil pumps. If pumps work satisfactorily, then renew oil tank cap as it is not venting properly.

If manual oil pump builds pressure when operated so plunger will not depress, then there is blockage at some point in output passage. Disconnect manual oil pump outlet line from manual pump fitting and operate both pumps. Manual pump should force oil from outlet fitting while auto pump should force oil from loose end of outlet line. Remove automatic oil pump body (4 – Fig. HL315) and disconnect manual pump outlet line from crankcase fitting. Blow air into guide bar pad oil outlet to possibly blow blocking material through pump body or through manual pump delivery passage. If blockage will not

blow free, then crankcase must be removed to clean passages in engine.

CLUTCH. Models 550, 550W and 550SL are equipped with clutch shown in Fig. HL317 while Models 450, 450W, 450HG and 450SL may be equipped with either clutch shown in Fig. HL318. Clutch hub on all models has left hand threads. Clutch shoes should be renewed only as a set. Inspect bearing and lubricate with Homelite®ALL-TEMP Multipurpose Grease (#24551) or a lithium base grease.

REWIND STARTER. Refer to Fig. HL313 for an exploded view of starter assembly.

To disassemble starter, hold cover (23) and unscrew retaining screws. Allow cover to turn until spring tension is relieved and remove cover.

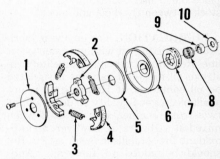

Fig. HL317 – View of Model 550, 550W and 550SL clutch.

1. Cover plate	6. Clutch drum
2. Hub	7. Sprocket
3. Spring	8. Bearing
4. Shoe	9. Inner race
5. Washer	10. Washer

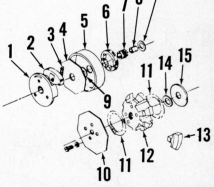

Fig. HL318 – Exploded view of two clutches which may be used on Models 450, 450W, 450HG and 450SL.

1. Hub	
2. Shoe	9. Washer
3. Spring	10. Cover
4. Plate	11. Garter spring
5. Clutch drum	12. Hub
6. Sprocket	13. Shoe
7. Bearing	14. Washer
8. Inner race	15. Washer

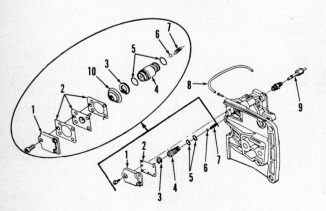

Fig. HL315 – Exploded view of automatic oil pump. Components in upper view are used on 550 series saws while components in lower view are used on 450 series saws.

1. Oil pump cover
2. Plunger & diaphragm
3. Snap ring
4. Pump body
5. "O" rings
6. Check ball
7. Spring
8. Oil line
9. Oil line
10. Spring

NOTE: If outer hook of spring catches on starter housing, pull cover away from housing until cover is allowed to turn.

Unscrew screw (13) to separate rope pulley (16) from cover. Remove snap ring (18) for access to rewind spring. If starter pawl assemblies must be removed, unscrew housing screws and remove starter housing (12). Threaded inserts are available if stud holes are damaged in flywheel.

Clean and inspect components. Lubricate sides of rewind spring with a small amount of Homelite® ALL-TEMP Multipurpose grease or a lithium base grease. Do not oil spring. Install inner spring shield (22), rewind spring (20) and spring lock (21) in cover with spring wound as shown in Fig. HL319. Install outer spring shield (19 – Fig. HL313) and snap ring (18). Insert bushings (15 and 17) in rope pulley (16) being sure knobs on bushings align with notches in pulley. Slide pulley onto post in cover and check to be sure splines on pulley

engage splines in spring lock. Install and tighten cap screw (13) to 45 in.-lbs. (5.1 N·m). Wind rope around pulley in clockwise direction as viewed from screw end of pulley. Set cover in housing. Pull rope handle and then allow rope to rewind so starter pawls will be forced open and pulley hub can slide between them into place. Turn cover clockwise 2 or 3 turns to preload rewind spring, snap plastic screen into place and install cover screws. Check starter operation.

CHAIN BRAKE. Model 450SL and 550SL are equipped with a chain brake mechanism (Fig. HL320 or HL321) to

stop saw chain motion in the event of kickback. In the event of kickback, the operator's left hand will force brake actuating lever forward and brake band will wrap around the clutch drum to stop clutch drum rotation. Chain brake effectiveness may be checked by running chain saw with chain turning but not cutting. Push chain brake actuating lever forward. Chain brake should stop chain instantly. If chain brake does not operate correctly, outer surface of clutch drum may be glazed. Remove glaze with emery cloth being sure to clean drum afterwards. Clutch drum and brake band must not be bent or nicked.

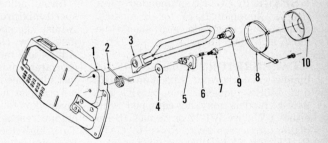

Fig. HL320 – Exploded view of chain brake used on Model 450SL.
1. Cover
2. Spring
3. Actuating lever
4. Washer
5. Latch
6. Roll pin
7. Shoulder screw
8. Brake band
9. Shoulder screw
10. Drum

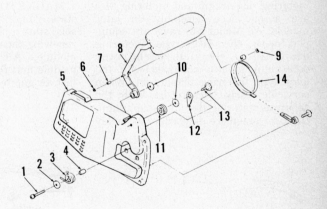

Fig. HL321 – Exploded view of chain brake used on Model 550SL.
1. Screw
2. Washer
3. Spring
4. Sleeve
5. Cover
6. "E" ring
7. Roller
8. Actuating lever
9. "E" ring
10. Washers
11. Spring
12. Latch
13. Shoulder screw
14. Brake band

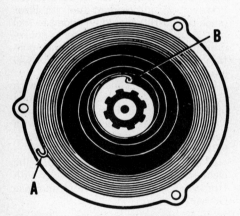

Fig. HL319 – View of rewind spring installation in starter cover. Hook outer loop (A) of spring in notch as shown. Inner loop (B) of spring must be curved inward to engage notch of spring lock.

HOMELITE

Model	Bore	Stroke	Displ.	Drive Type
240HG, 240SL, 245HG, 245SL	1.563 in. (40 mm)	1.250 in. (32 mm)	2.4 cu. in. (40 cc)	Direct

MAINTENANCE

SPARK PLUG. Recommended spark plug is Champion DJ7Y for all models. Spark plug electrode gap should be 0.025 inch (0.63 mm).

CARBURETOR. A Zama C1S-H4 diaphragm carburetor is used on 240HG and 240SL models while 245HG and 245SL models may be equipped with either a Walbro WT-19 or Zama C1S-H8 diaphragm carburetor. Refer to CARBURETOR SERVICE section for service procedures and exploded views.

As noted in the Zama service section, the metering diaphragm and metering disc are a one-piece assembly on later models. All Model 245 saws are equipped with the late type metering diaphragm. Service carburetor A-96352-A is also equipped with the later type metering diaphragm. When servicing early carburetors with the separate metering disc and diaphragm, the later one-piece diaphragm assembly (available in repair kit 96646-A) should be installed.

Initial adjustment of idle and high speed mixture screws is one turn open. Adjust idle speed screw so engine idles just below clutch engagement speed. Adjust idle mixture screw so engine accelerates smoothly. If necessary, readjust idle speed screw.

To adjust high speed mixture screw, proceed as follows. Run saw at idle until engine reaches operating temperature. Turn high speed mixture needle to obtain optimum performance with saw under cutting load.

MAGNETO AND TIMING. A solid state ignition is used on all models. The solid-state ignition system is serviced by renewing the spark plug and/or ignition module. Air gap between ignition module and flywheel is adjustable. Adjust air gap by loosening module retaining screws and place a 0.015 inch (0.4 mm) shim stock between flywheel and module.

LUBRICATION. The engine is lubricated by mixing oil with unleaded gasoline. Recommended oil is Homelite® two-stroke oil mixed at ratio as designated on oil container. If Homelite® oil is not available, a good quality oil designed for air-cooled two-stroke engines may be used when mixed at a 16:1 ratio, however, an antioxidant fuel stabilizer (such as Sta-Bil) should be added to fuel mix. Antioxidant fuel stabilizer is not required with Homelite® oils as they contain fuel stabilizer so the fuel mix will stay fresh up to one year.

Chain oil tank should be filled with Homelite® Bar and Chain Oil or a good quality SAE 30 oil. It may be necessary to use SAE 10 oil or oil mixed with kerosene if temperature is below 40°F (4°C).

Clutch needle bearing should be cleaned and lubricated periodically with Homelite® ALL-TEMP Multipurpose Grease.

MUFFLER. Outer screen of muffler should be cleaned of debris every week or after each 50 hours of use. Carbon should be removed from muffler and engine ports to prevent excessive car-

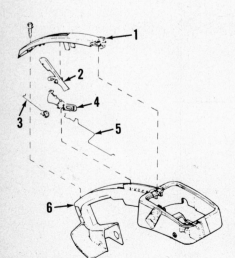

Fig. HL325 — View of trigger assembly used on 240HG and 240SL models.

1. Handle cover
2. Interlock
3. Spring
4. Throttle trigger
5. Throttle rod
6. Filter chamber

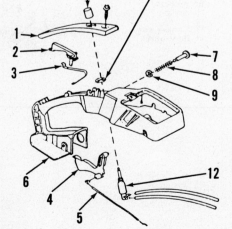

Fig. HL325S — View of trigger assembly and manual oil pump used on 245HG and 245SL models.

1. Handle cover
2. Interlock
3. Spring
4. Throttle trigger
5. Throttle cable
6. Filter chamber
7. Throttle lock pin
8. Spring
9. "E" ring
10. Button
11. Nut
12. Manual oil pump

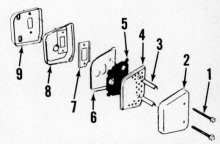

Fig. HL326 — Exploded view of muffler.

1. Screw
2. Cap
3. Spacer
4. Outer baffle
5. Screen
6. Inner baffle
7. Support
8. Body
9. Deflector

bon build-up and power loss. Do not allow loose carbon to enter cylinder and be careful not to damage exhaust port or piston. Refer to Fig. HL326 when reassembling muffler.

REPAIRS

TIGHTENING TORQUE VALUES.
Tightening torque values are listed in following table.

Carburetor retaining
  screws . . . . .18-33 in.-lbs.
    (2.0-3.7 N·m)
Chain brake band . . . . .27-44 in.-lbs.
    (3.1-5.0 N·m)
Chain brake lever . . . . . . .36-55 in.-lbs.
    (4.1-6.2 N·m)
Clutch hub . . . . .90-165 in.-lbs.
    (10.2-18.6 N·m)
Clutch nut . . . . .68-110 in.-lbs.
    (7.7-12.4 N·m)
Crankcase screws . . . . . . .54-82 in.-lbs.
    (6.1-9.3 N·m)
Flywheel . . . . .90-165 in.-lbs.
    (10.2-18.6 N·m)
Ignition module . . . . .27-44 in.-lbs.
    (3.1-5.0 N·m)
Muffler . . . . .63-88 in.-lbs.
    (7.1-9.9 N·m)

Spark plug . . . . .140-160 in.-lbs.
    (15.8-18.1 N·m)
Starter pulley screw . . . . . .36-55 in.-lbs.
    (4.1-6.2 N·m)
Vibration isolator . . . . .36-55 in.-lbs.
    (4.1-6.2 N·m)

COMPRESSION PRESSURE. For optimum performance of all models, cylinder compression pressure should be 130-160 psi (897-1104 kPa) with engine at normal operating temperature. Engine should be inspected and repaired when compression pressure is 90 psi (620 kPa) or below.

CYLINDER, PISTON, PIN AND RINGS. Cylinder may be removed after unscrewing socket head cap screws in bottom of crankcase (13 – Fig. H327). Be careful when removing cylinder as crankshaft assembly will be loose in crankcase. Care should be taken not to scratch or nick mating surfaces of cylinder and crankcase.

Inspect crankshaft bearings and renew if scored or worn. Thrust washers (9) should be installed with shoulder to inside. Bearings (10) should be installed with lettered end towards crankshaft. Crankshaft seals are installed with seal

lip to inside. Cylinder and crankcase mating surfaces should be cleaned then coated with room temperature vulcanizing (RTV) silicone sealer before assembly.

Early model cylinders are equipped with an open exhaust port while a bridged exhaust port is used on later model cylinders. Early model pistons are equipped with piston ring locating pins in ring groove. Later model pistons do not have piston ring locating pins and top piston ring should be installed so end gap is opposite exhaust port. End gap of bottom piston ring should be 90 degrees from top ring end gap. Piston ring end gap should be 0.003-0.017 inch (0.08-0.43 mm).

Bearings, seals and thrust washers must be positioned correctly on crankshaft before final assembly. Use the following procedure for crankshaft installation: With piston assembly installed on rod, insert piston in cylinder being sure piston rings are properly located. Install thrust washers (9), bearings (10), retaining rings (11) and seals (12) on crankshaft. Place 0.015 inch

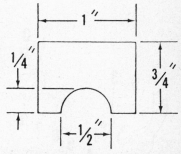

Fig. HL328 – Shims used in crankshaft assembly may be made by putting 0.015 inch thick plastic, metal, or other suitable material in the outline shown above. Refer to Fig. HL329 and text.

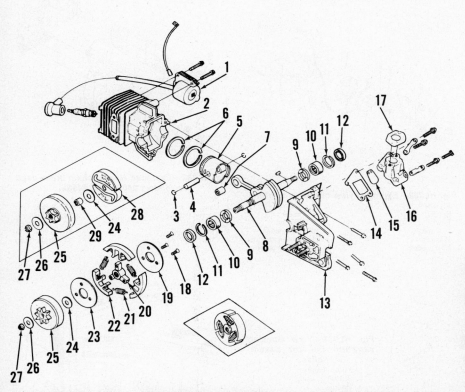

Fig. HL327 — Exploded view of engine and clutch assemblies. Models 245HG and 245SL are equipped with three-shoe clutch. Models 240HG and 240SL are equipped with "S" clutch (inset).

1. Ignition module		
2. Cylinder	9. Thrust washer	16. Intake manifold
3. Retainer	10. Needle bearing	17. Gasket
4. Piston pin	11. Retaining ring	18. Screw
5. Piston	12. Seal	19. Cover plate
6. Piston rings	13. Crankcase	20. Clutch hub
7. Needle bearing	14. Gasket	21. Clutch spring
8. Crankshaft	15. Reed petal	22. Clutch shoe

23. Cover plate	
24. Thrust washer	
25. Clutch drum/bearing	
26. Thrust washer	
27. Nut	
28. "S" clutch/hub	
29. Needle bearing	

Fig. HL329 — View showing placement of shims (Fig. HL328) between thrust washers (9 — Fig. HL327) and bearings (10) for correct crankshaft assembly. Refer to text.

thick shims shown in Fig. HL328 between thrust washers and bearings as shown in Fig. HL329. Gently push seals toward crankshaft counterweights until assemblies are snug. Remove shims and complete assembly being careful not to disturb position of thrust washers, bearings and seals. Before final tightening of crankcase screws, lightly tap both ends of crankshaft to obtain proper crankshaft end play, then tighten crankcase screws.

CLUTCH. Refer to Fig. HL327 for exploded view of clutch assemblies used. Models 240HG and 240SL are equipped with the "S" type centrifugal clutch (28) shown in inset while Models 245HG and 245SL are equipped with the three-type clutch (20, 21 and 22). On both types, clutch nut (27) and hub (20 or 28) have left-hand threads

NOTE: "OUTSIDE" marked on side of hub of "S" type clutch.

Clean and inspect clutch hub, drum and bearing for damage or excessive wear. Inspect crankshaft for wear or damage caused by defective clutch bearing. Clutch bearing contains 21 needle rollers which will fall out when bearing is removed if the following procedure is not followed. Roll a tube of paper approximately the size of the crankshaft and slide the clutch drum and bearing off the crankshaft and on to the rolled paper. The roll of paper will prevent the bearing needle rollers from falling out and the drum and bearing can be installed by reversing the procedure. If bearing is removed without using the above procedure, the needle bearings will fall out and a new bearing must be installed as needle rollers are too small.

NOTE: Be sure all 21 needle rollers are present in bearing race.

New bearings can be installed without using above procedure since wear has not yet loosened rollers.

CHAIN OIL PUMP. All models are equipped with a crankcase pulse actuated automatic chain oiler pump. Crankcase pulses actuate diaphragm and plunger (3 – Fig. HL330) to force oil out oil outlet (O). Inspect diaphragm (3) and "O" ring (2) for leaks.

Models 245HG and 245SL are also equipped with a manual oil pump (12 – Fig. HL325A) to supply additional lubrication when required. Individual manual oil pump components are not available and pump must be renewed as a unit assembly.

VIBRATION ISOLATORS. All models are equipped with vibration isolators between engine and engine housing. Vibration isolators may be renewed after removing handle bar (3 – Fig. HL331), starter housing (2) and air box (1). Use Fig. HL331 as a guide to reassemble vibration isolator components.

REWIND STARTER. To service recoil starter, remove starter housing from saw. Pull starter rope and hold rope pulley with notch in pulley adjacent to rope outlet. Pull rope back through outlet so it engages notch in pulley and allow pulley to completely unwind. Unscrew pulley retaining screw (8 – Fig. HL332) and remove rope pulley being careful not to dislodge rewind spring in housing. Care must be taken if rewind

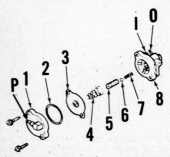

Fig. HL330 – Exploded view of automatic oil pump. Oil enters pump through inlet tube (I) and exits through tube (E). Diaphragm (3) is actuated by crankcase pulsations through pulse fitting (P).

1. Cover
2. "O" ring
3. Diaphragm & plunger
4. Spring
5. Stud
6. Check ball
7. Spring
8. Body

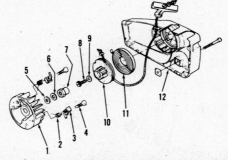

Fig. HL332 – Exploded view of rewind starter.

1. Flywheel
2. Spring
3. Pawl
4. Pawl pin
5. Washer
6. Lockwasher
7. Nut
8. Screw
9. Washer
10. Rope pulley
11. Rewind starter
12. Starter housing

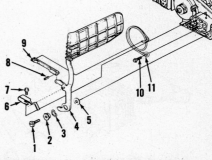

Fig. HL333 – Exploded view of chain brake used on Models 240SL and 245SL.

1. Screw
2. Cam
3. Curved washer
4. Brake lever
5. Thrust washer
6. Clip
7. Screw
8. Roll pin
9. Pivot link
10. Screw
11. Brake band

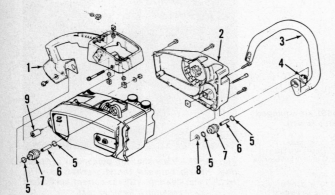

Fig. HL331 – View showing vibration isolator assemblies.

1. Filter chamber
2. Starter housing
3. Handle
4. Washer
5. Ring
6. Spacer
7. Isolator
8. Washer
9. Shear isolator

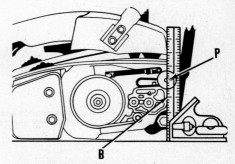

Fig. HL334 – Brake lever pin (P) is normally in line with front edge of guide bar pad (B). Refer to text for adjustment.

spring is removed to prevent injury if spring is allowed to uncoil uncontrolled.

Rewind spring is wound in clockwise direction in starter housing. Rope is wound on rope pulley in clockwise direction as viewed with pulley in housing. To place tension on rewind spring, pass rope through rope outlet in housing and install rope handle. Pull rope out and hold rope pulley so notch on pulley is adjacent to rope outlet. Pull rope back through outlet between notch in pulley and housing. Turn rope pulley clockwise to place tension on spring. Release pulley and check starter action. Do not place more tension on rewind spring

than is necessary to draw rope handle up against housing.

CHAIN BRAKE. Models 240SL and 245SL are equipped with a chain brake mechanism to stop saw chain motion in the event of kickback. In the event of kickback, the operator's left hand will force brake lever (4 – Fig. HL333) forward and brake band (11) will wrap around the clutch drum to stop clutch drum rotation. Chain brake should stop chain instantly. If chain brake does not operate correctly, outer surface of clutch drum may be glazed. Remove glaze with emery cloth being sure to

clean drum afterwards. Clutch drum and brake band must not be bent or nicked.

The force needed to actuate brake lever (4) is adjustable by rotating cam (2). Maximum force needed to actuate brake lever is obtained with cam down. Cam rotation will also alter position of brake lever. If brake lever must be repositioned after rotating cam, loosen retaining screw and relocate clip (6). The location of clip also determines the clearance between brake band (11) and clutch drum. Normal position for lever pin (P – Fig. HL334) is in line with front edge of guide bar pan (B).

HOMELITE

Model	Bore	Stroke	Displ.	Drive Type
330, 330SL, 330W	1.687 in. (43 mm)	1.464 in. (37 mm)	3.27 cu. in. (53.6 cc)	Direct

MAINTENANCE

SPARK PLUG. Recommended spark plug is Champion DJ7Y for all models. Spark plug electrode gap should be 0.025 inch (0.63 mm).

CARBURETOR. All models may be equipped with a Walbro WT or Zama diaphragm type carburetor. Refer to CARBURETOR SERVICE section for carburetor service and exploded views.

Initial adjustment of low speed mixture screw (L–Fig. HL340) and high speed mixture screw (H) is one turn open. Adjust idle speed screw so engine idles just below clutch engagement speed. Adjust low mixture screw to obtain maximum engine speed at idle and smooth acceleration. If necessary readjust idle speed screw.

To adjust high speed mixture screw, proceed as follows: Run saw at idle until engine reaches operating temperature. Turn high speed mixture needle to obtain optimum performance with saw under cutting load.

MAGNETO AND TIMING. A solid state ignition is used on all models. The solid-state ignition system is serviced by renewing the spark plug and/or ignition module. Air gap between ignition module and flywheel is adjustable. Adjust air gap by loosening module retain-

ing screws and place a 0.015 inch (0.38 mm) shim stock between flywheel and module.

Although ignition system malfunctions are usually caused by spark plug and/or ignition module failure, erratic enging operation, especially under load, may be due to ignition switch lead wire grounding on the cylinder or muffler. Make certain switch lead wire is routed and secured as shown in Fig. HL342 and wire connections at ignition switch are properly positioned to prevent contact with cylinder or muffler. Ignition switch ground wire should be secured to saw at a 45 degree angle from saw centerline (not straight back).

LUBRICATION. The engine is lubricated by mixing oil with unleaded gasoline. Recommended oil is Homelite® two-stroke oil mixed at ratio as designated on oil container. If Homelite® oil is not available, a good quality oil designed for air-cooled two-stroke engines may be used when mixed at a 16:1 ratio, however, an antioxidant fuel stabilizer (such as Sta-Bil) should be added to fuel mix. Antioxidant fuel stabilizer is not required with Homelite® oils as they contain fuel stabilizer so the fuel mix will stay fresh up to one year.

Chain oil tank should be filled with Homelite® Bar and Chain Oil or a good quality SAE 30 oil. It may be necessary to use SAE 10 oil or oil mixed with kerosene if temperature is below 40°F (4°C).

Clutch needle bearing should be removed, cleaned and lubricated periodically with Homelite® ALL-TEMP Multipurpose Grease.

MUFFLER. Muffler should be disassembled, cleaned of debris and inspected every week or as required. Renew muffler components that are cracked or worn excessively. Carbon should be removed from muffler and engine ports to prevent excessive carbon build-up and power loss. Do not allow loose carbon to enter cylinder and be careful not to damage exhaust port or piston. Refer to Fig. HL343 when reassembling muffler.

REPAIRS

TIGHTENING TORQUE VALUES. Tightening torque values are listed in following table.

Carburetor retaining screws	20-30 in.-lbs. (2.3-3.4 N·m)
Chain brake band	70-80 in.-lbs. (7.9-9.0 N·m)
Chain brake shield	40 in.-lbs. (4.5 N·m)

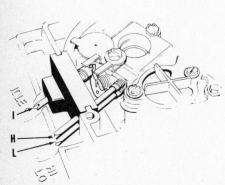

Fig. HL340 – View showing location of idle speed screw (I), low speed mixture screw (L) and high speed mixture screw (H).

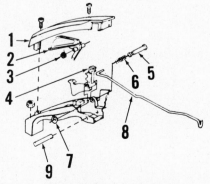

Fig. HL341 – View of trigger assembly.

1. Handle cover
2. Interlock
3. Spring
4. Throttle trigger
5. Throttle lock pin
6. Spring
7. "E" ring
8. Throttle rod
9. Groove pin

Fig. HL342 – Route and secure ignition switch lead as shown to prevent "shorting out" of ignition systems. Refer to text.

Chain stop . . . . .30-40 in.-lbs.
(3.4-4.5 N·m)
Clutch nut . . . . .100-120 in.-lbs.
(11.3-13.6 N·m)
Crankcase screws . . . . .60-70 in.-lbs.
(6.8-7.9 N·m)
Flywheel . . . . .250-300 in.-lbs.
(28.2-33.9 N·m)
Ignition module . . . . .70-80 in.-lbs.
(7.9-9.0 N·m)
Muffler . . . . .60-70 in.-lbs.
(6.8-7.9 N·m)
Spark plug . . . . .120-180 in.-lbs.
(13.6-20.3 N·m)
Starter pulley . . . . .40-50 in.-lbs.
(4.5-5.6 N·m)
Vibration isolator . . . . . . .40-50 in.-lbs.
(4.5-5.6 N·m)

COMPRESSION PRESSURE. For optimum performance of all models, cylinder compression pressure should be 130-160 psi (897-1104 kPa) with engine at normal operating temperature. Engine should be inspected and repaired when compression pressure is 90 psi (620 kPa) or below.

CYLINDER, PISTON, PIN AND RINGS. Cylinder may be removed after unscrewing socket head cap screws in bottom of crankcase (13 – Fig. H344). Be careful when removing cylinder as crankshaft assembly will be loose in crankcase. Care should be taken not to scratch or nick mating surfaces of cylinder and crankcase.

Inspect crankshaft bearings (10) and renew if scored or worn. Crankshaft seals are installed with seal lip to inside. Cylinder and crankcase mating surfaces should be flat and free of nicks and scratches. Mating surfaces should be cleaned then coated with room temperature vulcanizing (RTV) silicone sealer before assembly.

Bearings, seals and thrust washers must be positioned correctly on crankshaft before final assembly. Use the following procedure for crankshaft installation: With piston assembly installed on rod, insert piston in cylinder being sure piston rings are aligned on locating pins. Install thrust washers (9), bearings (10), retaining rings (11) and seals (12) on crankshaft. Place 0.015 inch thick shims shown in Fig. HL345

between thrust washers and bearings as shown in Fig. HL346.

Gently push seals toward crankshaft counterweights until assemblies are

Fig. HL346 — View showing placement of shims (Fig. HL345) between thrust washers (9 — Fig. HL344) and bearings (10) for correct crankshaft assembly. Refer to text.

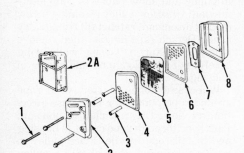

Fig. HL343 — Exploded view of muffler. Cap (2A) is used on Model 330W.

1. Screw
2. Cap
3. Spacer
4. Outer baffle
5. Screen
6. Inner baffle
7. Plate
8. Body

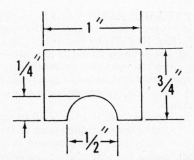

Fig. HL345 — Shims used in crankshaft assembly may be made by cutting 0.015 inch thick plastic, metal or other suitable material in the outline shown above. Refer to Fig. HL346 and text.

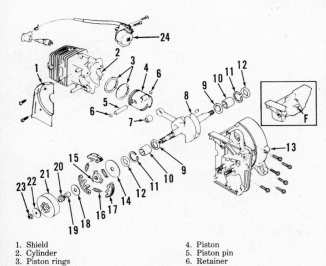

Fig. HL344 — Exploded view of engine and clutch assemblies. Pulse fitting (F) is connected to oil pump pulse hose.

7. Needle bearing
8. Crankshaft
9. Thrust washer
10. Needle bearing
11. Retainer ring
12. Seal
13. Crankcase
14. Thrust washer
15. Hub
16. Spring
17. Shoe
18. Thrust washer
19. Inner race
20. Roller bearing
21. Clutch drum
22. Thrust washer
23. Nut
24. Ignition module

1. Shield
2. Cylinder
3. Piston rings
4. Piston
5. Piston pin
6. Retainer

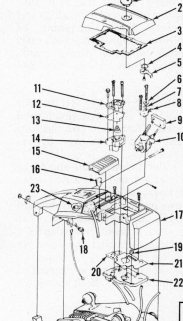

Fig. HL347 — Exploded view of oil pump and air box assemblies.

1. Choke knob
2. Cover
3. Gasket
4. Wave washer
5. Choke lever
6. Spacer
7. Wave washer
8. Choke plate
9. Grommet
10. Carburetor
11. Oil pump cover
12. Diaphragm & plunger
13. Spring
14. Oil pump body
15. Air filter
16. Grommet
17. Top engine housing
18. Ignition switch
19. Grommet
20. Gasket
21. Gasket
22. Plate
23. Retainer
24. Boot
25. Reed seat
26. Reed valve
27. Reed retainer

Homelite

CHAIN SAW

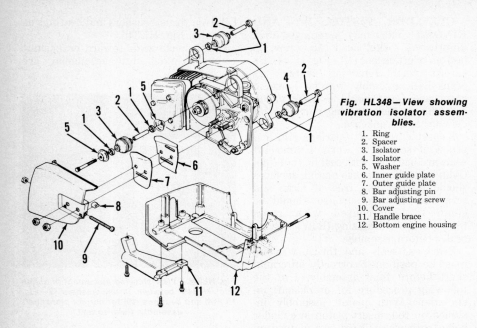

Fig. HL348—View showing vibration isolator assemblies.

1. Ring
2. Spacer
3. Isolator
4. Isolator
5. Washer
6. Inner guide plate
7. Outer guide plate
8. Bar adjusting pin
9. Bar adjusting screw
10. Cover
11. Handle brace
12. Bottom engine housing

chain oiler pump (11 through 14—Fig. HL347). Crankcase pulses actuate diaphragm and plunger (12) to force oil out oil outlet. Check oil pump assembly for leaks. Carefully inspect cover (11) and diaphragm (12). If oil pump is defective due to warpage of cover (11), sand cover until flat or renew cover.

VIBRATION ISOLATORS. All models are equipped with vibration isolators between engine and engine housing. Vibration isolators may be renewed after removing top engine housing (17—Fig. HL347) and bottom engine housing (12—Fig. HL348). Use Fig. HL348 as a guide to reassemble vibration isolator components.

REWIND STARTER. To service rewind starter, unscrew mounting screws and remove starter housing (11—Fig. HL349). Rotate ratchet (6) until it stops at end of shaft on pulley (8), then slide ratchet lever (7) off ratchet. Pull starter rope and hold rope pulley with notch in pulley adjacent to rope outlet. Pull rope back through outlet so it engages notch in pulley and allow pulley to completely unwind. Unscrew pulley retaining screw (4) and disengage ratchet (6) from pulley shaft. Detach rope handle, then remove pulley from starter housing while being careful not to dislodge rewind spring in housing.

When assembling starter, wind rope around rope pulley in a clockwise direction as viewed with pulley in housing. Pass rope through rope outlet in housing and install rope handle. Place pulley in housing. Reinstall ratchet (6) on pulley shaft and secure assembly with flat washer (5) and screw (4). To place tension on rewind spring, pull rope out and hold rope pulley so notch on pulley is adjacent to rope outlet. Pull rope back through outlet between notch in pulley

snug. Remove shims and complete assembly being careful not to disturb position of thrust washers, bearings and seals. Before final tightening of crankcase screws, lightly tap both ends of crankshaft to obtain proper crankshaft end play, then tighten crankcase screws.

CLUTCH. Refer to Fig. HL344 for exploded view of shoe type clutch used on all models. Clutch hub (15) has left-hand threads and is removed by unscrewing clockwise.

Needle roller bearing (20) should be removed, cleaned and lubricated after each 100 hours of operation. A high temperature grease such as Homelite® ALL-TEMP Multipurpose Grease should be used. Inspect crankshaft for wear or damage caused by defective clutch bearing.

If clutch slips with engine running at high speed under load, check the clutch

shoes for excessive wear. If chain continues to turn with engine running at idle speed (below normal clutch engagement speed), check for broken, weak or distorted clutch springs.

PYRAMID REED VALVE. A pyramid type reed intake valve seat (25—Fig. HL347) and four reeds (26) are used. Reeds are retained on pins projecting from the reed seat by retainer (27). Inspect reed seat, retainer and reeds for any distortion, excessive wear or other damage.

To reinstall, use a drop of oil to stick each reed to the seat, then push reed retainer down over the seat and reeds. Then install the assembly in crankcase; never install retainer, then attempt to install reed seat and reeds.

AUTOMATIC CHAIN OILER PUMP. All models are equipped with a crankcase pulse actuated automatic

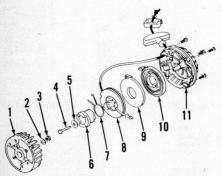

Fig. HL349—Exploded view of rewind starter.

1. Flywheel
2. Washer
3. Nut
4. Screw
5. Washer
6. Ratchet
7. Ratchet lever
8. Rope pulley
9. Spring case
10. Rewind spring
11. Starter housing

Fig. HL350—Exploded view of chain brake used on Model 330SL.

1. Chain stop
2. Shield
3. Washer
4. Brake lever
5. Bushing
6. Link
7. Screw
8. Spacer
9. Detent
10. Spring
11. Bracket
12. Brake band
13. Spring washer
14. Insert

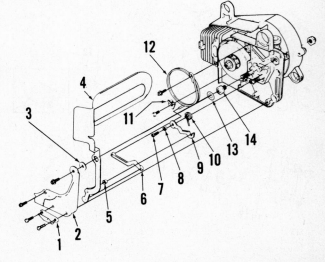

Illustrations Courtesy Homelite Div. of Textron, ©1987

and housing. Turn rope pulley clockwise to place tension on spring. Release pulley and check starter action. Do not place more tension on rewind spring than is necessary to draw rope handle up against housing. Slide ratchet lever (7) with hooked end up, on ratchet while guiding hooked end between posts of starter housing. Check operation of starter assembly before installing on saw.

CHAIN BRAKE. Model 330SL is equipped with a chain brake mechanism to stop saw chain motion in the event of kickback. In the event of kickback, the operator's left hand will force brake lever (4—Fig. HL350) forward and brake band (12) will wrap around the clutch drum to stop clutch drum rotation. Chain brake should stop chain instantly. If chain brake does not operate correctly, outer surface of clutch drum may be glazed. Remove glaze with emery cloth being sure to clean drum afterwards. Clutch drum and brake band must not be bent or nicked.

HOMELITE

Model	Bore	Stroke	Displ.	Drive Type
410	1.937 in. (49 mm)	1.375 in. (35 mm)	4.10 cu. in. (67 cc)	Direct

MAINTENANCE

SPARK PLUG. Recommended spark plug is Champion DJ7Y for all models. Spark plug electrode gap should be 0.025 inch (0.63 mm).

CARBURETOR. Model 410 is equipped with a Walbro WS diaphragm carburetor. Refer to Walbro section of CARBURETOR SERVICE section for carburetor overhaul and exploded view.

Remove carburetor cover to perform initial carburetor adjustments. Initial adjustment of idle speed screw (I–Fig. HL355) is ½-¾ turn clockwise after lobe on idle speed screw just contacts throttle stop lever (T). Initial adjustment of low speed mixture screw (L) is 1-1¾ turns open and high speed mixture screw (H) is 1-1¼ turns open. Install carburetor cover and start saw.

Adjust low mixture screw to obtain maximum engine speed at idle and smooth acceleration, then adjust idle speed screw so engine idles just below clutch engagement speed.

To adjust high speed mixture screw, proceed as follows: Run saw at idle until engine reaches operating temperature. Turn high speed mixture needle to obtain optimum performance with saw under cutting load.

Note check valve (20–Fig. HL356) and filter (19) which are used to vent fuel tank. Filter must be clean and valve must operate properly for required fuel flow to carburetor.

MAGNETO AND TIMING. Model 410 is equipped with a solid-state ignition. The solid-state ignition system is serviced by renewing the spark plug and/or ignition module. Air gap between ignition module and flywheel is adjustable. Adjust air gap by loosening module retaining screws and place a 0.015 inch (0.38 mm) shim stock between flywheel and module.

LUBRICATION. The engine is lubricated by mixing oil with unleaded gasoline. Recommended oil is Homelite® two-stroke oil mixed at ratio as designated on oil container. If Homelite® oil is not available, a good quality oil designed for two-stroke engines may be used when mixed at a 16:1 ratio, however, an antioxidant fuel stabilizer (such as Sta-Bil) should be added to fuel mix. Antioxidant fuel stabilizer is not required with Homelite® oils as they contain fuel stabilizer so the fuel mix will stay fresh up to one year.

Chain oil tank should be filled with Homelite® Bar and Chain Oil or a good quality SAE 30 oil. It may be necessary to use SAE 10 oil or oil mixed with kerosene if temperature is below 40°F (4°C).

Clutch needle bearing should be removed, cleaned and lubricated periodically with Homelite® ALL-TEMP Multipurpose Grease.

MUFFLER. Muffler should be disassembled and periodically cleaned. Renew muffler components that are cracked or worn excessively. Check engine exhaust port and remove excessive carbon build-up as required. Do not allow loose carbon to enter cylinder

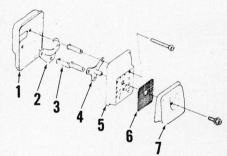

Fig. HL357—Exploded view of muffler.

1. Body
2. Plate
3. Spacer
4. Spacer plate
5. Cover
6. Screen
7. Cap

Fig. HL356—Exploded view of handle assembly.

1. Carburetor
2. Throttle rod
3. Plate
4. Spacer
5. Trigger lock
6. Pin
7. Throttle lock pin
8. Spring
9. Set screw
10. Trigger
11. Throttle rod
12. Cover
13. Air filter
14. Support
15. Stud
16. Ignition switch
17. Manual oil pump
18. Boot
19. Filter
20. Check valve
21. "E" ring
22. Choke rod
23. Retainer
24. Vibration isolator

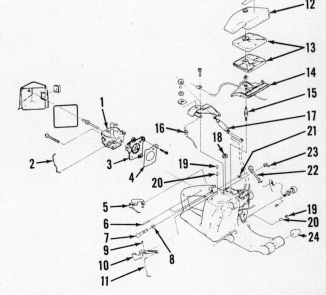

Fig. HL355—View of carburetor adjustment screws. Refer to text for adjustment.

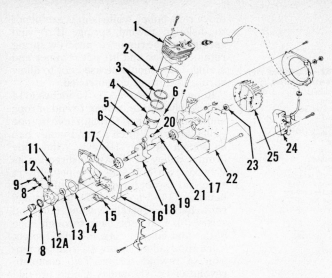

Fig. HL358 — Exploded view of engine and oil pump.

1. Cylinder
2. Gasket
3. Piston rings
4. Piston
5. Piston pin
6. Retainer
7. Worm
8. Felt seal
9. Cam screw
10. Gasket
11. Plunger & gear
12. Retainer
12A. Automatic oil pump body
13. Seal
14. Gasket
15. Chain stop
16. Crankcase half
17. Ball bearing
18. Crankshaft
19. Dowel pin (2)
20. Needle bearing
21. Key
22. Crankcase half
23. Seal
24. Ignition module
25. Flywheel

and be careful not to damage exhaust port on piston. Refer to Fig. HL357 when reassembling muffler.

REPAIRS

TIGHTENING TORQUE VALUES.
Tightening torque values are listed in following table.

Auto oil pump............40-50 in.-lbs.
    (4.5-5.6 N·m)
Auto oil pump cam screw..50-60 in.-lbs.
    (5.6-6.8 N·m)
Carburetor adapter......30-40 in.-lbs.
    (3.4-4.5 N·m)
Carburetor
  retaining screws ....40-50 in.-lbs.
    (4.5-5.6 N·m)
Chain stop.............30-40 in.-lbs.
    (3.4-4.5 N·m)
Clutch cover...........40-50 in.-lbs.
    (4.5-5.6 N·m)
Clutch hub...........350-450 in.-lbs.
    (39.5-50.8 N·m)
Crankcase screws.......80-90 in.-lbs.
    (9.0-10.2 N·m)

Flywheel............250-300 in.-lbs.
    (28.2-33.9 N·m)
Ignition module.........50-60 in.-lbs.
    (5.6-6.8 N·m)
Muffler...............80-90 in.-lbs.
    (9.0-10.2 N·m)
Muffler exhaust cap.....40-50 in.-lbs.
    (4.5-5.6 N·m)
Spark plug...........120-180 in.-lbs.
    (13.6-20.3 N·m)
Starter pulley..........10-20 in.-lbs.
    (1.1-2.2 N·m)
Vibration isolator.......60-70 in.-lbs.
    (6.8-7.9 N·m)

COMPRESSION PRESSURE. For optimum performance of all models, cylinder compression pressure should be 140-170 psi (966-1173 kPa) with engine at normal operating temperature.

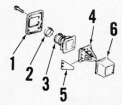

Fig. HL360 — Exploded view of reed valve assembly.

1. Retainer
2. Stiffener
3. Connector
4. Seal
5. Reed
6. Retainer

Engine should be inspected and repaired when compression pressure is 90 psi (620 kPa) or below.

PISTON, PIN, RINGS AND CYLINDER. The cylinder is secured to crankcase by four socket head screws. After removing cylinder, inspect cylinder bore for damage and excessive wear.

The piston pin is retained by clips at both ends of pin. The piston pin is supported by a renewable needle bearing in the connecting rod. Renew piston pin if worn or damaged.

The piston is equipped with two piston rings. Piston and cylinder are graded at factory according to size. Piston and cylinder are available only as a matched set.

Late models are equipped with a longer piston pin bearing (20 — Fig. HL358) than early models. Piston pin bosses on late model pistons are wider apart to accept the wider bearing. Long bearing cannot be installed in an early piston and short bearing must not be installed in a late piston as excessive side play will result in engine failure. Early bearing width is 0.506-0.512 inch (12.9-13.0 mm) while late bearing width is 0.568-0.574 inch (14.4-14.6 mm).

CONNECTING ROD, CRANKSHAFT AND CRANKCASE. Crankcase halves must be split for access to crankshaft. The crankshaft is supported by ball bearings at both ends of shaft. Connecting rod, crankpin and crankshaft are a pressed together assembly and separate components are not available. Rod and crankshaft must be serviced as a unit assembly.

CLUTCH. Refer to Fig. HL359 for an exploded view of clutch. Cover plate (2) is retained by Torx head screws (1). Clutch hub (3) has left-hand threads. Clutch shoes and springs should be renewed only as sets. Inspect bearing (9) and lubricate with Homelite® ALL-TEMP Multipurpose Grease.

REED VALVE. A pyramid type reed valve as shown in Fig. HL360 is used. Reeds are retained on pins projecting

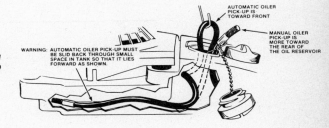

Fig. HL359 — Exploded view of clutch.

1. Torx screw
2. Plate
3. Clutch hub
4. Clutch shoe
5. Spring
6. Thrust washer
7. Clutch drum
8. Sprocket
9. Roller bearing
10. Inner race
11. Thrust washer

Fig. HL361 — View showing installation of oil pickup lines.

WARNING: AUTOMATIC OILER PICK-UP MUST BE SLID BACK THROUGH SMALL SPACE IN TANK SO THAT IT LIES FORWARD AS SHOWN.

AUTOMATIC OILER PICK-UP IS TOWARD FRONT

MANUAL OILER PICK-UP IS MORE TOWARD THE REAR OF THE OIL RESERVOIR

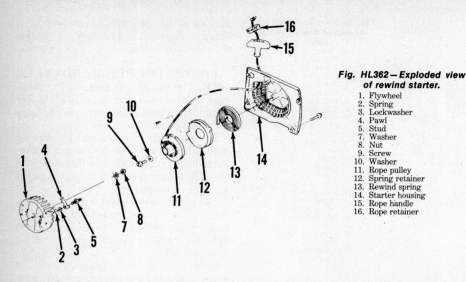

from the reed seat by a molded retainer (6). Inspect reed seat, retainer and reeds for any distortion, excessive wear or other damage.

To reinstall reed valve, use a drop of oil to stick each reed to the plastic seat, then push reed retainer down over the seat and reeds. Then install the assembly in the crankcase; never install retainer, then attempt to install reed seat and reeds.

AUTOMATIC CHAIN OILER PUMP. The automatic chain oiler pump used is shown in Fig. HL358. The pump can be removed after removing the clutch. Inspect all pump components and renew any part which is damaged or excessively worn. Oil pump output is not adjustable.

Note check valve (20–Fig. HL356) and filter (19) which are used to vent oil tank. Filter must be clean and valve must operate properly for oil to enter oil pumps. Refer to Fig. HL361 for view of correct installation of oil pickup lines.

VIBRATION ISOLATORS. The engine assembly is supported in the handle assembly by six vibration isolators (24–Fig. HL356). The vibration isolators are held in place with Torx head threaded pins. Renew split or otherwise damaged vibration isolators.

REWIND STARTER. To disassemble starter, remove starter from saw

then detach rope handle and allow rope to wind into starter. Unscrew pulley retaining screw (9–Fig. HL362) and re-

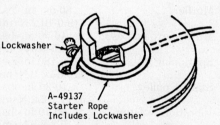

Fig. HL363—Insert rope through rope pulley hole and the rope around pulley hub as shown.

move rope pulley while being careful not to dislodge rewind spring. If rewind spring must be removed, unscrew spring retainer screw and lift out retainer and spring. Care should be used not to allow spring to unwind uncontrolled.

Rope length should be 45 inches (114 cm). Apply heat or cement to end of rope and insert rope end through hole in rope pulley and tie a hitch around pulley hub as shown in Fig. HL363. Wind rope around pulley in clockwise direction as viewed from hub side of pulley. Insert rope end through rope outlet of starter housing (14–Fig. HL362) and attach rope handle. Install washer (10) and screw (9). Pull rope back through rope outlet and engage rope in pulley notch. Turn rope pulley clockwise to apply tension to rewind spring. Two complete revolutions of the pulley should provide sufficient tension. Check starter operation, then install on engine.

CHAIN BRAKE. Refer to Fig. HL364 for an exploded view of chain brake. The chain brake will be triggered when the operator's hand forces brake lever (9) forward. The chain brake should stop saw chain instantly. If chain brake does not operate correctly, outer surface of clutch drum may be glazed. Remove glaze using emery cloth being sure to clean drum afterward. Clutch drum and brake band must not be bent or nicked.

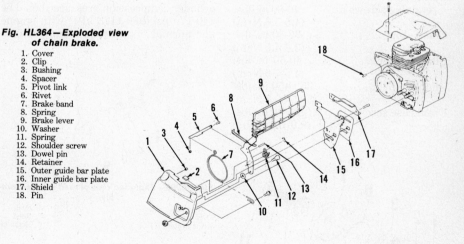

HOMELITE

Model	Bore	Stroke	Displ.	Drive Type
290	1.65 in. (42 mm)	1.34 in. (34 mm)	2.9 cu. in. (47.5 cc)	Direct
340	1.77 in. (45 mm)	1.34 in. (34 mm)	3.3 cu. in. (54.1 cc)	Direct

MAINTENANCE

SPARK PLUG. Recommended spark plug is Champion RCJ6Y, CJ6Y or equivalent. Specified electrode gap is 0.025 inch (0.63 mm) for CJ6Y plugs and 0.020 inch (0.51 mm) for RCJ6Y plugs.

CARBURETOR. A Tillotson HU diaphragm type carburetor is used. Refer to CARBURETOR SERVICE section for overhaul procedures and exploded view.

A view of the carburetor mixture screws is shown in Fig. HL370. Initial adjustment of the idle speed screw is ¾ to 1 turn clockwise after contacting the throttle stop lever. Initial adjustment of the idle speed mixture screw is 1½ turns counterclockwise from the seated position on Model 340 and 7/8 turn counterclockwise from the seated position on Model 290. Initial adjustment of the high speed mixture screw is 1 turn counterclockwise from the seated position on both models. Make final adjustments with engine warm and running. Adjust idle speed screw so engine idles just below clutch engagement speed. Adjust low speed mixture screw so engine will accelerate cleanly without hesitation. Adjust high speed mixture screw to obtain optimum performance under cutting load.

A view of the carburetor linkage is shown in Fig. HL371.

MAGNETO AND TIMING. A solid-state ignition system is used. Timing is fixed and set at 29 degrees BTDC. The solid-state ignition system is serviced by renewing the spark plug, ignition module (1 – Fig. HL375) or coil (3).

Two types of ignition systems have been used. Some early production units used a SEMS ignition system (blue module and black coil) while later and current production units use a Prufrex ignition system (blue module and blue coil). Components from one system are not compatible with the other. Service parts will only supply the Prufrex system. If an ignition system component fails on a SEMS system, the entire system will have to be replaced. The Prufrex module is part 98365 and the Prufrex coil is part 98366. Adjust rotor (flywheel)-to-module air gap to 0.008-0.012 inch (0.2-0.3 mm).

LUBRICATION. The engine is lubricated by mixing oil with unleaded gasoline. Recommended oil is Homelite® two-stroke oil mixed at the ratio designated on the oil container. If Homelite® oil is not available, a good quality oil designated for two-stroke engines may be used when mixed at a 16:1 ratio; however, an antioxidant fuel stabilizer (such as Sta-Bil) should be added to the fuel mix. Antioxidant fuel stabilizer is not required with Homelite® oils, as they contain fuel stabilizer so the fuel mix will stay fresh up to one year. Fuel tank capacity is 25.3 ounces (748 mL).

The chain oil tank should be filled with Homelite® Bar and Chain Oil or a good quality SAE 30 oil. Tank capacity is 16 ounces (473 mL). It may be necessary to use SAE 10 oil or oil mixed with kerosene if temperature is below 40°F (4°C).

REPAIRS

TIGHTENING TORQUE VALUES. Tightening torque values are listed in the following table:

Guide bar to crankcase . . . . . . 89 in.-lbs. (10.1 N·m)
Transfer port . . . . 27 in.-lbs. (3.1 N·m)
Engine to housing . . . . 62 in.-lbs. (7 N·m)
Spark plug . . . . 120-180 in.-lbs. (13.6-20.3 N·m)
Cylinder to crankcase . . . . 53 in.-lbs. (6 N·m)
Clutch to crankshaft . . . . 204 in.-lbs. (23 N·m)
Flywheel to crankshaft . . . . . 168 in.-lbs. (19 N·m)
Module to cylinder . . . . 44 in.-lbs. (5 N·m)

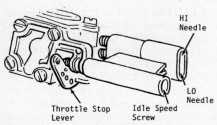

Fig. HL370 — View of carburetor adjustment screws.

Fig. HL371 — View of correct throttle linkage assembly.

Starter cover . . . . 10 in.-lbs.
(1.1 N·m)
Oil pump to engine . . . . 10 in.-lbs.
(1.1 N·m)

COMPRESSION PRESSURE. For optimum performance, cylinder compression pressure should be 140-170 psi (966-1173 kPa) with engine at normal operating temperature. Engine should be inspected and repaired when compression pressure is 90 psi (620 kPa) or below.

CONNECTING ROD, CRANKSHAFT AND CRANKCASE. Crankcase halves (1 and 16 – Fig. HL377) must be split for access to crankshaft. The crankshaft (12) is supported by ball bearings (13) at both ends. Connecting rod, crankpin and crankshaft are pressed-together assembly and separate components are not available. Rod and crankshaft must be serviced as a unit assembly.

When installing bearings onto crankshaft, heat the bearing(s) to a temperature of 350°F (177°C) in hot oil. The bearing retaining rings should align with the grooves in the bearing bore of the crankcase. Note that the tapered (rotor) end of the crankshaft should be on the same side of the cylinder as the port cover with the module mounting boss.

When assembling the lower crankcase half onto the cylinder, apply a light coat of sealant to the mating surface and outer edge of the bearing bore. Note that the two large mounting ears on the crankcase lower half should be on the clutch side. The outer surfaces of the seals should be flush with the outside edge of the bearing bores.

When installing the shortblock assembly into the engine housing, loosely install the two screws on the rotor side, then install the five screws on the clutch side. Tighten all shortblock mounting screws evenly.

PISTON AND RINGS. Model 290 uses two piston rings and Model 340 uses one piston ring. Specified ring end gap is 0.006-0.014 inch (0.15-0.35 mm) for Model 290 and 0.008-0.016 inch (0.2-0.4 mm) for Model 340.

Install piston with arrow pointing toward exhaust side of cylinder as shown in Fig. HL378.

A matched cylinder and crankcase assembly is used. The piston for Model 290 is serviced separately, while the piston for Model 340 is only available as an assembly along with the cylinder and the crankcase.

CLUTCH. Refer to Fig. HL379 for an exploded view of shoe type clutch used on both models. Clutch hub (9) has left-hand threads. Turn clockwise to remove from crankshaft. The clutch shoes should only be replaced in sets of three.

Needle roller bearing (4) should be removed, cleaned and lubricated periodically. A high temperature grease such as Homelite® ALL-TEMP Multipurpose Grease should be used. Inspect crank-

Fig. HL373 – Exploded view of handle and drive case assembly.

1. Handle	6. Spacer	10. Lever	14. Trigger
2. Spacer	7. Link	11. Spring	15. Spring
3. Isolator	8. Link	12. Lock assy.	16. Isolator
4. Strap	9. Lock	13. Cover	17. Guard
5. Isolator			18. Nut

Fig. HL374 – Exploded view of engine housing.

1. Cover	10. Chain adjusting	17. Rubber tubing	25. Support
2. Bumper plate	screw	18. Oil pump cover	26. Switch plate
3. Housing	11. Pin	19. Stud	27. Rubber tubing
4. Caps	12. Strainer	20. Plate	28. Fitting
5. Gaskets	13. Oil tube	21. Protector	29. Fuel line
6. Tube	14. Fitting	22. Tube	30. Clamp
7. Baffle	15. Elbow fitting	23. Rubber tubing	31. Weight
8. Plug	16. Clamp	24. Chain stop	32. Filter
9. Check valve			

shaft for wear or damage caused by a defective clutch bearing.

If clutch slips with engine running at high speed under load, check clutch shoes (8) for excessive wear. If chain continues to turn with engine running at idle speed (below normal clutch engagement speed), check for broken, weak or distorted clutch springs.

When reassembling clutch, hook spring ends together between any two of the clutch shoes.

AUTOMATIC CHAIN OILER PUMP. The gear driven, automatic chain oiler pump used on Models 290 and 340 is shown in Fig. HL379. Oil pump output is adjustable with five positions from 0.27-0.68 ounce (8-20 mL). A recessed screw is located at the bottom of the engine housing. Press screw inward with a flat screwdriver and rotate screw clockwise to increase flow and counterclockwise to reduce flow.

The oil pump may be removed after removing the clutch. When disassembling the pump, press spring-loaded plunger in while removing cam pin from pump housing as shown in Fig. HL380. Inspect all pump components. Renew any

Fig. HL375 — View of ignition components.
1. Module
2. Spacer
3. Coil
4. Switch

Fig. HL380 — When disassembling oil pump, press the spring-loaded plunger in while removing the cam pin from the pump housing.

Fig. HL378 — Install piston onto connecting rod with arrow pointing toward exhaust port.

Fig. HL379 — View of clutch and oil pump assemblies.
1. Hub
2. Felt seal
3. Drum
4. Bearing
5. Felt seal
6. Thrust washer
7. Spring
8. Shoe
9. Hub
10. Housing
11. Gear
12. Plate
13. Plunger
14. Spring
15. Plug

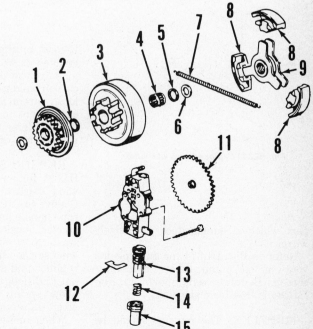

Fig. HL377 — Exploded view of engine. Install intake port insert (6) so notched corners face up.

1. Crankcase & cylinder
2. Spark plug
3. Cover
4. "O" ring
5. Insert
6. Insert
7. Piston ring(s)
8. Retainer clip
9. Piston pin
10. Piston
11. Bearing
12. Crankshaft assy.
13. Bearing
14. Retainer
15. Seal
16. Lower crankcase

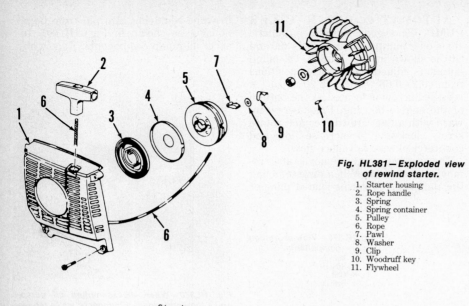

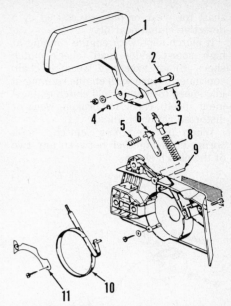

Fig. HL381—Exploded view of rewind starter.

1. Starter housing
2. Rope handle
3. Spring
4. Spring container
5. Pulley
6. Rope
7. Pawl
8. Washer
9. Clip
10. Woodruff key
11. Flywheel

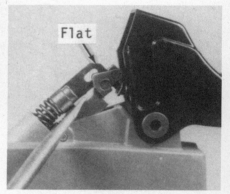

Fig. HL385—Exploded view of chain brake assembly.

1. Lever		7. Adjuster
2. Shoulder bolt		8. Spring
3. Pin		9. Pin
4. "E" ring		10. Brake band
5. Spring		11. Cover
6. Latch		

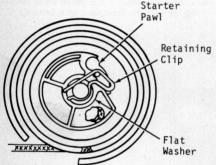

Fig. HL382—Pin on starter pawl must engage loop of retaining clip as shown.

Starter Pawl

Retaining Clip

Flat Washer

Fig. HL384—View of the guide bar pad showing location of the oil tank vent. Keep vent clear of sawdust.

Vent

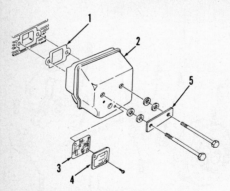

Fig. HL383 Exploded view of muffler.

1. Gasket
2. Muffler
3. Spark arrestor
4. Cover plate
5. Lockplate

Fig. HL386—View of chain brake mechanism. Insert a screwdriver as shown, then turn screwdriver to release adjuster from latch. When assembling components, position adjuster so flat is up as shown.

Flat

part which is damaged or excessively worn.

Refer to Fig. HL374 for an exploded view of oil pump tubing and filter screen. Be sure vent shown in Fig. HL384 is free from sawdust.

MUFFLER. The muffler should be disassembled and periodically cleaned.

Renew muffler components that are cracked or worn excessively. Check engine exhaust port and remove excessive carbon buildup as required. Do not allow loose carbon to enter cylinder, and be careful not to damage exhaust port or piston. Refer to Fig. HL383 for an exploded view of the muffler.

REWIND STARTER. Refer to Fig. HL381 for an exploded view of the rewind starter. To disassemble starter, remove starter from saw, then detach rope handle and allow rope to wind into starter housing. Remove clip (9) from starter post and remove pulley (5). If rewind spring (3) must be removed, lift out retainer and spring while being careful not to dislodge spring. Take care not to allow spring to unwind uncontrolled when separating spring from container.

When reassembling starter, note the following: Rewind spring must be in-

stalled in spring container (4) so spring is coiled in a counterclockwise direction from outer spring end. Rope length should be 35 inches (89.7 cm). Apply cement to rope end or fuse end with heat before installing rope. Insert rope into rope pulley and tie a knot at pulley end. Wrap rope around pulley in a clockwise direction as viewed from pawl side of pulley. Leave approximately 10 inches (25.4 cm) of rope unwrapped. Apply a light coat of grease to starter housing pulley post. Assemble starter, insert rope through rope outlet and install rope handle. See Fig. HL382 for proper installation of retaining clip. To prewind spring, position rope in notch in outside

Illustrations Courtesy Homelite Div. of Textron, ©1987

edge of rope pulley. While holding rope in notch, rotate rope pulley two turns clockwise, then remove rope from notch, release pulley and allow rope to wind onto pulley.

Before installing starter, check starter operation. Be sure spring is not bottomed out when starter rope is fully extended. It must be possible to rotate pulley clockwise with rope fully extended; if not, decrease spring prewind tension by one turn and recheck.

CHAIN BRAKE. Refer to Fig. HL385 for an exploded view of the chain brake. The chain brake will be triggered when the operator's hand forces brake lever (1) forward. The chain brake should stop the chain instantly. If chain brake does not operate correctly, outer surface of clutch drum may be glazed. Remove glaze using an emery cloth, being sure to clean drum afterward. Clutch drum and brake band (10) must not be bent or nicked.

Initial adjustment of the brake band adjusting screw is in 7 to 9 full turns.

HUSQVARNA

HUSQVARNA POWER PRODUCTS COMPANY
907 West Irving Park Road
Itasca, IL 60143

Model 33, 35, 35VR, 35VRA, 37	Bore	Stroke	Displ.	Drive Type
	1-7/16 in. (36.5 mm)	1.28 in. (32.5 mm)	2.1 cu. in. (34 cc)	Direct

MAINTENANCE

SPARK PLUG. Recommended spark plug is Champion CJ6. Spark plug electrode gap should be 0.025 inch (0.63 mm).

CARBURETOR. A Walbro WA diaphragm type carburetor is used on Models 35, 35VR, 35VRA and 37 and a Walbro WT diaphragm type carburetor is used on Model 33. Refer to CARBURETOR SERVICE section for service on Walbro carburetor.

Initial setting of both high and low speed mixture screws is 1⅛ turns open from a lightly seated position. Make final adjustment with engine warm and running. Adjust idle speed screw so engine idles just below clutch engagement speed. Adjust low speed mixture screw so engine will accelerate cleanly without hesitation. Adjust high speed mixture screw to obtain optimum performance under cutting load.

Note location of throttle link for Models 35, 35VR, 35VRA and 37 shown in Fig. H1.

IGNITION. Early models are equipped with a breaker-point type flywheel magneto ignition system while later models use a breakerless electronic ignition system.

Breaker-point gap should be 0.015 inch (0.38 mm) on models so equipped. Ignition timing is fixed on all models but breaker-point gap on applicable models should be set correctly or timing will be affected. On all models, air gap between flywheel magnets and ignition coil legs should be 0.016 inch (0.41 mm).

LUBRICATION. Engine is lubricated by mixing oil with fuel. Recommended fuel:oil ratio is 50:1 when using Husqvarna Two-Stroke Oil. If Husqvarna Two-Stroke Oil is not available, fuel:oil ratio should be 25:1 using a good quality SAE 30 oil designed for chain saw engines.

Fill chain oil tank with SAE 30 motor oil. Chain oil may be diluted up to 50 percent for winter usage by adding kerosene or diesel fuel to chain oil.

CARBON. Carbon should be removed from exhaust system and cylinder peri-

Fig. H1—On Models 35, 35VR, 35VRA and 37, throttle link (L) must be installed as shown when assembling handle.

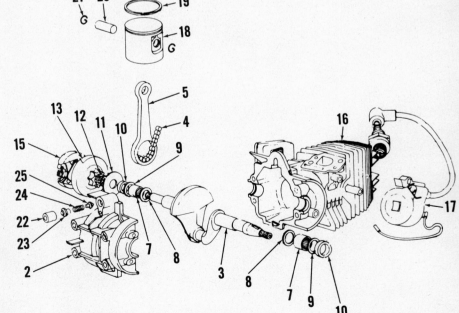

Fig. H2—Exploded view of early model engine. Later models are similar.

2. Crankcase	9. Retaining ring	16. Cylinder
3. Crankshaft	10. Seal	17. Ignition coil
4. Roller bearing	11. Thrust washer	18. Piston
5. Connecting rod	12. Bearing	19. Piston ring
7. Needle bearing	13. Clutch drum	20. Piston pin
8. Washer	15. Clutch assembly	21. Pin retainer
		22. Spacer
		23. Spring seat
		24. Spring
		25. Crankcase pressure valve

odically. Loose carbon should not be allowed to enter cylinder and care should be taken not to damage cylinder or piston.

REPAIRS

CYLINDER, PISTON, PIN AND RINGS. Cylinder (16–Fig. H2) is also upper crankcase half. Crankshaft is loose in crankcase when cylinder is removed. Care must be taken not to nick or scratch crankcase mating surfaces during disassembly.

Cylinder head is integral with cylinder and cylinder must be removed to remove piston. Piston is equipped with a single piston ring and floating type piston pin (20). Later models are equipped with needle bearings in connecting rod small end. On later models, piston and connecting rod are available as a unit assembly only. On all models, piston and ring are available in standard size only. Cylinder bore is chrome and should be inspected to determine if chrome is scored, peeling or excessively worn. Renew cylinder and piston if damaged or excessively worn.

Refer to CRANKSHAFT section for proper assembly of crankcase and cylinder.

CONNECTING ROD. To remove connecting rod, remove cylinder (16–Fig. H2). Note that cylinder is also upper crankcase half and crankshaft assembly is loose when cylinder is removed. Connecting rod (5) is one-piece and supported on crankpin by 11 loose bearing rollers (4). Be careful not to lose loose rollers that may fall out during disassembly. Rollers can be removed by sliding rod off rollers. To install rod bearing, hold rollers in place with heavy

grease or petroleum jelly and position rod over rollers. Be sure rollers do not fall out during assembly of crankcase.

CRANKSHAFT AND SEALS. Crankshaft is supported by needle roller bearings (7–Fig. H2) at both ends. Crankshaft assembly may be removed after removing stator plate, clutch and cylinder assemblies. Care should be

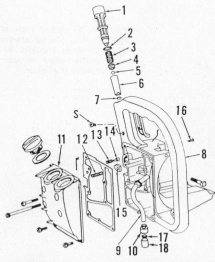

Fig. H4 — Exploded view of manual oil pump and front housing used on later models equipped with pulsation type automatic oiling system. Duckbill type valve (16) is used instead of early model valve components (22, 23, 24 & 25) shown in Fig. H2.

1. Piston	10. Fuel pickup
2. "O" ring	11. Front cover
3. Spring	12. Spring
4. Spring seat	13. Spring
5. Ball	14. Oil outlet valve
6. Pump body	15. Nut
7. Screen	16. Duckbill check valve
8. Front housing	17. Secondary filter
9. Fuel hose	18. Fuel filter

taken when removing cylinder as crankshaft will be loose in crankcase and connecting rod may slide off bearing rollers allowing them to fall into crankcase.

Before reassembling crankcases, apply a light coat of nonhardening sealant to crankcase mating surface. Be sure mating surfaces are not damaged during assembly. Retaining rings (9) must fit in ring grooves (G–Fig. H3) of crankcase and cylinder.

CLUTCH. A two-shoe centrifugal type clutch is used on all models. Clutch hub has left hand thread. Clutch bearing (12–Fig. H2) should be inspected for excessive wear or damage. Inspect clutch shoes and drum for signs of excessive heat.

OIL PUMP. All early models are equipped with a manual oil pump and automatic oiling system. Refer to Fig. H4 for exploded view of manual oil pump. Automatic oiling is accomplished by crankcase pulsations which pressurize oil tank and force oil to bar. A one-way valve (25–Fig. H2 on early models or 16–Fig. H4 on later models) prevents oil from entering crankcase.

NOTE: Early and late crankcases (2–Fig. H2) may not be interchanged unless valve type is also changed.

Later model saws are equipped with a positive displacement oil pump assembly located behind flywheel. Oil pump

Fig. H3 — Be sure retaining rings (R) are seated in grooves (G) of crankcase and cylinder.

Fig. H6 — On manual oil pump models, oil exhaust valve (14) and spring (13) are installed in hole (H) in tank.

assembly is driven by a worm gear on crankshaft. Remove oil pump plunger retaining roll pin and withdraw plunger, gear and spring to service. Use suitable tools to pry worm gear off crankshaft. Renew any component that is excessively worn or damaged. Plunger is available only with complete oil pump assembly.

REWIND STARTER. Refer to Fig. H7 for exploded view of pawl type starter typical of the type used on all models. Care should be taken when removing to remove rewind spring (12) to prevent spring from uncoiling uncontrolled.

Rewind spring (12) should be wound in clockwise direction in housing. Wind starter rope in clockwise direction around rope pulley (11) as viewed in starter housing (14).

CHAIN BRAKE. Model 33, 35, 35VRA and 37 are equipped with a chain brake designed to stop the saw chain quickly should kick-back occur. It is necessary to unlock the brake before removing or installing the clutch cover (1 – Fig. H8 or Fig. H9). Depending on cutting operation, dust shield should be occasionally removed so sawdust and debris can be cleaned from the brake mechanism.

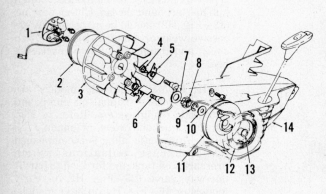

Fig. H7 — Exploded view of ignition and rewind starter used on early models. Rewind starter used on later models is similar.

1. Stator plate
2. Cover
3. Flywheel
4. Spring
5. Pawl
6. Pivot pin
7. Washer
8. Nut
9. Snap ring
10. Thrust washer
11. Rope pulley
12. Rewind spring
13. Bushing
14. Starter housing

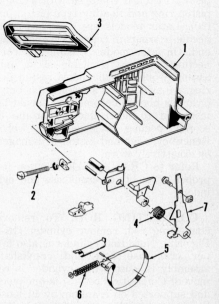

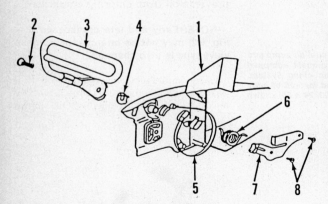

Fig. H8 — Exploded view of chain brake assembly typical of type used on 35, 35VRA and 37 models.

1. Clutch cover
2. Pivot pin
3. Trip lever
4. Stop plate
5. Brake band
6. Spring
7. Detent cover
8. Cap screw

Fig. H9 — Exploded view of chain brake assembly used on Model 33.

1. Clutch cover
2. Adjusting bolt
3. Guard
4. Spring
5. Brake band
6. Spring
7. Lever

HUSQVARNA

Model	Bore	Stroke	Displ.	Drive Type
40 Rancher, 140S, 240S, 240SE, 240SG, 340SE, 340SG	40 mm (1.575 in.)	32 mm (1.260 in.)	40 cc (2.4 cu. in.)	Direct
44, 444SE, 444SG	42 mm (1.654 in.)	32 mm (1.260 in.)	44 cc (2.7 cu. in.)	Direct

MAINTENANCE

SPARK PLUG. Recommended spark plug is Champion RCJ7Y. Spark plug electrode gap should be 0.5 mm (0.020 in.).

CARBURETOR. Late Model 44 is equipped with a Walbro Model HDA diaphragm carburetor. All other models are equipped with a Walbro Model HDC carburetor. Refer to CARBURETOR SERVICE section for carburetor service and exploded view.

On 140S models equipped with Walbro HDC 10 carburetors, initial setting of low speed mixture screw is ¾ turn open while initial setting of high speed mixture screw is ½ turn open. Initial setting for late Model 44 with Walbro Model HDA carburetor is 1¼ turns open for low and high speed mixture screws. Initial setting for all other models is one turn open for low speed and high speed mixture screws.

On all models, make final adjustment with engine warm and running. Adjust idle speed screw so engine idles just below clutch engagement speed. Adjust low speed mixture screw so engine will accelerate cleanly without hesitation.

Adjust high speed mixture screw to obtain optimum performance under cutting load.

Note that intake manifold must be installed with oval opening next to cylinder and round opening next to carburetor.

IGNITION. Models 40 Rancher, 140S and 240S are equipped with a breaker-point type flywheel magneto ignition system. Air gap between flywheel and coil legs should be 0.30-0.35 mm (0.012-0.014 in.). Breaker-point gap should be 0.3-0.4 mm (0.012-0.016 in.). Breaker-points should begin to open when mark on flywheel is 2.5 mm (0.1 in.) from upper edge of lower coil leg as shown in Fig. H10. Use a suitable test light or continuity meter to check breaker-point opening.

Models 240SE, 240SG, 340SE and 340SG are equipped with a two-piece breakerless electronic ignition system. An ignition module (6–Fig. H11) is located in the rewind starter housing. Models 44, 444SE and 444SG are equipped with a one-piece breakerless electronic ignition system. Air gap on both types of breakerless ignition systems, between flywheel and coil legs, should be 0.30-0.35 mm (0.012-0.014 in.).

On all models, flywheel may have two crankshaft key grooves. Key groove marked "P" is used on models equipped with Prufrex ignition systems while the

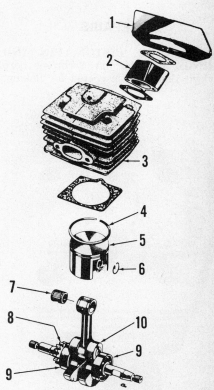

Fig. H12 – Exploded view of engine. Oil pump drive gear (8) is used on Models 140S, 240S, 240SE and 240SG. Note oil pump gear in Fig. H17 used on all other models.

1. Air baffle
2. Intake manifold
3. Cylinder
4. Piston ring
5. Piston & pin
6. Pin retainer
7. Bearing
8. Oil pump drive gear
9. Bearing
10. Crankshaft & rod assy.

Fig. H10 – Distance (D) from flywheel mark to edge of coil leg should be 2.5 mm (0.1 in.) when breaker-points open.

Fig. H11 – Exploded view of electronic ignition system used on Models 240SE, 240SG, 340SE and 340SG. Generating coil (3) is used on Models 240SG and 340SG with heated handles.

1. "O" ring
2. Seal retainer
3. Generating coil
4. Flywheel
5. Ignition coil
6. Ignition module

other key groove is used on models equipped with Bosch and breaker-point ignition systems. Tighten flywheel nut to 23.5-28.4 N·m (17-21 ft.lbs.).

LUBRICATION. Recommended fuel:oil ratio for engine lubrication is 50:1 when using Husqvarna Two-Stroke Oil. If Husqvarna Two-Stroke Oil is not available, fuel:oil ratio should be 25:1 using a good quality oil designed for use in two-stroke air-cooled engines.

The chain is lubricated by oil from an automatic chain oil pump. Clean automotive oil may be used. Oil viscosity should be chosen according to ambient temperature. Oil may be cut with up to 50 percent kerosene in extremely cold weather.

Oil pump output on 140S, 240S, 240SE and 240SG is not adjustable. Oil pump output on all other models is adjusted by exchanging cam screw (2—Fig. H17). Cam screw is available from the manufacturer in three color-coded sizes. A white cam screw indicates minimum oil output, a plain cam screw indicates standard oil output while a green cam screw indicates maximum oil output. Refer to OIL PUMP section for replacement procedure.

REPAIRS

CYLINDER, PISTON, PIN AND RINGS. Cylinder has a chrome bore which should be inspected for flaking,

cracking or other damage to chromed surface. Some pistons are equipped with one piston ring while others are equipped with two piston rings. Piston ring groove has a locating pin to prevent piston ring rotation. Arrow on piston crown must point toward exhaust port when installing piston.

Piston and cylinder are graded according to size to provide correct piston-to-cylinder clearance. Piston and cylinder bore sizes are indicated by a letter stamped on the piston crown or on the top of the cylinder. See Fig. H13. If cylinder is new or has very little use, piston and cylinder grade should be the same. If cylinder is used but not excessively worn, a piston with the same grade or a piston with the next largest grade may be installed. For instance, pistons with grade letters "B"or "C" may be installed in a used cylinder with grade letter "B." Grade letter "A" denotes smallest cylinder or piston while grade letter "E" denotes largest cylinder or piston. Tighten cylinder base screws to 8.8-9.8 N·m (78-87 in.-lbs.)

CRANKSHAFT, CONNECTING ROD AND CRANKCASE. Crankshaft and connecting rod are a unit assembly. It will be necessary to heat crankcase halves to remove or install crankshaft and main bearings. Care should be taken not to damage mating surfaces of crankcase halves. Check rotation of connecting rod around crankpin and renew crankshaft unit if roughness or other damage is found.

When reassembling crankshaft and crankcase halves, install main bearings allowing for installation of oil pump on drive side and crankshaft seal housing on flywheel side. A special tool is available from the manufacturer to properly position main bearings and crankshaft in crankcase. Tighten crankcase screws to 7-8 N·m (61-69 in.-lbs.). Make certain crankshaft is centered in crankcase and will rotate freely.

CLUTCH. All models are equipped with the two-shoe centrifugal clutch shown in Fig. H14. Clutch hub (1) has left hand threads. Inspect clutch shoes and drum for excessive wear or damage due to overheating. Clean and inspect clutch hub, drum and bearing for damage or excessive wear. Inspect clutch bearing lubrication hole in crankshaft end and clutch bearing contact surface on crankshaft for wear or damage.

AUTOMATIC OIL PUMP. Models 140S, 240S, 240SE and 240SG are equipped with the automatic oil pump shown in Fig. H15 and Fig. H16. Oil pump output is not adjustable. Access to oil pump components is obtained after removing guide bar plate (8—Fig. H15). Withdraw pin (14), unscrew plug (12) and withdraw plunger (15). Oil pump is

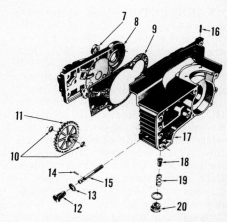

Fig. H15—Exploded view of early oil pump assembly.

7. Oil seal	14. Pin
8. Bar plate	15. Plunger
9. Gasket	16. Dowel pin
10. Washers	17. Right crankcase half
11. Oil pump gear	18. Screen
12. Plug	19. Spring
13. Washer	20. Plug

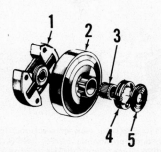

Fig. H14—Exploded view of clutch.

1. Clutch hub & shoes
2. Clutch drum
3. Bearing
4. Sprocket
5. Washer

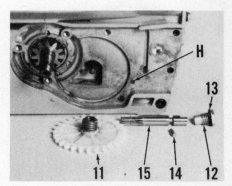

Fig. H16—View of oil pump components. Pin (14) is located in hole (H). Refer to Fig. H15 for parts identification.

The photo at lower left:

Fig. H13—View showing location of cylinder and piston grade letters. Grade "D" is shown.

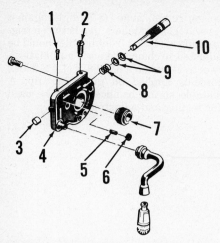

Fig. H17—Exploded view of oil pump used on Models 40 Rancher, 44, 340SE, 340SG, 444SE and 444SG.

1. Plug	6. Seal
2. Cam screw	7. Drive gear
3. Plug	8. Spring
4. Pump body	9. Washers
5. Tube	10. Plunger

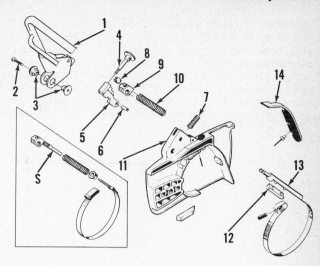

Fig. H19A—Exploded view of typical chain brake used on later models. Some models may have adjustable type brake band shown in inset.

1. Hand guard
2. Cap screw
3. Trunnion
4. Trigger button
5. Trigger lever
6. Pin
7. Spring
8. Nut
9. Latch
10. Spring
11. Housing
12. Guide
13. Brake band
14. Chain guard

driven by gear (8–Fig. H12) on crankshaft. A special tool is available from the manufacturer so gear can be removed without removing crankshaft.

Automatic oil pump used on all other models is shown in Fig. H17. Oil pump output is adjusted by exchanging cam screw (2–Fig. H17). Cam screw is available from the manufacturer in three color-coded sizes. A white cam screw indicates minimum oil output, a plain cam screw indicates standard oil output while a green cam screw indicates maximum oil output. Remove clutch for access to oil pump. Unscrew cam screw (2) before withdrawing pump plunger (10). Pump plunger (10) is driven by worm gear (7) on crankshaft. A special tool is available from the manufacturer for worm gear removal. Collar on worm gear must be toward oil pump when installed.

REWIND STARTER. To disassemble rewind starter on all models, first remove starter housing from saw. Pull starter rope and hold rope pulley with

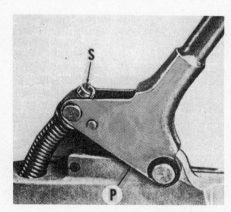

Fig. H19—Turn screw (S) to adjust chain brake on early models. Refer to text.

notch in pulley adjacent to rope outlet. Pull rope back through outlet so it engages notch in pulley and allow pulley to completely unwind. Unscrew pulley retaining screw (6–Fig. H18) and carefully remove rope pulley. If rewind spring must be removed, care should be taken not to allow spring to uncoil uncontrolled.

Install rewind spring in starter housing with spring coiled in clockwise direction from outer spring end. Wrap starter rope around rope pulley in a clockwise direction as viewed with pulley in starter housing. Turn rope pulley two turns clockwise before passing rope through rope outlet to place tension on rewind spring. Spring tension is correct if rope pulley can be rotated at least ½ turn further when rope is pulled completely out.

When installing starter assembly on saw, make sure starter pulley properly engages pawls on flywheel before tightening retaining cap screws.

CHAIN BRAKE. Some models may be equipped with a chain brake system designed to stop chain movement should kickback occur. Several types of chain brake systems have been used.

The chain brake on early models is activated when the operator's hand strikes the hand guard. To adjust chain brake on early models, pull back hand guard and be sure mechanism is cocked. Turn adjusting screw (S–Fig. H19) in until chain cannot be pulled around bar then turn screw out three or four turns. If screw has a square head, be sure screw head does not rest on side plates (P).

The chain brake on later models is activated either by the operator's hand striking the hand guard (1–Fig. H19A) or by sufficient force being applied to the guide bar tip during kickback to cause the front handle to contact the trigger button (4) resulting in automatic

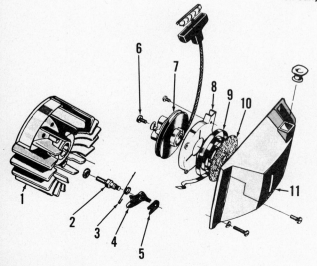

Fig. H18—Exploded view of Models 40 Rancher and 44 rewind starter. Other models are similar.

1. Flywheel
2. Pawl stud
3. Spring
4. Pawl
5. Clip
6. Screw
7. Rope pulley
8. Rope guide
9. Rewind spring
10. Washer
11. Starter housing

activation of brake mechanism. To adjust chain brake on later models, first pull back hand guard and be sure mechanism is cocked then determine if brake system has an adjustable brake band as shown in inset of Fig. H19A. If brake band is adjustable, turn adjusting screw (S) in until chain cannot be pulled around bar then turn screw out three or four turns. Chain should rotate freely around bar. Check brake band tension adjustment by starting saw and running at wide open throttle, then manually engage chain brake. Chain should stop rotating immediately. On models without adjustable brake band, be sure spring retaining nut (8) is tight against its seat. On all models, gap between trigger button (4) and front handle should be adjusted so chain brake will automatically activate when a 6.2-9.8 N (1.4-2.2 lbs.) force is applied on guide bar tip. A suitable spring balance should be used for testing and adjustment.

HUSQVARNA

Model	Bore	Stroke	Displ.	Drive Type
163S, 263CD	47 mm (1.85 in.)	36 mm (1.42 in.)	63 cc (3.8 cu. in.)	Direct
65, L65	48 mm (1.89 in.)	36 mm (1.42 in.)	65 cc (4.0 cu. in.)	Direct
77, L77, 280S, 380CD, 380S, 480CD	52 mm (2.05 in.)	36 mm (1.42 in.)	77 cc (4.7 cu. in.)	Direct
285CD	52 mm (2.05 in.)	40 mm (1.57 in.)	85 cc (5.2 cu. in.)	Direct
1100CD, 2100CD, 298XP, 2101XP	56 mm (2.2 in.)	40 mm (1.57 in.)	99 cc (6.0 cu. in.)	Direct

MAINTENANCE

SPARK PLUG. Recommended spark plug is Champion CJ6 for Models 285CD, 1100CD and 2100CD or Champion RC-J7Y for all other models. Electrode gap should be 0.5 mm (0.020 in.).

CARBURETOR. A Tillotson Model HS diaphragm carburetor is used on all models. Refer to CARBURETOR SERVICE section for service and exploded view of carburetor.

Initial adjustment of high speed mixture screw is one turn open for Models 285CS, 298XP, 2100CD and 2101XP and ¾ turn open for all other models. Initial adjustment of low speed mixture screw is one turn open on 65, 77 and 285CD models; 1¼ turns open on 298XP, 480CD, 2100CD and 2101XP models and ¾ turn open on all other models.

On all models, make final adjustment with engine warm and running. Adjust idle speed screw so engine idles just below clutch engagement speed. Adjust low speed mixture screw so engine will accelerate cleanly without hesitation. Adjust high speed mixture screw to obtain optimum performance under cutting load.

IGNITION. Models 77, 263CD, 285CD, 298XP, 380CD, 480CD, 1100CD, 2100CD, 2101XP and late L77 are equipped with breakerless capacitor discharge ignition systems while all other models are equipped with breaker point flywheel magneto ignition systems.

Ignition timing on Models 77, 263CD, 285CD, 298XP, 380CD, 480CD, 1100CD, 2100CD, 2101XP and late L77 is correct when mark on stator plate is aligned with mark on crankcase. Refer to Fig. H20 or H21. On 1100CD models, ignition timing may be checked with a power timing light by running engine at 8000 rpm. Mark on flywheel should align with mark on cylinder or crankcase.

Models equipped with breaker-points should have breaker-point gap of 0.3-0.4 mm (0.012-0.016 in.). Ignition timing is adjusted by loosening stator plate mounting screws and rotating stator plate. Ignition timing is adjusted as follows: Remove flywheel and attach Husqvarna timing tool 50 25 059-01 to end of crankshaft. Turn tool until pointer is aligned with mark (A—Fig. H22) on crankcase as shown in Fig. H22. Loosen stator plate mounting screws and rotate stator plate until coil leg contacts tang (B) on timing tool. Retighten stator plate mounting screws. Using a suitable continuity tester, adjust breaker-points to just open when timing tool pointer is aligned with mark on crankcase. Air gap between ignition coil legs and flywheel should be 0.2-0.3 mm (0.008-0.012 in.). To check air gap, affix tape to coil legs until thickness equals

Fig. H20—View of stator plate on early 1100CD models. Ignition timing is correct when mark (IM) on stator plate is aligned with mark (CM) on crankcase. Timing mark LM on cylinder should align with mark on flywheel at 8000 rpm if timing is checked with timing light.

Fig. H21—View of stator plate on 77, 263CD, 298XP, 380CD, 480CD, 2100CD, 2101XP and later L77 and 1100CD models with SEM ignition. Ignition timing is correct when mark (M) on stator is aligned with crankcase mark (arrow). Ignition timing procedure is the same for 263CD, 285CD and 380CD models with Bosch ignition system.

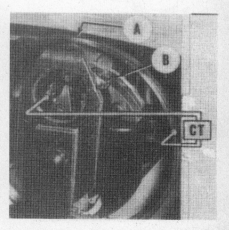

Fig. H22—View showing installation of timing tool 50 25 059-01 and connection of continuity tester (CT) on models with breaker-point ignition system. Refer to text for timing procedure.

desired air gap. Loosen coil mounting screws and push coil outward. Install flywheel and rotate slowly while noting if tape drags against flywheel. Remove flywheel and if tape dragged against flywheel, tighten coil screws to 4.0-4.5 N·m (35-40 in.-lbs.). If tape did not drag

Fig. H23 — View showing location of oil pump adjusting screw on models so equipped.

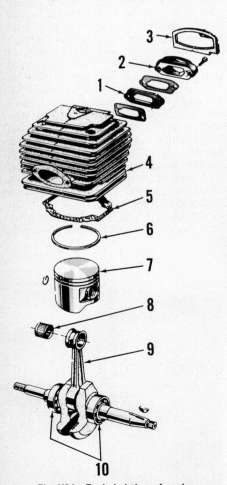

Fig. H24 — Exploded view of engine.

1. Insulator		
2. Intake manifold	7. Piston	
3. Baffle	8. Roller bearing	
4. Cylinder	9. Crankshaft & rod	
5. Gasket	assy.	
6. Piston rings (2)	10. Bearings	

against flywheel, elongate coil mounting holes and repeat procedure.

LUBRICATION. The engine is lubricated by mixing oil with the fuel. Recommended fuel:oil ratio is 50:1 when using Husqvarna Two-Stroke Oil. If Husqvarna Two-Stroke Oil is not available, fuel:oil ratio should be 25:1 using a good quality oil designed for use in air-cooled two-stroke engines.

All models are equipped with an automatic oil pump. On 65, L65, 77 and L77 models, oil pump output is determined by the stroke of plunger (17 – Fig. H27). Plunger is available from the manufacturer in two sizes, 1.2 mm and 1.4 mm. Refer to OIL PUMP section for identification and replacement procedure.

On all other models, oil pump output is determined either by turning an adjusting screw (S – Fig. H23) or by changing position of cam screw (CS – Fig. H29). On models equipped with adjusting screw (S – Fig. H23), number "1" indicates minimum oil output while number "4" provides maximum oil output. If oil pump does not have adjusting screw (S), then oil output is adjusted using cam screw (CS – Fig. H29) located on rear of pump. Refer to OIL PUMP section.

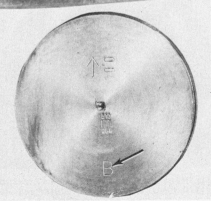

Fig. H25 — Arrows show location of piston and cylinder letter grades. Be sure arrow stamped in piston crown points toward exhaust port when installing piston. Grade "B" is shown.

REPAIRS

TIGHTENING TORQUES. Refer to the following table when tightening fasteners:

Fastener Diameter	
4 mm	4.5-5.5 N·m (40-50 in.-lbs.)
5 mm	5.5-6.8 N·m (50-60 in.-lbs.)
6 mm	10-11.8 N·m (90-105 in.-lbs.)
8 mm	28.2-32.8 N·m (250-290 in.-lbs.)
10 mm	36.7-42.4 N·m (325-375 in.-lbs.)

PISTON, PIN, RINGS AND CYLINDER. Cylinder bore is chrome plated and should be inspected for excessive wear and damage to chrome surface. Inspect piston and discard if excessive wear or damage is evident.

On Models 298XP, 2101XP and late 2100CD, new cylinders are available only with fitted pistons. On all other models and early 2100CD models, piston and cylinder are graded with a letter according to size. Piston is marked on piston crown while cylinder is marked on top as shown in Fig. H25. Letter sizes range from "A" to "C" on Models 285CD, 1100CD and 2100CD and from "A" to "E" on all other models, with "A" being smallest size. Piston and cylinder grades should match although one size larger piston may be installed in a used cylinder. For instance, a piston graded "C" may be used in a cylinder graded "B."

Piston must be installed with arrow on piston crown pointing toward exhaust port. Refer to Fig. H25. Piston is equipped with two piston rings. Locating pins are present in piston ring

Fig. H26 — Dogs (D) on oil pump drive gear must mesh with notches (N) on clutch drum.

grooves to prevent piston ring rotation. Be sure ring end gaps are around locating pins when installing cylinder.

CRANKSHAFT, CONNECTING ROD AND CRANKCASE. Crankshaft and connecting rod are a unit assembly. It will be necessary to heat crankcase halves to remove or install crankshaft and main bearings. Care should be taken not to damage mating surfaces of crankcase halves. Check rotation of connecting rod around crankpin and renew crankshaft unit if roughness or other damage is noted.

Reassemble crankshaft and crankcase halves as follows: Place a main bearing over flywheel end of crankshaft then press bearing inner race flush against bearing seat. Heat bearing seat area in corresponding crankcase half and install crankshaft. Make sure main bearing outer race seats fully in crankcase. Heat bearing seat area in drive half of crankcase and install drive side main bearing allowing for installation of oil pump. A special tool is available from the manufacturer to properly position drive side main bearing in crankcase. After assembling crankcase halves together, make certain crankshaft is centered in crankcase and will rotate freely.

CLUTCH. All models are equipped with a three-shoe centrifugal clutch. Clutch hub has left hand threads. Inspect clutch shoes and drum for excessive wear or damage due to overheating. Clean and inspect clutch hub, drum and bearing for damage or excessive wear. Inspect clutch bearing lubrication hole in crankshaft end and clutch bearing contact surface on crankshaft for wear or damage.

The oil pump is driven by clutch drum. Be sure notches on rear of clutch drum

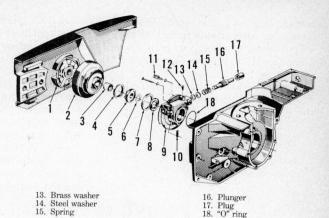

Fig. H28—Exploded view of oil pump and clutch assemblies used on all models except L65 and L77. Refer to Fig. H29 for view of non-adjustable oil pump used on some models.

1. Clutch shoes & hub
2. Clutch drum
3. Needle bearing
4. Seal
5. Oil pump drive gear
6. Washer
7. Seal
8. Seal
9. Oil pump housing
10. Gasket
11. Adjuster screw
12. Cam screw
13. Brass washer
14. Steel washer
15. Spring
16. Plunger
17. Plug
18. "O" ring

mesh with dogs (D–Fig. H26) of oil pump drive gear when installing clutch assembly.

OIL PUMP (Models 65, L65, 77 And L77.) All models are equipped with an automatic oil pump which is driven by the clutch drum. Notches on the back of the clutch drum engage dogs on oil pump drive gear (7–Fig. H27) which rides on the crankshaft. Plunger (17) is driven by worm gear (14), through driven gear (12) from drive gear (7). Pin (19) rides in cam groove of plunger (17) resulting in reciprocating motion of plunger. Oil pump output is determined by the stroke of plunger (17). Two plungers are available from the manufacturer to vary oil pump output and are marked for output identification. Maximum oil output is obtained if plunger marked 1.4 mm is installed while minimum oil output results if plunger marked 1.2 mm is installed.

Access to oil pump on 65, L65, 77 and L77 models is gained by removing oil pump cover plate (6). Remove pin (19),

plug (16), then withdraw plunger (17) and remove worm gear (14).

(All other models). Refer to Fig. H28 for exploded view of typical oil pump used. Two variations of pump have been produced and are identified by oil adjustment method. Oil pump shown in Fig. H28 is adjusted by turning screw (11) as shown in Fig. H23. Oil pump shown in Fig. H29 is adjusted by relocating cam screw (CS). Maximum oil output is obtained if cam screw is installed in hole "II" while minimum oil output results if cam screw is installed in hole "I." Screw (S) must be installed in remaining hole. On both types of pump, oil pump drive gear (5–Fig. H28) is driven by clutch drum (2).

To disassemble pump with adjusting screw (Fig. H28), unscrew adjusting screw (11) and, on models so equipped, cam screw (12). Remove plug (17) and plunger (16) by carefully tapping pump

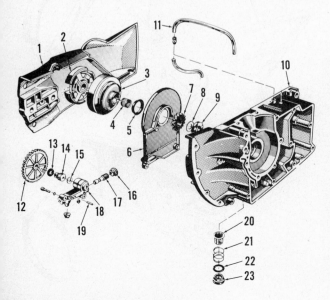

Fig. H27—Exploded view of oil pump and clutch assemblies used on Models 65, 77, L65 and 77.

1. Side cover
2. Clutch shoes & hub
3. Clutch drum
4. Needle bearing
5. Seal
6. Oil pump cover
7. Oil pump drive gear
8. Washer
9. Seal
10. Right crankcase half
11. Vent hose
12. Oil pump driven gear
13. Washer
14. Worm gear
15. Washer
16. Plug
17. Plunger
18. Oil pump housing
19. Cam pin
20. Screen
21. Spring
22. Gasket
23. Plug

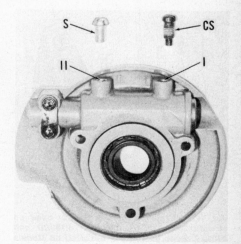

Fig. H29—View of oil pump used on some models. Oil pump output is determined by installation of cam screw (CS) in hole (I) or hole (II). Refer to text.

housing against a solid object. Withdraw remaining components from housing.

To disassemble pump with cam screw (CS – Fig. H29), remove cam screw (CS) and screw (S) then use the same procedure as previously outlined to withdraw plug and plunger.

On both types of pump, be sure crankshaft seal (8 – Fig. H28) and "O" ring (18) are not damaged or debris will enter main bearing.

REWIND STARTER. Refer to Fig. H30 or H31 for an exploded view of rewind starter. Note that starter used on 163S, 263CD, 285CD, 380CD, 380S and 480CD models has an intermediate plate (7 – Fig. H30) which retains rope handle. Rope handle may be knocked from notch in starter housing if plate is not held against housing during removal from saw.

To disassemble rewind starter on all models, first remove starter housing from saw. Pull starter rope and hold rope pulley with notch in pulley adjacent to rope outlet. Pull rope back through outlet so it engages notch in pulley and allow pulley to completely unwind. Unscrew pulley retaining screw and carefully remove rope pulley. If rewind spring must be removed, care should be taken not to allow spring to uncoil uncontrolled.

Install rewind spring in starter housing with spring coiled in clockwise direction from outer spring end. Wrap starter rope around rope pulley in a clockwise direction as viewed with pulley in starter housing. Turn rope pulley two turns clockwise before passing rope through rope outlet to place tension on rewind spring. Spring tension is correct if rope pulley can be rotated approximately ½ turn further when rope is pulled completely out.

When installing starter assembly on saw, make sure starter pulley properly engages pawls on flywheel before tightening retaining cap screws.

CHAIN BRAKE. Some models may be equipped with a chain brake system designed to stop chain movement should kickback occur. Several types of chain brake systems have been used.

The chain brake is activated either by the operator's hand striking the brake lever (1 – Fig. H33 or Fig. H34) or by sufficient force being applied to the guide bar tip during kickback to cause the front handle to contact trigger lever (6 – Fig H33) on so equipped models or trigger button (2 – Fig. H34) on 298XP

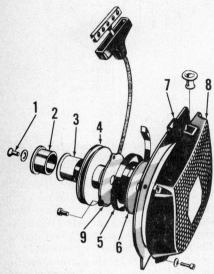

Fig. H30 — Exploded view of rewind starter used on all models except 280S, 298XP, 1100CD, 2100CD and 2101XP. Plate (9) is not used on all models.

1. Screw
2. Pivot
3. Bushing
4. Rope pulley
5. Rewind spring
6. Washer
7. Plate
8. Starter housing
9. Plate

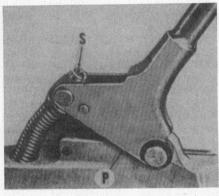

Fig. H32 — Turn screw (S) to adjust chain brake on early models. Refer to text.

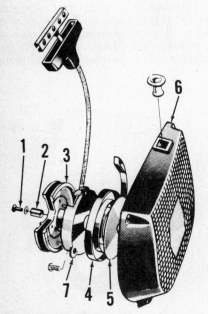

Fig. H31 — Exploded view of starter used on Models 280S, 298XP, 1100CD, 2100CD and 2101XP. Rope guide (7) is not used on Models 280S or 1100CD.

1. Screw
2. Bushing
3. Rope pulley
4. Rewind spring
5. Washer
6. Starter housing
7. Rope guide

Fig. H33 — Exploded view of typical chain brake used on later models except 298XP and 2101XP models.

1. Chain brake lever
2. Adjuster screw
3. Spring
4. Spring guide
5. Pin
6. Trigger lever
7. Side plates
8. Spring
9. Pin
10. Side cover
11. Spring
12. Brake rod & band
13. Trigger arm
14. Front handle

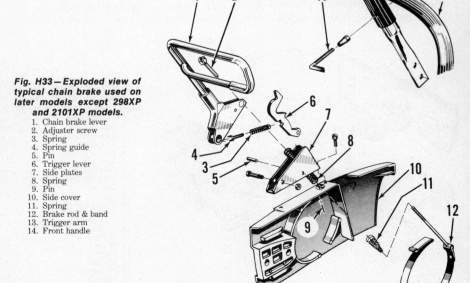

and 2101XP models resulting in automatic activation of brake mechanism.

To adjust chain brake shown in Fig. H33, pull back brake lever and be sure mechanism is cocked. Turn adjusting screw (2) in until chain cannot be pulled around bar then turn screw out approximately four turns. If screw has a square head, be sure screw head does not rest on brake lever side plates. Chain should rotate freely around bar. Check brake band tension adjustment by starting saw and running at wide open throttle, then manually engage chain brake. Chain should stop rotating immediately. Adjust gap between trigger lever (6) and trigger arm (13) so chain brake will automatically activate when a 12.4 N (2.8-3.4 lbs.) force is applied on guide bar tip. A suitable spring balance should be used for testing and adjustment.

On Models 298XP and 2101XP, be sure spring retaining nut (4–Fig. H34) is tight against its seat. Gap between trigger button (2) and front handle should be adjusted so chain brake will automatically activate when a 12.4-15.1 N (2.8-3.4 lbs.) force is applied on guide bar tip. A suitable spring balance should be used for testing and adjustment.

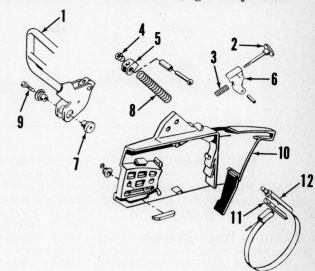

Fig. H34 — Exploded view of chain brake assembly used on Models 298XP and 2101XP.

1. Chain brake lever
2. Trigger button
3. Spring
4. Nut
5. Latch
6. Trigger lever
7. Trunnion
8. Spring
9. Allen screw
10. Housing
11. Guide
12. Brake band

HUSQVARNA

Model	Bore	Stroke	Displ.	Drive Type
61, 162SE, 162SG	48 mm (1.89 in.)	34 mm (1.34 in.)	61.5 cc (3.75 cu. in.)	Direct
266SE, 266SG 266XP, 268XP	50 mm (1.97 in.)	34 mm (1.34 in.)	66.7 cc (4.1 cu. in.)	Direct

MAINTENANCE

SPARK PLUG. Recommended spark plug is Champion RCJ7Y. Electrode gap should be 0.5 mm (0.020 inch).

CARBURETOR. A Tillotson Model HS diaphragm carburetor is used on all models except Model 61 which may be equipped with a Tillotson HS or Walbro WS carburetor. Refer to Tillotson or Walbro section of CARBURETOR SERVICE section for carburetor overhaul and exploded views.

On 268XP models, initial adjustment of low and high speed mixture screws is one turn open. On all other models, initial adjustment of low speed mixture screw is one turn open and high speed mixture screw is ¾ turn open. On all models, make final adjustment with engine warm and running. Adjust idle speed screw so engine idles just below clutch engagement speed. Adjust low mixture screw so engine will accelerate cleanly without hesitation. Adjust high speed mixture screw to obtain optimum performance under cutting load.

IGNITION. All models are equipped with an electronic breakerless ignition system. Ignition timing is not adjustable. Air gap between ignition coil and flywheel should be 0.30-0.35 mm (0.012-0.014 in.).

LUBRICATION. The engine is lubricated by mixing oil with the fuel. Recommended fuel:oil ratio is 50:1 when using Husqvarna Two-Stroke Oil. If Husqvarna Two-Stroke oil is not avaiable, fuel:oil ratio should be 25:1 using a good quality oil designed for use in air-cooled two-stroke engines.

All models are equipped with an adjustable automatic chain oil pump. Adjustment is possible after clutch removal. Turn screw (S–Fig. H41) for desired oil output–position "1" is minimum, position "4" is maximum.

REPAIRS

TIGHTENING TORQUES. Refer to the following table when tightening fasteners:

Fastener Diameter	
4 mm	4.5-5.5 N·m (40-50 in.-lbs.)
5 mm	5.5-6.8 N·m (50-60 in.-lbs.)
6 mm	10-11.8 N·m (90-105 in.-lbs.)
8 mm	28.2-32.8 N·m (250-290 in.-lbs.)

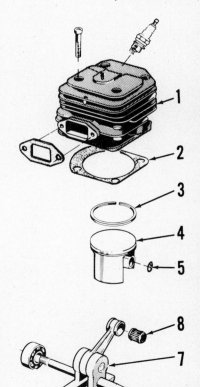

Fig. H42—Exploded view of engine used on 61 models. Other models are similar.

1. Cylinder	6. Bearing
2. Gasket	7. Crankshaft & rod assy.
3. Piston ring	8. Roller bearing
4. Piston	
5. Pin retainer	

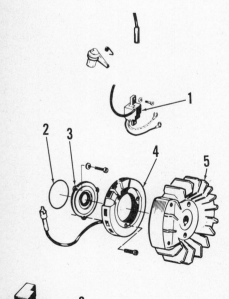

Fig. H40—Exploded view of ignition system. Generator coil (4) for heated handles is used on Model 162SG and Model 266SG.

1. Ignition coil	4. Generator coil
2. "O" ring	5. Flywheel
3. Seal & retainer	6. Ignition module

Fig. H41 — View showing location of oil pump adjusting screw (S). Adjusting screw shown is set at position 2.

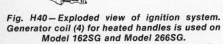

10 mm 36.7-42.4 N·m
(325-375 in.-lbs.)

PISTON, PIN, RINGS AND CYLINDER. Cylinder bore is Nicasil impregnated plated and should be inspected for excessive wear and damage to Nicasil surface. Inspect piston and discard if excessive wear or damage is evident.

On Models 266XP and 268XP, new cylinder are available only with fitted pistons but new pistons in grades "A" and "B" are available for installation in used cylinders. On all other models, piston and cylinder are graded with a letter according to size. Piston is

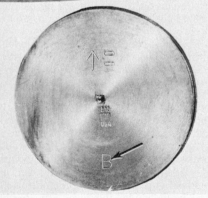

marked on piston crown while cylinder is marked on top as shown in Fig. H43. Letter sizes range from "A" to "C" with "A" being the smallest size. Piston and cylinder grades should match although one size larger piston may be installed in a used cylinder. For instance, a piston graded "C" may be used in a cylinder graded "B."

Piston must be installed with arrow on piston crown pointing toward exhaust port. Refer to Fig. H43. On Model 61 and early 162SE and 162SG models, piston is fitted with a single piston ring

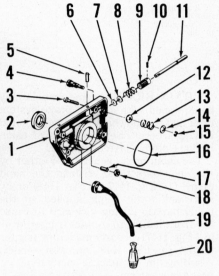

Fig. H45 — Exploded view of automatic oil pump. Note location of brass and steel washers (6 and 7).

1. Pump housing	11. Plunger
2. Oil seal	12. Washer
3. Screw	13. Spring
4. Adjusting screw	14. Washer
5. Pin	15. "E" ring
6. Brass washer	16. "O" ring
7. Steel washer	17. Tube
8. Spring	18. Seal
9. Driven gear	19. Oil hose
10. Screw	20. Oil pickup

while on later 162SE and 162SG models, piston is fitted with two piston rings. Models 266SE, 266SG, 266XP and 268XP are equipped with either a one-or two-ring piston. On all models, a locating pin is present in piston ring groove to prevent piston ring rotation. Be sure ring end gap is around locating pin when installing cylinder.

CRANKSHAFT, CONNECTING ROD AND CRANKCASE. Crankshaft and connecting rod are a unit assembly. It will be necessary to heat crankcase halves to remove or install crankshaft and main bearings from crankcase halves. Care should be taken not to damage mating surfaces of crankcase halves. Check rotation of connecting rod around crankpin and renew crankshaft unit if roughness or other damage is found.

CLUTCH. All models are equipped with a three-shoe centrifugal clutch. Clutch hub has left hand threads. Inspect clutch shoes and drum for excessive wear or damage due to overheating. Clean and inspect clutch hub, drum and bearing for damage or excessive wear. Inspect clutch bearing lubrication hole in crankshaft end and clutch bearing contact surface on crankshaft for wear or damage.

The oil pump is driven by the clutch drum. Be sure notches on rear of clutch drum mesh with dogs of oil pump drive gear when installing clutch assembly.

OIL PUMP. All models are equipped with an automatic oil pump which is driven by the clutch drum. Notches on the back of the clutch drum engage dogs on oil pump drive gear (4—Fig. H44) which rides on the crankshaft. The oil

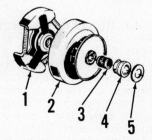

Fig. H43 — Arrows show location of piston and cylinder letter grades. Be sure arrow stamped in piston crown points towards exhaust port when installing piston. Grade "B" is shown.

Fig. H44 — Exploded view of clutch. Notches on back of clutch drum (2) engage dogs on oil pump drive gear (4).

1. Hub & shoes	
2. Clutch drum	4. Oil pump drive gear
3. Bearing	5. Washer

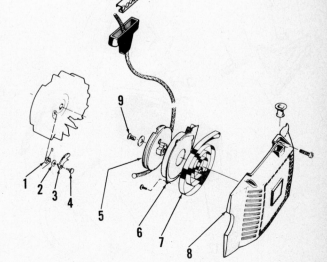

Fig. H46 — Exploded view of rewind starter.

1. Spring
2. Washer
3. Pawl
4. Pin
5. Rope pulley
6. Rope guide
7. Rewind spring
8. Starter housing
9. Screw

pump drive gear engages driven gear (9 – Fig. H45) which is secured to plunger (11) by set screw (10). Oil pump output is adjusted by turning screw (4).

To remove oil pump, first remove the clutch, chain, guide bar and oil pump retaining cap screws. Using two suitable screwdrivers, insert blade tips into notches provided in pump housing and carefully withdraw oil pump. To reinstall, manufacturer recommends placing special tool number 50 25 053-01 over crankshaft end to prevent damage to oil seal (2).

REWIND STARTER. To disassemble rewind starter, remove starter housing from saw. Pull starter rope and hold rope pulley (5 – Fig. H46) with notch in pulley adjacent to rope outlet. Pull rope back through outlet so it engages notch in pulley and allow pulley to completely unwind. Unscrew pulley retaining screw (9) and carefully remove rope pulley. If rewind spring must be removed, care should be taken not to allow spring to uncoil uncontrolled.

Install rewind spring in starter housing with spring coiled in clockwise direction from outer spring end. Wrap starter rope around rope pulley in a clockwise direction as viewed with pulley in starter housing. Turn rope pulley two turns clockwise before passing rope through rope outlet to place tension on rewind spring. Spring tension is correct if rope pulley can be rotated approximately ¼ turn further when rope is at its greatest length.

When installing starter assembly on saw, make sure starter pulley properly engages pawls on flywheel before tightening retaining cap screws.

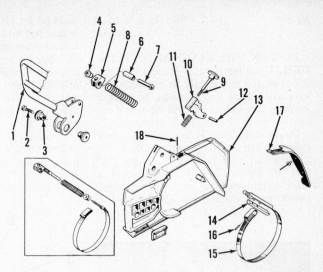

Fig. H48 – Exploded view of typical chain brake used on later models. Some models may have adjustable type brake band as shown in inset.

1. Hand guard
2. Cap screw
3. Trunnion
4. Nut
5. Latch
6. Bushing
7. Rivet
8. Spring
9. Trigger button
10. Trigger lever
11. Spring
12. Pin
13. Housing
14. Guide
15. Brake band
16. Pin
17. Chain guard
18. Pin

CHAIN BRAKE. Some models may be equipped with a chain brake system designed to stop chain movement should kickback occur. Several types of chain brake systems have been used.

The chain brake is activated either by the operator's hand striking the hand guard (1 – Fig. H47 or Fig. H48) or by sufficient force being applied to the guide bar tip during kickback to cause the front handle to contact trigger lever (6 – Fig. H47) on early models or trigger button (9 – Fig. H48) on later models resulting in automatic activation of brake mechanism.

To adjust chain brake on early models, pull back brake lever and be sure mechanism is cocked. Turn adjusting screw (2 – Fig. H47) in until chain cannot be pulled around bar then turn screw out approximately four turns. If screw has a square head, be sure screw head does not rest on hand guard side plates. Chain should rotate freely around bar. Check brake band tension adjustment by starting saw and running at wide open throttle, then manually engage chain brake. Chain should stop rotating immediately. Adjust gap between trigger lever (6) and trigger arm (10) so chain brake will automatically activate when a 6.2-9.8 N (1.4-2.2 lbs.) force is applied on guide bar tip. A suitable spring balance should be used for testing and adjustment.

To adjust chain brake on later models, first pull back hand guard and be sure mechanism is cocked then determine if brake system has an adjustable brake band as shown in inset of Fig. H48. If brake band is adjustable, follow early model brake band adjustment procedures as outlined in the previous paragraph. On models without adjustable brake band, be sure spring retaining nut (4) is tight against its seat. On all models, gap between trigger button (9) and front handle should be adjusted so chain brake will automatically activate when a 6.2-9.8 N (1.4-2.2 lbs.) force is applied on guide bar tip. A suitable spring balance should be used for testing and adjustment.

HANDLE HEATER. Models 162SG and 266SG are equipped with a front and rear handle heating system. A generating coil located underneath the flywheel produces approximately 20 volts at 8500 rpm to provide an electrical current to heating coils in front and rear handles. On early 162SG models, the heating system is controlled by a switch located to the right of rear handle. On later 162SG models and 266SG models, the heating system is regulated by a thermostat that closes at approximately 10°C (50°F).

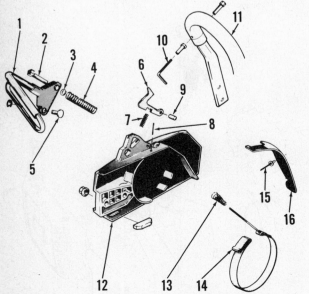

Fig. H47 – Exploded view of early model chain brake.

1. Chain brake lever
2. Adjusting screw
3. Washer
4. Spring
5. Pin
6. Trigger lever
7. Spring
8. Pin
9. Pin
10. Trigger arm
11. Front handle
12. Side cover
13. Sring
14. Brake rod & band
15. Rivet
16. Chain guard

HUSQVARNA

Model	Bore	Stroke	Displ.	Drive Type
133SE, 133SG	38 mm (1.496 in.)	30 mm (1.181 in.)	34 cc (2.1 cu. in.)	Direct
238SE, 238SG	40 mm (1.575 in.)	30 mm (1.181 in.)	37.4 cc (2.3 cu. in.)	Direct
242, 242G	42 mm (1.653 in.)	30 mm (1.181 in.)	42 cc (2.56 cu. in.)	Direct
181SE, 181SG, 281XP, 281XPG	52 mm (2.047 in.)	38 mm (1.496 in.)	80.7 cc (4.9 cu. in.)	Direct

MAINTENANCE

SPARK PLUG. Recommended spark plug for Models 133SE, 133SG, 238SE, 238SG, 242 and 242G is Champion CJ7Y. Recommended spark plug for Models 181SE and 181SG is Champion RCJ7Y. Recommended spark plug for Models 281XP and 281XPG is Champion RCJ6Y. Spark plug electrode gap should be 0.5 mm (0.020 in.) on all models.

CARBURETOR. Models 181SE, 281XP and 281XPG are equipped with a Tillotson HS diaphragm type carburetor. All other models are equipped with a Walbro HDA carburetor. Refer

to CARBURETOR SERVICE section for information and exploded views of Tillotson HS and Walbro HDA carburetors.

On all models, initial adjustment of both low and high speed mixture screws is 1 turn open from a lightly seated position. Make final adjustment with engine warm and running. Adjust idle speed screw so engine will accelerate cleanly without hesitation. Adjust high speed mixture screw to obtain optimum performance under cutting load. Do not adjust high speed mixture needle too lean as engine may be damaged.

IGNITION. All models are equipped with a breakerless electronic ignition system. Ignition timing is not adjustable. Air gap between ignition module core (2—Fig. H52) and flywheel magnets should be 0.4 mm (0.015 in.). Adjust air gap by loosening ignition module retaining screws.

LUBRICATION. The engine is lubricated by mixing oil with the fuel. Recommended oil is Husqvarna Two-Stroke Oil mixed at a ratio of 50:1. If Husqvarna Two-Stroke Oil is not available, a good quality oil designed for two-stroke engines may be used when mixed at a 25:1 ratio. Use a separate container when mixing the oil and gas.

All models are equipped with an automatic chain oil pump. Clean automotive oil may be used. Oil viscosity should be chosen according to ambient temperature. Oil pump output on 181SE, 181SG, 281XP and 281XPG models is adjustable; remove clutch to obtain access to adjusting screw. Adjust oil output by turning screw (11—Fig. H59)—position "1" is minimum, position "4" is maximum. Oil pump output on all other models is not adjustable.

REPAIRS

CYLINDER, PISTON, RINGS AND PIN. Cylinder has a chrome bore which should be inspected for flaking, cracking or other damage to chromed surface. Inspect piston and discard if excessive wear or damage is evident. New cylinders are available only with fitted pistons. On Models 133SE, 133SG, 181SE, 181SG, 281XP and 281XPG, new pistons are available for installation in used cylinders. Piston and cylinder are graded with a letter according to size. Piston is marked on piston crown while cylinder is marked on top as shown in Fig. H54. On Models 133SE, 133SG, 181SE and 181SG, letter sizes range from "A" to "C" with "A" being the smallest size. On Models 281XP and

Fig. H51—Exploded view of fuel tank/rear handle assembly used on 133SE models. Other models are similar.

1. Fuel tank/rear handle	9. Spring
2. Throttle trigger lock	10. Cover
3. Pin	11. Retainer
4. Throttle trigger	12. Hose
5. Spring	13. Fuel filter
6. Pin	14. Vent retainer
7. Throttle rod	15. Retainer filter
8. Pin	16. Vent orifice

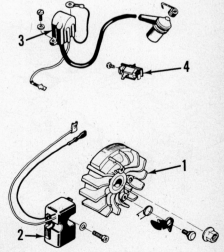

Fig. H52—Exploded view of ignition system typical of all models.

1. Flywheel	3. Coil
2. Module	5. Ignition switch

281XPG, letter sizes range from "A" to "B" with "A" being the smallest size. Piston and cylinder grades should match although one size larger piston may be installed in a used cylinder. For instance, a piston graded "B" may be used in a cylinder graded "A."

Piston has two piston rings on 181SE and 181SG models. Piston has a single piston ring on all other models. A locating pin is present in piston ring groove to prevent piston ring rotation. Be sure ring end gap is around locating pin when installing cylinder.

The piston pin is retained by wire retainers and rides in needle roller bearing in small end of connecting rod. Be sure piston is properly supported when removing piston pin to prevent damage to connecting rod. Arrow on piston crown must point toward exhaust port when installing piston.

CRANKSHAFT, CONNECTING ROD AND CRANKCASE. Crankshaft and connecting rod are a unit assembly. It will be necessary to heat crankcase halves to remove or install crankshaft and main bearings. Care should be taken not to damage mating surfaces of crankcase halves. Check rotation of connecting rod around crankpin and renew crankshaft unit if roughness or other damage is found.

Reassemble crankshaft and crankcase halves as follows: Place main bearing (8—Fig. H53) over flywheel end of crankshaft then press bearing inner race flush against bearing seat. Heat bearing seat area in corresponding crankcase half and install crankshaft. Make sure main bearing outer race seats fully in crankcase. Heat bearing seat

area in right crankcase half (16) and install drive side main bearing (12) allowing for installation of oil pump. A special tool is available from the manufacturer to properly position drive side main bearing in crankcase. On 133SE, 133SG, 238SE, 238SG, 242 and 242G models, drive side crankcase seal (13) seats directly in main bearing (12). On 181SE, 181SG, 281XP and 281XPG models, drive side crankcase seal (13—Fig. H59) seats in the oil pump housing. After assembling crankcase halves together, make certain

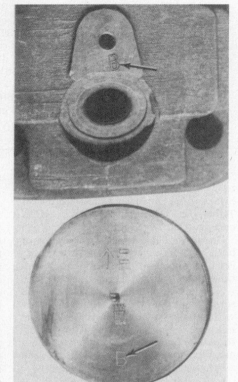

Fig. H54—Arrows show location of letter grades on a typical piston and cylinder. Be sure arrow stamped in piston crown points toward exhaust port when installing piston. Grade "B" is shown.

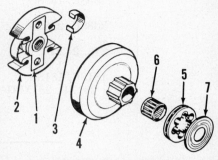

Fig. H56—Exploded view of clutch assembly used on 133SE, 133SG, 238SE, 238SG, 242 and 242G models.

1. Hub
2. Shoe
3. Spring
4. Drum
5. Sprocket
6. Needle bearing
7. Washer

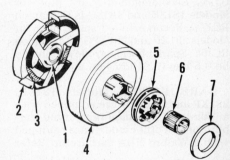

Fig. H57—Exploded view of clutch assembly used on 181SE, 181SG, 281XP and 281XPG models. Refer to Fig. H56 for parts identification.

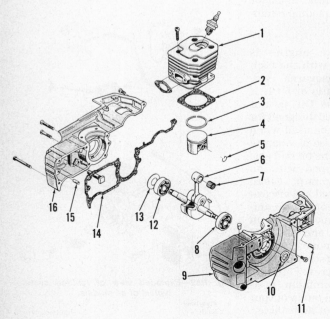

Fig. H53—Exploded view of 133SE and 133SG engine assembly. Other models are similar.

1. Cylinder
2. Gasket
3. Piston ring
4. Piston
5. Piston pin retainer
6. Crankshaft & rod assy.
7. Needle bearing
8. Ball bearing
9. Left crankcase half
10. Seal
11. Pin
12. Ball bearing
13. Seal
14. Gasket
15. Guide dowel
16. Right crankcase half

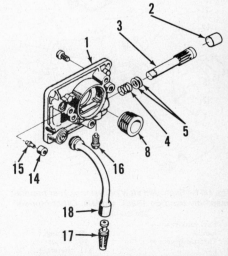

Fig. H58—Exploded view of automatic chain oiler pump used on 133SE, 133SG, 238SE, 238SG, 242 and 242G models. Refer to Fig. H59 for identification of components.

crankshaft is centered in crankcase and will rotate freely.

CLUTCH. Models 133SE, 133SG, 238SE, 238SG, 242 and 242G are equipped with the two-shoe centrifugal clutch shown in Fig. H56. Models 181SE, 181SG, 281XP and 281XPG are equipped with the three-shoe centrifugal clutch shown in Fig. H57. On all models, clutch hub (1) has left hand threads. Inspect clutch shoes and drum for excessive wear or damage due to overheating. Inspect clutch drum, bearing and crankshaft for damage.

On 181SE, 181SG, 281XP and 281XPG models, the oil pump is driven by the clutch drum. Be sure notches on rear of clutch drum mesh with dogs of oil pump drive gear when installing clutch assembly.

OIL PUMP. Models 133SE, 238SE, 238SG, 242 and 242G are equipped with the nonadjustable automatic oil pump shown in Fig. H58. Models 181SE, 181SG, 281XP and 281XPG are equip-

ped with the adjustable automatic oil pump shown in Fig. H59.

On 133SE, 133SG, 238SE, 238SG, 242 and 242G models, oil pump is driven by worm gear (8—Fig. H58) on crankshaft. Oil is then pumped by rotating plunger (3) as it reciprocates due to end of cam screw (16) riding in operating groove of plunger. Oil filter (17) is accessible after removing oil pump assembly. Oil pump may be disassembled for cleaning or renewal of individual components after removing cam screw (16) and withdrawing plunger (3). Make certain end of cam screw (16) properly engages groove in plunger (3) when reassembling pump.

On 181SE, 181SG, 281XP and 281XPG models, oil pump is driven by clutch drum. Notches on back of clutch drum engage dogs on oil pump drive gear (8—Fig. H59) which rides on the

crankshaft. Oil is then pumped as drive gear rotates reciprocating plunger (3). Oil pump output is adjusted by turning screw (11). Adjustment is possible after clutch removal. Turn screw (11—Fig. H60) for desired oil output—position "1" is minimum, position "4" is maximum. Oil filter (17—Fig. H59) is accessible after removing oil pump assembly and withdrawing hose (18) from crankcase. Oil pump may be disassembled for cleaning or renewal of individual components after removing cam screw (16), adjusting screw (11) and withdrawing plunger (3). When reassembling pump, make certain steel washer (5) and brass washer (6) are installed as shown in exploded view. Sleeve (7) must be installed with concave side out. Outer edge of sleeve (7) should be flush with oil pump housing surface.

REWIND STARTER. To disassemble rewind starter, remove starter housing from saw. Pull starter rope and hold rope pulley (4—Fig. H61) with notch in pulley adjacent to rope outlet. Pull rope back through outlet so it engages notch in pulley and allow pulley to completely unwind. Unscrew pulley retaining screw (1) and carefully remove rope pulley. If rewind spring (6) must be removed, care should be taken not to allow spring to uncoil uncontrolled.

Install rewind spring in starter housing with spring coiled in clockwise direction from outer spring end. Wrap starter rope around rope pulley in a clockwise direction as viewed with pulley in starter housing. Turn rope pulley two turns clockwise before passing rope through rope outlet to place

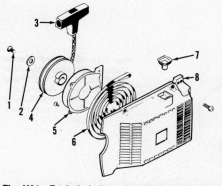

Fig. H61—Exploded view of rewind starter used on 181SE, 181SG, 281XP and 281XPG models. Other models are similar.

1. Screw	5. Spring retainer
2. Washer	6. Rewind spring
3. Rope handle	7. Rope guide
4. Rope pulley	8. Starter housing

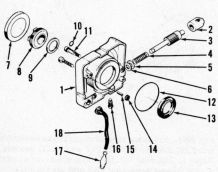

Fig. H59—Exploded view of adjustable oil pump used on 181SE, 181SG, 281XP and 281XPG models.

1. Pump housing	10. "O" ring
2. Plug	11. Adjusting screw
3. Plunger	12. "O" ring
4. Spring	13. Seal
5. Steel washer	14. Seal
6. Brass washer	15. Tube
7. Sleeve	16. Cam screw
8. Drive gear	17. Oil filter
9. Washer	18. Hose

Fig. H62—Exploded view of chain brake assembly used on 133SE and 133SG models.

1. Chain brake lever
2. Allen screw
3. Trunnion
4. Trigger lever
5. Spring
6. Pin
7. Latch
8. Sleeve
9. Rivet
10. Housing
11. Pin
12. Brake band
13. Spring guide
14. Brake spring
15. Spring seat

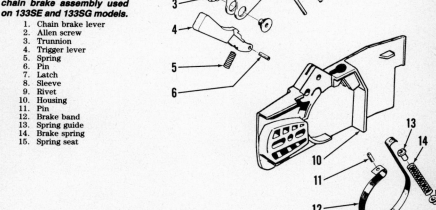

Fig. H60—View showing oil pump adjusting screw (11) on 181SE, 181SG, 281XP and 281XPG models.

tension on rewind spring or reverse the procedure used to relieve spring tension outlined in the previous paragraph. Spring tension is correct if rope pulley can be rotated approximately ¼ turn further when rope is at its greatest length.

When installing starter assembly on saw, make sure starter pulley properly engages pawls on flywheel before tightening retaining cap screws.

CHAIN BRAKE. All models are equipped with a chain brake system designed to stop chain movement should kickback occur. Refer to Fig.

H62 for chain brake system used on 133SE and 133SG models. Refer to Fig. H63 for chain brake system used on 181SE, 181SG, 281XP and 281XPG models. Refer to Fig. H64 for chain brake system used on Models 238SE, 238SG, 242 and 242G.

On all models, chain brake is activated either by the operator's hand striking the chain brake lever (1—Fig. H62, Fig. H63, or Fig. H64) or by sufficient force being applied to the guide bar tip during kickback. Pull back chain brake lever to reset mechanism.

On 133SE, 133SG, 238SE, 238SG, 242 and 242G models, adjustment of brake

mechanism is not required. On 181SE, 181SG, 281XP and 281XPG models, gap between trigger button (17—Fig. H63) and front handle should be adjusted so chain brake will automatically activate when a 7.6-11.1 N (1.7-2.5 lbs.) force is applied on guide bar tip. A suitable spring balance should be used for testing and adjustment.

HANDLE HEATER. Models 133SG, 238SG, 242G, 181SG and 281XPG are equipped with a front and rear handle heating system. A generating coil located underneath the flywheel produces approximately 20 volts at 8500 rpm to provide an electrical current to heating coils in front and rear handles. A switch located to the right of rear handle on 133SG, 238SG and 242G models controls the electric current. The heating system of 181SG and 281XPG models is regulated by a thermostat that closes at approximately 10° C (50° F).

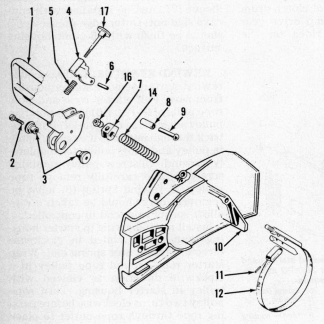

Fig. H63—Exploded view of chain brake assembly used on 181SE, 181SG, 281XP and 281XPG models. Refer to Fig. H62 for parts identification except for nut (16) and trigger button (17).

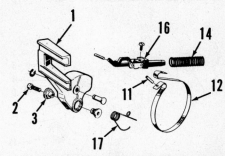

Fig. H64—Exploded view of chain brake assembly used on 238SE, 238SG, 242 and 242G models. Refer to Fig. H62 for parts identification except for trigger assembly (16) and spring (17).

HUSQVARNA

Model	Bore	Stroke	Displ.	Drive Type
50 Rancher, 50	44 mm (1.73 in.)	32 mm (1.26 in.)	49 cc (3.0 cu. in.)	Direct

MAINTENANCE

SPARK PLUG. Recommended spark plug is Champion RCJ7Y. Spark plug electrode gap should be 0.5 mm (0.020 in.).

CARBURETOR. A Walbro WA-82 diaphragm type carburetor is used. Refer to Walbro section of CARBURETOR SERVICE section for service and exploded views of carburetor.

Initial adjustment for both low speed and high speed mixture screws is one turn open from a lightly seated position. Make final adjustment with engine warm and running. Adjust idle speed screw so engine idles just below clutch engagement speed. Adjust low speed mixture screw so engine will accelerate cleanly without hesitation. Adjust high speed mixture screw to obtain optimum performance under cutting load.

Check fuel hose for cracks or splitting and renew as required. Total fuel hose length should be 230 mm (9 in.) and should protrude above fuel tank 138 mm (5-7/16 in.) when installed.

Fuel mixture is richened for cold starting purposes when the choke knob, located above rear handle on cylinder cover, is pushed upward. As knob moves upward a spring clip attached to the choke knob gradually depresses the center of the air filter thereby restricting air intake. If choke malfunctions, remove spring clip and check the distance across spring clip free ends. Distance should be 19 mm (3/4 in.) and may be adjusted by bending spring clip.

IGNITION. All models are equipped with a one-piece breakerless electronic ignition system. Two types of ignition systems have been used and are interchangeable. The color of the ignition module (2—Fig. H66) designates the manufacturer. Prufrex ignition modules are yellow and Electrolux ignition modules are black. On both types of ignition systems, air gap between ignition module core and flywheel magnets should be 0.4 mm (0.016 in.). Ignition timing is not adjustable.

LUBRICATION. Engine is lubricated by mixing oil with the fuel. Recommended oil is Husqvarna Two-Stroke Oil mixed at a ratio of 50:1. If Husqvarna Two-Stroke Oil is not available, a good quality oil designed for two-stroke air-cooled engines may be used when mixed at a 25:1 ratio. Use a separate container when mixing the oil and gas.

All models are equipped with an automatic chain oil pump. Clean automotive oil may be used. Oil viscosity should be chosen according to ambient temperature. Oil pump output is not adjustable.

REPAIRS

CYLINDER, PISTON, RINGS AND PIN. Cylinder has a chrome bore which should be inspected for flaking, cracking or other damage to chromed surface. Inspect piston and discard if excessive wear or damage is evident. New cylinders are available only with fitted pistons but new pistons are available for installation in used cylinders.

The piston is fitted with a single piston ring. A locating pin is present in piston ring groove to prevent piston ring rotation. Oversize pistons and rings are not available. Be sure ring end gap is around locating pin when installing cylinder.

The piston pin is retained by wire retainers and rides in needle roller bearing in small end of connecting rod. Be sure piston is properly supported when removing piston pin to prevent damage. Arrow on piston crown must point

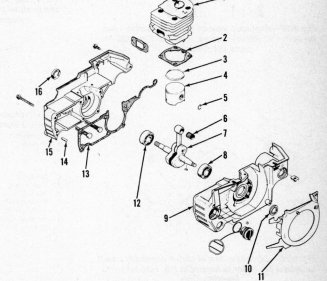

Fig. H67—Exploded view of engine assembly.

1. Cylinder
2. Gasket
3. Piston ring
4. Piston
5. Piston pin retainer
6. Needle bearing
7. Crankshaft & rod assy.
8. Ball bearing
9. Left crankcase half
10. Seal
11. Fan cover
12. Ball bearing
13. Gasket
14. Guide dowel
15. Right crankcase half
16. Seal

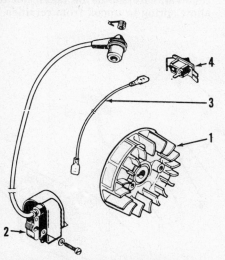

Fig. H66—Exploded view of ignition system.

1. Flywheel
2. Ignition module
3. Ground lead
4. Ignition switch

toward exhaust port when installing piston.

CRANKSHAFT, CONNECTING ROD AND CRANKCASE. Crankshaft and connecting rod are a unit assembly. It will be necessary to heat crankcase halves to remove or install crankshaft and main bearings. Care should be taken not to damage mating surfaces of crankcase halves. Check rotation of connecting rod around crankpin and renew crankshaft unit if roughness or other damage is found.

When reassembling crankshaft and crankcase halves, be sure main bearing outer races are bottomed against their seats in crankcase. A special tool is

available from the manufacturer to properly position main bearings and crankshaft in crankcase. Make certain crankshaft is centered in crankcase and will rotate freely. Clutch side crankshaft seal should be installed 1.58 mm (1/16 in.) below flush of crankcase face.

CLUTCH. Two types of two-shoe centrifugal clutches have been used on 50

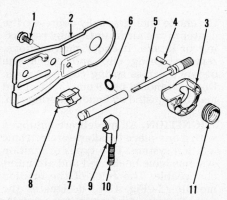

Fig. H71—Exploded view of oil pump assembly.

1. Cap screw
2. Cover plate
3. Gear protector
4. Pin
5. Plunger
6. "O" ring
7. Pump housing
8. Outlet tube
9. Inlet hose
10. Spring
11. Drive gear

Fig. H72—View of oil tank with left crankcase removed to show proper installation of oil pickup components (9 and 10).

Rancher models. Refer to Fig. H68 or Fig. H69 for exploded view of clutch assemblies. Refer to Fig. H70 for exploded view of two-shoe centrifugal clutch assembly used on Model 50. On all types of clutches, clutch hub (1) has left hand threads. Inspect clutch shoes and drum for excessive wear or damage due to overheating. Inspect clutch drum, bearing and crankshaft for damage. Clutch components are available individually.

OIL PUMP. All models are equipped with an automatic chain oiler pump which is driven by worm gear (11—Fig. H71) on crankshaft. Oil pump output is not adjustable.

Access to oil pump components is obtained after removing chain, guide bar, clutch and oil pump cover plate (2). Oil pump pickup hose (9) and filter spring (10) may be withdrawn from oil tank using a suitable screwdriver. When reassembling observe the following: Spring (10) must be completely installed on hose (9). After installing oil pickup assembly in oil tank, make certain spring (10) is perpendicular to oil tank bottom as shown in Fig. H72. Oil pickup assembly may be inspected through oil filler opening. "O" ring (6—Fig. H71) should be installed on gear end of housing (7) 10-12 mm (7/16 in.) from housing end. Notch in housing should engage locating lug in crankcase.

REWIND STARTER. To disassemble rewind starter, remove starter housing from saw. Pull starter rope and hold rope pulley (10—Fig. H73) with notch in pulley adjacent to rope outlet. Pull rope back through outlet so it engages notch in pulley and allow pulley to completely unwind. Unscrew pulley retaining cap screw (7) and remove rope pulley. If rewind spring requires removal, care should be taken not to allow spring to uncoil from retainer.

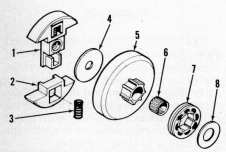

Fig. H68—Exploded view of clutch assembly used on some 50 Rancher saws. Some saws may be equipped with clutch assembly shown in Fig. H69.

1. Hub
2. Shoe
3. Spring
4. Washer
5. Drum
6. Needle bearing
7. Floating sprocket
8. Washer

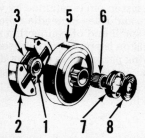

Fig. H69—Exploded view of clutch assembly used on some 50 Rancher saws. Refer to Fig. H68 for parts identification.

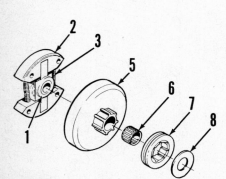

Fig. H70—Exploded view of clutch assembly used on Model 50. Refer to legend in Fig. H68 for parts identification.

Fig. H73—Exploded view of rewind starter.

1. Flywheel
2. Washer
3. Nut
4. Spring
5. Pawl
6. Retainer
7. Cap screw
8. Washer
9. Rope handle
10. Rope pulley
11. Rewind spring
12. Starter housing

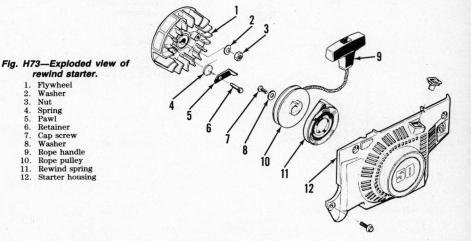

Reassembly is the reverse of disassembly while noting the following: Wrap starter rope around rope pulley in a clockwise direction as viewed with pulley in starter housing. Turn rope pulley two turns clockwise before passing rope through rope outlet to place tension on rewind spring or reverse the procedure used to relieve spring tension outlined in the previous paragraph. Spring tension is correct if rope pulley can be rotated approximately ½ turn further when rope is at its greatest length.

When installing starter assembly on saw, make sure starter pulley properly engages pawls on flywheel before tightening retaining cap screws.

CHAIN BRAKE. Refer to Fig. H74 for exploded view of chain brake assembly. The chain brake system is designed to stop chain movement should kickback occur. Chain brake is activated either by the operator's hand striking the hand guard (1) or by sufficient force being applied to the guide bar tip during kickback to dislodge trigger lever (6) and release brake spring (12) thereby pulling brake band (14) tight around clutch drum to stop chain. Pull back hand guard to reset mechanism.

Disassembly of chain brake for repair or renewal of individual components is evident after inspection of unit and referral to exploded view. Brake band adjustment should be checked after reassembly and installation of chain brake on saw. The distance between disengaged position (A—Fig. H75) and engaged position (B) of hand guard, as measured at point (P), should be 4 mm (0.157 in.). When brake mechanism is in the engaged position, gently pull back hand guard until resistance is felt before measuring. Adjustment is accomplished by varying the length of rod (10—Fig. H74).

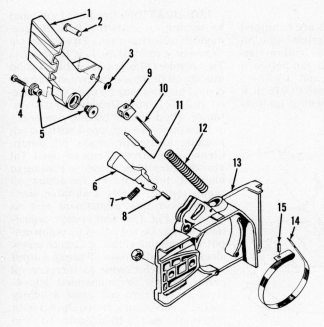

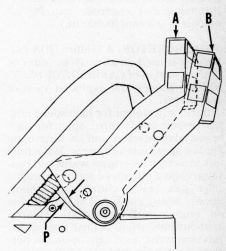

Fig. H74—Exploded view of chain brake assembly.

1. Hand guard
2. Pin
3. "E" ring
4. Allen screw
5. Trunnion
6. Trigger lever
7. Spring
8. Pin
9. Latch
10. Adjustment rod
11. Brake band retainer
12. Brake spring
13. Housing
14. Brake band
15. Pin

Fig. H75—Properly adjusted, hand guard travel between chain brake disengaged position (A) and engaged position (B) should be 4 mm (0.157 in.) when measured at point (P).

HUSQVARNA

Model	Bore	Stroke	Displ.	Drive Type
154SE, 154SG, 254, 254G	45 mm (1.771 in.)	34 mm (1.338 in.)	54cc (3.3 cu. in.)	Direct

MAINTENANCE

SPARK PLUG. Recommended spark plug for all models is Champion RCJ7Y. Recommended electrode gap for all models is 0.5 mm (0.020 in.).

CARBURETOR. A Walbro HDA carburetor is used on all models. Refer to Walbro section of CARBURETOR SERVICE for service and exploded view of carburetor.

Initial adjustment for high speed mixture screw is 1¼ turns open for high speed mixture screw and 1½ turns open for low speed mixture screw. Make final adjustment with engine warm and running. Adjust idle speed screw so engine idles just below clutch engagement speed. Adjust low speed mixture screw so engine will accelerate cleanly without hesitation. Adjust high speed mixture screw to obtain optimum performance under cutting load. Do not adjust high speed mixture screw too lean as overheating and engine damage could result.

IGNITION. All models are equipped with Electrolux breakerless ignition system shown in Fig. H85. Ignition timing is not adjustable. Air gap between ignition module core and flywheel magnets should be 0.4 mm (0.015 in.). Adjust air gap by loosening ignition

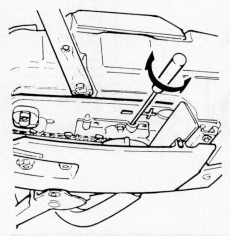

Fig. H86—Insert a suitable sized screwdriver as shown and refer to text for procedures to adjust automatic chain oil pump output.

module retaining screws and repositioning module.

LUBRICATION. Engine is lubricated by mixing oil with the fuel. Recommended oil is Husqvarna Two-Stroke Oil mixed at a ratio of 50:1. If Husqvarna Two-Stroke Oil is not available, a good quality oil designed for two-stroke air-cooled engines may be used when mixed at a 25:1 ratio. Use a separate container when mixing oil and gasoline.

All models are equipped with an adjustable automatic chain oil pump. Clean automotive oil can be used. Oil viscosity should be chosen according to ambient temperature. To adjust oil pump output, insert a suitable sized screwdriver into adjustment slot as shown in Fig. H86 and engage adjustment screw. Do not adjust oil pump output with engine running. Rotate screw clockwise to decrease oil pump output and counterclockwise to increase oil pump output. Recommended adjustment is one turn out from a lightly seated position on saws equipped with a 33.0-38.1 cm (13-15 in.) guide bar and two to three turns out from a lightly seated position on saws equipped with a 38.1-45.7 cm (15-18 in.) guide bar.

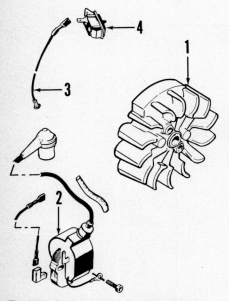

Fig. H85—Exploded view of ignition system.
1. Flywheel
2. Ignition module
3. Ground lead
4. Ignition switch

Fig. H87—Exploded view of engine assembly.
1. Cylinder
2. Gasket
3. Piston ring
4. Piston
5. Retainer
6. Needle bearing
7. Crankshaft & rod assy.
8. Ball bearings
9. Left crankcase half
10. Fan cover
11. Seal
12. "O" ring
13. Plate
14. Gasket
15. Tube
16. Guide dowel
17. Right crankcase half
18. Seal

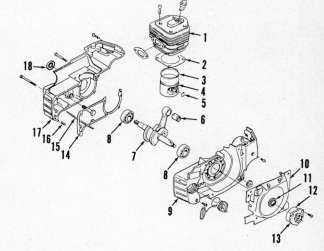

REPAIRS

CYLINDER, PISTON, RINGS AND PIN. Cylinder has a chrome bore which should be inspected for flaking, cracking or other damage to chromed surface. Inspect piston and discard if excessive wear or damage is evident. New cylinders are available only with fitted pistons. Piston is renewable only in standard size and as an assembly with piston ring, piston pin, needle roller bearing and retaining clips.

The piston is fitted with a single piston ring. On 254 and 254G models, a 1.0 mm (0.04 in.) and a 1.5 mm (0.06 in.) thickness ring have been used. Make sure correct size piston ring is used when renewing piston ring on a used piston. On all models, a locating pin is present in piston ring groove to prevent piston ring rotation. Be sure ring end gap is around locating pin when installing cylinder.

The piston pin is retained by wire retainers and rides in a needle roller bearing in small end of connecting rod. Be sure piston is properly supported when removing piston pin to prevent damage. Arrow on piston crown must point toward exhaust port when installing piston.

CRANKSHAFT, CONNECTING ROD AND CRANKCASE. Crankshaft and connecting rod are a unit assembly. It will be necessary to heat crankcase halves to remove or install crankshaft and main bearings. Care should be taken not to damage mating surfaces of crankcase halves. Check rotation of connecting rod around crankpin and renew crankshaft unit if roughness or other damage is noted.

When reassembling crankshaft and crankcase halves, be sure main bearing outer races are properly positioned in crankcase halves so crankshaft is centered in crankcase and will rotate freely.

CLUTCH. All models are equipped with two-shoe centrifugal clutch shown in Fig. H88. Clutch hub (1) has left hand threads. Inspect clutch shoes (2) and clutch drum (4) for excessive wear or damage due to overheating. Inspect clutch drum, needle bearing (5) and crankshaft end for damage. Clutch hub (1) and clutch shoes (2) are available as an assembly. Clutch drum (4) is available with components (5, 6 and 7).

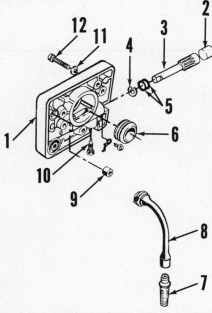

Fig. H89—Exploded view of adjustable, automatic oil pump.

1. Pump housing	7. Oil filter
2. Plug	8. Hose
3. Plunger	9. Seal
4. Washer	10. Adjusting screw
5. Washers	11. Washer
6. Drive gear	12. Screw

Spring (3), needle bearing (5), floating sprocket (6), washer (7) and washer (8) are available individually.

OIL PUMP. All models are equipped with the adjustable, automatic oil pump shown in Fig. H89. To adjust oil pump output, insert a suitable sized screwdriver into adjustment slot as shown in Fig. H86 and engage adjustment screw. Do not adjust oil pump output with engine running. Rotate screw clockwise to decrease oil pump output and counterclockwise to increase oil pump output. Recommended adjustment is one turn out from a lightly seated position on saws equipped with a 33.0-38.1 cm (13-15 in.) guide bar and two to three turns out from a lightly seated position on saws equipped with a 38.1-45.7 cm (15-18 in.) guide bar.

Oil filter (7—Fig. H89) is accessible after removing oil pump assembly. All components are renewable individually except for pump housing (1) which is renewable only as a complete oil pump assembly. Disassembly and reassembly of components is evident after referral to Fig. H89.

REWIND STARTER. To disassemble rewind starter, remove starter housing from saw. Pull starter rope and hold rope pulley (4—Fig. H90) with notch in pulley adjacent to rope outlet. Pull rope

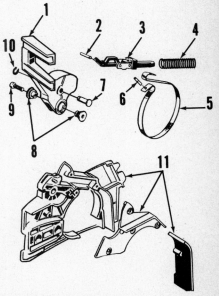

Fig. H91—Exploded view of chain brake assembly.

1. Brake lever	7. Pin
2. Pin	8. Trunnions
3. Trigger assy.	9. Allen screw
4. Spring	10. Retainer
5. Brake band	11. Side housing assy.
6. Band retainer	

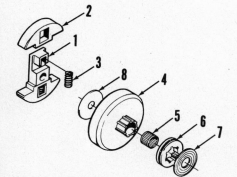

Fig. H88—Exploded view of clutch assembly.

1. Hub	5. Needle bearing
2. Shoe	6. Floating sprocket
3. Spring	7. Washer
4. Drum	8. Washer

Fig. H90—Exploded view of rewind starter.

1. Screw	5. Spring retainer
2. Washer	6. Rewind spring
3. Rope handle	7. Rope guide
4. Rope pulley	8. Starter housing

back through outlet so it engages notch in pulley and allow pulley to completely unwind. Remove pulley retaining screw (1) and carefully remove rope pulley. If rewind spring (6) must be removed, care should be taken not to allow spring to uncoil uncontrolled.

Install rewind spring in starter housing with spring coiled in a clockwise direction from outer spring end. Wrap starter rope around rope pulley in a clockwise direction as viewed with pulley in starter housing. Turn pulley two turns clockwise before passing rope through rope outlet to place tension on rewind spring or reverse the procedure used to relieve spring tension outlined in previous paragraph. Spring tension is

correct if rope pulley can be rotated approximately ½ turn further when rope is at its greatest length.

When installing starter assembly on saw, make sure starter pulley properly engages pawls on flywheel before tightening retaining screws.

CHAIN BRAKE. All models are equipped with a chain brake system designed to stop movement of chain should kickback occur. Refer to Fig. H91 for exploded view of chain brake system used.

On all models, chain brake is activated either by the operator's hand striking chain brake lever (1—Fig. H91) or by sufficient force being applied to bar tip

during kickback to dislodge trigger assembly (3) and release brake spring (4) thereby forcing brake band (5) tight around clutch drum to stop chain movement. Pull back chain brake lever to reset mechanism. Chain brake is set at factory and should need no further adjustment.

HANDLE HEATER. All models are equipped with front and rear handle heating system. A generating coil located under flywheel produces approximately 20 volts at 8500 rpm to provide an electrical current to heating coils in front and rear handles. A switch located to the right of rear handle controls the current.

HUSQVARNA

Model	Bore	Stroke	Displ.	Drive Type
40	40 mm	32 mm	40 cc	Direct
	(1.57 in.)	(1.26 in.)	(2.4 cu. in.)	
45	42 mm	32 mm	44 cc	Direct
	(1.65 in.)	(1.26 in.)	(2.7 cu. in.)	

MAINTENANCE

SPARK PLUG. Recommended spark plug for both models is Champion RCJ7Y with an electrode gap of 0.5 mm (0.020 in.).

CARBURETOR. A Walbro WT carburetor is used on both models. Refer to Walbro section of CARBURETOR SERVICE for service and exploded view of carburetor.

Initial adjustment for low speed and high speed mixture screws is one turn open from a lightly seated position. Make final adjustment with engine warm and running. Adjust idle speed screw so engine idles just below clutch engagement speed. Adjust low speed mixture screw so engine will accelerate cleanly without hesitation. Adjust high speed mixture screw to obtain optimum performance under cutting load. Do not adjust high speed mixture screw too lean as overheating and engine damage could result.

IGNITION. Both models are equipped with Electrolux breakerless ignition system shown in Fig. H94. Ignition timing is not adjustable. Air gap between ignition module core and flywheel magnets should be 0.3 mm (0.012 in.). Adjust air gap by loosening ignition module retaining screws and repositioning module.

LUBRICATION. Engine is lubricated by mixing oil with the fuel. Recommended oil is Husqvarna Two-Stroke Oil mixed at a ratio of 50:1. If Husqvarna Two-Stroke Oil is not available, a good quality oil designed for two-stroke air-cooled engines may be used when mixed at a 25:1 ratio. Use a separate container when mixing oil and gasoline.

Both models are equipped with an automatic chain oil pump. Clean automotive oil can be used. Oil viscosity should be chosen according to ambient temperature. Oil pump output is not adjustable.

REPAIRS

CYLINDER, PISTON, RING AND PIN. Cylinder has a chrome bore which should be inspected for flaking, cracking or other damage to chromed surface. Inspect piston and discard if excessive wear or damage is evident. New cylinders are available only with fitted pistons. Piston is renewable only in standard size and as an assembly with piston ring, piston pin, needle roller bearing and retaining clips.

The piston is fitted with a single piston ring. A locating pin is present in piston ring groove to prevent piston ring rotation. Be sure ring end gap is around locating pin when installing cylinder.

The piston pin is retained by wire retainers and rides in a needle roller bearing in small end of connecting rod. Be sure piston is properly supported when removing piston pin to prevent damage. Arrow on piston crown must point toward exhaust port when installing piston.

CRANKSHAFT, CONNECTING ROD AND CRANKCASE. Crankshaft and connecting rod are a unit assembly. Crankshaft main roller bearings (9—Fig. H95) are supported in interlocking bearing carriers (7). Separate bearing car-

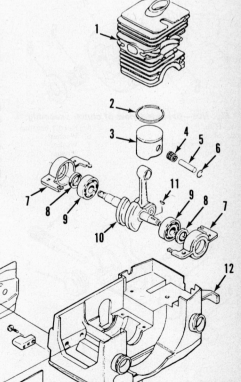

Fig. H95—Exploded view of engine assembly.
1. Cylinder
2. Piston ring
3. Piston
4. Needle roller bearing
5. Piston pin
6. Retainer
7. Bearing carriers
8. Seals
9. Roller bearings
10. Crankshaft & rod assy.
11. Key
12. Lower crankcase & saw body

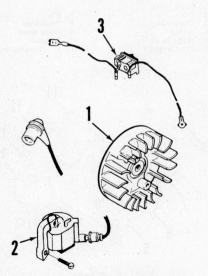

Fig. H94—Exploded view of ignition system.
1. Flywheel
2. Ignition module
3. Ignition switch

riers (7) and withdraw from crankshaft ends to service roller bearings (9) and seals (8). Make sure seals (8) are installed in bearing carriers with seal lip facing toward crankshaft assembly. Grease seal lips prior to assembling bearing carriers (7) onto crankshaft. Check rotation of connecting rod around crankpin and renew crankshaft unit if roughness or other damage is noted.

When installing crankshaft assembly, make sure mating surfaces of bearing carriers (7), lower crankcase (12) and cylinder (1) are clean and dry. Place a thin bead of a suitable form-in-place gasket compound onto sealing areas of lower crankcase (12) and cylinder (1). Lubricate piston and crankshaft assembly with engine oil and wipe off excess oil. Correctly install piston into cylinder bore and position bearing carriers (7) into crankcase area of cylinder (1). Position insulation block on cylinder, then correctly install cylinder with crankshaft assembly onto lower crankcase (12). Tighten the four mounting screws in a criss-cross pattern to 11 N·m (97 in.-lbs.). Make sure crankshaft rotates freely.

CLUTCH. Both models are equipped with three-shoe centrifugal clutch shown in Fig. H96. Clutch hub (1) has left-hand threads. Inspect clutch shoes (2) and clutch drum (4) for excessive wear or damage due to overheating. Inspect clutch drum, needle bearing (5) and crankshaft end for damage. Clutch hub (1) and clutch shoes (2) are available as an assembly. Clutch drum (4) is available with needle bearing (5). Spring (3), needle bearing (5), washer (6), washer (7) and washer (8) are available individually.

OIL PUMP. Both models are equipped with an automatic chain oiler pump which is driven by worm gear (5—Fig. H97) on crankshaft. Oil pump output is not adjustable.

Access to oil pump components is obtained after removing chain, guide bar and clutch. Oil pump suction pipe (6) and strainer (7) may be withdrawn from oil tank using a suitable screwdriver.

REWIND STARTER. To disassemble rewind starter, remove starter housing from saw. Pull starter rope (12—Fig. H98) out 15-20 cm (6-8 in.) and hold rope pulley (8). Pull rope back through outlet so rope engages an ear on pulley (8) and allow pulley to completely unwind. Unscrew pulley retaining screw (6) and remove rope pulley. If rewind spring (9) requires removal, care should be taken not to allow spring to uncoil from retainer.

Reassembly is the reverse of disassembly while noting the following: Wrap starter rope (12) around rope pulley (8) in a clockwise direction as viewed with pulley in starter housing (10). Turn rope pulley two turns clockwise before passing rope through rope outlet to place tension on rewind spring or reverse the procedure used to relieve spring tension outlined in the previous paragraph. Spring tension is correct if rope pulley (8) can be rotated

approximately ½ turn further when rope is at extended length.

When installing starter assembly on saw, make sure starter pulley properly engages pawls (4) on flywheel before tightening retaining cap screws.

CHAIN BRAKE. Both models are equipped with a chain brake system designed to stop movement of chain should kickback occur. Refer to Fig. H99 for exploded view of chain brake system used.

Chain brake is activated either by the operator's hand striking chain brake lever (1—Fig. H99) or by sufficient force being applied to bar tip during kickback to dislodge trigger assembly (3) and release brake spring (4) thereby forcing brake band (5) tight around clutch drum to stop chain movement. Pull back chain brake lever to reset mechanism. Chain brake is set at factory and should need no further adjustment.

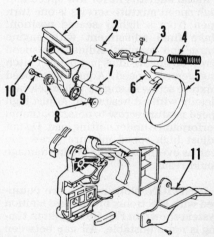

Fig. H99—Exploded view of chain brake assembly.

1. Brake lever
2. Pin
3. Trigger assy.
4. Spring
5. Brake band
6. Band retainer
7. Pin
8. Trunnions
9. Allen screw
10. Retainer
11. Side housing assy.

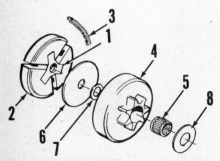

Fig. H96—Exploded view of clutch assembly.

1. Hub
2. Shoe
3. Garter spring
4. Drum
5. Needle bearing
6. Washer
7. Washer
8. Washer

Fig. H97—Exploded view of automatic oil pump assembly.

1. Pump housing
2. Plunger
3. Pressure pipe
4. Plunger housing
5. Worm gear
6. Suction pipe
7. Strainer

Fig. H98—Exploded view of rewind starter assembly.

1. Flywheel
2. Nut
3. Spring
4. Pawl
5. Retainer
6. Screw
7. Washer
8. Rope pulley
9. Rewind spring
10. Starter housing
11. Handle
12. Starter rope
13. Rope guide

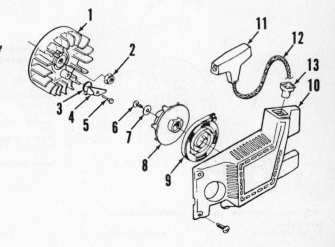

HUSQVARNA DISTRIBUTORS
(Arranged Alphabetically by States)

These franchised firms carry extensive stocks of repair parts. Contact them for name of nearest dealer who may have the parts you need.

Bee Tee Equipment Sales
P.O. Box 3037
21075 Alexander Court, Unit H
Hayward, CA 94540

Rocky Mountain Husky
P.O. Box 600
1437 East Second Ave.
Durango, CO 81302

Stull Power Equipment
10752 Tucker Street
Beltsville, MD 20705

Midwest Parts & Accessories
P.O. Box 8429
5000 36th Street SE
Grand Rapids, MI 49508

Dickerson Distributors, Inc.
127 NW Depot
P.O. Drawer 231
Durant, MS 39063

Northcentral Outdoor Equipment
1300 Ash Avenue N.E.
Brainerd, MN 56401

Ozark Equipment
Hwy. 63 & Black Street
P.O. Box 784
Rolla, MO 65401

Modern Distributing Co.
440 E. Tampa Street
Springfield, MO 65806

Midland Implement
P.O. Box 30358
402 Daniels Street
Billings, MT 59107

Huskipower Outdoor Equipment
2132 Hawkins Street
Charlotte, NC 28203

Trican American Corp.
P.O. Box 5258
Manchester, NH 03108

Lucky Distributing
P.O. Box 18000
8111 NE Columbia Blvd.
Portland, OR 97218

American Power Products
Monroeville Industrial Park
650 Seco Road
Monroeville, PA 15146

The Bill Voorhees Company
700 8th Avenue South
Nashville, TN 37203

Boswork Distributors
P.O. Box 2684
930 N. Fredonia
Longview, TX 75601

Husky of Virginia
P.O. Box 1704
Route 2, Box 533
Waynesboro, VA 22980

Timber Ridge Supply
19116 Spring Street
Union Grove, WI 53182

CANADA

Northern Titan Equipment Sales
14209 130th Avenue
Edmonton, Alberta T5L 4K8
CANADA

Pacific Equipment Ltd.
1420 East Georgia Street
Vancouver, BC V5L 2A8
CANADA

Scanfor, Inc.
106 Ferrier Street
Markham, Ontario L3R 2Z5
CANADA

Husqui Canada
Division of Buccaneer
520 Lafleur Street
Lachute, Quebec J8H 3X6
CANADA

JONSERED

JONSERED MOTOR AB
S-433 81 Partille 1, Sweden

Model	Bore	Stroke	Displ.	Drive Type
451E, 451EV	42 mm (1.654 in.)	32 mm (1.26 in.)	44 cc (2.7 cu. in.)	Direct
49SP	44 mm (1.734 in.)	32 mm (1.26 in.)	49 cc (3.0 cu. in.)	Direct
50, 51, 52, 52E, 521EV	44 mm (1.734 in.)	32 mm (1.26 in.)	49 cc (3.0 cu. in.)	Direct
60, 601, 62, 621	45 mm (1.77 in.)	35 mm (1.378 in.)	56 cc (3.4 cu. in.)	Direct
70E	50 mm (1.968 in.)	35 mm (1.378 in.)	69 cc (4.2 cu. in.)	Direct
75, 751	50 mm (1.968 in.)	38 mm (1.496 in.)	75 cc (4.6 cu. in.)	Direct
801	52 mm (2.047 in.)	38 mm (1.496 in.)	80 cc (4.9 cu. in.)	Direct
111	56 mm (2.2 in.)	45 mm (1.77 in.)	110 cc (6.7 cu. in.)	Direct

MAINTENANCE

SPARK PLUG. Recommended spark plug is Bosch WS7F for Models 50, 51, 52E, 521EV and 111 and Champion CJ7Y for all other models. Recommended spark plug electrode gap is 0.5 mm (0.020 in.).

CARBURETOR. All models are equipped with a Tillotson diaphragm carburetor. Refer to Tillotson section of CARBURETOR SERVICE section for exploded view and overhaul of carburetor.

Initial carburetor adjustment is one turn open from a lightly seated position for both low and high speed mixture screws. Make final adjustment with engine warm and running. Adjust idle speed screw so engine idles just below

clutch engagement speed. Adjust low speed mixture screw so engine will accelerate cleanly without hesitation. Adjust high speed mixture screw to obtain optimum performance under cutting load.

IGNITION. Models 451E, 451EV, 52E, 521EV and 70E are equipped with a breakerless capacitor discharge ignition system. All other models are equipped with a flywheel magneto ignition system with breaker-points located under the flywheel.

On all breaker-point models, point gap should be 0.4 mm (0.016 in.). Ignition timing for all breaker-point models is listed in the following table. Ignition timing is adjusted by loosening stator plate retaining screws and rotating stator plate. Rotate stator plate clockwise to advance timing and counterclockwise to retard timing.

Model	Ignition Timing BTDC
49SP	2.0 mm (0.079 in.)
50, 51, 52	2.0 mm (0.079 in.)
60, 601	3.2 mm (0.126 in.)
62, 621	2.7 mm (0.106 in.)
75, 751	2.5 mm (0.098 in.)
801	2.7 mm (0.106 in.)
111	3.8 mm (0.150 in.)

On electronic ignition models, ignition timing is fixed. Individual electronic ignition components are available separately on 451E, 451EV and 70E models while electronic components must be serviced as a unit assembly on 52E and

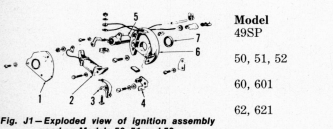

Fig. J1—Exploded view of ignition assembly used on Models 50, 51 and 52.

1. Cover
2. Ignition coil
3. Movable ignition breaker-point
4. Fixed ignition breaker-point
5. Condenser
6. Stator plate
7. Seal

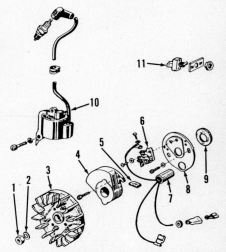

Fig. J2—Exploded view of ignition assembly used on 49SP models.

1. Nut
2. Washer
3. Flywheel
4. Cover
5. Oil wick
6. Fixed ignition breaker-point
7. Condenser
8. Stator plate
9. Seal
10. Ignition coil
11. Stop switch

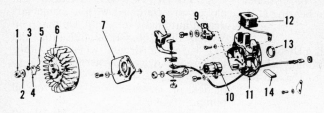

1. Nut
2. Washer
3. Snap ring
4. Starter dog
5. Spring
6. Flywheel

Fig. J3—Exploded view of ignition and flywheel assemblies used on Models 60, 601, 62, 621, 75, 751 and 801.

7. Cover
8. Movable ignition breaker-point
9. Fixed ignition breaker-point
10. Condenser
11. Stator plate
12. Ignition coil
13. Seal
14. Oil wick

521EV models. Air gap between flywheel magnets and ignition coil legs should be 0.3 mm (0.012 in.).

LUBRICATION. The engine is lubricated by mixing oil with the fuel. Recommend oil is Jonsered engine oil or a BIA certified air-cooled two-stroke engine oil approved for 40:1 fuel mixtures. Recommend fuel mixture ratio is 40:1 when using an approved engine oil. If a recommended oil is not available, a good quality oil designed for air-cooled two-stroke engines may be used when mixed with the fuel at a 20:1 ratio. Use a separate container when mixing the oil and gas.

All models are equipped with an automatic chain oiler. A good quality chain oil should be used according to ambient temperature. Automatic oil pump discharge on all models except Models 50 and 51 is adjusted by turning adjusting screw shown in Fig. J4 or Fig. J5. Initial setting is 1½ turns open. Turning screw

clockwise decreases oil flow. Automatic oil pump on Models 50 and 51 is not adjustable.

CARBON. Carbon deposits should be removed from muffler and exhaust ports at regular intervals. When scraping carbon, be careful not to damage engine cylinder. Do not allow loosened carbon into cylinder.

REPAIRS

CYLINDER, PISTON, PIN AND RINGS. Cylinder is chrome plated and oversize pistons are not available. Cylinders and pistons on all early models are graded during production according

to manufacturing tolerances. Pistons and cylinders may be graded "A, B, C, D, E, F and G." "A" pistons and cylinders are largest. Piston and cylinder should be of same grade. Later models do not have graded cylinders or pistons.

Cylinder should be checked for scoring, cracking or peeling of chrome surface. Install piston on all models so arrow on piston crown (Fig. J10) is pointing toward exhaust port. Care should be taken when installing cylinder on all models so piston rings are positioned correctly around piston ring locating pins. On some models, thrust washers are installed adjacent to the connecting rod small end bearing.

CONNECTING ROD, CRANK-SHAFT AND CRANKCASE. Connecting rod is equipped with a needle bearing in small end. Some models also have thrust washers on both sides of small end bearing. Connecting rod and crankshaft are a unit assembly on all models. Automatic oil pump should be removed prior to crankcase separation. Connecting rod, crankshaft and bearing should not be disassembled except by a shop equipped to realign crankshaft. Main bearings on Model 50 are roller type and are a press fit in crankcases. Bearings are installed with lettering on bearing

Fig. J4—View of oil pump adjusting screw on Models 60, 601, 62, 621, 75, 751 and 801.

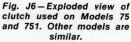

Fig. J6—Exploded view of clutch used on Models 75 and 751. Other models are similar.

1. Washer
2. Snap ring
3. Clutch shoe
4. Clutch hub
5. Spring
6. Washer
7. Clutch drum
8. Bearing
9. Bearing race
10. Washer
11. Washer
12. Nut

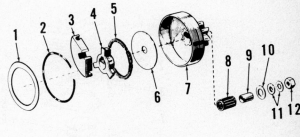

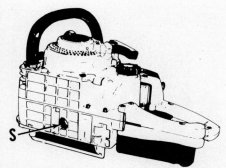

Fig. J5—View showing location of oil pump adjusting screw on Models 451E, 451EV, 495P, 52, 52E, 521EV, 70E and 111.

Fig. J8—Exploded view of engine used on Models 50, 51, 52, 52E and 521 EV. Models 451E, 451EV, 49SP and 70E are similar.

1. Cylinder
2. Gasket
3. Spacer
4. Gasket
5. Piston rings
6. Piston
7. Piston pin
8. Retainer
9. Washer
10. Bearing
11. Crankshaft & rod assy.
12. Seal
13. Bearing
14. Bearing
15. Oil pump drive gear
16. Dowel pin
17. Crankcase half
18. Oil cap
19. Fuel cap
20. Crankcase half
21. Gasket

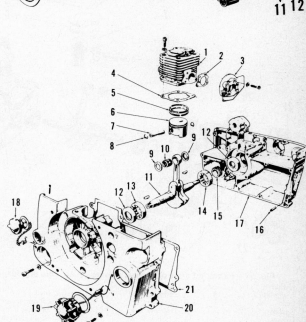

toward outside of crankcase. Bearings on all other models are pressed on crankshaft. Oil pump cam on Models 60, 75, 601, 621, 751 and 801 should be installed as shown in Fig. J11 with highest point of cam pointing toward crankpin.

Unthreaded end of oil pump worm gear (15–Fig. J8) used on Models 49SP, 52, 52E and 521EV must be installed against inner race of main bearing (14).

CLUTCH. Clutch on all models is retained by a nut. Clutch retaining nut has left hand threads. Refer to Fig. J6 for exploded view of clutch.

AUTOMATIC OIL PUMP. All models are equipped with a crankshaft driven automatic oil pump. Oil pump on Models 49SP, 50, 51, 52, 52E, 70E and 111 is worm driven while all other models are driven by a cam. Refer to Figs. J8A, J12, J13, J14 or J15 for exploded or cross-sectional view of oil pump.

Guide pin (4–Fig. J12) on Models 50 and 51 rides in a cam groove in piston (7) and must be removed before piston is withdrawn from housing (3). Worm gear (15–Fig. J8) and cam (14–Fig. J9) are pressed on crankshaft. Install cam so highest part is pointing toward crankpin as shown in Fig. J11. Unthreaded end of oil pump worm gear (15–Fig. J8) used on Models 49SP, 52, 52E, 70E and 521EV must be installed against inner race of main bearing (14).

REWIND STARTER. Refer to Fig. J17 for exploded view of rewind starter used on Models 60, 601, 75 and 751. To disassemble starter, remove rope handle and allow rope to rewind into starter. Remove starter housing (1) and starter assembly. Lift rope pulley and rope out of housing being careful not to disturb rewind spring (3). Outer end of rewind spring is retained by two slots in starter housing and is wound in clockwise direction. Inspect rope pulley bearing for wear or damage. Rope is wound on pulley in clockwise direction as viewed with pulley installed in housing. After

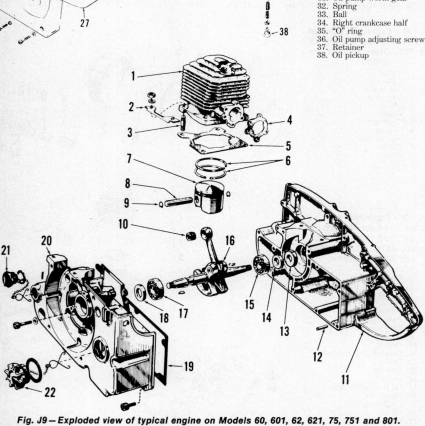

Fig. J8A – Exploded view of Model 111 engine assembly.

1. Screw
2. Washer
3. Spring
4. Ball
5. "O" rings
6. Manual oil pump housing
7. "O" ring
8. Piston
9. Spring
10. Washer
11. Snap ring
12. "O" rings
13. Automatic oil pump housing
14. Bushing
15. Spring
16. Piston
17. Spring
18. Compression release valve
19. Cylinder
20. Gasket
21. Piston rings
22. Pin retainer
23. Piston pin
24. Piston
25. Washer
26. Bearing
27. Left crankcase half
28. Seal
29. Bearing
30. Crankshaft & rod assy.
31. Oil pump worm gear
32. Spring
33. Ball
34. Right crankcase half
35. "O" ring
36. Oil pump adjusting screw
37. Retainer
38. Oil pickup

Fig. J10 – Install piston so arrow on piston crown on all models will point toward exhaust port.

Fig. J11 – Oil pump cam is installed on Models 60, 62, 75, 601, 621, 751 and 801 with high point of cam (arrow) toward crankpin.

Fig. J9 – Exploded view of typical engine on Models 60, 601, 62, 621, 75, 751 and 801.

1. Cylinder	7. Piston	13. Seal	17. Bearing
2. Lockplate	8. Piston pin	14. Oil pump cam	18. Seal
3. Stud	9. Retainer	15. Bearing	19. Gasket
4. Gasket	10. Bearing	16. Crankshaft & rod assy.	20. Crankcase half
5. Gasket	11. Crankcase half		21. Oil cap
6. Piston rings	12. Dowel pin		22. Fuel cap

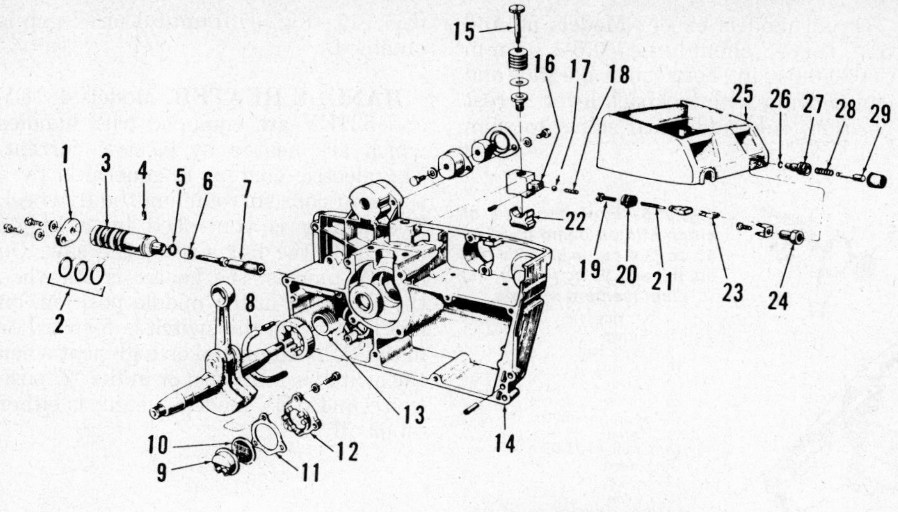

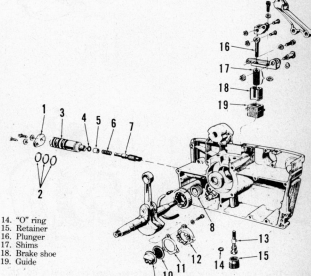

Fig. J12 — Exploded view of automatic oil pump and kickback mechanism used on Models 50 and 51.

1. Plate
2. "O" rings
3. Housing
4. Guide pin
5. "O" ring
6. Bushing
7. Piston
8. Oil line
9. Adapter
10. Screen
11. Gasket
12. Cover
13. Oil pump drive gear
14. Crankcase half
15. Kickback plunger
16. Housing
17. Hall
18. Spring
19. Ground wire
20. Grommet
21. Ground wire
22. Brake shoe
23. Terminal
24. Fitting
25. Air filter
26. Clip
27. Fitting
28. Spring
29. Kill button

starter assembly is fitted to fan housing and rope handle is installed, turn starter housing (1) until rope handle is pulled against rope outlet and turn starter housing (1) one complete turn and install housing retaining screws. This will place tension on the rewind spring so rope will rewind correctly.

Models 49SP, 50, 51, 52, 52E, 521EV, 62, 70E, 111, 621 and 801 are equipped with the rewind starter shown in Fig. J18. Starter assembly used on Models 451E and 451EV is similar. To disassemble starter, remove starter housing from engine. On Models 50 and 51 the ignition wire and spark plug lead to the high tension coil in the starter housing must be disconnected. Remove rope handle and allow rope to rewind in housing. Unscrew rope pulley retaining screw (15) and remove rope pulley (7). Rewind spring may be removed after removing cover (6). Care should be taken when removing spring as injury could result from uncontrolled spring removal.

Rewind spring is wound in clockwise direction. Install rope so it is wound in clockwise direction when rope pulley is installed in housing. To preload rewind spring, reassemble starter assembly in housing. Pull rope handle until there is approximately 30 cm (12 in.) of rope beyond rope outlet and notch in pulley is adjacent to outlet. Hold pulley and pull rope back through outlet. Insert rope in notch and rotate pulley one turn clockwise to preload spring. Pull rope handle and check starter operation.

KICKBACK MECHANISM. Models 451E, 451EV, 50, 51, 52E, 521EV and 70E are equipped with a kickback mechanism to stop the chain should the saw kickback while cutting. Mechanism is activated when operator's hand

Fig. J13 — Exploded view of automatic oil pump and chain brake used on 44 cc (2.7 cu. in.), 49 cc (3.0 cu. in.) and 69 cc (4.2 cu. in.) displacement models, except Models 50 and 51. Later model oil pump is equipped with four "O" rings (2) and bushing (5) is absent. Oil strainer (10) on 44 cc (2.7 cu. in.) models is located in bottom oil tank plug.

1. Retainer
2. "O" rings
3. Housing
4. "O" ring
5. Bushing
6. Spring
7. Piston
8. Oil pump worm gear
9. Adapter
10. Oil strainer
11. Gasket
12. Cover
13. Oil pump adjusting screw
14. "O" ring
15. Retainer
16. Plunger
17. Shims
18. Brake shoe
19. Guide

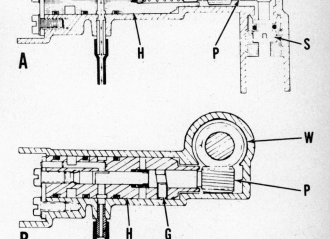

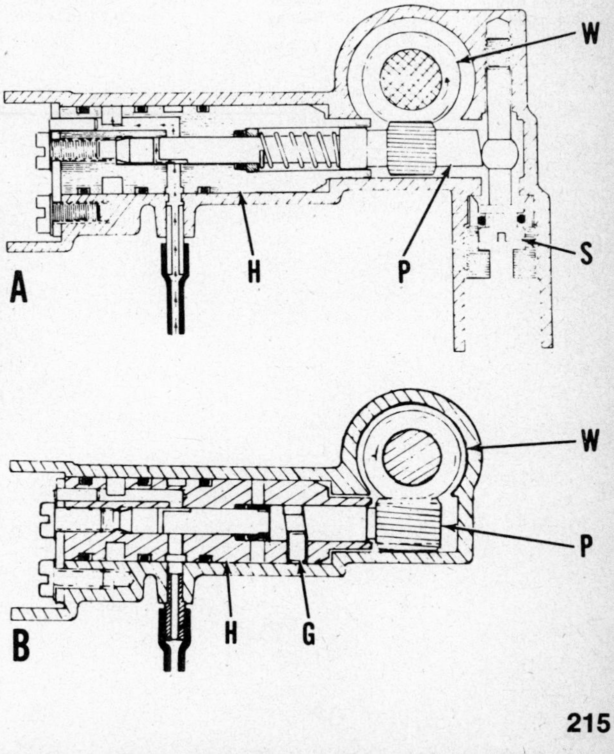

Fig. J14 — Cross-sectional view of worm gear driven automatic oil pumps. Adjustable pump (View A) is used on 44 cc (2.7 cu. in.), 49 cc (3.0 cu. in.), 69 cc (4.2 cu. in.) and 110 cc (6.7 cu. in.) displacement models except for Models 50 and 51 which use nonadjustable pump shown in (View B).

G. Guide pin
H. Housing
P. Piston
S. Adjusting screw
W. Worm gear

strikes kickback bar. Brake shoe (22 – Fig. J12 or 18 – Fig. J13) is forced against the clutch drum to stop chain. The ignition on Models 50 and 51 is also grounded to stop the engine.

On all models except Models 50 and 51, there should be 0.5-1.0 mm (0.020-0.040 in.) between brake shoe and clutch drum with kickback lever in rest position. Add additional shims to shim

pack (17 – Fig. J13) until desired gap is obtained.

HANDLE HEATER. Models 451EV and 521EV are equipped with handles which are heated by electric current. The electric current is generated by a series of coils surrounding the flywheel. The heater is controlled by a toggle switch on the left side of the saw. On 521EV models, the heater is off when the switch is in the middle position, on low heat when the switch is forward or in the "1" position and on high heat when the switch is rearward or in the "2" position. On 451EV models, heater is either on or off.

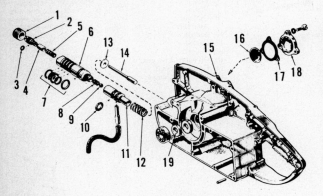

Fig. J15 — Exploded view of automatic oil pump used on 56 cc (3.4 cu. in.), 75 cc (4.6 cu. in.) and 80 cc (4.9 cu. in.) displacement models.

7. "O" rings
8. Spring
9. Check ball
10. "O" ring
11. Housing
12. Spring
13. Spring retainer
14. Piston
15. Crankcase half
16. Screen
17. Gasket
18. Cover
19. Pump drive cam

1. Plug
2. Adjuster
3. "O" ring
4. Valve
5. Spring
6. Housing

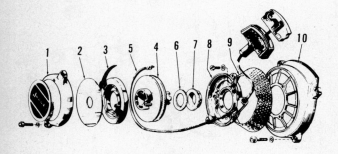

Fig. J17 — Exploded view of rewind starter used on Models 60, 75, 601 and 751.

1. Starter housing
2. Washer
3. Rewind spring
4. Rope pulley
5. Rope
6. Washer
7. Bearing
8. Base plate
9. Dirt guard
10. Fan housing

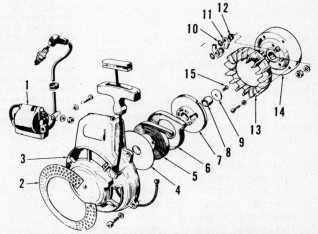

Fig. J18 — Exploded view of typical rewind starter assembly used on all models except Models 60, 601, 75 and 751.

1. High tension coil
2. Dirt guard
3. Starter housing
4. Washer
5. Rewind spring
6. Cover
7. Rope pulley
8. Bushing
9. Washer
10. Snap ring
11. Starter dog
12. Spring
13. Fan
14. Flywheel
15. Screw

JONSERED

Model 361, 361AV, 365, 370	Bore	Stroke	Displ.	Drive Type
	36.5 mm (1.44 in.)	32.5 mm (1.28 in.)	34.4 cc (2.1 cu. in.)	Direct

MAINTENANCE

SPARK PLUG. Recommended spark plug for Model 370 is Champion RCJ7Y. Recommended spark plug for all other models is Champion CJ6. Electrode gap for all models is 0.50 mm (0.020 in.).

CARBURETOR. A Tillotson HU or Walbro WA diaphragm type carburetor has been used on Models 361 and 361AV. Models 365 and 370 are equipped with a Walbro diaphragm type carburetor. Refer to CARBURETOR SERVICE section for service on Tillotson or Walbro carburetor.

Initial setting of both high and low speed mixture screws is 1⅛ turns open from a lightly seated position. Make final adjustment with engine warm and running. Adjust idle speed screw so engine idles just below clutch engagement speed. Adjust low speed mixture screw so engine will accelerate cleanly without hesistation. Adjust high speed mixture screw to obtain optimum performance under cutting load.

On 361AV models, throttle trigger (9 – Fig. J19) may occasionally become restricted by air filter connector (3). Should this occur, remove the air filter connector and trim off the required amount of material from the connector to allow free throttle trigger movement.

On all models, air leakage sometimes develops between heat shield (7) and cylinder making carburetor adjustment very difficult. If air leakage is suspected, remove carburetor and related components, then measure the thickness of gasket (8). If gasket (8) is 0.30-0.38 mm (0.012-0.015 in.) thick, then two gaskets of this thickness are required to stop air leakage. Current production models are equipped with on 0.63-0.72 mm (0.025-0.028 in.) thick gasket.

IGNITION. Early models are equipped with a breaker-point type flywheel magneto ignition system while later models use a breakerless electronic ignition system.

Breaker-point gap should be 0.38 mm (0.015 in.) on models so equipped. Ignition timing is fixed on all models but breaker-point gap on applicable models should be set correctly or timing will be affected. On all models, air gap between flywheel magnets and ignition coil legs should be 0.38 mm (0.015 in.).

LUBRICATION. The engine is lubricated by mixing oil with gasoline. Recommended oil is Jonsered engine oil or a BIA certified air-cooled two-stroke engine oil approved for 40:1 fuel mixtures. Recommended fuel mixture ratio is 40:1 when using an approved engine oil. If a recommended oil is not available,

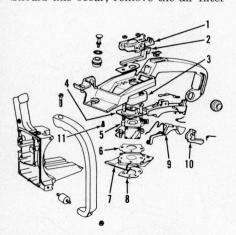

Fig. J19 – Exploded view of vibration isolated handles and air intake components used on 361AV models.

1. Choke retainer
2. Choke
3. Air filter connector
4. Connector guide
5. Carburetor
6. Gasket
7. Heat shield
8. Gasket
9. Throttle trigger
10. Throttle lock
11. Contact spring

Fig. J20 – Exploded view of early model engine assembly. Spacer (22), spring seat (23), spring (24) and pulse valve (25) are absent on Models 365 and 370. Washers (8) are absent on Model 370.

2. Crankcase
3. Crankshaft
4. Roller bearing
5. Connecting rod
7. Needle bearing
8. Washer
9. Retaining ring
10. Seal
11. Thrust washer
12. Bearing
13. Clutch drum
15. Clutch assy.
16. Cylinder
17. Ignition coil
18. Piston
19. Piston pin
20. Piston pin
21. Pin retainer
22. Spacer
23. Spring seat
24. Spring
25. Pulse valve

a good quality oil designed for air-cooled two-stroke engines may be used when mixed with the fuel at a 20:1 ratio.

Models 361 and 361AV are equipped with automatic and manual chain oil pumps. Models 365 and 370 are equipped with an automatic chain oil pump only. A good quality chain oil should be used with viscosity chosen according to ambient temperature. Automatic oil pump output is not adjustable.

CARBON. Carbon should be removed from exhaust system and cylinder periodically. Loose carbon should not be allowed to enter cylinder and care should be taken not to damage cylinder or piston.

REPAIRS

CYLINDER, PISTON, PIN AND RINGS. Cylinder (16–Fig. J20) on all models is also upper crankcase half. Crankshaft is loose in crankcase when cylinder is removed. Care must be taken not to nick or scratch crankcase mating surfaces during disassembly.

Cylinder head is integral with cylinder and cylinder must be removed to remove piston. Piston is equipped with a single piston ring and floating type piston pin (20). Later models are equipped with a needle bearing in connecting rod small end. On later models, piston and connecting rod are available as a unit

assembly only. On all models, piston and ring are available in standard size only. Cylinder bore is chrome and should be inspected to determine if chrome is scored, peeling or excessively worn. Renew cylinder and piston if damaged or excessively worn.

Refer to CRANKSHAFT section for proper assembly of crankcase and cylinder.

CONNECTING ROD. To remove connecting rod, remove cylinder (16–Fig. J20). Note that cylinder is also upper crankcase half and crankshaft assembly is loose when cylinder is removed. Connecting rod (5) is one-piece and supported on crankpin by 11 loose

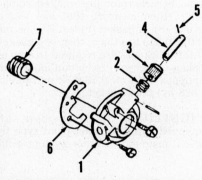

Fig. J22 – Exploded view of automatic oil pump used on Models 365 and 370.

1. Housing	
2. Spring	5. Pin
3. Driven gear	6. Gasket
4. Plunger	7. Worm gear

Fig. J23 – Exploded view of breaker-point ignition and rewind starter. Model 370 is equipped with one pawl (5).

1. Stator plate
2. Cover
3. Flywheel
4. Spring
5. Pawl
6. Pivot pin
7. Washer
8. Nut
9. Snap ring
10. Thrust washer
11. Rope pulley
12. Rewind spring
13. Bushing
14. Starter housing

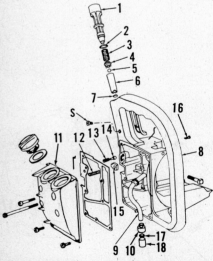

Fig. J21 – Exploded view of manual oil pump and front housing used on later Models 361 and 361AV. Duckbill type valve (16) is used instead of early model valve components (22, 23, 24 and 25) shown in Fig. J20.

1. Piston	10. Fuel pickup
2. "O" ring	11. Front cover
3. Spring	12. Spring
4. Spring seat	13. Spring
5. Ball	14. Oil outlet valve
6. Pump body	15. Nut
7. Screen	16. Pressure check valve
8. Front housing	17. Secondary filter
9. Fuel hose	18. Fuel filter

Fig. J24 – Exploded view of chain brake assembly used on all models except 370.

1. Clutch cover
2. Pivot pin
3. Trip lever
4. Stop plate
5. Brake band
6. Spring
7. Detent cover
8. Cap screws

bearing rollers (4). Be careful not to lose loose rollers that may fall out during disassembly. Rollers can be removed by sliding rod off rollers. To install rod, hold rollers in place with heavy grease or petroleum jelly and position rod over rollers. Be sure rollers do not fall out during assembly of crankcase.

CRANKSHAFT AND SEALS. Crankshaft is supported by needle roller bearings (7–Fig. J20) at both ends. Crankshaft assembly may be removed after removing stator plate, clutch and cylinder assemblies. Care should be taken when removing cylinder as crankshaft will be loose in crankcase and connecting rod may slide off bearing rollers allowing them to fall into crankcase.

Before reassembling crankcases, apply a light coat of nonhardening sealant to crankcase mating surface. Be sure mating surfaces are not damaged during assembly. Retaining rings (9) must fit in ring grooves of crankcase and cylinder.

CLUTCH. A two-shoe centrifugal type clutch is used on all models. Clutch hub has left hand thread. Clutch bearing (12–Fig. J20) should be inspected for excessive wear or damage. Inspect clutch shoes and drum for signs of excessive wear or damage due to overheating.

OIL PUMP. Models 361 and 361AV are equipped with a manual oil pump and automatic oiling system. Refer to Fig. J21 for exploded view of manual oil

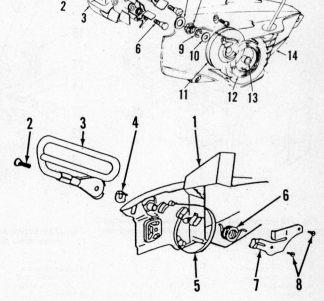

pump. Models 365 and 370 are equipped with an automatic oil pump only. Automatic oiling on Models 361 and 361AV is accomplished by crankcase pulsations which pressurize oil tank and force oil to bar. A one-way valve (25–Fig. J20 on early Models 361 and 361AV or 16–Fig. J21 on later models) prevents oil from entering crankcase.

NOTE: Early and late crankcase (2–Fig. J20) may not be interchanged unless valve type is also changed.

Models 365 and 370 are equipped with an automatic oil pump driven by worm gear (7–Fig. J22) on flywheel side of crankshaft. Oil pump output is not adjustable.

REWIND STARTER. Refer to Fig. J23 for exploded view of pawl type starter used on all models except 370. Model 370 is similar. Care should be taken if necessary to remove rewind spring (12) to prevent spring from uncoiling uncontrolled. Rewind spring (12) should be wound in clockwise direction in housing. On later models, rewind spring is contained in a cassette making

it unnecessary to uncoil spring during removal or installation. Wind starter rope in clockwise direction around rope pulley (11) as viewed in starter housing (14).

Check clearance between starter pawls (5) and head on pivot pin (6). Clearance should not exceed 0.5 mm (0.02 in.). Excessive clearance may cause premature wear of pawl engagement areas on rope pulley and unsatifactory operation during engine starting. Tight-

en pawls by carefully tapping pivot pins into the flywheel.

CHAIN BRAKE. A chain brake which can stop the saw chain quickly is available as an option on all models. It is necessary to unlock the brake before removing or installing clutch cover (1–Fig. J24 or 5–Fig. J24A). Sawdust and debris should be cleaned from around the brake mechanism as needed to ensure proper operation of chain brake.

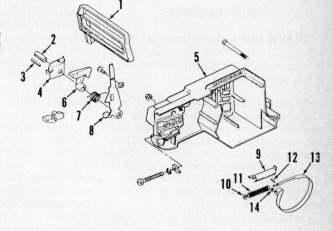

Fig. J24A — Exploded view of chain brake assembly used on Model 370.

1. Guard
2. Roll pin
3. Roll pin
4. Detent cover
5. Clutch cover
6. Inertia weight
7. Spring
8. Lever
9. Cover
10. Washer
11. Spring
12. Roll pin
13. Brake band
14. Pin

JONSERED

Model	Bore	Stroke	Displ.	Drive Type
510SP, 520SP	44 mm (1.732 in.)	32 mm (1.26 in.)	49 cc (3.0 cu. in.)	Direct
455	42 mm (1.65 in.)	32 mm (1.26 in.)	44.3 cc (2.7 cu. in.)	Direct
535	45 mm (1.77 in.)	32 mm (1.26 in.)	50.9 cc (3.1 cu. in.)	Direct

MAINTENANCE

SPARK PLUG. Recommended spark plug is Bosch WS7F for all models. Recommended spark plug electrode gap is 0.5 mm (0.020 in.).

CARBURETOR. Models 510SP and 520SP are equipped with a Tillotson HK diaphragm carburetor. Models 455 and 535 are equipped with a Walbro HDA diaphragm carburetor. Refer to Tillotson or Walbro section of CARBURETOR SERVICE section for exploded views and overhaul of carburetor.

Carburetors used on later 510SP models and all 520SP models are equipped with an additional jet (J – Fig. J25) located in the main fuel discharge port (P). The extra jet provides a more efficient fuel:air mixture through the carburetor venturi and stabilizes engine idle speed. Jet is available from the manufacturer and can be installed in early production 510SP model carburetors as follows: Remove carburetor from saw, then refer to exploded view of Tillotson HK type carburetor in CARBURETOR SERVICE section for parts identification. Invert carburetor and remove diaphragm cover plate and related components. Remove clip (C) from main fuel discharge port (P) and withdraw screen (S). Press jet into main fuel discharge port then reinstall screen and clip. The remainder of reassembly is the reverse of disassembly.

On all models, fuel tank vent hose and carburetor hoses should be routed as shown in Fig. J26. If hoses require renewal, they should be cut to the proper length to avoid kinked and pinched hoses. Recommended lengths are: fuel hose (F – Fig. J26) 120 mm (4.7 in.); pulse hose (P) 105 mm (4.1 in.); vent hose (V) 190 mm (7.5 in.).

Initial carburetor adjustment of both high and low speed mixture screws is one turn open from a lightly seated position. Make final adjustment with engine warm and running. Adjust idle speed screw so engine idles just below clutch engagement speed. Adjust low speed mixture screw so engine will accelerate cleanly without hesitation. Adjust high speed mixture screw to obtain optimum performance under cutting load.

IGNITION. A breakerless capacitor discharge ignition system is used on all models. Ignition timing is fixed. Individual electronic components are not available separately and must be serviced as a unit assembly. Air gap between flywheel magnets and ignition module core should be 0.30-0.40 mm (0.012-0.016 in.).

LUBRICATION. The engine is lubricated by mixing oil with the fuel. Recommended oil is Jonsered engine oil or a BIA certified air-cooled two-stroke engine oil approved for 40:1 fuel mixtures.

Recommended fuel mixture ratio is 40:1 when using an approved engine oil. If a recommended engine oil is not available, a good quality oil designed for air-cooled two-stroke engines may be used when mixed with the fuel at a 20:1 ratio. Use a separate container when mixing the oil and gas.

The chain is lubricated by oil from an automatic chain oil pump. Oil pump output on Models 510SP and 535SP is not adjustable. Oil pump output on Models 455 and 535 is adjustable by rotating screw (35 – Fig. J29) located on bottom

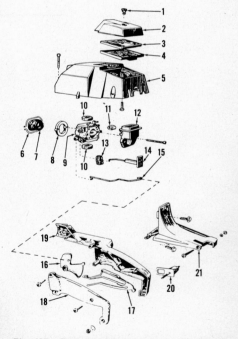

Fig. J27 — Exploded view of air box and throttle control assembly used on 520SP models. Air box components used on 510SP, 455 and 535 models are similar.

1. Nut
2. Filter cover
3. Upper air filter half
4. Lower air filter half
5. Engine cover
6. Clamp
7. Intake manifold
8. Mounting flange
9. Carburetor
10. Carburetor support
11. Mixture screw cover
12. Air filter connector
13. Grommet
14. Choke knob & link
15. Throttle link
16. Trigger
17. Trigger lock
18. Handle cover
19. Handle
20. Vibration isolator
21. Rear handle support

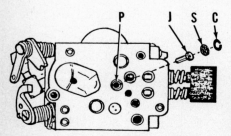

Fig. J25 — View of carburetor body showing location of jet (J) used on later 510SP model and all 520 SP model carburetors.

Fig. J26 — Fuel tank vent hose (V), pulse hose (P) and fuel supply hose (F) should be routed as illustrated.

of saw. Clean automotive oil may be used. Oil viscosity should be chosen according to ambient temperature.

Refer to OIL PUMP section for service information.

CARBON. Carbon deposits should be removed from muffler and exhaust ports at regular intervals. When scraping carbon, be careful not to damage engine cylinder. Do not allow loosened carbon into cylinder.

REPAIRS

CYLINDER, PISTON, PIN AND RINGS. The piston is accessible after removing the cylinder assembly. Piston is fitted with one piston ring. A locating pin is present in piston ring groove to prevent piston ring rotation. Oversize pistons and rings are not available. Piston, piston pin and cylinder are renewable as matched sets only. All models have needle type piston pin bearings. Install piston so arrow on piston crown points toward exhaust port.

On later 510SP models, the base flange on cylinder (2–Fig. J28) has been increased in thickness from 8 mm (0.315 in.) to 17.5 mm (0.689 in.) and the cylinder retaining bolts (1) lengthened from 60 mm (2.36 in.) to 70 mm (2.75 in.). Whenever cylinder assembly is renewed, measure cylinder base flange thickness to ensure proper retaining bolt length.

CONNECTING ROD, CRANKSHAFT AND CRANKCASE. Connecting rod is equipped with a needle bearing in small end. A roller bearing supports the connecting rod on the crankpin while the crankshaft rides in two ball bearings. Connecting rod and crankshaft are not available separately and must be serviced as a unit assembly.

To remove the crankshaft assembly, first remove the cylinder and piston assembly, then carefully pry upper crankcase half (8–Fig. J28 or Fig. J29) loose from lower crankcase half (18). Invert upper crankcase half to disconnect oil pressure hose (28–Fig. J28). On some early models, oil supply line (22) is connected directly to upper crankcase half and requires removal of oil pickup (23) so line may be pulled through opening in lower crankcase half. On all models, withdraw crankcase assembly from lower crankcase half.

Oil pump drive gear (13–Fig. J28 or Fig. J29) should be removed using special tool 504915505. Main bearings (14 and 15) may be removed with a suitable puller. Check rotation of connecting rod around crankpin and renew crankshaft unit if roughness or other damage is found. Carefully clean and inspect crankcase half mating surfaces, removing any burrs or nicks that may prevent an airtight seal.

Press main bearings on crankshaft until bottomed against bearing seats. Install oil pump drive gear on flywheel side of crankshaft using special tool 504905602. Apply a suitable high temperature grease on lips of crankshaft seals (12 and 17), then install locating washer (16) and crankshaft seals on crankshaft. Open side of seals should be facing each other. Place assembled crankshaft into lower crankcase half. Apply a thin coat of room temperature vulcanizing (RTV) silicone sealer on lower crankcase half, then install upper crankcase half. Position new cylinder base gasket (3) on crankcase. Base gas-

Fig. J28 – Exploded view of typical engine assembly used on 510SP and 520SP models.

1. Bolt	18. Lower crankcase half
2. Cylinder	19. Pin
3. Gasket	20. "O" ring
4. Piston ring	21. Oil pump plunger
5. Piston	22. Oil supply hose
6. Retainer	23. Oil pickup
7. Piston pin	24. Crankcase pulse hose
8. Upper crankcase half	25. Clamp
9. Bearing	26. Oil pressure line
10. Crankshaft & rod assy.	27. Grommet
11. Key	28. Oil pressure hose
12. Seal	29. Fitting
13. Oil pump drive gear	30. Oil tank vent
14. Main bearing	31. Fuel tank vent hose
15. Main bearing	32. Fuel pickup
16. Locating washer	33. Fuel hose
17. Seal	34. Clamp

Fig. J29 – Exploded view of engine assembly used on Models 455 and 535.

1. Bolt	19. Washer
2. Cylinder	20. "O" rings
3. Gasket	21. Oil pump plunger
4. Piston ring	22. Oil supply hose
5. Piston & pin assy.	23. Oil pickup
6. Retainer	24. Crankcase pulse hose
7. Bearing	25. Clamp
8. Upper crankcase half	26. Oil pressure line
9. Bearing	27. Grommet
10. Crankshaft & connecting rod assy.	28. Fuel cap
	29. Fitting
11. Key	30. Oil tank vent
12. Seal	31. Fuel tank vent hose
13. Oil pump drive gear	32. Fuel pickup
14. Main bearing	33. Fuel hose
15. Main bearing	34. Clamp
16. Locating washer	35. Oil pump adjuster
17. Seal	36. Oil pump retainer
18. Lower crankcase half	37. Spring

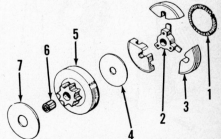

Fig. J30 – Exploded view of clutch assembly used on all models.

1. Spring	
2. Hub	5. Clutch drum
3. Shoe	6. Bearing
4. Washer	7. Washer

ket should be installed without sealer. Remainder of reassembly is the reverse of disassembly.

CLUTCH. Refer to Fig. J30 for exploded view of clutch assembly. To remove clutch, prevent flywheel rotation by removing the spark plug and inserting a loop of rope into the cylinder. Unscrew clutch hub (2) in clockwise direction as shown by arrow on hub.

Inspect clutch shoes (3) and drum (5) for signs of excessive heat. Clutch shoes should be renewed only as a set. Clutch bearing (6) should be inspected for excessive wear or damage. Lubricate clutch bearing with a lithium base grease prior to reassembly.

OIL PUMP. All models are equipped with an automatic oil pump driven by gear (13–Fig. J28 or Fig. J29) on crankshaft. Oil is pumped by plunger (21) as it rotates in pump bore. Oil pump output is not adjustable on Models 510SP and 520SP.

To obtain access to oil pump components on Models 510SP and 520SP, upper crankcase half (8–Fig. J28) must be removed as outlined in CONNECTING ROD, CRANKSHAFT AND CRANKCASE section. Remove pin (19) to withdraw plunger (21) from upper gearcase half.

On later models, pin (19) has been replaced with a cap screw and "O" ring seal. Early models can be changed to accept plunger retaining cap screw part 504020035 and "O" ring seal part 740420200 as follows: With pin and

plunger removed from upper crankcase half, enlarge pin bore using a 4.3 mm diameter drill bit, then thread a 5 mm tap into hole. Thoroughly clean upper crankcase half ensuring all metal particles have been removed before reassembly.

During reassembly make certain oil pressure hose (28) does not become pinched which can restrict oil delivery. Oil pressure hose length should be 85 mm (3.35 in.).

Models 455 and 535 are equipped with an adjustable automatic chain oil pump. Pump output is adjusted by rotating adjuster (35–Fig. J29) located on bottom of saw. Oil is pumped by plunger (21) which is driven by gear (13).

To disassemble pump, remove oil pump retainer (36). Using a suitable tool with a hooked end, withdraw adjuster (35), plunger (21), washer (19) and spring (37). Inspect "O" rings (20) for cracking or hardening. Inspect adjuster and plunger for excessive wear or other damage. Renew components as needed.

REWIND STARTER. Refer to Fig. J31 for an exploded view of starter assembly. To disassemble starter, first remove starter housing from saw. Pull starter rope and hold rope pulley with notch in pulley adjacent to rope outlet. Pull rope back through outlet so it engages notch in pulley and allow pulley to completely unwind. Unscrew pulley retaining screw and carefully withdraw rope pulley. If required, rewind spring and spring cassette (10 and 11) may now be renewed.

Reassemble starter components by reversing disassembly procedure while noting the following: Rope is wound on rope pulley in clockwise direction as viewed with pulley in housing. To place tension on rewind spring, pass rope through rope outlet in housing and install rope handle. Pull rope out and hold rope pulley so notch on pulley is adjacent to rope outlet. Pull rope back through outlet between notch in pulley and housing. Turn rope pulley clockwise to place tension on spring. Release pulley and check starter action. It should be possible to rotate rope pulley ½-turn clockwise with rope fully extended. Do not place more tension on rewind spring than is necessary to draw rope handle against housing.

CHAIN BRAKE. Some models may be equipped with a chain brake system designed to stop chain movement should kickback occur. The chain brake is activated when the operator's hand strikes the chain brake lever (1–Fig. J32) moving trigger (2) thereby forcing actuating lever (6) to release spring (10). Spring then draws brake band (11) tight around clutch drum to stop chain. Pull back chain brake lever to reset mechanism. Lightly lubricate actuating lever (6), inner cover plate (7) and trigger (2) with Molykote or equivalent grease when reassembling. No adjustment of brake mechanism is required.

Disassembly for repair or renewal of individual components is evident after inspection of unit and referral to Fig. J32.

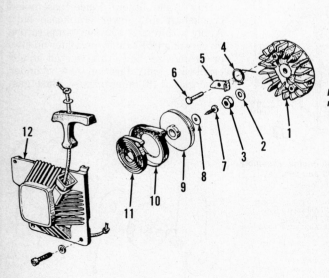

Fig. J31 – Exploded view of rewind starter assembly used on all models.

1. Flywheel
2. Washer
3. Flywheel nut
4. Spring
5. Pawl
6. Pin
7. Screw
8. Washer
9. Rope pulley
10. Rewind spring cassette
11. Rewind spring
12. Starter housing

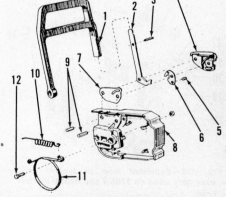

Fig. J32 – Exploded view of chain brake assembly used on some models.

1. Chain brake lever
2. Trigger
3. Roll pin
4. Outer cover plate
5. Pin
6. Actuating lever
7. Inner cover plate
8. Housing
9. Roll pin
10. Spring
11. Brake band
12. Cap screw

JONSERED

Model	Bore	Stroke	Displ.	Drive Type
625, 630 Super	48 mm (1.89 in.)	34 mm (1.34 in.)	61.5 cc (3.75 cu. in.)	Direct
670	50 mm (1.97 in.)	34 mm (1.34 in.)	66.8 cc (4.1 cu. in.)	Direct

MAINTENANCE

SPARK PLUG. Recommended spark plug is Bosch WS7F. Recommended spark plug electrode gap is 0.5 mm (0.020 in.).

CARBURETOR. A Tillotson HS diaphragm type carburetor is used. Refer to Tillotson section of CARBURETOR SERVICE section for exploded views and overhaul of carburetor.

Initial carburetor adjustment is 1¼ turn open from a lightly seated position for both low and high speed mixture screws. Make final adjustment with engine warm and running. Adjust idle speed screw so engine idles just below clutch engagement speed. Adjust low speed mixture screw so engine will accelerate cleanly without hesitation. Adjust high speed mixture screw to obtain optimum performance under cutting load.

IGNITION. All models are equipped with an electronic breakerless ignition system. Ignition timing is not adjustable. Air gap between trigger module (2–Fig. J34) and flywheel magnets should be 0.3-0.4 mm (0.012-0.016 in.).

LUBRICATION. The engine is lubricated by mixing oil with the fuel. Recommended oil is Jonsered engine oil or a BIA certified air-cooled two-stroke engine oil approved for 40:1 fuel mixtures. Recommended fuel mixture is 40:1 when using an approved engine oil. If a recommended engine oil is not available, a good quality oil designed for air-cooled two-stroke engines may be used

when mixed with the fuel at a 20:1 ratio. Use a separate container when mixing the oil and gas.

All models are equipped with an adjustable automatic chain oil pump. Adjustment is possible without clutch removal. Turn screw (S – Fig. J35) for desired oil output – position "1" is minimum, position "4" is maximum.

REPAIRS

PISTON, PIN, RINGS AND CYLINDER. Cylinder bore is chrome plated and should be inspected for excessive wear and damage to bore surface. Inspect piston and discard if excessive wear or damage is evident. Oversize pistons are not available.

Piston must be installed with arrow on piston crown pointing toward exhaust port. Piston on Model 630 is equipped with two piston rings. Piston on Models 625 and 670 is equipped with one piston ring. A locating pin is present in piston ring grooves to prevent piston ring rotation. Be sure ring end gap is around locating pin when installing cylinder.

Fig. J34 – Exploded view of electronic ignition components.

1. Flywheel
2. Trigger module
3. Ignition coil
4. Stop switch

Fig. J35 – View of oil pump with clutch removed. Oil pump adjusting screw (S) is set at position "2."

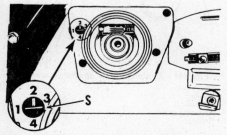

Fig. J36 – Exploded view of engine assembly. Models 625 and 670 are equipped with one piston ring (3).

1. Cylinder
2. Gasket
3. Piston rings
4. Piston & pin assy.
5. Piston pin retainer
6. Crankshaft assy.
7. Needle bearings
8. Ball bearing
9. Right crankcase half
10. Gasket
11. Left crankcase half
12. Seal
13. "O" ring
14. Seal housing
15. Hose
16. Oil strainer
17. Oil tank vent

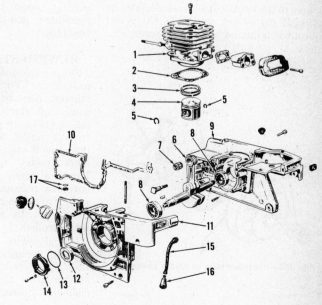

CONNECTING ROD, CRANK-SHAFT AND CRANKCASE. Connecting rod is equipped with a needle bearing in small end. Crankshaft and connecting rod are a unit assembly. It will be necessary to heat crankcase halves to remove or install crankshaft and main bearings. Care should be taken not to damage mating surfaces of crankcase halves. Check rotation of connecting rod around crankpin and renew crankshaft unit if roughness or other damage is found.

When reassembling crankshaft and crankcase halves, install main bearings allowing for installation of oil pump on drive side and crankshaft seal housing on flywheel side. A special tool is available from the manufacturer to properly position main bearings and crankshaft in crankcase. Tighten crankcase screws to 7-8 N·m (61-69 in.-lbs.). Make certain crankshaft is centered in crankcase and will rotate freely.

CLUTCH. A three-shoe centrifugal clutch is used. Clutch hub has left-hand threads. Inspect clutch shoes and drum for excessive wear or damage due to overheating. Clean and inspect clutch hub, drum and bearing for damage or excessive wear. Inspect clutch bearing lubrication hole in crankshaft end and clutch bearing contact surface on crankshaft for wear or damage.

The oil pump is driven by the clutch drum. Be sure notches on rear of clutch drum mesh with dogs of oil pump drive gear when installing clutch assembly.

AUTOMATIC OIL PUMP. All models are equipped with an automatic oil pump which is driven by the clutch drum. Notches on the back of the clutch drum engage dogs on oil pump drive gear (1 – Fig. J38) which rides on the crankshaft. The oil pump drive gear engages driven gear (6) which is secured to plunger (5) by set screw (7). Oil pump output is adjusted by turning screw (S).

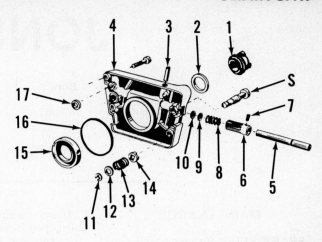

Fig. J38 – Exploded view of automatic oil pump.

S. Adjusting screw
1. Drive gear
2. Washer
3. Pin
4. Pump housing
5. Plunger
6. Driven gear
7. Set screw
8. Spring
9. Steel washer
10. Brass washer
11. "E" ring
12. Washer
13. Spring
14. Washer
15. Seal
16. "O" ring
17. Seal

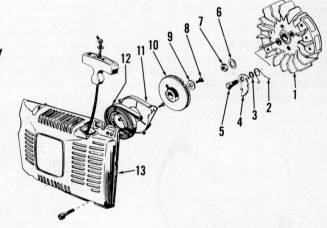

Fig. J40 – Exploded view of rewind starter assembly.

1. Flywheel
2. Pawl spring
3. Washer
4. Pawl
5. Pivot pin
6. Washer
7. Nut
8. Screw
9. Washer
10. Rope pulley
11. Spring cover
12. Rewind spring
13. Starter housing

To remove oil pump, first remove the clutch, chain, guide bar and oil pump retaining cap screws. Using two suitable screwdrivers, insert blade tips into notches provided in pump housing and carefully withdraw oil pump. To reinstall, manufacturer recommends placing special tool 502 50 53 01 over crankshaft end to prevent damage to oil seal (15).

REWIND STARTER. Refer to Fig. J40 for exploded view of rewind starter assembly. To disassemble rewind starter, remove starter housing from saw. Pull starter rope and hold rope pulley (10) with notch in pulley adjacent to rope outlet. Pull rope back through outlet so it engages notch in pulley and allow pulley to completely unwind. Unscrew pulley retaining screw (8) and carefully remove rope pulley. If rewind spring must be removed, care should be taken not to allow spring to uncoil uncontrolled.

Install rewind spring in starter housing with spring coiled in clockwise direction from outer spring end. Wrap starter rope around rope pulley in a clockwise direction as viewed with

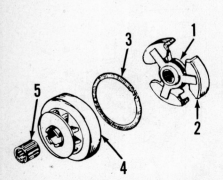

Fig. J37 – Exploded view of clutch assembly.

1. Hub
2. Shoe
3. Spring
4. Drum
5. Bearing

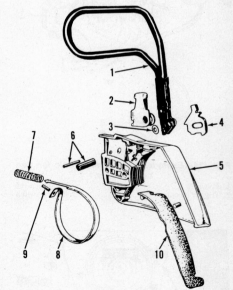

Fig. J41 – Exploded view of chain brake.

1. Chain brake lever
2. Sleeve
3. Washer
4. Actuating plate
5. Housing
6. Roll pin
7. Spring
8. Brake band
9. Pin
10. Chain guard

pulley in starter housing. Turn rope pulley two turns clockwise before passing rope through rope outlet to place tension on rewind spring. Spring tension is correct if rope pulley can be rotated approximately ½ turn further when rope is pulled completely out.

When installing starter assembly on saw, make sure starter pulley properly engages pawls on flywheel before tightening retaining cap screws.

CHAIN BRAKE. All models are equipped with a chain brake system designed to stop chain movement should kickback occur. Chain brake is activated when the operator's hand strikes the chain brake lever thereby forcing actuating plate (4 – Fig. J41) off of pin in housing releasing spring (7). Spring then draws brake band tight around clutch drum to stop chain. Pull back chain brake lever to reset mechanism. No adjustment of brake mechanism is required.

If brake requires disassembly for repair or renewal of individual components, it is recommended that a clutch drum be inserted in brake band and brake engaged, to facilitate removal of brake lever. When reassembling, make certain spring (7) is screwed completely on brake band and roll pins (6) are installed with split side toward front of saw.

HANDLE HEATER. Some models may be equipped with the handle heat-

ing system shown in Fig. J42. A generating coil (1) located under the flywheel produces an electric current which flows in series to the front handle (2), rear handle halves (3 and 5), heater control switch (6) and then grounded at the ignition stop switch (7) to complete the circuit.

The heating system may be tested using a suitable ohmmeter. Separate the wire connection from heater control switch (6) to ignition stop switch (7) and attach a tester lead to the wire. Ground other tester lead to the saw. Heating system may be considered satisfactory if tester reads 5-6 ohms resistance.

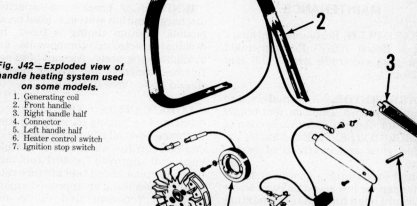

Fig. J42 – Exploded view of handle heating system used on some models.

1. Generating coil
2. Front handle
3. Right handle half
4. Connector
5. Left handle half
6. Heater control switch
7. Ignition stop switch

JONSERED

Model	Bore	Stroke	Displ.	Drive Type
820, 830	52 mm (2.047 in.)	38 mm (1.496 in.)	80.7 cc (4.9 cu. in.)	Direct
910E, 910EV, 920, 930 Super	54 mm (2.126 in.)	38 mm (1.496 in.)	87 cc (5.3 cu. in.)	Direct

MAINTENANCE

SPARK PLUG. Recommended spark plug is Bosch WS7F. Recommended spark plug electrode gap is 0.5 mm (0.020 in.).

CARBURETOR. All models are equipped with a Tillotson diaphragm carburetor. Refer to Tillotson section of CARBURETOR SERVICE section for exploded view and overhaul of carburetor.

Initial carburetor adjustment is 1¼ turns open for low speed mixture screw and 1 turn open for high speed mixture screw. Make final carburetor adjustment with engine warm and running. Adjust idle speed screw so engine idles just below clutch engagement speed. Adjust low speed mixture screw so engine will accelerate cleanly without hesitation. Adjust high speed mixture screw to obtain optimum performance under cutting load.

IGNITION. A breakerless capacitor discharge ignition system is used on all models. Ignition timing is fixed. Individual electronic components are available separately. Air gap between flywheel magnets and trigger module should be 0.3 mm (0.012 in.).

LUBRICATION. The engine is lubricated by mixing oil with the fuel. Recommended oil is Jonsered engine oil or a BIA certified air-cooled two-stroke engine oil approved for 40:1 fuel mixtures. Recommended fuel mixture ratio is 40:1 when using an approved engine oil. If a recommended oil is not available, a good quaity oil designed for air-cooled two-stroke engines may be used when mixed with the fuel at a 20:1 ratio. Use a separate container when mixing the oil and gas.

All models are equipped with an automatic chain oiler. A good quality chain oil should be used. Viscosity should be chosen according to ambient temperature. Automatic oil pump discharge is adjusted by turning adjusting screw through opening on bottom side of saw. Initial setting is 1½ turns open. Turning screw clockwise decreases oil flow. Models 830 and 930 Super may be equipped with an optional manual chain oil pump.

CARBON. Carbon deposits should be removed from muffler and exhaust ports at regular intervals. When scraping carbon, be careful not to damage engine cylinder. Do not allow loosened carbon into cylinder.

REPAIRS

CYLINDER, PISTON, PIN AND RINGS. Refer to Fig. J44 for exploded view of engine. Cylinder bore is chrome plates and should be inspected for excessive wear and damage to bore surface. Inspect piston and discard if excessive wear or damage is evident. Oversize pistons and rings are not available. Piston and cylinder are renewable as matched sets only. All models have needle type piston pin bearings. Models 910E and 910EV are also equipped with thrust washers on

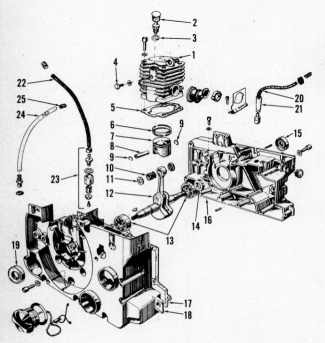

Fig. J44—Exploded view of engine assembly used on 910E and 910EV models. Models 820, 830, 920 and 930 Super are similar.

1. Cylinder
2. Decompression valve
3. Washer
4. Cap screw
5. Gasket
6. Piston rings
7. Piston
8. Piston pin
9. Piston pin retainer
10. Needle bearing
11. Thrust washer
12. Crankshaft assy.
13. Ball bearing
14. Oil pump drive gear
15. Right crankcase half
16. Right crankcase half
17. Gasket
18. Left crankcase half
19. Seal
20. Oil hose
21. Oil strainer
22. Fuel hose
23. Fuel filter assy.
24. Vent hose
25. Fitting

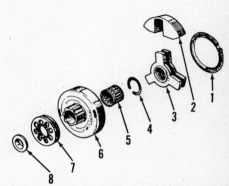

Fig. J45—Exploded view of typical clutch assembly. Ring (4) is not used on 820, 830, 920 and 930 Super models.

1. Spring
2. Shoe
3. Hub
4. Ring
5. Bearing
6. Drum
7. Sprocket
8. Washer

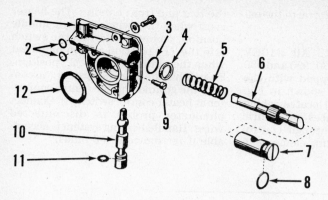

quired, rewind spring and cassette (11 and 12) may now be renewed.

Reassemble starter components by reversing disassembly procedure while noting the following: Rope is wound on rope pulley in clockwise direction as viewed with pulley in housing. To place tension on rewind spring, pass rope through rope outlet in housing and install rope handle. Pull rope out and hold rope pulley so notch on pulley is adjacent to rope outlet. Pull rope back through outlet between notch in pulley and housing. Turn rope pulley clockwise to place tension on spring. Release pulley and check starter action. Do not place more tension on rewind spring than is necessary to draw rope handle up against housing. With rope completely extended, it should be possible to rotate rope pulley an additional ½ turn if spring tension is correct.

CHAIN BRAKE. All models are equipped with a chain brake system designed to stop chain movement should kickback occur. Chain brake is

Fig. J47—Exploded view of automatic oil pump assembly used on all models.

1. Pump body
2. "O" rings
3. "O" ring
4. Washer
5. Spring
6. Plunger
7. Plug
8. "O" ring
9. Screw
10. Adjusting screw
11. "O" ring
12. Seal ring

both sides of connecting rod small end. On all models, install piston so arrow on piston crown points toward exhaust port.

Piston is equipped with two piston rings. A locating pin is present in piston ring grooves to prevent piston ring rotation. Be sure ring end gap is around locating pin when installing cylinder.

CYLINDER ROD, CRANKSHAFT AND CRANKCASE. Connecting rod is equipped with a needle bearing in small end. Crankshaft and connecting rod are a unit assembly. It will be necessary to heat crankcase halves to remove or install crankshaft and main bearings. Care should be taken not to damage mating surfaces of crankcase halves. Check rotation of connecting rod around crankpin and renew crankshaft unit if roughness or other damage is found.

CLUTCH. A three-shoe centrifugal type clutch is used on all models. Refer to Fig. J45 for exploded view of clutch assembly used on 910E and 910EV models. Models 820, 830, 920 and 930 Super clutch is similar. Inspect clutch

shoes and drum for excessive wear or damage due to overheating. Inspect clutch drum, bearing and crankshaft for damage. On 910E and 910EV models, a ring (4) has been installed between the crankshaft and hub (3) to prevent possible crankshaft breakage. Renew ring (4) everytime clutch hub is removed.

AUTOMATIC OIL PUMP. All models are equipped with a crankshaft driven automatic oil pump. Refer to Fig. J47 for exploded view of oil pump.

Oil pump operation is accomplished when plunger (6) is rotated by a worm gear installed on crankshaft. While rotating, the plunger reciprocates as the oblique end of plunger bears against adjuster (10) ball thereby pumping oil. Oil output is changed in turning adjuster (10). The oil pump assembly is accessible after clutch removal.

REWIND STARTER. Refer to Fig. J48 for exploded view of rewind starter assembly. To disassemble rewind starter, remove starter housing from saw. Pull starter rope and hold rope pulley (10) with notch in pulley adjacent to rope outlet. Pull rope back through outlet so it engages notch in pulley and allow pulley to completely unwind. Unscrew pulley retaining screw (7) and carefully remove rope pulley. If re-

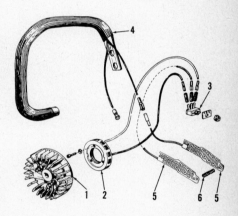

Fig. J50—Exploded view of handle heating system used on all 910EV models and some 820, 830, 920 and 930 Super models.

1. Flywheel
2. Generating coil
3. Heater control switch
4. Front handle
5. Rear handle heating elements
6. Spring connector

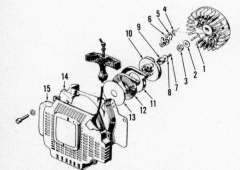

Fig. J48—Exploded view of rewind starter assembly used on all models.

1. Flywheel
2. Washer
3. Nut
4. Spring
5. Pawl
6. Snap ring
7. Screw
8. Washer
9. Bushing
10. Rope pulley
11. Spring cassette
12. Rewind spring
13. Washer
14. Shield
15. Starter housing

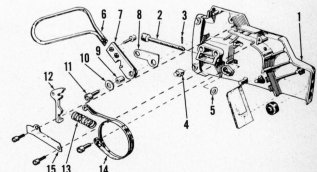

Fig. J49—Exploded view of chain brake.

1. Housing
2. Chain tensioner
3. Pin
4. Adjusting pin
5. Washer
6. Chain brake lever
7. Sleeve
8. Plate
9. Bushing
10. Washer
11. Socket head screw
12. Actuating plate
13. Spring
14. Brake band
15. Cover plate

activated when the operator's hand strikes the chain brake lever thereby forcing actuating plate (12—Fig. J49) off a pin in sleeve (7) releasing spring (13). Spring then draws brake band (14) tight around clutch drum to stop chain. Pull back chain brake lever to reset mechanism. No adjustment of brake mechanism is required.

Disassembly for repair or renewal of individual components is evident after inspection of unit and referral to the exploded view.

HANDLE HEATER. All 910EV models and some 820, 830, 920 and 930 Super models are equipped with the handle heating system shown in Fig. J50. A generating coil (2) located behind the flywheel (1) produces an electric current which flows through control switch and then to heating elements in the rear and front handles. The heater is off when the switch is in the middle position, on low heat when the switch is in the "1" position and on high heat when the switch is in the "2" position. To test handle heating system, disconnect the ground and the center connector at heater control switch (3). Connect ohmmeter probes to disconnected wires. Handle heating system is acceptable if resistance is 5-6 ohms.

JONSERED

Model	Bore	Stroke	Dislp.	Drive Type
490, 590	45 mm (1.77 in.)	32 mm (1.26 in.)	50.8 cc (3.1 cu. in.)	Direct

MAINTENANCE

SPARK PLUG. Recommended spark plug is Bosch WS7F. Recommended electrode gap is 0.5 mm (0.020 in.).

CARBURETOR. All models are equipped with a Walbro WA diaphragm type carburetor. Refer to Walbro section of CARBURETOR SERVICE section for service and exploded views.

Initial adjustment for both high and low speed mixture screws is 1-1/8 turns open from a lightly seated position. Make final adjustment with engine running at operating temperature. Adjust idle speed to just below clutch engagement speed. Adjust low speed mixture so engine will accelerate cleanly without hesitation. Adjust high speed mixture to obtain optimum full throttle performance under cutting load. Do not adjust high speed mixture too lean as overheating and engine damage could result.

IGNITION. A breakerless capacitor discharge ignition system is used on all models. Ignition timing is fixed. All electronic circuitry is contained in a one piece ignition module. Except for faulty wiring connections, repair of ignition system malfunctions is accomplished by component renewal. Air gap between ignition module and flywheel magnets should be 0.30-0.40 mm (0.012-0.016 in.).

LUBRICATION. The engine is lubricated by mixing oil with the fuel. The recommended oil is Jonsered engine oil or a BIA certified air-cooled two-stroke engine oil approved for 40:1 fuel mixtures. Recommended fuel mixture ratio is 40:1 when using an approved oil. If a recommended oil is not available, a good quality oil designed for air-cooled two-stroke engine may be used when mixed with the fuel at a 20:1 ratio.

All models are equipped with an adjustable automatic chain oil pump. A good quality chain oil should be used and viscosity chosen according to am-

bient temperature. Refer to AUTO-MATIC OIL PUMP section for service and adjustment procedures.

CARBON. Carbon deposits should be removed from muffler and exhaust ports at regular intervals. When removing carbon use caution not to damage piston or cylinder. Position piston to block exhaust ports to prevent loosened carbon from entering cylinder.

REPAIRS

CYLINDER, PISTON, PIN AND RINGS. Cylinder bore is chrome plated and should be inspected for cracking, flaking or other damage. Oversize pistons and rings are not available.

Piston must be installed on connecting rod with arrow on piston crown pointing toward exhaust ports. The piston pin rides in a needle roller bearing and is held in place by two wire retainers. Refer to Fig. J55 for exploded view of engine assembly.

The piston is fitted with a locating pin in piston ring groove to prevent ring rotation. Make certain ring end gap is around locating pin when installing cylinder. Tighten cylinder bolts to 9 N·m (80 in.-lbs.).

CONNECTING ROD, CRANKSHAFT AND CRANKCASE. Crankshaft and connecting rod (10—Fig. J55) are a unit assembly and are not available separately. Check rotation of connect-

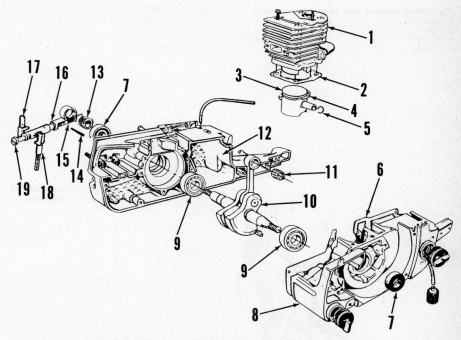

Fig. J55—Exploded view of engine assembly and automatic oil pump.

1. Cylinder
2. Cylinder gasket
3. Piston & pin assy.
4. Piston ring
5. Retainer
6. Gasket
7. Crankcase seal
8. Left crankcase half
9. Main bearing
10. Crankshaft & connecting rod assy.
11. Needle roller bearing
12. Right crankcase half
13. Worm gear
14. Cam pin
15. Plunger
16. Housing
17. Oil discharge hose
18. Oil suction hose
19. Adjusting screw

ing rod around crankpin and renew if roughness, excessive play or other damage is found.

The oil pump worm gear (13) must be removed before crankcase can be separated. The manufacturer recommends using special tool 50538187 (right-hand threads) to remove worm gears on early saws and special tool 502540102 (left-hand threads) to remove worm gears on late model saws. The manufacturer recommends using special tool 502516101 to separate crankcase halves (8 and 12).

To reassemble crankcase, press main bearings (9) onto crankshaft. Heat area around main bearing bore of flywheel side crankcase half (8) and install crankshaft assembly into crankcase half. Heat main bearing bore of clutch side crankcase half and assemble crankcase halves together. Tighten crankcase cap screws to 9 N·m (80 in.-lbs.). Make certain crankshaft turns freely in crankcase. Install crankcase seals flush with crankcase.

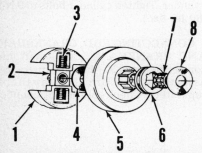

Fig. J56—Exploded view of clutch assembly.
1. Shoe
2. Hub
3. Spring
4. Washer
5. Drum
6. Sprocket
7. Needle roller bearing
8. Washer

CLUTCH. A two-shoe centrifugal clutch is used. Clutch hub (2—Fig. J56) has left-hand threads. Clutch shoes (1) and drum (5) should be inspected for excessive wear or damage due to overheating. Needle roller bearing (7) should be inspected for damage or discoloration and lubricated with Molykote or equivalent high temperature grease. Tighten clutch hub to 35 N·m (25 ft.-lbs.).

AUTOMATIC OIL PUMP. All models are equipped with an adjustable automatic chain oil pump driven by worm gear (13—Fig. J55). Oil is pumped by plunger (15) as it reciprocates due to cam pin (14) riding in operating groove of plunger. Pump output is adjusted by rotating adjusting screw (19).

Inspect discharge (17) and suction (18) hoses for cracking or hardening. Inspect plunger (15), worm gear (13) and cam pin for excessive wear. When installing oil pump, make certain notch in pump housing engages boss in crankcase casting.

REWIND STARTER. All models are equipped with the starter assembly shown in Fig. J57. To disassemble starter, pull out approximately 30 cm (12 in.) of rope and align notch in rope pulley (8) with rope guide (11). Insert rope into notch in pulley and carefully allow pulley to unwind, releasing tension on rewind spring (9). Remove screw (5) and washer (6) and carefully remove pulley. If rewind spring must be removed, depress tabs which secure rewind spring cover to starter housing (10) with a screwdriver or suitable tool.

To reassemble starter, lightly oil rewind spring and install into starter housing. Wind approximately five revolutions of rope onto rope pulley in a clockwise direction as viewed from flywheel side of pulley. Install rope pulley into starter housing and tighten screw (5) to 2.0 N·m (15 in.-lbs.). Pull out length of rope and position rope into notch of pulley. Turn rope pulley clockwise to preload rewind spring. Rope pulley should be able to rotate an additional ½ turn with rope fully extended. Do not place more tension on rewind spring than is necessary to draw rope handle up against housing.

CHAIN BRAKE. Some models are equipped with a chain brake system designed to stop chain movement should kickback occur. The chain brake is activated when operator's hand strikes chain brake lever (1—Fig. J58) tripping actuating plate (4) and allowing spring (7) to draw brake band (8) tight around clutch drum. Pull back chain brake lever to reset mechanism.

Disassembly for repair and component renewal is evident after referral to exploded view and inspection of unit.

When reassembling, make certain spring (7) is screwed completely onto brake band (8) and roll pins (3 and 5) are installed with split sides facing forward.

HANDLE HEATER. Some models are equipped with optional handle

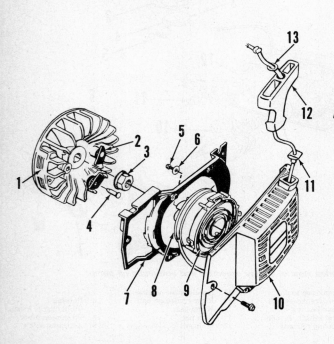

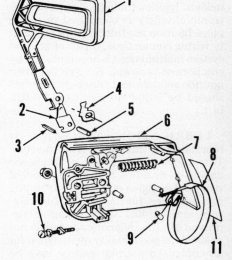

Fig. J57—Exploded view of rewind starter assembly.
1. Flywheel
2. Pawl
3. Nut
4. Pin
5. Screw
6. Washer
7. Shield
8. Rope pulley
9. Rewind spring & cover assy.
10. Housing
11. Rope guide
12. Rope handle
13. Washer

Fig. J58—Exploded view of chain brake system used on some models.
1. Chain brake lever
2. Sleeve
3. Roll pin
4. Actuating plate
5. Roll pin
6. Brake housing
7. Spring
8. Brake band
9. Pin
10. Chain adjuster assy.
11. Chain guard

heating system shown in Fig. J59. Handle heating system utilizes exhaust heat from muffler and directs heat to front and rear handles through heat tubes (5). Front handle temperature is controlled by adjusting screw (9) while rear handle temperature is controlled by adjusting screw (10). Turning adjusting screws completely in shuts off heat.

To service system, remove muffler and disassemble. Clean carbon deposits and soot from muffler (1) and valve assembly (6). Clean heat tubes with manufacturer's special tool 505382908 or equivalent long flexible probe. Inspect heat tubes for cracking or other damage and renew as necessary. Make certain heat tubes are not pinched or rubbing against sharp edges upon reassembly.

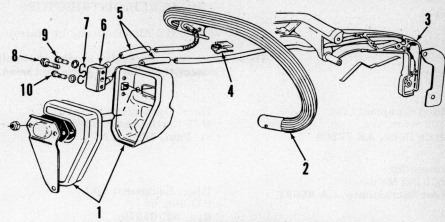

Fig. J59—Exploded view of handle heating system used on some models.

1. Muffler assy.	4. Clip	7. Wire bail	9. Adjuster screw
2. Front handle	5. Heat tubes	8. Cap screw	10. Adjuster screw
3. Rear handle	6. Valve assy.		

JONSERED DISTRIBUTORS

(Arranged Alphabetically by States)

These firms carry extensive stocks of repair parts.
Contact them for the parts you need.

Tilton Equipment Co.
6202 Sears Ave.
Little Rock, AR 72209

Scotsco Inc.
2601 Del Monte
West Sacramento, CA 95691

Scotsco Inc.
6767 East 50th
Commerce City, CO 80022

Tilton Equipment Co.
P.O. Box 1008
1295 Old Alpharetta Road
Alpharetta, GA 30201

Tilton Equipment Co.
1379 Jamike Ave.
Erlanger, KY 41018

Tilton Equipment Co.
4575 North Chatsworth Street
St. Paul, MN 55126

Tilton Equipment Co.
P.O. Box 68
Rye, NH 03870

Scotsco Inc.
9160 South East 74th Ave.
Portland, OR 97206

Tilton Equipment Co.
Lehigh Industrial Park Number One
2147 Ave. C
Bethlehem, PA 18017

CANADA

Josa Corp. Ltd.
Unit 3
1411 Walmont Way
Richmond, B.C. VGV 1Y3

Josa Corp. Ltd.
C.P./Box 5500, 180 Hamford
Lachute, Quebec J8H 4B5

Josa Corp. Ltd.
290 Baig Blvd.
Moncton, N.B. E1E 1C8

Josa Corp. Ltd.
630 Broadway
Cornerbrook, NFLD A2H 4O7

Josa Corp. Ltd.
1151 Russel Street
Thunder Bay, Ontario P7B 5M6

LOMBARD

SPRAY CARE INCORPORATED
4515 Reading Road
Cincinnati, Ohio 45229

Model	Bore	Stroke	Displ.	Drive Type
AP42, AP42-1, AP42SE	1.87 in. (47.5 mm)	1.50 in. (38.1 mm)	4.2 cu. in. (68.8 cc)	Direct
AP42D, AP42AV, AP42DAV	1.87 in. (47.5 mm)	1.50 in. (38.1 mm)	4.2 cu. in. (68.8 cc)	Direct
Comango	1.87 in. (47.5 mm)	1.50 in. (38.1 mm)	4.2 cu. in. (68.8 cc)	Direct
Comango Auto	1.87 in. (47.5 mm)	1.50 in. (38.1 mm)	4.2 in. (68.8 cc)	Direct
Super Comango	1.87 in. (47.5 mm)	1.50 in. (38.1 mm)	4.2 cu. in. (68.8 cc)	Direct
Super Comango Auto	1.87 in. (47.5 mm)	1.50 in. (38.1 mm)	4.2 cu. in. (68.8 cc)	Direct
Lightning II	1.87 in. (47.5 mm)	1.50 in. (38.1 mm)	4.2 cu. in. (68.8 cc)	Direct
Lightning III	1.87 in. (47.5 mm)	1.50 in. (38.1 mm)	4.2 cu. in. (68.8 cc)	Direct

MAINTENANCE

SPARK PLUG. Recommended spark plug is Champion CJ7Y for all the AP prefix models and CJ6 for all other models. Electrode gap should be 0.025 inch (0.63 mm).

CARBURETOR. Refer to CARBURETOR SERVICE section for servicing of Tillotson HS carburetor.

Initial adjustment of carburetor is as follows: Back out throttle stop screw until it no longer contacts throttle shaft lever, then turn stop screw in until it contacts throttle shaft lever and give it an additional ¾ turn. Turn idle and high speed mixture screws in until they seat lightly, then back out idle mixture screw ⅞-1 turn and the high speed mixture screw 1-1⅛ turns.

To make final adjustments, start engine and bring to operating temperature, adjust idle mixture screw until engine idles smoothly, then if necessary, adjust throttle stop screw until engine is operating at 2200-2500 rpm (just below clutch engagement). Following these adjustments, richen the idle mixture slightly (1/16-1/8 turn).

To adjust high speed mixture, load saw (make a cut) and adjust high speed mixture needle until saw operates smoothly, then richen mixture slightly by backing out high speed mixture screw about ⅛-turn.

IGNITION. Early models are equipped with a breaker-point type flywheel magneto ignition system while later models use a breakerless electronic ignition system.

Breaker-Point Models. Ignition timing for Lightning II and III models should be 30 degrees BTDC while ignition timing is fixed on all other models. Breaker-point gap on all models should be 0.015 inch (0.38 mm). Tighten flywheel nut to 190-200 in.-lbs. (21.5-22.6 N·m) torque.

Breakerless Models. Ignition timing is fixed on all models. Air gap between flywheel and ignition module should be 0.015 inch (0.38 mm). Tighten flywheel nut to 190-200 in.-lbs. (21.5-22.6 N·m) torque. Two types of ignition modules are used on later models and are not interchangeable. The module may be identified by its color and if required, must be renewed with the same color module.

LUBRICATION. Engine is lubricated by mixing lubricating oil with gasoline. Use a separate container when mixing the fuel and oil. Mix ½ pint (118 mL) of Lombard two-stroke engine oil (No. 1-1840) or SAE 30 motor oil with each gallon (3.7853 L) of regular gasoline.

Fill chain oil reservoir with SAE 30 motor oil. During cold weather, use lighter oil or dilute the SAE 30 oil up to 50 percent with kerosene as necessary.

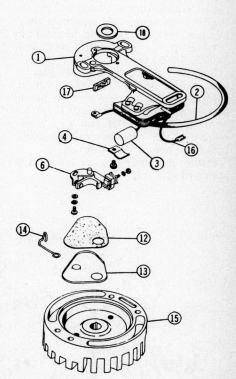

Fig. LO6 — Exploded view showing component parts of breaker-point type magneto used on models with adjustable ignition timing. Models with fixed timing are similar. See text.

1. Stator assy.
2. Coil & leadwire
3. Condenser
4. Clamp
6. Breaker-points
12. Gasket
13. Cover
14. Cover spring
15. Flywheel
16. Switch lead
17. Lubricating felt
18. Crankshaft seal

Clutch drum should be removed after every eight or ten cutting hours and a few drops of SAE 30 oil placed on drum bearing.

CARBON. Muffler and exhaust ports should be cleaned of carbon every thirty hours or less. To clean, remove muffler and turn engine until piston is at bottom of stroke. Use a blunt instrument, or wood scraper and remove all carbon from exhaust ports and surrounding chamber being careful not to damage exhaust ports. Remove spark plug. Shake out loosened particles and crank engine several times to blow out any remaining carbon. Clean muffler, then reinstall the muffler and spark plug.

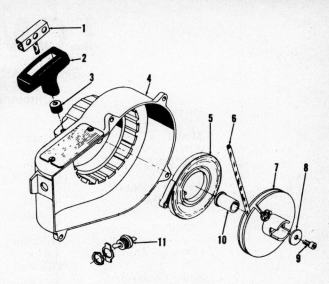

Fig. LO8—Exploded view showing component parts of starter assembly. Starter is mounted on a starter post (shaft) which is an integral part of blower housing.

1. Insert
2. Handle
3. Cushion
4. Blower (starter) housing
5. Rewind spring
6. Cord (rope)
7. Pulley
8. Washer
9. Socket head screw
10. Flange bushing
11. Switch

REPAIRS

PISTON, PIN AND RINGS. All models are fitted with two pinned rings. Standard sizes only are available for all models. Renew piston if clearance between piston skirt and cylinder exceeds 0.008 inch (0.20 mm), measured at right angle to piston pin, or if side clearance of new ring in top ring groove exceeds 0.010 inch (0.25 mm). Also inspect piston for cracks, scoring or loose fit of piston in piston bores. Piston and pin are available as a matched assembly only. Desired clearance between pin and pin bore in piston is 0.0001-0.0002 inch (0.0025-0.0051 mm).

Desired piston ring end gap is 0.008-0.018 inch (0.203-0.457 mm). Desired ring side clearance in piston groove is 0.005-0.008 inch (0.127-0.203 mm). Renew rings if end gap is excessive or side clearance exceeds 0.010 inch (0.25 mm) in new piston.

Piston, pin and rings are available in standard size only.

CYLINDER. Cylinder bore is chrome plated and must not be rebored. Renew cylinder if chrome plating is worn through to expose the softer base metal. Tighten cylinder retaining nuts to 73-83 in.-lbs. (8.2-9.4 N·m) torque.

CONNECTING ROD. Early models are equipped with a removable connecting rod. Late models are equipped with a connecting rod/crankshaft unit assembly which should not be disassembled.

On early models, connecting rod rides on 24 loose bearing rollers which must be renewed as a set. Use grease to hold rollers in place during assembly and place 12 rollers in cap and 12 rollers in rod. Assemble rod to cap with match marks aligned. Be sure surfaces of rod and cap mate properly and tighten rod screws to 60-65 in.-lbs. (6.8-7.3 N·m) torque.

On all models, piston pin is supported in connecting rod by a needle bearing. Bearing should not be removed as bearing and rod are available only as a unit assembly.

CRANKSHAFT. On all models, crankshaft is supported in two caged needle roller bearings except some earlier models which use a ball bearing and a needle roller bearing. Crankshaft end play is controlled by needle roller type thrust bearings. Crankshaft end play should be not less than 0.006 inch (0.15 mm) nor more than 0.027 inch (0.68 mm).

Renew the needle roller main bearings if any needle has flat spots or if rollers can be separated the width of one roller. Press only on lettered end of bearing during installation. If equipped with a ball bearing, inspect ball bearing for wear, pitting or scoring.

Renew crankshaft if any of the bearing surfaces are worn, scored or burned. Also check keyways and threads for signs of wear or damage.

CRANKSHAFT OIL SEALS. It is important that crankcase seals be maintained in good condition or loss of crankcase pressure and engine power will result.

Use extreme caution to prevent damage to seals during installation. If a sleeve installation tool is not available, use tape to cover any splines, shoulders or threads which the seals must pass over.

REED VALVE. The reed valve assembly can be removed after removing carburetor and air box. A flat reed valve assembly and a pyramid reed valve assembly have been used. Renew reeds if cracked or worn and be sure reeds are centered over openings of reed plate. Use all new gaskets during installation.

CLUTCH. The two-shoe centrifugal clutch (30—Fig. LO9) is threaded to

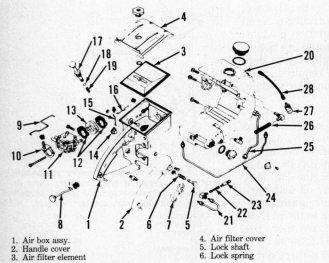

Fig. LO7—View showing typical air box and throttle handle assembly.

7. Throttle trigger
8. Choke lever
9. Throttle link
10. Cover bracket
11. Carburetor
12. Gasket
13. Spacer
14. Oil valve
15. Pull link
16. Push link
17. Oil pump assy.
18. "O" ring
19. Spring
20. Fuel & oil tank
21. Oil inlet line
22. Oil pickup tube
23. Oil pickup
24. Oil outlet line
25. Oil line
26. Fuel line
27. Fuel pickup
28. Fuel pickup tube

1. Air box assy.
2. Handle cover
3. Air filter element
4. Air filter cover
5. Lock shaft
6. Lock spring

crankshaft and is removed by locking crankshaft and turning clutch assembly in a clockwise direction.

If clutch slips under load at engine high speed, check for excessive wear of clutch shoes. If clutch will not disengage (chain creeps) at engine idle speed, check for broken, weak or distorted clutch springs.

Sprocket (drum) bushing is renewable and the drum should be removed after every eight or ten cutting hours and a few drops of SAE 30 oil placed on the bushing. Do not overlubricate bushing as excess oil could result in the clutch slipping.

STARTER. To disassemble starter, remove blower housing, then refer to Fig. LO8 and proceed as follows: Pull starter rope out fully, hold pulley and pry rope knot from pulley, then let pulley rewind slowly. Hold pulley and remove screw (9). Lift pulley and bushing (10) from starter post. Spring (5) can now be removed from housing but use caution as the rapidly uncoiling spring could cause injury.

Install spring in blower housing with loop in outer end over pin in blower housing and be sure spring is coiled in direction shown. Install bushing and spring and turn pulley clockwise until it engages spring. Insert new rope through handle and hole in blower housing. Knot both ends of rope and harden

the knots with heat or cement. Turn pulley eight turns clockwise and slide knot into slot of pulley and let pulley rewind slowly.

Starter pawls can be removed from flywheel after blower housing and starter assembly is removed and procedure is obvious.

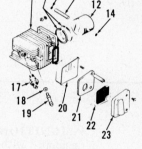
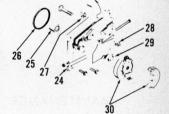

Fig. LO9 — Exploded view showing typical power head used on late models. Other models are similar.

1. Crankcase
2. Crankcase plug
3. Crankshaft & rod assy.
4. Thrust bearing
5. Bearing race
6. Main bearing
7. Oil seal
8. Felt seal
9. Reed valve assy.
10. Gasket
11. Gasket
12. Piston
13. Piston pin
14. Retaining ring
15. Piston rings
16. Cylinder
17. Spark plug
18. Washer
19. Decompression valve
20. Muffler body
21. Baffle plate
22. Screen
23. Muffler cover
24. Crankcase cover
25. Main bearing
26. "O" ring
27. Metering valve
28. Tensioner block
29. Oil seal
30. Clutch assy.
31. Stator assy.
32. Flywheel
33. Washer
34. Pawl spring
35. Starter pawl

LOMBARD

Model	Bore	Stroke	Displ.	Drive Type
Little Lightning	1.500 in. (38.1 mm)	1.250 in. (31.7 mm)	2.2 cu. in. (36.1 cc)	Direct
Little Lightning Deluxe	1.500 in. (38.1 mm)	1.250 in. (31.7 mm)	2.2 cu. in. (36.1 cc)	Direct
Little Lightning Super	1.562 in. (39.7 mm)	1.250 in. (31.7 mm)	2.4 cu. in. (39.3 cc)	Direct
Little Lightning Super Deluxe	1.562 in. (39.7 mm)	1.250 in. (31.7 mm)	2.4 cu. in. (39.3 cc)	Direct
AP22, AP22-1	1.500 in. (38.1 mm)	1.250 in. (31.7 mm)	2.2 cu. in. (36.1 cc)	Direct
AP22D, AP22D-1	1.500 in. (38.1 mm)	1.250 in. (31.7 mm)	2.2 cu. in. (36.1 cc)	Direct
AP24, AP24D, AP24SE	1.562 in. (39.7 mm)	1.250 in. (31.7 mm)	2.4 cu. in. (39.3 cc)	Direct

MAINTENANCE

SPARK PLUG. Recommended spark plug is Champion CJ7Y. Electrode gap should be 0.025 inch (0.63 mm).

CARBURETOR. A Tillotson Model HU or Walbro WA diaphragm carburetor has been used. Refer to CARBURETOR SERVICE section for an exploded view of carburetor and carburetor service.

Initial adjustment of idle and high speed mixture screws is 1 turn open. Make final adjustments with engine warm and running. Adjust idle mixture screw so engine will accelerate cleanly without stumbling. Adjust high speed mixture screw to obtain optimum performance with saw under cutting load. Adjust idle speed screw so engine idles just below clutch engagement speed.

IGNITION. Early models are equipped with a breaker-point type flywheel magneto ignition system while later models use a breakerless electronic ignition system.

Breaker-point gap should be 0.015 inch (0.38 mm) on models so equipped. Ignition timing is fixed on all models but breaker-point gap on applicable models should be set correctly or timing will be affected. Flywheel nut tightening torque is 100-125 in.-lbs. (11.3-14.1 N·m).

LUBRICATION. The engine is lubricated by mixing oil with the fuel. Recommended fuel:oil ratio is 16:1. Oil should be a good quality SAE 20 or SAE 30 oil designed for two-stroke air-cooled engines.

Clean SAE 20 or SAE 30 oil may be used for chain lubrication in warm weather. Dilute chain oil up to 50 percent with kerosene during cold weather operation.

REPAIRS

CYLINDER, PISTON, PIN AND RINGS. Cylinder is also upper crankcase half. Oil and fuel tank cover (34 – Fig. LO11) must be removed for access to cylinder screws. Crankshaft assembly will be loose when cylinder is separated from crankcase (24). Be careful not to nick or damage crankcase mating surfaces.

The piston is equipped with two piston rings. Piston pin (6) rides in caged needle roller bearing (8) in small end of connecting rod. Cylinder (3) has a chrome bore and oversize pistons and rings are not available. Inspect cylinder bore for excessive wear or damage to chrome surface. Tighten cylinder screws to 60-80 in.-lbs. (6.8-9.0 N·m). Refer to following paragraph for proper assembly of crankcase and cylinder.

CONNECTING ROD, CRANKSHAFT AND CRANKCASE. Cylinder (3 – Fig. LO11) must be removed for access to crankshaft assembly. Refer to previous section for cylinder removal.

Connecting rod and crankshaft are a unit assembly and must be serviced as such. Apply a light coat of nonhardening sealant to crankcase mating surfaces before assembly. Be sure retaining rings

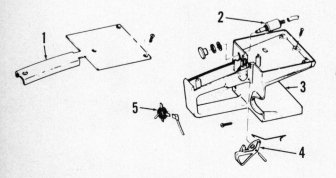

Fig. LO10 – Exploded view of rear handle assembly.
1. Cover
2. Manual oil pump
3. Rear handle
4. Throttle trigger
5. Ignition switch

(12) fit properly in grooves of crankcase and cylinder. Tighten cylinder-to-crankcase screws to 60-80 in.-lbs. (6.8-9.0 N·m).

CLUTCH. Saw may be equipped with a two-shoe or three-shoe centrifugal clutch. Clutch hub has left-hand threads. Clutch shoes and hub are available as a unit only. Inspect clutch components for excessive wear or damage.

REWIND STARTER. Refer to Fig. LO12 for an exploded view of rewind starter. To disassemble starter, remove rope handle and allow rope to wind into starter housing. Unscrew housing screws and detach starter housing (1) from left side cover (10). Remove "E" ring (8) and remove rope pulley. If necessary, remove wire retainer (6) and dislodge rewind spring from starter housing. Caution should be used to prevent spring from uncoiling uncontrolled.

Install rewind spring in starter housing with spring wound in clockwise direction from outer end. Wind rope around pulley in clockwise direction as viewed with rope pulley installed in housing. Pass end of rope through rope outlet in side cover (10) and install starter assembly on side cover without screws. Turn housing (1) clockwise until rope handle rests snugly against rope outlet. Install housing screws and check starter operation.

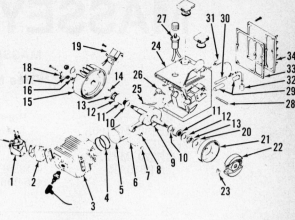
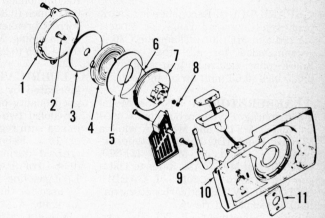

Fig. LO11—Exploded view of engine.

1. Carburetor
2. Spacer
3. Cylinder
4. Piston rings
5. Piston
6. Piston pin
7. Pin retainer
8. Bearing
9. Crankshaft & rod assy.
10. Thrust washer
11. Main bearing
12. Retainer
13. Seal
14. Key
15. Flywheel
16. Spacer
17. Pawl spring
18. Starter pawl
19. Ignition module
20. Washer
21. Clutch drum
22. Clutch hub & shoes
23. Clutch spring
24. Crankcase
25. Fuel line
26. Fitting
27. Oil regulator
28. Lubrication orifice
29. Valve & tube assy.
30. Oil line
31. Fuel pickup
32. Oil pickup
33. Gasket
34. Cover

Fig. LO12—Exploded view of rewind starter.

1. Housing
2. Spindle
3. Plate
4. Rewind spring
5. Plate
6. Wire retainer
7. Rope pulley
8. "E" ring
9. Choke plate
10. Side cover
11. Gasket

MASSEY-FERGUSON

MASSEY-FERGUSON INC.
P.O. Box 1813
Des Moines, Iowa 50306

Model	Bore	Stroke	Displ.	Drive Type
MF190, MF190A	1-3/8 in. (34.9 mm)	1-9/32 in. (32.5 mm)	1.9 cu. in. (31.1 cc)	Direct
MF370, MF370A, MF370AR	1-13/16 in. (46.0 mm)	1-7/16 in. (36.5 mm)	3.7 cu. in. (60.6 cc)	Direct

MAINTENANCE

SPARK PLUG. Recommended spark plug is a Champion DJ6J for Models MF190 and MF190A. Champion CJ6 is recommended for all other models. Spark plug electrode gap should be 0.025 inch (0.63 mm) for all models.

CARBURETOR. A Tillotson Model HS diaphragm type carburetor is used on Models MF190 and MF190A while a Walbro Model HDC diaphragm type carburetor is used on Models MF370, MF370A and MF370AR. Refer to Tillotson or Walbro sections of CARBURETOR SERVICE for carburetor overhaul and exploded views.

Initial adjustment of Tillotson carburetor is 1⅛ turns open for idle mixture screw and 1 turn open for high speed mixture screw. Initial adjustment of Walbro carburetor is 1 turn open for idle mixture screw and ¾-turn open for high speed mixture screw. Final adjustments should be made with engine warm. High speed mixture screw should be adjusted with engine under cutting load to obtain optimum performance. Do not adjust high speed mixture too lean as engine damage may result.

MAGNETO AND TIMING. A conventional flywheel magneto is used on all models. Ignition timing is fixed. Recommended breaker-point gap is 0.015 inch (0.38 mm) for all models. Incorrect breaker-point gap will affect ignition timing. Magneto air gap should be 0.008 inch (0.20 mm).

LUBRICATION. The engine is lubricated by mixing oil with fuel. A good quality oil designed for use in an air-cooled two-stroke engine should be mixed with regular gasoline at the ratio of 16:1. Fuel:oil ratio should be increased during break-in with ¾ pint (0.35 L) of oil added to one gallon (3.785 L) of gasoline. This break-in ratio should be used for the first four gallons (15.14 L) of fuel mixture.

Models MF190A, MF370A and MF370AR are equipped with an automatic chain oil pump. All models are equipped with a manual chain oil pump. Recommended chain oil is a good quality SAE 30 oil for summer use and SAE 20 for winter use. If saw is used in extremely cold weather, SAE 10 oil may be mixed with a small amount of kerosene.

REPAIRS

PISTON, PIN, RINGS AND CYLINDER. Before cylinder can be removed, crankcase end plate on Models MF190 and MF190A must be removed. Refer to CRANKCASE AND CRANKSHAFT section. Cylinder has chromed aluminum bore on all models with cylinder head integral with cylinder. Piston has two pinned piston rings. Piston pin is fully floating and retained by snap rings at each end. Piston pin on Models MF370, MF370A and MF370AR rides in a needle roller bearing in small end of connecting rod. Piston pin on Models MF190 and MF190A rides directly in small end of rod. Piston must be heated to remove and install piston pin.

Inspect chrome bore of cylinder for scoring, flaking, cracking or other signs of damage or excessive wear. Inspect piston pin, bearing and connecting rod small end. Install new piston pin bearing, on models so equipped, by pressing

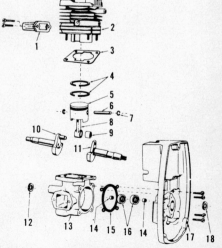

Fig. MF2 — Exploded view of engine used on Models MF190 and MF190A.

1. Muffler
2. Cylinder
3. Gasket
4. Piston rings
5. Piston
6. Piston pin
7. Snap rings
8. Connecting rod
9. Needle bearing
10. Crankshaft (drive end)
11. Crankshaft (flywheel end)
12. Seal
13. Crankcase
14. Roller bearings (Torrington B86)
15. Gasket
16. Roller bearing (Torrington DD40798)
17. End plate
18. Seal

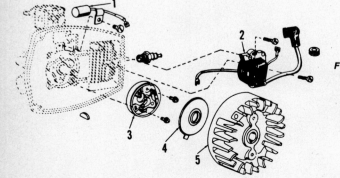

Fig. MF1 — Exploded view of magneto assembly.

1. Condenser
2. Ignition coil
3. Stator plate & breaker points
4. Cover
5. Flywheel

on lettered side of bearing. Be sure rod is properly supported when pressing against bearing to prevent damage to lower portion of rod if rod is still attached to crankshaft. Piston, pin and connecting rod are available only as a unit assembly on Models MF190 and MF190A.

Heat piston before installing piston pin which must be installed with closed end of pin towards exhaust port. Install piston with "EXH" marking on piston crown toward exhaust port of cylinder. Be sure piston rings are properly aligned with locating pins in ring grooves when installing cylinder. Tighten cylinder base nuts to 30-40 in.-lbs. (3.4-4.5 N·m) on Models MF190 and MF190A and to 80-100 in.-lbs. (9.0-11.3 N·m) on Models MF370, MF370A and MF370AR.

CONNECTING ROD. Connecting rod on Models MF370, MF370A and MF370AR can be removed after removing piston and unscrewing rod cap screws. Be careful not to lose bearing rollers (14–Fig. MF3) when removing rod and cap. To remove rod on Models MF190 and MF190A, crankshaft must be separated as outlined in CRANK-CASE AND CRANKSHAFT section.

Thirty-one loose bearing rollers are used in crankpin bearing on Models MF370, MF370A and MF370AR while a needle roller bearing is used on crankpin of Models MF190 and MF190A. Piston pin on Models MF190 and MF190A rides directly in small end of connecting rod. Piston rod on Models MF370, MF370A and MF370AR is supported by a needle roller bearing in connecting rod. Install roller bearing by pressing on lettered

side of bearing. Connecting rod, piston and piston pin on Models MF190 and MF190A are available only as a unit assembly.

Loose bearing rollers on Models MF370, MF370A and MF370AR can be held in place with heavy grease or wax on strip of new bearing rollers. Note match marks (M–Fig. MF4) on connecting rod and rod cap which must be aligned for installation. Install rod so match marks are toward flywheel end of crankshaft.

CRANKCASE AND CRANKSHAFT. Access to crankcase and crankshaft is possible after removing end plate (17–Fig. MF2 or 18–Fig. MF3). Flywheel end of crankshaft on all models is supported by a roller bearing. On Models MF190 and MF190A, two bearings (14 and 16–Fig. MF2) are used. Drive end of crankshaft is supported by two roller bearings on Models MF190 and MF190A and by a ball bearing on Models MF370, MF370A and MF370AR. Heat should be applied to crankcase or end plate to remove roller bearings. Ball bearing (8–Fig. MF3) is pressed on crankshaft and retained in crankcase by retainers (6). It may be necessary to apply heat to crankcase to remove bearing and crankshaft from crankcase.

Models MF190 and MF190A are equipped with a two-piece crankshaft (10 and 11–Fig. MF2). End plate (17), crankshaft half (11) and cylinder must be removed before connecting rod (8) can be removed. Drive end of crankshaft (10) may be removed after connecting rod (8) is removed. Drive (10) and flywheel (11) ends are available separately.

Ball bearing (8–Fig. MF3) on Models MF370, MF370A and MF370AR is pressed on crankshaft. Groove around outer race of bearing must be adjacent to crankpin. Heat crankcase (1) in bearing area and install crankshaft and bearing. Coat screw (7) threads with CV grade Loctite and install bearing retainers (6) and screws. Be sure screws do not contact crankshaft when shaft is turned.

REED VALVE. All models are equipped with a reed valve induction system. Refer to Figs. MF5 and MF6. Inspect reed petals for cracks or other damage. Inspect reed valve seats for pitting or other damage which may prevent petals from seating properly. Reed petals and seat are available only as a unit assembly.

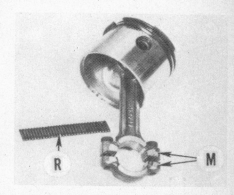

Fig. MF4—On Models MF370, MF370A and MF370AR, be sure connecting rod match marks (M) are aligned. Rod bearing has 31 rollers (R).

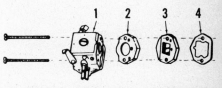

Fig. MF5—View of induction system used on Models MF190 and MF190A.

1. Carburetor   3. Reed valve assy.
2. Spacer   4. Gasket

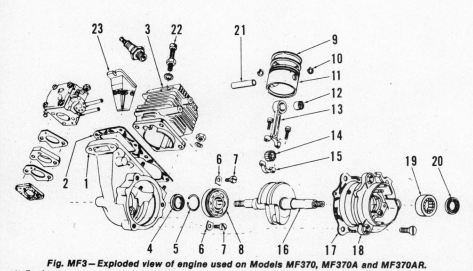

Fig. MF3—Exploded view of engine used on Models MF370, MF370A and MF370AR.

1. Crankcase	7. Screws	18. End plate
2. Gasket	8. Ball bearing	19. Roller bearing
3. Cylinder	9. Piston rings	20. Seal
4. Seal	10. Snap ring	21. Piston pin
5. Retainer	11. Piston	22. Compression release
6. Retainers	12. Needle bearing	23. Reed valve
	13. Connecting rod	
	14. Bearing rollers (31)	
	15. Rod cap	
	16. Crankshaft	
	17. Gasket	

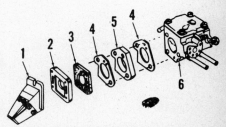

Fig. MF6—View of induction system used on Models MF370, MF370A and MF370AR.

1. Reed valve assy.   4. Gasket
2. Spacer   5. Heat insulator
3. Cork gasket   6. Carburetor

REWIND STARTER. Refer to Fig. MF7 for exploded view of rewind starter used on all models. To disassemble starter, proceed as follows: Remove starter housing from end plate. Remove rope handle and allow rope to rewind into starter. Remove "E" ring (6) and remove rope pulley (8) being careful not to dislodge rewind spring (9). If necessary, remove rewind spring being careful as injury may result if spring is allowed to uncoil uncontrolled.

Rewind spring is wound in clockwise direction in housing. Rope is wound on pulley in clockwise direction when viewing pulley installed in housing. Place tension on rewind spring by turning pulley clockwise before passing rope through rope outlet. Pulley should be turned a sufficient number of turns to draw rope handle against housing when rope is released, but not so many turns that rewind spring is fully extended when rope is completely withdrawn.

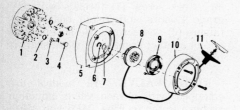

Fig. MF7 — Exploded view of rewind starter assembly.

1. Flywheel
2. Spring
3. Pawl
4. Pivot post
5. Fan shroud
6. "E" ring
7. Washer
8. Rope pulley
9. Rewind spring
10. Starter housing
11. Rope handle

McCULLOCH

McCULLOCH CORPORATION
900 Lake Havasu Avenue
Lake Havasu City, Arizona 86403

Model	Bore	Stroke	Displ.	Drive Type
10-10 Auto	1.75 in. (44.4 mm)	1.375 in. (34.92 mm)	3.3 cu. in. (54.0 cc)	Direct
7-10 Auto	2.0 in. (50.8 mm)	1.375 in. (34.92 mm)	4.3 cu. in. (70.5 cc)	Direct
PM700	2.0 in. (50.8 mm)	1.375 in. (34.92 mm)	4.3 cu. in. (70.5 cc)	Direct
PM10-10S, PM55, PM555	1.812 in. (46.02 mm)	1.375 in. (34.92 mm)	3.5 cu. in. (57.4 cc)	Direct
PM60, SP60	1.875 in. (47.62 mm)	1.375 in. (34.92 mm)	3.8 cu. in. (62.3 cc)	Direct
PM800, PM805, PM850, SP80, SP81, Double Eagle 80	2.06 in. (52.3 mm)	1.5 in. (38.1 mm)	5.0 cu. in. (81.9 cc)	Direct

MAINTENANCE

SPARK PLUG. Recommended spark plug is AC CS45T for Models 10-10 Auto, PM10-10S, PM55 and PM555. Recommended spark plug is AC CS42T on all other models. Recommended spark plug electrode gap is 0.025 inch (0.63 mm). Note spark plug has a conical seat which does not require a gasket. Tighten spark plug to 144-180 in.-lbs. (16.3-20.3 N·m) torque.

CARBURETOR. A McCulloch "W" series, Tillotson HS, Walbro SDC or Zama carburetor may be used. Refer to Tillotson, Walbro or Zama carburetor section in CARBURETOR SERVICE section for service on those carburetors.

Initial adjustment of mixture needles on Tillotson, Walbro and Zama carburetors is one turn open for both low and high speed mixture needles. Make final adjustment on Tillotson, Walbro and Zama carburetors with engine warm and running. Adjust idle speed screw so engine idles just below clutch engagement speed. Adjust low speed mixture screw so engine will accelerate cleanly without hesitation. Adjust high speed mixture screw to obtain optimum performance under cutting load. Some chain saws with Tillotson or Walbro carburetors are equipped with a throttle latch to advance the throttle opening to a fast idle position for starting. Throttle opening is adjusted by turning adjusting screw (S – Fig. MC6-3) on bottom of trigger.

McCulloch series "W" carburetor was manufactured as two different models. Early model is shown in Fig. MC6-4 and later model is shown in Fig. MC6-5. On early models, fuel is metered by an adjustable needle valve attached to the throttle shaft. On later models, this only adjusts idle mixture. High speed operation on early models is controlled by an adjusting screw which determines throttle plate opening. Later models utilize a fuel needle for high speed adjustment. Both models use a primer plunger for choking operation. Choking on early models is accomplished by forcing fuel past needle valve into the carburetor bore. Later models force fuel from a chamber into the carburetor bore.

Be sure primer operates correctly as fuel leaking into bore will change fuel mixture. Primer "O" rings must be installed correctly to prevent leakage. Some plungers shown in Fig. MC6-4

Fig. MC6-1 — Air cleaner cover and filter element removed to show carburetor adjustment points of early McCulloch Models "W" series carburetor. Later models are similar except for high speed mixture screw.

1. High speed mixture screw
2. Idle speed screw
3. Idle speed mixture screw
4. Throttle butterfly

Fig. MC6-2 — Keep finger on throttle butterfly as shown when adjusting carburetor. Refer to text for procedure.

Fig. MC6-3 — Fast idle adjustment on some models is performed by turning adjusting screw (S) on bottom of trigger.

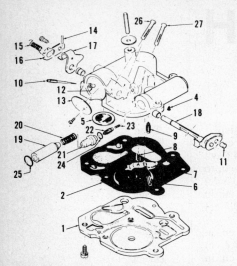

Fig. MC6-4 – Exploded view of early McCulloch Model "W" series carburetor. Refer to Fig. MC6-1 for view of carburetor installed.

1. Base plate	15. Idle governor spring
2. Diaphragm	16. Clip
4. Check valve	17. Throttle lever
5. Capillary seal	18. Throttle shaft
6. Inlet valve pin	19. Primer plunger
7. Inlet lever	20. Plunger spring
8. Spring	21. Seat
9. Inlet valve needle	22. Primer needle
10. Metering (low idle) mixture needle	23. Needle spring
11. Swivel	24. "O" ring
12. Air orifice	25. "O" ring
13. Throttle butterfly	26. Idle speed screw
14. Roll pin	27. High speed mixture screw

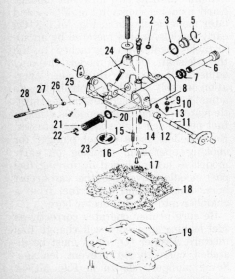

Fig. MC6-5 – Exploded view of later McCulloch Model "W" series carburetor. Refer to Fig. MC6-4 for view of early model.

1. High speed mixture needle	14. Fuel inlet valve
2. "O" ring	15. Spring
3. "O" ring	16. Inlet lever
4. Plug	17. Pin
5. Retainer	18. Diaphragm
6. Primer plunger	19. Base plate
7. "O" ring or "V" packing	20. "O" ring
8. Ball	21. Spring
9. Ball seat	22. Retaining ring
10. Valve	23. Seal
11. Throttle shaft	24. Idle speed screw
12. Bushing	25. Throttle plate
13. Valve	26. Fuel orifice
	27. Air orifice
	28. Idle metering needle

have a cup to retain "O" ring (25). Install cup 5/64 inch (1.98 mm) from end of primer housing bore as shown in Fig. MC6-6. Two types of primer plungers have been used on the carburetor shown in Fig. MC6-5. The rear groove of the plunger is 0.090 inch (2.29 mm) or 0.120 inch (3.05 mm) wide as shown in Fig. MC6-7. An "O" ring is used in the narrow groove while "V" packing is used in the wide groove as a service replacement.

If carburetor has been disassembled, make a preliminary adjustment prior to starting engine and make final adjustment after engine has been started and brught to operating temperature.

To make the preliminary adjustment on "W" series carburetors, refer to Fig. MC6-1 and proceed as follows: Turn the idle speed screw (2) counterclockwise until throttle butterfly (4) is completely closed. Hold a finger against the closed butterfly as shown in Fig. MC6-2 and turn the idle mixture screw (3 – Fig. MC6-1) clockwise until the butterfly starts to open, then turn the idle mixture needle three turns counterclockwise. Return to the idle speed screw (2) and while holding finger against butterfly (4), turn idle air screw clockwise until butterfly begins to open, then continue to turn the screw clockwise an additional ½ turn. Hold the throttle trigger in the wide open position, turn the high speed mixture screw (1) as required until throttle butterfly is in horizontal position.

Now turn screw (1) clockwise until throttle butterfly (4) starts to close, then turn the high speed mixture screw two turns counterclockwise. On later models, initial adjustment of main fuel needle (1 – Fig. MC6-5) is one turn. Do not attempt to adjust throttle plate opening.

With preliminary adjustment made as outlined, start engine and bring to operating temperature. Let engine run at idle rpm and if necessary, adjust idle speed screw until engine is operating just below chain creep speed. Now accelerate engine rapidly several times and check engine operation. If engine falters during acceleration, the mixture is too lean and idle mixture needle should be turned counterclockwise as necessary. If engine runs rough and smokes excessively during acceleration, the mixture is too rich and the idle mixture needle should be turned clockwise as necessary. Make this adjustment in small increments and check engine operation after each adjustment. If the idle mixture is changed it may also be necessary to readjust the idle speed screw to keep engine idle rpm below chain creep speed. Refer to Fig. MC6-8 and set the tension governor spring so engine idles smoothly in all positions. Reduce tension on spring if chain creeps.

With engine idle rpm and mixture adjusted, load engine (make a cut) and turn the high speed adjustment screw (1 – Fig. MC6-1) on early models counter-

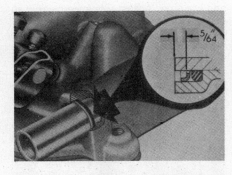

Fig. MC6-6 – Some early McCulloch "W" series carburetors have a seal cup which must be installed 5/64 inch (1.98 mm) inside primer bore as shown above.

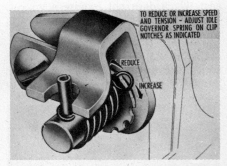

Fig. MC6-8 – View showing installation of idle governor spring. Later McCulloch "W" series carburetors do not have governor spring. Adjust spring as shown so engine will idle smoothly in any position.

Fig. MC6-7 – Primer plunger with narrow 0.090 inch (2.29 mm) groove (A) uses "O" ring (O). Primer plunger with wide 0.120 inch (3.05 mm) groove (B) uses "V" packing (V).

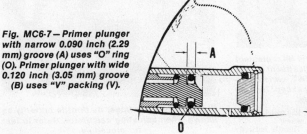

clockwise in small increments until engine operation begins to roughen, then turn the screw clockwise just enough to eliminate the engine roughness. On later models of "W" carburetor, the high speed mixture screw is turned clockwise to lean fuel mixture.

IGNITION. Early models are equipped with a breaker-point type flywheel magneto ignition system while later models use an electronic ignition system.

On models equipped with breaker-points, breaker-point gap should be 0.019 inch (0.48 mm). Clearance between ignition coil legs and flywheel magnets should be 0.010-0.012 inch (0.25-0.30 mm) and can be adjusted after loosening coil mounting screws. Ignition timing is 26 degrees BTDC and is not adjustable, however, incorrect breaker-point gap will affect ignition timing.

Clearance between ignition coil module legs and flywheel magnets should be 0.011-0.015 inch (0.28-0.38 mm) on models equipped with electronic ignition. Ignition timing is 26 degrees BTDC but is not adjustable.

Note that two different electronic systems have been used on later models. Individual components should not be interchanged. The different systems may be identified by noting color of components which are all black on one of the ignition systems.

LUBRICATION. Engine is lubricated by a mixture of regular gasoline and oil. The gasoline and oil should be mixed in a separate container before being put in the engine fuel tank. If using McCulloch engine oil, use 3 ounces (88.7 mL) of oil for each gallon (3.7853 L) of gasoline (approx. 1:40). If McCulloch oil is not available, use 6 ounces (177.4 mL) of SAE 40 two-stroke oil for each gallon (3.7853 L) of gasoline (approx. 1:20). Fill chain oiler tank each time fuel tank is filled. Use SAE 30 motor oil for temperatures above 40°F (4°C). When

cutting wood with a high sap or pitch content the chain oil may be diluted up to 50 percent with kerosene, if necessary. Adjust oil pump output on models with automatic chain oiler as shown in Fig. MC6-9.

On gear drive models, use SAE 140 all-purpose gear oil in transmission. With bar pointed down and filler plug removed, oil should be level with bottom of filler hole.

CARBON. If a noticeable lack of power or a decrease in the exhaust noise level is evident it is possible that the muffler and exhaust ports need cleaning. Use a wood scraper when cleaning exhaust ports to avoid damage to cylinder or piston.

REPAIRS

CONNECTING ROD. Removal of connecting rod requires separating cylinder and crankcase. To gain access to the cylinder and crankcase, remove clutch guard and starter assembly, clutch, fan housing, flywheel, ignition components, air cleaner cover and air cleaner screen, carburetor, spark arrester, cylinder shroud and fuel tank assembly.

With the above assemblies removed, drain chain oiler tank, if necessary, then remove the crankcase cover. Remove the four interior and four exterior cylinder retaining cap screws and separate crankcase from cylinder. Remove the

rod cap screws and remove rod and piston from crankshaft. Do not lose any of the 22 loose rollers used in PM800, PM805, PM850, SP80, SP81 and Double Eagle 80 or 20 loose rollers used in all other models. Heat piston evenly to about 200°F (93.4°C), support piston boss on a 9/16 inch deep socket and using a driver smaller than piston pin, press piston pin from rod.

NOTE: Piston support tool is P/N63093 and driver is P/N63094.

Inspect connecting rod for worn or scored bearing surfaces, bends or twists. If any of these defects are found, renew rod.

To reassemble, heat piston pin end of rod to about 300°F (149°C) and reinstall by reversing removal procedure. Install rod in piston with pips on rod and cap aligned. Use grease to hold rollers in crankshaft end of rod. Tighten rod cap screws to 65-70 in.-lbs. (7.3-7.9 N·m) with oiled threads.

PISTON, PIN, RINGS AND CYLINDER. Later models are equipped with a chrome cylinder bore. On these models, except Double Eagle 80, standard size pistons and rings only are available. Cylinder bore and piston on Models PM800, PM850 and Double Eagle 80 are graded. "A," "B" or "C" according to size. Letter size should be the same on piston and cylinder to obtain desired clearance. If cylinder is unmarked, use a

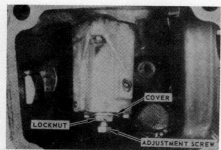

Fig. MC6-9 — Automatic oil pump output is adjusted by loosening locknut and turning adjustment screw. Locknut may be absent on later models. Adjustment should be made in small increments.

Fig. MC6-10 — Exploded view of typical engine assembly, and early type manual and automatic oil pumps. Later type manual and automatic oil pumps are shown in Fig. MC6-12A. Note that early models used insert (28) and snap ring (29) while late models use insert (25) and pin (12).

1. Roll pin
2. Manual oil pump housing
3. Spring
4. "O" ring
5. Roll pin
6. Boot
7. Gasket
8. Valve
9. Oil hose
10. Cylinder
11. Compression valve
12. Dowel pin
13. Oil seal
14. Snap ring
15. Ball bearing
16. Crankshaft
17. Needle bearing
18. Piston pin
19. Piston ring
20. Piston
21. Connecting rod
22. Roller bearing
23. Rod cap
24. Rod screws
25. Bearing insert
26. Roller bearing
27. Oil seal
28. Bearing insert
29. Snap ring
30. Oil tank cover
31. Gasket
32. Piston
33. Teflon washer
34. Piston ring
35. "O" ring
36. Spring
37. Adjustment sleeve
38. Automatic oil pump housing
39. Outlet ball valve
40. Spring
41. "O" ring
42. Valve cover
43. Locknut
44. Adjusting screw

piston marked "B." Piston letter size is marked on crown while cylinder is marked adjacent to compression release valve. Oversize pistons and rings are available on models with a cast iron liner in the cylinder.

Models with cast iron liner should conform to the following specifications: Piston-to-wall clearance should be 0.003-0.005 inch (0.08-0.13 mm) measured at piston skirt. Cylinder taper or out-of-round should not exceed 0.005 inch (0.13 mm). Piston ring end gap should be 0.006-0.017 inch (0.16-0.43 mm) on un-pinned rings and 0.051-0.066 inch (1.30-1.67 mm) on models with pinned piston rings. Maximum piston ring end gap should be 0.0055 inch (0.14 mm) on Model 10-10 Auto and 0.006 inch (0.15 mm) on Models 7-10 Auto and PM700. Minimum ring side gap is 0.003 inch (0.08 mm) for Models 10-10 Auto, 7-10 Auto and PM700. If cylinder is bored to an oversize, the tip of the compression release valve (DSP) must be cut one-half the amount of the oversize. For example, the compression release valve would be cut 0.010 inch (0.25 mm) if the cylinder is bored 0.020 inch (0.51 mm) oversize. Be sure valve does not protrude into cylinder and contact piston or piston rings.

Recommended piston-to-cylinder clearance is measured ⅜ inch (9.5 mm) from bottom of piston skirt. On models with chrome cylinder bore clearance should be 0.002-0.004 inch (0.06-0.10 mm) except for Models PM800 and PM850 which is 0.0024-0.0038 inch (0.061-0.096 mm) and Model Double Eagle 80 which is 0.009 inch (0.23 mm). Cylinder should be inspected and renewed if chrome has cracked, flaked or worn away and exposed soft base metal underneath. Pistons and rings are available in standard sizes only. Piston ring end gap should be 0.055-0.091 inch (1.40-2.31 mm) for Models PM555, PM700, PM800 and PM850. On Model Double Eagle 80, ring end gap should be 0.070 inch (1.78 mm). Piston rings used with chrome cylinder are tapered on some models and must be installed with taper pointing up as shown in Fig. MC6-11.

If needle bearings in piston require renewal, support piston on outer end of pin boss, place insert support or McCulloch special tool between piston bosses (in place of rod) and press top bearing out toward inside. Turn piston over and repeat operation on opposite bearing.

NOTE: Bearing enters hole in insert support as it is pressed out. Do not reuse any bearings that have been removed.

To install new bearings in piston, heat piston to about 200°F (93.4°C) and reverse procedure but use solid end of insert support and press bearing into piston until bearing butts against the insert support. This positions bearing inner end flush with inner ends of piston pin boss.

Pistons on all engines have piston pin offset in piston. Piston must be installed on connecting rod with large offset (O—Fig. MC6-12) toward clutch. The piston on most engines is also marked with "EX" and must be installed with "EX" side adjacent to exhaust port. Heat connecting rod eye to approximately 300°F (149°C) before installing piston and pressing in piston pin.

CRANKSHAFT. The crankshaft is supported by a ball bearing at flywheel end and a needle bearing at clutch end. Crankshaft should be discarded if it shows uneven or excessive wear, or any other signs of damage. When installing bearing on crankshaft, place shielded side of ball bearing next to counterweight of crankshaft and press bearing on shaft until it bottoms. When crankshaft and piston assembly is positioned in cylinder, be sure inner end of needle bearing is positioned ⅛ inch (3.17 mm) away from counterweight of crankshaft and that shaft seals are installed with lips facing inward. Tighten the four interior crankcase bolts to 55-60 in.-lbs. (6.3-6.8 N·m) and the four exterior crankcase bolts to 35-40 in.-lbs. (4.0-4.5 N·m) torque.

AUTOMATIC OILER. All models have an automatic chain oiler in addition to the manual chain oiler. The oil pump is operated by crankcase pulsations.

The oil pump is adjusted as shown in Fig. MC6-9. Chain oil is routed first through the manual oiler then through the automatic oiler before it exits at the bar pad. This allows the manual oiler to be used independently as well as providing priming for the automatic oiler. The oil pump is contained within the oil tank and may be removed after draining

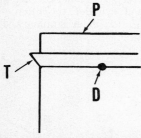

Fig. MC6-11—Tapered piston rings on some models must be installed so taper (T) is toward top of piston (P). Locating dot (D) on ring will be toward bottom when installed correctly.

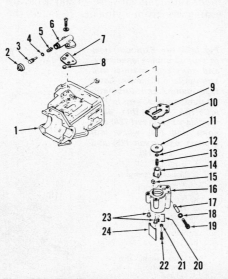

Fig. MC6-12A—Exploded view of later type manual and automatic chain oil pump. Locknut (21) may be absent on some models.

1. Crankcase	13. Spring
2. Boot	14. Adjustment sleeve
3. Plunger	15. Pad
4. "O" ring	16. Automatic oil pump
5. Spring	housing
6. Manual oil pump	17. Sleeve
housing	18. Washer
7. Gasket	19. Cap screw
8. Valve	20. Ball valve & spring
9. Gasket	21. Locknut
10. Piston	22. Adjusting screw
11. Piston ring	23. Eyelet
12. "O" ring	24. Spring clip

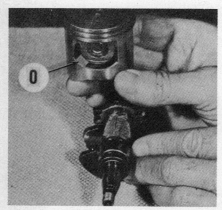

Fig. MC6-12—Install piston so large offset (O) at piston pin boss is toward clutch.

Fig. MC6-13—Flywheel may be locked in place on SP60, SP80, SP81, PM700 and PM850 Models by inserting ¼ inch locking pin through base plate into notch in flywheel.

oil tank and removing tank cover. Oil pump should be cleaned and inspected for damage or excessive wear. Be sure all oil passages are open and clean and renew piston disc if warped or cracked. Before starting chain saw, prime automatic oil pump by operating manual oiler several times.

CLUTCH. To remove clutch, remove clutch guard and starter assembly, bar, chain and fan (flywheel) housing. Lock flywheel by inserting a screwdriver between bossed portion of flywheel and leg of coil lamination (DO NOT use flywheel fin). Flywheel on SP60, SP80, SP81 and PM850 models is secured by inserting a ¼ inch (6.35 mm) locking pin through the base plate as shown in Fig. MC6-13 and rotating flywheel until pin engages notch in flywheel. Remove clutch retaining nut and pull clutch from crankshaft. Remove clutch drum and bearing, and shims. Refer to Figs. MC6-14 and MC6-15.

Inspect all parts for signs of excessive wear or other damage. Clutch shoes

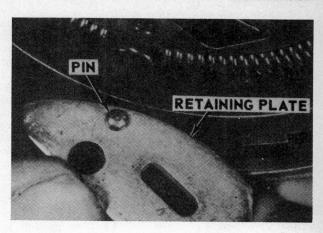

Fig. MC6-16—Install clutch spring (4—Fig. MC6-15) so spring ends will contact locating pin in clutch spring retaining plate.

must be renewed as a unit. Clutch spring(s) should also be renewed. Renew clutch rotor if it allows excessive play of clutch shoes. Renew shims if grooved or damaged. Inspect sprocket and renew if excessively worn. Inspect starter pawls on models equipped with recoil starter on clutch side of saw. Pawls can be renewed by removing rivets and installing new pawls and rivets.

Note that one retaining plate of clutch assembly used on Model SP80 has a pin which prevents the clutch spring from rotating. The clutch spring must be installed so that the ends of the spring will

be underneath retaining pin when the plate is installed on clutch shoe. Refer to Fig. MC6-16. The clutch drum on gear drive models is equipped with a seal which must be installed with lips of seal toward clutch bearing. Tighten clutch nut to 400-420 in.-lbs. (45.2-47.4 N·m) on Model SP80 and to 160-170 in.-lbs. (18.1-19.2 N·m) torque on all other models.

REWIND STARTER. Chain saw may be equipped with a rewind starter mounted on right or left side. Refer to Fig. MC6-18 for exploded view of recoil starter mounted on right side of chain saw. Rewind spring is wound in counterclockwise direction in housing and rope is wound in counterclockwise direction around rope pulley as viewed installed in housing. New rope length is 50 inches (127 cm). Early models have a hole in the rope pulley and a nail or other device can be inserted through the hole to hold the rewind spring on the rope pulley as shown in Fig. MC6-19. Note that the spring is wound clockwise if this method is used to install rewind spring.

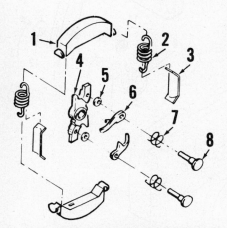

Fig. MC6-14—Exploded view of clutch used on all models except SP80.

1. Shoe	5. Washer
2. Spring	6. Pawl
3. Retainer	7. Spring
4. Rotor	8. Rivet

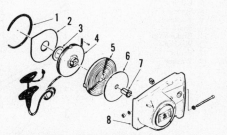

Fig. MC6-18—Exploded view of typical right hand rewind starter.

1. Snap ring	5. Rewind spring
2. Dust shield	6. Spring shield
3. Thrust washer	7. Nylon bushing
4. Rope pulley	8. Fan housing

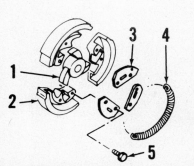

Fig. MC6-15—Exploded view of clutch shoe assembly used on Model SP80.

1. Rotor	
2. Clutch shoes	4. Clutch spring
3. Retainer plates	5. Cap screw

Fig. MC6-19—Some rope pulleys have a hole which allows the rewind spring to be held in position by inserting a nail or other device as shown.

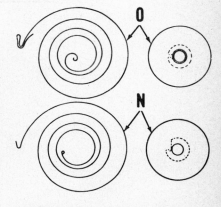

Fig. MC6-20—Note difference between old (O) and new (N) style rewind springs and rope pulleys. Refer to text.

An early and late type of rewind spring and rope pulley have been used. Refer to Fig. MC6-20. Early and late spring and pulley should not be interchanged. Early type spring and pulley must be used in early starter housing. Later type spring and pulley can be used in early or later starter housing.

Place tension on rope by pulling rope handle then hold rope pulley so notch on outer edge of pulley aligns with rope outlet. Pull loose rope into housing and

rotate rope pulley one or two turns in counterclockwise direction. Release rope and check starter operation.

Refer to Fig. MC6-21 for view of left hand starter found on saws manufactured in United States and some export models. Install rewind spring on fan housing in counterclockwise direction. Wind rope on rope pulley so it is wound in counterclockwise direction when viewed with pulley installed on housing. New rope length should be 42 inches (106.7 cm). Check operation of starter to be sure there is sufficient rewind spring tension to rewind rope, but rewind spring is bottomed when rope is pulled to its full length. Spring tension is altered by turning rope pulley while housing cover is removed.

Left-hand starter used on some saw models manufactured for export is

shown in Fig. MC6-22. Rewind spring is wound in clockwise direction as viewed with pulley installed in housing. Place tension on rope by pulling rope handle and then hold rope pulley so notch on outer edge of pulley aligns with rope outlet. Pull loose rope into housing and rotate rope pulley one or two turns in clockwise direction. Release rope and check starter operation.

CHAIN BRAKE. Some later models are equipped with the chain brake mechanism shown in Fig. MC6-25. The chain brake stops chain motion when the operator's hand contacts brake lever (11) and steel strap (3) tightens around the clutch drum thereby stopping chain motion. Chain brake components must operate freely for the chain brake mechanism to be effective.

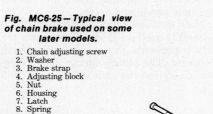

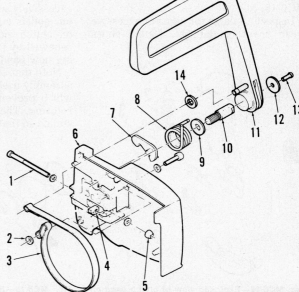

Fig. MC6-21 — Exploded view of left-hand rewind starter used on U.S. models and some export models.

1. Starter shaft
2. Wave washer
3. Fan housing
4. Sawdust guard
5. Spring shield
6. Rewind spring
7. Rope pulley
8. Cap screw
9. Rope roller
10. Cover
11. Rivet

Fig. MC6-25 — Typical view of chain brake used on some later models.

1. Chain adjusting screw
2. Washer
3. Brake strap
4. Adjusting block
5. Nut
6. Housing
7. Latch
8. Spring
9. Washer
10. Shaft
11. Brake lever
12. Washer
13. Screw
14. Washer

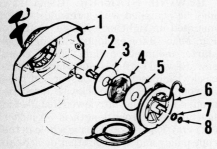

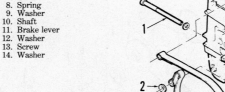

Fig. MC6-22 — Exploded view of left-hand rewind starter used on some export models.

1. Fan housing
2. Nylon bushing
3. Spring shield
4. Rewind spring
5. Dust shield
6. Rope pulley
7. Washer
8. Snap ring

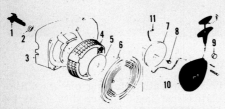

McCULLOCH

Model	Bore	Stroke	Displ.	Drive Type
Mini-Mac 25, Mini-Mac 30	1.375 in. (34.92 mm)	1.200 in. (30.48 mm)	1.78 cu. in. (29.1 cc)	Direct
Mini-Mac 35	1.438 in. (36.52 mm)	1.200 in. (30.48 mm)	2.0 cu. in. (32.8 cc)	Direct
Power Mac 6	1.438 in. (36.52 mm)	1.200 in. (30.48 mm)	2.0 cu. in. (32.8 cc)	Direct
PM510, PM515, SP40	1.562 in. (39.67 mm)	1.201 in. (30.50 mm)	2.3 cu. in. (37.7 cc)	Direct
*PM310, PM320, PM330, PM340, PM355, PM365, PM375, Eager Beaver 2.1	1.496 in. (37.99 mm)	1.200 in. (30.48 mm)	2.1 cu. in. (34.4 cc)	Direct
Mac 110, Mac 120, Mac 130, Mac 140	†1.375 in. (34.92 mm)	1.200 in. (30.48 mm)	†1.78 cu. in. (29.1 cc)	Direct
Eager Beaver, PM155, PM165	1.438 in. (36.52 mm)	1.200 in. (30.48 mm)	2.0 cu. in. (32.8 cc)	Direct

*NOTE: Metric and American fasteners are used on 2.1 cu. in. (34.4 cc) saws. Be sure correct fastener is installed.

†Later Mac 110 and 120 models have a 1.430 inch (36.32 mm) bore and 2.0 cu. in. (32.8 cc) displacement.

MAINTENANCE

SPARK PLUG. Recommended spark plug is AC CS42T or equivalent for SP40 models and AC CS45T or equivalent for all other models. On all models, spark plug electrode gap is 0.025 inch (0.63 mm). Note that plug has a tapered seat and does not require a gasket. Tighten spark plug to a torque of 144-180 in.-lbs. (16.3-20.3 N·m).

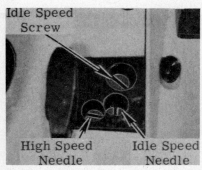

Fig. MC7-1 — View showing location of carburetor adjustment screws on Mac 110, 120, 130, 140 and Power Mac 6 and all Mini-Mac models.

CARBURETOR. Models may be equipped with either a Tillotson, Walbro or Zama diaphragm type carburetor.

Tillotson HU carburetors are used on some PM310, PM320, PM330 and PM340 models.

Walbro WA carburetors are used on some PM310, PM320, PM330, PM340 and PM510 models. Walbro MDC carburetors are used on Eager Beaver, Power Mac 6, PM155, PM165, all Mini-Mac models and some Mac 110, 120, 130 and 140 models.

Zama C1 carburetors are used on all PM355, PM365, PM375, PM515 and SP40 models and some PM310, PM320, PM330, PM340, PM510 and Eager Beaver 2.1 models. Zama M1 carburetors are used on some Mac 110, 120, 130 and 140 models.

Refer to CARBURETOR SERVICE section for overhaul and exploded views of Tillotson, Walbro and Zama carburetors. On all models except Walbro MDC and Zama M1, initial adjustment for idle and high speed mixture screws is one turn open.

On Walbro Model MDC, initial adjustment for idle and high speed mixture screws is ¾ turn open. On Zama Model M1, initial adjustment for idle and high speed mixture screws is 1¼ turns open.

On models equipped with Zama C1 carburetor, high speed mixture is not adjustable on some carburetors due to absence of high speed mixture screw.

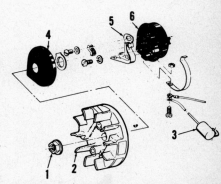

Fig. MC7-3 — Exploded view of ignition system used on all models except on 2.1 cu. in. (34.4 cc) saws.

1. Flywheel nut
2. Flywheel
3. Condenser
4. Cover
5. Ignition breaker-points
6. Breaker-box

On all types of carburetors, make final adjustment with engine warm and running. Adjust idle speed screw so engine idles just below clutch engagement speed. Adjust idle speed mixture screw so engine will accelerate cleanly without hesitation. Adjust high speed mixture screw to obtain optimum performance under cutting load.

IGNITION. All 2.1 cu. in. (34.4 cc) and late Eager Beaver (2.0 cu. in. [32.8 cc]) saws are equipped with an electronic ignition. Refer to Fig. MC7-4. Ignition coil and electronic circuitry are contained in a one-piece ignition module (1) which must be serviced as a unit assembly. Loosen ignition module retaining screws and position module so gap between flywheel (2) magnets and laminated coil legs is 0.012 inch (0.30 mm) then retighten screws.

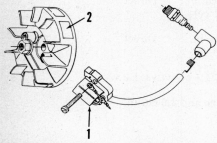

Fig. MC7-4 — Electronic ignition system used on all 2.1 cu. in. (34.4 cc) models and late Eager Beaver (2.0 cu. in. [32.8 cc]) models.

1. Ignition module & coil assy.
2. Flywheel

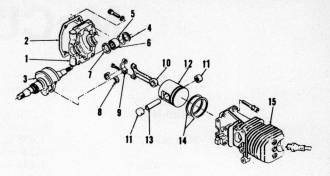

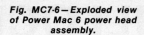

Fig. MC7-6 — Exploded view of Power Mac 6 power head assembly.

1. Crankcase bottom
2. Gasket
3. Crankshaft
4. Oil seal
5. Snap ring
6. Needle bearing
7. Thrust washer
8. Bearing rollers (20)
9. Connecting rod cap
10. Connecting rod
11. Bearing
12. Piston
13. Piston pin
14. Piston rings
15. Cylinder

All other models are equipped with a conventional breaker-point flywheel magneto ignition system with the breaker-points located in breaker-box (6 – Fig. MC7-3) located behind the flywheel. Breaker-point gap should be 0.018 inch (0.46 mm). Clearance between laminated coil legs and flywheel magnets should be 0.010 inch (0.25 mm) and can be adjusted after loosening coil mounting screws.

On all models, ignition timing is 26 degrees BTDC and is not adjustable.

LUBRICATION. The engine is lubricated with a mixture of regular gasoline and oil. Recommended fuel:oil ratio is 3 ounces (88.7 mL) of oil mixed with each gallon (3.7853 L) of gasoline (approx. 40:1) when using McCulloch oil. If McCulloch oil is not available, use 6 ounces (177.4 mL) of SAE 40 two-stroke air-cooled oil for each gallon (3.7853 L) of gasoline (approx. 20:1).

Fill chain oil tank each time fuel tank is filled. Use SAE 30 motor oil for temperatures above 40°F (4°C) and SAE 10 motor oil for lower temperatures.

Adjust oil pump output by turning adjusting screw (A – Fig. MC7-5 or MC7-13A). Turn screw in to decrease oil flow or out for increased oil flow.

NOTE: Late model oil pumps are nonadjustable. If an early type adjustable oil pump assembly must be renewed, then a nonadjustable oil pump assembly must be installed. Individual service components are available on each type oil pump assembly.

CARBON. If a noticeable lack of power or a decrease in the exhaust noise level is evident, it is possible that muffler and exhaust ports need cleaning. Use a wood scraper when cleaning exhaust ports to avoid damage to cylinder or piston.

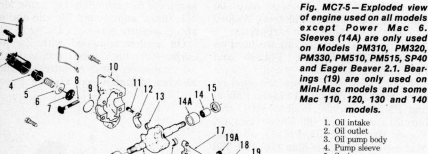

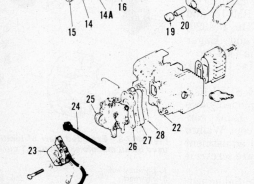

Fig. MC7-5 — Exploded view of engine used on all models except Power Mac 6. Sleeves (14A) are only used on Models PM310, PM320, PM330, PM510, PM515, SP40 and Eager Beaver 2.1. Bearings (19) are only used on Mini-Mac models and some Mac 110, 120, 130 and 140 models.

1. Oil intake
2. Oil outlet
3. Oil pump body
4. Pump sleeve
5. Spring
6. Washer
7. Pump piston
8. Chain bar mounting bolt
9. "O" ring
10. Crankcase
11. Cap screw
12. Rod cap
13. Bearing rollers (20)
14. Roller bearing
14A. Sleeve
15. Oil seal
16. Crankshaft
17. Connecting rod
18. Piston
19. Piston pin bearing
19A. Roller bearing
20. Piston pin
21. Piston rings
22. Cylinder
23. Ignition coil
24. Fuel hose
25. Carburetor
26. Gasket
27. Insulator
28. Gasket

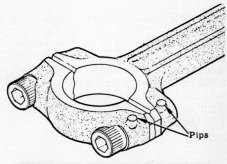

Fig. MC7-7 — For correct connecting rod assembly, pips must be aligned as shown.

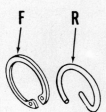

Fig. MC7-8 — Model PM510 may be equipped with flat (F) or round (R) pin retainers. Be sure retainer matches retainer groove.

REPAIRS

PISTON, RINGS AND CYLINDER. To remove piston it is necessary to separate crankcase and cylinder as outlined in CRANKSHAFT AND CRANKCASE section.

Piston pin on Mini-Mac 25, 30 and 35 models, Power Mac 6 models and some Mac 110, 120, 130 and 140 models is supported by needle bearings (19 – Fig. MC7-5) in piston and is a press fit in rod. Use McCulloch or other suitable tools to support piston then using a ¼ inch (6.35 mm) drift pin, press drift pin through metal end of one of the piston pin bearings and press pin and opposite bearing out of piston. Remove piston from rod and press out remaining bearing. Bearings must be renewed due to damage during removal. When assembling piston, pin and rod, care should be taken not to damage bearings or piston.

Piston pin on Models Eager Beaver, Eager Beaver 2.1, PM155, PM165, PM310, PM320, PM330, PM340, PM355, PM365, PM375, PM510, PM515, SP40 and some Mac 110, 120, 130 and 140 models rides in a roller bearing in the connecting rod. Piston pin may be pressed or driven out of piston after removing pin retainers while being careful not to lose loose bearing rollers in rod. Install a new bearing in rod so bearing cage is centered in rod small end.

Piston on Model PM510 may be equipped with flat (F – Fig. MC7-8) or round piston pin retainers. Be sure pin retainer matches retainer groove in piston pin bore.

Cylinder bore is chrome and no piston or piston ring oversizes are available. Ring end gap is 0.004-0.024 inch (0.11-0.61 mm) for 2.1 cu. in. (34.4 cc) models and 0.005-0.015 inch (0.13-0.38 mm) for all other models. Ring side clearance is 0.0045-0.0070 inch (0.115-0.178 mm) for Models PM510, PM515 and SP40 and 0.0030-0.0045 inch (0.077-0.115 mm) for all other models. Position piston rings on piston so end gaps are away from cylinder exhaust port.

CONNECTING ROD. Refer to PISTON section to remove piston from rod. Unscrew rod cap screws to remove rod from crankshaft. Rod bearing has 20 needle rollers.

Inspect connecting rod for worn or damaged bearing surfaces. Connecting rod should not be bent or twisted. Inspect crankshaft crankpin for wear or scoring.

To reassemble, hold bearing rollers using a heavy grease and install rod on crankshaft being sure pips on rod and cap shown in Fig. MC7-7 are aligned. Rod and cap are fractured and serrations must mate correctly. Tighten rod cap screws to 35-40 in.-lbs. (3.9-4.5 N·m).

CRANKSHAFT AND CRANKCASE. Crankshaft is supported by two needle roller bearings. Bearings on Models PM310, PM320, PM330, PM510, PM515, SP40, and Eager Beaver 2.1 are contained in sleeves (14A – Fig. MC7-5). Bearings on Power Mac 6 are retained by snap rings (5 – Fig. MC7-6). Thrust washers (7) on Power Mac 6 must be installed with chamfer on inside. Install crankshaft bearings on all models with lettered end of bearing out.

Crankcase and cylinder have mated surfaces and must not be interchanged. Use a suitable sealant on mating surfaces during assembly. Note that crankcase and cylinder must be renewed as a unit.

CLUTCH. To remove clutch, detach clutch guard, bar, chain and fan housing. The flywheel on some models may be locked by inserting a suitable tool in hole in backside of flywheel. Clutch nut has left-hand threads.

If necessary to renew clutch shoes, renew complete set of shoes. Check sprocket for worn rails and pins. Inspect sprocket needle bearing for wear. Clutch spring on all models except Power Mac 6 is retained by retainer plates (8 – Fig. MC7-9 or Fig. MC7-9A). A flat retainer plate or a plate with a bent corner has been used. Plates with a bent corner should be used in place of the flat retainer plates. Install clutch spring in clutch shoes with spring ends located where one of the retainer plates is to be installed. Install retainer plate adjacent to clutch spring ends with bent corner of plate up. Install other retainer plate with bent corner down contacting spring.

Tighten clutch nut to 125-150 in.-lbs. (14.2-16.9 N·m). Nut has left-hand threads and manufacturer does not recommend using an impact wrench to tighten clutch nut.

MANUAL CHAIN OILER. Refer to Fig. MC7-11 for exploded view of oil pump used on Eager Beaver, Mini-Mac

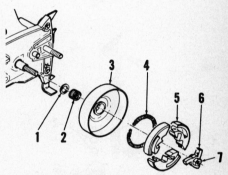

Fig. MC7-10 – Exploded view of Power Mac 6 clutch assembly.

1. Washer	
2. Bearing	5. Shoe
3. Drum & sprocket	6. Rotor
4. Garter spring	7. Nut

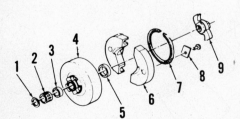

Fig. MC7-9 – Exploded view of early type clutch used on all models except Power Mac 6.

1. Washer	
2. Bearing	6. Clutch shoes
3. Spacer	7. Spring
4. Clutch drum	8. Retainer plates
5. Spacer	9. Rotor

Fig. MC7-9A – Exploded view of later type clutch assembly used on all models except Power Mac 6. Refer to Fig. MC7-9 for parts identification except for cover plate (10) and nut (11).

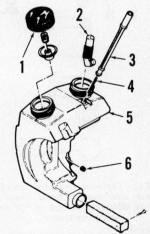

Fig. MC7-11 – View of manual oil pump used on Eager Beaver, Mini-Mac 25, 30, 35, Mac 110, 120, 130, 140, PM155, PM165, PM510, PM515 and SP40.

1. Fuel or oil fill cap	4. Spring
2. Pump body	5. Fuel & oil tank
3. Pump piston	6. Check valve

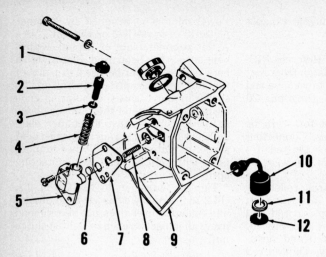

Fig. MC7-12 — Exploded view of manual oiler assembly used on some Power Mac 6 saws.

1. Cap
2. Pump plunger
3. "O" ring
4. Spring
5. Pump body
6. Valve
7. Diaphragm
8. Spring
9. Oil tank
10. Oil hose
11. Weight
12. Screen

25, 30, 35, Mac 110, 120, 130, 140, PM155, PM165, PM510, PM515 and SP40 with manual chain oiler. Three check valves (6) have been used and are colored black, green or gray. Recommended check valve is colored gray. Check valve is not renewable on some models. Be sure oil connector and oil discharge line are properly connected to prevent oil leaks.

Refer to Figs. MC7-12 and MC7-13 for exploded views of manual oil pumps used on Power Mac 6. Note that type shown in Fig. MC7-12 pumps oil using a diaphragm and spring while the manual oiler shown in Fig. MC7-13 uses a valve disc.

The manual oil pump on Models PM310, PM320, PM330, PM340, PM355, PM365, PM375 and Eager Beaver 2.1 is integral with automatic oil pump. Pump plunger (12 – Fig. MC7-13A) is operated by a remote button and push rod.

AUTOMATIC CHAIN OILER.
Refer to Fig. MC7-13 for exploded view of automatic chain oiler used on Power Mac 6. Oil pump cylinder (1) is removed by unscrewing in counterclockwise direction. Oil tank (19) must be removed to remove piston assembly. Check condi-

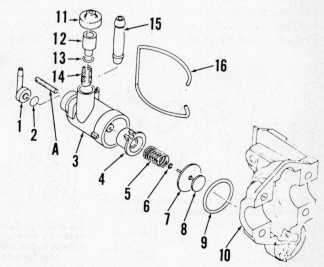

Fig. MC7-14 — Exploded view of rewind starter typical of all models.

1. Cover
2. Housing
3. Rewind spring
4. Pulley
5. Washer
6. Screw
7. Rope
8. Handle

tion of "O" rings and be sure oil and pressure passages are clear.

The automatic chain oiler used on PM155, PM165, PM510, PM515, SP40, Mini-Mac 25, 30, 35 Mac 110, 120, 130 and 140 is shown in Fig. MC7-5. Remove front cover and fuel tank to remove automatic oil pump. Some models are equipped with a washer to prevent movement of "O" ring (9). Washer must be sealed to crankcase (10) to prevent leakage. Later models have an "O" ring on the pump piston (7) and a piston ring with a smaller ID. These components should be installed in place of original components if low oil output occurs.

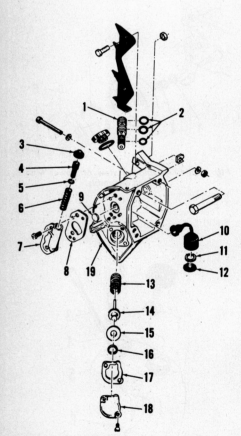

Fig. MC7-13 — Exploded view of automatic oiler and manual oiler used on some Power Mac 6 saws. Note difference in size of "O" rings (2) used on cylinder (1).

1. Oil pump cylinder
2. "O" rings
3. Cap
4. Pump plunger
5. "O" ring
6. Spring
7. Pump body
8. Gasket
9. Valve
10. Oil hose
11. Weight
12. Screen
13. Spring
14. Oiler piston
15. Piston ring
16. "O" ring
17. Gasket
18. Cover
19. Oil tank

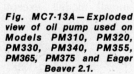

Fig. MC7-13A — Exploded view of oil pump used on Models PM310, PM320, PM330, PM340, PM355, PM365, PM375 and Eager Beaver 2.1.

1. Oil inlet
2. Check valve
3. Pump body
4. Sleeve
5. Spring
6. "O" ring
7. Washer
8. Piston
9. "O" ring
10. Crankcase
11. Cap
12. Plunger
13. "O" ring
14. Spring
15. Oil outlet
16. Retainer

Models PM310, PM320, PM330, PM340, PM355, PM365, PM375 and Eager Beaver 2.1 are equipped with automatic oil pump shown in Fig. MC7-13A. Oil tank cap is vented and must be unobstructed for proper oil pump operation. The oil pump uses two check valves which must function correctly for pump to operate. Check valve (2) is accessible after removing oil inlet (1). There is also a check valve located in pump body which is not available separately from body. Note bosses on pump body (3) when installing pump body on crankcase.

REWIND STARTER. To disassemble rewind starter, remove rope handle and allow rope to rewind into starter. Remove starter cover on all models. Remainder of disassembly is self-evident. Care should be taken when removing rewind spring to prevent injury.

Rewind spring should be wound in clockwise direction. Wind rope on pulley in clockwise direction when viewing pulley from screw (6 – Fig. MC7-14) side. To pre-tension rewind spring, complete starter assembly, pass rope through outlet and install rope handle. Pull a small amount of rope back through outlet and engage rope in notch of rope pulley (4).

Rotate pulley one turn clockwise with rope in notch. Pull rope handle and check rewind action. Repeat procedure until desired rewind action is obtained. Be sure excessive tension is not placed on spring as spring may break when rope is pulled to its full length. Proper tension can be determined by pulling rope to full length and then holding pulley. It should be possible to turn drum an additional ½ turn clockwise if spring is correctly tensioned.

CHAIN BRAKE. Models shown in Figs. MC7-15 and MC7-16 are equipped with a chain brake which stops chain motion when the operator's hand contacts chain brake lever. Refer to Fig. MC7-15 or MC7-16 for an exploded view of chain brake mechanism. Chain brake components must operate freely for mechanism to be effective.

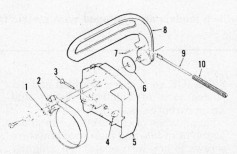

Fig. MC7-15 — Exploded view of chain brake mechanism used on Model SP40 and later Mini-Mac 25 models.

1. Springtip fastener
2. Brake strap
3. Chain adjusting screw
4. Adjusting nut
5. Clutch cover
6. Washer
7. Pin
8. Chain brake lever
9. Spring guide
10. Brake spring

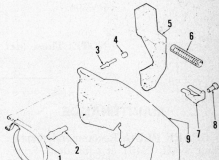

Fig. MC7-16 — Exploded view of chain brake used on Models Mac 110, 120, 130, 140, PM155, PM165, PM310, PM320, PM330, PM340, PM355, PM365, PM375, PM510, PM515, Eager Beaver and Eager Beaver 2.1.

1. Brake band
2. Pivot pin
3. Pin
4. Roller
5. Brake arm
6. Spring
7. Latch
8. Pivot pin
9. Clutch cover

McCULLOCH

Model	Bore	Stroke	Displ.	Drive Type
PM610, PM650, PM655, Super 610, Eager Beaver 3.7	47 mm (1.85 in.)	35 mm (1.38 in.)	60 cc (3.7 cu. in.)	Direct
PM605	40 mm (1.57 in.)	35 mm (1.38 in.)	58 cc (3.5 cu. in.)	Direct

NOTE: These McCulloch models are equipped with metric fasteners.

MAINTENANCE

SPARK PLUG. Recommended spark plug is AC CS45T or equivalent. Spark plug electrode gap is 0.025 inch (0.63 mm). Note that plug has a tapered seat and does not require a gasket. Tighten spark plug to 120 in.-lbs. (13.6 N·m).

CARBURETOR. Models PM650 and PM655 are equipped with a Walbro HDB diaphragm carburetor. Model PM610 may be equipped with a Tillotson HK, Walbro HDB or Zama C2S diaphragm carburetor. Models Super 610, Eager Beaver 3.7 and PM605 are equipped with a Zama C2S diaphragm carburetor. Refer to CARBURETOR SERVICE section for overhaul and exploded view of Tillotson, Walbro and Zama carburetors.

On all types of carburetors, initial adjustment of idle and high speed mixture screws is one turn open from a lightly seated position. Make final adjustment with engine warm and running. Adjust idle speed screw so engine idles just below clutch engagement speed. Adjust idle speed mixture screw so engine will accelerate cleanly without hesitation. Adjust high speed mixture screw to obtain optimum performance under cutting load.

IGNITION. All models are equipped with a capacitor discharge solid-state ignition system. Ignition components are contained in an ignition module located adjacent to flywheel. Ignition timing is 26 degrees BTDC and is not adjustable. Ignition module must be positioned by loosening retaining screws so there is 0.011-0.015 inch (0.28-0.38 mm) gap between module laminated legs and flywheel magnets.

LUBRICATION. The engine is lubricated by mixing oil with fuel. Recommended fuel:oil ratio is 40:1 if using McCulloch oil or 20:1 when using other two-stroke air-cooled oil. Regular grade gasoline is recommended.

All models are equipped with a manual and automatic oil pump. Oil output of automatic oil pump may be adjusted by removing air filter cover and turning adjusting screw (A – Fig. MC8-5).

REPAIRS

PISTON, RINGS AND CYLINDER. To remove piston, it is necessary to separate crankcase and cylinder as outlined in CRANKSHAFT AND CRANKCASE section.

The cylinder bore is chrome plated and should be inspected for flaking, cracking

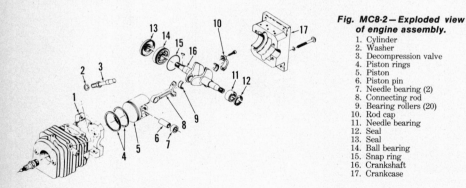

Fig. MC8-2 – Exploded view of engine assembly.
1. Cylinder
2. Washer
3. Decompression valve
4. Piston rings
5. Piston
6. Piston pin
7. Needle bearing (2)
8. Connecting rod
9. Bearing rollers (20)
10. Rod cap
11. Needle bearing
12. Seal
13. Seal
14. Ball bearing
15. Snap ring
16. Crankshaft
17. Crankcase

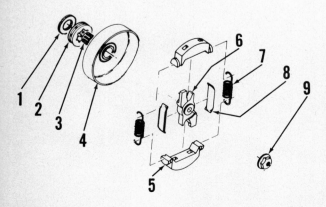

Fig. MC8-3 – Exploded view of clutch typical of all models.
1. Shim
2. Sprocket
3. Roller bearing
4. Clutch drum
5. Clutch shoe
6. Hub
7. Spring
8. Retainer
9. Nut (L.H.)

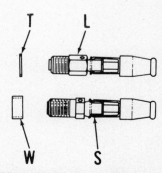

Fig. MC8-4 — Thin washer (T) must be used with long-nut decompression valve (L) while thick washer (W) is used with short-nut valve (S).

or other damage. Oversize pistons and rings are not available. Model PM610 saws built before February 1984 are equipped with a thicker piston ring than later models. Do not interchange piston rings.

The piston pin is a press fit in connecting rod small end. Piston pin rides in needle bearings which are a press fit in piston. The piston should be heated when removing or installing piston pin bearings.

Install piston so "E" on piston crown is toward exhaust port.

CONNECTING ROD, CRANK-SHAFT AND CRANKCASE.
For access to crankcase, remove air filter cover, air filter, carburetor, starter, chain brake, oil pump and left side cover. Remove fuel tank, handle, air box clutch and flywheel. Detach bottom shroud, muffler, oil tank and kill switch plate.

The connecting rod rides on 20 loose bearing rollers. Inspect rod and crankpin for excessive wear or damage. To assemble rod on crankshaft, hold bearing rollers with grease and install rod being sure pips on rod and cap are aligned. Rod and cap are fractured and serrations must mate correctly. Tighten rod screws to 65-70 in.-lbs. (7.4-7.9 N·m).

The crankshaft is supported by a ball bearing on the flywheel end and a needle roller bearing on the clutch end. To install ball bearing on crankshaft, heat bearing then press bearing on crankshaft with snap ring nearer crank pin and bottom bearing against crankshaft

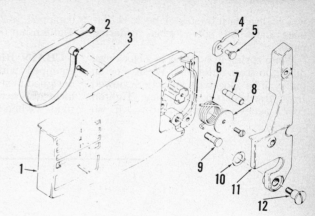

Fig. MC8-6 — Exploded view of chain brake.
1. Side cover
2. Brake band
3. Chain stop
4. Latch
5. Pivot pin
6. Spring
7. Pin
8. Washer
9. Brake band pin
10. Special washer
11. Brake lever
12. Pivot bolt

shoulder. Be sure bearing snap ring engages groove in crankcase and cylinder during assembly. Apply a suitable sealant to mating surfaces of crankcase and cylinder. Tighten crankcase screws to 70-75 in.-lbs. (7.9-8.5 N·m).

CLUTCH. Refer to Fig. MC8-3 for an exploded view of clutch. Clutch retaining nut (9) has left-hand threads. Clutch shoes, springs and retainers are available only as pairs.

DECOMPRESSION VALVE.
Models PM650 and PM655 are equipped with a decompression valve to aid engine starting. On Model PM650, two different valves have been used which are identified by nut length on the valve. Each valve must be installed with the proper thickness washer for correct fit in cylinder. Note that thin washer (T—Fig. MC8-4) must be installed on valve with long nut (L) while thick

washer (W) must be used with valve having short nut (S).

OIL PUMP. All models are equipped with the oil pump shown in Fig. MC8-5. The automatic oil pump is operated by crankcase pulsations directed against diaphragm (10) which moves piston (9). The manual oil pump is operated by forcing push rod against pump plunger (2).

REWIND STARTER. Rewind starter components are contained in starter housing on left side of saw. Detach rope handle, allow rope to wind into housing, unscrew retaining nut (2—Fig. MC8-7) or screw and disassemble starter. Use caution when removing rewind spring to prevent injury due to uncontrolled uncoiling of spring.

Note that some starters use a bolt and nut (6) to retain rope pulley while other starters are equipped with a screw

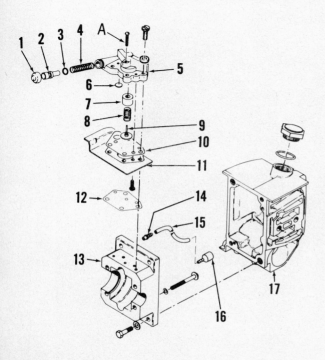

Fig. MC8-5 — Exploded view of manual and automatic oil pumps.

A. Adjusting screw
1. Cap
2. Manual pump plunger
3. "O" ring
4. Spring
5. Pump body
6. Check valve
7. Sleeve
8. Spring
9. Automatic pump piston
10. Pump diaphragm
11. Cover
12. Gasket
13. Crankcase
14. Fitting
15. Oil line
16. Oil pickup
17. Oil tank

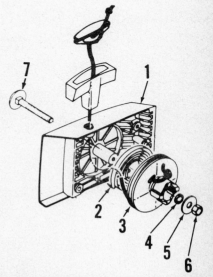

Fig. MC8-7 — Exploded view of rewind starter. A screw is used in place of bolt (7) and nut (6) on some models. Refer to text.

1. Starter housing
2. Rewind spring
3. Rope pulley
4. Spacer
5. Washer
6. Nut
7. Bolt

which threads into starter post. Difference must be noted when ordering parts.

Wrap spring in housing in a clockwise direction from outer end. Wrap rope on pulley in a clockwise direction viewed from flywheel side of pulley. Tighten rope pulley retaining screw, if so equipped, to 25-30 in.-lbs. (2.8-3.4 N·m). Tighten nut (6) to 35 in.-lbs. (3.9 N·m).

CHAIN BRAKE. Some models are equipped with a chain brake system designed to stop chain movement should kickback occur. The chain brake is activated when the operator's hand strikes chain brake lever (11 – Fig. MC8-6) tripping latch (4) and releasing spring (6) causing brake band (2) to be pulled tight around clutch drum. Pull back chain brake lever to reset mechanism. Disassembly and repair should be evident after observing exploded view and inspection of unit.

McCULLOCH

Model	Bore	Stroke	Displ.	Drive Type
PM1000	2.36 in. (60 mm)	1.42 in. (36 mm)	6.1 cu. in. (100 cc)	Direct

NOTE: This McCulloch model is equipped with metric fasteners.

MAINTENANCE

SPARK PLUG. Recommended spark plug is Bosch WS5F. Spark plug electrode gap should be 0.020 in. (0.5 mm).

CARBURETOR. A Tillotson HS diaphragm type carburetor is used. Refer to Tillotson section of CARBURETOR SERVICE section for service and exploded view of carburetor.

Initial adjustment of both low and high speed mixture screws is one turn open from a lightly seated position. Make final adjustment with engine warm and running. Adjust idle speed screw so engine idles just below clutch engagement speed. Adjust low speed mixture screw so engine will accelerate cleanly without hesitation. Adjust high speed mixture screw to obtain optimum performance under cutting load.

IGNITION. A breakerless capacitor discharge ignition system is used. Ignition timing is not adjustable. Air gap between ignition coil legs (2—Fig. MC9-1) and flywheel should be 0.014-0.018 inch (0.35-0.45 mm).

LUBRICATION. Engine is lubricated by mixing engine oil with gasoline. Recommended oil is McCulloch two-stroke oil mixed at ratio as designated on oil container. If McCulloch oil is not available, a good quality oil designed for two-stroke air-cooled engines may be used when mixed at a 25:1 ratio. Use a separate container when mixing the oil and gas.

An adjustable automatic chain oil pump is used. Adjustment screw is located on bottom of saw. Rotating screw clockwise decreases oil output. Refer to OIL PUMP section. Chain oil should be clean SAE 30 oil if ambient temperature is above 40°F (4°C) or SAE 10 at lower temperatures.

CARBON. If a noticeable lack of power or a decrease in the exhaust noise level is evident it is possible that the muffler and exhaust ports need cleaning. Use a wood scraper when cleaning exhaust ports to avoid damage to cylinder or piston.

REPAIRS

PISTON, PIN, RINGS AND CYLINDER. The piston is accessible after removing the cylinder assembly. The aluminum alloy piston is fitted with two pinned rings. Reject piston pin and piston if there is any visible up and down play of pin in the piston bosses. Piston and pin are not available separately. Piston pin rides in needle roller bearing in small end of connecting rod. Inspect and renew bearing if excessive wear or damage is evident. Install piston so arrow on piston crown points toward exhaust port.

Cylinder bore is chrome plated and no piston or piston ring oversizes are available. Maximum allowable ring end gap is 0.031 inch (0.8 mm). Renew rings or cylinder as required when service limit is exceeded. Make certain ring end gap is around locating pins when installing cylinder.

CONNECTING ROD, CRANKSHAFT AND CRANKCASE. The connecting rod and crankshaft are available only as a unit assembly. Crankshaft is supported by ball bearings at both ends.

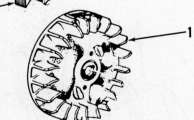

Fig. MC9-1—Illustrated view of ignition components.

1. Flywheel
2. Ignition coil
3. High tension wire
4. Ignition module
5. Ground lead
6. Right rear handle support

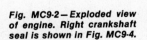

Fig. MC9-2—Exploded view of engine. Right crankshaft seal is shown in Fig. MC9-4.

1. Cylinder
2. Gasket
3. Piston rings
4. Piston
5. Piston pin
6. Pin retainer
7. Needle bearing
8. Crankshaft & rod assy.
9. Main bearing
10. Gasket
11. Left crankcase half
12. Seal
13. Main bearing
14. Bearing retainer
15. Guide pin
16. Right crankcase half

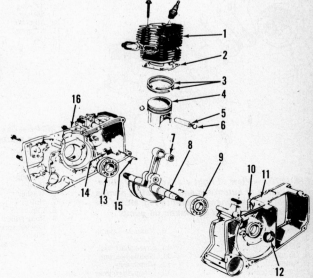

Clutch side main bearing is located by retainer (14–Fig. MC9-2) while flywheel side main bearing is located by a shoulder in crankcase. Care should be taken not to damage mating surfaces of crankcase halves. Check rotation of connecting rod around crankpin and renew crankshaft unit if roughness or other damage is found.

When reassembling, be sure flywheel side main bearing is flush against its seat in left crankcase half and that retainer (14) engages groove in clutch side main bearing. Heat may be applied to crankcase bearing bores to ease reassembly. Make certain crankshaft is centered in crankcase and will rotate freely. Clutch side crankshaft seal should be installed flush with crankcase face. Flywheel side crankshaft seal should protrude 0.04 inch (1 mm) from crankcase face when installed.

CLUTCH. To remove clutch, detach clutch guard, bar and chain. The flywheel may be locked by inserting a suitable tool through hole in left crankcase half and into drilling in flywheel. Clutch

hub (1–Fig. MC9-3) has left-hand threads. Inspect clutch shoes and drum for excessive wear or damage due to overheating. Inspect clutch drum, bearing and crankshaft for damage. Tighten clutch hub to 29 ft.-lbs. (40 N·m) torque.

OIL PUMP. A manual and an automatic oil pump is used. The manual oil pump (8–Fig. MC9-4) is attached to the right crankcase half behind the guide bar mounting studs. The manual pump may be removed for cleaning or renewal of components after removal of guide bar, chain and two retaining screws.

The automatic chain oil pump is located in right crankcase half and is driven by gear (13) on crankshaft. Oil pump operation is accomplished when plunger (7–Fig. MC9-5) is rotated by gear (13) and reciprocates as the oblique end of plunger bears against adjuster ball (10) thereby pumping oil. Oil output is changed by turning adjuster (10).

Automatic oil pump may be withdrawn from crankcase for repair or renewal of individual components after removing retainer (1). Drive gear (13) may be pulled off crankshaft after removing clutch assembly (12–Fig. MC9-4), seal (10) and spacer (9). Drive gear must be heated before installation on crankshaft to prevent crankshaft displacement.

REWIND STARTER. Rewind starter is shown in Fig. MC9-6. To dis-

assemble starter, remove rope handle and allow rope to wind around rope pulley. Disengage pulley retaining clip (8) and carefully remove rope pulley. Rewind spring is now accessible and may be removed.

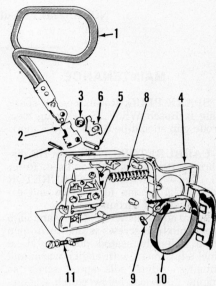

Fig. MC9-7 — Exploded view of chain brake assembly.

1. Chain brake lever
2. Sleeve
3. Washer
4. Housing
5. Pin
6. Trigger
7. Pin
8. Spring
9. Pin
10. Brake band
11. Chain tensioner

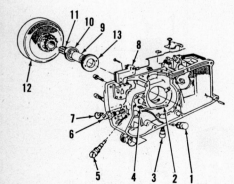

Fig. MC9-3 — Exploded view of clutch assembly.

1. Clutch hub
2. Clutch shoes
3. Garter spring
4. Clip
5. Sleeve
6. Drum
7. Needle bearing

Fig. MC9-5 — Exploded view of automatic oil pump.

1. Pump retainer
2. Plug
3. Washer
4. Orifice
5. Pump housing
6. "O" ring
7. Plunger
8. "O" ring
9. Spring
10. Adjuster
11. "O" ring
12. Cap
13. Drive gear

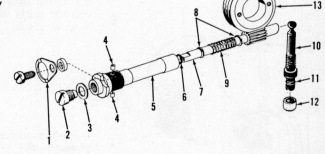

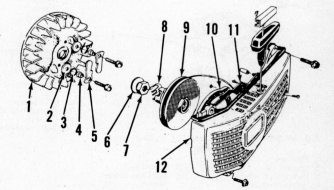

Fig. MC9-4 — View of right crankcase half showing location of automatic and manual oil pumps and related components. Refer to Fig. MC9-5 for exploded view of automatic oil pump.

1. Oil filter
2. Vent tube
3. Grommet
4. Oil pump adjuster
5. Oil pickup fitting
6. Automatic oil pump
7. Pump retainer
8. Manual oil pump
9. Spacer
10. Crankshaft seal
11. Needle bearing
12. Clutch assy.
13. Pump drive gear

Fig. MC9-6 — Exploded view of starter.

1. Flywheel
2. Washer
3. Spring
4. Bushing
5. Pawl
6. Washer
7. Nut
8. Clip
9. Rope pulley
10. Rewind spring
11. Shield
12. Starter housing

Install rewind spring in a clockwise direction viewed with spring installed in housing. Rope must be wrapped around rope pulley in a clockwise direction viewed with rope pulley in housing. Tension should be placed on starter rope by rotating rope pulley two turns clockwise.

CHAIN BRAKE. A chain brake system designed to stop chain movement should kickback occur is used. Refer to Fig. MC9-7 for an exploded view of chain brake. Chain brake is activated when the operator's hand strikes the chain brake lever thereby allowing trigger (6) to release spring (8). Spring then draws brake band tight around clutch drum to stop chain. Pull back chain brake lever to reset mechanism. No adjustment of brake mechanism is required.

Disassembly for repair or renewal of individual components is evident after inspection of unit and referral to the appropriate exploded view. It is recommended that a clutch drum be inserted in brake band and brake engaged, to facilitate removal of brake lever. When reassembling, make certain spring (8) is screwed completely on brake band and roll pins (5 and 7) are installed with split side towards front of saw.

McCULLOCH

Model	Bore	Stroke	Displ.	Drive Type
Double Eagle 50	1.72 in. (43.7 mm)	1.26 in. (32.0 mm)	3.1 cu. in. (50.0 cc)	Direct

MAINTENANCE

SPARK PLUG. Recommended spark pl,ug is Champion DJ8J. Spark plug electrode gap should be 0.025 inch (0.63 mm).

CARBURETOR. A Walbro HDA diaphragm type carburetor is used. Refer to CARBURETOR SERVICE section for overhaul and exploded view of Walbro carburetors.

Initial adjustment of low and high speed mixtures is one turn open from a lightly seated position. Make final adjustment with engine warm and running. Adjust idle speed screw so engine idles just below clutch engagement speed. Adjust low speed mixture so engine will accelerate cleanly without hesitation. Adjust high speed mixture to obtain optimum full throttle performance under cutting load. Do not adjust high speed mixture too lean as engine damage could result. Remove top cover to gain access to adjustment screws.

IGNITION. An electronic ignition system is used. Ignition coil and ignition circuitry are an integral part of an one-piece ignition module which must be serviced as a unit assembly. Air gap between ignition module core legs and flywheel magnets should be 0.010-0.012 inch (0.25-0.30 mm). Ignition timing is not adjustable.

LUBRICATION. The engine is lubricated by mixing gasoline with oil. The recommended oil is McCulloch two-

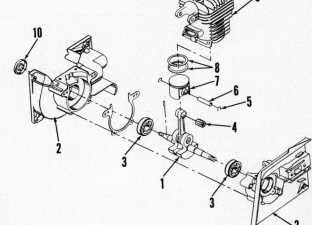

Fig. MC10-2 — Exploded view of engine assembly.

1. Crankshaft & connecting rod assy.
2. Crankcase halves
3. Ball bearings
4. Needle roller bearings
5. Piston pin retainer
6. Piston pin
7. Piston
8. Piston rings
9. Cylinder
10. Crankcase seal

stroke engine oil mixed at 40:1 ratio. If McCulloch two-stroke engine oil is not available, a good quality oil designed for use in two-stroke air-cooled engines can be used mixed at a 20:1 ratio.

An automatic as well as manual chain oil pump is used. Automatic oiler (5–Fig. MC10-1) is driven by worm gear (3) which is fitted on crankshaft (1). Note that right crankcase seal (6) is an integral part of oil pump. The automatic oil pump can be removed for inspection or repair after removing chain, guide bar and clutch assembly. The manual oil pump is a plunger type and is mounted to the left of trigger handle in saw body.

CARBON. If a noticeable lack of power or a decrease in the exhaust noise

lever is evident, it is possible the muffler and exhaust ports are restricted with carbon. Use a wooden scraper when cleaning carbon deposits from exhaust ports to avoid damaging piston or cylinder.

REPAIRS

PISTON, PIN, RINGS AND CYLINDER. The piston is accessible after removal of cylinder (9–Fig. MC10-2). The two piston rings (8) are pinned to prevent ring rotation. Piston pin (6) rides in needle roller bearing (4), in small end of connecting rod, and is retained in piston with two wire clips (5). Piston ring end gap should be 0.070 inch (1.78 mm). When installing piston, align "EX" on piston crown with exhaust port.

The cylinder bore is chrome plated and oversize pistons and cylinders are not available. Recommended piston-to-cylinder clearance is measured 3/8 inch (9.5 mm) from bottom of piston skirt. Clearance should be 0.004 inch (0.10 mm). Renew piston and cylinder assembly if flaking, cracking or other damage is noted in cylinder bore.

CONNECTING ROD, CRANKSHAFT AND CRANKCASE. The crankshaft is supported by two ball bearings (3–Fig. MC10-2) located in crankcase halves (2). Use care not to damage mating surfaces when splitting crank-

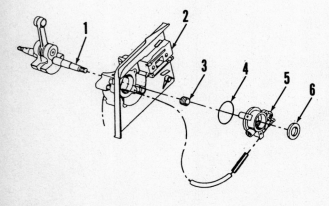

Fig. MC10-1 — Exploded view of automatic chain oil pump.

1. Crankshaft & connecting rod assy.
2. Right crankcase half
3. Worm gear
4. "O" ring
5. Oil pump assy.
6. Crankcase seal

case. Crankshaft and connecting rod are a unit assembly. Rotate connecting rod around crankpin to check for roughness, excessive wear or other damage. Renew as necessary.

Heat may be applied to bearing bores in crankcase halves to ease reassembling. Make certain crankshaft is centered in crankcase and will rotate freely.

CLUTCH. A three-shoe centrifugal clutch is used. Clutch rotor (6—Fig. MC10-3) has left-hand threads. Inspect clutch shoes (5) and drum (3) for excessive wear or damage due to overheating. Clutch shoes should be renewed as a set.

Periodically inspect clutch bearing (2) and lubricate with a suitable high temperature grease. When installing clutch spring (7), locate spring ends at rivet (9) to prevent spring rotation.

REWIND STARTER. Rewind starter shown in Fig. MC10-4 is used. To disassemble starter, remove rope handle (2) and carefully allow rope pulley (5) to turn counterclockwise to relieve tension on rewind spring. Remove screw (12) and lift off washer (11), pawl plate (10), pawl plate springs (9), pawls (7) and pawl springs (6). Be careful and withdraw rope pulley (5) noting how pulley engages with rewind spring and housing

assembly (4). Individual components can now be serviced.

Rope must be wrapped on pulley in a clockwise direction when reassembling. Turn rope pulley two turns clockwise before passing rope through rope guide to apply tension on rewind spring.

CHAIN BRAKE. A chain brake system designed to stop chain movement should kickback occur is used. The chain brake is activated when the operator's hand strikes chain brake lever (1—Fig. MC10-5), tripping latch (4), and releasing spring (8). The spring pulls brake band (11) tight around clutch drum, stopping chain movement. Pull back chain brake lever to reset mechanism.

Disassembly for repair or component replacement is evident after referral to exploded view and inspection of unit. No adjustment of chain brake system is required.

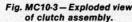

Fig. MC10-3 — Exploded view of clutch assembly.

1. Shim
2. Needle roller bearing
3. Drum & sprocket assy.
4. Shim
5. Shoes
6. Rotor
7. Spring
8. Shoe plate
9. Rivet

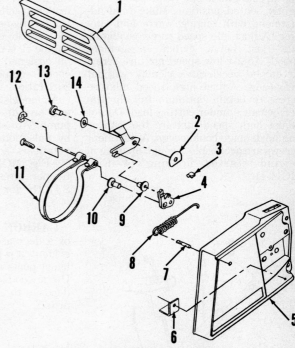

Fig. MC10-4 — Exploded view of rewind starter.

1. Washer
2. Rope handle
3. Housing
4. Rewind spring & housing assy.
5. Rope pulley
6. Pawl springs
7. Pawls
8. Pulley bushing
9. Pawl plate spring
10. Pawl plate
11. Washer
12. Screw

Fig. MC10-5 — Exploded view of chain brake system.

1. Chain brake lever
2. Washer
3. Clip
4. Latch
5. Housing
6. Chain stop
7. Pin
8. Spring
9. Latch slider
10. Pivot
11. Brake band
12. "E" clip
13. Pivot
14. Washer

McCULLOCH

Model	Bore	Stroke	Displ.	Drive Type
PM380, PM380AS, Eager Beaver 2.3	1.575 in. (40 mm)	1.181 in. (30 mm)	2.3 cu. in. (37.7 cc)	Direct

MAINTENANCE

SPARK PLUG. Recommended spark plug is AC CS45T or Champion DJ8. Spark plug electrode gap should be 0.025 inch (0.63 mm).

CARBURETOR. All models are equipped with a Tillotson diaphragm type carburetor. Refer to CARBURETOR SERVICE section for overhaul and exploded views.

Initial adjustment for high and low mixture screws is one turn open from a lightly seated position. Make final adjustment with engine warm and running. Adjust idle speed screw so engine idles just below clutch engagement speed. Adjust low speed mixture screw so engine accelerates cleanly without hesitation. Adjust high speed mixture screw to obtain optimum full throttle performance under cutting load. Do not adjust high speed mixture too lean as engine damage could occur. Adjustment screws are accessible through opening in rewind starter housing (4 – Fig. MC11-1).

IGNITION. All models are equipped with a solid state electronic ignition system. Ignition coil and all ignition circuitry are contained in an one-piece ignition module. Ignition module is serviced as a unit assembly only. Ignition timing is fixed at 26 degrees BTDC and is not adjustable. Air gap between ignition module core legs and flywheel magnets should be 0.010-0.012 inch (0.25-0.30 mm).

LUBRICATION. The engine is lubricated by mixing oil with regular leaded gasoline. Recommended oil is McCulloch two-stroke engine oil mixed at a 40:1 ratio. If McCulloch two-stroke engine oil is not available, a good quality oil designed for use in two-stroke air-cooled engines can be used mixed at a 20:1 ratio.

All models are equipped with a manual and an adjustable automatic chain oil pump. Automatic oil pump is actuated by pulsations from the crankcase and output is adjusted by turning screw (4 – Fig. MC11-2). Use SAE 30 oil for temperatures above 40°F (4°C) and SAE 10 for temperatures below 40°F (4°C).

CARBON. If noticeable lack of power or a decrease in exhaust noise level is evident, it is possible the muffler and exhaust ports are restricted with carbon. Use a wooden scraper to remove carbon deposits to avoid damaging cylinder or piston.

REPAIRS

PISTON, PIN, RINGS AND CYLINDER. The piston is fitted with two cast iron compression rings. Pins located in the piston ring grooves prevent ring rotation. When installing piston rings, make certain ring end gaps are around pins. Piston pin (7 – Fig. MC11-3) rides on needle roller bearing (5) fitted in the connecting rod small end and is held in place by two retainers (6). To remove piston, remove the piston pin retainers and tap out piston pin using a suitable driver. When installing piston, align the "EX" stamped on piston crown with exhaust port.

Cylinder bore is chrome plated and should be inspected for flaking, cracking, scoring or other damage. Oversize piston and cylinder assemblies are not available.

CONNECTING ROD, CRANKSHAFT AND CRANKCASE. Crankshaft and connecting rod are serviced as a unit assembly. Rotate connecting rod around crankpin to check for roughness, excessive wear or other damage. Renew as necessary.

The crankshaft is supported by two needle roller bearings (3 – Fig. MC11-3) located in crankcase halves.

When reassembling, apply a suitable sealer to crankcase mating surfaces. Make certain crankshaft is centered in crankcase and will turn freely.

CLUTCH. Refer to Fig. MC11-4 for a view identifying clutch assembly (7). Clutch shoes and rotor are serviced as a unit assembly only. Clutch rotor has left-hand threads. Clutch drum and sprocket assembly (8) is retained on crankshaft by

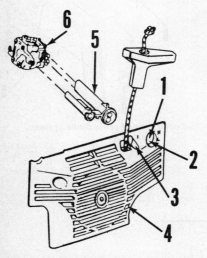

Fig. MC11-1 – View showing position of carburetor adjustment screws.

1. High speed mixture screw
2. Low speed mixture screw
3. Idle speed screw
4. Rewind starter housing
5. Guide tube
6. Carburetor

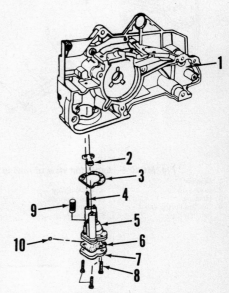

Fig. MC11-2 – Exploded view of automatic chain oil pump.

1. Right crankcase half
2. Gasket
3. Gasket
4. Adjusting screw
5. Pump body
6. Gasket
7. Cover
8. Screw
9. Filter screen
10. Check ball

snap ring (10). Note shield (6) used to prevent dirt or sawdust from centering clutch assembly. Tighten clutch rotor and shoe assembly to 125-150 in.-lbs. (14.2-17.0 N·m).

AUTO SHARP. Model PM380AS is equipped with automatic chain sharpening system shown in Fig. MC11-5. Except for knob (1) and spring (2), the auto sharp attachment is serviced as a unit assembly.

REWIND STARTER. All models are equipped with the rewind starter shown in Fig. MC11-6. To disassemble, fully extend rope, then pull slack rope back through rope guide and carefully allow rope pulley (6) to unwind relieving tension on rewind spring (5). Remove nut (9) and washer (8) and lift off rope pulley noting how pulley engages rewind spring. All components can now be serviced.

When reassembling, install rewind spring (5) into starter housing (2) making certain hook in outer coil engages notch in housing. Wind rope in a clockwise direction on rope pulley as viewed from pulley side of starter. When installing rope pulley, engage dog on pulley with hook on inner coil of rewind spring. To apply tension on rewind spring, sufficiently extend starter rope to allow rope pulley to be turned one turn clockwise. Then, carefully allow rope pulley to rewind rope. If rope handle is not tight against housing, repeat procedure one additional turn clockwise.

CHAIN BRAKE. All models are equipped with a chain brake system designed to stop chain movement should kickback occur. Chain brake is activated when operator's hand strikes chain brake lever (1–Fig. MC11-4), tripping latch (4), releasing spring (3) and pulling brake band (11) tight around clutch drum (8). Disassembly for repair or component renewal is evident after referral to exploded view and inspection of unit. No adjustment of chain brake system is required.

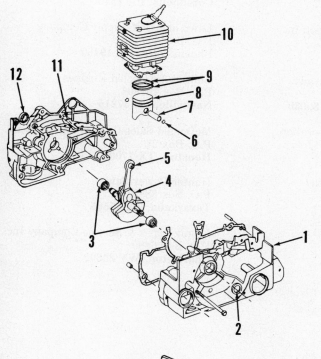

Fig. MC11-3 — Exploded view of engine.

1. Left crankcase half
2. Crankcase seal
3. Needle roller bearings
4. Crankshaft & connecting rod assy.
5. Needle roller bearing
6. Retainer
7. Piston pin
8. Piston
9. Piston rings
10. Cylinder
11. Right crankcase half
12. Crankcase seal

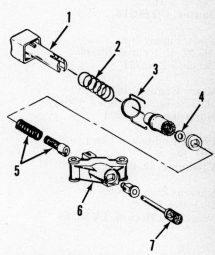

Fig. MC11-5 — Exploded view of auto sharp assembly used on Model PM380AS.

1. Knob
2. Spring
3. Wire bail
4. Washer
5. Springs
6. Housing
7. Grinding wheel

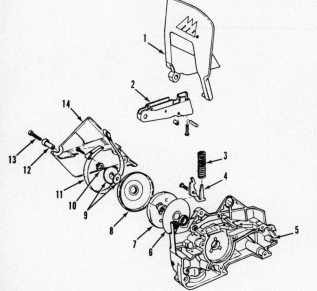

Fig. MC11-4 — Exploded view of clutch and chain brake assembly.

1. Chain brake lever
2. Brake box
3. Brake spring
4. Latch
5. Right crankcase half
6. Shield
7. Clutch assy.
8. Clutch drum & sprocket assy.
9. Washers
10. Snap ring
11. Brake band
12. Brake bushing
13. Screw
14. Clutch cover

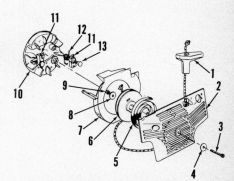

Fig. MC11-6 — Exploded view of rewind spring starter.

1. Rope handle
2. Housing
3. Screw
4. Washer
5. Rewind spring
6. Rope pulley
7. Fan baffle
8. Washer
9. Nut
10. Flywheel
11. Pawl
12. Pawl spring
13. Pawl pin

McCULLOCH DISTRIBUTORS

(Arranged Alphabetically by States)

These firms carry extensive stocks of repair parts.

Norton Corporation
P.O. Box 26450
Phoenix, AZ 85068

Lanco, Engines Service
13610 Gramercy Place
Gardena, CA 90249

West Star Distributing Co. Inc.
2438 Radley Court
Hayward, CA 94545

L. L. Johnson Distributing Co.
P.O. Box 16102
Denver, CO 80216

Cooks Supply Inc.
395 W. Enterprise Street
Ocoee, FL 32761

Metro Engines, Inc.
5695 Suite A, Oakbrook Pkwy.
Norcross, GA 30093

Power Equipment Company
P.O. Box 8
Elmhurst, IL 60126

Larsen-Olson of Iowa
P.O. Box 65530
West Des Moines, IA 50265

Crandall-Hicks
30 Oak Street
Westboro, MA 01581

Larsen-Olson of Minnesota
12811 16th Avenue, North
Plymouth, MN 55441

G.T.I. Distributing Inc.
727 Goddard Avenue
Chesterfield, MO 63017

Midwest Turf & Irrigation Inc.
8700 "J" Street
Omaha, NE 68127

Norton Corporation-Nevada
4420 Andrews Suite A
North Las Vegas, NV 89030

Eaton Equipment Corporation
23 Lake Street
Hamburg, NY 14075

Eaton Golf & Tractor Inc.
P.O. Box 1376
Syracuse, NY 13201

Porter Brothers Inc.
P.O. Box 520
Shelby, NC 28150

Century Equipment Inc.
4199 Leap Road
Hilliard, OH 43026

Bull Equipment Company Inc.
9525 S.W. Commerce Circle
Wilsonville, OR 97070

Stull Company
701 Fourth Avenue
Coraopolis, PA 15108

Lawn and Golf Supply Company
P.O. Box 447
Phoenixville, PA 19460

Chilton Air Cooled Engines
P.O. Box 150806
Nashville, TN 37215

McDonald Sales Corporation of Texas
P.O. Box 27
Houston, TX 77001

Hunter Power Saw
P.O. Box 5889
Texarkana, TX 75505

Engine Sales & Service Company Inc.
P.O. Box 6490
Charleston, WV 25302

OLYMPYK

OLEO-MAC s.p.a.
42011 Banolo In Piano
Reggio Emilia, Italy

Model	Bore	Stroke	Displ.	Drive Type
234AV	38 mm	30 mm	34 cc	Direct
	(1.50 in.)	(1.18 in.)	(2.1 cu. in.)	
240, 241, 244, 244AV	40 mm	30 mm	38 cc	Direct
	(1.57 in.)	(1.18 in.)	(2.3 cu. in.)	

MAINTENANCE

SPARK PLUG. Recommended spark plug for all models is Bosch WS7F. Spark plug electrode gap should be 0.63 mm (0.025 in.).

CARBURETOR. Tillotson HU and Walbro WA diaphragm type carburetors have been used. Refer to Tillotson and Walbro sections of CARBURETOR SERVICE section for service procedures and exploded views.

Initial adjustment for low and high speed mixture screws is one turn open from a lightly seated position. Final adjustment should be made with engine running at normal operating temperature. Adjust low speed mixture so engine will accelerate cleanly without hesitation. Adjust high speed mixture to obtain optimum full throttle performance under cutting load. Do not adjust high speed mixture too lean as overheating and engine damage could result. Adjust idle speed to just below clutch engagement speed.

IGNITION. Early Model 240 is equipped with a conventional flywheel magneto ignition system with breaker points located behind the flywheel. Breaker-point gap should be 0.40 mm

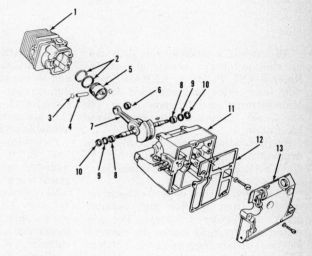

Fig. OL2 — Exploded view of engine assembly.
1. Cylinder
2. Piston rings
3. Retainer
4. Piston pin
5. Piston
6. Needle bearing
7. Crankshaft & connecting rod assy.
8. Main bearing
9. Thrust washer
10. Seal
11. Crankcase
12. Gasket
13. Cover

(0.016 in.). Breaker-point gap is adjusted by rotating stator plate. Breaker-point gap must be correctly adjusted as point gap affects ignition timing. Air gap between ignition coil legs and flywheel magnets should be 0.30 mm (0.012 in.).

Later Model 240 and all other models are equipped with a breakerless electronic ignition system. Ignition coil and all electronic circuitry are contained in an one-piece ignition module (2 – Fig. OL1) located outside of flywheel (1). Except for faulty wiring and wiring connections, repair of ignition system malfunctions is accomplished by component renewal. Use a process of elimination to trouble-shoot ignition module. Module to flywheel air gap shoud be 0.30 mm (0.012 in.). Ignition timing is fixed and not adjustable. Models 244 built before serial number 040440001 are equipped with a Phelon ignition system. Models 244 built after serial number 040440000 are equipped with a Selettra ignition system. The two ignition systems are interchangeable if entire system (module and flywheel) is exchanged.

LUBRICATION. The engine is lubricated by mixing oil with the fuel. The recommended oil is BIA certified two-stroke air-cooled engine oil. Fuel:oil ratio should be 40:1 when using a recommended oil. If BIA certified two-stroke air-cooled oil is not available, use a good quality oil designed for use in air-cooled two-stroke engines mixed at a 20:1 ratio. Use a separate container when mixing fuel and oil.

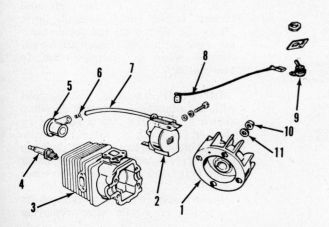

Fig. OL1 — Exploded view of electronic ignition system.
1. Flywheel
2. Ignition module
3. Cylinder
4. Spark plug
5. Boot
6. Spring connector
7. High tension lead
8. Primary lead
9. Ignition switch
10. Nut
11. Washer

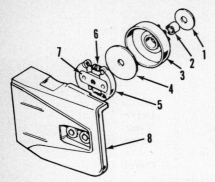

Fig. OL3—Exploded view of centrifugal clutch assembly.

1. Washer
2. Needle bearing
3. Drum
4. Washer
5. Shoe
6. Spring
7. Hub
8. Cover

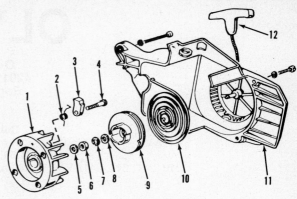

Fig. OL5—Exploded view of rewind starter. Two pawls (3), springs (2) and bolts (4) are used.

1. Flywheel
2. Spring
3. Pawl
4. Bolt
5. Washer
6. Nut
7. Snap ring
8. Washer
9. Rope pulley
10. Rewind spring
11. Starter housing
12. Rope handle

All models are equipped with adjustable automatic chain oil pumps. Refer to OIL PUMP in REPAIRS section for service and exploded views. Manufacturer recommends using oil specifically designed for saw chain lubrication.

Needle bearing (2–Fig. OL3) in clutch drum (3) should be lubricated with SAE 20 or SAE 30 oil at regular intervals.

CARBON. Carbon deposits should be removed from muffler and exhaust ports at regular intervals. Position piston at top dead center to prevent loosened carbon from entering cylinder. Use a wooden scraper to remove carbon. Use caution not to scratch piston or cylinder.

REPAIRS

CYLINDER, PISTON, PIN AND RINGS. Cylinder bore is chrome plated and should be renewed if cracking, flaking, scoring or other damage is noted. Cylinder (1–Fig. OL2) and crankcase (11) are a unit assembly and are not available separately.

Piston (5) and cylinder (1) are graded "A," "B," "C" or "D" during production with "A" being the largest size. Piston grade mark is stamped on piston crown while cylinder grade mark is stamped on cylinder head. Piston and cylinder marks should match although one size larger piston can be installed in a used cylinder, if matched piston is not available. For instance, piston marked "A" can be installed in a used cylinder marked "B."

Piston (5) is equipped with two piston rings (2). Locating pins are present in ring grooves to prevent ring rotation. Make certain ring end gaps are properly positioned around locating pins when installing cylinder. Piston pin (4) rides in needle bearing (6) and is held in place with two wire retainers (3). Inspect piston, pin and needle bearing for excessive wear or damage and renew as required. Install piston in cylinder with arrow on piston crown facing toward exhaust port.

CRANKSHAFT, CONNECTING ROD AND CRANKCASE. Crankshaft assembly is loose in crankcase when cylinder is removed. Crankshaft and connecting rod are a unit assembly. Check rotation of connecting rod around crankpin and renew crankshaft assembly if roughness, excessive play or other damage is noted.

Crankshaft is supported at both ends with needle type main bearings (8–Fig. OL2). Note location of thrust washers (9). Make certain thrust washers are properly located in grooves of crankcase and cylinder when reassembling. Use a suitable sealant on mating surfaces of crankcase and cylinder base.

CLUTCH. All models are equipped with the centrifugal clutch shown in Fig. OL3. Clutch hub (7) has left-hand threads. Inspect clutch shoes (5), drum (3), needle bearing (2) and needle bearing wear surface on crankshaft for excessive wear or damage due to overheating.

OIL PUMP. All models are equipped with the adjustable automatic oil pump shown in Fig. OL4. Oil is pumped by plunger (1) which is driven by a cam ground on engine crankshaft (21). Pump output is regulated by rotating adjusting screw (14). Clockwise rotation decreases output.

Pump assembly can be withdrawn for inspection or repair after removing

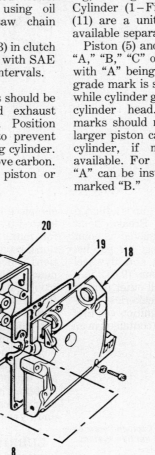

Fig. OL4—Exploded view of automatic oil pump and crankcase.

1. Plunger
2. Spring seat
3. Spring
4. "O" ring
5. Pump body
6. Check ball
7. Spring
8. "O" ring
9. Pump body
10. "O" ring
11. Spring
12. Pump fixture
13. "O" ring
14. Adjusting screw
15. Screw
16. Washer
17. Retainer
18. Cover
19. Gasket
20. Crankcase
21. Crankshaft

screw (15). Inspect all components for excessive wear or damage and renew as required. Check ball (6) must seat properly in pump body (5) for correct pump operation. Prime pump with clean oil prior to reassembly.

REWIND STARTER. To disassemble starter, pull out rope approximately 30 cm (12 in.) and hold rope pulley (9–Fig. OL5) from turning. Grasp rope and place into notch in rope pulley. Carefully allow pulley to unwind, relieving tension on rewind spring (10). Pry off snap ring (7) and remove rope pulley (9) being careful not to dislodge rewind spring (10). If rewind spring must be removed, use caution not to allow spring to uncoil uncontrolled.

During reassembly, lightly lubricate rewind spring and wind into starter housing in a clockwise direction starting with outer coil. Wind rope onto rope pulley in a clockwise direction as viewed from flywheel side of pulley. Preload rewind spring by placing rope into notch in rope pulley and rotating pulley in clockwise direction. Holding pulley firmly, allow tension on rewind spring to retract rope into starter housing. Spring tension is correct if rope handle is snug against housing with rope retracted and with rope fully extended, rope pulley will rotate one turn further.

CHAIN BRAKE. Some models are equipped with a chain brake system designed to quickly stop chain movement should kickback occur. Chain brake is activated when operator's hand strikes chain brake lever (1–Fig. OL6), tripping latch (4) to allow spring (6) to pull brake band (8) tight around clutch drum. Pull back chain brake lever to reset mechanism.

Disassembly for inspection or repair is evident after referral to exploded view and inspection of unit. Lubricate pivot points with a suitable grease. Do not lubricate brake band or outer diameter of clutch drum. No adjustment of chain brake system is required.

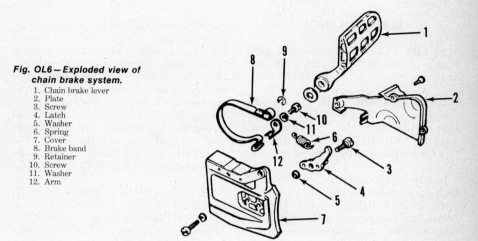

Fig. OL6 — Exploded view of chain brake system.
1. Chain brake lever
2. Plate
3. Screw
4. Latch
5. Washer
6. Spring
7. Cover
8. Brake band
9. Retainer
10. Screw
11. Washer
12. Arm

OLYMPYK

Model	Bore	Stroke	Displ.	Drive Type
945, 945AV	44 mm (1.73 in.)	30 mm (1.18 in.)	46 cc (2.8 cu. in.)	Direct
950, 950AV	45 mm (1.77 in.)	31 mm (1.22 in.)	50 cc (3.0 cu. in.)	Direct

MAINTENANCE

SPARK PLUG. Recommended spark plug is Bosch WS7F. Spark plug electrode gap should be 0.5 mm (0.020 in.).

CARBURETOR. All models are equipped with a Tillotson HK diaphragm type carburetor. Refer to Tillotson secton of CARBURETOR SERVICE section for service procedures and exploded views.

Initial adjustment for both low and high speed mixture screws is one turn open from a lightly seated position. Make final adjustment with engine running at operating temperature. Adjust low speed mixture so engine will accelerate cleanly without hesitation. Adjust high speed mixture to obtain optimum full throttle performance under cutting load. Adjust idle speed to just below clutch engagement speed.

IGNITION. All models are equipped with a breakerless electronic ignition system. Ignition coil and all electronic circuitry are contained in an one-piece ignition module (2–Fig. OL15). Except for faulty wiring and wiring connections, repair of ignition system malfunctions is accomplished by component renewal. Use a process of elimination to trouble-shoot ignition module. Ignition timing is not adjustable. Air gap between ignition module core laminations and flywheel magnets should be 0.35 mm (0.014 in.). Flywheel nut (9) should be tightened to 9.8 N·m (7 ft.-lbs.).

LUBRICATION. The engine is lubricated by mixing oil with the fuel. The recommended oil is BIA certified two-stroke air-cooled oil. Fuel:oil mixture should be a 40:1 ratio when using a recommended oil. If BIA certified two-stroke air-cooled oil is not available, use a good quality oil designed for use in two-stroke air-cooled engines mixed at a 20:1 ratio. Use a separate container when mixing fuel and oil.

All models are equipped with adjustable automatic chain oil pump assemblies. Refer to OIL PUMP in REPAIRS section for service, adjustment procedures and exploded views. Use clean SAE 30 or SAE 40 automotive oil for saw chain lubrication. During cold weather operation, chain oil may be diluted up to 50 percent with kerosene.

CARBON. Carbon deposits should be removed from muffler and exhaust ports at regular intervals. Use a wooden scraper to remove carbon to prevent damaging piston or cylinder. Position piston at top dead center to prevent loosened carbon from entering cylinder.

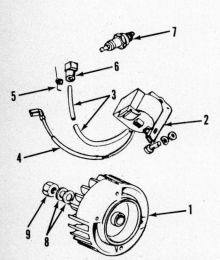

Fig. OL15 — Exploded view of ignition system used on all models.

1. Flywheel
2. Ignition module
3. High tension lead
4. Primary lead
5. Connector
6. Boot
7. Spark plug
8. Washers
9. Nut

Fig. OL16 — Exploded view of engine assembly.

1. Cylinder
2. Gasket
3. Piston rings
4. Piston pin
5. Retainer
6. Needle bearing
7. Crankshaft & connecting rod assy.
8. Right crankcase half
9. Seal
10. Main bearing
11. Main bearing
12. Seal
13. Gasket
14. Left crankcase half

REPAIRS

CYLINDER, PISTON, PIN AND RINGS. Cylinder bore is chrome plated and should be renewed if cracking, flaking, scoring or other damage is noted in cylinder bore. Inspect piston and renew if excessively worn or damaged. Piston and cylinder are marked "A," "B," "C" or "D" during production to obtain the desired piston-to-cylinder clearance with "A" being the largest size. Piston and cylinder grade marks should match although one size larger piston may be installed in a used cylinder. For instance, a piston marked "A" may be installed in a used cylinder marked "B." Piston is marked on piston crown while cylinder is marked adjacent to spark plug hole as shown in Fig. OL17. Piston is equipped with two piston rings. Locating pins are present in ring grooves to prevent ring rotation. Make certain ring end gaps are properly positioned around locating pins when installing cylinder. Piston pin rides in a needle roller bearing in connecting rod small end and is held in place with two wire retainers. Check needle bearing for excessive wear or discoloration due to overheating. Check fit of piston pin in

piston and renew pin and piston as required. Piston pin, pin retainers and piston rings are available separately, but piston is only available as an assembly with piston rings, pin and retainers. Install piston in cylinder with arrow on piston crown toward exhaust port. Apply Loctite 242 or a suitable equivalent on threads of cylinder screws and tighten to 11.8 N·m (9 ft.-lbs.).

CRANKSHAFT, CONNECTING ROD AND CRANKCASE. Crankcase halves must be split to remove crankshaft. Take care not to damage crankcase mating surfaces. Heat may be applied to crankcase to ease removal and installation of main bearings and crankshaft. Crankshaft and connecting rod are only available as a unit assembly. Check rotation of connecting rod around crankpin and renew crankshaft assembly if roughness, excessive play or other damage is noted. Use a suitable sealant on crankcase gasket upon reassembly.

CLUTCH. All models are equipped with the three-shoe centrifugal clutch shown in Fig. OL18. Clutch hub (2) has left-hand threads. Inspect shoes (1), drum (5) and needle bearing for wear or

damage due to overheating. Tighten clutch hub to 19.6 N·m (14 ft.-lbs.).

OIL PUMP. All models are equipped with an adjustable automatic chain oil pump. Oil is pumped by plunger (10 – Fig. OL19) which is driven by a cam ground on engine crankshaft. Oil pump output is regulated by rotating adjusting screw (2) located at front of engine next to guide bar. Clockwise rotation decreases oil output. Inspect plunger (10) and pump body (7) for excessive wear or damage. Inspect "O" rings for hardening or cracking. Check ball (6) must seat properly in pump body (7) for correct pump operation. Nut (1) should be tightened in pump body (7) to 20 N·m (15 ft.-lbs.). Tighten pump assembly in crankcase to 10 N·m (7 ft.-lbs.).

REWIND STARTER. All models are equipped with the rewind starter shown in Fig. OL20. To disassemble starter, pull out rope approximately 30 cm (12 in.) and hold rope pulley from turning. Place rope into notch (N) in rope pulley (10) and carefully allow pulley to unwind, relieving tension on rewind spring (11). Remove screw (5) and lift out rope

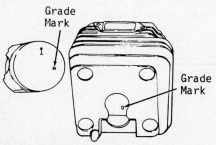

Fig. OL17 – View showing location of piston and cylinder grade marks. Grade "D" is shown.

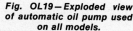

Fig. OL19 – Exploded view of automatic oil pump used on all models.

1. Nut
2. Adjusting screw
3. Spring
4. "O" ring
5. Spring
6. Check ball
7. Pump body
8. "O" rings
9. Spring
10. Plunger
11. "O" rings

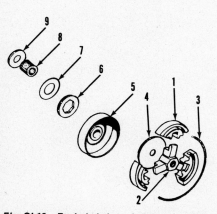

Fig. OL18 – Exploded view of clutch assembly.

1. Shoe
2. Hub
3. Spring
4. Washer
5. Drum
6. Sprocket
7. Washer
8. Needle bearing
9. Washer

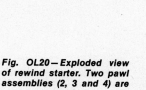

Fig. OL20 – Exploded view of rewind starter. Two pawl assemblies (2, 3 and 4) are used.

1. Flywheel
2. Spring
3. Pawl
4. Bolt
5. Screw
6. Washer
7. Washer
8. Washers
9. Nut
10. Rope pulley
11. Rewind spring
12. Plate
13. Starter housing
14. Rope handle
N. Notch

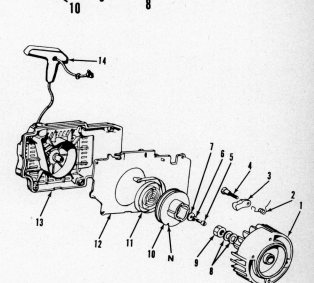

pulley being careful not to dislodge rewind spring. If rewind spring must be removed, use caution not to allow spring to uncoil uncontrolled.

Wind rewind spring into starter housing (13) in a clockwise direction starting from outer coil. New rope should be 96 cm (38 in.) long and 3 mm (1/8 in.) in diameter. Wind rope onto pulley in a clockwise direction as viewed from fly-

wheel side of pulley. Lightly grease pulley shaft in starter housing before installing pulley. Apply Loctite 242 or a suitable equivalent onto threads of screw (5). To preload rewind spring, place rope into notch (N) and rotate pulley clockwise. Tension on rewind spring is correct if rope handle is snug against starter housing with rope retracted and with rope fully extended,

rope pulley will rotate one additional turn clockwise. If rewind spring tension is not correct, repeat above procedure and either add more tension or remove tension as needed.

When installing rewind starter assembly onto saw, slowly pull out rope to engage pawls (3) with rope pulley. Tighten starter housing screws to 2 N·m (18 in.-lbs.).

CHAIN BRAKE. Some models are equipped with a chain brake system designed to quickly stop chain movement should kickback occur. Chain brake is activated when operator's hand strikes chain brake lever (1 – Fig. OL21). Forward movement of chain brake lever disengages arm (9), allowing spring (6) to draw band (4) tight around clutch drum. Pull back chain brake lever to reset mechanism.

Disassembly is evident after referral to exploded view and inspection of unit. Chain brake should be in the activated position when removing spring (6). Renew brake band (4) if band is worn beyond 3/4 of its original thickness at the most worn area. Chain brake should be kept clean and free of sawdust and dirt accumulation. Lightly lubricate pivot points being careful not to allow grease to get on working surface of brake band or clutch drum. No adjustment of chain brake system is required.

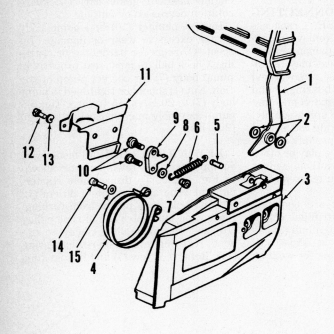

Fig. OL21 – Exploded view of chain brake system used on so equipped models.

1. Lever
2. Washers
3. Housing
4. Brake band
5. Pin
6. Spring
7. Spacer
8. Washer
9. Arm
10. Screws
11. Chain guide
12. Screw
13. Washer
14. Screw
15. Washer

OLYMPYK

Model	Bore	Stroke	Displ.	Drive Type
251, 251B, 252	44 mm (1.73 in.)	32 mm (1.26 in.)	49 cc (3.0 cu. in.)	Direct
251 Super, 254, 254AV, 355, 355AV	46 mm (1.81 in.)	32 mm (1.26 in.)	54 cc (3.3 cu. in.)	Direct
261, 264, 264AV	47 mm (1.85 in.)	35 mm (1.38 in.)	61 cc (3.7 cu. in.)	Direct
271, 272, 272AV	49 mm (1.93 in.)	35 mm (1.38 in.)	67 cc (4.1 cu. in.)	Direct
284, 284AV, 481 Super, 482AV, 482MP	52 mm (2.05 in.)	38 mm (1.50 in.)	82 cc (5.0 cu. in.)	Direct

MAINTENANCE

SPARK PLUG. Recommended spark plug for all models is Bosch WS7F or Champion CJ7Y. Electrode gap should be 0.5 mm (0.020 in.). Tighten spark plug to 29.4 N·m (22 ft.-lbs.).

CARBURETOR. All models are equipped with a Tillotson HS diaphragm type carburetor. Refer to Tillotson section of CARBURETOR SERVICE section for service procedure and exploded view.

Initial adjustment of low speed mixture screw is 1½ turns open from a lightly seated position. Initial adjustment of high speed mixture screw is one turn open from a lightly seated position. Final adjustment should be made with engine running at operating temperature. Adjust low speed mixture so engine will accelerate cleanly without hesitation. Adjust high speed mixture to obtain optimum full throttle performance under cutting load. Adjust idle speed to just below clutch engagement speed.

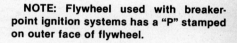
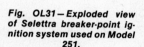

Fig. OL31—Exploded view of Selettra breaker-point ignition system used on Model 251.

1. Ignition coil
2. Stator plate
3. Condenser
4. Moveable breaker point
5. Fixed breaker point
6. Cover
7. Flywheel
8. Primary lead
9. Boot
10. Connector

IGNITION. Models 251, 261, 271, 481 Super, 482AV, 482MP and early 272 are equipped with a conventional breaker-point ignition system. Two types of breaker-point ignition systems are used: CEV (Fig. OL30) and Selettra (Fig. OL31). Models 261, 271, 481 Super, 482AV, 482MP and early 272 are equipped with a CEV ignition system and Model 251 is equipped with a Selettra ignition system.

Use Olympyk tool 60.00301 or equivalent puller to remove flywheel. Do not strike flywheel or flywheel magnets with hammer. It may be necessary to remove one starter pawl, if pawl hinders usage of flywheel puller.

NOTE: Flywheel used with breaker-point ignition systems has a "P" stamped on outer face of flywheel.

Breaker-point gap should be 0.45 mm (0.017 in.) on all models. On Model 251, air gap between flywheel magnets (7–Fig. OL31) and ignition coil (1) should be 0.35 mm (0.014 in.). There is no air gap adjustment on models equipped with CEV breaker-point ignition system.

Use Olympyk timing tool 60.00302 or a suitable dial indicator assembly to check ignition timing. Olympyk timing tool 60.00302 is equipped with an angle adapter used to hold dial indicator plunger at correct angle into spark plug hole. If angle adapter is used, set timing so breaker points just start to open at 2.2 mm (0.087 in.) BTDC for Model 251 and 2.6 mm (0.102 in.) BTDC for all other models. If angle adapter is not available,

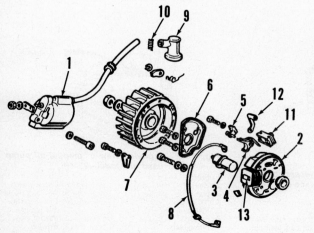
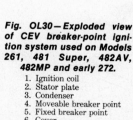

Fig. OL30—Exploded view of CEV breaker-point ignition system used on Models 261, 481 Super, 482AV, 482MP and early 272.

1. Ignition coil
2. Stator plate
3. Condenser
4. Moveable breaker point
5. Fixed breaker point
6. Cover
7. Flywheel
8. Primary lead
9. Boot
10. Connector
11. Insulator
12. Strap
13. Charge coil

fix dial indicator so plunger projects directly into spark plug hole and set timing so breaker points just start to open at 2.7 mm (0.106 in.) BTDC on Model 251 and 2.9 mm (0.114 in.) BTDC on all other models. Rotate stator plate to adjust ignition timing.

Models 251B, 251 Super, 252, 254, 254AV, 264, 264AV, 272AV, 284, 284AV, 355, 355AV and later 272 are equipped with a breakerless capacitor discharge ignition system. Olympyk module and coil tester 60.00893 may be used to test ignition module. If tester 60.00893 is not available, troubleshoot ignition module by process of elimination. Air gap between ignition module and flywheel magnets should be 0.35 mm (0.014 in.). Loosen ignition module mounting screws and move module to adjust air gap. Use Loctite 242 on threads of module mounting screws. Ignition timing is not adjustable. If flywheel requires removal, use Olympyk tool 60.00301 or a suitable equivalent puller to remove flywheel. Do not strike flywheel with hammer. It may be necessary to remove one starter pawl, if pawl hinders usage of flywheel puller.

NOTE: Flywheel used with capacitor discharge ignition systems have "E" stamped on outer face of flywheel.

LUBRICATION. The engine is lubricated by mixing oil with the fuel. The recommended oil is BIA certified two-stroke air-cooled engine oil. Fuel:oil mixture should be a 40:1 ratio when using recommended oil. If BIA certified two-stroke air-cooled engine oil is not available, use a good quality oil designed for use in air-cooled two-stroke engines mixed at a 20:1 ratio. Use a separate container when mixing fuel and oil.

Adjustable automatic chain oil pump assemblies are used on all models. Model 482MP is equipped with a manual pump in addition to the automatic oil pump. Refer to OIL PUMP in REPAIRS section for service and adjustment procedures.

Use clean SAE 30 or SAE 40 automotive oil for saw chain lubrication with viscosity chosen according to ambient temperature. Chain oil may be diluted with kerosene or diesel fuel by up to 25 percent during extreme cold temperature operation. Clutch needle bearing (6—Figs. OL34 or OL35) should be removed and lubricated with a suitable high temperature grease after every 24 hours of operation. Refer to CLUTCH in REPAIRS section.

CARBON. Carbon deposits should be cleaned from muffler and exhaust port at regular intervals. Position piston at top dead center to prevent loosened carbon from entering cylinder. Use a wooden scraper to remove carbon to prevent damage to piston or cylinder.

REPAIRS

CYLINDER, PISTON, PIN AND RINGS. Cylinder bore is chrome plated and should be renewed if cylinder bore is cracked, scored or excessively worn. Piston is equipped with two piston rings. Locating pins are present in ring grooves to prevent ring rotation. Make certain ring end gaps are properly positioned around locating pins when installing cylinder. Piston pin (5—Fig. OL33) rides in needle bearing (7) and is held in position with two wire retainers (6). Thrust washers (8) are used on all models except Models 264 and 264AV. Manufacturer recommends using Olympyk tool 60.00366 with the proper size drivers to remove and install piston pin.

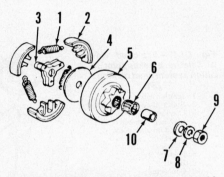

Fig. OL34—Exploded view of clutch assembly used on all models except 264 and 264AV.

1. Spring	6. Needle bearing
2. Shoe	7. Washer
3. Hub	8. Washer
4. Washer	9. Nut
5. Drum	10. Bushing

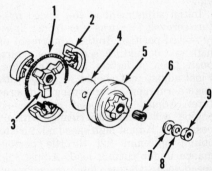

Fig. OL35—Exploded view of clutch assembly used on Models 264 and 264AV. Refer to Fig. OL34 for component identification.

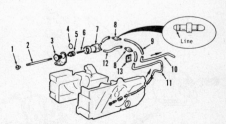

Fig. OL36—Exploded view of manual oil pump used on Model 482MP.

1. Button	8. Check valve
2. Rod	9. Discharge hose
3. Nut	10. Discharge line
4. "O" ring	11. Suction line
5. Piston	12. Suction hose
6. Spring	13. Bracket
7. Pump body	

Fig. OL33—Exploded view of engine assembly typical of all models. Thrust washers (8) are absent on Models 264 and 264AV. Models 481 Super, 482AV and 482MP use a worm gear in place of cam (15).

1. Cylinder	6. Retainer	10. Left crankcase half	
2. Gasket	7. Needle bearing	11. Gasket	15. Cam
3. Piston rings	8. Thrust washer	12. Seal	16. Seal
4. Piston	9. Crankshaft &	13. Main bearing	17. Right crankcase half
5. Piston pin	connecting rod assy.	14. Main bearing	18. Oil tank vent pin

Use a suitable support tool between piston skirt and top of crankcase when removing pin. Remove pin by pressing from flywheel side of engine toward clutch side. Install piston with arrow on piston crown pointing toward exhaust port. Press pin into piston from flywheel side. Use a drift pin or suitable tool to align piston with needle bearing (7) and thrust washers (8).

Piston and cylinder are graded during production to obtain desired piston-to-cylinder clearance. Piston and cylinder grade marks are "A," "B," "C" and "D" with "A" being the largest size. Piston grade mark is stamped on piston crown while cylinder grade mark is stamped on cylinder head. Piston and cylinder marks should match although one size smaller piston can be used if matched piston is not available. For instance, a piston marked "B" can be installed in a cylinder marked "A." Tighten cylinder screws to 10.8 N·m (8 ft.-lbs.).

CRANKCASE, CRANKSHAFT AND CONNECTING ROD.

Crankcase must be split on all models to remove crankshaft. Remove right side crankcase seal (16 – Fig. OL33) and cam (15) or worm gear (if so equipped) prior to separating crankcase halves. Refer to OIL PUMP for cam (or worm gear) removal. Use Olympyk tool 11283 or a suitable equivalent to separate crankcase halves. Use caution not to damage crankcase mating surfaces. Once crankcase is split, use a soft faced mallet to tap out crankshaft.

Crankshaft and connecting rod are available as a unit assembly only. Check rotation of connecting rod around crankpin and renew crankshaft assembly if roughness, excessive play or other damage is noted. Crankshaft is supported at both ends with ball type main bearings (13 and 14 – Fig. OL33). Use the proper size drivers to remove and install main bearings into crankcase halves. If main bearings remain on crankshaft during disassembly, use a suitable jaw-type puller to remove bearings from crankshaft. Install main bear-

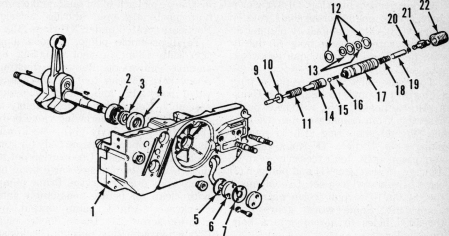

Fig. OL38 – Exploded view of piston type oil pump used on all models except 481 Super, 482AV and 482MP. Oil filter and pickup assembly (5, 6, 7 and 8) is typical of all models.

1. Right crankcase half	7. Gasket	12. "O" rings	17. Valve body
2. Main bearing	8. Cover	13. "O" rings	18. Spring
3. Cam	9. Piston	14. Pump body	19. Oil flow valve
4. Seal	10. Washer	15. Check ball	20. "O" ring
5. Gasket	11. Spring	16. Spring	21. Adjusting screw
6. Oil filter			22. Plug

ings into crankcase halves prior to reassembly.

NOTE: A new design crankshaft assembly with larger counterweights is used on 251 Super models starting with serial number 520200800 and 254 and 254AV models starting with serial number 540200800. Old design and new design crankshaft assemblies are not interchangeable.

Tighten crankcase screws in a crisscross pattern in small increments until a final torque of 10 N·m (7 ft.-lbs.) is obtained. Refer to OIL PUMP for installation of oil pump drive cam (or worm gear).

CLUTCH. Models 264 and 264AV are equipped with the three-shoe centrifugal clutch shown in Fig. OL35. All other models are equipped with the three-shoe clutch assembly shown in Fig. OL34. Clutch hub (3 – Fig. OL35) used on

Models 264 and 264AV screws onto crankshaft while hub (3 – Fig. OL34) used on all other models is a press fit on crankshaft with a Woodruff key. Hub (3 – Fig. OL35) and nut (9) on Models 264 and 264AV as well as nut (9 – Fig. OL34) on all other models have left-hand threads. Press on hub (3 – Fig. OL34) has three threaded holes to accomodate Olympyk tool 60.00301 or a suitable bolt-type puller.

Clutch shoes (2 – Figs. OL34 and OL35) should be renewed in complete sets to prevent an unbalanced condition. Springs (1 – Fig. OL34) should also be renewed as a set. Needle bearing (6 – Figs. OL34 and OL35) should be lubricated with a suitable high temperature grease. Tighten clutch nut (9 – Figs. OL34 and OL35) to 19.6 N·m (14 ft.-lbs.).

MANUAL OIL PUMP. Figure OL36 shows an exploded view of the manual oil pump used on Model 482MP. Install check valves (8) with line on valve (see inset) facing opposite of oil flow direction. Copper suction line (11) should be positioned under copper discharge line (10) when clamping lines to crankcase. Be sure suction hose (12) is connected to lower port of pump body (7). Prime pump and hose and line assemblies with clean oil during reassembly.

AUTOMATIC OIL PUMP. Models 481 Super, 482AV and 482MP are equipped with the gear type automatic oil pump shown in Fig. OL37. All other models are equipped with the piston type automatic oil pump shown in Fig. OL38.

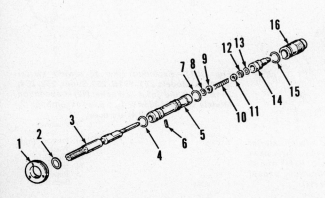

Fig. OL37 – Exploded view of gear plunger type oil pump used on Models 481 Super, 482AV and 482MP.

1. Worm gear
2. "O" ring
3. Plunger
4. "O" ring
5. Pump body
6. Cam pin
7. "O" ring
8. "O" ring
9. Washer
10. Spring
11. Washer
12. Snap ring
13. Washer
14. Adjuster
15. "O" ring
16. Plug

On gear type pump (Fig. OL37), worm gear (1) on engine crankshaft rotates plunger (3). Oil is pumped by plunger as it reciprocates in pump body (5) due to cam pin (6) riding in oblique groove in plunger.

To disassemble pump, remove plug (16) with Olympyk tool 82.00584. Using a suitable hooked tool, withdraw pump assembly from crankcase. Remove cam pin (6) and snap ring (12) to remove plunger (3). Inspect "O" rings, plunger and pump body for excessive wear or damage. Worm gear (1) and plunger (3) must be renewed as a set. Use Olympyk tool 82.00910 to pull worm gear from crankshaft. Some worm gears have threaded holes to accomodate a bolt-type puller.

NOTE: Oil pump assembly must be removed from crankcase prior to worm gear removal or installation.

Install worm gear with Olympyk tool 60.00576 or a suitable equivalent driver. Make certain worm gear is a tight fit on crankshaft. Prime pump with clean oil before installation into crankcase. Pump output is adjusted by rotating adjuster (14). Clockwise rotation decreases pump output.

Refer to Fig. OL38 for an exploded view of piston type oil pump. Oil is pumped by piston (9), driven by cam (3) on engine crankshaft. Oil is drawn into pump through hole in pump body (14). Pressurized oil forces check ball (15) off seat and oil is discharged through valve body (17). Two discharge ports are present in valve body. Port in center of valve body carries oil to guide bar and chain. Port located at end of valve body (toward adjusting screw) returns excess

discharge oil back to oil tank. Make sure both ports are open during service. Ports are located under "O" rings (13).

To disassemble pump, remove plug (22) with Olympyk tool 60.00542 or suitable equivalent. Remove adjusting screw (21). Thread tool 60.00542 into valve body (17) and withdraw pump assembly. Remainder of disassembly is accomplished by unscrewing valve body (17) from pump body (14). Check ball must seat properly in pump body for correct pump operation. Use caution not to nick, scratch or damage valve body or pump body during service. Prime pump with clean oil before reassembly into crankcase. Adjust pump output by rotating screw (21). Do not loosen plug (22) when adjusting output. Clockwise rototation decreases output.

Use Olympyk tool 60.00420 or a suitable jaw-type puller to pull cam (3) from crankshaft. Position jaws of puller at right angles to lobe of cam. Use Olympyk tool 60.00576 or suitable driver to install cam on crankshaft. Install cam with lobe facing away from crankshaft counterweights. Make certain cam is tight fit on crankshaft.

On all models, oil filter and pickup assembly can be serviced by removing cover (8) and withdrawing gaskets (5 and 7) and filter (6). Gaskets (5 and 7) should be renewed when reassembling filter and pickup assembly.

REWIND STARTER. Models 261, 271, 481 Super, 482AV, 482MP and early 272 are equipped with the rewind starter shown in Fig. OL39. Models 284, 284AV, 272AV and late 272 are similar except a baffle plate mounts on starter housing. On Models 261, 271, 481 Super, 482AV, 482MP and early 272, ignition coil (1 – Fig. OL30) is mounted on starter housing. Disconnect coil primary lead at ignition switch prior to removing starter housing.

Models 264 and 264AV are equipped with the rewind starter shown in Fig. OL40. All other models are equipped with the rewind starter shown in Fig. OL41. On Models 355 and 355AV, washer (12) is not used.

On all models, tension on rewind spring must be relieved before disassembling starter. Pull out rope approximately 30 cm (12 in.) and hold rope pulley firmly to keep from turning. Place rope into notch in outer circumference of pulley and carefully allow pulley to unwind, relieving rewind spring tension. Remove screw (7 – Figs. OL39, OL40 and OL41) and lift out rope pulley being careful not to dislodge rewind spring. If rewind spring must be removed, use caution not to allow spring to uncoil uncontrolled.

Rope should be 100 cm (39 in.) long and 3.5 mm (9/64 in.) in diameter on Models 251, 251B, 251 Super, 252, 254, 254AV, 355 and 355AV. On all other models, rope should be 120 cm (47.2 in.) long and 4 mm (5/32 in.) in diameter.

Install rewind spring into housing in a clockwise direction starting with outer coil. Wind rope onto rope pulley in a clockwise direction as viewed from flywheel side of pulley. When installing rope pulley into housing, make certain pulley properly engages rewind spring. Apply Loctite 242 or a suitable equivalent onto threads of screw (7 – Figs. OL39, OL40 and OL41). Tighten screw to 10 N·m (7 ft.-lbs.).

To preload rewind spring, place rope into notch in outer circumference of rope pulley and rotate pulley five turns clockwise on Models 251, 251B, 251

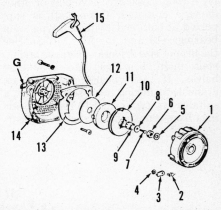

Fig. OL41 – Exploded view of rewind starter used on Models 251, 251B, 251 Super, 252, 254, 254AV, 355 and 355 AV. Washer (12) is absent on Models 355 and 355AV. Two pawl assemblies (2, 3 and 4) are used.

1. Flywheel	9. Bushing
2. Pawl spring	10. Rope pulley
3. Pawl	11. Rewind spring
4. Retainer	12. Washer
5. Washer	13. Baffle
6. Nut	14. Housing
7. Screw	15. Rope handle
8. Washer	G. Rope guide

Fig. OL39 – Exploded view of rewind starter used on Models 261, 271, 481 Super, 482AV and 482MP. Models 272, 272AV, 284 and 284AV are similar except a baffle within the starter housing is used. Two pawl assemblies (2, 3 and 4) are used. Refer to Fig. OL41 for component identification.

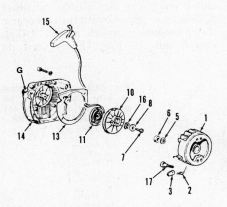

Fig. OL40 – Exploded view of rewind starter used on Models 264 and 264AV. Two pawl assemblies (2, 3 and 17) are used. Refer to Fig. OL41 for component identification except washer (16) and bolt (17).

Super, 252, 254, 254AV, 355 and 355AV. On all other models, rotate rope pulley seven turns clockwise. With rope retracted, rope handle should be snug against starter housing. With rope fully extended, rope pulley should rotate one turn further against spring tension. When installing starter assembly onto engine, pull out rope approximately 30 cm (12 in.) and slowly allow rope to rewind as starter is installed on engine to engage starter pawls.

CHAIN BRAKE. Some models are equipped with an optional chain brake system designed to quickly stop chain movement should kickback occur. Chain brake is activated when operator's hand strikes chain brake lever (1–Figs. OL42 and OL43). On Models 272, 272AV, 284 and 284AV, arm (13–Fig. OL43) disengages lever (12) allowing spring (2) to draw brake band (3) tight around clutch drum. On all other models, actuation lever (11–Fig. OL42) disengages pawl (8) from arm (7) allowing spring (2) to draw brake band (3) tight around clutch drum. Pull back chain brake lever to reset mechanism.

Disassembly is evident after inspection of unit and referral to appropriate exploded view. Renew any component found to be excessively worn or damaged in any other way. No adjustment of chain brake system is required.

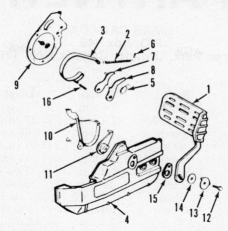

Fig. OL42 – Exploded view of optional chain brake system. System shown is used on all models so equipped except Models 272, 272AV, 284 and 284AV.

1. Lever
2. Spring
3. Brake band
4. Cover
5. Spring
6. Pin
7. Arm
8. Pawl
9. Cover
10. Cover
11. Actuation lever
12. Screw
13. Washer
14. Washer
15. Washer
16. Pin

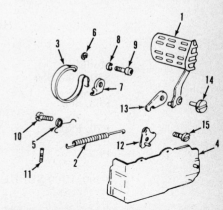

Fig. OL43 – Exploded view of optional chain brake system used on Models 272, 272AV, 284 and 284AV so equipped.

1. Lever
2. Spring
3. Brake band
4. Cover
5. Spring
6. "E" ring
7. Latch
8. Washer
9. Screw
10. Screw
11. Pin
12. Lever
13. Arm
14. Screw
15. Screw

PARTNER

EMAB CANADA
P.O. Box 549
Huron Park, Ontario, Canada N0M 1Y0

Model	Bore	Stroke	Displ.	Drive Type
S50, F55, S55	44 mm (1.73 in.)	36 mm (1.42 in.)	55 cc (3.36 cu. in.)	Direct
F65, S65	48 mm (1.89 in.)	36 mm (1.42 in.)	65 cc (3.97 cu. in.)	Direct
P70, P7000	50 mm (1.968 in.)	36 mm (1.42 in.)	70 cc (4.27 cu. in.)	Direct
P85	52 mm (2.05 in.)	36 mm (1.42 in.)	85 cc (5.2 cu. in.)	Direct
P100, P100 SUPER	60 mm (2.36 in.)	36 mm (1.42 in.)	100 cc (6.1 cu. in.)	Direct
R16	44 mm (1.73 in.)	36 mm (1.42 in.)	55 mm (3.36 cu. in.)	Direct
R420	48 mm (1.89 in.)	36 mm (1.42 in.)	65 cc (3.97 cu. in.)	Direct
R420T, R421T	48 mm (1.89 in.)	36 mm (1.42 in.)	65 cc (3.97 cu. in.)	Direct
R435	52 mm (2.05 in.)	36 mm (1.42 in.)	85 cc (5.2 cu. in.)	Direct
R440T	60 mm (2.36 in.)	36 mm (1.42 in.)	100 cc (6.1 cu. in.)	Direct
R417T, R517T	44 mm (1.73 in.)	36 mm (1.42 in.)	55 cc (3.36 cu. in.)	Direct

MAINTENANCE

SPARK PLUG. Recommended spark plug is Bosch WS5F for Models P100, P100 Super and R440T. Use Champion CJ6 or Bosch WS5E for all other models. Electrode gap is 0.5 mm (0.020 in.) for all models except P100 models equipped with a "Thyristor" ignition system which requires an electrode gap of 0.8 mm (0.031 in.).

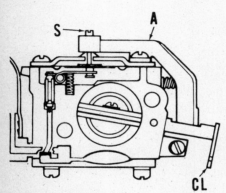

Fig. PT1—Some later models are equipped with an arm (A) on the carburetor that depresses the diaphragm thereby opening the fuel inlet valve when choke lever (CL) is turned. This allows fuel to enter carburetor if a vapor lock is present in diaphragm chamber.

CARBURETOR. A Walbro WS diaphragm type carburetor is used on P70, P7000, S50, S55 and S65 models while all other models are equipped with Tillotson HS diaphragm type carburetor. Refer to Tillotson or Walbro section of CARBURETOR SERVICE for service and exploded views of carburetors.

Some later models equipped with Tillotson carburetors may have the hot starting device shown in Fig. PT1. Should carburetor vapor lock, choke lever (CL) may be turned halfway to force arm (A) to depress the carburetor inlet valve. Connect a carburetor pressure checker to carburetor and adjust diaphragm movement by turning screw (S). Fuel inlet valve should just open when arm (A) rides up on choke shaft as choke lever is turned.

Normal needle settings for all models is one turn open for low and high speed mixture screws.

On all models, make final adjustment with engine warm and running. Adjust idle speed screw so engine idles just below clutch engagement speed. Adjust low speed mixture screw so engine will accelerate cleanly without hesitation. Adjust high speed mixture screw to obtain optimum performance under cutting load.

IGNITION. To check and adjust breaker-points on Models P85, R16, R420 and R435, remove top housing, fan housing, air strainer, and flywheel. Adjust breaker-point gap to 0.45 mm (0.018 in.). Ignition timing is fixed and cannot be adjusted, however, incorrect breaker-point gap setting will affect ignition timing. Edge gap (E – Fig. PT2) should be 8-12 mm (0.31-0.48 in.). Air gap between coil legs and flywheel should be 0.3-0.4 mm (0.012-0.016 in.).

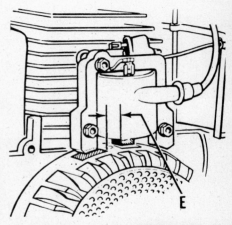

Fig. PT2—Edge gap (E) on later models with breaker points should be 8-12 mm (0.31-0.48 in.).

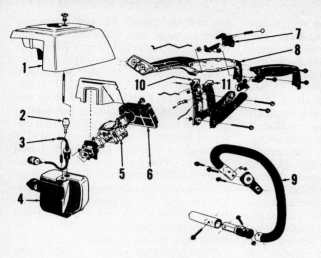

pin are not available separately. All models have needle type piston pin bearings.

Cylinder bore is chrome or Nickel-Sil impregnated. Inspect cylinder bore for excessive wear or damage to bore surface. Pistons and cylinders on later models are graded with a letter to designate size. Letter size is located on piston crown and top of cylinder. Letters on piston and cylinder should be the same to obtain desired piston-to-cylinder clearance. For instance, a piston with letter grade "B" should be used in a cylinder with letter grade "B." Install piston so arrow on piston crown points toward exhaust port.

CONNECTING RODS AND CRANKSHAFT. The connecting rod and crankshaft for all models are available only as a complete unit.

Main bearings of all models except R420, R420T and R421T are ball bearings. Roller bearings are used on both

Fig. PT3 — Exploded view of handle and fuel assemblies used on some later models.

1. Engine cover
2. Air vent
3. Fuel line
4. Fuel tank
5. Carburetor
6. Air filter
7. Throttle control
8. Rear handle
9. Front handle
10. Choke button
11. Stop button

All other models are equipped with a breakerless capacitor discharge ignition system. Early breakerless models have a "Thyristor" ignition system while later models have an "Ignitron" ignition system. On both types of ignition systems, ignition timing is not adjustable. Air gap between coil legs and flywheel should be 0.35-0.45 mm (0.014-0.018 in.).

LUBRICATION. Engine is lubricated by mixing engine oil with gasoline. Recommended oil is Beaird-Poulan engine oil approved for a fuel-to-oil mixture ratio of 40:1. If recommended oil is not available, a good quality oil designed for two-stroke air-cooled engines may be used when mixed at a 24:1 ratio. Use a separate container when mixing the oil and gas.

All models are equipped with an automatic chain oil pump. Oil output on P70, P85, P100, P100 Super, P7000, R435 and R440T models is adjustable by turning adjusting screw on bottom of saw. Oil output on early R16 models is adjusted by turning screw in control valve (22 — Fig. PT5). Oil output on later R16 models and on all other models is adjusted by replacing pump plunger (8 — Fig. PT10) with a plunger of different length. Refer to AUTOMATIC CHAIN OILER section. Chain oil should be clean SAE 30 oil if ambient temperature is above 40° F (4° C) or SAE 10 at lower temperatures.

CARBON. Carbon should be cleaned from muffler and exhaust ports at regular intervals. When scraping carbon, be careful not to damage the chamfered edges of the exhaust ports.

REPAIRS

PISTON, PIN, RINGS AND CYLINDER. The piston is accessible after removing the cylinder assembly. The aluminum alloy piston is fitted with two pinned rings. Reject piston pin and piston if there is any visible radial play of pin in the piston bosses. Piston and

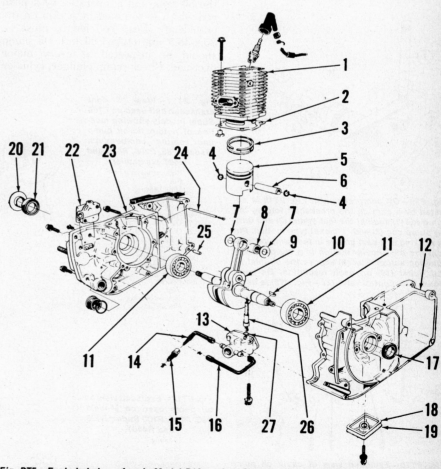

Fig. PT5 — Exploded view of early Model R16 engine. Other models are similar. Later models with 55cc (3.36 cu. in.) or 65cc (3.97 cu. in.) displacement do not use oil valve (22).

1. Cylinder	8. Needle bearing	14. Hose	21. Seal
2. Gasket	9. Crankshaft & rod assy.	15. Oil strainer	22. Oil control valve
3. Piston rings	10. Key	16. Hose	23. Crankcase half
4. Snap rings	11. Bearing	17. Seal	24. Vent hose
5. Piston	12. Crankcase half	18. Gasket	25. Pin
6. Piston pin	13. Oil pump	19. Oil pump cover	26. Push rod
7. Spacer		20. Washer	27. "O" ring

sides of crankshaft on Models R420, R420T and R421T. Outer races of the ball type main bearings are shrink fit in crankcase and if bearings fall from their bores by their own weight, bearings and crankcase assembly should be renewed.

To renew main bearings on Models F55, F65, P85, P100, P100 Super, R435, R440T, S55 and S65, remove cylinder and separate crankcase halves. Care should be taken not to damage mating surfaces of crankcase halves. On P85, P100, P100 Super, R435 and R440T models, clutch side main bearing is located by retainer (4 – Fig. PT11) while flywheel side main bearing is located by a shoulder in crankcase.

A shoulder in crankcase retains clutch side main bearing on F55, F65, S55 and S65 models. When reassembling, be sure main bearings are flush against their seats or when applicable, that retainer (4) engages groove in clutch side main bearing. Heat may be applied to crankcase bearing bores to ease reassembly. Make certain crankshaft is

centered in crankcase and will rotate freely. Clutch side crankshaft seal should be installed flush with crankcase face. Flywheel side crankshaft seal should protrude 1 mm (0.04 in.) from crankcase face when installed.

To renew main bearings on all other models, remove cylinder and separate crankcase halves. Remove crankshaft from crankcase half by tapping on opposite end of crankshaft. Heat crankcase halves to remove bearings. Bearing inner race will remain on crankshaft of Models R420, R420T, and R421T. Care should be used when removing inner race to prevent damage to crankshaft. Heat crankcase halves to install bearings. Carefully drive roller bearing inner races on crankshaft of models so equipped. Be sure internal hoses are installed before mating crankcase halves.

AUTOMATIC CHAIN OILER. The chain oiler pump for Models F55, F65, R16, R417T, R420, R420T, R421T, R517T, S50, S55 and S65 is located in the oil tank and is operated by a push rod which is actuated by a cam on the crankshaft. Push rod length must be 35.2-35.5 mm (1.38-1.39 in.). Oil pump should be inspected at every major overhaul. Check pump plunger, cylinder

pin and all springs for undue wear or other damage and make certain pump interlock spring set (9 – Fig. PT10) properly actuates the plunger (8).

Oil pump output on later Model R16 and on Models F55, F65, R417T, R420, R420T, R421T, R517T, S50, S55 and S65 is adjusted by replacing pump plunger with another pump plunger of a different length. Pump plunger 505317156 is standard and has a stroke of 1 mm (0.040 in.). Pump plunger 505317145 has a stroke of 0.8 mm (0.032 in.) and will reduce pump output 20 percent from standard plunger. Pump plunger 505317158 has a stroke of 1.5 mm (0.059 in.) and will increase pump output 50 percent more than standard plunger.

The chain oiler pump for P85, P100, P100 Super, R435 and R440T models is located in the right crankcase half and is driven by gear (13 – Fig. PT11) on crankshaft drive side. The chain oiler pump for P70 and P7000 models is located in the left crankcase half and driven by gear (13 – Fig. PT13) on crankshaft flywheel side. Oil pump operation on the above models is accomplished when plunger (7 – Fig. PT12 or Fig. PT14) is rotated by gear (13) and reciprocates as the oblique end of plunger bears against adjuster ball (10) thereby pumping oil.

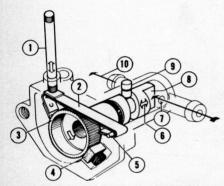

Fig. PT9 – Oil pump shown in Fig. PT10 is actuated by a cam on the crankshaft forcing the pump rod (1) against the leaf spring (2) and turning pump cog (3) with a racket type motion. Pin (9) working in a cam groove in the pump plunger converts the circular motion to a reciprocating pumping action. Slot (8) expose the oil inlet (7) and outlet (10) on each revolution. On early Model R16, control valve (22 – Fig. PT5) is used.

Fig. PT11 – View of right crankcase half used on P100 Super models showing location of automatic oil pump and related components. Models P85, P100, R435 and R440T are similar.

1. Right crankcase half
2. Pin
3. Main bearing
4. Bearing retainer
5. Vent tube
6. Grommet
7. Oil filter
8. Oil pickup fitting
9. Oil pump adjuster
10. Automatic oil pump
11. Pump retainer
12. Manual oiler
13. Drive gear
14. Spacer
15. Seal
16. Needle bearing
17. Clutch assy.

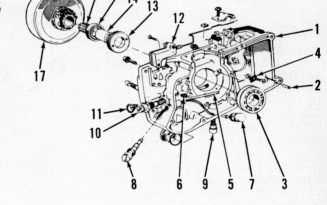

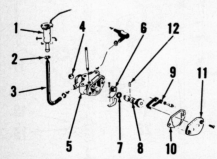

Fig. PT10 – Exploded view of chain oil pump used on all models except Models P85, P100, P100 Super, R435 and R440T. Refer to Fig. PT9 for operation of pump.

1. Oil cock	7. "O" ring
2. Lock ring	8. Plunger
3. Oil hose	9. Pump spring set
4. Cover (plug)	10. Gasket
5. Housing	11. Cover
6. Pump bar set	12. Cam pin

Fig. PT12 – Exploded view of oil pump used on Models P85, P100, P100 Super, R435 and R440T.

1. Retainer
2. Plug
3. Washer
4. Orifice
5. Pump housing
6. "O" ring
7. Plunger
8. "O" ring
9. Spring
10. Adjuster
11. "O" ring
12. Cap
13. Drive gear

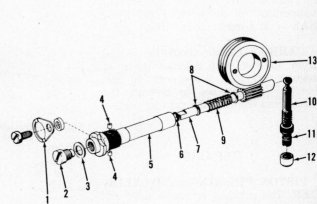

Oil output is changed by turning adjuster (10).

On models with oil pump in right crankcase half, drive gear (13–Fig. PT11) may be pulled off crankshaft after removing seal (15) and spacer (14). On models with oil pump in left crankcase half, drive gear (13–Fig. PT13) may be pulled off crankshaft after removing flywheel and seal housing (4). On all models, drive gear must be heated before installation on crankshaft to prevent crankshaft displacement.

REWIND STARTER. All models are equipped with the rewind starter shown in Fig. PT15. To disassemble starter, remove rope handle and allow rope to wind around rope pulley. Disengage pulley retaining clip (8) and carefully remove rope pulley. Rewind spring is now accessible and may be removed.

Install rewind spring in a clockwise direction viewed with spring installed in housing. Rope must be wrapped around rope pulley in a clockwise direction viewed with rope pulley in housing. Tension should be placed on starter rope by rotating rope pulley two turns clockwise.

CHAIN BRAKE. Some models may be equipped with a chain brake system designed to stop chain movement should kickback occur. Two types of chain

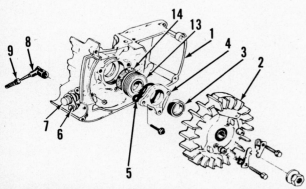

Fig. PT13—View of left crankcase half used on P70 and P7000 models showing location of automatic oil pump and related components.

1. Left crankcase half
2. Flywheel
3. Seal
4. Seal housing
5. Gasket
6. Pump retainer
7. Automatic oil pump
8. Pump pickup
9. Filter
13. Drive gear
14. Bushing

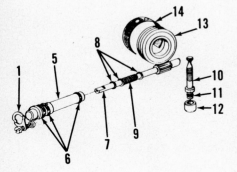

Fig. PT14—Exploded view of oil pump used on P70 and P7000 models.

1. Pump retainer
5. Pump housing
6. "O" ring
7. Plunger
8. "O" ring
9. Spring
10. Oil pump adjuster
11. "O" ring
12. Cap
13. Drive gear
14. Bushing

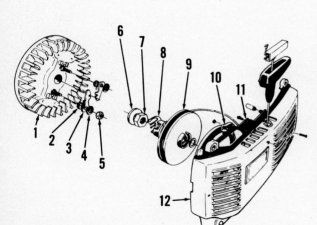

Fig. PT15—Exploded view of rewind starter assembly.

1. Flywheel
2. Spring
3. Pawl
4. Washer
5. Nut
6. Washer
7. Nut
8. Clip
9. Rope pulley
10. Rewind spring
11. Shield
12. Starter housing

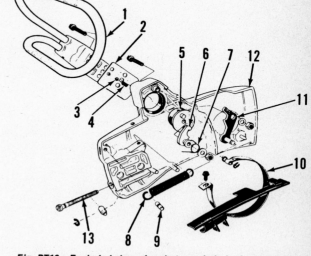

Fig. PT16—Exploded view of early type chain brake assembly.

1. Chain brake lever
2. Plate
3. Detent ball
4. Spring
5. Pivot
6. Trigger
7. Spring
8. Spring
9. Pin
10. Brake band
11. Actuating plate
12. Housing
13. Chain tensioner

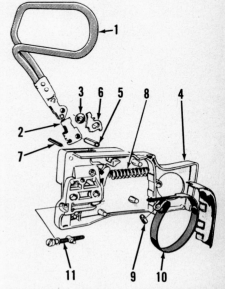

Fig. PT17—Exploded view of later type chain brake assembly.

1. Chain brake lever
2. Sleeve
3. Washer
4. Housing
5. Pin
6. Trigger
7. Pin
8. Spring
9. Pin
10. Brake band
11. Chain tensioner

brake systems have been used. Early type chain brake system is shown in Fig. PT16 and later type system is shown in Fig. PT17. On both types of chain brake systems, chain brake is activated when the operator's hand strikes the chain brake lever thereby allowing trigger (6) to release spring (8). Spring then draws brake band tight around clutch drum to stop chain. Pull back chain brake lever to reset mechanism. No adjustment of brake mechanism is required.

Disassembly for repair or renewal of individual components is evident after inspection of unit and referral to the appropriate exploded view. On later type chain brake (Fig. PT17), it is recommended that clutch drum be inserted in brake band and brake engaged, to facilitate removal of brake lever. When reassembling, make certain spring (8) is screwed completely on brake band and roll pins (5 and 7) are installed with split side toward front of saw.

PARTNER

Model	Bore	Stroke	Displ.	Drive Type
500, 5000, 5000H	44 mm (1.73 in.)	32 mm (1.26 in.)	49 cc (3.0 cu. in.)	Direct

MAINTENANCE

SPARK PLUG. Recommended spark plug is Champion DJ6Y for all models. Electrode gap should be 0.5 mm (0.020 in.).

CARBURETOR. Walbro WA-82 diaphragm type carburetors are used on all models. Refer to Walbro section of CARBURETOR SERVICE for service and exploded views of carburetor.

Initial adjustment for both low speed and high speed mixture screws is one turn open from a lightly seated position. Make final adjustment with engine warm and running. Adjust idle speed screw so engine idles just below clutch engagement speed. Adjust low speed mixture screw so engine will accelerate cleanly without hesitation. Adjust high speed mixture screw to obtain optimum performance under cutting load.

IGNITION. All models are equipped with a breakerless capacitor discharge ignition system. Ignition timing is not adjustable. Air gap between coil legs and flywheel should be 0.25-0.30 mm (0.009-0.012 in.).

LUBRICATION. Engine is lubricated by mixing engine oil with regular leaded gasoline. Recommended oil is Beaird-Poulan engine oil approved for a fuel-to-oil mixture ratio of 40:1. If recommended oil is not available, a good quality oil designed for two-stroke air-cooled engines may be used when mixed at a 24:1 ratio. Use a separate container when mixing the oil and gas.

All models are equipped with an automatic chain oil pump. Oil output on 500 models is not adjustable. Oil output on 5000 and 5000H models is adjusted by turning screw located behind guide bar. Refer to AUTOMATIC CHAIN OILER section.

REPAIRS

PISTON, PIN, RINGS AND CYLINDER. The piston is accessible after removing the cylinder assembly. Piston is fitted with two piston rings on 5000 and 5000H models and one piston ring on 500 models. Locating pins are present in piston ring grooves to prevent piston ring rotation. Oversize pistons and rings are not available. Reject piston pin and piston if there is any visible radial play of pin in the piston bosses. All models have needle type piston pin bearings. Install piston so arrow on piston crown points toward exhaust port.

Inspect cylinder bore for excessive wear or damage to bore surface. Cylinder should be renewed if new piston ring end gap in cylinder exceeds 0.8 mm (0.031 in.).

CRANKSHAFT, CONNECTING ROD AND CRANKCASE. Crankshaft and connecting rod are a unit assembly. When separating crankcase halves first remove cylinder, then withdraw oil pump drive gear from crankshaft using Partner special tool 505381816. Remove crankcase retaining cap screws and press crankshaft out of left crankcase half using Partner special tool 505-381811. Crankshaft may be driven out of right crankcase half using a suitable plastic mallet. Main bearings (11–Fig. PT21) can be pulled from crankshaft by using a bearing puller. Heat main bearings in oil to install on crankshaft. Heat crankcase halves on an electric hot plate prior to assembling crankcase. Oil pump drive gear (4–Fig. PT24) should be positioned on crank-

Fig. PT20 — Exploded view of throttle control and handle assemblies used on 5000 and 5000H models. Side protector (8) is not used on 500 models.

1. Vibration-damper	
2. Rear handle	9. Safety strap
3. Vibration-damper	10. Connector plug
4. Throttle lock	11. Cap screw
5. Throttle control	12. Coil spring
6. Throttle linkage	13. Housing
7. Rear handle cover	14. Washer
8. Side protector	15. Front handle

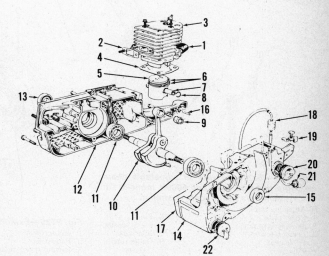

Fig. PT21 — Exploded view of engine used on 5000 and 5000H models. Model 500 is similar.

1. Intake manifold
2. Exhaust gasket
3. Cylinder
4. Gasket
5. Piston
6. Piston rings
7. Piston pin
8. Lock ring
9. Needle bearing
10. Crankshaft & rod assy.
11. Main bearings
12. Right crankcase half
13. Seal
14. Left crankcase half
15. Seal
16. Pin
17. Gasket
18. Fuel tank vent
19. Stop switch
20. Fuel cap
21. Fuel filter
22. Oil cap

shaft so outer gear face is 1 mm below flush of gear mounting land (L).

CLUTCH. All models are equipped with a two-shoe centrifugal clutch. Clutch hub has left-hand threads. Inspect clutch shoes and drum for excessive wear or damage due to overheating. Inspect clutch drum, bearing and crankshaft for damage. Clutch components are available individually or as a complete assembly.

AUTOMATIC CHAIN OILER. All models are equipped with an automatic chain oiler pump which is driven by gear (4 – Fig. PT23) on crankshaft. Oil pump output on 500 models is not adjustable while output on 5000 and 5000H models may be adjusted between 4-9 mL (0.13-0.30 oz.) per minute by turning screw (S) in end of pump housing (7).

Rotating screw counterclockwise provides maximum output.

Access to oil pump components is obtained after removing chain, guide bar, clutch and oil pump cover plate (1). When reassembling, make certain notch in pump housing (7 – Fig. PT24) engages locating lug in crankcase and that pin (2) is inserted in oil tank vent passage.

REWIND STARTER. All models are equipped with the rewind starter shown in Fig. PT25. To disassemble rewind starter, first remove starter housing from saw. Pull starter rope and hold rope pulley with notch in pulley adjacent to rope outlet. Pull rope back through outlet so it engages notch in pulley and allow pulley to completely unwind. Unscrew pulley retaining cap screw (1) and remove rope pulley. If rewind spring requires removal, unsnap tabs securing

spring retainer (3) to starter housing (5) and withdraw from housing. Care should be taken not to allow spring to uncoil from retainer.

Reassembly is the reverse of disassembly while noting the following: Wrap starter rope around rope pulley in a clockwise direction as viewed with pulley in starter housing. Turn rope pulley two turns clockwise before passing rope through rope outlet to place tension on rewind spring. Spring tension is correct if rope pulley can be rotated approximately ½ turn further when rope is at its greatest length.

When installing starter assembly on saw, make sure starter pulley properly engages pawls on flywheel before tightening retaining cap screws.

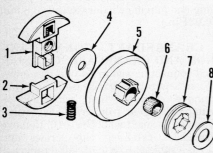

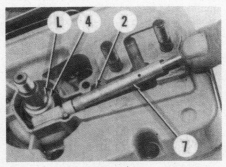

Fig. PT24—Install oil pump components as outlined in text. Refer to Fig. PT23 for parts identification.

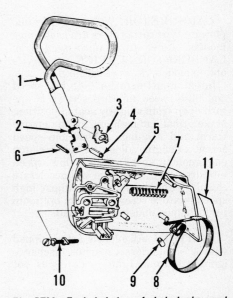

Fig. PT22—Exploded view of two-shoe type clutch assembly used on all models. On 500 models, chain drive sprocket is integral with clutch drum.

1. Hub
2. Shoe
3. Spring
4. Washer
5. Drum
6. Needle bearing
7. Rim sprocket
8. Washer

Fig. PT26—Exploded view of chain brake used on all models.

1. Chain brake lever
2. Sleeve
3. Actuating plate
4. Pin
5. Housing
6. Pin
7. Spring
8. Brake band
9. Pin
10. Chain tensioner
11. Chain guard

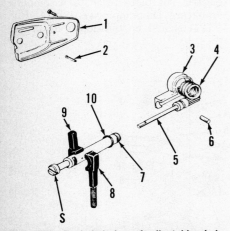

Fig. PT23—Exploded view of adjustable chain oil pump used on 5000 and 5000H models. Oil pump on 500 models is similar.

S. Adjusting screw
1. Cover plate
2. Oil tank vent pin
3. Gear protector
4. Drive gear
5. Plunger
6. Pin
7. Pump housing
8. Inlet tube
9. Outlet tube
10. "O" ring

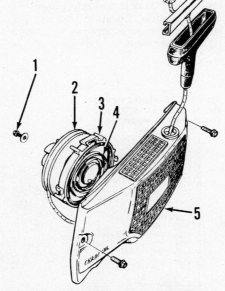

Fig. PT25—Exploded view of rewind starter.

1. Cap screw
2. Rope pulley
3. Rewind spring retainer
4. Rewind spring
5. Starter housing

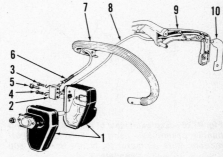

Fig. PT27—Exploded view of handle heating system used on 5000H models.

1. Muffler
2. Valve
3. Front handle temp. adjuster
4. Rear handle temp. adjuster
5. Cap screw
6. Hose
7. Front handle
8. Hose
9. Rear handle
10. Gasket

CHAIN BRAKE. Some models may be equipped with a chain brake system designed to stop chain movement should kickback occur.

The chain brake is activated when the operator's hand strikes the chain brake lever thereby forcing actuating plate (3–Fig. PT26) off of pin in housing releasing spring (7). Spring then draws brake band tight around clutch drum to stop chain. Pull back chain brake lever to reset mechanism. No adjustment of brake mechanism is required.

If brake requires disassembly for repair or renewal of individual components, it is recommended that a clutch drum be inserted in brake band and brake engaged, to facilitate removal of brake lever. When reassembling, make certain spring (7) is screwed completely on brake band and roll pins (4 and 6) are installed with split side towards front of saw.

HANDLE HEATER. Models 5000H are equipped with the front and rear handle heating system shown in Fig. PT27. Valve (2) is attached to the muffler allowing a small quantity of heated exhaust gas produced by the engine to flow through hoses (6 and 8) and enter chambers in front and rear handles. Front handle temperature is controlled by adjusting screw (3) while rear handle temperature is controlled by adjusting screw (4). Turning adjusting screws completely in shuts off heat.

Heating system should be periodically disassembled and carbon deposits removed. Inspect and renew hoses (6 and 8) if hoses are restricted due to carbon build up or show signs of cracking.

PIONEER

EMAB CANADA
P.O. Box 549
Huron Park, Ontario, Canada N0M 1Y0

Model	Bore	Stroke	Displ.	Drive Type
P10, P12, P12S	1-7/16 in. (36.5 mm)	1.28 in. (32.5 mm)	2.1 cu. in. (34 cc)	Direct

MAINTENANCE

SPARK PLUG. Recommended spark plug is Champion CJ6. Spark plug electrode gap should be 0.025 inch (0.64 mm). Tighten spark plug to 84-96 in.-lbs. (9.5-12.2 N·m).

CARBURETOR. A Tillotson HU diaphragm type carburetor is used on P10 models while a Walbro WA carburetor is used on P12 and P12S models. Initial setting for high and low speed mixture screws is 1⅛ turn open from a lightly seated position. Final adjustment of high speed mixture screw should be made with engine warm and under cutting load. High speed mixture must not be adjusted too lean as engine may be damaged.

IGNITION. Pioneer P10 models are equipped with standard magneto ignition with breaker points. A breakerless capacitor discharge magneto is used on P12 and P12S models.

On breaker-point models, breaker-point gap should be 0.015 inch (0.38 mm). Ignition timing is fixed but breaker-point gap will affect ignition timing and should be set correctly.

On all models, air gap between flywheel magnets and ignition coil legs should be 0.015 inch (0.38 mm).

LUBRICATION. Engine is lubricated by mixing engine oil with fuel. Recommended oil is Beaird-Poulan engine oil approved for a fuel-to-oil mixture ratio of 40:1. If recommended oil is not available, a good quality oil designed for two-stroke air-cooled engines may be used when mixed at a 24:1 ratio. Use a separate container when mixing the oil and gas.

The oil reservoir should be filled with Pioneer/Partner Chain Oil or, if not available, use a reputable brand SAE 10 to SAE 30 motor oil depending upon ambient temperature. The chain is automatically oiled by pressurizing the oil tank via check valve (16 – Fig. PR1-2).

The manual oil pump can be withdrawn after removing screw (S – Fig. PR1-3).

REPAIRS

CYLINDER, PISTON, RINGS AND PIN. The cylinder, cylinder head and rear crankcase half are one-piece (16 – Fig. PR1-4). Unit can be disassembled after removing the chain, flywheel, breaker points and the oil pump and front housing. The front crankcase half (2) is retained by the same four long screws that attach the front cover and tank and handle assembly. Be careful not to damage mating surfaces of crankcase halves.

The crankshaft, main bearings, seals, connecting rod and piston assembly can be withdrawn from the rear crankcase half and cylinder.

The 11 bearing rollers in connecting rod are loose and may fall out during disassembly. Be sure that all are removed and saved for assembly.

Piston is equipped with a single piston ring and a floating type piston pin (20). It may be necessary to heat piston to

Fig. PR1-1 – View of left side on a P10 model with starter, flywheel and breaker-point cover removed. Idle mixture needle is at (I); high speed mixture needle is at (H). Other models are similar.

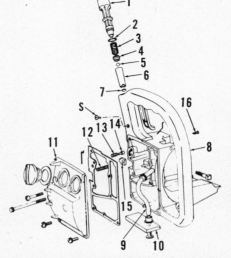

Fig. PR1-2 – Exploded view of manual pump and front housing.

1. Piston
2. "O" ring
3. Spring
4. Spring seat
5. Ball
6. Pump body
7. Screen
8. Front housing
9. Fuel hose
10. Filter
11. Front cover
12. Spring
13. Spring
14. Oil outlet valve
15. Nut
16. Pressure check valve

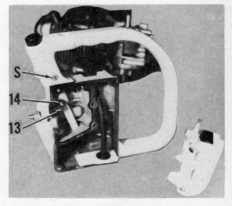

Fig. PR1-3 – View into front housing with cover removed. Oil outlet check valve (14) and spring (13) align with recess in cover. The manual oiler pump can be withdrawn after removing screw (S).

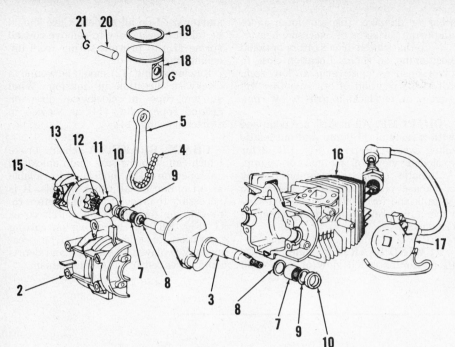

remove or install piston pin. Piston, pin and ring are available in standard size only. Cylinder bore is chrome plated and should be inspected to determine if chrome is scored, peeling or excessively worn. Renew cylinder and piston if damaged or excessively worn. If either half of crankcase requires renewal, then both halves must be renewed as they are a matched set.

Refer to CRANKSHAFT section for proper assembly of crankcase and cylinder.

CONNECTING ROD. To remove connecting rod, remove cylinder (16 – Fig. PR1-4). Note that cylinder is also upper crankcase half and crankshaft assembly is loose when cylinder is removed. Connecting rod (5) is one-piece and supported on crankpin by 11 loose bearing rollers (4). Be careful not to lose loose rollers that may fall out during disassembly. Rollers can be removed by sliding rod off rollers. To install rod bearing, hold rollers in place with heavy grease or petroleum jelly and position rod over rollers. Be sure rollers do not fall out during assembly of crankcase. It is recommended piston be assembled prior to rollers being installed.

CRANKSHAFT AND SEALS. Crankshaft is supported by needle roller bearings (7 – Fig. PR1-4) at both ends.

Fig. PR1-4 — Exploded view of power head and clutch.

2. Crankcase	8. Washer	12. Bearing
3. Crankshaft	9. Retaining ring	13. Clutch drum
4. Roller bearing	10. Seal	15. Clutch assy.
5. Connecting rod	11. Thrust washer	16. Cylinder
7. Needle bearing		

17. Ignition coil
18. Piston
19. Piston ring
20. Piston pin
21. Pin retainer

Fig. PR1-5 — Retaining rings (9) fit into grooves of case halves. Refer to Fig. PR1-4 for legend.

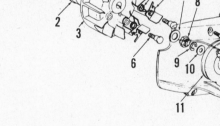

Fig. PR1-7 — Exploded view of rewind starter, flywheel and associated parts used on P10 models. Other models are similar.

1. Stator plate
2. Cover
3. Flywheel
4. Spring
5. Pawl
6. Pivot pin
7. Washer
8. Nut
9. Snap ring
10. Thrust washer
11. Rope pulley
12. Rewind spring
13. Bushing
14. Starter housing

Fig. PR1-6 — The clutch hub is stamped "OFF" and arrow indicates that hub and crankshaft have left-hand threads.

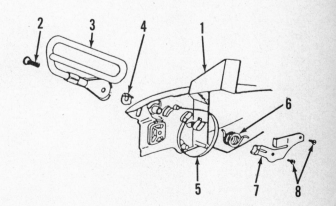

Fig. PR1-8 — Exploded view of chain brake assembly.

1. Clutch cover
2. Pivot pin
3. Trip lever
4. Stop plate
5. Brake band
6. Spring
7. Detent cover
8. Cap screw

Crankshaft assembly may be removed after removing flywheel, ignition breaker points, clutch and cylinder assemblies. Care should be taken when removing cylinder as crankshaft will be loose in crankcase and connecting rod may slide allowing the connecting rod roller bearings to fall.

Before reassembling crankcases, apply a light coat of nonhardening sealant to crankcase mating surface. Be sure mating surfaces are not damaged during assembly. Retaining rings (9 – Fig. PR1-5) must fit in ring grooves of crankcase and cylinder.

CLUTCH. A two-shoe centrifugal type clutch is used. Clutch hub has left-hand thread. Clutch bearing (12 – Fig. PR1-4) should be inspected for excessive wear or damage. Inspect clutch shoes and drum for signs of excessive heat.

Note that clutch driver offers optional positioning on shoes. Location close to pivot ensures more grip at low rpm. Alternate position offers smoother engagement, but lacks in grip at low rpm.

OIL PUMP. All models are equipped with a manual oil pump and automatic oiling system. Refer to Fig. PR1-2 for exploded view of manual oil pump. Automatic oiling is accomplished by crankcase pulsations which pressurize oil tank and force oil to bar. A one-way valve (16) prevents oil from entering crankcase.

REWIND STARTER. Refer to Fig. PR1-7 for exploded view of pawl type starter used on all models. Care should be taken if necessary to remove rewind spring (12) to prevent spring from uncoiling uncontrolled.

Rewind spring (12) should be wound in clockwise direction in housing. Wind starter rope in clockwise direction around rope pulley (11) as viewed in starter housing (14).

CHAIN BRAKE. A chain brake which can stop the saw chain quickly is equipped on P12S models and available as an option on all other models. It is necessary to unlock the brake before removing or installing the clutch cover (1 – Fig. PR1-8). Depending on cutting operation, dust shield should be occasionally removed so sawdust and debris can be cleaned from the mechanism.

PIONEER

Model	Bore	Stroke	Displ.	Drive Type
P-20, P-25	1.625 in. (41.3 mm)	1.5 in. (38.1 mm)	3.14 cu. in. (51.5 cc)	Direct

MAINTENANCE

SPARK PLUG. Champion CJ6 spark plug is recommeneded for both models. The electrode gap should be 0.030 inch (0.76 mm). Tighten spark plug to 84-96 in.-lbs. (9.5-10.9 N·m).

CARBURETOR. A Tillotson HU diaphragm type carburetor with integral fuel pump is used on both models. Refer to Tillotson section of CARBURETOR SERVICE for service and exploded view of carburetor.

Initial setting for low speed mixture needle is 7/8-1 turn open from a lightly seated position. The high speed mixture is determined by the size of a fixed orifice. Adjust idle speed screw (27—Fig. PR6-5) so engine idles just below clutch engagement speed. Adjust low speed mixture screw (6) so engine will accelerate cleanly without hesitation.

The choke valve is located in blowback tube (3—Fig. PR6-6).

MAGNETO. The breaker-points and condenser are located under the flywheel. Flywheel retaining nut is left-hand thread and should be tightened to 25 ft.-lbs. (34 N·m). The breaker-point gap should be 0.015 inch (0.38 mm). The breaker-point cam is ground into the engine crankshaft. The clearance between coil core and flywheel magnets (armature air gap) should 0.012 inch (0.30 mm). Check air gap using correct thickness of shim stock as shown in Fig. PR6-7. Edge gap setting should be 0.188-0.312 inch (4.78-7.92 mm). Ignition should occur (breaker-points just open) 30 degrees BTDC.

LUBRICATION. Engine is lubricated by mixing engine oil with gasoline. Recommended oil is Beaird-Poulan engine oil approved for a fuel-to-oil mixture ratio of 40:1. If recommended oil is not available, a good quality oil designed for two-stroke air-cooled engines may be used when mixed at a 24:1 ratio. Use a separate container when mixing the oil and gas.

The chain oiler reservoir should be filled with Pioneer/Partner Chain Oil or, if not available, use clean SAE 10 to SAE 40 motor oil depending upon ambient temperature. Both models are equipped with an automatic chain oiler pump (Fig. PR6-9). Worm gear (W) on crankshaft turns pump shaft and gear (5). Guide pin (6) rides in a cam slot (C) of pump shaft and causes pump shaft to move back and forth as it rotates. The back and forth movement pumps oil to the chain. Flat (F) on shaft acts as a valve to open the intake port on the outward stroke and the outlet port on the inward stroke. Felt washer (1) should be glued to pump cover (2).

CARBON. The muffler and cylinder exhaust ports should be cleaned periodically before any loss of power is noticed because of carbon build up. Remove the muffler and clean carbon from all parts of muffler. Turn engine crankshaft until piston is covering the exhaust port, then carefully clean carbon from the exhaust using a soft scraper. Be especially careful not to damage the piston. Do not attempt to clean exhaust with piston not covering the port. Hard carbon deposits can cause extensive damage if permitted to fall into the engine. The engine cooling fins should be cleaned at the same time that carbon is cleaned from exhaust.

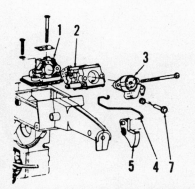

Fig. PR6-5 — View showing location of low speed mixture needle (6) and idle speed stop screw (27).

Fig. PR6-6 — Exploded view of induction components.

1. Insulating block
2. Carburetor assy.
3. Blowback tube
4. Throttle link
5. Throttle trigger
7. Choke knob

Fig. PR6-7 — Armature air gap should be checked and adjusted using correct thickness of shim stock (S).

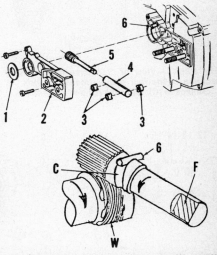

Fig. PR6-9 — View of chain oiler pump. Worm (W) is part of the engine crankshaft. Refer to text.

1. Felt washer
2. Pump cover
3. Sealing pads
4. Pump sleeve
5. Pump shaft & gear
6. Pin

REPAIRS

TIGHTENING TORQUES. Refer to the following for tightening torque values:

Crankcase (Tank) Halves . .25-35 in.-lbs.
(2.8-3.9 N·m)
Flywheel Nut . . . . .25 ft.-lbs.
(34 N·m)
Cylinder Base Nuts . . . . . . .70-80 in.-lbs.
(7.9-9.0 N·m)
Muffler-to-Cylinder . . . . .25-35 in.-lbs.
(2.8-3.9 N·m)
Clutch Driver . . . . .25 ft. lbs.
(34 N·m)

CYLINDER, PISTON, RINGS AND PIN. Compression pressure should be 150 psi (1035 kPa) on both models. The cylinder and head is one-piece and is attached to the crankcase with four screws. The cylinder bore is chrome plated and cylinder should be replaced if plating is worn away exposing the soft base metal. The piston should be heated to 300° F (149° C) before removing the piston pin. Use caution to prevent bending the connecting rod even after piston is heated. Mark the piston on exhaust port side if old piston is to be reinstalled. New pistons may be installed either way, but a used piston should be installed in the same position that it was first installed.

NOTE: The needle rollers may fall out of the piston pin bearing when the piston pin

is removed. **The needle rollers are not held in the cartridge of bearings used for original production. The bearing rollers of service piston pin bearings are held in the cartridge, but these rollers may fall out if extensively damaged.**

Press only on lettered end, when installing new piston pin bearing. Make sure none of the bearing rollers fall into the crankcase.

Piston ring end gap should be 0.088-0.098 inch (2.23-2.49 mm). The open end of piston pin retaining clips should be toward top (closed) end of piston.

CRANKSHAFT AND CONNECTING ROD. The crankshaft, crankpin and connecting rod are pressed together and are available only as a complete assembly. The crankshaft can be easily damaged by incorrect service procedures. Dropping crankshaft or pounding on the ends can easily knock crankshaft out of alignment. The crankshaft seals can be removed and installed without separating the crankcase (fuel tank) halves. Use Pioneer tool 471437 to remove seals and tool 429445 to install seals.

To separate the crankcase halves, remove handle bar, rewind starter, lower handle, carburetor, ignition coil, flywheel, ignition breaker-points, condenser, exhaust manifold, cylinder, piston, guide bar, saw chain, clutch and automatic chain oiler pump (Fig. PR6-9). Remove the 14 screws attaching crankcase halves together and

carefully separate halves. Heat crankcase halves before installing crankshaft main bearings.

The gasket surface between the two crankcase halves must be completely clean and free from nicks and burrs. The crankcase forms four different compartments when halves are joined together: (A–Fig. PR6-10) air box, (C) engine crankcase, (G) fuel tank and (O) chain oiler reservoir. Check the condition of fuel tank vent components (12, 13, 14, 15, 16 & 17–Fig. PR6-11). Insufficient fuel tank venting may be corrected by driving a small hole between plug (12) and "V" adjacent to plug. Vent assembly must be renewed as a unit.

Throttle trigger (3–Fig. PR6-11), throttle link (4), fuel pickup hose, handle brace nut (N), crankshaft assembly (8) and gasket (G) should all be located correctly between the crankcase halves before attaching the halves together. The handle brace nut can be held in place with the screw as shown in Fig. PR6-12 until the crankcase halves are together. The nut is captive between the halves after they are together.

CLUTCH. The clutch can be removed by unscrewing clutch driver from the end of the crankshaft. Special tool (part 473372) is available for turning clutch

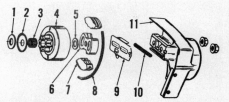

Fig. PR6-14 — Exploded view of clutch assembly.
1. Felt sealing washer
2. Thrust washer
3. Needle bearing
4. Clutch drum & sprocket
5. Thrust washer
6. Clutch driver
7. Clutch shoes
8. Spring
9. Tension adjusting screw
10. Adjusting block
11. Strut

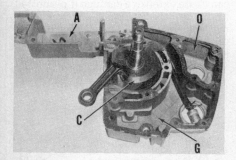

Fig. PR6-10 — View of crankcase half showing location of the four compartments: air box (A), crankcase (C), fuel tank (G) and oil tank (O).

Fig. PR6-12 — Nut (N — Fig. PR6-11) can be held in position with a screw while assembling.

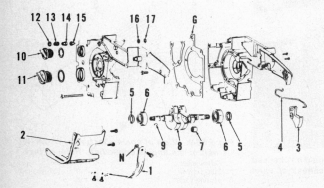

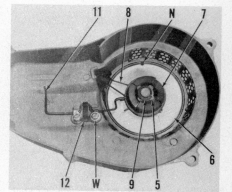

Fig. PR6-11 — Exploded view of engine assembly.
1. Rear handle brace
2. Lower shroud
3. Throttle trigger
4. Throttle link
5. Crankshaft seals
6. Main bearings
7. Piston pin bearing
8. Crankshaft assy.
9. Woodruff key
10. Oil cap
11. Fuel cap
12. Plug
13. Spring
14. Valve cap
15. Fuel vent check valve
16. Screen
17. Retaining ring

Fig. PR6-15 — View showing rewind starter assembled. Washer (W) should be on screw indicated. Refer to Fig. PR6-16 for legend.

driver. The clutch driver has left-hand thread. Felt dust seal washer (1 – Fig. PR6-9) should be glued onto pump cover (2).

Clutch slippage for as little as 30 seconds can generate enough heat to melt the clutch shoes and stick them to the drum.

When assembling the clutch, lubricate bearing (3 – Fig. PR6-14) and tighten the clutch driver to approximately 25 ft.-lbs. (34 N·m).

REWIND STARTER. Starter pinion (7 – Fig. PR6-15 and Fig. PR6-16) moves in to engage the lugs on the flywheel. Lever (11) is twisted by movement of the pinion and the lever pushes decompression valve, thus opening the valve.

New starter cord can be installed without removing the rewind spring.

Remove the housing and starter assembly (Fig. PR6-16). Remove the two screws attaching the decompression lever (11) and spring (12). Remove friction yoke (8) and starter pinion (7) by turning the pinion.

NOTE: Do not remove snap ring (9).

Remove handle (2) and allow cord to unwind if not broken. Remove the three screws and plate (6), then install new 0.130 inch (3.30 mm) diameter cord that is 43 inches (109 cm) long. The rewind spring should be preloaded approximately 2½ turns.

Starter pulley (5) and rewind spring (4) can be removed after snap ring (9) is withdrawn. The rewind spring will prob-

ably come out of housing when pulley is lifted out.

CAUTION: Use care to prevent injury.

To assemble, wind all but the last 5 to 6 inches (12.7 to 15.2 cm) of starter cord onto pulley, then locate the end out of notch (N – Fig. PR6-15) in plate. Stick the inner end of rewind spring through the housing and attach spring to pulley as shown in Fig. PR6-17. Position pulley over the center post and wind spring into starter housing as shown in Fig. PR6-18.

Allow the spring (and pulley) to unwind after the spring is wound into the housing. Preload the rewind spring 2½ turns and push end of starter cord out through the hole in housing. Install the brake spring, starter pinion and decompression lever as shown in Fig. PR6-15. Washer (W) should be on screw closest to starter pinion.

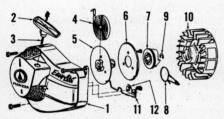

Fig. PR6-16 — Exploded view of rewind starter assembly.

1. Housing	7. Pinion
2. Handle	8. Friction yoke
3. Cord	9. Snap ring
4. Rewind spring	10. Flywheel
5. Pulley	11. Decompression link
6. Plate	12. Spring

Fig. PR6-17 — Rewind starter spring should be installed as shown through housing and attached to pulley.

Fig. PR6-18 — The rewind spring is wound into housing as shown.

PIONEER

Model	Bore	Stroke	Displ.	Drive Type
P40, Farmsaw, Farmsaw "S", P41, P41S	1.875 in. (47.6 mm)	1.437 in. (36.5 mm)	3.97 cu. in. (66 cc)	Direct·

MAINTENANCE

SPARK PLUG. Recommended spark plug is Champion CJ8 for Model P40, RCJ8 for Models Farmsaw and Farmsaw "S" and CJ7Y for Models P41 and P41S. Spark plug electrode gap should be 0.030 inch (0.76 mm). Tighten spark plug to 84-96 in.-lbs. (9.5-10.9 N·m).

CARBURETOR. A Tillotson HS carburetor is used. Refer to Tillotson section of CARBURETOR SERVICE for service and exploded view of carburetor.

Initial setting for low speed mixture needle (7–Fig. PR8-1) should be 1⅛ turns out from a lightly seated position and high speed mixture needle (8) should be ⅞ turn out from a lightly seated position. Clockwise rotation will lean the mixture.

Adjust high speed needle (8) just rich enough that engine will not stall when saw is loaded to a point where clutch slips. Adjust low speed needle (7) to the leanest setting that permits smooth acceleration from idle to high speed without faltering. Excessive smoking, lack of power and rough exhaust indicates carburetor is adjusted too rich. Lack of power and stalling under load (or cutting conditions) indicates mixture is adjusted too lean.

Idle speed is adjusted by turning stop screw (6). Engine should idle smoothly at less than clutch engagement speed.

CAUTION. Late P40 models and all other models are equipped with a speed limiter. Do not attempt to remove or alter this device to permit higher than normal engine speed. Overspeed could result in excessive wear and/or damage to the engine. Centrifugal force at excessive engine speeds can cause the flywheel to burst.

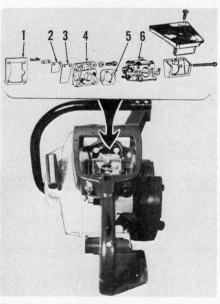

Fig. PR8-4 — View of reed valve assembly used on P40 models. Other models are similar.

1. Gasket
2. Reed stiffener
3. Reed pedal
4. Reed valve plate
5. Gasket
6. Carburetor

IGNITION SYSTEM. Model P40 is equipped with standard magneto ignition with breaker-points. A breakerless capacitor discharge magneto is used on all other models. Refer to the appropriate following paragraphs for service.

Breaker-Point Models. The ignition breaker-points are located under the flywheel. The flywheel retaining nut is left-hand thread and should be tightened to 25-30 ft.-lbs. (34-41 N·m) when reinstalling.

Breaker-point gap should be 0.015 inch (0.38 mm). When installing new breaker-points, it is suggested that point gap be set at 0.017-0.018 inch (0.43-0.46 mm) to allow for rubbing block initial wear (seating). The breaker-point cam is ground into engine crankshaft.

Clearance between coil core and flywheel magnets (armature air gap)

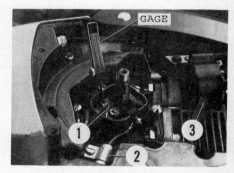

Fig. PR8-5 — View showing gage, breaker-points (1), condenser (2) and coil (3) with the flywheel removed from P40 model.

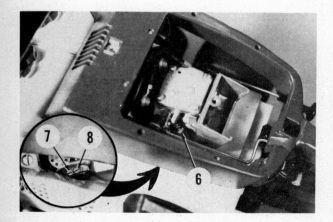

Fig. PR8-1 — View showing location of low speed mixture needle (7), high speed mixture needle (8) and idle speed stop screw (6).

Fig. PR8-6 — Armature air gap should be checked and adjusted using correct thickness of shim stock (S).

should be 0.012 inch (0.30 mm). Check air gap using correct thickness of shim stock as shown in Fig. PR8-6. Edge gap setting should be 0.188-0.312 inch (4.78-7.92 mm). Ignition should occur (breaker-points just open) at 30 degrees BTDC.

Breakerless Models. Ignition components are mounted outside the flywheel making it unnecessary to remove the flywheel for most ignition service. The flywheel retaining nut is right-hand thread and should be carefully tightened to 25-30 ft.-lbs. (34-41 N·m) when reinstalling.

A Wico Magneto Test Plug (Pioneer part 426814) or equivalent can be used as shown in Fig. PR8-9 to check the overall condition of the ignition.

To diagnose ignition troubles, first check for loose connections, shorted connections or wires and for faulty (shorted) stop switch. Stop switch (2–Fig. PR8-7 or PR8-8) is attached to wire (4) and stops engine by grounding the ignition system. On P41 and P41S models, wiring should be installed as

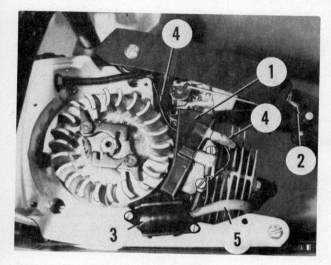

shown in Fig. PR8-7. If the test plug still will not fire after checking for shorts, install a new high tension coil (3–Fig. PR8-7) or one-piece ignition module (6–Fig. PR8-8) and recheck. If the test plug still will not fire on P41 and P41S models, install ignition module (1–Fig. PR8-7).

The only adjustment on the unit is the air gap between the ignition module core and the flywheel magnets (Fig. PR8-10). Clearance (air gap) should 0.012 inch (0.30 mm) and should be checked while pushing the flywheel toward the ignition module. Loctite 222 should be used on module retaining screws which should be tightened to 30-35 in.-lbs. (3.4-4.0 N·m) on Farmsaw and Farmsaw "S" models and 45-50 in.-lbs. (5.1-5.6 N·m) on all other models.

LUBRICATION. Engine is lubricated by mixing engine oil with gasoline. Recommended oil is Beaird-Poulan engine oil approved for a fuel-to-oil mixture ratio of 40:1. If recommended oil is not available, a good quality oil designed for two-stroke air-cooled engines may be used when mixed at a 24:1 ratio. Use a separate container when mixing the oil and gas.

The chain oiler reservoir holds approximately 0.69 pint (0.370 L) of oil should be filled with Pioneer/Partner Chain Oil

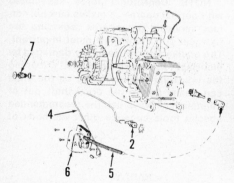

Fig. PR8-8 — Drawing of ignition components used on Farmsaw models. Refer to Fig. PR8-7 for legend except for one-piece ignition module (6) and compression release (7).

Fig. PR8-9 — View of test plug connected for testing the ignition system.

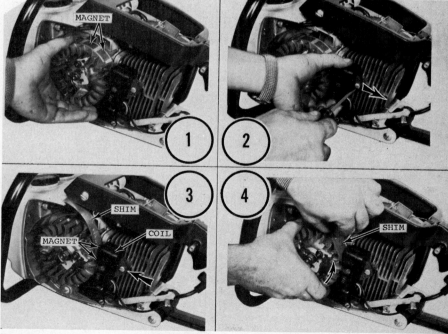

Fig. PR8-10 — Views showing typical armature air gap adjustment. View (1) shows magnets turned away from coil. View (2) shows moving the coil away from the flywheel. View (3) shows the correct thickness of shims positioned between magnets and armature (coil) core legs. Loosen the coil attaching screws and allow coil to move in toward magnets. Tighten the attaching screws, then roll shim out as shown in View (4).

or, if not available, use clean SAE 10 to SAE 30 motor oil depending upon ambient temperature.

NOTE: A metal plate is located directly under the oil filler opening and should not be mistaken for the oil level.

Turning adjusting screw (6–Fig. PR8-11) will change the volume of oil that is pumped to the bar and chain. Adjuster can only be turned approximately ¾ turn, but the volume is increased from about 0.17 ounce/minute to 0.37 ounce/minute (5 mL/minute to 11 mL/minute) within the adjusting range. Turning counterclockwise will increase the volume delivered. Set the adjusting screw at ⅜ turn open if 16 inch (40.6 cm) chain guide bar is used under average conditions. Adjustment may be altered at the discretion of the operator to meet various cutting conditions such as temperature, type of wood, size of wood, length of bar and oil viscosity. To check pump operation, increase engine speed several times and notice oil coming from nose of guide bar. A fine spray of oil should be observed.

Worm gear (7–Fig. PR8-12) on the crankshaft rotates and turns pump shaft and gear (3). End of pump shaft (5) is machined on an angle to provide a cam surface which rides against surface of adjuster (6). As the pump shaft turns the cam surface pushes the shaft in and out of pump body. The in and out movement

pumps oil to the chain. A flat on the pump shaft acts as a valve to open the intake port on the outward stroke and the outlet port on the inward stroke. A small amount of grease should be used to lubricate the pump gears. A special puller (Pioneer part 474329) is available for pulling the worm gear from crankshaft. When installing pump, be sure that oil pickup (1) is directed toward bottom of the tank.

REPAIRS

TIGHTENING TORQUES. Refer to the following for tightening torque values:

Air Filter	20-25 in.-lbs.
	(2.3-2.8 N·m)
Air Filter Cover Screw	25-30 in.-lbs.
	(2.8-3.4 N·m)
Carburetor Mounting	20-25 in.-lbs.
	(2.3-2.8 N·m)
Clutch Nut:	
Model P40	18-22 ft.-lbs.
	(24.4-29.8 N·m)
All Other	
Models	30-35 ft.-lbs.
	(40.7-47.5 N·m)
Crankcase Halves	45-50 in.-lbs.
	(5.1-5.6 N·m)
Cylinder Base Screws	90-100 in.-lbs.
	(10.2-11.3 N·m)
Flywheel Nut	25-30 ft.-lbs.
	(33.9-40.7 N·m)
Ignition Switch	15-20 in.-lbs.
	(1.8-2.3 N·m)
Isolator Mount Screws	40-50 in.-lbs.
	(4.5-5.6 N·m)
Muffler:	
Nuts	70-75 in.-lbs.
	(7.9-8.5 N·m)
Screw	45-50 in.-lbs.
	(5.1-5.6 N·m)
Oil Pump	25-30 in.-lbs.
	(2.8-3.4 N·m)
Reed Valve-to-Crankcase	25-30 in.-lbs.
	(2.8-3.4 N·m)
Spark Plug	84-96 in.-lbs.
	(9.5-10.9 N·m)
Trigger Mounting Screws	8-12 in.-lbs.
	(0.9-1.3 N·m)

CYLINDER, PISTON, RINGS AND PIN. Compression pressure should be 150 psi (1035 kPa) when checked with a gage while rotating crankshaft with re-

wind starter. Rewind starter, handle assembly and carburetor must be removed before removing the cylinder. The cylinder and head is one-piece and is attached to crankcase with four screws. Cylinder bore is chrome plated and cylinder should be renewed if the plating is worn away exposing the soft base metal. Piston should be heated to 300° F (149° C) before removing piston pin. Use care to prevent bending connecting rod even after piston is heated. On P40 models, piston pin is equipped with caged bearing (3–Fig. PR8-14) and specially shaped thrust washers (2). Notches on thrust washers must be toward sides of connecting rod. The thrust washers are not used on other models. On all models, pins located in piston ring grooves must be positioned toward flywheel as shown in Fig. PR8-14 or Fig. PR8-15, away from the exhaust port of cylinder. The ends of piston pin retaining clips must engage notch in piston.

NOTE: Incorrect installation of piston will cause extensive damage to the piston and cylinder.

CRANKSHAFT AND CONNECTING ROD. The crankshaft, crankpin and connecting rod are pressed together and are available only as a complete assembly.

NOTE: Centrifugal force associated with normal operation makes careful, correct servicing procedures regarding the flywheel and crankshaft most important. The crankshaft can be easily damaged by incorrect service procedures. Dropping the crankshaft or pounding on the ends can easily knock the crankshaft out of alignment. Always use the recommended special tools because other methods of

Fig. PR8-11—The adjuster (6) is visible behind strut. Turning adjuster counterclockwise will increase volume of oil delivered to the bar and chain.

Fig. PR8-12—Oil pickup (1) and hose (2) are located in tank through hole (H). Oil pressurized by the pump passes through ports (P) to lubricate the saw chain.

1. Oil pickup
2. Hose
3. Driven gear
4. Pump spring
5. Cam end
6. Adjuster
7. Worm gear
8. Gasket

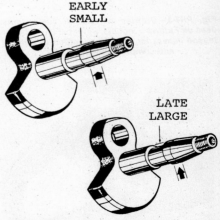

EARLY SMALL

LATE LARGE

Fig. PR8-13—The early crankshafts are small in diameter at the ignition cover gasket. Later models require ignition cover gasket with larger diameter hole.

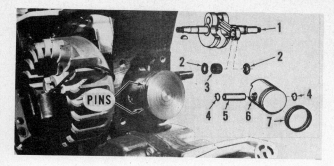

Fig. PR8-14—Install piston on connecting rod with ring locating pins toward flywheel side as shown. P40 model is shown.

1. Crankshaft
2. Thrust washers (P40 models only)
3. Needle bearing
4. Retaining rings
5. Piston pin
6. Piston
7. Rings

removing the crankshaft and main bearings can damage parts which may result in injury. Carefully inspect flywheel and renew if tapered seat, keyway or cooling fins are damaged. Install new flywheel if crankshaft has broken on magneto side or if engine has been operated with loose flywheel nut. Always tighten the flywheel nut to correct torque after each assembly.

Crankshaft seals can be removed and installed without separating the crankcase halves. Use Pioneer tool 430025 to hold the flywheel and remove flywheel nut (left-hand thread for Model P40; right-hand thread for all other models). Pull flywheel from tapered end of crankshaft using Pioneer tool 471439. Use Pioneer tool 471437 to remove seal from flywheel side and tool 429445 to install seal. The clutch and oil pump must be removed from right side before crankshaft seal can be renewed on that side. Use Pioneer tool 474329 to pull drive worm from crankshaft and tool 471437 to pull seal from crankcase. Use Pioneer tool 427407 to install seal on clutch side.

To separate crankcase halves, remove handle bar, rewind starter, handle assembly, carburetor, reed valve, flywheel, ignition coil, saw chain, guide bar, clutch, chain oiler pump, cylinder and piston. Remove screws (A & B – Fig. PR8-16) attaching crankcase halves together and carefully separate the halves. Fuel pickup line (L) should be withdrawn as shown for easier access to one of the screws.

Three different crankshafts have been used in P40 models. The first style crankshaft permitted both main bearings to stay in bores of crankcase. The second style crankshaft incorporated a thrust washer on the magneto side between crankshaft web and inner race of main bearing. The main bearing journal on the magneto side for the second type is large enough in diameter to require pressing the bearing onto journal. The third type is similar to the second type with the additional feature that crankshaft diameter is larger at the ignition cover gasket (Fig. PR8-13). The larger diameter requires a cover gasket with large diameter hole, the small diameter requires cover gasket with smaller diameter hole. Use special Pioneer tool 470335 and heat the crankcase to approximately 300° F (149° C) before attempting to remove main bearings from crankcase bores. Special Pioneer main bearing puller (part 471015) is necessary to remove magneto side main bearing from crankshafts with larger journals. Support crankshaft carefully in hand or with plate between webs before driving magneto side main bearing onto main journal.

NOTE: Be sure washer is installed between bearing and crankshaft web with radius on washer matching filler radius on crank web.

Both main bearings are press fit on Farmsaw, Farmsaw "S," P41 and P41S crankshaft. The magneto side main bearing is also a shrink fit in crankcase bore, while the drive side bearing is a slip fit in a cast iron liner of the drive side crankcase bore. Use special Pioneer tool 470335 and heat the crankcase to approximately 300° F (149° C) before attempting to remove or replace main bearing and crankshaft from magneto side of crankcase. Use special Pioneer main bearing puller (part 471015) to remove both main bearings from crankshaft. Support crankshaft carefully in hand or with plate between webs before driving bearings onto journals using Pioneer bearing driver (part 470335).

CAUTION: Be extremely careful while handling any of the three-piece crankshafts; because, hitting any part of the crankshaft and rod assembly can knock the unit out of alignment. Misalignment will result in early failure of some parts and may, because of the rotational speed involved, cause injury.

On all models, the gasket surface between the two crankcase halves must be completely clean and free from nicks, burrs and all parts of the old gasket. The crankcase forms three different compartments when the halves are joined together: Engine crankcase (C–Fig. PR8-17), Fuel tank (G) and Chain oiler reservoir (O).

Fig. PR8-15—View of P41 and P41S models showing correct location of ring locating pins. Farmsaw and Farmsaw "S" models are similar. Refer to Fig. PR8-14 for legend.

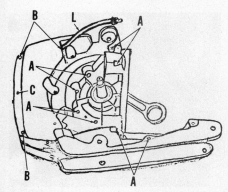

Fig. PR8-16—Screws (A) should be 1¼ inches (32 mm) long, screws (B) should be 2¼ inches (57 mm) long and screw (C) should be 2½ inches (64 mm) long. Fuel pickup line (L) should be withdrawn to facilitate removal and installation of one long screw.

Fig. PR8-17—View of Model P40 crankcase halves separated. Compartment (C) is crankcase, (O) is oil reservoir and (G) is the fuel tank. Be sure to clean gasket surface thoroughly and install new gasket before assembling. Other models are similar.

When assembling, the ten screws (A – Fig. PR8-16) should be 1¼ inches (32 mm) long; the three screws (B) should be 2¼ inches (57 mm) long; the screw (C) in dowel hole should be 2½ inches (64 mm) long.

NOTE: On P40 models, align the crankcase halves using a straightedge along top, machined surface (Fig. PR8-18) before tightening screws.

CLUTCH. All models are equipped with a direct-drive clutch. The clutch, typical of type used on Farmsaw, Farmsaw "S" and P40 models is shown in Fig. PR8-19; while Models P41 and P41S clutch is shown in Fig. PR8-22. Refer to the appropriate illustration while disassembling.

The clutch can be disassembled after removing strut and nut (6). The safety brake must be disengaged before removing strut from models so equipped.

NOTE: On Farmsaw, Farmsaw "S" and P40 models, use Pioneer flywheel holding fixture while removing and installing clutch nut. On P41 and P41S models, the clutch driver is provided with ¾ inch hex for use while removing clutch retaining nut.

On all models, clutch driver (8) should slide easily on the crankshaft splines. Inspect the crankshaft, bearing (15), drum (13) and washer (16) for wear and evidence of overheating. Inspect clutch shoes (9), driver (8), spring (10), drum (13) and sprocket (14) for damage. Clutch spring (10) originally used in

Fig. PR8-19 — Exploded view of clutch assembly used on P40 models. Farmsaw and Farmsaw "S" models are similar. Refer to text for assembly notes.

1. Strut
2. Chain tensioner
3. Tension adjuster screw
4. Outside guide plate
5. Inside guide plate
6. Self-locking nut
7. Cover
8. Clutch driver
9. Clutch shoe (3 used)
10. Garter spring
11. Plate (2½ inches OD)
12. Clutch drum
13. Clutch drum
14. Floating sprocket
15. Bearing
16. Washer (1¾ inch OD)

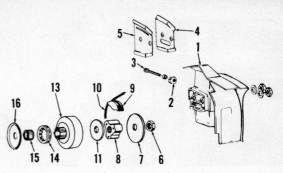

Model P40 clutch should be discarded and later spring color-coded yellow should be installed.

On all models, washer (16) should be installed with concave side toward crankcase. Lubricate bearing (15) with small amount of Mobil Sovarex No. 1W or Shell Alvania No. 2 before installing. Floating sprocket (14) should be installed with open side away from clutch drum as shown in Fig. PR8-15. Position drum and sprocket over bearing, then install plate (11 – Fig. PR8-19 or PR8-22). On Farmsaw, Farmsaw "S" and P40 models, driver (8 – Fig. PR8-19), shoes (9) and garter spring (10) should be assembled together correctly as shown in Fig. PR8-21. Outside of driver (O) is marked "OUTSIDE" and the cut-away edge (C) of the shoes should be trailing as shown. An assembling tool (Pioneer part 429923) is available to facilitate installation of clutch shoes (9 – Fig. PR8-19) and garter spring (10) around driver (8).

On P41 and P41S models, assemble driver (8 – Fig. PR8-22) with "X" mark facing up, shoes (9) and garter spring (10) correctly using Pioneer special tool (part 475212).

On all other models, install the subassembly that includes the driver, shoes and spring. Install cover (7 – Fig. PR8-19) on P40 models. Lubricate threads of all models and install a new nut (6 – Fig. PR8-19 or PR8-22). Tighten nut (6) to 18-22 ft.-lbs. (24.4-29.8 N·m) for P40 models and 30-35 ft.-lbs. (40.7-47.5 N·m) for all other models.

NOTE: The clutch nut (6) should be renewed each time it is removed and the threads should be lubricated to reduce chance of damaging the locking insert.

REWIND STARTER. Farmsaw, Farmsaw "S" and early P40 models are equipped with a Bendix type starter shown in Fig. PR8-24. Late P40 models and all P41 and P41S models are equipped with a pawl type starter shown in Fig. PR8-25. Refer to the appropriate following paragraphs for service.

BENDIX TYPE STARTER. Starter pinion (7 – Fig. PR8-24A) moves in to engage mating lugs on flywheel. To replace starter rope, use 0.130 inch (3.30 mm) diameter cord 43 inches (110 cm) long.

Rotate pinion (7) to remove friction yoke (8) and pinion. The friction yoke (8) should have silver cadmium coating. Install new friction yoke if early unplated unit is used. The later type features self lubrication and has less tension on spring so rope will recoil more easily.

Remove starter handle (2 – Fig. PR8-24) and allow spring to unwind slowly. Remove snap ring (9) or cap screw (14) and lift pulley (5) and rewind spring (4) from housing.

NOTE: If spring is not contained within a black plastic retainer, renew with com-

Fig. PR8-18 — Align crankcase halves of P40 models using a straightedge across machined surface shown, before tightening crankcase screws. All other models are equipped with alignment dowels.

Fig. PR8-20 — The open side of floating sprocket should be away from the clutch drum as shown.

Fig. PR8-21 — The clutch driver, shoes and spring must be assembled correctly. On Farmsaw, Farmsaw "S" and P40 models, side of driver marked "OUTSIDE" (O) should be out, and cutaway part of shoes should be trailing as shown at (C).

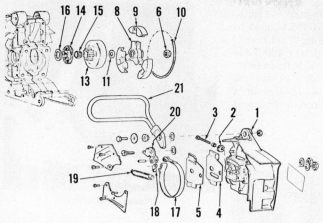

Fig. PR8-22 — Exploded view of clutch used on P41 and P41S models and chain brake used on Farmsaw "S" and P41S models.

1. Strut
2. Chain tensioner
3. Tension adjusting screw
4. Outside guide plate
5. Inside guide plate
6. Self-locking nut
8. Clutch driver
9. Clutch shoe
10. Spring
11. Plate
13. Clutch drum
14. Floating sprocket
15. Bearing
16. Washer
17. Brake band
18. Retaining tab
19. Brake spring
20. Engagement cam
21. Trip lever

NOTE: Observe the following when servicing chain brake:

• Periodically apply a small amount of grease to the point of contact between brake lever and cam face to ensure smooth operation.

• Brake band retainer tab is used in position by one of three cover screws. Ensure that screw is loctited and properly tightened to 45-50 in.-lbs. (5.1-5.6 N·m).

• Periodically oil pivot point (Arrow — Fig. PR8-27).

• Do not lubricate the brake band, as it would render brake ineffective.

• Do not substitute any parts within the brake system.

ponent 474828 which includes a spacer washer.

Clean rewind spring and housing area and repack with grease.

To assemble starter, fit rope through provided hole in pulley groove, knot end and apply grease to knot area to minimize fraying. Wind rope on pulley in direction shown, leaving approximately six inches (15.2 cm) free. Hook into groove provided. Locate inner end of spring to pulley and slide both over stater post ensuring spacer washer is in place.

Secure snap ring or cap screw, then turn pulley approximately 2½ turns to 3 turns to pretension the rewind spring. Fit rope through hole in housing and assemble handle. Install friction yoke and pinion as shown in (Fig. PR8-24A).

PAWL TYPE STARTER. Starter pawls (12 — Fig. PR8-25) are located on the flywheel and engage a notch in aluminum pulley (8) for starting. All models are equipped with two sets of pawls (12), pivots (11) and springs (13). Pawls and springs should be installed as shown in Fig. PR8-26. Starter must be

disassembled to renew rope (3 — Fig. PR8-25) or rewind spring (7). The 5/32 inch diameter (3.97 mm) diameter nylon cord should be 41 inches (104 cm) long. The rewind spring should be preloaded 2½-3 turns when assembling.

Use similar cleaning and assembly instructions as stated in Bendix Type Starter.

CHAIN BRAKE. A chain brake which can stop the saw chain quickly is originally installed on Farmsaw "S" and P41S and available as an option on Farmsaw and P41 models. A brake is also available for Model P40 under number 475100. It is necessary to unlock the brake before removing or installing the clutch cover (1 — Fig. PR8-22). Refer to Fig. PR8-27 for view of brake assembled in clutch cover. Depending on cutting operation, dust shield should be occasionally removed so sawdust and debris can be cleaned from the mechanism. The brake band retainer tab (Arrow — Fig. PR8-27) must be correctly located while installing dust shield over the spring.

COMPRESSION RELEASE. Farmsaw and Farmsaw "S" models are equipped with an "Easy-Arc" automatic decompression system. System is activated during recoil starter operation. One end of decompression link (11 — Fig. PR8-24) rides against starter pinion (7). Outward movement of starter pinion causes link (11) to pivot resulting in opposite end pushing compression release valve (7 — Fig. PR8-8) open. Compression release valve is a unit assembly and should be serviced as such.

SPECIAL TOOLS

Some special tools are available to facilitate servicing Pioneer Farmsaw, Farmsaw "S," P40, P41 and P41S models. Tool 430025 is used to hold flywheel while removing or installing the flywheel retaining nut. Flywheel puller 475501 is used to pull flywheel off tapered end of crankshaft. Flywheel damage is nearly always a result of incorrect removal practices. Tool 429923 or 432537 is used for guiding clutch shoes onto hub of Farmsaw, Farmsaw "S" and P40 models. Clutch plier assembly 47512 should be used to assemble clutch for P41 and P41S models. Tool 474329 is threaded onto oil pump drive gear, then puller screw is turned in to withdraw gear from shaft. The puller can also be used to hold drive gear while

Fig. PR8-23 — View of clutch assembled on crankshaft of P41 model.

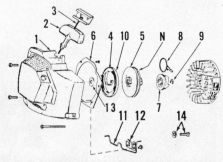

Fig. PR8-24 — Exploded view of Bendix type starter used on some P40 models. Compression release components (11 and 12) and cap screw (14) instead of snap ring (9) are used on Farmsaw and Farmsaw "S" models.

1. Housing
2. Handle
3. Cord
4. Rewind spring
5. Pulley
6. Plate
7. Pinion
8. Friction yoke
9. Snap ring
10. Spring cup
11. Decompression link
12. Spring
13. Washer (0.020 inch)
14. Cap screw

Fig. PR8-24A — Install friction yoke (8) and pinion (7) as shown.

pressing gear onto shaft. Use puller 471437 to remove crankshaft seals and driver 427407 to install crankcase seals on both ends. A 3/16 inch Allen wrench 4½ inches long (tool 429791) is necessary for removing the cylinder retaining screws. Piston pins can be installed using wrist pin loader assembly 474802. Bearing puller 471015 should be used to remove tight main bearings from crankshaft. Bearing driver 470335 is used to install bearings that are tight on crankshaft journals. Bearing driver 426023 is used to remove the drive side main bearing from the crankcase of P40 models. Heat should be applied to the area around the bearing while removing and installing.

Pioneer Tool 471437

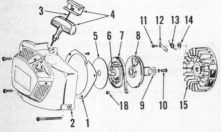

Pioneer Tool 470335

Fig. PR8-25 — Exploded view of pawl type starter used on some P40 models and all P41 and P41S models.

1. Baffle plate
2. Housing
3. Cord
4. Handle & anchor
5. Rewind spring washer
6. Bushing
7. Rewind spring
8. Pulley
9. Washer
10. Screw & lock washer
11. Pawl screw
12. Pawl
13. Spring
14. Washer
15. Flywheel
18. Ferrule

Pioneer Tool 430025

Pioneer Tool 475501

Fig. PR8-26 — The starter pawls and springs should be installed as shown.

Pioneer Tool 429923 or 432537

Fig. PR8-27 — View of safety brake assembly installed in strut. The retainer tab (arrow) holds end of brake band and is attached by one of the three screws for spring (19 — Fig. PR8-22) cover plate.

Pioneer Tool 474329

Pioneer Tool 475212

PIONEER

Model	Bore	Stroke	Displ.	Drive Type
P50, P51, P51S	2-1/16 in. (52.4 mm)	1½ in. (38.1 mm)	5.0 cu. in. (81.9 cc)	Direct
P60, P61, P61S	2¼ in. (57.1 mm)	1½ in. (38.1 mm)	6.0 cu. in. (98.3 cc)	Direct

MAINTENANCE

SPARK PLUG. Recommended spark plug is Champion CJ6 for Model P50 and CJ7Y for all other models. Spark plug electrode gap should be 0.030 inch (0.76 mm). Tighten spark plug to 84-96 in.-lbs. (9.5-10.9 N·m).

CARBURETOR. A Tillotson HS carburetor is used on P61 and P61S models while a Walbro SDC carburetor is used on all other models. Refer to Tillotson or Walbro section of CARBURETOR SERVICE for service and exploded views of carburetors.

On both types of carburetors, initial setting for low speed and high speed mixture needles should be one turn out from a lightly seated position. Idle speed is adjusted by turning throttle stop screw. Engine should idle smoothly at less than clutch engagement speed and should be able to accelerate to cutting speed without faltering.

The screws attaching reed valve plate (4–Fig. PR9-4) to crankcase can be removed after removal of carburetor. Be sure to clean all gasket surfaces and install new gaskets before assembling.

A felt filter is located on the fuel pickup inside the fuel tank. Fuel tank is integral with oil tank and engine crankcase.

IGNITION. A breakerless capacitor discharge ignition system is used on all models. Early P50 models are equipped with a multi-piece ignition system (Fig. PR9-5) while all other models are equipped with a one-piece ignition module.

A Wico test plug or equivalent can be used to check the overall condition of the ignition. Install test plug and check for fire. If plug does not fire, first check for loose connections, shorted connections or wires and for shorted stop switch. On early P50 models, wiring should be installed as shown Fig. PR9-5. If the test plug still will not fire, then ignition module should be renewed. Early P50 ignition is not available and if defective, will require renewal with one-piece ignition system.

On all models, air gap between the coil core and the flywheel magnets (Fig. PR9-7) should be 0.025-0.030 inch (0.63-0.76 mm).

LUBRICATION. Engine is lubricated by mixing engine oil with gasoline. Recommended oil is Beaird-Poulan en-

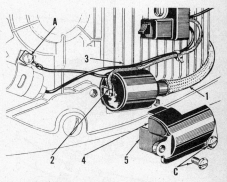

Fig. PR9-5 — Install ignition components and route wires as shown. The sleeve on the high tension lead should be snug against shoulder on coil (1). The red wire terminal should be connected as shown at (2) and the red wire should be at the top center of the coil. The black wire should be next to the red wire (3). The coil cover should be carefully installed with the top flange (4) over both the red and black wires. The end flange (5) should be between the crankcase and the red wire terminal. Tighten capacitor screw (A) to 20-25 in.-lbs. (2.3-2.8 N·m) and cover screws (C) to 25-30 in.-lbs. (2.8-3.4 N·m).

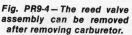

Fig. PR9-4 — The reed valve assembly can be removed after removing carburetor.

1. Gasket
2. Reed backing plate
3. Reed
4. Reed body
5. Gasket
6. Carburetor

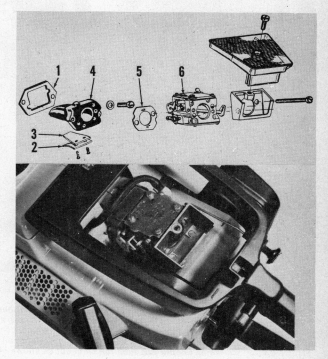

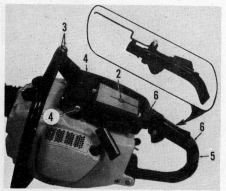

Fig. PR9-3 — View showing trigger assembly.

gine oil approved for a fuel-to-oil mixture ratio of 40:1. If recommended oil is not available, a good quality oil designed for two-stroke air-cooled engines may be used when mixed at a 24:1 ratio. Use a separate container when mixing the oil and gas.

All models are equipped with an adjustable automatic chain oiler (Fig.

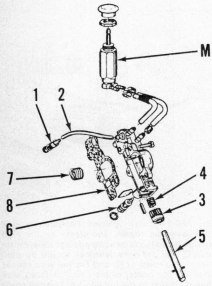

Fig. PR9-6—Exploded view of automatic oil pump assembly with manual pump (M) used on P60, P61 and P61S models. Refer to Fig. PR9-9 for parts identification.

PR9-9). Models P60, P61 and P61S are also equipped with manual oil pump (M – Fig. PR9-6).

The chain oiler reservoir holds approximately 0.88 pint (0.42 L) of oil and should be filled with Pioneer/Partner Chain Oil or, if not available, use clean SAE 10 to SAE 30 motor oil depending upon ambient temperature. Fill the oiler reservoir each time saw is refueled.

NOTE: A metal plate is located directly under the oil filler opening and should not be mistaken for oil level.

Turning adjusting screw (6 – Fig. PR9-8) will change the volume of oil that is pumped to the bar and chain. Adjuster can only be turned approximately one turn, but the volume is increased from 0.27 ounce/minute to 0.57 ounce/minute (8 mL/minute to 17 mL/minute) within the adjusting range. Turning counterclockwise will increase the volume delivered. The oil adjustment screw should be set wide open when first operating the saw to ensure that the bar and chain will receive an adequate supply of oil on the initial run. After the initial run, the setting can be decreased at the discretion of the operator to meet various cutting conditions such as temperature, oil viscosity, type of wood and size of wood.

Worm gear (7 – Fig. PR9-9) on the crankshaft rotates and turns pump shaft and gear (3). End of pump shaft (5) is

machined on an angle to provide a cam surface which rides against surface of adjuster (6). As the pump shaft turns, the cam surface pushes the shaft in and out of pump body. The in and out movement pumps oil to the chain. A flat on the pump shaft acts as a valve to open the intake port on the outward stroke stroke and the outlet port on the inward stroke. A small amount of grease should be used to lubricate the pump gears. A special puller (Pioneer part 474329) is available for pulling the worm gear from crankshaft. When installing pump, be sure that pickup (1 – Fig. PR9-9) is directed toward bottom of the tank while saw is held in upright position.

REPAIRS

TIGHTENING TORQUES. Refer to the following for tightening torque values:

Air Filter	20-25 in.-lbs. (2.3-2.8 N·m)
Air Filter Cover Screw	25-30 in.-lbs. (2.8-3.4 N·m)
Carburetor Mounting	20-25 in.-lbs. (2.3-2.8 N·m)
Clutch Nut	30-35 ft.-lbs. (40.7-47.5 N·m)
Crankcase Halves	45-50 in.-lbs. (5.1-5.6 N·m)
Cylinder Base Screws	90-100 in.-lbs. (10.2-11.3 N·m)
Flywheel Nut	25-30 ft.-lbs. (33.9-40.7 N·m)
Ignition Switch	15-20 in.-lbs. (1.8-2.3 N·m)
Isolator Mount Screws	40-50 in.-lbs. (4.5-5.6 N·m)
Muffler:	
Cap Screws	70-75 in.-lbs. (7.9-8.5 N·m)
Screw	45-50 in.-lbs. (5.1-5.6 N·m)
Oil Pump	25-30 in.-lbs. (2.8-3.4 N·m)

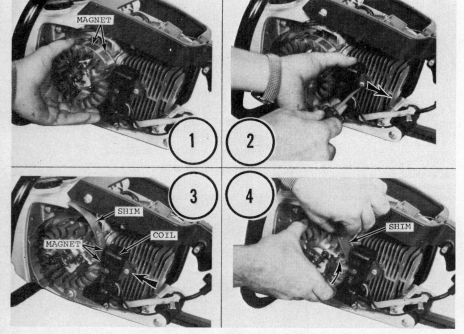

Fig. PR9-7 — Views showing armature air gap adjustment. View (1) shows magnets turned away from coil. View (2) shows moving the coil away from the flywheel. View (3) shows the correct thickness of shims positioned between magnets and armature (coil) core legs. Loosen the coil attaching screws and allow coil to move in toward magnets. Push flywheel toward coil, tighten the attaching screws using Loctite 222, then roll shim out as shown in view (4).

Fig. PR9-8 — Adjuster (6) is visible behind strut. Turning adjuster counterclockwise will increase volume of oil delievered to the bar and chain.

Reed Valve-to-Crankcase . . 25-30 in.-lbs.
(2.8-3.4 N·m)
Spark Plug . . . . 84-96 in.-lbs.
(9.5-10.9 N·m)
Starter Pawl Screws . . . 120-125 in.-lbs.
(13.6-14.1 N·m)
Trigger Mounting Screws . . 8-12 in.-lbs.
(0.9-1.3 N·m)

CYLINDER, PISTON RINGS AND PIN. Compression pressure should be 150 psi (1035 kPa) when checked with a gage while rotating crankshaft with rewind starter. Rewind starter and handle assembly must be removed before removing cylinder. The cylinder and head is one piece and is attached to crankcase with four screws. Cylinder bore is chrome plated and should be renewed if the plating is worn away exposing the soft base metal. Piston should be heated to 300° F (149° C) before removing the piston pin. Use care to prevent bending the connecting rod even after the piston is heated. The piston pin is equipped with a caged bearing (3 – Fig. PR9-10). Pins located in the piston ring grooves must be positioned toward flywheel as shown in Fig. PR9-10, away from exhaust port of cylinder.

NOTE: Incorrect installation of piston will cause extensive damage to the piston and cylinder. Use wrist pin loader 474802. The ends of the piston pin retaining clips must engage notch in piston.

CRANKSHAFT AND CONNECTING ROD. The crankshaft, crankpin and connecting rod are pressed together and are available only as a complete assembly. Crankshaft can be easily damaged by incorrect service procedures. Dropping the crankshaft or pounding on the ends can easily knock the crankshaft out of alignment. Crankshaft seals can be removed and installed without separating the crankcase halves. Use a small screwdriver between shaft and seal to remove and tool 427407 to install drive side seal and tool 429445 to install flywheel side seal.

To separate the crankcase halves, remove handle bar, rewind starter, handle assembly, carburetor, reed valve, flywheel, ignition coil, saw chain, guide bar, clutch, chain oiler pump, pump worm, cylinder and piston. Remove the screws attaching crankcase halves together and carefully separate the halves.

NOTE: Fuel pickup line should be withdrawn for easier access to one of the screws. Main bearing is a press fit on flywheel side of crankshaft. Bearing can be removed from shaft using 471015 bearing puller.

Heat crankcase halves before removing or installing the crankshaft main bearings.

Gasket surface between the two crankcase halves must be completely clean

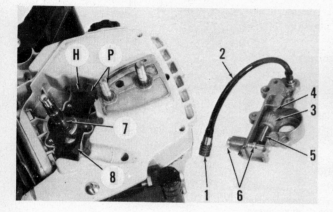

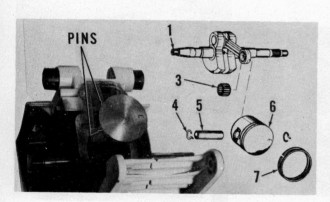

Fig. PR9-9 — Oil pickup (1) and hose (2) are located in tank through hole (H). Oil pressurized by the pump passes through ports (P) to lubricate the saw chain.

1. Oil pickup
2. Hose
3. Driven gear
4. Pump spring
5. Cam
6. Adjuster
7. Worm gear
8. Gasket

Fig. PR9-10 — Install piston on connecting rod with ring locating pins toward flywheel side as shown.

1. Crankshaft
3. Needle bearing
4. Retaining rings
5. Piston pin
6. Piston
7. Rings

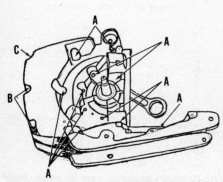

Fig. PR9-11 — Screws (A) should be 1¼ inches (32 mm) long, screws (B) should be 2¼ inches (57 mm) long and screw (C) should be 2½ inches (64 mm) long. Fuel pickup line should be withdrawn to facilitate removal and installation of one screw.

Fig. PR9-12 — View of crankshaft halves separated. Compartment (C) is crankcase, (O) is oil reservoir and (G) is the fuel tank. Be sure to clean gasket surface thoroughly and install new gasket before assembling.

and free from nicks and burrs. The crankcase forms three different compartments when the halves are joined together: Engine crankcase (C – Fig. PR9-12), Fuel tank (G) and Chain oiler reservoir (O).

When assembling, the two screws (B – Fig. PR9-11) should be 2¼ inches (57 mm) long; the screw (C) should be 2½ inches (64 mm) long and the remaining eleven screws (A) should be 1¼ inches (32 mm) long.

CLUTCH. The direct drive clutch is shown in Fig. PR9-14. Inset shows clutch components used on some P50 models and all P51S and P61S models. The clutch can be disassembled after removing strut (1) and nut (6). The clutch driver (8) should slide easily on the crankshaft splines. Inspect the crankshaft, bearing (15), drum (13) and washer (16) for wear and evidence of overheating. Inspect clutch shoes (9), driver (8), spring (10), drum (13) and sprocket (14) for damage.

Washer (16) should be installed next to crankcase. Lubricate bearing (15) with small amount of general purpose automotive grease before installing. Floating sprocket (14) should be installed with an open side away from clutch drum as shown in Fig. PR9-15. On some P50 models all P60 and P61 models, position drum and sprocket over bearing, then install plate (11 – Fig. PR9-14). Driver (8), shoes (9) and garter spring (10) should be assembled as shown in Fig. PR9-16. Outside of driver (O) is marked "OUTSIDE" and the cutaway edge (C) of the shoes should be trailing as shown. An assembling tool (Pioneer part 429923) is available to facilitate installation of clutch shoes (9 – Fig. PR9-14) and garter spring (10) around driver (8). Install driver (8), shoes (9) and spring (10) subassembly and cover (7). Lubricate threads, then install nut (6).

On models equipped with clutch assembly shown in inset of Fig. PR9-14, assemble driver (8) with hex nut side up, shoes (9) and spring (10) correctly using Pioneer special tool 475212.

REWIND STARTER. Starter pawls (12 – Fig. PR9-17) are located on the flywheel and engage a notch in pulley (8) for starting. All models are equipped with two sets of pawls (12), pivots (11) and springs (13). Pawls and springs should be installed as shown in Fig. PR9-18. Starter must be disassembled to renew rope (3 – Fig. PR9-17), or rewind spring (7). The 5/32 inch (3.97 mm) diameter nylon cord should be 41 inches (104 cm) long. The rewind spring should be preloaded three turns when assembling. Clean and apply automotive grease to spring.

CHAIN BRAKE. A chain brake which can stop the saw chain quickly is equipped on P51S and P61S models and available as an option on all other models. It is necessary to unlock the brake before removing or installing strut (1 – Fig. PR9-20). Refer to Fig. PR9-21 for view of brake assembled in

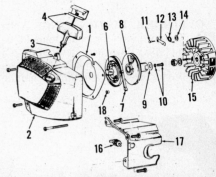

Fig. PR9-17 – Exploded view of rewind starter assembly. Two sets of pawls (11, 12, 13 & 14) are used.

1. Baffle plate
2. Housing
3. Cord
4. Handle & anchor
5. Bushing
7. Rewind spring
8. Pulley
9. Washer
10. Screw & lock washer
11. Pawl screw
12. Pawl
13. Spring
14. Washer
15. Flywheel
16. Stop switch
17. Cylinder shroud
18. Ferrule

Fig. PR9-15 – The open side of floating sprocket should be away from the clutch drum as shown.

Fig. PR9-16 – The clutch driver, shoes and spring must be assembled correctly. Side of driver marked "OUTSIDE" (O) should be out, and cutaway part of shoes should be trailing as shown at (C).

Fig. PR9-18 – The starter pawls and springs should be installed as shown.

Fig. PR9-14 – Exploded view of the clutch assembly. Refer to text for assembly notes. Some models are equipped with clutch components shown in inset.

1. Clutch cover
2. Chain tensioner
3. Tension adjuster screw
4. Outside guide plate
5. Inside guide plate
6. Self-locking nut
7. Cover (2½ inches OD)
8. Clutch driver
9. Clutch shoe (3 used)
10. Garter spring
11. Plate (2 inches OD)
13. Clutch drum
14. Floating sprocket
15. Bearing
16. Thrust washer (1.030 inches OD)

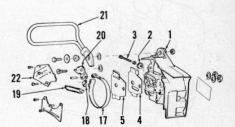

Fig. PR9-20 – Exploded view of chain brake assembly.

1. Strut
2. Chain tensioner
3. Tension adjusting screw
4. Outside guide plate
5. Inside guide plate
17. Brake band
18. Retaining tab
19. Brake spring
20. Engagement ca
21. Trip lever
22. Cover

strut. Depending on cutting operation, dust shield should be occasionally removed so sawdust and debris can be cleaned from the mechanism. The brake band retainer tab (Arrow—Fig. PR9-21) must be correctly located while installing dust shield over the spring.

NOTE: Observe the following when servicing chain brake:

• **Periodically apply a small amount of grease to the point of contact between brake lever and cam face to ensure smooth operation.**
• **Brake band retainer tab is held in position by one of three cover screws. Ensure that screw is loctited and properly tightened to 45-50 in.-lbs. (5.1-5.6 N·m).**
• **Periodically oil pivot point (Arrow—Fig. PR9-21).**

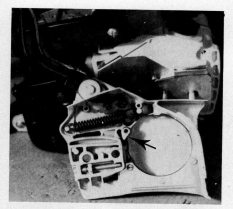

Fig. PR9-21—View of safety brake assembly installed in strut. The retainer tab (arrow) holds end of brake band and is attached by one of the three screws for cover (22—Fig. PR9-20).

• **Do not lubricate the brake band, as it would render brake ineffective.**
• **Do not substitute any parts within the brake system.**

SPECIAL TOOLS

Some special tools are available to facilitate servicing Pioneer saws. Tool 430025 is used to hold flywheel while removing or installing flywheel retaining nut. Flywheel puller 475501 is used to pull flywheel off tapered end of crankshaft. Flywheel damage is nearly always a result of incorrect removal practices. Tool 475212 or 432537 is used for guiding clutch shoes onto hub. Puller 474329 is threaded onto oil pump drive gear, then puller screw is turned in to withdraw gear from shaft. The puller can also be used to hold the drive gear while pressing gear onto shaft. Driver 427407 is used for installing crankcase seal on drive side. A 3/16 inch Allen

Pioneer Tool 475212

wrench 4½ inches long (tool 429791) is necessary for removing the cylinder retaining screws. Piston pins can be installed using the wrist pin loader assembly 475420. Bearing driver 470335 is used to install main bearings on the crankshaft. Driver 470335 is used to remove the drive side main bearing from the crankcase while heat is applied to the area around the bearing.

Pioneer Tool 475501

Pioneer Tool 432537

PIONEER

Model	Bore	Stroke	Displ.	Drive Type
1074	1.625 in. (41.3 mm)	1.5 in. (38.1 mm)	3.14 cu. in. (51.5 cc)	Direct
P21	1.625 in. (41.3 mm)	1.5 in. (38.1 mm)	3.14 cu. in. (51.5 cc)	Direct
P26, P26E	1.625 in. (41.3 mm)	1.5 in. (38.1 mm)	3.14 cu. in. (5.15 cc)	Direct
P28, P28E	1.625 in. (41.3 mm)	1.5 in. (38.1 mm)	3.14 cu. in. (51.5 cc)	Direct
P28S, P28ES	1.625 in. (41.3 mm)	1.5 in. (38.1 mm)	3.14 cu. in. (51.5 cc)	Direct

MAINTENANCE

SPARK PLUG. Recommended spark plug is Champion CJ8 for Models 1074 and P21 and RCJ8 for all other models. Spark plug electrode gap should be 0.030 inch (0.76 mm). Tighten spark plug to 84-96 in.-lbs. (9.5-10.9 N·m).

CARBURETOR. A Tillotson HU carburetor is used on most models, however, some models may be equipped with a Walbro WA carburetor. Refer to Tillotson or Walbro section of CARBURETOR SERVICE for service and exploded views of carburetors.

Initial setting for low speed mixture needle is 1¼ turns open from a lightly seated position for both type carburetors. The high speed mixture is determined by the size of a fixed orifice. Adjust idle speed screw (27–Fig. PR10-1) so engine idles just below clutch engagement speed. Adjust low speed mixture screw (6) so engine will accelerate cleanly without hesitation.

On all models, the choke valve is located in blowback tube (3–Fig. PR10-2).

NOTE: Be careful NOT to turn mixture needle in more than just lightly seated. The needle may be bent or broken and seats damaged if seated too hard.

IGNITION SYSTEM. Pioneer 1074, P21, P26, P28 and P28S models are equipped with standard magneto ignition with breaker-points. A breakerless capacitor discharge magneto is used on P26E, P28E and P28ES models. Refer to the appropriate following paragraphs for service.

Breaker-Point Models. The ignition breaker-points are located under the flywheel. The flywheel retaining nut is left-hand thread. Use special puller part 475501 or equivalent to remove flywheel from crankshaft taper. Tighten flywheel retaining nut to 20-25 ft.-lbs. (27-34 N·m).

Breaker-point gap should be 0.015 inch (0.38 mm). Breaker-point cam is ground into the engine crankshaft. Clearance between ignition coil core and flywheel magnets (armature air gap) should be 0.010-0.012 inch (0.25-0.30 mm). Check air gap using cor-

rect thickness of shim stock as shown in Fig. PR10-7.

Breakerless Models. Ignition components are mounted outside the flywheel making it unnecessary to remove the flywheel for most ignition service. The flywheel retaining nut is left-hand thread and should be carefully torqued to 20-25 ft.-lbs. (27-34 N·m) when reinstalling.

A Wico test plug or equivalent can be used to check the overall condition of the ignition. Install test plug and check for

Fig. PR10-5—A special puller (tool 475501) should be used to pull flywheel from taper on crankshaft. Failure to use puller will probably result in damage.

Fig. PR10-1 — View showing location of idle mixture needle (6) and idle speed stop screw (27) for models with Tillotson HU carburetor. Locations of idle mixture needle and idle stop screw for models with Walbro WA carburetor are similar.

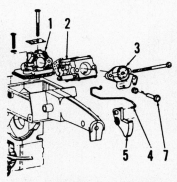

Fig. PR10-2 — Exploded view of induction components.

1. Insulating block
2. Carburetor assy.
3. Blowback tube
4. Throttle link
5. Throttle trigger
7. Choke knob

Fig. PR10-7 — Armature air gap should be checked and adjusted using correct thickness of shim stock (S).

fire. If plug does not fire, first check for loose connections, shorted connections or wires and for shorted stop switch. If the test plug still will not fire, then ignition module should be renewed.

Clearance between ignition module and flywheel magnets (armature air gap) should be 0.010-0.012 inch (0.25-0.30 mm). Check air gap using correct thickness of shim stock as shown in Fig. PR10-7.

LUBRICATION. Engine is lubricated by mixing engine oil with gasoline. Recommended oil is Beaird-Poulan engine oil approved for a fuel-to-oil mixture ratio of 40:1. If recommended oil is not available, a good quality oil designed for two-stroke air-cooled engines may be used when mixed at a 24:1 ratio. Use a separate container when mixing the oil and gas.

The chain oiler reservoir should be filled with Pioneer/Partner Chain Oil or, if not available, use SAE 10 to SAE 30 motor oil depending upon ambient temperature.

All models are equipped with an automatic chain oiler pump (Fig. PR10-9). Worm gear (W) on crankshaft turns pump shaft and gear (5). Guide pin (6) rides in a cam slot (C) of pump shaft and causes the pump shaft to move back and forth as it rotates. The back and forth movement pumps oil to the chain. Flat (F) on shaft acts as a valve to open the intake port on the outward stroke and the outlet port on the inward stroke. Felt washer (1) should be glued to pump cover (2).

REPAIRS

TIGHTENING TORQUES. Refer to the following for tightening torque values:

Crankcase (Tank) Halves . . 45-50 in.-lbs.
(5.1-5.6 N·m)
Flywheel Nut . . . . 20-25 ft.-lbs.
(27.1-34 N·m)
Cylinder Base Nuts . . . . 70-80 in.-lbs.
(7.9-9.0 N·m)
Muffler-to-Cylinder . . . . . . 45-50 in.-lbs.
(5.1-5.6 N·m)
Clutch Driver . . . . 18-22 ft.-lbs.
(24.4-29.8 N·m)

CYLINDER, PISTON, RINGS AND PIN. Compression pressure should be 150 psi (1035 kPa) with "Easy-Arc" starting decompression valve closed. The operating rod (11 – Fig. PR10-16) can be removed to check compression pressure. The cylinder and head is one piece and is attached to the crankcase with four screws. The cylinder bore is chrome plated and cylinder should be replaced if plating is worn away exposing the soft base metal. The piston should be heated to 300° F (149° C) before removing piston pin.

NOTE: Use care to prevent bending the connecting rod while removing piston pin, even after piston is heated.

Mark the piston on exhaust port side if old piston is to be reinstalled. New pistons may be installed either way, but a used piston should be installed in the same position that was first installed. The original needle rollers may fall out of the piston pin or wrist pin bearing when the pin is removed, as they are only retained by grease during assembly. The bearings used in service are of the shell type in which needles are contained. Press only on lettered end, when installing new piston pin bearing. Make

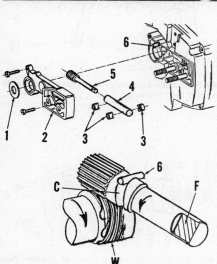

Fig. PR10-8 — View of ignition breaker-points (1), condenser (2) and coil (3) with the flywheel removed. Clip (C) is used to prevent the spark plug wire from holding decompression valve (D) open. The fuel tank vent valve is located at (V).

Fig. PR10-10 — View of crankcase halves showing location of the four compartments: Air box (A), Crankcase (C), Fuel tank (G) and Oil tank (O). Model P28 is shown but others are similar.

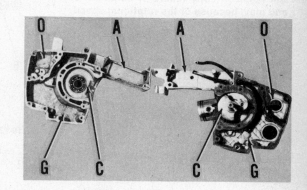

Fig. PR10-11 — Exploded view of crankshaft and crankcase typical of all models with integral handle. Refer to Fig. PR10-13 for exploded view of Model P28.

1. Rear handle brace
2. Lower shroud
3. Throttle trigger
4. Throttle link
5. Crankshaft seals
6. Main bearings
7. Piston pin bearing
8. Crankshaft assy.
9. Woodruff key
10. Oil cap
11. Fuel cap
12. Plug
13. Spring
14. Valve cap
15. Fuel vent check valve
16. Screen
17. Retaining ring

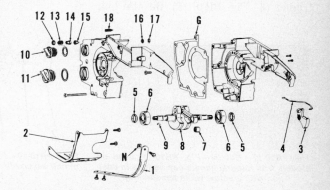

Fig. PR10-9 — Drawing of the chain oiler pump. Worm (W) is part of the engine crankshaft. Refer to text.

1. Felt washer
2. Pump cover
3. Sealing pads
4. Pump sleeve
5. Pump shaft and gear
6. Pin

sure that none of original bearing rollers fall into crankcase.

Piston ring end gap should be 0.088-0.098 inch (2.23-2.49 mm). The open end of piston pin retaining clips should be toward top of piston.

CRANKSHAFT AND CONNECTING ROD. The crankshaft, crankpin and connecting rod are pressed together and are available only as a complete assembly. The crankshaft can be easily damaged by incorrect service procedures. Dropping crankshaft or pounding on the ends can easily knock crankshaft out of alignment. The crankshaft seals can be removed and installed without separating the crankcase (fuel tank) halves. Use Pioneer tool 471437 to remove seals and tool 429445 to install seals.

To separate the crankcase halves, remove front handle, rewind starter, lower handle and cylinder shroud, carburetor, ignition coil, flywheel, ignition breaker-points, condenser, exhaust manifold, cylinder, piston, guide bar, saw chain, clutch and automatic chain oiler pump (Fig. PR10-9). Remove the 14 screws attaching crankcase halves together and carefully separate halves. Heat crankcase halves before installing crankshaft main bearings.

CAUTION: Be extremely careful while handling any of the three-piece crankshafts; because, hitting any part of the crankshaft and rod assembly can knock the unit out of alignment. Misalignment will result in early failure of some parts and may, because of the rotational speed involved, cause injury.

The gasket surface between the two crankcase halves must be completely clean and free from nicks and burrs. The crankcase forms four different compartments when halves are joined together: (A–Fig. PR10-10) Air box, (C) Engine crankcase, (G) Fuel tank and (O) Chain oiler reservoir. Check the condition of fuel tank vent components (12, 13, 14, 15, 16 & 17–Fig. PR10-11). Vent assembly must be renewed as a unit.

On all except P28 models, throttle trigger (3–Fig. PR10-11), throttle link

(4), fuel pickup hose, handle brace nut (N), crankshaft assembly (8) and gasket (G) should all be located correctly between the crankcase halves before attaching the halves together. The handle brace nut can be held in place with the screw as shown in Fig. PR10-12 until the crankcase halves are together. The nut is captive between the halves after they are together.

Model P28 is assembled similarly except that trigger assembly is located in the handle frame (Fig. PR10-13).

CLUTCH. Refer to Fig. PR10-14 or Fig. PR10-15 for exploded view of clutch assembly. The clutch can be removed by unscrewing the clutch driver from the end of the crankshaft. The clutch driver has left-hand threads. The felt dust seal washer (1–Fig. PR10-9) should be glued onto the pump cover (2).

NOTE: Use Pioneer flywheel holding fixture (part 430025) while removing and installing clutch driver. Other methods of stopping crankshaft rotation may result in damage.

Clutch slippage for as little as 30 seconds can generate enough heat to melt the clutch shoes and stick them to the drum.

When assembling clutch, lubricated bearing (3–Fig. PR10-15) and tighten clutch driver to approximately 20 ft.-lbs. (27 N·m).

REWIND STARTER. Starter pinion (7–Fig. PR10-16) moves in to engage the mating lugs on the flywheel. The decompression lever (11) is activated by the outward movement of the pinion resulting in the opposite end pushing valve (D–Fig. PR10-8) open.

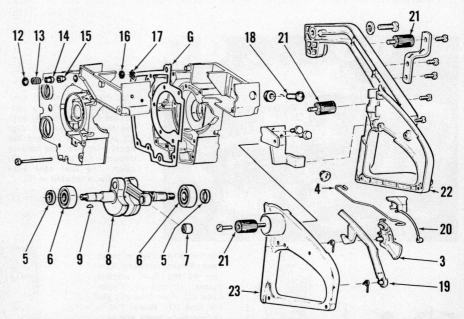

Fig. PR10-13 — Exploded view of crankcase, crankshaft and handle assembly for P28 models. Refer to Fig. PR10-11 for legend except the following.

18. Choke knob
19. Safety trigger
20. Throttle lock
21. Shock asorber
22. Handle frame
23. Frame cover

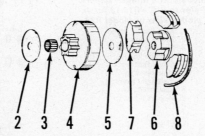

Fig. PR10-12 — Nut (N–Fig. PR10-11) used on models with integral handle can be held in position with a screw while assembling.

Fig. PR10-14 — Exploded view of three-shoe clutch assembly used on some models. Refer to Fig. PR10-15 for legend.

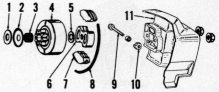

Fig. PR10-15 — Exploded view of typical two-shoe clutch assembly.

1. Felt sealing washer
2. Thrust washer
3. Needle bearing
4. Clutch drum & sprocket
5. Thrust washer
6. Clutch driver
7. Clutch shoes
8. Spring
9. Tension adjusting screw
10. Adjusting block
11. Strut

To replace starter cord, remove housing complete with starter assembly. Remove two screws securing the decompression lever (11–Fig. PR10-16) and spring (12). Remove friction yoke (8) and starter pinion (7) by rotating the pinion.

NOTE: If starter rope has broken, it is likely the rewind spring has been damaged at end joining pulley from over rotation. Spring should be replaced. Rope is 0.130 inch (3.30 mm) diameter nylon cord 43 inches (109 cm) long.

Providing rope has not broken, remove handle (2–Fig. PR10-17) and permit pulley (5) to slowly unwind to avoid spring damage.

Remove snap ring and lift off pulley. Rewind spring should be removed, wiped off and cavity cleaned and regreased.

To assemble, push rope end through provided hole in bottom of pulley groove, knot, then grease knot area to minimize rope fraying. Wind rope onto pulley in the direction of arrow leaving six inches (15.2 cm) of free end. Insert end piece in notch provided and tie loose end around helix area of pulley to avoid entanglement while winding up spring.

Place inner end of spring through slot provided in housing and hook into pulley cavity. Carefully place pulley over starter post and replace snap ring without dislodging end of spring.

Using a ¾ inch, 12 point socket (spark plug size), turn the rewind spring clockwise into place ensuring that outer end is hooked to housing. Relax spring, then pretension pulley 2½ to 3 turns. Poke rope end through housing and secure handle.

Install the pinion and yoke, decompression lever and spring.

Fig. PR10-18—Rewind starter spring should be installed as shown through housing and attached to pulley.

CHAIN BRAKE. A chain brake which can stop the saw chain quickly is originally installed on Models P28S and P28SE. This same brake assembly can be added to Models 1074, P21, P26, P26E and P28.

It is necessary to unlock brake before removing or installing strut (9–Fig. PR10-21). Refer to Fig. PR10-20 for view of brake assembled in clutch cover. Depending on cutting operation, dust shield should be occasionally removed so sawdust and debris can be cleaned from the mechanism. Brake band retainer tab (Arrow–Fig. PR10-20) must be correctly located while installing dust shield over spring.

NOTE: Observe the following when servicing chain brake:
- **Periodically apply a small amount of grease to point of contact between brake lever and cam face to ensure smooth operation.**
- **Brake band retainer tab is held in position by one of three cover screws. Ensure that screw is loctited and properly tightened to 45-50 in.-lbs. (5.1-5.6 N·m).**
- **Periodically oil pivot point (Arrow–Fig. PR10-20).**
- **Do not lubricate the brake band, as it would render brake ineffective.**
- **Do not substitute any parts within the brake system.**

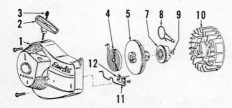

Fig. PR10-16—View showing rewind starter assembled. Washer (W) should be on screw indicated. Refer to Fig. PR10-17 for legend.

Fig. PR10-19—The rewind spring is wound into housing as shown.

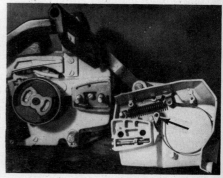

Fig. PR10-20—View of safety brake assembled without cover plate. Be sure that retainer tab (Arrow) is positioned before installing cover plate.

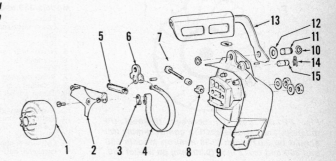

Fig. PR10-17—Exploded view of starter assembly used. Parts (11 and 12) are used to operate decompression valve for "Easy-Arc" starting.

1. Housing
2. Handle
3. Cord
4. Rewind spring
5. Pulley
6. Plate
7. Pinion
8. Friction yoke
9. Snap ring
10. Flywheel
11. Decompression link
12. Spring

Fig. PR10-21—Exploded view of safety brake used on P28S and P28ES models.

1. Clutch drum
2. Cover
3. Retaining tab
4. Brake band
5. Spring
6. Cam
7. Tension adjusting screw
8. Adjusting block
9. Strut
10. Snap rings
11. Pivot
12. Washer
13. Lever
14. Clip
15. Pin

PIONEER/PARTNER

EMAB CANADA
P.O. Box 549
Huron Park, Ontario, Canada N0M 1Y0

Model	Bore	Stroke	Displ.	Drive Type
330, 350, 360	1-7/16 in. (36.5 mm)	1.28 in. (32.5 mm)	2.1 cu. in. (34 cc)	Direct

MAINTENANCE

SPARK PLUG. Recommended spark plug is Champion CJ6 or RCJ6 with an electrode gap of 0.025 inch (0.63 mm) on Models 330 and 350. Recommended spark plug is Champion RCJ7Y with an electrode gap of 0.024 inch (0.60 mm) on Model 360.

CARBURETOR. A Walbro WT diaphragm type carburetor is used on all models. Refer to CARBURETOR SERVICE section for service on Walbro carburetor.

On Models 330 and 350, initial setting of both high and low speed mixture screws is 1⅛ turns open from a lightly seated position. On Model 360, initial setting of both high and low speed mixture screws is one turn open from a lightly seated position. Make final adjustment with engine warm and running. Adjust idle speed screw so engine idles just below clutch engagement speed. Adjust low speed mixture screw so engine will accelerate cleanly without hesitation. Adjust high speed mixture screw to obtain optimum performance under cutting load. High speed mixture must not be adjusted too lean as engine may be damaged.

IGNITION. All models are equipped with a Phelon type capacitor discharge ignition (CDI) system. Air gap (G–Fig. PP1) between flywheel magnets and module/ignition coil assembly should be 0.015 inch (0.38 mm) on Models 330 and 350 and 0.012 inch (0.30 mm) on Model 360.

LUBRICATION. Engine is lubricated by mixing engine oil with fuel. Recommended oil is Beaird-Poulan engine oil approved for a fuel-to-oil mixture ratio of 40:1. If recommended oil is not available, a good quality oil designed for two-stroke air-cooled engines may be used when mixed at a 24:1 ratio. Use a separate container when mixing the oil and gas.

The oil reservoir should be filled with Pioneer/Partner Chain Oil or, if not available, use a good quality SAE 10 to SAE 30 motor oil depending upon ambient temperature.

Early Model 330 is equipped with a manual oil pump and an automatic oiling system. Late Model 330 and Models 350 and 360 are equipped with a positive displacement oil pump assembly located behind flywheel.

CARBON. Carbon should be removed from exhaust system and cylinder periodically. Loose carbon should not be allowed to enter cylinder and care should be taken not to damage cylinder or piston.

REPAIRS

CYLINDER, PISTON, PIN AND RINGS. Cylinder (15–Fig. PP2) is also upper crankcase half. Crankshaft is loose in crankcase when cylinder is removed. Care must be taken not to nick or scratch crankcase mating surfaces during disassembly.

Cylinder head is integral with cylinder and cylinder must be removed to remove piston. Piston is equipped with a single piston ring and floating type piston pin (11). On Models 330 and 350, piston may need to be heated to remove or install piston pin. Needle bearings (12) are used in connecting rod small end on Model 360. On all models, piston and connecting rod are available as a unit assembly only. Piston and ring are available in standard size only. Cylinder bore is chrome plated and should be inspected to determine if chrome is scored, peeling or excessively worn. Renew cylinder and piston if damaged or excessively worn. If either half of crankcase requires renewal, then both halves must be renewed as they are a matched set.

Refer to CRANKSHAFT AND SEALS for proper assembly of crankcase and cylinder.

![Air gap diagram]

Fig. PP1-Air gap (G) between flywheel (F) magnets and module/ignition coil assembly (M) should be 0.015 inch (0.38 mm) on Models 330 and 350 and 0.012 inch (0.30 mm) on Model 360.

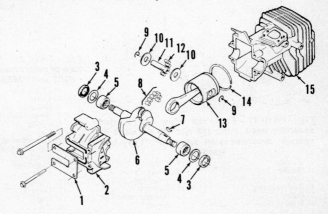

Fig. PP2 – Exploded view of engine assembly. Roller bearings (12) and thrust washers (10) are not used on Models 330 and 350.

1. Plate
2. Lower crankcase half
3. Seal
4. Retaining ring
5. Needle bearing
6. Crankshaft
7. Key
8. Roller bearings
9. Retaining clip
10. Thrust washer
11. Piston pin
12. Needle bearings
13. Piston & connecting rod assy.
14. Piston ring
15. Cylinder & upper crankcase half

CONNECTING ROD. To remove connecting rod, remove cylinder (15 – Fig. PP2). Note that cylinder is also upper crankcase half and crankshaft assembly is loose when cylinder is removed. Connecting rod (13) is one-piece and supported on crankpin by 11 loose bearing rollers (8). Be careful not to lose loose rollers that may fall out during disassembly. Rollers can be removed by sliding rod off rollers. To install rod bearing, hold rollers in place with heavy grease or petroleum jelly and position rod over rollers. Be sure rollers do not fall out during assembly of crankcase.

CRANKSHAFT AND SEALS. Crankshaft is supported by needle roller bearings (5 – Fig. PP2) at both ends. Crankshaft assembly can be removed after removing flywheel, oil pump (Late Model 330 and Models 350 and 360), clutch and cylinder. Care should be taken when removing cylinder as crankshaft will be loose in crankcase and connecting rod may slide off bearing rollers allowing them to fall into crankcase.

Before reassembling crankcases, apply a light coat of a form-in-place gasket compound on crankcase mating surface. Be sure mating surfaces are not damaged during assembly. Retaining rings (4) must fit in ring grooves (G – Fig. PP3) of lower crankcase and upper crankcase halves.

CLUTCH. A two-shoe centrifugal type clutch is used on all models. Clutch hub has left-hand threads. Clutch needle bearing (6 – Fig. PP4) should be inspected for excessive wear or damage. Inspect clutch shoes and drum for signs of excessive heat.

OIL PUMP. Early Model 330 is equipped with a manual oil pump and automatic oiling system. Refer to Fig.

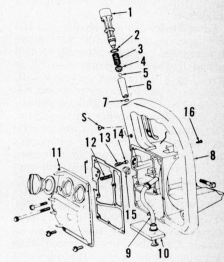

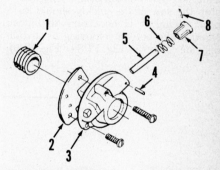

Fig. PP5 – Exploded view of manual pump and front housing on early Model 330.

1. Piston	9. Fuel hose
2. "O" ring	10. Filter
3. Spring	11. Front cover
4. Spring seat	12. Spring
5. Ball	13. Spring
6. Pump body	14. Oil outlet valve
7. Screen	15. Nut
8. Front housing	16. Pressure check valve

Fig. PP3 – Be sure retaining rings (R) are seated in grooves (G) of upper and lower crankcase halves.

Fig. PP6 – Exploded view of positive displacement oil pump assembly used on later Model 330 and Models 350 and 360.

1. Worm gear	5. Plunger
2. Gasket	6. Spring
3. Housing	7. Gear
4. Roll pin	8. Pin

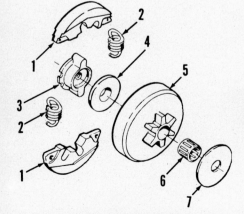

Fig. PP4 – Exploded view of clutch assembly.

1. Shoe half	
2. Spring	5. Drum
3. Hub	6. Needle bearing
4. Washer	7. Washer

Fig. PP7 – Exploded view of rewind starter, flywheel and associated parts used on Models 330 and 350. Components on Model 360 are similar except for starter housing (11).

1. Flywheel
2. Spring
3. Pawl
4. Pivot pin
5. Washer
6. Nut
7. Screw
8. Washer
9. Rope pulley
10. Rewind spring
11. Starter housing
12. Rope
13. Handle

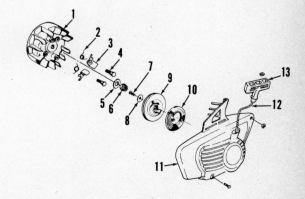

PP5 for exploded view of manual oil pump. Automatic oiling is accomplished by crankcase pulsations which pressurize oil tank and force oil to bar. One-way valve (16) prevents oil from entering crankcase.

Later Model 330 and Models 350 and 360 are equipped with a positive displacement oil pump assembly located behind flywheel. Oil pump assembly is driven by a worm gear on crankshaft. Remove oil pump plunger retaining roll pin (4 – Fig. PP6) and withdraw plunger (5), gear (7) and spring (6) to service. Use suitable tools to pry worm gear (1) off crankshaft. Renew any component that is excessively worn or damaged. Plunger (5) is renewable only with complete oil pump assembly.

REWIND STARTER. Refer to Fig. PP7 for exploded view of pawl type starter typical of the type used on all models. Care should be exercised when removing rewind spring (10) to prevent spring from uncoiling uncontrolled.

Rewind spring (10) should be wound in clockwise direction into housing. Wind starter rope in clockwise direction around rope pulley (9) as viewed in starter housing (11).

CHAIN BRAKE. All models are equipped with a chain brake designed to stop the saw chain quickly should kickback occur. It is necessary to unlock chain brake before removing or installing side cover (5 – Fig. PP8 or Fig. PP9).

Sawdust and debris should be cleaned from around the brake mechanism as needed to ensure proper operation of chain brake.

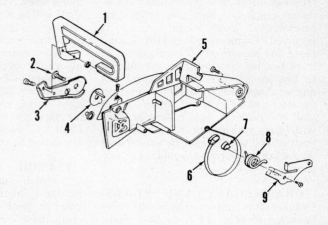

Fig. PP8 – Exploded view of chain brake assembly used on Models 330 and 350.
1. Guard
2. Pivot pin
3. Trip lever
4. Stop plate
5. Side cover
6. Brake band
7. Clip
8. Spring
9. Detent cover

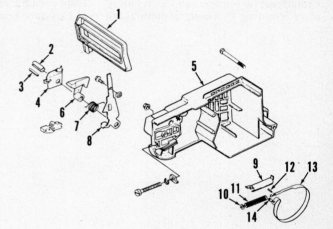

Fig. PP9 – Exploded view of chain brake assembly used on Model 360.
1. Guard
2. Roll pin
3. Roll pin
4. Detent cover
5. Side cover
6. Inertia weight
7. Spring
8. Lever
9. Cover
10. Washer
11. Spring
12. Roll pin
13. Brake band
14. Pin

PIONEER/PARTNER

Model	Bore	Stroke	Displ.	Drive Type
P39	1.875 in. (47.6 mm)	1.437 in. (36.5 mm)	3.97 cu. in. (65 cc)	Direct
P42	1.875 in. (47.6 mm)	1.437 in. (36.5 mm)	3.97 cu. in. (65 cc)	Direct
P45	1.97 in. (50 mm)	1.437 in. (36.5 mm)	4.38 cu. in. (72 cc)	Direct
P52	2.062 in. (52.4 mm)	1.5 in. (38.1 mm)	5.0 cu. in. (82 cc)	Direct
P62	2.25 in. (57.1 mm)	1.5 in. (38.1 mm)	6.0 cu. in. (98 cc)	Direct
P65	2.25 in. (57.1 mm)	1.5 in. (38.1 mm)	6.0 cu. in. (98 cc)	Direct

MAINTENANCE

SPARK PLUG. Recommended spark plug is a Champion KCJ7Y with an electrode gap of 0.025 inch (0.63 mm) on all models.

CARBURETOR. A Walbro WJ diaphragm type carburetor is used on all models. Refer to Walbro section of CARBURETOR SERVICE for service and exploded view of carburetor.

Initial adjustment for both low speed and high speed mixture screws is one turn open from a lightly seated position. Make final adjustment with engine warm and running. Adjust idle speed screw so engine idles just below clutch engagement speed. Adjust low speed mixture screw so engine will accelerate cleanly without hesitation. Adjust high speed mixture screw to obtain optimum performance under cutting load.

IGNITION. All models are equipped with a Phelon breakerless capacitor discharge ignition system. Ignition timing is not adjustable. Air gap between coil legs and flywheel should be 0.25-0.38 mm (0.010-0.015 in.).

LUBRICATION. Engine is lubricated by mixing engine oil with gasoline. Recommended oil is Beaird-Poulan engine oil approved for a fuel-to-oil mixture ratio of 40:1. If recommended oil is not available, a good quality oil designed for two-stroke air-cooled engines may be used when mixed at a 24:1 ratio. Use a separate container when mixing the oil and gas.

All models are equipped with an automatic chain oil pump. Models P62 and P65 are also equipped with a manual oil pump. Oil output is adjustable by turning adjusting screw on bottom of

saw. Refer to AUTOMATIC CHAIN OILER under REPAIRS section. Chain oil should be Pioneer/Partner Chain Oil or, if not available, use a good quality SAE 10 to SAE 30 motor oil depending upon ambient temperature.

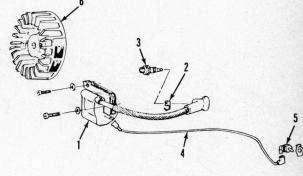

PP-11 — Exploded view of Phelon CD ignition system.
1. Ignition module/coil assy.
2. Terminal end
3. Spark plug
4. Lead
5. Run-stop switch
6. Flywheel

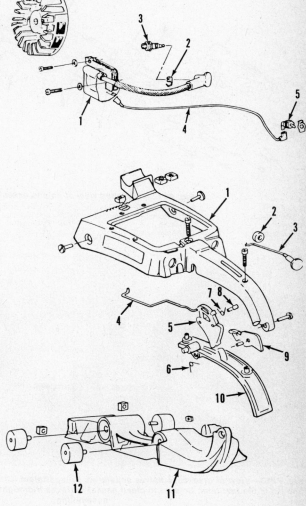

Fig. PP10 — Exploded view of rear handle assembly.
1. Rear handle
2. Grommet
3. Choke linkage & knob
4. Throttle linkage
5. Throttle control
6. Return spring
7. Return spring
8. Pin
9. Throttle lock
10. Rear handle cover
11. Base
12. Isolation mounts

CARBON. Carbon should be cleaned from muffler and exhaust ports at regular intervals. When scraping carbon, be careful not to damage the chamfered edges of the exhaust ports.

REPAIRS

PISTON, PIN, RINGS AND CYLINDER. Compression pressure should be 155 psi (1069 kPa) on P62 and P65 models and 150 psi (1035 kPa) on all other models when checked with a gage while rotating crankshaft with rewind starter. Rewind starter and handle as-sembly must be removed before removing the cylinder. The cylinder and head is one-piece and is attached to crankcase with four screws. Cylinder bore is chrome plated and should be renewed if the plating is worn away exposing the soft base metal. The aluminum alloy piston is fitted with two piston rings. Piston should be heated to 300° F (149° C) before removing the piston pin. Use care to prevent bending the connecting rod even after the piston is heated. The piston pin is equipped with a caged needle bearing (8–Fig. PP12). Pins located in the piston ring grooves must be positioned toward flywheel, away from cylinder exhaust port.

NOTE: Incorrect installation of piston will cause extensive damage to the piston and cylinder. Use Pioneer/Partner piston pin remover/installer tool 475420 when servicing piston pin. The ends of the piston pin retaining clips must engage notch in piston.

Tighten cylinder mounting screws to 90-100 in.-lbs. (10.2-11.3 N·m) using a criss-cross pattern.

CRANKSHAFT AND CONNECTING ROD. The crankshaft, crankpin and connecting rod are pressed together and are available only as a complete assembly. Crankshaft can be easily damaged by incorrect service procedures. Dropping the crankshaft or pounding on the ends can easily knock the crankshaft out of alignment. Crankshaft seals can be removed and installed without separating the crankcase halves. Use a small screwdriver between shaft and seal to remove and Pioneer/Partner tool 427407 to install drive side seal and Pioneer/Partner tool 429445 to install flywheel side seal.

To separate the crankcase halves, remove air filter assembly, handle bar, rewind starter, handle assembly, carburetor, reed valve, flywheel, ignition module/coil assembly, saw chain, guide bar, clutch, chain oiler pump, pump worm, cylinder and piston. Remove the screws attaching crankcase halves together. Use Pioneer/Partner flywheel and crankcase puller 475501 and carefully separate crankcase halves.

NOTE: Main bearings are a press fit on crankshaft. Bearings can be removed from crankshaft using Pioneer/Partner bearing puller 471015.

If main bearings remain in crankcase halves during separation, heat main bearing area of crankcase halves to approximately 200° F (93° C) and use Pioneer/Partner main bearing driver 470335 to drive bearings from each crankcase half.

Gasket surface between the two crankcase halves must be completely clean and free from nicks and burrs. The crankcase forms three different compartments when the halves are joined together: Engine crankcase (C–Fig. PP13), Fuel tank (G) and Chain oil reservoir (O).

When assembling, heat main bearing area of crankcase halves to approximately 200° F (93° C) prior to installing crankshaft assembly. The two screws (B–Fig. PP14) should be 2¼ inches (57.1 mm) long, screw (C) should be 2½

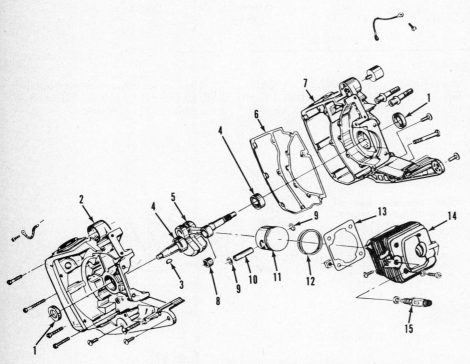

Fig. PP12—Exploded view of engine assembly.

1. Seal	5. Crankshaft & connecting rod assy.	8. Needle bearing	12. Piston rings
2. Crankcase half		9. Retainer clip	13. Gasket
3. Key	6. Gasket	10. Piston pin	14. Cylinder
4. Ball bearing	7. Crankcase half	11. Piston	15. Decompression valve

Fig. PP13—View of crankcase halves separated. Compartment (C) is crankcase, (O) is oil reservoir and (G) is the fuel tank. Be sure to clean gasket surfaces thoroughly and install new gasket before assembling.

inches (63.5 mm) long and the remaining eleven screws (A) should be 1¼ inches (31.7 mm) long.

REED VALVE. The reed valve assembly (Fig. PP15) can be removed after removing air filter assembly and carburetor. Renew reed petal (3) if cracked or worn and be sure reed petal is centered over opening of reed plate (4). Use new gaskets (1 and 5) during installation.

CLUTCH. The clutch can be disassembled after removing side cover, saw chain, guide bar and nut (8 – Fig. PP16). Clutch hub (6) should slide easily off crankshaft splines. Inspect the crankshaft, needle bearing (3) and drum (4) for wear and evidence of overheating. Inspect clutch shoes (5), hub (6), garter spring (7), drum (4) and floating sprocket (2) for damage.

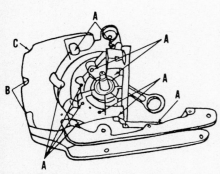

Fig. PP14—Screws (A) should be 1¼ inches (31.7 mm) long, screws (B) should be 2¼ inches (57.1 mm) long and screw (C) should be 2½ inches (63.5 mm) long. Fuel pickup line should be withdrawn to facilitate removal and installation of one screw.

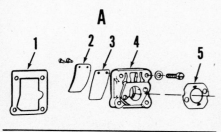

A

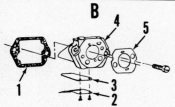

B

Fig. PP15—Exploded view of reed valve assembly. Components shown in view "A" are used on P39, P42 and P45 models. Components shown in view "B" are used on P52, P62 and P65 models.

1. Gasket
2. Reed stopper
3. Reed petal
4. Reed plate
5. Gasket

Washer (1) should be installed next to crankcase. Lubricate needle bearing (3) with a small amount of general purpose

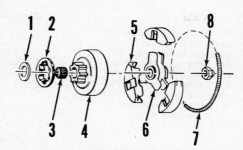

Fig. PP16—Exploded view of clutch assembly.
1. Washer
2. Floating sprocket
3. Needle bearing
4. Drum
5. Shoe
6. Hub
7. Garter spring
8. Nut

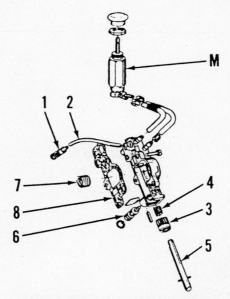

Fig. PP17—Exploded view of automatic oil pump assembly. Models P62 and P65 are also equipped with manual pump (M).
1. Oil pickup
2. Hose
3. Driven gear
4. Spring
5. Shaft
6. Adjuster screw
7. Worm gear
8. Gasket

Fig. PP18—Exploded view of rewind starter. Starter housing (1) shown is used on Models P42, P52, P62 and P65. Two pivots (16), pawls (17), springs (18) and washers (19) are used.

1. Starter housing
2. Shield
3. Handle
4. Starter rope
5. Baffle plate
6. Ferrule
7. Bushing
8. Rewind spring
9. Pulley
10. Washer
11. Lockwasher
12. Screw
13. Nut
14. Washer
15. Flywheel
16. Pivot
17. Pawl
18. Spring
19. Washer

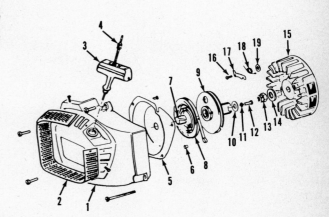

automotive grease before installing. Floating sprocket (2) should be installed with open side away from clutch drum (4). Install hub (6) with hex nut side facing toward outside (side cover). Pioneer/Partner tool 475212 is available to facilitate assembly of clutch shoes (5) and garter spring (7) around hub (6). Lubricate crankshaft threads and install hub and clutch shoe assembly, then install nut (8) and tighten to 30-35 ft.-lbs. (40.8-47.6 N·m).

OIL PUMP. All models are equipped with an automatic oil pump assembly. Models P62 and P65 are also equipped with manual pump (M – Fig. PP17).

Turning adjuster screw (6) will change the volume of oil that is pumped to the bar and chain. Adjuster can only be turned approximately one, but the volume is increased from 8 to 17 mL (0.27 to 0.57 oz.) per minute within this adjusting range. Turning counterclockwise will increase the volume delivered. The oil adjustment screw should be set wide open when first operating the saw to ensure that the bar and chain will receive an adequate supply of oil during initial operation. After initial operation, the setting can be decreased at the discretion of the operator to meet various cutting conditions such as temperature, oil viscosity, type of work and size of wood.

Worm gear (7) on the crankshaft rotates and turns pump shaft and gear (3). End of pump shaft (5) is machined on an angle to provide a cam surface which rides against surface of adjuster screw (6). As the pump shaft turns, the cam surface pushes the shaft in and out of pump body. The in and out movement pumps oil to the chain. A flat on the pump shaft acts as a valve to open the intake port on the outward stroke and the outlet port on the inward stroke. A small amount of grease should be used to lubricate the pump gears. Pioneer/Partner puller 474329 is available for pulling the worm gear from crankshaft.

When installing pump, be sure that pickup (1) is directed toward bottom of the tank while saw is held in an upright position.

REWIND STARTER. Starter pawls (17–Fig. PP18) are located on flywheel (15) and engage a notch in pulley (9) for starting. All models are equipped with two sets of pawls (17). Starter must be disassembled to renew rope (4) or rewind spring (8). The 5/32 inch (3.97 mm) diameter nylon cord should be 41 inches (104.1 cm) long. Clean and apply automotive grease on rewind spring (8). Rewind spring should be preloaded three turns during reassembly.

CHAIN BRAKE. All models are equipped with a chain brake designed to stop the saw chain quickly should kickback occur. It is necessary to unlock chain brake before removing or installing side cover (8–Fig. PP19). Sawdust and debris should be cleaned from around the brake mechanisim as needed to ensure proper operation of chain brake.

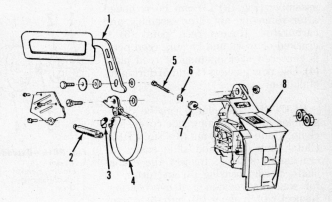

Fig. PP19 — Exploded view of chain brake typical of type used on Models P42, P45, P52, P62 and P65. Chain brake assembly used on P39 models is similar. On P39 models, make sure spring (2) is installed completely on brake band (4) end.

1. Brake lever
2. Spring
3. Retainer
4. Brake band & cam assy.
5. Tension adjusting screw
6. "E" clip
7. Tensioner plate
8. Side cover

PIONEER/PARTNER

Model	Bore	Stroke	Displ.	Drive Type
500, 5000 plus, 5000H plus	44 mm (1.73 in.)	32 mm (1.26 in.)	49 cc (3.0 cu. in.)	Direct

MAINTENANCE

SPARK PLUG. Recommended spark plug is Champion DJ6Y for all models. Electrode gap should be 0.5 mm (0.020 in.).

CARBURETOR. A Walbro WA diaphragm type carburetor is used on all models. Refer to Walbro section of CARBURETOR SERVICE for service and exploded views of carburetor.

Initial adjustment for both low speed and high speed mixture screws is one turn open from a lightly seated position. Make final adjustment with engine warm and running. Adjust idle speed screw so engine idles just below clutch engagement speed. Adjust low speed mixture screw so engine will accelerate cleanly without hesitation. Adjust high speed mixture screw to obtain optimum performance under cutting load.

IGNITION. All models are equipped with a breakerless capacitor discharge ignition system. Ignition timing is not adjustable. Air gap between coil legs and flywheel should be 0.25-0.30 mm (0.009-0.012 in.).

LUBRICATION. Engine is lubricated by mixing engine oil with regular leaded gasoline. Recommended oil is Beaird-Poulan engine oil approved for a fuel-to-oil mixture ratio of 40:1. If recommended oil is not available, a good quality oil designed for two-stroke air-cooled engines may be used when mixed at a 24:1 ratio. Use a separate container when mixing the oil and gas. when mixing the oil and gas.

All models are equipped with an automatic chain oil pump. Oil output on all models is adjusted by turning screw located behind guide bar. Refer to AUTOMATIC CHAIN OILER under REPAIRS section.

REPAIRS

PISTON, PIN, RINGS AND CYLINDER. The piston is accessible after removing the cylinder assembly. Piston is fitted with one piston ring on all models. A locating pin is present in piston ring groove to prevent piston ring rotation. Oversize pistons and rings are not available. Reject piston pin and piston if there is any visible radial play of pin in the piston bosses. All models have needle type piston pin bearings. Install piston so arrow on piston crown points toward exhaust port.

Inspect cylinder bore for excessive wear or damage to bore surface. Cylinder should be renewed if new piston ring end gap in cylinder exceeds 0.8 mm (0.031 in.).

CRANKSHAFT, CONNECTING ROD AND CRANKCASE. Crankshaft and connecting rod are a unit assembly. When separating crankcase halves first remove cylinder, then withdraw oil pump drive gear from crankshaft using Pioneer/Partner special tool 505 381816. Remove crankcase retaining cap screws and press crankshaft out of left crankcase half using Pioneer/Partner special tool 505 381811. Crankshaft may be driven out of right crankcase half using a suitable plastic mallet. Main bearings (11—Fig. PP21) can be pulled from crankshaft by using a bearing puller. Heat main bearing in oil to install on crankshaft. Heat crankcase halves on an electric hot plate prior to assembling crankcase. Oil pump drive gear (4—Fig. PP24) should be positioned on crankshaft so outer gear face is 1 mm (0.04 in.) below flush of gear mounting land (L).

Fig. PP20 — Exploded view of throttle control and handle assemblies used on 5000 and 5000H plus models. Side protector (8) is not used on 500 models.

1. Vibration-damper
2. Rear handle
3. Vibration-damper
4. Throttle lock
5. Throttle control
6. Throttle linkage
7. Rear handle cover
8. Side protector
9. Safety strap
10. Connector plug
11. Cap screw
12. Coil spring
13. Housing
14. Washer
15. Front handle

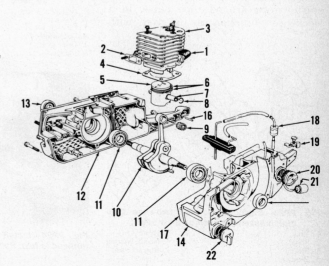

Fig. PP21 — Exploded view of engine used on all models.

1. Intake manifold
2. Exhaust gasket
3. Cylinder
4. Gasket
5. Piston
6. Piston rings
7. Piston pin
8. Lock ring
9. Needle bearing
10. Crankshaft & rod assy.
11. Main bearings
12. Right crankcase half
13. Seal
14. Left crankcase half
15. Seal
16. Pin
17. Gasket
18. Fuel tank vent
19. Stop switch
20. Fuel cap
21. Fuel filter
22. Oil cap

CLUTCH. All models are equipped with a two-shoe centrifugal clutch. Clutch hub has left-hand threads. Inspect clutch shoes and drum for excessive wear or damage due to overheating. Inspect clutch drum, bearing and crankshaft for damage. Clutch hub (1–Fig. PP22) and clutch shoes (2) are available as an assembly. Clutch drum (5) is available with needle bearing (6). Spring (3), washer (4), needle bearing (6), rim sprocket (7) and washer (8) are available individually.

AUTOMATIC CHAIN OILER. All models are equipped with an automatic chain oiler pump which is driven by gear (4–Fig. PP23) on crankshaft. Oil pump output on all models can be adjusted between 4-9 mL (0.14-0.30 oz.) per minute by turning screw (S) in end of pump housing (7). Rotating screw counterclockwise provides maximum output.

Access to oil pump components is obtained after removing chain, guide bar, clutch and oil pump cover plate (1). When reassembling, make certain notch in pump housing (7–Fig. PP24) engages locating lug in crankcase and that pin (2) is inserted in oil tank vent passage.

REWIND STARTER. All models are equipped with the rewind starter shown in Fig. PP25. To disassemble rewind starter, first remove starter housing from saw. Pull starter rope and hold rope pulley with notch in pulley adjacent to rope outlet. Pull rope back through outlet so it engages notch in pulley and allow pulley to completely unwind. Unscrew pulley retaining cap screw (1) and remove rope pulley. If rewind spring requires removal, unsnap tabs securing spring retainer (3) to starter housing (5) and withdraw from housing. Care should be taken not to allow spring to uncoil from retainer.

Reassembly is the reverse of disassembly while noting the following: Wrap starter rope around rope pulley in a clockwise direction as viewed with pulley in starter housing. Turn rope pulley two turns clockwise before passing rope through rope outlet to place tension on rewind spring. Spring tension is correct if rope pulley can be rotated approximately ½ turn further when rope is at its greatest length.

When installing starter assembly on saw, make sure starter pulley properly engages pawls on flywheel before tightening retaining cap screws.

CHAIN BRAKE. All models are equipped with a chain brake system designed to stop chain movement should kickback occur.

The chain brake is activated when the operator's hand strikes the chain brake lever thereby forcing actuating plate (3–Fig. PP26) off of pin in housing releasing spring (7). Spring then draws brake band tight around clutch drum to stop chain. Pull back chain brake lever to reset mechanism. No adjustment of brake mechanism is required.

If brake requires disassembly for repair or renewal of individual components, it is recommended that a clutch drum be inserted in brake band and brake engaged, to facilitate removal of brake lever. When reassembling, make certain spring (7) is screwed completely on brake band and roll pins (4 and 6) are installed with split side toward front of saw.

HANDLE HEATER. Model 5000H plus is equipped with the front and rear handle heating system shown in Fig. PP27. Valve (2) is attached to the muf-

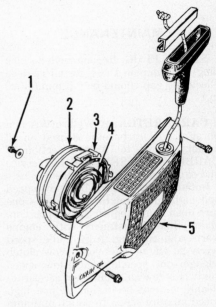

Fig. PP25 — Exploded view of rewind starter.

1. Cap screw
2. Rope pulley
3. Rewind spring retainer
4. Rewind spring
5. Starter housing

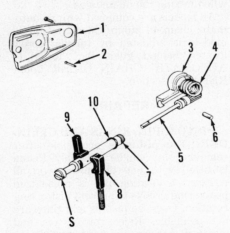

Fig. PP23 — Exploded view of adjustable chain oil pump used on all models.

S. Adjusting screw
1. Cover plate
2. Oil tank vent pin
3. Gear protector
4. Drive gear
5. Plunger
6. Pin
7. Pump housing
8. Inlet tube
9. Outlet tube
10. "O" ring

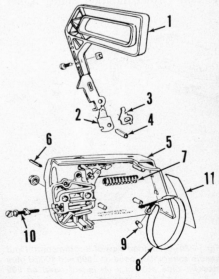

Fig. PP26 — Exploded view of chain brake used on all models.

1. Chain brake lever
2. Sleeve
3. Actuating plate
4. Pin
5. Housing
6. Pin
7. Spring
8. Brake band
9. Pin
10. Chain tensioner
11. Chain guard

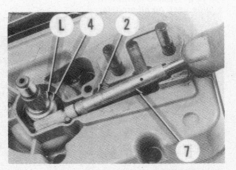

Fig. PP22 — Exploded view of two-shoe type clutch assembly used on all models.

1. Hub
2. Shoe
3. Spring
4. Washer
5. Drum
6. Needle bearing
7. Rim sprocket
8. Washer

Fig. PP24 — Install oil pump components as outlined in text. Refer to Fig. PP23 for parts identification.

fler allowing a small quantity of heated exhaust gas produced by the engine to flow through hoses (6 and 8) and enter chambers in front and rear handles. Front handle temperature is controlled by adjusting screw (3) while rear handle temperature is controlled by adjusting screw (4). Turning adjusting screws completely in shuts off heat.

Heating system should be periodically disassembled and carbon deposits removed. Inspect and renew hoses (6 and 8) if hoses are restricted due to carbon build up or show signs of cracking.

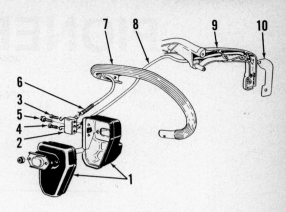

Fig. PP27 — Exploded view of handle heating system used on 5000H plus models.

1. Muffler
2. Valve
3. Front handle temp. adjuster
4. Rear handle temp. adjuster
5. Cap screw
6. Hose
7. Front handle
8. Hose
9. Rear handle
10. Gasket

PIONEER/PARTNER

Model	Bore	Stroke	Displ.	Drive Type
550	44 mm (1.73 in.)	36 mm (1.42 in.)	55 cc (3.36 cu. in.)	Direct
7000 plus	50 mm (1.968 in.)	36 mm (1.42 in.)	70 cc (4.27 cu. in.)	Direct

MAINTENANCE

SPARK PLUG. Recommended spark plug is Champion CJ6 or Bosch WS5E for both models with an electrode gap of 0.5 mm (0.020 in.).

CARBURETOR. A Walbro WJ or WS diaphragm type carburetor is used on both models. Refer to Walbro section of CARBURETOR SERVICE for service and exploded views of carburetors.

Initial adjustment for both low speed and high speed mixture screws is one turn open from a lightly seated position. Make final adjustment with engine warm and running. Adjust idle speed screw so engine idles just below clutch engagement speed. Adjust low speed mixture screw so engine will accelerate cleanly without hesitation. Adjust high speed mixture screw to obtain optimum performance under cutting load.

IGNITION. Both models are equipped with an Electrolux "EM" breakerless capacitor discharge ignition system. Ignition timing is not adjustable. Air gap between coil legs and flywheel should be 0.35-0.45 mm (0.014-0.018 in.).

LUBRICATION. Engine is lubricated by mixing engine oil with gasoline. Recommended oil is Beaird-Poulan engine oil approved for a fuel-to-oil mixture ratio of 40:1. If recommended oil is not available, a good quality oil designed for two-stroke air-cooled engines may be used when mixed at a 24:1 ratio. Use a separate container when mixing the oil and gas.

Both models are equipped with an automatic chain oil pump. Oil output is adjustable by turning adjusting screw on bottom of saw. Refer to AUTOMATIC CHAIN OILER under REPAIRS section. Chain oil should be Pioneer/Partner Chain Oil or, if not available, use a good quality SAE 10 or SAE 30 motor oil depending upon ambient temperature.

CARBON. Carbon should be cleaned from muffler and exhaust ports at regular intervals. When scraping carbon, be careful not to damage the chamfered edges of the exhaust ports.

REPAIRS

PISTON, PIN, RING AND CYLINDER. The piston is accessible after removing the cylinder assembly. The aluminum alloy piston is fitted with one pinned piston ring. Reject piston pin and piston if there is any visible radial play of pin in the piston bosses. Piston and pin are not available separately. A needle type piston pin bearing is used.

Cylinder bore is Nickel-Sil impregnated. Inspect cylinder bore for excessive wear or damage to bore surface. Pistons and cylinders are graded with a letter to designate size. Letter size is located on piston crown and top of cylinder. Letters on piston and cylinder should be the same to obtain desired piston-to-cylinder clearance. For instance, a piston with letter grade "B" should be used in a cylinder with letter grade "B." Install piston so arrow on piston crown points toward exhaust port.

CONNECTING ROD AND CRANKSHAFT. Crankshaft and connecting rod assembly (8 – Fig. PP31) is available only as a complete unit. Main bearings (10) are ball bearings. Outer races of the ball type main bearings are shrink fit in crankcase half and if bearings fall from their bores by their own weight, bearings and crankcase halves should be renewed.

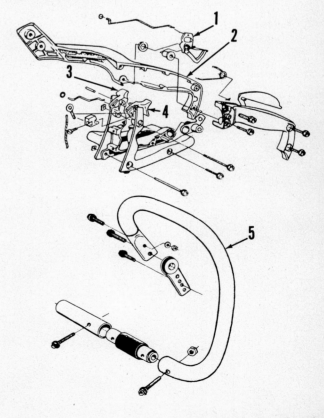

Fig. PP30 — Exploded view of handle assembly.
1. Throttle control
2. Rear handle
3. Choke button
4. Stop button
5. Front handle

To renew main bearings, first remove cylinder. Remove screws retaining crankcase halves together. Use Pioneer/Partner puller tool 505 381811 or a suitable equivalent and extract magneto side crankcase half from crankshaft and clutch side crankcase half. Remove crankshaft assembly from clutch side crankcase half by tapping on opposite end of crankshaft using a soft-faced mallet. Press ball bearings (10) off crankshaft ends using suitable tools. The manufacturer recommends renewing ball bearings (10) and seals (12 and 15) any time crankcase halves are split.

With ball bearings (10) installed on crankshaft assembly, heat bearing bores in crankcase halves to approximately 150° C (302° F) to install crankshaft assembly. Make sure a new gasket (16) is positioned between halves. Tighten crankcase halves retaining screws to 10 N·m (88 in.-lbs.). Make certain crankshaft is centered in crankcase and will rotate freely. Clutch side crankshaft seal should be installed flush with crankcase face. Flywheel side crankshaft seal should protrude 1 mm (0.04 in.) from crankcase face when installed.

CLUTCH. A two-shoe centrifugal type clutch is used. Clutch hub (1 – Fig. PP32) has left-hand threads. Clutch needle bearing (5) should be inspected for excessive wear or damage. Inspect clutch shoes and drum for signs of excessive heat.

AUTOMATIC CHAIN OILER. The chain oiler pump is located in the left (magneto side) crankcase half and is driven by gear (14 – Fig. PP33) on crankshaft flywheel side. Oil pump operation is accomplished when plunger (4) is rotated by gear (14) and reciprocates as the oblique end of plunger bears against adjuster (7) ball thereby pumping oil. Oil output can be adjusted between 5-15 mL (0.17-0.51 oz.) per minute by rotating adjuster (7). Drive gear (14) can be pulled off crankshaft after removing flywheel and seal (15 – Fig. PP31). Drive gear (14 – Fig. PP33) must be heated before installation on crankshaft to prevent crankshaft displacement.

REWIND STARTER. All models are equipped with the rewind starter shown in Fig. PP34. To disassemble starter, remove rope handle (12) and allow rope (9) to wind around rope pulley (8). Disengage pulley retaining clip (7) and carefully remove rope pulley (8). Rewind spring (10) is now accessible and may be removed.

Install rewind spring (10) in a clockwise direction viewed with spring in-

stalled in housing (11). Rope (9) must be wrapped around rope pulley (8) in a clockwise direction viewed with rope

pulley in housing (11). Tension should be placed on starter rope (9) by rotating rope pulley (8) two turns clockwise.

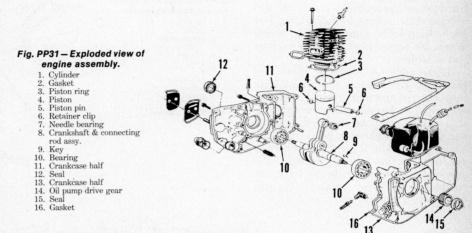

Fig. PP31 — Exploded view of engine assembly.
1. Cylinder
2. Gasket
3. Piston ring
4. Piston
5. Piston pin
6. Retainer clip
7. Needle bearing
8. Crankshaft & connecting rod assy.
9. Key
10. Bearing
11. Crankcase half
12. Seal
13. Crankcase half
14. Oil pump drive gear
15. Seal
16. Gasket

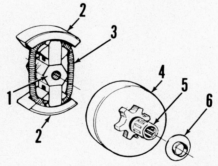

Fig. PP32 — Exploded view of two-shoe centrifugal clutch assembly.

1. Hub
2. Shoe
3. Garter spring
4. Drum
5. Needle bearing
6. Washer

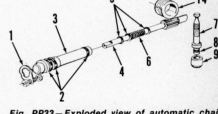

Fig. PP33 — Exploded view of automatic chain oiler.

1. Retainer
2. "O" rings
3. Housing
4. Plunger
5. "O" rings
6. Spring
7. Adjuster
8. "O" ring
9. Cap
14. Drive gear

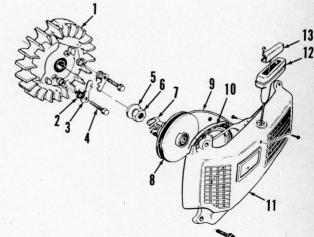

Fig. PP34 — Exploded view of rewind starter.
1. Flywheel
2. Spring
3. Pawl
4. Screw
5. Washer
6. Nut
7. Clip
8. Rope pulley
9. Rope
10. Rewind spring
11. Housing
12. Handle
13. Anchor

CHAIN BRAKE. Both models are equipped with a chain brake system designed to stop chain movement should kickback occur. Chain brake is activated when the operator's hand strikes chain brake guard (1–Fig. PP35) thereby allowing trigger (5) to release spring (9). Spring then draws brake band (10) tight around clutch drum to stop chain. Pull back chain brake guard to reset mechanism. No adjustment of brake mechanism is required.

Disassembly for repair or renewal of individual components is evident after inspection of unit and referral to exploded view. The manufacturer recommends that clutch drum be inserted in brake band (10) and brake engaged to facilitate removal of brake lever (2). When reassembling, make certain spring (9) is screwed completely on brake band and roll pins (6 and 7) are installed with split side toward front of saw.

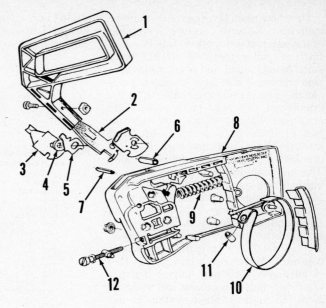

Fig. PP35 — Exploded view of chain brake assembly.
1. Guard
2. Lever
3. Detent cover
4. Washer
5. Trigger
6. Pin
7. Pin
8. Side cover
9. Spring
10. Brake band
11. Pin
12. Chain tensioner

PIONEER/PARTNER

Model	Bore	Stroke	Displ.	Drive Type
400	40 mm (1.57 in.)	32 mm (1.26 in.)	40 cc (2.4 cu. in.)	Direct
450	42 mm (1.65 in.)	32 mm (1.26 in.)	44 cc (2.7 cu. in.)	Direct

MAINTENANCE

SPARK PLUG. Recommended spark plug for both models is Champion RCJ7Y with an electrode gap of 0.5 mm (0.020 in.).

CARBURETOR. A Walbro WT carburetor is used on both models. Refer to Walbro section of CARBURETOR SERVICE for service and exploded view of carburetor.

Initial adjustment for low speed and high speed mixture screws is one turn open from a lightly seated position. Make final adjustment with engine warm and running. Adjust idle speed screw so engine idles just below clutch engagement speed. Adjust low speed mixture screw so engine will accelerate cleanly without hesitation. Adjust high speed mixture screw to obtain optimum performance under cutting load. Do not adjust high speed mixture screw too lean as overheating and engine damage could result.

IGNITION. Both models are equipped with Electrolux breakerless ignition system shown in Fig. PP41. Ignition timing is not adjustable. Air gap between ignition module core and flywheel magnets should be 0.3 mm (0.012 in.). Adjust air gap by loosening ignition module retaining screws and repositioning module.

LUBRICATION. Engine is lubricated by mixing engine oil with fuel. Recommended oil is Beaird-Poulan engine oil approved for a fuel-to-oil mixture ratio of 40:1. If recommended oil is not available, a good quality oil designed for two-stroke air-cooled engines may be used when mixed at a 24:1 ratio. Use a separate container when mixing the oil and gasoline.

Both models are equipped with an automatic chain oil pump. The oil reservoir should be filled with Pioneer/Partner Chain Oil or, if not available, use a good quality SAE 10 to SAE 30 motor oil depending upon ambient temperature. Oil pump output is not adjustable.

REPAIRS

CYLINDER, PISTON, RING AND PIN. Cylinder has a chrome plated bore which should be inspected for flaking, cracking or other damage to chromed surface. Inspect piston and discard if excessive wear or damage is evident. New cylinders are available only with fitted pistons. Piston is renewable only in standard size and as an assembly with piston ring, piston pin, needle roller bearing and retaining clips.

The piston is fitted with a single piston ring. A locating pin is present in piston ring groove to prevent piston ring rotation. Be sure ring end gap is around locating pin when installing cylinder.

The piston pin is retained by wire retainers and rides in a needle roller bearing in small end of connecting rod. Be sure piston is properly supported when removing piston pin to prevent damage. Arrow on piston crown must point toward exhaust port when installing piston.

CRANKSHAFT, CONNECTING ROD AND CRANKCASE. Crankshaft and connecting rod are a unit assembly.

Crankshaft main roller bearings (9 – Fig. PP42) are supported in interlocking bearing carriers (7). Separate bearing carriers (7) and withdraw from crankshaft ends to service roller bearings (9) and seals (8). Make sure seals (8) are installed in bearing carriers with seal lip facing toward crankshaft assembly. Grease seal lips prior to assembling bearing carriers (7) onto crankshaft. Check rotation of connecting rod around crankpin and renew crankshaft unit if roughness or other damage is noted.

When installing crankshaft assembly, make sure mating surfaces of bearing carriers (7), lower crankcase (12) and cylinder (1) are clean and dry. Place a thin bead of a suitable form-in-place gasket compound onto sealing areas of lower crankcase (12) and cylinder (1).

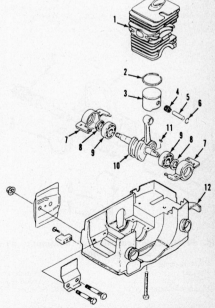

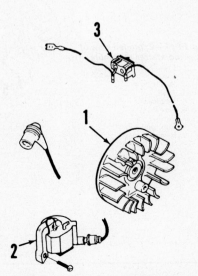

Fig. PP41 — Exploded view of ignition system.
1. Flywheel
2. Ignition module
3. Ignition switch

Fig. PP42 — Exploded view of engine assembly.
1. Cylinder
2. Piston ring
3. Piston
4. Needle roller bearing
5. Piston pin
6. Retainer
7. Bearing carriers
8. Seals
9. Roller bearings
10. Crankshaft & rod assy.
11. Key
12. Lower crankcase & saw body

Lubricate piston and crankshaft assembly with engine oil and wipe off excess oil. Correctly install piston into cylinder bore and position bearing carriers (7) into crankcase area of cylinder (1). Position insulation block on cylinder, then correctly install cylinder with crankshaft assembly onto lower crankcase (12). Tighten the four mounting screws in a criss-cross pattern to 11 N·m (97 in.-lbs.). Make sure crankshaft rotates freely.

CLUTCH. Both models are equipped with two-shoe centrifugal clutch shown in Fig. PP43. Clutch hub (1) has left-hand threads. Inspect clutch shoes (2) and clutch drum (5) for excessive wear or damage due to overheating. Inspect clutch drum, needle bearing (6) and crankshaft end for damage. Clutch hub (1) and clutch shoes (2) are available as an assembly. Clutch drum (5) is available

with needle bearing (6). Spring (3), needle bearing (6), washer (4) and washer (7) are available individually.

OIL PUMP. Both models are equipped with an automatic chain oiler pump which is driven by worm gear (5 – Fig. PP44) on crankshaft. Oil pump output is not adjustable.

Access to oil pump components is obtained after removing chain, guide bar and clutch. Oil pump suction pipe (6) and strainer (7) may be withdrawn from oil tank using a suitable screwdriver.

REWIND STARTER. To disassemble rewind starter, remove starter housing from saw. Pull starter rope (12 – Fig. PP45) out 15-20 cm (6-8 in.) and hold rope pulley (8). Pull rope back through outlet so rope engages an ear on pulley (8) and allow pulley to completely unwind. Unscrew pulley retaining screw (6) and remove rope pulley. If rewind spring (9) requires removal, care should be taken not to allow spring to uncoil from retainer.

Reassembly is the reverse of disassembly while noting the following: Wrap starter rope (12) around rope pulley (8) in a clockwise direction as viewed with pulley in starter housing (10). Turn rope pulley two turns clockwise before passing rope through rope outlet to place tension on rewind spring or reverse the procedure used to relieve spring tension outlined in the previous paragraph. Spring tension is correct if rope pulley (8) can be rotated approximately ½ turn further when rope is at extended length.

When installing starter assembly on saw, make sure starter pulley properly engages pawls (4) on flywheel before tightening retaining cap screws.

CHAIN BRAKE. Both models are equipped with a chain brake system designed to stop movement of chain should kickback occur. Refer to Fig. PP46 for exploded view of chain brake system used. It is necessary to unlock chain brake before removing or installing side cover (5). Sawdust and debris should be cleaned from around the brake mechanism as needed to ensure proper operation of chain brake.

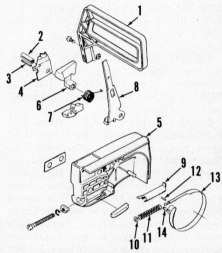

Fig. PP46—Exploded view of chain brake assembly.

1. Guard
2. Roll pin
3. Roll pin
4. Detent cover
5. Side cover
6. Inertia weight
7. Spring
8. Lever
9. Cover
10. Washer
11. Spring
12. Roll pin
13. Brake band
14. Pin

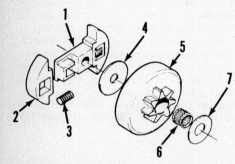

Fig. PP43 — Exploded view of clutch assembly.

1. Hub
2. Shoe
3. Spring
4. Washer
5. Drum
6. Needle bearing
7. Washer

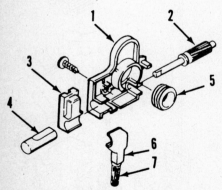

Fig. PP44—Exploded view of automatic oil pump assembly.

1. Pump housing
2. Plunger
3. Pressure pipe
4. Plunger housing
5. Worm gear
6. Suction pipe
7. Strainer

Fig. PP45 — Exploded view of rewind starter assembly.

1. Flywheel
2. Nut
3. Spring
4. Pawl
5. Retainer
6. Screw
7. Washer
8. Rope pulley
9. Rewind spring
10. Starter housing
11. Handle
12. Starter rope
13. Rope guide

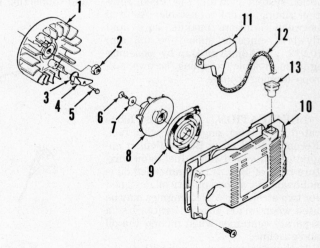

POULAN

BEAIRD-POULAN, INC.
5020 Flournoy Lucas Road
P.O. Box 9329
Shreveport, Louisiana 71129

Model	Bore	Stroke	Displ.	Drive Type
S25D, S25DA, S25CVA	....	....	2.3 cu. in. (38.0 cc)	Direct

MAINTENANCE

SPARK PLUG. Recommended spark plug is Champion CJ8. Spark plug electrode gap should be 0.025 inch (0.63 mm).

CARBURETOR. Most models are equipped with a Tillotson Model HU diaphragm carburetor. Some models are equipped with a Walbro WA diaphragm carburetor. Refer to Tillotson or Walbro section of CARBURETOR SERVICE section for operation and overhaul of carburetor.

Initial setting of idle mixture screw and high speed mixture screw is one turn open. Adjust idle speed screw until engine will idle just below clutch engagement speed. Adjust idle mixture screw so engine will accelerate without hesitation. High speed mixture screw should be adjusted to obtain optimum performance with engine under cutting load. Be sure mixture settings are not too lean as engine damage will result.

IGNITION. Conventional flywheel magneto ignition system with breaker-points located behind the flywheel is used on early models while a breakerless capacitor discharge ignition system is used on later models.

On models with breaker-points, breaker-point gap should be 0.017 inch (0.43 mm). Ignition timing is fixed but incorrect breaker-point gap will affect timing. Magneto air gap should be 0.010-0.014 inch (0.25-0.35 mm). Magneto air gap is adjusted by loosening screws (2–Fig. PN1) and placing 0.012 inch (0.30 mm) shim stock between lamination legs and flywheel magnets. Move coil assembly until lamination legs contact shim stock and tighten screws (2). Recheck air gap.

On breakerless models, ignition components are mounted outside the flywheel making it unnecessary to remove the flywheel for most ignition service.

The only adjustment of the unit is the air gap between the ignition module core and the flywheel magnets. Air gap should be 0.008-0.014 inch (0.20-0.35 mm). Air gap adjustment is similar to the procedures previously outlined for breaker point models.

On all models, flywheel nut should be tightened to 13-15 ft.-lbs. (17.6-20.3 N·m).

Fig. PN1 — View of flywheel and coil assembly. Note that washer (3) must have outer diameter contacting flywheel.

LUBRICATION. Engines on all models are lubricated by mixing oil with fuel. Recommended oil is Beaird-Poulan engine oil available in blends approved for 16:1 and 32:1 fuel mixtures. When using a recommended oil, follow mixing instructions on oil container. If a recommended oil is not available, a good quality oil designed for use in air-cooled two-stroke engines may be used when mixed at a 16:1 ratio. Use a separate container when mixing oil and gasoline.

Model S25D is equipped with a manual chain oil pump. All other models are equipped with manual and automatic chain oil pumps. Automatic pump output is not adjustable. A good quality SAE 30 oil should be used when ambient temperature is 40° F (4.4° C) or above or SAE 10 when ambient temperature is below 40° F (4.4° C).

CARBON. Carbon deposits should be removed from muffler and exhaust ports at regular intervals. Be careful not to damage engine cylinder, piston or ex-

Fig. PN2 — Exploded view of handle and gas tank assemblies.

1. Fuel cap
2. Gasket
3. Gasket
4. Fuel tank
5. Fuel pickup weight
6. Filter
7. Fuel line
8. Cylinder shroud
9. Choke knob
10. Cover
11. Wave washer
12. Choke lever
13. Manual oil pump button
14. Trigger
15. Oil pump rod
16. Trigger pin
17. Throttle link
18. Throttle link boot
19. Spacer
20. Wave washer
21. Choke shutter
22. Carburetor
23. Gasket
24. Air filter
25. Dust seal
26. Reed valve petal
27. Washer
28. Screw

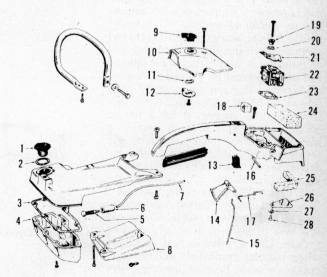

haust port when scraping carbon. Do not allow loosened carbon to enter cylinder.

REPAIRS

CYLINDER. Cylinder has a chrome plated bore which should be inspected and renewed if chrome is scored, cracked or excessively worn. Check for ring ridge at top of piston travel which may cause piston ring land to break when a new piston ring is installed.

PISTON, PIN AND RINGS. Piston should be heated to approximately 200° F (93.4° C) to aid in piston pin removal and installation. Closed end of piston pin must be toward exhaust port of cylinder. Snap ring on exhaust side of piston is sunk in retaining groove and will require use of a sharp hook type tool for removal. It may be necessary to drill a 1/8 inch hole (3.175 mm) hole into groove to gain access to snap ring. Manufacturer recommends discarding piston if a hole must be drilled to remove snap ring.

Piston is equipped with two piston rings. Piston rings are retained by a pin in each ring groove. Be sure piston rings are correctly aligned with pins and do not overlap pins when cylinder is installed. Install piston with ring locating pins on magneto side of engine. Piston and rings are available in standard sizes only.

CONNECTING ROD, CRANK-SHAFT AND CRANKCASE. Crankcase halves (1 and 20 – Fig. PN3) must be separated to remove crankshaft and to remove connecting rod from crankshaft. Be careful during disassembly not to nick or damage mating surfaces.

Unscrew connecting rod screws and remove rod and cap being careful not to lose loose bearing rollers (11). There are 28 bearing rollers in connecting rod bearing. Connecting rod small end bearing must be pressed out of rod. Be sure rod is properly supported when removing or installing bearing. Use heavy grease to hold bearing rollers (11) in rod and cap when installing connecting rod on crankshaft. Match marks on sides of rod and cap must be aligned during installation. Tighten connecting rod screws to 55-60 in.-lbs. (6.2-6.8 N·m). Crankshaft is supported by a needle roller bearing (17) in each crankcase half. Crankcase bearings must be pressed out of crankcase using a suitable driver. Install bearings by pressing bearings into crankcase until bearings are 1/32 inch (0.794 mm) below inner surface of crankcase. Thrust washers (6) may be installed with either side up and are held in place with a light coat of grease. Use a suitable seal protector when passing crankshaft end through crankcase seals. Be sure thrust washers

(6) do not dislodge during assembly. Tighten crankcase screws to 55-60 in.-lbs. (6.2-6.8 N·m).

CLUTCH. Refer to Fig. PN4 for exploded view of clutch assembly. Clutch hub has left-hand threads. Inspect clutch drum (6) and clutch shoes (5) for excessive wear or overheating and renew if required. Press clutch bushing (7) out of clutch drum and inspect bushing for roughness and wear.

REED VALVE. All models are equipped with a single reed valve petal (26 – Fig. PN2) beneath the carburetor. Reed valve is retained by screw (28) and washer (27). Sharp edge of washer (27) must be against reed petal. Tighten screw to 8-12 in.-lbs. (0.9-1.3 N·m). Reed petal should not stand open more than 0.010 inch (0.25 mm) from seat. Inspect reed petal for cracks and seat for burrs.

AUTOMATIC CHAIN OILER. Models S25DA and S25CVA are equipped with automatic chain oil pump

shown in Fig. PN3. Crankcase pulsations pass through impulse hole (1 – Fig. PN5) and actuate diaphragm and piston (31 – Fig. PN3), which forces chain oil out discharge line (28). Inspect pump components for wear or damage which may cause pump malfunction. Diaphragm piston (31) should move freely in hole of pump housing (27) for a stroke of approximately 1/4 inch (6.35 mm). Piston hole may be cleaned using a 0.063 inch drill bit in a hand drill. Do not use an electric drill. Do not insert drill bit more than 9/16 inch (14.3 mm) into hole. Be sure hole in diaphragm (31) for impulse passage in housing is aligned with passage as shown in Fig. PN5 during assembly.

REWIND STARTER. Refer to Fig. PN6 for exploded view of rewind starter used on all models. To disassemble starter, remove starter housing (17). Remove rope handle and allow rope to wind into rope pulley (15). Unscrew retaining screw (13) and remove rope pulley (15) being careful not to dislodge rewind spring (16). Rewind spring (16)

Fig. PN3 – Exploded view of engine. Automatic oil pump shown is not used on Model S25D.

1. Crankcase half
2. Gasket
3. Cylinder
4. Gasket
5. Crankshaft
6. Thrust washer
7. Washer
8. Nut
9. Rod cap
10. Connecting rod
11. Bearing rollers (28)
12. Piston
13. Bearing
14. Piston pin
15. Snap ring
16. Piston rings
17. Bearing
18. Seal
19. Gasket
20. Crankcase half
21. Intake oil line & valve
22. Cap
23. Manual pump plunger
24. "O" ring
25. Spring
26. Gasket
27. Pump housing
28. Exhaust oil line
29. Gasket
30. Spring
31. Diaphragm & piston
32. Cover

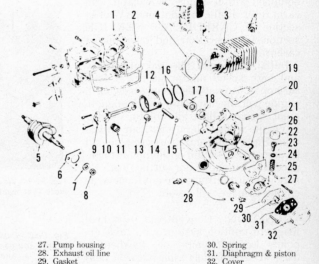

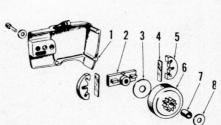

Fig. PN4 – Exploded view of clutch assembly.

1. Housing
2. Hub
3. Disc
4. Spring
5. Shoe
6. Drum
7. Bushing
8. Washer

Fig. PN5 – View of installation of diaphragm and piston in housing (2). Note use of wire (3) to align impulse hole in diaphragm with impulse passage (1).

can now be removed if necessary, but precaution should be taken not to allow spring to uncoil uncontrolled.

Rewind spring is wound in clockwise direction in housing. Wind rope on rope pulley (15) in clockwise direction when viewing pulley as installed in housing. Turn pulley (15) 1½-2 turns before passing rope through rope outlet in housing (17).

CHAIN BRAKE. Some models may be equipped with a chain brake system designed to stop chain movement should kickback occur. Chain brake is activated when operator's hand strikes chain brake lever (1 – Fig. PN7) releasing spring (5) and drawing brake band (6) tight around clutch drum (8). Pull back chain brake lever to reset mechanism.

Disassembly for repair and component renewal is evident after referral to exploded view and inspection of unit. No

adjustment of chain brake system is required.

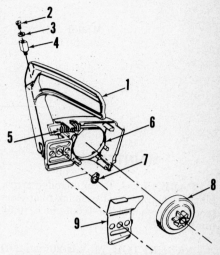

Fig. PN7 – Exploded view of chain brake system used on some models.

1. Chain brake lever
2. Screw
3. Washer
4. Anchor
5. Spring
6. Brake band
7. Snap ring
8. Clutch drum
9. Chain guard

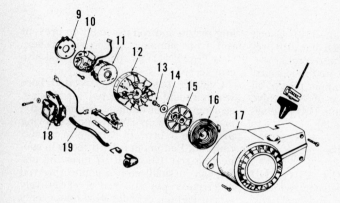

Fig. PN6 – Exploded view of ignition and rewind starter assemblies.

9. Base plate
10. Breaker-point assy.
11. Cover
12. Flywheel
13. Screw
14. Washer
15. Rope pulley
16. Rewind spring
17. Starter housing
18. Ignition coil
19. High tension wire

POULAN

Model	Bore	Stroke	Displ.	Drive Type
20, 20D	1.375 in. (34.92 mm)	1.250 in. (31.75 mm)	1.86 in. (30.48 cc)	Direct

MAINTENANCE

SPARK PLUG. Recommended spark plug is Champion CJ8. Spark plug electrode gap should be 0.025 inch (0.63 mm).

CARBURETOR. Models 20 and 20D are equipped with a Tillotson Model HU diaphragm carburetor. Refer to Tillotson section of CARBURETOR SERVICE for exploded view and service of carburetor.

Initial adjustment of idle mixture screw is one turn open. Carburetor has a fixed main fuel jet so high speed fuel mixture is not adjustable. Adjust idle mixture screw so engine will accelerate without hesitation. Adjust idle speed screw so engine idles just below clutch engagement speed.

MAGNETO AND TIMING. A flywheel magneto is used on all models. The ignition coil is located adjacent to the flywheel while the breaker-points are located on the right crankcase half.

Breaker-point gap should be 0.020-0.022 inch (0.51-0.56 mm) for new points and 0.017 inch (0.43 mm) for used points. Ignition timing is not adjustable and breaker-point gap must be set correctly or ignition timing will be affected. Air gap between coil legs and flywheel should be 0.010 inch (0.25 mm).

LUBRICATION. The engine is lubricated by mixing oil with the fuel. Recommended oil is Beaird-Poulan engine oil available in blends approved for 16:1 and 32:1 fuel mixture ratios. Follow manufacturers mixing instructions on oil container when using a recommended oil. If Beaird-Poulan engine oil is not available, a good quality oil designed for use in air-cooled two-stroke engines may be used when mixed at a 16:1 ratio. Use a separate container when mixing fuel and oil. Regular gasoline is recommended.

Both models are equipped with manual and automatic chain oil pumps. The manual oil pump is operated by pushing plunger (18 – Fig. PN10). The automatic oil pump is operated by crankcase pulsa-

tions through impulse line (10). Check valve (11) in end of impulse line (10) prevents entrance of oil into crankcase. Check valve must be located in slot just forward of filler hole in upper part of oil tank to prevent immersion of check valve in oil. Automatic oil pump (14) is available only as a unit assembly.

REPAIRS

CYLINDER, PISTON PIN AND RINGS. Cylinder can be removed after detaching fan housing, flywheel, carburetor, front handle, chain bar and muffler. Care must be used when hand-

ling piston and rod assembly to prevent rod from slipping off bearing rollers (12 – Fig. PN11) as rollers may fall into crankcase.

Cylinder has a chrome plated bore which should be inspected for flaking, scoring or other damage. Be sure piston is properly supported when removing piston pin to prevent damage to connecting rod. Piston pin rides directly in connecting rod. Check fit by inserting piston pin in small end of connecting rod and renew pin and rod if excessively worn. Tighten cylinder base nuts evenly to 100-110 in.-lbs. (11.3-12.4 N·m).

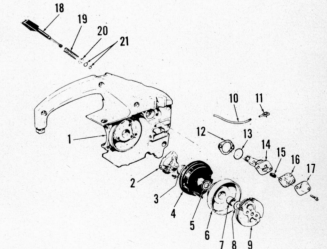

Fig. PN10 — Exploded view of right crankcase half.

1. Right crankcase half
2. Ignition breaker-points
3. Seal
4. Breaker-point cover
5. Spacer
6. Clutch drum
7. Bushing
8. Washer
9. Clutch assy.
10. Impulse line
11. Check valve
12. Gasket
13. "O" ring
14. Automatic oil pump
15. Filter
16. Gasket
17. Cover
18. Manual oil pump plunger
19. Spring
20. Washer
21. "O" rings

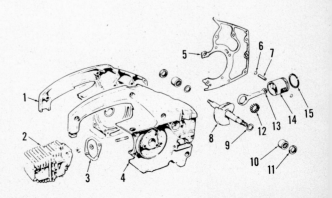

Fig. PN11 — Exploded view of engine.

1. Left crankcase half
2. Cylinder
3. Gasket
4. Right crankcase half
5. Gasket
6. Pin retainer
7. Piston pin
8. Crankshaft
9. Washer
10. Needle roller bearing
11. Seal
12. Bearing rollers (12)
13. Connecting rod
14. Piston
15. Piston ring

CONNECTING ROD, CRANKSHAFT AND CRANKCASE. Connecting rod is one-piece and rides on 12 loose bearing rollers (12 – Fig. PN11). Be careful not to lose any loose bearing rollers during disassembly. Bearing rollers can be removed after rod is slid off rollers. Bearing rollers may be held in place with petroleum jelly or heavy grease when installing connecting rod.

The crankshaft is supported by a needle roller bearing at each end. Install bearings so end of bearing is 0.6225-0.6265 inch (15.811-15.913 mm) from machined gasket surface. Washers (9 – Fig. PN11) must be installed with beveled edge nearest crankpin. Ignition coil-to-breaker point wire must be routed through crankcase halves and trigger assembly installed before crankcase halves are mated. Be sure crankcase impulse line and fuel pickup lines are properly located and not pinched. Be sure a fiber washer (2 – Fig. PN12) is installed on long crankcase screw. Absence of washer will result in oil leakage. Tighten crankcase screws to 30-35 in.-lbs. (3.4-3.9 N·m).

CLUTCH. Clutch hub has left-hand threads. Clutch hub, shoes and spring are available only as a unit assembly. Clutch drum (6 – Fig. PN10) and bushing (7) are available separately.

REWIND STARTER. The rewind starter is located on the left end of the crankshaft. Starter pawls are located on back side of flywheel (3 – Fig. PN13). Starter pawls are not available without renewing flywheel. Flywheel and starter pawls must be serviced as a unit assembly. Rope pulley (6) rides on needle roller bearing (5). Care should be used if rewind spring is removed to prevent spring from uncoiling uncontrolled. Install rewind spring (7) into rope pulley so outer end of spring is pointing in a clockwise direction. Wind rope around rope pulley in counterclockwise direction as viewed from flywheel side of pulley. Lubricate rope pulley bearing. Apply tension on rewind spring by turning rope pulley three turns clockwise before passing rope through rope outlet. Be sure spacer (4) is installed or starter pawls will rub against rope pulley. Align dot on flywheel shown in Fig. PN14 with keyway in crankshaft when installing flywheel. This will align key in crankshaft with corresponding slot in flywheel. Tighten flywheel nut to 8-10 ft.-lbs. (0.9-1.1 N·m).

Fig. PN12 – Long crankcase screw must be installed with fiber washer (2) to prevent oil leakage.

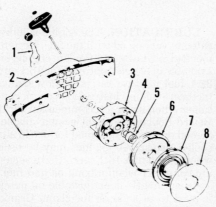

Fig. PN13 – Exploded view of rewind starter.
1. Choke plate
2. Left side cover
3. Flywheel
4. Spacer
5. Needle roller bearing
6. Rope pulley
7. Rewind spring
8. Spring plate

Fig. PN14 – Align dot on flywheel with crankshaft keyway to assist in mating key with flywheel slot.

POULAN

Model	Bore	Stroke	Displ.	Drive Type
M25, M25D, MS25D, MS25CVA, 1800	1.375 in. (34.92 mm)	1.250 in. (31.75 mm)	1.8 cu. in. (30.4 cc)	Direct
2000	....	....	2.0 cu. in. (32.7 cc)	Direct
2300, 2300AV, 2300CVA, 2350	....	....	2.3 cu. in. (37.7 cc)	Direct

MAINTENANCE

SPARK PLUG. Recommended spark plug is Champion CJ8. Spark plug electrode gap should be 0.025 inch (0.63 mm).

CARBURETOR. Models are equipped with either a Walbro WA or WT diaphragm carburetor. Refer to Walbro section of CARBURETOR SERVICE section for exploded view and service of carburetor.

Initial adjustment of idle and high speed mixture screws is one turn open. Adjust idle mixture screw so engine will accelerate without hesitation. Adjust high speed mixture screw to obtain optimum full throttle performance under cutting load. Adjust idle speed screw so engine idles just below clutch engagement speed.

IGNITION. A conventional flywheel magneto ignition system with breaker-points located behind the flywheel is used on early models while a breakerless capacitor discharge ignition system is used on later models.

On models with breaker-points, breaker-point gap should be 0.014-0.016 inch (0.36-0.41 mm). Ignition timing is not adjustable and breaker-point gap must be set correctly or ignition timing will be affected. Air gap between coil legs and flywheel should be 0.008-0.014 inch (0.20-0.36 mm).

On breakerless models, ignition components are mounted outside the flywheel making it unnecessary to remove the flywheel for most ignition service. The only adjustment of the unit is the air gap between the ignition module core and flywheel magnets. Air gap should be 0.008-0.014 inch (0.20-0.36 mm).

On all models, flywheel nut should be tightened to 13-15 ft.-lbs. (17.6-20.4 N·m).

LUBRICATION. The engine is lubricated by mixing oil with the fuel. Recommended oil is Beaird-Poulan engine oil available in blends approved for 16:1 and 32:1 fuel mixture ratios. Follow manufacturers mixing instructions on oil container when using a recommended oil. If Beaird-Poulan engine oil is not available, a good quality oil designed for use in air-cooled two-stroke engines may be used when mixed at a 16:1 ratio. Use a separate container when mixing oil and fuel.

An automatic nonadjustable oil pump is used to provide oil for chain. Crankcase pulsations pressurize oil tank to force oil through metering valve (4 – Fig. PN15) and oil line (8) to oil port. Be sure end of oil line does not extend past oil port opening or oil flow will be reduced. Check valve (5), located behind clutch, blocks chain saw oil entry into crankcase.

REPAIRS

CYLINDER, PISTON, PIN AND RING. Models M25, M25D, MS25D, MS25CVA and 2350 are equipped with a chrome plated cylinder bore. Cylinder bore should be inspected for cracking, flaking or other damage. All other models are equipped with a silicon impregnated cylinder bore. Oversize piston, ring or cylinder is not available. Piston on Model 2350 is equipped with two piston rings.

Use care when handling piston and connecting rod assembly to prevent rod from sliding off bearing rollers (7 – Fig. PN16 and PN17). Bearing rollers are

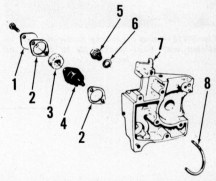

Fig. PN15 – View of automatic oil pump components.

1. Cover	5. Check valve
2. Gasket	6. Gasket
3. Filter	7. Crankcase (R.H.)
4. Metering valve	8. Oil line

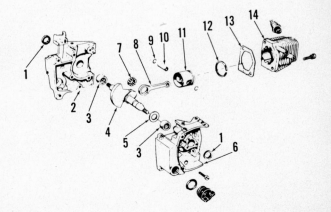

Fig. PN16 – Exploded view of engine used on Models M25, M25D, MS25D, MS25CVA, 1800 and early Model 2000.

1. Seal
2. Crankcase half (R.H.)
3. Bearing
4. Crankshaft
5. Thrust washer
6. Crankcase half (L.H.)
7. Bearing rollers (12)
8. Connecting rod
9. Pin retainer
10. Piston pin
11. Piston
12. Piston ring
13. Gasket
14. Cylinder

loose and may fall into crankcase. Be sure piston is properly supported when removing piston pin. Heat may be applied to piston crown to ease piston pin removal and installation. Piston pin rides directly in connecting rod on Models M25, M25D, MS25CVA, 1800 and early Model 2000. Check fit by inserting piston pin in small end of connecting rod. Renew piston pin and connecting rod if excessive play is evident. Piston pin on all other models and later Model 2000 rides in 21 loose roller bearings (16 – Fig. PN17). Note location of washers (15).

A locating pin is present in piston ring groove to prevent ring location. Install piston with locating pin toward flywheel side of crankshaft. Tighten cylinder base nuts to 100-110 in.-lbs. (11.3-12.4 N·m).

CONNECTING ROD, CRANK-SHAFT AND CRANKCASE.
Connecting rod is one-piece and rides on 12 loose bearing rollers (7 – Fig. PN16 and Fig. PN17). Be careful not to lose any loose bearing rollers during disassembly. Bearing rollers can be removed after rod is slid off rollers. Bearing rollers may be held in place with petroleum jelly or heavy grease when installing connecting rod.

The crankshaft is supported by a needle roller bearing at each end. Install bearings using Poulan tool 31064 or equivalent to crankcase mating surfaces and tighten crankcase screws to 45-50 in.-lbs. (5.1-5.6 N·m).

CLUTCH.
Clutch hub has left-hand threads. Clutch hub, shoes and spring are available only as a unit assembly. Clutch drum (3 – Fig. PN18) and bushing (7) are available separately.

REWIND STARTER.
Refer to Fig. PN19 for exploded view of starter assembly. To disassemble starter, extend rope and hold rope pulley (3) from turning. Pull rope back through side cover (5) and carefully allow pulley to unwind relieving tension on rewind spring (4). Remove screw (1) and lift off rope pulley. Use caution if removing rewind spring. Do not allow rewind spring to uncoil uncontrolled.

Rope is wound on rope pulley in a clockwise direction as viewed from flywheel side of side cover. Lightly lubricate pulley shaft with silicon grease. Rotate rope pulley clockwise to apply preload on rewind spring.

Starter pawls and flywheel are not available separately and are serviced on-ly as a unit assembly. Tighten flywheel nut to 13-15 ft.-lbs. (17.6-20.3 N·m).

REED VALVE.
A single-petal type reed valve is located under the carburetor and attached to the underside of the handle assembly. Maximum gap between reed petal and seating surface is 0.010 inch (0.25 mm). Renew reed if bent, broken or otherwise damaged. Inspect reed petal seat and renew carburetor housing if seat is damaged or warped. Washer under reed retaining screw serves as a reed stop and should be installed with sharp side against reed petal. Tighten reed petal screw to 8-10 in.-lbs. (0.9-1.1 N·m).

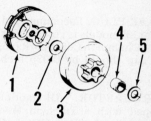

Fig. PN18 – View of clutch. Note hub, shoes and spring are available only as an assembly (1).

1. Hub & shoe assy.
2. Washer
3. Clutch drum
4. Bushing
5. Spacer

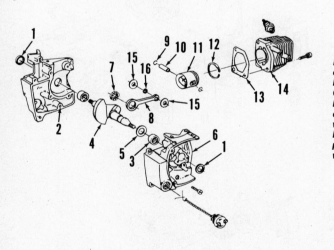

Fig. PN17 – Exploded view of engine assembly used on Models 2300, 2300AV, 2300 CVA and late Model 2000. Model 2350 engine is similar except piston (11) is equipped with two piston rings (12). Refer to Fig. PN16 for component identification except washers (15) and needle roller bearing (16).

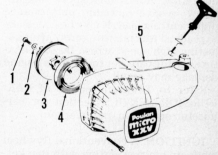

Fig. PN19 – Exploded view of rewind starter. Models 2300, 2300AV and 2300CVA are equipped with a fan baffle located between rewind spring (4) and side cover (5).

1. Screw
2. Washer
3. Rope pulley
4. Rewind spring
5. Side cover

POULAN

Model	Bore	Stroke	Displ.	Drive Type
306, 306A, 306SA	1.788 in. (45.41 mm)	1.437 in. (36.50 mm)	3.6 cu.in. (59.0 cc)	Direct
361	1.788 in. (45.41 mm)	1.437 in. (36.50 mm)	3.6 cu. in. (59.0 cc)	Direct
245A, 245SA	2.005 in. (50.92 mm)	1.437 in. (36.50 mm)	4.5 cu. in. (73.7 cc)	Direct
252A	2.005 in. (50.92 mm)	1.437 in. (36.50 mm)	4.5 cu. in. (73.7 cc)	Gear

MAINTENANCE

SPARK PLUG. Recommended spark plug for all models is Poulan spark plug 3014 or Champion CJ8. Spark plug electrode gap should be 0.025 inch (0.63 mm).

CARBURETOR. All models are equipped with a Tillotson Model HS diaphragm carburetor. Initial idle and high speed mixture settings are one turn open. Adjust idle speed screw so engine idles at engine speed just below clutch engagement speed. Adjust idle mixture screw so engine will accelerate without hesitation. Adjust high speed mixture screw to give optimum performance under cutting load. It may be necessary to readjust idle mixture screw after adjusting high speed screw. Be sure mixture settings are not too lean as engine damage may result.

Refer to Tillotson section of CARBURETOR SERVICE section for carburetor operation and overhaul.

IGNITION. A conventional flywheel magneto ignition system with breaker-point points located behind the flywheel is used on all models except later production 245A, 245S, 306A and 306SA models which are equipped with a breakerless capacitor discharge ignition system.

On breaker-point models, breaker point gap should be 0.015 inch (0.38 mm) on Model 361 and 0.017 inch (0.43 mm) on all other models. Magneto air gap should be 0.012 inch (0.30 mm) and may be adjusted by loosening coil mounting screws.

On breakerless models, ignition components are mounted outside the flywheel making it unnecessary to remove the flywheel for most ignition service. The only adjustment of the unit is the air gap between the ignition module core and the flywheel magnets. Air gap should be 0.008-0.014 inch (0.20-0.35 mm).

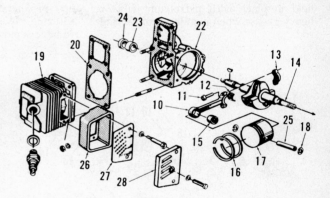

Fig. PN21—Exploded view of engine used on Model 361. Refer also to Fig. PN23. Refer to Fig. PN22 for parts identification except: 26. Muffler; 27. Muffler baffle; 28. Cover.

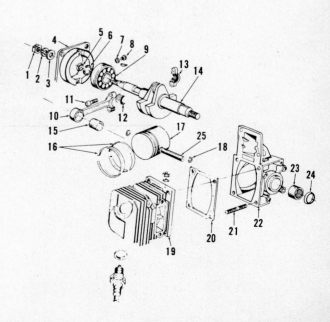

Fig. PN22—Exploded view of engine used on Models 245A, 245SA, 252A, 306, 306A and 306SA. Carrier (4) is a partial view showing rear of side cover (15—Fig. PN28).

1. Nut
2. Lockwasher
3. Washer
4. Bearing carrier
5. Seal
6. Snap ring
7. Washer
8. Cap screw
9. Bearing
10. Connecting rod
11. Socket head screw
12. Bearing rollers
13. Rod cap
14. Crankshaft
15. Bearing
16. Piston rings
17. Piston
18. Snap ring
19. Cylinder
20. Gasket
21. Stud
22. Crankcase
23. Bearing
24. Seal
25. Piston pin

Fig. PN20—View of Model 361 magneto.

1. Flywheel
2. Breaker points
3. Condenser
4. Stator
5. Ignition coil

LUBRICATION. All engines are lubricated by mixing oil with fuel. Recommended oil is Beaird-Poulan engine available in blends approved for 16:1 and 32:1 fuel ratios. Follow manufacturer's mixing instructions on oil container when using a recommended oil. If Beaird-Poulan engine oil is not available, a good quality oil designed for use in air-cooled two-stroke engines may be used when mixed at a 16:1 ratio. Use a separate container when mixing oil and fuel.

All models are equipped with a manual chain oiler. All models except 306 and 361 are equipped with an automatic chain oiler. Fill oiler reservoir with a good quality SAE 30 oil if ambient temperature is above 40°F (4.4°C) or SAE 10 if temperature is 40°F (4.4°C) or below.

CARBON. Carbon deposits should be removed from muffler and exhaust ports at regular intervals. When scraping carbon, be careful not to damage engine cylinder or piston. Do not allow loosened carbon to enter cylinder.

REPAIRS

CYLINDER. All models are equipped with a chrome plated cylinder. Renew cylinder if cylinder is scored, cracked or excessively worn. Only standard size piston and rings are available.

PISTON, PIN AND RINGS. Refer to Figs. PN21 and PN22. All models are equipped with two piston rings. Piston rings are retained by pins in ring grooves and must be aligned with pins when cylinder is installed. Install piston so ring locating pins are on magneto side of engine. Piston wrist pin has one closed end, which must be toward exhaust port. Heat piston to approximately 200°F (93.4°C) to aid in pin installation. Piston pin snap rings should be installed so sharp edge is out.

Pistons and rings are available in standard size only. Manufacturer does not specify piston or piston ring clearances.

CONNECTING ROD. Connecting rod may be removed after removing cylinder and piston. Unscrew connecting rod screws and remove rod and cap being careful not to lose loose bearing rollers. There are 25 bearing rollers in connecting rod on Model 361. All other models are equipped with 28 bearing rollers. Connecting rod small end bearing must be pressed out of rod. Be sure rod is properly supported when removing or installing bearing.

Use heavy grease to hold roller bearings in rod and cap. Match marks on sides of rod and cap must be aligned during installation.

CRANKSHAFT AND CRANKCASE. Crankshaft is supported in antifriction bearings at both ends. Flywheel end of crankshaft on Model 361 is supported by needle roller bearing (23—Fig. PN21) in the crankcase while ball bearing (9—Fig. PN22) contained in side cover (4) is used to support flywheel end of crankshaft on all other models. Clutch end of crankshaft on Model 361 is supported by ball bearing (3—Fig. PN23) in bearing carrier (7) while needle roller bearing (23—Fig. PN22) in crankcase (22) supports clutch end of crankshaft on all other models.

Fuel, oil, ignition, starter and clutch assemblies must be removed from engine to remove crankshaft. Remove cylinder, piston and connecting rod. On all models except 361, remove bearing carrier (4), bearing (9) and crankshaft (14) from crankcase. Unscrew retaining cap screws (8) and separate bearing (9) and crankshaft from bearing carrier (4). Remove snap ring (6) and pull bearing (9) off crankshaft. To remove crankshaft from Model 361, unscrew bearing carrier (7—Fig. PN23) screws and remove bearing carrier and crankshaft from crankcase. Remove crankshaft from bearing (3). Unscrew two retaining screws (1) and separate bearing from carrier (7). To reassemble, reverse disassembly procedure. Install ball bearing with groove in outer race adjacent to crankshaft counterweight. Bearing carrier (4—Fig. PN22) and bearing carrier (7—Fig. PN23) must be heated to 200°F (93.4°C) before installing bearing.

CLUTCH. Clutch hub is equipped with left-hand threads. Clutch hub bearing is available for all models. Refer to Figs. PN23, PN24 or PN25 for exploded view of clutch.

Fig. PN23—Exploded view of clutch and bearing housing carrier used on Model 361.

1. Cap screw
2. Washer
3. Bearing
4. "O" ring
5. Oil line
6. Oil fitting
7. Bearing housing carrier
8. Oil line
9. Seal
10. Sleeve
11. Clutch cover
12. Clutch shoe
13. Clutch hub
14. Spring
15. Thrust washer
16. Bearing race
17. Clutch drum
18. Bearing
19. Washer
20. Washer
21. Nut

Fig. PN24—Exploded view of Models 245A, 245SA, 306A and 306SA manual and automatic oil pump and clutch assemblies.

1. Plunger
2. Plunger rod
3. Spring
4. Manual oil pump housing
5. Intake valve
6. Spring
7. Oil pump button
8. Oil tank
9. Gasket
10. Gasket
11. Oil outlet valve
12. Washer
13. Spring
14. Piston
15. Lever
16. Quad ring
17. Disc
18. Cam
19. Gear
20. Auto. oil pump cover
21. Seal
22. Thrust washer
23. Bearing
24. Bearing race
25. Clutch drum
26. Clutch shoe
27. Thrust washer
28. Clutch hub
29. Clutch spring
30. Retaining ring
31. Spirolox

Poulan

CHAIN SAW

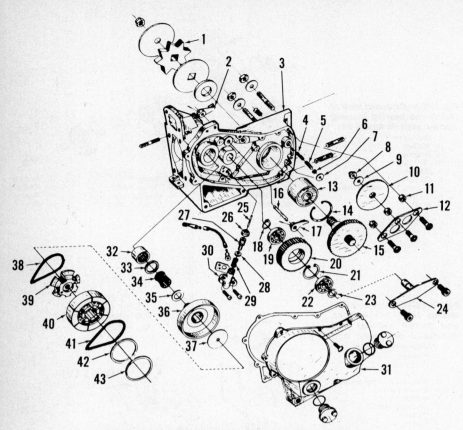

1. Sprocket
2. Manual oil pump lever
3. Crankcase
4. Spring
5. Auto. oil pump piston
6. Quad ring
7. Washer
8. Nut
9. Washer
10. Auto. oil pump cam & gear
11. Spacer
12. Plate
13. Bearing
14. Snap ring
15. Chain drive gear
16. Shaft
17. Manual oil pump lever
18. Snap ring
19. Bearing
20. Idler gear
21. Snap ring
22. Bearing
23. Spacer
24. Idler gear plate
25. Plunger rod
26. Cap
27. Plunger
28. Quad ring
29. Spring
30. Manual oil pump housing
31. Cover
32. Bearing
33. Seal
34. Clutch bearing
35. Thrust washer
36. Clutch drum
37. Thrust washer
38. Spring
39. Clutch hub
40. Clutch shoe
41. Spring
42. Retaining ring
43. Spirolox

TRANSMISSION. Gear transmission on Model 252A may be disassembled after removing gearcase cover. Remove clutch assembly and disassemble transmission. Note that bearings (19 and 22—Fig. PN25) are separated by a snap ring (21) and cannot be driven out of idler gear (20) simultaneously. Automatic oil pump drive gear must be adjusted to mesh with chain drive gear (15). Pump drive gear plate (12) has an adjusting slot to adjust gear mesh so gears turn freely without binding.

Fig. PN25—Exploded view of Model 252A gear transmission.

REED VALVE. All models are equipped with reed valve induction (Fig. PN26) with four reed petals on a pyramid reed block. Inspect reed block (3) for nicks, chips or burrs. Be sure reed petal (4) lays flat against seat.

AUTOMATIC CHAIN OIL PUMP. The following models are equipped with an automatic oil pump: 245A, 245SA, 252A, 306A and 306SA.

Oil pump on Model 252A is driven by a cam on gear (10—Fig. PN25). Pump drive gear plate (12) has an adjusting slot to adjust gear mesh so pump gear and chain drive gear will turn freely.

Oil pump on remainder of automatic chain oiler models is driven by cam (18—Fig. PN24) on engine crankshaft. Inspect bronze gear (19) and renew if gear teeth are broken or excessively worn. If button on lever (15) is worn, renew lever. Pack oil pump cavity with a suitable grease before reassembly. Install seal (21) in cover and carefully install cam (18) in seal with step of cam toward seal until seal seats against shoulder of cam. Be careful not to damage seal. Install pump lever (15) in cover and gear (19) on cam (18). Place disc (17) in housing and install washer (12), spring (13), piston (14) and quad ring (16). Install cover (20) and pump components in cover on crankshaft.

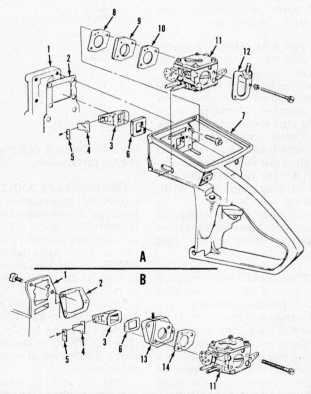

Fig. PN26—View "A" identifies location of reed valve components on Model 361 and view "B" identifies location of reed valve components on all other models.

1. Crankcase
2. Gasket
3. Reed block
4. Petal
5. Stopper
6. Gasket
7. Rear handle assy.
8. Gasket
9. Spacer
10. Gasket
11. Carburetor
12. Bracket
13. Adapter
14. Gasket

328

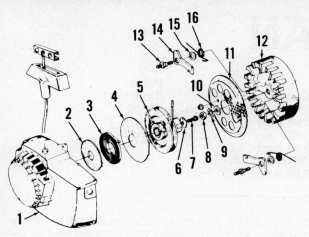

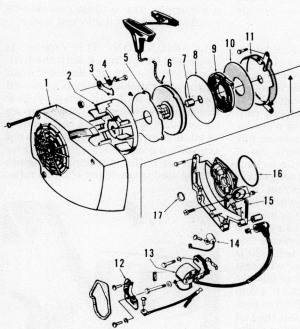

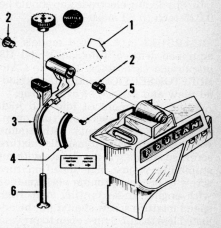

Fig. PN27—Exploded view of rewind starter used on Model 361.

1. Starter housing
2. Spring plate
3. Rewind spring
4. Spring cover
5. Rope pulley
6. Washer
7. Screw
8. Flywheel nut
9. Lockwasher
10. Washer
11. Flywheel cover
12. Flywheel
13. Stud
14. Starter pawl
15. Washer
16. Spring

Fig. PN28—Eploded view of rewind starter and ignition assembly used on all models except Model 361. Later 245A, 245SA, 306A and 306SA models have breakerless ignition.

1. Fan housing
2. Flywheel
3. Starter pawl
4. Spring
5. Plate
6. Rope pulley
7. Bearing
8. Spring plate
9. Rewind spring
10. Spring plate
11. Starter housing
12. Breaker points
13. Coil & armature
14. Condenser
15. Side cover
16. "O" ring
17. Seal

REWIND STARTER. Refer to Figs. PN27 and PN28 for exploded views of rewind starters. Rewind spring on models shown in Fig. PN27 should be wound in clockwise direction when viewed installed in housing. Rewind spring should be wound in counterclockwise direction on models shown in Fig. PN28. Starter rope on models shown in Fig. PN27 should be wound on rope pulley in clockwise direction when viewed installed in starter housing. Starter rope should be wound in counterclockwise direction on models shown in Fig. PN28. Turn rope pulley sufficient turns to place tension on rewind spring before passing rope through outlet so rope will rewind into housing.

Fig. PN29—Exploded view of chain sharpener offered on some models.

1. Spring
2. Nylon bearing
3. Arm
4. Sharpening stone
5. Lock screw
6. Adjusting screw

POULAN

Models	Bore	Stroke	Displ.	Drive Type
4200, 4400, 6900	1.845 in. (46.86 mm)	1.5626 in. (39.69 mm)	4.2 cu. in. (68.8 cc)	Direct
4900, 7700	1.957 in. (49.70 mm)	1.5626 in. (39.69 mm)	4.7 cu. in. (77.0 cc)	Direct
5200, 5400, 8500	2.066 in. (52.48 mm)	1.5626 in. (39.69 mm)	5.2 cu. in. (85.2 cc)	Direct

MAINTENANCE

SPARK PLUG. Recommended spark plug for Models 6900, 7700 and 8500 is Champion CJ6. Recommended spark plug for all other models is Champion CJ8. Spark plug electrode gap should be 0.025 inch (0.63 mm).

CARBURETOR. Listed models are equipped with a Tillotson Model HS diaphragm carburetor. Refer to CARBURETOR SERVICE section for exploded view and service of carburetor.

Initial adjustment of idle and high speed mixture screws is one turn open. Make final adjustments with engine warm and running. Adjust idle mixture screw so engine will accelerate without stumbling. Adjust high speed mixture screw to obtain optimum performance with engine under cutting load. High speed mixture screw should not be adjusted less than 7/8 turn open to prevent engine from running too lean, as engine damage could result. Adjust idle speed screw so engine idles just below clutch engagement speed.

IGNITION. All models are equipped with a solid state capacitor discharge ignition system. Ignition timing is not adjustable. Air gap between ignition module (IM—Fig. PN50) and flywheel should be 0.012-0.015 inch (0.30-0.38 mm). Loosen module mounting screws and move module to obtain desired air gap.

If ignition is malfunctioning, use the following procedure to locate faulty component: Check spark plug. Disconnect ignition switch wire and check ignition switch operation. Be sure ground strap (G—Fig. PN51) between handle and right crankcase half is properly connected. If engine does not stop when ignition switch is in "OFF" position, but ignition switch operates properly, check for short to ground in module to ignition switch lead. To check the ignition module, disconnect transformer lead from module and replace it with a lead from a continuity test light. Connect remaining lead of test light to a cylinder fin. Note if test light is on, reverse test light leads and again note if test light is on. A dim light should appear with test light leads connected one way but not when the leads are reversed. If a dim light is not present with either connection, renew the module. Repeat the test light connection that resulted in a dim light from the test light and carefully install the starter housing. Be sure leads do not contact housing (test light will glow brightly if leads contact housing). Pull starter rope. Test light should flash brightly on and off, if not, renew module. If module operation is satisfactory, inspect wire between module and transformer. The ignition coil may be checked using a suitable coil tester.

LUBRICATION. The engine is lubricated by mixing oil with the fuel. Recommended oil is Beaird-Poulan engine oil available in blends approved for 16:1 and 32:1 fuel ratios. Follow manufacturer's mixing instructions on oil container when using a recommended oil. If Beaird-Poulan engine oil is not available, a good quality oil designed for use in air-cooled two-stroke engines may be used when mixed at a 16:1 ratio.

Fig. PN51—Ground strap (G) must be connected as shown for proper operation of ignition system.

Fig. PN50—View of ignition module (IM) and transformer (T).

Fig. PN52—View showing location of oil pump adjusting screw (S).

Use a separate container when mixing oil and fuel.

All models are equipped with an automatic chain oil pump. Oil output is adjusted by turning screw (S—Fig. PN52). Turn screw counterclockwise to increase oil output. Use clean automotive oil only for chain oil. SAE 30 oil is recommended for warm weather operation while SAE 10 is recommended for cold weather operation.

REPAIRS

CYLINDER, PISTON, PIN AND RINGS. All models are equipped with a cylinder which has a chrome plated bore. Inspect cylinder bore for excessive wear or damage to chrome surface. The piston is equipped with two piston rings. Piston and rings are available in standard size only. Piston ring grooves have a locating pin in each groove to prevent piston ring rotation. Be sure ring end gap is properly aligned with locating pin when installing cylinder.

The connecting rod is aligned by two thrust washers (10—Fig. PN53) which are each 0.032 inch (0.81 mm) thick. The piston must be installed with "EXH" on piston crown toward exhaust port. See Fig. PN54. Heat may be applied to piston crown to ease removal and installation of piston pin.

CRANKSHAFT, CONNECTING ROD AND CRANKCASE. Crankshaft is supported at both ends by a ball bearing. Crankshaft and connecting rod are a unit assembly and are not available separately. Heat crankcase halves to remove or install main bearings. Tighten

crankcase screws to 55-60 in.-lbs. (6.2-6.8 N·m).

CLUTCH. All models are equipped with the three shoe clutch shown in Fig. PN55. Clutch hub (19) has left-hand threads. Inspect clutch shoes and drum for excessive wear or damage due to excessive slippage. Inspect bearing (16) inner race (15) and clutch drum for wear and damage.

AUTOMATIC OIL PUMP. Refer to Fig. PN55 for an exploded view of automatic chain oil pump. Oil pump may be disassembled after removing roll pin (11). Manufacturer recommends renewing both gears if either gear requires renewal. Note that worm gear (2) is driven by crankshaft only if clutch hub is sufficiently tight to hold worm gear against shoulder on crankshaft.

REED VALVE. All models are equipped with a reed valve induction system. Reed valve is accessible after removing carburetor. Check gap between end of each reed valve petal and petal seat. If gap exceeds 0.010 inch (0.25 mm), renew reed petal. Renew any petal which is cracked, bent, rusted or will not seal against seat.

REWIND STARTER. Refer to Fig. PN56 for an exploded view of rewind starter. To disassemble starter, remove rope handle and allow rope to wind into starter. Unscrew socket head screw (7) and remove rope pulley (9) being careful not to dislodge rewind spring (11). Care should be used if rewind spring is removed to prevent spring from uncoiling uncontrolled. Install re-

wind spring in starter housing with spring coils in a clockwise direction from outer end. Rope length should be 45 inches (114 cm). Wind rope around rope pulley in clockwise direction as viewed with pulley in starter housing. Place tension on rewind spring by turn-

Fig. PN54—Piston must be installed with arrow and "EXH" toward exhaust port.

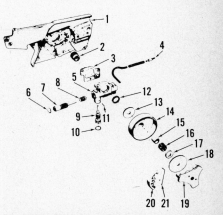

Fig. PN55—Exploded view of oil pump and clutch assemblies.

1. Right crankcase half
2. Oil pump worm gear
3. Gasket
4. Oil pickup
5. Oil pump housing
6. Plug
7. Plunger
8. Spring
9. Adjuster
10. "O ring
11. Pin
12. Seal
13. Washer
14. Clutch drum
15. Inner race
16. Bearing
17. Washer
18. Washer
19. Clutch hub
20. Clutch shoe
21. Spring

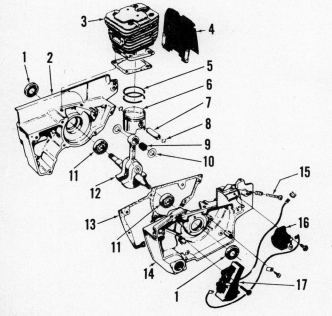

Fig. PN53—Exploded view of engine and ignition components.

1. Oil seal
2. Right crankcase half
3. Cylinder
4. Air baffle
5. Piston rings
6. Piston
7. Piston pin
8. Piston retainer
9. Roller bearing
10. Thrust washer
11. Bearing
12. Crankshaft & rod assy.
13. Gasket
14. Left crankcase half
15. Idle speed screw
16. Transformer
17. Ignition module

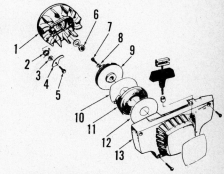

Fig. PN56—Exploded view of rewind starter used on all models.

1. Flywheel
2. Spring
3. Washer
4. Pawl
5. Screw
6. Nut
7. Screw
8. Washer
9. Rope pulley
10. Washer
11. Rewind spring
12. Washer
13. Starter housing

ing rope pulley three turns clockwise before passing rope through rope outlet.

CHAIN BRAKE. Some models are equipped with a chain brake system designed to stop chain movement should kickback occur. Chain brake is activated when operator's hand strikes chain brake lever (1—Fig. PN57) releasing latch (4) allowing spring (6) to draw brake band (9) tight around clutch drum. Pull back chain brake lever to reset mechanism.

Disassembly for repair and component renewal is evident after referral to exploded view and inspection of unit. To adjust brake, rotate screw (14) in ½ turn increments until chain brake engages with minimal effort but will not engage itself from vibration of engine running under cutting load.

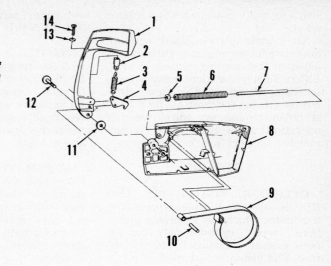

Fig. PN57—Exploded view of chain brake system used on some models.
1. Chain brake lever
2. Anchor
3. Spring
4. Latch
5. Washer
6. Spring
7. Guide rod
8. Chain guard
9. Brake band
10. Pin
11. Washer
12. Screw
13. Washer
14. Adjusting screw

POULAN

Model	Bore	Stroke	Displ.	Drive Type
5500	2.047 in. (52 mm)	1.654 in. (42 mm)	5.4 cu. in. (89 cc)	Direct
6000, S6000	2.165 in. (55 mm)	1.654 in. (42 mm)	6.1 cu. in. (100 cc)	Direct

MAINTENANCE

SPARK PLUG. Recommended spark plug is Champion CJ4. Spark plug electrode gap should be 0.025 inch (0.63 mm).

CARBURETOR. All models are equipped with a Tillotson Model HS diaphragm carburetor. Refer to CARBURETOR SERVICE section for overhaul and exploded view of carburetor.

Initial setting of idle and high speed mixture screws is one turn open. Make final adjustments with engine warm and running. Adjust idle mixture screw so engine will accelerate without stumbling. Adjust high speed mixture screw to obtain optimum engine performance with egine under cutting load. Adjust idle speed screw so engine idles just below clutch engagement speed.

IGNITION. Model 5500 is equipped with a flywheel magneto ignition system while all other models are equipped with a capacitor discharge solid state ignition system. Ignition timing marks are located on fan as shown in Fig. PN60. Fan and flywheel may be separated and should be marked before disassembly so timing marks on fan will correspond with piston position for correct ignition timing. Spark should occur when mark (EL) on fan is aligned with mark shown in Fig. PN60. Ignition timing is adjusted by loosening stator plate mounting screws and moving stator plate. Initial ignition timing setting is provided by aligning crankcase mark with mark on stator. See Fig. PN61. Breaker-point gap is 0.012-0.016 inch (0.30-0.40 mm) on Model 5500. Air gap between coil legs and flywheel on Model 5500 is 0.0010-0.0015 inch (0.020-0.038 mm).

LUBRICATION. The engine is lubricated by mixing oil with the fuel. Recommended oil is Beaird-Poulan engine oil available in blends approved for 16:1 and 32:1 fuel ratios. Follow manufacturer's mixing instructions on oil container when using a recommended oil. If Beaird-Poulan engine oil is not available, a good quality oil designed for use in air-cooled two-stroke engines may be used when mixed at a 16:1 ratio. Use a separate container when mixing fuel and oil.

All models are equipped with an automatic chain oil pump. Oil pump output is adjusted by turning adjusting screw adjacent to bar spike on Models 5500 and 6000 or adjacent to clutch on Model S6000. Turning screw clockwise will decrease oil output while turning screw counterclockwise will increase oil output.

REPAIRS

PISTON, PIN, RINGS AND CYLINDERS. The cylinder may be removed after removal of airbox cover, air cleaner, carburetor, cylinder shroud and muffler. The cylinder is chrome plated and should be inspected for excessive wear or damage to chrome plating.

Piston pin is retained by wire retainers and rides in a roller bearing in the small end of the connecting rod. The piston is equipped with two piston rings which are retained in position by locating pins in the ring grooves. The piston must be installed with the arrow on the piston crown pointing toward the exhaust port. See Fig. PN62. Some pistons have a letter "A" stamped near the arrow which must not be confused with letter stamped on piston crown to indicate piston size.

Cylinder and piston are marked "A," "B" or "C" during production to obtain desired piston-to-cylinder clearance. Cylinder and piston must have same letter marking to obtain proper clearance. Cylinders are stamped on top of cylinder or on cylinder flange. Pistons are stamped on piston crown but letter indicating piston size should not be confused with letter "A" which is stamped on some piston crowns to indicate which side of piston must be installed adjacent to exhaust port.

CONNECTING ROD, CRANKSHAFT AND CRANKCASE. Crankcase halves must be split on all models to remove crankshaft assembly. The crankshaft is supported at both ends by ball bearings.

Fig. PN60—View of ignition marks: CM—crankcase mark; EL—flywheel timing mark; TD—top dead center.

Fig. PN61—Arrow shows alignment of stator plate mark and crankcase mark.

Fig. PN62—View showing location of piston and cylinder grade letters. Note that arrow on piston crown must point toward exhaust port.

Connecting rod and crankshaft are a pressed together assembly which should be disassembled only by a shop with the tools and experience necessary to assemble and realign crankshaft. Connecting rod, bearing and crankpin are available as a unit assembly.

On Models 5500 and 6000, the automatic oil pump is driven by worm (2—Fig. PN64) located between main bearing and oil seal. On these models, worm should be pressed on crankshaft prior to installing crankshaft assembly in crankcase. Heat worm gear to 210°F (99°C) to ease reassembly of worm to crankshaft.

CLUTCH. Four- and six-shoe clutches have been used. The clutch on all models is retained by a nut with left-hand threads. A puller should be used to remove clutch hub from crankshaft. Models 5500 and 6000 are equipped with two springs (15—Fig. PN64) which should be renewed in pairs.

Tighten clutch nut to 22 ft.-lbs. (30 N·m) on Models 5500 and 6000 or to 19 ft.-lbs. (26 N·m) on S6000 models.

CHAIN OILER. All models are equipped with an automatic chain oil

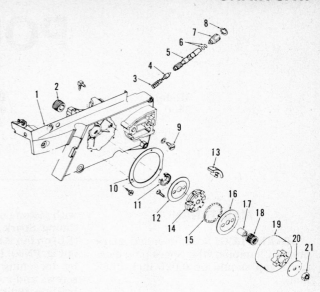

Fig. PN64—Exploded view of Model 5500 and 6000 oil pump and clutch assemblies. Two garter springs (15) are used. Oil pump worm gear (2) is pressed on crankshaft.

1. Right crankcase half
2. Oil pump worm gear
3. Spring
4. Thrust pin
5. Oil pump plunger
6. "O" rings
7. Adjusting screw
8. Snap ring
9. Cam screw
10. Cover plate
11. Seal
12. Guide plate
13. Clutch shoe
14. Clutch hub
15. Garter spring
16. Guide plate
17. Inner bearing race
18. Needle bearing
19. Clutch drum
20. Washer
21. Nut

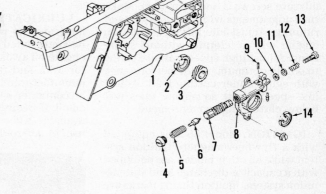

Fig. PN65—Exploded view of oil pump used on S6000 models.

1. Right crankcase half
2. Oil seal
3. Worm
4. Plug
5. Spring
6. Thrust pin
7. Plunger
8. Pump housing
9. Pin
10. Rubber washer
11. Spring seat
12. Spring
13. Adjusting screw
14. Seal

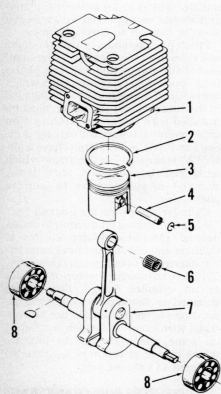

Fig. PN63—Exploded view of engine. Piston is equipped with two piston rings.

1. Cylinder
2. Piston rings
3. Piston
4. Piston pin
5. Pin retainer
6. Needle bearing
7. Crankshaft & rod assy.
8. Ball bearing

pump. The oil pump on Model S6000 is contained in a removable oil pump housing (8—Fig. PN65) with plunger (7) driven by worm (3) located outside the right crankcase oil seal. The oil pump on all other models is contained in the right crankcase half. The oil pump plunger (5—Fig. PN64) is driven by worm (2) which is located between main bearing and oil seal (11).

To disassemble oil pump on Models 5500 and 6000, remove chain, bar and clutch. Remove snap ring (8) and unscrew adjusting screw (7). Remove cam screw (CS—Fig. PN66) and withdraw oil pump components. When reassembling, be sure cam screw (CS) is correctly meshed with groove in plunger (5—Fig. PN64).

Worm gear (2—Fig. PN64 or 3—Fig. PN65) may be extracted without removing crankshaft by using a suitable puller. Mark position of worm gear on Models 5500 and 6000 prior to removal. On

Fig. PN66—View showing location of cam screw (CS) which must be unscrewed before oil pump plunger (5—Fig. PN64) can be withdrawn.

S6000 models, install seal (14—Fig. PN65) so seal lip will be toward clutch.

REWIND STARTER. Refer to Fig. PN67 for exploded view of rewind starter. To disassemble starter, remove starter housing from saw, remove rope handle and allow rope to wind into starter. Remove snap rings and pawl springs (8) and withdraw rope pulley being careful not to dislodge rewind

spring. If necessary to remove rewind spring, precautions should be taken to prevent spring from uncoiling uncontrolled.

Install rewind spring in starter housing in clockwise direction from outer end. Wind rope around rope pulley in clockwise direction as viewed with pulley in starter housing. Pawl springs (8) must be positioned against spring spacer (7) as shown in Fig. PN68. To place tension on starter rope, rotate rope pulley clockwise six turns before passing rope through outlet. Check operation of rewind starter. Rope handle should rest snugly against starter housing with rope released. It should be possible to turn rope pulley ¼ turn clockwise with rope fully extended. Readjust spring tension if rope handle is loose against starter housing or rewind spring is coil bound with rope fully extended.

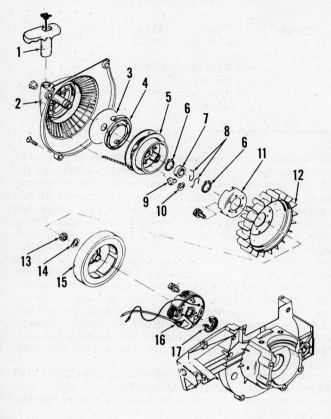

Fig. PN67—Exploded view of rewind starter and ignition assemblies. Refer to Fig. PN68 for installation of pawl springs (8).

1. Rope handle
2. Starter housing
3. Spacer
4. Rewind spring
5. Rope pulley
6. Snap ring
7. Spacer
8. Pawl springs
9. Pawl
10. "E" ring
11. Starter cup
12. Fan
13. Nut
14. Spring washer
15. Flywheel
16. Stator plate
17. Seal

Fig. PN68—View showing installation of spring spacer (7), pawl springs (8) and pawls (9).

POULAN

Model	Bore	Stroke	Displ.	Drive Type
3400	....	....	3.4 cu. in. (56 cc)	Direct
3700	....	....	3.7 cu. in. (61 cc)	Direct
4000	....	....	3.9 cu. in. (64 cc).	Direct

MAINTENANCE

SPARK PLUG. Recommended spark plug is Champion CJ8Y. Spark plug electrode gap should be 0.025 inch (0.63 mm).

CARBURETOR. All models are equipped with a Walbro HDB-8 diaphragm carbureter. Refer to Walbro section of CARBURETOR SERVICE section for overhaul and exploded view of carburetor.

Initial setting of low and high speed mixture screws is one turn open from a lightly seated position. Make final adjustments with engine warm and running. Adjust low speed mixture screw so engine will accelerate without stumbling. Adjust high speed mixture screw to obtain optimum engine performance with engine under cutting load. Adjust idle speed screw so engine idles just below clutch engagement speed.

IGNITION. All models are equipped with a solid state capacitor discharge ignition system. Ignition timing is not adjustable. Air gap between ignition module (2—Fig. PN71) and flywheel magnets should be 0.010-0.014 inch (0.25-0.35 mm). Loosen module mounting screws and move module to obtain desired air gap.

LUBRICATION. The engine is lubricated by mixing oil with the fuel. Recommended oil is Beaird-Poulan engine oil available in blends approved for 16:1 and 32.1 fuel ratios. Follow manufacturer's mixing instructions on oil container when using a recommended oil. If Beaird-Poulan engine oil is not available, a good quality oil designed for use in air-cooled two-stroke engines may be used when mixed at a 16:1 ratio. Use a separate container when mixing the fuel and oil.

Saw chain is lubricated by oil from the automatic and manual chain oil pump shown in Fig. PN74. Oil pump used on early 3400 models is equipped with an oil output adjustment screw. Adjustment screw is accessible from under saw and should be set two turns open from seated position. Later 3400 models and all 3700 and 4000 models have nonadjustable oil pumps. Use clean automotive oil only for chain oil. SAE 30 oil is recommended for warm weather operation while SAE 10 is recommended for cold weather operation.

REPAIRS

CYLINDER, PISTON, PIN AND RINGS. All models are equipped with a cylinder which has a chrome plated bore except later Model 3400 which is equipped with a silicon impregnated cylinder bore. Inspect cylinder bore for excessive wear or damage to chrome surface. The piston is equipped with two piston rings. Piston and rings are available in standard size only. Piston grooves have a locating pin in each groove to prevent piston ring rotation. Be sure ring end gap is properly aligned with locating pin when installing cylinder. The piston is a press fit in connecting rod small end and should be removed and installed with special tools 31069 and 31077 to prevent damage. The piston must be installed with piston ring locating pins toward the inlet port.

CRANKSHAFT, CONNECTING ROD AND CRANKCASE. Crankshaft is supported at both ends by a roller bearing.

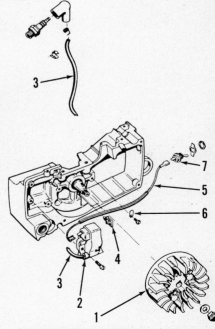

Fig. PN71—Exploded view of ignition components used on all models.

1. Flywheel
2. Ignition module
3. High tension lead
4. Lead retainer
5. Ground wire
6. Wire retainer
7. Stop switch

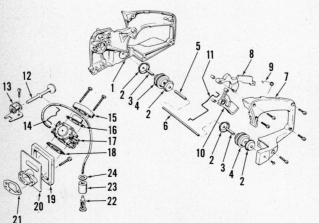

Fig. PN70—Exploded view of rear handle assembly and related components.

1. Right handle half
2. Cup
3. Spacer
4. Isolator
5. Center spacer
6. Shaft
7. Left handle half
8. Throttle lock
9. Spring
10. Throttle trigger
11. Throttle linkage
12. Choke button
13. Choke bracket
14. Choke linkage
15. Seal
16. Seal adapter
17. Carburetor
18. Gasket
19. Seal
20. Intake manifold
21. Gasket
22. Fuel pickup
23. Fuel filter
24. Washer

Crankshaft and connecting rod are a unit assembly and are not available separately. Care should be taken not to damage mating surfaces of crankcase halves when removing crankshaft unit. Check rotation of connecting rod around crankpin and renew crankshaft unit if roughness or other damage is found. Check main bearing contact surfaces on crankshaft for damage or excessive wear. If main bearings (9—Fig. PN72) require renewal, remove seals (12) and drive out main bearings toward center of crankcase using special tools 31033 and 3158 or equivalent.

Install main bearings in bearing bores from inside of crankcase using support tool 31033 and bearing locating tool number 31074. Bearing lettered end should be toward crankshaft. Install crankshaft seals (12) with open side toward main bearings, flush to 0.015

inch (0.38 mm) below flush of outer crankcase bearing bosses. Thrust washers (8) should be placed on crankshaft with stepped side toward main bearings. Using sealant part 30054, apply a 1/32 inch (0.8 mm) diameter bead to left crankcase half (11) mating surface, then assemble the crankshaft and crankcase halves. The manufacturer does not recommend the use of a substitute sealant. Tighten crankcase cap screws to 45-50 in.-lbs. (5.0-5.6 N·m).

CLUTCH. All models are equipped with the three-shoe clutch shown in Fig. PN73. Clutch hub (1) has left-hand threads. Inspect clutch shoes and drum for excessive wear or damage due to excessive slippage. Inspect bearing (6), clutch drum (5) and bearing contact surface on crankshaft for wear and damage.

CHAIN OILER PUMP. Refer to Fig. PN74 for exploded view of automatic and manual oil pump used on all models. Oil pump may be removed for disassembly and repair after removing clutch assembly and oil pump cover plate.

Inspect and renew any questionable components. Oil pump used on early 3400 models is equipped with an oil output adjustment screw. Adjustment screw is accessible from under saw and should be set two turns open from seated position. Later 3400 models and all 3700 models have nonadjustable pumps.

REWIND STARTER. Refer to Fig. PN75 for exploded view of rewind starter. To disassemble rewind starter, first remove starter housing from saw. Remove air baffle (5) then pull starter

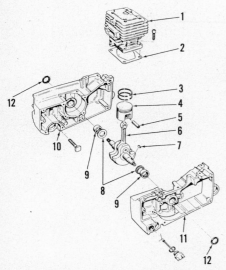

Fig. PN72—Exploded view of engine assembly.

1. Cylinder	7. Woodruff key
2. Gasket	8. Thrust washers
3. Piston rings	9. Main bearings
4. Piston	10. Right crankcase half
5. Piston pin	11. Left crankcase half
6. Crankshaft & rod assy.	12. Crankshaft seals

Fig. PN74—Exploded view of manual and automatic oil pump assembly used on all models. Pumps used on early 3400 models have an output adjustment screw on underside of saw (not shown). Refer to text.

1. Lever retainer
2. Manual pump lever
3. Right crankcase half
4. Manual pump rod
5. Boot
6. Cap
7. Snap ring
8. Pump piston
9. Quad ring
10. Washer
11. Spring
12. Housing
13. Spring
14. Pintle
15. Diaphragm
16. Gasket
17. Cover
18. Filter
19. Gasket
20. Oil pickup
21. Oil outlet

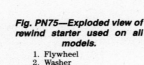

Fig. PN73—Exploded view of clutch assembly used on all models.

1. Clutch hub	5. Clutch drum
2. Clutch shoes	6. Needle bearing
3. Spring	7. Thrust washer
4. Plate	

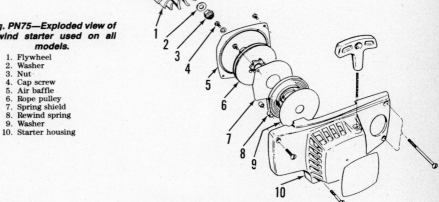

Fig. PN75—Exploded view of rewind starter used on all models.

1. Flywheel
2. Washer
3. Nut
4. Cap screw
5. Air baffle
6. Rope pulley
7. Spring shield
8. Rewind spring
9. Washer
10. Starter housing

rope and hold rope pulley (6) with notch in pulley adjacent to rope outlet. Pull rope back through outlet so it engages notch in pulley and allow pulley to completely unwind. Unscrew pulley retaining cap screw (4) and remove rope pulley. If rewind spring requires removal, remove shield (7) and carefully withdraw rewind spring from starter housing. Care should be taken to prevent spring from uncoiling uncontrolled.

Reassembly is the reverse of disassembly while noting the following: Install rewind spring in starter housing with spring coils in a clockwise direction from outer end. Rope length should be 48 inches (122 cm). Wrap starter rope around rope pulley in clockwise direction as viewed with pulley in starter housing. Place tension on rewind spring by turning rope pulley three turns

clockwise before passing rope through rope outlet.

CHAIN BRAKE. Some models are equipped with a chain brake system designed to stop chain movement should kickback occur. Chain brake is activated when operator's hand strikes chain brake lever (1—Fig. PN76), tripping latch (2) and allowing spring (3) to draw brake band (6) tight around clutch drum. Pull back chain brake lever to reset mechanism.

Disassembly for repair and component renewal is evident after referral to exploded view and inspection of unit.

To adjust chain brake, rotate adjustment screw (11) in ½ turn increments until chain brake engages with minimal effort but will not activate itself due to engine vibration.

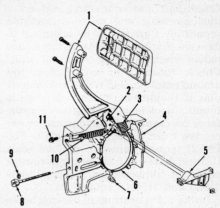

Fig. PN76—Exploded view of chain brake system used on some models.

1. Chain brake lever
2. Latch
3. Spring
4. Housing
5. Guard
6. Brake band
7. Bar adjusting screw anchor
8. Bar adjusting screw
9. "E" ring
10. Spring
11. Adjusting screw

POULAN

Model	Bore	Stroke	Displ.	Drive Type
2800	....	....	2.8 cu. in. (46 cc)	Direct
3000	....	....	3.0 cu. in. (49 cc)	Direct

MAINTENANCE

SPARK PLUG. Recommended spark plug is Champion CJ4. Spark plug electrode gap should be 0.025 inch (0.63 mm).

CARBURETOR. Both models are equipped with a Walbro HDA diaphragm type carburetor. Refer to Walbro section of CARBURETOR SERVICE section for overhaul and exploded view of carburetor.

Initial adjustment for both high and low speed mixture screws is one turn open from a lightly seated position. Make final adjustment with engine running at operating temperature. Adjust low speed mixture screw so engine will accelerate without hesitation. Adjust high speed mixture screw to obtain optimum full throttle performance under cutting load. Adjust idle speed screw so engine idles just below clutch engagement speed.

IGNITION. Both models are equipped with a breakerless capacitor discharge ignition system. Ignition timing is not adjustable. Air gap between ignition module and flywheel magnets should be 0.012 inch (0.30 mm). Loosen module mounting screws and move module to obtain desired air gap.

LUBRICATION. The engine is lubricated by mixing oil with fuel. Recommended oil is Beaird-Poulan engine oil available in blends approved for 16:1 and 32:1 fuel ratios. Follow manufacturer's mixing instructions when using a recommended oil. If Beaird-Poulan engine oil is not available, a good quality oil designed for use in air-cooled two-stroke engines may be used when mixed at a 16:1 ratio. Use a separate container when mixing the fuel and oil.

Both models are equipped with adjustable automatic chain oil pumps. Use clean automotive oil only for chain oil. SAE 30 is recommended for warm weather operation and SAE 10 for cold weather operation.

REPAIRS

CYLINDER, PISTON, PIN AND RINGS. Model 2800 is equipped with a silicon impregnated cylinder bore. Model 3000 is equipped with a chrome plated cylinder bore. On Model 3000, cylinder bore should be inspected for flaking, cracking or other damage to chrome surface.

The piston is equipped with two piston rings. Oversize piston and piston rings are not available. Locating pins are present in ring grooves to prevent ring rotation. Make certain ring end gaps are properly aligned with locating pins when installing cylinder. Piston pin (5—Fig. PN86) rides in needle roller bearing (7) and is held in place by two wire retainers (6). When installing piston, align arrow on piston crown with exhaust ports.

CRANKSHAFT, CONNECTING ROD AND CRANKCASE. Crankshaft is supported by ball bearing (9—Fig. PN86) on both ends. Clutch side ball bearing is located in crankcase with snap ring (13). Crankshaft and connecting rod (11) are a unit assembly and are not available separately. Check rotation of connecting rod around crank pin and renew if roughness, excessive play or other damage is found. Care should be taken not to damage crankcase mating surfaces when separating crankcase halves (10 and 12). Use sealant part 30054 when reassembling crankcase. Apply a 1/32 inch (0.8 mm) bead on sealing surface of one crankcase half, then assemble crankshaft and crankcase halves. Manufacturer does not recommend usage of a substitute sealant.

CLUTCH. Both models are equipped with the two-shoe centrifugal clutch shown in Fig. PN87. Clutch shoes and

Fig. PN86—Exploded view of engine assembly.

1. Cylinder
2. Gasket
3. Piston rings
4. Piston
5. Piston pin
6. Retainer clip
7. Needle roller bearing
8. Woodruff key
9. Ball bearing
10. Left crankcase half
11. Crankshaft & connecting rod assy.
12. Right crankcase half
13. Snap ring
14. Seal

Fig. PN87—Exploded view of clutch and automatic oil pump assemblies. Sprocket (5) is absent on Model 2800.

1. Clutch shoes & hub assy.
2. Plate
3. Clutch drum
4. Needle roller bearing
5. Sprocket
6. Thrust washer
7. Oil pump housing
8. Gasket
9. Pin
10. Adjusting screw
11. "O" ring
12. Spring
13. Spur gear
14. Plunger
15. Plug
16. Seal
17. Worm gear
18. Right crankcase half
19. Oil tank vent wire
20. Oil filter & pickup assy.
21. Oil suction line
22. Oil discharge line

hub assembly (1) have left-hand threads. Inspect clutch shoes (1) and drum (3) for excessive wear or damage due to overheating. Clutch shoes, garter spring and hub are available as a unit assembly only. Inspect bearing (4) for damage or discoloration. Inspect bearing contact surface on crankshaft for excessive wear or other damage.

AUTOMATIC OIL PUMP. Refer to Fig. PN87 for view of automatic chain oil pump used on both models. Remove guide bar and clutch assembly to gain access to oil pump. Plunger (14) is actuated by spur gear (13) which is driven by worm gear (17). All pump components should be inspected and renewed if excessive wear or damage is found.

Pump output is adjusted by rotating adjusting screw (10) located on bottom of saw. Remove pin (9) to remove adjusting screw for inspection or renewal.

REWIND STARTER. Refer to Fig. PN88 for exploded view of rewind starter. To disassemble starter, remove rope handle (13) and carefully allow rope pulley (9) to unwind relieving tension on rewind spring (10). Remove screw (4), wave washer (5), cam (6), retainer (7) and starter pawls (8). Remove rope pulley using caution not to dislodge rewind spring. Note how pulley engages rewind spring. If rewind spring must be removed, do not allow spring to uncoil uncontrolled.

Reassembly is the reverse of disassembly while noting the following: Make certain hook on outer coil of rewind spring properly engages starter housing (12). Wind rope in a clockwise direction on rope pulley as viewed from flywheel side of pulley. Rotate rope pulley clockwise before passing rope through rope guide to preload rewind spring. Rope handle will be snug against starter housing if rewind spring preload is correct.

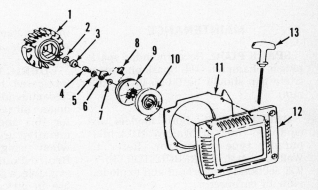

Fig. PN88—Exploded view of rewind starter.
1. Flywheel
2. Washer
3. Nut
4. Screw
5. Wave washer
6. Cam
7. Retainer
8. Pawl
9. Rope pulley
10. Rewind spring
11. Baffle
12. Starter housing
13. Rope handle

PROKUT

ZIP PENN LASER SALES
9946 Mills Station Road No. 2
Sacramento, CA 95827

Model	Bore	Stroke	Displ.	Drive Type
32	36.5 mm (1.44 in.)	30.4 mm (1.2 in.)	32 cc (1.9 cu. in.)	Direct
38	39.7 cc (1.56 in.)	30.4 cc (1.2 in.)	38 cc (2.3 cu. in.)	Direct

MAINTENANCE

SPARK PLUG. Recommended spark plug is Champion CJ7Y for both models. Spark plug electrode gap should be 0.5 mm (0.020 in.).

CARBURETOR. Both models are equipped with a Walbro WA diaphragm type carburetor. Refer to Walbro section of CARBURETOR SERVICE section for service procedure and exploded view.

High speed mixture is not adjustable. Initial setting of low speed mixture screw is 1-3/8 turns open on Model 32 and 1-1/2 turns open on Model 38.

Final adjustment should be made with engine running at operating temperature. Adjust engine idle speed to just below clutch engagement speed. Adjust low speed mixture so engine will accelerate cleanly without hesitation.

IGNITION. Both models are equipped with a breakerless electronic ignition system. Ignition coil and all electronic circuitry are contained in a one-piece ignition module. Ignition timing is not adjustable. Air gap between ignition module legs and flywheel magnets should be 0.35 mm (0.014 in.). Loosen ignition module mounting screws and move module to adjust air gap. Use a suitable thread locking solution on module screws to prevent screws from vibrating loose. If flywheel requires removal, use ProKut tool 3630260 or a suitable equivalent to withdraw flywheel. Tighten flywheel nut to 34.3 N·m (26 ft.-lbs.).

LUBRICATION. The engine is lubricated by mixing oil with the fuel. Use a good quality oil designed for use in air-cooled two-stroke engines. Fuel:oil ratio is 16:1 for all models. Use a separate container when mixing fuel and oil.

Both models are equipped with an automatic oil pump which utilizes crankcase pulsations to pressurize oil tank. Pump output is adjustable. Refer to OIL PUMP under REPAIRS section for service procedures and exploded views. Use clean automotive oil for saw chain lubrication. Oil viscosity must be chosen according to ambient temperature. For example, use SAE 30 for warm weather operation and SAE 15 for cold weather operation.

REPAIRS

CYLINDER, PISTON, PIN AND RINGS. Cylinder is chrome plated and should be renewed if cracking, scoring or other damage is noted in cylinder bore.

NOTE: Piston aligns connecting rod on rod bearing rollers (25—Fig. PK1). Excessive piston movement during or after cylinder removal may allow rod bearing rollers to fall into crankcase.

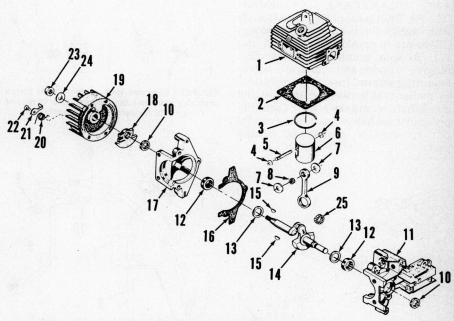

Fig. PK1—Exploded view of engine assembly. Two pawl assemblies (20, 21 and 22) are used.

1. Cylinder
2. Gasket
3. Piston ring
4. Snap ring
5. Piston pin
6. Piston
7. Thrust washer
8. Bearing rollers
9. Connecting rod
10. Seal
11. Right crankcase half
12. Main bearing
13. Thrust washer
14. Crankshaft
15. Key
16. Gasket
17. Left crankcase half
18. Counterweight
19. Flywheel
20. Spring
21. Pawl
22. Pin
23. Nut
24. Washer
25. Bearing rollers

Piston and cylinder are marked during production to obtain desired piston-to-cylinder clearance of 0.02 mm (0.0008 in.). Original piston and cylinder are marked "A." Factory renewal piston and cylinder assemblies are marked "B." Piston or cylinder marked "C" is 0.127 mm (0.005 in.) oversize while piston or cylinder marked "D" is 0.127 mm (0.005 in.) undersize. Piston and cylinder markings should match, however, a new piston marked "B" can be installed in a used cylinder marked "A."

NOTE: Do not install a new piston marked "B" or "C" into a new cylinder marked "A."

Piston is equipped with one piston ring. A locating pin is present in ring groove to prevent ring rotation. Maximum allowable piston ring end gap is 1.0 mm (0.039 in.). Piston pin (5—Fig. PK1) rides on 18 loose bearing rollers (8). Use ProKut tool 4180010 or a suitable equivalent with proper size drivers to remove and install piston pin. Hold bearing rollers (8) in place with heavy grease and place thrust washer (7) on each side of rod before installing piston. Install piston with arrow on piston crown facing toward exhaust side of cylinder. Make certain piston ring end gap is properly positioned around locating pin in ring groove before installing cylinder. Tighten cylinder screws to 8.8 N·m (78 in.-lbs.).

CRANKSHAFT, CONNECTING ROD AND CRANKCASE. Crankshaft (14—Fig. PK1) is supported at both ends with caged roller bearings (12). Bearings (12) locate in crankcase halves (11 and 17). To split crankcase halves, first remove cylinder and crankcase halves mounting screws. Insert a screwdriver or similar tool between crankcase and crankshaft counterweight. Carefully pry crankcase halves apart being careful not to damage crankcase mating surfaces.

NOTE: Crankshaft runout can be checked before disassembly of engine. To check runout, remove clutch and flywheel. Mount a dial indicator on both ends of crankshaft as close as possible to bearings (12). Check runout while rotating crankshaft. Runout should not exceed 0.07 mm (0.0027 in.).

Connecting rod rides on 12 loose bearing rollers (25). Connecting rod can be removed from crankshaft after crankcase halves are separated. Hold bearing rollers on crankpin with heavy grease when installing connecting rod. Note location of thrust washers (13). Do not use gasket sealing compounds on crankcase gasket (16). Tighten crankcase screws using a crisscross pattern to 6.9 N·m (61 in.-lbs.).

CLUTCH. Both models are equipped with the centrifugal clutch shown in Fig. PK2. Early models are equipped with the centrifugal clutch shown in Fig. PK3. Complete clutch assemblies are interchangeable, although, individual components are not. Clutch hub (2) has left-hand threads. Inspect shoes, hub, drum and needle bearing for excessive wear or damage due to overheating. Clutch shoes are available only as a complete set. Tighten clutch hub to 18.6 N·m (14 ft.-lbs.).

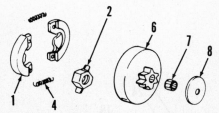

Fig. PK3—Exploded view of centrifugal clutch assembly used on early models. Refer to legend in Fig. PK2 for component identification.

OIL PUMP. Both models are equipped with the pressure-type chain oiling system shown in Fig. PK4. Impulse hose (3) connects to crankcase. Crankcase pulsations pressurize oil tank (1). Check valve (4) prevents chain oil from entering crankcase. Pump output is regulated by rotating screw (8). Clockwise rotation decreases output. Shut-off valve (10) is linked to throttle trigger, preventing oil flow at idle speed.

Oil tank (1) must hold pressure for proper operation of system. Pressurize oil tank to 34.5 kPa (5.0 psi) to check for leakage in tank or leak-back of check valve (4). Malfunctions are often due to check valve (4) stuck closed preventing crankcase pulsations from entering oil tank.

REWIND STARTER. Both models are equipped with the rewind starter shown in Fig. PK7. Remove starter housing (7) to disassemble starter. Withdraw housing (7) sufficiently to disconnect ignition switch wires then remove housing. Remove rope handle and allow rope to slowly wind into starter housing to relieve tension on rewind spring. Remove screw (1) and carefully remove rope pulley (4). If rewind spring (6) must be removed, care should be taken to prevent personal injury due to uncontrolled uncoiling of spring.

Install rewind spring (6) into housing (7) in a clockwise direction starting with outer coil end. Wrap starter rope around rope pulley in a clockwise direction as viewed from flywheel side of pulley. To preload rewind spring, pull out a loop of rope from notch in rope pulley and rotate pulley ½ turn clockwise. Rope handle should be snug against housing with rope retracted. With rope fully extended, rope pulley should be able to rotate ½ turn further to prevent rewind spring breakage.

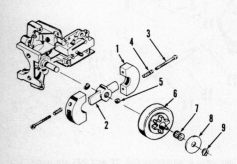

Fig. PK2—Exploded view of centrifugal clutch assembly used on later models.

1. Shoe	6. Drum
2. Hub	7. Needle bearing
3. Screw	8. Washer
4. Spring	9. Snap ring
5. Nut	

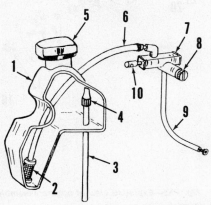

Fig. PK4—View showing automatic oiling system.

1. Oil tank	6. Hose
2. Oil filter	7. Metering valve assy.
3. Impulse hose	8. Adjusting screw
4. Check valve	9. Discharge hose
5. Cap	10. Shut-off valve

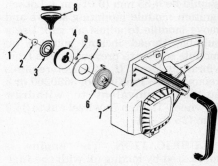

Fig. PK7—Exploded view of rewind starter assembly.

1. Screw	6. Rewind spring
2. Washer	7. Housing
3. Rope	8. Rope handle
4. Rope pulley	9. Eyelet
5. Spring cover	

Starter pawls (21—Fig. PK1) are secured on flywheel with pins (22). Drive pins out from inside of flywheel to remove pawls. Use ProKut tool 3630260 or a suitable equivalent to remove flywheel. Use a suitable thread locking solution on pins (22) when reassembling pawls. Tighten flywheel nut to 34.4 N·m (26 ft.-lbs.).

CHAIN BRAKE. Both models are equipped with the chain brake system shown in Fig. PK9. Chain brake is actuated when operator's hand strikes hand guard (15). Forward movement of actuator (13) trips latch (11) allowing spring (4) to pull brake band (2) tight around clutch drum (6). Pull back hand guard (15) to reset chain brake.

To adjust chain brake, disengage brake by pulling hand guard (15) to rearmost position (toward engine). Install guide bar and saw chain and properly adjust chain tension. Rotate brake tension adjustment screw (between brake arm mounting studs at front of actuator) clockwise, while pulling saw chain around guide bar, until chain movement becomes difficult. Back off adjustment screw (counterclockwise) until chain moves freely around guide bar. Make certain brake band does not contact clutch drum with brake in the disengaged position.

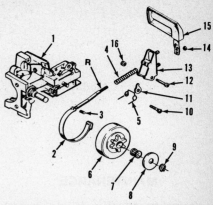

Fig. PK9—Exploded view of chain brake system. Brake tension screw (not shown) is located at front of actuator (13) between hand guard (15) mounting studs.

1. Right crankcase half	
2. Brake band	10. Screw
3. Pin	11. Latch
4. Spring	12. Shoulder screw
5. Spring	13. Actuator
6. Drum	14. Nut
7. Needle bearing	15. Hand guard
8. Washer	16. Nut
9. Snap ring	R. Rod

PROKUT

Model	Bore	Stroke	Displ.	Drive Type
45	41 mm (1.61 in.)	33.8 mm (1.33 in.)	45 cc (2.74 cu. in.)	Direct

MAINTENANCE

SPARK PLUG. Recommended spark plug is Champion CJ7Y. Electrode gap should be 0.5 mm (0.020 in.).

CARBURETOR. A Tillotson HU diaphragm carburetor is used on early models. A Del'Orto C16.12 diaphragm carburetor is used on late models. Refer to Tillotson and Del'Orto sections of CARBURETOR SERVICE section for service procedures and exploded views.

Initial adjustment is 1-3/4 turns open for low speed mixture screw and 1-1/4 turns open for high speed mixture screw.

Final adjustment should be made with engine running at operating temperature. Adjust idle speed to just below clutch engagement speed. Adjust low speed mixture screw so engine will accelerate cleanly without hesitation. Adjust high speed mixture screw to obtain maximum no-load speed of 12,400 rpm.

IGNITION. A breakerless electronic ignition system is used. Refer to Fig. PK16. Ignition coil and all electronic circuitry are contained in a one-piece ignition module (8). Ignition timing is not adjustable. Air gap between ignition module and flywheel magnets should be 0.35 mm (0.014 in.).

Use ProKut tool 4180100 or a suitable equivalent bolt-type puller to remove flywheel. Remove starter pawl bolts (4) to accommodate puller bolts. Use a suitable thread locking solution on pawl bolts upon reassembly. Tighten flywheel nut to 28.4 N·m (21 ft.-lbs.). Use a suitable thread locking solution on ignition coil/module attaching screws if air gap is adjusted.

LUBRICATION. The engine is lubricated by mixing oil with the fuel. Use a good quality oil designed for use in air-cooled two-stroke engines. Fuel:oil mixture should be a 16:1 ratio. Use a separate container when mixing fuel and oil.

The automatic oil pump shown in Fig. PK23 is used. Pump output is not adjustable. Use clean automotive oil for saw chain lubrication.

REPAIRS

CYLINDER, PISTON, PIN AND RINGS. Cylinder bore is chrome plated and should be renewed if cracking, scoring or other damage is noted in cylinder bore.

Piston and cylinder are marked during production to obtain desired piston-to-cylinder clearance of 0.02 mm (0.0008 in.). Original equipment piston and cylinder are marked "A." Factory renewal piston and cylinder assemblies are marked "B." Piston or cylinder marked "C" is 0.127 mm (0.005 in.) oversize. Piston or cylinder marked "D" is 0.127 mm (0.005 in.) undersize. Piston and cylinder markings should match, however, a new piston marked "B" can be installed into a used cylinder marked "A."

NOTE: Do not install a new piston marked "B" or "C" into a new cylinder marked "A."

Piston is equipped with two piston rings. Maximum piston ring end gap should not exceed 1.0 mm (0.039). Locating pins are present in ring grooves to prevent ring rotation. Make certain ring end gaps are properly positioned around locating pins when installing cylinder.

Piston pin (5—Fig. PK17) rides in needle bearing (7) and is retained with two snap rings (6). Use ProKut 4180010 or a suitable equivalent to press out pin. Piston may be heated to approximately 110°-120°C (230°-248° F) to ease installation of piston pin.

NOTE: Use electric oven or hot oil bath to heat piston. Do not use an open flame.

Install piston into cylinder with arrow on piston crown facing toward exhaust port.

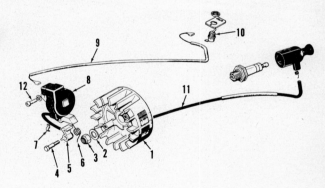

Fig. PK16—Exploded view of electronic ignition system. Two pawl assemblies (4, 5 and 6) are used.

1. Flywheel
2. Washer
3. Nut
4. Bolt
5. Pawl
6. Spring
7. Clamp
8. Ignition module
9. Primary lead
10. Ignition switch
11. High tension lead
12. Screw

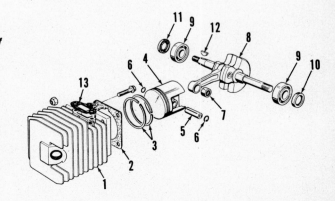

Fig. PK17—Exploded view of engine assembly.

1. Cylinder
2. Gasket
3. Piston rings
4. Piston
5. Piston pin
6. Snap ring
7. Needle bearing
8. Crankshaft & connecting rod assy.
9. Main bearings
10. Seal
11. Seal
12. Key
13. Gasket

and 3—Fig. PK20). Use the proper size drivers to remove and install main bearings. Use ProKut tool 4180900 to install crankshaft assembly into main bearing. Refer to Fig. PK21. Do not use gasket sealer on crankcase gasket. Tighten crankcase screws using a crisscross pattern to 6.9 N·m (61 in.-lbs.).

CLUTCH. The centrifugal clutch assembly shown in Fig. PK22 is used. Clutch hub (1) has left-hand threads.

Inspect shoes (2), drum (7), needle bearing (6) and bushing (5) for excessive wear or damage due to overheating and renew if needed. Shoes (2) are available only as a complete set. Tighten clutch hub (1) to 28.4 N·m (21 ft.-lbs.).

OIL PUMP. The automatic oil pump assembly shown in Fig. PK23 is used. Pump output is not adjustable. Oil is pumped by plunger (2) which is driven by worm gear (3) on end of engine crankshaft. Pump plunger (2) reciprocates in pump body (1) due to cam bolt (14) riding in oblique groove in plunger. Plunger can be removed from housing after removing cam bolt (14) and bushing (4). Inspect worm gear (3),

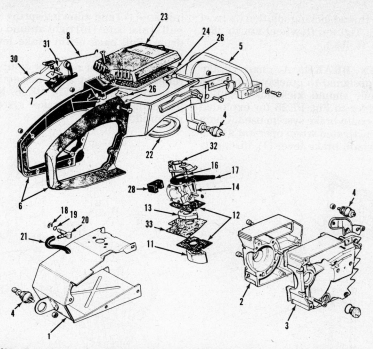

Fig. PK20—Exploded view of crankcase, handle assemblies, carburetor and related components.

1. Cylinder cover	12. Gaskets	22. Seal
2. Left crankcase half	13. Heat shield	23. Cover
3. Right crankcase half	14. Carburetor	24. Air filter
4. Vibration isolator	16. Spacer	26. Support
5. Front handle	17. Choke valve	28. Seal
6. Rear grip assy.	18. "E" ring	30. Safety lever
7. Throttle trigger	19. "O" ring	31. Spring
8. Throttle rod	20. Fitting	32. Air intake
11. Intake spacer	21. Fuel hose	33. Gasket

CRANKSHAFT, CONNECTING ROD AND CRANKCASE.

Crankshaft and connecting rod are available as a unit assembly only. Check rotation of connecting rod around crankpin and renew crankshaft assembly if roughness, excessive play or other damage is noted. Check crankshaft runout by supporting crankshaft assembly between two counterpoints such as a lathe. Make certain no damage exists to centering holes

at each end of crankshaft. Maximum allowable runout is 0.08 mm (0.0031 in.).

NOTE: Crankshaft runout can be checked while still assembled in crankcase. Remove clutch and flywheel and mount dial indicators on both sides of crankshaft as close to main bearings as possible. Measure runout while rotating crankshaft. Renew crankshaft assembly if runout exceeds 0.07 mm (0.0027 in.), when measured in this manner.

Crankshaft is supported at both ends with ball-type main bearings (9—Fig. PK17) and locate in crankcase halves (2

Fig. PK21—View showing installation procedure of crankshaft and connecting rod assembly into crankcase using ProKut tool 4180900. Main bearing (9—Fig. PK17) is pressed into crankcase half prior to installation of crankshaft assembly.

ProKut Tool 4180900

Crankshaft Assembly

Crankcase Half

Fig. PK22—Exploded view of centrifugal clutch assembly.

1. Hub	5. Bushing
2. Shoes	6. Needle bearing
3. Spring	7. Drum
4. Spring guide	8. Washer

Fig. PK23—Exploded view of automatic oil pump.

1. Pump body
2. Plunger
3. Worm gear
4. Bushing
5. Felt plug
6. Thrust washer
7. Banjo bolt
8. Pickup & filter assy.
9. Suction line
10. Oil line
11. Seal
12. Seal
13. Banjo bolt
14. Cam bolt
15. Plug
16. Washer
17. Screw
18. Washers
19. Plate

plunger (2) and pump body (1) for excessive wear or damage. Always renew seal (12) and washers (18) during reassembly of pump.

REWIND STARTER. Refer to Fig. PK24 for exploded view of rewind starter.

To disassemble starter, remove starter housing (1) from saw. Remove rope handle (3) and carefully allow rope to wind into housing (1). Remove nut (6) and washer (5). Rope pulley (4) and rewind spring and case assembly (2) can now be removed from housing.

Install rewind spring (2) into housing (1) with open side of case facing housing (1). Wind rope onto rope pulley (4) in a clockwise direction as viewed from flywheel side of pulley. Lubricate shaft (S) with a suitable low temperature grease. Rotate rope pulley ½ turn clockwise before passing rope through rope guide (G) to preload rewind spring. Rope handle should be snug against housing with rope retracted. If not, lift a loop of rope from pulley and place into notch (N) in pulley. While holding rope in notch, rotate pulley clockwise to increase rewind spring tension. With rope fully extended, rope pulley should be able to rotate ½ turn further. If not, repeat above procedure, only rotate pulley counterclockwise to decrease rewind spring tension.

Refer to Fig. PK16 for exploded view of starter pawl assemblies. Use a suitable thread locking solution on pawl bolts (4). Tighten flywheel nut to 28.4 N·m (21 ft.-lbs.).

CHAIN BRAKE. A chain brake system designed to quickly stop chain movement should kickback occur is used. Refer to Fig. PK25 for exploded view of chain brake system used. Chain brake is activated when operator's hand strikes chain brake lever (1), disengaging latch (7) and allowing spring (14) to pull brake band (10) tight around clutch drum. Pull back chain brake lever to reset mechanism.

Disassembly for repair or component renewal is evident after inspection of unit and referral to Fig. PK25. No adjustment of chain brake system is required.

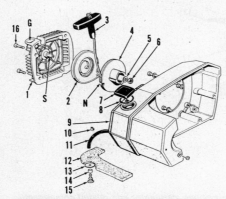

Fig. PK24—Exploded view of rewind starter, left engine cover and fuel tank assembly and related components. Refer to Fig. PK16 for view of flywheel and starter pawls.

G. Rope guide	7. Fuel cap
N. Notch	8. Seal
S. Shaft	9. Left engine cover &
1. Starter housing	fuel tank assy.
2. Rewind spring & case	10. Clamp
assy.	11. Fuel hose
3. Rope handle	12. Felt
4. Rope pulley	13. Washer
5. Washer	14. Fuel screen
6. Nut	15. Fuel pickup

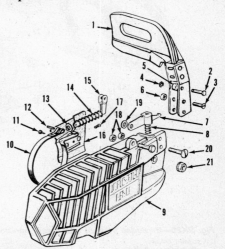

Fig. PK25—Exploded view of chain brake assembly.

1. Chain brake lever	11. Screw
2. Pin	12. Pin
3. Screw	13. Washer
4. "E" ring	14. Spring
5. Spacer	15. Arm
6. Nut	16. Guide plate
7. Latch	17. Screw
8. Spring	18. Nuts
9. Housing	19. Washer
10. Brake band	20. Screw

PROKUT

Model	Bore	Stroke	Displ.	Drive Type
55	44 mm (1.73 in.)	36 mm (1.42 in.)	49 cc (3.4 cu. in.)	Direct
65	47 mm (1.85 in.)	37.3 mm (1.47 in.)	65 cc (4.0 cu. in.)	Direct

MAINTENANCE

SPARK PLUG. Recommended spark plug for both models is Champion CJ7Y. Electrode gap should be 0.5 mm (0.020 in.).

CARBURETOR. Both models are equipped with a Tillotson HK diaphragm carburetor. Refer to Tillotson section of CARBURETOR SERVICE section for service procedure and exploded view.

Initial adjustment of low speed mixture screw is 1-1/2 turns open on Model 55 and 1-3/8 turns open on Model 65. Initial adjustment of high speed mixture screw is ¾ turn open for both models.

Final adjustment should be made with engine running at operating temperature. Adjust idle speed to just below clutch engagement speed. Adjust low speed mixture screw so engine will accelerate cleanly without hesitation. Adjust high speed mixture screw to obtain maximum no-load speed of 12,000 rpm for Model 55 and 11,600 rpm for Model 65.

IGNITION. Model 55 manufactured prior to 1985 and Model 65 manufactured prior to 1984 are equipped with a breaker-point ignition system. Breaker-point gap should be 0.45-0.50 mm (0.018-0.020 in.). Air gap between ignition coil legs and flywheel magnets should be 0.45 mm (0.018 in.). Loosen coil attaching screws and move coil to adjust air gap. Use a suitable thread locking solution on coil attaching screws. Ignition timing is not adjustable, however, breaker-point gap will affect timing. Be sure breaker-point gap is adjusted correctly as a gap too wide will advance timing and a gap too close will retard timing.

Model 55 manufactured after 1984 and Model 65 manufactured after 1983 are equipped with a breakerless electronic ignition system. Some models are equipped with a standard ignition coil with an electronic module located behind flywheel. On other models, ignition coil and all electronic circuitry are contained in a one-piece ignition module/coil (2—Fig. PK35). Air gap between ignition module/coil and flywheel magnets should be 0.35-0.40 mm (0.014-0.016 in.). Use a suitable thread locking solution on module/coil attaching screws.

On both models, use ProKut 4180140 to remove flywheel. If ProKut tool 4180140 is not available, remove starter pawl assemblies (6, 7, 8 and 9) to accommodate a bolt-type puller. Use a suitable thread locking solution on pawl bolts (6) upon reassembly. Tighten flywheel nut (10) to 34.8 N·m (26 ft.-lbs.).

LUBRICATION. The engine is lubricated by mixing oil with the fuel. Use a good quality oil designed for use in air-cooled two-stroke engines. Fuel:oil mixture should be a 16:1 ratio. Use a separate container when mixing fuel and oil.

Both models are equipped with an automatic chain oil pump. Oil pump is driven by a worm gear coupled to clutch drum. Pump output is not adjustable. Refer to OIL PUMP under REPAIRS section for service and exploded view. Use clean automotive oil for saw chain lubrication.

REPAIRS

CYLINDER, PISTON, PIN AND RINGS. Cylinder bore is chrome plated and should be renewed if cracking, scoring or other damage is noted in cylinder bore.

Piston and cylinder are marked during production to obtain desired piston-to-cylinder clearance of 0.02 mm (0.0008 in.). Original equipment piston and cylinder are marked "A." Factory renewal piston and cylinder assemblies are marked "B." Piston or cylinder marked "C" is 0.127 mm (0.005 in.) oversize. Piston or cylinder marked "D" is 0.127 mm (0.005 in.) undersize. Piston and cylinder markings should match, however, a new piston marked "B" can be installed into a used cylinder marked "A."

NOTE: Do not install a new piston marked "B" or "C" into a new cylinder marked "A."

Piston is equipped with two piston rings. Maximum piston ring end gap should not exceed 1.0 mm (0.039 in.). Locating pins are present in ring grooves to prevent ring rotation. Make certain ring end gaps are properly positioned around locating pins when installing cylinder.

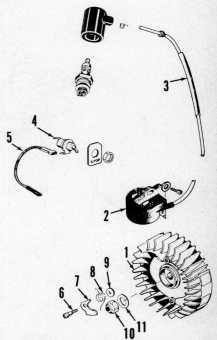

Fig. PK35—Exploded view of breakerless electronic ignition system typical of type used. Refer to text.

1. Flywheel
2. Ignition module/coil
3. High tension lead
4. Ignition switch
5. Primary lead
6. Pawl bolt
7. Pawl
8. Spring
9. Washer
10. Nut
11. Washer

Piston pin (7—Fig. PK36) rides in needle bearing (6) and is retained with two snap rings (5). Use ProKut tool 4180010 or a suitable equivalent to press out pin. Piston may be heated to approximately 110°-120° C (230°-248° F) to ease piston pin installation.

NOTE: Use electric oven or hot oil bath to heat piston. Do not use an open flame.

Install piston into cylinder with arrow on piston crown facing toward exhaust port.

CRANKSHAFT, CONNECTING ROD AND CRANKCASE. Crankshaft and connecting rod (8—Fig. PK36) are available as a unit assembly only. Check

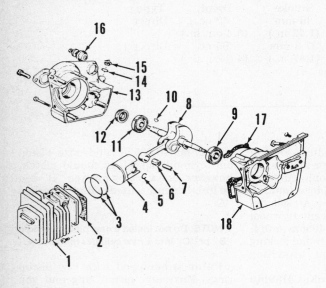

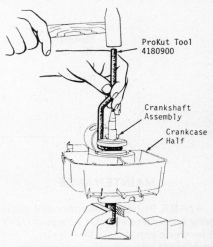

Fig. PK36—Exploded view of typical engine assembly.

1. Cylinder
2. Gasket
3. Piston rings
4. Piston
5. Retainer
6. Needle bearing
7. Piston pin
8. Crankshaft & connecting rod assy.
9. Right main bearing
10. Woodruff key
11. Left main bearing
12. Seal
13. Left crankcase half
14. Seal
15. Oil cap
16. Vibration isolator
17. Gasket
18. Right crankcase half

Fig. PK37—View showing installation of crankshaft and connecting rod assembly into crankcase using ProKut tool 4180900. Main bearing (9—Fig. PK36) is pressed into crankcase half prior to installation of crankshaft assembly.

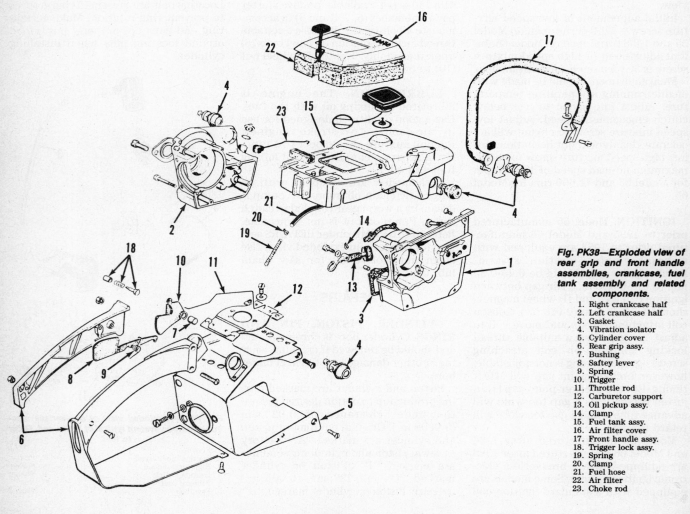

Fig. PK38—Exploded view of rear grip and front handle assemblies, crankcase, fuel tank assembly and related components.

1. Right crankcase half
2. Left crankcase half
3. Gasket
4. Vibration isolator
5. Cylinder cover
6. Rear grip assy.
7. Bushing
8. Saftey lever
9. Spring
10. Trigger
11. Throttle rod
12. Carburetor support
13. Oil pickup assy.
14. Clamp
15. Fuel tank assy.
16. Air filter cover
17. Front handle assy.
18. Trigger lock assy.
19. Spring
20. Clamp
21. Fuel hose
22. Air filter
23. Choke rod

rotation of connecting rod around crankpin and renew crankshaft assembly if roughness, excessive play or other damage is noted. Check crankshaft runout by supporting crankshaft assembly between two counterpoints such as a lathe. Make certain no damage exists to centering holes at each end of crankshaft. Maximum allowable runout is 0.08 mm (0.0031 in.).

NOTE: Crankshaft runout can be checked while still assembled in crankcase. Remove clutch and flywheel and mount dial indicators on both sides of crankshaft as close to main bearings as possible. Measure runout while rotating crankshaft. Renew crankshaft assembly if runout exceeds 0.07 mm (0.0027 in.) when measured in this manner.

Crankshaft is supported at both ends with ball-type main bearings (9 and 11). Main bearings locate in crankcase halves (13 and 18). Use the proper size drivers to remove and install main bearings. Use ProKut tool 4180900 to install crankshaft assembly into main bearing. Refer to Fig. PK37. Do not use gasket sealer on crankcase gasket (17—Fig. PK36). Tighten crankcase screws using a crisscross pattern to 6.4 N·m (57 in.-lbs.).

CLUTCH. Refer to Fig. PK39 for an exploded view of clutch assembly used on both models. Clutch hub (4) has left-hand threads. Inspect shoes (5), drum (3) and needle bearing (2) for excessive wear or damage due to overheating. Shoes (5) are available only as a complete set. Tighten clutch hub (4) to 41.2 N·m (31 ft.-lbs.).

OIL PUMP. Both models are equipped with the automatic oil pump shown in Fig. PK40. Oil is pumped by plunger (6)

which is rotated by worm gear (1). Drive lugs (L) on worm gear (1) engage clutch drum, therefore oil is pumped only when saw chain is rotating.

To disassemble pump, remove cam bolt (5), plug (8) and bushing (7). Plunger (6) can now be removed for inspection or renewal. Carefully inspect seal (2) and seal surface on worm gear (1). Note that slight wear on seal or worm gear may allow pump to draw air causing pump malfunction. It is recommended to renew seal (2) any time pump is disassembled.

REWIND STARTER. All models are equipped with the rewind starter shown in Fig. PK41. To disassemble starter, remove starter housing (5) from saw. Remove rope handle (4) and carefully allow rope to wind into starter, relieving tension on rewind spring (2). Starter drive (6) is a press fit in rope pulley (3). Remove rope and tap drive (6) out of pulley (3) toward flywheel side of housing (5) using a proper size punch and hammer.

Rewind spring (2) is retained in a plastic case. Install spring with open side of case toward starter cover (1). Install starter drive (6) with hole in drive aligned with hole in rope pulley. Wind rope onto rope pulley in a clockwise direction as viewed from flywheel side of pulley.

Rotate starter cover (1) clockwise before installing cover screws to engage rope pulley and preload rewind spring. Preload spring only enough to pull rope handle snug against housing. Rope pulley should be able to rotate an additional ½ turn clockwise with rope fully extended to prevent rewind spring breakage.

Refer to Fig. PK35 for view of starter pawls. Use a suitable thread locking solution on pawl bolts (6).

CHAIN BRAKE. Some models are equipped with a chain brake system designed to stop chain movement should kickback occur. Chain brake is activated when operator's hand strikes hand guard (12—Fig. PK39), tripping lever (16) and allowing spring (15) to draw brake band (14) tight around clutch drum (3). Pull back hand guard to reset mechanism.

Disassembly is evident after inspection of unit and referral to exploded view. Renew any component excessively worn or damaged. Chain brake should be clean and free of sawdust and dirt accumulation. No adjustment of chain brake is required.

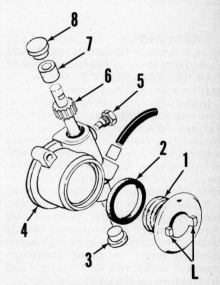

Fig. PK40—Exploded view of automatic oil pump assembly.

1. Worm gear	
2. Seal	6. Plunger
3. Plug	7. Bushing
4. Housing	8. Plug
5. Cam bolt	L. Drive lugs

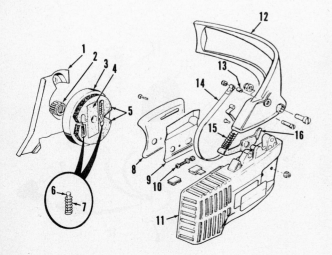

Fig. PK39—Exploded view of clutch and chain brake. Chain brake is optional on both models.

1. Plate
2. Needle bearing
3. Drum
4. Hub
5. Shoes
6. Spring guide
7. Spring
8. Inner guide plate
9. Outer guide plate
10. Bar adjusting screw
11. Cover
12. Hand guard
13. Spacer
14. Brake band
15. Spring
16. Lever

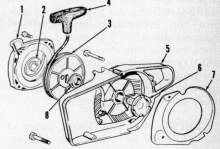

Fig. PK41—Exploded view of rewind starter assembly.

1. Starter cover	5. Housing
2. Rewind spring	6. Starter drive
3. Rope pulley	7. Baffle
4. Rope handle	8. Bushing

PROKUT

Model	Bore	Stroke	Displ.	Drive Type
70	51 mm	34.5 mm	70 cc	Direct
	(2.0 in.)	(1.36 in.)	(4.3 cu. in.)	
120	58 mm	45.5 mm	120 cc	Direct
	(2.28 in.)	(1.79 in.)	(7.3 cu. in.)	

MAINTENANCE

SPARK PLUG. Recommended spark plug for both models is Champion CJ7Y. Electrode gap should be 0.5 mm (0.020 in.).

CARBURETOR. All models are equipped with a Tillotson HS diaphragm carburetor. Refer to Tillotson section of CARBURETOR SERVICE section for service and exploded views.

Initial adjustment of low speed mixture screw is 1-7/8 turns open on Model 120 and 1-3/4 turns open on Model 70. Initial adjustment of high speed mixture screw is 7/8 turn open on Model 120 and ¾ turn open on Model 70. Final adjustment should be made with engine running at operating temperature. Adjust idle speed to just below clutch engagement speed. Adjust low speed mixture screw so engine will accelerate cleanly without hesitation. Adjust high speed mixture screw to obtain maximum speed of 10,300 rpm on Model 120 and 10,500 rpm on Model 70.

IGNITION. Model 70 manufactured prior to 1984 is equipped with a breaker-point ignition system. Model 120 and Model 70, manufactured after 1983, are equipped with a breakerless electronic ignition system.

BREAKER-POINT IGNITION. Breaker-point gap should be 0.45-0.50 mm (0.018-0.020 in.). Air gap between ignition coil lamination and flywheel magnets should be 0.45 mm (0.018 in.). Use a suitable thread locking solution on coil attaching screws. Ignition timing is not adjustable, however, breaker-point gap will affect timing. Be sure breaker-point gap is adjusted correctly.

ELECTRONIC IGNITION. Refer to Fig. PK51 for exploded view of electronic ignition system used on so equipped Model 70. Note that coil (8) is located outside of flywheel (1) while ignition module (13) is located behind flywheel (1). Model 120 is equipped with

the electronic ignition system shown in Fig. PK52. Ignition coil and all electronic circuitry are contained in a one-piece ignition module (13).

Except for faulty wiring or wiring connections, repair of ignition system malfunctions is accomplished by component renewal.

On Model 120, air gap between ignition module and flywheel magnets should be 0.65 mm (0.026 in.). Air gap between ignition coil and flywheel magnets on all other models should be 0.40 mm (0.016 in.). Use a suitable thread locking solution on module (or coil) attaching screws. Ignition timing is not adjustable on all models.

Starter pawl assemblies (2, 3, 4 and 7—Fig. PK51) can be removed to accommodate a suitable bolt-type puller to remove flywheel on all models. Use a suitable thread locking solution on bolts (2) when reassembling pawls. Tighten flywheel to 39.2 N·m (29 ft.-lbs.) on Model 120 and 28.4 N·m (21 ft.-lbs.) on Model 70.

LUBRICATION. The engine is lubricated by mixing oil with the fuel. Use a good quality oil designed for use in air-cooled two-stroke engines. Fuel:oil mixture should be a 16:1 ratio.

Use a separate container when mixing fuel and oil.

Models 70 and 120 are equipped with an automatic chain oil pump. Automatic oil pump output is only adjustable on Model 120. Refer to OIL PUMP under REPAIRS section for service and exploded views of manual and automatic oil pump assemblies. Use clean automotive oil for saw chain lubrication.

REPAIRS

CYLINDER, PISTON, PIN AND RINGS. Cylinder bore is chrome plated and should be renewed if cracking, scor-

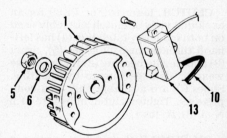

Fig. PK52—Exploded view of electronic ignition system used on Model 120. Refer to Fig. PK51 for component identification.

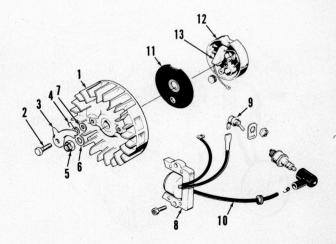

Fig. PK51—Exploded view of electronic ignition system used on Model 70 manufactured after 1983. Note two pawl assemblies (2, 3, 4 and 7) are used.

1. Flywheel
2. Bolt
3. Pawl
4. Spring
5. Nut
6. Washer
7. Washer
8. Ignition coil
9. Ignition switch
10. High tension lead
11. Cover
12. Module case
13. Module

ing or other damage is noted in cylinder bore. Note that cylinder used on Model 120 is equipped with decompression valve (28—Fig. PK54) to ease starting.

Piston and cylinder are marked during production to obtain desired piston-to-cylinder clearance of 0.02 mm (0.0008 in.). Original equipment piston and cylinder are marked "A." Factory renewal piston and cylinder assemblies are marked "B." Piston or cylinder marked "C" is 0.127 mm (0.005 in.) oversize. Piston or cylinder marked "D" is 0.127 mm (0.005 in.) undersize. Piston and cylinder markings should match, however, a new piston marked "B" can be installed into a used cylinder marked "A."

NOTE: Do not install a new piston marked "B" or "C" into a new cylinder marked "A."

Piston is equipped with two piston rings. Piston should be inspected and renewed if cracking or scoring is noted. Maximum allowable piston ring end gap is 1.0 mm (0.039 in.). Locating pins are present in ring grooves to prevent ring rotation. Be certain ring end gaps are properly positioned around locating pins when installing cylinder. Tighten cylinder screws to 11.8 N·m (9 ft.-lbs.) on all models.

On Model 70, piston pin (8—Fig. PK53) is a press fit in connecting rod small end.

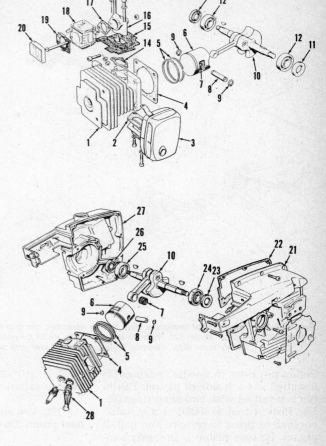

Fig. PK53—Exploded view of engine assembly, carburetor and related components used on Model 70. Two needle bearings (7) are used. Refer to text.

1. Cylinder
2. Gasket
3. Muffler
4. Gasket
5. Piston rings
6. Piston
7. Needle bearing
8. Piston pin
9. Snap ring
10. Crankshaft & connecting rod assy.
11. Seal
12. Main bearing
13. Seal
14. Gasket
15. Gasket
16. Intake manifold
17. Gasket
18. Carburetor
19. Plate
20. Screen

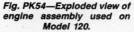

Fig. PK54—Exploded view of engine assembly used on Model 120.

1. Cylinder
4. Gasket
5. Piston rings
6. Piston
7. Needle bearing
8. Piston pin
9. Wire clip
10. Crankshaft & connecting rod assy.
21. Right crankcase half
22. Gasket
23. Seal
24. Main bearing
25. Main bearing
26. Seal
27. Left crankcase half
28. Decompression valve

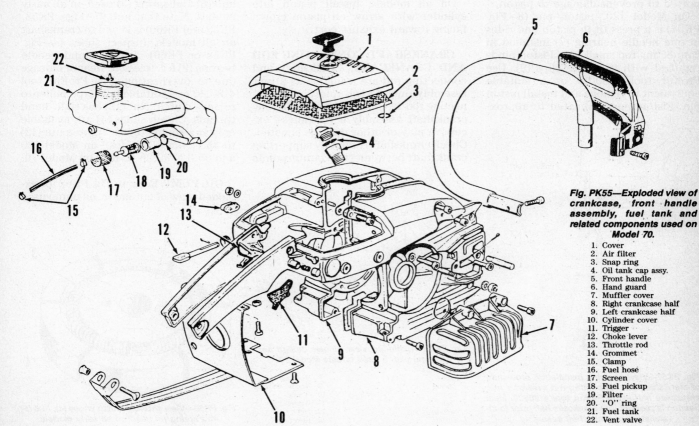
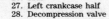

Fig. PK55—Exploded view of crankcase, front handle assembly, fuel tank and related components used on Model 70.

1. Cover
2. Air filter
3. Snap ring
4. Oil tank cap assy.
5. Front handle
6. Hand guard
7. Muffler cover
8. Right crankcase half
9. Left crankcase half
10. Cylinder cover
11. Trigger
12. Choke lever
13. Throttle rod
14. Grommet
15. Clamp
16. Fuel hose
17. Screen
18. Fuel pickup
19. Filter
20. "O" ring
21. Fuel tank
22. Vent valve

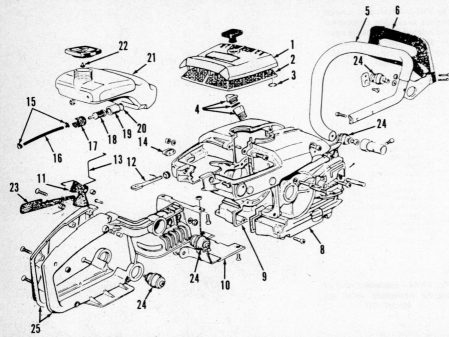

Fig. PK56—Exploded view of crankcase, front handle assembly, rear grip assembly, fuel tank and related components similar to Model 120. Refer to legend in Fig. PK55 for component identification except, safety lever (23), vibration isolator (24) and rear grip assembly (25).

such as a lathe. Make certain no damage is present in centering holes at each end of crankshaft. Renew crankshaft assembly if runout exceeds 0.08 mm (0.0031 in.).

NOTE: Crankshaft runout can be checked while still assembled in crankcase. Remove clutch and flywheel and mount dial indicators on each side of crankshaft as close to main bearings as possible. Measure runout while rotating crankshaft. Renew crankshaft assembly if runout exceeds 0.07 mm (0.0027 in.) when measured in this manner.

Crankshaft is supported with ball-type main bearings (12—Fig. PK53) or (24 and 25—Fig. PK54) at both ends. Main bearings are a press fit into crankcase halves. Use the proper size drivers to remove and install main bearings. Use ProKut tool 4180900 or a suitable equivalent to install crankshaft assembly into crankcase. Refer to Fig. PK57. Do not use gasket sealer on crankcase gasket. Tighten crankcase screws using a crisscross pattern to 7.8 N·m (69 in.-lbs.) on Model 120 and 7.3 N·m (65 in.-lbs.) on Model 70.

CLUTCH. Late Model 70 is equipped with the clutch assembly shown in Fig. PK58. Late Model 120 is equipped with the clutch assembly shown in Fig. PK60. Refer to Fig. PK59 for view of shoes (4), hub (5) and spring (3) used on all early models. Note that hub (5—Figs. PK58, PK59 and PK60) is keyed to crankshaft on all models. Inspect shoes (4—Fig. PK58 or PK60), drum (7) and needle bearing (9) for excessive wear or damage due to overheating. Use ProKut tool 4180110 or a suitable bolt-type puller to remove clutch. Nut (12) has right-hand threads. Clutch shoes (4) are available only as a complete set. Tighten nut (12) to 45.1 N·m (33 ft.-lbs.) on Model 120 and 35.3 N·m (26 ft.-lbs.) on Model 70.

OIL PUMP. Refer to Fig. PK62 for exploded view of automatic oil pump used

Piston pin rides in needle bearings (7) installed in each side of piston. Piston pin is retained with two snap rings (9). Use ProKut tool 4180020 or a suitable equivalent press to remove and install piston. Be sure piston is properly supported to prevent damage to piston.

On Model 120, piston pin (8—Fig. PK54) is a press fit in piston and rides in one needle bearing (7) installed in connecting rod small end. Piston pin is retained with two wire clips (9). Use ProKut tool 4180010 or a suitable equivalent to remove and install piston pin. Piston may be heated to approx-imately 110°-120° C (230°-248° F) to ease installation of piston pin.

NOTE: Use an oven or a hot oil bath to heat piston. Do not use an open flame.

On all models, install piston into cylinder with arrow on piston crown facing toward exhaust port.

CRANKSHAFT, CONNECTING ROD AND CRANKCASE. Crankshaft and connecting rod are available as a unit assembly only. Check rotation of connecting rod around crankpin and renew crankshaft assembly if roughness, excessive play or other damage is noted. Check crankshaft runout by supporting crankshaft between two counterpoints

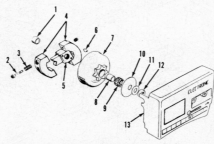

Fig. PK57—View showing installation procedure of crankshaft and connecting rod assembly into crankcase half using ProKut tool 4180900. Main bearing is pressed into crankcase half prior to installation of crankshaft assembly.

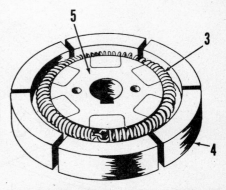

Fig. PK58—Exploded view of new design centrifugal clutch used on late Model 70.

1. Bushing
2. Screw
3. Spring
4. Shoes
5. Hub
6. Woodruff key
7. Drum
8. Bushing
9. Needle bearing
10. Washer
11. Washer
12. Nut
13. Cover

Fig. PK59—View showing clutch shoes (4), hub (5) and spring (3) used on all early models.

on Model 70. Oil is pumped by piston (5) which is rotated by drive plate (10). Drive plate is cycled up and down by plunger (15) which rides on cam of engine crankshaft. Piston (5) rotates one notch with each down stroke of drive plate (10). Spring (12) forces piston brake (13) against piston (5), preventing piston (5) from backing up during drive plate (10) return stroke.

Plunger (15) is 31 mm (1.22 in.) long when new. Renew plunger if worn shorter than 30.3 mm (1.193 in.). Renew drive plate (10) if wear at piston contact area exceeds 1.5 mm (0.059 in.) when compared with a new drive plate. Reservoir (R) should be filled with high temperature lithium base grease and capped with felt plug (20). Pump output is not adjustable.

Refer to Fig. PK63 for exploded view of adjustable automatic oil pump used on Model 120. Oil is pumped by piston

(5) which is rotated by worm gear (23) mounted on engine crankshaft. Pump output is regulated by turning adjusting lever (28). Renew piston and worm gear if excessive wear or damage is noted. Closely inspect seal (30) and seal surface on worm gear (23). Note that slight wear on seal or worm gear may allow pump to draw air causing pump malfunction. It is recommended to renew seal (30) any time pump is disassembled.

REWIND STARTER. To disassemble starter, remove rope handle (10—Fig. PK64) and carefully allow rope to wind into housing, relieving tension on rewind spring (5). Remove screw (9) and rope pulley (6) using caution not to dislodge rewind spring (5). If rewind spring (5) must be removed, use caution not to allow spring to uncoil uncontrolled.

Install rewind spring (5) into housing (2) in a clockwise direction starting with outer coil. Install rope onto rope pulley (6) in a clockwise direction as viewed from flywheel side of pulley. Rotate pulley (6) clockwise to apply tension on rewind spring. Apply only enough tension on rewind spring (5) to pull rope handle snug against housing. Rope pulley should be able to rotate an additional ½ turn with rope completely extended.

Refer to Fig. PK51 for exploded view of starter pawl assemblies. Use a suitable thread locking solution on pawl bolts (2).

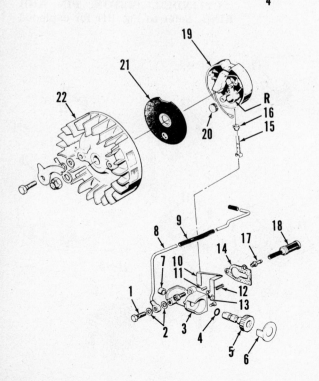

Fig. PK60—Exploded view of centrifugal clutch used on late Model 120.

2.	Screw
3.	Spring
4.	Shoes
5.	Hub
7.	Drum
9.	Needle bearing
10.	Washer
11.	Washer
12.	Nut
14.	Washer

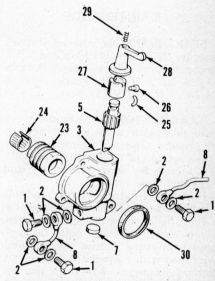

Fig. PK63—Exploded view of adjustable automatic oil pump used on Model 120.

1.	Banjo bolt	24.	Collar
2.	Washers	25.	Pin
3.	Pump body	26.	Pin
5.	Piston	27.	Bushing
7.	Plug	28.	Adjusting lever
8.	Tube	29.	Spring
23.	Worm gear	30.	Seal

Fig. PK62—Exploded view of automatic oil pump used on Model 70.

1.	Banjo bolt
2.	Washers
3.	Pump body
4.	"O" ring
5.	Piston
6.	Cover
7.	Plug
8.	Tube
9.	Hose
10.	Drive plate
11.	Pin
12.	Spring
13.	Piston brake
14.	Gasket
15.	Plunger
16.	Seal
17.	Fitting
18.	Oil pickup
19.	Module case
20.	Felt plug
21.	Cover
22.	Flywheel
R.	Reservoir

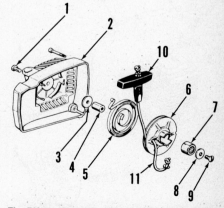

Fig. PK64—Exploded view of rewind starter used on Model 70. Model 120 is similar except, washer (11) is not used and shaft (4) is part of housing (2).

1.	Bolt		
2.	Housing		
3.	Washer	7.	Needle bearing
4.	Shaft	8.	Washer
5.	Rewind spring	9.	Screw
6.	Rope pulley	10.	Rope handle
		11.	Washer

REDMAX

KOMATSU ZENOAH AMERICA, INC.
4405 International Boulevard, Suite B-119
Norcross, GA 30093

Model	Bore	Stroke	Displ.	Drive Type
G300T, G300TS, G300AV, G300AVS	36 mm (1.42 in.)	28 mm (1.10 in.)	28.5 mm (1.74 cu. in.)	Direct

MAINTENANCE

SPARK PLUG. Recommended spark plug for all models is Champion CJ8Y. Recommended electrode gap is 0.6 mm (0.024 in.). Tighten spark plug to 14.7-17.6 N·m (11-13 ft.-lbs.).

CARBURETOR. All models are equipped with a Zama Z1 or Z1A diaphragm type carburetor. Refer to Zama section of CARBURETOR SERVICE section for service procedure and exploded view.

Initial adjustment for models equipped with a Zama Z1 carburetor is 1-1/8 turns open for low speed mixture screw and 1-3/8 turns open for high speed mixture screw. On models equipped with a Zama Z1A carburetor, initial adjustment is 1-1/4 turns open for low and high speed mixture screws.

Final adjustment should be made with engine running at operating temperature. Adjust low speed mixture so engine will accelerate cleanly without hesitation. Adjust high speed mixture to obtain optimum full throttle performance under cutting load. Adjust idle speed so engine operates at 2,700-3,100 rpm or just below clutch engagement speed.

IGNITION. All models are equipped with an electronic capacitor discharge ignition system. Ignition coil and all electronic circuitry are contained in a one-piece ignition module (3—Fig. R10) located outside of flywheel. Except for faulty wiring or connections, repair of ignition system malfunction is accomplished by component renewal. Ignition timing is not adjustable. Air gap between ignition module (3) and flywheel magnets (2) should be 0.3-0.4 mm (0.012-0.016 in.). If removed, tighten flywheel nut to 14.7-16.7 N·m (11-12 ft.-lbs.).

LUBRICATION. The engine is lubricated by mixing oil with the fuel. Recommended oil is Redmax two-stroke engine oil. Fuel and oil mixture should be a 40:1 ratio when using the recommended oil. If Redmax two-stroke engine oil is not available, a good quality oil designed for use in air-cooled two-stroke engines may be used when mixed at a 25:1 ratio.

All models are equipped with an automatic chain oil pump. Pump output is not adjustable. Refer to OIL PUMP in REPAIRS section for service and exploded views.

Redmax genuine chain oil is recommended for saw chain lubrication. If Redmax genuine chain oil is not available, clean SAE 10W-30 automotive oil may be used.

REPAIRS

CYLINDER, PISTON, PIN AND RING. Refer to Fig. R11 for exploded

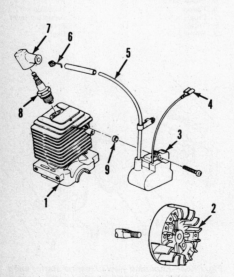

Fig. R10—Exploded view of ignition system used on all models.

1. Cylinder
2. Flywheel
3. Ignition module
4. Primary ignition wire
5. High tension lead
6. Spring connector
7. Boot
8. Spark plug

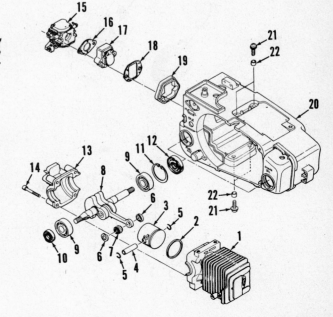

Fig. R11—Exploded view of engine assembly, engine case and related components.

1. Cylinder
2. Piston ring
3. Piston
4. Piston pin
5. Clip
6. Washer
7. Needle bearing
8. Crankshaft & connecting rod assy.
9. Main bearing
10. Seal
11. Snap ring
12. Seal
13. Crankcase
14. Screw
15. Carburetor
16. Gasket
17. Reed valve assy.
18. Gasket
19. Seal
20. Engine case
21. Screw
22. Spacer

view of engine assembly. After removing mounting screws, tap cylinder (1) and crankcase (13) with a soft-faced mallet to split crankcase from cylinder. Take care not to damage mating surfaces. Note that cylinder is also part of engine crankcase. Inspect cylinder bore and renew cylinder if cracking, flaking or other damage is noted in cylinder bore plating. Maximum cylinder bore diameter is 36.05 mm (1.419 in.). Piston is equipped with one piston ring (2). Minimum piston diameter is 35.7 mm (1.40) and maximum ring end gap is 0.7 mm (0.027 in.). Piston pin (4) is supported in connecting rod small end by needle bearing (7) and is retained in piston pin bore with two wire clips (5). Note location of washers (6). Closed end of piston pin (4) must be installed facing exhaust port. Piston may be installed in either direction.

CRANKSHAFT AND CONNECTING ROD.
Crankshaft is loose in crankcase with cylinder removed. Crankshaft and connecting rod (8—Fig. R11) are a unit assembly and supported at both ends with ball type main bearings (9). Rotate connecting rod around crankpin and renew assembly if roughness, excessive play or other damage is noted.

Check crankshaft runout by supporting crankshaft at points (A—Fig. R-12) and measuring at points (B). Maximum crankshaft runout should not exceed 0.07 mm (0.0027 in.).

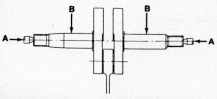

Fig. R12—Measure crankshaft runout by supporting crankshaft at points (A). Runout measured at points (B) should not exceed 0.07 mm (0.0027 in).

Fig. R13—View of reed valve assembly. Refer to text for service procedures.

Main bearings (9—Fig. R11) and seals (10 and 12) should be installed on crankshaft when reassembling cylinder and crankcase. Clutch side seal (12) should be against snap ring (11). Starter side seal (10) should be installed with outer face of seal flush with outer face of cylinder and crankcase. Use a suitable form-in-place gasket compound on mating surfaces of cylinder and crankcase. Tighten crankcase screws (14) to 4.9-7.8 N·m (43-69 in.-lbs.).

Install engine assembly into engine case (20). Use a suitable thread locking solution on screws (21) and tighten screws to 2.9-3.9 N·m (26-35 in.-lbs.).

REED VALVE.
The reed valve assembly (17—Fig. R11) should be inspected whenever the carburetor is removed. Reed petal (P—Fig. R13) should seat very lightly against insulator block (B) throughout its entire length with the least possible tension. Tip of reed petal must not stand open more than 0.7 mm (0.027 in.). Reed stop (S) opening should be 5.3-5.7 mm (0.209-0.224 in.). Adjust reed stop opening by bending reed stop (S).

CLUTCH.
All models are equipped with the two-shoe centrifugal clutch shown in Fig. R14. Use Redmax tool 3330-97110 to remove and install clutch. Clutch hub (3) has left-hand threads. Shoes (1) should be renewed in sets to prevent an unbalanced condition. Clutch springs (2) should be renewed if stretched, broken or damaged or if clutch engagement speed is below 4,200 rpm. Springs should be renewed in pairs. Install shoes with recess in shoes facing outward. Make certain oil pump drive plate (7) properly engages clutch drum (5) and notches in oil pump worm gear (1—Fig. R15 or R16). Tighten clutch hub to 21.6-25.5 N·m (16-19 ft.-lbs.).

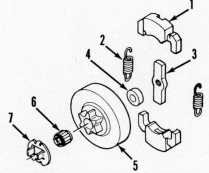

Fig. R14—Exploded view of clutch assembly used on all models.

1. Shoe	5. Drum	
2. Spring	6. Needle bearing	
3. Hub	7. Oil pump plate	
4. Spacer		

OIL PUMP.
All models are equipped with a nonadjustable automatic chain oil pump. Refer to Fig. R15 or R16 for views of pump. Oil pump (2—Fig. R15) is a unit assembly and cannot be disassembled. Oil pump drive plate (7—Fig. R14) is driven by clutch drum (5) and engages worm gear (1—Fig. R15 and R16). Worm gear (1) rotates plunger (4—Fig. R16). Oil is pumped by plunger (4) as it reciprocates due to cam pin (3) riding in oblique groove in end of plunger.

Apply a suitable grease on worm gear prior to reassembly. Prime oil pump by

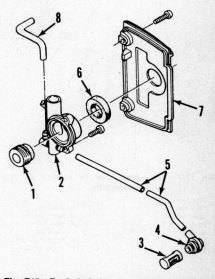

Fig. R15—Exploded view of automatic oil pump.

1. Worm gear	5. Suction line
2. Pump assy.	6. Seal
3. Filter	7. Cover
4. Grommet	8. Discharge

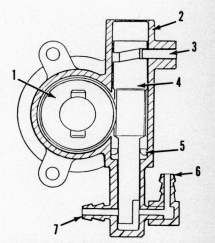

Fig. R16—Cross-sectional view of automatic oil pump.

1. Worm gear	5. Seal
2. Housing	6. Discharge
3. Cam pin	7. Inlet port
4. Plunger	

adding clean oil to inlet port (7) before attaching suction line to suction port. Be certain oil pump drive plate properly engages worm gear before installing clutch.

REWIND STARTER. All models are equipped with the rewind starter shown in Fig. R17. To disassemble starter, remove starter housing (11), rope handle (3) and slowly allow rope to wind into starter housing, relieving tension on rewind spring (10). Remove screw (7)

and lift out rope pulley (9) being careful not to dislodge rewind spring (10). If rewind spring must be removed, use caution not to allow spring to uncoil uncontrolled. Flywheel (1) must be removed to disassemble pawl assembly (4 and 5). Note location of "E" ring on back side of flywheel. Renew any components found to be excessively worn or damaged. Tighten flywheel nut to 14.7-16.7 N·m (11-12 ft.-lbs.).

Lightly lubricate rewind spring (10) and bore of rope pulley (9) with a suitable low temperature grease prior to installing rewind spring into starter housing. Install rope pulley with rope attached into housing. Run rope through rope guide (12) and install handle (3). Place rope into notch in rope pulley and rotate pulley five turns clockwise to preload rewind spring. Carefully allow rewind rope onto pulley. If rewind tension is correct, rope pulley will be able to rotate at least one turn further with

rope fully extended and rope handle will be held against housing by spring tension in released position.

CHAIN BRAKE. Models G300TS and G300AVS are equipped with a chain brake system designed to quickly stop chain movement should kickback occur. Chain brake is activated when operator's hand strikes hand guard (1—Fig. R18), lifting latch (3) thereby allowing spring (4) to draw brake band (6) tight around drum. Pull back hand guard to reset mechanism.

Disassembly for inspection or repair is evident after referral to exploded view and inspection of unit. Renew any component found to be excessively worn or damaged. Chain brake mechanism should be clean and free of sawdust and dirt accumulation. Lightly lubricate all moving parts and pivot points. No adjustment of chain brake system is required.

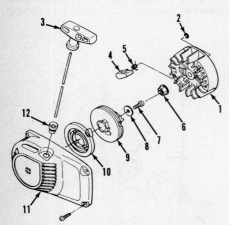

Fig. R17—Exploded view of rewind starter assembly.

1. Flywheel
2. "E" ring
3. Rope handle
4. Pawl
5. Spring
6. Nut
7. Screw
8. Washer
9. Rope pulley
10. Rewind spring & case assy.
11. Starter housing
12. Rope guide

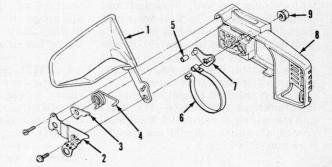

Fig. R18—Exploded view of chain brake system used on Models G3300TS and G300AVS.

1. Hand guard & lever assy.
2. Bracket
3. Latch
4. Spring
5. Roller
6. Brake band
7. Lever
8. Cover
9. Nut

REDMAX

Model	Bore	Stroke	Displ.	Drive Type
G561AV, G561AVS, G561AVSH	44 mm (1.73 in.)	35 mm (1.38 in.)	53.2 cc (3.25 cu. in.)	Direct
G621AV, G621AVS, G621AVSH	47.5 mm (1.87 in.)	35 mm (1.38 in.)	62.0 cc (3.78 cu. in.)	Direct

MAINTENANCE

SPARK PLUG. Recommended spark plug for all models is Champion CJ7Y or RCJ7Y. Spark plug electrode gap should be 0.60-0.70 mm (0.024-0.027 in.)

CARBURETOR. All models are equipped with a Walbro HDA diaphragm type carburetor. Refer to Walbro section of CARBURETOR SERVICE section for service procedure and exploded view.

Initial adjustment of the low speed mixture screw is 1-1/4 to 1-1/2 turns open from a lightly seated position. Initial adjustment of the high speed mixture screw is 1-1/4 to 1-3/4 turns open from a lightly seated position.

Make final adjustment with engine running at operating temperature. Adjust low speed mixture screw to obtain maximum idle speed. Once maximum idle speed is obtained, open low speed mixture screw an additional ¼ turn. Adjust idle speed screw so engine operates at 2,400-2,600 rpm. Repeat this procedure until best possible idling condition is achieved. A tachometer should be used to make final adjustment of high speed mixture to prevent exceeding maximum allowable speed. Adjust high speed mixture to obtain clean acceleration and optimum full throttle performance under cutting load. Maximum allowable no-load speed is 12,000 rpm for Models G561AV, G561AVS and G561AVSH and 12,500 rpm for all other models. If necessary, readjust idle speed to 2,400-2,600 rpm.

IGNITION. All models are equipped with a breakerless electronic ignition system. Refer to Fig. R28. Except for faulty wiring and connections, repair of ignition system malfunction is accomplished by component renewal.

Ignition module can be checked with an ohmmeter. Module primary resistance should be approximately 0.72-0.98 ohm. Coil secondary resistance should be approximately 5,490-6,710 ohms. Ignition timing is not adjustable. Air gap between module lamination and flywheel magnets should be 0.4-0.5 mm

(0.016-0.020 in). Flywheel nut should be tightened to 14.7-19.6 N·m (11-14 ft.-lbs.).

LUBRICATION. The engine is lubricated by mixing oil with the fuel. Recommended oil is Redmax two-stroke engine oil mixed at a 40:1 ratio. If Redmax two-stroke engine oil is not available, a good quality oil designed for use in air-cooled two-stroke engines may be used when mixed at a 25:1 ratio. Use a separate container when mixing oil and fuel.

All models are equipped with the automatic chain oil pump shown in Fig. R29. Oil pump output is adjusted by rotating adjusting shaft (8). Clockwise rotation of shaft decreases pump output.

Redmax genuine chain oil is recommended for saw chain lubrication. If Redmax genuine chain oil or suitable equivalent is not available, clean SAE 10W-30 automotive oil may be used.

REPAIRS

CYLINDER, PISTON, PIN AND RINGS. Cylinder (1—Fig. R30) bore is chrome plated and should be renewed if cracking, flaking or other damage to

cylinder bore is noted. Oversize piston and rings are not available. Piston (4) is equipped with two piston rings (3). Maximum ring end gap is 0.6 mm (0.024 in.) on 561 series engines and 0.7 mm (0.028 in.) on 621 series engines. Maximum allowable piston ring side clearance is 0.13 mm (0.005 in.) for all models. Locating pins are present in ring grooves to prevent ring rotation. Make certain ring end gaps are properly positioned around locating pins before installing cylinder. Piston pin (5) rides in needle bearing (7) and is retained in position with two wire clips (6). Once removed, wire clips should not be reused. New wire clips should be installed with end gaps facing upward. It should be possible to push out piston pin (5) by hand. If pin is stuck, tap out with a suitable hammer and driver while properly supporting piston to prevent damage to connecting rod. Install piston with arrow on piston crown toward exhaust port. Note location of thrust washers (8) when installing piston. Tighten cylinder screws to 6.9-8.8 N·m (61-78 in.-lbs.).

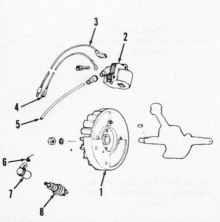

Fig. R28—Exploded view of ignition system used on all models.
1. Flywheel
2. Ignition module
3. Primary lead
4. Ground lead
5. High tension lead
6. Connector
7. Boot
8. Spark plug

Fig. R29—Exploded view of automatic oil pump used on all models.
1. Pump assy.
2. Pickup filter
3. Clip
4. Discharge hose
5. Suction hose
6. Clip
7. "O" ring
8. Adjusting shaft
9. Connector
10. Grommet
11. Worm gear
12. Gasket

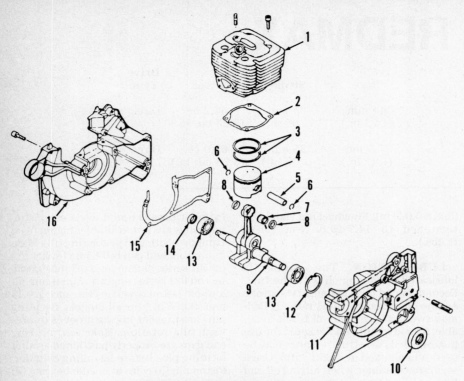

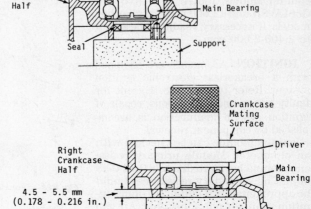

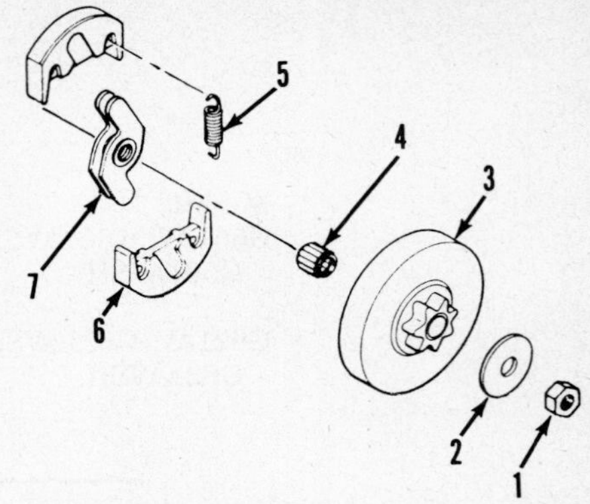

*Fig. R34—Exploded view of two-shoe clutch
assembly used on models so equipped.*

1. Nut
2. Washer
3. Drum
4. Needle bearing
5. Spring
6. Shoe
7. Hub

Fig. R30—Exploded view of engine assembly.

1. Cylinder
2. Gasket
3. Piston rings
4. Piston
5. Piston pin
6. Wire clip
7. Needle bearing
8. Thrust washer
9. Crankshaft &
   connecting rod assy.
10. Seal
11. Right crankcase half
12. Snap ring
13. Main bearing
14. Seal
15. Gasket
16. Left crankcase half

right side crankcase seal (10) into bearing bore until it contacts snap ring (12).
Make certain oil suction hose is properly installed before reassembling crankcase. Tighten crankcase screws to
6.9-9.3 N·m (61-82 in.-lbs). Make certain
crankshaft is centered in crankcase and
rotates freely.

CLUTCH. A two-shoe (Fig. R34) and
a three-shoe (Fig. R35) clutch have been
used. Clutch nut and hub have left-hand
threads on all models. Shoes and hub are
a unit assembly on all models and are
not available separately. Clutch drum
rides on a needle roller bearing. Shoes,
drum and needle bearing should be inspected for excessive wear or damage
due to overheating. Renew excessively
worn or damaged components. Tighten
clutch hub to 24.5-29.4 N·m (18-22 ft.-
lbs.) on all models. Tighten clutch nut
to 14.7-19.6 N·m (11-14 ft.-lbs.) on all

**CRANKSHAFT, CONNECTING ROD
AND CRANKCASE.** Crankcase halves
(11 and 16—Fig. R30) must be split to
remove crankshaft (9). Use a soft-
faced mallet to tap crankcase halves
apart. Do not damage crankcase mating surfaces. Crankshaft and connecting rod are a unit assembly and are
not available separately. Rotate connecting rod around crankpin and renew
assembly if roughness, excessive play or
other damage is noted. Crankshaft is
supported at both ends with ball type
main bearings (13).

Check crankshaft runout by supporting crankshaft at points (A—Fig. R31)
and measuring at points (B). Maximum
allowable runout is 0.1 mm (0.004 in.).

Use a press and the proper size drivers
and supports when removing and installing main bearings (13—Fig. R30) and
seals (10 and 14). Install left side main

bearing 14.8-15.0 mm (0.583-0.591 in.)
below crankcase mating surface. Refer
to Fig. R32. Install right side main bearing 4.5-5.5 mm (0.178-0.216 in.) from
outer surface of bearing bore. Refer to
Fig. R33. Install left side crankcase seal
(14—Fig. R30) 3.5 mm (0.138 in.) below
outer surface of crankcase bore. Press

*Fig. R32—View showing in-
stallation of left side main
bearing.*

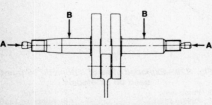

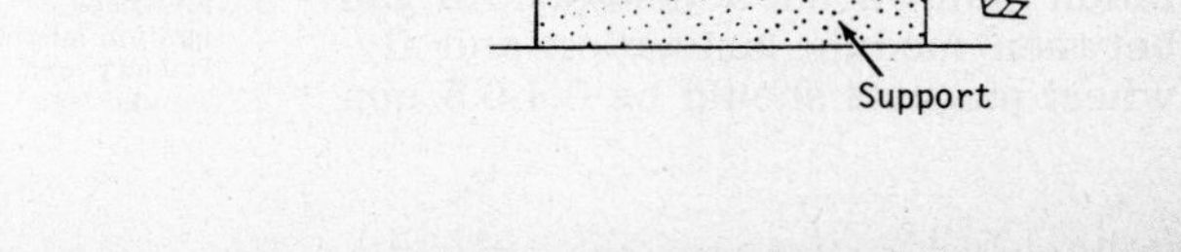

*Fig. R31—Measure crankshaft runout by support-
ing crankshaft at points (A). Runout measured at
points (B) should not exceed 0.1 mm (0.004 in.).*

*Fig. R33—View showing in-
stallation of right side main
bearing.*

models. Use Redmax tool 3356-96210 to remove and install two-shoe clutch assemblies and Redmax tool 2616-96210 to remove and install three-shoe clutch assemblies.

OIL PUMP. All models are equipped with an adjustable automatic chain oil pump. Oil pump output is adjusted by rotating adjusting shaft (8—Fig. R29). Pump is driven by worm gear (11) located on engine crankshaft. Inspect pump plunger and worm gear for excessive wear or damage. Pump plunger is not available separately from pump body. Inspect suction and discharge hoses and renew if cracking or other damage is noted. Apply a suitable grease on pump plunger upon reassembly. Oil tank vent valve is located behind ignition module and is retained in tank with a snap ring.

REWIND STARTER. All models are equipped with the rewind starter shown in Fig. R36. To disassemble starter, remove rope handle (14) and carefully allow rope to wind into starter housing (12) relieving tension on rewind spring (11). Remove screw (7) and lift out rope pulley (9) noting how pulley engages inner coil of rewind spring. If rewind spring must be removed, use caution not to allow spring to uncoil uncontrolled. Renew any component found to be excessively worn or damaged.

Lightly lubricate rewind spring and rope pulley shaft in starter housing with a suitable low temperature grease. Wind rewind spring into spring case (10) in a counterclockwise direction starting with outer coil as viewed from spring side of case. Assemble rope pulley to rewind spring case making certain hook on inner coil of rewind spring properly engages slot in rope pulley. Install rope pulley with rewind spring and case into starter housing and install washer (8) and screw (7). Make sure pulley turns freely. Pass rope through rope guide

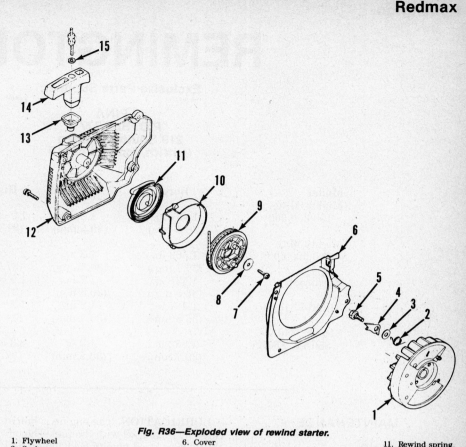

Fig. R36—Exploded view of rewind starter.

1. Flywheel	6. Cover	11. Rewind spring
2. Spring	7. Screw	12. Starter housing
3. Washer	8. Washer	13. Rope guide
4. Pawl	9. Rope pulley	14. Rope handle
5. Pivot screw	10. Rewind spring case	15. Washer

(13). Place rope into notch in outer edge of rope pulley and rotate pulley clockwise until spring is coil bound. Back off pulley one-full turn and carefully allow pulley to rewind rope onto pulley. If spring tension is correct, rope pulley should be able to rotate 1-1/2 to 2 turns clockwise with rope fully extended.

CHAIN BRAKE. Models G561AVS, G561AVSH, G621AVS and G621AVSH are equipped with a chain brake system designed to quickly stop chain movement should kickback occur. Chain brake is activated when operator's hand strikes hand guard (1—Fig. R37). For-

ward movement of brake lever (5) causes stopper (4) to disengage arm (11) allowing spring (10) to draw brake band (9) tight around clutch drum. Pull back hand guard to reset mechanism.

Disassembly for inspection or repair is evident after referral to exploded view and inspection of unit. Renew any component found to be excessively worn or damaged. Lightly lubricate pivot points with a suitable grease. No adjustment of chain brake system is required.

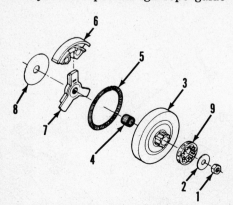

Fig. R35—Exploded view of three-shoe clutch assembly used on models so equipped. Refer to Fig. R34 for component identification except washer (8) and sprocket (9).

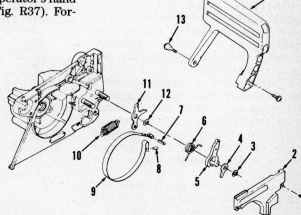

Fig. R37—Exploded view of chain brake system.

1. Hand guard
2. Cover
3. "E" ring
4. Stopper
5. Lever
6. Spring
7. Pin
8. Roller
9. Brake band
10. Spring
11. Arm
12. "E" ring
13. Shoulder screw

REMINGTON

Exclusive Parts Supplier:

ALPINA
P.O. Box 777
219 South Lindberg
Griffith, Indiana 46319

Model	Bore	Stroke	Displ.	Drive Type
Mighty Mite 100,200,300	1.437 in. (36.5 mm)	1.2 in. (30.5 mm)	1.9 cu. in. (31.1 cc)	Direct
Mighty Mite 400,500,600	1.562 in. (39.7 mm)	1.2 in. (30.5 mm)	2.3 cu. in. (37.7 cc)	Direct
Yardmaster	1.437 in. (36.5 mm)	1.2 in. (30.5 mm)	1.9 cu. in. (31.1 cc)	Direct
812,814,816	1.437 in. (36.5 mm)	1.2 in. (30.5 mm)	1.9 cu. in. (31.1 cc)	Direct
816AV, 840AV, 850AV, 860AV	1.562 in. (39.7 mm)	1.2 in. (30.5 mm)	2.3 cu. in. (37.7 cc)	Direct

MAINTENANCE

SPARK PLUG. Recommended spark plug for all models is Champion CJ7Y. Spark plug electrode gap should be 0.025 inch (0.63 mm).

CARBURETOR. All models are equipped with a Walbro WA diaphragm carburetor. Refer to CARBURETOR SERVICE section for carburetor servicing.

High speed mixture is not adjustable. Initial setting of idle mixture screw is 1¼ turns open. Adjust idle speed screw so engine idles just below clutch engagement speed.

If intake spacer between carburetor and cylinder is removed, be sure to install spacer so larger opening is nearest cylinder.

IGNITION. Models 812, 814, 816, 816AV, 840AV, 850AV, 860AV and all other later production models, are equipped with a breakerless capacitor discharge ignition system. Ignition timing is not adjustable.

All other models are equipped with a conventional flywheel magneto ignition system having breaker points located under the flywheel. Breaker-point gap should be 0.015 inch (0.38 mm). Breaker points, condenser, felt wiper, breaker box and cover are available only as a unit assembly.

On all models, air gap between coil legs and flywheel magnets should be 0.010 inch (0.25 mm).

LUBRICATION. The engine is lubricated by mixing oil with the fuel. The oil should be a good quality SAE 30 oil designed for use in chain saw or air-cooled two-stroke engines. Fuel: oil ratio is 16:1 for all engines.

An automatic nonadjustable oil pump is used on all models. Recommended chain oil is SAE 20 for warm climate or SAE 10 for winter usage.

REPAIRS

CYLINDER, PISTON, PIN AND RINGS. To remove cylinder, remove air filter and unscrew seven screws securing housing halves. Separate halves sufficiently to disconnect ignition switch wires then remove left housing half. Remove flywheel and ignition coil and disconnect oil line from housing. Detach throttle and oil control linkage and remove chain brake handle. Unscrew two nuts securing right housing half to engine and remove housing half. Partially disassemble chain brake for access to adjacent cylinder screw. Unscrew cylinder screws and carefully remove cylinder.

NOTE: Piston aligns connecting rod on rod bearing rollers. Excessive piston movement during or after cylinder removal may allow connecting rod bearing rollers to fall off crankpin.

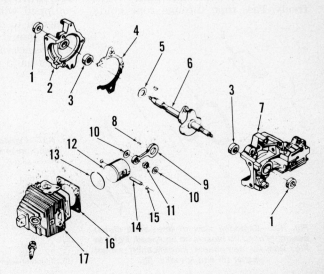

Fig. RE10 — Exploded view of engine.
1. Seal
2. Crankcase half (L.H.)
3. Bearing
4. Gasket
5. Thrust washer
6. Crankshaft
7. Crankcase half (R.H.)
8. Bearing rollers (12)
9. Connecting rod
10. Thrust washers
11. Bearing rollers (18)
12. Piston
13. Piston ring
14. Piston pin
15. Pin retainers
16. Gasket
17. Cylinder

Reverse disassembly to install cylinder and refer to CHAIN BRAKE section for adjustment.

Cylinder is chrome plated and oversize pistons and rings are not available. Inspect cylinder bore for scoring or excessive wear which may expose soft base metal underneath chrome.

Eighteen loose roller bearings are used in small end of connecting rod. Hold bearing rollers in place with grease and place a thrust washer on each side of rod before installing piston. Install piston so "EXH' on piston crown is toward exhaust port and with closed end of piston pin toward exhaust port. Tighten cylinder mounting screws to 90-115 in.-lbs (10.2-13.0 N·m).

CONNECTING ROD, CRANKSHAFT AND CRANKCASE.
The connecting rod is one-piece type which may be removed from crankshaft after crankcase halves are separated.

Inspect all components for damage and excessive wear. Check crankshaft runout and renew if bent. Note thrust washer (5–Fig. RE10) between crankshaft arm and main bearing. When installing connecting rod, hold 12 bearing rollers on crankpin with grease then direct connecting rod over flywheel end of crankshaft and onto bearing rollers. Install crankshaft seals with numbered or lettered side toward crankshaft end. Tighten crankcase screws to 110-135 in.-lbs (12.4-15.2 N·m).

If removed, install antivibration shock mounts on crankcase with stud end marked "-" threaded into crankcase.

CLUTCH. All models are equipped with a two-shoe centrifugal type clutch. The clutch hub has left-hand threads. Clutch bearing (6–Fig. RE11) should be inspected and renewed if damaged. Inspect shoes and drum for signs of excessive heat.

OIL PUMP. An automatic oil pump is used on all models. Crankcase pulsations are used to pressurize oil tank. Oil flow is regulated by throttle. On early models, the oil outlet tube is pinched by a rod mechanism connected to the throttle while on later models the throttle operates a shut-off valve.

A one-way valve (6–Fig. RE12) attached to the oil tank prevents oil from entering engine crankcase. Valve can be checked by pressurizing oil tank to 5 psi (34.5 kPa) with throttle closed. If tank will not hold pressure, be sure oil outlet tube is closed before suspecting one-way valve.

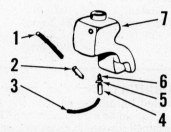

Fig. RE12 — Exploded view of oil tank assembly.

1. Oil line
2. Oil pickup
3. Crankcase pressure line
4. Fitting
5. "O" ring
6. Valve
7. Oil tank

REWIND STARTER. Refer to Fig. RE13 for an exploded view of rewind starter. To disassemble starter, remove air filter and unscrew seven screws securing housing halves. Separate halves sufficiently to disconnect ignition switch wires then remove left housing half. Remove rope handle and allow rope to wind into starter. Unscrew rope pulley retaining screw (5) and carefully remove rope pulley (4). If rewind spring (2) must be removed, care should be used to prevent personal injury due to uncontrolled uncoiling of spring.

Install rewind spring (2) with coils wrapped in clockwise direction from outer spring end. Wrap rope around rope pulley in clockwise direction as viewed with pulley installed in left housing half. Rewind spring should be preloaded by turning rope pulley three turns clockwise before passing rope through rope outlet in housing.

CHAIN BRAKE. Some models are equipped with the chain brake shown in Fig. RE14. To adjust chain brake, pull chain brake to rearmost position (toward engine) and check chain for ease of movement. If chain does not move freely, turn brake rod end (R–Fig. RE14) counterclockwise so clutch drum can rotate freely. Make sure chain tension is adjusted correctly. Turn brake rod end (R) clockwise so it is difficult to pull chain around bar then turn brake rod end counterclockwise to point just after chain will move freely around bar.

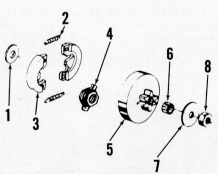

Fig. RE11 — Exploded view of clutch. Clutch hub (4) has left-hand threads.

1. Washer
2. Springs
3. Clutch shoes
4. Hub
5. Clutch drum
6. Bearing
7. Washer
8. Nut

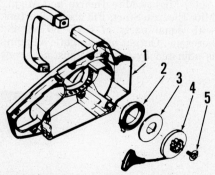

Fig. RE13 — Exploded view of rewind starter.

1. Housing half
2. Rewind spring
3. Spring cover
4. Rope pulley
5. Screw

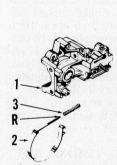

Fig. RE14 — View of chain brake assembly.

1. Crankcase half (R.H.)
2. Brake band & rod
3. Spring
4. Spring
5. Pivot pin
6. Latch
7. Shoulder bolt
8. Actuator
9. Chain brake arm

REMINGTON

Model	Bore	Stroke	Displ.	Drive Type
Mighty Mite Auto	1.5 in. (38.1 mm)	1.2 in. (30.5 mm)	2.1 cu. in. (34.4 cc)	Direct
Mighty Mite Bantam	1.5 in. (38.1 mm)	1.2 in. (30.5 mm)	2.1 cu. in. (34.4 cc)	Direct
Mighty Mite Deluxe	1.5 in. (38.1 mm)	1.2 in. (30.5 mm)	2.1 cu. in. (34.4 cc)	Direct
Mighty Mite Electric Start	1.5 in. (38.1 mm)	1.2 in. (30.5 mm)	2.1 cu. in. (34.4 cc)	Direct
SL-4A	1.81 in. (46.0 mm)	1.38 in. (35.1 mm)	3.6 cu. in. (59.0 cc)	Direct
SL-7A	2.25 in. (57.1 mm)	1.44 in. (36.6 mm)	5.7 cu. in. (93.4 cc)	Direct
SL-9, SL-9A	1.69 in. (42.9 mm)	1.25 in. (31.7 mm)	2.8 cu. in. (45.9 cc)	Direct
SL-11, SL-11A	1.91 in. (48.5 mm)	1.38 in. (35.1 mm)	4.0 cu. in. (65.5 cc)	Direct
SL-14A	1.69 in. (42.9 mm)	1.25 in. (31.7 mm)	2.8 cu. in. (45.9 cc)	Direct
SL-16A	1.69 in. (42.9 mm)	1.25 in. (31.7 mm)	2.8 cu. in. (45.9 cc)	Direct
SL-55A	2.06 in. (52.3 mm)	1.5 in. (38.1 mm)	5.0 cu. in. (81.9 cc)	Direct

MAINTENANCE

SPARK PLUG. Recommended spark plug for all models is Champion CJ6. Spark plug electrode gap should be 0.025 inch (0.63 mm).

CARBURETOR. All models are equipped with a Tillotson Model HS or HU diaphragm carburetor. Initial adjustment of idle and high speed adjusting needles is one turn open. High speed adjusting screw should be adjusted so optimum performance is obtained when saw is under cutting load. High speed screw should not be adjusted too lean as engine may be damaged.

Refer to Tillotson section of CARBURETOR SERVICE section for carburetor operation and overhaul.

MAGNETO AND TIMING. A flywheel magneto is used on all models. Ignition timing is fixed at 30 degrees BTDC and is nonadjustable. Breaker point gap should be 0.015 inch (0.38 mm). Be sure breaker-point gap is correct as incorrect gap setting will affect ignition timing.

Air gap setting on all Mighty Mite models should be 0.010 inch (0.25 mm). To adjust air gap, loosen coil lamination mounting screws and insert 0.010 inch (0.25 mm) thick shim or feeler gage between lamination and flywheel. Tighten mounting screws when correct gap is obtained.

LUBRICATION. The engine is lubricated by mixing oil with the fuel. The oil should be a good quality SAE 30 oil designed for use in chain saw or air-cooled two-stroke engines. Fuel: oil ratio is 16:1 for all engines.

A manual chain oiler is used on all models. An automatic chain oiler is also used on Models SL-4A, SL-7A, SL-9A, SL-11A, SL-14A, SL-16A, Mighty Mite Auto, Mighty Mite Deluxe and Mighty Mite Electric Start. Fill chain oiler tank with equal parts of SAE 30 oil and kerosene. Output of automatic oil pump is adjusted by turning adjusting screw located near trigger or near front handle. Turning screw clockwise decreases oil flow while turning the screw counterclockwise will increase oil flow. Oil pump screen or filter on automatic oil pump models should be removed and cleaned periodically.

CARBON. Carbon deposits should be removed from muffler and exhaust ports at regular intervals. Be careful not to damage cylinder when scraping carbon. Do not allow loosened carbon into cylinder.

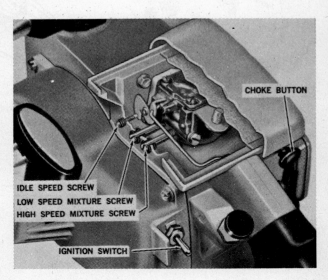

Fig. RE30 — View showing location of carburetor adjusting screws on most models except Mighty Mite models.

CHOKE BUTTON

IDLE SPEED SCREW
LOW SPEED MIXTURE SCREW
HIGH SPEED MIXTURE SCREW

IGNITION SWITCH

REPAIRS

CYLINDER, PISTON, PIN AND RINGS.

To remove cylinder on all Mighty Mite models, remove chain guard, starter housing and carburetor cover. Disconnect choke linkage and compression release rod, if so equipped. Remove carburetor and disconnect throttle linkage and fuel line. Remove rear handle assembly, unscrew cylinder base screws and remove cylinder. Remove muffler from cylinder.

To remove cylinder on all other models, remove starter housing, flywheel and stator. Remove carburetor, disconnect oil lines and detach rear handle cover. Remove compression release rod on models so equipped and remove rear handle assembly. Unscrew cylinder base nuts and remove cylinder.

Cylinder is chrome plated and oversize pistons and rings are not available. Inspect cylinder bore for scoring or excessive wear which may expose soft base metal underneath chrome.

Piston rings on all models except late Mighty Mite models are pinned to prevent rotation. Late Mighty Mite models are equipped with a single piston ring which is not pinned. Pinned and unpinned rings may not be interchanged. Piston rings on all models must be installed with inner bevel toward top of piston. Pistons with two rings are marked "EXH" on piston crown and must be installed with "EXH" toward exhaust port of cylinder. Insert piston pin with solid end of pin toward exhaust port on all models except Mighty Mite models. Model SL-7A has spacers between connecting rod and piston. Install spacers with recess toward piston pin bearing. Place piston pin snap rings in piston with sharp edge out and gap toward piston skirt. Tighten cylinder base nuts to 60 in.-lbs. (6.8 N·m).

CONNECTING ROD.

To remove connecting rod, remove cylinder and piston as previously outlined. Unscrew connecting rod screws and remove rod being careful not to lose loose bearing rollers. Models SL-7A, SL-55A and all Mighty Mite models have 24 bearing rollers. Models SL-9, SL-9A, SL-14A and SL-16A have 26 bearing rollers, and all other models have 28 bearing rollers.

The connecting rod is fractured and has match marks on one side of rod and cap. Be sure rod and cap are correctly meshed and match marks are aligned during assembly. Tighten connecting rod screws to 35 in.-lbs. (3.9 N·m) on Mighty Mite models and to 50 in.-lbs. (5.6 N·m) on all other models.

CRANKSHAFT AND CRANKCASE.

To remove crankshaft on Mighty Mite models, remove clutch and flywheel. Remove rear handle. Remove connecting rod as previously outlined. Remove crankcase cover (1 – Fig. RE33). Crankshaft may now be removed.

To remove crankshaft on all other models, remove clutch and rear handle. Remove connecting rod as previously outlined. Remove right crankcase cover and remove crankshaft. On Models SL-4A, SL-7A, SL-11 and SL11A, crankcase may be separated from fuel tank. On Models SL-55A, SL-9, SL-9A, SL-14A and SL-16A, crankcase is integral with fuel tank.

Inspect bearings and seals for damage or excessive wear. Crankshaft bearings should be installed so numbered side of bearing is inward. Press on inward side of bearing so bearing is flush with recessed shoulder. Seals should be flush with surface.

AUTOMATIC CHAIN OILER.

All models except Mighty Mite Bantam, SL-9 and SL-11 are equipped with an automatic chain oiling system. The oil tank is pressurized by crankcase or cylinder pressure to force oil to chain. Check valve operation should be checked if excessive oil smoke is produced by the engine. Check valve on Mighty Mite Auto, Mighty Mite Deluxe and Mighty Mite Electric Start models is located in oil tank cavity shown in Fig. RE32. Check valve on all other models with automatic chain oiler is located in oil line fitting in oil tank. All models with

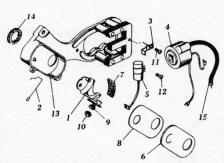

Fig. RE31—Exploded view of typical magneto assembly used on all models except Mighty Mite models.

1. Breaker points	5. Condenser
2. Clamp	6. Cover
3. Coil clip	13. Core & stator
4. Coil	14. Felt washer

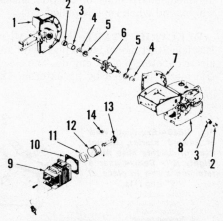

Fig. RE33—Exploded view of engine used on Mighty Mite series models.

1. Crankcase cover			
2. Seal			
3. Bearing		9. Cylinder	
4. Thrust washer		10. Gasket	
5. Thrust bearing		11. Piston rings	
6. Crankshaft		12. Piston	
7. Gasket		13. Connecting rod & cap	
8. Crankcase & frame		14. Bearing	

Fig. RE32—View showing location of check valve (C) in oil tank of Mighty Mite Auto, Mighty Mite Deluxe and Mighty Mite Electric Start models.

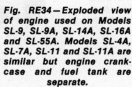
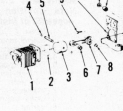

Fig. RE34—Exploded view of engine used on Models SL-9, SL-9A, SL-14A, SL-16A and SL-55A. Models SL-4A, SL-7A, SL-11 and SL-11A are similar but engine crankcase and fuel tank are separate.

1. Cylinder		
2. Piston rings		
3. Piston		
4. Snap ring		
5. Piston pin	12. Bearing	15. Thrust bearing
6. Bearing	13. Crankcase & fuel tank	16. Crankshaft
7. Connecting rod & cap	14. Thrust washer	17. "O" ring
8. Bearing		18. Crankcase cover
9. Screw		
10. Gasket		
11. Seal		

automatic oiler except Mighty Mite Auto, Mighty Mite Deluxe and Mighty Mite Electric Start are equipped with a shut-off valve to stop oil flow when engine is stopped or at slow idle. Oil shut-off valve on Model SL-55A is built into manual oil pump body and is actuated by the throttle trigger. Shut-off valve on other models so equipped is located adjacent to manual oil pump and is controlled by a link from the throttle trigger.

CLUTCH. An inboard type clutch is used on Model SL-7A and all Mighty Mite models. All other models have clutch drum mounted outside of clutch hub. Clutch hub is screwed on crankshaft with left-hand threads. Models with clutch drum mounted outboard have a right hand threaded nut to retain drum. Tighten clutch nut to 175 in.-lbs. (19.8 N·m) on Models SL-4A, SL-11, SL-11A and SL-55A. Tighten clutch nut on Models SL-9, SL-9A, SL-14A and SL-16A to 100 in.-lbs. (11.3 N·m).

REED VALVES. All models except Mighty Mite models are equipped with reed valve induction. Reed valve petals should be inspected for warpage, cracks or nicks. Reed valve seat should also be inspected for damage. Reed petals are available separately from reed valve housing.

REWIND STARTER. Refer to Fig. RE38 for exploded view of typical rewind starter used on all models except Mighty Mite Electric Start. To disassemble starter, remove starter housing from saw. Remove rope handle and allow rope to rewind into starter. Unscrew retaining screw on Mighty Mite Auto or "E" ring (11) on all other models. Remove friction shoe assembly. Remove rope pulley being careful not to disturb rewind spring. If necessary to remove rewind spring, be careful not to allow spring to uncoil uncontrolled.

Edges of friction shoes (9) should be sharp. Renew friction shoes if excessively worn. Renew fiber washers (8 and 10) if glazed or oil soaked. To reassemble starter, reverse disassembly procedure. Install rewind spring so that windings are in clockwise direction. Wrap rope around pulley and install pulley being sure inner hook of rewind spring engages pulley. Place tension on rewind spring by turning pulley three turns before passing rope through hole in housing. Be sure that friction shoe assembly is installed correctly. If properly installed, sharp ends of friction shoes will extend when rope is pulled.

ELECTRIC START. Mighty Mite Electric Start model is equipped with an electric motor to start engine. The electric motor is driven by an external 12

volt battery which may be recharged. Starter mechanism is gear driven by electric motor as shown in Fig. RE39.

Wires for electric starter should be connected as follows: One white lead of battery connector (6) should be connected to rear pole of switch (4) while other white lead should be connected to positive "+" terminal of starter motor. A black wire should be connected between negative "-" terminal of starter motor and middle pole of switch (4). A green wire should be connected to middle pole of switch (4) and grounded to starter housing (5). A blue wire should be connected to the front pole of switch (4) and the ignition coil primary wire.

Battery should be discarded if minimum voltage level of 12.8 volts is not attained after 48 hours of charging. The battery charger may be checked by connecting a voltmeter to battery connector of charger—exposed pin is negative. With battery charger plugged into a 110 volt circuit, battery charger output should be in excess of 7.5 volts. If battery and charger operate satisfactorily, remove starter cover and note if starter motor will turn freely. If starter motor is not binding, connect battery to starter housing plug and using a voltmeter and appropriate voltage checks, determine if starter switch, starter motor or wiring is defective.

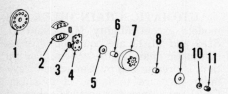

Fig. RE35—Exploded view of typical clutch used on all models except SL-4A, SL-11, SL-11A and SL-55A. Clutch drum is mounted inboard on all Mighty Mite models.

1. Cover
2. Clutch shoe
3. Spring
4. Clutch hub
5. Thrust washer
6. Sprocket race
7. Clutch drum
8. Bearing
9. Washer
10. Washer
11. Nut (L.H.)

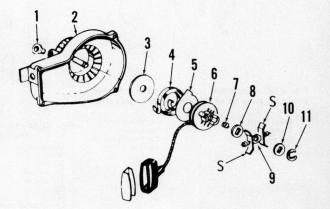

Fig. RE38—Exploded view of rewind starter. Starter used on Mighty Mite Auto, Mighty Mite Deluxe uses a retaining screw in place of "E" ring (11).

1. Rope bushing
2. Starter housing
3. Spring shield
4. Rewind spring
5. Dust shield
6. Rope pulley
7. Brake spring
8. Fiber washer
9. Friction shoe assy.
10. Fiber washer
11. "E" ring

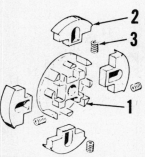

Fig. RE37—Exploded view of clutch hub (1), shoes (2) and springs (3) used on Models SL-4A, SL-11 and SL-11A.

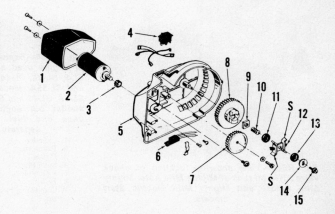

Fig. RE39—Exploded view of electric starter used on Mighty Mite Electric Start. Note position of sharp edges (S) of friction shoes.

1. Cover
2. Starter motor
3. Pinion gear
4. Starter switch
5. Starter housing
6. Battery connector
7. Idler gear
8. Starter gear
9. Drive washer
10. Spring
11. Fiber washer
12. Friction shoe assy.
13. Fiber washer
14. Washer
15. SEMS screw

ROPER

ROPER SALES CORP.
1905 West Court Street
Kankakee, IL 60901

Model	Bore	Stroke	Displ.	Drive Type
C110, C121	1-3/8 in. (34.9 mm)	1-9/32 in. (32.5 mm)	1.9 cu. in. (31.1 cc)	Direct
C332, C343, C354	1-13/16 in. (46.0 mm)	1-7/16 in. (36.5 mm)	3.7 cu. in. (60.6 cc)	Direct

MAINTENANCE

SPARK PLUG. Recommended spark plug is a Champion DJ6J for Models C110 and C121. Champion CJ6 is recommended for all other models. Spark plug electrode gap should be 0.025 inch (0.63 mm) for all models.

CARBURETOR. A Tillotson Model HS diagphragm type carburetor is used on Models C110 and C121 while a Walbro Model HDC diaphragm type carburetor is used on Models C332, C343 and C354. Refer to Tillotson or Walbro sections of CARBURETOR SERVICE section for carburetor overhaul and exploded views.

Initial adjustment of Tillotson carburetor is 1⅛ turns open for idle mixture screw and one turn open for high speed mixture screw. Initial adjustment of Walbro carburtor is one turn open for idle mixture screw and ¾-turn open for high speed mixture screw. Final adjustments should be made with engine warm. High speed mixture screw should be adjusted with engine under cutting load to obtain optimum performance. Do not adjust high speed mixture too lean as engine damage may result.

MAGNETO AND TIMING. A conventional flywheel magneto is used on all models. Ignition timing is fixed. Recommended breaker-point gap is 0.015 inch (0.38 mm) for all models. Incorrect breaker-point gap will affect ignition timing. Magneto air gap should be 0.005-0.010 inch (0.13-0.25 mm).

LUBRICATION. The engine is lubricated by mixing oil with fuel. A good quality oil designed for use in an air-cooled two-stroke engine should be mixed with regular gasoline at the ratio of 16:1. Fuel:oil ratio should be increased during break-in with ¾-pint (0.35 L) of oil added to one gallon (3.785 L) of gasoline. This break-in ratio should be used for the first gallon (3.785 L) of fuel mixture.

Models C121, C343 and C354 are equipped with an automatic chain oil pump. All models are equipped with a manual chain oil pump. Recommended chain oil is a good quality SAE 30 oil for summer use and SAE 20 for winter use. If saw is used in extremely cold weather, SAE 10 oil may be mixed with a small amount of kerosene.

REPAIRS

PISTON, PIN, RINGS, AND CYLINDER. Before cylinder can be removed, crankcase end plate must be removed. Refer to CRANKCASE AND CRANKSHAFT section. Cylinder has chromed aluminum bore on all models with cylinder head integral with cylinder. Piston has two pinned piston rings. Piston pin is fully floating and retained by snap rings at each end. Piston pin on Models C332, C343 and C354 rides in a needle roller bearing in small end of connecting rod. Piston pin on other models rides directly in small end of rod. Piston must be heated to remove and install piston pin.

Inspect chrome bore of cylinder for scoring, flaking, cracking or other signs of damage or excessive wear. Inspect piston pin, bearing and connecting rod small end. Install new piston pin bearing, on models so equipped, by pressing on lettered side of bearing. Be sure rod is properly supported when pressing against bearing to prevent damage to lower portion of rod if rod is still attached to crankshaft. Piston, pin and connecting rod are available only as a unit assembly on Models C110 and C121.

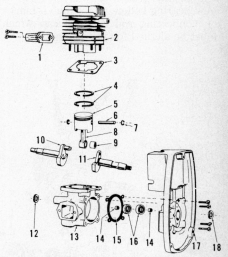

Fig. RP2—Exploded view of engine used on Models C110 and C121.

1. Muffler
2. Cylinder
3. Gasket
4. Piston rings
5. Piston
6. Piston pin
7. Snap rings
8. Connecting rod
9. Needle bearing
10. Crankshaft (drive end)
11. Crankshaft (flywheel end)
12. Seal
13. Crankcase
14. Roller bearings (Torrington B86)
15. Gasket
16. Roller bearings (Torrington DD40798)
17. End plate
18. Seal

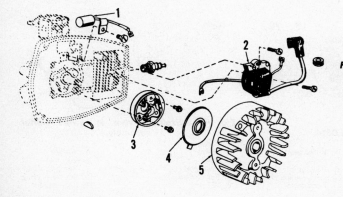

Fig. RP1—Exploded view of magneto assembly.

1. Condenser
2. Ignition
3. Stator plate & breaker points
4. Cover
5. Flywheel

Heat piston before installing piston pin which must be installed with closed end of pin toward exhaust port. Install piston with "EXH" marking on piston crown toward exhaust port of cylinder. Be sure piston rings are properly aligned with locating pins in ring grooves when installing cylinder. Tighten cylinder base nuts on Models C110 and C121 to 30-40 in.-lbs. (3.4-4.5 N·m) and to 80-100 in.-lbs. (9.0-11.3 N·m) on all other models.

CONNECTING ROD. Connecting rod on Models C332, C343 and C354 can be removed after removing piston and unscrewing rod cap screws. Be careful not to lose bearing rollers (14–Fig. RP3) when removing rod and cap. To remove rod on Models C110 and C121, crankshaft must be separated as outlined in CRANKCASE AND CRANKSHAFT section.

Thirty-one loose bearing rollers are used in crankpin bearing on Models C332, C343 and C354 while a cartridge roller bearing is used on Models C110 and C121. Piston pin rides directly in small end of connecting rod Models C110 and C121. Piston pin is supported by a needle roller bearing in connecting rod on Models C332, C343 and C354. Install roller bearing by pressing on lettered side of bearing. Connecting rod, piston and piston pin are available only as a unit assembly on Models C110 and C121.

On Models C332, C343 and C354, loose bearing rollers can be held in place with heavy grease or wax on strip of new bearing rollers. Note match marks on connecting rod and rod cap which must be aligned for installation.

CRANKCASE AND CRANKSHAFT. Access to crankcase and crankshaft is possible after removing end plate (17–Fig. RP2 or 18–Fig. RP3). Flywheel end of crankshaft on all models is supported by a roller bearing. Two bearings (14 and 16–Fig. RP2) are used on Models C110 and C121. Drive end of crankshaft is supported by two roller bearings on Models C110 and C121 and by a ball bearing on Models C332, C343 and C354. Heat should be applied to crankcase or end plate to remove roller bearings. Ball bearing (8–Fig. RP3) is pressed on crankshaft and retained in crankcase by retainers (6). It may be necessary to apply heat to crankcase to remove bearing and crankshaft from crankcase.

Models C110 and C121 are equipped with a two-piece crankshaft (10 and 11–Fig. RP2). End plate (17), crankshaft half (11) and cylinder must be removed before connecting rod (8) can be removed Drive end of crankshaft (10) may be removed after connecting rod (8) is removed. Drive (10) and flywheel (11) ends are available separately.

Ball bearing (8–Fig. RP3) on Models C332, C343 and C354 is pressed on crankshaft. Groove around outer race of bearing must be adjacent to crankpin. Heat crankcase (1) in bearing area and install crankshaft and bearing. Coat screw (7) threads with Loctite 222 or 242 and install bearing retainers (6) and screws. Be sure screws do not contact crankshaft when shaft is turned.

REED VALVE. All models are equipped with a reed valve induction system. Refer to Figs. RP4 and RP5. Inspect reed petals for cracks or other damage.

Inspect reed valve seats for pitting or other damage which may prevent petals from seating properly. Reed petals and seat are available only as a unit assembly.

REWIND STARTER. Refer to Fig. RP6 for exploded view of rewind starter used on all models. To disassemble starter, proceed as follows: Remove starter housing from end plate Remove rope handle and allow rope to rewind into starter. Remove "E" ring (6) and remove rope pulley (8) being careful not to dislodge rewind spring (9). If necessary, remove rewind spring being careful as injury may result if spring is allowed to uncoil uncontrolled.

Rewind spring is wound in clockwise direction in housing. Rope is wound on pulley in clockwise direction when viewing pulley installed in housing. Place tension on rewind spring by turning pulley clockwise before passing rope through rope outlet. Pulley should be turned a sufficient number of turns to draw rope handle against housing when rope is released, but not so many turns that rewind spring is fully extended when rope is completely withdrawn.

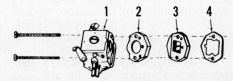

Fig. RP4—View of induction system used on Models C110 and C121.

1. Carburetor
2. Spacer
3. Reed valve assy.
4. Gasket

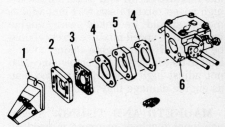

Fig. RP5—View of induction system used on Models C332, C343 and C354.

1. Reed valve assy.
2. Spacer
3. Cork gasket
4. Gasket
5. Heat insulator
6. Carburetor

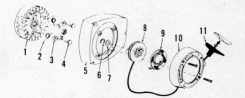

Fig. RP6—Exploded view of rewind starter assembly.

1. Flywheel
2. Spring
3. Pawl
4. Pivot post
5. Fan shroud
6. "E" ring
7. Washer
8. Rope pulley
9. Rewind spring
10. Starter housing
11. Rope handle

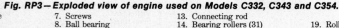

Fig. RP3—Exploded view of engine used on Models C332, C343 and C354.

1. Crankcase
2. Gasket
3. Cylinder
4. Seal
5. Retainer
6. Retainers
7. Screws
8. Ball bearing
9. Piston rings
10. Snap ring
11. Piston
12. Needle bearing
13. Connecting rod
14. Bearing rollers (31)
15. Rod cap
16. Crankshaft
17. Gasket
18. End plate
19. Roller bearing
20. Seal
21. Piston pin
22. Compression release
23. Reed valve

ROPER

Model	Bore	Stroke	Displ.	Drive Type
C611, C625, C636	1.562 in. (39.7 mm)	1.312 in. (33.3 mm)	2.5 cu. in. (41 cc)	Direct

MAINTENANCE

SPARK PLUG. Recomended spark plug is Champion DJ6J. Spark plug electrode gap should be 0.025 inch (0.63 mm).

CARBURETOR. A Tillotson HK diaphragm carburetor is used on all models. Refer to CARBURETOR SERVICE section for overhaul procedures.

Initial setting of idle and high speed mixture screws is one turn open. Adjust idle mixture screw so engine will accelerate without hesitation. Adjust high speed mixture screw to obtain optimum performance with saw under cutting load.

MAGNETO AND TIMING. A breaker-point type flywheel magneto is used on all models. Ignition timing is fixed. Recommended breaker-point gap is 0.015 inch (0.38 mm) for all models. Incorrect breaker-point gap will affect ignition timing. Magneto air gap should be 0.008 inch (0.20 mm). Tighten flywheel nut to 130-150 in.-lbs. (14.7-16.9 N·m).

LUBRICATION. The engine is lubricated by mixing oil with the fuel. A good quality oil designed for use in air-cooled two-stroke engines should be mixed with regular gasoline at a ratio of 16:1. Fuel:oil ratio should be increased during break-in with ¾-pint (0.35 L) of oil added to one gallon (3.785 L) of gasoline. This break-in ratio should be used for the first gallon (3.785 L) of fuel mixture.

All models are equipped with an automatic chain oil pump while Model C636 is also equipped with a manual oil pump. Recommended chain oil is a good quality SAE 30 oil for summer use and SAE 20 for winter use. If saw is used in extremely cold weather, SAE 10 oil may be mixed with a small amount of kerosene.

REPAIRS

CYLINDER, PISTON, PIN AND RINGS. Cylinder (23 – Fig. RP10) on all models is also upper crankcase half. Crankshaft is loose in crankcase when cylinder is removed. Care must be taken not to nick or scratch crankcase mating surfaces during disassembly.

Cylinder head is integral with cylinder and cylinder must be removed to remove piston. Piston is equipped with two piston rings and a floating type piston pin. It may be necessary to heat piston to remove or install piston pin. Piston, pin and rings are available in standard size only. Cylinder bore is chrome and should be inspected to determine if chrome is scored, peeling or excessively worn. Renew cylinder and piston if damaged or excessively worn.

Refer to CRANKSHAFT section for proper assembly of crankcase and cylinder.

CONNECTING ROD, CRANK-SHAFT AND CRANKCASE. The connecting rod is supported on crankshaft by 26 bearing rollers. Tighten connecting rod screws to 45-55 in.-lbs. (5.1-6.2 N·m).

Two needle roller bearings (12 – Fig. RP10) support crankshaft. Inspect crankshaft and renew if worn, bent or damaged. Crankcase and cylinder mating surfaces must be free of nicks and gouges or other damage which will prevent crankcase sealing.

Before reassembling crankcase and cylinder, apply a light coat of non-hardening sealant to crankcase and cylinder mating surfaces. Be sure retaining rings (11) mesh with grooves in crankcase and cylinder. Tighten crankcase screws to 60-75 in.-lbs. (6.8-8.5 N·m).

CLUTCH. All models are equipped with a two-shoe centrifugal clutch. Clutch hub (1 – Fig. RP10) has left-hand threads. Clutch shoes and hub are available only as a unit assembly. Clutch drum (5) is supported by bearings (4 and 7).

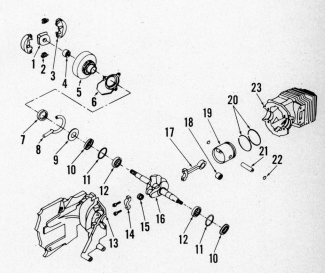

Fig. RP10 – Exploded view of engine and clutch.

1. Clutch hub
2. Springs
3. Shoes
4. Bearing
5. Clutch drum
6. Cover
7. Bearing
8. Oil outlet line
9. Washer
10. Seal
11. Retainer ring
12. Bearing
13. Crankcase
14. Rod cap
15. Bearing rollers (26)
16. Crankshaft
17. Conecting rod
18. Bearing
19. Piston
20. Piston rings
21. Piston pin
22. Pin retainer
23. Cylinder

OIL PUMP. All models are equipped with an automatic chain oil pump. Crankcase pulsations pressurize the oil tank through a check valve to force oil to the chain. Note that oil outlet line (8–Fig. RP10) is routed around crankshaft. Be sure check valve in oil tank operates correctly or oil may enter crankcase.

REWIND STARTER. Refer to Fig. RP11 for an exploded view of rewind starter. To disassemble starter, detach starter housing from saw, remove rope handle and allow rope to rewind into housing. Remove "E" ring (1) and washer (2) then carefully remove rope pulley (3) being careful not to dislodge rewind spring (4). If spring must be removed, care must be taken not to allow spring to uncoil uncontrolled.

Install spring so coils are wrapped in a clockwise direction from outer end. Wind rope on pulley in a clockwise direction as viewed with pulley installed in housing. Turn rope pulley two turns clockwise before passing rope through rope outlet so spring is preloaded.

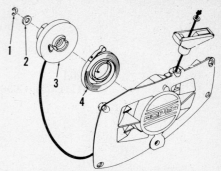

Fig. RP11—Exploded view of rewind starter.

1. "E" ring
2. Washer
3. Rope pulley
4. Rewind spring

SACHS-DOLMAR

SACHS-DOLMAR DIVISION
1022 Hawn Avenue
Shreveport, Louisiana 71107

Model	Bore	Stroke	Displ.	Drive Type
CT	56 mm (2.20 in.)	48 mm (1.89 in.)	118 cc (7.2 cu. in.)	Direct

MAINTENANCE

SPARK PLUG. Recommended spark plug is Bosch WSR6F. Spark plug electrode gap should be 0.51 mm (0.020 in.)

CARBURETOR. Model CT is equipped with a Tillotson HL diaphragm carburetor. Initial setting of idle and high speed mixture screws is 1¼ turns open from a lightly seated position. Adjust low speed mixture so engine will accelerate cleanly without hesitation. The high speed screw should be adjusted to give optimum performance under load. Adjust idle speed to just below clutch engagement speed.

The carburetor used on Model CT is equipped with a ball valve type governor which enrichens the fuel mixture at the governed speed and prevents engine overspeeding. Original governor assembly is tuned for each engine and cannot be renewed. If damaged, a fiber disk must be used in place of the governor spring and ball valve.

Refer to Tillotson section of CARBURETOR SERVICE section for carburetor operation and overhaul.

IGNITION TIMING. Early models were equipped with a breaker-point ignition system while later models are equipped with a breakerless electronic ignition system. Breaker-point gap on models so equipped should be 0.4 mm (0.016 in.)

Ignition timing on models equipped with breaker points should be 3.4 mm (0.134 in.) BTDC. Timing on models with electronic ignition should be 2.6 mm (0.102 in.) BTDC.

Ignition timing on electronic ignition is correct if marks on flywheel, crankcase and ignition base plate are aligned. Refer to Fig. D1. If flywheel, crankcase or ignition base plate has been renewed or altered, use the following procedure to time engine: Position piston at ignition firing position using a dial indicator assembly protruding into spark plug hole. Make a mark on crankcase which is aligned with mark on

flywheel. Remove flywheel and loosen ignition base plate screws. Align mark on ignition base plate with mark on crankcase and tighten base plate screws.

Air gap between poles of ignition coil and flywheel and trigger coil and flywheel should be 0.25-0.39 mm (0.010-0.015 in.).

TROUBLE-SHOOTING ELECTRONIC IGNITION. If spark plug will not fire and spark plug and wiring are not faulty, proceed as follows: Remove flywheel and check for loose, corroded or damaged connections and wires. Discharge condenser by shorting to ground.

Fig. D1– Electronic ignition is correctly timed when marks on crankcase and ignition base plate are aligned.

To check ignition coil, disconnect ignition coil leads. Connect ohmmeter leads to primary wire of coil and to ground. Resistance should be 1 ohm. Connect ohmmeter leads to high tension wire and to ground. Resistance should be 1,000-3,000 ohms. Renew coil if shorted or open windings are found or ohmmeter readings do not agree with specifications.

To check charging coil, disconnect coil leads. Some charging coils have a diode connected to coil. Connect ohmmeter leads to coil leads and read resistance. If coil does not have a diode connected to coil, resistance should be 500-1600 ohms. If coil has a diode connected, connect ohmmeter leads to coil leads, take reading, then reverse ohmmeter leads and take another reading. Second reading should be ten times greater or smaller than first reading. Renew coil if any readings are incorrect.

Capacitance of storage condenser should be 0.6-0.9 mfd. Condenser is mounted integrally with base plate and must be renewed as a unit.

Trigger coil may be checked by substituting a new or good coil in place of original coil. Ignition timing must be checked and readjusted if necessary when trigger coil or ignition coil is renewed.

Fig. D4– Exploded view of Model CT engine.

1. Cylinder
2. Piston ring
3. Piston
4. Snap ring
5. Piston pin
6. Gasket
7. Bearing
8. Washer
9. Clutch drum
10. Bearing race
11. Bearing
12. Retainer plate
13. Clutch springs
14. Clutch hub
15. Retainer plate
16. Clutch shoe
17. Bearing
18. Nut
19. Crankshaft & rod assy.
20. Washer
21. Slotted nut
22. Bearing

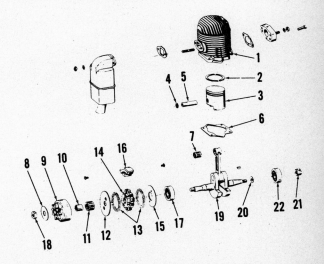

LUBRICATION. The engine is lubricated by mixing oil with the fuel. Recommended oil is Sachs-Dolmar two-stroke engine oil. Fuel mixture should be a 40:1 ratio when using recommended oil. During break-in period (first the hours of operation), mix oil and fuel at a 30:1 ratio. If Sachs-Dolmar two-stroke engine oil in not available, a good quality oil designed for use in air-cooled two-stroke engines may be used when mixed at a 25:1 ratio after break-in period or 20:1 ratio during break-in period. Use a separate container when mixing fuel and oil.

Model CT is equipped with an automatic chain oil pump. Oil pump is driven by worm gear on engine crankshaft. Oil pump output may be varied by turning adjusting screw (16–Fig. D6). Turning screw clockwise will decrease oil output while turning screw counterclockwise will increase oil output.

CARBON. Carbon deposits should be removed from muffler and exhaust ports at regular intervals. When scraping carbon, be careful not to damage cylinder or piston. Do not allow loosened carbon into cylinder.

REPAIRS

PISTON, PIN, RINGS AND CYLINDER. To remove cylinder on Model CT, remove front handle and carburetor cover. Disconnect oil lines and remove starter housing assembly. Remove carburetor and muffler. Remove cylinder.

CONNECTING ROD, CRANKSHAFT AND CRANKCASE. The crankcase must be split to remove connecting rod and crankshaft assembly. To disassemble crankcase, remove chain, clutch, handle assembly, rewind starter,

ignition assembly, cylinder and piston. Remove any other components which prevent disassembling crankcase. Remove clutch side crankcase half first from crankshaft. Separate crankshaft and remaining crankcase.

Connecting rod and crankshaft are a pressed together assembly which should be disassembled only by a shop with the tools and experience necessary to assemble and realign crankshaft. Connecting rod and bearing are available. Crankshaft runout should not exceed 0.015 mm (0.0006 in.). Heat crankcase before installing crankshaft and bearings.

CLUTCH. Refer to Fig. D4 for exploded view of clutch. Clutch nut has left-hand threads. A puller should be used to remove hub (14–Fig. D4). Clutch springs should be renewed in pairs. Tighten clutch nut to 39.4 N·m (29 ft.-lbs.)

CHAIN OILER. Model CT is equipped with an automatic chain oiler driven by a worm gear.

The pump shaft and worm gear (4–Fig. D6) is driven by a notch in flywheel retaining nut (21–Fig. D4). Oil pump may be disassembled by removing starter housing and referring to Fig. D4.

REWIND STARTER. Refer to Fig. D6 for exploded view of rewind starter. When disassembling starter, be sure rewind spring is not allowed to uncoil uncontrolled as spring may cause personal injury. Heat starter housing to remove and install pivot pin (26). Install pin so snap ring groove stands above pin bore shoulder 18.1 mm (0.713 in.) Rewind spring should be installed with windings in clockwise direction as viewed with spring in housing. Rope should be wound on pulley in clockwise direction as viewed with pulley installed in starter housing.

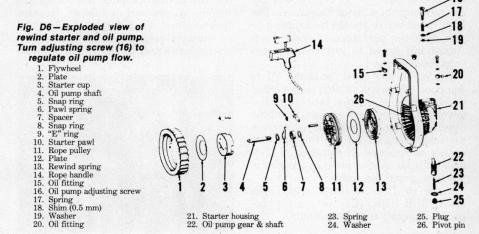

Fig. D6 — Exploded view of rewind starter and oil pump. Turn adjusting screw (16) to regulate oil pump flow.

1. Flywheel
2. Plate
3. Starter cup
4. Oil pump shaft
5. Snap ring
6. Pawl spring
7. Spacer
8. Snap ring
9. "E" ring
10. Starter pawl
11. Rope pulley
12. Plate
13. Rewind spring
14. Rope handle
15. Oil fitting
16. Oil pump adjusting screw
17. Spring
18. Shim (0.5 mm)
19. Washer
20. Oil fitting
21. Starter housing
22. Oil pump gear & shaft
23. Spring
24. Washer
25. Plug
26. Pivot pin

SACHS-DOLMAR

Model	Bore	Stroke	Displ.	Drive Type
122 Super, 123	47 mm (1.850 in.)	40 mm (1.575 in.)	70 cc (4.2 cu. in.)	Direct
133, 133 Super	52 mm (2.047 in.)	40 mm (1.575 in.)	85 cc (5.2 cu. in.)	Direct
143MX	55 mm (2.165 in.)	40 mm (1.575 in.)	95 cc (5.8 cu. in.)	Direct
152, 153	55 mm (2.165 in.)	42 mm (1.654 in.)	100 cc (6.1 cu. in.)	Direct

MAINTENANCE

SPARK PLUG. Recomended spark plug for Model 122 Super is Bosch HS5E. Recommended spark plug for all other models is Bosch WSR6F. Spark plug electrode gap should be 0.51 mm (0.020 in.)

CARBURETOR. All models are equipped with a Tillotson HS diaphragm carburetor. Refer to Tillotson section of CARBURETOR SERVICE section for overhaul and exploded view of carburetor.

Initial setting of idle and high speed mixture screws is approximately one turn open from a lightly seated position. Final adjustment should be made with engine running at operating temperature. Adjust low speed mixture so engine will accelerate cleanly without hesitation. Adjust high speed mixture to obtain optimum performance under a cutting load. Adjust idle speed screw so engine idles just below clutch engagement speed.

IGNITION. Early 122 Super, 152 and 153 models are equipped with a conventional flywheel magneto ignition system. Breaker-point gap on models so equipped should be 0.3-0.4 mm (0.012-0.016 in.). Later 122 Super, 152 and 153 models and 133, 133 Super and 143 MX models are equipped with a breakerless ignition system. Ignition timing should be 2.1-2.5 mm (0.083-0.098 in.) BTDC on Models 152 and 153 and 2.2 mm (0.086 in.) BTDC on all other models. Individual components of the breakerless ignition system used on all models so equipped are not available separately.

Ignition timing on Model 122 Super is set using Dolmar tool 956 007 000 as shown in Fig. D9. With right side of timing tool resting against base of stator plate, left side of timing tool should be aligned with mark on stator plate. If mark and edge of timing tool are not aligned, loosen stator plate screws and rotate stator plate until mark is aligned with tool.

To check timing on all other models, position engine at recommended ignition point using a dial indicator assembly protruding into spark plug hole. Make reference marks on flywheel and starter housing. Check timing with a power timing light at 8,000 rpm. If reference marks are not aligned at 8,000 rpm, rotate stator plate to adjust.

LUBRICATION. The engine is lubricated by mixing oil with regular grade gasoline. Recommended oil is Sachs-Dolmar two-stroke engine oil.

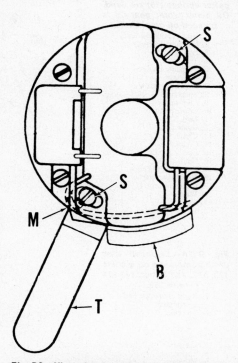

Fig. D9 — View showing location of timing gage (T) when setting ignition timing on Model 122 Super. Mark (M) on stator plate should align with left edge of gage (T) when right edge of gage is against stator plate base (B). Loosen stator plate screws (S) and rotate stator plate if mark (M) and gage are not aligned.

Fuel and oil mixture should be a 40:1 ratio when using recommended oil. During break-in period (first ten hours of operation), mix fuel and oil at a 30:1 ratio. If Sachs-Dolmar two-stroke engine oil is not available, a good quality oil designed for use in air-cooled two-stroke engines may be used when mixed at a 25:1 ratio after break-in period or 20:1 ratio during break-in period. Use a separate container when mixing oil and fuel.

All models are equipped with an automatic chain oil pump. Oil pump is driven by a worm gear on engine crankshaft. Oil pump output is varied by turning adjusting screw adjacent to clutch on Models 123 and 153 or adjacent to chain bar spike on all other models. Turning screw clockwise will decrease oil output while turning screw counterclockwise will increase oil output.

REPAIRS

PISTON, PIN, RINGS AND CYLINDER. The cylinder may be removed after removal of airbox cover, air cleaner, carburetor, cylinder shroud and muffler. The cylinder is chrome plated and should be inspected for excessive wear or damage to chrome plating.

Piston pin is retained by wire retainers and rides in roller bearing in the small end of the connecting rod. The piston is equipped with two piston rings which are retained in position by locating pins in the ring grooves. The piston must be installed with the arrow on the piston crown pointing toward the exhaust port. Some pistons have a letter "A" stamped near the arrow which must not be confused with letter stamped on piston crown to indicate piston size.

Cylinder and piston are marked "A," "B" or "C" during production to obtain desired piston-to-cylinder clearance. Cylinder and piston must have same letter marking to obtain proper clearance. Cylinders are stamped on top of cylinder or on cylinder frame. Pistons are stamped on piston crown but letter indicating piston size should not be confused with letter "A" which is stamped on some piston crowns to indicate which side of piston must be installed adjacent to exhaust port. Tighten cylinder screws to 10 N·m (88 in.-lbs.).

CONNECTING ROD, CRANK-SHAFT AND CRANKCASE. Crankcase halves must be split on all models to remove crankshaft assembly. The crankshaft is supported at both ends by ball bearings. Connecting rod and crankshaft are a pressed together assembly which should be disassembled only be a shop with the tools and experience necessary to assemble and realign crankshaft. Connecting rod, bearing and crankpin are available as a unit assembly.

Heat crankcase to ease installation of main bearings. Heat main bearing inner races to install crankshaft. Tighten crankcase screws to 7 N·m (62 in.-lbs.).

On Models 122 Super and 152, the automatic oil pump is driven by worm (2 – Fig. D11) located between main bearing and oil seal. On these models, worm must be pressed on crankshaft prior to installing crankshaft assembly in crankcase.

CLUTCH. Three, four and six-shoe clutches have been used. The clutch on all models is retained by a nut with left-hand threads. A puller should be used to remove clutch hub from crankshaft. Models 122 Super and early 152 are equipped with two springs (15 – Fig. D11) which should be renewed in pairs.

Tighten clutch nut to 26 N·m (19 ft.-lbs.) on all models.

CHAIN OIL PUMP. All models are equipped with an automatic chain oil pump. The oil pump on Models 123, 133, 133 Super, 143 MX and 153 is contained in a removable oil pump housing (10 – Fig. D11A) with plunger (9) driven by worm gear (2) located outside the right crankcase oil seal. The oil pump on 122 Super and 152 models is contained in the right crankcase half as shown in Fig. D11. Plunger (5) is driven by worm gear (2) which is located between main bearing and oil seal (11).

Worm gear (2 – Fig. D11 or D11A) may be extracted without removing crankshaft by using special Sachs-Dolmar tool 957 434 00. Use a thrust cap over crankshaft to prevent damage to crankshaft or threads. Mark worm gear

location on Models 122 Super and 152 prior to removal. Heat worm gear approximately 104° C (220° F) prior to installation. Install Model 152 worm so smooth end abuts main bearing. Install Model 123 worm so outer edge is 11.8-12.4 mm (0.465-0.488 in.) from pump mounting surface on crankcase.

On Models 122 Super and 152, be sure cam screw (9 – Fig. D11) is correctly meshed with groove in plunger (5) during assembly. Install seal (11 – Fig. D11A) on Models 123, 133, 133 Super, 143 MX and 153 with seal lip facing toward clutch.

REWIND STARTER. Refer to Fig. D12 or D13 for exploded views of rewind starters. To disassemble starter, remove starter housing from saw, remove rope handle and allow rope to wind into starter. Remove snap ring(s) and withdraw rope pulley, being careful not to dislodge rewind spring, precautions should be taken to prevent spring from uncoiling uncontrolled.

Install rewind spring in starter housing in clockwise direction from outer end. Starter rope length is 100 cm (39.4 in.) for Models 122 Super, 123, 133, 133

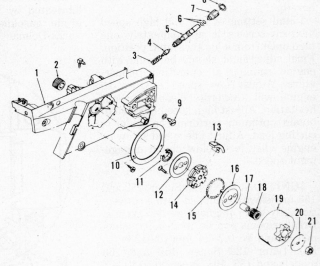

Fig. D11 – Exploded view of Model 152 oil pump and clutch assemblies. Model 122 Super is similar. Two garter springs (15) are used. Oil pump worm gear (2) is pressed on crankshaft.

1. Right crankcase half
2. Oil pump worm gear
3. Spring
4. Thrust pin
5. Oil pump plunger
6. "O" rings
7. Adjusting screw
8. Snap ring
9. Cam screw
10. Cover plate
11. Seal
12. Guide plate
13. Clutch shoe
14. Clutch hub
15. Garter spring
16. Guide plate
17. Inner bearing race
18. Needle bearing
19. Clutch drum
20. Washer
21. Nut

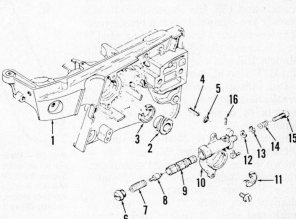

Fig. D11A – Exploded view of oil pump used on Models 123, 133, 133 Super, 143 MX and 153.

1. Right crankcase half
2. Worm gear
3. Oil seal
4. Pin
5. "O" ring
6. Plug
7. Spring
8. Thrust pin
9. Plunger
10. Pump housing
11. Seal
12. Rubber washer
13. Spring seat
14. Spring
15. Adjusting screw
16. Pin

Fig. D10 – Exploded view of engine. Two piston rings (2) are used on all models.

1. Cylinder
2. Piston rings
3. Piston
4. Piston pin
5. Pin retainer
6. Needle bearing
7. Crankshaft & rod assy.
8. Ball bearing

Super and 143 MX, and 115 cm (45¼ in.) for Models 152 and 153. Wind rope around rope pulley in clockwise direction as viewed with pulley in starter housing. Pawl springs (8 – Fig. D13) on Models 152 and 153 must be positioned against spring spacer (7) as shown in Fig. D14. To place tension on starter rope, rotate rope pulley clockwise 4½ turns on Models 122 Super, 123, 133, 133 Super and 143 MX and 5 turns on Models 152 and 153 before passing rope through outlet. Check operation of rewind starter. Rope handle should rest snugly against starter housing with rope released. It should be possible to turn rope pulley clockwise at least ¼ turn with rope fully extended. Readjust spring tension if rope handle is loose against starter housing or rewind spring is coil bound with rope fully extended.

CHAIN BRAKE. Some models are equipped with a chain brake system designed to stop chain movement should kickback occur. Chain brake is activated when operator's hand strikes hand guard (1 – Fig. D15) causing chain brake lever (2) to disengage brake band and lever assembly (6) allowing spring (8) to draw brake band tight around clutch drum (9). Pull back hand guard to reset mechanism.

Disassembly for repair or component renewal is evident after referral to exploded view and inspection of unit. No adjustment of chain brake system is required.

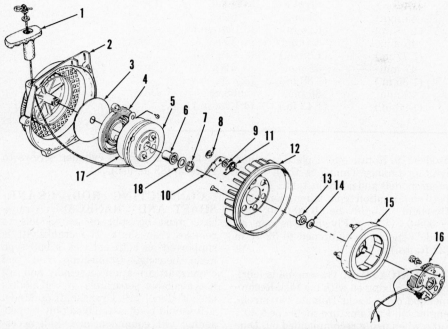

Fig. D12 — Exploded view of rewind starter and ignition assemblies used on Models 123, 133, 133 Super and 143MX. Model 122 Super is similar.

1. Rope handle	6. Bushing	11. Spring
2. Starter housing	7. Snap ring	12. Fan
3. Spacer plate	8. "E" ring	13. Nut
4. Rewind spring	9. Washer	14. Spring washer
5. Rope pulley	10. Pawl	15. Flywheel
		16. Stator plate & ignition assy.
		17. Spacer plate
		18. Washer

Fig. D14 — View showing installation of spring spacer (7), pawl springs (8) and pawls (9).

Fig. D13 — Exploded view of rewind starter and ignition assemblies used on Model 152. Model 153 is similar. Refer to Fig. D14 for installation of pawl springs (8).

1. Rope handle
2. Starter housing
3. Spacer
4. Rewind spring
5. Rope pulley
6. Snap ring
7. Spacer
8. Pawl springs
9. Pawl
10. "E" ring
11. Starter cup
12. Fan
13. Nut
14. Spring washer
15. Flywheel
16. Stator plate & ignition assy.
17. Seal

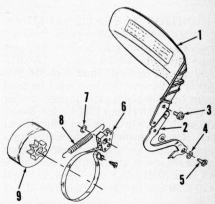

Fig. D15 — Exploded view of chain brake system typical of type used on all models.

1. Hand guard	6. Brake band & lever assy.
2. Brake lever	7. "E" ring
3. Screw	8. Spring
4. Wave washer	9. Clutch drum
5. Shoulder bolt	

SACHS-DOLMAR

Model	Bore	Stroke	Displ.	Drive Type
112, 113, 114	45 mm (1.77 in.)	32 mm (1.26 in.)	51 cc (3.1 cu. in.)	Direct
116	45 mm (1.77 in.)	35 mm (1.38 in.)	56 cc (3.4 cu. in.)	Direct
117, 119, 120	47 mm (1.85 in.)	35 mm (1.38 in.)	61 cc (3.7 cu. in.)	Direct
120 Super	49 mm (1.93 in.)	36 mm (1.42 in.)	68 cc (4.1 cu. in.)	Direct

MAINTENANCE

SPARK PLUG. Recommended spark plug is Bosch WSR6F. Electrode gap should be 0.51 mm (0.020 in.)

CARBURETOR. Bing 48B102, Tillotson HK and HS and Walbro HD and HDA diaphragm type carburetors have been used. Refer to appropriate sections of CARBURETOR SERVICE section for service procedures and exploded views.

Initial setting of low speed mixture screw and high speed mixture screw is one turn open on Models 114, 117 and 119. Initial adjustment on all other models is 1½ turns open for low speed mixture and one turn open for high speed mixture. Final adjustment should be made with engine running at operating temperature. Adjust low speed mixture screw so engine will accelerate cleanly without hesitation. Adjust high speed mixture screw to obtain optimum performance with saw under cutting load. Do not adjust high speed mixture too lean as overheating and engine damage could result. Adjust idle speed to just below clutch engagement speed.

IGNITION. Models 112 and 117 are equipped with a breaker-point flywheel magneto ignition system. Breaker-point gap should be 0.3-0.4 mm (0.012-0.016 in.). Special Sachs-Dolmar tool 956 009 000 or a cutaway flywheel must be used to set breaker-point gap. Ignition timing is 1.8 mm (0.071 in.) BTDC for Model 112 and 2.2 mm (0.087 in.) for Model 117. Rotate stator plate to adjust ignition timing. Air gap between ignition coil laminations and flywheel should be 0.3 mm (0.012 in.) on Model 117 and 0.20-0.30 mm (0.008-0.012 in.) on Model 112.

Models 113, 114, 116, 119, 120 and 120 Super are equipped with a breakerless solid-state ignition system. Ignition timing is 1.8 mm (0.071 in.) BTDC for Model 114 and 2.2 mm (0.087 in.) for

Model 119. Rotate stator plate to adjust ignition timing. Timing is fixed on all other models and not adjustable. Air gap between ignition coil laminations and flywheel should be 0.20-0.30 mm (0.008-0.012 in.). Flywheel nut on all models should be tightened to 30 N·m (22 ft.-lbs.).

LUBRICATION. The engine is lubricated by mixing oil with the fuel. Recommended oil is Sachs-Dolmar two-stroke engine oil. Fuel mixture should be a 40:1 ratio when using recommended oil. During break-in period (first ten hours of operation), mix oil and fuel at a 30:1 ratio. If Sachs-Dolmar two-stroke engine oil is not available, a good quality oil designed for use in air-cooled two-stroke engines may be used when mixed at a 25:1 ratio after break-in period or 20:1 ratio during break-in period. Use a separate container when mixing oil and fuel.

All models are equipped with an automatic chain oil pump. The oil pump is driven by a worm gear on engine crankshaft. Oil pump output is varied by turning adjusting screw on saw underside. Turning screw clockwise decreases oil flow while turning screw counterclockwise increases oil flow.

REPAIRS

PISTON, PIN, RINGS AND CYLINDER. The piston pin is retained by wire retainers and rides in a roller bearing in connecting rod small end. Two piston rings are used on Models 117, 119, 120 and 120 Super while a single piston ring is used on all other models.

Cylinder is chrome plated and cannot be bored oversize. Cylinder and piston are marked "A," "B," or "C" during production to obtain desired piston-to-cylinder clearance. Cylinder and piston must have same letter marking to obtain proper clearance. Cylinder is stamped near spark plug hole while piston is stamped on crown. Install piston so arrow on piston crown points toward ex-

haust port. Tighten cylinder screws to 10 N·m (88 in.-lbs.).

CONNECTING ROD, CRANKSHAFT AND CRANKCASE. Crankcase must be split on all models to remove crankshaft. The crankshaft is supported on both ends by a ball type main bearing. Connecting rod and crankshaft are a unit assembly and are not available separately on all models except Model 119. Crankshaft on Model 119 should be disassembled only by personnel with equipment and skills necessary to assemble and realign crankshaft assembly.

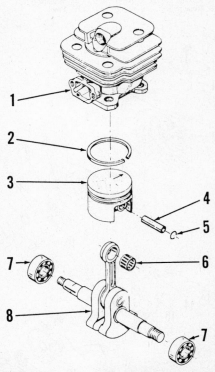

Fig. D20—Exploded view of engine. Two piston rings (2) are used on Models 117 and 119.

1. Cylinder
2. Piston ring
3. Piston
4. Piston pin
5. Pin retainer
6. Needle bearing
7. Ball bearing
8. Crankshaft & rod assy.

Crankcase should be heated to 99°-121° C (210°-250° F) to install main bearings. Clutch side main bearing inner race should be heated to approximately 104° C (220° F) to ease installation of bearing onto crankshaft. Flywheel side main bearing is a sliding fit on crankshaft. Install crankcase seals with open side facing inward and outer diameter flush with outer surface of crankcase.

Upon reassembly, tighten crankcase screws to 5 N·m (44 in.-lbs.). Install cylinder and retighten crankcase screws to 7 N·m (62 in.-lbs.).

CLUTCH. Clutch hub on all models has left-hand threads. Clutch on Models 112, 113, 114, 116, 120 and 120 Super has two shoes while three clutch shoes are used on Models 117 and 119. Tighten clutch hub to 55 N·m (40 ft.-lbs.) on Models 112, 113, 114, 116, 120 and 120 Super or to 48 N·m (35 ft.-lbs.) on Models 117 and 119.

CHAIN OIL PUMP. All models are equipped with the chain oil pump shown in Fig. D22. Plunger (8) is driven by worm gear (4) mounted on crankshaft. On early models, crankcase oil seal lip seals against a shoulder on worm while on later models shoulder on worm gear is absent and oil seal lip rides against crankshaft. Be sure correct worm gear and oil seal are used. Worm gear may be extracted without removing crankshaft. Use Sachs-Dolmar special tool 957 430 000 when removing or installing worm with a shoulder. Shoulder of worm gear should contact with main bearing. On models equipped with shoulderless worm gear, use Sachs-Dolmar special tool 957 433 000 to remove and install worm gear. When removing worm gear, be sure to use a protective cap over crankshaft to prevent damage to crankshaft. Worm gear should be heated to approximately 104° C (220° F) prior to installation. Install seal (15) so seal lip is toward clutch.

REWIND STARTER. Refer to Fig. D21 for exploded view of rewind starter. To disassemble starter, remove starter housing from saw, remove rope handle and allow rope to rewind into starter. Detach snap ring (6) and remove rope pulley being careful not to dislodge rewind spring. If rewind spring must be removed, caution should be taken not to allow spring to uncoil uncontrolled.

Install rewind spring in starter housing in clockwise direction from outer spring end. Starter rope length should be 100 cm (39½ inches). Wind rope around rope pulley in clockwise direction as viewed with pulley in starter housing. Place sufficient tension on rope

by turning rope pulley approximately four turns before passing rope through outlet so handle will rest snugly against starter housing with rope released. It should be possible to turn rope pulley clockwise with rope fully extended. Readjust spring tension if rope handle is loose against starter housing or rewind

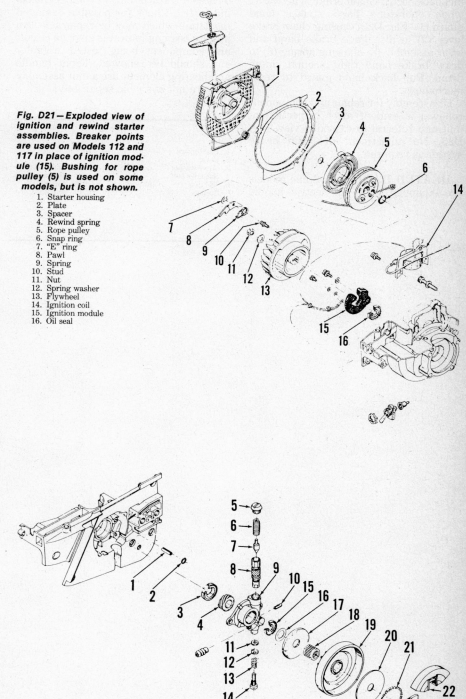

Fig. D21—Exploded view of ignition and rewind starter assemblies. Breaker points are used on Models 112 and 117 in place of ignition module (15). Bushing for rope pulley (5) is used on some models, but is not shown.

1. Starter housing
2. Plate
3. Spacer
4. Rewind spring
5. Rope pulley
6. Snap ring
7. "E" ring
8. Pawl
9. Spring
10. Stud
11. Nut
12. Spring washer
13. Flywheel
14. Ignition coil
15. Ignition module
16. Oil seal

Fig. D22—Exploded view of oil pump and clutch assemblies.

1. Pin	7. Thrust pin	13. Spring	18. Bearing
2. "O" ring	8. Plunger	14. Adjusting screw	19. Clutch drum
3. Oil seal	9. Pump housing	15. Seal	20. Washer
4. Worm gear	10. Pin	16. Thrust washer	21. Spring
5. Plug	11. Rubber washer	17. Washer	22. Clutch shoe
6. Spring	12. Spring seat		23. Clutch hub

spring is coil bound with rope fully extended.

CHAIN BRAKE. Some models are equipped with a chain brake system designed to stop chain movement should kickback occur. Chain brake is activated when operator's hand strikes hand guard (1 – Fig. D23) causing chain brake lever (2) to disengage brake band and lever assembly (8) allowing spring (6) to draw brake band tight around clutch drum. Pull back hand guard to reset mechanism.

Disassembly for repair and component renewal is evident after inspection of unit and referral to exploded view Fig. D23. No adjustment of chain brake system is required.

HEATED HANDLES. Some models are equipped with an electric handle heating system. A generator located behind the flywheel supplies an electrical current to heating elements in front handle and rear grip.

Test generator and heating elements with an ohmmeter. A zero reading indicates a short circuit in component being tested. Check for possible damaged insulation which may be repairable. An infinity reading indicates an open circuit and component being tested is faulty and should be renewed. Front handle and heating element are a unit assembly and are not available separately.

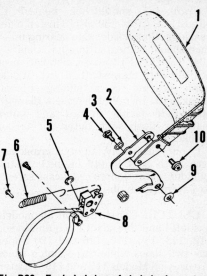

1. Hand guard
2. Lever
3. Wave washer
4. Shoulder bolt
5. "E" ring
6. Spring
7. Pin
8. Brake band & lever assy.
9. Washer
10. Screw

Fig. D23 — Exploded view of chain brake system.

SACHS-DOLMAR

Model	Bore	Stroke	Displ.	Drive Type
100, 100 Super	37 mm (1.46 in.)	31 mm (1.22 in.)	33 cc (2.0 cu. in.)	Direct
102	40 mm (1.57 in.)	31 mm (1.22 in.)	39 cc (2.38 cu. in.)	Direct
103, 105, 108	42 mm (1.65 in.)	29 mm (1.14 in.)	40 cc (2.44 cu. in.)	Direct

MAINTENANCE

SPARK PLUG. Recommended spark plug for Models 100, 100 Super and 102 is Champion RDJ7Y. Recommended spark plug for Models 103, 105 and 108 is Champion RCJ8. Electrode gap on Models 100 and 100 Super should be 0.6 mm (0.024 in.). Electrode gap on all other models should be 0.51 mm (0.020 in.).

CARBURETOR. Models 100, 100 Super and 102 are equipped with a Walbro WT diaphragm carburetor. Models 103, 105 and 108 are equipped with a Walbro WA diaphragm carburetor. Refer to Walbro section of CARBURETOR SERVICE section for exploded views and service procedures.

Initial adjustment on Model 100 is 1¼ turns open for high speed mixture screw and 1⅛ turns open for low speed mixture screw. Initial adjustment for Model 100 Super is ¾ turn open for high speed mixture screw and 1½ turns open for low speed mixture screw. On all other models, initial adjustment is one turn open for both high and low speed mixture screws.

Final adjustment should be made with engine running at operating temperature. Adjust low speed mixture so engine will accelerate cleanly without hesitation. Adjust high speed mixture to obtain optimum full throttle performance under cutting load. Do not adjust high speed mixture too lean as overheating and engine damage could result. Adjust idle speed to just below clutch engagement speed.

IGNITION. All models are equipped with a breakerless electronic ignition system. All electronic circuitry is contained in a one-piece ignition module assembly (6—Figs. D35 and D36). Air gap between ignition module lamination and flywheel (3) should be 0.2-0.3 mm (0.008-0.012 in.) on all models. Ignition timing is fixed and not adjustable.

LUBRICATION. The engine is lubricated by mixing oil with the fuel. Recommended oil is Sachs-Dolmar two-stroke engine oil. Fuel mixture should be a 40:1 ratio when using the recommended oil. During break-in period (first ten hours of operation), mix fuel and oil at a 30:1 ratio. If Sachs-Dolmar two-stroke engine oil is not available, a good quality oil designed for use in air-cooled two-stroke engines may be used when mixed at a 25:1 ratio after break-in period or 20:1 ratio during break-in period. Use a separate container when mixing fuel and oil.

All models are equipped with an automatic chain oil pump. Oil pump is driven by a worm gear on engine crankshaft. Oil pump output is adjustable on all models except Model 100. Refer to OIL PUMP in REPAIRS section for service, adjustment procedures and exploded views.

Manufacturer recommends using Sachs-Dolmar saw chain oil. If Sachs-Dolmar saw chain is not available, use a good quality oil designed specifically for saw chain lubrication.

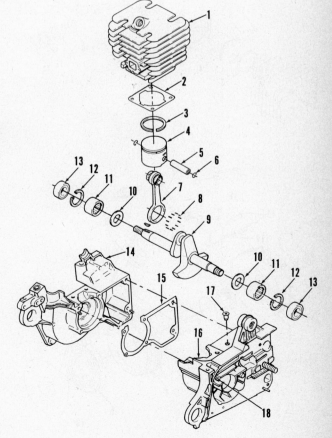

Fig. D33—Exploded view of engine assembly used on Models 100, 100 Super and 102.

1. Cylinder
2. Gasket
3. Piston ring
4. Piston
5. Piston pin
6. Pin retainer
7. Connecting rod
8. Bearing rollers
9. Crankshaft
10. Thrust washer
11. Main bearing
12. Snap ring
13. Seal
14. Left crankcase half
15. Gasket
16. Right crankcase half
17. Oil tank vent
18. Guide pin

REPAIRS

PISTON, PIN, RING AND CYL-INDER. Piston is equipped with one piston ring on all models. The piston pin rides in a needle roller bearing in rod small end and is held in place with two wire retainers. Cylinder has a Nikasil impregnated bore and should be renewed if excessively worn or damaged. Piston, ring and cylinder are available in standard size only on Models 100, 100 Super and 102. Piston and cylinder on Models 103, 105 and 108 are marked "A," "B" or "C" during production to obtain desired piston-to-cylinder clearance. Cylinder and piston must have like markings to maintain proper clearance. Cylinders are marked on top of cylinder or on cylinder frame. Pistons are marked on piston crown. Install piston with arrow on piston crown toward exhaust port.

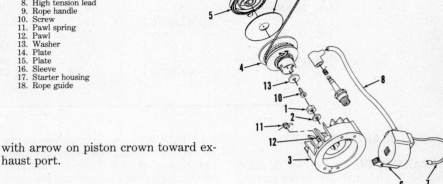

Fig. D36 – Exploded view if ignition and rewind starter assemblies used on Models 103, 105 and 108.

1. Nut
2. Washer
3. Flywheel
4. Rope pulley
5. Rewind spring
6. Ignition module
7. Short circuit wire
8. High tension lead
9. Rope handle
10. Screw
11. Pawl spring
12. Pawl
13. Washer
14. Plate
15. Plate
16. Sleeve
17. Starter housing
18. Rope guide

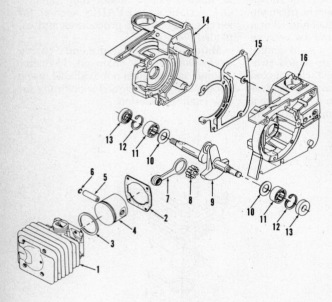

Fig. D34 – Exploded view of engine assembly used on Models 103, 105 and 108. Refer to Fig. D33 for component identification.

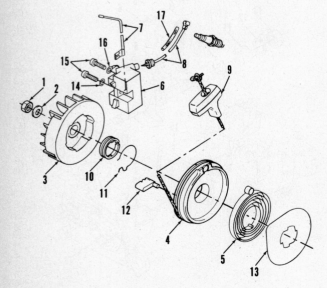

Fig. D35 – Exploded view of ignition and rewind starter assemblies used on Models 100, 100 Super and 102.

1. Nut
2. Washer
3. Flywheel
4. Rope pulley
5. Rewind spring
6. Ignition module
7. Short circuit wire
8. High tension lead
9. Rope handle
10. Retainer ring
11. Brake spring
12. Pawl
13. Plate

NOTE: Use care when handling piston and rod assembly to prevent rod from slipping off bearing rollers as rollers are loose and may fall into crankcase.

Tighten cylinder screws to 6-8 N·m (53-71 in.-lbs.).

CONNECTING ROD, CRANK-SHAFT AND CRANKCASE. On early models, connecting rod (7 – Figs. D33 and D34) is separate from crankshaft (9) and rides in 12 loose bearing rollers (8). Connecting rod and needle bearing in rod small end are a unit assembly. Loose bearing rollers (8) at crankpin can be removed after rod is slipped off rollers. Bearing rollers may be held in place with a heavy grease during rod installation.

The crankshaft is supported at both ends with caged needle roller main bearings (11). Main bearings locate against snap rings (12). Note location of thrust washers (10) at both ends of crankshaft. On some later models, crankshaft, connecting rod and crankpin bearing are a unit assembly.

Heat may be applied to crankcase halves (14 and 16) to ease installation of main bearings. On Models 103, 105 and 108, manufacturer recommends using Loctite 242 or a suitable equivalent on outer diameter of crankcase seals (13) before installing seals.

CLUTCH. Refer to Fig. D37 for exploded view of clutch assembly used on Models 100, 100 Super and 102. Refer to Fig. D38 for exploded view of clutch used on Models 103, 105 and 108. Clutch assembly (1 – Fig. D37 and Fig. D38) has left-hand threads on all models. Clutch drum (2 – Fig. D37) on Models 100, 100 Super and 102 is available only with a fitted needle bearing. Shim (3) is used on Model 100 Super only. Clutch shoes and hub are available only as a complete assembly. Manufacturer recommends using special Sachs-Dolmar tool 950 500 020 to remove and install clutch assembly.

Clutch drum (2–Fig. D38) is separate from needle bearing (4) on Models 103, 105 and 108. Note location of spacers (3 and 5). Install thin spacer (3) between engine and clutch assembly (1) and thick spacer (5) between clutch drum (2) and snap ring (6). Manufacturer recommends using special Sachs-Dolmar tool 950 500 020 to remove and install clutch assembly.

OIL PUMP. All models are equipped with automatic chain oil pumps. Pump output is adjustable on all models except Model 100.

Pump plunger (11–Fig. D37) on Models 100, 100 Super and 102 is driven by worm gear (5) on crankshaft. Use special Sachs-Dolmar tool 950 500 010 to remove and install worm gear on crankshaft. After oil pump has been removed, suction line (6) can be removed for inspection or renewal. Pump plunger (11) and body (7) should be renewed only as a complete unit.

When installing pump assembly, be certain guide bore (G) in pump body properly engages guide pin (18–Fig. D33) in right crankcase half (16).

Adjust oil pump output on late 100 Super and 102 models by rotating adjusting screw (14–Fig. D37) located under saw. On early 100 Super and 102 models, adjust oil pump output by pulling down adjustment pin with a hooked wire or other suitable tool and sliding adjusting bushing forward or rearward. Forward position is maximum output. Refer to Fig. D39 for view of adjustment procedure.

Refer to Fig. D38 for exploded view of automatic oil pump used on Models 103, 105 and 108. Oil is pumped by plunger (16), driven by worm gear (15) which is rotated by drive spring (7). When installing pump, make certain drive spring (7) properly engages clutch drum (2) and worm gear (15). Pump output is adjusted by rotating adjusting screw (9) located at top right of saw.

REWIND STARTER. Flywheel must be removed to gain access to starter on Models 100, 100 Super and 102. To relieve tension on rewind spring, remove rope handle (9–Fig. D35) and carefully allow rope pulley (4) to unwind relieving tension on spring. To disassemble starter, pry off brake spring (11) and remove retainer ring (10). Lift off rope pulley (4) being careful not to dislodge rewind spring.

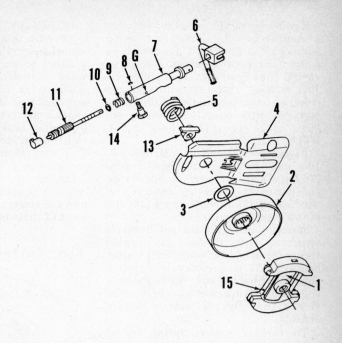

Fig. D37—Exploded view of clutch assembly used on Models 100, 100 Super and 102 and chain oil pump assembly used on Models 100 Super and 102. Oil pump shown is used on later models. Refer to Fig. D39 for adjustment procedure on early model pumps. Nonadjustable pump used on Model 100 is similar. Shim (3) is used on Model 100 Super only.

G. Guide bore
1. Clutch assy.
2. Clutch drum
3. Shim
4. Plate
5. Worm gear
6. Suction line assy.
7. Pump body
8. "O" ring
9. Spring
10. Washer
11. Plunger
12. Plug
13. Seal
14. Adjusting screw
15. Clutch spring

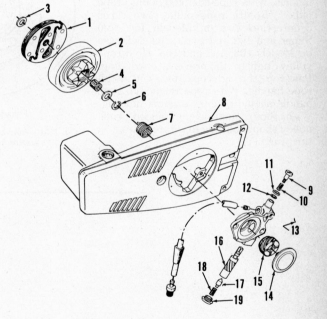

Fig. D38—Exploded view of clutch assembly and chain oil pump assembly used on Models 103, 105 and 108.

1. Clutch assy.
2. Clutch drum
3. Spacer
4. Needle bearing
5. Spacer
6. Snap ring
7. Drive spring
8. Chain guard & oil tank assy.
9. Adjusting screw
10. Spring
11. Washer
12. "O" ring
13. Pump body
14. Cap & shaft assy.
15. Worm gear
16. Plunger
17. Thrust pin
18. Spring
19. Plug

Fig. D39—View showing oil pump output adjustment procedure on early Models 100 Super and 102. Refer to text.

Rewind spring (5) should be wound in a counterclockwise direction starting with outer coil. Wind rope onto rope pulley in a counterclockwise direction as viewed from flywheel side of pulley. Install retainer ring (10) with end gap pointing toward ignition coil (6). Make certain starter pawl (12) properly engages brake spring (11). Refer to Fig. D40.

To disassemble starter on Models 103, 105 and 108, remove rope handle (9 – Fig. D36) and carefully allow rope pulley to unwind, relieving tension on rewind spring (5). Remove screw (10) and lift off rope pulley (4).

Starter pawls (12) are not available separately from flywheel (3). Rewind spring (5) should be wound into starter housing (17) in a clockwise direction starting with outer coil. Wind rope onto rope pulley (4) in a clockwise direction as viewed from flywheel side of starter housing.

To preload rewind spring on all models, wind rope completely onto rope pulley. Rotate rope pulley two turns counterclockwise on Models 100, 100 Super and 102 and two turns clockwise on Models 103, 105 and 108. Hold rope pulley tightly to prevent unwinding. Pass rope through rope guide and install rope handle. With rope retracted, rope handle should be snug against housing. With rope completely extended, rope pulley should be able to rotate at least ¼ turn further.

CHAIN BRAKE. Some models are equipped with a chain brake system designed to stop chain movement should kickback occur. Chain brake is activated when operator's hand strikes chain brake lever (1 – Fig. D41). Forward movement of chain brake lever disengages brake latch (4) and allows spring (8) to draw brake band (10) tight around clutch drum stopping chain movement. Pull back chain brake lever to reset mechanism.

Disassembly for repair or component renewal is evident after inspection of unit and referral to Fig. D41. No adjustment of chain brake system is required.

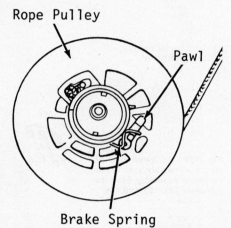

Fig. D40 — View showing proper engagement of starter pawl and brake spring.

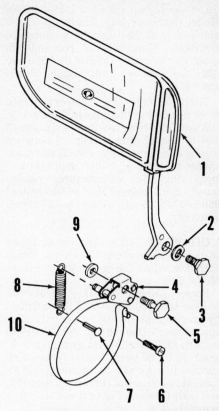

Fig. D41 — Exploded view of chain brake system used on models so equipped.

1. Chain brake lever	6. Screw
2. Wave washer	7. Pin
3. Shoulder bolt	8. Spring
4. Latch	9. Spacer
5. Shoulder bolt	10. Brake band

SACHS-DOLMAR

Model	Bore	Stroke	Displ.	Drive Type
110	40 mm (1.57 in.)	34 mm (1.34 in.)	43 cc (2.6 cu. in.)	Direct
111	44 mm (1.73 in.)	34 mm (1.34 in.)	51 cc (3.1 cu. in.)	Direct
115	44 mm (1.73 in.)	34 mm (1.34 in.)	52 cc (3.2 cu. in.)	Direct

MAINTENANCE

SPARK PLUG. Recommended spark plug is Champion RDJ7Y. Electrode gap should be 0.5 mm (0.020 in.) on all models.

CARBURETOR. Model 110 is equipped with a Tillotson HU diaphragm type carburetor. Models 111 and 115 are equipped with a Walbro WT diaphragm type carburetor. Refer to Tillotson or Walbro sections of CARBURETOR SERVICE section for service and exploded views.

Initial adjustment for both high and low speed mixture screws is one turn open from a lightly seated position.

Final adjustment should be made with engine running at operating temperature. Adjust low speed mixture so engine will accelerate cleanly without hesitation. Adjust high speed mixture to obtain optimum full throttle performance under cutting load. Adjust idle speed to just below clutch engagement speed. Do not adjust high speed mixture too lean as overheating and engine damage could result.

IGNITION. All models are equipped with a breakerless electronic ignition system. All electronic circuitry is contained in a one-piece ignition module assembly located outside of flywheel.

Air gap between ignition module and flywheel magnets should be 0.2-0.3 mm (0.008-0.012 in.). Ignition timing is fixed at 1.8 mm (0.07 in.) BTDC and is not adjustable. Flywheel nut should be tightened to 30 N·m (22 ft.-lbs.).

LUBRICATION. The engine is lubricated by mixing oil with the fuel. Recommended oil is Sachs-Dolmar two-stroke engine oil. Fuel and oil mixture should be a 40:1 ratio when using the recommended oil. During break-in period (first ten hours of operation), mix fuel and oil at a 30:1 ratio. If Sachs-Dolmar two-stroke engine oil is not available, a good quality oil designed for use in air-cooled two-stroke engines maybe used when mixed at a 25:1 ratio after break-in period or 20:1 ratio during break-in period. Use a separate container when mixing fuel and oil.

All models are equipped with an adjustable automatic chain oil pump. Oil pump output is adjusted by rotating screw (10 – Fig. D53) under saw on clutch side.

Manufacturer recommends using Sachs-Dolmar saw chain oil. If Sachs-Dolmar saw chain oil is not available, use a good quality oil designed specifically for saw chain lubrication.

REPAIRS

PISTON, PIN, RINGS AND CYLINDER. Refer to Fig. D51 for exploded view of engine assembly. Model 111 and early Model 110 are equipped with one piston ring (2). Late Model 110 and Model 115 are equipped with two piston rings. Piston rings are pinned to prevent ring rotation. Piston pin (4) rides in needle bearing (15) in connecting rod small end and is held in position by two wire retainers (5). Install piston (3) with arrow on piston crown toward exhaust ports. Always use new wire retainers (5).

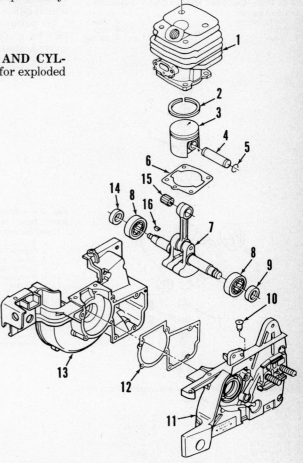

Fig. D51 – Exploded view of engine assembly.

1. Cylinder
2. Piston ring
3. Piston
4. Piston pin
5. Retainer
6. Gasket
7. Crankshaft & connecting rod assy.
8. Main bearing
9. Right crankcase seal
10. Oil tank vent valve
11. Right crankcase half
12. Gasket
13. Left crankcase half
14. Left crankcase seal
15. Needle bearing
16. Key

Cylinder (1) bore should be inspected for excessive wear or damage. Oversize pistons and rings are not available. If cylinder requires renewal, piston should also be renewed. Pistons are graded "A" or "B" but either "A" or "B" pistons may be used in all cylinders. Tighten cylinder screws to 5.9-6.1 N·m (52-54 in.-lbs.)

CRANKSHAFT, CONNECTING ROD AND CRANKCASE. Tap crankcase with a soft faced hammer to separate crankcase halves. Crankshaft and connecting rod are a unit assembly and are not available separately. Rotate connecting rod around crankpin and re-

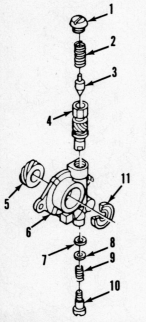

Fig. D52—Exploded view of clutch assembly.

1. Thrust washer
2. Needle bearing
3. Drum
4. Spacer
5. Shoe
6. Hub
7. Spring

new entire assembly if roughness, excessive play or other damage is noted. Crankshaft and connecting rod assembly is supported in crankcase by two caged roller main bearings (8—Fig. D51).

Heat crankcase halves (11 and 13) to approximately 100° C (212° F) to install main bearings. Special Sachs-Dolmar tool 950 500 050 must be used when installing main bearings to ensure proper crankshaft end play of 0.50 mm (0.020 in.). Tighten crankcase screws to 5.9-6.1 N·m (52-54 in.-lbs.).

CLUTCH. All models are equipped with the two-shoe centrifugal clutch shown in Fig. D52. Clutch hub (6) has left-hand threads. Clutch shoes (5) and hub (6) are available as an assembly only.

Manufacturer recommends using special Sachs-Dolmar tool 944 500 690 to remove and install clutch. Lightly lubricate needle bearing (2) when reassembling clutch assembly. Tighten clutch hub to 45-55 N·m (33-40 ft.-lbs.).

OIL PUMP. All models are equipped with the automatic chain oil pump shown in Fig. D53. Oil is pumped by plunger (4) which is driven by worm gear (5). Oil pump output is adjusted by rotating screw (10) located under saw on clutch side.

Oil pump suction and discharge hoses can be inspected after oil pump is removed. Renew hoses if cracks or other

damage is noted. Use a suitable sealant on suction hose pickup when installing into oil tank to prevent leakage.

Inspect plunger (4), worm gear (5) and bore in pump body (6) for excessive wear or damage. Always renew plunger and worm gear as a complete set. If wear on plunger or worm gear is extreme, it is recommended to renew entire pump assembly. Manufacturer recommends using special Sachs-Dolmar tool 957 433 000 to remove and install worm gear. Be sure to use a protective cap on stub of crankshaft to prevent tool from damaging crankshaft.

To install worm gear in the proper position, screw worm gear into special tool 957 433 000 until worm gear is flush with inner face of tool. Heat worm gear and tool to approximately 100° C (212° F). Quickly push worm gear onto crankshaft until tool bottoms on crankcase. Allow to cool, then unscrew tool from worm gear.

REWIND STARTER. Early models are equipped with the starter shown in Fig. D54. Later models are equipped with the starter shown in Fig. D55. Note carrier (6—Fig. D55) used in place of pawl assembly (8, 9 and 13—Fig. D54). Also note differences in rope pulley (5—Fig. D54 and Fig. D55).

To disassemble starter on all models, pull out rope approximately 20 cm (8 in.) and hold rope pulley firmly. Unwind three turns of rope from rope pulley and allow pulley to slowly unwind, relieving

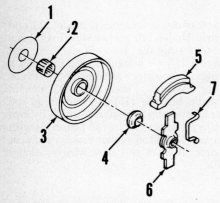

Fig. D53—Exploded view of automatic chain oil pump.

1. Plug
2. Spring
3. Thrust pin
4. Plunger
5. Worm gear
6. Pump body
7. "O" ring
8. Washer
9. Spring
10. Adjusting screw
11. Seal

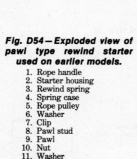

Fig. D54—Exploded view of pawl type rewind starter used on earlier models.

1. Rope handle
2. Starter housing
3. Rewind spring
4. Spring case
5. Rope pulley
6. Washer
7. Clip
8. Pawl stud
9. Pawl
10. Nut
11. Washer
12. Flywheel
13. Pawl spring

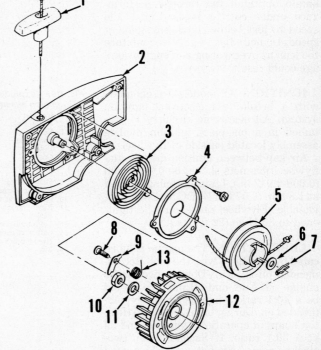

tension on rewind spring. Pry off clip (7–Fig. D54) or brake spring (7–Fig. D55). All other components can now be removed. Note that care should be exercised so not to allow rewind spring (3–Fig. D54 and Fig. D55) to uncoil uncontrolled.

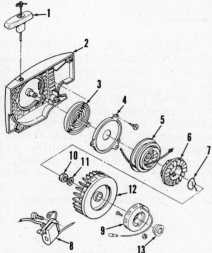
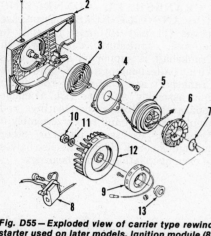

Fig. D55—Exploded view of carrier type rewind starter used on later models. Ignition module (8) is used on all models. Generator (9) and centering guide (13) are used on models equipped with handle heating systems.

1. Rope handle
2. Starter housing
3. Rewind spring
4. Spring case
5. Rope pulley
6. Carrier
7. Brake spring
8. Ignition module
9. Generator
10. Nut
11. Washer
12. Flywheel
13. Centering guide

If rewind spring is removed, wind spring into spring case (4) in a counter-clockwise direction starting with outer coil. Wind rope onto rope pulley (5) in a clockwise direction as viewed from flywheel side of starter housing (2). On later models, be sure brake spring (7–Fig. D55) is properly seated in notch in rope pulley (5) and knot in rope does not extend beyond face of rope pulley.

To preload rewind spring on all models, insert rope through rope guide in starter housing (2–Fig. D54 and Fig. D55) and install rope handle (1). Wind rope clockwise on rope pulley as far as possible. Pull out rope handle approximately 50 cm (20 in.) and firmly hold pulley to prevent pulley rotation. Pull extended rope back through rope guide and wind onto pulley. Allow spring tension to wind remainder of rope onto pulley. Rope handle should be snug against starter housing with rope retracted. Rope pulley should be able to rotate a minimum of ¼ turn against spring tension with rope fully extended.

CHAIN BRAKE. Some models are equipped with a chain brake system designed to quickly stop chain movement should kickback occur. Chain brake is activated when operator's hand strikes hand guard (1–Fig. D56) or when sudden upward movement of chain guide bar causes weight (24) to trip weight holder (11). When brake system is activated, spring (28) draws brake band

(13) tight around clutch drum. Pull back hand guard to reset mechanism.

Chain brake must be in the released position before brake housing (6) can be removed. Disassembly for inspection or component renewal is evident after referral to exploded view and inspection of unit. Lightly lubricate all pivot points with a suitable low temperature grease. No adjustment of chain brake system is required.

HEATED HANDLES. Some models are equipped with electrically heated handles. An electrical current is supplied by generator (9–Fig. D57), located behind flywheel, to heating elements in front handle (3) and rear grip.

Heating elements and wiring can be checked with an ohmmeter. Check for continuity across heating elements. Front heating element is not available separately from front handle. Be sure generator mounting surfaces are clean and mounting screws are tight to ensure a proper ground connection. Renew generator if no other component is found faulty.

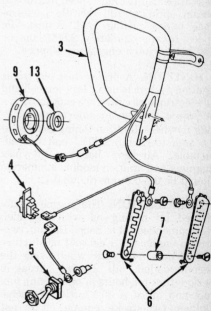

Fig. D56—Exploded view of chain brake system.

1. Hand guard
2. Pin
3. Shoulder screw
4. Latch
5. Spring
6. Housing
7. Pin
8. Nut
9. Cover
10. "E" ring
11. Weight holder
12. Spring
13. Brake band
14. Brake band retainer
15. Screw
16. Brake band retainer
17. Screw
18. "E" ring
19. Screw
20. Plate
21. Brake lever
22. Spring stop
23. Spring
24. Weight
25. Pin
26. Wave washer
27. Pin
28. Spring
29. Pin

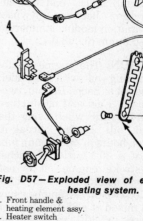

Fig. D57—Exploded view of electric handle heating system.

3. Front handle & heating element assy.
4. Heater switch
5. Ignition switch
6. Rear grip heating elements
7. Connector
9. Generator
13. Centering guide

SACHS-DOLMAR

Model	Bore	Stroke	Displ.	Drive Type
166	56 mm (2.20 in.)	48 mm (1.89 in.)	118 cc (7.2 cu. in.)	Direct

MAINTENANCE

SPARK PLUG. Recommended spark plug is Bosch WSR6F. Electrode gap should be 0.5 mm (0.020 in.).

CARBURETOR. A Walbro WB diaphragm type carburtor is used. Refer to Walbro section of CARBURETOR SERVICE for service and exploded view.

Initial adjustment is 1¼ turns open for low speed mixture screw and 1½ turns open for high speed mixture screw. Final adjustment should be made with engine running at operating temperature. Adjust low speed mixture so engine will accelerate cleanly without hesitation. Adjust high speed mixture to obtain optimum full throttle performance under cutting load. Adjust idle speed to approximately 2,800 rpm or just below clutch engagement speed.

IGNITION. A breakerless electronic ignition system is used. Ignition coil and all electronic circuitry are contained in a one-piece ignition module located outside flywheel. Ignition timing is fixed at 3.0 mm (0.12 in.) BTDC and not adjustable. Air gap between flywheel magnets and ignition module lamination should be 0.2-0.3 mm (0.008-0.12 in.).

LUBRICATION. The engine is lubricated by mixing oil with the fuel. Recommended oil is Sachs-Dolmar two-stroke engine oil. Fuel and oil mixture should be a 40:1 ratio when using the recommended oil. During break-in period (first ten hours of operation), mix fuel and oil at a 30:1 ratio. If Sachs-Dolmar two-stroke engine oil is not available, a good quality oil designed for use in air-cooled two-stroke engines may be used when mixed at a 25:1 ratio after break-in period or 20:1 ratio during break-in period. Use a separate container when mixing fuel and oil.

Manual and automatic chain oil pumps are used. Automatic oil pump output is adjustable. Refer to OIL PUMP section for service and adjustment procedure. Manufacturer recommends using Sachs-Dolmar saw chain oil. If Sachs-Dolmar saw chain oil is not available, use a good quality oil designed specifically for saw chain lubrication.

REPAIRS

CYLINDER, PISTON, PIN AND RINGS. Cylinder (2 – Fig. D67) may be equipped with a decompression valve (1) to ease engine starting. Cylinder bore should be inspected for excessive wear or damage. Oversize piston and rings are not available. Piston (4) is equipped with two piston rings (3). Piston rings are pinned in ring grooves to prevent ring rotation. Make certain ring end gaps are properly positioned around locating pins when installing cylinder. Piston pin (5) rides in needle bearing (8) in connecting rod small end and is held in position with two wire retainers (6). Install piston with arrow on piston crown toward exhaust port.

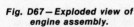

Fig. D67 – Exploded view of engine assembly.
1. Decompression valve
2. Cylinder
3. Piston rings
4. Piston
5. Piston pin
6. Retainer
7. Gasket
8. Needle bearing
9. Crankshaft & connecting rod assy.
10. Seal
11. Left crankcase half
12. Gasket
13. Ball bearing
14. Key
15. Ball bearing
16. Right crankcase half
17. Seal

CRANKSHAFT, CONNECTING ROD AND CRANKCASE.
Crankcase halves (11 and 16) must be split to remove crankshaft assembly (9). Crankshaft is supported at both ends with ball bearings (13 and 15). Crankshaft and connecting rod are a unit assembly and are not available separately. Rotate connecting rod around crankpin and renew assembly if roughness, excessive play or other damage is noted. Heat crankcase halves to ease installation of ball bearings.

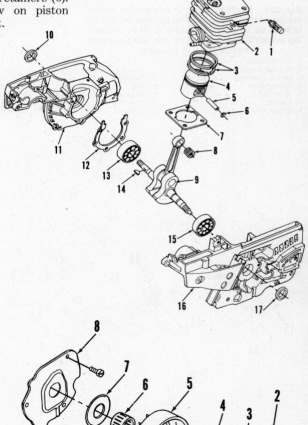

Fig. D68 – Exploded view of clutch assembly.
1. Hub
2. Shoe
3. Spring
4. Plate
5. Drum
6. Needle bearing
7. Thrust washer
8. Plate

CLUTCH. Refer to Fig. D68 for exploded view of the four shoe centrifugal clutch used. Clutch hub (1) has left-hand threads. Manufacturer recommends using Sachs-Dolmar tool 944 500 670 to remove and install clutch hub. Always renew shoes (2) as a complete set.

OIL PUMP. Refer to Fig. D69 for exploded view of manual and automatic oil pump assemblies. Worm gear (18) on engine crankshaft drives pump plunger (4). Automatic oil pump output is adjusted by rotating adjusting screw (10) located on bottom of saw on clutch side. Turn screw clockwise to decrease output. Use Sachs-Dolmar tool 957 434 000 to remove and install worm gear. Be sure to use protective cap 950 228 010 or a suitable equivalent over stub of crankshaft when pulling off worm to prevent damaging crankshaft. Install seal (6) with seal lip toward clutch.

REWIND STARTER. Refer to Fig. D70 for exploded view of rewind starter. To disassemble starter, remove rope handle (3) and allow rope to rewind into rope pulley (9). Remove snap ring (15), brake springs (14), compression ring (11) and snap ring (10). Do not interchange snap rings (10 and 15). Remove rope pulley (9) being careful not to dislodge rewind spring (7). If rewind spring must be removed, use caution not to allow spring to uncoil uncontrolled.

Install rewind spring into starter housing in a clockwise direction starting from outer coil. Starter rope should be 100 cm (39.5 in.) in length and 4 mm (5/32 in.) in diameter. Wind rope around rope pulley in a clockwise direction as viewed from flywheel side of starter housing. With rewind starter reassembled, preload rewind spring as follows:

Wind as much rope as possible around rope pulley. Pull out rope handle approximately 50 cm (20 in.) and secure rope pulley from turning. Rewind slack rope back onto pulley and release pulley allowing rewind spring tension to retract remainder of rope. Rope handle should be snug against housing with rope fully retracted.

CHAIN BRAKE. Some models are equipped with a chain brake system designed to quickly stop chain movement should kickback occur. Chain brake is activated when operator's hand strikes hand guard (1 – Fig. D71) causing brake lever (2) to disengage lever assembly (15) allowing spring (14) to draw brake band (8) tight around clutch drum. Pull back hand guard to reset mechanism.

Disassembly for repair or inspection is evident after referral to exploded view and inspection of unit. Lightly lubricate all pivot points. No adjustment of chain brake system is required.

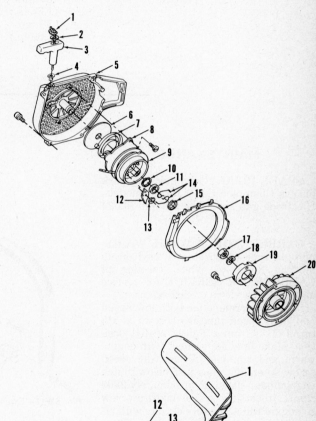

Fig. D70—Exploded view of rewind starter assembly.

1. Rope
2. Washer
3. Rope handle
4. Rope guide
5. Starter housing
6. Plate
7. Rewind spring
8. Cover
9. Rope pulley
10. Snap ring
11. Compression ring
12. Pawl
13. "E" ring
14. Brake spring
15. Snap ring
16. Baffle
17. Nut
18. Washer
19. Starter cup
20. Flywheel

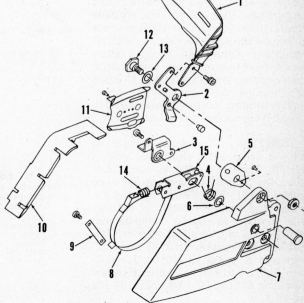

Fig. D71—Exploded view of chain brake system.

1. Hand guard
2. Brake lever
3. Bracket
4. Spring
5. Lock plate
6. Spacer
7. Cover
8. Brake band
9. Brake band retainer
10. Cover
11. Guide plate
12. Shoulder bolt
13. Wave washer
14. Spring
15. Lever assy.

Fig. D69—Exploded view of automatic and manual oil pump assemblies.

1. Plug
2. Spring
3. Thrust pin
4. Plunger
5. Pump body
6. Seal
7. Seal
8. Washer
9. Spring
10. Adjusting screw
11. Suction hose
12. Oil hose
13. "T" fitting
14. "O" ring
15. Manual pump assy.
16. Oil hose
17. Oil pickup
18. Worm gear
19. "O" ring

SHINDAIWA

SHINDAIWA, INC.
P.O. Box 1090
Tualatin, OR 97062

Model	Bore	Stroke	Displ.	Drive Type
345	34 mm (1.34 in.)	33 mm (1.30 in.)	33.6 cc (2.0 cu. in.)	Direct
350	35 mm (1.38 in.)	33 mm (1.30 in.)	35.5 cc (2.2 cu. in.)	Direct
416	37 mm (1.46 in.)	33 mm (1.30 in.)	39.4 cc (2.4 cu. in.)	Direct
451	39 mm (1.54 in.)	33 mm (1.30 in.)	43.6 cc (2.7 cu. in.)	Direct
500	43 mm (1.69 in.)	33 mm (1.30 in.)	47.9 cc (2.9 cu. in.)	Direct

MAINTENANCE

SPARK PLUG. Recommended spark plug is Champion CJ8Y for all models. Electrode gap should be 0.6 mm (0.024 in.).

CARBURETOR. A Walbro WA diaphragm type carburetor is used on all models. Refer to Walbro section of CARBURETOR SERVICE for service and exploded views of carburetor.

Initial adjustment for both low speed and high speed mixture screws is 1¼ turns open from a lightly seated position. Make final adjustment with engine warm and running. Adjust idle speed screw so engine idles just below clutch engagement speed (approximately 2800 rpm). Adjust low speed mixture screw so engine will accelerate cleanly without hesitation. Adjust high speed mixture screw to obtain optimum performance under cutting load. During first 10 hours of operation, the manufacturer recommends rotating mixture screws an additional ⅛ turn toward rich setting.

IGNITION. All models are equipped with a breakerless electronic ignition system. Ignition timing is not adjustable. On Model 345, air gap between pulser coil (1 – Fig. SW12) legs and flywheel and exciter/module coil (3) legs and flywheel should be 0.30-0.35 mm (0.012-0.014 in.). On all other models, air gap between ignition coil (8 – Fig. SW13) legs and flywheel should be 0.30-0.35 mm (0.012-0.014 in.). Tighten flywheel retaining nut to 11.7-13.8 N·m (104-122 in.-lbs.).

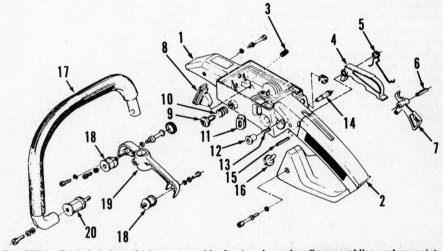

Fig. SW11 — Exploded view of trigger assembly, front and rear handle assemblies and associated components.

1. Rear handle
2. Handle grip
3. Spring
4. Lock lever
5. Spring
6. Spring pin
7. Trigger
8. Grommet
9. Adjuster screw
10. Spring
11. Grommet
12. Stop knob
13. Spring
14. Stopper
15. Spring pin
16. Run/stop switch
17. Front handle
18. Vibration damper
19. Bracket
20. Vibration damper

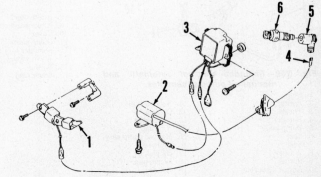

Fig. SW12 — Exploded view of breakerless electronic ignition components used on Model 345.

1. Pulser coil
2. Ignition coil
3. Exciter/module coil
4. Terminal
5. Spark plug boot
6. Spark plug

LUBRICATION. Engine is lubricated by mixing engine oil with premium grade unleaded gasoline. Recommended oil is Shindaiwa Premium 2-Cycle Oil mixed at a ratio of 40:1. If Shindaiwa Premium 2-Cycle Oil is not available, a good quality oil designed for air-cooled two-stroke engines may be used when mixed at a 25:1 ratio. Use a separate container when mixing the oil and gas.

All models are equipped with an automatic chain oil pump. Recommended chain oil is Shindaiwa Bar and Chain Oil or a good quality bar and chain oil. Oil output on all models is adjusted by turning oil pump adjuster shaft. Access hole is located on top of saw. Refer to AUTOMATIC CHAIN OILER under REPAIRS section.

CARBON. Carbon should be cleaned from muffler and exhaust ports at regular intervals. When scraping carbon, be careful not to damage the chamfered edges of the exhaust ports.

REPAIRS

CYLINDER, PISTON, PIN AND RINGS. Cylinder (20–Fig. SW14) bore is chrome plated and should be renewed if cracking, flaking or other damage to cylinder bore is noted. Recommended piston-to-cylinder clearance is 0.025-0.061 mm (0.0010-0.0024 in.) with a maximum limit of 0.18 mm (0.0071

in.). Lower crankcase half (1) is renewable with cylinder and upper crankcase half (20). Oversize piston and rings are not available. Piston (14) is equipped with two piston rings (16). Locating pins are present in ring grooves to prevent ring rotation. Make certain ring end gaps are properly positioned around locating pins before installing cylinder. Piston pin (15) rides in needle bearing (12) and is retained in position with two wire retainer clips (13). Once removed, wire clips should not be reused. Install piston on connecting rod so arrow on piston crown points

toward exhaust port. Note location of thrust washers (11) when installing piston.

CRANKSHAFT AND CONNECTING ROD. Crankshaft is loose in crankcase when cylinder is removed. Cylinder and upper crankcase half are a unit assembly. Crankshaft and connecting rod (10–Fig. SW14) are a unit assembly and supported at both ends with roller type main bearings (6). Rotate connecting rod around crankpin and renew assembly if roughness, excessive play or other damage is noted.

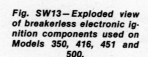

Fig. SW13—Exploded view of breakerless electronic ignition components used on Models 350, 416, 451 and 500.

4. Terminal
5. Spark plug boot
6. Spark plug
7. Module assy.
8. Ignition coil

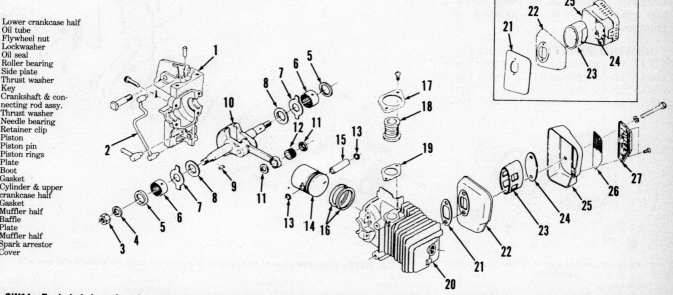

1. Lower crankcase half
2. Oil tube
3. Flywheel nut
4. Lockwasher
5. Oil seal
6. Roller bearing
7. Side plate
8. Thrust washer
9. Key
10. Crankshaft & connecting rod assy.
11. Thrust washer
12. Needle bearing
13. Retainer clip
14. Piston
15. Piston pin
16. Piston rings
17. Plate
18. Boot
19. Gasket
20. Cylinder & upper crankcase half
21. Gasket
22. Muffler half
23. Baffle
24. Plate
25. Muffler half
26. Spark arrestor
27. Cover

Fig. SW14—Exploded view of engine and muffler assemblies. Inset shows muffler assembly used on Model 350. Gasket (19) and side plates (7) are not used on Model 345.

Maximum crankshaft runout measured on main bearing journals and supported between lathe centers is 0.068 mm (0.0027 in.).

New seals (5) should be installed on crankshaft when reassembling upper and lower crankcase halves. Oil holes in roller bearings (6) must face toward cylinder. With crankshaft assembly installed in lower crankcase half (1), crankshaft-to-side plate clearance should be 0.07-0.24 mm (0.003-0.009 in.) on all models. Renew side plate (7) or thrust washer (8) as necessary to obtain recommended clearance. Use a suitable form-in-place gasket compound on mating surfaces of upper and lower crankcase halves. Be sure mating surfaces are not damaged during assembly. Tighten screws securing lower crankcase half (1) to cylinder (20) to 6.9-7.9 N·m (61-70 in.-lbs.) after first applying a suitable thread fastening solution on threads of screws.

CLUTCH. A three-shoe centrifugal type clutch is used on all models. Clutch hub has left-hand threads. Clutch needle bearing (1 – Fig. SW15) should be inspected for excessive wear or damage. Inspect clutch shoes and drum for signs of excessive heat.

AUTOMATIC CHAIN OILER. All models are equipped with an automatic chain oil pump assembly. Oil pump assembly is driven by clutch drum via gears. Oil pump assembly (9 – Fig. SW16) is not serviceable and renewable only as a complete assembly.

Initial setting of oil pump output is the midrange position between minimum and maximum output. To adjust, use a suitable tool and rotate adjuster shaft (8) clockwise to decrease oil pump output and counterclockwise to increase oil pump output.

REWIND STARTER. Refer to Fig. SW17 for exploded view of pawl type starter used on Model 345. Refer to Fig. SW18 for exploded view of pawl type starter used on Models 350 and 416.

Refer to Fig. SW19 for exploded view of pawl type starter used on Models 451 and 500. Care should be exercised when

removing rewind spring (2 – Fig. SW17 or 15 – Fig. SW18) to prevent spring from uncoiling uncontrolled.

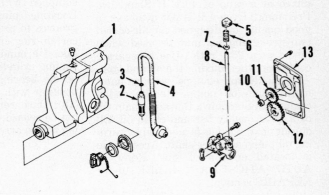

Fig. SW16 — Exploded view of automatic oil pump assembly and associated components. A dust plate is used between oil pump assembly (9) and gears (11 and 12) on Models 350, 416, 451 and 500.

1. Oil tank
2. Strainer
3. Retainer
4. Pickup hose
5. Grommet
6. Spring
7. Washer
8. Adjuster shaft
9. Oil pump assy.
10. Collar
11. Drive gear
12. Oil pump input gear
13. Cover

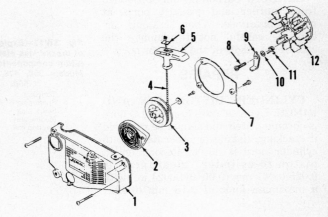

Fig. SW17 — Exploded view of rewind starter assembly used on Model 345.

1. Housing
2. Rewind spring & cassette
3. Rope pulley
4. Rope
5. Handle
6. Anchor
7. Baffle
8. Pivot screw
9. Pawl
10. Washer
11. Return spring
12. Flywheel

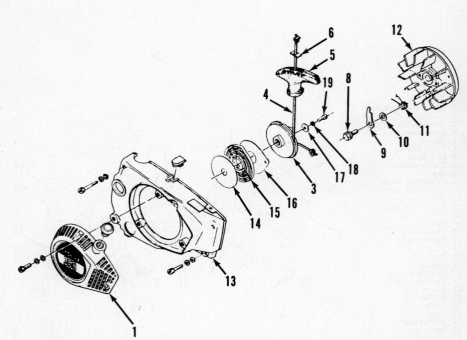

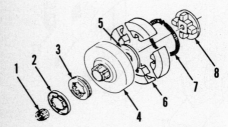

Fig. SW15 — Exploded view of three-shoe clutch assembly.

1. Needle bearing	5. Washer
2. Cover	6. Shoe
3. Floating sprocket	7. Garter spring
4. Drum	8. Hub

Fig. SW18 — Exploded view of rewind starter assembly used on Models 350 and 416.

1. Housing	8. Pivot screw	12. Flywheel	16. Plate
3. Rope pulley	9. Pawl	13. Side cover	17. Flat washer
4. Rope	10. Washer	14. Plate	18. Lockwasher
5. Handle	11. Return spring	15. Rewind spring	19. Screw
6. Anchor			

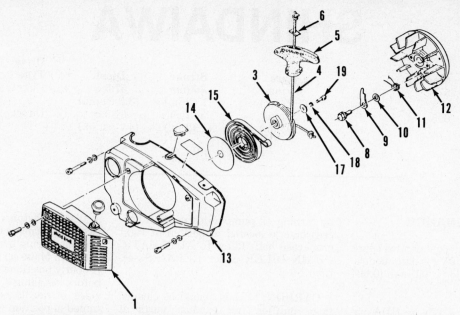

Fig. SW19—Exploded view of rewind starter assembly used on Models 451 and 500. Refer to legend in Fig. SW18 for identification of components.

During reassembly, do not apply anymore tension on rewind spring than required to properly draw rope handle up against starter housing in relaxed position.

CHAIN BRAKE. All models are equipped with a chain brake designed to stop the saw chain quickly should kickback occur. Chain brake is activated when operator's hand strikes lever (1–Fig. SW20), releasing latch (2) thereby allowing spring (6) to draw brake band (12) tight around clutch drum. Pull back lever (1) to reset mechanism.

Disassembly for inspection or repair is evident after referral to exploded view and inspection of unit. Renew any component found to be excessively worn or damaged. Chain brake mechanism should be clean and free of sawdust and dirt accumulation. Lightly lubricate all moving parts and pivot points.

To adjust chain brake, first remove spark plug boot from spark plug and properly ground terminal end. Place chain brake lever (1) in released position. Use a suitable size screwdriver and rotate adjuster (5) clockwise until saw chain cannot be rotated around guide bar by hand pressure. Then rotate adjuster (5) counterclockwise noting when brake band (12) does not contact outside surface of clutch drum. Normal adjustment is 2-4 turns counterclockwise from saw chain bound position. Make sure brake band does not drag on outside of clutch drum with brake lever in released position. With brake lever in applied position, saw chain should not be free to rotate around guide bar.

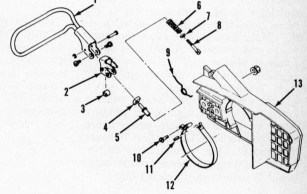

Fig. SW20—Exploded view of chain brake assembly.
1. Lever
2. Latch
3. Spacer
4. Cover
5. Adjuster
6. Spring
7. Washer
8. Adjustment rod
9. Spring
10. Pivot screw
11. Pin
12. Brake band
13. Housing

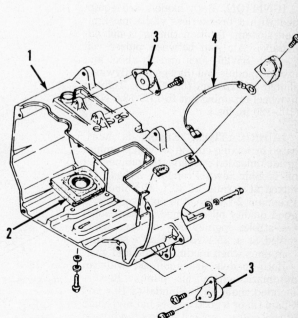

Fig. SW21—Exploded view of engine housing and related components. Ground wire (4) is used on Model 345.
1. Engine housing
2. Seal
3. Vibration damper
4. Ground wire

SHINDAIWA

Model	Bore	Stroke	Displ.	Drive Type
575	45 mm (1.77 in.)	36 mm (1.42 in.)	57.3 cc (3.5 cu. in.)	Direct
695	49 mm (1.93 in.)	36 mm (1.42 in.)	67.9 cc (4.1 cu. in.)	Direct

MAINTENANCE

SPARK PLUG. Recommended spark plug is Champion CJ6Y for both models. Electrode gap should be 0.6 mm (0.024 in.).

CARBURETOR. A Walbro HDA diaphragm type carburetor is used on both models. Refer to Walbro section of CARBURETOR SERVICE for service and exploded views of carburetor.

Initial adjustment for both low speed and high speed mixture screws is 1¼ turns open from a lightly seated position. Make final adjustment with engine warm and running. Adjust idle speed screw so engine idles just below clutch engagement speed (approximately 2800 rpm). Adjust low speed mixture screw so engine will accelerate cleanly without hesitation. Adjust high speed mixture screw to obtain optimum performance under cutting load. During first 10 hours of operation, the manufacturer recommends rotating mixture screws an additional ⅛ turn toward rich setting.

IGNITION. Both models are equipped with a breakerless electronic ignition system. Ignition timing is not adjustable. Air gap between pulser coil (1–Fig. SW26) legs and flywheel and exciter/module coil (3) legs and flywheel should be 0.5 mm (0.020 in.). Tighten flywheel retaining nut to 11.9-13.5 N·m (105-120 in.-lbs.).

LUBRICATION. Engine is lubricated by mixing engine oil with premium grade unleaded gasoline. Recommended oil is Shindaiwa Premium 2-Cycle Oil mixed at a ratio of 40:1. If Shindaiwa Premium 2-Cycle Oil is not available, a good quality oil designed for air-cooled two-stroke engines may be used when mixed at a 25:1 ratio. Use a separate container when mixing the oil and gas.

Both models are equipped with an automatic chain oil pump. Recommended chain oil is Shindaiwa Bar and Chain Oil or a good quality bar and chain oil. Oil output on both models is adjusted by turning oil pump adjuster shaft. Access hole is located in bottom of right crankcase half. Refer to AUTOMATIC CHAIN OILER under REPAIRS section.

CARBON. Carbon should be cleaned from muffler and exhaust ports at regular intervals. When scraping carbon, be careful not to damage the chamfered edges of the exhaust ports.

REPAIRS

CYLINDER, PISTON, PIN AND RINGS. Cylinder (15–Fig. SW27) bore is chrome plated and should be renewed if cracking, flaking or other damage to cylinder bore is noted. Recommended piston-to-cylinder clearance is 0.074-0.102 mm (0.0029-0.0040 in.) with a maximum limit of 0.18 mm (0.0071 in.). Oversize piston and rings are not available. Piston (11) is equipped with two piston rings (13). Locating pins are present in ring grooves to prevent ring rotation. Make certain ring end gaps are properly positioned around locating pins before installing cylinder. Piston pin (12) rides in needle bearing (8) and is retained in position with two wire retainer clips (10). Once removed, wire clips should not be reused. Install piston on connecting rod so arrow on piston crown points toward exhaust port. On Model 575, note location of thrust washers (7 and 9) when installing piston. Tighten screws securing cylinder (15) to crankcase to 6.9-7.9 N·m (61-70 in.-lbs.) after first applying a suitable thread fastening solution on threads of screws.

CRANKSHAFT AND CONNECTING ROD. Cylinder (15–Fig. SW27) must be removed and crankcase halves (1 and 16) must be split to remove

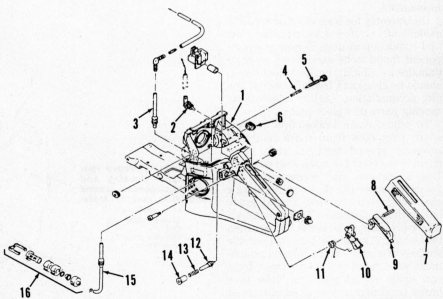

Fig. SW25 – Exploded view of trigger assembly, rear handle assembly and associated components.

1. Rear handle	5. Adjuster screw	9. Lock lever	13. Spring
2. Run/stop switch	6. Grommet	10. Trigger	14. Stop knob
3. Vent tube	7. Handle grip	11. Spring	15. Fuel pickup hose
4. Spring	8. Spring pin	12. Stopper	16. Fuel strainer assy.

crankshaft and connecting rod assembly. Crankshaft and connecting rod (6) are a unit assembly and supported at both ends with ball type main bearings (4). Rotate connecting rod around crankpin and renew assembly if roughness, excessive play or other damage is noted. Renew ball bearings (4) if roughness, excessive play or other damage is noted. Maximum crankshaft runout measured on main bearing journals and supported between lathe centers is 0.068 mm (0.0027 in.).

New seals (3) should be installed into crankcase halves and gaskets (2 and 14) renewed during reassembly. After reassembly, slowly rotate crankshaft assembly to be sure crankshaft assembly and piston rotate freely without binding otherwise damage to engine could result. Tighten screws securing crankcase halves (1 and 16) to 6.9-7.9 N·m (61-70 in.-lbs.) after first applying a suitable thread fastening solution on threads of screws.

CLUTCH. A three-shoe centrifugal type clutch is used on both models. Clutch hub has left-hand threads. Clutch needle bearing (4 – Fig. SW28) should be inspected for excessive wear or damage. Inspect clutch shoes and drum for signs of excessive heat.

AUTOMATIC CHAIN OILER. All models are equipped with an automatic chain oil pump assembly. Oil pump assembly is driven by clutch drum via gear (5 – Fig. SW29). Oil pump assembly (2) is not serviceable and renewable only as a complete assembly.

Initial setting of oil pump output is ⅔ open position between minimum and maximum output. To adjust, use a suitable tool and rotate adjuster shaft (3) clockwise to decrease oil pump output and counterclockwise to increase oil pump output.

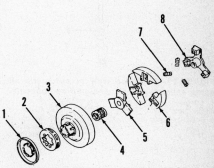

Fig. SW28 – Exploded view of three-shoe clutch assembly.

1. Cover
2. Floating sprocket
3. Drum
4. Needle bearing
5. Outer hub
6. Shoe
7. Spring
8. Inner hub

Fig. SW26 – Exploded view of breakerless electronic ignition components.

1. Pulser coil
2. Ignition coil
3. Exciter/module coil
4. Terminal
5. Spark plug boot

Fig. SW27 – Exploded view of engine, intake and muffler assemblies. Model 695 does not use thrust washers (7 and 9). Adapter plate (17) is not used on Model 575.

1. Crankcase half
2. Gasket
3. Seal
4. Bearing
5. Key
6. Crankshaft & connecting rod assy.
7. Thrust washer
8. Needle bearing
9. Thrust washer
10. Retainer clip
11. Piston
12. Piston pin
13. Piston rings
14. Gasket
15. Cylinder
16. Crankcase half
17. Adapter plate
18. Gasket
19. Boot
20. Plate
21. Sleeve
22. Gasket
23. Muffler assy.
24. Guard
25. Spark arrestor
26. Cover

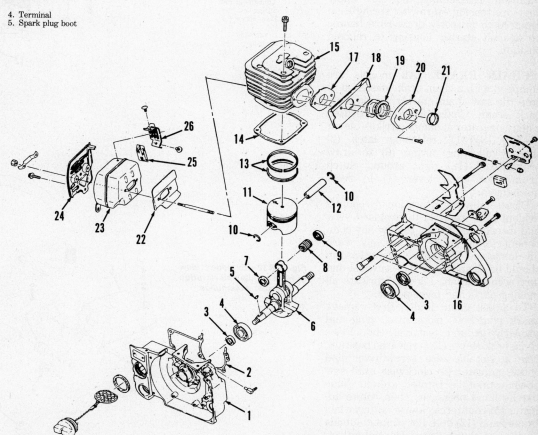

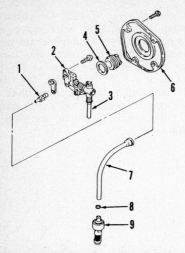

Fig. SW29—Exploded view of automatic oil
pump assembly and associated components.
1. Fitting
2. Oil pump assy.
3. Adjuster shaft
4. Thrust washer
5. Drive gear
6. Cover
7. Pickup hose
8. Retainer
9. Strainer

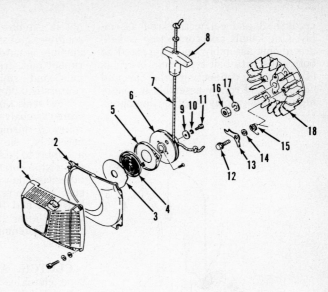

Fig. SW30—Exploded view
of rewind starter assembly.
1. Housing
2. Baffle
3. Plate
4. Rewind spring
5. Cassette
6. Rope pulley
7. Rope
8. Handle
9. Flat washer
10. Lockwasher
11. Screw
12. Pivot screw
13. Pawl
14. Washer
15. Return spring
16. Nut
17. Lockwasher
18. Flywheel

REWIND STARTER. Refer to Fig.
SW30 for exploded view of pawl type
starter used on both models. Care
should be exercised when removing rewind spring (4) to prevent spring from
uncoiling uncontrolled.

During reassembly, do not apply
anymore tension on rewind spring than
required to properly draw rope handle
up against starter housing in relaxed
position.

CHAIN BRAKE. All models are
equipped with a chain brake designed to
stop the saw chain quickly should kickback occur. Chain brake is activated
when operator's hand strikes lever
(1–Fig. SW31), releasing latch (2)
thereby allowing spring (6) to draw
brake band (12) tight around clutch
drum. Pull back lever (1) to reset
mechanism.

Disassembly for inspection or repair is
evident after referral to exploded view
and inspection of unit. Renew any component found to be excessively worn
or damaged. Chain brake mechanism
should be clean and free of sawdust and
dirt accumulation. Lightly lubricate all
moving parts and pivot points.

To adjust chain brake, first remove
spark plug boot from spark plug and
properly ground terminal end. Place
chain brake lever (1) in released position.
Use a suitable size screwdriver and
rotate adjuster (5) clockwise until saw
chain cannot be rotated around guide
bar by hand pressure. Then rotate adjuster (5) counterclockwise noting when
brake band (12) does not contact outside
surface of clutch drum. Normal adjust-

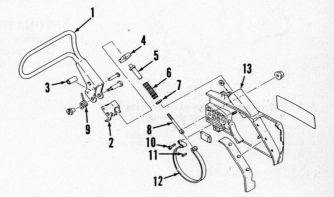

Fig. SW31—Exploded view
of chain brake assembly.
1. Lever
2. Latch
3. Spacer
4. Cover
5. Adjuster
6. Spring
7. Washer
8. Adjustment rod
9. Spring
10. Pivot screw
11. Pin
12. Brake band
13. Housing

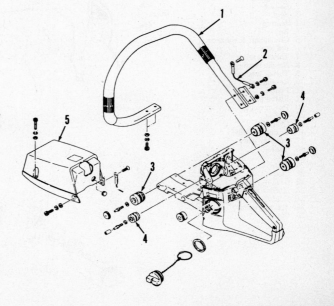

Fig. SW32—Exploded view
of front handle and vibration
damper assemblies.
1. Front handle
2. Ground wire
3. Vibration damper
4. Vibration damper
4. Cylinder cover

ment is 2-4 turns counterclockwise from saw chain bound position. Make sure brake band does not drag on outside of clutch drum with brake lever in released position. With brake lever in applied position, saw chain should not be free to rotate around guide bar.

HANDLE HEATER. Some 695 models are equipped with the handle heating system shown in Fig. SW33. Generating coil (2) located behind flywheel (18) produces an electric current which flows through on/off switch (3) and then to heating elements in rear handle (4) and front handle (1).

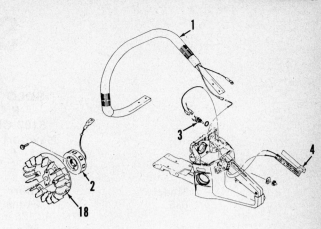

Fig. SW33—Exploded view of handle heating assembly on so equipped 695 models.
1. Front handle heating element
2. Generating coil
3. On/off switch
4. Rear handle heating element
18. Flywheel

SOLO

SOLO MOTORS, INC.
P.O. Box 5030
5100 Chestnut Avenue
Newport News, Va. 23605

Model	Bore	Stroke	Displ.
635	54 mm	40 mm	92 cc
	(2.126 in.)	(1.575 in.)	(5.6 cu. in.)
642	58 mm	40 mm	106 cc
	(2.283 in.)	(1.575 in.)	(6.47)

MAINTENANCE

SPARK PLUG. A Bosch W175 spark plug is recommended. Recommended equivalent is Champion J8J. Set electrode gap to 0.6 mm (0.025 in.).

CARBURETOR. A Tillotson diaphragm carburetor with integral fuel pump is used on both models. Early Model 635 uses an HL-239A while Model 642 and late Model 635 use a Model HL-296A.

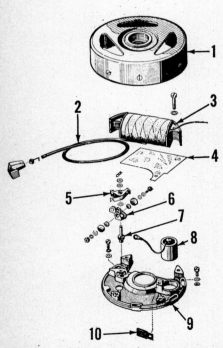

Fig. SO1—Exploded view of Bosch magneto used on Model 635 chain saws. Model 642 is similar.

1. Rotor	6. Breaker point base
2. High tension wire	7. Pivot bolt
3. Ignition coil	8. Condenser
4. Insulating guard	9. Stator plate
5. Breaker point-lever	10. Cam wiper

Refer to Tillotson section of CARBURETOR SERVICE for carburetor service and exploded views. Initial setting of idle mixture screw is ¾ turn open while high speed mixture screw is 1½ turns open. Make final adjustment with engine warm and running. Set the fuel needle for smoothest idle operation and adjust idle speed stop screw so that engine idles at just below clutch engagement speed. Open main fuel needle until engine four-cycles (fires only on every other stroke) then, turn needle in slowly until engine two-strokes (fires on every stroke) at operating speed.

MAGNETO AND TIMING. Refer to Fig. SO1 for exploded view of Bosch flywheel type magneto. Breaker-point gap should be 0.5 mm (0.020 in.).

To check or adjust timing remove blower fan so that flywheel openings are exposed. If Solo timing gage (Part No. 00 80 162) is available, screw gage finger tight into spark plug hole. Turn engines so that timing gage indicates piston is at top dead center. Breaker point gap should then be 0.25-0.3 mm (0.010-0.012 in.). If not, check maximum breaker point opening to be sure that point gap is properly adjusted to 0.5 mm (0.020 in.). If gap is correct and point opening with piston at TDC is not 0.25-0.3 mm (0.010-0.012 in.), adjust stator position in slotted mounting holes to obtain correct measurement. Then, turn engine clockwise so that timing gage indicator falls 3 marks; breaker points should then be just starting to open. (Three marks on timing gage equals approximately 2.5 mm piston travel BTDC or 0.1 inch BTDC).

LUBRICATION. Engine is lubricated by mixing oil with fuel. During the first 20 hours of operation (break-in period),

mix one part of oil with 20 parts of gasoline; thereafter, mix one part of oil with 25 parts of gasoline. Use a good grade of SAE 30 motor oil and regular grade gasoline.

Both models are equipped with automatic chain oilers depicted in Fig. SO2. Exploded views are shown in Fig. SO3. Chain oilers used on Models 635 and 642 are pump driven by a cam or crankshaft end. All oil chain reservoirs should be filled with SAE 30 oil.

Both models are equipped with a manual chain oiler system. It is possible to unclog the automatic system by operating the manual system.

Needle roller bearing in clutch drum should be removed, cleaned and lubricated with Lubriplate or similar grease occasionally.

REPAIRS

CONNECTING ROD. The connecting rod is of one-piece construction and is serviced only as an assembly with the

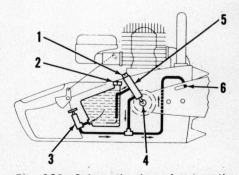

Fig. SO2—Schematic view of automatic chain oiler used on Models 635 and 642. The oil pump (5) is driven by a cam on the crankshaft end (4) thus forcing oil to the chain (6). A manual pump (3) will also force oil to the chain. To vary amount of oil going to chain from automatic pump (5), turn outer control screw (1).

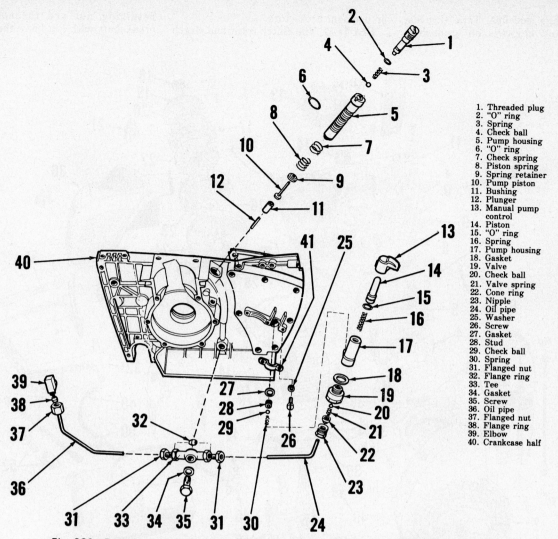

1. Threaded plug
2. "O" ring
3. Spring
4. Check ball
5. Pump housing
6. "O" ring
7. Check spring
8. Piston spring
9. Spring retainer
10. Pump piston
11. Bushing
12. Plunger
13. Manual pump control
14. Piston
15. "O" ring
16. Spring
17. Pump housing
18. Gasket
19. Valve
20. Check ball
21. Valve spring
22. Cone ring
23. Nipple
24. Oil pipe
25. Washer
26. Screw
27. Gasket
28. Stud
29. Check ball
30. Spring
31. Flanged nut
32. Flange ring
33. Tee
34. Gasket
35. Screw
36. Oil pipe
37. Flanged nut
38. Flange ring
39. Elbow
40. Crankcase half

Fig. SO3—Exploded view of automatic chain oil pump assembly as used on Models 635 and 642. Refer to Fig. SO2 for schematic view. Be sure to install "O" rings (6) in original position when reassembling.

crankshaft. If crankpin bearing is rough, burned or excessively worn, renew the crankshaft and connecting rod assembly.

Connecting rod upper end is fitted with a needle bearing. Use drivers of proper size and adequately support connecting rod when removing and installing bearing.

PISTON, PIN AND RINGS. Piston, pin and rings are available in standard size only. Piston and piston pin are available only as a fitted assembly. The two compression rings are available separately.

To remove piston from rod and crankshaft assembly, remove the pin retaining rings, support piston and tap or press the pin from piston and connecting rod.

When installing piston, arrow on piston crown should point towards

exhaust port.

CRANKSHAFT AND MAIN BEARINGS. The crankshaft is supported by two ball bearing type mains. The main bearings can be renewed after removing the cylinder and separating the split type crankcase. Crankcase halves should be heated in oven or under heat lamp to about 250° F (121° C) to remove bearing or to install crankshaft and bearing assembly in crankcase.

As with all two-stroke engines, maintenance of crankshaft oil seals is to utmost importance. When installing seals or crankshaft assembly, be careful

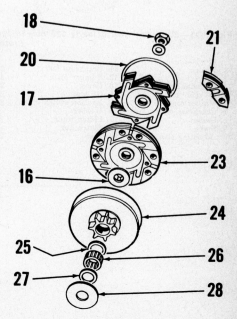

Fig. SO4—Exploded view of Model 635 and 642 clutch assembly. Refer to Fig. SO5 for parts identification.

not to damage seal lips. Tape threads, shoulders and keyways on crankshaft or use seal protectors.

CLUTCH. The clutch rotor and clutch retaining nut are threaded to the crankshaft with left-hand threads.

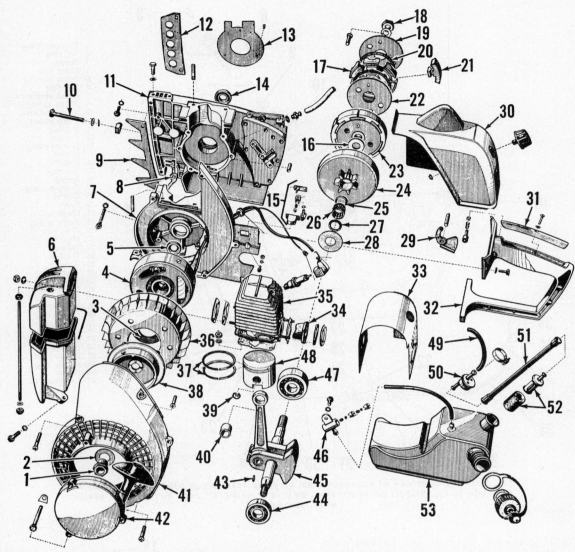

Fig. SO5—Exploded view of early 635 powerhead. Model 642 and later 635 are similar. Refer to Fig. SO1 for exploded view of magneto (4). Clutch assembly for 635 and 642 is shown in Fig. SO4.

1. Flywheel nut	20. Clutch springs	28. Washer	37. Piston rings
2. Washer	21. Clutch shoes	29. Throttle trigger	38. Starter cup
3. Spacer	11. Crankcase half	22. Disc	30. Cover	39. Snap rings	46. Breather valve
4. Magneto assy.	12. Bumper plate	23. Clutch assembly	31. Insert	40. Bushing	47. Ball bearing
5. Oil seal	13. Cover	24. Clutch assembly &	32. Handle	41. Blower housing	48. Piston & pin assy.
6. Muffler assy.	14. Oil seal	sprocket assy.	33. Shield	42. Starter assy.	49. Fuel line
7. Crankcase half	15. Ignition switch	25. Felt ring	34. Carburetor port	43. Key	50. Hose connector
8. Gasket	16. Washer	26. Needle bearing	35. Cylinder	44. Ball bearing	51. Hose
9. Spike	17. Clutch rotor	27. Felt ring	36. Blower fan	45. Crankshaft & rod	52. Fuel pickup
10. Adjusting screw	18. Clutch nut			assy.	53. Fuel tank
	19. Disc				

SOLO

Model	Bore	Stroke	Displ.
600, 605, 631K, 632AVK	38 mm (1.496 in.)	28 mm (1.102 in.)	32 cc (1.95 cu. in.)
606, 638AVK	42 mm (1.653 in.)	28 mm (1.102 in.)	38 cc (2.32 cu. in.)

MAINTENANCE

SPARK PLUG. Recommended spark plug is Bosch WKA175T6 or Champion RCJ6. Electrode gap should be 0.5 mm (0.020 in.).

CARBURETOR. Models 600, 605 and 606 are equipped with a Walbro HDC 29 diaphragm carburetor. Models 631K, 632AVK and 638AVK are equipped with a Walbro HDC 10 diaphragm carburetor. Some models may be equipped with a Tillotson HK55-96A carburetor. Refer to Walbro or Tillotson section of CARBURETOR SERVICE section for service and exploded views.

For initial carburetor adjustment, back idle speed screw out until throttle valve is completely closed, then turn screw back in until screw tip contacts stop plus ½ turn. Turn both mixture screws in until lightly seated, then back high speed mixture screw (H – Fig. SO10) out about one turn and back idle mixture screw out about ¾ turn. On Models 631K, 632AVK and 638AVK, back out high speed mixture screw ⅝ turn and low speed mixture screw 1⅛ turns. Start engine, readjust idle speed screw and mixture screws so engine idles just below clutch engagement speed. With engine running full throttle, readjust high speed mixture screw so engine will run at highest obtainable speed without excessive smoke.

IGNITION. A conventional flywheel magneto ignition system is used on early model saws. Breaker-point gap should be 0.35-0.45 mm (0.014-0.017 in.) Air gap between flywheel and ignition coil should be 0.25 mm (0.010 in.). Timing is fixed but will be affected by breaker point setting. Later model saws are equipped with an electronic ignition system built into the ignition coil. Flywheels for electronic ignition models cannot be interchanged with breaker point models. The coil to flywheel air gap on electronic ignition models should be 0.25-0.30 mm (0.009-0.011 in.). Timing is not adjustable on electronic ignition models.

LUBRICATION. The engine is lubricated by mixing oil with gasoline. Recommended oil is Castrol Super TT or Castrol TTS mixed at a 40:1 ratio during break-in period and normal operation. If Castrol Super TT or Castrol TTS is not available, use a good quality oil designed for use in air-cooled two-stroke engines mixed at a 20:1 ratio during break-in period, and a 25:1 ratio for normal operation.

All models are equipped with a non-adjustable automatic chain oil pump. Refer to Fig. SO11 for an exploded view of pump.

The needle roller bearing in the clutch drum should be removed occasionally, cleaned and lubricated with Lubriplate or a similar grease.

REPAIRS

CONNECTING ROD, CRANK-SHAFT AND CRANKCASE. The connecting rod is one-piece construction and is serviced only as an assembly with the crankshaft. If crankpin bearing is rough, burned or excessively worn, renew crankshaft and connection rod assembly.

The upper end of the connecting rod is fitted with a needle bearing. Use drivers of proper size and adequately support rod when installing or removing bearing.

Crankshaft is supported on two roller bearings. Inspect crankcase bearing bores for damage due to movement of bearing race.

PISTON, PIN, RINGS, AND CYLINDER. Models 600, 600K, 605AV, 631K and 632AVK are equipped with an aluminum cylinder with an iron sleeve. All other models have an aluminum cylinder with a chrome bore. Pistons and cylinders are graded according to size with a letter stamped on top of cylinder

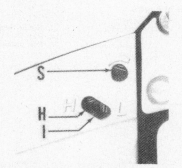

Fig. SO10 — View of idle speed screw (S), high speed mixture screw (H) and idle mixture screw (I).

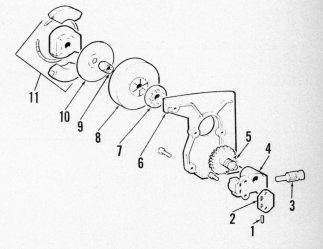

Fig. SO11 — Exploded view of clutch and oil pump assembly.

1. Roller
2. Gasket
3. Piston
4. Oil pump body
5. Worm & gear
6. Plate
7. Oil pump drive gear
8. Clutch drum
9. Bearing
10. Washer
11. Clutch assy.

and piston. Piston and cylinder letter sizes should be the same for proper fit of piston in cylinder. Install piston with arrow on piston crown toward exhaust port.

CLUTCH. The clutch hub is threaded on the crankshaft with left-hand threads. Clutch drum rides on bearing (9 – Fig. SO11) and drives oil pump drive gear (7).

REWIND STARTER. To disassemble starter, remove rope handle and allow rope to rewind into starter. Remove "E" ring (24 – Fig. SO13) and remove rope pulley being careful not to dislodge rewind spring. If rewind spring must be removed, care should be used not to allow spring to uncoil uncontrolled.

Install rewind spring in housing in a clockwise direction from outer spring end. To place tension on rewind spring, install rope pulley and pawl assembly with rope unwound, pass rope through outlet in starter housing and attach handle. Rotate rope pulley in a clockwise direction without winding rope on pulley until rewind spring is coil bound. Allow pulley to unwind one full turn and then allow rope to wind on pulley. Rope handle should fit snugly against rope outlet.

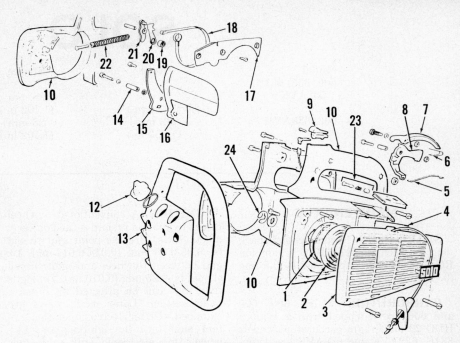

Fig. SO13 — Exploded view of starter and chain brake assemblies.

1. Rope pulley	7. Lever	13. Tank housing	17. Plate	22. Brake spring
2. Rewind spring	8. Throttle trigger	14. Spacer	18. Brake band	23. Retainer button,
3. Starter housing	9. Ignition switch	15. Plate	19. Spacer	pin & spring
4. Air filter	10. Side covers	16. Chain brake	20. Brake lever	24. "E" ring
5. Throttle link	12. Tank cap	actuator	21. Cam	
6. Spring				

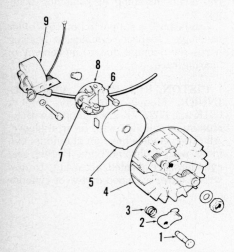

Fig. SO12 — Exploded view of ignition system.

1. Stud
2. Starter pawl
3. Spring
4. Flywheel
5. Ignition box
6. Condenser
7. Breaker points
8. Breaker plate
9. Ignition coil

Fig. SO14 — Exploded view of engine.

1. Oil hose	6. Crankcase	11. Pin retainers	16. Adapter	21. Needle bearing
2. Strainer	7. Seal	12. Piston pin	17. Carburetor	22. Key
3. Impulse nipple	8. Washer	13. Piston	18. Gaskets	23. Fuel pickup
4. Nipple	9. Needle bearing	14. Piston ring	19. Intake manifold	24. Filter
5. Gasket	10. Crankshaft	15. Muffler	20. Cylinder	

SOLO

Model	Bore	Stroke	Displ.
616	*42 mm	32 mm	*45 cc
	(1.654 in.)	(1.260 in.)	(2.75 cu. in.)

*Models produced after serial number 8999 are equipped with a 45 mm (1.77 in.) bore and a 52 cc (3.17 cu. in.) displacement.

MAINTENANCE

SPARK PLUG. Recommended spark plug for this model is Bosch WKA 175 T6 or Champion RCJ6. Electrode gap should be 0.5 mm (0.020 inch).

CARBURETOR. Model 616 is equipped with a Walbro HDC 29 diaphragm carburetor. Refer to Walbro section of CARBURETOR SERVICE section for service and exploded views.

For initial carburetor adjustment, back idle speed adjusting screw out until throttle valve is completely closed then turn screw back in until it contacts idle stop plus ½ turn additional. Turn both fuel adjusting needles shown in Fig. S020 in until lightly seated, then back main fuel needle out about one turn and back idle mixture screw out about ¾ turn. Start engine, readjust idle speed and fuel needles so that engine idles at just below clutch engagement speed. With engine running at full throttle, readjust main fuel needle so that engine will run at highest obtainable speed under cutting load.

IGNITION. A conventional flywheel magneto ignition system is used. Breaker point gap should be 0.35-0.45 mm (0.014-0.017 inch). Air gap between flywheel and ignition coil legs should be 0.25 mm (0.010 inch). Timing is fixed but will be affected by breaker points setting.

LUBRICATION. Engine is lubricated by mixing oil with fuel. During the first 20 hours of operation (break-in period), mix one part oil with 20 parts of gasoline; thereafter, mix one part oil with 25 parts gasoline. Use a good grade of SAE 30 motor oil and regular grade gasoline.

Model 616 is equipped with an automatic adjustable chain oiler shown in Fig. S021. The gear driven piston type pump flow can be adjusted by the screw below the chain tightening screw. Turn screw towards "+" to increase, counter-clockwise toward "-" to reduce oil flow. To shut off oil flow completely (as when using other attachments) turn adjusting screw to neutral position (Fig. S022). Reduce oil flow only when using a very short bar, or if

a lightweight oil must be used on a hot day.

Needle roller bearing in clutch drum should be removed, cleaned and relubricated with Lubriplate or similar grease occasionally.

REPAIRS

CONNECTING ROD. The connecting rod is one-piece construction and is serviced only as an assembly with the crankshaft. If crankpin bearing is rough, burned or excessively worn, renew the crankshaft and connecting rod assembly.

The upper end of the connecting rod is fitted with a needle bearing. Use drivers of proper size and adequately support rod when installing or removing bearing.

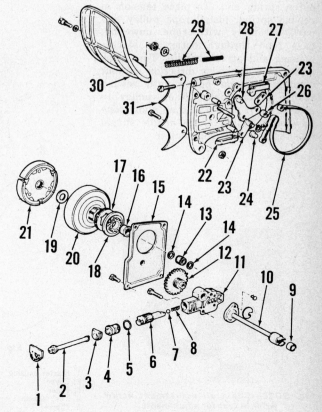

Fig. SO21—Exploded view of oil pump, clutch assembly and chain brake.

1. Plate
2. Adjuster shaft
3. Spacer
4. Oil adjuster
5. "O" ring
6. Piston
7. Ball
8. Spring
9. Oil strainer
10. Hose
11. Housing
12. Worm & gear
13. Needle bearing
14. Felt ring
15. Pump cover
16. Bushing
17. Sprocket
18. Oil pump drive gear
19. Washer
20. Clutch drum
21. Clutch assy.
22. Guide shoe
23. Lever
24. Pin
25. Brake band
26. Spacer
27. Spring seat
28. Lever
29. Springs
30. Hand guard
31. Bucking spikes

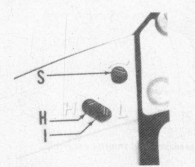

Fig. SO20—View of idle speed screw (S) high speed mixture screw (H) and idle mixture screw (I).

PISTON, PIN, RINGS AND CYLINDER. Model 616 is equipped with a chromed bore aluminum cylinder. Pistons and cylinders are graded with a letter stamped on the top of the cylinder and top of piston. Piston and cylinder should be marked with some letter grade for proper fit. Install pistons with arrow on piston crown towards exhaust port.

CRANKSHAFT AND CRANKCASE. Crankshaft is supported on two roller bearings. It may be necessary to heat crankcase around bearings to facilitate removal of crankshaft and bearings from crankcase halves. For ease of installation of crankshaft assembly, apply heat around main bearing bores.

CLUTCH. The clutch drum is retained by an "E" ring. Clutch hub has left hand threads. Clutch hub, shoes and springs are available only as a unit assembly.

REWIND STARTER. To disassemble starter, remove rope handle and allow rope to rewind into starter. Detach "E" ring (16—Fig. S024) and remove rope pulley (17) being careful not to dislodge rewind spring. If rewind spring (19) must be removed, care should be used not to allow spring to uncoil uncontrolled.

Install rewind spring so coils are wrapped in clockwise direction from outer spring end. To place tension in rewind spring, install rope pulley and pawl assembly with rope unwound, pass rope through outlet in starter housing and attach handle. Turn rope pulley in a clockwise direction without winding rope on pulley until rewind spring is coil bound. Allow pulley to unwind ¼-½ turn and then allow rope to wind on pulley. Rope handle should fit snugly against rope outlet.

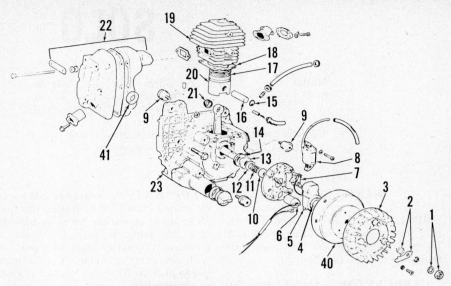

Fig. SO23—Exploded view of engine used on Model 616.

1. Nut & lockwasher	8. Ignition coil	14. Seal	20. Piston
2. Spring & pawl	9. Motor mount	15. Pin retainer	21. Needle bearing
3. Fan	10. Cam	16. Piston pin	22. Muffler assembly
4. Felt ring	11. Spring	17. Piston rings	23. Crankcase and
5. Breaker box	12. Felt ring	18. Gasket	crankshaft assy.
6. Condenser	13. Spacer	19. Cylinder	40. Flywheel
7. Breaker points			41. Seal

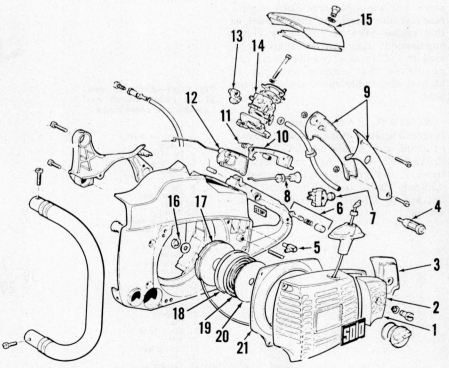

Fig. SO24—Exploded view of starter assembly and throttle assembly.

1. Starter housing	6. Retainer button, pin	11. Spring	17. Rope pulley
2. Cover	& spring	12. Throttle	18. Spring cover
3. Filter	7. Stop button	13. Spacer	19. Spring
4. Fuel pick-up	8. Choke link	14. Carburetor	20. Washer
5. Nipple	9. Handle grips	15. Air filter and cover	21. Plate
	10. Lever	16. "E" ring	

Fig. SO22—Chain oil adjustment screw. Refer to text for adjustments.

SOLO

Model	Bore	Stroke	Displ.
610	40 mm (1.57 in.)	28 mm (1.10 in.)	35 cc (2.1 cu. in.)
615	42 mm (1.65 in.)	32 mm (1.26 in.)	44 cc (2.7 cu. in.)
620	44 mm (1.73 in.)	34 mm (1.34 in.)	52 cc (3.1 cu. in.)
650	48 mm (1.89 in.)	34 mm (1.34 in.)	62 cc (3.7 cu. in.)
655	48 mm (1.89 in.)	38 mm (1.50 in.)	70 cc (4.2 cu. in.)
660	52 mm (2.05 in.)	38 mm (1.50 in.)	81 cc (5.0 cu. in.)

MAINTENANCE

SPARK PLUG. Recommended spark plug for all models is Bosch WKA175T6 or equivalent. Electrode gap should be 0.5 mm (0.020 inch).

CARBURETOR. Models 610 and 615 are equipped with a Tillotson Model HU diaphragm carburetor while all other models are equipped with a Tillotson Model HS diaphragm carburetor. Refer to Tillotson section of CARBURETOR SERVICE section for service and exploded views.

Initial setting of idle mixture screws is ¾ turns open on all models. Initial setting of high speed mixture screw is 1 turn open on Models 610 and 615 and 1¼ turns open on all other models. Idle mixture screw should be adjusted so that engine will accelerate cleanly without stumbling. High speed mixture screw should be adjusted to provide optimum performance with saw under a cutting load. Adjust idle speed screw so that engine idles just below clutch engagement speed.

IGNITION. Early models are equipped with a conventional flywheel magneto ignition system while later models are equipped with an electronic breakerless ignition system.

Breaker-point gap on models so equipped should be 0.35-0.45 mm (0.014-0.017 in.) Air gap between flywheel and ignition coil legs should be 0.25 mm (0.010 in.). Ignition timing is fixed but will be affected by ignition breaker point setting.

LUBRICATION. Oil is mixed with the fuel to lubricate engine. Recommended fuel:oil ratio is 20:1 during the first 20 hours of operation (break-in period) and 25:1 thereafter. Oil should be designed for air-cooled two-stroke engines.

All models are equipped with a gear driven piston type automatic chain oil pump. Oil pump output is adjustable by moving lever on side of clutch cover on Models 610 and 615 or by turning adjusting screw on top of clutch cover on all other models. Chain oil should be

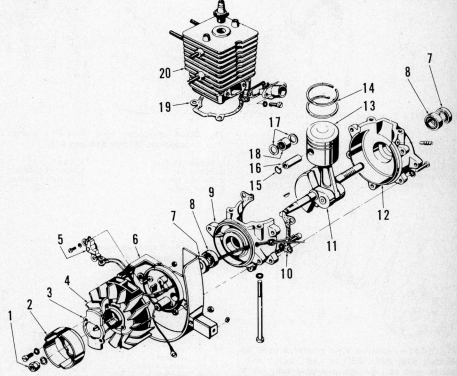

Fig. SO30—Exploded view of engine used on Models 610 and 615.

1. Nut
2. Starter cup
3. Spacer
4. Flywheel
5. Breaker points
6. Air shroud
7. Seal
8. Bearing
9. Left crankcase half
10. Gasket
11. Crankshaft assy.
12. Right crankcase half
13. Piston
14. Piston rings
15. Pin retainer
16. Piston pin
17. Thrust washers
18. Needle bearing
19. Gasket
20. Cylinder

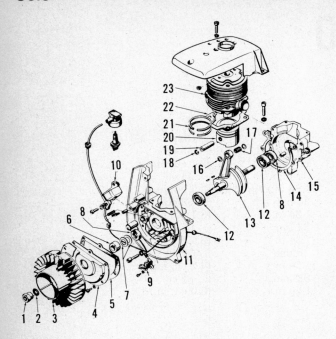

Fig. SO31—Exploded view of engine used on Models 620, 650, 655 and 660. Later models are equipped with electronic ignition in place of breaker points (9).

1. Nut
2. Washer
3. Flywheel
4. Breaker point cover
5. Gasket
6. Breaker point cam
7. Spring discs
8. Seal
9. Breaker points
10. Ignition coil
11. Left crankcase half
12. Bearing
13. Crankshaft assy.
14. Gasket
15. Right crankcase half
16. Thrust washers
17. Needle bearing
18. Pin retainer
19. Piston pin
20. Piston
21. Piston rings
22. Gasket
23. Cylinder

stamped with the same letter. Cylinders stamped "B" may use pistons stamped "B or A"; cylinders stamped "C" may use pistons stamped "A, B or C"; cylinders stamped "D" may use pistons stamped "B, C or D"; cylinders stamped "E" may use pistons stamped "C, D or E". Install pistons with arrow on piston crown towards exhaust port.

CRANKSHAFT, CONNECTING ROD AND CRANKCASE. Crankshaft is supported on two ball bearings. It may be necessary to heat crankcase around bearings to facilitate removal of crankshaft and bearings from crankcase halves. Crankshaft and connecting rod are available only as a unit assembly and should not be disassembled. Apply heat around main bearing bores if crankcase halves to ease installation of crankshaft assembly.

CLUTCH. The clutch drum on all models is retained by an "E" ring (11—Fig. SO32 or 9—Fig. SO33). Clutch hub has left hand threads. Clutch hub, shoes and springs on Models 620, 650, 655 and 660 are available only as a unit assembly.

REWIND STARTER. Refer to Fig. SO34 or Fig. SO35 for an exploded view of rewind starter. To disassemble starter, remove rope handle and allow rope to rewind into starter. Remove spring clip and remove rope pulley and pawl assembly being careful not to dislodge rewind spring. If rewind spring must be removed, care should be used not to allow spring to uncoil uncontrolled. Rewind spring on Models 610 and 615 is located in starter housing while rewind spring on all other models is located in left side of rope pulley (6—Fig. SO35).

Rope length should be 85 cm (33½ in.) on Models 610 and 615 or 95 cm (37½ in.) on all other models. Install rewind spring in a clockwise direction

clean and the viscosity determined by ambient temperature.

REPAIRS

PISTON, PIN, RINGS AND CYLINDER. Models 610 and 620 are equipped

with aluminum cylinders which have a steel sleeve. All other models are equipped with chromed bore aluminum cylinders. Pistons and cylinders on all models are graded with a letter stamped on the top of the cylinder the top of the piston. Letters on cylinders stamped "A, N or U" must use pistons

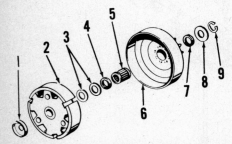

Fig. SO32—Exploded view of clutch used on Models 610 and 615.

1. Washer
2. Clutch shoe
3. Clutch hub
4. Spring
5. Washer
6. Felt seal
7. Needle bearing
8. Clutch drum
9. Felt seal
10. Washer
11. "E" ring

Fig. SO34—Exploded view of rewind starter used on Models 610 and 615.

1. Starter housing
2. Spring cup
3. Rewind spring
4. Rope pulley
5. Pawl
6. Slotted washers
7. Serrated washer
8. Spring clip

Fig. SO33—Exploded view of clutch used on Models 620, 650, 655 and 650. Clutch hub, shoes and springs are available only as a unit.

1. Cup washer
2. Clutch assy.
3. Washers
4. Felt seal
5. Needle bearing
6. Clutch drum
7. Felt seal
8. Washer
9. "E" ring

Fig. SO35—Exploded view of starter used on Models 620, 650, 655 and 660.

1. Starter housing
2. Felt seal
3. Spring cup
4. Rewind spring
5. Plate
6. Left pulley half
7. Rope
8. Right pulley half
9. Pawl
10. Felt seal
11. Slotted washer
12. Pawl hub
13. Washer
14. Serrated washer
15. Spring clip

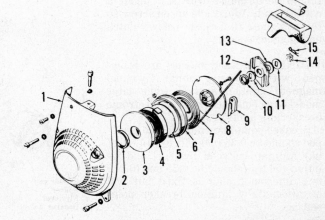

in starter housing of Models 610 and 615 and in a counter-clockwise direction in left rope pulley half on all other models. To place tension in rewind spring, install rope pulley and pawl assembly with rope unwound, pass rope through outlet in starter housing and attach handle. Wind rope pulley in a clockwise direction without winding rope on pulley until rewind spring is coil bound. Allow pulley to unwind ¼-½ turns and then allow rope to wind on pulley. Rope handle should fit snugly against rope outlet.

OIL PUMP. All models are equipped with an automatic oil pump driven by the chain sprocket. Refer to Fig. S036 or S037 for an exploded view of oil pump.

Oil pump used on Models 610 and 615 is driven by a series of gears. Steel gears were used on early models while later models are equipped with plastic gears. Steel and plastic gears may not be interchanged unless the whole set of gears is replaced. Drive gear (16—Fig. S036) screws into pump driver (5) on later models with plastic gears but is pressed into driver on early models with steel gears.

Oil pump adjuster (11) must be installed with high point towards idler gear (18). Oil pump flow may also be adjusted by turning screw in oil tank cover (1) adjacent to "MAX" letters on cover.

Models 620, 650, 655 and 660 are equipped with a worm drive reciprocating type pump. Loctite should be applied to screw (1—Fig. S037) threads.

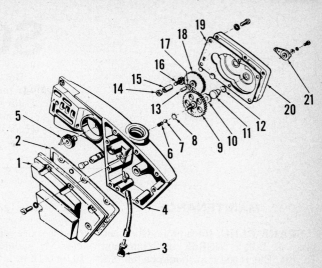

Fig. SO36—Exploded view of oil pump assembly used on Models 610 and 615.

1. Oil tank cover
2. Gasket
3. Oil pick-up
4. Oil tank housing
5. Pump driver
6. Spring
7. Check ball
8. Washer
9. Pump gear
10. Disc
11. Adjuster
12. "O" ring
13. Pin
14. Seal
15. Bushing
16. Pump drive gear
17. Washer
18. Idler gear
19. Gasket
20. Pump cover
21. Adjusting lever

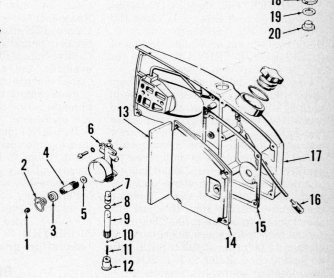

Fig. SO37—Exploded view of oil pump used on Models 620, 650, 655 and 660.

1. Set screw
2. Drive spring
3. Gasket
4. Worm
5. Washer
6. Oil pump housing
7. Beveled plug
8. "O" ring
9. Plunger
10. Ball
11. Spring
12. Plug
13. Plate
14. Oil tank cover
15. Gasket
16. Oil pick-up
17. Cover
18. Retainer
19. Washer
20. Adjuster

SOLO

Model	Bore	Stroke	Displ.
647	42 mm (1.65 in.)	34 mm (1.34 in.)	47 cc (2.9 cu. in.)
654	45 mm (1.77 in.)	34 mm (1.34 in.)	54 cc (3.3 cu. in.)

MAINTENANCE

SPARK PLUG. Recommended spark plug is Bosch WSR6F or Champion RCJ64. Electrode gap should be 0.5 mm (0.020 in.).

CARBURETOR. Models 647 and 654 are equipped with either a Tillotson HU or a Walbro WT diaphragm carburetor. Refer to Tillotson or Walbro section of CARBURETOR SERVICE section for service and exploded views.

For initial adjustment, turn high speed and low speed mixture screws in until lightly seated. Back out low speed screw 1¼ turns and high speed screw one full turn. Rotate idle speed screw out until throttle valve is completely closed, then turn back in until screw tip contacts stop plus ½ turn. Make final adjustments with engine warm and running. Adjust low speed screw to obtain the highest possible rpm. Readjust idle speed screw to obtain 2,700-2,800 rpm. Adjust high speed screw so engine operation is 12,000 rpm at full throttle with no load applied. Refer to Fig. SO47 for view locating adjustment screws.

IGNITION. All models are equipped with electronic ignition system shown in Fig. SO48. Ignition timing is not adjustable. Air gap between ignition module core legs (2) and flywheel magnets (1) should be set at 0.2-0.3 mm (0.08-0.12 in.).

LUBRICATION. Engine is lubricated by mixing oil with gasoline. Recommended oil is Castrol Super TT or Castrol TTS mixed at a 40:1 ratio during break-in period and normal operation. If Castrol Super TT or Castrol TTS is not available, use a good quality oil designed for use in air-cooled two-stroke engines mixed at a 20:1 ratio during break-in period and a 25:1 ratio for normal operation.

Models 647 and 654 are equipped with an adjustable, automatic, gear driven oil pump. Refer to Fig. SO49. Clean automotive oil may be used with viscosity determined by ambient conditions.

Periodically the needle roller bearing in clutch drum should be removed, cleaned and lubricated with MOBILTEM 78 or an equivalent high temperature grease.

REPAIRS

PISTON, PIN, RINGS, AND CYLINDER. Model 647 is equipped with an aluminum cylinder with a steel sleeve. There are two sizes of pistons and cylinders available. The standard size will have a "N" stamped on cylinder head while the piston will be unmarked. Oversize piston and cylinder will have a "U"

stamped on the cylinder head and piston crown. Only piston and cylinder which corresponds should be used together.

The cylinder wall on Model 654 is Nikasil impregnated. Three sizes of pistons and cylinders are available. The pistons and cylinders are identified with the markings "A," "B" or "C" stamped on the cylinder head and piston crown with "A" being the smallest and "C" being the largest. On new assemblies, a piston marked "A" can be used in a cylinder marked "A" or "B." A piston marked "B" can be used in a cylinder marked "B" or "C."

Piston marked "C" can only be used in a cylinder marked "C." When installing a used cylinder, a piston marked "A" can

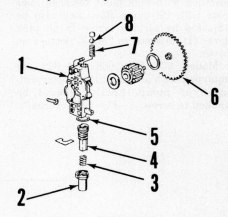

Fig. SO49 – Exploded view of oil pump assembly.

1. Pump body
2. Adjuster
3. Spring
4. Intermediate adjuster
5. "O" ring
6. Driven gear
7. Spring
8. Check ball

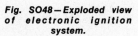

Fig. SO47 – Idle speed screw is accessible through opening (S). High speed mixture screw and low speed mixture screw are accessible through opening (M). "L" and "H" on side cover identify location of screws.

Fig. SO48 – Exploded view of electronic ignition system.

1. Flywheel
2. Ignition module
3. Ignition switch
4. Ignition coil

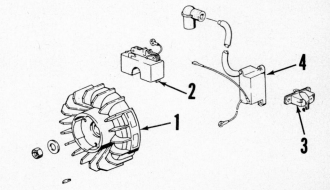

be used in a cylinder marked "A" or "B." A piston marked "B" can be used in a cylinder marked "A," "B" or "C." Pistons marked "C" can be used in a cylinder marked "B" or "C." Locating pins are used in piston ring grooves to prevent piston ring rotation. Be sure ring end gaps are around locating pins when installing cylinder. Install piston with arrow on piston crown pointing toward exhaust port. Refer to Fig. SO50 for exploded view of engine assembly.

CRANKSHAFT, CONNECTING ROD AND CRANKCASE. Crankshaft is supported by two ball bearings pressed on the crankshaft. Ball bearings (10 – Fig. SO50) must be removed using a jaw type bearing puller. Once a bearing has been removed, the bearing should be discarded and a new one installed. Crankshaft and connecting rod are available as a unit assembly only and should not be disassembled.

CLUTCH. All models are equipped with a three-shoe centrifugal clutch. Clutch hub is threaded with left-hand threads. Clutch drum rides on needle roller bearing (6 – Fig. SO51) and drives oil pump. Clutch hub, shoes and spring are available as a unit assembly only.

REWIND STARTER. To disassemble starter, extend rope until one full turn is unwound. Pull slack rope back through rope guide and carefully let pulley (4 – Fig. SO52) unwind, unloading tension on rewind spring (2). After removing spring clip (6), starter pawl (7), washer (5) and rope pulley (4) can be lifted off starter assembly. If rewind

spring (2) is to be removed, care should be taken not to let rewind spring unwind uncontrolled. Install rewind spring (2) into spring cup (3) in a clockwise direction starting with outer coil. Install rewind spring and spring cup into starter housing making sure hook in outer coil engages notch in starter housing.

Starter rope length should be 90 cm (35.4 in.). To install starter rope, wind four turns of rope onto rope pulley and lay pulley on spring cup making sure hook on inner spring coil engages notch in pulley. Install starter pawl (7), washer (5) and spring clip (6). Insert rope into notch on pulley and rotate a pulley approximately 1½ turns in a clockwise direction to apply tension on rewind spring. Carefully let pulley rewind to retract rope. Rope tension is correct if rope pulley is able to tighten one full turn after rope is fully extended.

OIL PUMP. Models 647 and 654 are equipped with an adjustable, automatic, piston type pump. The oil pump is driven by a drive gear on chain sprocket (9 – Fig. SO51).

CHAIN BRAKE. Models 647 and 654 are equipped with a chain brake system designed to stop chain movement should kickback occur. The chain brake is activated when the operator's hand strikes chain brake lever (1 – Fig. SO53) tripping lock lever (4) and releasing spring (5) and plunger (2) pulling brake band (8) tight around clutch drum. Pull back chain brake lever to reset mechanism.

If disassembly is required, chain brake must be in off position before chain guard can be removed. Inspect lock lever and plunger for excessive wear

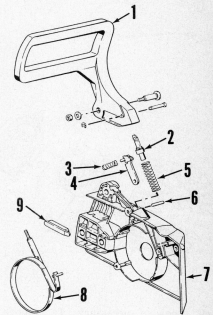

Fig. SO53—Exploded view of chain brake system.

1. Chain brake lever
2. Plunger
3. Spring
4. Lock lever
5. Spring
6. Pin
7. Chain guard
8. Brake band
9. Guide shoe

Fig. SO51—Exploded view of clutch assembly.

1. Clutch shoe
2. Hub
3. Spring
4. Washer
5. Felt ring
6. Needle roller bearing
7. Clutch drum
8. Washer
9. Oil pump drive gear
10. Washer

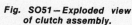

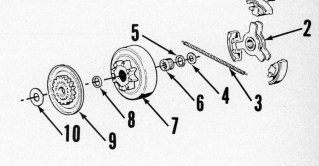

Fig. SO52—Exploded view of starter assembly.

1. Starter housing
2. Rewind spring
3. Spring cup
4. Rope pulley
5. Washer
6. Spring clip
7. Pawl
8. Rope handle

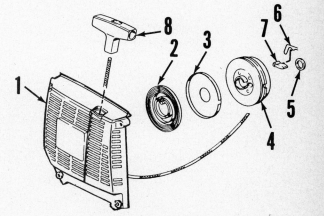

Fig. SO50—Exploded view of engine assembly.

1. Cylinder
2. Muffler
3. Gasket
4. Cover
5. Piston ring
6. Piston
7. Crankshaft & connecting rod assy.
8. Crankshaft seal
9. Washer
10. Ball bearing
11. Crankcase half
12. Needle roller bearing
13. Piston pin
14. Pin retainer

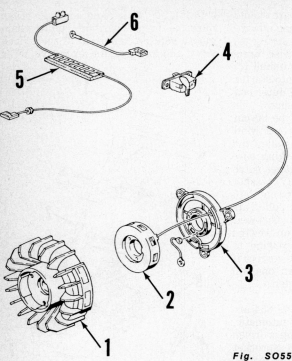

Fig. SO54—Exploded view of handle heating system on models so equipped.

1. Flywheel
2. Generator
3. Generator seat
4. Switch
5. Heating element
6. Lead

and renew if necessary. To remove plunger (2), trip lock lever (4) with a screwdriver. Use caution when releasing spring as spring is under high load. When reassembling plunger (2), screw plunger into connector 7-9 full turns. The brake band must come in contact with the retaining edges of spring seat. If not, screw plunger in or out to adjust.

To test chain brake adjustment, position assembly in a soft-jawed vise so handle is parallel with top of vise jaws. The chain brake should engage when a weight of 4.4 kg (9.7 lbs.) is suspended from the chain brake lever. If engagement is above or below this specification, inspect for worn lock lever and plunger or weak or broken spring. Renew components as necessary.

HEATED HANDLE. Some models are equipped with a front and rear handle heating system. Generating coil (2–Fig. SO54) located under the flywheel provides an electrical current to heating coils (5) in front and rear handles. The heating coils are wired in series. Switch (4) opens or closes a common ground. Refer to Fig. SO55 for schematic drawing.

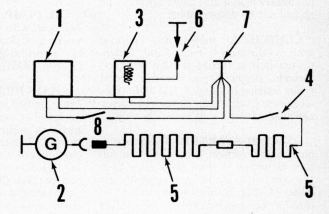

Fig. SO55—Schematic drawing of ignition system and handle heating system on models so equipped.

1. Ignition module
2. Generator
3. Ignition coil
4. Heater switch
5. Heating elements
6. Spark plug
7. Ground connection
8. Ignition switch

SOLO

Model	Bore	Stroke	Displ.
662	46 mm	38 mm	63 cc
	(1.81 in.)	(1.50 in.)	(3.84 cu. in.)
667	48 mm	38 mm	69 cc
	(1.89 in.)	(1.50 in.)	(4.2 cu. in.)
670	48 mm	38 mm	69 cc
	(1.89 in.)	(1.50 in.)	(4.2 cu. in.)
680	52 mm	38 mm	81 cc
	(2.05 in.)	(1.50 in.)	(5.0 cu. in.)
603	56 mm	42 mm	103 cc
	(2.2 in.)	(1.7 in.)	(6.3 cu. in.)

MAINTENANCE

SPARK PLUG. Recommended spark plug is Bosch WSR6F or Champion RCJ64. Spark plug electrode gap should be 0.5 mm (0.020) for all models.

CARBURETOR. Models 662 and 667 are equipped with a Walbro diaphragm type carburetor. Models 670, 680 and 603 are equipped with either a Walbro WJ3 or a Tillotson diaphram type carburetor. Refer to CARBURETOR SERVICE section for service and exploded views.

For initial adjustment, carefully screw in high and low speed mixture screws until lightly seated. Rotate low and high speed mixture screws out one full turn. Rotate idle speed screw out until throttle valve is completely closed, then rotate screw back in until throttle valve is slightly cracked open. Final adjustment should be made with engine warm and running. Adjust idle speed to just below clutch engagement (approximately 2,400 rpm). Adjust low speed mixture screw to obtain highest possible rpm, then readjust idle speed to approximately 2,400 rpm. Adjust high speed

mixture screw to obtain 12,000 rpm maximum at full throttle with no load applied. Do not adjust high speed mixture too lean as engine damage could result. Refer to Fig. SO65 for view locating adjustment screws.

IGNITION. All models are equipped with an electronic ignition system. Ignition timing is not adjustable. Air gap should be set at 0.2-0.3 mm (0.008-0.012 in.) between ignition coil core and flywheel magnets. Refer to Fig. SO66 for exploded view of ignition system used on Models 670, 680 and 603. Ignition system on Models 662 and 667 is similar to type shown in Fig. SO66.

LUBRICATION. The engine is lubricated by mixing oil with gasoline. The recommended oil is Castrol Super TT or Castrol TTS mixed at a 40:1 ratio during break-in period and normal operation. If Castrol Super TT or Castrol TTS is not available, a good quality oil designed for use in air-cooled two-stroke engines can be used mixed at a 20:1 ratio during

break-in period and 25:1 ratio for normal operation.

All models are equipped with an automatic, piston type oil pump. Oil pump output is adjustable by turning screw (8–Fig. SO67) located on bottom of saw on clutch side. The oil pump is driven by worm gear (8–Fig. SO69) located inside of clutch drum (7). The clutch drum rides on needle roller bearing (6) which should be disassembled, cleaned and lubricated periodically using MOBILTEM 78 or an equivalent high temperature grease.

REPAIRS

CYLINDER, PISTON, RINGS AND PIN. Model 662 is equipped with an aluminum cylinder with a steel sleeve. Model 667 is equipped with an aluminum cylinder with Nikasil impregnated cylinder walls. Models 662 and 667 have two sizes of pistons and cylinders assemblies available. Standard size assemblies will have a "N" stamped on the cylinder head while the piston will be un-

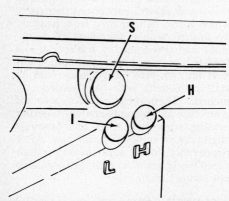

Fig. SO65—View identifying location of idle speed screw (S), high speed mixture screw (H) and low speed mixture screw (I).

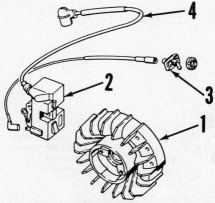

Fig. SO66—View showing ignition system components used on Models 670, 680 and 603. Ignition system components on Models 662 and 667 are similar.

1. Flywheel
2. Ignition coil
3. Ignition switch
4. Spark plug lead

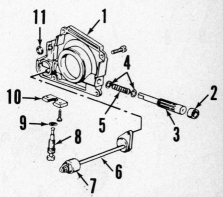

Fig. SO67—Exploded view of automatic oil pump.

1. Pump housing
2. Plug
3. Piston
4. Washers
5. Spring
6. Hose
7. Oil strainer
8. Adjuster
9. "O" ring
10. Adjuster check plate
11. "O" ring

marked. Oversize assemblies will have a "U" stamped on the cylinder head and the piston crown. Only piston and cylinder which correspond should be used together.

Models 670, 680 and 603 are equipped with an aluminum cylinder with Nikasil impregnated cylinder walls. Three sizes of piston and cylinder assemblies are available. Size designations will be marked "A," "B" or "C" stamped on the cylinder head and piston crown. When using new parts, piston marked "A" can be used in cylinder marked "A" or "B." Piston marked "B" can be used in cylinder marked "B" or "C." Pistons marked "C" can be used only in cylinders marked "C." When installing a used cylinder, piston marked "A" can be used in cylinder marked "A" or "B." Piston marked "B" can be used in cylinder marked "A," "B" or "C." Piston marked "C" can be used in cylinder marked "B" or "C."

To remove piston from connecting rod, remove piston pin retaining clips (9 – Fig. SO68) and carefully push out piston pin (10).

Locating pins are used in piston ring grooves to prevent piston ring rotation. When installing piston rings, make sure ring end gaps are placed around locating pins.

When installing piston on connecting rod, align arrow on piston crown with exhaust port.

CRANKSHAFT, CONNECTING ROD AND CRANKCASE. Crankshaft and connecting rod are a unit assembly and should not be disassembled. Check rotation of connecting rod around crankpin. If roughness or other damage is noted, renew crankshaft and connecting rod assembly. The upper end of connecting rod is fitted with needle roller bearing (15 – Fig. SO68). Use drivers of the proper size and adequately support connecting rod when removing or installing bearing.

Crankcase halves (7) can be separated using Solo tool 0080460 or a suitable flywheel puller. Be careful not to damage crankcase mating surfaces. The crankshaft is supported by two ball bearings (6). The ball bearings can be removed from crankshaft using a suitable bearing puller. If bearings are removed from crankshaft or remain in crankcase halves during separation, they should be renewed. To install ball bearings on crankshaft, heat bearings approximately 130° C (266° F) using either a hot plate or an oil bath. Do not use an open flame to heat bearings.

The crankcase halves will require heating to ease reassembly. Be sure to remove all plastic, rubber or other parts which would be damaged from heating. To ensure proper alignment of crankshaft during reassembly, use special tool 0080462 or a suitable equivalent. First heat ignition side of crankcase and install crankshaft with ball bearings attached. Then heat clutch side of crankcase and assemble halves together making sure crankshaft ball bearings align with openings in crankcase. After reassembly, make sure the crankshaft turns freely and that counterweights do not contact crankcase.

CLUTCH. All models are equipped with a three-shoe centrifugal clutch as shown in Fig. SO69. Clutch hub (1) is

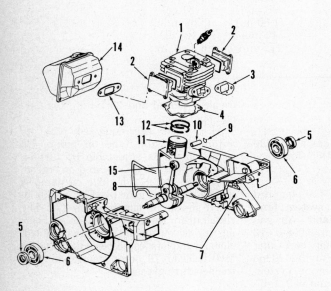

Fig. SO68 — Exploded view of engine assembly.
1. Cylinder
2. Cover
3. Intake gasket
4. Cylinder gasket
5. Seal
6. Ball bearing
7. Crankcase halves
8. Crankshaft & connecting rod assy.
9. Pin retainer
10. Piston pin
11. Piston
12. Piston rings
13. Exhaust gasket
14. Muffler
15. Needle roller bearing

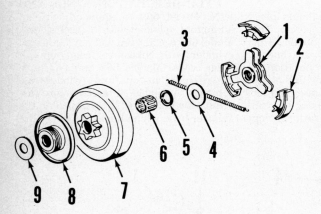

Fig. SO69 — Exploded view of clutch assembly.
1. Hub
2. Shoe
3. Spring
4. Washer
5. Gasket
6. Needle roller bearing
7. Clutch drum
8. Worm gear
9. Washer

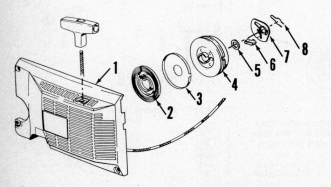
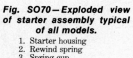

Fig. SO70 — Exploded view of starter assembly typical of all models.
1. Starter housing
2. Rewind spring
3. Spring cup
4. Rope pulley
5. Washer
6. Starter pawl
7. Plate
8. Spring clip

threaded on crankshaft with left-hand threads. Use special Solo tool 0080456 or a suitable equivalent to prevent crankshaft from turning while removing clutch hub. The clutch drum rides on needle roller bearing (6) and drives worm gear (8) which in turn drives the chain oil pump.

OIL PUMP. All models are equipped with a piston type, automatic oil pump. Oil pump output is adjustable. The crankshaft seal for the clutch side of crankcase is located in oil pump housing. Oil pump can be removed for inspection or component renewal after clutch assembly has been removed. Refer to Fig. SO67 for exploded view of oil pump assembly.

REWIND STARTER. To disassemble starter, extend rope one full turn of rope pulley (4–Fig. SO70). Pull slack rope back through rope guide and place rope in recess of rope pulley. Carefully turn pulley counterclockwise to release spring tension. Remove spring clip (8), plate (7) and starter pawl (6). Rope pulley can now be removed. New starter rope should be 110 cm (43.3 in.) in length and 4.0 mm (5/32 in.) in diameter. If re-

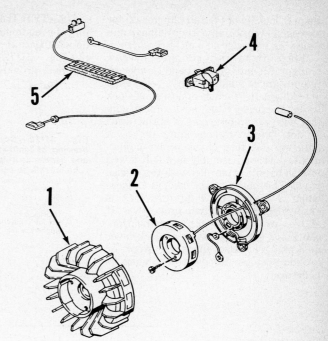

Fig. SO72—Exploded view of handle heating system used on some models.
1. Flywheel
2. Generator
3. Generator seat
4. Switch
5. Heating coil

wind spring (2) is to be removed, use care not to let rewind spring unwind uncontrolled.

To reassemble, wind spring into spring cup (3) in a clockwise direction starting with outer coil. If rewind spring is to be renewed, the new spring will come wound in a new cup. Lightly lubricate rewind spring and starter shaft and place spring cup into starter housing (1) with open side facing toward housing. Make sure hook in outer coil engages notch in starter housing. Wind rope five turns onto rope pulley. Place rope pulley onto spring cup making sure hook on inside coil engages notched recess of pulley. Install plate (7), starter pawl (6) and spring clip (8). Insert rope into recess of pulley and load spring by turning pulley approximately two turns clockwise. Carefully allow pulley to rewind taking up slack in rope. Rope handle should be tight against starter housing. The rope pulley must be able to turn one-half to one full turn after rope is fully extended.

CHAIN BRAKE. All models are equipped with a chain brake system designed to stop chain movement should kickback occur. The chain brake is activated when the operator's hand strikes chain brake lever (1–Fig. SO71) tripping lock lever (4), releasing spring (5) and plunger (2) allowing brake band (10) to be pulled tight around clutch drum. Pull back chain brake lever to reset mechanism.

If disassembly is required, the chain brake must be in off position before the chain guard can be removed. To remove plunger (2), first trip lock lever (4) with a screwdriver. Use caution when tripping lock lever as spring is under high load.

Fig. SO71—Exploded view of chain brake system.
1. Chain brake lever
2. Plunger
3. Spacer
4. Lock lever
5. Spring
6. Pin
7. Spring
8. Guide shoe
9. Chain guard
10. Brake band
11. Chain brake cover

Inspect lock lever (4) and plunger (2) for excessive wear or any other damage and renew as necessary.

When installing plunger, screw plunger (2) into brake band connector five full turns making sure beveled edge of plunger is facing opposite of lock lever. The brake band must come in contact with retaining edges of spring seat. If not, adjust by changing depth of plunger. To test chain brake adjustment, position assembly in a soft-jawed vise so handle is parallel with top of vise jaws. The chain brake should engage when a weight of 4 kg (8.8 lbs.) is suspended from the chain brake lever. If above or below this specification, check for excessive wear on lock lever and plunger. Also check for weak or broken springs. Renew components as necessary.

HEATED HANDLES. Some models may be equipped with front and rear handle heating system. Generating coil (2 – Fig. SO72) located under the flywheel provides an electrical current to heating coils (5) in front and rear handles. The heating coils are wired in series. Switch (4) opens or closes a common ground. Refer to Fig. SO73 for a schematic drawing of heating circuit.

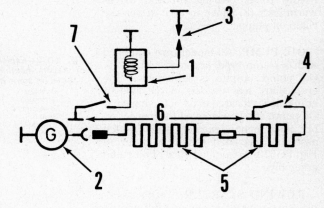

Fig. SO73 – Schematic drawing of ignition system and handle heating system on models so equipped.

1. Ignition module
2. Generator
3. Spark plug
4. Heater switch
5. Heating coils
6. Ground connection
7. Ignition switch

STIHL

STIHL INC.
536 Viking Drive
Virginia Beach, Virginia 23452

Model	Bore	Stroke	Displ.	Drive Type
015, 015AV, *015AVE, 015L, *015LE	1.496 in. (38 mm)	1.102 in. (28 mm)	1.96 cu. in. (32 cc)	Direct

*Models denoted by suffix letter "E" are "Electronic" models.

MAINTENANCE

SPARK PLUG. Recommended spark plug is Bosch WKA175T6 or equivalent. Electrode gap should be 0.020 inch (0.51 mm).

CARBURETOR. A Walbro Model HDC diaphragm carburetor is used on all models. Refer to CARBURETOR SERVICE section for repair and an exploded view of carburetor.

Initial adjustment of idle and high speed mixture screws is ¾ turn open. Adjust idle speed screw so engine idles just below clutch engagement speed. Adjust high speed mixture screw to obtain optimum performance with chain saw under cutting load. Final adjustments should be made with engine warm and running.

IGNITION. Models 015, 015AV and 015L are equipped with a conventional flywheel magneto ignition system while Models 015AVE and 015LE are equipped with a breakerless transistor ignition system. Refer to the appropriate following paragraphs for service.

FLYWHEEL MAGNETO IGNITION. Ignition breaker-point gap should be 0.014-0.016 inch (0.35-0.40 mm). Ignition timing is not adjustable except by adjusting breaker-point gap. Ignition timing should occur at 0.09 inch (2.3 mm) BTDC. Magneto edge gap ("E" gap) shown in Fig. ST1 should be 0.12-0.29 inch (3.0-7.3 mm). Magneto edge gap may be adjusted slightly by loosening flywheel nut and rotating flywheel on crankshaft as there is a small clearance between flywheel groove and crankshaft key.

TRANSISTOR IGNITION. Models 015AVE and 015LE are equipped with a Bosch breakerless transistor ignition. The transistor circuit is designed to take the place of breaker-points in a conventional ignition system. The system is triggered magnetically by a magnet in the flywheel.

To check ignition timing, install Stihl timing tool 0000 850 4000 on chain bar studs. Using either a piston locating tool or a timing light note whether mark on clutch hub is aligned with pointer on timing tool. Ignition timing should be 0.087 inch (2.2 mm) BTDC. Ignition timing

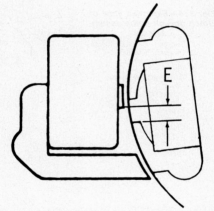

Fig. ST1 — Magneto edge gap (E) on Models 015, 015AV and 015L should be 0.12-0.29 inch (3.0-7.3 mm).

Fig. ST2 – Exploded view of engine. Thrust washers (T) are used on models produced after 1978.

1. Cylinder
2. Piston ring
3. Piston pin
4. Pin retainer
5. Piston
6. Connecting rod
7. Bearing rollers (12)
8. Oil seal
9. Retaining ring
10. Needle bearing
11. Crankshaft
12. Needle bearing
13. Retaining ring
14. Oil seal
15. Crankcase
16. Gasket
17. Handle assy.
18. Oil pickup
T. Thrust washer

may be adjusted slightly by loosening flywheel nut and rotating flywheel on crankshaft as there is a small clearance between flywheel groove and crankshaft key.

Recommended air gap between ignition coil armature legs and flywheel is 0.006-0.008 in. (0.15-0.2 mm). Loosen ignition coil mounting screws and move ignition coil to adjust air gap.

LUBRICATION. The engine is lubricated by mixing oil with the fuel. Fuel:oil ratio is 40:1 when using STIHL two-stroke engine oil. If STIHL two-stroke engine oil is not available, a good quality oil designed for two-stroke air-cooled engines may be used when mixed at a 25:1 ratio. Use a separate container when mixing the oil and gasoline.

All models are equipped with an automatic chain oiler system. Manufacturer recommends the use of approved oils designed specifically for saw chain lubrication. If necessary, clean automotive oil may be used to lubricate saw chain. Chain oil may be diluted with kerosene during cold weather. Oil:kerosene mixture ratio should not exceed 4 parts oil to 1 part kerosene.

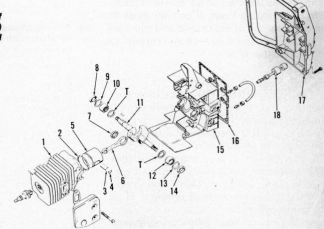

MAINTENANCE

CYLINDER, PISTON, PIN AND RINGS. Cylinder and front crankcase are one-piece. Crankshaft and bearings are loose when the cylinder is removed. Care must be taken not to damage mating surfaces of crankcase halves.

Cylinder head is integral with cylinder. Piston is equipped with a single piston ring and the piston pin rides directly in the piston and small end of connecting rod. Cylinder is chrome plated and should be inspected for damage or excessive wear. Cylinder (1 – Fig. ST2) and front crankcase half (15) are available only as a unit assembly.

Piston pin (3) must be installed with closed end of pin toward "A" side of piston crown shown in Fig. ST3 and piston must be installed with "A" side toward exhaust port in cylinder. Piston and piston pin are available in standard sizes only.

Refer to CRANKSHAFT section for assembly of crankcase and cylinder.

CRANKSHAFT AND SEALS. The crankshaft rides on needle bearings (10 and 12 – Fig. ST2) held between the cylinder and front crankcase half. Care should be taken when removing cylinder as crankshaft will be loose in crankcase and connecting rod may slide off bearing rollers (7) allowing them to fall into crankcase.

Before reassembling crankcases, apply a light coat of nonhardening sealant to crankcase mating surfaces.

NOTE: Large diameter needle bearing (10), retaining ring (9) and seal (8) on later models must be installed on flywheel end of crankshaft while smaller diameter bearing retaining ring and seal must be installed on clutch end. Models produced after serial number 5628679 are also equipped with thrust washers (T) located between crankshaft bearings and crankshaft. Bearings, retaining rings and seals on early models have same outer diameter and may be installed on either end of crankshaft. Retaining rings (9 and 13) must fit in ring grooves of crankcase and cylinder. Tighten cylinder-to-crankcase screws to 60 in.-lbs. (6.8 N·m).

CONNECTING ROD. To remove connecting rod, remove crankshaft as outlined in previous section. Connecting rod (6 – Fig. ST2) is one-piece and supported on crankpin by 12 loose bearing rollers. Be careful not to lose rollers that may fall out during disassembly. Inspect connecting rod, bearing rollers and crankpin for excessive wear or damage. Hold bearing rollers in position with heavy grease or petroleum jelly during assem-

bly. Be sure all twelve bearing rollers are in position before assembling crankcase.

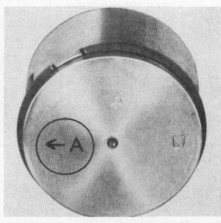

Fig. ST3 — Install piston on connecting rod with "A" on piston crown toward exhaust port in cylinder.

CLUTCH. Models without chain brake are equipped with the two-shoe centrifugal type clutch shown in Fig. ST4 while models with chain brake are equipped with the three-shoe type clutch shown in Fig. ST6. On both types, clutch hub has left hand thread. Clutch needle bearing should be inspected for excessive wear or damage. Inspect clutch shoes and drum for signs of excessive heat.

OIL PUMP. All models are equipped with a plunger type automatic chain oil pump. Oil pump is driven by the clutch through gear (7 – Fig. ST4) mounted on crankshaft. A worm attached to driven gear (5) turns pump plunger (3). The plunger reciprocates in pump housing as cam groove in end of plunger rides against pin (4). Pin (4) must be removed before plunger can be withdrawn from pump housing.

REWIND STARTER. Refer to Fig. ST5 for exploded view of pawl type re-

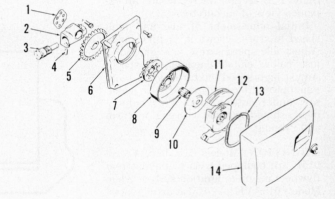

Fig. ST4 — Exploded view of clutch and oil pump assemblies.

1. Gasket
2. Oil pump housing
3. Pump plunger
4. Pin
5. Driven gear & worm
6. Cover
7. Drive gear
8. Clutch drum
9. Bearing
10. Washer
11. Clutch shoe
12. Clutch hub
13. Garter spring
14. Housing

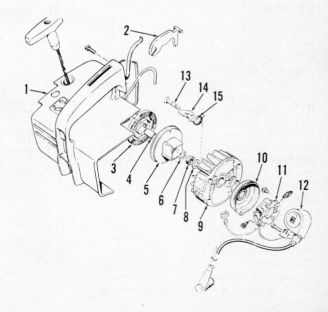

Fig. ST5 — Exploded view of rewind starter and ignition.

1. Rear housing
2. Trigger interlock
3. Rewind spring
4. Bushing
5. Rope pulley
6. "E" ring
7. Flywheel nut
8. Washer
9. Flywheel
10. Cover
11. Breaker or trigger plate
12. Ignition coil
13. Stud
14. Pawl
15. Spring

wind starter used on all models. Care should be taken if it is necessary to remove rewind spring (3) to prevent spring from uncoiling uncontrolled.

Rewind spring must be wound in clockwise direction in housing. Wind starter rope in clockwise direction around rope pulley (5) as viewed with pulley installed in starter housing. Turn rope pulley three or four turns in clockwise direction before passing rope through rope outlet to place tension on rewind spring. To check spring tension, pull starter rope to full length. It should be possible to rotate rope pulley in clockwise direction with rope fully extended.

Starter pawl studs (13) are driven into flywheel. To renew pawl stud or spring, remove flywheel and drive stud out of

flywheel. Apply "Loctite" to stud before installation.

CHAIN BRAKE. Some models may be equipped with a chain brake system designed to stop chain movement should kickback occur. The chain brake is activated when the operator's hand strikes hand guard (1 – Fig. ST6) thereby allowing brake lever (3) to release spring (7). Spring then draws brake band (9) tight around clutch drum to stop chain. Pull back hand guard to reset mechanism. No adjustment of brake mechanism is required.

Disassembly for repair or renewal of individual components is evident after inspection of unit and referral to the exploded view.

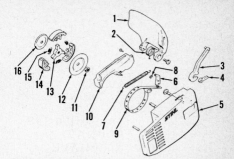

Fig. ST6 — Exploded view of optional chain brake and clutch assembly available on all models.

1. Hand guard	9. Brake band
2. Spring	10. Shield
3. Brake lever	11. Nut
4. Actuating lever	12. Washer
5. Housing	13. Clutch hub
6. Pivot	14. Clutch shoe
7. Spring	15. Clutch spring
8. "E" ring	16. Washer

STIHL

Model	Bore	Stroke	Displ.	Drive Type
020AV, *020AVPE	1.496 in. (38 mm)	1.102 in. (28 mm)	1.96 cu. in. (32 cc)	Direct
040, 041, 041FB, 041AV, *041AVE	1.73 in. (44 mm)	1.57 in. (40 mm)	3.72 cu. in. (61 cc)	Direct
*041AVE Super	1.89 in. (48 mm)	1.57 in. (40 mm)	4.4 cu. in. (72.0 cc)	Direct
041G	1.73 in. (44 mm)	1.57 in. (40 mm)	3.72 cu. in. (61 cc)	Gear
050AV, 051AV, *051AVE, *051AVEQ	2.05 in. (52 mm)	1.65 in. (42 mm)	5.42 cu. in. (89 cc)	Direct
*075AVE, *076AVE	2.28 in. (58 mm)	1.65 in. (42 mm)	6.77 cu. in. (111 cc)	Direct

*Models denoted by suffix letter "E" are "Electronic" models.

MAINTENANCE

SPARK PLUG. Recommended spark plug is Bosch WSR6F for all models. Spark plug electrode gap should be 0.020 inch (0.5 mm).

CARBURETOR. Models are equipped with either a Tillotson or Walbro diaphragm carburetor. Refer to the appropriate section of CARBURETOR SERVICE section for carburetor overhaul and exploded views.

Carburetor model designation is stamped on carburetor. Initial adjustment of mixture screws from a lightly seated position should be 1¼ turns open for idle mixture screw and 1 turn open for high speed mixture screw. Make final adjustments with engine warm and running. Adjust idle speed screw just below clutch engagement speed. Adjust idle mixture screw so engine will accelerate cleanly without hesitation. Adjust high speed mixture screw to obtain optimum performance under cutting load. Do not adjust high speed mixture needle too lean as engine may be damaged.

IGNITION. Models 020AV, 040, 041, 041FB, 041AV, 050AV and 051AV are equipped with a conventional flywheel magneto ignition system. Models 041AVE, 041AVE Super and 041G are equipped with a breakerless capacitor discharge ignition system while Models 020AVEP, 051AVE, 051AVEQ, 075AVE and 076AVE are equipped with breakerless transistor ignition system.

Breaker-Point Ignition. Breaker-point gap on models so equipped should

be 0.014-0.016 inch (0.35-0.40 mm). Ignition timing should occur as follows: 0.080-0.087 inch (2.0-2.2 mm) BTDC on Model 020AV; 0.095-0.102 inch (2.4-2.6 mm) BTDC on Models 040, 041, 041FB and 041AV; 0.090-0.106 inch (2.3-2.7 mm) BTDC on Models 050AV and 051AV to serial number 2981245 and 0.075-0.083 inch (1.9-2.1 mm) BTDC after serial number 2981245. Loosen magneto base plate screws and rotate magneto base plate to adjust ignition timing.

Ignition edge gap should be checked whenever ignition timing is adjusted. Edge gap should also be checked if engine is difficult to start or misfires at full throttle. To check edge gap, rotate flywheel counterclockwise until breaker-points just start to open. Measure edge gap between trailing edge of flywheel magnet and edge of adjacent ignition coil leg. Edge gap on Models 040, 041, 041FB and 041AV should be 0.24-0.35 inch (6-9 mm). On 050AV and 051AV models to serial number 2981245, edge gap should be 0.35-0.51 inch (9-13 mm) and 0.47-0.63 inch (12-16 mm) on 050AV

and 051AV models after serial number 2981245. Adjust edge gap by changing breaker-point gap.

Air gap between flywheel magnets and ignition coil should be 0.008-0.012 inch (0.20-0.30 mm) on Models 020AV, 040, 041, 041FB and 041AV and 0.006-0.012 inch (0.15-0.30 mm) on all other models.

Capacitor Discharge Ignition. Early Models 041AVE and 041G are equipped with Bosch capacitor discharge ignition systems shown in Fig. ST12. Later model Bosch ignition is identical in function,

Fig. ST12 – View of Bosch capacitor discharge ignition found on early Models 041AVE and 041G. Trigger module (T) contains diodes and thyristor. All components are sealed in stator plate casting on later models. Refer to text.

CA. Condenser
CC. Charging coil
IC. Ignition coil
S. Stator mounting screws
T. Trigger module

Fig. ST11 – Diagram of Bosch capacitor discharge ignition used on Models 041AVE and 041G. Refer to text for operation. Operation of SEM capacitor discharge ignition is similar.

but all components are sealed in stator plate casting and are not individually serviceable. If malfunction occurs, entire stator assembly must be renewed. Models after serial number 9158250 are equipped with SEM capacitor discharge ignition. Operation of SEM and Bosch ignitions are basically the same and are interchangeable if entire ignition systems are exchanged. SEM ignition can be identified by a removable ignition coil. Refer to schematic in Fig. ST11 and to following paragraph for operation of capacitor discharge ignition system.

Charging coil (CC–Fig. ST11) charges capacitor (CA) after current is rectified by diode (D1). Thyristor (T) does not pass current until sufficient voltage is applied at its gate. The primary windings of ignition coil (IC) also serves as a trigger coil and will supply current through diode (D2) to the gate of thyristor (T). When the voltage at the thyristor gate reaches proper level, the thyristor will allow current to flow through it thereby discharging the capacitor through thyristor (T) and primary windings of ignition coil (IC). The sudden surge of current through the primary windings will induce sufficient voltage into the secondary windings of the ignition coil to cause a spark at spark plug (S).

To properly time early model Bosch ignition, trigger coil (ignition coil-IC) must be in correct relationship with flywheel magnet. Ignition timing should be 0.075 inch (1.9 mm) for Models 041AVE and 041G. To check ignition timing, install a timing gage in spark plug hole and rotate engine until piston is at ignition position as indicated above. Note if flywheel mark (F–Fig. ST13) is aligned with mark (C) on crankcase. Remove flywheel and note if mark on stator plate is aligned with crankcase mark (Fig. ST14). If either of these marks is not aligned, ignition must be adjusted.

To adjust ignition, rotate engine with flywheel installed until correct piston position is indicated by timing gage.

Make a mark on a crankcase adjacent to mark on flywheel. Remove flywheel, loosen stator plate mounting screws (S–Fig. ST12) and rotate stator plate until mark on plate is aligned with previously made mark on crankcase. Retighten stator plate mounting screws. A timing light may also be used to check ignition timing as follows: Remove spark plug, install timing gage and rotate engine until correct piston position for ignition is indicated. Make two aligned marks on rotating screen and starter housing cover. Recheck piston position to be sure marks are correct. Install spark plug and connect timing light. Using a tachometer, run engine at 6000 rpm and check alignment of previously made marks with time light. Loosen stator plate mounting screws and adjust timing as required. Recheck timing with light.

If early model Bosch ignition is defective, check spark plug, high tension lead, ignition switch and all terminals and ground connections. To check for a faulty ignition coil (IC), connect an ohmmeter lead to high tension lead and other ohmmeter lead to ground. Ohmmeter reading should be 1,000-3,000 ohms. To check primary windings, disconnect yellow wire at terminal "B" on stator plate and connect one lead of ohmmeter to yellow wire and other ohmmeter lead to ground. Ohmmeter reading should be less than one ohm. To check charging coil (CC), disconnect coil wire from terminal "C" on stator plate. Connect one lead of ohmmeter to coil wire and other lead to ground. Note reading. Reverse lead connections of ohmmeter and note reading. One reading should be at least ten times larger or smaller than the other reading. Condenser capacitance should be 0.6-0.9 mfd. Condenser and stator plate must be renewed as an assembly. Air gap between ignition coil and flywheel magnets on early Bosch ignition should be 0.010-0.014 inch (0.25-0.35 mm). Individual components cannot be tested on later Bosch ignition. Com-

plete stator plate assembly must be renewed if malfunction is noted.

To test ignition coil primary winding on SEM ignition, disconnect primary wire and connect ohmmeter to primary connection and ground. Reading should be 0.4-0.5 ohm. To test secondary winding, connect ohmmeter to spark plug end of high tension lead and ground. Reading should be 2,700-3,300 ohms. Renew ignition coil if correct readings are not obtained. Air gap between ignition coil and flywheel magents should be 0.008-0.011 inch (0.2-0.3 mm).

To check ignition timing on later Bosch and SEM ignitions, remove spark plug and install dial indicator into spark plug hole. Remove saw chain and guide bar and install special tool part 0000 850 4000 on guide bar studs with pointer toward clutch as shown in Fig. ST15. Rotate flywheel clockwise and make a reference mark (M) on clutch shoe (3) opposite of pointer (2) at 0.075 inch (1.9 mm) BTDC on models up to serial number 2783541 and 0.098 inch (2.5 mm) BTDC on models after serial number 2783541. Replace spark plug and connect a suitable power timing light. Using a tachometer, check ignition timing at 6000 rpm. If reference marks do not align, adjust by rotating stator plate. Recheck timing after adjusting.

Transistor Ignition. Models 020 AVPE, 051AVE, 075AVE and 076AVE are equipped with a Bosch breakerless transistor ignition. The transistor circuit is designed to take the place of breaker-points in a conventional ignition system. The transistor ignition system is triggered magnetically by a magnet in the flywheel.

To check ignition timing, install Stihl timing tool 0000 850 4000 on chain bar studs. Using either a piston locating tool or a timing light note whether mark on clutch hub is aligned with pointer on timing tool. Ignition timing should be 0.090 inch (2.3 mm) BTDC on Model 020AVPE

Fig. ST13—Flywheel mark (F) and crankcase mark (C) should be aligned for correct ignition timing on early models with earlier style Bosch capacitor discharge ignition. Most later models with breaker-point ignition have similar marks.

Fig. ST14—View of stator plate and crankcase timing marks (T) on early Bosch capacitor discharge models.

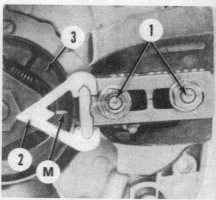

Fig. ST15—View showing reference mark (M), guide bar studs (1), special tool 0000 850 4000 (2) and clutch shoe (3).

and 0.098 inch (2.5 mm) BTDC on all other models. Ignition timing may be adjusted slightly by loosening flywheel nut and rotating flywheel on crankshaft as there is a small clearance between flywheel groove and crankshaft key.

Recommended air gap between ignition coil armature legs and flywheel is 0.006-0.010 inch (0.15-0.25 mm) on all models. Loosen ignition coil mounting screws and move ignition coil to adjust air gap.

LUBRICATION. The engine is lubricated by mixing oil with the fuel. Fuel:oil ratio is 40:1 when using STIHL two-stroke engine oil. If STIHL two-stroke engine oil is not available, a good quality oil designed for two-stroke air-cooled engines may be used when mixed at a 25:1 ratio. Use a separate container when mixing the oil and gasoline.

Fill chain oiler tank with SAE 30 non-detergent motor oil. All models are equipped with an automatic chain oiler system. The chain oiler pump used on all models except Models 020AV and 020AVPE, is gear driven off clutch end of crankshaft as shown in Fig. ST16 and Fig. ST17. Adjust output on Models 040, 041, 041FB, 041G, 041AV, 041AVE and 041AVE Super by turning control screw (11 – Fig. ST16) found under air filter. Models 050AV, 051AV, 051AVE, 051AVEQ, 075AVE and 076AVE oil output is adjusted by moving control lever underneath grip frame on exhaust side.

Plunger type oil pump used on Models 020AV and 020AVPE is not adjustable.

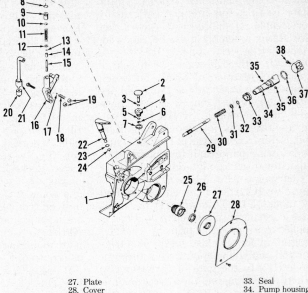

Fig. ST17— *Exploded view of chain oiler components used on later 051AVE and 051AVEQ models and all 075AVE and 076AVE models. Manual oil pump components (2 through 19) are used on 075AVE and 076AVE models.*

1. Right crankcase half
2. Button
3. "O" ring
4. Cap
5. "O" ring
6. Circlip
7. Seal
8. "O" ring
9. Pump piston
10. Spring retainer
11. Spring
12. Washer
13. "O" ring
14. Bushing
15. Rod
16. Housing
17. Check ball
18. Spring
19. Seals
20. Hose
21. Oil pump pickup
22. Oil control lever
23. "O" ring
24. "O" ring
25. Worm gear
26. Seal
27. Plate
28. Cover
29. Pump piston
30. Spring
31. Washer
32. "O" ring
33. Seal
34. Pump housing
35. Bushing
36. Snap ring
37. Plug
38. Cap screw

Refer to Fig. ST18 for exploded view of oil pump.

Model 041G is equipped with a gear reduction assembly which should be lubricated with SAE 30 oil. Fill drive housing until oil reaches lower edge of fill plug hole.

CARBON. The muffler assembly should be removed from the engine and the carbon scraped from the exhaust ports and muffler periodically.

REPAIRS

TIGHTENING TORQUES: The following torque values should be observed:

Clutch Nut
050AV, 051AV, 051AVE, 051AVEQ,
 075AVE, 076AVE . . . . 44 ft.-lbs.
 (60 N·m)

Other models . . . . 22 ft.-lbs.
 (29.4 N·m)

Clutch Hub
050AV, 051AV, 051AVE, 051AVEQ,
 075AVE, 076AVE . . . . 55 ft.-lbs.
 (75 N·m)

Other models . . . . 25 ft.-lbs.
 (34.3 N·m)

Clutch Hub Carrier (9 – Fig. ST23)
Models so equipped except for 020AV
 and 020AVPE . . . . 55 ft.-lbs.
 (75.1 N·m)

020AV, 020AVPE . . . . 21 ft.-lbs.
 (28.5 N·m)

Flywheel Nut
040, 041, 041FB, 041AV, 041AVE,
 041AVE Super, 041G . . . . 22 ft.-lbs.
 (29.4 N·m)

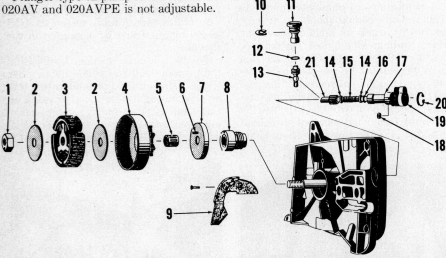

Fig. ST16— *Exploded view of clutch and automatic chain oiler assemblies used on Models 040, 041, 041AV, 041AVE, 041AVEQ, 041G, 050AV, 051AV and early 051AVE and 051AVEQ. Pump operates only when clutch is engaged. As clutch engages, pressed pin in plate (7) transmits motion to worm gear (8) which revolves pump assembly (17). Oil output is adjusted by turning control screw (11) except on Model 050AV, 051AV, 051AVE and 051AVE. Output is adjusted on Models 050AV, 051AV, 051AVE and 051AVEQ by moving lever under grip frame on exhaust side. Be sure outer edges of washers (2) are away from clutch shoes when installed.*

1. Nut
2. Washer
3. Clutch rotor & shoes
4. Clutch drum
5. Bearing
6. Pin
7. Plate
8. Worm gear
9. Plate
10. Washer
11. Oil control screw
12. "O" ring
13. Control bolt
14. Washer
15. Spring
16. "O" ring
17. Pump housing
18. Ring
19. Rubber ring
20. Snap ring
21. Pump piston

050AV, 051AV, 051AVE, 051AVEQ,
  075AVE, 076AVE . . . . 26 ft.-lbs.
              (35 N·m)

020AV, 020AVPE . . . . 18 ft.-lbs.
              (24.4 N·m)

RINGS, PISTON, PIN AND CYLINDER. The aluminum alloy piston is equipped with two piston rings. The floating piston pin is retained in the piston with a snap ring at each end. The pin bore of the piston is unbushed; the connecting rod has a caged needle roller piston pin bearing. An oversize piston pin is not available.

Cylinder and cylinder head are cast in one-piece. The cylinder is available only with a fitted piston. Piston and cylinder on Models 040, 041, 041AV, 041AVE, 041AVE Super and 041G and on 050AV models prior to 1971, are grouped into different size ranges with approximately 0.0002 inch (0.005 mm) difference between each range. Each group is marked with letters "A" to "E"; some of the earlier models may be marked "A" to "K." Letter "A" denotes smallest size with "E" or "K" being largest. The code letter is stamped on the top of the piston on all models, at the bottom of the cylinder on earlier models, and at the top of the cylinder on later models. The code letter of the piston and the cylinder must be the same for proper fit of a new piston in a new cylinder. However, new pistons are available for installation in used cylinders. Select proper new piston size to fit used cylinder size listed in the following table.

NEW PISTON CODE	USED CYLINDER CODE
A	A, B
B	A, B, C
C	B, C, D
D	C, D, E
E	D, E

The piston and cylinder matching code has been simplified on later 050AV models and 051AV, 051AVE, 051AVEQ, 075AVE and 076AVE models. New cylinder and piston assemblies are coded "A," "B" and "C" with new pistons for installation in used cylinders available in code "B" only.

Cylinder bore on all models except some 075AVE and 076AVE models, is chrome plated. Cylinders that do not have chrome plated bores are identified by the letters "SIL" on cylinder base. Pistons for use with "SIL" cylinders are identified by a circle around the cylinder matching code letter stamped in the piston crown. Do not interchange pistons used with chrome bore cylinders with pistons used in "SIL" cylinders.

To reinstall piston on connecting rod, proceed as follows: Install one snap ring in piston. Lubricate the piston pin needle bearing with motor oil and slide bearing into pin bore of connecting rod. Install piston on rod so arrow on piston crown points toward exhaust port. Push piston in far enough to install second snap ring. Locating pins are present in piston ring grooves to prevent ring rotation. Make certain ring end gaps are properly positioned around locating pins when installing cylinder.

After piston and rod assembly is attached to crankshaft, install cylinder as follows: Turn crankshaft to top dead center and support piston with a wood block that will fit between piston skirt and crankcase when cylinder gasket is in place. A notch should be cut in the wood block so that it will fit around the connecting rod. Lubricate piston and rings with motor oil and compress rings with compressor that can be removed after cylinder is pushed down over piston. On

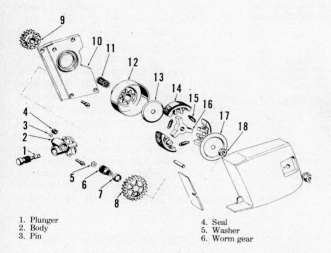

Fig. ST18 — Exploded view of Model 020AV and 020AVPE automatic oil pump and clutch assembly. Refer to Fig. ST22 for view of clutch used on models with chain brake.

7. Seal
8. Driven gear
9. Drive gear
10. Cover
11. Clutch bearing
12. Clutch drum
13. Washer
14. Clutch shoe
15. Spring
16. Clutch hub
17. Washer
18. Nut

1. Plunger
2. Body
3. Pin
4. Seal
5. Washer
6. Worm gear

Fig. ST19 — Exploded view of engines used on Models 050AV, 051AV and early 051AVE. Models 040, 041, 041FB, 041AV, 041AVE and 041AVE Super are similar, but are not equipped with compression release valve (components 16 through 23).

1. Spark plug
2. Cylinder
3. Head gasket
4. Snap ring
5. Piston
6. Piston pin
7. Bearing
8. Crankshaft & connecting rod assy.
9. Circlip
10. Gasket
11. Bearing
12. Seal
13. Crankcase half
14. Snap ring
15. Bearing
16. Knob
17. Pin
18. Spring
19. Check ball
20. Spring
21. Tab washer
22. Housing
23. Plunger
24. Pin
25. Crankcase half
26. Circlip

some models, it may be necessary to remove the cylinder and install an additional gasket between the cylinder and crankcase if piston strikes top of cylinder.

CONNECTING ROD. The connecting rod and crankshaft are a unit assembly and must be removed and serviced as a unit. Refer to Figs. ST19, ST20 and ST21 for an exploded view of engine.

Crankshaft and connecting rod unit type assembly should not be disassembled. Connecting rod big end rides on a roller bearing and should be inspected for excessive wear or damage. If rod, bearing or crankshaft is damaged, complete crankshaft assembly must be renewed.

CRANKSHAFT AND CRANKCASE. All models are equipped with a split type crankcase that is separable from the cylinder, but is available only as a complete crankcase assembly.

On 050AV and 051AV models and early 051AVE models, crankshaft is supported by a ball bearing at the flywheel end and a roller bearing at the clutch end as shown in Fig. ST19. Ball bearing (11) is secured to crankshaft by circlip (9). End play should be 0.008-0.012 inch (0.2-0.3 mm). Later 051AVE models and all other models, are equipped with ball bearings at both crankshaft ends. End play is not adjustable.

Crankcase halves on all models may be heated to ease reassembly of main bearings into crankcase halves. Main bearing inner races should also be heated to ease reassembly of crankshaft into main bearings.

CLUTCH. All models are equipped with a three-shoe centrifugal type clutch. Refer to Figs. ST16, ST18, ST22 and ST23 for exploded views of clutch assemblies used. A locking bolt is screwed into the spark plug hole to prevent crankshaft rotation when removing clutch nut or hub. Clutch nut and hub have left hand threads. Make certain drive plate (7 – Fig. ST16 and 27 – Fig. ST17) properly engages oil pump worm gear (8 – Fig. ST16 and 25 – Fig. ST17) before installing clutch.

Install clutch retaining washers on all models so inner face of washers is against clutch hub. A new design clutch is used on 041, 041AV, 041FB and 041AVE models after serial number 9647305. Washer (2 – Fig. ST16) is absent and nut (1) is an integral part of clutch rotor (3). On new design clutch assemblies, tighten clutch rotor to 29 ft.-lbs. (39.2 N·m). Clutch shoes and springs should be renewed as a unit to prevent unbalanced clutch operation.

GEAR TRANSMISSION. Model 041G is equipped with a gear drive transmission. Refer to Fig. ST24 for exploded view of Model 041G transmission. Disassembly is evident with inspection of unit. A suitable puller should be used to remove chain sprocket and gear from shaft (9).

Inspect components for excessive wear or damage. Refill drive housing with

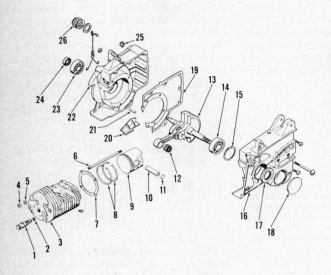

Fig. ST20 — Exploded view of engine assembly used on later 051AVE and 051AVEQ models and all 075AVE and 076AVE models. Decompression valve (1) is optional on 051AVE and 051AVEQ models.

7. Gasket
8. Piston rings
9. Piston
10. Piston pin
11. Pin retainer
12. Needle bearing
13. Crankshaft & rod assy.
14. Ball bearing
15. Snap ring
16. Right crankcase half
17. Seal
18. Cover
19. Gasket
20. Insert
21. Dowel pin
22. Left crankcase half
23. Ball bearing
24. Seal
25. Oil tank vent
26. Oil tank cap

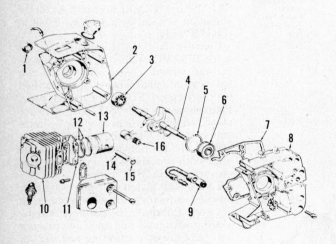

Fig. ST21 — Exploded view of Model 020AV and 020AVPE engine.

1. Seal
2. Crankcase half
3. Bearing
4. Crankshaft & rod assy.
5. Snap ring
6. Bearing
7. Gasket
8. Crankcase half
9. Oil pickup
10. Cylinder
11. Gasket
12. Piston rings
13. Piston
14. Piston pin
15. Pin retainer
16. Roller bearing

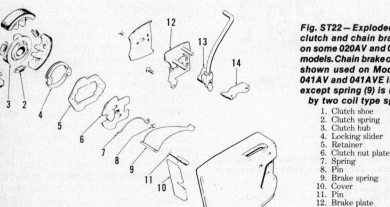

Fig. ST22 — Exploded view of clutch and chain brake used on some 020AV and 020AVPE models. Chain brake of the type shown used on Models 041, 041AV and 041AVE is similar except spring (9) is replaced by two coil type springs.

1. Clutch shoe
2. Clutch spring
3. Clutch hub
4. Locking slider
5. Retainer
6. Clutch nut plate
7. Spring
8. Pin
9. Brake spring
10. Cover
11. Pin
12. Brake plate
13. Brake rod
14. Brake shoe

SAE 30 oil until oil level reaches lower edge of oil fill hole.

REWIND STARTER. Friction shoe type and pawl type starters have been used. Refer to Fig. ST25 for an exploded view of pawl type starter used on 020AV and 020AVPE models, Fig. ST26 for an exploded view of pawl type starter used on 076AVE models, and to Fig. ST27 for an exploded view of friction shoe type starter typical of all other models.

On all models, disassembly of starter for renewal of individual components is evident after inspection of unit and referral to the appropriate exploded view.

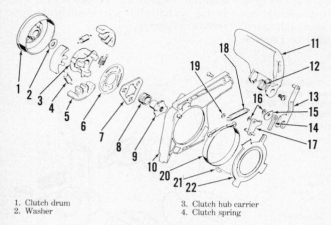

1. Clutch drum
2. Washer
3. Clutch hub carrier
4. Clutch spring

Fig. ST23 — Exploded view of clutch isolating chain brake system used on some models.

5. Clutch shoe
6. Spring plate
7. Drive plate
8. Needle bearing
9. Hub
10. Side cover
11. Hand guard
12. Spring
13. Brake lever
14. Actuating lever
15. Washer
16. "E" ring
17. Cam
18. Brake spring
19. "E" ring
20. Brake band
21. Release plate spring
22. Release plate

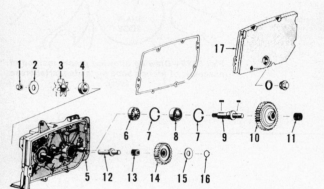

Fig. ST24 — Exploded view of gear transmission used on Model 041G.

1. Nut
2. Washer
3. Sprocket
4. Spacer
5. Gearcase
6. Bearing
7. Snap ring
8. Seal
9. Shaft
10. Gear
11. Bearing
12. Shaft
13. Bearing
14. Gear
15. Washer
16. Snap ring
17. Cover

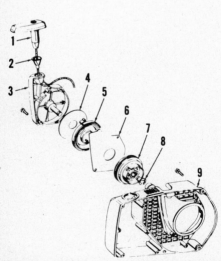

Fig. ST25 — Exploded view of pawl type rewind starter used on Models 020AV and 020AVPE. Pawls on flywheel are not shown.

1. Rope handle
2. Bushing
3. Housing
4. Washer
5. Rewind spring
6. Cover
7. Rope pulley
8. "E" ring
9. Fan housing

Fig. ST26 — Exploded view of rewind starter and fuel pickup components used on 076AVE models.

1. Fuel tank
2. Fuel tank cap
3. Connector
4. Hose
5. Pickup body
6. Insert
7. Strainer
8. Filter
9. Rope handle
10. Rewind spring
11. Rope pulley
12. Pawl
13. Washer
14. Spring clip
15. Nut
16. Flywheel

Fig. ST28 shows correct assembly of starter shoes on brake lever. Be sure assembly is installed as shown in exploded views and leading edges of friction shoes are sharp or shoes may not properly engage drum.

To place tension on rope of Models 020AV and 020AVPE, pull starter rope and hold rope pulley to prevent spring from rewinding rope on pulley. Pull rope back through rope outlet and wrap two additional turns of rope on pulley without moving pulley. Release pulley and allow rope to rewind. Rope handle should be snug against housing and rope pulley must be able to rotate a minimum of ½ turn further with rope completely extended.

To place tension on rope of all other models, proceed as follows: Pull rope out of handle until notch in pulley is adjacent to rope outlet and hold pulley to prevent rope from rewinding. Pull rope back through outlet and out of notch in pulley. Turn rope pulley two turns clockwise and release rope back through notch. Check starter operation. Rope handle should be snug against housing in released position and rope pulley must be able to rotate a minimum of ½ turn further with rope completely extended.

CHAIN BRAKE. Some models are equipped with a chain brake system designed to stop chain movement should kickback occur. On models equipped with chain brake system shown in Fig. ST22, brake is activated when operator's hand strikes hand guard pushing brake rod (13) forward. Forward movement of brake rod allows spring (9) to force brake shoe (14) tight against clutch drum. At the same instant, retainer (5) and locking slider (4) disengage clutch allowing engine to continue running freely. To reset brake mechanism, allow engine to return to idle speed and pull back hand guard.

Chain brake must be in the disengaged position before chain cover can be removed. Manufacturer recommends using special tool 1113 890 3600 to remove clutch nut plate (6). Clutch nut plate has left hand threads. Further disassembly is evident after referral to Fig. ST22 and inspection of unit.

Clean and inspect all components for excessive wear and damage and renew as necessary.

Make certain retainer (5) and locking slider (4) will move easily and clutch rotates freely with locking slider (4) disengaged when reassembling.

Models 041, 041AV and 041AVE use coil springs instead of flat brake spring (9). When reassembling coil springs, install large diameter spring to the front directly above brake shoe lining. Install small diameter spring toward rear of brake shoe. Lightly lubricate moving parts with a suitable grease upon reassembly. No adjustment of brake system is required.

On models equipped with chain brake shown in Fig. ST23, drive plate (7) engages dogs on clutch hub carrier (3). Spring plate (6) holds drive plate against release plate (22) causing inner teeth of drive plate to engage clutch hub (9). When chain brake is activated, actuating lever (14) releases cam (17) allowing spring (18) to draw brake band (20) tight around clutch drum. At the same time release plate (22) pushes drive plate (7) into flat spring plate (6) disengaging hub (9) allowing engine to continue to run freely. To reset brake mechanism, return engine to idle speed and pull back hand guard.

Chain brake must be in the disengaged position before chain cover can be removed. Manufacturer recommends using special tool 1111 893 1303 to remove clutch hub. Hub has left hand threads. Further disassembly is evident after referral to Fig. ST23 and inspection of unit.

When reassembling spring plate (6), make certain spring tabs are facing outward. Lightly lubricate moving parts with a suitable grease upon reassembly. Tighten clutch hub to 55 ft.-lbs. (75 N·m). No adjustment of chain brake system is necessary.

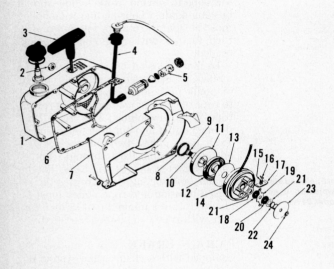

Fig. ST27 — Exploded view of typical rewind starter used on all models exept 020AV, 020AVPE and 076AVE.

1. Fuel tank
2. Nut
3. Rope handle
4. Fuel pickup
5. Filter
6. Gasket
7. Fan cover
8. Felt ring
9. Spring washer
10. Pulley shaft
11. Cover
12. Rewind spring
13. Washer
14. Rope pulley
15. Spring
16. Spring retainer
17. Friction shoe
18. Slotted washer
19. Brake lever
20. Slotted washer
21. Washer
22. Spring
23. Washer
24. "E" ring

Fig. ST28 — Drawing showing proper method of assembly of friction shoe plates to starter brake lever.

STIHL

Model	Bore	Stroke	Displ.	Drive Type
08S, 08SQ, S-10	1.85 in. (47 mm)	1.26 in. (32 mm)	3.39 cu. in. (56 cc)	Direct
070, 070AV	2.30 in. (58 mm)	1.57 in. (40 mm)	6.47 cu. in. (106 cc)	Direct
090G	2.30 in. (58 mm)	1.57 in. (40 mm)	6.47 cu. in. (106 cc)	Gear
090, 090AV, 090R	2.60 in. (66 mm)	1.57 in. (40 mm)	8.36 cu. in. (137 cc)	Direct

MAINTENANCE

SPARK PLUG. Spark plug gap should be 0.020 inch (0.5 mm). Recommended spark plug for Models 08S and 08SQ is Bosch W7A, WS7E for Model S-10 and Bosch WS7F for all other models.

CARBURETOR. All models are equipped with a Tillotson Model HL or HS diaphragm carburetor. Refer to Tillotson section of CARBURETOR SERVICE for carburetor overhaul and exploded views.

Carburetor model designation is stamped on carburetor. Initial adjustment of HL and HS carburetors is 1 turn open for idle and high speed mixture needles. Adjust idle mixture and idle speed screws so engine idles just below clutch engagement speed and will accelerate without hesitation. Adjust high speed mixture screw to obtain optimum performance with saw under cutting load. Final adjustments should be made with engine warm and running. Do not adjust high speed mixture needle too lean as engine may be damaged.

GOVERNOR. Models listed below under governing speed are equipped with an air vane type governor. The governor linkage is attached to the carburetor choke shaft lever. Thus maximum speed is controlled by the air vane governor closing the choke disc.

Governed speed is adjustable by changing the tension of the governor spring. On all models, the adjusting plate is mounted to the engine behind the starter housing as shown in Fig. ST32. After maximum governed speed is adjusted at factory, position of spring is secured by a lead seal. If necessary to readjust governor, new position of governor spring should be sealed or wired securely. Maximum no-load governed speed on Models 070, 070AV, 090, 090AV, 090G and 090R should be 7500 rpm. On Models 08S and 08SQ, maximum no-load governed speed should be 8000 rpm.

IGNITION. All models are equipped with a conventional flywheel magneto ignition system.

Ignition breaker-point gap should be set at 0.014-0.016 inch (3.5-4.0 mm). Ignition timing is adjusted by loosening stator mounting screws and rotating stator plate. Ignition timing should occur as follows: 0.08 inch (2.0 mm) BTDC on Models 08S, 08SQ and S-10; and 0.12 inch (3.0 mm) BTDC on all other models.

LUBRICATION. The engine is lubricated by mixing oil with the fuel. Regular leaded gasoline is recommended.

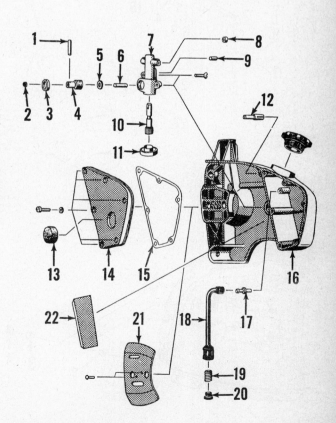

Fig. ST33 — Exploded view of automatic chain oiler pump used on Models 08S, 08SQ and S-10. Pump plunger (10) is actuated by pin (1 — Fig. ST44) on clutch retaining nut. Pump plunger (10) and pump body (7) are serviced as a complete pump assembly only. Pump output is nonadjustable.

1. Pin
2. Plug
3. Washer
4. Bushing
5. Washer
6. Pin
7. Pump body
8. Seal
9. Pin
10. Plunger
11. Cap
12. Pin
13. Pad
14. Cover
15. Gasket
16. Chain cover
17. Connector
18. Hose
19. Screen
20. Plug
21. Guide plate
22. Plate

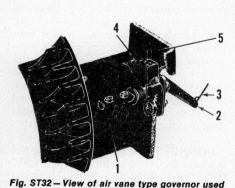

Fig. ST32 — View of air vane type governor used on some models.

1. Air vane
2. Lever
3. Throttle link
4. Notched plate
5. Governor spring

Recommended oil is STIHL two-stroke engine oil mixed at a 40:1 ratio. If STIHL two-stroke engine oil is not available, a good quality oil designed for use in air-cooled two-stroke engines may be used when mixed at a 25:1 ratio. Use a separate container to mix oil and gasoline.

Fill chain oiler tank with SAE 30 non-detergent motor oil. All models are equipped with an automatic chain oiler system. Models shown in Fig. ST36 use pumps that are actuated by crankcase pulsations against diaphragm (3) which is connected to the engine crankcase. The oil pump used on Models 08S, 08SQ and S-10 is acuated by pin (1–Fig. ST44) in clutch retaining nut. Adjust oil output by turning screw (1–Fig. ST37) on diaphragm pump models. Saws with diaphragm pumps are also equipped with a manually operated pump as shown in Fig. ST36. Oil pump on Models 08S, 08SQ and S-10 is not adjustable.

Model 090G is equipped with a gear reduction assembly which should be lubricated with SAE 30 oil. Fill drive housing until oil reaches lower edge of fill plug hole.

CARBON. The muffler assembly should be removed from the engine and the carbon scraped from the exhaust ports and muffler periodically.

REPAIRS

TIGHTENING TORQUES. The following torque values should be observed:

Clutch Nut
070, 070AV, 090,
  090AV, 090G . . . . 32 ft.-lbs. (44 N·m)
Other models . . . . . . 22 ft.-lbs. (30 N·m)
Flywheel Nut
070, 070AV, 090,
  090AV, 090G . . . . 25 ft.-lbs. (34 N·m)
Other models . . . . . . 22 ft.-lbs. (30 N·m)

Fig. ST36 — Exploded view of oil pump used on Models 070, 070AV, 090, 090AV, 090G and 090R. Turn screw (1 – Fig. ST37) to adjust pump output.

1. Oil tank
2. Washer
3. Diaphragm
4. Plug
5. Spring
6. Check ball
7. Washer
8. Pump plunger
9. Spring
11. Oil pickup
12. Pump body
13. Roller
14. Spring
15. Pumping element
16. Notched washers
17. Annular rings
18. Washer
19. Snap ring
20. Pin
21. Manual pump rod
22. "O" ring
23. Washer

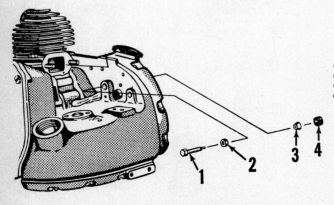

Fig. ST37 — View showing location of automatic chain oiler adjustment screw on diaphragm actuated oiler models.
1. Adjustment screw
2. Locknut
3. Stop
4. Rubber cap

RINGS, PISTON, PIN AND CYLINDER. The aluminum alloy piston is equipped with two piston rings. The floating piston pin is retained in the piston with a snap ring at each end. The pin bore of the piston is unbushed; the connecting rod has a caged needle roller piston pin bearing. An oversize piston pin is not available. However, on early models with the color code (either a black or white mark) on the piston and pin must be the same for proper fit of pin in bore.

Cylinder and cylinder head are cast in one piece. The cylinder bore is chrome plated. The cylinder is available only with a fitted piston. Piston and cylinder are grouped into different size ranges with approximately 0.0002 inch (0.0051 mm) difference between each range, and each group is marked with letter "A" to "E"on late models, or "A" to "K" on early models. Letter "A" denotes smallest size with "E" or "K" being largest. The code letter is stamped on the top of the piston and the bottom of the cylinder on early models, and at the top of the cylinder on later models. The code letter of the piston and the cylinder must be the same for proper fit of a new piston in a new cylinder. However, a new piston may be used in a worn cylinder if clearance is satisfactory.

To reinstall piston on connecting rod, proceed as follows: Install one snap ring in piston. Lubricate the piston pin needle bearing with motor oil and slide bearing into pin bore of connecting rod. Install piston on rod so arrow on piston crown points toward exhaust port. Push piston pin in far enough to install second snap ring.

Locating pins are present in piston ring grooves to prevent ring rotation. Make certain ring end gaps are properly positioned around locating pins when installing cylinder.

After piston and rod assembly is attached to crankshaft, install cylinder as follows: Turn crankshaft to top dead center and support piston with a wood block that will fit between piston skirt and crankcase when cylinder gasket is in place. A notch should be cut in the wood block so that it will fit around connecting rod. Lubricate piston and rings with motor oil and compress rings with compressor that can be removed after cylinder is pushed down over piston. On some models, it may be necessary to remove the cylinder and install an additional gasket between the cylinder and crankcase if piston strikes top of cylinder.

CONNECTING ROD. Connecting rod is a two-piece component on 070, 070AV, 090, 090AV, 090G and 090R models and may be removed without removing crankshaft. On 08S, 08SQ and S-10 models, the connecting rod and crankshaft are a

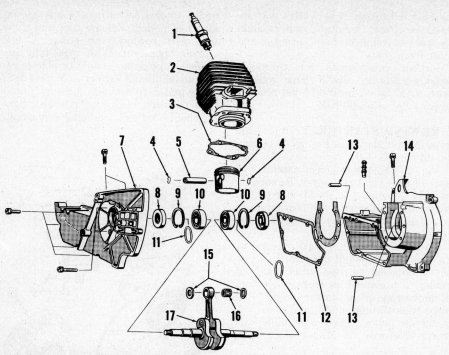

Fig. ST39 – View of engine used on Models 08S, 08SQ and S-10. Shims (11) are used on S-10 models. Washers (15) are absent on later Models 08S and 08SQ.

1. Spark plug		14. Crankcase half
2. Cylinder	6. Piston	10. Ball bearing	15. Washers
3. Head gasket	7. Crankcase half	11. Shim	16. Bearing
4. Circlip	8. Seal	12. Gasket	17. Crankshaft &
5. Piston pin	9. Snap ring	13. Dowel pin	connecting rod assy.

unit assembly and must be removed and serviced as a unit. Refer to Figs. ST39 and ST40 for exploded views of engine assemblies.

Crankshaft and connecting rod unit type assembly should not be disassembled. Connecting rod big end rides on a roller bearing and should be inspected for excessive wear or damage. If rod, bearing or crankshaft is damaged, complete crankshaft assembly must be renewed.

On models with removable connecting rod, color coding is used to match connecting rod to crankshaft. Colors (red or green) must match on connecting rod and crankshaft for proper clearance. Rod and shaft dimensions are as follows:

Crankpin	**Rod Bore**
Green	
17.996-18.000 mm	24.010-24.014 mm
(0.7085-0.7087 in.)	(0.9453-0.9454 in.)
Red	
18.001-18.005 mm	24.015-24.019 mm
(0.7087-0.7088 in.)	(0.9455-0.9456 in.)

Tighten connecting rod cap screws to 86 in.-lbs. (9.7 N·m).

CRANKCASE, CRANKSHAFT AND SEALS. All models are equipped with a two-piece crankcase that is separable from the cylinder, but is available only as a complete crankcase assembly.

Models 08S, 08SQ and S-10 are equipped with ball type main bearings which

locate in crankcase with snap rings (9 – Fig. ST39). Do not obstruct main bearing oil hole in crankcase when installing snap rings. Crankshaft end play is controlled by shims (11) on S-10 models. Shims are available in thicknesses of 0.004 inch (0.1 mm) and 0.008 inch (0.2 mm); desired end play of crankshaft is 0.008 inch (0.2 mm).

Models 070, 070AV, 090, 090AV, 090G and 090R are equipped with needle roller type main bearings at each end of the crankshaft; crankshaft end play is controlled by plastic check plates (23 – Fig. ST40) which locate between shoulder on crankshaft (21) and roller bearings (16). Check plates are available in varied thicknesses to obtain desired end play of 0.008-0.016 inch (0.20-0.30 mm).

To remove or install main bearings from the crankcase halves, first heat the crankcase to 194-212° F (90-100° C); then, drive bearings into or out of crankcase halves with proper size driver.

CLUTCH. All models are equipped with a three- or six-shoe centrifugal type clutch. Refer to Figs. ST43, ST44 and ST45 for exploded views of clutch assemblies used.

A crankshaft locking bolt is inserted in plug (26 – Fig. ST40) to prevent crankshaft rotation while unscrewing clutch

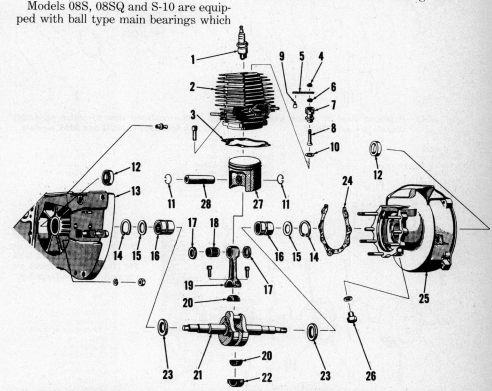

Fig. ST40 – Exploded view of Model 090 engine. Models 070, 070AV, 090AV, 090G and 090R are similar.

1. Spark plug	8. Insert	15. Washer	22. Connecting rod cap
2. Cylinder	9. Rivet	16. Roller bearing	23. Check plate
3. Head gasket	10. Washer	17. Washer	24. Gasket
4. Retainer	11. Snap ring	18. Bearing	25. Crankcase half
5. Flat spring	12. Seal	19. Connecting rod	26. Plug
6. Retainer	13. Crankcase half	20. Bearing	27. Piston
7. Valve	14. Snap ring	21. Crankshaft	28. Piston pin

nut on Models 070, 070AV, 090, 090AV, 090G and 090R. A locking bolt is screwed into the spark plug hole to prevent crankshaft rotation on all other models. Clutch nut has left hand threads. A puller may be required to remove clutch assembly from crankshaft.

On Models 08S, 08SQ and S-10, clutch nut holds pin (1 – Fig. ST44) to drive automatic chain oil pump contained in chain cover (16 – Fig. ST33). Be sure pin is not damaged and meshes correctly with pump.

Install clutch retaining washers so outer rim of washers is against clutch hub. On 070, 070AV, 090, 090AV, 090G and 090R models, sleeve (4 – Fig. ST43 and ST45) swells when tightening nut (1) to ensure tight fit of rotor (5) on crankshaft. Be certain sleeve is clean and dry prior to installing. Clutch shoes and springs should be renewed as a unit to prevent unbalanced clutch operation.

GEAR TRANSMISSION. Model 090G is equipped with a gear drive trans-

mission. Disassembly is evident with inspection of unit. A suitable puller should be used to remove chain sprocket and gear from shaft.

Inspect components for excessive wear or damage. Refill drive housing with SAE 30 oil until oil level reaches lower edge of oil fill hole.

REWIND STARTER. Friction shoe type starter shown in Fig. ST48 is used on all models.

Fig. ST49 shows correct assembly of starter shoes on brake lever. Be sure assembly is installed as shown in exploded views and leading edges of friction shoes are sharp or shoes may not properly engage drum.

To place tension on rope proceed as follows: Pull rope out until notch in pulley is adjacent to rope outlet and hold pulley to prevent rope from rewinding. Remove rope from starter handle. Pull rope back through outlet and place into notch in pulley. Turn rope pulley six turns clockwise on Models 08S, 08SQ

and S-10 and seven turns clockwise on all other models. Release rope and allow to slowly rewind onto pulley. Check starter operation. With rope fully extended, rope pulley should be able to rotate an additional ½ turn on Models 08S, 08SQ and S-10 and one full turn on all other models. With rope released, handle should be held snug against housing.

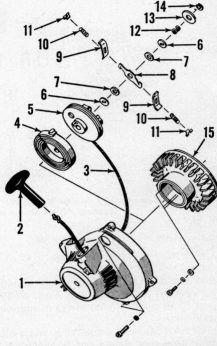

Fig. ST48 – Exploded view of typical friction shoe starter. Position of washers (6 and 7) is reversed on later models. Refer to Fig. ST49 for assembly of friction shoe plates (9) to brake lever (8).

1. Starter housing	9. Friction shoe plate
2. Rope handle	10. Springs
3. Rope	11. Retainers
4. Rewind spring	12. Spring
5. Rope pulley	13. Washer
6. Washers	14. Snap ring
7. Washers	15. Blower fan & starter cup
8. Brake lever	

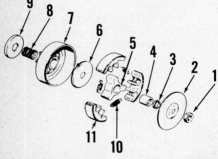

Fig. ST43 – Exploded view of clutch used on Models 070 and 070AV.

1. Nut	
2. Washer	
3. Washer	7. Drum
4. Spieth adapter sleeve	8. Bearing
5. Rotor	9. Plate
6. Retainer	10. Springs
	11. Shoes

Fig. ST45 – Exploded view of clutch assembly used on 090, 090AV, 090G and 090R models.

1. Nut	
2. Washer	7. Drum
3. Spacer	8. Needle roller bearing
4. Sleeve	9. Plate
5. Rotor	10. Spring
6. Washer	11. Shoe

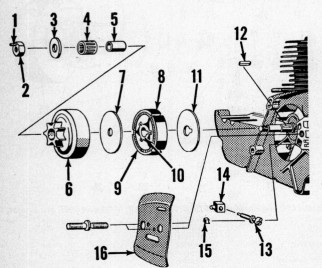

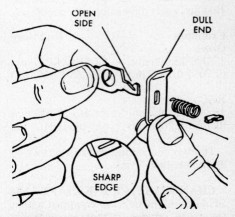

Fig. ST44 – Exploded view of clutch assembly used on Models 08S, 08SQ and S-10. Pin (1) and nut (2) drives automatic chain oiler pump.

1. Pin
2. Nut
3. Washer
4. Needle bearing
5. Bearing race
6. Clutch drum & sprocket assy.
7. Washer
8. Clutch shoes
9. Clutch springs
10. Clutch rotor
11. Washer
12. Drive key
13. Chain adjusting screw
14. Adjusting nut
15. Clamping piece
16. Guide bar plates

Fig. ST49 – Drawing showing proper method of assembly of friction shoe plates to starter brake lever.

CHAIN BRAKE. Model 08SQ is equipped with a chain brake system designed to stop chain movement should kickback occur. Chain brake is activated when the operator's hand strikes hand guard (1 – Fig. ST50) thereby allowing cam (7) to release spring (14). Spring then draws brake band tight around clutch drum to stop chain. Pull back hand guard to reset mechanism. No adjustment of brake mechanism is required.

Disassembly for repair or renewal of individual components is evident after inspection of unit and referral to the exploded view.

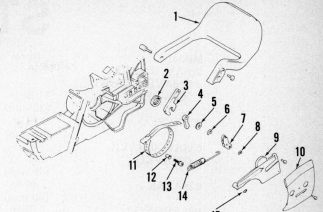

Fig. ST50 — Exploded view of chain brake system used on 08SQ models.

1. Hand guard
2. Spring
3. Connector
4. Actuating lever
5. Washer
6. "E" ring
7. Cam
8. "E" ring
9. Cover
10. Plate
11. Brake band
12. Sleeve
13. Cap screw
14. Spring
15. Clip

STIHL

Model	Bore	Stroke	Displ.	Drive Type
028AV, 028AVE, 028AVEQ, 028WB, 028WBE	*1.65 in. (42 mm)	1.22 in. (31 mm)	*2.62 cu. in. (43 cc)	Direct
028AVSEQ	1.81 in. (46 mm)	1.22 in. (31 mm)	3.14 cu. in. (51.4 cc)	Direct
038AV, 038AVE, 038AVEQ	1.89 in. (48 mm)	1.34 in. (34 mm)	3.72 cu. in. (61 cc)	Direct
038AVSE	1.97 in. (50 mm)	1.34 in. (34 mm)	4.09 cu. in. (67 cc)	Direct
038AVMEQ	2.05 in. (52 mm)	1.34 in. (34 mm)	4.4 cu. in. (72.1 cc)	Direct
042AVE	1.93 in. (49 mm)	1.42 in. (36 mm)	4.15 cu. in. (68 cc)	Direct
048AVE, 048AVES, 048AVSEQ	2.05 in. (52 mm)	1.42 in. (36 mm)	4.64 cu. in. (76 cc)	Direct

*028 series saws produced after serial number 6111990 have a 1.73 in. (44 mm) bore and a 2.87 cu. in. (47 cc) displacement.

MAINTENANCE

SPARK PLUG. Recommended spark plug is Bosch WSR6F. Spark plug electrode gap should be 0.020 inch (0.51 mm).

CARBURETOR. Series 028 saws are equipped with a Tillotson HU diaphragm carburetor. Series 038 saws are equipped with a Tillotson HK diaphragm carburetor. Model 042AVE and 048 series saws are equipped with a Walbro WS diaphragm carburetor. Refer to CARBURETOR SERVICE section for carburetor overhaul.

Initial setting of low and high speed mixture scews for all models is one turn open from a lightly seated position. Make final adjustments with engine warm and running. Adjust idle speed screw just below clutch engagement speed. Adjust idle mixture screw so engine will accelerate cleanly without hesitation. Adjust high speed mixture screw to obtain optimum performance with saw under cutting load.

IGNITION. Breaker-Point Ignition. Models 028AV, 028WB and 038AV are equipped with breaker-points while all other models use a breakerless ignition system.

Breaker-point gap should be 0.014-0.016 inch (0.35-0.40 mm) on Models 028AV, 028WB and 038AV while air gap between flywheel magnets and coil legs should be 0.008-0.012 inch (0.2-0.3 mm). Edge gap between trailing edge of flywheel north (N) magnet and upper edge of middle ignition coil leg should be 0.157-0.315 inch (4-8 mm) at ignition. Ignition timing is 0.083-0.090 inch (2.1-2.3 mm) BTDC on 028AV and 028WB models and 0.090-0.106 inch (2.3-2.7 mm) BTDC on Model 038AV. Timing marks are located on flywheel and crankcase. Vary breaker-point position to adjust timing.

Breakerless Ignition (All Models Except 028AV, 028WB and 038AV). Models 042AVE, 048AVE, 048AVES and 048AVSEQ are equipped with a SEM breakerless ignition system while Models 028AVE, 028AVEQ, 028WBE, 028AVSEQ, 038AVE, 038AVEQ, 038AVSE and 038AVMEQ may be equipped with either a Bosch or SEM breakerless ignition system. The Bosch system is identified by the ignition module (6 – Fig. ST51) located behind the flywheel and an external ignition coil (2) while the SEM ignition module and ignition coil are a one-piece externally mounted unit (1).

NOTE: Replacement flywheels for some models have two keyways for use with Bosch or SEM ignition systems. When viewed from finned side of flywheel, keyway (S – Fig. ST52) should mate with crankshaft key on SEM equipped models while keyway (B) should be used on Bosch equipped models.

Air gap between flywheel magnets and coil legs on models with electronic

Fig. ST51 — Components (2, 3, 4 and 5) are used on models with breaker-point ignition, components (2, 3 and 6) are used on models with Bosch electronic ignition and components (1 and 3) are used on models with SEM ignition system.

1. SEM ignition module
2. Ignition coil
3. Flywheel
4. Condenser
5. Breaker-points
6. Bosch ignition module

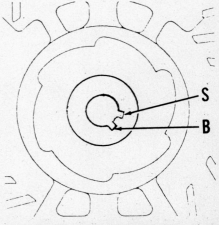

Fig. ST52-View showing location of replacement flywheel keyways for Bosch (B) or SEM (S) ignition system. See text.

ignition should be 0.008-0.012 inch (0.2-0.3 mm). Ignition timing is not adjustable, but should be checked periodically to ensure proper ignition module operation. Timing should be 0.098 inch (2.5 mm) BTDC on 028 series saws, 042AVE models and 048 series saws, and 0.114 inch (2.9 mm) BTDC on 038 series saws. Check timing at 8,000 rpm with a power timing light.

Bosch ignition coil can be tested using an ohmmeter. Primary resistance should be 0.7-1.0 ohm. Secondary resistance should be 7,700-10,300 ohms.

LUBRICATION. The engine is lubricated by mixing oil with the fuel. Recommended oil is STIHL two-stroke engine oil. Recommended fuel and oil ratio is 40:1 when using STIHL two-stroke engine oil. If STIHL two-stroke engine oil is not available, a good quality oil designed for use in air-cooled two-stroke engines may be used when mixed at a 25:1 ratio. Recommended fuel is regular leaded gasoline. Use a separate container when mixing oil and gasoline.

Manufacturer recommends use of saw chain lubricating oil; clean automotive type oil may be used as an alternative. Automatic oil pump output on 028 series saws is not adjustable while oil pump output on all other models is adjusted by turning screw on saw underside.

REPAIRS

TIGHTENING TORQUES. Refer to following table of torque values when tightening fasteners.

Flywheel Nut (All Models) . . . 22 ft.-lbs.
(30 N·m)

Clutch Hub or Hub Carrier
028AV, 0208AVE, 028AVEQ,
  028WB, 028WBE . . . . 37 ft.-lbs.
(50 N·m)
038AV, 038AVE, 038AVEQ,
  038AVMEQ . . . . 44 ft.-lbs.
(60 N·m)
042AVE, 048AVE, 048AVES,
  048AVSEQ . . . . 43 ft.-lbs.
(59 N·m)

Cylinder
028AV, 028AVE, 28AVEQ,
  028WB, 028WBE, 038AV,
  038AVE, 038AVSE,
  038AVMEQ . . . . 6 ft.-lbs.
(8 N·m)
042AVE, 048AVE, 048AVES,
  048AVSEQ . . . . 7 ft.-lbs.
(10 N·m)

Crankcase
028AV, 028AVE, 028AVEQ,
  028WB, 028WBE . . . . 6 ft.-lbs.
(8 N·m)

All other models . . . . 4 ft.-lbs.
(5 N·m)

PISTON, PIN, RINGS AND CYLINDER. The piston is accessible after removing the cylinder. Extract snap rings then drive out piston pin to separate piston from connecting rod.

The cylinder is available only with a fitted piston. However, a new standard size piston is available and may be used in a worn cylinder if clearance is satisfactory.

All models are equipped with two piston rings. On all models, a locating pin is present in piston ring groove to prevent ring rotation. Be sure piston ring end gap is properly positioned around locating pin when installing cylinder.

Install piston so arrow on piston crown points toward cylinder exhaust port.

CONNECTING ROD, CRANKSHAFT AND CRANKCASE. All models are equipped with a connecting rod, bearing and crankshaft which are pressed together and available only as a unit assembly. The crankshaft is supported by a ball bearing at each end. Heat crankcase halves prior to installation of bearings and install bearings so outer race abuts snap ring (9 – Fig. ST53) or crankcase shoulder. Heat main bearing inner races to ease installation of crankshaft. On all models except 038 series saws, oil seal recess of clutch side main bearing should face outward. Note that clutch side oil seal (7) seats in outer flange of main bearing (6).

On 038 series saws, crankshaft seal (7) shown in inset of Fig. ST53, is positioned on the outside of snap ring (9) and seats in right crankshaft half (8).

On all models, tighten crankcase screws using a diagonal pattern.

CLUTCH. Early 028 series saws without chain brake are equipped with the clutch shown in Fig. ST56. Install plate (1) so concave side is toward clutch hub (4). Clutch hub has left hand threads and

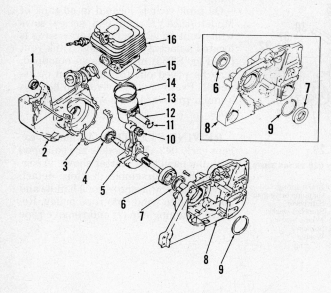

Fig. ST53 — Exploded view of Model 042AVE engine. Other models are similar. Right main bearing, snap ring and seal used on 038 series saws are shown in inset. Refer to text.

1. Oil seal
2. Crankcase half (L.H.)
3. Gasket
4. Bearing
5. Crankshaft & rod assy.
6. Bearing
7. Oil seal
8. Crankcase half (R.H.)
9. Snap ring
10. Needle bearing
11. Pin retainer
12. Piston pin
13. Piston
14. Piston rings
15. Gasket
16. Cylinder

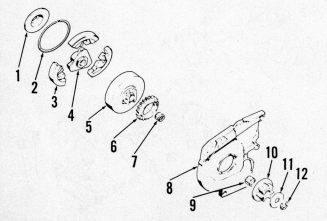

Fig. ST56 — Exploded view of clutch used on early 028 series saws without a chain brake.

1. Plate
2. Spring
3. Clutch shoe
4. Hub
5. Clutch drum
6. Oil pump drive gear
7. Bearing
8. Side cover
9. Bearing
10. Sprocket
11. Washer
12. "E" ring

should be tightened to 37 ft.-lbs. (50 N·m). Install oil pump drive gear (6) so gear teeth are toward clutch drum.

Early 028 series saws with chain brake and 042AVE models with chain brake use the clutch shown in Fig. ST57. Hub carrier (11) has left hand threads and screws onto crankshaft. Special socket 1118 893 1300 for early 028 series or special socket 1117 893 1300 may be used to remove or install hub carrier. Carrier teeth engage teeth of drive plate (12) which has slots to accept clutch hub

(17) dogs. Spring plate (14) is located between drive plate (12) and clutch hub and must be installed so spring leaves extend toward drive plate (12) as shown in Fig. ST58. Clutch hub (17 – Fig. ST57) is retained by snap ring (19) and supported by needle bearing (13) which rides on carrier (11). Clutch drum (20) is supported on crankshaft by needle bearing (21). The automatic oil pump is driven by drive gear (26) which is mounted on clutch drum (20) with gear teeth toward drum.

Most later 028 series saws and 038 series saws are equipped with clutch assembly shown in Fig. ST59. Clutch hub (17) has left hand threads. Clutch drum (20) is supported by needle bearing (21). The automatic oil pump is driven by drive gear (26) which is mounted on clutch drum (20) with gear teeth toward drum. Washer (33) and snap ring (34) retain oil pump drive gear in position.

All other models, with or without chain brake systems are equipped with a clutch assembly typical of the type shown in Fig. ST60. Clutch hub (17) has left hand threads. Plate (18) is absent on so equipped 028 series and 038 series saws.

OIL PUMP. All models are equipped with the gear driven chain oil pump shown in Fig. ST63 or ST64. The oil pump drive gear mounted on the clutch drum meshes with driven gear (4) and worm on gear backside rotates oil plunger (6). Oil plunger (6) reciprocates in pump body due to cam on plunger riding against adjuster (10 – Fig. ST63) or pin (12 – Fig. ST64) on nonadjustable pumps.

Oil tank vent is located in oil tank of Model 042AVE and 048 series saws while vent on 028 and 038 series saws is located adjacent to bar studs. Tank vent (V – Fig. ST65) on models so equipped, may be pried out for inspection or renewal. Press or drive vent into bore so annular groove is flush with top edge of bore.

REWIND STARTER. All models except early 042AVE models are equipped with the pawl type starter shown in Fig. ST66. To disassemble starter, detach starter housing, remove rope handle and allow rope to wind onto rope pulley. Remove retaining clip (7) and remove rope

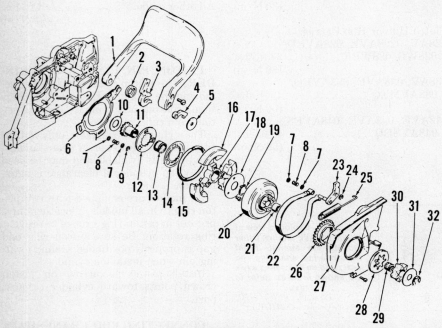

Fig. ST57—Exploded view of clutch and chain brake used on Model 042AVE. Early 028 series saws are similar.

1. Brake lever	9. "E" ring	17. Hub	25. Brake spring
2. Spring	10. Washer	18. Plate	26. Oil pump drive gear
3. Brake arm	11. Hub carrier	19. Snap ring	27. Side cover
4. Latch	12. Drive plate	20. Clutch drum	28. Sprocket washer
5. Washer	13. Needle bearing	21. Needle bearing	29. Needle bearing
6. Plate	14. Spring plate	22. Brake strap	30. Sprocket
7. Washer	15. Spring	23. Brake strap lever	31. Washer
8. Spring	16. Clutch shoe	24. "E" ring	32. "E" ring

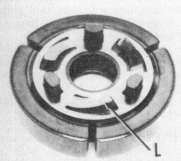

Fig. ST58—Install spring plate on clutch hub so spring leaves (L) extend toward drive plate (12 – Fig. ST57).

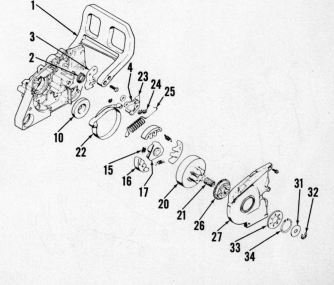

Fig. ST59—Exploded view of clutch assembly used on most later 028 series saws and 038 series saws. Refer to Fig. ST57 for parts identification except for washer (33) and snap ring (34). Chain brake system is used on 028AVEQ and 038AVEQ models.

pulley. Care should be used when removing rewind spring and case as uncontrolled uncoiling of spring may be harmful. Rope length should be 41¾

inches (106 cm). Wind rope around rope pulley in a clockwise direction as viewed with pulley installed in housing. Note that clip (7) retains pulley and pawl (6).

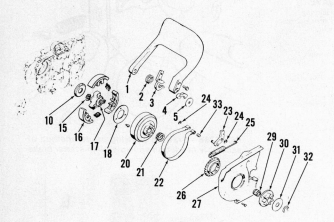

Fig. ST60 — Exploded view of clutch and chain brake used on 048 series saws and some 028 and 038 series saws. Refer to Fig. ST57 for parts identification.

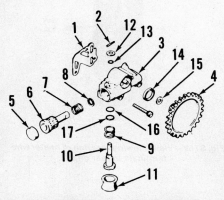

Fig. ST63 — Exploded view of Model 042AVE and 038 and 048 series automatic oil pumps.

1. Gasket	9. Spring
2. Adjuster pin	10. Adjuster
3. Pump body	11. Boot
4. Oil pump driven gear	12. Spring washer
5. Plug	13. "O" ring
6. Plunger	14. Seal
7. Spring	15. Washer
8. Washer	16. "O" ring
	17. Washer

Fig. ST65 — View of oil tank vent (V) used on 028 and 038 series saws. Vent may be pryed from bore as shown.

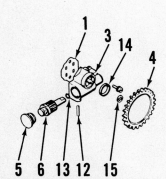

Fig. ST64 — Exploded view of typical oil pump used on 028 series saws. "O" ring (13) and seal (14) are absent on some pumps.

1. Gasket	
3. Pump body	12. Pin
4. Oil pump drive gear	13. "O" ring
5. Plug	14. Seal
6. Plunger	15. Washer

Fig. ST66 — Exploded view of typical pawl type rewind starter used on all models except early 042AVE models which use starter shown in Fig. ST67.

1. Starter housing	4. Bushing
2. Rewind spring & case	5. Washer
3. Rope pulley	6. Pawl
	7. Clip

Turn rope pulley three turns clockwise when preloading rewind spring. Rewind spring tension is correct if rope pulley will rotate an additional ½ turn with rope fully extended and, if rope handle is pulled snug against housing with rope fully retracted.

Early Model 042AVE is equipped with the friction shoe type starter shown in Fig. ST67. To disassemble starter, detach starter housing, remove rope handle and allow rope to wind onto rope pulley. Remove "E" ring (13) and remove friction shoe assembly and rope pulley. Care should be used when removing rewind spring and case as uncontrolled uncoiling of spring may be harmful. If removed, install rewind spring in case so coils are in a counterclockwise direction from outer spring end as viewed from open side of case. Rope length should be 45¼ inches (115 cm) long. Wind rope around rope pulley in a clockwise direction as viewed with pulley installed in housing. Refer to Fig. ST68 when assembling friction shoe plates on brake lever. Install friction shoe assembly on rope pulley so hook ends of brake lever point in clockwise direction. Turn rope pulley three turns clockwise when preloading rewind spring. With rope fully retracted, rope pulley should be snug against housing. With rope full extended, rope pulley should be able to turn an additional ½ turn.

CHAIN BRAKE. Models 028AVEQ and 038AVEQ are equipped with chain brake systems shown in Fig. ST59 while remaining models may be equipped with chain brake systems shown in Figs. ST57 or ST60.

On all models, chain brake is activated when operator's hand strikes brake lever (1) causing latch (4) to disengage brake strap lever (23) releasing spring (25). Spring (25) then, through the pivoting action of lever (23), pulls brake strap (22) around clutch drum to stop chain movement.

Check chain brake operation and renew any components which inhibit rapid stoppage of saw chain.

HANDLE HEATER. Some models are equipped with an electric handle heating system. An electric current generated by a coil module located under the flywheel passes through a switch and then to heating elements in the handlebar and rear grip.

To check system, remove carburetor cover and rear grip insert. Using an ohmmeter perform the following checks: Disconnect wire from switch and check switch. To perform remaining checks, disconnect generator wire (G — Fig. ST69) from terminal (T1). Connect ohmmeter leads to terminals (T1 and T2).

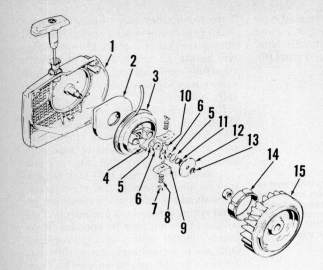

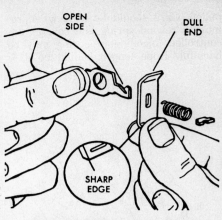

Fig. ST67—Exploded view of friction shoe type rewind starter used on early Model 042AVE.

1. Starter housing
2. Rewind spring & case
3. Rope pulley
4. Pin
5. Washer
6. Slotted washer
7. Retainer
8. Spring
9. Friction shoe plate
10. Brake lever
11. Spring
12. Thrust washer
13. "E" ring
14. Starter cup
15. Flywheel

Fig. ST68—Drawing showing proper method of assembly of friction shoe plates to starter brake lever.

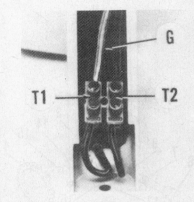

Fig. ST69—View showing location of heater wire terminals in rear grip.

Ohmmeter should read approximately 1 ohm. If ohmmeter reads infinity, heating element in rear grip is faulty and must be renewed. If ohmmeter reads zero ohms, insulation of rear grip heating element is damaged and must be repaired. Connect ohmmeter leads to terminal (T2) and ground. Ohmmeter reading should read approximately 2 ohms. If ohmmeter reads infinity, handlebar heating element is faulty and handlebar must be renewed as heating element is

not available separately. If ohmmeter reads zero ohms, insulation is damaged and must be repaired. Connect ohmmeter leads to generator lead (G) and ground. Ohmmeter should read approximately 0.6 ohms. If ohmmeter reads infinity, generator must be renewed. If ohmmeter reads zero, insulation is damaged and must be repaired.

When installing generator be sure generator is centered on crankshaft and coils do not contact flywheel.

STIHL

Model	Bore	Stroke	Displ.	Drive Type
030AV	1.65 in. (42 mm)	1.26 in. (32 mm)	2.7 cu. in. (45 cc)	Direct
031AV, *031AVE	1.73 in. (44 mm)	1.26 in. (32 mm)	3.2 cu. in. (48 cc)	Direct
032AV, *032AVE	1.77 in. (45 mm)	1.26 in. (32 mm)	3.11 cu. in. (51 cc)	Direct
045AV, *045AVE	1.97 in. (50 mm)	1.50 in. (38 mm)	4.58 cu. in. (75 cc)	Direct
*056AVE	2.05 in. (52 mm)	1.50 in. (38 mm)	4.94 cu. in. (81 cc)	Direct
*045AVSE, *056AVSE, *056AVSEQ	2.13 in. (54 mm)	1.50 in. (38 mm)	5.3 cu. in. (87 cc)	Direct
*056AVME, *056AVMEQ	2.2 in. (56 mm)	1.50 in. (38 mm)	5.7 cu. in. (93.4 cc)	Direct

*Models denoted by suffix letter "E" are "Electronic" models.

MAINTENANCE

SPARK PLUG. Recommended spark plug is Bosch WSR6F. Spark plug electrode gap should be 0.020 inch (0.5 mm).

CARBURETOR. All models are equipped with either a Walbro WA, Walbro WJ, Tillotson HS or Tillotson HU diaphragm type carburetor. Carburetor model numbers are stamped on carburetor for identification purposes. Refer to Tillotson or Walbro sections of CARBURETOR SERVICE for carburetor overhaul and exploded views.

On all models, initial adjustment of mixture screws from a lightly seated position should be 1-1¼ turns open for idle speed mixture screw and 1¼-1½ turns open for high speed mixture screw. Make final adjustment with engine warm and running. Adjust idle speed screw just below clutch engagement speed. Adjust idle mixture screw so engine will accelerate cleanly without hesitation. Adjust high speed mixture screw to obtain optimum engine performance with engine under cutting load. Do not adjust high speed mixture too lean as engine damage could result.

IGNITION. Models 030AV, 031AV, 032AV and 045AV are equipped with a conventional flywheel magneto ignition system. Models 031AVE and 032AVE are equipped with a breakerless transistor ignition system while all other models are equipped with a breakerless capacitor discharge ignition system.

Flywheel-Magneto Ignition. Ignition breaker-point gap on models so equipped should be set at 0.014-0.016 inch (0.35-0.40 mm). Ignition timing is adjusted by loosening stator mounting screws and rotating stator plate. On models not equipped with a stator plate, vary breaker-point gap to adjust timing. Ignition timing should occur 0.08-0.09 inch (2.0-2.3 mm) BTDC on Models 030AV and 031AV; 0.083-0.090 inch (2.1-2.3 mm) BTDC on Model 032AV; and 0.098-0.106 in. (2.5-2.7 mm) on 045AV models.

Air gap between ignition coil and flywheel magnets should be 0.008-0.012 inch (0.2-0.3 mm) on all models. Loosen ignition coil attaching screws and move coil to adjust air gap.

Edge gap is the distance between the trailing edge of the north (N) flywheel magnet and the adjacent edge of the center ignition coil leg. Edge gap on Models 030AV and 031AV should be 0.14-0.15 inch (3.5-3.7 mm); 0.18-0.33 inch (4.7-8.5 mm) on Model 032AV and 0.24-0.35 inch (6.0-9.0 mm) on Model 045AV. To check edge gap, rotate flywheel in a counterclockwise direction and measure edge gap at the instant breaker-points begin to open. Vary breaker-point gap and ignition timing to adjust edge gap.

Capacitor Discharge Ignition. Models 045AVE, 045AVSE, 056AVE, 056AVSE, 056AVSEQ, 056AVME and 056AVMEQ are equipped with a capacitor discharge ignition system. Ignition must be serviced as a unit assembly as individual components are not available separately.

To properly time ignition, trigger coil must be in correct relationship with flywheel magnet. Ignition timing should be 0.098-0.106 inch (2.5-2.7 mm) BTDC for all models. To check ignition timing, install a timing gage in spark plug hole and rotate engine until piston is at ignition position as indicated above. Note if mark on flywheel is aligned with mark on crankcase. Remove flywheel and note if mark on stator plate is aligned with crankcase mark. If either of these marks is not aligned, ignition must be adjusted.

To adjust ignition, rotate engine with flywheel installed until correct piston position is indicated by timing gage. Make a mark on crankcase adjacent to mark on flywheel. Remove flywheel, loosen stator plate mounting screws and rotate stator plate until mark on plate is aligned with previously made mark on crankcase. Retighten stator plate mounting screws. A timing light may also be used to check ignition timing as follows: Remove spark plug, install timing gage and rotate engine until correct piston position for ignition is indicated. Remove guide bar and install special tool 0000 850 4000 on guide bar studs. Make a reference mark opposite of arrow on tool 0000 850 4000 on clutch plate or clutch shoe on earlier models. Recheck piston position to be sure marks are correct. Install spark plug and connect timing light. Using a tachometer, run engine at 6000 rpm and check alignment of previously made reference mark and arrow on special tool 0000 850 4000 with timing light. Loosen stator plate mounting screws and adjust timing as required. Recheck timing with light.

Transistor Ignition. Models 031AVE and 032AVE are equipped with a Bosch breakerless transistor ignition. The transistor circuit is designed to take the place of breaker-points in a conventional ignition system. The transistor ignition system is triggered magnetically by a magnet in the flywheel.

To check ignition timing, install Stihl timing tool 0000 850 4000 on chain bar

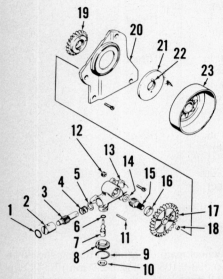

Fig. ST75 — Exploded view of automatic oil pump assembly used on early Models 030AV, 031AV, 031AVE, 032AV and 032AVE.

1. "O" ring
2. Bushing
3. Plunger
4. Spring
5. Washer
6. "O" ring
7. Adjusting screw
8. Segments
9. Retainer
10. Dirt seal
11. Pin
12. Seal
13. Pump body
14. Washer
15. Worm gear
16. Seal
17. Gear
18. Plug
19. Gear
20. Cover
21. Drive plate
22. Drive pin
23. Clutch drum

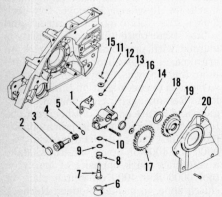

Fig. ST76 — Exploded view of automatic oil pump assembly used on later 030AV, 031AV and 031 AVE models and Models 032AV, 032AVE, 045AV, 045AVE, 045AVSE, 056AVE, 056AVSE, 056AVSEQ, 056AVME and 056AVMEQ.

1. Gasket
2. Plug
3. Plunger
4. Spring
5. Washer
6. Grommet
7. Adjusting screw
8. Spring
9. Washer
10. "O" ring
11. Special washer
12. "O" ring
13. Pump body
14. Washer
15. Stepped pin
16. Seal
17. Gear
18. Washer
19. Gear
20. Cover

studs. Using either a piston locating tool or a timing light note whether mark on clutch hub is aligned with pointer on timing tool. Ignition timing should be 0.078-0.090 inch (2.0-2.3 mm) BTDC on Model 031AVE and 0.106 inch (2.7 mm) BTDC on Model 032AVE. Ignition timing may be adjusted slightly by loosening flywheel nut and rotating flywheel on crankshaft as there is a small clearance between flywheel groove and crankshaft key.

Recommended air gap between coil armature legs and flywheel is 0.008-0.012 inch (0.2-0.3 mm). Loosen ignition coil mounting screws and move ignition coil to adjust air gap.

Tighten flywheel nut on all models to 22 ft.-lbs. (30 N·m).

LUBRICATION. The engine is lubricated by mixing oil with the fuel. Fuel:oil ratio is 40:1 when using STIHL two-stroke engine oil. If STIHL two-stroke engine oil is not available, a good quality oil designed for two-stroke air-cooled engines may be used when mixed at a 25:1 ratio. Use a separate container when mixing the oil and gasoline.

Fill chain oiler tank with SAE 30 nondetergent motor oil. All models are equipped with an automatic chain oiler system. Early Models 030AV, 031AV, 031AVE, 032AV and 032AVE are equipped with plunger type pump shown in Fig. ST75 while all other models are equipped with plunger type pump shown in Fig. ST76. On all models, oil pump output is determined by adjusting screw (7). Turning adjusting screw changes stroke of plunger (3). Slot of adjusting screw (7) is found on bottom of saw and may be turned ¼ turn.

CARBON. The muffler assembly should be removed from the engine and the carbon scraped from the exhaust ports and muffler periodically.

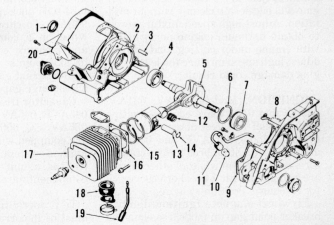

Fig. ST77 — Exploded view of engine used on Models 045AV 045AVE, and 045AVSE. Other models are similar.

1. Seal
2. Crankcase half
3. Dowel pin
4. Ball bearing
5. Crankshaft & rod assy.
6. Snap ring
7. Ball bearing
8. Crankcase half
9. Gasket
10. Oil pickup
11. Oil hose
12. Roller bearing
13. Piston pin
14. Pin retainer
15. Piston rings
16. Gasket
17. Cylinder
18. Intake manifold
19. Crankcase pulse hose
20. Fan cover

REPAIRS

PISTON, PIN, RINGS, AND CYLINDER. The aluminum alloy piston is equipped with two piston rings. The floating piston pin is retained in the piston with a snap ring at each end. The piston pin is supported in the connecting rod small end by a caged needle roller bearing. An oversize piston pin is not available.

Cylinder and cylinder head are cast in one piece. The cylinder bore is chrome plated. The cylinder is available only with a fitted piston. On 030AV, 031AV, 031AVE, 032AV and 032AVE models, piston and cylinder are grouped into different sizes with approximately 0.0002 inch (0.0051 mm) difference between each size. Each group size is marked with code letter "A" to "E." Letter "A" denotes smallest size with "E" being largest. The code letter is stamped on the top of the piston and the bottom of the cylinder on early models, and at the top of the cylinder on later models. On early models, the code letter of the piston and the cylinder must be the same for proper fit of a new piston in a new cylinder. On later models, the piston and cylinder grouping system has been simplified. Pistons are marked either "B" or "C" with a "B" piston fitting "A," "B" or "C" cylinders and a "C" piston fitting "D" or "E" cylinders.

To reinstall piston on connecting rod, proceed as follows: Install one snap ring in piston. Lubricate the piston pin needle bearing with motor oil and slide bearing into pin bore of connecting rod. Install piston on rod so arrow on piston crown points toward exhaust port. Push piston pin in far enough to install second snap ring.

After piston and rod assembly is attached to crankshaft, install cylinder as follows: Turn crankshaft to top dead center and support piston with a wood block that will fit between piston skirt and crankcase when cylinder gasket is in place. A notch should be cut in the wood block so it will fit around connecting rod. Locating pins are present in piston ring grooves to prevent ring rotation. Make certain ring end gaps are properly positioned around locating pins when installing cylinder. Two sizes of piston rings are used on 045 and 056 series saws. Be certain to install the thicker ring in the second (bottom) piston ring groove. Lubricate piston and rings with motor oil and compress rings with a ring compressor that can be removed after cylinder is pushed down over piston. Tighten cylinder screws to 71 in.-lbs. (8 N·m) on Models 030AV, 031AV, 031AVE, 032AV and 032AVE. On 045 and 056 series saws, tighten cylinder screws to 64 in.-lbs. (7.2 N·m).

CONNECTING ROD, CRANKSHAFT AND CRANKCASE.

All models are equipped with a connecting rod, bearing and crankshaft which are pressed together and available only as a unit as-

sembly. The crankshaft is supported by a ball bearing at each end. Flywheel side main bearing (4–Fig. ST77) is held in position by a shoulder in crankcase half (2) while snap ring (6) retains clutch side main bearing (7). On early 031AV and 031AVE models and all 030AV, 045AV, 045AVE, 045AVSE, 056AVE, 056AVSE, 056AVSEQ, 056AVME and 056AVMEQ models, snap ring (6) is installed in groove on main bearing (7). On all other models, snap ring is installed in crankcase half (8). Heat crankcase halves prior to installation of bearings. Heat bearing inner races with a soldering gun prior to installing crankshaft. Tighten crankcase screws using a diagonal pattern.

CLUTCH. Fig. ST78 is an exploded view of clutch assembly typical of all models except for models equipped with an isolating clutch chain brake system which uses clutch assembly shown in Fig. ST79.

On models equipped with clutch shown in Fig. ST78, clutch hub (8) and nut (10) have left hand threads. Install clutch retaining washers so face of inner diameter is against clutch hub. On some later models, washer (9) is absent and nut (10) is incorporated with clutch hub (8). Clutch shoes and springs should be renewed as a unit to prevent unbalanced clutch operation. When installing clutch on models equipped with nut (10), clutch hub (8) should be tightened to 36 ft.-lbs. (49 N·m) and nut (10) should be tightened to 25 ft.-lbs. (34 N·m). On models with integral nut and hub assembly, hub and nut assembly should be tightened to 29 ft.-lbs. (40 N·m).

On models equipped with clutch shown in Fig. ST79, clutch components are retained by drive plate (6). Drive plate has left hand threads. Use Stihl tool 1113 890 3600 or equivalent to remove or install drive plate. Drive plate should be tightened to 29 ft.-lbs. (40 N·m).

REWIND STARTER. Two types of rewind starters may be used. Friction shoe type starter used on early 045AV, 045AVE and 045AVSE models is shown in Fig. ST81. Pawl type starter used on

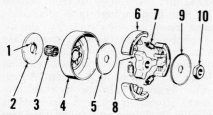

Fig. ST78—Exploded view of clutch used on most early models. Washer (9) and nut (10) are absent on all later models except 045 series. Refer to text.

1. Drive pin
2. Drive plate
3. Bearing
4. Clutch drum
5. Washer
6. Shoe
7. Spring
8. Clutch hub
9. Washer
10. Nut

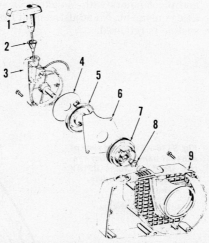

Fig. ST81—Exploded view of friction shoe type starter used on early Models 045AV, 045AVE and 045AVSE. Refer to Fig. ST84 for assembly of friction shoe plates (10) and brake lever (9).

1. Handle
2. Starter rope
3. Housing
4. Fan cover
5. Rewind spring
6. Rope pulley
7. Washer
8. Slotted washer
9. Brake lever
10. Friction shoe
11. Spring
12. Spring retainer
13. Slotted washer
14. Washer
15. Spring
16. Washer
17. "E" ring

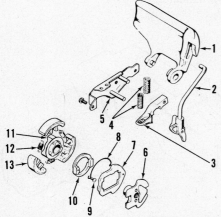

Fig. ST79—Exploded view of isolating clutch chain brake assembly used on some models.

1. Hand guard
2. Brake rod
3. Brake shoe
4. Brake spring
5. Plate
6. Drive plate
7. Retainer
8. Wire spring
9. Pin
10. Locking slider
11. Clutch hub
12. Clutch spring
13. Clutch shoe

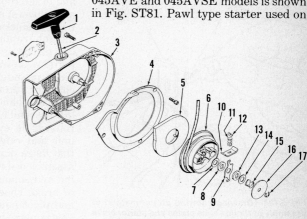

Fig. ST82—Exploded view of pawl type rewind starter used on Models 030AV, 031AV and 031AVE. Pawls on flywheel are not shown.

1. Rope handle
2. Bushing
3. Housing
4. Washer
5. Rewind spring
6. Cover
7. Rope pulley
8. "E" ring
9. Fan housing

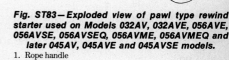

Fig. ST83—Exploded view of pawl type rewind starter used on Models 032AV, 032AVE, 056AVE, 056AVSE, 056AVSEQ, 056AVME, 056AVMEQ and later 045AV, 045AVE and 045AVSE models.

1. Rope handle
2. Starter rope
3. Housing
4. Rewind spring
5. Rope pulley
6. Pawl
7. Washer
8. Spring clip
9. Fan cover

030AV, 031AV and 031AVE models is shown in Fig. ST82 while pawl type starter used on 032AV, 032AVE, 056 AVE, 056AVSE, 056AVSEQ, 056 AVME, 056AVMEQ and later 045AV, 045AVE and 045AVSE models is shown in Fig. ST83.

On early Models 045AV, 045AVE and 045AVSE, assemble starter shoes on brake lever as shown in Fig. ST84. Be sure assembly is installed as shown in exploded views and leading edges of friction shoes are sharp or shoes may not properly engage drum.

To place tension on rope of Models 030AV, 031AV and 031AVE, assemble starter components but do not install starter on saw. Pull starter rope and hold rope pulley to prevent spring from rewinding rope on pulley. Pull rope back through rope outlet and wrap two additional turns of rope on pulley without moving pulley. Release pulley and allow rope to rewind. Rope handle should be pulled against housing and rope pulley should be able to rotate ½ turn further when rope is pulled to greatest length.

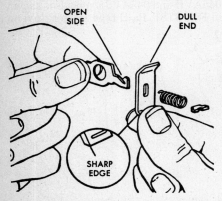

Fig. ST84 – Drawing showing proper method of assembly of friction shoe plates and starter brake lever.

To place tension on rope of all other models, proceed as follows: Pull rope out of handle until notch in pulley is adjacent to rope outlet and hold pulley to prevent rope from rewinding. Pull rope back through outlet and place into notch in pulley. On pawl type starter assemblies shown in Fig. ST83, turn rope pulley three turns clockwise and release rope back through notch. On friction shoe type starter assemblies shown in Fig. ST81, turn rope pulley seven turns clockwise. Check starter operation. Rope handle should be held against housing by spring tension and rope pulley should be able to rotate ½ turn further when rope is extended to greatest length.

CHAIN BRAKE. Some models are equipped with a chain brake system designed to stop chain movement should kickback occur.

On models equipped with the chain brake and isolating clutch system shown in Fig. ST79, brake is activated when operator's hand strikes hand guard (1). Forward movement of hand guard (1) and brake rod (2) releases brake shoe (3) and allows springs (4) to push brake shoe tight against clutch drum. At the same instant, retainer (7) and locking slider (10) disengage drive plate (6) and clutch hub (11) allowing engine to continue running unhindered. To reset brake mechanism, return engine to idle speed and pull back hand guard.

Disassembly for repair and component renewal is evident after inspection of unit and referral to Fig. ST79 noting that large diameter spring (4) should be assembled directly over brake shoe lining and smaller diameter spring to rear of brake shoe. Lubricate moving parts and pivot points with Molykote or suitable equivalent. No adjustment of brake system is required.

Models equipped with the chain brake system shown in Fig. ST85 use a brake band (10) instead of brake shoe (3 – Fig. ST79). Forward movement of hand guard (2 – Fig. ST85) and brake rod (3) release actuating lever (4) and cam (6) allowing spring (9) to draw brake band (10) tight around clutch drum. Pull back hand guard to reset mechanism.

Disassembly for repair or component renewal is evident after inspection of unit and referral to Fig. ST85. Lubricate moving parts and pivot points with Molykote or suitable equivalent. No adjustment of chain brake system is required.

Both chain brake systems should be kept clean and free from dirt and sawdust accumulation which could hinder proper operation. Renew any components found to be excessively worn or damaged.

HEATED HANDLES. Some 031AV and 031AVE models are equipped with a handle heating system which utilizes heat from engine exhaust gases. Hot exhaust from muffler enter valve (4 – Fig. ST86) and are routed to front handle and rear grip through heat tubes. Exhaust gases are then vented to the atmosphere. Rotate valve (3) to regulate heat.

Some models are equipped with an electrical handle heating system. A generator located under the flywheel creates an alternating current which passes through a switch and to heating elements in front handle and rear grip.

Check heating elements, switch and generator with an ohmmeter. Rear heating element should have a resistance of approximately one ohm. Front heating element should have a resistance of approximately two ohms and generator approximately 0.6 ohm.

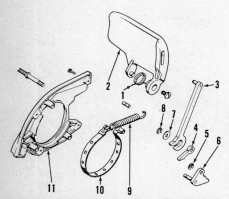

Fig. ST85 – Exploded view of band type chain brake system used on some 032AV and 032AVE models and on some 045 and 056 series saws.

1. Spring	7. Washer
2. Hand guard	8. "E" ring
3. Brake rod	9. Spring
4. Actuating lever	10. Brake band
5. "E" ring	11. Cover
6. Cam	

Fig. ST86 – Exploded view of exhaust handle heating system used on some 031AV and 031AVE models.

1. Heat tube
2. Hose
3. Adjusting valve
4. Valve body
5. Clamp
6. Wire clip

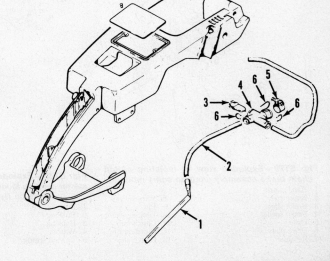

STIHL

Model	Bore	Stroke	Displ.	Drive Type
009, 009E, 009EQ, 010AV, 010AVE	1.42 in. (36 mm)	1.42 in. (36 mm)	2.26 cu. in. (37 cc)	Direct
009LES, 011AV, 011AVE, 011AVEQ, 011AVTEQ	1.50 in. (38 mm)	1.42 in. (36 mm)	2.50 cu. in. (41 cc)	Direct
012AVE, 012AVEQ, 012AVTEQ	1.57 in. (40 mm)	1.42 in. (36 mm)	2.74 cu. in. (45 cc)	Direct

MAINTENANCE

SPARK PLUG. Recommended spark plug is Bosch WSR6F or equivalent. Spark plug electrode gap should be 0.020 inch (0.5 mm).

CARBURETOR. A Walbro WA or WT diaphragm type carburetor or Zama C1S diaphragm type carburetor is used on all models. Refer to Walbro or Zama sections of CARBURETOR SERVICE section for repair and an exploded view of carburetor.

Initial adjustment of idle and high speed mixture screw is 1 turn open from a lightly seated position. Make final adjustments with engine warm and running. Adjust idle speed screw just below clutch engagement speed. Adjust idle mixture screw so engine will accelerate cleanly without hesitation. Adjust high speed mixture screw to obtain optimum performance under cutting load. Do not adjust high speed mixture needle too lean as engine may be damaged.

IGNITION. Models 009, 010AV and 011AV are equipped with a conventional flywheel magneto ignition system. All other models are equipped with a breakerless capacitor discharge ignition system.

Flywheel-Magneto Ignition. Ignition breaker-point gap on models so equipped should be 0.012-0.016 inch (0.3-0.4 mm). Ignition should occur at 0.071-0.083 inch (1.8-2.1 mm) BTDC. Ignition timing is adjusted by varying breaker-point gap. Some models have timing marks located on flywheel and crankcase as shown in Fig. ST87. A dial indicator should be used to check timing.

Recommended air gap between ignition coil and flywheel magnets should be 0.008 inch (0.2 mm). Loosen ignition coil mounting screws and move coil to adjust air gap.

Magneto edge gap should be 0.020 inch (0.5 mm) at ignition. As proper edge gap is preferred over breaker-point gap and ignition timing, vary breaker-point gap if edge gap should require adjustment.

Capacitor-Discharge Ignition. Models 009E, 009EQ, 009LES, 010AVE, 011AVE, 011AVEQ, 011AVTEQ, 012AVE, 012AVEQ and 012AVTEQ are equipped with a breakerless capacitor discharge ignition system. All electronic components are contained in a one-piece ignition module and must be serviced as unit assembly. Air gap between ignition module and flywheel magnets should be 0.006-0.008 inch (0.15-0.20 mm). Loosen ignition module mounting screws and move module to adjust air gap. Ignition timing should be 0.071-0.087 inch (1.8-2.2 mm) BTDC. Ignition timing is not adjustable but should be checked periodically to ensure proper ignition module operation.

LUBRICATION. The engine is lubricated by mixing oil with the fuel. Fuel:oil ratio is 40:1 when using STIHL two-stroke engine oil. If STIHL two-stroke engine oil is not available, a good quality oil designed for two-stroke air-cooled engines may be used when mixed at a 25:1

ratio. Use a separate container when mixing the oil and gasoline.

All models are equipped with an automatic chain oiler system. Manufacturer recommends the use of approved oils designed specifically for saw chain lubrication. If necessary, clean automotive oil may be used to lubricate saw chain. Chain oil may be diluted with kerosene during cold weather. Oil:kerosene mixture ratio should not exceed 4 parts oil to 1 part kerosene.

REPAIRS

CYLINDER, PISTON, PIN AND RINGS. Cylinder head is integral with cylinder. Cylinder can be removed after detaching fan housing, muffler, front handle and rear handle. Care must be taken when handling piston and rod assembly to prevent rod from slipping off bearing rollers (8 – Fig. ST88) as rollers

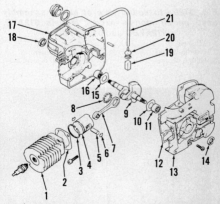

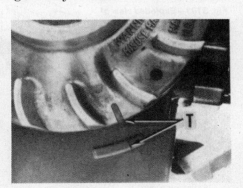

Fig. ST87 — Timing marks (T) on models so equipped, may be used to check ignition timing. Refer to text.

Fig. ST88 — Exploded view of engine assembly typical of all models.

1. Cylinder
2. Gasket
3. Piston ring
4. Piston
5. Piston pin
6. Pin retainer
7. Connecting rod
8. Needle rollers
9. Crankshaft
10. Thrust washer
11. Needle bearing
12. Gasket
13. Right crankcase half
14. Seal
15. Thrust washer
16. Needle bearing
17. Left crankcase half
18. Seal
19. Fuel filter
20. Fuel pickup
21. Hose

may fall into crankcase. Cylinder has a chrome bore which should be inspected for flaking, scoring, or other damage.

The aluminum alloy piston is equipped with one piston ring. The piston pin is retained by wire retainers and rides in a needle roller bearing in the connecting rod small end. Be sure piston is properly supported when removing piston pin to prevent damage to connecting rod. Piston must be installed with arrow on piston crown facing toward exhaust port in cylinder. Piston pin must move freely in piston upon reassembly. Piston and piston pin are available in standard sizes only. Tighten cylinder screws in two steps, initially to 53-62 in.-lbs. (6-7 N·m) and then to a final torque of 84-106 in.-lbs. (9.5-12 N·m).

CONNECTING ROD, CRANKSHAFT AND CRANKCASE. Connecting rod is one-piece and rides on 12 loose bearing rollers (8 – Fig. ST88). Be careful not to lose any loose bearing rollers during disassembly. Bearing rollers can be removed after rod is slid off rollers. Bearing rollers may be held in place with petroleum jelly or heavy grease when installing connecting rod. Manufacturer

recommends using special clamping tool 1120 893 9100 to secure connecting rod in place during disassembly and reassembly.

The crankshaft is supported by a needle roller bearing (11 and 16) in each crankcase half. Crankcase bearings must be renewed using Stihl press arbor 1120 893 7200 or equivalent. When installed, bearings should not interfere with installation of crankshaft seals (14 and 18)

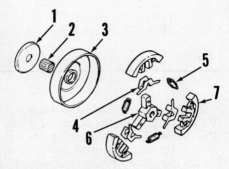

Fig. ST91—Exploded view of three-shoe type clutch assembly used on 012 series saws.

1. Washer
2. Needle bearing
3. Clutch drum
4. Retainer
5. Spring
6. Clutch hub
7. Clutch shoe

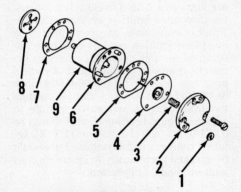

Fig. ST92—Exploded view of automatic chain oiler pump.

1. "C" ring
2. Cover
3. Spring
4. Diaphragm & plunger
5. Gasket
6. Body
7. Gasket
8. Filter retainer
9. Oil filter

and thrust washers (10 and 15). Install crankshaft seals, with seal lip toward bearing, flush with crankcase surface. Insert thrust washers into recesses in crankcase halves. Use a suitable seal protector when passing crankshaft end through crankcase seals. Be sure thrust washers (10 and 15) do not dislodge during assembly. Tighten crankcase screws to 44 in.-lbs. (5 N·m).

CLUTCH. All models except 012 series saws are equipped with the one-piece "S" configuration clutch shown in Fig. ST89. Clutch hub (5) has left hand threads and must be installed with retainer (4) positioned as shown in Fig. ST90. Clean and inspect clutch hub, drum and bearing for damage or excessive wear. Inspect crankshaft for wear or damage caused by clutch bearing. Clutch hub should be tightened to 22 ft.-lbs. (30 N·m).

Models 012AVE, 012AVEQ and 012AVTEQ are equipped with the three-shoe centrifugal clutch shown in Fig. ST91. Clutch hub (6) has left hand threads. Clutch drum rides on needle bearing (2). Inspect needle bearing for excessive wear or other damage and lubricate periodically with a suitable high temperature grease. Clutch shoes (7) and springs (5) should be renewed as complete sets only.

OIL PUMP. All models are equipped with a diaphragm type automatic chain oiler pump. Crankcase pulses move diaphragm and plunger (4 – Fig. ST92) to force oil out oil outlet. Oil tank vent, located below oil outlet, should be cleaned regularly to prevent oil flow restriction. Oil pump should be occasionally disassembled and cleaned with a suitable solvent to remove oil deposits and foreign material which may prohibit pump operation. Inspect and renew diaphragm (4), gaskets (5) and filter (9) if signs of deterioration or cracking are evident.

Fig. ST89—Exploded view of clutch assembly used on all models except Models 012AVE, 012AVEQ and 012AVTEQ.

1. Washer
2. Needle bearing
3. Clutch drum
4. Retainer
5. Hub & shoe assy.

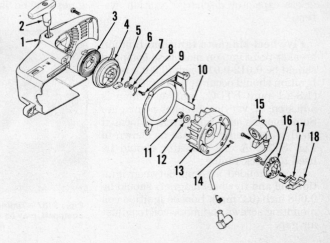

Fig. ST93—Exploded view of rewind starter and breaker-point ignition used on 010AV models. Rewind starter on all other models is similar.

1. Starter housing
2. Rope handle
3. Rewind spring
4. Rope pulley
5. Pawl
6. Washer
7. Grooved spacer
8. Clip
9. Screw
10. Fan cover
11. Nut
12. Washer
13. Flywheel
14. Woodruff key
15. Ignition coil
16. Breaker plate
17. Contact spring
18. Cable clamp

Fig. ST90—View showing correct installation of retainer (4) and clutch and shoe assembly (5) for clutch assembly shown in Fig. ST89.

REWIND STARTER. All models are equipped with a pawl type rewind starter typical of the type shown in Fig. ST93. To disassemble starter, detach starter housing, remove rope handle and allow rope to wind onto rope pulley. Remove retaining clip (8) and remove rope pulley. Care should be used when removing rewind spring as uncontrolled uncoiling of spring may be harmful. Rope length should be 37¾ inches (96 cm). Wind rope around rope pulley in a clockwise direction as viewed with pulley installed in housing. Note that clip (8) retains pulley and pawl (5). Turn rope pulley two turns clockwise when preloading rewind spring. Rope handle should be pulled against housing with rope retracted and rope pulley should be able to rotate ½ turn further with rope fully extended.

CHAIN BRAKE. Some models may be equipped with a chain brake system designed to stop chain movement should kickback occur. The chain brake is activated when the operator's hand strikes hand guard (1 – Figs. ST94 and ST95)

thereby allowing brake lever (3) to release spring (6). Spring then draws brake band (8) tight around clutch drum to stop chain. Pull back hand guard to reset mechanism. No adjustment of brake mechanism is required.

Disassembly for repair or renewal of individual components is evident after inspection of unit and referral to Fig. ST94 or Fig. ST95.

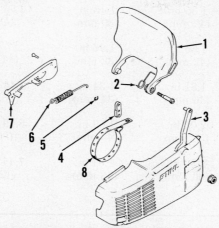

Fig. ST94 — Exploded view of optional chain brake assembly used on earlier models.

1. Hand guard
2. Spring
3. Brake lever
4. Pivot
5. "E" ring
6. Spring
7. Shield
8. Brake band

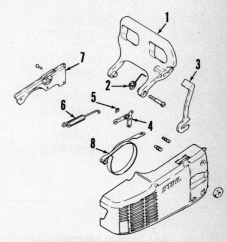

Fig. ST95 — Exploded view of chain brake system used on some later models. Refer to Fig. ST94 for component identification.

STIHL

Model	Bore	Stroke	Displ.	Drive Type
024AVE, 024AVEQ	1.65 in. (42 mm)	1.18 in. (30 mm)	2.56 cu. in. (42 cc)	Direct
024AVSE, 024AVSEQ	1.65 in. (42 mm)	1.26 in. (32 mm)	2.7 cu. in. (44.3 cc)	Direct
034AVE, 034AVEQ	1.81 in. (46 mm)	1.34 in. (34 mm)	3.44 cu. in. (56.4 cc)	Direct
064AVE, 064AVEQ	2.05 in. (52 mm)	1.57 in. (40 mm)	5.19 cu. in. (85 cc)	Direct
084AVE, 084AVEQ	2.36 in. (60 mm)	1.69 in. (43 mm)	7.44 cu. in. (122 cc)	Direct

MAINTENANCE

SPARK PLUG. Recommended spark plug is Bosch WSR6F or equivalent. Recommended electrode gap is 0.020 inch (0.50 mm).

CARBURETOR. All models are equipped with an all position diaphragm type carburetor. Series 024 saws are equipped with a Tillotson HU or a Walbro WT carburetor. Series 034 saws are equipped with either a Tillotson HK or a Zama C3A carburetor. Series 064 saws use Walbro WJ carburetors. Models 084AVE and 084AVEQ may be equipped with either a Tillotson HT-1 or HT-2 diaphragm carburetor. Refer to Tillotson, Walbro or Zama sections of CARBURETOR SERVICE section for carburetor overhaul and exploded views.

Initial adjustment on all models except 084AVE and 084AVEQ models equipped with Tillotson HT-2 carburetor is one turn open for low and high speed mixture screws. On 084AVE and 084AVEQ models equipped with a Tillotson HT-2 carburetor, initial adjustment of low speed mixture screw is 1¼ turn open. High speed mixture is fixed and high speed screw should be turned down completely and left in that position.

On all models, final adjustment should be made with engine running at operating temperature. Adjust low speed mixture so engine will accelerate cleanly without hesitation. High speed mixture should be adjusted using an accurate tachometer. On 064AVE and 064AVEQ models and 084AVE and 084AVEQ models with a Tillotson HT-1 carburetor, adjust high speed mixture to obtain a maximum speed of 12,000 rpm. On all other models, adjust high speed mixture

to obtain a maximum speed of 13,000 rpm. Do not exceed maximum rpm limits as overheating and engine damage could result. If an accurate tachometer is not available, do not vary high speed mixture from initial setting.

IGNITION. All models are equipped with a breakerless transistor controlled ignition system. Except for faulty wiring connections, repair of ignition system malfunctions is accomplished by component renewal.

On Models 034AVE, 034AVEQ, 064AVE, 064AVEQ and some 024 models, electronic circuitry is contained in a one-piece ignition module. Refer to Fig. ST100. Models 084AVE and 084AVEQ and some 024 models use a two-piece ignition coil (3—Fig. ST101) and trigger module (4) which can be serviced separately. On 024 series engines both ignition systems are interchangeable and use the same flywheel.

Air gap between ignition module or ignition coil and flywheel magnets should be 0.008-0.012 inch (0.2-0.3 mm) on all models.

Ignition timing is not adjustable but may be checked with a power timing light to ensure proper ignition module or trigger module operation. Ignition timing should be as follows: 0.083 inch (2.1 mm) BTDC on 024AVE and 024AVEQ models, 0.09 inch (2.3 mm) BTDC on 024 AVSE and 024AVSEQ models, 0.09-0.12 inch (2.4-3.2 mm) BTDC on all other models.

Flywheel nut should be tightened to 22 ft.-lbs. (30 N·m) on 024 series saws, 25 ft.-lbs. (34 N·m) on 034 series saws and 33 ft.-lbs. (45 N·m) on all other models.

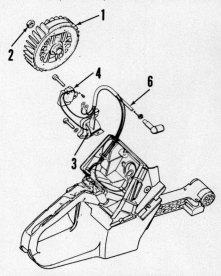

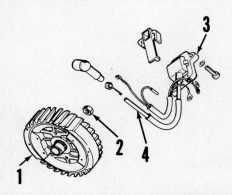

Fig. ST100—Exploded view of ignition system used on 034AVE and 034AVEQ. Models 064AVE and 064AVEQ and some 024 series ignition systems are similar.

1. Flywheel
2. Nut
3. Ignition module
4. High tension lead

Fig. ST101—Exploded view of ignition system used on 084AVE and 084AVEQ models. Ignition system on some 024 models is similar.

1. Flywheel
2. Nut
3. Ignition coil
4. Trigger module
6. High tension lead

LUBRICATION. The engine is lubricated by mixing oil with the fuel. Recommended oil is STIHL two-stroke engine oil. Recommended fuel mixture when using STIHL two-stroke engine oil is a 40:1 ratio. If STIHL two-stroke engine oil is not available, a good quality oil designed for use in air-cooled two-stroke engines may be used when mixed at a 25:1 ratio. Use a separate container when mixing oil and gasoline.

All models are equipped with automatic chain oil pumps. Oil pump output is adjustable on all models except 024AVE, 024AVEQ, 024AVSE, 024AVSEQ and some early 034AVE and 034AVEQ models. Refer to OIL PUMP under REPAIRS section for service and adjustment procedures.

Manufacturer recommends the use of approved oil designed specifically for saw chain lubrication. If an approved oil is not available, clean automotive oil may be used with viscosity chosen according to ambient temperature.

REPAIRS

CYLINDER, PISTON, PIN AND RINGS. The aluminum alloy piston is equipped with two piston rings. The floating piston pin is retained in the piston with two wire retainers. The piston pin is supported in the connecting rod small end by a caged needle bearing. New cylinders are available only with a fitted piston. If only the piston requires renewal, pistons marked "B" on piston crown may be used in all "broken in" cylinders.

To separate piston from connecting rod, remove one piston pin retainer (5—Fig. ST102) and push piston pin (4) out by hand. If pin is stuck, tap out with a hammer and a suitable driver. Be sure to properly support piston to prevent damage to connecting rod. Install piston with arrow on piston crown toward exhaust port. Piston pin must slide easily into bore. Manufacturer recommends using Stihl tool 5910 890 8200 to install piston pin retainers on 024 and 034 series engines and Stihl tool 5910 890 2213 to install piston pin retainers on all other models. Install piston pin retainers with end gap facing either top or bottom of piston. Piston is equipped with locating pins to prevent piston ring rotation. Be certain ring end gap is properly positioned around locating pins before installing cylinder. When installing cylinder, support piston with a wooden block that will fit between piston skirt and top of crankcase. A notch should be cut into the wooden block so block will fit around connecting rod. Tighten cylinder screws to 11 ft.-lbs. (15 N·m) on 064 and 084 series engines and 7 ft.-lbs. (10 N·m) on all other models.

CRANKCASE, CRANKSHAFT AND CONNECTING ROD. All models are equipped with a two-piece split type crankcase that is separate from the cylinder but available as a complete crankcase assembly only.

The crankshaft and connecting rod are a unit assembly and are not available separately. Rotate connecting rod around crankpin and renew entire assembly if roughness or other damage is noted.

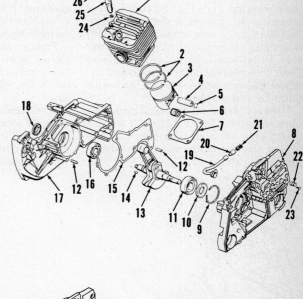

Fig. ST102—Exploded view of engine assembly typical of all models. Snap ring (9) and decompression valve assembly (24, 25 and 26) is used on Models 084AVE and 084AVEQ only.
1. Cylinder
2. Piston rings
3. Piston
4. Piston pin
5. Pin retainer
6. Needle bearing
7. Gasket
8. Right crankcase half
9. Snap ring
10. Seal
11. Right main bearing
12. Dowel pin
13. Crankshaft & connecting rod assy.
14. Key
15. Gasket
16. Left main bearing
17. Left crankcase half
18. Seal
19. Oil hose
20. Oil pickup
21. Oil filter
22. Oil tank vent
23. Split pin
24. Seal
25. Decompression valve
26. Grommet

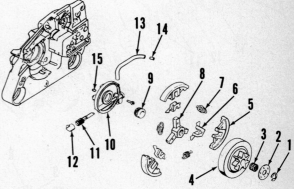

Fig. ST103—Exploded view of clutch and oil pump assemblies used on Models 024AVE, 024AVEQ, 024AVSE and 024AVSEQ.
1. "E" clip
2. Thrust washer
3. Needle bearing
4. Clutch drum
5. Clutch shoe
6. Retainer
7. Spring
8. Clutch hub
9. Worm gear
10. Oil pump body
11. Plunger
12. Plug
13. Oil hose
14. Sleeve
15. Cam pin

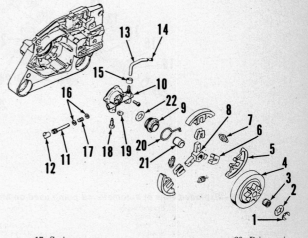

Fig. ST104—Exploded view of clutch and oil pump assemblies used on Models 304AVE, 034AVEQ, 064AVE and 064AVEQ. Sleeve (21) and washers (16 and 22) are absent on 064AVE and 064 AVEQ models. Some early Models 034AVE and 034AVEQ were equipped with a cam pin in place of adjusting screw (18) and were nonadjustable.
1. "E" clip
2. Thrust washer
3. Needle bearing
4. Clutch drum
5. Clutch shoe
6. Retainer
7. Spring
8. Clutch hub
9. Worm gear
10. Pump body
11. Plunger
12. Plug
13. Hose
14. Sleeve
15. Collar
16. Washers
17. Spring
18. Adjusting screw
19. Adjusting screw anchor
20. Drive spring
21. Sleeve
22. Washer

Stihl

Stihl

Manufacturer recommends using Stihl tools ZS5910 890 2220 and AS5910 890 2205 to separate crankcase halves and to remove and install crankshaft on 034, 064 and 084 series engines. Follow tool manufacturer's instructions for proper usage of tools.

Crankshaft is supported by ball roller type main bearings at both ends. On 084 AVE and 084AVEQ models, clutch side main bearing (11 – Fig. ST102) locates against snap ring (9) in right crankcase half (8). Clutch side crankcase seal (10) seats into outer flange of main bearing (11). Install seal with outer face of seal flush with bearing outer race. Install flywheel side crankcase seal (18) flush with outer face of crankcase.

Heat crankcase halves on all models to approximately 250° F (120° C) to ease installation of main bearings. Use the proper size drivers to install main bearings and seals.

CLUTCH. All models are equipped with a three-shoe centrifugal clutch. Refer to Figs. ST103, ST104 and ST105. Clutch hub (8) has left hand threads.

New design clutch springs (7) with a white color code should be installed on all models to obtain a 3,500 rpm clutch engagement speed. Clutch springs should be renewed in complete sets only.

Inspect needle bearing (3) for excessive wear, damage or discoloration due to overheating. Lubricate bearing with a suitable high temperature grease.

Tighten clutch hub to 37 ft.-lbs. (50 N·m) on all 024 series saws, 35 ft.-lbs. (48 N·m) on 034 and 064 series saws and 52 ft.-lbs. (71 N·m) on all 084 series saws.

When installing clutch drum on 034 and 064 series saws, rotate clutch drum (4 – Fig. ST104) back and forth to engage notch in circumference of clutch drum with oil pump drive spring (20). On 084

AVE and 084AVEQ models, clutch drum (4 – Fig. ST105) must properly engage oil pump drive plate (10). Using a small screw driver or similar tool, rotate oil pump drive plate to a horizontal position and center notch in drive plate with cutout in crankcase to ease installation of clutch drum. Align mark on outer face of clutch drum with lower edge of crankcase cutout. Rotate clutch drum to be certain clutch drum and oil pump drive plate are properly engaged.

OIL PUMP. Models 024AVE, 024 AVEQ, 024AVSE and 024AVSEQ are equipped with the automatic chain oil pump shown in Fig. ST103. Oil pump output is not adjustable. Pump plunger (11) is driven by worm gear (9). Plunger reciprocates due to cam pin (15) riding in groove of plunger.

To disassemble pump, remove cam pin (15) with a magnet and pry out plug (12). Plunger can then be removed.

Use suitable grease on all moving parts upon reassembly. Make certain cam pin properly engages groove in plunger and does not extend beyond pump body.

Models 034AVE, 034AVEQ, 064AVE and 064AVEQ are equipped with the adjustable automatic chain oil pump shown in Fig. ST104.

NOTE: Sleeve (21) and washers (16 and 22) are absent on 064AVE and 064AVEQ models.

Early Models 034AVE and 034AVEQ were equipped with a cam pin in place of adjusting screw (18) and were nonadjustable.

Oil is pumped by plunger (11) which is driven by worm gear (9). Worm gear (9) is driven by drive spring (20) which engages notch in clutch drum (4).

To disassemble pump, remove adjusting screw (18), pry out plug (12) and remove plunger (11). Renew any components with excessive wear or damage.

Apply a suitable grease to all moving parts upon reassembly. Make certain drive spring (20) is properly installed on worm gear (9). Oil pump output is adjusted by rotating adjusting screw (18).

Models 084AVE and 084AVEQ are equipped with the adjustable automatic oil pump shown in Fig. ST106. Clutch drum (4 – Fig. ST105) rotates oil pump drive gear (12) which meshes with oil pump driven gear (2 – Fig. ST106). Driven gear (2) is pressed on worm gear (4) which rotates plunger (13). Oil pump output is adjusted by rotating adjusting pin (22) or by moving lever attached to cable (17). Cable (17) actuates adjusting slide (14).

To disassemble pump, remove cable (17), snap ring (19), washer (16), spring

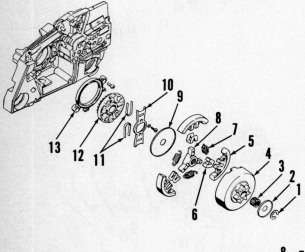

Fig. ST105 – Exploded view of clutch assembly used on 084AVE and 084AVEQ models.

1. "E" clip
2. Thrust washer
3. Needle bearing
4. Clutch drum
5. Clutch shoe
6. Retainer
7. Spring
8. Clutch hub
9. Washer
10. Oil pump drive plate
11. Springs
12. Oil pump drive gear
13. Cover

Fig. ST106 – Exploded view of automatic oil pump used on Models 084AVE and 084AVEQ.

1. Cover	8. Spring washer	15. Spring	22. Adjusting pin
2. Driven gear	9. "O" ring	16. Washer	23. Grommet
3. Seal	10. "O" ring	17. Adjusting cable	24. Pin
4. Worm gear	11. Washer	18. "O" ring	25. Retainer
5. Washer	12. Spring	19. Snap ring	26. Oil hose
6. Washer	13. Plunger	20. Spring	27. Screw
7. Pump body	14. Adjusting slide	21. "O" ring	

(15) and adjusting slide (14). Using pliers or suitable tool, compress adjusting pin (22) against pump body (7) and withdraw pin (24). Remove adjusting pin (22) with "O" ring (21) and spring (20). Plunger (13), spring (12), washer (11) and "O" ring (10) can now be removed. Pry driven gear (2) off worm gear (4). Place worm gear (4) into a vise with protective jaws and pry pump body (7) away from worm gear. Any excessively worn or damaged components should be renewed.

Reassembly is the reverse of disassembly. Worm gear seal (3) should always be renewed if worm gear is removed.

NOTE: Before installing worm gear (4) and seal (3), fill pump body with clean oil to prime pump. If it becomes necessary to prime pump after pump is assembled, pry back plug at adjusting cable (17). Inject clean oil through small hole in driven gear (2) until oil flows from pump body at plug of adjusting cable.

Apply a suitable sealant on threads of front mounting screw (27) before installing pump.

On all models, oil tank vent (22 – Fig. ST102) is located in oil tank and may be removed for inspection or renewal. Insert a long punch inside oil tank and drive out vent from inside. When installing vent, press into oil tank 0.03 inch (0.7 mm) below surface of crankcase on 024 series saws, 0.04 inch (1.0 mm) on 034 and 064 series saws and 0.06-0.08 inch (1.5-2.0 mm) on all other models.

REWIND STARTER. Models 084 AVE and 084AVEQ are equipped with the rewind starter shown in Fig. ST107. All other models are similar noting that rewind starters on 024 and 034 series saws use one pawl (2) instead of two shown in Fig. ST107. Cover (6) is absent on 024 and 034 series starters.

To disassemble starter, extend rope approximately 12 inches (30 cm). While holding rope pulley (4), unwind three or four complete turns of rope from pulley. Carefully allow pulley to unwind, relieving tension on rewind spring. Pry off wire clip (1) and remove rope pulley using caution not to dislodge rewind spring (5). If rewind spring must be removed, use caution not to allow spring to uncoil uncontrolled.

Rewind spring is wound into case in a counterclockwise direction starting with outer coil. Be sure hook on outer coil of spring engages lug of starter housing. Lubricate starter shaft (12) with a suitable low temperature grease before installing rope pulley. Wind rope onto rope pulley in a clockwise direction as viewed from flywheel side of starter housing.

To preload rewind spring, rotate rope pulley counterclockwise until rope handle (10) is approximately eight inches (20 cm) from starter housing. Make a loop in rope between pulley and housing and grip loop of rope close to pulley. Use loop of rope to rotate pulley three complete turns clockwise. Carefully allow pulley to rewind taking up slack in rope.

With rope fully retracted, rope handle should be snug against housing. With rope fully extended, rope pulley should be able to rotate ½ turn further.

CHAIN BRAKE. Some models are equipped with a chain brake system designed to stop chain movement should kickback occur. Chain brake is activated when operator's hand strikes chain brake lever (1 – Fig. ST108), tripping latch (6) thereby allowing spring (10) to

draw brake band (8) tight around clutch drum. Pull back chain brake lever to reset mechanism.

Disassembly is evident after inspection of unit and referral to exploded view. No adjustment of chain brake system is required. Renew any component found to be excessively worn or damaged. Lubricate all pivot points with Molykote or suitable equivalent.

HANDLE HEATER. Some models are equipped with an electric handle heating system. A generator located behind the flywheel supplies an electrical current to a switch and heating elements in front handle and rear grip.

To test handle heating system on 024, 034 and 064 series saws, remove carburetor cover and rear grip insert. Disconnect wire from heater switch and con-

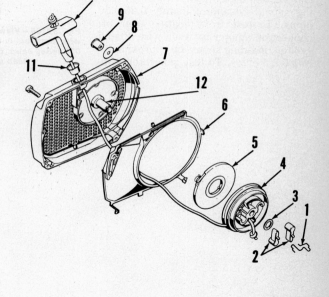

Fig. ST107 – Exploded view of rewind starter used on Models 084AVE and 084 AVEQ. Other models are similar.

1. Wire clip
2. Pawls
3. Washer
4. Rope pulley
5. Rewind spring & case
6. Cover
7. Starter housing
8. Washer
9. Sleeve
10. Rope handle
11. Rope guide
12. Shaft

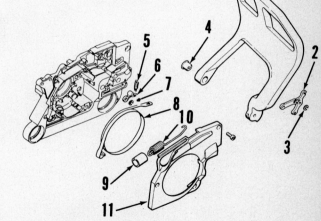

Fig. ST108 – Exploded view of chain brake system typical of all models.

1. Chain brake lever
2. Lever assy.
3. "E" ring
4. Bushing
5. Spring
6. Latch
7. "E" ring
8. Brake band
9. Sleeve
10. Spring
11. Cover

nect ohmmeter between switch and ground. Reading should be zero ohms with switch in the "ON" position. To perform the remaining checks, disconnect the generator wire (G–Fig. ST109) from terminal (T1). Connect ohmmeter to terminals (T1 and T2) to test heating element in rear grip. Reading should be approximately one ohm. Connect ohmmeter between terminal (T2) and ground to test heating element in front handle. Reading should be approximately two ohms. Connect ohmmeter between generator lead (G) and ground. Reading should be approximately 0.6 ohm.

On all checks, if reading is zero ohms, look for damaged insulation causing a short in circuit being tested. An infinity reading indicates an open circuit component being tested should be renewed.

Refer to Fig. ST110 to test handle heating system on Models 084AVE and 084AVEQ. To test heating element in rear grip, disconnect wires (3 and 4) and connect ohmmeter between wires. Reading should be approximately 0.25-0.30 ohms. To test front heating element, connect ohmmeter between wire (2) and ground. Reading should be approximately 1.6-2.2 ohms. To test generator, con-

nect ohmmeter between generator wire (G) and ground. Reading should be approximately 0.6 ohms. On all tests, a zero reading indicates damaged insula-

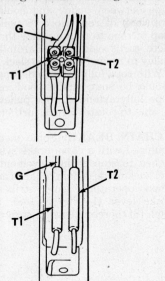

Fig. ST109—View showing location of heater wire terminals in rear grip used on 024, 034 and 064 series saws. Both styles of connectors have been used. Refer to text.

tion causing a short in circuit being tested. Insulation may be repaired. An infinite reading indicates an open circuit and component should be renewed.

Front handle heating element and front handle are not available separately on all models.

Be sure generator is centered on crankshaft and use a suitable thread locking solution on threads of retaining screws.

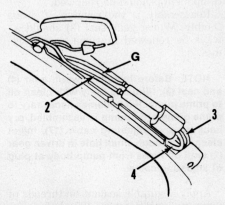

Fig. ST110—View showing location of heater wires in rear grip on 084AVE and 084AVEQ models. Refer to text.

TANAKA

TANAKA KOGYO (USA) CO.
22121 Crystal Creek Blvd. S.E.
Bothell, WA 98012

Model	Bore	Stroke	Displ.	Drive Type
ECS-290, ECS-300	35 mm (1.4 in.)	30 mm (1.2 in.)	29 cc (1.8 cu. in.)	Direct

MAINTENANCE

SPARK PLUG. Recommended spark plug is NGK BMR6A for both models. Electrode gap should be 0.6 mm (0.024 in.).

CARBURETOR. A Walbro WT diaphragm type carburetor is used on both models. Refer to Walbro section of CARBURETOR SERVICE for service and exploded views of carburetor.

Initial adjustment for both low speed and high speed mixture screws is one turn open from a lightly seated position. Make final adjustment with engine warm and running. Adjust idle speed screw so engine idles just below clutch engagement speed (approximately 2800 rpm). Adjust low speed mixture screw so engine will accelerate cleanly without hesitation. Adjust high speed mixture screw to obtain maximum no-load speed of 11,800 rpm.

IGNITION. Both models are equipped with a breakerless electronic ignition system. Ignition timing is not adjustable. Air gap between ignition module/coil assembly (17—Fig. TK3) legs and flywheel (21) should be 0.35 mm (0.014 in.).

LUBRICATION. Engine is lubricated by mixing engine oil with leaded or unleaded gasoline having an octane rating of at least 87. Recommended oil is Tanaka Two-Stroke Oil mixed at a ratio of 50:1. If Tanaka Two-Stroke Oil is not available, a good quality oil designed for air-cooled two-stroke engines and for mixture ratios between 25:1-to-50:1 may be used when mixed as outlined by oil manufacturer. Use a separate container when mixing the oil and gasoline.

Both models are equipped with an automatic chain oil pump. Recom-

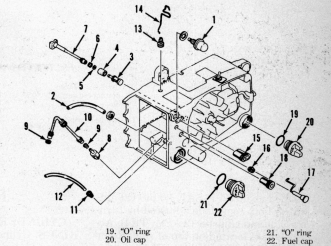

Fig. TK-1—Exploded view of fuel system components and oil pump system components used on both ECS-290 and ECS-300 models. Model ECS-300 uses a throttle cable instead of throttle link (14).

1. Priming pump
2. Hose
3. Oil filter body
4. Oil filter
5. Washer
6. Clip
7. Oil pump suction hose
8. Fuel filter
9. Clip
10. Carburetor supply hose
11. Fitting
12. Return hose
13. Boot
14. Throttle link
15. Carburetor mixture screws grommet
16. Choke knob grommet
17. Choke knob
18. Idle speed screw grommet
19. "O" ring
20. Oil cap
21. "O" ring
22. Fuel cap

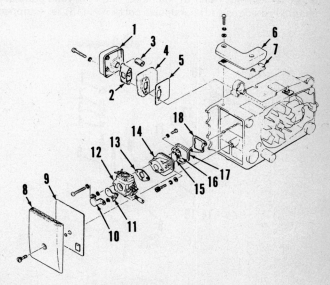

Fig. TK2—Exploded view of intake and muffler components.

1. Muffler half
2. Baffle
3. Spark arrestor
4. Muffler half
5. Gasket
6. Upper cover
7. Lower cover
8. Front cover
9. Air cleaner element
10. Redirection bracket
11. Choke valve
12. Carburetor assy.
13. Gasket
14. Intake manifold
15. Reed petal
16. Reed stopper
17. Insulator rubber
18. Gasket

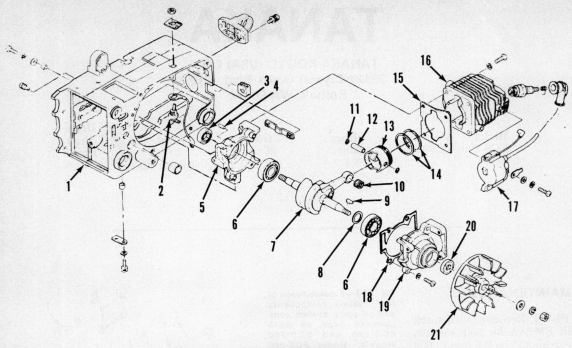

Fig. TK3 — Exploded view of engine assembly.

1. Case
2. Run/Stop switch
3. Seal
4. Needle roller
5. Crankcase half
6. Bearing
7. Crankshaft & connecting rod assy.
8. Shim
9. Key
10. Needle bearing
11. Retainer clip
12. Piston pin
13. Piston
14. Piston rings
15. Gasket
16. Cylinder
17. Ignition module/coil assy.
18. Gasket
19. Crankcase half
20. Seal
21. Flywheel

mended chain oil is SAE 30 oil. Oil output on both models is adjusted by turning oil pump adjuster (2–Fig. TK4). Access hole is located on top of saw. Refer to AUTOMATIC CHAIN OILER under REPAIRS section.

CARBON. Carbon should be cleaned from muffler and exhaust ports at regular intervals. When scraping carbon, be careful not to damage the chamfered edges of the exhaust ports.

REPAIRS

CYLINDER, PISTON, PIN AND RINGS. Cylinder (16 – Fig. TK3) bore is chrome plated and should be renewed if cracking, flaking or other damage to cylinder bore is noted. Oversize piston and rings are not available. Cylinder (16) should be renewed if bore is out-of-round or tapered 0.10 mm (0.004 in.) beyond standard bore dimension. Piston (13) is equipped with two piston rings

(14). Piston ring end gap should be 0.1-0.3 mm (0.004-0.012 in.). Locating pins are present in ring grooves to prevent ring rotation. Make certain ring end gaps are properly positioned around locating pins before installing cylinder. Piston pin (12) rides in needle bearing

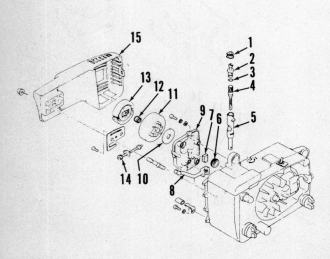

Fig. TK4 — Exploded view of clutch and oil pump assemblies.

1. Grommet
2. Oil pump output adjuster
3. "O" ring
4. Plunger
5. Pump body
6. Worm gear
7. Air vent sponge
8. Oil pump discharge hose
9. Cover
10. Washer
11. Clutch drum
12. Needle bearing
13. Clutch assy.
14. Saw chain tension adjuster
15. Side cover

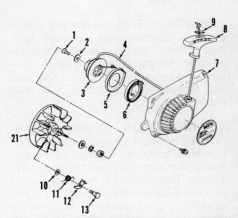

Fig. TK5 — Exploded view of rewind starter assembly.

1. Screw
2. Washer
3. Rope pulley
4. Rope
5. Rewind spring case
6. Rewind spring
7. Housing
8. Handle
9. Anchor
10. Washer
11. Spring
12. Pawl
13. Pivot screw
21. Flywheel

(10) and is retained in position with two wire retainer clips (11). Once removed, wire clips should not be reused. Install piston on connecting rod so arrow on piston crown points toward exhaust port.

CRANKSHAFT AND CONNECTING ROD. Crankcase halves must be split to remove crankshaft assembly. Crankshaft and connecting rod (7 – Fig. TK3) are a unit assembly and supported at both ends with roller type main bearings (6). Rotate connecting rod around crankpin and renew assembly if roughness, excessive play or other damage is noted.

New seals (3 and 20) should be installed in crankcase halves prior to installing crankshaft assembly. Recommended crankshaft end play is 0.3 mm (0.012 in.). Adjust thickness of shim (8) to obtain correct end play. Shim (8) is available in thicknesses of 0.05, 0.10, 0.15 and 0.20 mm.

CLUTCH. A two-shoe centrifugal type clutch is used on both models. Clutch hub has left hand threads. Clutch needle bearing (12 – Fig. TK4) should be inspected for excessive wear or damage. Inspect clutch shoes and drum for signs of excessive heat. Clutch assembly (13) is only renewable as a complete unit.

AUTOMATIC CHAIN OILER. Both models are equipped with an automatic chain oil pump assembly. Oil pump plunger (4 – Fig. TK4) is driven by worm gear (6) mounted on crankshaft end. Rotate oil pump output adjuster (2) clockwise to increase oil flow and counterclockwise to decrease oil flow.

REWIND STARTER. Refer to Fig. TK5 for exploded view of pawl type starter used on both models. Care should be exercised when removing rewind spring (6) to prevent spring from uncoiling uncontrolled.

During reassembly, do not apply any more tension on rewind spring than required to properly draw rope handle up against starter housing in relaxed position.

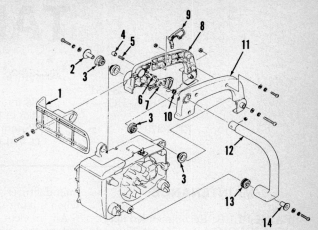

Fig. TK6—Exploded view of front and rear handle assemblies used on Model ECS-290.

1. Hand guard
2. Collar
3. Vibration dampers
4. Cap
5. Spring
6. Push pin
7. Throttle lever
8. Rear handle half
9. Throttle lock lever
10. Return spring
11. Rear handle half
12. Front handle
13. Vibration damper
14. Collar

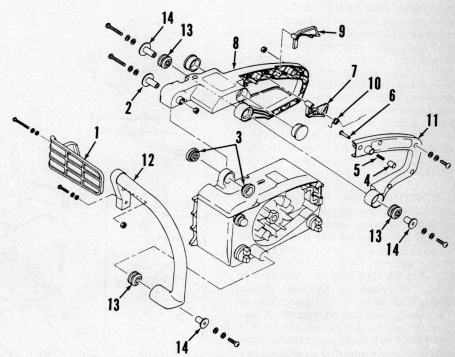

Fig. TK7—Exploded view of front and rear handle assemblies used on Model ECS-300. Refer to legend in Fig. TK6 for identification of components.

TANAKA

Model	Bore	Stroke	Displ.	Drive Type
ECS-350, ECS-351, ECS-355, ECS-356	38 mm (1.5 in.)	30 mm (1.2 in.)	34 cc (2.1 cu. in.)	Direct
ECS-370	38 mm (1.5 in.)	32mm (1.3 in.)	36 cc (2.2 cu. in.)	Direct

MAINTENANCE

SPARK PLUG. Recommended spark plug is NGK BM7A for Model 370 and NGK BM6A of all other models. Electrode gap should be 0.6 mm (0.024 in.).

CARBURETOR. A Walbro WA diaphragm type carburetor is used on all models. Refer to Walbro section of CARBURETOR SERVICE for service and exploded views of carburetor.

Initial adjustment for both low speed and high speed mixture screws is one turn open from a lightly seated position. Make final adjustment with engine warm and running. Adjust idle speed screw so engine idles just below clutch engagement speed (approximately 2800 rpm). Adjust low speed mixture screw so engine will accelerate cleanly without hesitation. Adjust high speed mixture screw to obtain maximum no-load speed of 11,800 rpm.

IGNITION. Early models ECS-350 and ECS-351 are equipped with a breaker-point ignition system. All other models are equipped with a breakerless electronic ignition system. On breaker-point ignition models, breaker-points (32 – Fig. TK11) should just start to open when "M" mark on flywheel surface aligns with raised mark (approximately 10 o'clock position) on crankcase surface. Breaker-point gap should be 0.35 mm (0.014 in.). Make sure breaker-point gap is properly adjusted as ignition timing will be affected.

On all models with a breakerless electronic ignition system, ignition timing is not adjustable. Air gap between ignition coil assembly (28) legs and flywheel (27) should be 0.35 mm (0.014 in.).

LUBRICATION. Engine is lubricated by mixing engine oil with leaded or unleaded gasoline having an octane rating of at least 87. Recommended oil is Tanaka Two-Stroke Oil mixed at a ratio of 50:1. If Tanaka Two-Stroke Oil is not available, a good quality oil designed for air-cooled two-stroke engines and for mixture ratios between 25:1-to-50:1 may be used when mixed as outlined by oil

manufacturer. Use a separate container when mixing the oil and gasoline.

All models are equipped with an automatic chain oil pump. Recommended chain oil is SAE 30 oil. Oil output on all models, except early Model ECS-350, is adjusted by turning oil pump output adjuster (1 – Fig. TK11). Refer to AUTOMATIC CHAIN OILER under REPAIRS section.

CARBON. Carbon should be cleaned from muffler and exhaust ports at regular intervals. When scraping carbon, be careful not to damage the chamfered edges of the exhaust ports.

REPAIRS

CYLINDER, PISTON, PIN AND RINGS. Cylinder (18 – Fig. TK11) bore is chrome plated and should be renewed if cracking, flaking or other damage to cylinder bore is noted. Oversize piston and rings are not available. Cylinder (18) should be renewed if bore is out-of-round or tapered 0.10 mm (0.004 in.) beyond standard bore dimension. Piston (15) is equipped with two piston rings (16). Piston ring end gap should be

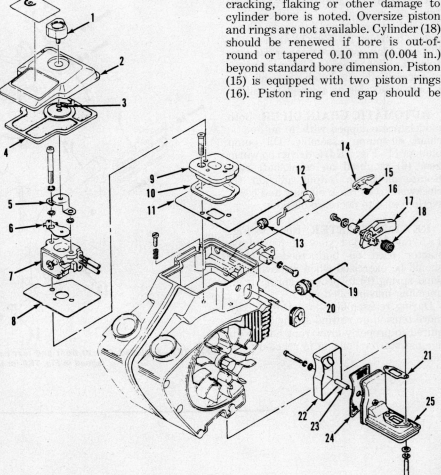

Fig. TK10—Exploded view of intake and muffler components.

1. Knob	8. Gasket	14. Throttle lock	20. Grommet
2. Upper cover	9. Insulator block	15. Spring	21. Gasket
3. "O" ring	10. Insulator block rubber	16. Spacer	22. Muffler half
4. Air cleaner element	11. Heat shield	17. Throttle lever	23. Spacer
5. Redirection bracket	12. Choke knob	18. Spring	24. Spark arrestor
6. Choke valve	13. Grommet	19. Throttle link	25. Muffler half
7. Carburetor assy.			

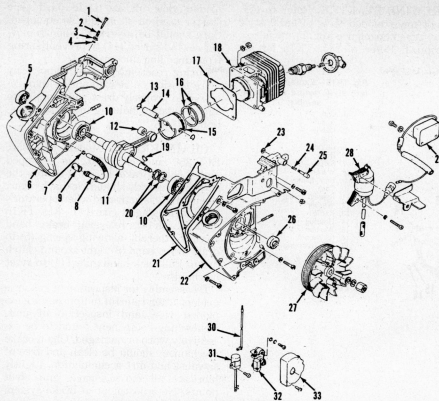

Fig. TK11 — Exploded view of engine assembly and related components. Oil pump output is nonadjustable on Model ECS-350. Magneto breaker-point ignition is used on early ECS-350 and early ESC-351 models.

1. Oil pump adjuster
2. Spring
3. Washer
4. "O" ring
5. Seal
6. Crankcase half
7. Retainer
8. Oil pump suction hose
9. Strainer
10. Bearing
11. Crankshaft & connecting rod assy.
12. Needle bearing
13. Retainer clip
14. Piston pin
15. Piston
16. Piston rings
17. Gasket
18. Cylinder
19. Key
20. Shim or shims
21. Gasket
22. Crankcase half
23. Clip
24. Spring
25. Push pin
26. Seal
27. Flywheel
28. Ignition coil
29. Ignition module
30. Primary lead
31. Condenser
32. Breaker-point assy.
33. Cover

Fig. TK12 — Exploded view of three-shoe clutch assembly.

1. Hub & shoe assy.
2. Drum
3. Needle bearing
4. Washer

Fig. TK13 — Exploded view of automatic oil pump assembly.

1. Cover
2. Seal
3. Body
4. Grommet
5. Plunger
6. Worm gear
7. Pin
8. Grommet
9. Air pipe
10. Discharge hose
11. Jet

0.1-0.3 mm (0.004-0.012 in.). Locating pins are present in ring grooves to prevent ring rotation. Make certain ring end gaps are properly positioned around locating pins before installing cylinder. Piston pin (14) rides in needle bearing (12) and is retained in position with two wire retainer clips (13). Once removed, wire clips should not be reused. Install piston on connecting rod so arrow on piston crown points toward exhaust port.

CRANKSHAFT AND CONNECTING ROD.
Crankcase halves must be split to remove crankshaft assembly. Crankshaft and connecting rod (11 – Fig. TK11) are a unit assembly and supported at both ends with roller type main bearings (10). Rotate connecting rod around crankpin and renew assembly if roughness, excessive play or other damage is noted.

New seals (5 and 26) should be installed in crankcase halves prior to installing crankshaft assembly. Recommended crankshaft end play is 0.3 mm (0.012

in.). Adjust thickness of shim or shims (20) to obtain correct end play. Shim or shims (20) are available in thicknesses of 0.05, 0.10, 0.15 and 0.20 mm.

CLUTCH. A three-shoe centrifugal type clutch is used on all models. Clutch hub has left hand threads. Clutch needle bearing (3 – Fig. TK12) should be inspected for excessive wear or damage.

Fig. TK14 — Exploded view of early style rewind starter assembly.

1. Cap
3. Handle
5. Guide
6. Rope
7. Screw
8. Washer
9. Rope pulley
10. Case
11. Rewind spring
12. Washer
14. Housing
15. Washer
16. Castle nut
17. Return spring
18. Washer
19. Pawl
20. Washer
21. Pivot screw
27. Flywheel

Inspect clutch shoes and drum for signs of excessive heat. Clutch assembly (1) is only renewable as a complete unit.

AUTOMATIC CHAIN OILER. All models are equipped with an automatic chain oil pump assembly. Oil pump plunger (5 – Fig. TK13) is driven by worm gear (6) mounted on crankshaft end. On all models, except early Model

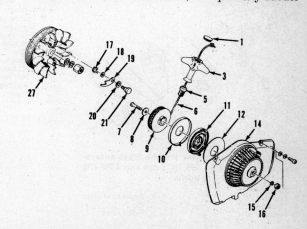

ECS-350, rotate oil pump output adjuster (1–Fig. TK11) clockwise to increase oil flow and counterclockwise to decrease oil flow.

REWIND STARTER. Refer to Fig. TK14 for exploded view of early style pawl type starter used on all models so equipped. Refer to Fig. TK15 for exploded view of late style pawl type starter used on all models so equipped. Care should be exercised when removing rewind spring (11) to prevent spring from uncoiling uncontrolled.

During reassembly, do not apply any more tension on rewind spring than required to properly draw rope handle up against starter housing in relaxed position.

CHAIN BRAKE. Models ECS-355, ECS-356 and ECS-370 are equipped with a chain brake designed to stop the saw chain quickly should kickback occur. Chain brake is activated when operator's hand strikes hand guard (1–Fig. TK16 or Fig. TK17), releasing brake band lever (6) thereby allowing spring (5) to draw brake band (8) tight around clutch drum. Pull back hand guard (1) to reset mechanism.

Disassembly for inspection or repair is evident after referral to appropriate exploded view and inspection of unit. Renew any component found to be excessively worn or damaged. Chain brake mechanism should be clean and free of sawdust and dirt accumulation. Lightly lubricate all moving parts and pivot points. No adjustment of brake system is required.

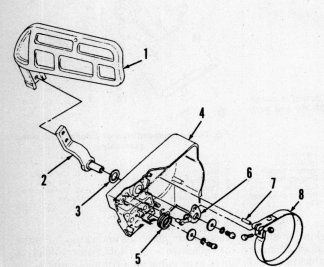

Fig. TK15—Exploded view of late style rewind starter assembly.

1. Cap
2. Anchor
3. Handle
4. Clip
5. Guide
6. Rope
7. Screw
8. Washer
9. Rope pulley
10. Case
11. Rewind spring
12. Washer
13. Baffle
14. Housing
15. Washer
16. Castle nut
17. Return spring
18. Washer
19. Pawl
20. Washer
21. Pivot screw
27. Flywheel

Fig. TK16—Exploded view of chain brake assembly used on early ECS-355, ECS-356 and ECS-370 models.

1. Hand guard
2. Lever
3. Washer
4. Side case
5. Spring
6. Brake band lever
7. Pin
8. Brake band

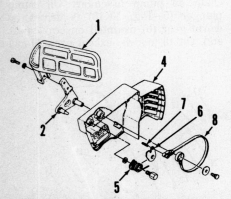

Fig. TK18—Exploded view of front and rear handle assemblies.

1. Run/stop switch
2. Handle grip
3. Right handle half
4. Vibration dampers
5. Vibration dampers
6. Collar
7. Safety lever
8. Left handle half
9. Front handle
10. Front handle vibration damper
11. Cover

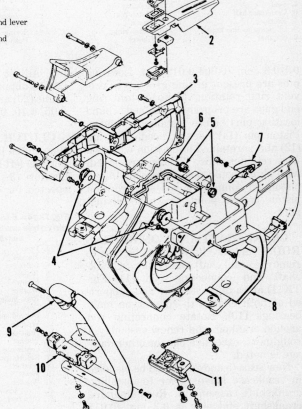

Fig. TK17—Exploded view of chain brake assembly used on late ECS-355, ECS-356 and ESC-370 models.

1. Hand guard
2. Lever
4. Side case
5. Spring
6. Brake band lever
7. Pin
8. Brake band

TANAKA

Model	Bore	Stroke	Displ.	Drive Type
ECS-415	40 mm (1.6 in.)	32 mm (1.3 in.)	40 cc (2.4 cu. in.)	Direct

MAINTENANCE

SPARK PLUG. Recommended spark plug is NGK BPM7A. Electrode gap should be 0.6 mm (0.024 in.).

CARBURETOR. A Walbro WT diaphragm type carburetor is used. Refer to Walbro section of CARBURETOR SERVICE for service and exploded views of carburetor.

Initial adjustment for both low speed and high speed mixture screws is one turn open from a lightly seated position. Make final adjustment with engine warm and running. Adjust idle speed screw so engine idles just below clutch engagement speed (approximately 2800 rpm). Adjust low speed mixture screw so engine will accelerate cleanly without hesitation. Adjust high speed mixture screw to obtain maximum no-load speed of 11,800 rpm.

IGNITION. A breakerless electronic ignition system is used. Ignition timing is not adjustable. Air gap between ignition coil assembly (21 – Fig. TK21) legs and flywheel (20) should be 0.35 mm (0.014 in.).

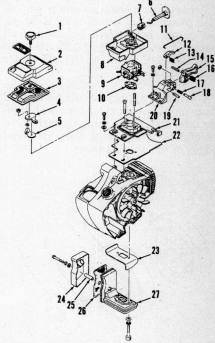

Fig. TK20 — Exploded view of intake and muffler components.

1. Knob
2. Upper cover
3. Air cleaner element
4. Redirection bracket
5. Choke valve
6. Chock knob
7. Grommet
8. Lower cover
9. Carburetor assy.
10. Gasket
11. Link
12. Throttle lock lever
13. Spring
14. Spring pin
15. Throttle lever
16. Spring
17. Spring
18. Push pin
19. Spring pin
20. Bracket
21. Insulator block
22. Heat shield
23. Gasket
24. Muffler half
25. Spacer
26. Spark arrestor
27. Muffler half

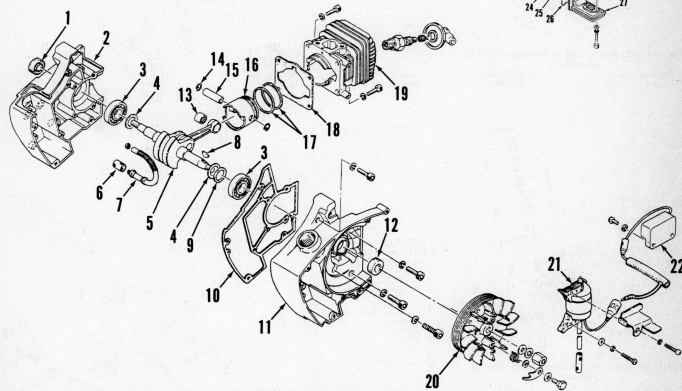

Fig. TK21 — Exploded view of engine assembly.

1. Seal
2. Crankcase half
3. Bearing
4. Thrust washer
5. Crankshaft & connecting rod assy.
6. Strainer
7. Oil pump suction hose
8. Key
9. Shim
10. Gasket
11. Crankcase half
12. Seal
13. Needle bearing
14. Retainer
15. Piston pin
16. Piston
17. Piston rings
18. Gasket
19. Cylinder
20. Flywheel
21. Ignition coil
22. Ignition module

LUBRICATION. Engine is lubricated by mixing engine oil with leaded or unleaded gasoline having an octane rating of at least 87. Recommended oil is Tanaka Two-Stroke Oil mixed at a ratio of 50:1. If Tanaka Two-Stroke Oil is not available, a good quality oil designed for air-cooled two-stroke engines and for mixture ratios between 25:1-to-50:1 may be used when mixed as outlined by oil manufacturer. Use a separate container when mixing the oil and gasoline.

An automatic chain oil pump is used. Recommended chain oil is SAE 30 oil. Oil output is adjusted by turning oil pump adjuster (2 – Fig. TK23). Refer to AUTOMATIC CHAIN OILER under REPAIRS section.

CARBON. Carbon should be cleaned from muffler and exhaust ports at regular intervals. When scraping carbon, be careful not to damage the chamfered edges of the exhaust ports.

REPAIRS

CYLINDER, PISTON, PIN AND RINGS. Cylinder (19 – Fig. TK21) bore is chrome plated and should be renewed if cracking, flaking or other damage to cylinder bore is noted. Oversize piston and rings are not available. Cylinder (19) should be renewed if bore is out-of-round or tapered 0.10 mm (0.004 in.) beyond standard bore dimension. Piston (16) is equipped with two piston rings (17). Piston ring end gap should be 0.1-0.3 mm (0.004-0.012 in.). Locating pins are present in ring grooves to prevent ring rotation. Make certain ring end gaps are properly positioned around locating pins before installing cylinder. Piston pin (15) rides in needle bearing (13) and is retained in position with two wire retainer clips (14). Once removed, wire clips should not be reused. Install piston on connecting rod so arrow on piston crown points toward exhaust port.

CRANKSHAFT AND CONNECTING ROD. Crankcase halves must be split to remove crankshaft assembly. Crankshaft and connecting rod (5 – Fig. TK21) are a unit assembly and supported at both ends with roller type main bearings (3). Rotate connecting rod around crankpin and renew assembly if roughness, excessive play or other damage is noted.

New seals (1 and 12) should be installed in crankcase halves prior to installing crankshaft assembly. Recommended crankshaft end play is 0.3 mm (0.012 in.). Adjust thickness of shim (9) to obtain correct end play. Shim (9) is available in thicknesses of 0.05, 0.10, 0.15 and 0.20 mm.

CLUTCH. A three-shoe centrifugal type clutch is used. Clutch hub has left hand threads. Clutch needle bearing (3 – Fig. TK22) should be inspected for excessive wear or damage. Inspect clutch shoes and drum for signs of excessive heat. Clutch assembly (1) is only renewable as a complete unit.

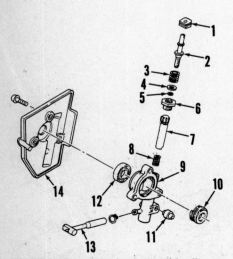

Fig. TK22 – Exploded view of three-shoe clutch assembly.

1. Hub & shoe assy.
2. Drum
3. Needle bearing
4. Washer

Fig. TK24 – Exploded view of rewind starter assembly.

1. Handle
2. Guide
3. Clip
4. Rope
5. Screw
6. Washer
7. Rope pulley
8. Rewind spring case
9. Rewind spring
10. Washer
11. Baffle
12. Housing
13. Toothed lockwasher
14. Castle nut
15. Return spring
16. Washer
17. Pawl
18. Washer
19. Pivot screw
20. Flywheel

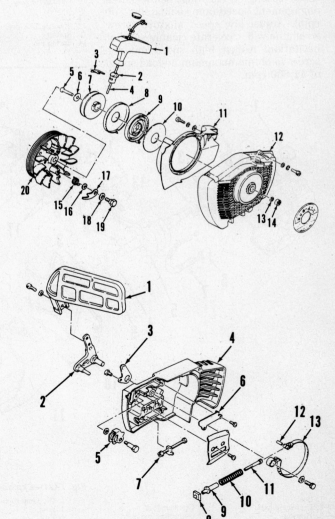

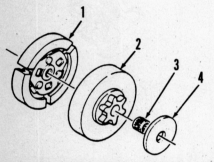

Fig. TK23 – Exploded view of automatic oil pump assembly.

1. Grommet
2. Output adjuster
3. Spring
4. Washer
5. "O" ring
6. Cap
7. Plunger
8. Spring
9. Body
10. Worm gear
11. Air pipe
12. Seal
13. Discharge hose
14. Cover

Fig. TK25 – Exploded view of chain brake assembly.

1. Hand guard
2. Lever
3. Detent
4. Side case
5. Arm
6. Spring holder
7. Saw chain tension adjuster
8. Lockplate
9. Adjuster
10. Spring
11. Rod
12. Pin
13. Brake band

AUTOMATIC CHAIN OILER. An automatic chain oil pump assembly is used. Oil pump plunger (7–Fig. TK23) is driven by worm gear (10) mounted on crankshaft end. Rotate oil pump output adjuster (2) counterclockwise to increase oil flow and clockwise to decrease oil flow.

REWIND STARTER. Refer to Fig. TK24 for exploded view of pawl type starter. Care should be exercised when removing rewind spring (9) to prevent spring from uncoiling uncontrolled.

During reassembly, do not apply any more tension on rewind spring than required to properly draw rope handle up against starter housing in relaxed position.

CHAIN BRAKE. A chain brake designed to stop the saw chain quickly should kickback occur is used. Chain brake is activated when operator's hand strikes hand guard (1–Fig. TK25), releasing arm (5) thereby allowing spring (10) to draw brake band (13) tight around clutch drum. Pull back hand guard (1) to reset mechanism.

Disassembly for inspection or repair is evident after referral to appropriate exploded view and inspection of unit. Renew any component found to be excessively worn or damaged. Chain brake mechanism should be clean and free of sawdust and dirt accumulation. Lightly lubricate all moving parts and pivot points.

To adjust chain brake, first remove spark plug boot from spark plug and properly ground terminal end. Place chain brake lever (2) in released position. Use a suitable sized screwdriver and rotate adjuster (9) clockwise until saw chain cannot be rotated around guide bar by hand pressure. Then rotate adjuster (9) counterclockwise noting when brake band (13) does not contact outside

surface of clutch drum. Make sure brake band does not drag on outside of clutch drum with brake lever in released position. With brake lever in applied position, saw chain should not be free to rotate around guide bar.

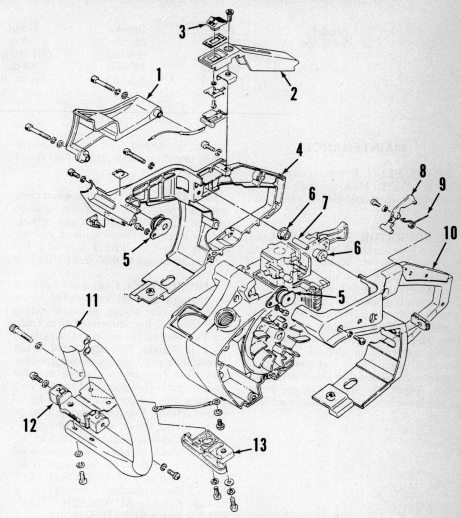

Fig. TK26—Exploded view of front and rear handle assemblies.

1. Guard
2. Handle grip
3. Run/stop switch
4. Rear handle half
5. Vibration damper
6. Damper
7. Collar
8. Safety lever
9. Spring
10. Rear handle half
11. Front handle
12. Front handle vibration damper
13. Cover

TANAKA

Model	Bore	Stroke	Displ.	Drive Type
ECS-506	41 mm (1.6 in.)	38 mm (1.5 in.)	50 cc (3.1 cu. in.)	Direct
ECS-650	46 mm (1.8 in.)	38 mm (1.5 in.)	63 cc (3.8 cu. in.)	Direct

MAINTENANCE

SPARK PLUG. Recommended spark plug is NGK BPM7A for both models. Electrode gap should be 0.6 mm (0.024 in.).

CARBURETOR. A Walbro HDA diaphragm type carburetor is used on both models. Refer to Walbro section of CARBURETOR SERVICE for service and exploded views of carburetor.

Initial adjustment for both low speed and high speed mixture screws is 1¼ turns open from a lightly seated position. Make final adjustment with engine warm and running. Adjust idle speed screw so engine idles just below clutch engagement speed (approximately 2800 rpm). Adjust low speed mixture screw so engine will accelerate cleanly without hesitation. Adjust high speed mixture screw to obtain maximum no-load speed of 11,800 rpm.

IGNITION. Both models are equipped with a breakerless electronic ignition system. Ignition timing is not adjustable. Air gap between ignition coil assembly (21 – Fig. TK31) legs and flywheel (20) should be 0.35 mm (0.014 in.).

LUBRICATION. Engine is lubricated by mixing engine oil with leaded or unleaded gasoline having an octane rating of at least 87. Recommended oil is Tanaka Two-Stroke Oil mixed at a ratio of 50:1. If Tanaka Two-Stroke Oil is not available, a good quality oil designed for air-cooled two-stroke engines and for mixture ratios between 25:1-to-50:1 may be used when mixed as outlined by oil manufacturer. Use a separate container when mixing the oil and gasoline.

Both models are equipped with an automatic chain oil pump. Recommended chain oil is SAE 30 oil. Oil output is adjusted by turning oil pump adjuster (3 – Fig. TK33). Access hole is located on top of saw. Refer to AUTOMATIC CHAIN OILER under REPAIRS section.

CARBON. Carbon should be cleaned from muffler and exhaust ports at regular intervals. When scraping carbon, be careful not to damage the chamfered edges of the exhaust ports.

REPAIRS

CYLINDER, PISTON, PIN AND RINGS. Cylinder (14 – Fig. TK31) bore is chrome plated and should be renewed if cracking, flaking or other damage to cylinder bore is noted. Oversize piston and rings are not available. Cylinder (14) should be renewed if bore is out-of-round or tapered 0.10 mm (0.004 in.) beyond standard bore dimension. Piston

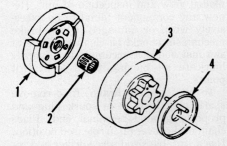

Fig. TK32 — Exploded view of three-shoe clutch assembly.

1. Hub & shoe assy.
2. Needle bearing
3. Drum
4. Sprocket washer

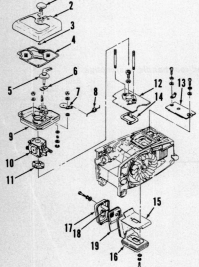

Fig. TK30 — Exploded view of intake and muffler components.

1. Knob
2. Upper cover
3. "O" ring
4. Air cleaner element
5. Choke knob
6. Choke actuating bracket
7. Choke valve
8. Choke link
9. Lower cover
10. Carburetor assy.
11. Gasket
12. Insulator block
13. Plate
14. Gasket
15. Bracket
16. Muffler half
17. Muffler half
18. Spacer
19. Spark arrestor

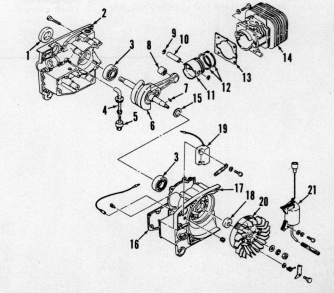

Fig. TK31 — Exploded view of engine assembly.

1. Seal
2. Crankcase half
3. Bearing
4. Oil pump suction hose
5. Strainer
6. Crankshaft & connecting rod assy.
7. Key
8. Needle bearing
9. Retainer clip
10. Piston pin
11. Piston
12. Piston rings
13. Gasket
14. Cylinder
15. Shim
16. Gasket
17. Crankcase half
18. Seal
19. Ignition module
20. Flywheel
21. Ignition coil

(11) is equipped with two piston rings (12). Piston ring end gap should be 0.1-0.3 mm (0.004-0.012 in.). Locating pins are present in ring grooves to prevent ring rotation. Make certain ring end gaps are properly positioned around locating pins before installing cylinder. Piston pin (10) rides in needle bearing (8) and is retained in position with two wire retainer clips (9). Once removed, wire clips should not be reused. Install piston on connecting rod so arrow on piston crown points toward exhaust port.

CRANKSHAFT AND CONNECTING ROD. Crankcase halves must be split to remove crankshaft assembly. Crankshaft and connecting rod (6 – Fig. TK31) are a unit assembly and supported at both ends with roller type main bearings (3). Rotate connecting rod around crankpin and renew assembly if roughness, excessive play or other damage is noted.

New seals (1 and 18) should be installed in crankcase halves prior to installing crankshaft assembly. Recommended crankshaft end play is 0.3 mm (0.012 in.). Adjust thickness of shim (15) to obtain correct end play. Shim (15) is available in thicknesses of 0.05, 0.10, 0.15 and 0.20 mm.

CLUTCH. A three-shoe centrifugal type clutch is used on both models. Clutch hub has left hand threads. Clutch needle bearing (2 – Fig. TK32) should be inspected for excessive wear or damage. Inspect clutch shoes and drum for signs of excessive heat. Clutch assembly (1) is only renewable as a complete unit.

AUTOMATIC CHAIN OILER. Both models are equipped with an automatic chain oil pump assembly. Oil pump plunger (16 – Fig. TK33) is driven by worm gear (7) via sprocket washer (4 – Fig. TK32). Oil pump is operational only when clutch drum (3) is rotating. Rotate oil pump output adjuster (3 – Fig. TK33) clockwise to increase oil flow and counterclockwise to decrease oil flow.

REWIND STARTER. Refer to Fig. TK34 for exploded view of pawl type starter. Care should be exercised when removing rewind spring (8) to prevent spring from uncoiling uncontrolled.

During reassembly, do not apply any more tension on rewind spring than required to properly draw rope handle up against starter housing in relaxed position.

CHAIN BRAKE. Both models are equipped with a chain brake designed to stop the saw chain quickly should kickback occur. Chain brake is activated when operator's hand strikes hand guard (1 – Fig. TK35), releasing arm (5)

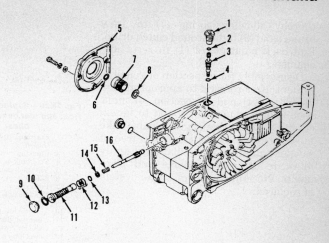

Fig. TK33 — Exploded view of automatic oil pump assembly.

1. Cap
2. "O" ring
3. Output adjuster
4. "O" ring
5. Cover
6. Seal
7. Worm gear
8. Thrust washer
9. Cap
10. Snap ring
11. Plunger body
12. "O" rings
13. "O" ring
14. Washer
15. Spring
16. Plunger

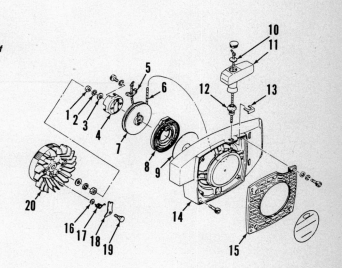

Fig. TK34 — Exploded view of rewind starter assembly.

1. Nut
2. Lockwasher
3. Washer
4. Cup
5. Anchor
6. Rope
7. Rope pulley
8. Rewind spring & case
9. Plate
10. Anchor
11. Handle
12. Guide
13. Clip
14. Housing
15. Cover
16. Washer
17. Return spring
18. Pawl
19. Pivot screw
20. Flywheel

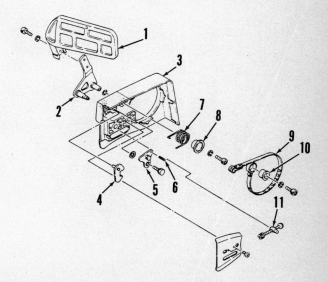

Fig. TK35 — Exploded view of chain brake assembly.

1. Hand guard
2. Lever
3. Side case
4. Reset plate
5. Arm
6. Spring pin
7. Spring
8. Bushing
9. Brake band
10. Band retainer
11. Saw chain tension adjuster

thereby allowing spring (7) to draw brake band (9) tight around clutch drum. Pull back hand guard (1) to reset mechanism.

Disassembly for inspection or repair is evident after referral to appropriate exploded view and inspection of unit. Renew any component found to be excessively worn or damaged. Chain brake mechanism should be clean and free of sawdust and dirt accumulation. Lightly lubricate all moving parts and pivot points. No adjustment of brake system is required.

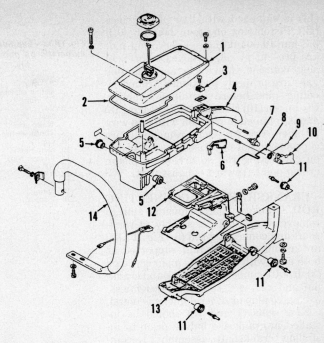

Fig. TK36 — Exploded view of front and rear handle assemblies.

1. Fuel tank cover
2. Gasket
3. Run/stop switch
4. Fuel tank & rear handle
5. Vibration damper
6. Safety lever
7. Push pin
8. Throttle link
9. Spring
10. Throttle lever
11. Vibration damper
12. Cylinder cover
13. Lower brace
14. Front handle

MM.	INCHES			MM.	INCHES			MM.	INCHES		
1	0.0394	1/32	+	51	2.0079	2.0	+	101	3.9764	3 31/32	+
2	0.0787	3/32	−	52	2.0472	2 1/16	−	102	4.0157	4 1/32	−
3	0.1181	1/8		53	2.0866	2 3/32	−	103	4.0551	4 1/16	
4	0.1575	5/32	+	54	2.1260	2 1/8	+	104	4.0945	4 3/32	+
5	0.1969	3/16	+	55	2.1654	2 5/32	+	105	4.1339	4 1/8	+
6	0.2362	1/4	−	56	2.2047	2 7/32	−	106	4.1732	4 3/16	−
7	0.2756	9/32	−	57	2.2441	2 1/4	−	107	4.2126	4 7/32	−
8	0.3150	5/16	+	58	2.2835	2 9/32	+	108	4.2520	4 1/4	+
9	0.3543	11/32	+	59	2.3228	2 5/16	+	109	4.2913	4 9/32	+
10	0.3937	13/32		60	2.3622	2 3/8	−	110	4.3307	4 11/32	−
11	0.4331	7/16	−	61	2.4016	2 13/32	−	111	4.3701	4 3/8	−
12	0.4724	15/32	+	62	2.4409	2 7/16	+	112	4.4094	4 13/32	+
13	0.5118	1/2	+	63	2.4803	2 15/32	+	113	4.4488	4 7/16	+
14	0.5512	9/16	−	64	2.5197	2 17/32	−	114	4.4882	4 1/2	−
15	0.5906	19/32		65	2.5591	2 9/16	−	115	4.5276	4 17/32	
16	0.6299	5/8	+	66	2.5984	2 19/32	+	116	4.5669	4 9/16	+
17	0.6693	21/32	+	67	2.6378	2 5/8	+	117	4.6063	4 19/32	+
18	0.7087	23/32	−	68	2.6772	2 11/16	−	118	4.6457	4 21/32	−
19	0.7480	3/4	−	69	2.7165	2 23/32	−	119	4.6850	4 11/16	−
20	0.7874	25/32	+	70	2.7559	2 3/4	+	120	4.7244	4 23/32	+
21	0.8268	13/16	+	71	2.7953	2 25/32	+	121	4.7638	4 3/4	+
22	0.8661	7/8	−	72	2.8346	2 27/32	−	122	4.8031	4 13/16	−
23	0.9055	29/32	−	73	2.8740	2 7/8	−	123	4.8425	4 27/32	−
24	0.9449	15/16	+	74	2.9134	2 29/32	+	124	4.8819	4 7/8	+
25	0.9843	31/32	+	75	2.9528	2 15/16	+	125	4.9213	4 29/32	+
26	1.0236	1 1/32	−	76	2.9921	3.0	−	126	4.9606	4 31/32	−
27	1.0630	1 1/16	+	77	3.0315	3 1/32	+	127	5.0000	5.0	
28	1.1024	1 3/32	+	78	3.0709	3 1/16	+	128	5.0394	5 1/32	+
29	1.1417	1 5/32	−	79	3.1102	3 1/8	−	129	5.0787	5 3/32	−
30	1.1811	1 3/16		80	3.1496	3 5/32		130	5.1181	5 1/8	
31	1.2205	1 7/32	+	81	3.1890	3 3/16	+	131	5.1575	5 5/32	+
32	1.2598	1 1/4	+	82	3.2283	3 7/32	+	132	5.1968	5 3/16	+
33	1.2992	1 5/16	−	83	3.2677	3 1/4	−	133	5.2362	5 1/4	−
34	1.3386	1 11/32	−	84	3.3071	3 5/16	−	134	5.2756	5 9/32	−
35	1.3780	1 3/8	+	85	3.3465	3 11/32	+	135	5.3150	5 5/16	+
36	1.4173	1 13/32	+	86	3.3858	3 3/8	+	136	5.3543	5 11/32	+
37	1.4567	1 15/32		87	3.4252	3 7/16	−	137	5.3937	5 13/32	
38	1.4961	1 1/2	−	88	3.4646	3 15/32	−	138	5.4331	5 7/16	−
39	1.5354	1 17/32	+	89	3.5039	3 1/2	+	139	5.4724	5 15/32	+
40	1.5748	1 9/16	+	90	3.5433	3 17/32	+	140	5.5118	5 1/2	+
41	1.6142	1 5/8	−	91	3.5827	3 19/32	−	141	5.5512	5 9/16	−
42	1.6535	1 21/32		92	3.6220	3 5/8		142	5.5905	5 19/32	
43	1.6929	1 11/16	+	93	3.6614	3 21/32	+	143	5.6299	5 5/8	+
44	1.7323	1 23/32	+	94	3.7008	3 11/16	+	144	5.6693	5 21/32	+
45	1.7717	1 25/32	+	95	3.7402	3 3/4	+	145	5.7087	5 23/32	+
46	1.8110	1 13/16	−	96	3.7795	3 25/32	−	146	5.7480	5 3/4	−
47	1.8504	1 27/32	+	97	3.8189	3 13/16	+	147	5.7874	5 25/32	+
48	1.8898	1 7/8	+	98	3.8583	3 27/32	+	148	5.8268	5 13/16	+
49	1.9291	1 15/16	−	99	3.8976	3 29/32	−	149	5.8661	5 7/8	−
50	1.9685	1 31/32		100	3.9370	3 15/16		150	5.9055	5 29/32	−

MM.	INCHES			MM.	INCHES			MM.	INCHES		
151	5.9449	5 15/16	+	201	7.9134	7 29/32	+	251	9.8819	9 7/8	+
152	5.9842	5 31/32	+	202	7.9527	7 15/16	+	252	9.9212	9 29/32	+
153	6.0236	6 1/32	−	203	7.9921	8.0	−	253	9.9606	9 31/32	−
154	6.0630	6 1/16	+	204	8.0315	8 1/32	+	254	10.0000	10.0	
155	6.1024	6 3/32	+	205	8.0709	8 1/16	+	255	10.0393	10 1/32	+
156	6.1417	6 5/32	−	206	8.1102	8 1/8	−	256	10.0787	10 3/32	−
157	6.1811	6 3/16	−	207	8.1496	8 5/32	−	257	10.1181	10 1/8	−
158	6.2205	6 7/32	+	208	8.1890	8 3/16	+	258	10.1575	10 5/32	+
159	6.2598	6 1/4	+	209	8.2283	8 7/32	+	259	10.1968	10 3/16	+
160	6.2992	6 5/16	−	210	8.2677	8 1/4	−	260	10.2362	10 1/4	−
161	6.3386	6 11/32	−	211	8.3071	8 5/16	−	261	10.2756	10 9/32	
162	6.3779	6 3/8	+	212	8.3464	8 11/32	+	262	10.3149	10 5/16	+
163	6.4173	6 13/32	+	213	8.3858	8 3/8	+	263	10.3543	10 11/32	+
164	6.4567	6 15/32	−	214	8.4252	8 7/16	−	264	10.3937	10 13/32	−
165	6.4961	6 1/2	−	215	8.4646	8 15/32	−	265	10.4330	10 7/16	−
166	6.5354	6 17/32	+	216	8.5039	8 1/2	+	266	10.4724	10 15/32	+
167	6.5748	6 9/16	+	217	8.5433	8 17/32	+	267	10.5118	10 1/2	+
168	6.6142	6 5/8	−	218	8.5827	8 19/32	−	268	10.5512	10 9/16	−
169	6.6535	6 21/32	−	219	8.6220	8 5/8	−	269	10.5905	10 19/32	−
170	6.6929	6 11/16	+	220	8.6614	8 21/32	+	270	10.6299	10 5/8	+
171	6.7323	6 23/32	+	221	8.7008	8 11/16	+	271	10.6693	10 21/32	+
172	6.7716	6 25/32	−	222	8.7401	8 3/4	−	272	10.7086	10 23/32	−
173	6.8110	6 13/16	+	223	8.7795	8 25/32	−	273	10.7480	10 3/4	−
174	6.8504	6 27/32	+	224	8.8189	8 13/16	+	274	10.7874	10 25/32	+
175	6.8898	6 7/8	+	225	8.8583	8 27/32	+	275	10.8268	10 13/16	+
176	6.9291	6 15/16	−	226	8.8976	8 29/32	−	276	10.8661	10 7/8	−
177	6.9685	6 31/32	−	227	8.9370	8 15/16	−	277	10.9055	10 29/32	−
178	7.0079	7.0	+	228	8.9764	8 31/32	+	278	10.9449	10 15/16	+
179	7.0472	7 1/16	−	229	9.0157	9 1/32	−	279	10.9842	10 31/32	+
180	7.0866	7 3/32	−	230	9.0551	9 1/16		280	11.0236	11 1/32	−
181	7.1260	7 1/8	+	231	9.0945	9 3/32	+	281	11.0630	11 1/16	+
182	7.1653	7 5/32	+	232	9.1338	9 1/8	+	282	11.1023	11 3/32	+
183	7.2047	7 7/32	−	233	9.1732	9 3/16	−	283	11.1417	11 5/32	−
184	7.2441	7 1/4	−	234	9.2126	9 7/32	−	284	11.1811	11 3/16	−
185	7.2835	7 9/32	+	235	9.2520	9 1/4	+	285	11.2204	11 7/32	+
186	7.3228	7 5/16	+	236	9.2913	9 9/32	+	286	11.2598	11 1/4	+
187	7.3622	7 3/8	−	237	9.3307	9 11/32	−	287	11.2992	11 5/16	−
188	7.4016	7 13/32	−	238	9.3701	9 3/8	−	288	11.3386	11 11/32	−
189	7.4409	7 7/16	+	239	9.4094	9 13/32	+	289	11.3779	11 3/8	+
190	7.4803	7 15/32	+	240	9.4488	9 7/16	+	290	11.4173	11 13/32	+
191	7.5197	7 17/32	−	241	9.4882	9 1/2	−	291	11.4567	11 15/32	−
192	7.5590	7 9/16	−	242	9.5275	9 17/32	−	292	11.4960	11 1/2	−
193	7.5984	7 19/32	+	243	9.5669	9 9/16	+	293	11.5354	11 17/32	+
194	7.6378	7 5/8	+	244	9.6063	9 19/32	+	294	11.5748	11 9/16	+
195	7.6772	7 11/16	−	245	9.6457	9 21/32	−	295	11.6142	11 5/8	−
196	7.7165	7 23/32	−	246	9.6850	9 11/16	−	296	11.6535	11 21/32	−
197	7.7559	7 3/4	+	247	9.7244	9 23/32	+	297	11.6929	11 11/16	+
198	7.7953	7 25/32	+	248	9.7638	9 3/4	+	298	11.7323	11 23/32	+
199	7.8346	7 27/32	−	249	9.8031	9 13/16	−	299	11.7716	11 25/32	−
200	7.8740	7 7/8	−	250	9.8425	9 27/32	−	300	11.8110	11 13/16	−

NOTE. The + or − sign indicates that the decimal equivalent is larger or smaller than the fractional equivalent.

NOTES

19-70 CARBURATURE ADJUSTMENT—OVER HAUL—

324 POULAN C—SAW
318 —CARBUR
320 REED
18—WALBRO—CARB—22 CLEAN